PUBLICATIONS

OF THE

NAVY RECORDS SOCIETY

VOL. 145

THE MARITIME BLOCKADE OF GERMANY IN THE GREAT WAR: THE NORTHERN PATROL, 1914–1918

THE NAVY RECORDS SOCIETY was established in 1893 for the purpose of printing unpublished manuscripts and rare works of naval interest. The Society is open to all who are interested in naval history, and any person wishing to become a member should apply to the Hon. Secretary, Department of War Studies, King's College London, Strand, London WC2R 2LS. The annual subscription is £30, which entitles the member to receive one free copy of each work issued by the Society in that year, and to buy earlier issues at much reduced prices.

SUBSCRIPTIONS and orders for back volumes should be sent to the Membership Secretary, 5 Goodwood Close, Midhurst, West Sussex GU29 9JG.

THE MARITIME BLOCKADE OF GERMANY IN THE GREAT WAR: THE NORTHERN PATROL, 1914–1918

Edited by

JOHN D. GRAINGER

PUBLISHED BY ASHGATE
FOR THE NAVY RECORDS SOCIETY
2003

Published by
Ashgate Publishing Limited
Gower House
Croft Road
Aldershot
Hants GU11 3HR
England

Ashgate Publishing Company
Suite 420
101 Cherry Street
Burlington, Vermont 05401-4405
USA

Ashgate website: http://www.ashgate.com

British Library Cataloguing in Publication Data

Grainger, John D.
The maritime blockade of Germany in the Great War : the northern patrol, 1914–1918. – (Navy Records Society publications)
1. Great Britain. Royal Navy. Cruiser Squadron, 10th – History 2. World War, 1914–1918 – Blockades – North Atlantic Ocean 3. World War, 1914–1918 – Naval operations, British
I. Title II. Navy Records Society
940.4'52

Library of Congress Cataloging-in-Publication Data
Grainger, John D., 1939–
The maritime blockade of Germany in the Great War : the Northern Patrol, 1914–1918 / John D. Grainger.
p. cm. – (Navy Records Society publications)
Includes bibliographical references and index.
1. Great Britain. Royal Navy. Cruiser Squadron, 10th – History. 2. World War, 1914–1918 – Blockades – Germany. 3. World War, 1914–1918 – Naval operations, British.
I. Title. II. Publications of the Navy Records Society

D581.G68 2003
940.4'52–dc21

2002036803

ISBN 0 7546 3536 8

Printed on acid-free paper

Typeset in Times by Bournemouth Colour Press, Parkstone and printed in Great Britain by MPG Books Ltd, Bodmin.

This book is dedicated to
the memory of my grandfather,
John Downie Chapman, 1864–1915,
Chief Engineer, Clan Line,
Engineer Commander RNR, who
died in the *Clan MacNaughton*, February 1915,
and of my mother
Sarah Elizabeth Grainger, 1904–1999,
who mourned her father all her life
and whose questions provoked this book.

CONTENTS

ACKNOWLEDGEMENTS

This book has benefited from the assistance of archivists at the Public Record Office, the Imperial War Museum, the National Maritime Museum in London, the Royal Naval Museum at Portsmouth, the Scottish Record Office in Edinburgh, and the County Record Offices of Shetland and Orkney.

Much needed financial assistance was provided by an award from The Scouloudi Foundation in association with the Institute of Historical Research and a Research Grant from the British Academy, for which I am most grateful.

ABBREVIATIONS

The following abbreviations and editorial conventions are employed in the documents; I exclude compass directions.

AMC	Armed Merchant Cruiser
AT	Armed Trawler
CMO	Confidential Monthly Order
D-of-T	Director of Transports
DR	Directional Radio
DTD	Director of Trade Division
GMT	Greenwich Mean Time
GPO	General Post Office
HMT	His Majesty's Trawler
mag.	magnetic
OW	Officer of the Watch
PMO	Principal Medical Officer
PV	paravane
RMLI	Royal Marines Light Infantry
RN	Royal Navy
RNR	Royal Naval Reserve
RNVR	Royal Naval Volunteer Reserve
SCW	Superintendent of Contact Work
SNO	Senior Naval Officer
SO	Senior Officer
TBD	Torpedo Boat Destroyer
Ty	Temporary
W/T	Wireless Telegraph
***	signifies a paragraph is omitted
...	signifies the omission of one or more words (except in lists)
[ ]	numbers in square brackets refer to other documents in this collection

Spellings

Spelling of, particularly, proper names of non-English ships and places can be haphazard. I have not altered any of these in the documents, but I have noted the 'correct' form as occasions offer, for example in the footnotes. The officers who wrote these documents had better things to do with their time than consult foreign gazetteers; the Admiralty documents, on the other hand, compiled in a more leisurely manner, are taken as 'correct'.

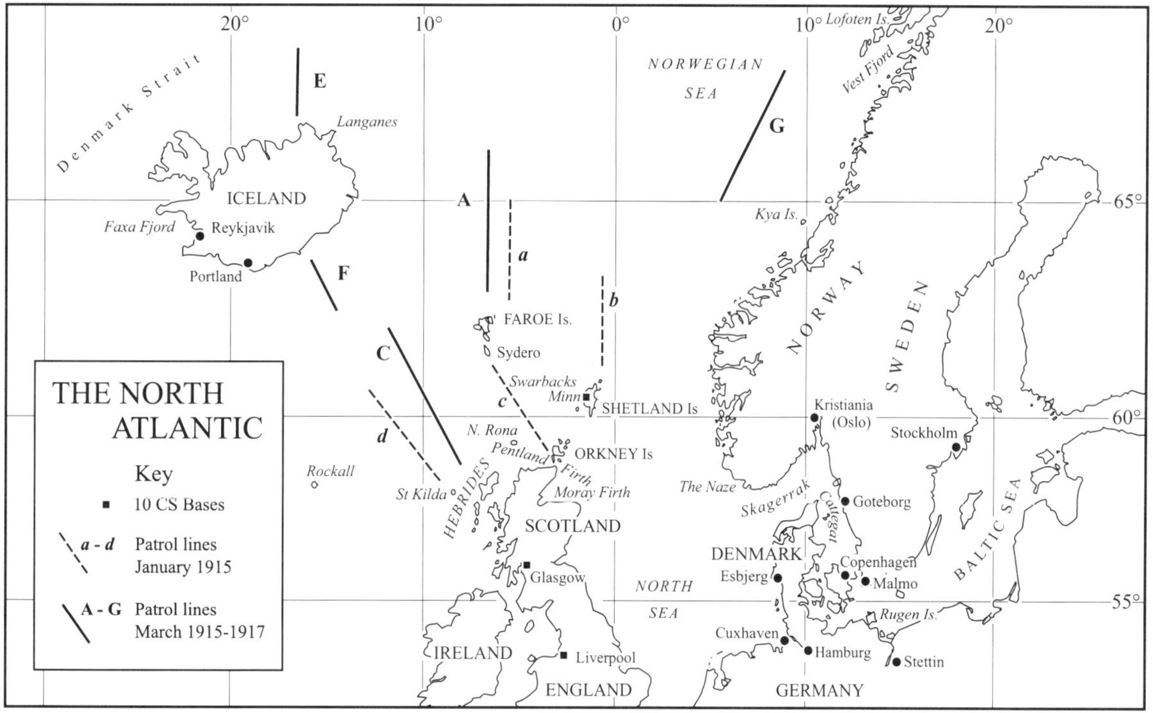
THE NORTH ATLANTIC
Key
10 CS Bases
a - d Patrol lines January 1915
A - G Patrol lines March 1915-1917
20°
10°
0°
10°
20°
65°
60°
55°
Denmark Strait
NORWEGIAN SEA
NORTH SEA
BALTIC SEA
ICELAND
Reykjavik
Portland
Faxa Fjord
Langanes
Lofoten Is.
Vest Fjord
Kya Is.
NORWAY
SWEDEN
FAROE Is.
Sydero
Swarbacks Minn
SHETLAND Is
ORKNEY Is
N. Rona
Pentland Firth
Moray Firth
St Kilda
HEBRIDES
Rockall
SCOTLAND
Glasgow
IRELAND
Liverpool
ENGLAND
Kristiania (Oslo)
Stockholm
The Naze
Skagerrak
Cattegat
Goteborg
DENMARK
Esbjerg
Copenhagen
Malmo
Rugen Is.
Cuxhaven
Hamburg
Stettin
GERMANY
A
a
b
c
d
C
E
F
G

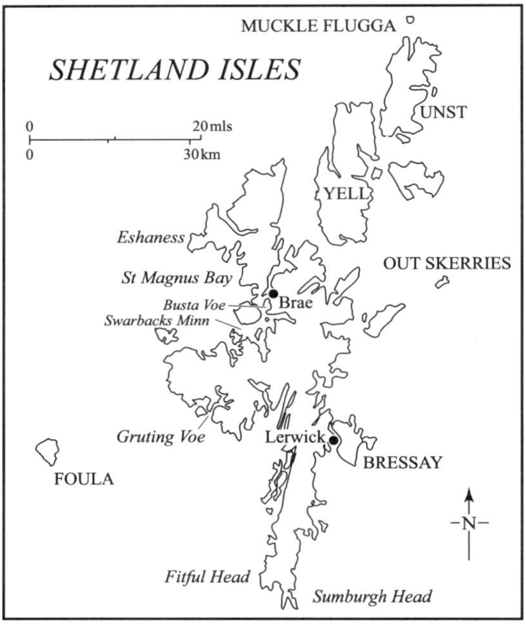
SHETLAND ISLES
MUCKLE FLUGGA
UNST
0
20 mls
0
30 km
YELL
Eshaness
OUT SKERRIES
St Magnus Bay
Brae
Busta Voe
Swarbacks Minn
Gruting Voe
Lerwick
BRESSAY
FOULA
N
Fitful Head
Sumburgh Head

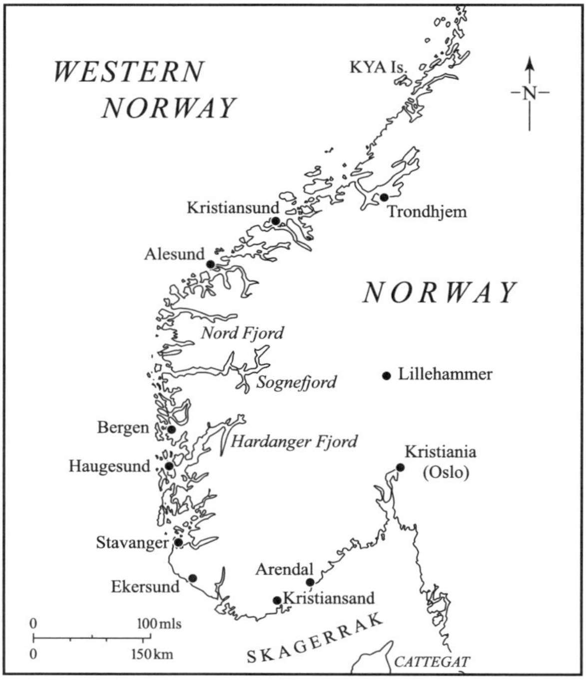
WESTERN NORWAY
KYA Is.
N
Kristiansund
Trondhjem
Alesund
NORWAY
Nord Fjord
Sognefjord
Lillehammer
Bergen
Hardanger Fjord
Haugesund
Kristiania
(Oslo)
Stavanger
Arendal
Ekersund
Kristiansand
0
100 mls
0
150 km
SKAGERRAK
CATTEGAT

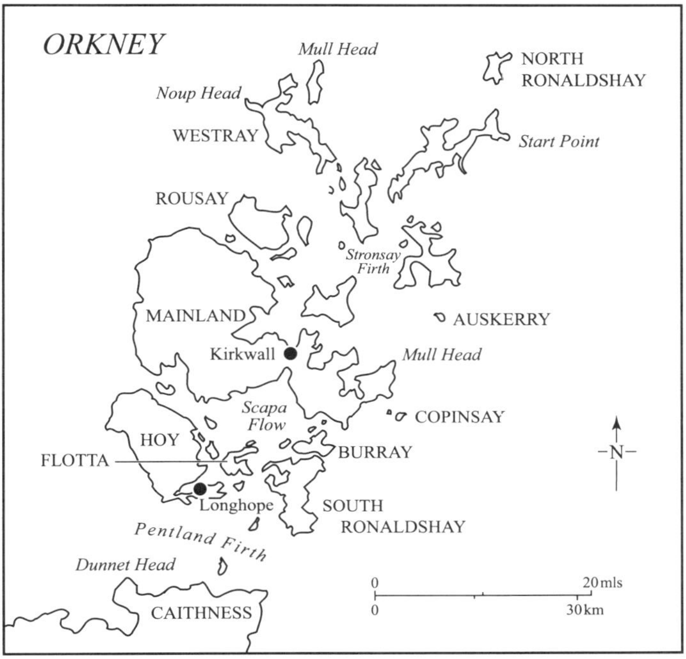
ORKNEY
Mull Head
NORTH
RONALDSHAY
Noup Head
WESTRAY
Start Point
ROUSAY
Stronsay
Firth
MAINLAND
AUSKERRY
Kirkwall
Mull Head
Scapa
Flow
COPINSAY
HOY
FLOTTA
BURRAY
N
Longhope
SOUTH
RONALDSHAY
Pentland Firth
Dunnet Head
0
20 mls
0
30 km
CAITHNESS

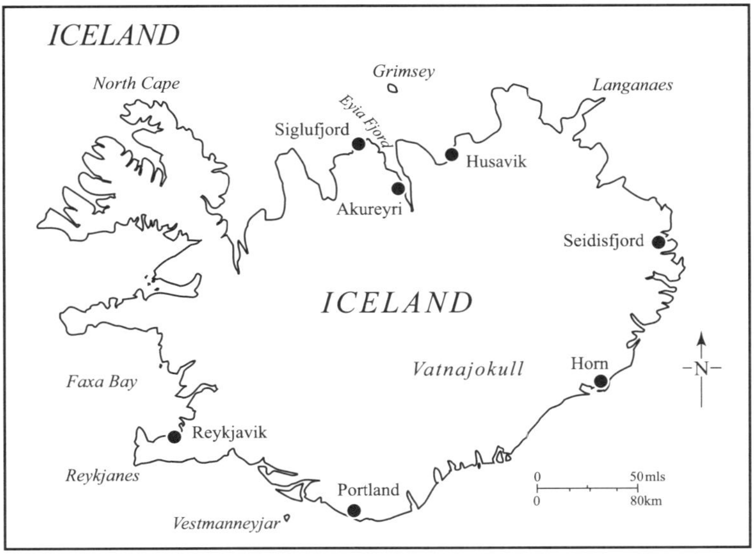
ICELAND
Grimsey
North Cape
Langanaes
Eyia Fjord
Siglufjord
Husavik
Akureyri
Seidisfjord
ICELAND
Horn
N
Vatnajokull
Faxa Bay
Reykjavik
0
50 mls
Portland
Reykjanes
0
80km
Vestmanneyjar

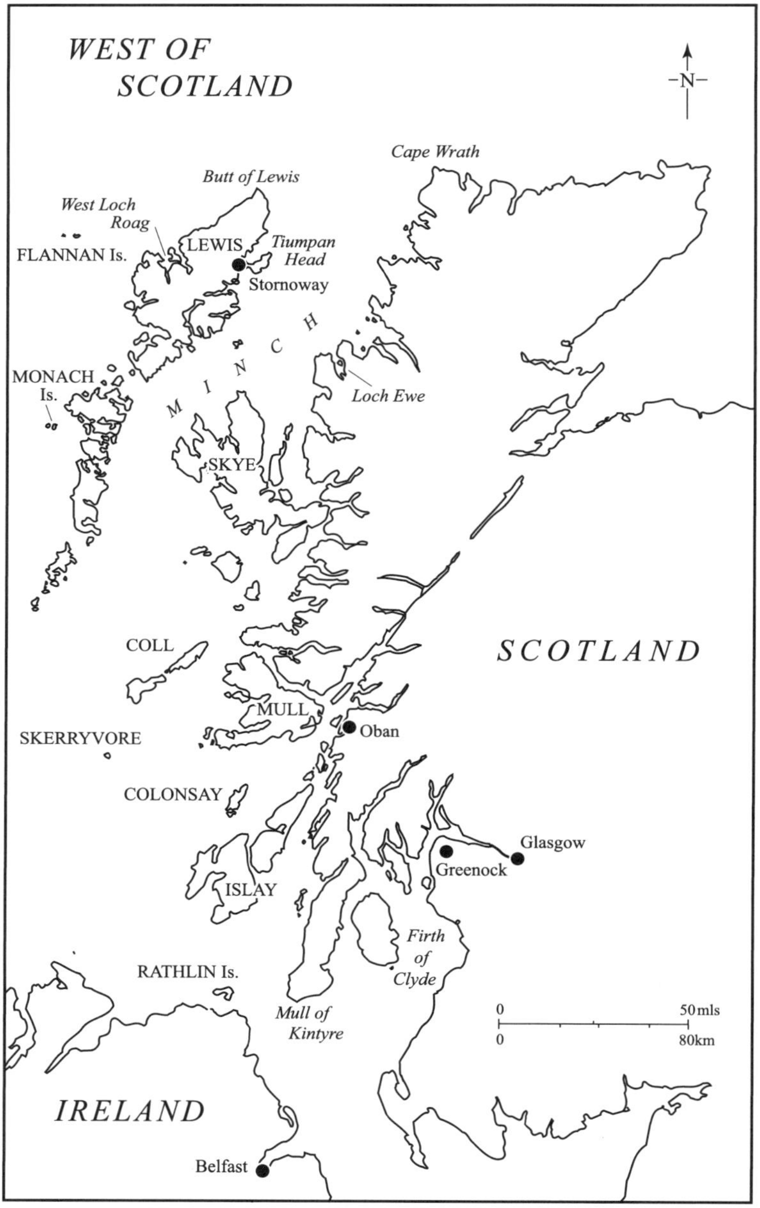
WEST OF
SCOTLAND
N
Cape Wrath
Butt of Lewis
West Loch
Roag
LEWIS
Tiumpan
Head
FLANNAN Is.
Stornoway
M I N C H
MONACH
Is.
Loch Ewe
SKYE
COLL
SCOTLAND
MULL
Oban
SKERRYVORE
COLONSAY
Glasgow
Greenock
ISLAY
Firth
of
Clyde
RATHLIN Is.
Mull of
Kintyre
0
50 mls
0
80km
IRELAND
Belfast

INTRODUCTION

The blockade of Germany and its allies in the Great War was part of the strategy which brought about their defeat, and the responsibility for enforcing that blockade rested firmly with the Royal Navy. Operating within a gradually changing network of rules and practices, the Tenth Cruiser Squadron, a force of ships which grew from eight to over forty vessels, asserted an increasingly firm control over all the maritime traffic sailing the waters north of the British Isles. For three and a half years the Northern Patrol was the most continuously active naval force of any participant in the Great War.

The assumption when war began in August 1914 was that the naval war would consist of great battles between the main fleets of the two naval powers, Britain and Germany. However, the failure of the great battles to materialise forced a general rethinking. The Tenth Cruiser Squadron, originally set to patrol part of the North Sea, became instead a force designed to prevent enemy vessels escaping from that sea, and then one intended to prevent raw materials and other supplies from reaching Germany.

The first patrol of old cruisers was replaced in the winter of 1914/15 by a fleet of requisitioned Armed Merchant Cruisers. They were lightly armed but capable of keeping at sea for a long time and better adapted to survive in the vicious northern waters. They were also more suited to the new role of the patrol: intercepting all ships to check that they were not carrying goods deemed 'contraband' by the British government.

The Blockade Policy

During the first three months of the patrol it was gradually realised that the war would last a long time. The prospect of a short war had meant that only the most obvious precautions needed to be taken to prevent materials of war reaching Germany, and that only goods of direct military use needed to be intercepted. The original list of prohibited goods, published in an Order-in-Council on 4 August 1914, consisted of two types: those whose import into the enemy countries was absolutely prohibited, and those whose import was permitted on condition that they were not destined for the enemy armed forces. The absolute list comprised arms, warships, aircraft, animals suitable for use in war, and 'implements and apparatus designed exclusively for the manufacture of munitions'. The conditional list included foodstuffs, forage, fuel, gold, silver, vehicles, and so on. The term used for these items was 'contraband', a term whose connotations of smuggling and illegality was designed, perhaps unconsciously at first, to place the enforcement of the import ban on a quasi-legal basis. The two lists, of absolute and conditional contraband, were generally in harmony with the Declaration of London of 1909, even though the United Kingdom had not ratified that agreement. Any good not on the two lists could be traded freely. If intercepted a ship destined for an enemy or enemy-occupied port could be detained; if her cargo was absolute contraband, the goods could be seized; if conditional, only if they were consigned to the enemy government.

There was plenty of room for doubt and interpretation, and the original policy was modified very quickly; on 20 August 1914, a second Order-in-Council made it more difficult to trade conditional contraband into a neutral country, where it might be consigned to an agent of the enemy for re-export. On 26 August it was reported that the German government had taken control of all foodstuffs, and the British government used this as an excuse to vary its original lists. More items were added to the conditional list on 21 September, mainly metals, but also glycerine, hides, and rubber; and on 29 October still more adjustments were made, with many conditional items being moved to the absolute list.[1] This process of expansion went on through another dozen Orders-in-Council. In each case more items were added to both lists, and conditional items were moved on to the absolute list.

The System of Control

Soon after the Order-in-Council of 29 October, which was issued partly in response to neutral complaints about the earlier British measures, the Admiralty made an attempt to establish control over the North Sea. On 2 November the North Sea was declared a military area, and all neutral vessels entering it were to be subject to Admiralty direction. It had been supposed that neutral ships were laying German mines, and the new

[1]The full texts of the Orders-in-Council of 4 August, 21 September and 29 October are in Appendix II of A.C. Bell, *A History of the Blockade of Germany and the Central Powers* (London, 1937) – henceforth 'Bell'.

regulations were intended to allow some sort of naval inspection to be made of suspected neutrals. In particular all Scandinavian ships were ordered to pass through the Straits of Dover rather than go north of Scotland. This did not suit these ships and the various Scandinavian shipping lines involved asked for, and usually received, permission to go northabout so long as they called at Kirkwall in the Orkneys to be examined.[1]

It was about this time that a combination of submarine attacks and winter storms destroyed the original cruiser force and it was not until early January that the Northern Patrol was properly reconstituted as a force of Armed Merchant Cruisers, which then had the task of intercepting the merchant vessels which were travelling northabout. This interception had to be done before the ships entered the 'military zone' of the North Sea, and hence between Scotland and Iceland. The new patrol lines were thus in the North Atlantic rather than the North Sea or Norwegian Sea; in effect the squadron had been driven out of the North Sea by the German submarine fleet. The German response was to extend that 'military area' of the North Sea to cover the waters all round Britain and Ireland, specifically pointing out that this excluded the waters north of the Shetlands and a thirty-mile-wide area along the Norwegian coast.[2] This was exactly the area where the Tenth Cruiser Squadron had now to be most vigilant.

The patrol lines of the squadron were arranged so that a reasonable attempt could be made to intercept all approaching ships. The preliminary line was west of the Hebrides, based on St Kilda and extending northwestwards towards Iceland. This was backed up by other patrol lines, one extending north of the Shetlands, one based on the Faeroe Islands and a third in the waters north of the Faeroes. (The straits between Shetland and Orkney, between Orkney and Caithness, and the waters round the Hebrides were supervised by Auxiliary Patrols.) This still left the waters around Iceland unpatrolled, and once a ship had passed the Faeroes there was only a small chance of its being intercepted.[3] For the winter this was not very important, since the waters north and west of Iceland were blocked by ice, but the issue would have to be addressed in the spring.

Before that came, the issue of 'contraband' was reconsidered yet again and a new Order-in-Council appeared, that of 11 March. This was

[1] *The Tenth Cruiser Squadron I*, Monograph 19 of Admiralty Naval Staff (1921), para. 21.

[2] Ibid., para. 30, quoting the German announcement in translation.

[3] The *Rio Negro*, carrying survivors from the sunk German cruiser *Karlsruhe*, passed through the patrol area late in November.

to be the basis of British policy with regard to trade conditions for the rest of the war. It established a complete blockade of Germany. In legal terms a blockade had to be established by a public proclamation and by naval patrols directly outside the ports. With the development of the long-range land-based artillery this ceased to be feasible, and the invention of the submarine made it quite impossible. There then was made a distinction between a 'close blockade' and a 'distant blockade', the latter of which had no international legal force.[1] In the Great War, therefore, for a time, the term blockade was avoided in official language among the Allies, though in everyday speech it was common. By 1916 it had become official as well, and Lord David Cecil became Minister for Blockade.

By the system finally set up by the Order-in-Council of 11 March 1915, though it had effectively been in operation for several months, no vessel would be allowed to go to a German port; any vessel leaving Germany with a cargo would be compelled to hand over that cargo to the Allies; goods in any ship which were ultimately destined for Germany were liable to the same treatment; any ship which tried to conceal a cargo destined for Germany was liable to be condemned if intercepted later.

Ships which were intercepted were now to be examined much more rigorously, and most were sent in to Kirkwall, or later to Lerwick or Stornoway, for the Customs Service to investigate; details of cargo, destination, ownership (of goods and ships), consignees, origins and anything else were telegraphed to London where a network of committees considered the evidence, made further enquiries and finally rendered a decision. This system was fairly economical with manpower, though the Customs had to expand their presence in the ports of examination. The London committees were kept small, so that a decision might be quick, if that was desired. The work of the Enemy Exports Committee, for goods exported from Germany, very quickly dried up; that of the Contraband Committee, on the other hand, for goods heading for Europe, where destinations were more varied, was onerous and continuous.

The membership of the Contraband Committee brought together men from the Foreign Office, which was officially in charge of contraband matters, the Admiralty Trade Division, the Board of Trade and the Treasury Solicitor's Office, enabling an input of information from many areas, including the Intelligence Department and British

[1]M.S. Partridge, 'The Royal Navy and the End of the Close Blockade, 1885–1905', *Mariners' Mirror* 75, 1989, 119–136.

embassies and consulates overseas. The decision on each case would be to release ship and cargo, or to send both to the Prize Court for being enemy property or of enemy origin; frequently only part of the cargo was of prohibited goods, in which case the ship would be sent to a better-equipped port to discharge the goods condemned. There was clearly plenty of scope for discussion, argument and dispute in all this, and plenty of scope for diplomatic pressure, artful delay and negotiation. In fact, one of the purposes of the bureaucratic procedure was to be able to impose delay and so make it uneconomic for suspect cargoes to be carried.

This structure had been developed by the time the Order-in-Council of 11 March 1915 was issued, and it remained the main means of controlling trade until the United States came into the war two years later. Yet it was only able to operate because the vessels at sea were intercepted efficiently and regularly by the Tenth Cruiser Squadron, and by other forces in the Channel, or because ships went voluntarily into various ports for examination. The Channel was controlled fairly easily, especially at the Dover choke-point, so it was through the northern waters that a ship would sail if it wished to avoid inspection – or 'evade' the blockade, as the sailors put it.

The Neutral States

The North Sea and North Atlantic coasts from the northern border of Belgium to the western border of Russia were controlled by neutral states, except for the short German stretch on the North Sea. These neutrals, The Netherlands, Denmark, Sweden and Norway, all had substantial maritime trades and mercantile marines. Denmark and The Netherlands were neighbours of Germany and could be easily dominated by her; Sweden was in many respects sympathetic to Germany. The merchants of all four of these states could be expected to do their best to profit from the economic demands of both sides in the conflict, while at the same time remaining neutral. But all four might easily be pushed into belligerency by inconsiderate or hostile actions on the part of one side or the other.[1]

The Dutch ships, at least for the first two years of the war, used the sea route through the Straits of Dover, and so the Northern Patrol had to deal in the main with ships of the Scandinavian countries. Each of these had its own reaction to the war and to the blockade, arising out of its

[1]For an overall view of Scandinavia at the time, cf. J.T. Shotwell, ed., *Sweden, Norway, Denmark, and Iceland in the World War* (New Haven, 1930).

particular geographical situation and its own internal political dynamics.

Norway was both the furthest from Germany and the most dependent on trade with Britain and on its own extensive mercantile marine. Yet distance from Germany was not much protection where that could be cancelled by a short steamship voyage. The Admiralty imagined that the intricate Norwegian coastline harboured German warships, particularly submarines, or submarine bases. Norway was a new country, only having gained full independence from Sweden nine years before the war; its population was small, its navy minimal, its diplomats inexperienced. Above all it was wholly dependent on Britain for coal for domestic, industrial and steamship use. It showed its friendliness by such gestures as swiftly returning the British officers and men of armed guards who found themselves driven to take refuge in Norwegian ports, where they could have been detained – as several hundred Germans and as the crew of the *India* were. But Norway never showed any wish to exchange its neutrality for belligerency.[1]

Sweden was the Scandinavian state which was least susceptible to British pressure: it was the most distant, the least sea-oriented, the largest and the most industrially developed. But it was also the most divided internally over the question of participation in the fighting. Much of the ruling elite was pro-German, and the participation of unpopular Tsarist Russia on the Allied side was an added incentive to support the Central Powers. This pro-German sentiment was not confined to a few important individuals, but had considerable political support in the country. At the same time the more democratic groups in Sweden tended to be pro-Allied, and between these extremes, the majority just wished to remain neutral. The participation of Russia on the Allied side was thus a complicating factor which helped paralyse Swedish decision-making for long enough for it to be clear that neutrality was the best option.[2]

Denmark's dilemma was the most awkward of them all. Geographically bordering on Germany, unlike the others, and with a longstanding quarrel with that state over the loss of southern Jutland (Schleswig) in the war of 1864, it was closely tied to both Germany and Britain by its exports of agricultural goods, and by its necessary imports of manufactured goods and fuel. Both great powers supplied coal, and Denmark had a substantial merchant marine, which could be and was

[1]T.K. Derry, *A History of Modern Norway 1814–1972* (Oxford, 1973), chapter 9; P.G. Vigress, *The Neutrality of Norway in the World War* (Stanford, 1932); the crew of the *India* was held because they were actively belligerent when the ship was sunk.

[2]F.D. Scott, *Sweden, the Nation's History* (Minneapolis, 1977), chapter 17.

hostage to the country's policy. As a small country Denmark was susceptible to pressure from both sides, and the political situation in Denmark was delicate and volatile. British pressure in late 1914 produced a strong, if momentary, anti-British feeling, but that pressure also brought the Danish shipping companies to submit to British demands. Yet the proximity of Germany gradually brought the Danes into that country's orbit, and during the war German exports of coal in exchange for the import of Danish agricultural products largely replaced British trade in these goods.[1]

Denmark had a colonial empire: the Faeroe Islands, Iceland, Greenland and three islands in the West Indies. The Faeroes and Iceland were of particular concern to Britain, given their geographical situation athwart the northabout sea-route and the rich fisheries in the nearby seas; both of these colonies slid into dependence on Britain during the war. Iceland used the situation to expand its autonomy during these years, so that by 1918 it was linked to Denmark only by the person of the king both countries acknowledged. Both Britain and Germany made serious plans to occupy the Faeroes; these may have been secret, but the Faeroese feared such occupation, and it would not have taken much to make the islands a battleground. Greenland was the source of some useful products, cryolite in particular, which featured repeatedly in interceptions by the Northern Patrol. The Virgin Islands were sold to the United States in 1917, in a deal which also included US recognition of Danish sovereignty over all Greenland.[2]

The pressure of the blockade on the three Scandinavian states – or perhaps, with Iceland, four – thus produced differing reactions. Denmark was trapped in a painful dilemma which brought it into near-dependence on Germany while its colonial empire was diminished and weakened, even though Denmark was neutral; Sweden was very resistant to domination by anyone; Norway was reinforced in its neutrality, but with pro-Allied feelings;[3] Iceland was rendered heavily dependent on Britain. For Norway, Sweden and Iceland, moreover, the economic results of the warfare at first produced unaccustomed prosperity for two years, which helped mask the wider problems;[4] but this came at a cost of fuelling inflation, and as pressure from both sides grew, 1917 and 1918 were years of hardship in all Scandinavia, an

[1]T. Kaarstad, *Great Britain and Denmark 1914–1920* (Odense, 1979), 99–122.

[2]Ibid., 123–131.

[3]This is the burden of O. Riste, *The Neutral Ally* (Oslo and London, 1965), but the case is somewhat overstated.

[4]Derry, op. cit., 271; Scott, op. cit., 471; T. Thorsteinsson in Shotwell, ed., op. cit., chapter IV.

unpleasant experience all the more galling for being so outside their control.[1]

The Northern Patrol ships were heavily involved in these international complications by being the instrument of British policy. Not all the sailors on the Patrol understood the wider diplomatic dimensions to their work, though the Admirals and Commodores certainly did. (Indeed, in one extraordinary memorandum, Admiral Oliver at the Admiralty appeared to believe that even the Commander-in-Chief had failed to understand the wider situation and that he should 'be informed of the political difficulties involved'.)[2] The delicacy with which ships of these neutral states had to be dealt with was all the more necessary when American vessels were intercepted, for, if the northern neutrals could be awkward and difficult to deal with, the United States had real power.

Merchants in the USA had seized on the chance to make money from the war as quickly and avidly as any other neutral, or any British or French war-profiteer. Companies extended themselves to establish new branches in Scandinavian countries with the intention of passing goods through to Germany; the Hamburg–America Line reinvented itself as the American Exporters Line, and established itself in Denmark; the German branch of Standard Oil sold its oil tankers to Standard Oil companies in the USA by means of a back-dated contract. The British moved very gingerly to cope with this, and carefully avoided any serious disagreement with the American government – the Standard Oil ship transfer was agreed to by the British government, for example. This was encouraged by the attitude of the USA to the northern neutrals. Repeated attempts were made by all four states to get the USA to join with them in asserting 'neutral rights', but every time the USA ignored them. It was clear that the USA was not going to be involved in an aggressive neutrality, which could only mean a willingness, despite President Wilson's apparent policy, to become involved as a belligerent.

[1]As an example which would approximately apply to all four northern states (and perhaps all Europe), Thorsteinsson in Shotwell, ed., op. cit., quotes the following cost of living indices (I add annual figures for Britain and Germany for comparison):

	Iceland	Britain	Germany
October 1914	108	100	100
Autumn 1915	123	125	125
Autumn 1916	155	161	165
Autumn 1917	248	204	246
Autumn 1918	333	210	304

The similarity of these trends, and even of the figures, is worth remarking.

[2]ADM 137/1101, 210, minute by Admiral H.T. Oliver, 16 August 1915.

It behoved all British institutions, therefore, to avoid angering the USA, an aspect of policy which Germany did not fully appreciate.[1]

The activities of the Tenth Cruiser Squadron were, therefore, of much wider significance than merely stopping and boarding merchant ships and sending them in for further examination. Most immediately, of course, they were men and ships at war interfering with men and ships who were neutral and at peace; mutual suspicion was inevitable, and care and courtesy on the part of the boarding parties was absolutely essential to avoid incidents which could have wider repercussions, since the most obvious point of friction between Britain and the northern neutrals was in the activities of this squadron. On the whole, despite what many sailors saw as provocations, the courtesy was maintained. The most persistent irritant was the Norwegian–America Line, whose ships defied the blockade for as long as possible, being branded as 'evaders' and 'blockade-runners'. Yet both 'sides' in the argument clearly saw the matter as a sort of game, even to the extent taken by the British of keeping a score.

The intermittent German submarine campaigns of the first two and a half years of the war were much less obnoxious to these neutral ships than British interference: neutral ships were certainly sunk, perhaps more often by mines than by torpedoes, but this happened far less frequently than the continual and repeated chasing, stopping, diversion, searching of ships and confiscation of cargoes by the Northern Patrol. And yet, it was clear early on that between British and German methods those of the British were infinitely preferable – the Northern Patrol only sank ships by accident; German submarines could scarcely do anything else.

This difference in methods was vastly more important when the neutral state involved was the United States of America. It is clear that the British government applied a different standard to American ships, which were often permitted to go through with only a cursory examination or none at all, where a Danish or Norwegian ship would be treated far more rigorously. The diplomatic weight of the United States and its capacity for effective outrage was shown by the reaction to the sinkings of the *Lusitania* and *Arabic*; the British procedures were less oppressive precisely because that weight and capacity were fully appreciated.

The result of the British procedures and sense of the diplomatic delicacies was that the scope for independent action by British captains

[1]A.S. Link, *Wilson* (5 vols, New York, 1947–1962), particularly volumes 2 and 3. P. Devlin, *Too Proud to Fight: Woodrow Wilson's Neutrality* (Oxford, 1974).

– and admirals – was very much less than it was for German U-boat skippers. In stopping a ship the captain on the Northern Patrol knew that all he had to do was to decide whether the ship he had intercepted was in any way 'suspicious'; if it was, he would put an armed guard on board and send the ship to a port where someone else would examine it, and from where a decision on its treatment could be passed on to yet another group, the Contraband Committee in London – which met in the Foreign Office, not even at the Admiralty.

This committee had members from the Foreign Office, the Admiralty and the legal departments, and received information from British diplomats overseas, from the Customs department and anyone else with anything to contribute, including the Secret Service and the Admiralty's code-breaking office, Room 40. It met virtually every day, and would render a decision almost instantly if necessary. The fact that the committee met in the Foreign Office makes it clear that the whole blockade system was an instrument of British foreign policy, in which the Admiralty had a say, but which was not under final Admiralty control.

The whole process in the case of every individual ship could be conducted with courtesy and apparent legality, spread over a sufficient length of time for any bad tempers to cool. By contrast, a U-boat captain had to decide for himself whether a ship should be sunk or not, or, occasionally, be sent towards Germany as a prize. The British procedures had a more leisurely aspect, were much less dangerous to the neutral – they were not going to be shot at – and there was plenty of room for discussion and argument. What is more, all the men involved knew all that. On the other side, the decision of a U-boat captain could not be predicted, because it was that of an individual interpreting orders and policy which only he of the participants knew.

The Admirals

The spread of responsibility through the various authorities on the British side lessened the burden on the squadron commanders, who could thus concentrate on their command duties, leaving the larger issues elsewhere. The first commander, Rear-Admiral Dudley de Chair,[1]

[1]De Chair, Dudley Rawson Stratford, KCB, KCMG, MVO (1864–1958), joined the navy in 1878, was prisoner of war for six weeks in the Egyptian War of 1882, Lieutenant 1884, Commander 1896, specialised as torpedo officer 1890–1900, Captain 1902, Naval Attache at Washington 1902–1905, Captain of cruisers *Bacchante* and *Cochrane* 1905–1909, Naval Secretary to the First Lord 1913–1914, Rear-Admiral 1914, Commander of Tenth Cruiser Squadron 1914–1916, Naval Adviser at the Foreign Office 1916–1917, Vice-Admiral 1917, commanded Third Battle Squadron 1917–1918, Admiral

held the post until February 1916, when he was succeeded by Vice-Admiral Reginald Tupper.[1] The two admirals had contrasting command styles, no doubt a result of their differing characters and experiences, but they were equally effective. De Chair had achieved a measure of fame as far back as the Egyptian war of 1882; Tupper was five years older than de Chair, without his renown. Both were experienced ship commanders but had also made their marks as administrators, de Chair as Naval Attache in Washington, Tupper as Deputy Commissioner of the Western Pacific territories; both had spent their time in the Admiralty, de Chair at a rather higher level than Tupper, and both had commanded the big ships. For several crucial years before the Great War, however, their experiences had differed: de Chair was in the Admiralty from 1910, first as the Assistant to the Controller of the Navy (Jellicoe was then the Controller) then as Naval Secretary to the First Lord (Winston Churchill); Tupper had been Rear-Admiral in the Home Fleet and at the outbreak of the war was in post as Rear-Admiral for the West Coast of Scotland and the Hebrides, which in peacetime had the air of a post preliminary to retirement. De Chair was thus available for a sea-going command, whereas Tupper, his senior in the list, was already employed. When de Chair's ships moved to the waters west of the Northern and Western Isles, therefore, they became neighbours.

Both men became fully familiar with the difficult waters north and west of Scotland during the first year of the war. De Chair had to set up the new squadron, organise its processes and replenishments. Tupper, based at Stornoway, had command of a set of small patrol craft, trawlers and yachts, in the narrow waters of the Scottish west coast. When Tupper took over command of the Tenth Cruiser Squadron, the organising work had been done, and in a sense he only had to operate the system.

De Chair certainly had a difficult start. The first squadron, the old cruisers of the *Edgar* class, was destroyed in the first winter storms of

in Command of Coastguards and Reserves 1918–1920, Admiral 1920, retired 1923, Governor of New South Wales 1923–1930, Home Guard 1940–1942; he published his autobiography *The Sea is Strong* (London, 1954), in which chapters 20 and 21 recount his Northern Patrol experiences.

[1]Tupper, Reginald Godfrey Otway, GBE, KCB, CVO (1859–1945), joined navy in 1873, Lieutenant 1882, Commander 1894, Naval Intelligence Department Admiralty 1898, Deputy Commissioner Western Pacific 1898–1901, Captain 1901, Assistant Director of Naval Ordnance 1901–1903, Captain of *Excellent* 1907–1910, Rear-Admiral 1910, Rear-Admiral Home Fleet 1912–1913, and of West Coast of Scotland and Hebrides 1913–1916, Vice-Admiral 1916, commander Tenth Cruiser Squadron 1916–1918 and Second Cruiser Squadron 1918–1919, Commander-in-Chief Western Approaches at Queenstown 1919–1921, retired 1921; he published his *Reminiscences* (London, 1929), in which Chapter 8 discusses his Northern Patrol work.

late 1914, and he had to organise a new one, consisting of the Armed Merchant Cruisers. This took some time, and was not made easier by continuing losses of ships – three of the new vessels were sunk within the first three months. These losses also marked out several other Armed Merchant Cruisers as potential casualties, and four more were paid off – and two more sunk – in the next year. Tupper did not have all this work to do, and acquired a full establishment of ships, plus a group of Armed Trawlers as well.

The Operation of Blockade Policy

The protracted procedures on the British side were not wholly to the taste of the men on the Northern Patrol. Fairly frequently the complaint was made that a ship had been intercepted and sent in for what the captains and men thought were good reasons, only for the ship to be released with cargo intact. The sailors therefore felt that they had undergone hardship, and perhaps danger, for no reason. The basis for the annoyance which this occasioned was not simply pusillanimity among Foreign Office officials – a constant target – but also the widespread feeling that the neutrals, by not actually fighting on the British side, were really sympathetic towards the enemy. To some extent this was true for some, but the dominant feeling among all neutrals, at least early in the war, was a determination to remain neutral, and an intention to make a profit at the expense of both sides.

So the elimination of German overseas trade was perceived in all the northern neutrals as a fine opportunity for profiting by supplying those goods from overseas which German ships and merchants could not supply. In this they were aided, at least at first, by British merchants and shippers, who enthusiastically provided substantial quantities of goods to the enemy. For example, British exports to Denmark rose from £1.5m in the first quarter of 1913 to £1.7m in the corresponding period of 1915; and re-exports rose from £119,000 to £1.5m in the same period. Exports and re-exports from Britain to all four northern neutrals (The Netherlands, Denmark, Sweden, Norway) rose from £11.5m to £16.5m. This was partly a response to the war emergency, in that all countries were stocking up, but it was also partly in response to demand from Germany for imports from those states. The official British account was unable to distinguish particular commodities in these figures, but some items showed such extraordinary increases that 'the inference proper to be drawn was not doubtful'.[1] Exports of cocoa multiplied more than

[1]Bell, 267–272.

three times, those of meat doubled, grain and flour quadrupled, lubricating oil doubled, and so on. These were exports sold by British firms, but they were also exported by permission of the British authorities. A sharp protest from France soon brought the British to heel.

Thus this profit-taking by British firms was brought under some control, but it was much more difficult to control the neutrals. Statistical evidence was compiled comparing the trade of the last year or years of peace with that of the first year of war for each neutral state. This could not become clear until sufficient evidence was collected, but by the time of the Order-in-Council of 11 March it was fairly obvious what was happening.[1]

The answer was to restrain neutral supplies to the quantities needed for each country only – a system which became called 'rationing' – which would then prevent re-exports to the enemies. Neutrals were reluctant, of course, seeing it as a coercion, which it was. Britain, however, had the whip hand, in that most of the northern neutrals relied on British coal supplies. In particular, this applied to the supplies for steamships. The only alternative sources were Germany and the United States. German supplies were not usable, since a ship fuelled by German coal would fall foul of the British blockade rules; United States supplies were certainly available, but most steamships expected to carry only sufficient coal to make a single transatlantic crossing, and carrying enough for a return voyage would seriously reduce the cargo space and was scarcely practical. Further, the British government could hold out the carrot of a rapid inspection and release of ships from any neutral country whose government accepted the rationing regime. Already in November 1914 an agreement had been reached with Captain Cold[2] of the Danish United Shipping Company by which agents of the company would liaise with consular officials in America over goods shipped through them, and in Denmark the company would investigate consignees of those goods. In return the company's ships were given accelerated treatment by the British system. Cold even agreed to hold suspected goods in Danish warehouses, or return them for condemnation in the British Prize Courts.[3]

[1]Note that it was not just the northern neutrals which were involved; Bell's statistics on British exports also looked at Greece, and Italy and Switzerland were other important neutral traders, at least until Italy entered the war in May 1915. The French, of course, attended to the disciplining of Switzerland.

[2]Cold, Captain Christian Magdalus Thestrup (1863–1934), member of a prominent Danish political family, Captain in Danish Navy 1901, Administrative Director of Det Forenede Dampskibs-Selskap 1908–1921, Foreign Minister 1922–1924.

[3]Bell, 255.

The Netherlands adopted the solution of putting all its import business into the hands of the Netherlands Overseas Trust, which negotiated with the Allied governments over the issue of trade.[1] This relieved The Netherlands government of the responsibility and gave it a viable excuse to present to Germany. From the British point of view this was the perfect solution, for the Trust operated the British contraband rules on its behalf; in the matter of trade, therefore, The Netherlands had become a British satellite, and the Trust was exceptionally careful to give no grounds for suspicion.[2] Little could be done, on the other hand, to control the export of Dutch home products to Germany, a well-established traditional trade which expanded during the war. The only answer was for the British to buy the produce, mainly food, themselves. Denmark was in much the same situation. Eventually the Danish Merchants' Guild made an agreement over trade, but this agreement never worked as well as that with the Dutch.

In various guises, such agreements became the pattern for other neutrals. Denmark only made its agreement after some resistance, and some of the trades made agreements themselves rather than nationally. The British presented their statistics and stated what quantities of goods they proposed the Danes should import. The Danish government disputed the figures, suggested higher ones, and the British tended to agree.[3] The generosity was sensible; in this case, of course, the enforcement was a British responsibility.

Over the years 1915 and 1916 these agreements were extended to many products and to all four northern neutrals. It had to be a continuous process, if only because of the repeated expansion of the lists of contraband goods.[4] Sometimes the agreement was with a group of companies in a particular trade, sometimes with a single company – as with each individual Norwegian shipping company – and sometimes with a government. In Iceland by 1916 the Acting Consul Eric Cable[5]

[1]Bell, 262–272; the agreement was reached on 26 December 1914.

[2]Bell, 266, makes this point, showing that Dutch exports were in fact lower than 'normal'.

[3]There was an agreement with Denmark in February 1915: Bell, 290.

[4]The 11 March 1915, Order-in-Council meant early agreements had to be reworked; the addition of cotton to the contraband list on 20 August 1915 (delayed because of the sensitivity of United States cotton exports, but decided on eventually because of its use in munitions), was rapidly followed by cotton agreements with Denmark (21 August), Norway (31 August), and The Netherlands (1 September).

[5]Cable, Eric Grant, CMG (1887–1970), Acting Consul at Helsingfors 1909, 1911, Vice-Consul at Hamburg 1913, Rotterdam 1914, Acting Consul and Consul in Iceland 1914–1919 (and in charge of French Vice-consulate 1916–1917), Consul Riga 1920, Oslo 1922–1926, Danzig 1926–1929, Portland Oregon 1929–1931, Seattle 1932–1933, Copenhagen 1933–1939, Consul General Cologne 1939, Rotterdam 1939–1940, Ministry of Home Security 1940–1941, Northern Department Foreign Office 1941–1942, Consul-General Zurich 1942–1947, retired 1947.

was virtually directing economic policy on behalf of the local government.[1] In Sweden the pro-German government could not be persuaded to an agreement, and refused to consider The Netherlands solution; some individual agreements were made with firms or trades and the export of British coal was restricted; at the same time the Swedes had a strong negotiating weapon in that there was an important trans-Sweden trade between the western Allies and Russia which Britain was anxious not to see interrupted, at least until after the Bolshevik seizure of power in November 1917. In the end a government agreement was made in May 1918, by which time, with the collapse of Russia and the entry of the USA into the war, it had become more or less irrelevant.[2]

By then the problem of controlling the import trade to the northern neutrals had been solved in a different way. Early in the war some merchant captains had tried to gain exemption from search and sending-in by acquiring a certificate from British consular representatives at their port of loading. These, from the point of view of the Contraband Committee and the Northern Patrol captains, were all but useless since they were not specific, either to the goods carried or to their origin, and there were suspicions that they were simply purchased. But the idea was perhaps the basis for the Navicert, or 'Letter of Assurance' as it was officially called. This was a document which was given as a result of a careful investigation at the point of loading, showing that the goods were as stated, that they were consigned to acceptable recipients, and were within the ration for the particular destination country.

It was a vastly elaborate scheme – each item in a cargo required its own Navicert – but it was wholly effective because the goods were inspected before loading, and shippers knew that any items without a Navicert would be viewed with very great suspicion, and so they could legitimately reject such cargoes. By telegraphing copies of manifests, with Navicert numbers, to the Contraband Committee, a ship would be assured of rapid consideration, and perhaps even of an undisturbed passage, since the Committee could indicate that the ship should not be sent in. The British and Allied governments also could be assured that their rules were being enforced – by the neutrals.

The beauty of the system lay in the fact that all these measures – the Netherlands Trust, agreements with individual firms, control of coal, rationing, Navicerts, and so on – were actually by and large operated by the neutrals themselves. The neutrals retained a sense of participation

[1]T. Thorsteinsson, 'Iceland and the War', in Shotwell, ed., op. cit.
[2]Bell, 651–669.

and power which was wholly absent when a neutral ship was stopped and sunk by a German U-boat. The British, in effect, enlisted the neutrals as their satellites in the war, which may well be one reason for the anger felt by the Germans when they contemplated the blockade: it was not something they could strike against with any ease, and it looked very much like a continually elaborating cobweb of measures, which bound the neutrals ever more tightly to the Allies and their interests. The only measure the Germans had which could counter this system was the blunt weapon of unrestricted submarine warfare, a cure for the problem which was worse than the disease.

The final refinement of the system was the Navicert, which marked the beginning of the end for the Northern Patrol. If every ship had a Navicert for every item of its cargo there was no point in intercepting them. In the last year of the Patrol's life the number of ships sent in for examination gradually reduced. The only problem then were the 'blockade-runners', which were few by this stage in the war. The Navicert system was taken over in its entirety by the USA once that country declared war. Since North America was the source of most of the merchandise which sailed eastwards across the Atlantic this meant that the Northern Patrol could be dispensed with. Most of the ships went to convoy duty.

The Effectiveness of the Blockade

The efficacy and war-winning utility of the blockade became an article of faith in British accounts of the war. Certainty was not complete during the war, but afterwards, especially when it was seen that the German civilian population was on the verge of starvation in 1918, the blockade of the wartime years was credited with decisive effect.[1] This interpretation was accepted by many Germans, for whom the continuation of the blockade after the Armistice prolonged the agony.[2] It was bolstered by statistical evidence, first by the account of Admiral Consett in 1923, based on his experiences as naval attaché in Sweden during the war, whose book bore the unambiguous title *The Triumph of Unarmed Forces*, and by an internal British government account by A.C. Bell, which was completed in 1937 and under the title *The*

[1]E.g., E. Lipson, *Europe 1914–1939* (London, 1st edn, 1940, 8th edn, 1960), 306: 'Through the blockade the British navy exercised a silent but fatal pressure ...', is fairly typical.

[2]E.g., H. Bohme, *An Introduction to the Social and Economic History of Germany*, trans. W.R. Lee (Oxford, 1978, originally published in German in 1972), 100: by 1918 'Germany was on the brink of collapse. The country's economic and military resources had been exhausted', which is a sideways compliment to the blockade.

Blockade of the Central Powers. In 1939, when war began again, the British government's strategy under Prime Minister Neville Chamberlain was predicated on the theory of blockade being an effective weapon, and was implemented with many assurances that Nazi Germany's economy was on the verge of collapse, and that the institution of a blockade would soon tip it over the edge.[1]

Such a policy was soon overtaken by events, of course, but the assumption that the blockade had been decisive in the Allied victory in the Great War continued unchallenged, and is repeated in textbooks to this day. Some doubts do surface, however. The area under blockade was a very large proportion of a continent, not simply one country, for Austria-Hungary, Bulgaria and Ottoman Turkey were included with Germany, and during the war these countries conquered Belgium, northern France, Serbia, Romania, Poland and western Russia. By 1917 the area under blockade was half Europe, and included the rich industrial resources of Germany, Belgium, northern France and Bohemia, and the productive agricultural lands of Hungary, Romania and Poland. The mineral resources of Sweden and the agricultural resources of Denmark and The Netherlands were also largely available to the Central Powers. One of the reasons for the idea of blockade falling out of favour as an explanation for Allied victory in Hitler's war is the manifest nonsense of attempting to blockade a whole continent – yet that is essentially what the Great War blockade did.

There is no doubt that German foreign trade was disrupted by the blockade, at least extra-European trade, and, since that trade was very largely by sea, there is equally no doubt that it was the work of the Tenth Cruiser Squadron which was the effective instrument in its disruption.[2]

[1]Lord Chatfield, Minister for the Co-ordination of Defence in Chamberlain's Cabinet, is reported as saying 'It might be that eventually Germany would have to capitulate owing to her condition, without any great land fighting. Our great weapon, as he had remarked at previous meetings, was our sea power and blockade, and we were ever tightening the screw' (PRO, CAB 65/56, 7 March 1940, minutes of a meeting, quoted in D. French, *Raising Churchill's Army* (Oxford, 2000), 158). Or as Chamberlain himself put it more pithily: 'Hitler missed the bus'. Chatfield, of course, was a sailor, an Admiral of the Fleet, but that is no excuse for such a statement as he had made. It can only be a result of the navy's interpretation of the events of 1914–1918, combined with a wilful misunderstanding of what had happened on the Western Front. It was, however, an accurate statement of the policy of the Chamberlain government in 1939–1940.

[2]German imports fell to 40% of their value (in gold marks) by 1918 (from 1913); exports fell even more, to less than 30%. Yet this is an ambiguous change, since the freed manufacturing capacity (and workers) was converted to war production: '... the tremendous economic decline of the Central Powers between 1914 and 1918 was caused less by the blockade than by the excessive demands made on their economies by the war', G. Hardach, *The First World War*, trans. P. and B. Ross (London, 1977), table 6 and pp. 32–34. But the 'excessive demands' were partly the result of the blockade! And it was not just an economic matter.

Germany had been becoming increasingly dependent on imports of food and some raw materials before 1914 and so the elimination of its seaborne trade was a serious blow.[1] But its effects were inevitably slow in appearing, and it was not for a year and half that any real shortages showed themselves – and then those shortages were not so much in the industrial materials which the blockade had been originally directed against, but in the supply of food to the civilian population. It has been pointed out, however, by Offer in particular, that the food shortage was in large part the result of the inefficient organisation of food production and distribution within Germany.[2]

Thus it is possible to argue away the blockade's effectiveness – industrial production continued and the army was scarcely incommoded, food was short because of government inefficiency.[3] To discern the fallacy of this view it is only necessary to imagine the difference to the German war effort which the absence of an Allied blockade would have made. Continued German overseas trade would have permitted the continued import of food and scarce raw materials, the continued earning of foreign exchange, an openness to overseas influences and a more confident German foreign policy; above all, it would not have been necessary to resort to unrestricted submarine warfare. The absence of the U-boat campaign of 1917–18 would have meant that the United States would not have needed to come into the war on the Allied side – and it would also have meant the continuation of American trade with Germany and the continued ability of the German state to raise loans on the American money market, rather than the restriction of both of these to the Allies. It does not need any further imagining to see the result: German victory. To that extent the blockade was certainly a war-winning weapon.

It was not, however, the decisive weapon, as its vaunters imply. That was the Allied armies on the Western Front, if any 'weapon' must be singled out. The effects of the blockade took time to reach deep into the German economy and society, in part because of the reserves which existed, and in part because the blockade was only partly effective for a long time. Further, the most effective part was clearly the denial of adequate food supplies to the German civilian population, which had not even been the prime target of the Allied planners. Indeed it seems probable that the great majority would have been horrified at the

[1]German imports of food and raw materials from overseas and outside Europe fell to 45% of the total in 1914.

[2]A. Offer, *The First World War: an Agrarian Interpretation* (Oxford, 1989).

[3]N. Ferguson, *The Pity of War* (London, 1998), 252–255, deliberately iconoclastic in all things, almost argues the blockade into complete ineffectiveness.

thought that the blockade would hit women and children first and worst. But neither did the submarine's inventors and developers imagine or plan that it would be used to make attacks on civilian vessels.

A further reason for the blockade's slowness to have an effect was the necessity for the Allies to avoid seriously annoying the United States. Until the various U-boat campaigns, it was the Allied blockade which particularly annoyed the American government, and the declaration of unrestricted submarine warfare in February 1917 came just in time to prevent a serious rupture in Allied–US relations, in which the blockade figured as a major element. Not for the first time a German move rescued the Allies from an approaching predicament, for they had faced an American embargo on financial resources which would have had serious effects.[1]

At a different level, the effectiveness of the blockade is measurable by the number of ships intercepted by the Tenth Cruiser Squadron, and, even more, by the numbers which they failed to intercept. The former is known and is reported by the admirals in their regular reports, with totals annually, with understandable pride. The number of failed interceptions is necessarily less precise. Estimates were made in the Admiralty, but, despite apparent precision, they must be regarded as the lowest likely numbers: ships undoubtedly got through which the British never knew about. Those which were known to have got through were recorded, presumably by British diplomats and spies in the neutral countries, who could discover them perhaps by looking them up in the newspaper lists of arrivals, perhaps by relying on local informants, perhaps even by going to the docks themselves, but there is plenty of scope in all this for non-recording, since it was in the interests of captains, merchants, consignees, and even neutral governments, to keep success secret. Similarly any ship which got through to Germany would remain unknown, unless the Germans announced it, as they sometimes did. It must be assumed, therefore, that a considerable number of vessels got through which the Admiralty were never aware of.

Further, there is no guarantee that those vessels which were intercepted and examined did not carry goods which eventally reached Germany, despite the elaborate British system designed to prevent it. The neutrals were treated as gently as the British could devise, consistent with their incurable suspicion, but the neutrals' priority was to make a profit and they had no loyalty to either side. Concealment of

[1]In late 1916 and early 1917, there were serious problems between the Allies and the USA over finance and trade, including a run on the Bank of England in February 1917; cf. K. Burk, *Britain, America and the Sinews of War 1914–1918* (London, 1985); Ferguson, *Pity of War*, 326–329, downplays this.

contraband would be instinctive – and there was a strong incentive to do so. As the Brazilian captain explained when he was detained with a cargo of rubber, he had heard of the high price rubber was fetching in Europe and wished to take advantage [204 para. 4]. Other goods besides rubber commanded high prices too – cotton, oil, food, metals – and there were plenty of methods for getting goods through. False manifests, colluded captures by German ships in Danish waters, a sequence of consignees, were only some of the methods which were discovered by the British. And any goods not discovered had obviously got through, though the fact would not be announced. It must be concluded that, while the blockade was largely effective in the end, it was by no means as tight as the British assumed, then and later.

Yet the German economy clearly suffered. The lengths to which the Germans went to get supplies through is evidence of that. The neutral ships which made regular runs across the Atlantic were obvious methods, in which small high-value goods might be carried as personal luggage. Consigning goods from German firms overseas to front men in neutral states was a method more suited to bulk goods, which could only be countered by extensive investigations by the Allies. No government which was not suffering would go to the expense of constructing special U-boats to carry valuable cargoes – *Deutschland* and *Bremen* – if it was not in desperate need of those goods. Nickel, rubber, oil, tobacco, coffee, were all recorded in the documents in this volume as requiring special treatment, and this is clearly a minimal list.

There was one tactic which, surprisingly, the German Navy did not adopt. The ships of the Tenth Cruiser Squadron were large, and their approximate location was known. They were originally civilian vessels, but were certainly acting as armed warships. To U-boats they should surely have been obvious targets. In 1917 several were in fact sunk, though they were not apparently targeted as vessels of the Northern Patrol, only as victims of the indiscriminate sinking policy. But a deliberate concentration on these ships earlier in the war would have surely reaped a good harvest. Not only would a warship have been sunk, but the Tenth Cruiser Squadron would then have been reduced in strength, perhaps opening a gap in the blockade, and it would have to be replaced by another cruiser taken from its primary task of transporting goods and people. When the *Moewe* escaped into the Atlantic in 1916, four ships were detached from the Tenth Cruiser Squadron to join the twenty-strong flotilla which went to hunt for it. They failed to find it, even though the *Moewe* haunted the shipping lanes. This was a clear bonus for the German tactic, quite apart from the 25 ships captured or sunk, and a large number of ships delayed by remaining in port for fear of being caught. And part of that bonus was the weakening of the Northern Patrol for several months.

Of course, it was not easy to locate individual ships at sea, as *Moewe*'s career showed, but the location of Tenth Cruiser Squadron patrol lines was predictable within fairly narrow limits, and these cannot have been much of a secret in Scandinavian merchant naval circles. When *India* was sent to watch the Norwegian coast near the Vest Fjord in August 1915, it proved to be very easy to sink her. A concentration on the blockaders would surely have damaged the blockade very seriously.

It must be concluded, therefore, that the blockade had only a limited effectiveness, though one whose effects increased with time, and which became wholly effective only with the entry of the USA into the war, combined with the universal use of the Navicert. The effects on Germany were perhaps marginal overall, but with a deeper impact on the availability of certain goods, some of which were crucial to the war economy. The effectiveness of the blockade was, however, multiplied by the poor organisation instituted by the German government. Better distribution of food and a more sensible allocation system would have mitigated much of the blockade's effects.[1] And, of course, by blaming the British blockade for the shortages in Germany, the German government both transferred the blame to the enemy and missed the real problem, which was itself.

There is, however, a further, less tangible effect which is customarily ignored in the passion for quantifiable evidence. One of Germany's complaints before the war had been of the 'encirclement' which the Triple Entente of Britain, France, and Russia appeared to be enforcing. The addition of Romania, Serbia and Italy to Germany's enemies in 1914 to 1916 reinforced that effect, and the blockade completed the encirclement geography. Contact with the rest of the world was not wholly eliminated, but psychologically the dreaded encirclement appeared to have come about in fact as well as accusation. The inability of the German Navy to break through the blockade increased the sense of being stifled, as did the complete failure of any other state to join the Central Powers after the accession of Bulgaria in 1915. At the same time the Allied powers received regular accretions to the list of their allies, even if many of them were of little military value.[2] The squeeze

[1]This is the burden of Offer's work (op. cit.).

[2]After the end of 1914, only Bulgaria joined the Central Powers in active warfare; by contrast the Allies were joined by Italy in 1915, by Albania, Portugal and Romania in 1916, by the USA, Cuba, Panama, Greece, Thailand, Liberia, China and Brazil in 1917 – and these were spaced out, not all at once.

on resources, the spreading hunger, the cessation of foreign trade, the military stalemate, were all made worse by the steady drip of declarations of war from all quarters of the world.

The effectiveness of the blockade was thus neither so great as the British navalists claimed nor so minimal as the latest revisionists suggest. Its effect was, above all, cumulative, and it could only be made approximately complete if and when the USA participated in it fully. So until 1917 there were gaps and leaks and holes through which supplies could reach Germany, but from 1915 onwards the quantities were decreasing. The British could certainly have tightened up their blockade in that time if they had wished, but only at the cost of alienating the USA, and while the USA might not have gone so far as to declare war on Britain over the issue, it would certainly have been able to make life very unpleasant for the Allies. It was a triumph for Allied diplomacy, and no less a triumph for the behaviour of the enforcers of the blockade, above all the sailors of the Northern Patrol, that US–Allied relations were no more than disturbed over the issue. The upheavals which afflicted US–German relations were much more spectacular and much of that affliction was the result of the behaviour of individual German officers, diplomats and U-boat captains. It was an indication of just what could have gone wrong for the Allies if the conduct of the Tenth Cruiser Squadron had been less seamanlike, courteous and intelligent.

The Documents

The main sequence of documents in this collection is the Reports of Proceedings by Admirals de Chair and Tupper as commanders of the Tenth Cruiser Squadron, forming an almost continuous account of events from the start of the war to the dismantling of the Northern Patrol at the end of 1917. The only gaps in the sequence come when the Admirals returned to a southern base, leaving command to one of their subordinates, whose reports are not always incorporated. Attached to this sequence are a variety of other documents emanating from several sources. The Admiralty, as always, was a profuse source of letters, minutes, memoranda and telegrams, but many of those documents are of very limited interest, so that only those pertaining to the overall work of the squadron are included. The Commander-in-Chief, particularly when that office was held by Jellicoe, produced more material, as did the commanders in Orkney and Shetland. Replies to these by de Chair and Tupper are included where worthwhile and relevant.

Below the level of control, policy and command there are three types of document. Several ships' captains produced worthwhile documents, notably Captain Vivian in *Patia* during 1915, which illustrate at a stage closer to events the work being done. The Reports of Proceedings by Captain Vivian and by Captain Walter in *Victorian* suggest the sort of material which formed the bases for the Admirals' own reports, and indicate the very varied reports which could be made. Then there are reports written by boarding officers, officers in charge of armed guards who were put on board the intercepted ships to take them into a British port. To a degree these are somewhat misleading since such reports were only made when something out of the ordinary happened – the ship was sunk, say, or driven to a Norwegian port. Nevertheless almost all of them are remarkable human documents, showing the high qualities of these junior officers, usually RNR or RNVR men, in very unpleasant and difficult circumstances. For the regular routine of the patrol there are extracts from diaries by a variety of officers.

For the conditions of the seamen there is much less to go on. Some information may be inferred from comments by officers, but only one document produced by a sailor has been discovered: by Able Seaman Style in *Alcantara*. It is a diary, not very revealing, but one which indicates an ordinary sailor coping as well as he can with a very boring life, one where intercepting a ship was an event, and the northern lights, or a visit ashore on Shetland, a milestone. The diary is continuous, but here it has been separated into monthly sections. For the men working in the worst conditions, the stokers, it is necessary to rely on comments by Tupper (not de Chair) in his inspections as noted in his Reports, or the savage remarks by Commodore Benson [210], and the hapless 'mutiny' by eight men in *Teutonic* in 1916. For this it seems clear that ultimate responsibility must lie with the lackadaisical response of the Admiralty to the problems of pay and food, both of which assumed abnormally great importance to men in hot, dirty places, doing physically demanding work. In the less stressful spaces of Admiralty offices, they were, no doubt, thought to be of minor importance.

Two further sources have been resorted to. The majority of the intercepted ships were sent in for examination at three ports, Kirkwall in Orkney, Lerwick in Shetland, and Stornoway in the Hebrides. There they were examined by Customs officers, who reported on them to the Contraband Committee in London. No worthwhile documents from the Customs records from Stornoway were located, but there are several from Kirkwall and Lerwick which show the sort of work done and the conditions of work.[1] The Contraband Committee, as befits such a

[1]The Stornoway records, such as they are, are kept in the Scottish Record Office in Edinburgh; the Kirkwall and Lerwick Records are in the local Record Offices in those

bureaucratic organisation, compiled comprehensive and detailed minutes, which were printed and bound and indexed, and these have also yielded a number of documents.[1] These two sources have been used mainly for the purpose of following up the individual ships mentioned in the various reports made by the Admirals (and some captains) on the Tenth Cruiser Patrol. It was one of the regular complaints by these men, and by others, that they were working hard and in dangerous conditions to locate and intercept the ships, only to discover that the Committee or the Customs had released them. An attempt has been made to follow up each and every ship mentioned as being detained – though this is not the whole number sent in – to discover its fate; similarly the deeds of the German submarines are frequently referred to, and they are identified as far as possible (based on the detailed itineraries of the individual U-boats in Spindler's book).[2]

cities. I am grateful to the record keepers in all three places for their assistance – particularly at Lerwick where it seemed for a time that the records might be closed for a hundred years; this turned out to have been reduced, much to my relief after the journey there.

[1]A copy is in the PRO, TS series.

[2]A. Spindler, *Der Handelskrieg mit U-booten* (5 vols, Berlin and Frankfurt-on-Main, 1932–1966).

1

THE FIRST PATROL: THE *EDGARS*, AUGUST–NOVEMBER 1914

The initial intention of the Tenth Cruiser Squadron, as laid out in the War Book, was to intercept enemy ships, civilian and naval, in the North Sea. Since so few German warships could be found there, by default the squadron had to concentrate on other tasks. More than once it was taken up by the Grand Fleet and used in a scouting or screening role [4]. Otherwise the ships investigated any other vessels, which were overwhelmingly British; neutrals were examined for enemy trade. Gradually the focus of the squadron shifted from combating enemy ships to enforcing the contraband trade rules, a shift which had begun by the end of August 1914 but which was not formalised until mid-October [11], by the alteration of the patrol area from the northern North Sea to the waters north and west of Shetland.

This change only briefly anticipated the effective destruction of the squadron by the winter storms in October. The *Edgars* were ships built in the early 1890s, when the Navy's centre of gravity and operations were the Channel and the Mediterranean, and they could not cope with the North Atlantic [12, 13]. Partly repaired and returned to their home ports, they were replaced in the north by armed liners [15–16]. *Hawke*'s sinking by *U 9* [10] was another enlightening moment, and from that time submarines were a major preoccupation of all surface ships, to the extent that many 'sightings' of submarines cannot be believed; see, for example, the reaction of *Antrim* to a shoal of 'black fish' [9 para. 16]. The endurance and strength of the few Armed Merchant Cruisers stands out all the more, as the *Edgars* succumbed at the first real storm.

This initial period of the Northern Patrol must be counted as a failure. The original intention was, of course, in part foiled by the German ships' failure to co-operate by coming out, but any consistency in work was also prevented by the repeated interruption of patrolling to accompany the Grand Fleet or a Battle Squadron on a sweep, and by alterations in bases, in areas, and, of course, by the emergence of the new purpose, trade control. The Admiralty's instruction [16] as a result was that the new Patrol was to 'be employed exclusively for patrol duty'.

1. *Rear-Admiral de Chair to Admiralty*

HMS *Crescent*, 27 August 1914

Report of Proceedings, 1–27 August 1914

I have the honour to make the following report of my proceedings for the information of Their Lordships:

1. Saturday, 1st August – On receipt of the order to mobilise at 2 p.m., I left the Admiralty and proceeded to Portsmouth where I hoisted my Flag on board H.M.S. *Crescent* as Rear Admiral Commanding Tenth Cruiser Squadron.

2. On my arrival the disposition of the Squadron was as follows:

Crescent, *Edgar*, *Grafton* ... at Portsmouth.
Endymion, *Theseus*, *Gibraltar* ... at Devonport.
Royal Arthur ... at Chatham.
Hawke ... at Queenstown, refitting.

3. Sunday, 2nd August – I received from the Commander-in-Chief Portsmouth,[1] my War Orders together with a copy of the General War Plans ... under which the Squadron under my orders, together with *Dryad*, which was placed under my orders, was constituted as Cruiser Force B. *Dryad* was at Portsmouth at the time.

4. The order to 'Mobilise Naval Reserves' having been issued at 2.00 a.m. on 2nd August, ranks and ratings for the Squadron at once began to arrive on board, and continued to do so at intervals all day.

5. Monday, 3rd August – Finding that the ships under my orders were nearly complete with crews I obtained permission from the Commander-in-Chief to leave Portsmouth and proceed in execution of previous orders, leaving *Dryad* behind to bring on late arrivals and stores. *Crescent* and *Grafton* accordingly proceeded in company, and *Edgar*, after communicating with Cowes to enable an officer to join, followed and joined my Flag in the early morning of 4th August.

6. Tuesday, 4th August – As a majority of the remaining ships of my Squadron were at Devonport, I proceeded down Channel (with the intention of picking them up off Plymouth) and up the West Coast to Scapa Flow. *Endymion*, *Theseus* and *Gibraltar* were not, however, completed in time to accompany me.

7. Midnight, 4/5th August – Orders were received to commence hostilities against Germany, and at 8.35 a.m. on 5th August when off the Mull of Cantire,[2] I directed *Grafton* to capture the German steamer

[1]Admiral the Hon. Sir Hedworth Meux.

[2]This is the regular spelling (or 'Cantyre') at this time for 'Kintyre'. No effort has been made to 'correct' spellings of place names, even when they appear in several guises.

Wilhelm Behrens, 750 tons, and send her into port. This steamer was sent into Greenock.[1]

8. Thursday, 6th August – I arrived at Scapa Flow with *Edgar* and *Grafton* at 8.30 a.m. and at once commenced coaling. At 4.45 p.m. *Endymion* and *Theseus* arrived, having been delayed by orders of the Commander-in-Chief Devonport,[2] to proceed to Falmouth on the 4th August to watch the *Kron Princessin Cecilie*. As this steamer was found not to be the vessel of that name carrying bullion, she was released by order of the Admiralty together with another German Steamer also detained at Falmouth.

9. *Crescent* and *Edgar* having completed with coal I left Scapa at 6.30 p.m. after directing the remainder of my ships to rejoin me at a rendezvous marked R.1 (on plan) as soon as they had finished coaling. *Gibraltar* arrived as I was leaving, having been detached off the Isle of Man on 5th August to capture the German Steamer *Marie Glaesar* and send her to Greenock.[3]

10. In accordance with directions from the Commander-in-Chief Grand Fleet, I proceeded by way of the westward of Orkneys to patrol the southern portion of the area laid down in my War Orders ...

11. Friday 7th August – *Grafton* joined me at noon, and *Endymion* and *Theseus* at 4 p.m. Various vessels were examined but no captures were made.

12. Saturday, 8th August – Two German sailing trawlers (*Geeste* BV 17 and *Delme* BV 25) were captured. The crews were taken off and the boats sunk by gun fire. At noon I directed *Edgar* to take *Theseus* and *Gibraltar* under her orders and proceed to northern portion of patrol in the vicinity of Norwegian Coast (between Lat. 61.30´N and 62.30´N).

13. Sunday, 9th August – Various Steamers were examined by *Endymion* and *Grafton*. News was obtained of the presence of the *Prinz Friedrich Wilhelm* at Bergen together with 22 German Trawlers.[4] She was reported in Norwegian Papers as making warlike preparations. *Dryad* arrived off Sunburgh Head[5] about 7 p.m. with Officers and ratings and a few mails, and I sent her back to Scapa Flow with 27 prisoners taken from the two German Trawlers captured and sunk on Saturday 8th August.

[1]The *Wilhelm Behrens* was condemned by the Prize Court.

[2]Admiral Sir George le C. Egerton.

[3]The *Marie Glaesar* was condemned by the Prize Court.

[4]*Prinz Friedrich Wilhelm*, a 17,000 ton liner, would not be likely, in a neutral port, to be able to make any 'warlike preparations'. When *Berlin* took refuge in Trondheim she was swiftly disarmed by the Norwegians.

[5]This is the normal spelling, at least by Englishmen, for what is now 'Sumburgh'.

14. Monday, 10th August – *Dryad* joined me from Scapa Flow, and later in the day *Royal Arthur*, which had escorted two Colliers (for 10th Cruiser Squadron) to Busta Voe, St. Magnus Bay, met me off Muckle Flugga. I sent *Endymion* to Busta Voe to coal the same evening.

15. Tuesday 11th August – I met my Second Division at X 6. and reorganised the Squadron in two Divisions as follows:

First Division	Second Division
Crescent (Flag)	*Edgar* (Senior Officer)
Grafton	*Royal Arthur*
Endymion	*Gibraltar*
Theseus	*Hawke*

I then proceeded with First Division to sweep to SW and directed Second Division to return to Northern portion of patrol and sweep to NE.

Gibraltar was detached from Second Division and proceeded to Busta to coal.

16. Arrangements for coaling Squadron were worked out so that two ships, one from each Division, would be in harbour together, and the strength of the patrolling divisions would be maintained at three ships each so far as practicable.

17. Wednesday, 12th August – In accordance with orders from Commander-in-Chief Grand Fleet, I detached *Endymion* and *Gibraltar* to join Rear-Admiral Grant[1] at Faroe Islands. They left Busta Voe complete with coal during the afternoon, *Grafton* was detached from First Division and proceeded to Busta Voe to coal.

18. Thursday, 13th August – Orders were received about midnight to commence hostilities against Austria. I met the Second Division at X.4 at 8 a.m., *Edgar* was detached from Second Division and proceeded to Busta Voe to coal, while *Royal Arthur* and *Hawke* returned to northern portion of patrol and continued with First Division (i.e., *Crescent* and *Theseus*) on the southern portion of patrol.

19. Friday, 14th August – After ordering *Theseus* to continue patrol, I proceeded into Lerwick Harbour, arriving at 2 p.m. Here I found *Dryad* with mails and provisions, and the colliers *Tweed* and *Needwood*. *Crescent* completed with coal from the former. While at Lerwick I

[1]Grant, William Lowther, RN, Captain 1902, Rear-Admiral 1909, Home Fleet 1910–1911, Commanded Sixth Cruiser Squadron 1914, Vice-Admiral 1915, Commander-in-Chief China Station 1915–1918, Admiral 1918, Commander-in-Chief North America and West Indies 1918–1919. Grant was in command of the Sixth Cruiser Squadron from 1 August, an appointment which put Beatty's nose out of joint (*Beatty Papers* I, 54).

communicated with Colonel Evans, RMLI,[1] and learnt from him the progress of the RNR Force which has been organised for the defence of the Islands. In accordance with directions from the Commander-in-Chief, I left Lerwick at 10.30 p.m., and proceeded to rendezvous R.3 where I directed *Edgar*, *Grafton* and *Theseus* to meet me.

20. Saturday, 15th August – Having been joined by *Grafton* and *Theseus* at R.3, at 6.0 a.m. I proceeded to Lat. 59 N, Long. 0.30´E, where I arrived and met the Flag of the Commander-in-Chief at 8 a.m. *Edgar*, which had been coaling at Busta Voe, joined me at 10 a.m. After receiving orders by signal I proceeded with my Cruisers to a position four miles ahead of the Grand Fleet. At 5[1]p.m., I moved to a position bearing SSE 12 miles from 'Flag' where I continued until dawn on Sunday 16th August when I commenced to get into a position 30 miles on Eastern Flank, spread on a N and S line 10 miles apart, off the Skagerack.

21. Sunday, 16th August – At 9.30 a.m. in accordance with Commander-in-Chief's order to retire, Squadron under my command altered course to N by W and proceeded at 13 knots, 12 miles apart on a line N 82° E, from Battle Fleet, the nearest Cruiser (*Crescent*) being 10 miles on Starboard beam. At 6 p.m. *Theseus* was detached to Lerwick to coal, steering N at 12 knots. At 8 p.m. course of Squadron was altered in accordance with signal to N 17° W, speed 11 knots, and at 11 p.m. Squadron was proceeding N ½ E speed 10 knots, ships spread 5 miles apart on a line E ½ S.

22. Monday, 17th August – On receipt of Commander-in-Chief's orders at 4 15 p.m., I proceeded with *Grafton* and *Edgar* to rendezvous at T.4 where I met *Royal Arthur*, *Hawke* and *Dryad* at 5.30 p.m. After communicating I detached *Royal Arthur* and *Hawke* to the northern portion of patrol (off coast of Norway) and proceeded with the remainder of Squadron to Lerwick to coal.

23. Tuesday, 18th August – I landed three field guns from Squadron for the use of the local Defence Force under Colonel Evans, RMLI. *Theseus* and *Grafton* having completed with coal sailed at 10 p.m. to southern portion of patrol. *Dryad* sailed with me for Scapa Flow at noon. *Edgar* having completed with coal sailed at 6 p.m. for northern portion of patrol off Norwegian Coast. At 7.45 p.m., the Armed Merchant Ship *Alsatian* (commanded by Captain Valentine Phillimore,

[1]Evans, Horace C., Lieutenant-Colonel, RMLI, in command of RNR troops in the Shetlands from August 1914.

RN)[1] arrived. Having given him orders to proceed on southern portion of patrol at 9 a.m. on 19th August, I left Lerwick in *Crescent* which had completed with coal and proceeded to join the Division on southern portion of patrol.

24. Wednesday, 19th August – Having been joined by *Grafton* and *Theseus* at W.6, I proceeded towards Nord Fjord on the Norwegian Coast. At 1.30 p.m. *Edgar*, *Hawke* and *Royal Arthur* were met with and the whole Squadron then steered SW to meet *Alsatian* at X.7. *Alsatian* was sighted at 4.15 p.m. and steamed in company with Squadron. The ships of Norwegian patrol parted company at 6 p.m. and returned to their station, and *Alsatian* was detached to patrol from northern point of Shetlands to X.6. I proceeded with First Division S 75° W to resume duty on Shetland Patrol.

25. In consequence of the addition of Armed Merchant Ships to the Squadron under my Command I considered it desirable to somewhat revise the arrangements for carrying out the 'Northern Patrol'. I therefore issued the enclosed orders for information of the Squadron [2].

26. Thursday, 20th August – *Dryad* arrived 10 miles SW of V.3 noon with mails, and returned to Scapa Flow. At 4 p.m. the Norwegian Steamer *Bergensfjord*, New York to Bergen, was met with and visited in Lat. 60.41´N, Long. 0.30´E. The Master stated that in the event of falling in with a German Ship of War he expected to be captured on account of his cargo which largely consisted of flour. As, however, the ship was not proceeding to a Dutch port, I did not detain her.[2] Various other vessels were visited but without result as regards news or contraband.

27. Friday, 21st August – *Endymion* and *Gibraltar* rejoined my Flag after service with 6th Cruiser Squadron. During the forenoon all ships present carried out practice with aiming rifle. The *Gibraltar* left to rejoin Second Division on Norwegian Patrol, releasing *Royal Arthur* which proceeded to Busta Voe to coal, and *Grafton* was detached from First Division to Lerwick for the same purpose. At 6 p.m., the

[1]Phillimore, Valentine Egerton Bagot, CBE, DSO, RN (1873–1945); Lieutenant 1894, Commander 1905, Captain 1913, Captain in *Alsatian* and *Motagua* 1914–1915, in command of Auxiliary Patrol area 1915–1916, SNO West Coast of Africa 1916–1919, SNO Genoa 1918–1919, retired 1922.

[2]It is interesting, to say the least, that as early as this de Chair should single out the *Bergensfjord* for particular mention; the ship, and its sisters in the Norwegian–America Line, became notorious in the patrol for ignoring British demands, or, as the British put it, 'evading' the patrol. De Chair's comment on the ship's destination is also an indication that British preoccupations with stopping German trade were still limited to one neutral state, The Netherlands.

Norwegian Steamer *Norueca* from Galveston to Amsterdam was boarded by *Crescent* in Lat. 60.44´N, Long. 1.20´E. The Captain stated he had received orders by wireless during the morning diverting his ship to Christiania whither he proposed to proceed. Two German Stokers found on board were made prisoners, and the ship was allowed to continue her voyage.

28. Saturday, 22nd August – Aiming rifle practice was again carried out during the forenoon by 1st Division, and *Alsatian* reported satisfactory trial of gun mountings. *Dryad* arrived (10 miles SW of V.3) with despatches and mails from Scapa Flow and was again detached for that Port.

29. Sunday, 23rd August – I quitted Southern area of patrol at 8 a.m., leaving *Endymion* and *Theseus*, and proceeded to the Norwegian area where I met and communicated with my Second Division and learned from the Senior Officer that according to reports from vessels boarded very few ships remained in White Sea. He had also been informed that a large number of German Steamers were lying inside the Islands with no crews or cargoes and that these ships would probably remain there during the war. After leaving the Second Division I proceeded to meet *Alsatian* at a rendezvous N 65° E, 10 miles from W.6, where I gave her instructions to proceed as directed by Commander-in-Chief to rendezvous 20 miles west from Udsire Island Lighthouse at 6 a.m. on Monday, 24th August, and place herself under the orders of the Rear-Admiral Commanding Sixth Cruiser Squadron. I then returned to the Southern area and rejoined my First Division.

30. Monday, 24th August – *Royal Arthur* having completed with coal rejoined Second Division on Norwegian patrol, relieving *Hawke* which proceeded to Lerwick to coal and receive supplies. *Grafton* having completed with coal at Lerwick rejoined First Division. At 8.30 a.m. I parted company with *Endymion* and *Grafton*, and proceeded with *Theseus* to Lerwick where I found *Forward* and Supply Ship No 16 (*Alcinous*). The Armed Merchant Ship *Mantua* (Captain Charles Tibbits, MVO)[1] arrived at 9 p.m. She was ordered to patrol on the Parallel 60° N from 0 to 4.30´E at 14 knots (Area M.C.3.) leaving Lerwick at 2 p.m. on 25th August. I remained the night at Lerwick to enable *Crescent* to receive her stores from Supply Ship, and took the opportunity to consult with Lieut. Colonel Evans, RMLI, as to the

[1]Tibbitts, Charles, CBE, MVO, RN (1872–1947); Commander 1905, Captain 1914, Captain in *Mantua*, August 1914 and April 1916, Captain of *Cyclops* and in charge of repair work 1916 at Scapa, Captain of Portsmouth Dockyard 1920, Rear-Admiral (retired) 1924, Vice-Admiral 1929.

berthing of seaplanes and the general scheme of defence of the Shetlands. He informed me that satisfactory arrangements could be made for berthing two seaplanes in the harbour, and that he had now enrolled some 70 men in the Special RNR Force for defence and look-out purposes. These with the local Territorial Detachment, made up a total of some 240 men who with the help of the Field Guns already landed would be able to offer an effective resistance to a raiding force until help should be forthcoming.

31. Tuesday, 25th August – *Hawke* arrived Lerwick at 6 a.m. and commenced coaling and receiving stores from Supply Ship. Before leaving I went on board *Mantua* and inspected her fighting arrangements and Ship's Company. These ships have a great deal of unused accommodation which could easily be fitted up for the conveyance of wounded after a fleet action. I left Lerwick in *Crescent* at 10.0 a.m and rejoined my First Division at V.4. at 4.0 p.m. proceeding on Shetland patrol area.

32. Wednesday, 26th August – In compliance with orders from Commander-in-Chief [5] to withdraw Northern Patrol except Merchant Auxiliaries, I took steps to concentrate the ships of 10th Cruiser Squadron and proceeded with *Endymion* and *Grafton* by way of Muckle Flugga and West Coast of Shetlands or Scapa Flow. Owing to dense fog met with to the North and West of Shetlands it was not possible to assemble the whole Squadron, and I therefore directed Second Division and *Hawke* to proceed independently to Scapa Flow, and to arrive during forenoon of 27th August. Supply Ship No. 16 (*Alcinous*) and colliers at Lerwick and Busta Voe were also ordered to proceed to Scapa Flow.

33. Thursday, 27th August – I arrived at Scapa Flow at 7.0 a.m. where I found the Flag of the Commander-in-Chief. *Hawke* had already anchored. *Theseus* arrived at 8.0 a.m., and *Edgar*, *Royal Arthur* and *Gibraltar* at 9.30 a.m. All ships proceeded to coal and complete with stores from Supply Ship which arrived from Lerwick.

2. *Revised Arrangements for Cruiser Force B.*

19 August 1914

Cruiser Force B
Ships available ... Eight '*Edgar*' Class.
Four Armed Merchant Ships.[1]
'*Dryad*'.

General Remarks

As ships of Cruiser Force B, except the Armed Merchant ships, have only slow speed and require time to gain full speed they should not be spread more than five miles apart, day or night. This will enable a concentration to be effected before getting into effective gun range with enemy war vessels.

Patrols

The Norwegian Patrol
The number of ships available is four *Edgar* class. (Note, one will always be away coaling.)
Disposition. The Eastern ship will work on a line N 37° E and S 33° W (Mag). The southern position of this ship to be Lat 61.30´N, Long 4.8´E. The other ships to be spread on a line of bearing west (Mag) approximately from the eastern ship.

The northern limit of the patrol to be Lat. 62.30'N. During darkness ships should turn together at pre-arranged times so as to preserve their time of bearing. Distance apart 5 miles.

This disposition will enable a close watch to be kept on the coast of Norway.

The Shetland Patrol
Ships available ... Four *Edgar* class. (One will always be away coaling.)

This patrol will work in the neighbourhood of the Outer Skerries in a north easterly direction, and as far as Lat. 61.30´N, Long. 3.00´E to enable it to meet the Norwegian Patrol. Ships five miles apart in line ahead. Cruise N 76° E and S 76° W (Mag).

Armed Merchant Ships
Number available ... Four.

One will coal at a time, probably at Liverpool.

These ships will patrol from the Northern point of the Shetlands to Lat.

[1]Only *Alsatian* was present at this time, and *Mantua* from 24 August.

61.30´N, Long. 2.00´E at economical speed (about 16 knots). With two ships available they will patrol between Northern point of the Shetlands and Lat. 62 N, Long. 3.00´E. With more than two ships available, one or two will be placed on a more southerly patrol line running East and West. These ships have considerable speed and small fighting value; their duty is to report and shadow enemy war vessels and stop and examine all merchant shipping. They are to divide the area to be patrolled by them. *Dryad* will be used for communication between Cruisers and the base at Scapa Flow.

Coaling

Ships of Shetland Patrol will coal at Lerwick, those of Norwegian Patrol at Busta Voe. This arrangement will, however, depend on the weather.

3. *Rear Admiral de Chair to 'The Officers Commanding HM Ships and Vessels under my orders'*

HMS *Crescent*, 22 August 1914

The following details of limits of areas to be patrolled by HM Ships under my orders are promulgated for consideration and guidance:-

Area Y

Northern Limit 62.30´

Southern Limit 61.30´

Eastern Limit N 26° E from Long. 4.00´E.

Western Limit N 36° E from Long. 2.00´E.

The Areas SD 1 & 2, MC 1, 2 & 3 are formed by parallelograms whose adjacent sides are as follows:

Area SD 1

N 59° E 125 miles and S 29° E from Out Skerries light.

Area SD 2

N 18° E 90 miles and S 72° E 20 miles from Lat. 59.32´N, Long. 1.20´W.

Area MC 1

N 20° W 10 miles and N 65° E 94 miles from Muckle Flugga light.

Area MC 2

N 55° E 105 miles and North 10 miles from Lat. 61.30´N, Long. 00.00´.

Area MC 3

East 120 miles and North 10 miles from Lat. 60.00´N, Long. 00.00´.

All bearings are true.

4. *Commander-in-Chief Grand Fleet to Rear-Admiral de Chair*

HMS *Iron Duke*, 26 August 1914

The Tenth Cruiser Squadron has been withdrawn from the Northern Patrol [1 para. 32].

2. Area VI. Base line N 50° E (true) from Buchan Ness. Ends of base 20 to 150 miles from Buchan Ness; the area to extend 50 miles S 40° E from the base.

3. The Sixth and Tenth Cruiser Squadrons will work in Area VI under Rear-Admiral Commanding Sixth Cruiser Squadron ('*Drake*') who will arrange that under normal conditions two ships are at Scapa coaling and eight are working in the area.

***

7. *Alsatian* and *Mantua* and any other armed cruisers added to the Grand Fleet will form the Northern Patrol and cover the Shetlands. *Forward* and four destroyers will be based on the Shetlands for patrol duties as herebefore. The Rear-Admiral Commanding Tenth Cruiser Squadron is requested to give the necessary instructions to the Senior Officer of the Armed Merchant Cruisers.

5. *Rear-Admiral de Chair to Admiralty*

HMS *Crescent*, 1 October 1914

Report of Proceedings, 28 August–30 September 1914

***

1. Friday, 28th August – At 9.30 a.m. in accordance with orders received from the Commander-in-Chief [4], I left Scapa Flow in *Crescent* with *Grafton*, *Theseus*, *Royal Arthur* and *Hawke* to patrol Area VII, working with the 6th Cruiser Squadron for the purpose. *Endymion* and *Edgar* remained at Scapa to complete with coal and stores, and *Gibraltar* was under orders to proceed the same afternoon to Hebburn to dock. *Oceanic* sailed from Scapa Flow for Northern Patrol at 10.30 a.m. The *Alsatian* and *Mantua* were already on their beat. Supply ship No. 16 (*Alcinous*) left for Cromarty at 11.30 a.m. During the afternoon I received a message from *Gibraltar* informing me that in compliance with further Admiralty orders, the ship was sailing for Rosyth. At 7.00 p.m. I parted company with my Second Division which proceeded to the Eastern half of Area VI.

2. Saturday, 29th August – At 4.00 a.m. both Divisions commenced patrol ... In compliance with directions from the Commander-in-Chief, I detached *Theseus* at 6.30 a.m. to proceed to Scapa to coal preparatory to convoying steamers loaded with coal and other munitions of war to the White Sea for the use of the Russians. During the afternoon the Second Cruiser Squadron passed through Area VI proceeding towards the Norwegian Coast to take up station in Area V. *Gibraltar* reported arrival at Queensferry at 4.53 p.m. She also informed me that on examination the combustion chamber of one boiler was nearly closed, everything being clinkered including lowest tube.

3. Sunday, 30th August – *Endymion* re-joined First Division and *Edgar* Second Division.

4. Monday, 31st August – *Grafton* and *Royal Arthur* were detached from First and Second Divisions respectively and proceeded to Cromarty for Coal and Stores. Sixth Cruiser Squadron which had been patrolling to northward of my Squadron was withdrawn from Area VI, and from noon the area itself was re-constituted as follows by signal from Commander-in-Chief:

Baseline N 30° E (true) from a point 20 miles N 50° E (true) Buchan Ness. Ends of base 20 to 130 miles from Buchan Ness; the area to extend 50 miles S 60° E (true) from the base.

This adjustment was made in order to cover the area throughout which minelayers proceeding to mine the vicinity of the Pentlands would pass a few hours before dark and after daylight. Cruisers occupying the area were directed to be on the outer limit at 4.00 a.m. steaming towards Scapa Flow, and on the inner limit at 6.00 p.m. steaming to seaward, at other times cruising as necessary. During the forenoon *Crescent* and *Endymion* carried out practice with Aiming Rifle and Small Guns. At 4.00 p.m. I was joined by my Second Division (*Edgar* and *Hawke*). Squadron proceeded in company. The Armed Merchant Ship *Alsatian* quitted Northern Patrol and proceeded to Liverpool to coal.

5. Tuesday, 1st September – At 4.00 a.m. in accordance with orders received from the Commander-in-Chief, I arrived at a rendezvous Lat. 57.10´N, Long. 1.0´E. Supported by Third Battle Squadron, 10 miles in rear, I proceeded to sweep towards Pentland Firth, ships spread N 48° E and S 48° W at 10 knots. At 9.30 a.m. First Battle Cruiser Squadron was observed ahead. At noon I received orders to return to Eastern half of Area VI, and I accordingly altered course with my Squadron to S 42° E and proceeded at 8 knots. During the afternoon the weather became thick. From date of taking station in Area VI many vessels were boarded, mostly of Norwegian nationality. The Armed Merchant

Cruiser *Oceanic* proceeded to Thurso in compliance with directions from the Commander-in-Chief, to convey passengers to Faroe Islands [7]. *Gibraltar* reported departure from Rosyth to dock at Hebburn.

6. Wednesday, 2nd September – *Endymion* and *Dryad*, the latter bringing despatches and mails from Cromarty, joined me at 4.30 a.m. at the extreme SE limit of area. *Dryad* returned to Cromarty and Squadron proceeded on patrol, ships spread. In compliance with orders from the Commander-in-Chief, I proceeded to a rendezvous Lat. 58.30´N, Long. 00 W at 3.30 p.m. when I met Second and Third Cruiser Squadrons and Second Flotilla of Destroyers and communicated, receiving despatches. At 6.30 p.m. Sixth Cruiser Squadron was sighted and arrangements for continuing the combined patrol were made by signal. These arrangements provided for the patrol of SE portion of area by Tenth Cruiser Squadron supported by Sixth Cruiser Squadron 30 miles in rear. *Oceanic* reported her departure from Thurso for Faroe Islands at 6.30 a.m., and *Gibraltar* her arrival in Tyne at 7.30 a.m. The latter also reported that an attempt to dock her at Hebburn had failed, fortunately without accident, and she hoped to dock on Friday, 4th September. *Theseus* reported departure from Scapa for White Sea at 2.40 p.m. *Royal Arthur* and *Grafton* left Cromarty to rejoin my Flag at 5.00 p.m.

7. Thursday, 3rd September – *Royal Arthur* and *Grafton* rejoined my Flag from Cromarty at 6.00 a.m. After communicating for transfer of despatches and mails the patrol was resumed at 10 knots and zig-zagging to avoid submarines as directed by Commander-in-Chief. At 4.00 p.m. further orders were received from the Commander-in-Chief in compliance with which the Squadron under my command proceeded to patrol in SW portion of Area VI supported by Sixth Cruiser Squadron. Many vessels were boarded during the day but no news of importance was obtained.

8. Friday, 4th September – *Hawke* was detached from the Squadron at 10.15 p.m., to complete with coal at Cromarty.

9. Saturday, 5th September – *Edgar* was detached to Cromarty to coal at 5.00 a.m. In compliance with an urgent message from the Commander-in-Chief, received at 7.30 a.m., I spread my Squadron and proceeded with all despatch to eastward in search of an enemy's cruiser reported by *Naiad* and *Thetis* in Lat. 58.54´N, Long. 2.13´W. At 10.30 a.m. Commander-in-Chief ordered chase to be abandoned, and I thereupon resumed patrol. The vessel reported would appear to have been HMS *Swift*. At noon I received a message from the Commander-in-Chief stating that *Drake* would leave Area VI at 2.00 a.m. 6th September, leaving *King Alfred* under my orders. Large numbers of vessels – mostly of Norwegian or Danish nationality – were boarded

without result. *Dryad* arrived from Cromarty at 12.30 p.m., with despatches and mails for Squadron and returned to that port. During the afternoon *Endymion* carried out Torpedo Practice. At 1.00 p.m. the First Light Cruiser Squadron passed, steering for Rosyth.

10. Sunday, 6th September – At 5.14 p.m. *Gibraltar* rejoined Squadron from Hebburn where she had been docked. *Dryad* arrived with despatches and mails for Squadron at 6.30 p.m., and returned to Cromarty. *King Alfred* joined me at rendezvous Lat. 58 N, Long. 1 W at 1.00 p.m. when I gave her necessary orders for cruising in support of Tenth Cruiser Squadron. I left Squadron in *Crescent* at 10.00 p.m. and shaped course for Cromarty.

11. Monday, 7th September – At 10.00 a.m. *Crescent* arrived and anchored off Invergordon and proceeded to coal. Second and Third Cruiser Squadrons and *Edgar* were in harbour. The latter sailed to rejoin Tenth Cruiser Squadron at 6.00 p.m.

12. Tuesday, 8th September – Second and Third Cruiser Squadrons left Cromarty at 7.30 a.m. *King Alfred* was directed by me to proceed to Scapa Flow to complete with coal at midnight. At 1.00 p.m. I received information that *Oceanic* was ashore at Hoevdi Grund, 2½ miles E by S from Southness, Foula Island, Shetlands. I at once sent a message to the Commander-in-Chief asking whether I should send a ship of the Tenth Cruiser Squadron to assist her, but he informed me that a battleship had been ordered to the scene.[1] *Dryad* sailed at 6.20 p.m. with despatches and mails for Tenth Cruiser Squadron, and *Endymion* arrived to coal at 7.30 p.m.

13. Wednesday, 9th September – During the early morning a signal was received from the Armed Cruiser *Alsatian* stating that *Oceanic* had become a total wreck, and that crew were on board *Alsatian*. I informed the Commander-in-Chief, and he approved of my sending *Alsatian* to Liverpool to land crew. Later in the morning *Endymion* reported that *Royal Arthur* when proceeding to examine the Swedish Steamer *Tua* of Gothenburg, had rammed and sunk that vessel. Two of the crew were reported missing. I directed *Endymion* to send *Royal Arthur* to Cromarty with the survivors. I left Cromarty in *Crescent* at 10.00 a.m. and proceeded to Area VI, arranging a rendezvous with Squadron at Q.4, at 6.00 a.m. on Thursday, 10th September.

14. Thursday, 10th September – At 6.00 p.m. I rejoined Squadron at rendezvous and proceeded on patrol, boarding merchant ships and

[1] *Oceanic* was the largest ship wrecked in the Shetlands until that time. A single blade of her propeller is displayed, set in concrete, outside the Shetland Museum in Lerwick.

searching for floating mines in accordance with directions from the Commander-in-Chief. I was informed by *Edgar* that Squadron had been searching for mines the previous day in area indicated by Commander-in-Chief, but that none had been found. Numerous fishing buoys similar to those reported as 'floating mines' had however, been seen, and several sunk or picked up. *Dryad* returned to Cromarty at 7.00 a.m. and *Grafton* was detached to that port to coal at 5.00 p.m.

15. Friday, 11th September – At 5.00 p.m. *Gibraltar* was detached from Squadron and proceeded to Cromarty to coal. Several fishing buoys were sunk during the day.

16. Saturday, 12th September – *King Alfred* and *Endymion*, the former from Scapa, and the latter from Cromarty, joined me at Q.4 at 5.20 a.m. I directed *King Alfred* to proceed to Lat. 59.19´N, Long. 0.52´E and search for Buoys, Casks or Floats and then patrol on base line A.B.C. *Dryad* arrived from Cromarty with despatches, mails and provisions for Squadron and returned. *Royal Arthur* rejoined Squadron from Cromarty at 8.30 a.m. and *Edgar* was detached to coal at that port at 5.40 p.m.

17. Sunday, 13th September – Having received orders from the Commander-in-Chief to look out for Norwegian Steamer *Klosterfos* I proceeded on a N by W Course. Squadron passed through a supposed mine area in Lat. 59.25´N, Long. 10.30´E during the forenoon. Many fishing buoys were sighted and sunk by rifle fire, but no actual signs of mines were discovered. These buoys which as a rule were conical wooden ones with a length of two inch rope attached had probably broken adrift from fishing nets or had been abandoned by fishing boats. They were in several cases marked 'O.B.33' and some had 'R.F.' and a crowned eagle cut or burned on inside of wood. At noon *Endymion* boarded a Norwegian sailing vessel bound for Hamburg with a cargo of salted hides. She produced a Green Certificate from Customs Authorities at Falmouth dated 4th September. Before allowing her to proceed I communicated with the Commander-in-Chief who directed that she should not be detained. The Armed Merchant Ships *Alsatian* and *Mantua* received orders from the Commander-in-Chief to patrol on a line 120 miles long from Muckle Flugga, one ship being sent every three days to patrol for one day during daylight to west of line joining Orkneys and Sogne Voen Fjord.

18. Monday, 14th September – *Grafton* rejoined Squadron from Cromarty at 5.00 a.m. and *Hawke* was detached to coal at Cromarty at 7.30 a.m.

19. Tuesday, 15th September – *Gibraltar* rejoined Squadron from Cromarty at 8.0 a.m. The state of the weather precluded boarding until

the evening, but few vessels were met with during the day. Ships spread.

20. Wednesday, 16th September – After communicating with the Rear-Admiral of the 6th Cruiser Squadron and with *Edgar* which had arrived in patrol area from Cromarty I proceeded in *Crescent* to Cromarty arriving before dark. Second Cruiser Squadron and *Hawke* were in harbour.

21. Thursday, 17th September – *Crescent* completed with coal. *Hawke* sailed during the afternoon to rejoin patrol.

22. Friday, 18th September – *Endymion* arrived at 9.0 a.m., and completed with coal. At 6.30 p.m. *Dryad* proceeded to sea with despatches, mails and provisions for Tenth Cruiser Squadron.

23. Saturday, 19th September – *Sappho* arrived Cromarty at 8.0 a.m., having been directed by the Commander-in-Chief to place herself under my orders. She proceeded to complete with coal and I gave her orders to join Tenth Cruiser Squadron on patrol on Tuesday 22nd September. *Royal Arthur* arrived at 5.30 p.m. to coal, and I left in *Crescent* at 5.45 p.m., and proceeded to Area VI to join Squadron.

24. Sunday, 20th September – *King Alfred* having reported that she had been ordered to return into harbour on my arrival on patrol area, I directed her to proceed to Scapa Flow to coal, arriving there before dark. I rejoined my Squadron at 11.0 a.m. and proceeded to patrol to NNW. The weather was very rough with heavy seas and *Edgar* reported that it had been impossible to board ships since the previous Thursday night. Finding that *Dryad* had been unable to communicate with Squadron on account of the weather conditions I sent her to Peterhead with orders to return to Cromarty.

At 6.30 p.m. I detached *Edgar* to dock and coal in the Tyne (directing her to call at Rosyth for orders as to approaching Tyne) and *Grafton* to Cromarty to coal. *Teutonic* informed me that she would be on cruising ground during the night and gave her position at 8.0 p.m. Lat. 60.36´N, Long. 00.36´W. I therefore concluded that she had joined the Armed Merchant Vessels under my orders on Northern Patrol, though I had received no orders on the subject.

25. Monday, 21st September – *Endymion* rejoined my Flag from Cromarty at 3.0 p.m. She reported having boarded ten ships since leaving Cromarty.

26. Tuesday, 22nd September – *Gibraltar* was detached at 5.0 a.m. to coal at Cromarty, and *Sappho* joined Squadron from Cromarty at 10.0 a.m. Squadron carried out aiming rifle practice during forenoon. Several vessels were boarded and information was given by the Captain of a Danish Steamer which frequently visited the Baltic that the Germans appeared to have recently abandoned those waters.

27. Wednesday, 23rd September – At 3.0 a.m. signal from the Commander-in-Chief was passed to *Teutonic* directing that Armed Merchant Ships should at once move to a position off Trondhjem to intercept the German Liner *Brandenburg* which was reported likely to sail from that port. *Teutonic* reported that *Alsatian* had been detached from Northern Patrol to coal at Liverpool. *Royal Arthur* rejoined from Cromarty at 10.0 a.m. and target practice was carried out, ships spread five miles apart. Squadron resumed patrol at noon at 10 knots, course S 74° W zig-zagging to avoid submarines reported proceeding in direction of area. In compliance with signal from the Commander-in-Chief I continued on course S 52° W until 10.0 p.m. when altered to NNE.

28. Thursday, 24th September – Several fishing and other vessels were examined and boarded. Those fishing outside the limits laid down were ordered out of the prohibited area. *Grafton* rejoined Squadron from Cromarty at 10.30 a.m. and *Hawke* was detached to that port to coal at 12.30 p.m.

29. Friday, 25th September – In compliance with directions received from the Commander-in-Chief Home Fleets, *Sappho* was detached from Squadron with orders to proceed to Scapa Flow, and *Dryad* which was at Cromarty was directed to proceed to the same destination. Target Practice with heavy and light guns was carried out during the forenoon.

30. Saturday, 26th September – *Gibraltar* rejoined Squadron from Cromarty at 8.0 a.m., and *Edgar* from Newcastle-on-Tyne at 9.0 a.m. *Endymion* was detached to Cromarty to coal at 10.0 a.m. Several vessels were boarded until state of weather (strong north easter with blinding rain squalls) precluded lowering of boats when examination only was carried out.

31. Sunday, 27th September – The weather continuing bad no boarding was carried out but various steamers and fishing craft were examined.

32. Monday, 28th September – I parted company with my Squadron at 8.0 a.m. and proceeded to Cromarty to coal and repair defects. I was unable to make the harbour during daylight as it became necessary to ease speed on account of the heavy sea running and the racing of the main engines.

33. Tuesday, 29th September – *Crescent* arrived at Cromarty at 8.0 a.m. and proceeded to coal. *Hawke* had left to rejoin Squadron the previous evening and *Endymion* was in harbour, but left to rejoin Squadron at 6.0 p.m. The Second Cruiser Squadron was also present.

34. Wednesday, 30th September – *Royal Arthur* arrived to coal and repair defects.

***

6. *Commander-in-Chief Home Fleets to Rear Admiral 10th Cruiser Squadron*

29 August 1914

Admiralty telegraph by wire as follows – Begins

'The Russians are placing a large order for coal from Blyth and Cardiff, one of the Colliers left on 18th for Archangel, others are leaving Blyth today, stop. Archangel is their only free port, they are also sending important consignment of guns, stop. You are to send one of the *Edgar* class to complete with coal forthwith and then order her to proceed North calling at Alexandrovsk[1] for information as to whether any enemy's ships have been in the White Sea. If there are no signs of the enemy, ship can return, rendering all assistance possible to vessels en route. List of vessels will be sent by post'.[2] Ends.

Detail a Ship with reliable engines, sending her to Scapa to coal at once and report her name.

7. *Captain W.J. Slayter[3] to the Rear-Admiral Commanding the 10th Cruiser Squadron*

HMS *Oceanic*, at Lerwick, 6 September 1914

I have the honour to report that on Tuesday, 1st September, in accordance with orders received from the Commander-in-Chief I embarked at 6.30 p.m. Mr Cable from Thurso, for passage to the Faroe Islands. It was necessary for *Oceanic* to remain at Thurso until 6 a.m. on the 2nd September to receive charts of the Faroe Islands, which were delivered at that hour by HM Destroyer *Ure*. At 6.30 a.m., *Oceanic* weighed and proceeded to the Faroe Islands, where she arrived 5.30 a.m. on the 3rd September.

I communicated with Mr Coats, the Consul, who informed me that

[1]Alexandrovsk is the pre-revolutionary name for Murmansk, which was developed as a port at British request during the war; cf. N. Stone, *The Eastern Front 1914–1917* (London, 1975), 158–159.

[2]In the event no list was sent: Commander-in-Chief to *Theseus*, 2 September: 'Proceed at once without waiting for list of vessels' (ADM 137/1943, 177). This is the first of a long series of detachments which the C-in-C or the Admiralty imposed on the Squadron. *Theseus* was sent in this case and had a confusing time in northern Russia, beset by Admiralty errors and changes of instructions (cf ADM 137/2943, 177–187).

[3]Slayter, W.J., RN, Captain 1907, Captain of *Oceanic* 1914, Captain HM Dockyard Rosyth 1915–1918, Rear-Admiral 1918, Admiral Superintendent Tyne and Liverpool ports 1918–1920.

no German Man-of-War or Merchant ships had visited the Faroe Islands recently. He also informed me that he was in telephonic communication with the outlying Islands and there was no report of any German craft having been in the vicinity lately. The only part of which he could not be sure was the Island of Sydero, to which there was no telephone. I requested leave from the Governor to be allowed to proceed round about the Islands, but the Governor expressed the wish that the strict Law of Neutrality should be observed, and that I should leave the Faroe Islands twenty-four hours after arrival. Under the circumstances I got away at 4 p.m. and proceeded to Sydero, where I arrived at 6.20 p.m. and sent an Officer to interview the acting Sheriff, who was able to tell him that no German Man-of-War or Merchant ships had been in the vicinity of the Island recently.

At 5 a.m. on the morning of the 4th September in accordance with the wish of the Governor of the Faroe Islands, I proceeded out of Trangisvaag at 14 knots, and returned to my Patrol off Muckle Flugga, where I have since remained until 11.39 a.m. on the 6th September, when I proceeded into Lerwick to pick up mails and communicate with *Mantua*.

I am proceeding at 6 p.m. 6th September to Patrol on a line 30 miles West of Fair Island; the *Mantua* is proceeding at the same hour to the Muckle Flugga patrol where she will remain until 8 p.m. on the 7th September, or until relieved by HMS *Alsatian*.

On the arrival of HMS *Alsatian*, the *Mantua* proceeds to Liverpool to complete with coal.

HMS *Forward* and four destroyers are employed on the Orkneys Patrol, and have nothing to report as to the presence of the enemy in those waters.[1]

8. *Commander-in-Chief Grand Fleet to Rear-Admiral Commanding Tenth Cruiser Squadron*

HMS *Iron Duke*, 18 September 1914

The Northern Patrol (Cruiser Force B) consists of the Tenth Cruiser Squadron and such Armed Merchant Cruisers as may be attached to it, at present *Teutonic*, *Mantua* and *Alsatian*, the whole force being under the orders of the Rear-Admiral Commanding Tenth Cruiser Squadron.

[1]Coates had been consul in Iceland and the Faeroes since 1907; Cable was now appointed to Iceland; Coates remained in the Faeroes until 1916. Cable's work in Iceland effectively brought the island into satellite status of Britain for the duration of the war.

2. The Tenth Cruiser Squadron is temporarily withdrawn from the Northern Area, and is working in Area VI off Cromarty Firth ...

In the absence of the Rear-Admiral Commanding Tenth Cruiser Squadron, the senior officer of the armed cruisers will take charge of the Northern Area and may receive orders either from the Rear-Admiral Commanding Tenth Cruiser Squadron or direct from the Commander-in-Chief.

3. The Armed Cruisers will patrol a line 120 miles east (magnetic) from Muckle Flugga, one ship being detached every three days to patrol for one day during daylight to the eastward of the line joining the Orkneys and Shetlands, this ship may call for mails at Lerwick on the way.

4. The Armed Cruisers are to coal at Liverpool and the Senior Officer is to inform the Rear-Admiral Commanding Tenth Cruiser Squadron and the Commander-in-Chief at least 48 hours before it is necessary for a ship to quit the Northern Area for this purpose.

5. The *Alsatian* and *Mantua* will be temporarily employed with the Rear-Admiral HMS *Drake* between the 19th and the 21st, patrolling the Norwegian coast.[1]

9. *Rear-Admiral de Chair to Admiralty*

HMS *Crescent*, 1 November 1914

Report of Proceedings, 2–31 October 1914

***

1. Friday, 2nd October – *Crescent* having coaled and repaired defects in main engines I proceeded with 10th Cruiser Squadron to comply with signal received from Commander-in-Chief of September 30th directing that stations ordered by Operations Order No. 14 should be taken up at 8.0 a.m. on Saturday 3rd October. Ships were ordered to be in the following positions by the time stated.

Crescent *Grafton*	Lat. 58.32´N, Long. 2.19´E.
Edgar *Hawke* *Endymion*	12 miles S 67° W (true) from *Crescent*.

[1]*Drake* was Rear-Admiral Grant's flagship (see p. 28 note 1).

Gibraltar } 24 miles S 67° W (true) from *Crescent*.

Edgar reported the following proceedings of Squadrons during my absence: 'Weather remained very bad on Monday, slightly improved on Tuesday. We were ordered to look out for enemy's submarine parent ship at S end of Area I on Tuesday morning without success. Tuesday at 11.0 a.m. ordered to return to Area VI, shortly afterwards to intercept a strange cruiser reported at 9.30 a.m. 7 miles off Grumbriggs near Stonehaven steering to the northward at full speed. *Nottingham* and Minelayers also joined in but nothing was seen by nightfall. Since then have been patrolling Area VI; very few steamers met with, no news ...'

The movements of the Armed Merchant Ships on Northern Patrol from last reports received appear to be as follows:

Teutonic ... 30th September – Patrolling 30 miles off probable exit of Bergen, stopping close in at night, in order to intercept *Prince Frederick Wilhelm*.

Mantua ... Northern Patrol.

Alsatian ... 23rd September, left Northern Patrol to coal at Liverpool.

2. Saturday, 3rd October – At 8.0 a.m. my Squadron was disposed as ordered and course was shaped S 8° E speed 12 knots, zig-zagging to avoid submarines until 1.30 p.m., when speed was reduced to 11 knots owing to state of weather. Squadron turned 16 points and proceeded N 8° W at 9 knots in order to cross Northern Base Line of Area 5 at 10 a.m. on 4th October, as ordered by Commander-in-Chief's signal.

3. Sunday, 4th October – *Royal Arthur* rejoined Squadron at 6.15 a.m. taking the place of *Grafton* which was detached to Cromarty to coal at 6.40 a.m. Course and speed of Squadron were arranged with a view to crossing the northern base line of Area V Latitude 58.19´N, Longitude 2 E and Squadron proceeded at full speed. Signal was however negatived a quarter of an hour later. The Northern base line of Area V was again crossed – going north – at 10.0 p.m. going south at 10.0 a.m. and the sweep to the southwards was continued until 4.0 p.m., when I turned and proceeded N 12° W.

4. Monday, 5th October – At 8.30 a.m. squadron turned to S 5° E, and proceeded at 12 knots, zig-zagging. In accordance with orders from Commander-in-Chief the northern base line of Area V was crossed at noon and course was continued for 40 miles. At 4.0 p.m., Squadron again turned to N 8° W. At Noon *Gibraltar* was detached to coal and make good defects at Scapa Flow.

At 10.0 a.m. *Crescent* boarded the British SS *Manchester Civilian* bound from Buenos Ayres to Gothenburg with 6800 tons of maize and 500 tons of bran, consigned to orders. The Captain stated that he had been detained for three days at Kirkwall by the orders of the Commander-in-Chief and released on 4th October. While at Kirkwall he received a telegram from his owners urging him to proceed, he also stated that he had been chased by the *Cap Trafalgar* on leaving the American Coast.[1] In view of the fact that the ship had been detained and released I allowed her to proceed though there appeared little doubt as to the ultimate destination of the cargo as it is known that large shipments of cereals for Germany are being obtained from South America.

5. Tuesday, 6th October – The Northern Base Line of Area V was crossed at 11.00 a.m., and the Squadron proceeded to the Southward until 4.30 p.m. when course was shaped N 8° W. *Edgar* and *Royal Arthur* changed places in the line.

At 5.0 p.m. orders were received to chase towards Latitude 58.19´N, Longitude 2 E and squadron proceeded at full speed. Signal was however recaptured a quarter of an hour later. The Northern base line of Area V was again crossed – going North – at 10.00 p.m.

6. Wednesday, 7th October – At 5.0 a.m. Squadron turned to south and crossed northern base line of Area V at 11.30 a.m. Second Cruiser Squadron having been detached to Cromarty to coal the southern line of patrol now consisted of First Light Cruiser Squadron, Tenth Cruiser Squadron (five ships), *Russell* class (three ships) and Third Cruiser Squadron – from West to East in the order given. Ships turned to the north in time to recross northern base line at 9.0 p.m.

At 10.0 a.m. I detached *Edgar* to Cromarty to complete with coal.

A report was received from *Hawke* that she had sighted a copper cylinder about 10 feet long and 20 inches in diameter floating vertically about 3 feet out of the water, painted white at upper end. After examination it was sunk by gun fire. It was considered probable that this was part of the petrol tank of a wrecked aeroplane.

7. Thursday, 8th October – In accordance with orders from the Commander-in-Chief, Squadron turned to South at 6.0 a.m. crossing northern base line of Area V at 2.0 p.m., and recrossing – going north – at 6.0 p.m. *Hawke* reported that she had picked up a large pontoon similar to that carried by large passenger ships, consisting of a batten framework round six copper air vessels like the cylinder mentioned in para. 6.

Hawke was detached to Cromarty to coal at 9.30 p.m.

[1]*Cap Trafalgar* was a German merchant ship, of the Hamburg–America line, armed by *Karlsruhe*, and so became an Armed Merchant Cruiser; she had only a brief career, being caught in the midst of coaling off Trinidad Island, Brazil, by the AMC *Carmania*, and sunk.

8. Friday, 9th October – In compliance with a signal from the Commander-in-Chief I directed *Gibraltar* to remain at Scapa Flow and await orders and reported her ready for service at 9.0 a.m.

In consequence of thick fog the Squadron reduced to 8 knots but increased speed on fog lifting. *Grafton* rejoined Squadron at 7.0 a.m.

The northern base line of Area V was crossed to southward at 1.0 p.m., and to northward at 3.0 p.m.

The weather continued foggy with bright intervals.

At 6.35 p.m. orders were received from the Commander-in-Chief to return to Area VI and I accordingly proceeded arranging a rendezvous at P.6. at 10.0 a.m. on 10th October.

9. Saturday, 10th October – At 7.30 a.m. *Endymion* boarded the British Steamer *Transport* from Elsinore to Barry, whose Captain reported that German line of patrol of Cruisers and Torpedo craft was established between Rugen Island and Swedish mainland, stopping and examining all trade.[1]

The patrol of Area VI as now arranged by the Commander-in-Chief comprised 2nd, 3rd, and 10th Cruiser Squadrons and *Liverpool* and Destroyers. Second Cruiser Squadron was ordered to form a line ahead patrol near a line drawn N 66° E true from Latitude 59.30´N, Longitude 1.30´E to within 20 miles of Norwegian Coast, varying the position by at least 20 miles daily. Third Cruiser Squadron was ordered to Cromarty to coal, and *Liverpool* and Destroyers were detailed to South part of Area VI.

In order to conform to these movements I directed Tenth Cruiser Squadron to patrol the NE half of Area VI on lines running N 60° W and S 60° E (true), twelve miles apart, the general plan being for ships to be on the southern line at daylight proceeding NW during the day and turning about dark to SE for the night.

Endymion was detached to Cromarty to coal and make good defects.

10. Sunday, 11th October – After turning over general orders for continuance of patrol to *Grafton* I proceeded in *Crescent* to meet *Edgar* which had left Cromarty at 8.30 a.m., and communicated to her directions to take charge of Tenth Cruiser Squadron during my absence. I then proceeded for Cromarty.

Royal Arthur was detached to Queenstown to dock with orders to rejoin Squadron in Area VI.

At 5.0 p.m. *Liverpool* and two Destroyers were sighted making for Scapa Flow.

[1]Thus, on this relatively small scale, the German Navy was already doing what the Royal Navy eventually did through the Northern Patrol.

11. Monday, 12th October – I arrived at Cromarty in *Crescent* at 8.30 a.m. to coal and repair engines. *Endymion*, *Hawke* and Third Cruiser Squadron were in harbour. *Crescent* completed with coal and took in hand urgent defects. *Hawke* left Cromarty at 6.0 p.m. to rejoin Squadron on patrol.

12. Tuesday, 13th October – *Theseus* and *Hawke* rejoined Squadron in Area VI and continued examining and boarding steamers.

13. Wednesday, 14th October – *Endymion* left Cromarty at 10 a.m. to rejoin Squadron, and *Grafton* was detached from patrol to coal. *Royal Arthur* reported arrival at Queenstown to dock.

14. Thursday, 15th October – *Grafton* arrived at Cromarty at 7.0 a.m. and proceeded to coal.

At 1.20 p.m. *Theseus* reported Submarines and that a torpedo had been fired at her but missed astern. Captain of *Edgar* being Senior Officer on Patrol promptly ordered *Theseus*, *Endymion* and *Hawke* to proceed NW at full speed. *Hawke* was not then in sight and *Theseus* reported she was last seen at 11.15 a.m. steaming to SW to examine a steamer. The Commander-in-Chief then ordered ships of the Tenth Cruiser Squadron to leave SW portion of Area VI and concentrate at Northern part.

At 4.30 p.m. having informed *Edgar* I was rejoining the Squadron I left Cromarty and endeavoured to get in touch with *Hawke* by W/T but without result [10].

The Commander-in-Chief ordered 4th Flotilla of Torpedo Boat Destroyers to vicinity where submarines had been seen and to search for *Hawke*, and directed me to proceed with Tenth Cruiser Squadron to Northern Patrol.

15. Friday, 16th October – At 1.30 p.m. I rejoined the Squadron consisting of *Edgar*, *Endymion* and *Theseus* at Lat. 60.30´N, Long. 0.40´E and shaped course NNE to join Second Battle Squadron in accordance with orders from Commander-in-Chief.

Endymion was detached to Lat. 61.20´N, Long. 1.20´E to tow the Norwegian Sailing Vessel *Nordsee* to Lerwick.

At 4.0 p.m. Second Battle Squadron was sighted and at 5.20 p.m. I joined *Russell*, *Edgar* joined *Exmouth* and *Theseus* joined *Albemarle* and proceeded to patrol SSE crossing a line ENE from Muckle Flugga at 8.0 p.m. going South and midnight going North.

At 9.25 p.m. *Endymion* reported that she had joined *Boadicea* which was standing by Sailing Ship *Nordsee* and would take the latter in tow at daylight.

16. Saturday, 17th October – At 8.30 a.m. the Second Battle Squadron having left the patrol line the Rear-Admiral (*Russell*) took charge of the patrol disposed as follows from W to E:

Tenth Cruiser Squadron (3 ships).
Russell class (4 ships).
Third Cruiser Squadron (4 ships).

and continued on same area till 10.0 a.m. when *Antrim* reported that she was being attacked by submarines. The Senior Officer thereupon ordered all ships to proceed N at 14 knots. A subsequent signal from *Antrim* indicated that supposed submarines were probably black fish.

At 12.30 p.m. *Russell* class ships left the patrol and I assumed charge. *Alsatian* was escorting SS *Rolf* (Danish) to Lerwick, *Endymion* was towing Sailing Ship *Nordsee* (Norwegian) to Lerwick, and *Theseus* was examining SS *United States* (Danish). This left Third Cruiser Squadron and two ships of Tenth Cruiser Squadron on patrol. The *Rolf* and *Nordsee* were eventually sent into Lerwick with prize crews on board.[1]

In compliance with orders from the Commander-in-Chief [11] a patrol was organised on a base line NW (mag.) from Muckle Flugga, ships spread 10 miles apart, steering W by S and E by N not passing to eastward of base line; speed during day 12 knots zig-zagging and making good 10 knots, during night 9 knots.

At 3.30 p.m. *Crescent* captured SS *Prosper II* (Norwegian) put a prize crew on board and sent her to Lerwick.[2]

17. Sunday, 18th October – During the morning *Endymion*, *Theseus* and *Alsatian* joined the patrol which was disposed in following order from S to N:

Tenth Cruiser Squadron (4 ships), *Alsatian*, Third Cruiser Squadron (4 ships), inner ship 7 miles from Muckle Flugga, remaining ships 10 miles apart, turning 16 points every two hours, keeping to westward of base line.

Gibraltar reported arrival at Busta Voe in compliance with orders from the Commander-in-Chief.

18. Monday, 19th October – *Grafton* joined Squadron from Cromarty at 5 p.m., *Dryad* also joined from Busta Voe and in accordance with orders from the Commander-in-Chief I ordered her to Hillswick to tow two Battle Practice Targets to Busta Voe.

The patrol line for the day was shifted W by S 10 miles and parallel to the original line.

19. Tuesday, 20th October – The patrol line was shifted (during the

[1]*Rolf* and *Nordsee* were not detained.

[2]*Prosper II* was transferred to the Prize Court for a decision on it and its cargo (TS 14/1 of 2 November 1914).

night 19/20 October), and ships were ordered to be in position at 6.0 a.m. ten miles apart on a line N (mag.) from Muckle Flugga, inner ship 7 miles from shore. The same patrol courses were preserved, ships altering course 6 points every three hours. From noon ships were ordered to continue W by S till 6.0 p.m., when they turned to E by N for the night.

At 6.0 p.m. *Alsatian* was ordered to proceed to Lat. 62.15´N, Long. 5.0´W and patrol four miles N and S (true) from the position to intercept ships passing north of Faroe Islands.

20. Wednesday, 21st October – At 6.0 a.m. ships were on a line N 10° E (true) from Muckle Flugga, inner ship 10 miles distant, remainder 12 miles apart, course W by S. The wind and sea increasing precluded boarding but at 4.30 p.m. in Lat. 60.13´N, Long. 3.58´W the SS *Christopher Kurdsen* was intercepted and captured, and *Endymion* was ordered to take her into Scapa Flow.[1]

In accordance with directions from the Commander-in-Chief I ordered *Alsatian* to a position between Lat. 61.0´N and 61.40´N in Long. 5.0´W in order to intercept trade.

At 7.30 p.m. I received a signal from *Dryad* informing me that ship was ashore in Hoy Sound off Skerry of Ness.[2]

21. Thursday, 22nd October – At 6.0 a.m. ships were on a line parallel to but 10 miles West of line of patrol of 21st, only three ships remaining as Third Cruiser Squadron had proceeded to Busta Voe to coal. The weather was thick with strong wind and considerable sea.

22. Friday, 23rd October – Patrol as yesterday was continued, but as Third Battle Squadron was guarding approach to Fair Island Channel Westward I disposed the ships on a WNW course. *Gibraltar* joined from Busta Voe and *Theseus* was detached thither to coal, thus leaving three ships for patrol besides *Alsatian* which was carrying out separate patrol in vicinity of Sydero Island. At 2.30 p.m. the Norwegian Sailing Ship *Sophie* was boarded in Lat. 60.35´N, Long. 2.28´W she had a cargo of wheat from Albany to Hull, and as the Master produced a 'War clearance' from the Customs Authorities at Queenstown she was allowed to proceed. At the same time enquiry was made by telegram to Queenstown as to the ultimate destination of this cargo and a reply was received that ship was all correct.

23. Saturday, 24th October – The patrol line was altered, northern end being thrown back to the eastward. *Edgar* and *Royal Arthur* having

[1]*Christopher Knudsen* (correct name) was not detained.
[2]*Dryad* survived, was refloated, and returned to duty.

joined the Squadron from Busta Voe and Queenstown respectively, the patrol consisted of five ships disposed 15 miles apart, the inner ship 10 miles from Muckle Flugga, visibility being very good. Patrol course was W by N until 6.0 p.m.; nothing was seen. Third Cruiser Squadron left Busta Voe at daylight to take up station for intercepting ships passing north of Faroe Islands. *Alsatian* was in position to take part in this patrol at 6.0 a.m. At noon the weather in this locality was reported thick.

24. Sunday, 25th October – Leaving directions with *Edgar* to take charge of Tenth Cruiser Squadron ships on patrol I proceeded in *Crescent* to Busta Voe, Swarbacks Minn, to coal and make good defects. *Endymion* and *Theseus* were in harbour. *Zealandia* called and took away a battle practice target.

25. Monday, 26th October – In accordance with directions from the Commander-in-Chief ships of the Tenth Cruiser Squadron on patrol were spread on a line N 20° E from Lat. 62.20´N, Long. 1.0´W sweeping N 70° W turning 16 points together to starboard every four hours. *Edgar* put into Busta Voe at 8.0 a.m. with an urgent hospital case and returned to patrol. *Teutonic* reported rejoining Northern Patrol at 8.0 a.m.

26. Tuesday, 27th October – *Theseus* having coaled and made good defects left Busta Voe and returned to patrol. Third Cruiser Squadron arrived on Olna Firth and commenced coaling.

27. Wednesday, 28th October – Signal was received from the Commander-in-Chief, addressed to the Senior Officers Third and Tenth Cruiser Squadrons and SNO Scapa at 2.38 p.m. to spread Tenth and Third Cruiser Squadrons to endeavour to intercept enemy minelayer probably passing between Faroe and Orkney Islands to North Sea. A further signal was received from the Commander-in-Chief that the minelayer would probably attempt to return well to northward of the Shetlands. I ordered Tenth Cruiser Squadron consisting of *Edgar*, *Endymion*, *Theseus*, *Gibraltar* and *Royal Arthur* to proceed to take up positions on a line NE (true) from Muckle Flugga, inner ship seven miles distant, remainder 10 miles apart, ships to cross base line steering SE (true) at midnight, altering course 16 points every two hours. I directed Third Cruiser Squadron to sail as soon as possible to prolong the line of patrol to NE; they accordingly left Olna Firth at 5.0 p.m.[1]

[1]The minelayer was the armed merchant ship *Berlin*, which eventually took refuge in Bergen, and was there interned.

Endymion having left Busta Voe to return to patrol at 2.0 p.m. *Grafton* arrived to coal &c.

28. Thursday, 29th October – *Royal Arthur* arrived at Busta Voe at 8.0 a.m. to coal and I left in *Crescent* at 1.0 p.m. Tenth and Third Cruiser Squadrons had been ordered to patrol, on a base line N (true) from Muckle Flugga, southern ship 30 miles distant, remainder 10 miles apart, steering E (true) at 5.0 p.m., altering course 16 points every two hours. *Grafton* reported main condenser leaking and fear that copper expansion ring at back of port H.P. Slide fractured, also funnels showing signs of weakness. At 4.24 p.m. I received a signal from *Edgar* that she had increased to 14 knots and was endeavouring to intercept a suspicious steamer with two funnels sighted by *Endymion* in Lat. 61.20´N, Long. 0.53´W steering NE. At 4.56 p.m. in answer to my signal *Endymion* informed me that steamer had altered course to SE at 4.30 p.m. I immediately proceeded full speed to the eastward to endeavour to cut the chase off. My position then was just north of Muckle Flugga. At 5.10 p.m. *Endymion* informed me that steamer was funnels down and gaining although *Endymion* was steaming 18 knots. At 5.45 p.m I ordered general chase to SE. At 6.26 p.m. *Theseus* reported she had broken down and had to ease speed as it was not safe for her to proceed faster owing to engine defects. At 7.5 p.m. *Endymion* reported she was gaining on the chase and could see her stern light. At 10.45 p.m. signal was received from the Commander-in-Chief that First Light Cruiser Squadron was to assist Tenth Cruiser Squadron if required. I ordered Senior Officer 1st Light Cruiser Squadron to endeavour to intercept stranger who would probably make the Coast of Norway and proceed south.

29. Friday, 30th October – At 12.27 a.m. *Endymion* reported that she had overtaken the steamer. I at once ordered Senior Officers of the Third Cruiser Squadron and 1st Light Cruiser Squadron to abandon chase as steamer was captured; Tenth Cruiser Squadron to return to patrol line, Third Cruiser Squadron to proceed in execution of previous orders received from the Commander-in-Chief. The steamer was boarded by *Endymion* in Lat. 60.28´N, Long. 3.22´E, and proved to be the SS *Bergensfiord*, having on board the German Consul General from Seoul, Korea, and six German stowaways. Ship was from New York to Bergen with mails and passengers, a general cargo, crude rubber and coffee. A president of the Norwegian Parliament was also on board and protested against being detained. I informed him that I much regretted the inconvenience to passengers but the orders from the British Government were that the ship was to be sent in for examination. The Captain of the *Bergensfiord* also requested permission to inform his

owners by W/T that the ship had been boarded by a Man-of-War and detained; I replied I regretted I could not allow any W/T signals to be made but on arrival at Kirkwall he should ask permission to cable. *Endymion* was ordered to place a prize crew on board and escort steamer to Kirkwall. The arrival of the *Bergensfiord* at Kirkwall was reported at 5.15 p.m.[1] and *Endymion* proceeded to Scapa Flow to coal. I detached *Gibraltar* to Busta Voe to coal at 1.39 a.m. and Tenth Cruiser Squadron returned to patrol north of Muckle Flugga. Third Cruiser Squadron reported arrival at Olna Firth at 5.30 p.m.

30. Saturday, 31st October – Patrol consisting of *Crescent*, *Edgar*, *Theseus*, *Grafton* were spread 20 miles apart NNW (true) from Muckle Flugga, in line ahead at 10 knots, altering course 16 points every two hours. *Edgar* was detached after dark to proceed to Swarbacks Minn (Busta Voe) to coal. As *Theseus* reported serious defect, rupture of inner bottom above reserve feed water tanks, bilge water leaking into feed tanks and density of boilers rapidly increasing, I detached her at midnight to proceed to Swarbacks Minn to make good defects. *Endymion* reported arrival at Scapa Flow at 10.30 a.m. and requested permission (which was approved) to remain in order to repair serious defects in engines and fore bridge, and to complete with coal. *Crescent* reported leaky condenser.

Signal was passed from Commander-in-Chief to *Teutonic* to take an occasional stretch over to Iceland, and she reported intended movements accordingly.

At 6.6 p.m. Admiralty Orders were received to commence hostilities against Turkey.

10. *Lieutenant-Commander R. Rosoman*[2] *to Rear-Admiral F.S. Miller HMS* Cyclops[3]

on board MEA *Soudan*, Hospital Ship No. 1, Scapa, 17 October 1914

I regret to report the loss of HMS *Hawke* under the following

[1]*Bergensfjord* was held up for a month over the question of rubber in her cargo – carrying a group of official Germans cannot have helped her case – but was eventually released (TS 14/1 of 3 December 1914).

[2]Rosoman, Robert R., DSO, RN, Lieutenant-Commander 1907, Commander 1918, Captain (retired) 1922.

[3]Miller, Francis Spurstow, CB, RN (1863–1954); Lieutenant 1887, Commander 1897, Captain 1903, assistant Hydrographer at Admiralty 1909–1912, Rear-Admiral 1913, in administrative charge of Scapa Flow 1914–1916, in command of Northern Division of Coast of Ireland 1917–1919, Vice-Admiral 1918, Admiral (retired) 1923.

conditions. On Thursday morning 15 October the ship was on her usual patrol with the *Endymion* spread ten miles to starboard, *Theseus*, *Edgar* and *Grafton* at ten mile intervals to port. At or about 9.30 *Endymion* was ordered to close to enable *Hawke* to get mails brought out to her. Both ships stopped, *Hawke* lowered a boat and fetched the mails. *Endymion* proceeded across *Hawke*'s stern to go and close other ships with the same object in view. After hoisting the sea boat *Hawke* proceeded twelve knots or possibly thirteen to rejoin station, all water tight doors being closed. At or about 10.30 a.m. the *Hawke* was struck by something abreadst of the foremost funnel on the starboard side. The engines were at once stopped and the ship started to list to starboard. I was on the aft deck at the time and rushed up the after ladder and climbed on to the after bridge to get out boom boats. This could not be done as steam was never put on the boat hoist. Both sea boats were lowered and the port one drifted away astern with some people in her.

I imagine the starboard one was crushed by the ship. All this time the ship was listing more and more to starboard until she came bottom upwards, hesitated for a brief period and disappeared bow first. Three rafts on the quarter deck and one from for'd were in the water. The picket boat which [was] stowed the port side [was] somehow got into the water and floated for a time but was probably badly holed and soon went down.

After the ship disappeared the sailing pinnace came to the surface floating bottom up. She soon went down. When in the water I passed the Captain floating and said, 'Mine, I suppose, Sir', he replied, 'No, sub, I saw the track of torpedo after we had been struck.[1] After swimming about for some considerable time I got to one of the rafts and was picked up by HMS *Swift* the following morning with about nine others at roughly 11.30 a.m. I estimate from the time the ship was struck until she disappeared the time elapsed was fifteen minutes. My watch stopped at 10.45 which was the time I took to the water.

I submit I may be allowed to proceed on leave until I can get a kit together as I lost everything.

[1]*Hawke* was sunk by *U 9*, which was probably the boat which fired earlier at *Theseus*. *Hawke*'s captain, Captain Bernhard A. Pratt-Barlow, died in the sinking. It was the attack on *Hawke* which persuaded Admiral Jellicoe to withdraw the Grand Fleet from the North Sea.

11. *Commander-in-Chief Home Fleet to Rear Admiral Commanding Tenth and Third Cruiser Squadrons and HMS* Alsatian

HMS *Iron Duke*, 17 October 1914

Tenth Cruiser Squadron, Third Cruiser Squadron and Armed Merchant Cruisers to intercept trade to North Westward of Shetlands, varying position constantly. Ships not to be south of a line North-West by North from Ossa Skerry during dark hours, so as to clear battle fleet. Senior Officer arrange details. My 2 a.m. position will be Lat. 60.50´N, Long. 3.25´W.[1]

12. *Rear-Admiral de Chair to Admiralty*

HMS *Crescent*, 3 December 1914

Report of Proceedings, 1 November–3 December 1914

***

1. Sunday, 1st November – Weather being clear, line ahead patrol in a NNW (true) direction was carried out by *Crescent*, *Grafton*, *Royal Arthur*, from a point 20 miles S 70° W (true) from Muckle Flugga, ships steering NNW and SSE altering course every two hours in order to intercept vessels passing North of Shetland.

The dispositions of the vessels of Cruiser Force B were as follows:

Crescent	On patrol
Grafton	
Royal Arthur	
Edgar	Coaling and making good defects at Swarbacks Minn.
Gibraltar	
Theseus (broken down)	
Endymion	Rejoining from Kirkwall where she had taken a Prize.
Teutonic	Patrolling north of Faroe Island.
Alsatian	Coaling at Liverpool.
Mantua	Detached.
Dryad	Docking at Aberdeen.

2. Monday, 2nd November – The line of patrol was shifted 10 miles to the Westward and ships proceeded on a W by S course 10 miles apart,

[1]This instruction is the definitive change in the purpose of the Northern Patrol, from an interception of enemy warships to control of trade.

turning 16 points at 6.0 p.m. Weather threatening and visibility 5 to 6 miles. *Gibraltar* rejoined at 6.0 p.m. from Swarbacks Minn and was detached to Lat. 60.30´N, Long. 4.30´W to tow the Norwegian sailing ship *Sorfareren* captured by Third Battle Squadron, to Kirkwall.[1]

3. Tuesday, 3rd November – Shifted position of patrol again. Ships were disposed on a base line N by W (true) from Lat. 60.51´N, Long. 1.32´W 10 miles apart, steering west. Sea too rough for boarding. *Crescent* left the patrol line at 5.0 a.m. and proceeded to Swarbacks Minn to enable me to meet the SNO Lerwick (Commander Startin, RNR)[2] to settle the position of lookout stations and position of boom for the defence of the base. She left again for patrol at 11.30 a.m. but at 2.30 p.m. signal was received from the Commander-in-Chief ordering the Tenth Cruiser Squadron to return to Busta Voe at full speed to coal. *Endymion* at 2.15 p.m. reported having intercepted the Norwegian SS *Baltimore* with rye consigned to Trondhjem on order. I requested instructions from the Commander-in-Chief, and the ship was released on his orders. *Crescent* arrived at Swarbacks Minn at 5.0 p.m. The remainder of the Squadron arrived during the night. No difficulty was experienced in making the harbour after dark on this particular night but it is difficult to make at night as a rule, owing to the poor light at the entrance and the abnormal currents that sweep this coast.

Ships prepared to fill up with coal with all despatch, when at 11.0 p.m. a signal was received from the Commander-in-Chief ordering the Tenth Cruiser Squadron to resume patrol.

4. Wednesday, 4th November – The following ships sailed during the morning: *Edgar*, *Endymion*, *Grafton*, *Gibraltar* and *Royal Arthur*. *Crescent* remained in harbour to coal and repair engines and *Theseus* to repair inner bottom &c. which had given way over Reserve Feed Tanks. I ordered patrol to form on a base line 349 from Lat. 60.48´N, Long. 1.50´W, ships 10 miles apart, steering W and E altering course 16 points every 3 hours.

5. Thursday, 5th November – Ordered patrol to steer W at 7.0 a.m. until 6.0 p.m. then to alter course 16 points. The following ships were intercepted, Prize Crews put on board and sent to Lerwick:
SS *Brakar* (Norwegian) with Linseed, Oil, Flour, and consigned to various firms in Christiana and Copenhagen.

[1]*Sorfararen* became the subject of a Prize Court case.

[2]Startin, James, KCB, RN (1855–1948); joined Navy 1869, Commander 1891, Captain 1897, Rear-Admiral 1907, Rear-Admiral of Channel and Home Fleets, 1908–1909, Vice-Admiral retired 1911; Lieutenant-Commander RNR 1914, Commander RNR 1914, Captain RNR 1914, Admiral (retired) 1915, Commodore RNR 1916.

SS *Alfred Nobel* (Norwegian) with meat & grain.[1]

6. Friday, 6th November – Patrol base line was 349 from Lat. 60.44´N, Long. 2.10´W. This shifted the line 10 miles to westward.

By order of the Commander-in-Chief the Armed Merchant Ship patrol was placed under the orders of the Rear-Admiral Commanding the Sixth Cruiser Squadron.

Grafton arrived at base to complete with coal and make good defects.

7. Saturday, 7th November – Ships were ordered to cross the same base line at 7.0 a.m. steering to make good 250°.

Theseus, which had been repairing inner bottom and other defects and taking in fresh water for boilers, now completed the work. Using ship's boats and obtaining water from a stream flowing into the harbour she took in 253 tons in four days. *Grafton* reported that a number of rivets connecting furnace and combustion chamber in one boiler had been found loose. This, in addition to engine defects, necessitated ship leaving patrol for five days.

A lookout station commanding a view of the harbour entrance and of the ships in Busta Voe had been arranged with Commander Startin, RNR, who sent the Steam Yacht *Vagrant* from Lerwick to superintend the erection of a suitable hut. This, when completed, was to be manned by six Signalmen RNR from Lerwick.

8. Sunday, 8th November – *Theseus* having made good defects sailed to join patrol which was arranged from a position Lat. 60.30´N, Long. 2.50´W in a S to N direction in accordance with instructions from the Commander-in-Chief, course 240°, ships turning 16 points at dark.

Royal Arthur arrived at 9.0 a.m. and commenced coaling. As *Endymion* reported several perforations in inner bottom over feed tanks I directed her to leave the patrol and proceed to Busta Voe. She arrived about 5.0 p.m. and made a full report of defects. After communication with the Commander-in-Chief I directed *Endymion* to sail for Scapa in order that the work might be taken in hand by *Cyclops*.

9. Monday, 9th November – I left Swarbacks Minn in *Crescent* at 8.0 a.m. and rejoined patrol from position Lat. 60.30´N, Long. 2.50´W, line bearing from S to N. A heavy sea and strong wind necessitated speed being reduced to 8 knots, making good about 4 knots. At 9.0 p.m. ships were ordered to heave to. *Gibraltar* left patrol and proceeded to the base to coal and make good defects.

[1]*Brakar* was not detained; for *Alfred Nobel*, see [19]; the ship was the subject of a Prize Court case.

10. Tuesday, 10th November – A heavy sea and strong wind still prevailing, speed was restricted to 8 knots. *Theseus* reported having intercepted the Norwegian SS *Fram* bound from Charleston to Nyborg with a cargo of oil-cake consigned to order. On the instructions of the Commander-in-Chief I directed *Theseus*, as it was too rough to lower a boat, to escort vessel to Yell Sound, and under the lee to place a prize crew on board and send her to Lerwick for examination.[1] At 11.0 a.m. instructions were received from the Commander-in-Chief for Squadron to take up position on a line Noup Head Light–Foula Island by 3.30 p.m. and to fall back to a line NW from Noup Head after dark with a view to intercepting German Minelayer which it was considered possible might attempt operations that night. I accordingly ordered *Edgar* to proceed to a position 25 miles S 50° W from Foula Island, and *Crescent* took up station 10 miles S 50° W from *Edgar*.

11. Wednesday, 11th November – Nothing having been seen on patrol line ordered, I was directed by the Commander-in-Chief to return to Northern Patrol at 8.30 a.m. and ordered *Edgar* who had reported serious engine defects to proceed to the base when weather moderated and make them good. While proceeding, the Squadron encountered a severe gale with heavy sea; wind working from W to NW. Squadron hove to. During forenoon heavy seas came over forecastle of *Crescent*, wrecking fore bridge, sweeping overboard Admiral's Sea Cabin, carrying away ventilating cowl of foremost stokehold (a considerable amount of water getting down and putting fires out), breaking hammock nettings and damaging beyond repair Port Cutter which was turned in, removing bodily a whaler at davits abaft cutter; various hawser reels and other fittings fastened to the deck were torn away from their securings owing to woodwork being rotten.

Edgar reported the loss of an Able Seaman swept overboard and also a cutter damaged and other items [13]. *Theseus* which was nearer the Shetlands reported only minor damage.

12. Thursday, 12th November – *Crescent* proceeded to Swarbacks Minn to repair damage, sailing again at 4.0 p.m. for Scapa Flow to meet the Commander-in-Chief.

Grafton and *Royal Arthur* having completed with coal and repaired defects proceeded on patrol, and *Edgar* arrived at base to coal and make good engine defects and damage caused by severe weather.

13. Friday, 13th November – I arrived at Scapa Flow in *Crescent* at 8.0 a.m. The Commander-in-Chief informed me that it had been

[1] *Fram* was not detained.

decided to send half Tenth Cruiser Squadron to Clyde Yards for refit, and I accordingly directed *Grafton* and *Royal Arthur* to leave patrol and proceed to the Clyde. *Edgar* was placed in charge of the patrol during my absence.

14. Saturday, 14th November – *Crescent* left Scapa Flow at 7.0 a.m. and proceeded to the Clyde.

15. Sunday, 15th November – I arrived at Greenock at 4.0 p.m. *Royal Arthur* was already anchored there and *Grafton* at Govan.

16. Monday, 16th November – *Crescent* proceeded to the works of Messrs John Brown & Co., Clydebank, and was secured alongside. After consultation with the Captain Superintendent of Contract built ships, Mr Pine, Constructor, and the Manager and officials of Messrs John Brown, who inspected the defects and damage caused by the gale of 11th instant, it was decided to proceed with the important items while making a survey of the ship generally. The same procedure was also adopted as regards *Royal Arthur* and *Grafton*.

17. Tuesday, 17th November – The Director of Dockyards (Sir James Marshall, KCB)[1] having arrived, a further consultation with all the officials present was held and detailed directions were given as to the work to be undertaken on each of the three ships. The point aimed at was to put the ships in a seaworthy and efficient state for service in the North Sea within a time limit of three weeks. The principal items which proved the governing factors as regards time were found to be:

> *Crescent* – Inner Bottom, Deck, Suction and Bilge pumps Battening down arrangements, Rudder.
> *Royal Arthur* – Inner Bottom.
> *Grafton* – Condensers.

The engine defects of all three ships generally, though serious, were considered repairable within the prescribed period, and it was decided to take in hand such other items as could be dealt with provided they did not delay the completion of the ships for sea.

18. Wednesday, 18th November – The work of repairing the three ships in the Clyde was now fully in hand and it was hoped to make them thoroughly seaworthy by 7th December. From this date the proceedings of the squadron can best be described by the following telegrams which passed between the Commander-in-Chief, the Admiralty and myself:[2]

***

[1]Marshall, James Brown, KCB, Director of Dockyards, 1906–1917; he entered the Royal Dockyard at Portsmouth in 1867 and rose. He died in 1922.

[2]For the preliminary report see [15] and [17].

20th Nov. From Admiralty to RAC 10th CS. 'Seven *Edgars* of 10th Cruiser Squadron are to return to their Home Ports forthwith and pay off. Only sufficient work is to be done for *Crescent*, *Royal Arthur* and *Grafton* now repairing at Clyde yards to enable them to return to Home Ports. Commander-in-Chief, Home Fleets informed.'

***

20th Nov. From C-in-C H.F. to RAC 10th CS. '... When will ships with you be ready to proceed (stop). I will order remainder to leave their station tonight and *Edgar* when defects have been made good (stop). Obstruction at your late base will be kept down send me plan of it also list of stores for its construction (stop). Have ordered your supply ship and all colliers there except two to return to my base (stop). Your Engineer Officer will be sent to rejoin *Crescent* (stop). *Plassy* has been ordered here (stop). *Dryad* will remain north.'

20th Nov. RAC 10th CS to C-in-C H.F. '... Owing to much work being commenced *Grafton*'s Sailing date is November 30th *Crescent* and *Royal Arthur* December 7th working day and night (stop). No obstruction at base yet in place. Vice-Admiral Orkneys and Shetlands had been asked to provide boom similar to that at Cromarty placed between Gillarona Ness and Papa Little Island the narrow channel to the east of Papa Little Island to be blocked. Two armed Trawlers patrol entrance day and night. Look out huts connected by telephone are erected and working (stop). Propose to visit Admiralty on Monday 23rd Nov. to push forward new arrangements for patrol.'

22nd Nov. From Admiralty to Rear-Admiral 10th CS. '... *Crescent*, *Royal Arthur* and *Grafton* are to be paid off at Clyde yards and laid up with care and maintenance parties under charge of Captain Superintendent Clyde. Commander-in-Chief, Home Fleets has been informed.'

25th Nov. From RAC 10th CS to Admiralty. 'Following dates are proposed for paying off ships of 10th Cruiser Squadron at the Clyde. *Crescent* 4th December, *Royal Arthur* 7th December, *Grafton* 9th December.'

27th Nov. From Admiralty to RAC 10th CS. '... drafts of men will be withdrawn before the dates mentioned (stop). These withdrawals will probably not include Engine Room ratings.'

19. My Flag was hauled down in *Crescent* at Clydebank on evening of 3rd December and will be hoisted tomorrow in *Alsatian* at Liverpool.

13. *Journal of Commander H. T. Bowen.*[1]

Only mine and torpedo had added two new dangers which few of our ships had been built to resist. The *Edgar* and her sister ships were particularly vulnerable. They were the oldest ships that joined the Home ... Fleet, and they were so little subdivided that it required only one mine or torpedo to send them instantly to the bottom.

The weather that autumn was very bad and gradually the old ships got knocked to pieces. I remember one night when I had been on the bridge practically all day, and the Captain sent me down to my cabin about midnight to try to get some rest. It was blowing a full gale and it looked doubtful if the ship would weather it. My cabin was on the upper deck (in the after superstructure) and I lay down on my bunk in my clothes and being very tired I dozed off. I was awakened by a terrific crash and my cabin door was burst open and water poured in. All I could see outside was a swirling mass of foam on the upper deck. I thought the ship must be sinking. I swung myself out of my bunk and, up to my knees in water, waded up the slope through the doorway. The ship seemed on her beam ends and it looked as if nothing could save her. As I watched she slowly – miraculously – righted herself. A minute later another great wave swept her from stem to stern. It was then that a midshipman was carried overboard from the foremost gun and on over the nettings aft and laid almost at my feet. After that there was a lull and I could take in the scene. The gun crews were clinging to the guns or whatever they could hold on to, while live ammunition rolled with the ship across the deck ... [W]hen dawn broke the weather moderated and we were able to take stock of our damage: one man lost, several injured, and one boiler room flooded, and all our boats either lost or damaged. When later in the day we were able to turn round and run for the shelter of our Shetland Islands base, we found in Swarbacks Minn some other ships of the squadron which had suffered even worse damage. The great gale put an end to the use of these old cruisers on the Northern Patrol ...

14. *Commander-in-Chief Home Fleets to Admiralty*

HMS *Iron Duke*, 7 November 1914

Report from British trawler(s) from Iceland indicates numerous large steamers passed between Faroe Isles and Iceland Store Depot.

[1]Bowen, Harold T., RN, Lieutenant 1907, Commander 1919, Commander (retired) serving in *Victory*, 1940.

Two large armed liners much required to strengthen this patrol 200 miles long.

15. *Commander-in-Chief Home Fleets to Admiralty*

HMS *Iron Duke*, 11 November 1914

Experience last gale makes it doubtful whether ships of Tenth Cruiser Squadron can be made seaworthy.

They are not so now.

Crescent, *Royal Arthur* and *Grafton* being sent Greenock.

Have you arranged with Director of Dockyards for Admiralty officers to visit and inspect ships[?]

Decision can then be given whether it is worth attempting to patch them up.

Without them or efficient sea-going substitutes I can no longer control neutral trade in contraband passing north of Shetland Islands.

16. *Admiralty to Commander-in-Chief Home Fleets*

18 November 1914

The following arrangements are in hand and will be completed with the utmost despatch in order to put the Northern Patrol on a more satisfactory footing.

The patrol will consist of 24 armed liners constituted as follows:

Three – Already on patrol.

Four – Now commissioning with full crews and armament.

Seventeen – Further vessels which are now being taken up. Their speed will be 14 to 17 knots. Tonnage 4,000 to 6,000 tons a somewhat reduced armament. These vessels will be manned by the crews of the *Edgar*s, supplemented where possible by RNR firemen. The *Edgar*s will be paid off as the liners become available.

These 24 vessels will be under the command of Rear-Admiral de Chair and will be employed exclusively for patrol duty.

17. *Admiralty to Commander-in-Chief Home Fleets and Rear-Admiral HMS* Crescent

20 November 1914

Seven *Edgar*s of Tenth Cruiser Squadron are to return to their home ports forthwith and pay off. Only sufficient work to be done on *Crescent*, *Royal Arthur* and *Grafton* now repairing at Clyde Yards to enable them to return to home ports.

Commander-in-chief only:

This is preparatory to commissioning the 17 armed liners. Meanwhile it is recognised that patrol line will necessarily be weak and several important cargoes copper, aluminium, and rubber are expected to be on their way shortly. Anticipate that vessels trying to get through will try to pass between Orkney and Shetland.

2

THE ARMED MERCHANT CRUISERS, DECEMBER 1914–MARCH 1915

The replacement of the *Edgars* by Armed Merchant Cruisers took two months, during which time the Northern Patrol was effectively suspended. The ships had to be designated, collected, converted and manned [18, 33, 42], and gradually came on patrol during December 1914 and January 1915. The fact that it was the northern winter when they went on patrol for the first time was not calculated to assist efficiency. The problems were illustrated by *Caribbean*'s and *Patia*'s experiences [20, 23, 46]. Two of the ships – *Viknor* and *Clan MacNaughton* – were soon sunk, and the internal account of the process of selection shows evidence of haste and lack of preparation, which were clearly two of the main causes for the losses [33, 42].

The work of the patrol was not made any easier by the uncertain legal and political situation. No blockade was actually instituted – indeed, legally, no blockade was ever instituted – and the list of goods which the British government decided should be denied the enemy constantly increased. Hence the problem with the *Denver* [24] and the *Trondhjemsfjord* [37], among others, and the evident confusion over the usefulness of various certificates [28 paras 26 and 29; also 5 para. 17]. The Contraband Committee in London had also to devise its own procedures and explore its powers against the same changing background.

Yet in that time the patrol system became properly established. Between them Rear Admiral de Chair, the Commander-in-Chief [22], and Captain Webb at the Admiralty [21], devised a system of patrols which produced successive lines of ships past which the cargo and passenger vessels had to sail. At least one of the lines could be expected to intercept them. For this work the Armed Merchant Cruisers were much better suited than the naval warships, being generally faster and of greater endurance, as well as having greater capacity for the large crews needed. Despite the difficulties of the first winter, therefore, the Northern Patrol was fully operational by the time a clear policy on blocking trade with Germany was devised in March 1915.

18. *Rear-Admiral de Chair to Admiralty*

HMS *Alsatian*, 25 January 1915

Report of Proceedings, 4 December 1914–25 January 1915

***

1. In compliance with directions from Admiralty I hoisted my Flag in the *Alsatian* in command of the Tenth Cruiser Squadron consisting of twenty-four Armed Merchant Cruisers on Friday, 4th December at Liverpool.

2. The composition of the Squadron and the positions of the ships on that date were as follows:

Alsatian (Flag)	Rearming with 6" guns at Liverpool.
Eskimo *Caribbean* *Ambrose* *Oropesa* *Hilary* *Hildebrand* *Virginian* *Cedric*	Fitting out at Liverpool.
Orotava *Clan MacNaughton* *Digby* *Otway*	Fitting out at London.
Patia *Patuca* *Bayano* *Motagua* *Changuinola*	Fitting out at Avonmouth.
Calyx	Fitting out at Hull.
Viknor	Fitting out on the Tyne.
Columbella	Fitting out on the Clyde.

Teutonic *Mantua*	On Northern Patrol.
Laurentic	Was employed on special service proceeding to West Coast of Africa with orders to join my Flag on her return.

3. During my stay at Liverpool every effort was made to expedite the work of fitting out the ships, but delays were constant, chiefly owing to labour troubles and the state of the labour market generally. At Liverpool the quality of the labour was most inferior and Contractors experienced great difficulty in obtaining sufficient hands and continuous labour. At London and Avonmouth similar conditions appeared to exist and continual hastening measures were necessary on the part of the Commanding Officers and the Officers superintending the work at all the Ports. The following ships have been completed (and are at sea or coaling) to date:

Cedric	11 December.
Virginian *Oropesa* *Otway*	15 December.
Hilary *Eskimo*	16 December.
Columbella	17 December.
Hildebrand *Ambrose*	18 December.
Calyx	20 December.
Patuca	22 December.
Alsatian	23 December.
Caribbean	24 December [20].
Clan MacNaughton	25 December.
Viknor	29 December.
Bayano	2 January.
Orotava	3 January.
Digby	4 January.
Changuinola	7 January.
Patia	6 January [23].
Motagua	16 January.

4. In order to carry out the administrative work on the Squadron it was found necessary to establish a Base Office at Liverpool, from which orders and communications could be distributed to the ships

which it was decided should use that port for coaling and repairs.

5. Monday, 21st December – Work on *Alsatian* still being incomplete, I proceeded overland to Scapa Flow to report to Commander-in-Chief and receive from him details of the duties to be carried out by the Squadron under my orders ...

6. Friday, 25th December – *Alsatian* arrived at Scapa Flow where I re-embarked and proceeded North.

7. Saturday, 26th December – I arrived on A Patrol (North of Faroes) and found the disposition of the ships on patrol to be as follows:[1]

A Patrol (North of Faroes) ... *Teutonic*, *Cedric*, *Columbella*, *Mantua*, *Virginian*.
B Patrol (North of Shetlands) ... Nil.
C Patrol (South of Sydero) ... *Otway*, *Oropesa*, *Hilary*.
D Patrol (West of Hebrides) ... *Hildebrand*, *Patuca*, *Calyx*, *Ambrose*.

Caribbean was on passage North from Liverpool, and *Eskimo* arrived at Scapa Flow being detailed for special service by Commander-in-Chief.

Teutonic being due to coal was despatched to Liverpool.

8. I learned from *Teutonic* that very few ships had been intercepted North of the Faroe Islands, but the nights being long at this time of year it was difficult to say whether much traffic was passing.

9. Sunday, 27th December – I ordered *Cedric* and *Caribbean* to patrol North of Shetlands, and to intercept all ships passing as far North as Lat. 62 N. It now became necessary to despatch the first batch of ships to Liverpool to coal in order that a proper rotation should be established. For this purpose I detached *Columbella* from A, *Oropesa* from C, and *Ambrose* from D which, with *Teutonic* detached the day before from B, made one ship from each patrol. The weather on all patrols was bad, blowing a gale from SW with driving snow and hail, and ships were in many cases forced to ease down or lie to.

10. Monday, 28th December – Weather moderated, and several steamers were intercepted.

11. Tuesday, 29th December – I left A patrol in *Alsatian* and proceeded South of Faroe Islands to B patrol in order to get in touch with *Cedric* and *Hildebrand*. *Calyx* searched for mines (probably one of those laid off Tory Island) reported West of Hebrides. Information was received of arrival of *Teutonic* at Liverpool, and sailing of *Viknor* from Tyne.

[1]See also, for a rationale of this disposition, document [21].

12. Wednesday, 30th December – Wind from SSW backing to SSE, force 7 and squally, heavy sea, but several neutral steamers were intercepted by Squadron. It was too rough to board but ships were taken under lee of the land and prize crews put onboard. They were then sent in to Kirkwall.

13. Thursday, 31st December – Wind still Southerly, blowing hard, hail and snow squalls, heavy sea. Eleven ships on patrol, 5 coaling and 4 not yet joined. Ships at Tilbury and Avonmouth still delayed by labour disputes and strikes.

14. Friday, 1st January 1915 – Heavy gale from South backing to SE. Glass fell to 28.50,[1] very heavy sea. I detached *Virginian* to patrol North of Iceland to see if shipping were passing that way and also to report if passage were blocked by ice. *Mantua* patrolling passage between Iceland and Faroes. *Alsatian* reinforced C Patrol as *Otway* was escorting ships to Kirkwall. *Hilary* was ordered to stand by dismasted Norwegian sailing ship till gale moderated. *Viknor* joined B Patrol, but owing to damage sustained in gale, had to take shelter in Burra Sound. Impressed the importance on Armed Merchant Cruisers of not interfering with neutral ships' colours, and also of treating them with courtesy.

15. Saturday, 2nd January – Wind in SE, force 9, heavy sea. Glass fell to 28.10.[2] *Hilary* reported that at 1.15 a.m., while towing Norwegian barque *Marietta* which had been dismasted, the vessel sprang a leak and foundered. Her crew took to the boats but one boat capsized and only six men were saved. Among those drowned were Sub-Lieutenant Osmund E. Miles, R.N.R., and Frank Scott, Signalman, ... of *Hilary*. *Cedric* was lying to with prize, weather being too bad to board. *Hilary* proceeded to Kirkwall to land survivors of Norwegian barque.

16. Sunday, 3rd January – Gale moderating, glass rising, weather clearing. Each ship of D Patrol having two prize crews away, also several prize crews being away from ships of B and C patrols, arranged for *Hilary* to bring them out and distribute them. I consider it necessary to have a small vessel attached for this duty (i.e., of bringing out prize crews from Kirkwall) as it is not safe to send the Armed Merchant Cruisers through the submarines area outside Kirkwall to recover their crews. I was informed by the Admiral at Queenstown that *Orotava* had left that port to join my Flag. This Armed Merchant Cruiser had left London about 24th December but owing to incomplete state and defects developed she had put into Queenstown for necessary repairs &c.

[1]965 mbs, the lowest pressure of the 'normal' range.
[2]952 mbs.

17. Monday, 4th January – *Bayano* arrived and was placed under orders of *Otway* C Patrol. *Virginian* was detached to Liverpool to coal, with orders to return as soon as possible in readiness to join special patrol with *Teutonic* and *Mantua* off Norway, ordered by Commander-in-Chief for 10th January. *Digby* reported sailing from Thames to join my Flag.

18. Tuesday, 5th January – *Mantua* was detached to Liverpool to coal, with orders similar to those given to *Virginian*. I directed the Senior Officers of B and C Patrols to shift their respective base lines 20 miles to the westward at 8.0 a.m., at the same time warning them of the reported presence of submarines off the Shetlands. As an additional precaution they were ordered to zig-zag by day. *Hildebrand* reported that in consequence of the submarine menace she was unable to go to Kirkwall, and that Destroyers were being sent to bring in the Steamer *Denver* which she was escorting [24]. I therefore directed *Hilary* which was still at Kirkwall, to bring out all prize crews and distribute them to their own ships, leaving the harbour after dark.

19. Wednesday, 6th January – *Orotava* joined B patrol and *Oropesa* returned to C patrol. *Patia* was reported leaving Avonmouth [23] and *Virginian* arrived at Liverpool. I detached *Caribbean* to Liverpool to coal. *Hilary* proceeded to St Kilda where she transferred D Patrol prize crews to *Hildebrand*. *Alsatian* was working to westward of C Patrol on a track approximating to the Atlantic route used by vessels passing north of Shetlands.

20. Thursday, 7th January – *Changuinola* was reported leaving Avonmouth, and *Mantua* arrived at Liverpool. *Alsatian* proceeded to westward as far as St Kilda to communicate with D Patrol and returned towards B Patrol at night. *Cedric* reported an accident which occurred when hoisting in her motor boat; four seamen were injured and the boat had to be abandoned as a total wreck.

21. Friday, 8th January – I directed the Senior Officer of C Patrol (*Otway* temporarily) to extend his patrol from Lat. 59.30´N to Lat. 61.10´N. During the forenoon I communicated by boat with *Cedric* and gave her the necessary instructions for carrying out her patrol. After carrying out Aiming Practice *Alsatian* proceeded to A Patrol.

22. Saturday 9th January. With the approval of the Commander-in-Chief I remained South of the Faroe Islands in order to direct patrol, and with the special purpose of insuring the interception of the Norwegian Mail Steamer *Bergensfjord* which was expected to pass through patrol areas between 9th and 13th January and was reported to have German Reservists on board travelling under neutral passports. *Hildebrand* reported that all prize crews had been distributed

to their ships. *Clan MacNaughton* was reported to be unable to attain a speed of more than 11½ knots.

Mantua at Liverpool informed me that she had developed a leak which necessitated docking her; she would not be ready to sail till about 19th. *Digby* arrived from London and joined B Patrol.

I find it very difficult to keep touch with other patrols when I am North of Faroes due to the short range and small power of the Marconi W/T apparatus with which the Armed Merchant Cruisers are fitted.

23. Sunday, 10th January – *Teutonic* joined B Patrol from Liverpool, and Patia joined B Patrol from Avonmouth. The general disposition of the Armed Merchant Cruisers under my orders, the patrols of which were arranged more especially for the interception of the *Bergensfjord* are as follows:

Alsatian ... To the E. of B Patrol on the Bergen track.
B Patrol ... *Cedric*, *Patia*, *Teutonic*, *Viknor*, *Orotava*.
C Patrol ... *Otway*, *Bayano*, *Oropesa*, *Hilary*, *Digby*.
D Patrol ... *Hildebrand*, *Patuca*, *Clan McNaughton*.
Proceeding to join ... *Ambrose*, *Changuinola*.
Coaling at Liverpool ... *Columbella*, *Virginian*, *Mantua*, *Calyx*, *Caribbean*.
Completing at Avonmouth ... *Motagua*.
Detached for special service ... *Eskimo*.

At 6.30 a.m., *Oropesa* reported that *Bergensfjord* had been heard communicating with Bergen, but her signals were faint.

24. Monday, 11th January – *Ambrose* rejoined D Patrol; *Virginian* left Liverpool. In accordance with directions from the Commander-in-Chief, patrols were moved further to the northward in order to keep clear of Battle Squadrons which were passing through their areas. At 8.30 a.m., *Viknor* reported that she had intercepted the Norwegian Steamer *Bergensfjord* in Lat. 62.10´N, Long. 2.24´W. I proceeded in *Alsatian*, with *Patia* and *Teutonic* in company, to the position given. On sighting *Viknor*, standing by *Bergensfjord* I detached *Patia* and *Teutonic* to chase an oil steamer reported by *Viknor*. *Viknor* reported having boarded *Bergensfjord* and arrested a passenger travelling under the name of Spero with a neutral passport. I directed *Viknor* to arrest Spero and any German Reservists discovered and take them on board *Viknor* and to request the Captain of *Bergensfjord* to assist him to obtain their documents. *Viknor* then reported that Spero owned to being the man wanted (Baron Hans

Adam von Wedel)[1] but claimed American Citizenship. It was also stated that the *Bergensfjord* had been examined before leaving New York and that all known Germans had been taken ashore. Six stowaways and one passenger aged 60 were thought to be German Reservists but they would not acknowledge it. These individuals were all taken on board *Viknor* and under arrest. No documents could be discovered and it was reported that papers had been destroyed by a German Doctor.

As the *Bergensfjord* had passed north of Faroe Islands by night, apparently with the direct purpose of avoiding our patrols, and with no intention of calling at Kirkwall although she is one of the vessels permitted to use the North about route, I directed *Viknor* to put a prize crew on board and escort her to Kirkwall, afterwards proceeding to Liverpool to land prisoners and complete with coal.

At 3.0 p.m. *Viknor* reported that the Captain of *Bergensfjord* had written protesting against being taken into harbour on the plea that he was carrying international mails, and also that he would not give any assistance in the navigation of his ship. However, the presence of the prize crew on board and *Alsatian* and *Viknor*, one on each beam, soon put matters right and *Bergensfjord* proceeded to Kirkwall.[2]

In order to intercept two suspicious ships (*California* and *Mjolnir*) reported to be going west, I directed the Senior Officer of D Patrol to place one of his ships between St Kilda and Monarch Islands and to arrange the remainder in line ahead patrol on a line 334° from St Kilda, southern position of southern ship 10 miles from that Island.

The Senior Officer of B Patrol was directed to arrange his ships on a line ahead patrol on a line 340° from Lat. 61 N, Long. 1.20´W, southern position of southern ship being on that point, with ships 30 miles apart.

25. Tuesday 12th January – *Viknor* escorted *Bergensfjord* as far as Fair Isle channel, where she was met by *Garry*, which took charge of *Bergensfjord*. *Viknor* then proceeded to Liverpool to coal and dispose of her prisoners. *Calyx* having completed with coal left Liverpool to rejoin patrol. *Changuinola* arrived from Avonmouth and joined C Patrol. Much difficulty has been experienced in communicating by W/T with

[1]Wedel, Hans Adam von, Baron, Prussian officer and American notary, travelled from Berlin to the United States in 1914 where he organised the purchase of passports which were altered and then issued to German reserve officers for travel to Europe. He hurriedly left the USA when the first disclosures of this practice appeared. His forgeries were clearly poor: his own altered passport gave him away.

[2]*Bergensfjord* was delayed while the Customs inspected her cargo and made enquiries of the Board of Agriculture over some items. The ship was only then allowed to go on (TS 14/1 of 14 January 1915).

Commander-in-Chief and Senior Officers of Patrols when *Alsatian* is north of the Faroe Islands. I consider that a more powerful installation with a musical note would improve matters, and have represented the desirability of making the alteration during the next visit of *Alsatian* to Liverpool.

26. Wednesday, 13th January – *Hildebrand* was detached to Liverpool to coal, and *Patuca* took charge of D Patrol in her absence. *Virginian* rejoined after coaling and was placed on A Patrol from 15 to 60 miles 315° from Myggenoes Light in the Faroe Islands. *Clan MacNaughto*n reported having put into Loch Ewe for fresh water for boilers. *Columbella* left Liverpool after coaling.

27. Thursday, 14th January – I detached *Cedric* and *Otway* to Liverpool to coal and directed *Patia* and *Bayano* to take charge of B and C Patrols respectively. *Calyx* rejoined D Patrol after coaling. *Teutonic* reported that a 6" Common Shell which had been unshipped from ready rack by heavy sea, exploded against the bulwarks. No one was injured and damage was repairable by ship's artificers. A W/T message from the steamer *Bergensfjord* to Bergen was intercepted[1] in which it was suggested that the route of the *Kristianiafjord* (one of the same Company's Steamers) due about 7th February, should be altered, presumably with a view to avoiding our patrols. This would appear to indicate the probability that this line of Steamers would not abide by their undertaking to call at Kirkwall. I think it desirable here to mention the difficulty of adequately dealing with westbound vessels, more especially as several of these may be considered potential minelayers. At this season of the year it is often impossible to examine ships by boarding and all that can be done is to advise them to call at Kirkwall, a course which few if any of them are likely to follow without compulsion.

28. Friday, 15th January – *Columbella* returned to A Patrol after coaling, *Clan MacNaughto*n was detached from D Patrol to coal, *Hildebrand* arrived at Liverpool. In accordance with directions from the Commander-in-Chief I ordered *Ambrose* to be in a position 4 miles SSE of Tiumpan Head at midnight to meet *Conqueror*.

29. Saturday, 16th January – *Motagua* was reported to be leaving Avonmouth to join my Flag. This was the last of the Armed Merchant Cruisers to be completed. *Otway* arrived at Liverpool.

During the night B and C Patrols were shifted 25 miles to the

[1]This was clearly one of *Bergensfjord*'s first actions after being released (see previous note).

westward. I was informed by the Senior Naval Officer Liverpool that *Viknor* had not arrived in port. She had last been heard of on Wednesday 13th January when she made her position through Malin Head Signal Station. At noon I arrived on a rendezvous north of Faroe Islands and communicated visually with *Columbella* and *Virginian* giving them full instructions as to Norway Patrol.

30. Sunday, 17th January – *Cedric* and *Clan McNaughton* arrived at Liverpool to coal, and *Patuca* was detached from patrol to proceed to Liverpool. In compliance with directions from the Commander-in-Chief *Columbella* and *Virginian* were moved to B Patrol and *Patia* and *Orotava* were placed on A Patrol. B Patrol was then formed on a base line 334° from Lat. 60.50´N, Long. 2 W, line ahead patrol, ships 30 miles apart. A Patrol was formed on a base line 320° from Myggenoes Light, south eastern ship 20 miles from Light, remainder 20 miles apart. C Patrol was formed on a base line Sydero to Butt of Lewis, northern ship 40 miles from Sydero, ships 20 miles apart.

31. Monday, 18th January – *Caribbean* left Liverpool and *Patuca* arrived there to coal. *Motagua* joined C Patrol on arrival from Avonmouth. Prize Crews belonging to *Oropesa* and *Hilary* embarked at Kirkwall in *Royal Scott* for return to their ships, but owing to state of weather they could not be transferred.

32. Tuesday, 19th January – *Hilary* left patrol and proceeded to Liverpool to coal. *Caribbean* which was on her way north from Liverpool, put into Belfast. As previously directed by the Commander-in-Chief, the ships working on B Patrol, viz: *Columbella*, *Virginian*, *Teutonic* and *Oropesa*, were ordered to a position off the coast of Norway with a view to intercept the German Steamer *Brandenburg* which was expected to leave Thorshavn.[1] Ships were disposed as follows: *Teutonic* on parallel 62.20´N, 4 to 14 miles from Svino Light, *Columbella* and *Oropesa* on parallel 62.10´N, from 5 to 20 miles from Langfled, *Columbella* being in eastern half. *Virginian* on parallel 62 N, 5 to 15 miles from shore. All ships were directed to keep out of sight of land by day taking up positions by night and in thick weather.

I was informed by the Commander-in-Chief that bodies and wreckage from *Viknor* had been washed ashore at Portrush. Nothing had been heard of this ship which was conveying Baron von Wedel and seven other German prisoners taken from *Bergensfjord* to Liverpool, since she reported her position through Malin Head on Wednesday, 13th January, and it may be assumed that her loss occurred on or about that

[1]This is clearly a mistake, *Brandenburg* was not at Thorshavn (in the Faeroes).

date. I fear she may have foundered in the gale, as she was considered a poor sea boat and not on Lloyds' List as A.1.

33. Wednesday, 20th January – *Ambrose* which had been waiting off Butt of Lewis for *Conqueror* was ordered to rejoin D Patrol. A new centre line for A Patrol was arranged, extending 80 miles in direction of 360° from Lat. 62.20´N, Long. 10 W, ships 30 miles apart. A new centre line for C Patrol was arranged, extending 80 miles in direction of 360° from Lat. 59.40´´N, Long. 9°W ships 25 miles apart. The eastern line of D Patrol was ordered to extend from St. Kilda 80 miles in direction of 335°, ships 35 miles apart. On account of submarine menace, orders were given to all patro1s to zigzag by day and on moonlight nights, maintaining a speed of 13 knots.

34. Thursday, 21st January – heavy gale from north. *Mantua* and *Hildebrand* sailed from Liverpool after coaling. *Orotava* was detached from B Patrol to coal, and *Hilary* arrived at Liverpool. *Caribbean* reported that she was anchored off Bangor (Ireland) repairing steering gear, and would probably proceed north during the day.

I arranged a rendezvous with *Motagua* and communicated by visual signal the orders as regards Norway patrol on which I directed her to relieve *Oropesa*. *Bayano* was placed in charge of C Patrol temporarily.

At 10.45 p.m. orders were received from Commander-in-Chief to abandon Norway Patrol and assume new B Patrol area, the centre line of which was to lie on meridian 1.15´E between Lat. 61.10´N and 62.30´N.

35. Friday, 22nd January – On the resumption of B Patrol as ordered *Motagua* returned to C Patrol as Senior Officer.

Information was received from Senior Naval Officer, Liverpool, that *Caribbean* had grounded slightly and required docking at Belfast.

36. Saturday, 23rd January – *Mantua* rejoined A Patrol and *Hildebrand* D Patrol as Senior Officers respectively. *Otway* left Liverpool. *Oropesa* and *Calyx* were detached to coal.

I proceeded in *Alsatian* to the Southward. Course was afterwards shaped for Barra Head.

Calyx reported having visited St Kilda to ascertain what progress had been made with work on W/T Station. This appeared to have been delayed by bad weather, and would not be completed for a month.

37. Sunday, 24th January – The disposition of Tenth C.S. for the ensuing week was as follows:

A Patrol ... *Otway*, *Mantua*, *Patia*.
B Patrol ... *Columbella*, *Virginian*, *Teutonic*.
C Patrol ... *Motagua*, *Bayano*, *Changuinola*, *Digby*.

D Patrol ... *Hildebrand*, *Ambrose*, *Clan MacNaughton*.
Proceeding to coal ... *Alsatian*, *Orotava*, *Oropesa*, *Calyx*.
At Liverpool ... *Cedric*, *Hilary*, *Patuca*.
At Belfast ... *Caribbean*.
Special service ... *Eskimo*.

Off Skerryvore *Otway* and *Clan MacNaughton* were passed steaming to the Northward. Orders were given them by signal, *Otway* being directed to proceed to A Patrol, taking charge as Senior Officer of all patrols.

At 5.0 p.m. a message was received from *Tara* that a submarine had been reported in the vicinity of Larne.

38. Monday, 25th January – *Alsatian* anchored off the bar in the Mersey at 1.20 a.m.

19. *Contraband Committee to Sir Cecil Spring-Rice,*[1] *British Ambassador at Washington, DC*

4 December 1914

We have ample evidence that the major part of the enormous imports of meat into Denmark from the United States is finding its way into Germany. So great has this trade become that several American meat firms have opened offices in Copenhagen since the war began. In regard to the meat cargoes on these ships [*Alfred Nobel*, *Bjornsen*, *Fridland*], we are authoritatively informed that American shippers have approached meat merchants in Copenhagen without success in order to persuade them to appear as legitimate owners of cargoes. The cargoes are in the Prize Court, where proof of innocent destination must be produced by owners. Please obtain for us at once statistics showing exports of meat and lard from U.S.A. to Norway, Sweden and Denmark respectively for each of the years 1912 and 1913 (if possible showing monthly figures) and figures for last three months from official government returns.

[1]Spring-Rice, Cecil Arthur, GCMG, GCVO (1869–1918), British Ambassador to Washington 1913–1918; earlier postings had been to Washington (three times), Brussels, Berlin, Constantinople, Teheran (twice), Egypt, St Petersburg, and Minister at Stockholm (1908–1913); author of the poem 'I vow to thee, my country'.

20. *Commander F.H. Walter*[1] *to Rear-Admiral Commanding Tenth Cruiser Squadron*

HMS *Caribbean*, Liverpool, 9 January 1915

Report of Proceedings, 12 December 1914–6 January 1915

I have the honour to report proceedings as follows:

1. On Saturday 12th December 1914 I commissioned HMS *Caribbean* with 1 Lieutenant, R.N., and 183 Naval ratings from Devonport, and on the 14th ultimo the Mercantile Crew signed on.

2. On the 17th December ship proceeded out of Brocklebank Dock and anchored in the River Mersey for the night.

3. On the 18th December ship proceeded for Gunnery Trials and for adjustment of Compasses; the former were quite satisfactory, but the Compass adjustment was done under difficulties, and was rendered useless owing to a Resistance Coil having been put within 6 feet of the Compass.

4. Great trouble was experience[d] with the Search Lights and Dynamos – the lights frequently going out due to overload on Dynamos. Ship anchored at 3.30 p.m. and defects were taken in hand, which were not finished until Thursday 23rd ult., p.m.

5. During the week ship was at anchor for completion of defects, no leave at all was given to the Officers or men, and the ship was kept ready for sea – steam being on the Engines all the time. This was necessary owing to the strong tide and the constant traffic during dense fog. A collision took place within three cables of ship (at about midnight) on the 17th ultimo (the first night at anchor). On another occasion at about 11.30 p.m. *Eskimo* signalled 'Am dragging both anchors, will you keep clear'. Weather was very bad all this time.

6. On Thursday 24th December, ship proceeded to B Patrol when the fog cleared, and at 11.30 p.m. Telemotor gear broke down rendering ship Not Under Control for half an hour, weather at the time being very bad.

7. On Christmas Day at 2 p.m. ship rolled 40° each way, and steering gear again gave trouble about midnight. Weather still very bad – a heavy SE gale blowing most of the day.

8. On 27 December a small Danish Steamer called *Rodfaxe* was sighted and hove to. The wind had increased to a very heavy

[1]Walter, Frederick Henry, RN, (1872–1949), Lieutenant 1894, Commander 1905, Captain of *Caribbean* 1914–1915, of *Victorian* 1915–1916, Captain 1918, Captain of *Teutonic* 1918–1919.

SSE gale-force 10, and ship again rolled 40°–45°. The Aeriel was carried away, and ship was at times unmanageable.

9. At 8.45 a.m. on the 29th ult., closed on a Norwegian Steamer *Ranulf Hansen*, with Barley from New York 18 days out. Took her into Burra Firth at SNO's orders (*Cedric*) and boarded her, and all being correct she was ordered to proceed. The *Rodfaxe* was also ordered by *Cedric* to proceed at 10 a.m. Ship remained at Burra Firth for the night to repair damage and overhaul steering gear.

10. Ship returned to her patrol at daylight the following morning (30th) and Sub-calibre practice was carried out by all guns' crews in the forenoon; ship steaming round a target, and ship was swung for deviations at the same time. Ship was never off her Patrol again, but very bad weather was experienced and though the ship is a very good seaboat, rolls very heavily, and steers badly, unless going Full Speed.

Cedric was sighted and communicated with on 1st January, and also on 6th, and final orders to leave Patrol were received from her at 2.30 p.m. on 6th inst.

11. Several defects require to be made good, the Telemotor gear being the principal item, and the alteration of the Seaboats' davits which are at present a most dangerous fitting, the distances between the boat's slings being 10 feet shorter than the distance between the davits.

12. Ship left Liverpool 200 tons of coal short and to arrive with 20 per cent on board, or 300 tons, cuts her working days down to 15 days at 12 knots.

Coal expenditure appears to be excessive since leaving Liverpool ship has steamed 3028 miles on 1200 tons of coal.

21. *Memorandum by Captain Richard Webb,*[1] *Director of Trade Division*

Admiralty, 24 December 1914

Northern Patrol (24 Armed Liners)

This patrol assumes that the Pentland Firth and the passage between Orkneys and Shetlands is watched by yachts and trawlers &c. under a separate command from that of the 10th Cruiser Squadron.

[1]Webb, Richard, KCMG, CB, RN (1870–1950), Commander 1902, Captain 1907, Captain of *Amethyst* on East Coast of South America 1909–1911, of *Illustrious* 1913, Director of Trade Division 1914–1917, Captain of *New Zealand* 1917–1918, Rear-Admiral 1918, Assistant High Commissioner in Turkey 1918–1920, Rear-Admiral in Fourth Battle Squadron in the Mediterranean 1920–1922, Vice-Admiral 1924, Head of Naval Mission to Greece 1924–1925, President Royal Naval College Greenwich 1926–1929, Admiral 1928, retired 1929.

Assuming the Line Ahead Patrol be adopted on the grounds of economy of ships, two lines – a night's run apart – are essential.

There are two positions in which the line can be placed:

(a) With the advanced line between Shetlands and the East Coast of Iceland, and the retired line between Hebrides and the West coast of Iceland.
(b) The advanced line between Shetlands and Norway, the retired line in two parts, one between Faroe and the Hebrides, and one on a line NE from Faroes.

Method (a) is less exposed to submarine attack, but the total length of line to be watched is 850 miles as compared with 450 in method (b).

Owing to the approaching winter weather which will reduce the efficiency of the enemy's submarines, and the fact that the Patrol lines will never occupy the same position on two successive days, it is considered that the extra risk of submarine attack involved in method (b) should be adopted.

The positions of the lines should, therefore, it is suggested, be as follows:

Line X.	Between the Shetlands and Norway.
Line Y	Between Lewis and Syderoe.
Line Z.	On a line from Faroe between NNE and ENE about 100 miles in length.

The position of these lines should be constantly varied within the limits of about 100 miles.

The majority of the ships available should be equally divided between lines X and Y, lighter and less valuable ships being stationed on X. Three or four of the largest vessels should be used on Line Z.

Certain neutrals have been allowed to use the Northern Route provided that they approach from the West to the Northward of latitude 60 N until they arrive at longitude 3 W when they are to steer for Kirkwall, passing to the Eastward of N. Ronaldshay. These will be shepherded in by the vessels watching the Fair Island Channel.

It is considered that Liverpool should be the base for supplies, subject to such modification as the Commander-in-Chief thinks fit.

It is possible that vessels might attempt to pass North of Iceland, but this is considered unlikely in view of the extra distance and dangerous navigation. In any case, a patrol would be ineffective, as the hours of daylight are only approximately 4 to 5.

Assuming that 24 ships are available, and that 4 of these are required for line Z (NE of Faroes) then 7 ships should be continually available on each of the patrol lines X and Y. In this case, if the speed of Patrol be 12 knots, and the average visibility be 5 miles, there will be an even chance of sighting ships passing in and out.

This patrol should prove fairly efficient against merchant ships, but it is undoubtedly much exposed to sudden attack by the enemy's cruisers which at present are free to leave the Skagerak at any time, and which can enter or leave their own North Sea ports at night without much risk.

This exposure to attack must be accepted, and in the event of enemy cruisers escaping out of their ports, successfully evading any watching vessels and attacking the patrol line, the latter must endeavour to escape in the darkness and thick weather, or make use of territorial waters.

It is desirable that these patrols should be occasionally backed up by an Armoured Cruiser Squadron, and that in any case there should be a squadron within supporting distance.

17 Armed Merchant Vessels are now completing for sea and are expected to be available early in January to reinforce the Northern Patrol, making 24 Vessels in all ... Rear-Admiral de Chair has been appointed to command the Squadron with his flag in HMS *Alsatian*.

It is contemplated that these ships shall be employed to prevent enemy or neutral merchant vessels entering or leaving the North Sea contrary to the regulations which have been issued to control the movements of merchant vessels within the North Sea area, and also to give timely warning should any of the enemy's cruisers attempt to break out by the North-about route.

In carrying out these duties, it is contemplated that the Squadron will work in close association with the Yacht and Trawler Patrol in the Fair Island passage and with the Cruiser Squadrons of the Grand Fleet.

***

22. *Commander-in-Chief Home Fleets to Admiralty*

HMS *Iron Duke*, 1 January 1915

***

2. The Tenth Cruiser Squadron is divided into four divisions, and is organised at present as follows:

Area	Eastern Base line of Area	Ships allotted to area
A. Between Faroes and Iceland	Meridian of 5.30´W	*Alsatian* *Mantua* *Otway* *Virginian* *Columbella*

B.	North of Shetland Islands	Meridian of 1.0´W	*Teutonic* *Cedric* *Caribbean* *Patia* *Orotava* *Viknor*
C.	South of Faroe Islands	Line joining Sydero and Sule Skerry	*Motagua* *Oropesa* *Bayano* *Changuinola* *Digby* *Hilary*
D.	West of Hebrides	N ½ W from St Kilda	*Hildebrand* *Calyx* *Eskimo* *Ambrose* *Clan McNaughton* *Patuca*

Ships in rotation coal at Liverpool, and when they are in routine at least four vessels will be on each patrol.

On the armed merchant cruiser *Laurentic* joining the squadron, she will be detailed to area A.

3. The actual base line of each patrol and the area patrolled is constantly moved, in order that the actual position of the patrols may not become known to the enemy. Each patrol conforms to the movements of the remainder, so that the distance apart conforms to the distances run during the dark hours by the trading steamers at nine knots.

4. After a time the whole of the patrol areas will be shifted considerably, as otherwise a cruiser raid by the enemy might meet with some success.

5. ... [I]t is contemplated that the Tenth Cruiser Squadron will work in association with the Yacht and Trawler Patrol in the Fair Island passage, and with the cruiser squadrons ... [but these] ... cruiser squadrons have not as yet been stationed in support of the Tenth Cruiser Squadron.

It is proposed, however, to keep one cruiser squadron generally in the vicinity of Latitude 60 N, Longitude 5 W, to support the Tenth Cruiser Squadron.

6. As regards the Trawler Patrol, it has been found necessary, on account of the vulnerability of Scapa Flow to submarine attack, to concentrate a large number of the Northern Patrol trawlers in the Hoxa, Switha, Hoy and Holm entrances.

7. The mercantile traffic through the Pentlands is dealt with chiefly by the armed boarding steamers which are stationed forty to fifty miles to the eastward of Pentland Skerries; owing to the presence of submarines a position closer in than this is dangerous. It may be noted that when the Loch Ewe trawler patrol is up to its authorised strength, these vessels will be able to render some assistance.

8. I would add that, while the daylight hours remain as short as at present (about five hours north of the Faroes), some vessels probably pass without being examined. When the patrols are at full strength, however, and the days become longer, complete control of shipping should be established.

23. *Captain G.A. Vivian[1] to Rear-Admiral Commanding Tenth Cruiser Squadron*

HMS *Patia*, 2 February 1915

Report of Proceedings, 5–31 January 1915

I have the honour to submit herewith a report of my proceedings. I left Avonmouth on the morning of the 5th of January to carry out gun-trials, which were quite satisfactory. After anchoring in Walton Bay to land Lieut. (G) etc., I sailed at 9 p.m. for Milford Haven to adjust my compasses there in accordance with orders received from the Admiralty. I arrived at Milford Haven at daylight on the 6th and swung for compass adjustment, sailing again at 3.30 for my destination. Going up the West Coast of Ireland a moderate gale and heavy sea were experienced. On the 8th I sighted and stopped the Norwegian steamer *Sverresborg* of Bergen bound for Kirkwall from Baltimore. The sea was too heavy for boarding.[2] On January 10th stopped and examined British collier *Lena*. At 1.30 sighted *Cedric* and communicated with her. At 2.40 proceeded in chase of a steamer which was overtaken at 3.45 and found to be the Norwegian steamer *Mexican[o]* [25] bound for Kirkwall. Too much sea to board. At 7 a.m. on the 11th observed a steamer steering to the East,

[1]Vivian, Gerald W., CMG, RN (1869–1921), Lieutenant 1894, Commander 1904, Captain 1912; qualified in flying 1913, Captain of *Patia* 1914–1915.

[2]The *Sverresborg* was inspected and allowed to proceed.

remained with her until daylight and then stopped her. Found her to be the Swedish steamer *Lapland* bound for Narvik in water-ballast. This ship was not boarded as there was too much sea and we have no boat fitted with dropping-gear. This ship I think should have been sent in, but she was very obviously in ballast (her screw and fore-foot being nearly out of the water) and therefore could not have any contraband, and the only way I could send her in was by convoying her to Kirkwall myself. As this meant leaving station and also the possibility of submarine attack, I did not consider such a course advisable and therefore allowed her to proceed. At 11.15 I sighted your flag-ship and took station on her Starboard beam. On the 15th at noon sighted a steamer, stopped her and found her to be the Norwegian steamer *Bragin* from Ardrossan to Bergen with bunker coal. Too much sea to board her. On the 16th experienced a very heavy Northerly gale with a very heavy sea, hove to until 6 a.m. the 17th when weather moderated and by your orders I proceeded to A Patrol sighting your flagship on the way. On the 19th sighted and communicated with the *Orotava* by signal. On the 21st experienced a very heavy Northerly gale, hove to until 4 a.m. on the 23rd when weather moderated and proceeded on patrol. At 1 p.m. stopped British trawler *Lord Knollys* bound for Hull. At 5 p.m. on the 27th stopped British trawler *Yokohama* of Hull going North. At 4 a.m. on the 29th in accordance with your orders, I left patrol and proceeded for Liverpool. At 4 a.m. on the 30th I received orders not to go to Liverpool but to proceed to Lough Swilly, when within about 60 miles of Lough Swilly orders were received from C. in C. Grand Fleet to proceed to Loch Ewe. Course was altered accordingly. At 7 p.m. the same day when I was just north of the Monach Light Orders were received to proceed to the Firth of Clyde to coal, owing to hostile submarines. Course was again altered. In view of the fact that I had been informed that enemy's submarines were believed to be off Larne, speed was adjusted so as to pass through the North Channel with the maximum favourable tide, and the engines were run at full speed. I passed through the North Channel at a speed over the ground of something over 18 knots and continued at full speed until I anchored at the Tail of the Bank at 4 p.m. on the 31st. The weather was thick with driving hail-storms and occasional clearings. A constant zig-zag was maintained and all precautions taken against submarine attack, but no submarines were observed.

After a month's experience of this ship the following remarks are submitted: When full up with coal and down by the head, as is for normal trim under these conditions, she is not a particularly good sea-boat and is sluggish and wet. When however the forward coal is out or to an extent out, the ship behaves extremely well in a sea-way and is buoyant and dry when hove to in a heavy sea. She is extremely economical in coal and the engines and boilers are most satisfactory. Her weak point from a structural point of view is that the two large holds have no subdivision at all and no real decks; they are in fact large tanks, the flooding of either being sufficient to sink the ship, and owing to the extremely small pumping power available for clearing these spaces the flooding of them is a comparatively easy matter. This point has been represented to the Admiralty, but if it is intended to retain these ships for service in the Navy, they would undoubtedly be very vastly improved by the fitting of a thwartship watertight bulkhead in each hold, and this would not be a matter of much time or money. Many of the fittings in the ship are poor, the majority of the swing-doors open to the roll of the ship for instance, which though in itself not of great importance, may show the ship up by the lights exposed, as very few of the automatic arrangements for putting the lights out work properly. I hope to rectify this matter before going to sea again. The ship has no boat fitted with dropping-gear, which in view of the work she is employed on she most certainly should have. When fitting out I asked for Montagu whalers with dropping-gear, I got two ordinary whalers without dropping-gear. These boats are stowed on crutches in the after well-deck, and can only be hoisted out by the derricks and winches. In a sea-way this is not a satisfactory method at all, and these boats should be at davits (which can easily be fitted) with dropping-gear. The W/T is unsatisfactory and we get no range and most inaccurate messages, partially perhaps owing to the plant, but mainly to the inexperience of the operators. This has improved recently and will I think improve more.

24. *Contraband Committee Minutes*
Statement by Captain Richard Webb, Director of Trade Division

Admiralty, 9 January 1915

The *Denver* was brought into Kirkwall in order that her papers, and if necessary her cargo, should be examined [18, para. 18].

It is, of course, obvious that a vessel which is avowedly going direct to an enemy port cannot be allowed to pass through the British patrol line without examination. This examination in these days of large vessels cannot be properly carried out at sea, especially in the stormy waters round the Orkneys. It is therefore necessary to take ships into Kirkwall.

The vessel arrived at Kirkwall at 11.50 a.m. on the 5th January, and the telegram from His Majesty's Customs at Kirkwall presumably reached the Foreign Office that evening.

The Admiralty telegraphed the Foreign Office at 9.45 a.m. on the 6th January, asking if any steps had been taken, and if not, that a telegram should be sent to His Majesty's Customs at Kirkwall to release the vessel if the Foreign Office were satisfied that the vessel and cargo were innocent.

At the same time a telegram was sent to the Admiral Commanding the Orkneys and Shetlands[1] stating that orders had been sent to the Customs to give the vessel a clearance.

The vessel was cleared by the Customs at 3 p.m. 6th January. She left to continue her voyage at 5.30 p.m. on the 6th January.

25. *Contraband Committee Minutes*

12 January 1915

A telegram dated the 11th January from the Customs at Lerwick [gave a list of the cargo on the *Mexicano*] [23]. A telegram should be sent to the Customs instructing them to allow this vessel to proceed. She has on board two consignments of 166 tons and 83 tons respectively of rosin for Christiania. The Commissioners recommend that a telegram should be sent to His Majesty's Ministers at Copenhagen, Christiania and Stockholm, instructing them to urge the governments to which they are accredited to place rosin and resinous substances on their prohibition of exports list, and intimating that these two consignments have been allowed to proceed, as His Majesty's Government do not wish to delay the vessel; but that in the event of rosin and resinous substances not being put on the prohibition of exports list His Majesty's Government will be impelled to hold up future shipments of these articles, as they are now absolute contraband ....[2]

[1]The Admiral Commanding Orkneys and Shetlands was Admiral S.C. Colville (Chapter 3, p. 175 note 3).

[2]This is an excellent example of the blackmail used by the Committee, with the full approval of the Foreign Office and the Admiralty, which was designed to compel the neutral governments of northern Europe to act as British agents for the enforcement of British policy – always referred to as 'regulations', as though there was never any doubt as to the legality or acceptability of such policy.

26. *Contraband Committee Minutes*

18 January 1915

A note from the Danish Minister stating that part of the cargo on board this vessel [*United States*] consists of 220 tons of copper to the Nordske Kabel Traadfabriker Valsevarkar and 100 tons of lead to Hermann Raffel of Copenhagen. The Danish Minister states that the first of these two firms has solemnly declared that the copper is for consumption in Denmark and Norway and will not in any way be re-exported to countries at war with Great Britain. Messrs Raffel have given a similar declaration with regard to the lead which is for consumption in Denmark. The Danish Minister hopes that the *United States* will be allowed to proceed on the 17th January with an undertaking by Captain Cold that the pig-lead, dried hides, machinery, telegraph poles, vulcanised fibre, rubber packing, automobile, bearing instruments will be returned to Great Britain as soon as the steamer is unloaded. As regards the copper and lead, the Danish Minister should be informed that the guarantees given are satisfactory, and that there will be no need to return these two items. The other items mentioned must, however, be returned failing satisfactory guarantees as to their destination.

A telegram was received from the Customs at Kirkwall dated the 17th January, giving details of the cargo on board this vessel, which is of a miscellaneous character. A copy of the telegram should be sent to the Board of Agriculture.

27. *Surveyor F.G. Haughton to [Board of Customs and Excise]*

Kirkwall, 18 January 1915

The Master of the SS *Kronprinsessen Margarita* was subjected to conditions as to landing and communications similar to all other alien masters. These conditions ... did not at any time contemplate placing masters in custody while the conditions were complied with, and were a compromise between the wish of the Admiral Commanding for total prohibition as to landing ... and representations made by me to the Admiralty ... that reasonable opportunity for the carrying on of the Master's business should be afforded. The Admiral's consent was given to the proposed conditions ...

Kirkwall being in the centre of a naval activity it is imperative that no opportunity should be given to any alien, friendly or otherwise, for gleaning information, and the restriction ... preventing masters from passing beyond the shore end of Kirkwall Pier was added as a result of the Admiral's letter ...

A censorship is exercised over all communications from alien masters by the King's Harbour Master, ... and presumably if any telegrams from the Master of the *Kronprinsessen Margarita* was not allowed to pass, the telegram must have contained forbidden matter.

28. *Rear-Admiral de Chair to Admiralty*

HMS *Alsatian*, 9 March 1915

Report of Proceedings, 25 January–9 March 1915

***

1. On arrival in the Port of Liverpool on 25th January I gave all necessary orders to Captain Benson[1] as regards conduct of patrol during my absence, and *Cedric* then left for the North.

2. During my stay in Liverpool I reorganised the Base Office, and arranged for better facilities for coaling and watering ships of Tenth Cruiser Squadron in order to enable them to return to their patrols more expeditiously. Arrangements were also made with the G.P.O. to install telephones on board ships while in the docks with a view to eatablishing communication as visual signalling is not practicable.

3. *Alsatian* completed with coal and Stores on Sunday 31st January, but on account of the presence of hostile submarines off the Bar Lightship the sailing of all Armed Merchant Cruisers was delayed.

4. On 3rd February I requested permission from Admiralty for Armed Merchant Cruisers to proceed to their stations and in reply received orders to wait till there was less moonlight.

5. In the meantime it became necessary to make arrangements for coaling other Armed Merchant Cruisers, and with the concurrence of the Commander-in-Chief, *Digby*, *Ambrose*, *Columbella* and *Changuinola* were detached to Loch Ewe, and *Teutonic*, *Virginian* and *Patia* to the Clyde.

6. On 4th February I wired to the Admiralty saying I proposed sailing at 6 p.m. on 6th February and received approval the same day.

7. Saturday, 6th February – The following ships left Liverpool after

[1]Benson, Robert Edmund Ross, CB, RN (1864–1927), Lieutenant 1887, Commander 1900, Captain 1906, Inspecting Captain of Mechanical Training Establishments 1912–1914, Captain of *Cedric* 1914–1916, Commodore 2nd Class in Tenth Cruiser Squadron and Captain in *Teutonic* 1916, Rear-Admiral (retired) 1918, Vice-Admiral 1923.

dark and proceeded to rejoin their patrols, giving the Isle of Man a wide berth to avoid the two German submarines reported waiting there: *Alsatian*, *Caribbean*, *Bayano*, *Oropesa* and *Calyx*, the latter with special orders from the Commander-in-Chief to call at Loch Ewe for signal books for St Kilda W/T Station. *Orotava* remained at Liverpool to make good a defect developed when coming out of dock.

8. Sunday, 7th February – Information having been received that a Norwegian Steamer had been reported laying mines on the 3rd instant between Barra Head and Coll Island, and *Virginian* having reported exploding a mine by gunfire on 6th February in Lat. 56.15´N, Long. 7.59´W, I warned all ships on passage to keep a good look out. When in Lat. 56.19´N, Long. 7.37´W *Alsatian* sighted a floating mine. *Bayano* also reported sighting two floating mines in Lat. 56.33´N, Long. 7.43´W. In both cases attempts were made to explode these mines, but they were lost sight of in heavy sea and mist before this could be done. When in W/T touch with *Hildebrand* on D Patrol I enquired whether there was any news of *Clan McNaughton*. This ship had not been heard of since the evening of 2nd February and *Hildebrand* and *Patuca* had been searching for her, but without success. When last communicated with by W/T, *Clan McNaughton* would appear to have been in Lat. 58.41´N, Long. 9.27´W carrying out patrol duties.

9. Monday, 8th February – On arrival within W/T touch of the various patrols I ascertained their positions and orders and made such additional dispositions as seemed necessary in view of the increased number of ships available:

A Patrol ... *Alsatian*, *Otway*, *Mantua*.
B Patrol ... *Cedric*, *Caribbean*.
C Patrol ... *Bayano*, *Hilary*, *Oropesa*, *Changuinola*.
D Patrol ... *Hildebrand*, *Patuca*, *Digby*.
Proceeding to Clyde ... *Motagua*.
Proceeding to Loch Ewe ... *Calyx*.
Oon passage to Liverpool ... *Orotava*.
Coaling in Clyde ... *Ambrose*, *Patia*, *Teutonic*, *Virginian*.
Coaling in Loch Ewe ... *Columbella*.
Coaling at Scapa Flow ... *Eskimo*.
Missing ... *Clan MacNaughton*.

The ships working on D Patrol were searching for *Clan MacNaughton* and reported sighting several small pieces of wreckage such as hatchway cover, griping spar, door, battens, life belts, &c.

10. Tuesday, 9th February – *Changuinola* rejoined C Patrol, *Hilary* left C Patrol for Clyde to coal and make good defective steering gear.

Columbella left Loch Ewe; *Ambrose* arrived in Clyde. The following orders were given to Senior Officer, C Patrol: Cross base line Sydero–Sule Skerry steering to make good 245° at 7 a.m. daily, southern ship 45 miles from Sule Skerry, ships 20 miles apart, speed 13 knots, zigzag, altering course 16 points at 6 p.m. daily. A new base line was ordered for B Patrol–360° from Lat. 61.10´N, Long. 1 W, ships 20 miles apart, base line to be crossed at 7 a.m. daily, steering to make good 250°, speed 13 knots, zigzag, altering course 16 points at 6 p.m. daily.

During the afternoon closed *Hildebrand* within visual signalling distance and obtained from her the latest news of *Clan MacNaughton*. It appears probable that she foundered on the night of 2nd February, between 1.30 and 9.15, to the westward of the Hebrides, possibly by striking a floating mine of which there were many drifting north. As *Hildebrand*, *Patuca* and *Digby* had been searching in the vicinity since 6 a.m. on 3rd February, and the painting of wreckage observed pointed to the fact that the fragments belonged to an Armed Merchant Cruiser, I directed *Hildebrand* to abandon search and resume patrol as follows: Cross base line 335° from St Kilda Steering to make good 235° at 7 a.m. daily, southern ship 15 miles from St Kilda, ships 20 miles apart, speed 13 knots, zigzag, altering course 16 points at 6 p.m. daily. The following orders were given for A Patrol: Cross base line 360° from Lat. 62.45´N, Long, 5 W steering to make good 270° at 7 a.m. daily, southern ship in Lat. 62.45´N, Long. 5 W, ships 20 miles apart, speed 19 knots, zigzag, altering course 16 points at 6 p.m. daily. These base lines are being continually shifted in order to avoid submarines.

11. Wednesday, 10th February – *Columbella* and *Orotava* returned to B Patrol after coaling at Loch Ewe and Liverpool respectively. *Columbella* reported the facilities at Loch Ewe very poor for coaling and watering. *Eskimo* left Scapa where she had been making good engine defects to join D Patrol. *Motagua* arrived in Clyde to coal. The Armed Boarding Steamer *Caesarea* left Kirkwall with Prize Crew for ships of 10th Cruiser Squadron. This has supplied a long felt want as there are sometimes as many as 18 prize crews away at one time.

12. Thursday, 11th February – *Patia* left Clyde and *Hilary* arrived there to coal and repair broken rack to steering gear. At 11 a.m. *Cedric* reported that she had chased a two funnel steamer for 3 hours which drew away from her at 16½ knots, and patrols were disposed to intercept her. At 5.15 p.m. she was caught and boarded by *Digby* and was found to be *Frederick VIII* of the Danish United Shipping Co. She informed *Digby* that *Kristianiafjord* was to the northward and westward of her position (Lat. 60.26´N, Long. 6.12´W) steaming west. *Frederick VIII* was allowed to proceed after examination. She gave as her reason

for not calling at Kirkwall that her voyage had already been delayed two days by mines off Christiansund and that she was unaware of necessity of calling at Kirkwall when westward bound. Captain also stated that it was commonly reported at Christiansund that German submarines were lying in wait there for ships of Wilson Line.[1] Arranged new base lines of patrols as follows:

A ... 360° from Lat. 62.40´N, Long. 6 W, line to be crossed at 7 a.m. daily, steering to make good 270°.

B ... 350° from Lat. 61 N, Long. 1.15´W, line to be crossed at 7 a.m. daily, steering to make good 240°.

13. Friday, 12th February – *Eskimo* joined D Patrol from Scapa where she had been coaling and making good defects after carrying out special service duties by order of Commander-in-Chief.

The weather being favourable, opportunity was taken by several ships to carry out Gunnery Practices.

14. Saturday, 13th February – *Mantua* was detached to Clyde to coal. *Patia* rejoined B Patrol. *Caesarea* brought out prize crews from Kirkwall and transferred them to *Bayano*, *Oropesa* and *Caribbean*. *Otway* intercepted *Trondhjemsfjord* of the Norwegian–American Line proceeding east. She evidently endeavoured to avoid our patrols by passing to north of Faroe Islands, and had no intention of calling at Kirkwall. Her cargo included fuses and detonators. She was sent to Kirkwall with a prize crew [37]. With a view to intercepting the Danish Steamer *Oscar II* which was reported to have left New York on 4th February, the base line of B Patrol was shifted forty miles to the eastward during the night as there were signs from intercepted W/T messages from *Oscar II* to Bergen that she had managed to slip through C Patrol.

15. Sunday, 14th February – The shifting of B Patrol turned out to be a fortunate move, for *Cedric* and *Caribbean* shortly afterwards sighted her, and after a four hour chase *Cedric* reported that she had captured *Oscar II* at 3 a.m., in Lat. 61 N., Long. 1.20´W. and had sent her to Kirkwall with a prize crew. This ship had many passengers on board, several of whom appeared to be travelling under assumed names, and were probably German Reservists, and the Captain forwarded a written protest against being sent to Kirkwall. She belongs to one of the

[1]An example of a practice, or an attitude, very common throughout the war: neutrals were constantly willing to report rumours, facts, guesswork, and to relate information of all sorts to the British. There is no reason to suppose that they were any less reticent with the Germans or less willing to discuss the British ships, though submarines were viewed much less favourably than the British surface ships when intervention occurred.

Steamship Lines which are allowed to use the Northabout route on the understanding that their vessels will call at Kirkwall, which, however, they appear not to have the slightest intention of doing [34]. General disposition of Squadron was as follows:

A Patrol ... *Alsatian*, *Otway*, *Columbella*.
B Patrol ... *Cedric*, *Caribbean*, *Patia*, *Orotava*.
C Patrol ... *Bayano*, *Oropesa*, *Changuinola*, *Digby*.
D Patrol ... *Hildebrand*, *Patuca*, *Calyx*, *Eskimo*.
Proceeding to Clyde to coal ... *Mantua*.
Coaling in Clyde ... *Teutonic*, *Virginian*, *Hilary*, *Ambrose*, *Motagua*.

The number of Vessels intercepted during the week was 39, of which 15 were sent into port for examination. During the afternoon *Alsatian* intercepted a Norwegian sailing Ship *Olav*. The Captain of this ship stated that he felt sure the cargo, which was bran, was intended for Germany. There were three Germans among the crew. She had cleared from Falmouth, where, it appears, the Officials told the Captain that if caught by Northern Patrol he would be sent to Kirkwall. These details I reported to Commander-in-Chief, as I consider the action of the Falmouth Officials would appear to assist the enemy. It is not understood how they could have let her proceed as the most casual examination must have raised their suspicions [39].

16. Monday, 15th February – *Caribbean*, after being warned of the presence of submarines in the Minch, was detached to Loch Ewe, and *Patuca* to Clyde, to coal. *Mantua* arrived in Clyde.

Bayano reported having sighted a ship's life boat, outside painted grey, inside white, in Lat. 59.1´N, Long. 7.46´W. Several planks were painted black and covered in grey paint, and name was missing.

17. Tuesday, 16th February – Got into visual touch with *Cedric* and after giving her necessary orders etc. detached her to Liverpool to coal. *Caribbean* arrived at Loch Ewe to coal, and *Virginian*, *Motagua* and *Teutonic* left the Clyde after coaling. Second Light Cruiser Squadron was met with at 4 p.m. steaming S 74° E.

During the night Patrols were re-arranged as follows:

A ... 330° from Lat. 62.38´N, Long. 7 W steering to make good 240°, ships 20 miles apart.

B ... 350° from Lat. 61 N, Long. 10 W, steering to make good 240°, ships 20 miles apart.

C ... 335° from Lat. 59.40´N, Long. 5.25´W, steering to make good 245°, ships 25 miles apart.

At 6 p.m. *Changuinola* reported that she had boarded American Oil Tank *Pioneer* of New York, formerly the German ship *Kiow* of

Hamburg. She had a cargo of petrol and was proceeding to Goteburg and Copenhagen. Her owners were the Standard Oil Co. and her Captain, who was American, did his best to pass the patrol. The ship was on her first voyage under American Colours, having been purchased since the outbreak of war. She was sent in to Kirkwall with a prize crew.[1]

18. Wednesday, 17th February – *Hilary* left Clyde, *Patuca* arrived there to coal. *Virginian* and *Motagua* rejoined patrol. A heavy gale from SE, backing to E by N was experienced. Glass fell rapidly from 29.80 to 28.56,[2] snow and hail. Ships were directed to lie to if necessary. *Columbella* reported unable to steer course and ship lying to. *Calyx* proceeded to west of Loch Tarbert for shelter.

Five German submarines were reported 8 miles SW of Cape Wrath. It would appear they are making for the neighbourhood of west coast ports to intercept British shipping.

19. Thursday, 18th February – *Cedric* arrived at Liverpool to coal. This ship carries 6000 tons of coal and can keep the sea for 43 days at 13 knots, but *Caribbean* who left Loch Ewe today to rejoin patrol is a very poor sea boat and carries only enough coal to keep the sea 11 days. *Motagua* reported having passed *Bergensfiord* east bound. She was allowed to proceed in accordance with Admiralty order. Blowing hard from ESE at the time with snow squalls, too rough to lower a boat.

20. Friday, 19th February – *Eskimo* was detached to Clyde to coal and repair a head eccentric sheave. Her stability is doubtful, and water supply is small as she has no evaporator. *Caribbean* and *Hilary* rejoined patrol, and *Ambrose* left the Clyde, having completed restowage of ballast to improve her stability.

The Commander-in-Chief having informed me of an expected mine-laying expedition by German trawlers, I directed B Patrol to alter course 16 points at 11.30 a.m. in order to intercept vessels coming from eastward. At 2.30 p.m. C Patrol was also turned to the east. Later B Patrol was ordered to prolong to the northward a line 360° from Muckle Flugga formed by First Cruiser Squadron, sweeping to eastward at daylight on Saturday 20th, and turning so as to arrive at base line again before daylight on Sunday 21st, and C Patrol was ordered to work on southwest side of line Sydero – Lat. 60 N, Long. 5 W, altering course 16 points at midnight and every two hours. The weather, which had been bad all the week, prevented ships boarding and made it necessary

[1] *Pioneer* was inspected and allowed to proceed (TS/1 of 19 February 1915).
[2] 29.80" = 1009 mbs; 28.56" = 967 mbs.

to postpone the sailing of *Caesarea* from Scapa with prize crews for Squadron as there was no possibility of transferring them to their proper ships. Speed of Squadron was reduced and in many cases ships were compelled to lie to.

21. Saturday, 20th February – Weather again became worse, heavy gale from NE with snow squalls. *Otway* left patrol to coal in the Clyde. She carries 3150 tons of coal and can keep the sea 30 days. *Caesarea* (having sailed from Scapa before my signal postponing her departure was received) arrived at rendezvous with thirteen prize crews for eight ships but was unable to communicate on account of the state of the weather, and had to return to Scapa.

In accordance with directions from Commander-in-Chief I ordered B Patrol on arrival at 2 E to return to base line and to resume original patrol for eastbound ships at 7 a.m. on 21st February. All ships were directed to lie to till weather moderated if necessary. Later in the day information was received that two German Trawlers were leaving Bergen, and A Patrol was directed to form a line ahead patrol on base line 350° from Lat. 62.38´N, Long. 7 W steering to make good 350° at 7 a.m.; B Patrol to form line ahead patrol on base line to prevent them passing N of Shetlands, steering to make good 350° at 7 a.m. from Lat. 61 N, Long. 10 W, both patrols altering course 16 points every two hours, ships 15 miles apart.

22. Sunday, 21st February – Disposition of Squadron was as follows:

A Patrol ... *Alsatian*, *Columbella*, *Virginian*.
B Patrol ... *Patia*, *Teutonic*, *Motagua*, *Caribbean*, *Orotava*.
C Patrol ... *Bayano*, *Oropesa*, *Changuinola*, *Hilary*, *Digby*.
D Patrol ... *Hildebrand*, *Calyx*, *Ambrose*.
Proceeding to Clyde to coal ... *Otway*.
Coaling in Clyde ... *Mantua*, *Patuca*, *Eskimo*.
Coaling at Liverpool ... *Cedric*.

The number of Merchant Ships intercepted during the past week was 51 of which 12 were sent into port with prize crews.

Fifteen prize crews were away from their ships and could not get back on account of bad weather prevailing.

Submarine attack being expected a new area was arranged for B Patrol, the centre line of which was on Meridian of 10.15´E, between Lat. 61.10´N and 62.30´N, ships 25 miles apart, centre line to be crossed at Noon daily, steering to make good 270°.

C Patrol was ordered to move to a new area the centre line of which was 360° from Lat. 59.40´N, Long. 9 W, ships 25 miles apart, centre line to be crossed at noon daily, steering to make good 260°.

Hilary reported having intercepted the American SS *Cushing* with petroleum. This vessel, which was originally German, had been transferred to the American Flag on 14th October. She was sent in to Kirkwall with a prize crew.[1]

A considerable number of British Trawlers was reported more than ten miles north of Muckle Flugga and in vicinity of Faroe Islands. In view of the expected minelaying by German Trawlers I suggested to the Commander-in-Chief that the area should be prohibited to fishing craft.

23. Monday, 22nd February – *Orotava* and *Oropesa* were detached to Loch Ewe to coal, their small coal capacity and slow speed making it undesirable to send them a long distance for this purpose. *Otway* arrived in the Clyde.

A Patrol was moved to a new area, centre line 360° from Lat. 62.20´N, Long. 10 W, to be crossed at noon daily steering to make good 245°, ships 25 miles apart.

D Patrol was disposed 335° from St Kilda, ships 35 miles apart, nearest ship 15 miles from St Kilda. *Cambria* arrived at St Kilda with prize crews for *Alsatian*, *Bayano*, *Digby*, *Hildebrand*, *Orotava*, *Calyx*, *Patia*, *Changinola* and transferred them to ships sent to meet her there. With a North Westerly wind this little harbour gives a good lee.

24. Tuesday, 23rd February – *Orotava* arrived at Loch Ewe to coal. *Hildebrand* was detached to the Clyde. On her way South she reported having exploded a horned mine by gunfire in Lat. 56.47´N, Long. 7.50´W.

A Steamer boarded by *Bayano* reported sighting a hospital ship in Lat. 60 N, Long. 9 W but this was probably the Danish Steamer *United States* which was seen to have an ensign painted forward and aft on both sides with her name in between, presumably as a protection against submarine attack. *Calyx* anchored at St Kilda and proceeded with the installation of wireless telegraphy station. *Bayano* reported that a number of mercantile ratings who had signed on T.124 for three months were unwilling to re-engage and requested instructions. This system of short engagements is undoubtedly a mistake and likely to lead to difficulties in filling up crews. Men are now signed on for the period of

[1]The *Cushing* was carrying a large cargo of petroleum and Colza oil for Copenhagen. The Contraband Committee enquired of the Customs as to the bill of sale, for the transfer of ownership took place after the war began (the ship was previously the *Prometheus*). Yet only a day later, 24 February, the Committee gave leave for the ship to continue her voyage (TS 14/1 of 23 and 24 February 1915). This attitude is significant, for the purchaser was the American Standard Oil Company of New Jersey. The unwillingness of the British government to ruffle any American feathers is evident already; the German attitude was very different with regard to transferred ownership [107].

the war but many of those who joined ships for three months only will in all probability not be willing to serve longer and ships may be delayed before they can be replaced.

25. Wednesday, 24th February – *Oropesa* arrived at Loch Ewe, and *Hildebrand* arrived in the Clyde to coal. *Mantua* and *Patuca* left Clyde. *Columbella* and *Changuinola* were met by me at a pre-arranged rendezvous for visual signal communication and *Alsatian*'s prize crew was received from the latter. *Caribbean* reported that she was repairing one dynamo completely disabled, and that her foremost funnel had shifted, due to heavy rolling; she reported rolling over 40° each way and sometimes gunwale under. All her boilers had a very high density. I have reported elsewhere [41] ... that this ship is unsuitable, being old and slow and rolling badly in the heavy weather generally experienced in these latitudes.

The Danish Steamer *Ester* which was boarded by *Digby* reported having passed two floating mines 20 miles SE of Muckle Flugga.

W/T. Naval procedure is now in general use in the Squadron, and the Marconi Operators who have been obtained for many of the ships are on the whole very fairly proficient in it. In view of the impossibility of other means of communication, and of the length of time taken to promulgate information to the Squadron by letter, a vast amount of W/T communication is necessary, involving much work in the coding and W/T offices. Difficulty exists in obtaining suitable Officers for coding, and the large number of codes now in use renders this an important matter.

In accordance with Grand Fleet W/T Orders Art. XV Armed Merchant Cruisers now keep watch on S Wave, calling on S but shifting to Q for communicating except in the case of urgent messages. This organisation has not worked as well as had been expected, and would appear to have the following disadvantages:

(a) The range of most of the Armed Merchant Cruisers on S does not exceed 150 miles.
(b) Signals made by *Alsatian* on Q are not intercepted by ships of the Squadron.
(c) By keeping watch on S, information of the approach of merchant vessels (which has hitherto proved of much value) is missed.

26. Thursday, 25th February – *Columbella* was detached to proceed to Liverpool ... relative to her unsatisfactory loading and bad steering. *Calyx* having completed work on W/T installation at St Kilda was sent to the Clyde to coal. In the severe weather prevailing during her presence with D patrol I was glad that the duty assigned to her kept *Calyx* in close proximity to St Kilda where she was able to obtain

shelter. The SS *Denver* of New York intercepted by *Ambrose* with cargo of cotton for Bremen reported that the *Dacia* was 200 miles astern of her. Patrols were disposed with the special object of intercepting this vessel.[1] Several vessels from United States Ports intercepted had their cargo sealed and certified by British Diplomatic and Consular Authorities. I considered it advisable, however, to make no exception in their case to the rule that all vessels using north about route should call at Kirkwall, and they were accordingly sent in with prize crews. I may here remark that many more vessels than those authorised are using the north about route, and few, if any of them, would call at Kirkwall unless sent there in charge of prize crews. *Patia* reported that in Lat. 61.10´N, Long. 2.16´E she sank floating mines which exploded. No horns were visible. *Teutonic* sank a spherical floating mine in Lat. 61.58´N, Long. 2.18´E and another in Lat. 61.58´N, Long. 1.48´E also a third in Lat. 61.32´N, Long. 1.58´E. *Motagua* sank one mine and *Oiler No. 4* reported passing several mines in same vicinity. In view of the dangerous nature of the area and in order to keep in touch by W/T I shifted the centre line of B patrol (to which *Patia* and *Teutonic* belonged) to Long. 3 W with the Commander-in-Chief's approval.

27. Friday, 26th February – *Mantua* and *Patuca* rejoined A and D patrols respectively after coaling in Clyde. *Cedric* left Liverpool 800 tons of coal short of full stowage in consequence of coal strike at that port. In compliance with signal from Commander-in-Chief I gave orders that west bound ships should only be taken into Stornoway for examination if they were suspected of laying mines or acting as tenders to hostile submarines. This was done primarily with a view to preventing the more westerly patrols from sending ships back long distances when clearly on their course towards America.

The Centre Line of B Patrol was shifted to 350° from Lat. 60.40´N, Long. 3 W, ships 20 miles apart, steering to make good 240°. *Patia* reported that a large spherical floating mine had been passed at 4.30 a.m. in Lat. 61.50´N, Long. 00 and the patrol was stopped until daylight. The weather continuing bad – a heavy southerly gale with big sea – the sailing of *Cambria* with prize crews was again postponed, and patrols were ordered to lie to till weather moderated.

28. Saturday, 27th February – *Columbella* arrived at Liverpool and *Calyx* in Clyde.

With a view to intercepting the SS *Dacia* which was expected to

[1]The Contraband Committee asked that *Dacia* be seized and taken to Liverpool for examination (TS 14/1 of 26 February 1915); the ship was apparently not caught.

attempt the north about passage, A Patrol was ordered to form a line ahead patrol 300° from Myggenoes Light, and B Patrol base line was shifted to 350° from Lat. 60.35´N Long. 3 W, steering to make good 240°. *Caribbean* reported having rolled very heavily in recent rough weather. Her lee roll as registered by pendulum which could not go any further was 50° which brought her gunwale under. Ship recovered very quickly however.

At 2.25 a.m. *Patuca* intercepted the American SS *Navahoe* from Bremen bound for Norfolk (USA) steering west with side lights but no steaming lights. On being sighted she altered course 16 points. On being overhauled she stopped, but as it was too rough to board she was signalled to follow *Patuca* under lee of the land where examination of papers might be carried out. On this the Captain reported his condenser broken and would take three hours to repair. Later he made the following signal: 'Condenser ready, no contraband, refuse to follow you'. I ordered *Patuca* to retain her until the weather moderated, and to board and examine her when possible. At 5 p.m. *Patuca* reported that *Navahoe* had signalled 'Lead', and was following him towards St Kilda.

29. Sunday, 28th February – At 3.50 a.m. *Patuca* boarded *Navahoe* under the lee of St Kilda. In a very heavy squall the boarding boat was swamped alongside and had to be cut adrift, but the officers and crew managed to get on board the steamer. *Patuca* then proceeded with *Navahoe* and hove to 33 miles north of the Island. As the state of the weather – a gale was blowing from NW – prevented hatches being lifted for examination, and the Captain said that he would require drinking and boiler water shortly, I directed *Patuca* to take *Navahoe* to Stornoway the nearest Port, and carry out examination there, informing the Senior Naval Officer of her suspicious character. It was reported to me later that no mines or oil fuel were discovered at this examination and the ship appeared to be in ballast. A separate report in writing has been ordered.[1]

Patuca also informed me of the death of her Commanding Officer, Commander France-Hayhurst, RN,[2] which took place at Glasgow on Wednesday 24th February. He had apparently been sent to hospital during the last visit of *Patuca* to the Clyde.

Cedric returned to patrol and *Caribbean* was detached to Clyde to coal. The latter had only been on patrol nine days since last coaled but

[1]*Navahoe* is not mentioned in the Contraband Committee minutes; the decision was clearly made at Stornoway by the Customs.

[2]France-Hayhurst, C.R., Commander, Captain of *Patuca* 1914–1915.

her extravagant consumption and defective state made it necessary to send her in without delay. Disposition of Squadron was as follows:

A Patrol ... *Alsatian*, *Mantua*, *Virginian*.
B Patrol ... *Cedric*, *Patia*, *Motagua*, *Teutonic*.
C Patrol ... *Bayano*, *Changuinola*, *Hilary*, *Digby*.
D Patrol ... *Patuca*, *Ambrose*.
Coaling in Clyde ... *Otway*, *Hildebrand*, *Eskimo*, *Calyx*.
Coaling at Liverpool ... *Columbella*.
Coaling at Loch Ewe ... *Orotava*, *Oropesa*.
Proceeding to Clyde ... *Caribbean*.

During the last week 67 vessels were intercepted of which 18 were sent into port with prize crews.

30. Monday, 1st March – *Teutonic* intercepted the Danish Steamer *Hellig Olav* from New York with 99 German passengers including a judge and a governor from New Guinea. She was allowed to proceed in accordance with Admiralty Telegram of 26th February.

Prize crews for *Bayano*, *Hilary* and *Changuinola* were received from *Duke of Albany* which had been sent to St Kilda from Scapa Flow.

Bayano was detached to Clyde to coal, and *Virginian* was directed to take her place as Senior Officer of C Patrol which was further reinforced by the return of *Oropesa* from Loch Ewe. *Orotava* returned to B patrol.

31. Tuesday, 2nd March – The Russian Icebreaker *Canada* and the Steamer *Dwinsk*, both on their way from Archangel to Barrow were met with, and the former, whose Captain appeared to be doubtful of his position (he made Faroe Islands but thought he was off Out Skerries) and reported his engines in a bad way, was advised as to his course. Both vessels were given a safe route and instruction as directed by the Commander-in-Chief, and they proceeded in company.

At 2.0 p.m. I communicated with *Cedric* at a pre-arranged rendezvous and gave her all necessary orders visually. *Digby* and *Changuinola* after distributing and receiving prize crews respectively sailed for the Clyde to coal.

32. Wednesday, 3rd March – *Otway* having returned from the Clyde I placed her in charge of D Patrol which was reduced to two ships, viz: *Ambrose* and *Patuca*. B Patrol was extended in line ahead patrol on the meridian of 3 W from Lat. 60.50´N to Lat. 62.20´N to look out for a Danish Steamer reported to be leaving Faroe Islands with 700 barrels of whale oil for Germany.

33. Thursday, 4th March – Information having been received from the Commander-in-Chief that a suspicious steamer under British

Colours was reported to have anchored off Haskier Island at 6.0 p.m. on Wednesday 3rd March, I directed *Ambrose* to proceed thither. *Ambrose* passed round the Island but found nothing there.

Patia proceeded to Clyde to coal, and *Orotava* was detached to work with Sixth Cruiser Squadron to eastward of Shetlands as directed by Commander-in-Chief. *Hildebrand* should have left the Clyde after coaling but was detained owing to a fractured high pressure piston.

34. Friday, 5th March – Patrols were disposed to intercept the Danish Steamer *Frederick VIII* which had been heard calling by W/T.

B Patrol ... Line ahead patrol 360° from Lat. 62.20´N, Long. 3 W, ships 40 miles apart.

C Patrol ... Line ahead patrol 360° from Lat. 60.30´N, Long. 9 W to Lat. 61 N, Long. 9 W, ships 30 miles apart.

D Patrol ... Line ahead patrol 335° 15 miles from St Kilda, ships 30 miles apart.

Duke of Albany which met *Motagua* at a pre-arranged rendezvous, transferred three prize crews for that ship and one for *Hilary*.

I am forwarding a separate submission as regards the allowance of hard-lying money to Prize Crews who suffer much damage to clothing when boarding vessels, and are put to great discomfort especially in sailing ships, when conducting merchant ships into Port for examination.

35. Saturday, 6th March – A Patrol was temporarily shifted on to the Meridian of Greenwich.

At 3.15 a.m. *Virginian* reported that she was in pursuit of a steamer which she intercepted at 5 a.m. This proved to be *Frederick VIII* and she was at once boarded and examined as directed [44]. A German named Schmidt, aged 65, and R. Lang claiming to be a Russian Finn, who however could not speak Russian and had a strong German accent and no passport, were removed, and ship was allowed to proceed.

The Norwegian Steamer *Drammensfjord* with a cargo of Ferrotungsten, and the Swedish Steamer *Ottawa* which was suspected to have 21 Germans among the crew, were also intercepted by *Hilary* and *Mantua* respectively and sent in to Kirkwall with Prize Crews. From her position when intercepted the *Ottawa* was evidently trying to evade patrol and although on the list of Steamers permitted to use northabout route she did not intend to call at Kirkwall. *Mantua* had to escort *Ottawa* under lee of Faroes as it was too rough to board her where she was caught.[1]

[1] *Drammensfjord* and *Ottawa* were investigated and allowed to continue on 10 March.

From time to time W/T Signals are intercepted from American ships approaching the North Sea, signalling between themselves as to their position and destination; this is most useful information and generally leads to their capture.

36. Sunday, 7th March – At 8.45 a.m. *Teutonic* reported that she had sunk by gunfire a mine of German pattern with five horns on top in Lat. 61.21´N, Long. 2.52´W. A six pounder was used for the purpose and the mine did not explode. The special rifle ammunition for sinking mines failed to penetrate.

Disposition of Squadron was as follows:

A Patrol ... *Alsatian*, *Otway*, *Mantua*.
B Patrol ... *Cedric*, *Motagua*, *Teutonic*.
C Patrol ... *Virginian*, *Oropesa*, *Hilary*.
D Patrol ... *Ambrose*, *Patuca*.
Coaling in Clyde ... *Patia*, *Bayano*, *Caribbean*, *Changuinola*, *Digby*.
Detained in Clyde ... *Eskimo*, considered to lack stability (Admiralty order), *Hildebrand* (replacing fractured H.P. Piston).
At Liverpool ... *Columbella* (being re-ballasted).
Proceeding to rejoin patrol ... *Calyx*.
Detached for service with 6th Cruiser Squad ... *Orotava*.

Of 62 vessels intercepted and examined during the past week, 12 have been sent in with prize crews.

37. Monday, 8th March – Having given all necessary orders to *Cedric* for continuance of Patrol, I proceeded in *Alsatian* for Liverpool. *Motagua* was also detached to the Clyde to coal.

38. Tuesday, 9th March – *Alsatian* arrived at Liverpool at 2.15 a.m.

29. *Captain G.A. Vivian to Rear-Admiral Commanding Tenth Cruiser Squadron*

HMS *Patia*, At Sea, 7 March 1915

Report of Proceedings, 1 February–6 March 1915

***

On Feb. 1st I proceeded into the James Watt Dock at Greenock and made the necessary arrangements for making good such minor defects as I had and completing with coal. Coaling was completed by the evening of the 5th and all defects by the 9th. Orders having been received from the Admiralty that I was not to sail until ordered I reported the ship ready and then was directed to proceed to sea [28, paras 4 and 6]. I left the Dock on the morning of the 11th and anchored on the Tail of the Bank sailing that afternoon at 3.30. Early on the morning of the 12th I sighted a battleship steering South. At 6.15 a.m. on the 13th I sighted your Flagship and communicated after which in accordance with your orders I proceeded to join B Patrol. On the 15th in the morning I stopped a British trawler the *Elf-King* from Iceland to Lerwick and in the afternoon the trawler *Strathmaree* from the Faeroes to Aberdeen. On the 16th I received your orders to take charge of B Patrol. At 7 a.m. I sighted a steamer which I stopped and boarded and found to be the Norwegian steamer *Aquila* from Savannah to Norkopping with a cargo of cotton-seed cake. A prize-crew was placed on board and this ship was sent in to Kirkwall.[1] On the 17th I sighted the Second Light Cruiser Squadron and communicated with *Liverpool*, during the day a strong South-Easterly gale was experienced. On the 19th at 8.30 a.m. sighted a large sailing ship and found her to be the Norwegian ship *Bennetsvat* from Christiansand to Mobile in ballast and very light. Too much sea to board. At 2 p.m. sighted and at 3 p.m. stopped the Danish steamer *Alexandra* from Christiania to New York. Boarded her and found she had cleared from Newcastle and had also been boarded the previous day by a Torpedo-Boat. Cargo sulphite and general. Allowed her to proceed. On the 21st I saw a considerable number of trawlers all of which appeared to be British but it was impossible to examine them all. At 5 p.m. I sighted a steamer under the land and proceeded at full speed to cut her off. Stopped and boarded her at 6 p.m. and found her to be the Danish steamer *Botnia* from Iceland to Leith with fish (400 tons for Leith and 80 tons for Copenhagen) and 30 bags of mails for Leith. Allowed her to proceed. On the 22nd, 23rd, 24th examined various trawlers all British. On the 25th in the early morning I sighted the Norwegian high land. At 9.10 passed a floating object about 40 yards off and turned to examine it, finding it to be a floating mine. Hit it several times with rifle bullets without any apparent effect and finally sunk it with a 3 pdr projectile, mine did not explode. This mine appeared to be one of our own mines or similar to them, cylindrical with lug on top.[2] At 9.30 *Teutonic* reported having sunk a black spherical mine with three electric cables on top and a small chain secured to one cable, and at 10.45 she reported having sunk another similar mine. At 2.25 *Motagua* reported having sunk a black spherical mine with three lifting lugs which she thought was one of our own. As

[1]*Aquila* was allowed to go on after examination at Kirkwall.

[2]De Chair reports a similar difficulty elsewhere [see 28 para. 26].

there were apparently some number of mines drifting about in this vicinity I decided not to recross this area during the night but to do a line ahead patrol to the northward and return to my patrol line in the morning. That evening in accordance with your orders *Caribbean* was directed to proceed to St Kilda for further orders and at 2.30 a.m. *Motagua* was directed to proceed to the rendezvous ordered. During the night *Teutonic* and myself proceeded North at 13 knots zig-zagging there being some moon. At 3.30 I turned South again. At 4.30 a.m. a black spherical mine was seen from the bridge passing down the Port side of the ship. Port engine was at once stopped and helm put hard to Starboard, no explosion occurred. I do not think this mine ever actually touched the ship, though it was impossible to be certain in the very dim light. This ship having a rather bluff entry makes a considerable bow-wave, and I think this bow-wave probably washed the mine clear of the ship, when seen from the bridge it was about 4 to 6 feet from the side under the bridge and the roll of the ship towards it seemed to be almost on top of it. When ship was well clear engines were stopped and *Teutonic* was directed to stop also, as there seemed to be too many mines about for comfort. Proceeded again at daylight and at 6 a.m. observed another floating object. Approached this and found it to be a large iron drum or cask with two chain strops round it, floating light and not apparently any form of mine. Could not make out that there was anything underneath it. Fired at it with a rifle when after being hit three or four times it filled and sank. Proceeded to new base-line in accordance with your orders. Strong South-Westerly gale in the afternoon with heavy seas, so hove the ship to. Weather moderated during the night and I increased speed and resumed the patrol on the morning of the 27th. Examined two British trawlers during the day. At 4 sighted a steamer going East and at 4.50 stopped and boarded her, found her to be the Danish steamer *Kalo* from Baltimore to Esbjerg with 700 tons of barley and 8854 quarters of wheat. Esbjerg being only 5 or 6 miles from the German frontier and not being a grain-importing centre, the ultimate destination of this cargo seemed fairly obvious. Put a prize-crew on board with some difficulty and sent her in to Kirkwall.[1] The Captain of this ship like the *Aquila* had a British Consular Certificate, but what value is to be attached to this certificate is quite unknown to me. Certainly the Captains of ships which have this certificate seem to be under the impression that having obtained this

[1]Despite Captain Vivian's insinuation, the *Kalo* was permitted to continue her voyage by decision of the Contraband Committee (TS 14/1 of 1 March 1915).

certificate they are exempt from further search or detention. Apparently it costs them a certain sum of money and it would seem desirable that there should be a clearer understanding on this point, and that HM Consuls who grant these certificates should make it clear whether the certificate does or does not exempt ships from further search. On March 1st sighted a large steamer, *Teutonic* in sight at the same time. Both ships closed to intercept steamer. *Teutonic* boarded steamer which was the *Hellig Olaf*, the subject of a recent communication from the Admiralty.[1] At 12.45 sighted a sailing ship and found her to be the *Pass of Balmaha* with a prize-crew from *Cedric* on board.[2] At 4.20 sighted *Orotava* and communicated with her, receiving from her one of our prize-crews. At 9.30 on March 2nd sighted a steamer which was found to be the Danish steamer *Jommsborg* with a prize-crew from *Motagua* on board.[3] At 9.40 p.m. sighted a steamer and at 11 stopped and boarded her, found her to be the Danish steamer *Kallundborg* from Huelva to Norresundby with a cargo of sulphur ore and with a customs clearance pass from Ardrossan where she had coaled. Allowed her to proceed. On the 3rd the weather changed and a moderate South-East to Southerly gale occurred with a moderate sea. On the 4th at 4 p.m. I left the patrol and proceeded for the Firth of Clyde, where I arrived and anchored at the Tail of the Bank at 8 p.m. on the 6th.

I would again submit that the efficiency of the ship would be very materially improved by the fitting of a thwartship bulkhead in each of the two holds. The want of a good sea-boat with a suitable dropping gear is constantly felt, the old type of service whaler is not in my opinion a good sea-boat and having to hoist her in and out with a derrick and lower her from a winch is not a satisfactory method in a sea-way. As boarding is the principal work these ships have to do, they should have I submit the best sea-boats and disengaging gear possible, both for the better performance of the work the ship is employed on and also for the safety of the boats' crews.

The health of the Ship's Company has not been as satisfactory as I could wish, and this matter has formed the subject of a separate communication.

[1]Apparently the *Hellig Olav* was not sent in; note de Chair's comment [28 para. 30].

[2]*Pass of Balmaha*, with a cargo of coffee for Bremen, was allowed to proceed there by the Contraband Committee (TS 14/1 of 9 March 1915), coffee not yet being on the contraband list.

[3]*Jomsborg* was allowed to go on after examination (TS 14/1 of 5 March 1915).

30. *Rear-Admiral de Chair to Admiralty*

HMS *Alsatian*, 5 February 1915

Be pleased to inform Their Lordships that I do not consider the *Calyx* is suitable for service as an Armed Merchant Cruiser of the Northern Patrol.

This ship has a gross tonnage of 2876, her coal capacity is 525 tons and her speed is only 12 knots. With this limited coal stowage she can only keep the sea for eleven days, and on account of her small size she frequently has to lie to on account of the bad weather generally experienced in the areas under patrol.

As the coaling base for Armed Merchant Cruisers is Liverpool her period on patrol is limited to eight days at the most, during several of which she is unable to maintain her station on account of weather and slow speed.

The ship rolls heavily in the seas encountered in the Atlantic, and the stiffening added to her structure to take the strain of gunfire causes the decks to work and leak. Moreover the constant motion of the ship during the comparatively long periods spent at sea has a deleterious effect on the health of the crew.[1]

31. *Commander-in-Chief Home Fleets to Admiralty*

Invergordon, 10 February 1915

Following message rec[eive]d: from RAC 10th CS dated 9th inst – begins –

'*Hildebrand*, *Hilary* and *Patuca* searched since 3rd for *Clan MacNaughton*.

Wreckage found on Monday in 60.25´N, 9.37´W consisting of life-belts, grating, griping gear, hatch covers. Marks of hatch covers corresponded to those in *Clan MacNaughton*.'

Last signal from *Clan MacNaughton* rec[eive]d 2nd referred to Leading Seaman being lost overboard – weather was very bad at that time.

I fear she foundered during night 2nd inst.

Search discontinued & Patrol resumed. 2215 – ends

[1]See also the comment by one of *Calyx*'s crew, Able Seaman Style [150].

32. *W.H. Whiting,*[1] *Superintendent of Contract Work, to First Sea Lord*[2]

10 February [1915]

We have fitted out about 100 ships, besides 190 trawlers, drifters, etc.

We have about 30 more in hand.

All of these ships at sea (other than the trawlers and drifters) have had careful investigation made of their stability.

In each case instructions as to lading to secure adequate metacentric height have been furnished to the commanding officer.

So far as is known, and apart from trawlers and fleet sweepers lost by mines, the total casualties or missing vessels up to the present time are

Oceanic ... Wrecked
Roedean ... Wrecked[3]
Viknor ... (Missing Lost in mine field)
Clan Macnaughton ... Missing in heavy weather.

This is for seven months' work, including winter gales in the North Atlantic.

The 17 vessels of the Northern Patrol were like the rest of these ships, the best we could get at the moment they were urgently wanted. They are of all classes, and naturally not all of them what we should most desire for cruiser work in these latitudes.

33. *Superintendent of Contract Work to Third Sea Lord*

14 February 1915

1. On ... 24/11/[1914] ... an order was given that 17 ships were to be taken up as Armed Merchant Cruisers for Northern Patrol.

They were to be of moderate size – 4,000 to 5,000 tons gross register – fair speed, and were to be taken up and completed in one week. They were not to be of the largest Passenger Type ...

2. The selection was made in the first place by Officers representing –

[1]Whiting, William Henry, CB, Naval Constructor at Chatham and Hong Kong, Chief Constructor at Admiralty, 1897–1912, Superintendent of Contract Work 1912–1917, retired 1917, died 1927.

[2]The First Sea Lord was Lord Fisher.

[3]*Roedean*, a minesweeper, the former *Roebuck*, sank on 13 January 1915 at Longhope; the cause was never determined.

Director of Trade Division ... Capt Margesson, RN,[1] Superintendent of Contract Work ... Mr Dennis, Constructor,[2] from lists, prepared by Mr Kemball Cook of D-of-T's Dept.,[3] of vessels in English Ports at the moment, or likely to arrive immediately, and most nearly satisfying the conditions named, as far as could be seen from the general plans of the vessels. There were extremely few vessels from which to make the selection.

They were not inspected before taking up. To have inspected the ships before selection was quite impossible in view of imperative orders as to urgency; and the vessels were, or had been, recently in actual running.

***

The first list of 9 vessels including *Viknor* and *Clan MacNaughton*, was submitted on 18th November and approved by Third Sea Lord on same day. The second list of 8 vessels was submitted on 19th and approved by him on that or the following day.

4. The work mainly consisted of:

(a) Fitting of guns, magazines, signalling, and other Military arrangements, as well as plate and coal protection to Machinery and Steering Gear.
(b) Stripping of woodwork and cabins which could be dispensed with.
(c) Making arrangements for necessary additional coal where required, and fitting of additional accommodation.
(d) Making good any defects apparent while fitting out, and putting ship into condition for Sea.

***

Where the original data was incomplete, or there was any reason to doubt its accuracy at the present time, an Inclining experiment on the vessel was made in order to get reliable data as to actual stability conditions. From the information thus obtained stability calculations

[1]Margesson, Wentworth Henry Davies, CB, RN (1869–1950), Commander 1903, Captain (retired) 1910, representing Director of Trade Division, February 1915; retired to farm in Southern Rhodesia.

[2]Dennis, R., Constructor in Contract Work Department 1914–1915, at Portsmouth 1916–1918.

[3]Kemball-Cook, Basil Alfred (1876–1949), CB, KCMG, joined Admiralty 1900 in the Trade Division, Director of Naval Sea Transport, Ministry of Shipping 1917–1920, Reparation Commission 1920–1926, retired 1926, Managing Director of British Tanker Company 1927–1935, Director of British Guiana Goldfields, 1936–1938, air-raid warden 1939–1945, Divisional Food Officer for London 1942–1948.

were made by S.C.W's Staff at Admiralty. Where considered necessary ballast was put into the vessel.

A short paper of instructions as to loading and working out coal was in every case given to the Commanding Officer of the ship, which ensured adequate stability of the vessel in all conditions of lading.

***

34. *Contraband Committee Minutes*

15 February 1915

This vessel [*Oscar II*] was allowed to proceed [from Kirkwall] as she had 600 passengers and Danish mails.

35. *Contraband Committee Minutes*

15 February 1915

Sailing vessel *Olav* (Norwegian). A signal has been received from the Commander-in-chief to say that the Norwegian sailing vessel *Olav* has been intercepted and ordered to Kirkwall. She has on board three Germans, and the master states that the cargo is for Germany. The same statement of the master was reported to the Contraband Committee by the Collector at Falmouth, and is recorded in the minutes referred to above. The Committee decided to take no action in this case until the Customs' telegram from Kirkwall has been received [39].

36. *Contraband Committee Minutes*

15 February 1915

Steamship *Santiago* (American). In a despatch ... of the 29th January, the British consul-general at New York, transmits the manifest of this vessel. He states that she has been loaded under inspection, and will call at Kirkwall for examination.

The following memorandum in regard to the cargo on this vessel has been prepared from the manifest by the Admiralty:

'*Santiago*. The entire cargo of this ship, with the exception of a few small items only, is consigned to firms against which we have information of the most definite kind. The manifest shows not less than 2,500 tons (approximately) of lard, of which over 1,000 tons is from

Sulzberger to Leopold Gyth, and over 1,000 from Armour to Armour (500,000 kilog. of Armour's lard have been brought by the Rubervoidwerke roofing material manufacturers) of Hamburg, and are expected during February. We have also the most positive information against Sulzberger and Leopold Gyth. These shipments are now addressed to Malmo instead of to Copenhagen, as in previous cases, in order to avoid the Danish prohibition of export of foreign lard. It is true that Sweden also has just prohibited the export of lard.

'There is also a great quantity of meat, etc from Swift and Hammond to O. Hansen, Paul Buch, Christensen Thorgersen, all of whom are on the black list.

'The hides and tanning extract on the ship are mostly to S.N. Mayer, of Copenhagen, who advertised 10,000 skins for sale in a recent issue of the *Hamburger Nachrichten*, having obtained permission to export them.

'There is a consignment of belt knives and machine blades to Carl Lassen (of Hamburg), and another including belt knives and electrical grinding machinery from Knauth, Nachod and Kuhue (German) to Paul Lehmann, who is on the black list. We have copies of two insurance policies on "knives" and other iron goods to Hamburg, referring to other ships now on their way. There is also cocoa from Muller Schall to Harry Levin, of which we have information in wireless from Berlin. Lastly, there is a great quantity of machinery and miscellaneous goods from Joseph Spiero to J.M. Bohm. This includes twelve lathes of the shipment, of which notification was sent to Stockvis and Zonen, of Rotterdam, German agents.'

The Committee would draw attention to the enormous quantity of lard and meat which are still being imported into Scandinavia from America. From articles 5 and 6 of the agreement with Denmark it will be seen that it was hoped at an early date to reach an agreement with the American meat packers in regard to the export of meat from the United States to Scandinavian countries, and it is understood that negotiations have been proceeding between a representative of the meat packers, Mr. Urion, and the Restriction Committee. The Contraband Committee would be glad to be informed whether there is a prospect of an early and favourable conclusion of these negotiations.

37. *Contraband Committee Minutes.*

16 February 1915

Steamship *Trondhjemsfjord* (Norwegian). A telegram from the Customs at Kirkwall, dated the 15th February. This vessel has no mails and no passengers, and carries a [varied] cargo ...

***

... The names of the consignees, most of whom have recently opened establishments in Norway, are as follows – Morris, Armour, Herskind, Beck, Thorgessen, Gyth and Vay. Several of these consignees are on the black list.

On the 13th February ... His Majesty's Minister at Christiania, referring to this vessel, stated that there was a great deal of lard on the manifest, and that he would try and get lard put on the prohibited list before the vessel arrived at a Norwegian port.

Foreign lard is on the Danish prohibition list, but the Danish Foreign Office informed His Majesty's Minister at Copenhagen, on the 15th February ... that considerable difficulty is anticipated when consignments of foreign lard, at present afloat, reach Denmark. This may be taken to indicate that there is some probability of the Danish prohibition of export of American lard being withdrawn when stocks accumulate in Denmark. It will not be overlooked that, in the absence of a prohibition of export, lard may now be exported direct from Norway to Germany, and even if the prohibition of export is enforced in Norway, the Scandinavian countries reserve the right of sending articles on their prohibition lists to other Scandinavian countries. There are, therefore, at present, two dangers: the first, that the lard consigned to Norway may be exported direct to Germany if the prohibition of export is not enforced before the vessel arrives at a Norwegian port; the second, that this lard may be sent from Norway to Denmark, that stocks may there accumulate, and that the Danish prohibition of exports of foreign lard will then be removed. The names of the consignees rather point to the conclusion that the lard will be sent to Germany for the use of the German troops.[1]

The following telegram should be sent to His Majesty's Minister at Christiania:

[1]This long section on lard is odd: the cargo included other elements of more immediately obvious military application, such as oil, tyres, steel, firearms, ferro-tungsten, and blasting machinery and fuses.

'Norwegian steamship *Trondhjemsfjord* has arrived at Kirkwall. She carries 1,757 tons of lard for named consignees in Christiania. Having regard to the names of the consignees, many of whom are known to be agents of the German Government, the vessel is being detained pending information from you that lard has been added to the Norwegian prohibition of export list.'

We understand that the Norwegian prohibitions of export do not apply to exports to Denmark. There is at present in Denmark prohibition of export of American lard, but the Danish Government have confidentially informed us that they anticipate considerable difficulty when the consignments of lard at present afloat reach Denmark. We should, therefore, in this case desire an assurance from the Norwegian Government that none of the lard on board the *Trondhjemsfjord* will be allowed to be re-exported from Norway to any other country.

The following telegram should be sent to the Customs

'Norwegian steamship *Trondhjemsfjord*. The telegram, dated the 15th February, from the Customs at Kirkwall, does not give the destination of several consignments. Please furnish full particulars by telegraph. The telegram from Kirkwall states that in several instances no address of the consignees is given, but possibly the port of destination is stated at the top of each sheet of the manifest. It is essential that the Foreign Office should know whether the goods are destined for Norway, Sweden or Denmark.

'What is the nature of the certificates given by the Norwegian and Swedish Ministers in Washington? Are they guarantees on behalf of the Norwegian and Swedish Governments that the articles referred to will not be re-exported, or are they merely attesting the signatures of the exporters or the consignees that there will be no re-exportation?'

A telegram ... of the 15th February, has been received from His Majesty's Minister at Copenhagen, in which he states that the question of export of Danish lard is being used for purely political purposes by opponents of the Danish Government. As regards foreign lard, M. Clan anticipate considerable difficulty when the consignments at present afloat reach Denmark. The Committee recommend that, subject to the approval of Sir E. Crowe,[1] the following reply should be sent to Sir H.

[1]Crowe, Eyre, GCB, GCMG, CB (1864–1925), Clerk in Foreign Office from 1885, Senior Clerk 1906, Assistant Under Secretary of State 1912, Permanent Under Secretary of State 1920–1925; Crowe was the official placed in charge of matters concerning the blockade from 1915.

Lowther:[1]

'His Majesty's Government are greatly disturbed by the final paragraph of your telegram. Are they to understand that the removal of the Danish prohibition of export of foreign lard is being contemplated? Please press for early and precise information on this point in order that we may, in such an event, reconsider our attitude.'

38. *Contraband Committee Minutes*

16 February 1915

Steamship *Bergensfjord* (Norwegian). The following telegram ... has been received from His Majesty's Minister, Christiania:

'Norwegian–American Line informs me that they have received a wireless message from *Bergensfjord*, to the effect that she was loaded under the inspection of British consul-general, New York, who certified her manifest. Captain of vessel asked if she had received permission to pass without detention.'

The following telegram was sent to His Majesty's Ambassador at Washington, on the 30th January:

'I have been in Communication with Managing Director of Norwegian-American Line, with a view to concluding an arrangement similar to that made with Captain Cold, whose name however has not been mentioned.

'Norwegian–American Line cannot agree not to engage cargo without our consent. They agree, however, that all steamers owned and chartered by them shall be laden under the control of His Majesty's consul-general in New York, in order to ensure that cargoes are in conformity with the manifests. Their agents at New York, Messrs Benham and Boyce, will be authorised to arrange with consul-general for all work relating to the inspection to be performed at the company's expense. A copy of each manifest will be sent to the consul-general for transmission to Foreign Office. If destination or character of any part of cargo be considered suspicious, it will be unloaded in New York, or if this is inconvenient, it will either remain in Norway under guarantee of

[1]Lowther, Henry Crofton, KCMG, GCVO (1858–1939), British Minister at Copenhagen, 1913–1916; previous postings had been to The Hague, Stockholm, Berlin, Rio de Janeiro and Constantinople; he had been Chargé d'Affaires at Madrid, Berne and Rio de Janeiro. After a posting to Tokyo he was Minister at Santiago 1909–1913; he retired in 1917.

Norwegian Government, or be shipped back to the United States of America on next voyage of ship concerned.

'All steamers in question sail from New York.

'Please instruct consul-general to endeavour to come to working arrangement on these lines with agents, after consultation with Sir R. Crawford.'[1]

When Mr Henriksen called at the Foreign Office on that date, he stated that he could not agree that his passenger vessels should put into Kirkwall, as he said he was afraid of the danger to life owing to the lack of accommodation at Kirkwall and the presence of mines. He was informed by the Foreign Office that if he wished his vessels not to put into Kirkwall, or in the alternative to be brought into Kirkwall, he should write a letter stating fully his reasons. Two days afterwards a letter was received from him, saying that he did not propose to write to the Foreign Office, as he had had an interview with the Director of the Trade Division of the Admiralty, and there was now no necessity to write to America.

Early in November an order was issued recommending vessels to use the Channel on account of the danger of mines. Certain lines – seven in number – asked permission to use the north-about route. Permission was granted on the distinct understanding that the vessels called at Kirkwall for examination. The Norwegian-American Line, which was one of those which asked permission, have consistently endeavoured to avoid this obligation, and many of their ships have been brought into Kirkwall by His Majesty's vessels under circumstances creating considerable friction. They are now seeking to avoid this obligation altogether. It will be recollected that on more than one occasion the passenger vessels of this line have carried German reservists. No information has been received from His Majesty's consul-general at New York in regard to the cargo of the *Bergensfjord*. A telegram marked 'Immediate' should be sent to His Majesty's Ambassador at Washington as follows:

'We have received no information from the consul-general at New York, respecting the cargo of the *Bergensfjord* which was loaded under his inspection. Please instruct him to telegraph immediately any contraband cargo which she carries.'

The above telegram should be repeated to His Majesty's Minister at Christiania.

[1]Crawford, Sir Richard Frederick, KCMG, employed in the Ottoman financial service until 1914, honorary Minister Plenipotentiary in the Diplomatic Service from 1914, commercial adviser in Washington 1915–1918.

39. *Contraband Committee Minutes*

20 February 1915

Telegram from Messrs Botterell and Roche reporting that the vessel [*Olav*], which has been allowed to proceed from Falmouth, has been brought into Kirkwall [28, para. 15] and asking that she should be allowed to proceed at once. The representative of the Admiralty communicated the following telegram from the Vice-Admiral Commanding First Battle Squadron:

'*Olaf* (Norway) cargo of bran sent to Kirkwall. Her captain states that certain cargo going to Germany, three Germans amongst crew. She was given special clearance from Falmouth the 28th January. Officials told Captain that if he was caught by north patrol he would be sent to Kirkwall (?) [*sic*] other ship with linseed from Falmouth at the same time. Falmouth procedure would apparently assist enemy's ends.'

In view of this information the Committee decided that this vessel should be detained pending the result of the enquiries which should be made by His Majesty's Minister at Christiania with regard to the ultimate destination of its cargo. The following telegram should be sent to His Majesty's Minister at Christiania:

'The naval authorities at Kirkwall report that they have been informed by her captain that he is certain that the cargo on this vessel is going to Germany. In view of this statement it has been decided to detain the vessel pending enquiries as to the ultimate destination of the cargo. You should communicate these statements to the Norwegian Government and endeavour to obtain from them a definite guarantee that the cargo will not be allowed to leave Norway.' [40]

40. *Contraband Committee Minutes*

22 February 1915

The action indicated [on] 20th February [39] was cancelled on receipt of a telegram from the Customs at Kirkwall, stating that the objections raised by the naval authorities had been removed and the *Olav* permitted to clear for Aarhus and Aalborg.

41. *Rear-Admiral de Chair to Admiralty*

23 February 1915

***

1. *Viknor*, which was built in 1888, was the tourist yacht *The Viking* lately employed in cruising in the Norwegian Fjords. She was a comparatively small ship (gross tonnage 5386) and of somewhat slow speed. From her dimensions she was evidently difficult to load as an armed Cruiser, especially as she had a large low well deck forward, and was probably full of special fittings as regards W/T doors and bulkheads for the convenience of tourists. Almost immediately on her arrival on patrol for the first time she found it necessary to shelter from the weather, and on the occasion when I saw her standing by the *Bergensfjord* [18, para. 24] I formed the opinion that she was not suitable for the work of an Armed Merchant Cruiser in these latitudes during the winter months. It was generally considered that she was a very heavy roller.

2. As regards the sea-keeping qualities of the ships composing the Squadron under my command and their suitability for the service upon which they are engaged I beg to offer the following remarks after an experience of two months spent on patrol:

(a) *Alsatian*, *Otway*, *Cedric*, *Hilary*, *Mantua*, *Hildebrand* – very good indeed, so far as I have been able to ascertain.
(b) *Patia*, *Bayano*, *Patuca*, *Motagua*, *Changuinola* – very good indeed, and very economical steamers, but they have a weak point structurally, viz: the two large holds have no sub-division, being only two large tanks, and the flooding of either would be sufficient to sink the ship.
(c) *Virginian* – good, but has poor coal capacity and is a somewhat extravagant steamer.
(d) *Teutonic* – good, but has no double bottoms and carries no boiler feed water.
(e) *Columbella* – unsuitable. Very extravagant with coal, using 4% daily, with small capacity, viz: 2900 tons. This gives her a range of 16 days steaming at 12 knots. She steers very badly, carrying 20° weather helm and at times becomes unmanageable. Her loading is most unsatisfactory, she is 1'9" down by the bow instead of 4' by stern when full up with coal and stores.
(f) *Caribbean* – unsuitable. Old and slow and of small coal capacity. Difficult to load and rolls badly [46].

(g) *Orotava* – unsuitable. Old and of small coal capacity – 17 days at 12 knots. She has a quick roll.
(h) *Ambrose* – fairly suitable. She is old and has been badly maintained. Her stability is not satisfactory and her loading has lately been altered with a view to improving it.
(i) *Digby* – good, but difficult to steer as she holds much wind. Single screw, maximum speed 13³/₄ knots appears to require loading down to get her propeller under water.
(j) *Oropesa* – unsuitable. Old and slow, of small coal capacity and an extravagant steamer. Has had considerable trouble with her condensers.
(k) *Calyx* – unsuitable. A small ship and very extravagant steamer, cannot remain on patrol 12 days. She has only one water tight bulkhead in the ship, viz: no shaft alley. She rolls heavily in the long Atlantic seas and her well deck forward is a considerable danger. More suitable for use as a boarding steamer, having been built for short passages in North Sea.
(l) *Eskimo* – The above remarks apply to this ship and in addition, she has no evaporator and must be frequently sent into port for boiler water.

3. The *Clan McNaughton*, which has been missing since 2nd February and must, I regret, be given up as lost, was a new ship with very large hold spaces, and a flush deck with exceptionally large hatchways. Her deep tank (No. 3 hold) was ballasted with 1518 tons of salt water. On 18th January I represented through the Senior Naval Officer, Liverpool that it was undesirable that this tank should be used for water ballast, but the reply from *Clan McNaughton* was that it was placed there by Admiralty order which directed that the tank should be permanently filled [29, 30]. The speed of this ship was reported to be 11 knots, and her draught when she left the Thames was 16'1" forward, 22'3" aft. The whole weight of her coal, water, stores &c. appears to have been in the middle of the ship.

42. *Note by W.H. Whiting, Superintendent of Contract Work*

24 February 1915

Numerous complaints as to the behaviour of the steamers for the Northern Patrol seem to raise the question whether the severe conditions under which these vessels are employed were fully realised when deciding on the type of vessel for the work.

It is understood that it was originally contemplated that First Class Protected Cruisers of the *Edgar* type should be used, but that their entire suitability was doubted. Directives were given to select seventeen Merchant Vessels of 4 or 5 thousand tons gross register for the work. The need for fair speed for overhauling other vessels, combined with this very moderate size, gave little opportunity for choice. As a matter of fact there were barely sufficient vessels suitable at the time.

As the complaints respecting the behaviour of these vessels affect most of the types chosen, the presumption is that the vessels are rather small for the work.

It may perhaps be considered that vessels which can make thoroughly satisfactory trans-Atlantic passages in the heavy weather frequently met with may nevertheless be found inadequate to the work of cruising to and fro in the direction broadside to the heaviest gales. This may be accentuated by the inability of the vessels to heave to for fear of torpedo attack, or by the necessity to steam a zigzag course along a particular line. There can be little doubt that such conditions as these constitute a severe test for any vessel, and it is submitted for consideration whether it is not desirable, in view of the experience gained during the last two months, and of the fact that the season of heavy weather in the North Atlantic has by no means ended, to carry on the work with vessels of a somewhat larger type averaging, say, gross register tonnage of 10,000 tons.

The report called for from the Rear-Admiral Commanding [41] as to the behaviour of the Squadron may perhaps help a decision on this question to be reached.

43. *Contraband Committee Minutes*

26 February 1915

It is reported that this vessel [*Dacia*] will probably reach British waters very shortly. A letter should be sent to the Admiralty asking that when the vessel is seized, in accordance with the instructions given, she shall be brought to Liverpool.

44. *Contraband Committee Minutes*

1 March 1915

This vessel [*Frederick VIII*] has a cargo of foodstuffs, machinery and cocoa. The Admiralty are requested to take steps to have this vessel brought in.

45. *Rear-Admiral de Chair to Admiralty*

HMS *Alsatian*, 5 March 1915

Having now been in command of the Armed Merchant Ships forming the Northern Patrol (known as Cruiser Force B or Tenth Cruiser Squadron) for three months, I consider it desirable to bring to Their Lordships' notice the necessity for augmenting the force by the addition of six large ships.

2. The force as originally contemplated was to consist of 24 vessels, but this number has never been reached as the *Laurentic* did not join my flag.

3. The loss of the *Viknor* and *Clan McNaughton* has further reduced the numbers to 21, and ... several of the smaller and older ships are unsuitable for the work required of them, notably *Calyx*, *Eskimo* and *Caribbean* [46].

4. With the advent of summer the need for a large number of ships to carry out an efficient patrol becomes more pressing for two reasons:

(a) Increased area to be patrolled consequent on the passage north of Iceland being free of ice.

(b) Longer periods of daylight necessitating longer periods of steaming at high speed and consequent increased coal consumption and more frequent absence of ships from patrol (at the present moment nine ships are absent from patrol coaling).

5. Since the patrol commenced several articles have been added to the list of contraband and a larger number of merchant vessels is using the northabout route. The work of the patrol has thus materially increased and many more prize crews have to be detached from their ships to take vessels into port.

6. It also happens from time to time that an Armed Merchant Cruiser is required to assist one of the other Cruiser Squadrons in boarding work. At present the *Orotava* is detached from my command to augment the Sixth Cruiser Squadron operating to the eastward of the Shetlands.

7. I would therefore submit that at least six large ships should be added to Cruiser Force B without delay as the need for their services becomes more pressing from day to day.

46. *Commander F.H. Walter to Rear-Admiral Commanding Tenth Cruiser Squadron*

HMS *Caribbean*, 6 March 1915

In accordance with your Memorandum no. 25 of 1st February 1915 regarding rolling of ship under my command, I have the honour to further report as follows:

Very heavy weather has been experienced during the last three weeks and the ship rolled in my opinion more than she should under the circumstances. She rolled 43° each way eleven times on the night of 26th February. I personally saw a roll of 50° on the bridge with a very heavy sea running. Her period is from five to ten seconds, but there is considerable difficulty in recording the rolls accurately as the only Clinometer on deck is the very small pendulum on the standard Compass. Application has been made for a Mattock Rolling Indicator. I think the ballast is too low down and should be shifted one deck higher. The ship is otherwise an admirable seaboat, but a single screw ship of her length is naturally not handy. She scarcely takes on board any water at all and is very tight below, but this constant heavy rolling will I fear in such an old ship strain her badly. I will endeavour to alter the ballasting if possible.[1]

47. *Minute by Captain Richard Webb, Director of Trade Division*

12 March 1915

Six vessels are reported as unsuitable:

	Tons
Columbella	(8,300)
Caribbean	(5,800)
Orotava	(6,000)
Oropesa	(5,300)
Calyx	(2,870)
Eskimo	(3,320)

The paying off of the *Calyx* and *Eskimo* have been dealt with on other papers.

[1]De Chair classified *Caribbean* as ‘not efficient’ later in the month, and this assessment by Commander Walter was surely one good reason for the ship’s paying-off in June.

It is suggested that further ballasting may correct some of the faults in the other 4 vessels, or at any rate in the *Columbella* and, possibly, in the *Orotava*.

If two of the 4 vessels are withdrawn, the addition of the six new vessels will only bring the Squadron up to 24 vessels, which is regarded by the R.A. 10th Cruiser Squadron as a minimum.

[Note by Admiral H.F. Oliver,[1] 13 March 1915]: I think we should make every effort to try and find suitable ships and widen the search for them if necessary.

The Japanese have some good steamers and so have the Union Company which ply round Australia and New Zealand where the weather is much worse than it is on this side.

[1]Oliver, Henry Francis, GCB, KCMG, MVO, RN (1865–1965), Lieutenant 1888, Commander 1899, Captain 1903, Naval Assistant to the First Sea Lord 1908–1913, Rear-Admiral 1913, Director of Naval Intelligence 1913–1914, Acting Vice-Admiral and Chief of Admiralty War Staff, 1914–1917, Deputy Chief of Naval Staff 1917, Rear-Admiral commanding First Battle Cruiser Squadron, 1918, Vice-Admiral 1919 in command of Home Fleet, commanded Reserve Fleet 1919–1920, Second Sea Lord 1920–1924, Admiral 1923, commanded Atlantic Fleet 1924–1927, Admiral of the Fleet 1928, retired 1933, returned to active list 1940.

3

THE PATROL ESTABLISHED, MARCH–JUNE 1915

The mishaps of the first seven months were compounded by the loss of yet another ship, *Bayano*, early in March 1915 [49 para. 2], but the later arrival of six new Armed Merchant Cruisers [49 para. 35; 65] brought the squadron to near its full establishment; the removal of two of the least suitable ships was a net gain. The patrol system was now fully operational, and the better weather posed fewer dangers. Yet this also opened up more passages for ships to pass, as the ice receded from the northern coast of Iceland. The investigation of the ice condition became a regular spring preoccupation, and new patrol lines were needed when the passage opened up [71 para. 8].

Even with more favourable conditions it was difficult to maintain more than half the ships on patrol at any one time. Passages to and from Glasgow and Liverpool, the time taken there for refreshment, and repairs and accidents, meant that the actual patrols seldom had more than a dozen ships on duty. The recession of the ice made it necessary to search a greater area of ocean. In turn the greater number of ships intercepted made it necessary to detach large numbers of men as 'prize-crews', or 'armed guards'. These were commanded by junior officers, often very young, who thus had large reponsibilities. The dilemmas they faced are illustrated by the account of Sub-Lieutenant Maclure [83, also 55], and they provoked reactions as high as the Commander-in-Chief and the Admiralty [55, 85, 86]; the dilatoriness of the Admiralty in reaching a decision is notable, and ominous for other, similar matters.

The distance of the Patrol's patrol-lines from the Glasgow and Liverpool bases, and the dangers of mines and submarines off the western coasts, brought up the idea of a more northern base. De Chair went to inspect West Loch Roag in Lewis in the Outer Hebrides [64], but preferred Swarbacks Minn in Shetland, already being used occasionally [70, 76]. A base was thereupon developed there; it was a recognition that the war was to be a long-drawn-out affair.

48. *Captain G.W. Vivian to Rear-Admiral Commanding Tenth Cruiser Squadron*

HMS *Patia*, At Sea, 14 April 1915

Report of Proceedings, 6 March–14 April 1915

***

I proceeded to Glasgow at midnight on the 6th and secured in the Princes dock. On the 8th I completed with coal and discharged the Enteric cases I had to hospital. The Admiralty Medical Department sent an officer down to hold an enquiry on the outbreak of Enteric we had had, but nothing definite was ascertained as all the water supplies were free of infection, 15 of my men (besides those already in hospital) including the Gunner's Mate and Sergeant of Marines were discharged to Chatham and Haslar Hospitals as possible typhoid carriers which was most disorganising for the ship. On March 17th I was ready for sea but had to wait as it was intended to send another Medical Officer from the Admiralty to visit the ship, this was however eventually not carried out, and I left on the 29th for Rothesay Dock, and put to sea at midnight that night. A fairly strong Westerly wind was blowing which, if there were any submarines about, would most probably have caused them to shelter under the Irish Coast. I maintained my maximum speed and a constant ten minutes zig-zag and saw nothing of any submarines. At 3.30 p.m. on the 21st I passed the *Mantua* and at 5.30 intercepted a steamer which I found to be one of our own colliers. At 10.30 a.m. on the 22nd I sighted and spoke to the *Changuinola*, and at 12.15 the *Digby*. At 6.30 a.m. on the 23rd I sighted and closed a steamer which was a trawler (GY 2) bound for Lerwick. On the 24th at 10 a.m. I sighted and closed a steamer and found her to be the Norwegian steamer *Henrik* from New York to Bergen or Christiania, boarded her with some difficulty and found she had a general cargo of very considerable value, mainly copper ingots and wire, aluminium, flour, petroleum, motor-car parts, castings, etc, in fact most things which Germany is believed to want. It was more or less of a chance that I sighted this ship as I happened to be a good bit North of my line, and I do not think that there is much doubt that this ship was trying to get through unseen, for when I first saw her and stood towards her she altered course and was apparently inclined to run, but finally decided not to. Her captain was somewhat indignant at being boarded at all, and he produced the inevitable British Consular Certificate which he seemed to think cleared him of any further trouble. It is I think most desirable that the value to be attached to this certificate should be more clearly made known both to Masters of neutral vessels and also to Captains of HM Ships. A further point that seems to arise is this, if the British Consul or his representative examined and inspected this ship's cargo, as the certificate apparently implies, surely the importance of preventing this cargo going into wrong hands must have been apparent and all HM Ships on this work might have been warned to look out for this ship, possibly the Consul did send information, but certainly no information reached me. The mere fact that this ship was bound for Bergen or Christiania with such a cargo seems to me to be in itself gravely suspicious, and from what I gathered from my boarding officer as to the demeanour of the Captain and Mate I do not think there is much doubt that they were quite aware that they were running a very doubtful cargo and their indignation was doubtless mainly due to the prospective loss of their bonus for getting safely through. This ship's cargo was some 5000 tons or more, the bulk of which as far as we had time to examine the manifest (which the Master was extremely loth to show) was material and goods which Germany is said to be badly in need of, and the value of which to that country would have been very considerable, and that we stopped her at all was only due to the fact that I was North of my line and almost in sight of the Faeroes. I had not time to make a careful examination of the manifest as the weather was threatening and I was anxious to get a prize-crew on board before the sea got up.[1] At 5 p.m. I closed and examined the British trawler *King Emperor* of Hull (H 202) from Iceland to Lerwick. On the 25th at 9.30 a.m. I stopped the Swedish steamer *Ran* from Philadelphia to Odense with a cargo of Indian corn. Too much sea to board at the time, but at 3 p.m. I decided to try to board her though there was an unpleasant breaking sea. The boat was very skilfully handled by the officer in charge and the prize-crew were safely put on Board and the *Ran* proceeded to Kirkwall.[2] On the 27th I examined the British trawler *Neptunian* of Hull (H 626) and later the British trawler *Ben Strome*. At 8 p.m. I stopped and examined the Danish steamer *Douro* from Iceland to Leith with fish. Allowed her to proceed. *Cedric* left B Patrol at 7 p.m. On the 28th at 10 a.m. I

[1]This ship was the subject of a long dispute and discussion. Part of the cargo was vouched for by the French government, which urged the speedy release of the ship from Kirkwall. But part of the cargo was judged to be 'prize' and the ship was ordered to Sunderland to discharge it. The ship was thus delayed all through April as a result (TS 14/1 March and April).

[2]The *Ran*'s cargo was part maize and part rye; the ship was allowed to go on from Kirkwall (TS 14/1 of 14 March 1915).

boarded the Danish three-masted schooner *Activ* from Barcelona to Copenhagen with a small cargo of oil-cake. While I was boarding this ship observed a large steamer south of me, so left the schooner and went after the steamer, which I came up with at noon. Found this ship to be the Danish steamer *Transvaal*, a new and very fine ship. She was from the Chilean ports and had come back through the Panama Canal, had only seen one ship since leaving the West Indies and was bound for Aarhus and Copenhagen. She had a large and valuable cargo, particularly for warlike purposes, consisting of 5400 tons of Chilian nitrate, 1000 tons of bran, 240 tons of cotton-seed cake, 500 rolls of leather and some general cargo. The nitrate was to be unloaded at Aarhus, which in view of its proximity to the German frontier and the reported shortage of nitrates in Germany seemed to point to its ultimate destination. Put a prize-crew on board and sent her in to Kirkwall[1] [63], and then went back to look for the schooner *Activ*. Sent a prize-crew on board her at 2 p.m. and sent her in to Kirkwall [60]. At 5.30 sighted and closed a large steamer which was the Danish steamer *Oscar*[2] which had been previously boarded, allowed to proceed. *Motagua* joined patrol at 3 p.m. On the 29th sighted *Teutonic* in the morning joining up with the patrol. On the 30th at noon I shaped course for Stornoway to pick up prize-crews from *Duke of Cornwall* in accordance with your orders. At 2 p.m. I sighted and boarded a large Norwegian steamer the *Sverre* from San Francisco to Copenhagen with 5400 tons of barley. This ship had come through the Panama Canal and had seen no ships coming across the Atlantic, she had made North Rona and was going through the Fair Island Channel. Put a prize-crew on board and sent her into Kirkwall.[3] This made our fifth prize-crew away. At 10 p.m. I anchored outside Stornoway and at midnight having received various prize-crews I weighed and proceeded to the rendezvous to meet *Digby*. On the 31st I sighted a large Russian steamer (*Baltica*) and shortly afterwards the Danish steamer *Tula* from Falmouth to Copenhagen. At noon met *Digby* and transferred prize-crews for A, C, D patrols to her, shaping course for my patrol at 1 p.m. At 5 p.m. stopped and boarded Swedish steamer *Loke* with a cargo of salt and cork from Gibraltar to Stockholm.

[1]Several items in *Transvaal*'s cargo were deemed 'contraband' (leather, wool, wheat bran, cottonseed cake, nitrate of soda) and destined for a merchant on the Black List; these items were sent for adjudication in the Prize Court (TS 14/1 of 30 March 1915). There ensued much discussion between Copenhagen and London over the nitrate of soda.

[2]Presumably *Oscar II*; it was not detained on this voyage.

[3]*Sverre*'s cargo of barley was on the Danish list of prohibited exports and the ship was allowed to go on (TS 14/1 of 7 April 1915).

Allowed her to proceed. On April 1st proceeded to the rendezvous where I had directed *Teutonic* and *Motagua* to meet me to get their prize-crews. It was blowing hard with a heavy sea and no boarding was feasible when we met, but after dinner the sea moderated a bit and both ships' prize-crews were transferred, and the three ships resumed the patrol. On April 3rd I met *Motagua* at rendezvous and received from her my other two prize-crews. On April 4th at 9 a.m. stopped Danish steamer *Vladimir Reitz* from Galveston to Kirkwall with oil-cake. Too much sea to board. Ship allowed to proceed. At noon stopped a large Danish steamer the *Chumpon* from New Orleans to Goteborg with a cargo of cotton. Too much sea to board, so she was taken under the lee of Muckle Flugga where a prize-crew was put on board and the ship sent in to Kirkwall.[1] In the afternoon of the 5th sighted and boarded the Norwegian barque *Sigurd* of Sandnaes from Stavanger to Talcahuana with a general cargo. This ship originally left Hamburg last September, ran ashore on the coast of Denmark, was repaired at Stavanger and finally sailed from there. Her cargo was therefore presumably German. A prize-crew was placed on board and she was sent into Stornoway.[2] On the 6th examined two Norwegian sailing-ships, the *Sokoto* with a prize-crew already on board[3] and the *Baron Holberg* bound for Swansea with timber. On the 8th intercepted the Norwegian steamer *Imo* with a prize-crew on board.[4] On the 9th examined several British trawlers, the Norwegian barque *Zanrak* bound for Birkenhead with timber and the British steamer *Frimley* from Dundee to New York. On the 10th I met *Patuca* at the rendezvous and prize-crews were transferred from her to this ship, *Orotava* and *Teutonic*. On the morning of the 11th I proceeded in accordance with your orders to C Patrol, examining the Norwegian barque *Desideria* bound for Newport with timber on the way. Allowed to proceed. On the 12th at daylight I sighted a *Dreadnought* type of battleship at daylight, probably the *Warspite*, and shortly afterwards stopped the Norwegian steamer *Brakar* from Baltimore to Copenhagen with 8700 tons of Indian corn. During the process of getting my boat out

[1]*Chumpon* was allowed to proceed (TS 14/1 of 7 April 1915).

[2]Despite Captain Vivian's suspicions the *Sigurd* was not detained and proceeded on her voyage without reference to the Contraband Committee. Since the cargo had presumably already been paid for, any loss would fall on the Norwegian owners or their customers or their insurers, and only resentment in a neutral country would be the result.

[3]*Sokoto*'s cargo was nitrate of soda; the Contraband Committee decided to let it go on, since a licence would be needed to re-export it (TS 14/1 of 12 April 1915).

[4]The master of *Imo* is quoted as having refused a large bribe to take petroleum to Rotterdam; despite the fact that the vessel's charterer was on the British Black List, it was allowed to proceed; the cargo was cottonseed cake (TS 14/1 of 10 April 1915).

a collision ... occurred between *Brakar* and *Patia* which was very nearly extremely serious as there was a heavy sea running at the time. As it was, comparatively little damage was done to either ship and what damage was done was above the water-line. Prize-crew were put on board *Brakar* and she was sent into Kirkwall.[1] At 1 p.m. I intercepted the Norwegian sailing-ship *Zanrak* which I had previously seen. Allowed to proceed. At 2 p.m. I stopped and boarded the Danish steamer *Johan Siem* from Charleston to Aalborg with oil-cake. Prize-crew put on board and sent in to Kirkwall.[2] There was a heavy sea running and the whaler was very nearly swamped. On the 13th at 10 a.m. I left the patrol and proceeded for Belfast in accordance with your orders. During this patrol that is from March 22nd to April 15th, twenty-five ships were intercepted and stopped not counting trawlers, of which nine were sent in with prize-crews. I arrived in Belfast Lough at 11 p.m. on the 14th and proceeded direct to Belfast.

Much of the boarding carried out on this trip has been undertaken in heavy seas, this work has been admirably carried out by the R.N.R. officers of this ship, who are all excellent officers, capable seamen and very keen.

49. *Rear-Admiral de Chair to Admiralty*

HMS *Alsatian*, 20 April 1915

Report of Proceedings, 9 March–20 April 1915

***

1. The installation of a 3 Kilowatt Wireless set in *Alsatian* was taken in hand soon after arrival on 9th March and at the same time the ship was completed with coal and stores and small defects were made good.

2. On Thursday, 11th March I received information that the *Bayano* which had left the Clyde the previous night, had been sunk at 5.15 a.m. 10 miles SE by E from Corsewall Point.[3] The remaining Armed Merchant Cruisers in the Clyde (viz *Digby*, *Hildebrand*, *Changuinola*, *Patia*) were detained there pending further orders from Admiralty until 15th March.

3. *Ambrose* arrived at Liverpool on the afternoon of 12th March and

[1] *Brakar* was allowed to proceed without reference to the Contraband Committee.
[2] *Johan Siem* was allowed to go on (TS 14/1 of 14 April 1915).
[3] *Bayano* was torpedoed by *U 27*.

reported that on the preceding day when off Oversay Island he was attacked by a submarine on three separate occasions. Commander Bruton,[1] who undoubtedly saved his ship by skilful manoeuvring, was of opinion that the first two attacks were delivered by the same boat. Two torpedoes were fired, one in the first and one in the second attack, but on the third occasion the conning tower of the submarine was seen about 400 yards on the Port Quarter, and fire was at once opened, and the object appeared to have been hit after about 8 or 9 rounds. The first apparent hit threw up a thick water mist, and on two projectiles subsequently striking the water in the same place a thick oily looking spray appeared, also a spray rainbow in colour. The guns' crews were convinced that the object aimed at had been hit and an Officer who was watching the firing from the boat deck was also of that opinion. Nothing more was seen. The low speed of *Ambrose* placed her in great danger on this occasion; had the weather been at all unfavourable for high steaming it is extremely improbable that she would have escaped.[2]

4. 15th March, while proceeding north from the Clyde *Digby* was chased by a submarine 25 miles S of Skerryvore.[3] She took refuge in Tobermory Harbour and after obtaining a Destroyer escort from Larne proceeded to her patrol on 16th March.

5. Orders were received on 12th and 19th March that *Calyx* and *Eskimo* respectively were to be paid off. *Calyx* left patrol for Hull on 13th March. *Eskimo* prepared to pay off at Liverpool.

***

8. Sunday, 21st March – The fitting of the 3 Kilowatt Wireless set in *Alsatian* having been completed and tested with satisfactory results I left Liverpool at midnight and proceeded at 18 knots to rejoin patrol.

9. Monday, 22nd March – At 6 a.m. I was joined by the Torpedo Boat Destroyer *Dove* at a rendezvous 53 degrees – 9 miles from South Rock Light Vessel, whence *Alsatian* proceeded under escort until well clear of Rathlin Island.

10. Tuesday, 23rd March – During the afternoon *Cedric* joined me at a pre-arranged rendezvous and I communicated information as regards patrols &c.

[1]Bruton, Charles William, RN (1875–1952), Commander 1908, Captain 1915, Captain in *Ambrose* 1915, Rear-Admiral (retired) 1922.

[2]The submarine was neither hit nor sunk.

[3]This was probably *U 27* which passed Skerryvore on 14 March. No other submarine was in the area at the time.

Disposition of Squadron was as follows:

A Patrol ... *Otway*.
B Patrol ... *Cedric*, *Columbella*, *Caribbean*, *Patia*.
C Patrol ... *Alsatian*, *Changuinola*, *Digby*.
D Patrol ... *Hildebrand*, *Motagua*.
Coaling at Liverpool ... *Teutonic*, *Oropesa*, *Orotava*, *Hilary*, *Patuca*, *Ambrose*.
Coaling in Clyde ... *Mantua*.
Proceeding to rejoin patrol ... *Virginian*.
Ordered to pay off ... *Calyx*, *Eskimo*.

Arrangement of Patrol lines was as follows:-
A Patrol – Cross centre line 360° from Lat. 62.20´N, Long. 10 W daily at noon, steering to make good 245°, ships from South to North 20 miles apart.
B Patrol – Cross centre line 350° from Lat. 60.35´N, Long. 3 W daily at 8 a.m., steering to make good 240°, Ships from South to North 20 miles apart.
C Patrol – Cross centre line 360° from Lat. 59.20´N, Long. 9 W daily at 9 a.m., steering to make good 240°, ships from South to North 25 miles apart.
D Patrol – Line ahead patrol 335° from St Kilda, ships 35 miles apart, southern position of southern ship 15 miles from St Kilda, ships from South to North.

Special temporary disposition of patrols were also made by me with a view to intercepting the Swedish Steamer *Forsvick* (ex German *Neuenfels*) which was reported to have left Vigo with a cargo of rice for Goteborg [53].

Duke of Cornwall brought out prize crews from Kirkwall for *Columbella*, *Changuinola*, and *Digby*, and transferred them to the latter ship at a pre-arranged rendezvous.

11. Wednesday, 24th March – *Patia* reported having intercepted the Norwegian Steamer *Henrik* from New York to Bergen and Christiania with a valuable cargo consisting of copper ingots and wire, oil, aluminium, flour, motor accessories &c. She was sent in to Kirkwall with a Prize Crew [54, 57, 58].[1]

The increasing number of Ships sent in to port with prize crews causes a considerable depletion among the ships' companies, and the additional Seamen, Stoker and Marine ratings which I am informed by

[1]See p. 121, note 1.

the Commander-in-Chief are to be sent to the Squadron are much needed. When the six large ships (asked for to augment the patrol) have joined the difficulty should be largely removed.

C and D patrols being now very short of ships (consequent on loss of *Bayano* and paying off of *Calyx* and *Eskimo*) I directed *Otway* and *Virginian* to join C patrol, having previously ascertained that few if any ships were passing north of the Faroe Islands.

From information gained by officers boarding Norwegian ships it appears that while articles imported into the country are carefully retained for home consumption, Norwegian grown foodstuffs &c., are freely exported to Germany.

12. Thursday, 25th March – Eleven Steamers were intercepted, of which seven were sent in to Kirkwall with prize crews. In order to avoid excessive depletion of ships' companies it was necessary in some cases to order prize crews to be provided by ships other than those which actually intercepted.

13. Friday, 26th March – *Duke of Cornwall* brought out seven prize crews from Kirkwall and transferred them to *Hildebrand* for return to their ships.

14. Saturday, 27th March – B Patrol being now reduced to two ships, viz: *Cedric* and *Patia* (the former under orders to leave patrol to coal) I directed a line ahead patrol to be formed on meridian 3.30´W, ships 30 miles apart, south to north, southern position of southern ship Lat. 60.30´N. *Motagua* was ordered to join this patrol.

Information was received from the Senior Naval Officer Humber, that *Calyx* had been paid off. This (with the prospective paying off of *Eskimo*) reduces the number of ships under my command to eighteen, which is insufficient to adequately carry out the duties required of the Northern Patrol.

15. Sunday, 28th March – With a view to intercepting the Norwegian Mail Steamer *Bergensfjord* which I was directed to send in to Kirkwall when met with, line ahead patrols were ordered for D and C patrols, and B patrol was ordered to resume the same patrol as arranged yesterday with *Patia*, *Teutonic*, and *Motagua*.

Otway which was in charge of C Patrol intercepted *Oscar II* which was allowed to proceed in accordance with Admiralty orders after it had been ascertained that she carried no contraband or German Reservists. Disposition of ships of Squadron was as follows:

A Patrol ... *Alsatian*.
B Patrol ... *Patia*, *Teutonic*, *Motagua*.
C Patrol ... *Virginian*, *Changuinola*, *Digby*.

D Patrol ... *Hildebrand.*
Coaling at Liverpool ... *Oropesa*, *Orotava*, *Ambrose.*
Coaling in Clyde ... *Mantua*, *Caribbean.*
Proceeding to Coal ... *Cedric*, *Columbella.*
Rejoining patrol ... *Hilary*, *Patuca.*

During the past week 49 vessels were intercepted, of which 23 were sent into port with prize crews.

Patia intercepted the Danish Steamer *Transvaal* loaded with nitre, bran, cotton seed cake, and leather &c., for Aalsund and Copenhagen. She was sent in to Kirkwall with a prize crew.[1]

The Captain of the Steamer *Grodno* which was intercepted going West by *Teutonic* reported that when passing south of Fair Isle about 7.30 p.m. on Saturday 27th March, he was followed for half an hour by a brillant light close to the water. At 9.30 p.m. he heard a heavy explosion astern; a large vessel had passed to the eastward shortly before.[2] I reported the matter by wireless to the Commander-in-Chief. In accordance with directions the Senior Naval Officer Larne was requested to furnish a destroyer escort for *Cedric* on passage to Liverpool, but I was informed that none were available.

Patuca reported that while returning to patrol from Liverpool at 7.0 a.m. she sighted the periscope of a submarine 6.5 miles N 32 E from the Maidens, steering N by E.

16. Monday, 29th March – Orders having been received from Admiralty to send into port the Norwegian Steamers *Bergensfjord*, *Romsdalsfjord* and *Romsdal*, B and C Patrols were disposed to intercept them, and *Bergensfjord* was intercepted by *Otway* and sent to Kirkwall with a prize crew [59]. *Otway* reported that the Captain of the *Bergensfjord* had sent a strong written protest against ship being taken into war zone and dangerous waters near Kirkwall, stating that his cargo was vouched for by the British Consul-General, and all contraband goods were guaranteed not to be re-exported. All Germans on board except one had Australian Government passports. The Captain also requested permission to send a message by W/T to Christiania, but by direction of the Commander-in-Chief this was not allowed.

Cedric which was on passage to Liverpool reported that she had exploded by gunfire a spherical mine with horns in Lat. 55.46´N, Long. 9.48´W.

[1]See p. 122, note 1.

[2]There is no record of a ship sinking in this area at this time; no submarine had been in the area since 15 March.

17. Tuesday, 30th March – Information was received that the Armed Yacht *Vanessa* had fired on a strange grey steamer with no colours steaming SW from Cape Wrath. This was probably *Duke of Cornwall* proceeding from Scapa to Stornoway with Prize Crews for Tenth Cruiser Squadron.

18. Wednesday, 31st March – *Virginian* reported that in boarding the Danish Schooner *Julianna* she had fouled her and carried away her mizzen topmast, jibboom and some running gear, but the damage was not such as to prevent her proceeding to Kirkwall in charge of a prize crew.

19. Thursday, 1st April – *Motagua* reported that a fire had occurred in her linen store the contents of which were burnt, and considerable damage was done by fire and water in wardroom and adjacent cabins, but the fighting efficiency of the ship was not impaired. The cause of the outbreak was being investigated. She was ordered to remain on patrol.

Orotava reported having intercepted Norwegian SS *Romsdalsfjord*, New York to Bergen with general cargo in Lat. 61.20´N, Long. 3.30´W. The weather was too rough to allow of boarding at the time but I directed *Orotava* to take her under the lee of the land and place a prize crew on board as soon as possible. This was safely accomplished at 8.0 p.m., and the vessel was sent in to Kirkwall.[1]

Teutonic reported that when boarding the American Steamer *Herman Frasch* on 28th March the Captain of that vessel made a statement as to the examination of his cargo at Kirkwall on 8th March on his previous voyage eastward bound for Bremen. He said the cargo was examined by entering hold through manhole door in hatch. The seals were not broken. The cargo was discharged at Bremen. He also stated that German Steamers were running cargoes to Bremen via the Kiel Canal from Copenhagen and other ports.

20. Friday, 2nd April – At 1.40 a.m. *Hilary* reported that she had chased the Norwegian Steamer *Romsdal* bound from New York to Christiania with a cargo of wheat, and had sent her in with a prize crew.[2]

I met *Digby* at a pre-arranged rendezvous and *Alsatian* received from her three prize crews which had been brought out from Kirkwall by

[1]*Romsdalfjord*, along with her sister ship *Bergensfjord*, was deliberately detained to bring pressure on the Norwegian government to conform to British wishes on exports. The ship was still held at Sunderland at the end of April, despite a Norwegian assurance that the copper on board would not be re-exported, and that exports of copper products were prohibited (TS 14/1 of 5 April 1915 *et al.*).

[2]*Romsdal* was not detained.

Duke of Cornwall.

21. Saturday, 3rd April – The weather became very bad and prevented boarding in the open sea, but by taking ships under the lee of the nearest land prize crews were put on board where required and all vessels intercepted were dealt with. In some cases it was necessary to turn an intercepted vessel over from one ship to another of the patrol as no more prize crews could be spared from the first ship's company. *Patia* had six prize crews away [48]. In all 21 prize crews were away from the Squadron.

In consequence of the reported presence of a submarine off St Kilda, I moved D patrol from 10 to 20 miles from land, and later directed a line ahead patrol 335° 10 miles from Flannan Islands.

Oropesa reported she had intercepted a Norwegian Sailing Ship, also a Norwegian Steamer. She kept in company with both until under the lee of Shetlands and sent them to Kirkwall with prize crews. This I consider was a good piece of work in view of the South Westerly gale and heavy sea prevailing at the time.

Alsatian intercepted the American Oil tanker *Llama* with mineral oil. This vessel which was originally the German *Brilliant* had been intercepted on a previous voyage and sent in to Kirkwall on 8th January. The actual date of her transfer to the United States Flag is not given, but in 'Alterations to Lloyds' Register No. 13 dated 19th Nov–3rd Dec.' the change of name is shewn.[1] Heavy sea from SW. Gale moderating.

22. Sunday, 4th April – B Patrol centre line was shifted to 360° from Lat. 60.35´N, Long. 3 W, ships steering to make good 240°.

Disposition of Squadron was as follows:

A Patrol ... *Mantua*, *Teutonic*.
B Patrol ... *Patia*, *Motagua*, *Caribbean*, *Orotava*.
C Patrol ... *Alsatian*, *Virginian*, *Oropesa*, *Hilary*.
D Patrol ... *Hildebrand*, *Patuca*.
Proceeding to Clyde to coal ... *Changuinola*.
Proceeding to Liverpool to coal ... *Digby*.
At Liverpool ... *Otway*, *Cedric*, *Ambrose*.
In the Clyde ... *Columbella*.

During the past week 80 ships were intercepted, of which 29 were sent into port with prize crews.

[1]*Llama* was permitted to sail on when the Danish government gave an assurance that her cargo was intended for Danish internal consumption (TS 14/1 of 7 and 12 April 1915). The ship was another of those acquired in September 1914 by Standard Oil of New Jersey from their original German owners, with the deed of sale dated 'May'.

Teutonic was detached to endeavour to intercept the Swedish SS *Sir Ernest Cassel* which had left Narvik (Lat. 68.27´N) on the night of Saturday, 3rd April for Rotterdam. *Motagua* having arrived at a pre-arranged rendezvous with my Flag, I directed her to take charge of SS *Llama* from *Alsatian*, putting a prize crew on board when under the lee of the Shetlands. The work of the Squadron has been rendered more difficult by the continued heavy gales which prevent boarding in the open sea, but vessels have been taken under the lee of Faroes or Shetlands and none of those intercepted have been allowed to escape without examination, while all those suspected of carrying contraband have been sent in with prize crews.

23. Monday, 5th April – In accordance with directions from Admiralty I proceeded in *Alsatian* to West Loch Roag in the Island of Lewis, Hebrides, with a view to reporting on the suitability of the anchorage as a base for coaling Tenth Cruiser Squadron. Rear-Admiral Tupper, Senior Naval Officer Stornoway, met me on arrival and I conferred with him on the subject. A full report is contained in my submission No. 72/028 of 6th April 1915 [64].

Columbella on rejoining patrol after coaling reported that the heavy sea of last night had carried away gun shelter and put out of action ammunition supply and communications on the forecastle. Jury gear was being fitted. She also reported that the 270 tons of ballast put into the ship according to Admiralty directions with a view to bringing her down by the stern, had the effect of trimming her two feet by the head.

24. Tuesday, 6th April – A report was received from St Kilda through Senior Naval Officer Stornoway, that a submarine had been sighted at 6.0 p.m. on 5th 10 miles SE of St Kilda steering east, and that at midnight a red light was seen but disappeared suddenly. A submarine was also reported in Lat. 55.24´N, Long. 5.11´W at 4.0 a.m. today. *Motagua* which was on passage to Clyde was warned and directed to pass Mull of Cantyre in the dark and to use full speed.

Teutonic reported the capture of the Swedish Steamer *Sir Ernest Cassel* with a cargo of 10,600 tons of Magnetic Ore in Lat. 62.3´N, Long. 4.42´E. She was sent to Kirkwall with a prize crew[1] and *Teutonic* was directed to remain on her present detached patrol to look out for another Swedish Steamer, the *Vanda*, loaded with copper reported to have arrived at Aalesund [65].

I left West Loch Roag in *Alsatian* at 6.0 p.m. The gale throughout the

[1]The Contraband Committee decreed that the ore itself was not contraband, but since the ship's destination was Rotterdam, the ore's destination was obviously Germany; the ore was thus to be discharged to the Prize Court (TS 14/1 of 9 April 1915).

day set up a considerable sea in the anchorage and boat work was difficult.

25. Wednesday, 7th April – The gale continued, blowing from WSW with very high sea and heavy squalls of rain and hail. *Alsatian* intercepted Swedish SS *Zamora*, New York to Stockholm, and kept in company with her through the night.

26. Thursday, 8th April – The wind and sea having decreased *Zamora* was boarded and sent in to Kirkwall with prize crew in accordance with Admiralty Orders.[1] *Teutonic* which was still on detached duty to the eastward of Shetlands reported that during the night she had been followed by a suspicious vessel which she considered to be a German Cruiser. She endeavoured to draw the vessel towards Muckle Flugga till daylight but lost sight of her in a rain squall at 2.0 a.m. *Teutonic* was ordered to return to B patrol by Commander-in-Chief.

The Norwegian Steamer *Imo* from Norfolk (USA) to Aarhus was intercepted by *Oropesa* and sent to Kirkwall with prize crew in accordance with Admiralty orders.[2]

***

Several Steamers and Sailing Ships were intercepted, among the former the Norwegian Steamer *Lapland* with a cargo of lead, bacon, cotton seed, oil, and cocoa beans from New York to Bergen and Copenhagen. She was sent in to Kirkwall.[3]

27. Friday, 9th April – *Oropesa* intercepted the American Steamer *Ogeechee* bound from Bremen to New York with general cargo and sent her in to Stornoway.[4] The Chief Engineer of the ship, a British subject, informed the Boarding Officer that German Men-of-War at Bremen were being re-armed with guns at least 6 centimeters larger, and that heavier armour was being fitted.

In accordance with directions from Commander-in-Chief, I detached *Caribbean* from B Patrol to work with *Lancaster* to the eastward of the Shetlands.

28. Saturday, 10th April – Some anxiety was felt at the non-arrival of

[1] *Zamora*'s cargo was copper, wheat and oats, and both ship and cargo were sent to the Prize Court, and a thorough search of the ship ordered (TS 14/1 of 12 April 1915).

[2] See p. 123, note 4.

[3] Most of *Lapland*'s cargo was immediately sent to the prize court, and the rest was regarded as suspicious; the ship itself was not 'prize-courted', though the idea was considered (TS 14/1 of 10 April 1915).

[4] This ship was allowed to proceed despite the origin of the cargo, a clear indication of the very great care being exercised not to annoy the USA.

Ambrose which had left Liverpool on Wednesday evening, and it was not till 2.0 p.m. that she was heard calling Malin Head. She had put into Belfast on account of heavy weather and had remained there until Friday night.

29. Sunday, 11th April – In accordance with the wishes of the Commander-in-Chief, and in order to meet the altered conditions caused by short nights and the passage of shipping north of Iceland during the summer months the patrol areas were changed and ships re-distributed as follows:

A Patrol ... Cross base line 360° from Lat. 62.55´N, Long. 5 W at 8.0 a.m. daily, steering to make good 225°, ships 25 miles apart from S to N – *Otway*, *Columbella*, *Mantua*, *Teutonic*, *Alsatian*. To be increased to six ships when available.
B Patrol ... Withdrawn.
C Patrol ... Cross centre line 13° from Lat. 58.30´N, Long. 8 W at noon daily, steering to make good 240°, ships 25 miles apart from S to N – *Ambrose*, *Patuca*, *Hilary*, *Patia*, *Virginian*, *Orotava*, *Oropesa*.
D Patrol ... Withdrawn.
E Patrol ... North of Iceland. Six ships when available.
F Patrol ... South of Iceland. Four ships when available.
G Patrol ... On Meridian 3 E between Lat. 62 and 63½ N. Three ships when available and one Cruiser from Grand Fleet. As a temporary measure *Caribbean* was working on this patrol ... This re-arrangement requires 27 Armed Merchant Cruisers of which only 18 were available, and of these
Cedric ... was rejoining patrol.
Hildebrand ... was proceeding to coal in Clyde.
Motagua, *Changuinola* ... were coaling in Clyde.
Digby ... was coaling at Liverpool.

During the past week the number of vessels intercepted by the Tenth Cruiser Squadron was 66, of which 20 were sent into port with prize crews and 3 without prize crews.

30. Monday, 12th April – *Patia* reported that when boarding the Norwegian Steamer *Brakar* bound from Baltimore to Copenhagen with Indian Corn, a slight collision occurred, the Steamer touching *Patia* on starboard quarter, starting a plate and bending a frame. *Brakar* was slightly damaged under forecastle; she proceeded to Kirkwall with prize crew.[1] I have directed *Patia* to forward a full report of the occurrence.

[1]The ship was not detained.

Warspite in Lat. 60.35´N, Long. 10.2´W was carrying out turret gun trials.

I met *Cedric* at a pre-arranged rendezvous and communicated visually giving her necessary orders for change of C Patrol.

31. Tuesday, 13th April – *Otway* reported that she had intercepted the Swedish Steamer *Oscar Frederick*, Buenos Aires to Goteburg with coffee and grain, in Lat. 62.47´N, Long. 60.56´W. She was sent to Kirkwall with a prize crew.[1] Her Captain protested against being sent in on account of the danger of meeting German submarines.

Ambrose was detached for service on G patrol, relieving *Caribbean* which proceeded to Clyde to coal.

32. Wednesday, 14th April – *Cedric* intercepted the Swedish Steamer *Carolina* from Charleston to Goteborg with cotton.[2] She reported having sighted a large submarine in Lat. 59.55´N, Long. 7.38´W steering SW at 4 a.m. C Patrol was temporarily moved to the eastward as a precautionary measure, as this position is in their working area.

33. Thursday, 15th April – *Patuca* intercepted the Danish Steamer *Spigerborg*, Huelva to Aalborg with pyrites. This vessel had cleared from Ardrossan with a green customs pass but was ordered to be detained if met with as she had attempted to pass through the North Channel at night after being given written instructions showing route to be used. She was sent to Kirkwall with a prize crew, and the Admiral Commanding Orkneys and Shetlands was informed of her capture and of the advisability of detaining her pending instructions from Admiralty.[3]

From information received from Commander-in-Chief it appears that a Reserve Officer and 16 other Germans of military age succeeded by the use of false Norwegian passports in reaching Christiania by the Norwegian Steamer *Bergensfjord* which (as already reported) was boarded by *Otway* on 29th March, and sent in to Kirkwall with a prize crew. It was a great surprise to hear that this ship had been released with Germans onboard. This was the third occasion she had been sent into port by Tenth Cruiser Squadron; she is an old offender and has tried to evade our patrols. It has always been understood that the sending of a

[1]At Kirkwall much of *Oscar Frederick*'s cargo was deemed to be of enemy origin (that is, from German firms in Brazil) and the ship discharged those items at West Hartlepool (TS 14/1 of 17 and 29 April 1915).

[2]*Carolina* was sent in to Kirkwall; the Contraband Committee recommended that the cargo of 2600 tons of cotton should be purchased rather than go on to Sweden; the purchase was recorded as going through on 28 April (TS 14/1 of 16 and 28 April 1915).

[3]The Danish government provided assurances that the *Spigerborg*'s cargo would not be re-exported.

ship into Port with a prize crew ensured a thorough examination of her passengers and cargo such as could not very well be made by any ship at sea especially in the heavy weather usually met with in these waters, and the limited time at our disposal.[1]

34. Friday, 16th April – In reply to an enquiry by Commander-in-Chief, as to number of ships intercepted by G Patrol (off coast of Norway) during the week I informed him that none had been intercepted and suggested the provision of two submarines to operate with the patrol working close in shore to stop ships going south. Submarines not being available however it was necessary to relinquish the idea of intercepting coastal trade for the present.

35. Saturday, 17th April – In anticipation of the completion of six additional Armed Merchant Cruisers, to be added to the 10th CS, the re-arranged patrols were organised as follows:

A Patrol
(North of Faroe Islands)
Alsatian (Flag)
Otway
Orcoma
Mantua
Alcantara
Teutonic

C Patrol
(South of Faroe Islands)
Cedric (SO)
Patia
Orotava
Oropesa
Changuinola
Motagua
Digby
Patuca

E Patrol
(North of Iceland)
Columbella (SO)
Virginian
Andes
Arlanza

F Patrol
(South of Iceland)
Hildebrand
India
Ebro
Hilary

G Patrol
(Coast of Norway)
Caribbean (SO)
Ambrose

Information was received from the Captain Superintendent, Clyde, that *Virginian* was ashore in the Clyde opposite Govan Ferry. This delayed the departure of *Oropesa* as the river was blocked.

[1]*Bergensfjord* was considered by the Contraband Committee on 3 April, and released to continue her voyage on the 5th; the ship was thus at Kirkwall for at least three days.

36. Sunday, 18th April – *Virginian* was towed off by tugs at 2 a.m. and *Oropesa* was able to leave the Clyde. The disposition of Squadron was as follows:

A Patrol ... *Alsatian, Otway, Mantua.*
C Patrol ... *Cedric, Columbella, Teutonic, Changuinola, Hilary.*
G Patrol ... *Ambrose.*
Rejoining Patrol ... *Motagua, Oropesa.*
Proceeding to Belfast to coal ... *Patuca.*
At Belfast ... *Patia* (coaling), *Digby* (making good machinery defects).
In Clyde ... *Virginian, Hildebrand, Caribbean, Orotava.*

During the past week A Patrol intercepted 10 ships (besides 23 Trawlers) and sent in two with prize crews; C Patrol intercepted 35 ships and sent in 18 with prize crews.

37. Monday, 19th April – I left patrol in *Alsatian* and proceeded for Liverpool. At 11.30 a.m. *Oropesa* reported that in Lat. 56 N, Long. 7.8´W she encountered and fired on a submarine. At 12.20 p.m. she burst a shell close to the submarine which disappeared. When *Alsatian* passed over the position a few hours later large quantities of oil were observed on the surface.[1]

38. Tuesday, 20th April – *Alsatian* arrived in the Mersey at 6.0 a.m.

50. *Rear-Admiral de Chair to Admiralty*

HMS *Alsatian*, 13 March 1915

In compliance with the directions contained in paragraph 2 of your letter M 0753 dated 10th February, to report as to the steps which I consider should be taken to render the northern patrol efficient against the passage of minelayers, I beg to state for Their Lordships' information that in my view the only way is to send all ships to which the slightest suspicion is attached, whether proceeding east or west, into port (either Kirkwall or Lerwick whichever is most convenient) with Prize Crews, in order that their cargo may be thoroughly examined.

With the increasing list of articles rendered contraband, the numbers of vessels to be sent in on that account will form a majority of those intercepted, and the remainder which are mostly in ballast, should be rummaged for mines or other hostile cargo such as might be carried by a submarine tender. This can seldom be done efficiently at sea.

[1] *U 22* was in the area at the time; she was not sunk.

51. *Commander-in-Chief Home Fleets to Admiralty*

HMS *Iron Duke*, 15 March 1915

***

2. In order to deal satisfactorily with the enemy and neutral shipping proceeding by the North about route, four lines of patrols are essential so as to ensure the interception of ships during daylight hours, and four ships on each patrol are considered the minimum number which can efficiently cope with the work, five being more desirable.

The work will be considerably increased when the policy of intercepting all supplies going to Germany is put into force.

3. In considering the suitability of the ships at present employed on this duty, they have been divided into five classes:

Class	Ship	Tons	Knots	
A	*Cedric*	2,100	17–16	
	Alsatian	18,500	19–18	
	Otway	12,000	18–17	
	Mantua	10,900	17–16	
	Hildebrand	7,000	15–14	
B	*Hilary*	6,300	15–14	
	Patia	6,100	15–14	Very economical, but the flooding of one of the 2 large holds would in all probability sink the ship. The *Bayano* was another of this class.
	Patuca	6,100	15–14	
	Motagua	6,200	15–14	
	Changuinola	6,200	15–14	
C	*Teutonic*	10,000	19–18	Has no double bottom or feed water.
	Virginian	11,000	17–16	Poor coal capacity and is an expensive stmr.
D	*Digby*	3,960	14–13	Steers badly. Requires loading.
	Ambrose	4,590	15–14	Poor coal capacity and doubtful stability.
E	*Columbella*	8,290	18–16½	
	Caribbean	5,820	16–15	
	Orotava	5,980	15–14	
	Oropesa	5,960	14½–13½	
	Eskimo	3,320	17–16	

Those included in classes A, B and C are efficient for the work for which they are required; those in class D are fairly efficient. Ships in class E are not efficient and should, I submit, be relieved.

Calyx	Is now being paid off.
Clan MacNaughton *Viknor* *Bayano*	Have been lost.

It should be noted that the ships in Class B are sisters to the *Bayano*; the Rear-Admiral Commanding Tenth Cruiser Squadron, points out how vulnerable they are to torpedo attack, and the rapid sinking of the *Bayano* has proved this to be the case.

4. It is submitted that those in Class D should be withdrawn until their stability and loading have been carefully enquired into and adjusted, and those in Class E should be paid off as being unsuitable. Ten more ships will then be required to complete the squadron.

5. With reference to the losses of *Viknor* and *Clan McNaughton*, there is no evidence to show how this occurred.

That of the former may have been due to the ship drifting on to the North of Ireland minefield when hove to in the gale that was blowing at the time, or to striking a floating mine.

It seems improbable that the *Clan McNaughton* struck a mine or was torpedoed, the ship being well clear of mines and submarine areas. A heavy gale was blowing at the time and the distribution of weights referred to in the Rear-Admiral Commanding Tenth Cruiser Squadron's Submission no. 32/73 of the 23rd February 1915 [41], may have affected her seaworthiness. It has also been suggested that a large wooden booby hatch, built over the forward cargo hatch, may have been washed away, resulting in the flooding of the forehold in consequence.

6. Unless the submarine blockade off Liverpool and the Clyde can be raised, it may be necessary to establish a secure base elsewhere, with facilities for engine repairs and for coaling this class of vessel.

Loch Ewe is suggested for consideration, but it will be necessary to render it safe against submarine attack before use and to organise coaling from Lighters by shore labour.

52. *Rear-Admiral de Chair to Admiralty*

HMS *Alsatian*, 20 March 1915

… [A]s the *Clan McNaughton* went down at night and in one of the worst gales experienced by the ships of the 10th Cruiser Squadron and as no signal by W/T was received from her that she was in distress, it is feared her sinking must have been very sudden, more so than if struck by mine or submarine. Apart from this it was too rough at the time for a submarine to operate and she was rather out of the track of floating mines.

In my opinion, it is more probable that she rolled over, as it is considered an explosion would have liberated more wreckage than was afterwards found.

It is understood that the deep tank contained 1,500 tons of salt water which is a matter worthy of notice for should either the forward or after bulkhead of this tank have given away it would have been a serious matter.

I have no reason to suspect foul play.

It might be desirable to enquire from the owners of the vessel what they thought of her stability, trimmed, and ballasted as she was at the time of her loss.

53. *Contraband Committee Minutes*

22 March 1915

It appears from telegrams received [from the Customs at Stornoway] that this rice [on *Forsvik*] was loaded at Virgo [*sic*: i.e. Vigo] from the German vessel *Neuenfels*. The consignee is on the black list. The Customs should be informed that this cargo is to be placed in the Prize Court, and the Procurator-General, the Admiralty Marshal, the Swedish Minister and His Majesty's Minister in Stockholm should be informed.

54. *Contraband Committee Minutes*

22 March 1915

In view of secret agreement between French government and Norwegian Hydro Company, French Minister requests that certain consignments from New York per *Fram*, *Henrik* and *Romsdalfjord* may be allowed to pass.

55. *Commander-in-Chief Home Fleets to Admiral Commanding Orkneys and Shetlands and Rear-Admiral Commanding Tenth Cruiser Squadron*

HMS *Iron Duke*, 28 March 1915

The question having been raised as to the procedure to be adopted by the officer in charge of a prize crew engaged in conducting a neutral ship into port for examination, in the event of a neutral ship encountering an enemy submarine, the matter has been referred to the Admiralty for decision.

2. In the meantime the following rules are to be observed:

(a) The officer must endeavour to arrange for the neutral ship to escape.
(b) The officer must not use the neutral ship as a weapon for attacking the submarine unless attacked by her.
(c) The prize crew must not fight on the deck of the neutral ship, unless the submarine has committed a hostile act against the neutral ship. In the latter event the prize crew are justified in fighting to the last.

56. *Contraband Committee Minutes*

29 March 1915

The Committee decided that it was unnecessary to telegraph to His Majesty's Ministers in Scandinavia in order that they might obtain guarantees with regard to the ultimate destination of the suspicious items on board this vessel [the *United States*], as Captain Cold had pointed out, when in London, that he was much more likely to be able to return suspicious items to London if no official communications were made to the Scandinavian governments in regard to any consignments on board his vessels.

57. *Contraband Committee Minutes*

30 March 1915

Telegram from Customs at Kirkwall: 'In accordance with your wire of 28th I wrote master [of *Henrik*] that the machinery marked VL, Eabvl, WS, in cases in addition to item 163 required to be examined by the Customs, and asked him to place the cases accessible for such examination. He writes me through consul that all the cases are at the bottom of No. 2 hold and cannot be placed in a position accessible for examination without discharging a great part of the cargo, but he is willing, provided facilities can be provided, but he states that it seems to be impracticable here, and that in the circumstances he awaits our further instructions. From cargo plan master's statement appears correct, as all the heavy machinery is stored at the bottom of No. 2 hold. The vessel draws 22 ft, and could not come alongside here, as we can only berth vessels drawing 13 ft. There is no labour here apart from a coal merchant who may be asked to stevedore a small undertaking. There are no lighters for putting cargo overside. Under the circumstances I concur with the master that the examination of the machinery here is impracticable, and I await your further instructions' [54, 58].

58. *Contraband Committee Minutes*

31 March 1915

Telegram from Mr Findlay [Minister at Christiania],[1] 30 March 1915: 'French Minister says it is important there should be no delay of delivery of goods consigned to Norsk Hydro Electrisk Kvaelstof Company on board *Henrik*.' [54, 57].[2]

59. *Contraband Committee Minutes*

31 March 1915

[*Bergensfjord*] New York to Bergen, Stavanger, Christiansand, and Christiania. All cargo loaded at New York. British consul-general New York certifies vessel loaded under consular supervision.

A telegram should be sent to His Majesty's Minister at Christiania stating that the steamship *Bergensfjord* must be detained for enquiries and search unless the Norwegian-America line will undertake that no cargo shall be discharged until they have been informed of the consignments to the delivery of which His Majesty's Government takes

[1]Findlay, Mansfeldt de Cardonnel, GBE, KCMG, CB (1861–1932), British Minister at Christiania (i.e. the Norwegian capital, now Oslo), 1911–1923; earlier postings had been to Stockholm, Constantinople, Vienna, Buenos Aires, Belgrade, Sofia, Cairo, Saxony and as Minister to Bulgaria, 1909–1911.

[2]See p. 121, note 1.

exception, and in the event of exception being taken to any consignment they will return those consignments to this country.

60. *Contraband Committee Minutes*

31 March 1915

The Customs should be requested to thoroughly examine this vessel [*Activ*] to see whether she carries any cargo other than specified and to obtain an explanation as to the origin of the oil-cake [67].

61. *Commander-in-Chief Home Fleets to Admiralty*

HMS *Iron Duke*, 4 April 1915

... It will be seen that the numbers of ships intercepted varies directly with the number of armed merchant cruisers on patrol ... As the days become longer a larger number of vessels carrying contraband will probably try to get through and the routes which they take are likely to be more varied. If the number of those which evade the patrols should increase proportionately, neutrals will more likely embark on contraband trade and greater numbers of vessels will endeavour to get through.

In the circumstances it is strongly urged that the Tenth Cruiser Squadron be brought up to its full strength of 24, ... as soon as possible.

62. *Contraband Committee Minutes*

5 April 1915

Telegram from Mr Findlay, Christiania, 3 April: 'As regards items of which export is prohibited from Norway, Norwegian government will not grant any dispensations. This covers all the foodstuffs, including apples, oils and leather. Lard consigned to Buch is possible German property already ... but is not likely to find its way there, and if far down, it appears hardly worth delaying the ship for it [59].

'As regards other items the Norwegian-America line have received satisfactory guarantees against re-export in all cases except that of the machinery consigned to Wingo, whose office is closed for holidays. As regards this consignment, line can give undertaking proposed in my telegram immediately following.'

The Committee decided that in view of this telegram from Mr

Findlay ... the *Bergensfjord* should be allowed to proceed and the Customs should be informed accordingly. His Majesty's Minister at Christiania should be informed, and he should be asked to take special care to watch the consignment of 54 tons of machinery, which were mentioned in the Foreign Office telegram no. 78, and endeavour to trace its destination [49 para. 33].

63. *Contraband Committee Minutes*

5 April 1915

Telegram from Lowther in Copenhagen: 'Commercial attaché understands that Denmark is a large consumer of nitrate for agricultural purposes. These nitrates were formerly brought over Germany, while now attempt is being made to capture this trade both for Danish home consumption and for re-export to Norway and Sweden.'

There seems no doubt that nitrate on *Transvaal* really is for Danish consumption only [48].[1]

64. *Rear-Admiral de Chair to Admiralty*

HMS *Alsatian*, 6 April 1915

I have the honour to report for Their Lordships' information that I have visited Loch Roag and find it is a harbour capable of holding eight ships of the Armed Merchant Cruiser Type.

Three of the berths are completely landlocked, and if provided with suitable moorings would take the ships with coaling ports close to the water such as *Alsatian*, *Cedric*, *Virginian*, *Teutonic*, *Mantua*, and *Columbella*. The remaining billets would allow the rest to be at single anchor. It would appear that Nos 2, 3 and 5 billets would be liable to be affected by the swell rolling in from Northward in the event of a Northerly gale, as they are open to the horizon.

In No.3 billet to-day, with the wind from South blowing 6 a short broken sea has been set up, with waves 2 feet high, making it impossible to open *Alsatian*'s coaling ports. Coaling from colliers could however be carried on.

With these long ships there is not sufficient swinging room at single anchor and steam on the engines appears necessary at all times.

[1]The ship was accordingly permitted to sail on.

It is estimated that six ships will always be in harbour coaling and repairing at the same time, at an average of 1,000 tons per diem for each ship, but eight ships must be provided for.

Two tugs would be required to bring ships from Du Beg to their anchorage as they would be very light and in this condition difficult to handle in a high wind, especially the single screw ships.

The coal supply for the squadron of at present eighteen ships whose total stowage is 54,000 tons and daily expenditure 1,500 tons, would need a considerable number of colliers and lighters, and there should never be less than eight colliers available at one time for coaling ship, as each large ship would need two colliers alongside forward owing to the coal having to be taken into the forward holds, there being no after holds. Ships with side ports could have lighters alongside as well. Large working parties would be necessary, owing to the small complement, if the speed of coaling at Liverpool is to be attained.

The question of water supply is one of difficulty. The total stowage for eighteen ships is 14,000 tons and the estimated expenditure 750 tons per diem. (With 24 ships it would approximately be 1,000 tons per diem.) Necessary transport and pumping plant would be required if time is to be saved. At Liverpool watering ship goes on all the time the ship is coaling, from shore hoses. The *Alsatian* takes 1,200 tons of water each time she visits Liverpool and it requires three days to put it on board. This large amount is required because the boiler water after thirty days out attains a certain density necessitating emptying and refilling boilers. The cleaning of fresh water tanks which have been used for salt water ballast also requires the expenditure of a large amount of water.

The local water, owing to peat bog, would probably be bad for drinking and most of the ships are not at all well supplied with distilling plant for which they have little use in their ordinary employment, nor do they carry water injectors for emptying tanks alongside the ship.

Although boiler cleaning can be done by the firemen it is not usually the custom, and the scaling of boilers is always done by a specially trained gang of men who come on board on arrival of ship at Liverpool, as it has been found that the firemen do more harm than good if used for this purpose.

A Repair Ship with suitable appliances for dealing with Engine Room defects should be provided to meet the following requirements:

Most ships have Triple Expansion Engines and all ships have cylindrical boilers with pressure from 160 up to 220 lbs.

Two ships have Quadruple Expansion Engines.

Two ships have turbines (Parson's).

The largest engine cylinder is 110" diameter.

Boilers are up to 17ft long and 12ft diameter.

Fire bars are usually of cast iron type.

Repairs to boiler casings and Fireirons.

Testing, renewing tubes, repacking glands of tubes of condensers. (Tubes are larger than service pattern).

Straightening of bent eccentric rods.

Auxiliary Machinery. Casting work. Renewing of broken valve spindles and worn out valves. Pump rods, plunger and piston rings of ballast pumps.

Portable boreing bar for cylinders of Auxiliary Machinery.

Ash ejector parts. Telemotor steering parts to be overhauled. There are 54 dynamos fitted in the eighteen ships with voltages from 65 to 220.

Coppersmith work on pipes and flanges up to 6" diameter.

There is at present very little capstan work and no Air Compressors, but repairs to capstan engines must be provided for; and there is very little gun mounting work other than examination.

There is a good deal of repair work to deck structure in exposed places, and to boats due to boarding in rough weather.

Wireless (Marconi) repairs seem fairly frequent.

With regard to submarine menace it is considered that it would not be long before West Loch Roag as a coaling base became known and submarines would be operating off there more freely than off Liverpool. Within the last week two submarines have been reported off St Kilda.

In conclusion I consider that Busta Voe and Olna Firth in Swarbacks Minn are better protected and landlocked and suitable for a coaling base for ships of the Northern Patrol than West Loch Roag. The harbour of the former is very much easier of entrance and exit and the berthing of the ships would not require tugs. I also consider the water supply at those places is infinitely better and more abundant than at West Loch Roag.

Table showing Steaming Capacity, Coal and water Stowage, &c.

Ship	Days Out	Tons of Coal Bunkers &c	Tons of Water
Alsatian	30	6500	1400
Cedric	30	6700	850
Hilary	28	1950	1020
Hildebrand	28	2000	1180
Otway	27	3150	1500
Mantua	26	2500	1100
Virginian	23	4490	1100

Teutonic	23	5000	190
Digby	19	1350	750
Patia	18	2140	440
Motagua	18	1650	500
Patuca	18	2140	440
Ambrose	18	1450	790
Changuinola	18	1650	500
Columbella	15	2900	490
Orotava	15	1850	600
Oropesa	15	1580	710
Caribbean	12	1910	480

65. *Minute by Captain Richard Webb, Director of Trade Division*

12 April 1915

It is approved for *Victorian* to take the place of *Caribbean*, and when the ships now fitting out are complete, viz: *India*, *Andes*, *Arlanza*, *Alcantara*, and *Ebro* ... and *Orcoma* ... the ships in the Tenth Cruiser Squadron will be 24 in number.

***

As regards paragraph 2 in Commander-in-Chief's letter [61] there can be no doubt that the activities of prospective blockade runners will increase in the near future. Very few vessels have so far avoided the patrol, and only one of them, the *Vanda*, was carrying much contraband [49 para. 24]. But the Iceland–Coast of Norway route will undoubtedly be tried by vessels anxious to avoid visit and search, and a patrol will probably become imperative between Iceland and Greenland. This will mean still more vessels to effectively carry out the patrol.

As Germany gets more and more pinched for supplies she will do her utmost, by paying abnormal prices and by other means, to get vessels to try and run the blockade. It may therefore reasonably be expected that a further increase of the Northern Patrol will be asked for by Commander-in-Chief in the near future.

66. *Contraband Committee Minutes*

14 April 1915

The following clause appears on the face of all bills of lading [on the *Hellig Olav*, now at Kirkwall]: 'Consignees of within goods are under obligation to furnish Det Forende Dampskibs Selskat at Copenhagen, promptly and on demand, a written declaration that within are for consumption in country of destination shown on this bill of lading and will not be re-exported. Failure to provide such a declaration gives shipowner right to withhold delivery of goods or discharge them at any place whereupon liability of shipowner shall cease.'

67. *Contraband Committee Minutes*

8 April 1915

Telegram from Customs at Kirkwall: 'These vessels [*Activ* and *Laura*] have been thoroughly examined and have no other cargoes than oil-cake. I am unable to obtain any information as to origin of oil-cake. Reference has been made to the consignee, Asmussen, Copenhagen, who is on the black list, and he has cabled to the consul here that the Danish Foreign Office has cabled all necessary particulars, presumably direct to London.

'Re *Activ*, the bills of lading show two kinds of cake, Turto de Cabra and Turto do Cacahuete. The vessel is usually in the Newfoundland–Spain fish carrying trade. Re *Laura* there are three varieties of cake as per bills of lading, Turto do Cacahuete, Turto de Coco di Sesano. Samples of the varieties of oil-cake from each vessel have this day been forwarded to you. There are no marks on the cakes and only a miscellaneous lot on some of the bags, e.g., Dunkirk, Marseilles. Probably a lot of old bags have been used. The masters of these vessels can give me no information whatever regarding the origin of the cake and nothing can be learned from the crew.'

The Customs should be informed that both these schooners may be allowed to proceed.

68. *Diary of Dr J. Shaw*[1]

[Wednesday] 14 April 1915. If they [the boarding party] find anything suspicious they let the captain know. Sometimes a signaller which we send with the boarding party signals to our ship by semaphore. If the boat is suspicious an armed party, i.e., the officer and four or five marines or seamen, are sent to take the boat into Kirkwall.

[1]Shaw, John, Dr, RNVR, Surgeon Probationer on *Druid*, *Changuinola* and *Lydiard*; later he served as a doctor in various practices in Scotland and England.

69. *Captain G.W. Vivian to Rear-Admiral Commanding Tenth Cruiser Squadron*

HMS *Patia*, 20 May 1915

Report of Proceedings, 14 April–20 May 1915

***

On arrival at Belfast I went alongside Messrs Workman and Clark's yard and the work of putting in the bulkheads as ordered by the Admiralty was at once taken in hand. Messrs Workman and Clark having built this ship had everything ready, and the work was expeditiously carried out. At the same time I fitted up the extra accommodation necessary for the additional officers and men we were to carry, made good the damage caused by collision with the steamer *Brakar*, and completed a few other minor defects. All work was completed by the 25th and after embarking 13 guns and a large quantity of ammunition for Glasgow I sailed on the evening of the 25th and arrived in the Clyde at daylight the following morning, proceeding straight into Princes Dock. After disembarking the guns and ammunition I filled up with coal which was rather a slow process and was not completed until the evening of the 28th. I left Glasgow at 1 p.m. on the 29th and anchored at the Tail of the Bank till dark when I sailed to rejoin the Patrol. Full speed and a constant zig-zag were maintained. On the 30th I met the Swedish steamer *Atlantic*[1] and the Norwegian steamer *Artemis*[2] both with prize-crews on board. On May 2nd at 10 a.m. I stopped and boarded the Swedish steamer *Ludwig Peyron* from Boston to Malmo with a cargo of wheat. Put a prize-crew on board and sent her to Kirkwall.[3] At 10 p.m. sighted a large steamer going West, stopped her and found her to be the *Frederick VIII* from Copenhagen to New York. She had been previously stopped by *Cedric*. Allowed her to proceed. At 10.30 p.m. on the 9th May I stopped and examined the Norwegian steamer *Siljestad* from Burntisland to Halifax N.S. in ballast. Allowed to proceed. On May 6th at 9.00 p.m. I stopped the Norwegian steamer *Augusta*. When my boat was halfway to her, she

[1]*Atlantic* was detained at Kirkwall and some of the cotton in her cargo was compulsorily purchased while satisfactory guarantees were obtained for the rest. She also carried rosin, which was subject to question (TS 14/1 of 19, 26 and 27 April 1915).

[2]Many items of *Artemis*' cargo were prize-courted (meat, oleo oil, grease, lard); the cotton in her cargo was guaranteed against re-export by the Danish Minister (TS 14/1 of 26 April 1915).

[3]The *Ludwig Peyron* was released on 4 May 1915 (TS 14/2 of that date).

signalled that she had a prize-crew from *Teutonic* on board.[1] On May 7th at 8 a.m. I stopped the Swedish sailing ship *Signal*, she either would not or could not answer my signals as to where she was from etc, but hoisted her colours and also the single flag signal 'L', which I took to mean according to the signal book that she had some infectious disease on board. She appeared to have an unusually large tank on the upper deck, but as it might have been oil or petrol I decided to board her. She had no infectious disease and had been boarded a week before by a patrol trawler which had told him to fly 'L', and according to the captain of the *Signal* also told him that if he flew 'L' he would not be boarded again during his voyage. He was in ballast from Halsingborg to Halifax N.S. Allowed to proceed. At 8.45 proceeded after a steamer whose smoke I had seen a long distance away. At 10.45 I met your flagship and after communicating and receiving my prize-crew proceeded to intercept a large sailing ship I had seen in the morning. Boarded this ship at 6.15 and found her to be the Norwegian ship *Alonso* from Sandesfiord to Be[n]guela with a cargo of coal. This ship was a whaler parent-ship. Allowed her to proceed. At 7.30 examined the Norwegian sailing ship *Staut* from Hull to Halifax N.S. in ballast. Allowed her to proceed. On May 8th at 6.20 a.m. sighted and stopped the Danish steamer *London* from Philadelphia to Copenhagen with lubricating oil and gasoline. The manifesto did not clearly show how much cargo this ship had and the captain did not seem to know either, but he said his ballast tanks were full of petrol in bulk. Sent into Kirkwall with a prize-crew.[2] Later intercepted Norwegian sailing ship *Som* Christiansand to Halifax in ballast and the Danish steamer *Ivoreyri* from Ibeza to Trangisvaag with salt. Both allowed to proceed. On May 9th sighted Russian sailing ship *Mareichen* from Finland to Pensacola in ballast. Allowed to proceed. In the afternoon chased a steamer going West and found her to be a Norwegian flying the 'previously boarded flag'. On May 10th intercepted Russian sailing ship *Avio*, and on the 12th the Russian barque *Diaz* from Lowestoft to Canada. Both in ballast and allowed to proceed. On May 13th I stopped and boarded the Danish steamer *Chumpon* last from Kirkwall, bound to Genoa and Bangkok

[1]The *Augusta*'s cargo was the subject of a long dispute. The cargo was wheat, oats, nickel and copper. The nickel was prize-courted at once (TS 14/2 of 8 May 1915) and the guarantees were demanded over the copper. This was complicated by the knowledge that Germany had instituted an examination policy in the Baltic [77]. In the end the copper was retained under the Copper Agreement (TS 14/2 of 1 June 1915).

[2]There were no consignees for the cargo, which was at first ordered to the Prize Court (TS 14/2 of 11 May 1915); three days later this was cancelled; the ship was cleared to continue to Copenhagen on 7 June (TS 14/2 of that date).

with a general cargo. This ship having called at Kirkwall and having sailing orders from the King's Harbour-Master there was allowed to proceed. At 4.30 p.m. I met and communicated with *Hildebrand* and received from her my prize-crew. On May 14th I intercepted and boarded the Swedish steamer *Thai* from Salvador to Christiania with a cargo of coffee. This ship had called at Punta Delgada in the Azores. She had gone out to Salvador and had come back through the Panama Canal and had then called at the Azores. Her movements between Magellan and Salvador seemed somewhat mysterious and she may perhaps have been employed in connection with the German Squadron on that coast at that time. Her captain positively danced with indignation when he was informed he would have to go to Kirkwall. Altogether this ship seemed rather suspicious. Sent to Kirkwall with prize-crew.[1] At 5 p.m. intercepted Norwegian sailing ship *Ladas* from Amsterdam to Miramichi in ballast. Allowed to proceed. At 9.00 p.m. stopped and boarded American steamer *Pioneer* of New York from Copenhagen to New York and boarded the Danish steamer *Esrom* from Middlesborough to Newport News in ballast. Allowed to proceed. *Columbella* left the patrol late last night, and *Changuinola* joined the patrol early this morning.

On May 16th at 5.30 a.m. intercepted the Russian steamer *Claudius Aulagnon* from Cardiff to Archangel. Allowed to proceed. At 9.00 p.m. sighted smoke on the Starboard bow and proceeded to investigate it. This ship was however faster than I was though I was going full-speed and drew ahead rapidly. Signalled the patrol North of me to cut her off. Shortly afterwards *Virginian* informed me this ship was the Danish steamer *United States* bound West.[2] At 3.30 a.m. on the 17th intercepted and boarded the Swedish steamer *Sydland* from New York to Goteborg. This ship had a very valuable cargo both intrinsically and also from a contraband point of view, consisting mainly of 1000 tons of bar copper, 2000 barrels of lubricating oil, a quantity of nickel and aluminium, leather, motor-cars, machinery and many other things. Sent in to Kirkwall with armed guard.[3] At 3.30 a.m. on the 18th intercepted

[1]Some of the items in *Thai*'s cargo were sent to the Prize Court; the ship was not released until June (TS 14/2 of 17 May and 3 June 1915).

[2]Many items in *United States*' cargo were marked to be retained; by agreement with Captain Cold of the shipping line, the ship completed its voyage and then either returned the contraband cargo to Britain or placed it in storage in Denmark.

[3]Some items in *Sydland*'s cargo were deemed contraband and the ship was sent to West Hartlepool to discharge these. The whole process took a long time, no doubt as a means of bringing pressure to bear on the Swedish line and government (TS 14/2 of 19 May 1915 *et al.*).

Norwegian steamer *King Haakon* from Newcastle bound West. Previously boarded and allowed to proceed.

In accordance with your orders I left the patrol on the evening of the 18th for the Firth of Clyde.

During the patrol, that is from April 29th to May 19th the following ships were intercepted. 15 steamers of which three had armed guards on board already, one was Russian, and all were West-bound in ballast except one en route to Benguela. None were sent in. In spite of the longer daylight and the greatly increased visibility, these results are less than were obtained on the last patrol, which seems to indicate either that there is less traffic between the Faeroes and Shetlands or which is more probable that the traffic passing between these Islands makes either Sydero or Muckle Flugga and consequently the ships in the centre of the patrol line see less of the traffic than those at the ends of the line. I arrived at Greenock at 4.30 a.m. on May 20th after an unpleasant passage with thick weather, which made the route round Cantyre difficult owing to the low visibility of the lights.

70. *Commander-in-Chief Home Fleets to Admiralty*

HMS *Iron Duke*, 16 April 1915

... I concur in Rear-Admiral de Chair's view that Swarbacks Minn would be far more suitable for the purpose than Loch Roag [64], and consider that if all the necessary facilities could be provided the former would be a most useful base.

2. Failing Swarbacks Minn, I am of opinion that Loch Ewe would be preferable to Loch Roag.

71. *Rear-Admiral de Chair to Admiralty*

HMS *Alsatian*, 31 May 1915

Report of Proceedings, 20 April–31 May 1915.

***

1. Six additional ships were fitting out to join my command and steps were taken while *Alsatian* was at Liverpool to hasten their completion. These vessels were:

Alcantara at Liverpool, commissioned 16th April.

Orcoma at Liverpool, commissioned 20th April.

Andes at Liverpool, commissioned 22nd April.

Arlanza at Liverpool, commissioned 24th April.

India in the Thames. She had commissioned 12th April, and left Tilbury to join patrol on 26th April.

Ebro in the Thames. She had commissioned 12th April.

The necessary Sailing and General Orders were prepared for these ships as directed in M.02656 dated 8th April.

I personally inspected the *Alcantara* and *Orcoma* and found them much superior to *Calyx* and *Eskimo* which they supersede. They were, however, shorthanded, and were waiting for the completion of their complement.

2. While at Liverpool I learned that the Oil Tank Steamer *Energie* had been discovered to be carrying an undue amount of oil in her water tanks. There was 12 to 14 inches of oil found floating on top of the water; a clever device, as water came out of the cocks when tanks were tested. The Senior Naval Officer (Rear-Admiral Stileman)[1] ordered several tons of this to be pumped out before the ship left (which she did under Admiralty permission) but on 27th April she was observed off the Calf of Man with wireless apparatus rigged (she had none in harbour) and exhibiting two black balls. The patrol boat which sighted her asked if she required assistance but she stated she required none. A message was sent by the Senior Naval Officer, Liverpool to *Cedric* that she was to be boarded if met with, but she had already been intercepted and released by *Orotava*. However, on 23rd April, she was again intercepted and taken into Kirkwall.[2]

As submarines were reported to be in the vicinity of Calf of Man, Colonsay, Ailsa Craig, St Kilda and Butt of Lewis about this time the action of this oil steamer appears to have been most suspicious.

3. From a report received from one of the boarding officers of the Squadron it appears that three Swedish Steamers which had been taken into Kirkwall recently and released were met by German Cruisers off Point Malmo at the Southern entrance of Sound leading into Baltic and escorted to a German port where their cargo was discharged after which the vessels continued their voyage to Sweden ...

4. The following information obtained from officers of the White Star Line forms an interesting sequel to the examination and release

[1]Stileman, Harry Hampson, KBE, RN (1860–1938), Lieutenant 1883, Commander 1898, Captain 1903, Rear-Admiral (retired) 1919, SNO Liverpool from October 1914; Lay Deputation Secretary Bible Churchmen's Missionary Society after retirement.

[2]*Energie* was a ship, according to *Lloyd's Register*, which was registered at Hamburg; presumably its ownership had changed since August 1914. She was not detained at Kirkwall, nor did the Customs feel the need to refer her to the Contraband Committee.

from Kirkwall of the American SS *Greenbrier* in January last:

'Fourteen Germans were taken out of the ship on her arrival in Bremen, and the Chief Engineer, who was English was interned there. The American papers at first expressed indignation at the capture of the ship, but later, when they learned she was full of contraband cargo and had Germans on board they marvelled at the fact that she had been released and allowed to proceed to Bremen'.

In fact, as one officer expressed it – 'The case of the *Greenbrier* became the laughing stock of the ports of the Southern States'.[1]

5. Wednesday, 28th April – *Alsatian* having completed with coal and effected necessary repairs, I left Liverpool at 8.30 p.m. and proceeded at 18 knots to rejoin patrol.

6. Thursday, 29th April – As a submarine was reported to be operating in the neighbourhood of Ailsa Craig the route via Rathlin Sound was used.

Further reports of presence of submarines off St Kilda were received through Malin Head which also repeated a report from *India* that at 9.0 a.m. she had sighted a submarine in Lat. 54.53´N, Long. 11.7´W.

7. Friday, 30th April – I met *Cedric* at a pre-arranged rendezvous and gave necessary orders and instructions on resuming direction of patrols. *India* was also met with and directed as to her patrol duties.

8. Saturday, 1st May – In accordance with orders received from the Commander-in-Chief *Hildebrand* was detached to patrol south of Iceland on a line 35 miles 135° from Osterhorn to intercept ships passing to Southward of Iceland.

The Danish Steamer *United States* from New York was intercepted by *Cedric* having on board 4 Germans with safe passports from Australia, 6 German women and one Austrian stowaway. As it seemed probable that the passports were forged and the men (and possibly the women) were German Reservists, I directed *Cedric* to put a prize crew on board and send the ship to Kirkwall. At the same time I communicated my suspicions to the Admiral Commanding Orkneys and Shetlands, and suggested that the ship should be well searched and passports examined by an expert. I learned later that at least one German had proved to be a Reserve Officer (Aviator) and another with an American passport had no naturalization papers.[2]

Digby which I met at a pre-arranged rendezvous, reported having

[1]*Greenbrier* had been released by Kirkwall Customs without reference to the Contraband Committee.

[2]See p. 150, note 2.

visited Reykjavik on 25th April and delivered safe and confidential packets to HM Consul. He stated that a serious fire during night of 24/25 April had destroyed ten buildings including British Consulate, a bank and an hotel. As regards the passage north of Iceland, Denmark Strait was reported navigable although drift ice was coming from Greenland intermittently. North and north east coast of Iceland free from ice, passage north of Iceland therefore practicable, but the Consul had no knowledge whether it was being used. This information was confirmed by the Danish Senior Naval Officer of Fishery Protection Cruiser.

The Commander of the *Digby* (Commander Mahon)[1] also informed me that as a result of his visit he had formed a strong opinion of the friendliness of the Icelanders of Reykjavik towards England, and this feeling had been reflected in the newspapers which under a form of home rule had even been permitted to anticipate British intervention. He thought that occasional visits of British men-of-war at this juncture could do no harm and might lead to much closer relations.

9. Sunday, 2nd May – In view of submarine activity in Northern Waters the Commander-in-Chief directed me to move C Patrol 40 miles to the westward, and this was done. *India* was also detached from that patrol to work off the Norwegian coast in the vicinity of Lundo Light in order to intercept Norwegian steamers proceeding from Kirknaes to Rotterdam with ore for Germany.

Disposition of Squadron was as follows:

A Patrol ... *Alsatian*, *Otway*, *Digby*.
C Patrol ... *Cedric*, *Columbella*, *Motagua*, *Patia*, *Orotava*, *Virginian*, *Oropesa*.
F Patrol ... *Hildebrand*.
G Patrol ... *Caribbean*, *India*.
At Liverpool ... *Teutonic*, *Arlanza*, *Andes*, *Alcantara*, *Orcoma*.
At London ... *Ebro*.
In Clyde ... *Mantua*, *Ambrose*, *Patuca*, *Hilary*, *Changuinola*.

During the past week 65 vessels were intercepted and examined, of which 10 were sent in to Kirkwall with contraband. Seventeen of these were west bound ships in ballast.

At 12.35 p.m. I received a further message from Commander-in-Chief to the effect that a submarine attack was possible

[1]Mahon, Richard Faulkner Herbert Hartland, Lieutenant 1896, Commander 1908, captain of *Digby* 1914–1915, and of *Patia* 1915, Captain (retired) 1922.

during the next forty eight hours. Patrols were accordingly warned to zig-zag at high speeds.

10. Monday, 3rd May – I met *Hildebrand* at a rendezvous off SE Coast of Iceland and gave her further orders as regards patrol.

Tuesday, 4th May.

11. Wednesday, 5th May – With a view to ascertaining the suitability of Swarbacks Minn as a northern base for the Squadron I anchored in Busta Voe where I was met by Commander Alston,[1] Senior Naval Officer, Lerwick, who had come over at my request to discuss the question of the defence of the harbour and resources for supply of water &c. There is no doubt that this anchorage is more suitable than West Loch Roag as a base, both on account of berthing room and facilities for supplies, while the question of adequate defence presents no great difficulties. There is room for seven of the 10th Cruiser Squadron to lie at single anchor, and colliers and auxiliaries can be easily berthed closer in shore.

Swarbacks Minn possesses also the great advantage of being central, and a ship leaving there is at once on patrol.

12. Thursday, 6th May – *Jupiter* having reported that she had sighted the US Oil Tank Steamer *Petrolite* steering NE in Lat. 60.30´N, Long. 4.20´W I left Busta Voe at 9.0 a.m. and proceeded at 18 knots in order to intercept this vessel which had apparently evaded the patrol. The *Petrolite* (late German *Excelsior* of the Standard Oil Co.) was captured by *Alsatian* at 3.30 p.m. and sent into Kirkwall with a prize crew. She had a cargo of 4,300 tons of oil. This shows the advantage of having a base so central.[2]

Teutonic reported having sent in the Swedish steamer *Augusta* and *Alcantara* the Norwegian Steamer *Otterstad*.[3] Both these vessels were specially directed by Admiralty to be captured, though the former had the usual Certificate from the British Consul General at New York, and the latter a Canadian Green clearance.

13. Friday, 7th May – *Patia* which I met at a pre-arranged rendezvous, reported that while at Belfast water tight bulkheads had been fitted in fore and main holds, and cabin accommodation had been provided for additional officers. *Virginian* and *Hilary* were also

[1]Alston, Hubert G., CB, RN, 1866–1939, Lieutenant 1895, Commander, SNO Lerwick, May 1915, Captain (retired) 1919.

[2]The Danish Minister made an immediate request that *Petrolite*'s case should be expedited; the ship and cargo were released quickly (TS 14/2 of 7 and 8 May 1915).

[3]For *Augusta* see p. 149, note 1; *Otterstad* was allowed to continue her voyage (TS 14/2 of 10 May 1915).

communicated with and Prize Crews returned to them.

A submarine was reported off Fair Isle steering west at 15 knots. C Patrol was warned accordingly.

Columbella's Armed Guard on board Norwegian Steamer *Gudron* sighted a large submarine steering W by N ½ N which passed two miles off and paid no attention to the Steamer. This occurred in Lat. 59.36´N, Long. 5.45´W.[1]

14. Saturday, 8th May – The Swedish Steamer *Gotland* loaded with ore from Narvik to Rotterdam which was ordered by Admiralty Telegram to be sent in, was intercepted and dealt with by *India*.[2]

A submarine was reported at 4.40 a.m. in Lat. 58.6´N, Long. 1.9´W probably the same as that seen by the *Columbella*'s Armed Guard yesterday.

The *Oscar II* of the Danish United Shipping Co. was once more intercepted on her homeward voyage and sent in to Kirkwall. *Patuca* (which intercepted her) reported that the Captain had lodged a protest. There were 9 men and 14 women – Germans – among the passengers, all provided with American papers.[3]

15. Sunday, 9th May – The disposition of the Squadron was as follows:

A Patrol ... *Alsatian*, *Teutonic*, *Digby*.
C Patrol ... *Cedric*, *Patia*, *Columbella*, *Patuca*, *Virginian*, *Hilary*.
E Patrol ... *Alcantara*.
F Patrol ... *Hildebrand*.
G Patrol ... *India*, *Ambrose*.
Proceeding to Clyde to coal ... *Oropesa*, *Caribbean*.
Coaling in Clyde ... *Motagua*, *Orotava*, *Mantua*, *Changuinola*.
At Liverpool ... *Otway*, *Arlanza*, *Andes*, *Orcoma*.
At London ... *Ebro*.

During the past week 83 vessels were intercepted, of which 20 were sent into port with Armed Guards.

In consequence of the reported presence of a submarine off Butt of Lewis proceeding to eastward, C Patrol was shifted to Long. 9 West.

16. Monday, 10th May – I proceeded to North of Iceland, met *Alcantara* and steamed towards Denmark Strait to investigate the ice field reported there. I found a large field of closely packed ice drifting

[1]*Gudron* was sent in to Kirkwall, but released (TS 14/2 of 10 May 1915).

[2]The cargo in *Gotland* went to the Prize Court (TS 14/2 of 11 May 1915).

[3]*Oscar II* was owned by the same line as the *United States*, and was treated in the same way – see p. 150, note 2 (TS 14/2 of 10 May 1915).

SE. The edge was traced from Lat. 66.48´N, Long. 16.12´W to Lat. 68 N, Long. 13.2´W and no passage could be discovered. This was confirmed by the Captain of a Sealer who stated that no vessels were passing north of Iceland.

A submarine was reported to have been chased by an Armed Boarding Trawler at 1 a.m. in Lat. 58.33´N, Long. 6.12´W steering NW.[1] C Patrol was shifted to Meridian 10 W remaining in Lat. 61.

17. Tuesday, 11th May – *Columbella* reported having intercepted the Norwegian Steamer *Vinland* from Cape Breton Island to Kirkwall, cargo maize, with green clearance from Customs at Cape Breton Island. As this ship, whose original name was *Rago*, was one of those purchased by Albert Jensen of Copenhagen financed by Hugo Stinnes a German millionaire, I directed *Columbella* to put an Armed Guard on board and send her in to Kirkwall. This was done.[2]

Submarines were reported off Arran Island and off the Bar Lightship, Liverpool.

18. Wednesday, 12th May – *Alcantara* having further investigated the extent of the ice pack to the north of Iceland reported that the southern end was in Eyia Fjord and there was no passage through. The pack appeared to have considerable breadth and to be moving eastward.

On receipt of Admiralty Telegram No. 185 I warned patrols to look out for a light grey steamer with Danish Flags painted on both sides, which was reported to have left Bremerhaven on 11th May carrying W/T installations and operators, probably for use with submarines. Ships were directed to examine all west bound vessels in ballast very carefully and send them into Stornoway with Prize Crews.

Submarines were reported in Lat. 58.37´N, Long. 1.42´W, also off Ferriman Point, Anglesea, and off Tramore Head.

19. Thursday, 13th May – *Alcantara* was withdrawn from patrol off north coast of Iceland and directed to relieve *India* off Lundo Island with a view to intercepting steamers passing to Rotterdam with ore.

A submarine was reported off Thurso, going east.

20. Friday, 14th May – *India* reported having intercepted and sent to Kirkwall the Swedish Steamers *Volrath Than* and *Nordland* from Narvik to Rotterdam with ore. *Hilary* reported having intercepted the Swedish Steamer *Scandinavia* from Malaga to Goteborg with Olive Oil.

[1]This was probably *U 20*, fresh from sinking *Lusitania*; it is known to have passed west of the Hebrides on the 10th.

[2]*Vinland* was allowed to go on; the purchase having been completed, there was little point in punishing the neutrals (TS 14/2 of 14 May 1915).

She was also sent to Kirkwall. All three vessels had been ordered to be sent in by Admiralty Telegram.[1]

In reply to an enquiry from the Commander-in-Chief, as to the probable reason for falling off in numbers of ships sent in by the Tenth Cruiser Squadron, I informed him that I considered this was due to there being only one patrol south of Faroe Islands, and suggested the re-establishment of B Patrol north of the Shetlands. With the Commander-in-Chief's concurrence this was done and *Teutonic* and *Patuca* were detailed to form the patrol.

Patia reported having intercepted and sent to Kirkwall the Swedish Steamer *Thai* from Salvador via Azores to Christiania. The Captain of this vessel was unreasonably excited at being sent to Kirkwall and her previous movements appeared uncertain.[2]

21. Saturday, 15th May – Submarines were again reported active off Liverpool, and the Norwegian Steamer *Heim* on passage to Kirkwall in charge of an Armed Guard from *Patuca* [78][3] reported having sighted two submarines together in Lat. 60.20´N, Long. 6.4´W at 5 p.m. on 14th May, proceeding in the direction of Butt of Lewis.

22. Sunday 16th May – The disposition of the Squadron was as follows:

A Patrol ... *Alsatian*, *Orcoma*.
B Patrol ... *Teutonic*, *Patuca*.
C Patrol ... *Patia*, *Orotava*, *Changuinola*, *Hilary*, *Motagua*, *Virginian*.
F Patrol ... *Hildebrand*.
G Patrol ... *Alcantara*, *Ambrose*.
Proceeding to Clyde to coal ... *India*, *Columbella*.
In Clyde ... *Mantua*, *Caribbean*, *Oropesa*, *Digby*.
At Liverpool ... *Cedric*, *Otway*, *Arlanza*, *Andes*.
Proceeding from London ... *Ebro*.

During the past week 62 ships were intercepted of which 18 were sent in to port with armed guards.

Patuca reported having intercepted the American Steamer *City of Macon* proceeding west with stone ballast. Her Captain stated that when

[1]The cargoes of *Volrath Than* and *Nordland* (magnetic ore) went to the Prize Court; *Scandinavia* was released (TS 14/2 of 17 May 1915).

[2]See p. 150, note 1, and Captain Vivian's account [69].

[3]*Heim*'s cargo was 650 tons of tobacco from Santo Domingo. The Contraband Committee were suspicious. A long telegram from Santo Domingo finally concluded that the shippers were Dominicans though it was acknowledged that the whole of the Dominican crop went to Germany before the war [79].

bound east he had slipped through our patrols in thick weather but was sighted later by a four-funnel cruiser which did not board, and the cargo reached Germany safely. In view of the previous record of this ship she was sent in to Stornoway for close examination.[1]

Teutonic intercepted and sent in to Kirkwall the Swedish Steamer *Kronprinz Gustaff* from Teneriffe to Christiania and Malmo with a cargo of coffee and cocoa. This ship had previously been intercepted by Cruiser Force E which directed her to call at Kirkwall but did not place an Armed Guard on board. She was sent in to Kirkwall in accordance with directions contained in Admiralty Telegram of 14th May.[2]

Submarines were reported off Little Ormes Head and The Maidens in the Liverpool district.

23. Monday, 17th May – *Patia* intercepted and sent in to Kirkwall the Swedish Steamer *Sydland* which was reported full of contraband for Germany ...[3]

In order to avoid submarines which were reported to be coming from Norway past Muckle Flugga to west coast of Ireland B Patrol was shifted to Long. 8 W and C Patrol to Long. 11 W.

Virginian on passage to Liverpool intercepted a message reporting a submarine off the Mull of Cantyre. She accordingly altered her route and proceeded via Rathlin Sound.

Submarines were also reported off Skerryvore and in Pentland Firth.

24. Tuesday, 18th May – Submarines were reported 6 miles WNW from Liverpool Bar and 2 miles from Turnberry Light.

25. Wednesday, 19th May – Norwegian SS *Heim* reported sighting a submarine going south through the Minch.

Thick weather in the patrol areas made the work of intercepting vessels difficult and it is probable that some ships evaded the Squadron.

26. Thursday, 20th May – The weather in the area covered by patrols became very thick, visibility decreasing in places to less than a mile.

Alcantara reported the capture of the Swedish Steamer *Malmland* with ore from Narvik to Rotterdam.[4]

27. Friday, 21st May – *Oropesa* reported having intercepted and sent

[1]The *City of Macon* was not detained.

[2]The *Kronprins Gustaf Adolf* (correct name) had a cargo which produced many questions. That it was a Swedish ship did not speed the process of investigation. Much of the cargo was referred to the Prize Court, then discharge was halted, guarantees for some items were received, yet others were consigned to firms on the Black List. The ship was sent in on 16 May and was still not released on 30 June (TS 14/2 of 19 May to 30 June 1915 *passim*).

[3]See p. 150, note 3.

[4]The cargo went to the Prize Court (TS 14/2 of 24 May 1915).

in to Kirkwall the Danish Steamer *Excellence Pleske* from Galveston to Aarhus with oil cake [82].

With some difficulty on account of the thick weather prevailing I met *Otway* and communicated with her, receiving among other despatches a packet from the Admiralty for conveyance to HM Consul, Thorshavn.

28. Saturday, 22nd May – Dense fog.

With a view to covering the route of vessels proceeding south of Rockall to eastward I detailed the *Changuinola* to patrol on a 30 mile line 135° from Lat. 58.40´N, Long. 9.30´W.

Hildebrand on passage to the Clyde sank two floating mines in Lat. 55.52´N, Long. 3.20´W. These mines had horns and one exploded when sunk.

A submarine was reported off Butt of Lewis going West.

29. Sunday, 23rd May – Weather thick. Visibility under one mile.

Arlanza intercepted the Norwegian Steamer *Drammensfjord* in Lat. 63.53´N, Long. 12.55´W from New York to Bergen on Great Circle. She had a cargo of explosives, food stuffs, copper, brass, rubber with the usual guarantees against transhipment by Norwegian and British Ambassadors, which however did not include explosives, arms or minerals. She was sent in to Kirkwall with an armed guard.[1]

Ebro was detailed to work off Lundo Light, relieving *Alcantara* which returned to north coast of Iceland.

Disposition of Squadron was as follows:

A Patrol ... *Alsatian*, *Otway*, *Orcoma*.
B Patrol ... *Teutonic*, *Digby*.
C Patrol ... *Motagua*, *Oropesa*, *Orotava*, *Changuinola*, *Hilary*.
E Patrol ... *Alcantara*.
F Patrol ... *Arlanza*.
G Patrol ... *Caribbean*, *Ebro*.
Proceeding to Clyde ... *Hildebrand*, *Patuca*, *Ambrose*.
Coaling etc. in Clyde ... *Mantua*, *Columbella*, *Patia*, *India*.
Coaling etc. at Liverpool ... *Andes*, *Virginian*.
Rejoining Patrol ... *Cedric*.

During the past week 36 ships were intercepted of which 12 were sent in to port with armed guards. The small number was undoubtedly due to the thick weather prevailing on all except one clear day.

In reply to my enquiry as to when *Andes* would be ready to join

[1]*Drammensfjord* was allowed to proceed, though the agent was required to provide guarantees against re-export, which he did (TS 14/2 of 27 May and 10 June 1915).

patrol the Senior Naval Officer Liverpool informed me that that vessel was delayed owing to shortage of Firemen.

In a general report as to steamers intercepted, *Alcantara*, which had been working off Lundo Light on the Norwegian Coast, stated that south bound steamers were passing inside the islands.

Submarines were reported 15 miles NW of Bar Lightship Liverpool, and 3 miles E of Flannan Islands.

30. Monday, 24th May – Weather still misty, low visibility.

Teutonic intercepted the Danish Sailing Vessel *Skandia*, Gothenburg to Morocco, cargo wood, with a French Bill of Lading. The Master reported that when in Lat. 58.57´N, Long. 5.14´W at 10 a.m. on 22nd May, he was boarded by a German Submarine which also spoke a Danish Schooner named *Fulton*, bound for Liverpool. The submarine which appeared to have no number, came alongside the *Skandia* and asked if he had seen any British ships. I directed *Teutonic* to send this vessel to Stornoway with an armed guard and instructions that she should be well searched on arrival.[1]

Changuinola intercepted the British Steamer *Whitefield* which reported having seen two mines on Stanton Bank on 23rd May, approximate position Lat. 56.12´N, Long. 7.51´W.

Submarines were reported off Ormes Head, Larne Harbour and the Maidens in the Liverpool district, and also off Fair Isle.

31. Tuesday, 25th May – *Cedric*, *Digby* and *Teutonic* were met with and orders and information passed. I directed Commodore Benson to take charge of B and C Patrols.

Digby, whose mainmast had been removed experimentally in accordance with directions from Commander-in-Chief, reported that it was considered the W/T transmitting range had been reduced by the alteration, but it was doubtful how much. Full aerial as originally proposed had not been rigged on account of the ship's short stay in harbour, but it was intended to improve the fitting on the occasion of her next visit. I despatched *Digby* to Thorshavn (Faroe Islands) with a secret package for British Consul there, directing him to obtain information of the visits of German ships or other matters of interest.

32. Wednesday, 26th May – *Orcoma* intercepted the Norwegian Steamer *Susanna* from Iceland to Bergen and Copenhagen with a cargo of whale oil. The Master stated that it was necessary for him to coal in Faroe Islands before he could proceed to Kirkwall, but later he said he could proceed to Lerwick. I directed *Orcoma* to send him to Lerwick

[1]Nothing was found which required reference to the Contraband Committee.

with an armed guard. The Admiralty order to send this vessel into port was not received till 27th May.[1]

Submarines were reported in Lat. 59.23´N, Long. 4.25´W where a ship was boarded and her papers examined, also one mile off Brims Ness, Caithness.

33. Thursday, 27th May – I proceeded to NE of Iceland and communicated with *Alcantara* receiving further information as regards the state of the ice pack. ... Though shewing signs of breaking up there did not appear to be any passage through it to the Westward. Commander Wardle[2] also gave details as regards the route of vessels southward bound from Narvik he had obtained while on patrol off Lundo Light (Norway). Ships were passing inside the islands coming out near Kya Island 20 miles off Homter where he personally observed five ships which however kept within neutral waters. He suggested that in order to intercept the Narvik trade the patrol should be just south of Lofoten Islands.

India intercepted *Frederick VIII* on passage from New York to Copenhagen and sent her to Kirkwall with an armed guard. So far as could be ascertained the man of the name of 'Isaac Woolf' referred to in Admiralty Telegram No. 198, was not on board.[3]

Submarines were reported off Hvidingso and also NW of Hebrides.

34. Friday, 28th May – In consequence of the reported presence of hostile submarines off the Norwegian coast in Lat. 62.25´N, I directed the *Ebro* and *Caribbean* which formed G Patrol in those waters, to withdraw to Long. 2 E.

India having reported that she had not been supplied with Cypher X, I directed her to meet me at a rendezvous, and provided her with a copy from *Alsatian*.

Ebro reported having intercepted the Norwegian Steamer *Tyr* from New York bound ostensibly for Archangel with a cargo of copper,

[1]The *Susanna*'s cargo was cylinder oil, roe, fish and cloth. The ship was at first allowed to go on, but when the agent the Contraband Committee referred to replied that he had nothing to do with the ship, it was detained by the Admiral at Longhope; but then, 'for political reasons', the ship was released. These reasons were undisclosed but are not difficult to discern. *Susanna* was a Danish ship plying between Denmark and Iceland, a Danish colony; relations between these two, and between both and Britain were delicate, and were not worth jeopardising for such a cargo (TS 14/2 of 31 May 1915).

[2]Wardle, Thomas Erskine, CB, DSO, RN (1859–1945), Lieutenant 1897, Commander 1908, Captain 1915, Captain of *Alcantara* 1915–1916, Chief of Staff British Naval Mission to Greece 1921–1923, SNO Nore Reserve Fleet, 1923–1924, Commodore 1st Class in command of Royal Australian Fleet 1924–1926, Rear-Admiral (retired) 1926, Vice-Admiral 1931.

[3]The ship was quickly released.

nickel and other important contraband consigned to Petrograd. She had some *bona fide* papers, but also others which were suspicious, and as her real destination appeared doubtful she was sent in to Kirkwall with an armed guard.[1]

35. Saturday, 29th May – Larger number of eastward bound vessels, both steam and sail, have been met with during the past few days which have been generally clear, but I consider the volume of trade is decreasing and the number of ships using the northern route is not so great as formerly. This may be due either to the action of our patrols or the enemy's submarines – or both.

Instances have lately occurred of German submarines boarding and examining neutral vessels within the area patrolled by Tenth Cruiser Squadron, and it appears that with their increased radius of action these boats are establishing a surveillance of ships passing north of Scotland.

36. Sunday, 30th May – *Alsatian* quitted patrol and proceeded for Liverpool.

The disposition of the Squadron was as follows:

A Patrol ... *Otway*, *Alcantara*, *Orcoma*, *Virginian*.
B Patrol ... *Cedric*, *India*, *Digby*.
C Patrol ... *Columbella*, *Patia*, *Motagua*, *Oropesa*, *Changuinola*.
F Patrol ... *Arlanza*.
G Patrol ... *Caribbean*, *Ebro*.
Rejoining from Clyde ... *Mantua*.
Proceeding to Clyde to coal ... *Hilary*, *Orotava*.
Proceeding to Liverpool ... *Alsatian*.
Coaling etc. at Liverpool ... *Teutonic*, *Andes*.
Coaling in Clyde ... *Hildebrand*, *Patuca*, *Ambrose*.

During the past week 67 Vessels were intercepted of which 19 were sent in with armed guards.

Although *Andes* was commissioned on 22nd April she has remained at Liverpool waiting completion for sea and only left today. I understand this delay is due to inability to obtain sufficient firemen.

37. Monday, 31st May – *Alsatian* arrived at Liverpool at 9.0 a.m.

[1] *Tyr* was regarded with deep suspicion, the fear being that she would discharge part of the cargo in Norway before completing her voyage to Archangel. Assurances came from New York, Russia and Norway before the ship was released (TS 14/2 of 29 May, 15 and 24 June 1915).

72. *Diary of Dr J. Shaw*

Friday 23rd April [1915]. It was decided to board a trawler. Lieutenant Clarke,[1] Sub-Lieutenant Inglis[2] and crew entered white boat at bow. In lowering her some mistake made because we were going 6 knots at the time. At any rate she capsized and all crew were thrown into water. Lieut. Clarke was under boat under water but managed to get hold of her rudder which came loose. But he had an awful struggle to get at it. He had heavy clothes and was wearing sword and revolver. He managed to relieve himself of revolver. Sub-Lieut. Inglis with one or two of the crew got aft and were in danger from the propellers ... One man hung onto a rope like grim death until pulled up.

73. *Extract from a Memorandum of Mr A.L. Hudson (British subject living in Bergen) of a conversation with Mr Baker and Mr Rasmussen of the American Consular Service*

[no date, but probably 25 April 1915]

Mr Baker came across in the *Kristianiafjord* which arrived at Bergen yesterday midday [24 April?] after the Germans had been taken off at Kirkwall. There were altogether four Germans on board, but a doctor and a priest were allowed to proceed to Bergen. One of the passengers taken off, a German officer, had a Swedish pass, for which he had paid 25 dollars in New York, but he could not speak a word of Swedish. The other had no pass and said he had been naturalised in California, but was very vague about that district on examination, and even on his own story had not been there long enough to be naturalised.

The *Kristianiafjord* used the new Marconi Indicator to great advantage, as owing to having this instrument on board she was able to pick her way through the British cordon without being seen [74]. A lookout was also stationed at the masthead when she got near the British lines. She came north up under Iceland and got through two lines of cruisers safely by the help of the indicator and fogbanks. It was only owing to one of the latter that she was eventually caught by a small auxiliary cruiser fifty miles off the Bergen entrance.

[1]Clarke, Francis H.D., RNR, Lieutenant 1913.
[2]Inglis, Henry U., RNR, Sub-Lieutenant 1914, Lieutenant 1916.

74. *Note by Philip Dumas,*[1] *ADT, for DNO*

3 May 1915

This is probably the same apparatus as is installed in *Iron Duke* and *Alsatian* [73].

The one in *Iron Duke* is not of much use. That in *Alsatian* has not been tried properly yet. There is nothing very new in detecting the direction of wireless signals but the simplest apparatus to do so requires expert attention. The lamentable deficiency in personnel will not permit of its installation to any great extent in the Fleet; in incompetent hands it is worse than useless. It is dangerous [87].[2]

75. *Captain G.W. Vivian to Admiralty (for Director of Victualling)*

HMS *Patia*, 4 May 1915

***

There have been very considerable complaints from the men since we left port this time as to their food and after going very carefully into the whole question it seems to me those complaints have a good deal in them. Briefly the complaints are these:

(1) An insufficiency of meat.
(2) The inferior quality of the food supplied.
(3) The extreme monotony of the diet.[3]

***

[1]Dumas, Philip Kylie, RN (1869–1948), Lieutenant 1889, Commander 1900, Captain 1906, Assistant Director of Torpedoes 1914–1918, Rear-Admiral 1918, Vice-Admiral (retired) 1924, Admiral 1928.

[2]For an outline of the development of this aspect of radio, cf. Vice-Admiral A. Hezlett, *The Electron and Sea Power*, London 1975, 96–110. The problem of the equipment in *Iron Duke* was that the ship was usually surrounded by many other ships; that in *Alsatian* (and that in the Norwegian ships) was, as became clear later [182], effective because the ship was usually patrolling at some distance from potential interference.

[3]Captain Vivian continues by going into great detail on these subjects, for several pages.

76. *Rear-Admiral de Chair to Admiral H.F. Oliver*

HMS *Alsatian*, 5 May 1915

I have again visited Swarbacks Minn and there is no doubt in my mind but that it is far more suitable for my purposes than Loch Roag [64, 70]. I would ask you to let me have the *Gibraltar* or some such ship with 200 or 300 firemen, ship should retain her wireless and guns. She should be moved as in plan to command entrance. The defence nets against submarines could go either as in plan A or B, the latter has the shoal water round about 21 fathoms which makes it easier for mooring but requires two lots of nets and trawlers, plan A shows the net defence in deeper waters but protecting a bigger part of the harbour. Whichever you think most practicable I would ask you to put in hand at once as it should be ready early in June or July [78].

This ship was quite easy to handle and manoeuvre in the harbour, whereas in Loch Roag it was quite difficult and at times dangerous.

I will send you a W/T officially recommending Swarbacks Minn.

PS. It will be necessary to have an officer appointed in charge of this base, some one who has experience and authority to deal with important cases as they arise. I shall be busy on patrol and cannot afford the time to run in and settle difficulties. I am of opinion that Rear Admiral W.B. Fawkener[1] would be the best man now available. He has dockyard experience of handling and berthing ships, and has been in charge of the coaling station at Perim since retiring, and in fact he possesses just the experience that is required. He should be appointed as soon as possible so as to be on the spot from the beginning of the development of the base, so that it can be pressed forward with all despatch. His address is RN Club, Portsmouth. I saw him at Liverpool not long ago and he is in full possession of his strength, activity and wits. He might be given a call sign, SNO Swarbacks Minn, same as Tupper is SNO Stornoway. I could always get him by W/T through the *Gibraltar*. Commander Alston at Lerwick should remain there as he [is] in charge of all trawlers, yachts, etc, on patrol round Shetlands and is very busy with that.

[1]Fawckner, William Blewett, RN, Lieutenant 1882, Commander 1895, Captain 1902, Rear-Admiral 1912, SNO Swarbacks Minn 1915–1917, Vice-Admiral (retired) 1917.

77. *Contraband Committee Minutes*

8 May 1915

[The Committee] desire to point out that orders are known to have been given to German war vessels in the Baltic to take all ships trading between Sweden and oversea countries into Swinemunde for examination, and they would be glad to know whether, in view of the extreme probability of the copper being allowed to proceed the Admiralty consider that this vessel [*Augusta*] should be allowed to proceed to Stockholm. The Committee have reason to believe that the cargo of this vessel has been insured for a very large amount by Messrs Bleichroder of Hamburg.

78. *Note by F. Learmonth,*[1] *CSD*

15 May 1915

1. The question of providing a Submarine Boom Defence for Swarbacks Minn was fully considered by this Department in December last.

2. The scheme then proposed – which is practically identical with project A of the Rear-Admiral Commanding Tenth Cruiser Squadron [76] – was as follows:

Swarbacks Minn. An anti-submarine net of the Cromarty type to be laid between Gillarona Ness and the north-western corner of Papa Little Island. This necessitates mooring Trawlers in depths approaching fifty fathoms, which is considered practicable. An anti-submarine net in The Rona to be laid between the south part of Papa Little Island and the passage South-West; and in order to protect ships in Aith Voe it should be laid from Moo Ness, if this situation is found to be not too exposed. The narrow channel eastward of Little Papa Island to be blocked in the most suitable manner, either by nets or ships.

It is considered that there are berths for three large-size vessels in Busta Voe, three in Olna Firth, and three in Aith Voe – making nine berths in all – which would be thus protected from submarine attack.

3. The principal objection to scheme B of Rear-Admiral

[1] Learmonth, Frederick Charles, KBE, CB, RN (1866–1941), Commander 1900, Captain 1906, Superintendent of Charts 1908, Rear-Admiral 1918, Director of Fixed Defences 1918–1919, Hydrographer of the Navy 1919–1924, retired 1921, Nautical Assessor to the House of Lords 1925–1933.

Commanding Tenth Cruiser Squadron, providing for Booms across the channels on either side of Linga Island, is that vessels in Busta Voe would not be immune from Torpedo attack by vessels seaward of the Boom.

It is considered that any scheme would be incomplete unless Aith Voe – which affords a lurking place for hostile submarines – was protected. The Booms in Busta Voe and Olna Firth to be given priority in construction.

4. The site selected for mooring the *Gibraltar* seems dangerously near to the shore, and her safety would be jeopardised in the 'williwaws' that prevail, Possibly she would be better moored, swinging to two anchors in the central part of the basin south of Linga Island.

***

79. *Contraband Committee Minutes*

17 May 1915

The tobacco [on board *Heim*] may, of course, be ultimately destined for Germany, as that country has been accustomed in former years to handle the entire crop [from Santo Domingo], but, as far as I know, there is no evidence of this.

In view of the recent communications from the French Government it is desirable to stop tobacco reaching Scandinavia in large quantities – an entirely new trade since the outbreak of war – the Committee decided to telegraph to His Majesty's Minister at Copenhagen to inquire what is known of the consignee and whether it is likely that this enormous quantity of tobacco will be smoked in Denmark.

The Admiralty and the War Trade Department possess intercepted telegrams, indicating that the whole of the cargo on this vessel [*Heim*] is destined for Germany, and the Committee decided to place the cargo in the Prize Court ... .[1]

[1]See p. 158, note 3. This is a good example of the pressures on the Committee, and of the varied sources of information available to it.

80. *Commander-in-Chief to Admiralty*

21 May 1915

I have not yet received a reply to my submission 574 of 28th March ... [55]

In view of the German threats and the fact that the neutral ships will be in no worse position if prize crews attack submarine first, I submit they may be supplied with bombs lanced for dropping on submarine when she comes alongside, and that prize crews be directed to attack at once.

Is this approved?

81. *Admiralty to Commander-in-Chief Home Fleet*

21 May 1915

It is approved to establish coaling base at Swarbacks Minn for Tenth Cruiser Squadron to be protected by boom defence [76].

Rear-Admiral Fawkener has been appointed as SNO at this base.

82. *Contraband Committee Minutes*

24 May 1915

The Customs should be instructed to make as complete and rapid examination of this vessel [the *Excellence Pleske*] as is possible without discharging her as there is reason to suspect that she may be carrying concealed munitions of war. In the event of nothing being discovered she may be allowed to proceed.

Customs at Kirkwall: '... examination ... was made of ship and cargo on arrival without anything being discovered. Judging by straightforward demeanour of master and officers who were questioned I am of opinion that cargo is entirely innocent as far as their knowledge goes'.

83. *Sub-Lieutenant W. MacLure, RNR, to Commander Down, RN,*[1] *King's Harbour Master, Kirkwall*

26 May 1915

I have the honour to submit to you the following report. I boarded with armed guard from HMS *Oropesa* the Norwegian sailing ship *Glendoon* in Lat. 59.20´N, Long. 9.43´W at 4 p.m. May 22nd.

I steered the various courses necessary, according to the wind, which was generally very light with spells of dead calms and thick fog.

At 6 p.m. yesterday I was taken in tow by HMT *Sarah Alice* about 5 miles off Auskerry and towed into harbour where I anchored at 9 o'clock last night.

At 3 a.m. 24th May in about Lat. 59.33´N, Long. 4.20´W whilst lying becalmed with dense fog a German Submarine came alongside and ordered the Captain to put out a boat and send his papers. The Captain did so and when asked if he had any British subjects on board or if he had seen any British Men of War he said he had not.

The answer was accepted and after examining papers the submarine left steering West.

In shielding us the Captain took a very grave risk of losing his ship and crew, more especally on account of him having his daughter and son on board.

The submarine was about 250 feet long, with a freeboard of about 8 feet and 6 feet aft. His conning tower was long and oval shaped, with one periscope and signal mast, and he had a gun, apparently about 3 inch, mounted about 30 feet abaft his conning tower. This gun he kept trained on us all the time. There were two Officers and three men in the conning tower and three men at the gun.[2]

Captain Larssen of the *Glendoon* went in the boat himself with his papers, as he was afraid to trust anyone else, with regard to denying our presence on board.

Having had this experience, I beg to state that the presence of an armed guard on board a neutral sailing ship places both the crew of the ship and the armed guard in an extremely helpless position if met by an enemy submarine.

As I was placed at that time, lying becalmed and in a dense fog, and

[1]MacLure, William McW., RNR, Sub-Lieutenant 1915, Lieutenant 1917.

Down, William L., RN, Commander (retired) 1898, King's Harbour Master Kirkwall 1915, Captain (retired) 1918; Honorary Captain in the Army.

[2]The identity of the submarine is not known.

had the Commander of the Submarine found out I was on board with an armed guard, I had no means of escape or defence other than firing on the submarine with our rifles and thereby jeopardising the lives of the Captain, his daughter and son and his crew, all of whom were neutrals. Had they attempted to board us the same thing would have applied. We could have captured or shot the boarding party but at the risk of the lives of all these neutrals.

I considered the situation from every point I could think of, and have come to the conclusion that an armed guard is absolutely helpless unless willing to sacrifice the lives of neutrals in their own defence.

I believe that Captain Larssen of the *Glendoon* intended calling at Kirkwall of his own accord, as his Log-book from Savannah was headed 'From Savannah towards Kirkwall' but he saw as he thought the chance of being relieved of expense and did not mention this fact.

I beg to suggest from this and other passages on ships in charge of armed guard, that if all ships bound East and intercepted by Patrol ships, were given orders to call at Kirkwall, they would do so, without putting a Prize Crew on board, as the Captains know that the orders would be sent by wireless telegraph from intercepting ship, and are afraid to try and evade orders in case they are met again in the North Sea and their ship captured altogether as a penalty for not obeying the orders of a Government ship. Captain Larssen stated to me that he did not object in the least being sent to Kirkwall but he did object to having an armed guard put on board, as they only endangered his ship and crew.

At 7 p.m. yesterday (25th) while again lying becalmed in the middle of Fair Island channel, HMT *Sarah Alice* came up to us. I requested the Officer Commanding to take us in tow, but he refused on the grounds that it was against his regulations, but offered to go to Fair Isle and wire for a tow-boat to come out to us. Being foggy I pointed out that the tow-boat would never find us, and informed him about the submarine. When Captain Larssen learned that HM Trawler refused to tow us, he became very angry, and stated that now we had had the chance of being towed in by one of our own government's ships, and they refused to do so, he would no longer shield us in the event of being met by another enemy submarine.

HMT *Sarah Alice* left us and went in the direction of Fair Island, coming back to us at 6 p.m. and then taking us in tow, brought us into Harbour.[1]

[1]The *Glendoon* was allowed to proceed (TS 14/2 of 26 May 1915).

84. *Captain G.W. Vivian to Rear-Admiral Commanding Tenth Cruiser Squadron*

HMS *Patia*, 17 June 1915

Report of Proceedings, 20 May–17 June 1915

***

Having completed with coal and made good a few minor defects, I left Glasgow on the evening of the 26th to rejoin the patrol. On the morning of the 27th I passed HMS *Black Prince*. On the 29th having rejoined C Patrol, I stopped the Norwegian sailing ship *Sorfararen* of Christiansand from Fernandina to Malmo with 4000 tons of phosphate rock. There was too much sea at the time to board, but an armed guard was put on board a few hours later and the ship was sent into Stornoway.[1] On June 1st at 4 a.m. I intercepted the Danish barque *Anna* from Cuba to Rotterdam with a cargo of cedar and granadillo wood. This small cedar is I believe extensively used in the manufacture of pencils, a large Bavarian and Austrian industry, so it seemed possible that this cargo had an ultimate destination for that purpose. She was 68 days out and short of provisions, so I gave her what was necessary, put an armed guard on board and sent her in to Kirkwall.[2] From the captain of this ship I received the following information, which is rather involved and of little value now. When he was at Maceio in South America, three Germans shipped on his ship through the German and Norwegian Consuls. These men left the ship again in Cuba. One of those three was a seaman from the *Karlsruhe*, who had been sent on shore sick and had then apparently deserted. This man gave the Captain of the *Anna* the following information as regards *Karlsruhe*. In November *Karlsruhe* captured a British steamer named, according to him, *Edrany* (probably the *Indrani*), but did not sink her anyhow for some time as she had coal (which presumably *Karlsruhe* utilised). The day after this (so this man said) the *Karlsruhe* took a Dutch steamer and

[1]*Sorfararen*'s cargo was 3,964 tons of hard rock phosphate. The Contraband Committee wondered if Germany was really the destination since the consignees used only half that amount each month. Phosphate was not on the contraband list, so the surplus could be re-exported legally, and it was source for the manufacture of 'poison gas and other gases'. After a fortnight the Committee decided on a pre-emptive purchase (TS 14/2 of 1 and 15 June 1915).

[2]*Anna*'s cargo was assigned to the Netherlands Overseas Trust as a way of preventing re-export from The Netherlands; when the Trust accepted it the ship was allowed to proceed (TS 14/2 of 7 and 15 June 1915).

made her captain take charge of *Indrani*. This captain found on board *Indrani* what the man described as a British Naval Code or Cypher Book (possibly the MV Code), which was said to have be left on board *Indrani* by a British Naval Officer and which the Captain of the *Indrani* had not thrown overboard prior to capture. This book was given to the Captain of *Karlsruhe*. The man also stated that the *Karlsruhe* always had very precise information as to the whereabouts of *Glasgow* and other British Men-of-War and that *Karlsruhe* and the ships with her (presumably prizes, colliers, etc.) always kept 60 miles apart. He also told the Captain that the *Karlsruhe* had been sunk, and he must have told him this some time in February or early March, as the *Anna* left Cuba late in March. This would be, as far as I recollect, before we had anything very definite about the loss of the *Karlsruhe* in England, though of course the Authorities may have known more than was made known generally, but it rather looks as if there was an intention of sinking the *Karlsruhe* at some definite time or another, as the man could not conceivably have got the information after leaving Maceio in November.

Of course this is very ancient history now and I merely give it for what it is worth, the seizing of the Dutch ship seems improbable, and why this man who said himself that he was a deserter should have been shipped in a Danish ship by the German Consul at Maceio seems also rather difficult to understand.[1]

On June 3rd I intercepted the Norwegian steamer *John Blumer* from Arendal to Montreal in ballast, and allowed her to proceed. On June 4th intercepted the Norwegian steamer *Olaf Kyne* from Newcastle to Loui[s]burg NS in ballast. Allowed to proceed. On June 5th at 3 a.m. stopped the British trawler *Phoebe* from Iceland with fish, she had been previously stopped. Allowed to proceed. At 5.40 p.m. stopped and boarded the Norwegian steamer *Nordkyn* from Baltimore to Aarhus with a cargo of Indian corn. This steamer had gone from Baltimore to Sydney (Cape Breton) to coal, and at Sydney had obtained a green clearance pass, signed by the Customs Officer at Sydney. As far as I am aware, in accordance with the specimen green clearance supplied to the ship, these passes can only be issued from a Port in the United Kingdom. I do not know whether arrangements have been made with the Canadian Authorities as to the issue of these passes, nor do I know

[1] *Karlsruhe* had been in the West Indies at the outbreak of war and had raided British commerce off Pernambuco for a time before sinking near Barbados in November 1914. Many of the survivors returned to Germany in December, at a time before the Northern Patrol was operational. Captain Vivian's information was well out-of-date.

what value is to be attached to them. The pass is identically the same as our own, except that the word 'Canada' is used instead of the words 'United Kingdom'. Sent the ship into Kirkwall with an armed guard.[1] On June 6th I communicated with *Mantua* and received four of my absentees from her.

On June 7th at 5 p.m. I intercepted the Swedish barque *Frigga* from Burntisland to St John (New Brunswick) in ballast. Allowed her to proceed. On June 8th intercepted the Russian steamer *Bangpuhtis* who had already been boarded. On June 9th at 7 a.m. stopped and boarded the American oil-tank *Platuria* from New York to Karlshamn with 4000 tons of petroleum. Sent in to Kirkwall with an armed guard.[2] At 7 p.m. intercepted the Danish steamer *Ulrik Holm* from Copenhagen to New York in ballast. Allowed to proceed. At 11.30 p.m. stopped and boarded the Danish Motor ship *California*, from New York to Copenhagen, with a large general cargo of 6400 tons composed of corn, hides and many other items. Captain said he was going to Kirkwall anyhow, but he showed so much anxiety as to the positions of the other patrols (which of course he did not get) that I thought it as well to make certain that he did go to Kirkwall, so put an armed guard on board and sent him in.[3] On June 9th I met *Digby* at 5 p.m. and received from her one of my armed guard. Fog and mist were experienced for the next two days and on the 12th, though the *United States* and *Rio de Janeiro*, which were both wanted, were fairly close to us, judging by the strength of their W/T signals, we did not see either of them.[4] On June 13th I intercepted two Norwegian sailing ships, the *Fingal* for New York in ballast, and the *Glenlora* from Christiania to Genoa with scrap-iron. Both allowed to proceed. At 10 p.m. intercepted the Norwegian steamer *Liv*, flying the

[1]The consignee of the cargo ('mixed corn' according to the Customs) was regarded with suspicion, so, despite a Danish prohibition on export of such goods, the cargo was sent to the Prize Court, on the conjecture that it was really destined for Germany (TS 14/2 of 8 June 1915).

[2]*Platuria* was yet another formerly German oil-tanker sold to Standard Oil of New Jersey in September 1914. The destination of the cargo, Karlshamn, on Sweden's southern coast, raised suspicions that it would either go to Germany or be intercepted by the German patrols in the Baltic, but a plan to insist on the discharge of the cargo north of the Sound was foiled because of an absence of 'cisterns' to store it. The ship was therefore allowed to continue, and the British Minister in Stockholm asked to watch its arrival and discharge at Karlshamn (TS 14/2 of 11, 17 and 30 June 1915).

[3]After guarantees against re-export were given, *California* was allowed to go on (TS 14/2 of 12 and 18 June 1915).

[4]*Rio de Janeiro* was sent in by another ship. She had provided a declaration of willingness to insist on abiding by British conditions, but several items went to the Prize Court and the ship was still at Avonmouth at the end of June while discussions continued (TS 14/2 of 9 to 30 June 1915).

'previously boarded flag'.[1] On June 14th at 3 a.m. intercepted the Swedish steamer *Augusta* also flying the 'previously boarded flag'.[2] At 4 p.m. communicated with *Patuca* and received from her three of my armed guards.

On June 15th at 8 p.m. I left the patrol in accordance with your orders and proceeded for the Clyde.

During this patrol, that is from May 26th to June 16th, the following ships were intercepted. Seven sailing ships, of which one was Russian, one was bound for Genoa, three were in ballast and bound West and two were sent in with Armed Guards. Eight steamers, of which three were bound West in ballast, two had been previously boarded, and three were sent in with Armed Guards. These results are not very great, but we seem to have been very much out of the track of the East-bound traffic. I passed Cantyre at 11 p.m., and arrived in the Clyde at 4 a.m. on June the 17th.

85. *Admiral S.C. Colville*[3] *to Commander-in-Chief Home Fleets*

HMS *Cyclops*, 29 May 1915

With reference to my signal to the Vice-Admiral Commanding the Second Battle Squadron of 26th May ... informing him of the circumstances of the examination of the ship's papers of the Norwegian Sailing Ship *Glendoon* (Master L.A. Larssen – cargo Cotton seed cake) by a German Submarine, an armed guard in charge of Sub-Lieutenant MacLure, RNR, of HMS *Oropesa* being on board at the time, I have the honour to submit Sub-Lieutenant MacLure's and Captain Larssen's reports of the incident [83].

***

2. This incident brings into prominence the position of Armed Guards on board Neutral Ships and the action to be taken by them if attacked by a hostile submarine ...

3. On this occasion the ship (being a sailing craft) and the armed

[1]*Liv* was allowed to proceed after Customs examination.

[2]There is no record of *Augusta*'s examination on this voyage.

[3]Colville, Hon. Stanley Cecil James, GCB, GCMG, GCVO, CB, RN (1861–1939), Lieutenant 1882 (involved in Zulu and Egyptian Wars), Commander 1892, Captain 1896, Flag Captain in China, North America and Mediterranean stations, Rear-Admiral 1906, Vice-Admiral 1911 in command of First Battle Squadron 1912–1914, Admiral 1914, Vice-Admiral Orkney and Shetland 1914–1916, Commander-in-Chief Portsmouth 1916–1919, retired 1922.

guard were in a particularly hopeless position and the young Officer in charge was faced with a very difficult and delicate problem. The courses open to him were:

(a) to surrender and not compromise the crew of the vessel.
(b) to put up some sort of a fight (2 Officers and 6 men were on the deck of the submarine) and thus sacrifice the ship and neutrals on board.
(c) to leave matters to the Master.

4. The question was however happily settled for him by the generosity (which can be better appreciated from the fact that he had his son and daughter on board) of this neutral Master who ran an extremely grave risk in shielding the Armed Guard. For had the Germans discovered that they had been 'bluffed' they would certainly have destroyed the ship and not taken much thought for the safety of those on board. A steamship has some power of resistance and chance of escape, but a becalmed sailing ship none.

5. The King's Harbour Master at Kirkwall thanked Captain Larssen very cordially on my behalf for his generous and brave action, and I submit that he should be very handsomely rewarded by the British Government, but that the matter be kept as confidential as possible to prevent the Germans hearing of the incident, not only for the *Glendoon*'s sake but also to save the possibility of serious reprisals in the future. The incident may, however, become Public in Norway and the necessity for definite orders for Armed Guards placed in like positions is apparent.

6. My own views in regard to the courses open to the Officers in charge of an armed guard (Paragraphs 3 (a), (b) and (c)) are that his duties are simply to see that the ship is navigated into port, and that on no account should he attempt any belligerent act under a Neutral Flag. It could do no good as half a dozen rifles are useless against a submarine and it is highly improbable that the submarine will come alongside so that bombs could be dropped on board her, or will place herself in a position in which she could be rammed. Even if the submarine were to do either of these and the bombs and ramming failed, it would immediately become known to the Germans with the result that they would make reprisals.[1]

[1]Of course, Captain Larssen – and any other neutral skippers so caught – was in as awkward a position as MacLure. Had he revealed the presence of the British Armed Guard, his ship could have been sunk, for it was, from the German point of view, under British control; so lying about the presence of the guard was protecting himself and his ship. It is perhaps characteristic of the Royal Navy to assume that Captain Larssen was actually protecting the sub-lieutenant and his men.

86. *Commander-in-Chief Home Fleets to Admiralty*

HMS *Iron Duke*, 4 June 1915

***

2. After consideration of the whole matter I agree with the remarks of the Admiral Commanding Orkneys and Shetlands in paragraph 6 of his letter No. 159 of 29 May [85].

3. The question is of great difficulty, however. If, as seems probable German submarines place themselves in a position to intercept vessels between Fair Island and Kirkwall, and carry out this policy of sinking all neutrals having armed guards on board, they will reap a rich harvest, unless the destroyer force in the locality should be so strengthened as to make the work too dangerous for hostile submarines.

4. Meanwhile it is essential to increase the number of ports to which neutral vessels may be sent for examination, and I propose that the establishment of such a station at once at Gruting Voe in the Shetlands be considered, and the necessary personnel provided. This must include interpreters.

87. *Rear-Admiral Commanding Tenth Cruiser Squadron to Commander-in-Chief Home Fleets*

HMS *Alsatian*, 7 June 1915

It appears to be a very difficult matter to render this instrument at all accurate.[1] Errors occur which can only be discovered and rectified by constant trials, by someone who has a good knowledge of the instrument. So that if *Kristianiafjord* has been newly fitted, such accurate results would hardly be expected [73, 74].

To obtain the position of any ship on patrol, it is necessary for that ship to transmit. It is not considered that ships on patrol have all used their W/T installations with such regularity that a merchant vessel can fix their positions and still less their course. The possibility of such a thing being done, however, under a chain of delicate circumstances, must be admitted. W/T signalling by ships on patrol has now been much reduced, and it is hoped to reduce it still further.

It is considered far more probable that *Kristianiafjord* avoided the patrol owing to the thick weather then prevailing.

[1]I.e., the Radio Direction Finder.

4

A NEW BASE; SUBMARINES, JUNE–AUGUST 1915

The new base at Swarbacks Minn took all summer to be completed, but it was in use before the defences were fully installed [88 para. 10, 98, 104, 106 para. 14]. It is worth noting the effort involved, which was increased by the use of Lerwick as an examination port [102, 103]. The patrol's ships were stretched by the opening of the passage north of Iceland, and by rumours, apparently originating with a German naval officer in Scandinavia, of Jan Mayen Island, Bear Island, Iceland and Spitzbergen being used clandestinely by German submarines. None of this was true, as a little thought demonstrated, but it all had to be checked [88, paras 22, 26].

Submarines were certainly more active in this period of better weather. The attempt to re-establish a patrol close to the Norwegian coast [88 paras 7 and 8, 89] was countered by the sinking of *India* by a submarine [106 para. 27, 129, 130]; her replacement by a trawler patrol was only partly successful [114]; the vigorous trangressions of Lt Randell brought him a high reputation, and eventual promotion, but did little good for Britain's standing in Scandinavia [88, para. 21, 107–109, 132].

The sinking of *Trondhjemsfjord*, however, may well have been a rapid corrective [106 para. 15, 118]. Shock is clearly evident in Andrew Johnsen's letter on the subject [120], and the British could scarcely fail to point out the obvious contrast between the Royal Navy's practice of stop-and-search and the policy of sinking available to the German submarines [125]. It was correct, however, that the ship had been diverted from its course by British intervention, which enabled the submarine to stop and sink her. The fact that other ships in the same situation (the *Drammensfjord*, particularly) were not sunk, suggests that it was the initiative of the submarine commander which was decisive.

The first anniversary of the outbreak of war impelled Admiral Jellicoe to discuss the effectiveness of the Northern Patrol's work, and the policy of 'blockade' as a whole [121, 122]. His figures were supported by those of the Trade Division, Admiralty [127], and gave rise to the Order-in-Council of 15 August 1915.

88. *Rear-Admiral de Chair to Admiralty*

HMS *Alsatian*, 9 July 1915

Report of Proceedings, 10 June–9 July 1915

***

1. Thursday, 10th June – *Alsatian* having completed with coal and carried out necessary repairs I left Liverpool and proceeded to rejoin the Squadron.

Motagua which was on passage from Clyde to rejoin patrol reported sighting the periscope and conning tower of a submarine in Lat. 56.27´N, Long. 7.48´W (off Barra Head). The boat came to the surface steering SE and dived immediately. Submarines were also reported off the Butt of Lewis where a Danish Steamer was stopped and boarded.

2. Friday, 11th June – *Alsatian* intercepted the Danish Steamer *Arabien* in Lat. 56.59´N, Long. 9.32´W on passage from Vladivostock to Copenhagen with a general cargo. Her Master stated that he intended to proceed through Pentland Firth and to call at Kirkwall as ordered. As she had a tricolour clearance from Algiers she was allowed to proceed.[1]

3. Saturday, 12th June – Thick weather prevailed in the patrol areas, and it was with some difficulty that *Cedric* was met and communicated with for the purpose of turning over orders and receiving information.

Patrols were re-arranged as necessary, *Motagua* being placed to the southward of C Patrol (Lat. 58.40´N, Long. 9.30´W) for the purpose of intercepting traffic making for the Pentland Firth.

4. Sunday, 13th June – The disposition of the Squadron was as follows:

A Patrol ... *Alsatian*, *Hilary*, *Orcoma*, *Virginian*, *Otway*.
B Patrol ... *Cedric*, *Orotava*, *Motagua*.
C Patrol ... *Patia*, *Mantua*, *Hildebrand*, *Changuinola*, *Patuca*.
E Patrol ... *Andes*.
F Patrol ... *Arlanza*.
G Patrol ... *Teutonic*, *Ambrose*.
Proceeding to Clyde to coal ... *Digby*, *India*.
Coaling in Clyde ... *Columbella*, *Oropesa*, *Ebro*.
Coaling etc. at Liverpool ... *Victorian*, *Alcantara*.

Of 82 ships intercepted and examined during the past week, 21 were sent into port with armed guards.

[1]*Arabien* was not detained (TS 14/2 of 14, 15 and 21 June 1916) once satisfactory guarantees were obtained through the agent.

Changuinola reported having intercepted the Norwegian Steamer *Signe*, New York to Archangel with a cargo of copper, steel and minerals. She had a green clearance for coal only – in itself a suspicious matter – and her destination might well be doubted. She was sent to Kirkwall with an armed guard.[1]

As it seemed probable that the Norwegian Steamer *Rio de Janeiro* which was ordered to be sent in ... had evaded our more western patrols, aided by thick weather, I directed *Teutonic* which was on G Patrol to endeavour to intercept her, East of Muckle Flugga.

Submarines were reported in the Minch and to the westward of St Kilda where they stopped two steamers. They were also reported off Great Ormes Head in the Liverpool district.

5. Monday, 14th June – *Cedric* reported having intercepted the Danish Steamer *Frederick VIII* from Copenhagen to New York. She had on board 718 passengers, among whom were many Germans, and was sent to Stornoway with an armed guard. The Master made the usual protest in writing against being sent in.[2]

Teutonic cleverly managed to capture the Norwegian Steamer *Rio de Janeiro* in Lat. 61.32´N, Long. 3.48´E from Cape St Vincent to Bergen and Malmo with a cargo of linseed, cocoa, grease cake and tobacco. She was sent to Kirkwall with an armed guard ... .[3]

Motagua reported that while boarding the British Steamer *Goathland* in Lat. 58.22´N, Long. 8.15´W she observed an unknown steamer being sunk by a large submarine. She proceeded at once towards the steamer, driving the submarine off by gun fire, not in time unfortunately to save the ship. The steamer sunk appeared to be about 1500 tons, had no flags painted on the sides; so was probably British and looked like a collier.[4] She was steering N at the time. After the incident two boats were observed pulling ESE for the Flannan Islands which were in sight. The Senior Naval Officer, Stornoway was informed. *Motagua* then returned and protected *Goathland* till she was safely out of range of submarine [93].

[1]*Signe*, with a 'full cargo of contraband for Archangel' – a curious use of the word 'contraband' – was only permitted to sail on after an enquiry in New York as to whether it was a 'a genuine cargo' and assurances from the Norwegian government that the ship was not to call at any port before Archangel (TS 14/2 of 15, 21 and 29 June 1915).

[2]*Frederick VIII* was detained until 28 June, when a suspicious cargo of tobacco was released (TS 14/2 of 28 June 1915).

[3]*Rio de Janeiro* was subsequently sent to Avonmouth – see Chapter 3, page 174, note 4.

[4]This was actually a Norwegian ship, *Davager*, sunk by *U 33*.

As a matter of precaution I moved B and C Patrols to the north westward temporarily.

Hilary reported having intercepted in Lat. 63.29´N, Long. 12.43´W the United States Steamer *Sea Connet* from New York to Scandinavian ports with a cargo which included rifles, copper, armour plating and ammunition. She was sent to Kirkwall with an armed guard ... .[1]

At 10.30 p.m. signal was received from *India* that she was attacked by a submarine in Lat. 59.20´N, Long. 7.52´W. The periscope was sighted right aft on the port quarter, and a torpedo just missed the ship. The submarine then dived.[2] I directed *India*, which was bound for the Clyde to coal, to keep clear of other patrols and to steer to the southward.

Submarines were reported 3 miles west of Rathlin O'Bierne Island, off Barra Head and to westward of Flannan Islands.

6. Tuesday, 15th June – At 12.35 p.m. *Orotava* reported that she had sighted a submarine in Lat. 59.57´N, Long. 7.00´W close to a Danish Steamer named *Russ* which was stopped and had boats half lowered as if about to abandon ship. *Orotava* at once went to the rescue, opened fire on the submarine and drove it away. *Orotava* then escorted Danish Steamer to a place of safety keeping between her and submarine.[3]

The steamer, which was in ballast from Copenhagen to Baltimore, proceeded, steering NW.

In consequence of the presence of submarines in the patrol areas as far north as Lat. 60 it was considered advisable to shift the patrols northward and westward temporarily. There appears to be a fair amount of trade passing St Kilda and Butt of Lewis to eastward.

7. Wednesday, 16th June – Reporting on the condition of the route north of Iceland *Andes* stated that the field-ice had increased considerably and now extended to Eyia Fjord past Grimsey Island to Grove Bank, then East to Lat. 67.9´N, Long. 16.27´W and northwards for miles. Navigation was considered impracticable at present, but the conditions were exceptional and liable to daily change.

The route given ... for British and Allied Vessels bound for Archangel from British Ports south of Holyhead now appears to be unsafe on account of the increasing range and activity of hostile submarines, therefore suggested to the Commander-in-Chief that the following route should be substituted: Bass South and West of Ireland, 90 miles from

[1]Many items of *Sea Connet*'s cargo were questioned; the ship was sent to North Shields and investigations took time (TS 14/2 of 17 and 29 June 1915).

[2]The identity of the submarine is not known.

[3]This was *U 33* again.

land, thence to Lat. 63 N, Long. 12 W, thence to Archangel. I learned later that the British SS *Strathnairn* from Cardiff to Archangel with coal had been sunk by a submarine off St David's Head on the night of 15th June.[1]

8. Thursday, 17th June – I proceeded in *Alsatian* to the eastward in order to get in touch with G Patrol and ascertain the amount of trade intercepted on the areas G. 1, 2, 3 and 4. I also hoped to intercept the Norwegian Steamer *Kristianiafjord* which was reported to have left Bergen on 16th June and was ordered to be sent in if met with.

The *Kristianiafjord* was heard signalling with Bergen at about 10.0 a.m., and at frequent intervals from then onwards. Orders to cease W/T signalling in *Alsatian* were given.

It was noticed that *Kristianiafjord*'s replies to Bergen were very short, and quickly made; this made it difficult to obtain a reading on the direction finder fitted in *Alsatian*. It was also observed that the strength of *Kristianiafjord*'s signals did not alter appreciably throughout the day. This was probably purposely arranged for, so as to prevent an estimate of her proximity from being formed.

After about 5 hours, during which time *Kristianiafjord* was also working with a Norwegian Ship with Call Sign LFM, the line she was on was roughly located by means of the direction finder, but not her exact position, i.e., it was impossible to say whether she was on the port bow or starboard quarter.

At 9.45 p.m. a message from *Kristianiafjord* was intercepted stating that she was 370 miles from Bergen. *Alsatian* then recommenced signalling on full power, and ships of C Patrol were directed to make no W/T signals. *Kristianiafjord* was consequently given no opportunity of locating the positions of ships on C Patrol by means of her direction finder, and as it transpired, in trying to avoid *Alsatian*, she ran into C Patrol.

9. Friday, 18th June – *Kristianiafjord* proceeding west with 544 passengers was intercepted in Lat. 60.42´N, Long. 11.37´W at 10.30 a.m. by *Mantua* of C Patrol. The Master strongly protested, saying it was most unwarrantable conduct to Neutrals with clear papers, but the ship was sent in to Stornoway with an Armed Guard ... .[2]

In compliance with signal from the Commander-in-Chief, I proceeded for Swarbacks Minn in the Shetlands to meet Rear-Admiral Fawckner.

[1]By *U 22*.

[2]Andrew Johnsen, the agent in London for the Norwegian–America Line, had sent in advance guarantees for several items in *Kristianiafjord*'s cargo, but still others were questioned (TS 14/2 of June 1915 *passim*).

10. Saturday, 19th June – I arrived at Swarbacks Minn in *Alsatian* and anchored in Busta Voe. Rear-Admiral Fawckner who had proceeded from Scapa in *Sappho* met me and we consulted as to arrangements for using Swarbacks Minn as a northern base for Tenth Cruiser Squadron [98] ... Representatives of Works and Store Departments were also met and arrangements made for coaling and watering 24 ships.

It was considered that with the large consumption of the Squadron (1600 tons per diem), four colliers should always be available for use at once, and a moored coal hulk would be required for supplying yachts, drifters and harbour craft. Wooden stages will also be necessary to prevent colliers from damaging side ports of ships. The question of water supply was gone into and local resources were inspected. A loch above the Whaling Station in Olna Firth was selected as yielding a fair drinking water of peaty character, and as far as could be ascertained free from sources of contamination from sewage &c. It is estimated that 150 tons a day for boilers will be required and this could be obtained by means of a pipe line to the shore whence lighters would convey it to ships. Four 100 ton steam hoys fitted with the necessary hoses should be supplied for this purpose.

The *Gibraltar* now being fitted as a depot and repair ship should arrive during the first week in July and will be moored so that her gun can command the boom. She will have 200 to 300 firemen in addition to her reduced complement, for assisting in the coaling, and be fitted with W/T in order that the Senior Naval Officer, Swarbacks Minn may be able to communicate with me and receive information of ships arriving to coal.

Look out stations connected by telephone are being put up and a Hospital Ship and Frozen Meat Ship will be required.

As it is probable that the enemy will lay mines off the entrance a pair of Sweeping Trawlers will be required to keep the channel open.

The Danish steamer *Oscar II* from New York to Christiansund was intercepted by *Hildebrand* and sent to Kirkwall with an Armed Guard ... .[1]

Submarines were reported to the northward of St Kilda, and off Great Ormes Head in the Liverpool district.

11. Sunday, 20th June – *Motagua* intercepted the Norwegian

[1]Some items of *Oscar II*'s cargo were consigned to firms on the Black List but sufficient guarantees were forthcoming that, combined with the past performance of the line, the ship was allowed to proceed at once (TS 14/2 of 21 June 1915).

Steamer *Bergensfjord* from New York to Bergen in Lat. 61.49´N, Long. 12.50´W. She had on board 473 passengers including 2 German Naval Officers, 7 German women and Dr Dernburg.[1] Her cargo was general and mostly contraband. In spite of strenuous protests by the Master she was sent in to Kirkwall with an Armed Guard ... .[2] This is now the fourth time the *Bergensfjord* has been captured and sent into port by the Tenth Cruiser Squadron on account of unneutral service.

Having received Prize Crews by *Caesarea* which sailed again for Scapa with despatches for the Commander-in-Chief, I left Swarbacks Minn in *Alsatian* and proceeded to rejoin patrol.

The disposition of the Squadron was as follows:

A Patrol ... *Orotava*, *Motagua*, *Hilary*.
B Patrol ... (Temporarily suspended in view of Submarine menace.)
C Patrol ... *Alcantara*, *Cedric*, *Oropesa*, *Hildebrand*.
E Patrol ... *Andes*.
F Patrol ... *Changuinola*.
G Patrol ... *Teutonic*, *Victorian*.
Proceeding to Clyde ... *Mantua*, *Ambrose*.
Coaling in Clyde ... *Columbella*, *Digby*, *India*, *Patia*, *Patuca*.
Rejoining from Clyde ... *Ebro*.
Proceeding to Liverpool ... *Arlanza*.
Coaling at Liverpool ... *Otway*, *Orcoma*, *Virginian*.

Of 69 ships intercepted and examined 12 were sent into port with Armed Guards.

12. Monday, 21st June – *Alsatian* intercepted the Norwegian Sailing Ship *Bessfield* with wheat from South America for Norway. Her Master reported that on 6th June when making for Queenstown, 90 miles from Mizzen Head, she passed close to a British two-funnelled cruiser which however did not board. On the next day when 30 miles from Mizzen Head she was stopped by the German Submarine *U 34* and ordered not to call at any British Port. The submarine stopped the ship by exploding a shell above her deck, bits of which came on board. Before being released by the submarine the Master was given written orders to proceed to Bergen and told that if

[1]Dernburg, Bernhard Jakob Ludwig (1865–1937), Minister for Colonies in Imperial German Government 1907, Vice-Chancellor April–June 1919 as leader of Democratic Party, active in politics in the 1920s.

[2]The Contraband Committee received a barrage of information in advance of *Bergensfjord*'s arrival (TS 14/2 of 4, 9, 11, 12 June 1915), and a full list on 22 June, but the ship was only cleared to proceed on 28 June.

he was found off his course he would be shot. *Bessfield* was sent into Lerwick with an Armed Guard.[1]

A submarine was reported off Great Orme's Head chasing a ship which however escaped.

13. Tuesday, 22nd June – *Teutonic* who was on Patrol off the Norwegian Coast reported that she had sighted the German Steamer *Konsul Schultze* off Kya Island (Lat. 64.28´N, Long. 10.13´E) and immediately gave chase. On being sighted the Steamer altered course and ran for territorial waters to the north east of the island. I directed *Teutonic* to keep her in sight and to call up *Victorian* to watch the other side of the island. *Teutonic* reported later that the *Konsul Schultze* had proceeded NE towards Folden Fjord. The Commander-in-Chief was informed of the matter and *Teutonic* was ordered to patrol about Lat. 64.22´N, Long. 9.34´E with *Victorian* backing her up to try and get the steamer to come out.

There is little doubt that a submarine well handled in place of *Teutonic* would have captured or sunk the *Konsul Schultze*.

14. Wednesday, 23rd June – *Teutonic* continued on patrol as ordered but *Konsul Schultze* was not sighted, and it was ascertained later she had gone to Trondhjem.

The Commander-in-Chief informed me that he was sending the Armed Trawler *Tenby Castle* to assist in watching for this steamer in order to enable *Teutonic* or *Victorian* to remain in the offing in case German submarines arrived on the scene.

Some difficulty was experienced in communicating with *Teutonic* by W/T on account of interference from Bergen which was so persistent as to appear clearly intentional.

A submarine was reported 8 miles NNW of Butt of Lewis intercepting ships passing there. If the ships could be warned to pass well clear of both Butt of Lewis and St Kilda it would save many losses. It is interesting to note how successful the German submarines are in intercepting ships, neutral and otherwise; in clear weather they can always see one of our patrols coming in time to get away.

15. Thursday, 24th June – *Andes* reporting as to the passage north of Iceland informed me that on 19th June the ice was breaking up as it neared the coast, but the main pack extended one mile from Cape Revsnals to Lat. 67.14´N and Long. 15.50´W and as far north as could be seen from that position.

[1]*Bessfield*'s cargo of wheat was originally for Britain, hence no doubt the submarine's instructions; the ship was thus unable to sail on because of the change (TS 14/2 of 23 June 1915).

16. Friday, 25th June – The Commander-in-Chief informed me that an E Class submarine would proceed from Yarmouth to cruise off Stadlandet in Lat. 62.10´N for a week. This will supply a long felt want and should be very successful; submarines are most suitable for this work in such a locality.

Three Steamers, *Polcirkeln* (Swedish), *Steinstad* (Norwegian) and *Inger Johanne* (Norwegian) with iron ore from Narvik and Kirkness to Middlesboro were sent in to Kirkwall by G Patrol,[1] but though German steamers were sighted they remained in territorial waters and evaded capture.

Hilary reported having intercepted the Norwegian Steamer *Noreuga* with cotton seed oil from Newport News to Copenhagen. She was sent to Kirkwall ... .[2]

Since 25th December 1914 – a period of six months – the distance covered by my Flagship has been 35,758 miles, the number of days' steaming being 138. The expenditure of coal and water for the same period amounts to 20,796 tons and 13,322 tons respectively. This is fairly typical of the work performed by the Squadron as a whole. It is estimated that the total annual expenditure of coal of this Squadron of 24 ships should work out at 598,000 tons.

17. Saturday, 26th June – *Hildebrand* reported having intercepted the British Trawler *Egret* of Grimsby on passage to Iceland. This vessel when 64 miles WNW of Dunnet Head on Thursday, 24th June sighted a submarine and a quantity of wreckage close to.[3]

A submarine was reported to have been engaged by an Armed Trawler off Butt of Lewis, but she disappeared, no doubt coming up somewhere else equally suitable for her patrol.

18. Sunday, 27th June – The disposition of the Squadron was as follows:

A Patrol ... *Alsatian*, *Otway*, *Orotava*, *Hilary*.
B Patrol ... *Motagua*.
C Patrol ... *Columbella*, *Changuinola*, *Oropesa*, *Orcoma*.

[1]Given their destination, the Kirkwall Customs sent these ships on immediately.

[2]*Noruega*'s cargo was cotton, cottonseed cake, tobacco, lumber and other things, consigned to a variety of Scandinavian firms. Some of the cotton was ordered to be sent to the Prize Court at once, and other items were queried. After some discussion the ship was allowed to go on with its full cargo on condition that the suspect items were not to be delivered until the British government agreed. In other words, these goods would be stored in Scandinavia, at the shipping line's expense (TS 14/2 of 26 and 30 June 1915).

[3]No submarine was in the area, but the tide and currents are fierce there; the debris could have moved some distance.

E Patrol ... *Alcantara.*
F Patrol ... *Hildebrand.*
G Patrol ... *Teutonic*, *Victorian*, *Tenby Castle*, *Ebro* (proceeding to relieve *Teutonic*).
Proceeding to Liverpool ... *Andes.*
Returning to patrol from Liverpool ... *Virginian.*
Coaling at Liverpool ... *Cedric*, *Arlanza.*
Coaling in Clyde ... *Digby*, *India*, *Patia*, *Patuca*, *Mantua*, *Ambrose.*

Of 71 vessels intercepted and examined during the past week, 14 were sent into port with Armed Guards.

In accordance with directions received from the Commander-in-Chief to strengthen G Patrol I ordered *Orcoma* to leave C Patrol and proceed to the coast of Norway. Although G Patrol has so far been unsuccessful in capturing any German ships proceeding to and from Narvik, four neutral vessels loaded with iron ore were sent into Kirkwall last week.

As this patrol, which is of some importance, practically detaches six ships from the east and west trade route patrols it appears most desirable in order that the efficiency of the northern patrol generally may not be impaired, that additional ships or submarines should be added to the Squadron under my command; the latter could work from my Northern base with excellent results.

19. Monday, 28th June – *Victorian* on G Patrol reported that one Norwegian vessel and two ships without colours had passed to the southward by the route inside the islands at 8.0 a.m. in Lat. 64.30´N. Shortly afterwards she reported a steamer going North by the same route.

Digby in reporting her position mentioned that on evening of 27th June she fell in with five armed trawlers searching for a submarine which had been sighted half an hour previously.

When to the NW of St Kilda she sighted life belts, hatch covers, cotton bales and other wreckage which appeared to have been in the water about 48 hours.[1]

I met *Teutonic* at a pre-arranged rendezvous and received details as regards the escape of *Konsul Schulze* from G Patrol. When first sighted by *Teutonic* the steamer was about 13 miles distant. She altered course when *Teutonic* was still 8 miles away so that it was not possible to stop her by gunfire.

[1]The origin of this debris is unknown.

20. Tuesday, 29th June – *Orcoma* was met at a pre-arranged rendezvous and given orders for Senior Officer of G Patrol as regards G.4 on which the best approximate positions for ships were considered to be as follows:

No. 1. Between Skomvaer Light and Taes Islets.
No. 2. About 20 miles 270° from Rust Island.
No. 3. About 15 miles 320° from Andenaes Light.

The Senior Officer was directed to vary these as the circumstances of the case required, ships closing in in misty weather or during hours of darkness, and exercising all their ingenuity to catch the German steamers.

Orcoma proceeded to join G Patrol.

Alcantara reported from position Lat. 66.23´N, Long. 17.35´W that the ice extended northward from Flatey Island and also filled bay toward Melrakka. She was informed by a vessel that there was no channel to the westward and that the ice would probably remain some time.

Reporting further as regards wreckage, cotton bales &c., sighted *Digby* stated that the bales recovered were labelled 'Leon Owaloff & Sons, Moscow' at the ends. They were also marked 'Wogan & Co.' above, and 'Zerega' at the bottom. No indication of the name of the ship from which they came could be found.

The Armed Boarding Steamer *Royal Scot* joined C Patrol in place of *Orcoma*.

Teutonic on passage to Liverpool to coal reported having picked up a lifebuoy newly painted and marked '*Cubano*, Tonsberg' in Lat. 59.5´N, Long. 7.2´W. This was presumably from the Norwegian Steamer sunk off the Flannan Islands by a submarine on 2nd June.[1]

21. Wednesday, 30th June – Many ships appeared to be passing Butt of Lewis proceeding east from southern ports, and I suggested to the Commander-in-Chief the desirability of establishing a patrol 330°, 90 miles from that point. As this area, however, is occupied by German Submarines it may be considered preferable to use destroyers, Torpedo Boats or submarines with Head quarters at Stornoway or Loch Roag in preference to ships of 10th Cruiser Squadron.

At 1.25 p.m. I received a message from *Victorian* on G Patrol reporting that she was alongside the German Steamer *Pallas* which had been seized by Armed Trawler *Tenby Castle* who had damaged her steering gear by gunfire. Unfortunately this took place within

[1]*Cubano* was sunk by *U 35*.

Norwegian Territorial Waters and was witnessed by several other vessels including the Norwegian patrol boat *Freya* whose Captain requested that the *Pallas* should be released in accordance with international law. I directed *Victorian* to detain the steamer pending further orders and referred the matter to the Commander-in-Chief. Meanwhile *Victorian* had released the *Pallas*, and as the seizure took place well within territorial waters (Lat. 64.35´N, Long. 10.40´E approximately) no other course appeared practicable. It may be interesting to note that the Norwegian Officer in command of *Freya* explained to the Commanding Officer of *Victorian* that he would probably not have insisted on the ship's release had not two other steamers – a Norwegian and a Swede – passed close to the prize and seen what was going on [107].

In a detailed report *Victorian* stated that the *Pallas* was first sighted about 11.45 a.m., approximate position being Lat. 64.45´N, Long. 10.40´E so that she was inside territorial waters throughout the incident. No casualties occurred, and the vessel was able to proceed under her own steam.

22. Thursday, 1st July – At 2.0 a.m. *Patuca* reported that she had been in collision with the Swedish Steamer *Oscar II* 2637 tons, Buenos Aires to Christiania with a cargo of coffee, hides &c. in Lat. 59.17´N, Long. 10.40´W.[1] This vessel was ordered to be sent in if met with ... She struck the *Patuca* on the starboard bow, crushing her own bows, then rubbing alongside was holed in engine room by *Patuca*'s propeller. The damage to *Patuca* included bulged-in plates on side, and flange of propeller badly bent, but temporary repair by means of collision mat, shoring up of side and filling spaces between plates with cement made her sufficiently seaworthy to steam 14 knots and I ordered her to proceed to the Clyde.

The damage to *Oscar II* proved serious and she started making water badly. The crew abandoned her and went on board *Patuca* and the engine room filled, putting fires out.

Columbella and *Digby* which were ordered to proceed to the assistance of *Patuca* quickly arrived on the scene, and *Royal Scot* was detached to tow *Oscar II* to Stornoway. At 10 a.m. *Royal Scot* started towing with *Digby* escorting. Meanwhile I had reported the circumstances to the Commander-in-Chief who informed me that destroyers would meet the ships off the Butt of Lewis. I had also requested the Senior Officer at Stornoway to send a tug, and he

[1]This is a different ship from the *Oscar II* in para. 10.

despatched two yachts and six trawlers to assist. At 1.0 p.m. *Digby* reported that the upper deck of *Oscar II* was awash and the tow had parted. At 4.0 p.m. *Royal Scot* again had the steamer in tow but speed was only 4 knots so that Stornoway could not be reached till Saturday, 3rd July. At 10.15 p.m. *Digby* reported position Lat. 59.25´N, Long. 9.45´N, steering 108° at 4.5 knots.

India was met at a pre-arranged rendezvous and given orders to relieve *Victorian* on G Patrol. *Alcantara* was also met and directed to proceed to Jan Mayen Island and search for evidence of the truth of a report as to its exploitation by a company which was suspected to be a German subterfuge to establish a submarine depot or W/T station there. *Alcantara* was also ordered to report whether there appeared to be a passage to the north of the ice field.

23. Friday, 2nd July – At 5.0 a.m. *Digby* reported that another tackle had given out on board the *Oscar II* and that the wind and sea were rising. The tug *Plover* was despatched from Stornoway to tow the *Oscar II* but for some reason she failed to locate her, and though *Digby* and the Yacht *Lolaire* searched for the tug she could not be met with. At 11.0 a.m. *Digby*'s position was Lat. 59.9´N, Long. 8.14´W, steering 108°, making good 3½ knots with steamer in tow of *Royal Scot*. At 11.30 a.m. the condition of *Oscar II* became such that all hands had to leave her, but she remained in tow. At 1.30 p.m the tow parted but was again picked up by *Royal Scot*. Meanwhile the Torpedo Boat Destroyers *Staunch* and *Fury* had joined the escort. At 5.0 p.m. towing operations again had to be suspended, and also at 6.0 p.m. when tow parted. At 8.35 p.m. *Digby* reported great difficulty in towing as all wires had gone except that attached to cable of derelict, and there was no steam or hand gear on her capstan.

Mantua reported having intercepted and sent to Kirkwall with an Armed Guard the Danish Steamer *Hellig Olaf* from New York to Christiania and Denmark, with 440 passengers and a general cargo. Her Master made the usual protest against being sent in.[1] This capture was made in thick fog.

... [I]t appears that large quantities of salted and fresh fish are being conveyed in Norwegian line-fishing vessels from Iceland to Aalsund consigned to the owners of the vessels. I consider that all such vessels should be sent into Kirkwall or Lerwick, or that they should be required to obtain permits from the British Government before engaging in this

[1]Some items in *Hellig Olaf*'s cargo were for black-listed consignees, but the ship was not detained long (TS 14/4 of 5 July 1915).

trade. Large numbers of Dutch Trawlers from Ymuiden are also fishing off Iceland and should, I think, be sent in as they are not above suspicion in the matter of espionage. In both cases it appears probable that much of the fish finds its way to Germany.

24. Saturday, 3rd July – Fog and mist, visibility 1 to 2 miles.

At 2.0 a.m. *Digby* reported that *Oscar II* though completely waterlogged was still in tow of *Royal Scot*. At 8.0 a.m. they had reached a position Lat. 59.11´N, Long. 7.42´W when steering became exceedingly difficult through yawing of derelict. At 9.0 a.m. the tow again parted, bollards having drawn and wires gone, and as further towing by *Royal Scot* was impracticable she was sent to Stornoway to fill up with water. Though search was made by *Lolaire* and *Staunch* nothing could be seen of the promised Tug, and at 5.20 p.m. an attempt by *Digby*, assisted by *Fury*, to pick up the tow proved unsuccessful. The *Oscar II* had now developed a list of 40 degrees and the seas were sweeping her and at 7.0 p.m. she sank in Lat. 59.11´N, Long. 7.37´W. I ordered *Digby* to return to Patrol, and *Royal Scot* returned to Scapa Flow.

G Patrol intercepted the Swedish Steamer *Narvik* with iron ore for Philadelphia, and sent her to Kirkwall with an Armed Guard.[1]

25. Sunday, 4th July – Thick fog was experienced, particularly in the more northern patrol areas. Visibility 300 yards.

The Armed Boarding Steamer *Fiona* joined C Patrol, replacing *Royal Scot*.

Oropesa reported that when in Lat. 58.42´N, Long. 9.9´W she picked up two wooden ladders, with cotton entangled in the rungs. One of these ladders was stamped with the word 'Ceylon'.[2]

The disposition of the Squadron was as follows:

A Patrol ... *Alsatian*, *Otway*, *Patia*, *Hilary*, *Digby*.

C Patrol ... *Columbella*, *Mantua*, *Virginian*, *Ambrose*, *Oropesa*, *Fiona*.

E Patrol ... *Alcantara*.

F Patrol ... *Arlanza*.

G Patrol ... *India*, *Orcoma*, *Ebro*.

Proceeding to Liverpool to coal ... *Victorian*.

Coaling at Liverpool ... *Cedric*, *Teutonic*, *Andes*.

Coaling in Clyde ... *Hildebrand*, *Patuca*, *Changuinola*, *Orotava*, *Motagua*.

[1] *Narvik* was not detained.

[2] This could be debris from the *Cubano* (page 188, note 1).

Of 55 ships intercepted and examined during the past week 8 were sent in with Armed Guards.

Oropesa reported having intercepted the Swedish Steamer *Grekland* from Christiania to Boston with fish, wood pulp and matches. The Master stated that he passed through the Fair Island Channel and saw the patrol but that he was not boarded or hailed by them.[1]

26. Monday, 5th July – *Alcantara* having carried out my orders to visit Jan Mayen Island, reported that a party landed there and searched the Island but no persons or suspicious building were seen. The ice pack was found in Lat. 71.12´N, Long. 6.29´W and traced to Lat. 70.20´N, Long. 16.54´W, but further investigation was prevented by fog which was prevalent generally in the patrol areas. Visibility – approximately 1 mile.

27. Tuesday, 6th July – Fog clearing. *Mantua* reported having intercepted the Norwegian sailing ship *Sirius*. She was sent to Kirkwall with an Armed Guard ... .[2]

Cedric which rejoined patrol from Liverpool, was met and I communicated to the Commodore the necessary orders and information for carrying on patrol during my absence.

The Danish Sailing Ship *Maren* on passage to Kirkwall with an Armed Guard from *Columbella* was intercepted in Lat. 60.3´N, Long. 2.45´W by a large German submarine fitted with W/T apparatus, which enquired as to her destination. The submarine appeared to have come from the direction of Fair Island.[3]

A submarine was also reported in Lat. 59.12´N, Long. 6.20´W steaming west about 14 knots.

28. Wednesday, 7th July – In compliance with directions from the Commander-in-Chief the Armed Trawler *Tenby Castle* was ordered to leave G Patrol and return to the base. As the ships carrying ore to Germany from Narvik appeared to be keeping inside territorial waters I suggested that the Armed Merchant Cruisers on G Patrol should be placed as previously arranged, viz: to work G.2, G.3 and G.4 alternately two or three days at a time, spread 15 miles apart.

Ships on G Patrol were warned of the reported presence of

[1]*Grekland* does not seem to have been sent in.

[2]*Sirius* had a cargo of rosin for Petrograd; it was allowed to go on with the condition that it call only at Archangel (TS 14/4 of 9 and 19 June 1915). On 15 July, however, the British Vice-Consul at Narvik reported that the ship intended to land goods there for onward transmission through Sweden. From the shippers' and consignees' point of view that made sense but made a nonsense of the British conditions – this time.

[3]*Maren* was not detained; the identity of the submarine is not known.

submarines in Folden Fjord (Lat. 64.25´N, Long. 11.30´E).

I quitted patrol in *Alsatian* and proceeded to Liverpool.

Thursday, 8th July.

29. Friday, 9th July – I arrived at Liverpool in *Alsatian*.

89. *Commander F.H. Walter to Rear-Admiral Tenth Cruiser Squadron*

HMS *Victorian*, 6 July 1915

Report of Proceedings, 9 June–7 July 1915

I have the honour to report proceedings as follows:

1. On 9 June *Victorian* was commissioned, with Officers and men mostly from *Caribbean*.

2. The ship was in a very dirty state, having only recently finished coaling, all the ports and ventilators had been left open. Fireman's quarters and part of Mess Deck had to be disinfected.

3. Monday night 14 June ship undocked and proceeded to River, swinging ship early on Tuesday morning, and left for patrol at 9 p.m. on the 15th June, the same night.

4. At 4.15 a.m. Petty Officer 1 cl William Batteris fell overboard and was apparently drowned off Calf of Man. There was no reason for this accident that I have been able to find. A Court of Enquiry was held into the circumstances, all particulars of which have been forwarded to you.

5. On 17th June picked up Prize Crews and swung ship, a totally different Deviation Table being the result.

6. On 18th June met *Orotava*, *Changuinola*, *Motagua*, and *Cedric*.

7. Met *Teutonic* at 5 a.m. on Monday 21st June on G IV Patrol, and proceeded on G II Patrol on 23rd.

8. Sent in Swedish SS *Polirken*, with Armed Guard under Sub-Lieutenant W.A. Wheable at 4 a.m. on 24th June, and at 9.30 a.m. sent in Norwegian SS *Steinstad* with Lieutenant John Humphrey, RNR on board.[1]

9. Met Armed Trawler *Tenby Castle* at 8 a.m. on 26th June and on 27th at 6 p.m. took over patrol as *Teutonic* left for coal.

10. Patrolled round Kea Id.

11. Armed Trawler *Tenby Castle* captured German SS *Pallas* and reported he had shot away her steering gear. Shortly after my arrival

[1]Wheable, Henry A., RNR, Midshipman 1914, Lieutenant 1918.

Humphrey, John, OBE, RNR (1879–1956), Lieutenant in *Victorian* June 1915, Member of Bombay Legislative Council 1932–1937, Chairman Karachi Chamber of Commerce 1940, 1941, 1943. See page 186, note 1, for the result of the sending-in.

Norwegian Navy Patrol Boat *Fr[e]ya* came along and protested against the capture, which was in territorial waters. After hearing the evidence of Lieutenant Randell RNR,[1] the Norwegian Pilot in charge of *Pallas*, the Norwegian Commanding Officer, and taking into consideration the probabilities of the case, I ordered the prize to be abandoned, as Lieutenant Randell had placed himself considerably inside the Territorial Limit. A report of this occurrence has been forwarded [97].

12. On evening of 30th June *Orcoma* joined Patrol and all units moved North to G IV. En route the Chief Petty Officer of Armed Trawler *Tenby Castle* was hoisted on board with a fractured thigh, and a PO 1 was sent in his place temporarily.

13. Swedish SS *Narvick* was sent in to Kirkwall with an Armed Guard on board – Sub-Lieutenant Honeyman RNR in command. 2nd July.[2]

14. At midnight on 2nd July *India* arrived and took over G Patrol, *Victorian* proceeding to Liverpool to coal.

15. 3rd July. A surprise periscope attack was carried out, one round being fired from each gun in the ship to test gun mountings.

16. Received Armed Guards from *Virginian*.

17. Arrived in River Mersey at 7 p.m. on the 6th July and docked at 7 a.m. on Wednesday 7th July.

18. The number of ships intercepted since leaving Liverpool was 19 of which three were sent in.

90. *Captain Charles Royds*[3] *to Captain G.W. Vivian*

Longhope, 13 June 1915

I expect you will get a complaint from your armed guards which are just going out to rejoin you [94], so thought I would let you know my version. Under ordinary conditions, as soon as the armed guards are freed from the vessel which they have brought into Kirkwall, they are sent across to Longhope, and accommodated on board the *Cambria*. At one time they used to be billetted in Kirkwall, but on account of so

[1]Randell, John T., DSC, RNR, Lieutenant 1915, Acting Lieutenant-Commander in command of Trawlers 1917–1918.

[2]Honeyman, Frederick S., RNR, Sub-Lieutenant 1915, Lieutenant 1917; for *Narvick*, see page 191, note 1.

[3]Royds, Charles William Rawson, KBE, CMG, RN (1876–1931), Lieutenant 1898, Commander 1909, Captain 1914, Flag Captain to Admiral Colville at Longhope 1915, Captain of *Emperor of India* 1915–1919, Rear-Admiral (retired) 1926, Vice-Admiral 1930, Deputy Commissioner of the Metropolitan Police, 1926–1931.

much drunk[en]ness and rows in the town and at the hotel, this had to be stopped. When the vessel which is taking these armed guards to rejoin their ships is ordered to sail, the armed guards are sent on board; lately this vessel has been the *Duke of Cornwall*. It happens this time that the *Cambria* is employed in taking troops from Lerwick to Thurso, also that the *Duke of Cornwall* is required for patrol duty, and her relief the *Duke of Albany* is on the beach, consequently the *Caesarea* is being employed. I am perfectly well aware that the *Caesarea* has not got the accommodation, that is to say, there is not cabin accommodation for these Officers sent on board. Anyhow, one of your Officers has complained that they are not being treated properly, and states that they were not received at the gangway by the 1st Lieutenant, that they had to climb on board by means of a rope ladder, that they are not allowed to use the Officers' smoking room, and that they cannot get enough drink, or any at all, I forget which. I won't remark on the two first objections; with reference to the Officers' smoking room, I understand that on another occasion when the *Caesarea* was taking armed guards, the furniture was broken, and chessmen and draughtsmen were lost, books lent were taken away by the Officers taking passage and never returned, nor were the bills for drinks paid. The Officers have practically no wine on board, and what they have would be soon finished if these Officers taking passage were allowed what they want, also the smoking room is very small and there is not enough room for both lots of Officers. I have seen the accommodation which has been given over to the use of the Officers taking passage, and they have one place all to themselves on the boat deck, as well as the use of the Saloon, in which they have permission to smoke. I think that it is a great pity that these Officers should start growling and complaining and making themselves objectionable to the Officers in which ship they are taking passage.

Everyone knows and realizes that there is not much joy connected with the duties carried out by the 10th CS and also that those duties are being extremely well carried out; they certainly have one bit of 'percks' which no one stationed up here gets, namely in getting to their, or some, home port about every 3 weeks, which is a consideration. Anyhow I don't want to make a row, but thought that I would let you know the other side of the question, in case the complaint was sent in to you officially [95].

91. *Diary of Dr J. Shaw*

Monday 14 June 1915. I have just returned from a stroll on deck, 11 p.m., and my nerves are somewhat tense with excitement. Going on deck I observed that the Jack Tars were wearing their life-saving apparatus. I also noticed that they were all looking past the port side of the stern. On enquiring of one of the petty officers he told me that a torpedo had just been observed passing our stern. I immediately ran back to my cabin and informed Baker. We both donned out lifesaving belts and went on deck again. Baker was inclined to laugh at me but we both questioned some of the old hands who had seen torpedoes fired in their day and they declared there could be no mistake about it. The G.I. (Gunnery Instructor) informed me that the wash was just like the time when a torpedo missed the boat he was in – the *Edgar* – which was the time the *Hawke* was sunk.

92. *Captain G.W. Vivian to Admiralty*

HMS *Patia*, 14 June 1915

With reference to my letter of the 4th May reporting the unsatisfactory nature of the messing of the Ship's Company [75] and to my further letter of May ...[1] reporting that I had made certain alterations and arrangements which I hoped would remedy this unsatisfactory state of affairs:

I have the honour to report that the messing is now much improved, and the men are satisfied and contented. The quality of the food is very much better and the monotony has been considerably reduced. I have a new Chief Steward who takes a great deal of trouble to find out what the men want and as far as possible to meet their views, with the result that the messing has improved all round, and the men realize that every effort is being made to feed them properly and to give them a certain amount of variety in their diet; and I see no reason why this state of affairs should not continue.

93. *Captain J.A. Webster[2] to Rear-Admiral Commanding Tenth Cruiser Squadron*

HMS *Motagua*, 14 June 1915

I have the honour to report that at 8.00 a.m. to-day I sighted two

[1]Blank in the copy in the National Maritime Museum.

[2]Webster, John A., MVO, CBE, RN (1874–1924), Commander 1907, Captain 1914, Captain in *Motagua* June 1915, Director of Navigation 1917–1919, retired 1922.

steamers steering North and altered course to intercept them. At 8.52 a.m. in Lat. 58.22´N, Long, 8.11´W, I stopped and sent a boat away to board the SS *Goathland* of Whitby, bound from Cardiff to Archangel with coal.

The boat had got a little more than half-way, and this ship was getting headway again, when the Officer of the Watch called my attention to the other steamer, then bearing South and four to five miles off, which appeared to have something wrong with her. A good look convinced me that she was settling by the stern and I, at once, hoisted the signal for 'Submarine in vicinity' and signalled my boarding Officer to tell *Goathland* to steer north as fast as able, at the same time increasing to full speed myself.

As it appeared most probable that the submarine would make for the *Goathland* as soon as he saw his torpedo hit the other ship, and not knowing how much time had elapsed since then, I turned to NNE to reduce the target I offered, as it was possible that we were within torpedo range. This proved not to be the case, however, as at 8.59 a.m., when nearly steady on this course, the submarine rose about nine or ten thousand yards from me and half a mile or so from the steamer which sank almost immediately afterwards stern first.

The submarine was moving through the water heading about NW (i.e. I was on his starboard bow) but never rose higher than to upper deck awash, so I had no hope of reducing the range by turning towards him. Being in diving trim, he could go under immediately he realised my action and I should only have lost time as my intention was to force him to dive as soon as I could and prevent him using any of his superior surface speed to close *Goathland*. I, therefore, opened fire with the stern gun, but the range being so great (over 9000 yards) there was little chance of hitting. Had he shown any inclination to remain up I should have turned, and had given orders for the guns to be trained accordingly, but after the second round he dived and was not seen again. Both shots fell short, the elevation at 9000 yards being the limit for the gun.

I estimated that if I could get the submarine down and keep him under it would take over an hour, at the least, for him to get near enough to *Goathland* to fire. Moreover doing this would necessitate using full battery power for the whole of that time, which I doubted his willingness to do.

Goathland steamed North at full speed, about $9^1/_2$ knots, towing the boarding boat and I proceeded at 15 knots zigzagging ahead of her in a position where I could open fire if the submarine came again to the surface and also act as a screen in case there was another to the northward. When I considered that danger of attack from astern was practically over I increased my distance ahead and covered a wider area. By 2.00 p.m. I dropped astern, picked up my boat, and parted company with *Goathland* whom I last saw about 1.00 p.m. in Lat. 59.55´N, Long. 8.30´W steering about N by E, to pass west of the Faeroes.

The submarine was one of the larger type, as far as could be seen, but the distance was too great to see details clearly.

The sunken steamer appeared to be about 1500 tons, was flying an ensign with red in it, probably British. She had no name or national colours on her side and generally looked like a collier.

After she sank, two boats were seen pulling about ESE for the Flannan Isles, which were in sight, and SNO Stornoway was informed accordingly.

She appeared to have been torpedoed on the starboard quarter, but I cannot say exactly when it occurred. When I looked at her, just before stopping to board, there was nothing unusual about her, but as she was then end on, any trim by the stern would not have been noticeable. The Master of *Goathland* could give no information about her.[1]

94. *Lieutenant W. Clark, RNR*[2] *to Captain G.W. Vivian, RN*

HMS *Patia*, At Sea, 15 June 1915

I have the honour to submit the following report regarding the treatment of officers in charge of armed guards on board HMS *Caesarea* from June 12th to June 14th.

At 2 p.m. on Saturday June 12th, together with a number of Armed Guards from the 10th Cruiser Squadron, I was transferred from HMS *Duke of Cornwall* to HMS *Caesarea*. The sleeping accommodation provided for us in HMS *Caesarea* was on the Settees in the Chart Room, on which it was impossible to sleep while the ship was under way; the only bedding provided was two blankets each and no pillows, the blankets being in a dirty condition. We also found it exceedingly difficult to obtain sufficient water for washing purposes.

On arrival on board, we were informed that on no account would officers in charge of Armed Guards be allowed to use the smoking-room used by the officers of the ship, and on one occasion when an officer requested a steward to bring him a drink, he was informed by the steward that orders had been given that no drinks whatever were to be

[1]This was the *Davager* again, sunk by *U 33*.
[2]Clarke, William, DSC, RNR, Sub-Lieutenant 1914, Lieutenant 1916.

supplied to officers of Armed Guards; with reference to the above statements the 1st Lieutenant informed us that the reason for refusing to serve us with drinks and debarring us from the use of the smoking-room was, that some four months ago a party of Midshipmen RNR had misbehaved themselves while on board HMS *Caesarea*, and another reason given was that there was not a sufficient stock of wines on board the ship to supply officers not belonging to the ship.

The Officers in charge of Armed Guards during the time of war naturally do not mind any inconvenience or hardship when necessary, but could not understand why restrictions were placed on them, not usually placed on commissioned officers in His Majesty's Navy or Naval Reserve, I therefore as senior officer of Armed Guards requested to see the Commanding Officer.

On asking the Commanding Officer if matters could be improved he replied 'I can do nothing for you, and refuse to interest myself in the matter'. I then asked permission to see the Flag Captain of HMS *Cyclops* which was granted.

On arrival on board HMS *Cyclops* I was informed that the Flag Captain was on shore and an officer took me to see Rear Admiral Millar RN, who informed me that the matter would be investigated by Commdr Knox RN[1] of HMS *Sappho*.

The following day I was ordered to proceed to Longhope Hotel, where I was severely admonished by Captain Royds RN for making any complaints at all.

I therefore forward this report to you.

95. *Captain G.W. Vivian to Captain Charles Royds*

HMS *Patia*, 16 June 1915

Re your letter of the 13th [90]: I did get a complaint from the senior of the Officers of my Armed Guards, relative to *Caesarea*, but I think there is some misunderstanding about what occurred. This officer did not complain himself, at least not on the points you mention, but as the senior officer of the Armed Guards he was requested by the other officers to represent their complaints.

To take the points you mentioned in your letter: (1) that they were not received at the gangway by the 1st Lieutenant. My officer says that he heard no such complaint, but he did hear one officer (a Sub-lieut, he

[1]Knox, Gerald V.C., RN, Lieutenant 1896, Commander 1907, Captain (retired) 1919.

thinks) say 'they might send someone to show us where to go'.

(2) That they had to climb on board by means of a rope-ladder. My officer says he never heard any complaint of that nature, and on the face of it it seems rather improbable, as none of our ships here use or can use anything but rope-ladders both in our own ships and ships boarded.

(3) That they were not allowed to use the officers smoking-room. No doubt there is a good deal to be said on both sides in this matter, but I do not gather that actually not being allowed to use the smoking-room was the real cause of complaint. My officer informs me that the real grievance of the Armed Guard officers was that they were as he describes it 'boycotted' the moment they got on board, the reason given being that on some previous occasion some Armed Guard officers misbehaved themselves and broke the furniture etc. As the *Caesarea* and yourself are doubtless aware the culprits on that occasion were RNR midshipmen. Personally I think sending midshipmen away with Armed Guards, unless unavoidable, is a mistake, and I never do it. My Armed Guard officers until quite recently (I have lately had four Temporary Sub-Lieuts RNR sent me) have been as follows:

1. Captain of a Cable ship, aged 32.
2. Third Officer of a White Star Liner, aged 30.
3. Chief Officer of a P. and O. Liner, aged 36.
4. Second Officer of a Furness Liner, aged 29.
5. Chief Officer in a Royal Mail Steamer, aged 33.

and a better and more zealous lot of officers I have never had to deal with. Assuming that *Caesarea*'s previous experience of the misconduct of certain boys, which one would almost think might have been checked, was as stated, it seems to be palpably wrong to visit the sins of these midshipmen upon the heads of other experienced and older officers. These officers resent, and rightly so in my opinion, being treated in this way, they have many of them given up a very great deal to serve their country (one of my officers gave up the command of a ship at £510 a year to serve as a Sub Lieut, and he is a married man with a family). It is not their fault that they are on board *Caesarea*, they are there in the performance of their duties, and duties which, I speak for my own officers, they do and have done extraordinarily well. As showing to what extent this 'boycott' was carried, it appears that the officers of *Caesarea* would hardly speak to the officers of the Armed Guards, and that the officers of the Armed Guards were not even allowed to mess at the same table as the officers of *Caesarea*, though there was ample room, but had to mess at a separate table, and further than that one senior officer of the Armed Guards was actually informed by one of the officers of *Caesarea* that 'it was no use his complaining to the Flag-Captain, as the Admiral, Flag-Captain, and Captain of *Sappho* were personal friends of Captain of *Caesarea*', which was a truly deplorable thing to say, and calculated to do infinite harm.

Recently in this ship it fell to my lot to embark Armed Guards at Stornoway for the 10th Cruiser Squadron, I had approximately 15 officers and 60 men, and no cabins or indeed accommodation of any sort, and these officers and men had to be on board one or two nights. What happened? All my officers cheerfully gave up the settees in their cabins, clean blankets etc., were issued, and anything feasible was done to make both officers and men comfortable, and they *were* made comfortable, and said so too. I do not say that a similar procedure is possible in *Caesarea*, it probably is not, but the contrast is most marked, and to treat these Armed Guard officers as outcasts and interlopers is neither fair to them nor in the best interests of the Service, and may produce entirely unlooked for results in the Naval Reserve.

(4) That they cannot get enough drink or none at all. As far as my officer was concerned this cannot in any way apply as he happens to be a total abstainer, but as regards other officers he tells me that some officers did ask whether they could have a drink and were informed by a steward that the officers of Armed Guards could not be served with any drink, a most gratuitous and unnecessary form of insult, implying as it did that none of these officers were considered to be sufficiently trustworthy to be served with liquor in any form: and this to officers who had commanded or had anyhow been Chief Officers of their own ships. Not a word was said until later about there being no liquor on board the *Caesarea*, but merely that officers of the Armed Guards were not to be served, as if they were on the Parish Prohibition list.

To me it seems a most lamentable and deplorable fact that zealous, capable and patriotic officers such as mine are should come back from their various trips with the one complaint that they are far better treated and far more comfortable in any prize-ship they take in, even the most humble of tramps or sailing-ships than they are in the *Caesarea*, one of HM Ships. They do not mind how long they are away in tramps and such-like, living on very little, as long as they do not have to go on board *Caesarea*. No complaint is made about the *Duke of Cornwall*, where the officers endeavour as far as I can ascertain to make things as comfortable as circumstances will permit.

My RNR Officers are neither children, drunkards or fools, they resent and resent very deeply, and I think very naturally, their treatment in *Caesarea*, for they are competent and capable men of a mature age. They fully recognise that in a state of war they cannot expect to have the ordinary comforts of peace-time; they do not look for or expect anything of the sort, but they do expect to be treated as officers holding commissions in HM Service should be treated, and they do not expect to be treated as outcasts, merely because some boys on a previous occasion misbehaved themselves.

I am the last person in the world to want to make trouble on such matters, especially in war-time, but I do honestly think that the whole of this matter should be looked into very carefully, for feeling is high, not only amongst my own officers, but also I understand amongst the Reserve Officers of other ships.

As I do not wish to raise this question officially, unless it becomes absolutely imperative, I am sending you this letter together with a copy of my officer's complaint, privately, in the hope that this state of affairs may be rectified, but of course if further complaints on the same subject come to me, I shall have no option but to raise the whole matter officially, and the reports I have received as to what has occurred on board the *Caesarea* as regards the officers of the Armed Guards are such as to leave a very unpleasant taste in my mouth.

I have no objection to your showing this letter to any senior officer concerned in the administration of *Caesarea*, should you so wish.

96. *Diary of Dr J. Shaw*

Thursday 17 June 1915. Our own boat the *Changuinola* seems to have more social life aboard of her than any of the others as we found out from the officers of prize crews so probably I am fortunate in getting aboard her. Three of these prize crew officers were P. and O. officers and I never saw such a glum-looking lot. They would have no part in our sports and I hear that one of them ... remarked to one of our officers that we should have been looking after our guns instead of fooling about or something to that effect. In spite of this we are about the crack ship for lowering boats, etc., on the patrol.

97. *Captain G.W. Vivian to Rear-Admiral Commanding Tenth Cruiser Squadron*

HMS *Patia*, 26 July 1915

Report of Proceedings, 17 June–26 July 1915

***

On my passage down to the Clyde the Port Engine developed a serious knock which increased as we went on, so that I had to stop the Engine for a time. It was evident that there was something very much amiss with the stern coupling. On June 18th I proceeded into dry-dock. On examination of the Port propeller and shafting it was found that all the stern coupling bolts were loose in their holes and that one had sheared, and further that the propeller had apparently not been originally home on the shaft when the nut was screwed up, as though the nut could not shift there was a space between the nut and the boss (we eventually got five and a half inches circumferentially on the nut when the propeller was replaced). Owing to this space between the nut and the boss, water had got in and set up so much rust etc that very considerable difficulty was experienced in getting the propeller off at all. The Port shaft was drawn and sent up to the shop to have the flanges for the coupling, which were in bad order, trued and to have the holes reamed out and new bolts fitted. We were I think very fortunate in not losing the propeller, as it certainly would not have stood very much longer.

All defects were completed by the 26th, when we undocked and started coaling, which was completed on the 28th. I intended to sail that evening, but when raising steam a joint of the main steam-pipe gave out and I had to shut off again to make this defect good, which delayed me till the 29th. I left the Clyde on the evening of the 29th to rejoin the patrol. On the 30th I intercepted the Danish schooner *Leif* for Fredrickshald to Torquay with timber. Allowed to proceed. In the afternoon I passed a number of bales of cotton and some floating wreckage. On July 1st I joined A Patrol in accordance with your orders. On July 3rd at 9.30 a.m. I sighted a large motor-vessel. When steering to intercept her we both got into a thick fog and I lost her. An hour later the fog thinned and I made for where she should be if she had not altered course, and finally picked her up again and boarded her. She was the *Pedro Christopherson* from Christiania to West Coast of America Ports via Panama Canal, though what she was doing up North of the Faeroes on her way to Panama was not quite clear, unless it was to avoid submarine attack. She had a general cargo, mainly paper. Altogether this ship seemed rather doubtful, and as the fog had again shut down, placed an Armed Guard on board and sent her in to Stornoway.

On July 4th I stopped and examined the British trawler *Elf-King* for Hull to Iceland. Allowed to proceed. On July 5th intercepted Danish sailing ship *Maagen* flying the 'previously boarded' flag. On July 8th in accordance with your orders, I left A Patrol after being relieved by *Changuinola*, and proceeded to relieve *Columbella* on C Patrol, communicating with *Ambrose* on the way. On July 9th I intercepted and boarded the Norwegian steamer *Uluband* from New Orleans to

Copenhagen with a cargo of oil-cake. Sent in to Kirkwall with an armed guard. On July 13th I intercepted and stopped the Danish steamer *Florida* from Baltimore to Stockholm with a cargo of coal. Sent in to Kirkwall with an Armed Guard.[1] On July 14th intercepted the Russian steamer *General Suworow* from Cardiff to Archangel with coal. Allowed to proceed. Shortly afterwards stopped and boarded the Danish auxiliary sailing-ship *Ivigtut* from Greenland to Copenhagen with a cargo of cryolite. Sent in to Kirkwall with an Armed Guard.[2] At 10 p.m. stopped and boarded the Danish steamer *Antwerpen* from Swedish ports to Baltimore, having coaled at Newcastle. Her cargo was mainly wood-pulp and iron angle-bar. This seemed a curious cargo to be going to America, which has all her own iron and exports her surplus, and gets or used to get anyhow her wood-pulp from Canada and Newfoundland. However this ship had a green clearance from Newcastle, so presumably had been examined there. Allowed to proceed. On July 1st intercepted the British trawler *Frolic* flying the 'previously boarded' flag. On July 16th communicated with *Mantua* and received from her one of my Armed Guards. At 7 p.m. intercepted the Norwegian steamer *Peter Jobson* flying the 'previously boarded' flag.[3]

On July 17th chased and came up with the Danish steamer *Gurre* with an Armed Guard already on board, but flying the wrong flag of the day.[4] On July 19th at 10.30 p.m. sighted a steamer without lights, and proceeded to intercept her. On approaching her about midnight she signalled to say she was the Swedish steamer *Anna*. The *Anna* in Lloyds list was very obviously smaller than this ship, so boarded her and found her to be the British steamer *Whitefields* for Archangel from Brest with a cargo of Munitions consigned to the Russian Government. Told to proceed. On the 21st passed the Danish steamer *California* bound for Stornoway with an Armed Guard on board.[5] On the 22nd stopped and boarded the Norwegian steamer *Imo* last from Tynemouth to Baltimore in ballast. This ship was chartered by the Norwegian government to bring grain from Baltimore, and had a green clearance from Tynemouth. Told to proceed. At 10 p.m. intercepted the Norwegian sailing-ship *Cairnsmore* with an Armed Guard already on board.[6] On July 24th I met

[1] *Pedro Christopherson*, *Maagen*, *Uluband* and *Florida* were not detained.

[2] Greenland being a Danish colony, this was a delicate intervention. The Contraband Committee at first asked for a guarantee against re-export, but on the advice of Lowther in Copenhagen, let *Ivigtut* sail on (TS 14/4 of 19, 21, 23 July 1915).

[3] *Peter Jobson* was not detained.

[4] *Gurre* was examined at Kirkwall then allowed to sail on.

[5] *California* was not detained.

[6] *Cairnsmore*'s cargo was consigned to firms on the Black List and it was sent in to the Prize Court (TS 14/4 of 27 and 28 July 1915).

and communicated with *Cedric*, who took over charge of the patrol, after which I left for the Clyde.

During this patrol that is from June 29th to July 25th the following ships were intercepted. Three sailing-ships, of which two had been previously boarded and one was bound for an English Port. Eleven steamers of which one was Russian, one British, one in ballast bound West, three had been previously boarded, one had a green clearance, and four were sent in with Armed Guards.

As regards Armed Guards sent in in ships to Stornoway, it is submitted that it would seem desirable if feasible that they should proceed to Scapa to return to their ships. The two last Armed Guards that I sent in there were as follows: (1) May 29th, Sailing-ship *Sorfararen*. Arrived Stornoway May 30th. Armed Guard left for Glasgow June 1st and arrived the same day. Rejoined ship on June 17th, when she arrived at Glasgow. Therefore for 16 days the Guard were living in Glasgow at the Government expense, when they might probably have been able to rejoin their ship had they been sent to Scapa. (2) Steamer *Pedro Christopherson*, July 3rd. Probably arrived at Stornoway July 4th. Guard have not rejoined up to this date (July 25th) and will probably rejoin on our arrival in the Clyde on July 26th, having been away 23 days. I am not at present aware whether this Guard was sent down to Glasgow from Stornoway on arrival or not.

I passed Cantyre at 10.30 p.m. on the 26th and arrived in the Clyde at 3 a.m. on July 26th.

98. *Rear-Admiral H.D. Fawckner, Senior Naval Officer Swarbacks Minn, to Admiralty*

c/o SNO Office, Lerwick, 19 June 1915

After consultation with the Rear-Admiral Commanding Tenth Cruiser Squadron [88 para. 10], I beg to submit the following recommendations which are absolutely necessary to start the base at Swarbacks Minn.

Coal. A blockship to be sent to Swarbacks Minn with a cargo of coal to remain as a Coal Depot for yachts, Pilot vessels, Drifters, etc. After Coaling vessels of the Cruiser Squadron, vessel could be discharged as a Block ship releasing the Colliers for further supplies.

Floating Stages. Twelve in No. 14' x 6' x 2' it is presumed these dimensions are the same as those now in use at Scapa to facilitate the coaling of ships fitted with side coaling ports.

Baskets of 1 cwt and 2 cwt will be required for this purpose.

Colliers with long derricks should be sent in view of the great height of the hatches above the water line of the ships of the Tenth Cruiser Squadron.

1 Tug for general purposes.

1 Steam Drifter for transfer of *Gibraltar* working parties and for general use of Coaling Officer.

It is understood that the Admiral Commanding Orkneys and Shetlands has forwarded his suggestions as to an efficient Patrol Service being provided, and it is further concluded for the necessary examination service.

Water. The probable average requirements of boiler water for Tenth Cruiser Service when base is first started will be about 100 tons daily.

It is estimated that small vessels will require about 50 tons daily. It is submitted that a supply of water be obtained from the Hill Lake near the Whaling Station in Olna Firth.

The Water is suitable for Boiler Water, and it is believed also for drinking purposes, as the Whalers take their supplies from this source. A hulk is moored at the end of the pier in sufficient depth of water for tank and other small vessels to lay alongside at any time of tide. The Representative of the Works Department has been consulted and he is dealing with the matter through the Civil Engineer at Rosyth. Until the supply is available it is suggested that Boiler Water be sent in the double bottom compartments of the Colliers.

When the port is further developed the daily requirements of water will be greatly increased, and it will be necessary most probably to have an additional source of supply.

Voe Lake appears to be the most suitable for the purpose, but it entails a considerable amount of piping and the extension of the pier at Voe, and the erection of staging to carry the pipes into a sufficient depth of water for tank vessels to load.

2 Tank Vessels of 100 tons for supply of Cruisers.

1 Tank Vessel of 50 tons for supply of small vessels.

The latter can be obtained locally.

Secretary. The Admiral Commanding Orkneys and Shetlands has highly recommended to me Assistant Paymaster H.B. Tuffill, RNR,[1] now serving in his office, for this post. I shall be glad to avail myself of his services if the appointment has not been previously filled. I have taken rooms at Busta, Beal, but pending Admiralty instructions, letters and telegrams for me are being sent c/o Senior Naval Office, Lerwick.

[1]Tuffill, Harold Birch, CBE, RD, RNR (1870–1950), Assistant Paymaster 1904, Accounts Officer and Secretary RNR 1914–1915, Secretary to Admiral Fawckner at Swarbacks Minn, 1915–1917, Paymaster Lieutenant-Commander May 1917, Secretary Port and Transit Executive Committee 1917–1920, Commander 1920.

99. *Captain J.A. Webster to Rear-Admiral Commanding Tenth Cruiser Squadron*

HMS *Motagua*, 19 June 1915

I have the honour to report that at about 10.43 a.m. today a submarine was sighted in Lat. 56.27´N, Long. 7.48´W, steaming to the South West.

The feather of the periscope was first sighted and then the wash of the conning tower, as it was coming to the surface, about 4000 yards away. The hull was never seen as the submarine dived immediately, probably on sighting the ship.

HMS *Changuinola*, who was six miles or so to the North East had shortly before warned me of a suspicious wake and oil on the water, and I am of the opinion that the submarine had dived for her and was coming to the surface to continue its voyage when I saw it. Although the guns were manned, the submarine was not up long enough to permit of fire being opened.[1]

100. *Diary of Dr J. Shaw*

Monday 21st June 1915. Ship's sports were held today. Some of the events were as follows: Tug of war, obstacle race for men, officer's obstacle race, potato race, bun race, bolster fight, sack race, blindfold boxing, officer's bottle race, etc.

In Tug-of-war the marines beat the petty officers. In turn the officers beat the marines (the Jacks seemed to take the officers' part in this struggle with the marines). The officers in their turn were beaten by the firemen. The quarterdeck beat fo'c'sle and firemen beat quarterdeck and so on, so that firemen came out best ...

22nd June. The distribution of prizes was made by the captain ... The winners of the various events among the men received presents of money, 5/-, 2/-, and so on. (This money was got up by subscription from the officers and captain.)

The winners of the officers' events received iron crosses (made of tin and enamelled black). This gave rise to cheering and laughter among the men.

[1]The identity of the submarine is not known.

101. *Commander-in-Chief Home Fleets to Admiral Commanding Orkneys and Shetlands, and Rear-Admiral Commanding Tenth Cruiser Squadron*

HMS *Iron Duke*, 21 June 1915

***

3. [replacing para (c) of letter of 28 March 1915] [55]: The Officer must not attempt any belligerent act under the neutral flag; should the neutral crew desert the ship, however, and the submarine open fire, the Armed Guard will then be at liberty to defend themselves on board the neutral ship.

102. *Admiral S.C. Colville to Commander-in-Chief Home Fleets*

HMS *Cyclops*, 25 June 1915

***

2. The staff, etc., required [at Swarbacks Minn] would be:
Naval Examination Staff. 1 Commander, RN retired.
1 German interpreter.
1 Scandinavian Interpreter.
1 Assistant Paymaster, RNR
4 Messengers.
Guards for ships and prisoners.

(Good interpreters are an absolute necessity. The messengers and guards could be drawn from the Shetlands, RNR).

Customs Staff. 2 or 3 Civil Servants.
2 or 3 Preventive Officers.

(A female searcher is also a necessity: one might possibly be obtained locally).

Accommodation required. Living quarters for above Officers,
Building to remove suspects to.
Accommodation for Armed Guards.

It is not known what dwelling houses there are in the neighbourhood of Gruting Voe, but it is highly improbable that the accommodation required could be found on shore. A suitable hulk or vessel would however solve the difficulty.

Protection of harbour. A yacht as guardship and a boom would be necessary.

Communications. As there is a good deal of telegraphing the land telegraph arrangements would require perfecting and elaborating.

Communication with 10th Cruiser Squadron would be by W/T through *Cyclops*, land wire and cable to Lerwick and then to Gruting Voe. This is rather a roundabout method and a W/T station on shore or in the hulk would be desirable. The yacht guardship's installation would not be sufficiently powerful.
Consuls for neutral countries. Would be required.
Harbour Service Craft. Tugs, drifters or steamboats with necessary crews would be required.
The number of Neutral Merchant Vessels sent in, taking half the number now sent to Kirkwall, would be about 50 monthly. The period of detention is anything from two days to a month.

3. Although the many advantages of instituting an examination centre for neutral vessels on the West Coast of the Shetlands are fully recognised, it would undoubtedly be a considerable undertaking. As an alternative I would suggest that more use should be made of Lerwick where, although the anchorage accommodation (about 12 ships) is less than half of Gruting Voe, there are already in existence a Custom House, a large telegraph office, Armed Guards (Shetlands RNR), living and office accommodation could be obtained and, I expect, the necessary Consuls exist, in any case they could be easily appointed. All that would be required would be the Examining Staff, Interpreters, guardship, tugs and protection to the harbour. If necessary ships proceeding to Lerwick from the West could have their route periodically changed Northabout and Southabout of Shetlands [103].

103. *Commander-in-Chief Home Fleets to the Admiralty*

HMS *Iron Duke*, 29 June 1915

After consideration of the letter No. 15 of 25th instant from the Admiral Commanding Orkneys and Shetlands [102] I am of opinion that the proposal made in clause 3 of his letter to use Lerwick as the examination centre is the best to adopt.

2. It is recommended that immediate steps be taken to provide the necessary staff, guard ship and troops.

3. For the present the submarine construction might stand over, but it is considered that it should be provided by September next.

104. *Admiralty to Commander-in-Chief HM Ships and Vessels Devonport*

30 June 1915

I am commanded by My Lords Commissioners of the Admiralty to acquaint you that they have decided to detail HMS *Gibraltar* for service as a Depot ship at Swarbacks Minn.

2. HMS *Gibraltar* is to be commissioned at Devonport with a Chatham crew, the complement including a coaling party of 200 RNR stokers. The scheme of complement is attached.[1]

3. HMS *Gibraltar* is to be fitted with Net Defence for the port side only: this is to be extemporised in the first instance and will be got in place after arrival at Swarbacks Minn. It is understood that the Torpedo Net defence fittings have been removed except heel sockets, and that Admiralty Superintendent Devonport should therefore arrange to restore one side or provide a raft or target from which the defence could be hung, whichever can be done most expeditiously.

4. As regards machinery, the *Gibraltar* will require to steam to her base at moderate speed and maintain herself in harbour after arrival.

5. Accommodation for a full complement should be arranged and for a reasonable number of supernumeraries. HMS *Gibraltar* should have three 6" or 4.7" guns and two searchlights. (The complement is drawn up on the assumption that only one gun need be continuously manned and both searchlights at night.) It is understood that the openings in deck left by the removal of 9.2" guns have not been made watertight. These openings are to be closed watertight.

6. Wireless Telegraphy is to be fitted.

7. Work is to be put in hand forthwith and a date for completion submitted as soon as possible. The proposed date of commissioning is also to be reported in due course.

[1]The scheme of complement comprised: 1 Captain, 2 Officers, 7 Petty Officers, 18 Seamen, 3 Telegraphists, 4 Engineers, 15 Stokers, 200 RNR Firemen, 29 others, 12 Royal Marines, a total of 296 men.

105. *Commander F.H. Walter to Rear-Admiral Tenth Cruiser Squadron*

HMS *Victorian*, 12 August 1915

Report of Proceedings, 7 July–10 August 1915

I have the honour to report proceedings as follows:

1. Ship docked at 6 a.m. on Wednesday 7th July, and leave was granted to one Watch of the Crew.

Arrangements were made to take more coal in No. 2 and No. 4 holds, and ship left with 4080 tons on 14th July, dropping the Pilot at 11.30 p.m. Ship proceeded to Patrol Draft: 30ft 7in forward and 29ft 5in aft. Mean draft 31ft. Displacement: 13037 tons.

2. Sunday 18th ultimo relieved *Ambrose* on C Patrol and on 23rd received Armed Guards for *Motagua*, *Andes* and *Arlanza*.

3. At 2.40 p.m. chased Danish steamer *United States* until about 4 a.m. when *Mantua* was observed to intercept her.[1]

4. On 27th July changed to A Patrol, and swung ship on 31st for correcting compasses.

5. On 30th July chased *Kristianiafjord* for three hours and found *India* intercepting her.[2]

6. Received two Armed Guards for *Alsatian* at 10 p.m. on 31st July.

7. On 1st August rendezvoused with *Andes* and gave him his Armed Guards.

8. On 7th August sighted Iceland, having chased a trawler for over 50 miles.

9. Orders were received to meet *Patuca* and receive Armed Guards on Monday 9th August. Owing to dense fog this was not done until 10 a.m. Tuesday, when fog lifted. One Armed Guard for *Victorian*, one for Andes, and one for *Hildebrand* were received.

10. At 2 p.m. on Tuesday 10th August orders were received to proceed to our base for coal.

Ships intercepted (not trawlers)	18
Ships intercepted (Trawlers)	7
Ships sent in (3 being sailing ships)	8
Number of days at sea	28¾
Number of miles steamed	7600

[1]The *United States* was not detained.

[2]*Kristianiafjord* was held up all through August with queries about various cargo items (TS 14/4 *passim*).

Coal expended	3596 tons
Average speed for the distance	11 knots

11. Arrived River Mersey 7.45 p.m. on 12th August.

106. *Rear-Admiral de Chair to Admiralty*

HMS *Alsatian*, 21 August 1915

Report of Proceedings, 9 July–21 August 1915

***

1. During the stay of *Alsatian* in Liverpool a W/T. Direction Finder designed by the National Physical Laboratory was fitted on board under the superintendence of Mr F.E. Smith of that department. Trials will be made with this instrument as opportunity offers, and a report of the result will be forwarded.

2. Information was received of the sinking of the German Steamer *Freidrich Arp* by the Armed Trawler *Tenby Castle* on 8th July. This took place off the Huso and Haran Islands on the Norwegian Coast. The *Tenby Castle* on sighting the steamer fired a shot across her bows and ordered her to steer SW by W. This the Captain refused to do and steamed towards the land. *Tenby Castle* fired a shot into the steamer's stern when she stopped but still refused to steer as directed, and after being warned that she would be sunk unless she obeyed orders, she again made for the shore. Sixteen rounds were then fired into her starboard quarter and she sank in Lat. 67.47´N, Long. 14.15´E. The crew and pilot were rescued and transferred to *India*. The *Friedrich Arp* was bound to Stettin from Narvik with a cargo of magnetic ore [109].

From a report by *Teutonic* it appears that, steamers at Narvik are kept informed of the noon positions of ships on G Patrol, the intelligence being sent out by the Norwegian Gunboat *Frithjof*.

3. On 11th July signal was made by *India* that *Ebro* had sighted submarine in Lat. 69.22´N, Long. 15.15´E on 9th July.

4. On 18th July *Andes* intercepted and sent to Kirkwall in accordance with Admiralty Orders the Danish Steamer *Sterling* from Reykjavik to Thorshavn and Copenhagen with a general cargo including wool.[1] The *Sterling* reported that only two Danish Steamers had, up to the present,

[1]Lowther, the Minister in Copenhagen, stated that the wool on board *Sterling* was destined for Germany; it was accordingly condemned by the Prize Court (TS 14/4 of 21 July 1915).

passed round the north coast of Iceland from East to West.

5. Monday, 19th July – *Alsatian* having completed with coal and carried out necessary repairs left Liverpool and proceeded to rejoin the Squadron.

6. Tuesday, 20th July – *Orcoma* boarded British Steamer *Colenso*, Blyth to Archangel. Her Master reported passing a complete deck cargo of wood at 2.40 a.m. on 19th July in Lat. 59.58´N, Long. 1.25´E.

7. Wednesday, 21st July – *Alsatian* rejoined A Patrol and I took charge of the Squadron, the disposition of ships being as follows:

A Patrol ... *Alsatian*, *Andes*, *Hildebrand*, *Hilary*, *Changuinola*, *Oropesa*.
B Patrol ... *Cedric*.
C Patrol ... *Columbella*, *Victorian*, *Mantua*, *Patia*, *Motagua*, *Royal Scot* (Armed Boarding Steamer).
E Patrol ... *Alcantara*.
F Patrol ... *Arlanza*.
G Patrol ... *Teutonic*, *Patuca* relieving *Orcoma*.
Proceeding to Clyde ... *Ambrose*, *Ebro*.
Coaling in Clyde ... *India*, *Digby*.
Proceeding to Liverpool ... *Otway*.
Coaling at Liverpool ... *Virginian*.

In compliance with orders from the Commander-in-Chief, *Columbella* was detached from C Patrol to Scapa Flow with a view to proceeding to Spitzbergen.[1]

Otway was met at pre-arranged rendezvous and given orders as regards docking and repairs.

Alcantara on E Patrol (north of Iceland) reported having experienced twelve days nearly continuous fog and mist.

Information was received from the Grimsby Trawler *Aralia* that a merchant in Reykjavik had stated that German submarines were being supplied from Seidisfjord.[2]

8. Thursday, 22nd July – At 6.45 a.m. *Columbella* reported that she was being attacked by a submarine in Lat. 60.26´N, Long. 4.42´W. The submarine apparently dived after making the attack and came up five miles astern. A Danish Schooner of about 600 tons was in the vicinity at the time. At 7.20 a.m. *Columbella* reported that the submarine had

[1]Another investigation by one of de Chair's ships, which yielded nothing: ADM 137/1101, 279–291.

[2]This again proved to be unfounded.

been avoided.[1]

Andes reported having intercepted and sent to Kirkwall the Danish SS *Botnia* from Reykjavik to Copenhagen with a general cargo including wool.[2] Her master reported the north passage clear close to the land, and fishing boats and sealers coming that way.

A submarine was reported to have sunk a trawler in Lat. 60.36´N, Long. 4 W and the Russian Collier *Rubonia* was sunk in Lat. 60.20´N, Long. 5.19´W[3]

9. Friday, 23rd July – *Cedric* was met at a pre-arranged rendezvous and given special orders. The Commodore then took command of C Patrol.

Alcantara was also met and given necessary orders. Reports of her visit to Jan Mayen Island and as regards the condition of the ice on North Coast of Iceland, are forwarded herewith ... .[4]

Andes reported having intercepted the Norwegian Steamer *Wacousta*, New York to Archangel with machinery and general cargo. As the whole cargo was consigned to Archangel the ship was allowed to proceed.

Two submarines were operating in Lat. 59.15´N, Long. 7.20´W where they sank the French ship *Danae*.[5]

10. Saturday, 24th July – *Patuca* reported having intercepted the British SS *Grangewood* returning from Archangel. The Master stated that Archangel was full of German Agents. A firm known as Haunevig trading as the London and Archangel Transport Company of Leadenhall Street London, was ostensibly selling coal, but this he believed to be merely a blind. Among others connected with this firm was an Englishman named Jenner of Southend, a suspicious character who had recently travelled through Germany.

I ordered *Patuca* to direct *Grangewood* to pass north of the Faroes and west of 10 West, to avoid submarines operating off the Shetlands, unless she had received other instructions from Admiralty. *Mantua* reported having intercepted and sent in to Kirkwall the Danish SS *United States*, New York to Copenhagen with 39 passengers and a

[1]The submarine was probably *U 36*; it sank the *Star of Peace* trawler nearby on the same day.

[2]*Botnia* in fact was brought into Stornoway; it was released on agreeing that the wool cargo (from Iceland) should be stored 'until the end of the war' in Copenhagen, and that a bond for double the current value be deposited (TS 14/4 of 7, 13 and 30 August 1915).

[3]Both victims of *U 36*.

[4]At ADM 137/185, 267–271, summarised by E. Keble Chatterton, *The Big Blockade* (London, 1932), 166–169.

[5]*U 36* again; there is no indication that more than one U-boat was involved.

general cargo. Her master stated she had a case of small pox on board.[1]

From reports from various ships boarded it was ascertained that on 17th July submarines were working both to the eastward and westward of the Shetlands. As this area appeared to be dangerous vessels sent in with Armed Guards were directed to pass to the northward of Lat. 61 N till in Long. 3 W or alternatively by North Rona and Sule Skerry.

11. Sunday, 25th July – The disposition of the Squadron was as follows:

A Patrol ... *Alsatian*, *Hildebrand*, *Oropesa*, *Andes*, *Changuinola*.
C Patrol ... *Cedric*, *Motagua*, *Victorian*, *Orotava*.
E Patrol ... *Hilary*.
F Patrol ... *Arlanza*.
G Patrol ... *Teutonic*, *Patuca*.
Proceeding to Clyde ... *Patia*, *Mantua*.
Proceeding to Liverpool ... *Orcoma*, *Alcantara*.
Proceeding to Scapa ... *Royal Scot*.
Coaling at Liverpool ... *Otway*.
Coaling in Clyde ... *India*, *Digby*, *Ebro*, *Ambrose*.
Rejoining from Liverpool ... *Virginian*.
Special service ... *Columbella*.

During the past week 115 vessels have been intercepted, of which 17 were sent in to port with Armed Guards.

Information was received that the British SS *Grangewood* which had been intercepted by *Patuca* on 24th instant, had been sunk by a submarine in Lat. 60.55´N, Long. 3 E.[2]

12. Monday 26th July – The Danish SS *Frederick VIII* from Copenhagen to New York was intercepted by *Motagua*, but was allowed to proceed in accordance with directions from Admiralty. From information received it appears possible that large numbers of American Bonds may be sent to the United States by Germany in the passenger ships of this line (Danish United Steamship Co.). It might hamper German financial intercourse with neutrals if these ships were sent in and searched when westward bound with a view to the confiscation of such bonds.

Teutonic reported having intercepted the Norwegian Steamer *Bianca*, Manchester to Pet Shora, Russia, in ballast. She had been

[1]See page 211, note 1.

[2]Sunk by *U 41*; *Grangewood*'s master clearly paid no heed to the advice of de Chair and the *Patuca*'s captain (para. 10).

stopped by a German submarine carrying two guns 25 miles NW by W from Foula Island at 5 p.m. on Sunday 25th July. Her Master was ordered on board the submarine and interrogated as to whether he had seen any British Cruisers. The submarine proceeded W by S at full speed on the surface.[1]

Patuca reported having intercepted the Norwegian Steamer *Baune*, Liverpool to Archangel with green clearance. She had been stopped by a German submarine in Lat. 60.28´N, Long. 6.25´W on the morning of 24th July when her papers were examined and she was asked if there were any other steamers in Liverpool loading for Archangel. The submarine also enquired whether a three-masted steamer had been seen. The *Baune* was allowed to proceed by the submarine owing to the fact that she carried copper consigned to Schmidt of Archangel. This individual is reported to have been interned in Archangel. In these circumstances, and as the *Baune* was steering an incorrect course for Archangel, I ordered her to be sent to Kirkwall with an Armed Guard.[2]

Information was received from the Commander-in-Chief that the Norwegian SS *Fimreite* which was proceeding to Kirkwall with an Armed Guard from *Motagua* had been sunk by gun fire by a small submarine at 4 a.m. on 22rd July in Lat. 60.15´N, Long. 8.45´W.[3] The crew and guard were picked up at 3 p.m. the same day by the Norwegian barque *Springbank* which transferred them to the Trawler *Caliban*, for conveyance to Kirkwall.

Virginian was met at a pre-arranged rendezvous and given orders to proceed to F Patrol, keeping a special look out for ships carrying wool from Iceland.

Information was received of the sinking of the American Steamer *Leelanaw* on 25th July in Lat. 60.58´N, Long. 4.50´W when westward bound from Kirkwall. The submarine which sank the ship apparently towed the survivors of the crew in their boats towards Kirkwall where they eventually landed. Several Trawlers were also sunk in the neighbourhood of the Orkneys on the same day.[4]

Teutonic reported that she had intercepted the British Steamer *Thurso* from Immingham to Archangel with a general cargo including 30 casks of chalk, and 104 barrels of asphalt consigned to Schmidt of Archangel, apparently the same person to whom cargo in *Baune* was

[1]This was probably *U 36*, soon after sinking *Danae*, *Rubonia* and so on (page 214, notes 1, 3, 5).

[2]The ship was released at once; the submarine was probably *U 36*.

[3]*U 36* again.

[4]All this was the work of *U 41*.

consigned. As she was provided with a Green Clearance from Immingham and carried a large quantity of lead and motor cars for the Russian Government she was allowed to proceed.

13. Tuesday 27th July – *Hildebrand* reported having intercepted and sent into Kirkwall with an Armed Guard in accordance with Admiralty orders the Norwegian Steamer *Trondhjemsfjord* from New York to Bergen with general cargo.

Andes reported having intercepted and sent to Kirkwall with an Armed Guard in accordance with Admiralty orders the Danish motor Schooner *Venus* with a cargo of wool from Stockseyri, Iceland, for Copenhagen.

The Armed Yacht *Vanessa* reported chasing a submarine in Lat. 58.15´N, Long. 8.12´W and sighting a suspicious steamer steering to SW from same position. *Orotava* proceeded to intercept the steamer but did not succeed in sighting her.

The American Oil Steamer *Llama*, New York to Stockholm was stopped by a submarine in Lat. 58.55´N, Long. 7.26´W. She was afterward intercepted and sent to Kirkwall by *Sappho* which was working on C Patrol.[1]

14. Wednesday, 28th July – *Orotava* reported sighting a submarine in Lat. 57 N, Long. 9 W steering S at 5.10 a.m., distance about 7 miles. She maintained a steady converging course for about twenty minutes when the submarine dived.

The British Steamer *Benshaw* boarded by *Patuca* reported having seen a ship blown up on 27th July in the neighbourhood of Lat. 61.39´N, Long. 1.6´E.[2]

I anchored at Swarbacks Minn in *Alsatian* and conferred with Rear-Admiral Fawckner as to the development of the Base. The Boom Defence between Papa Little Island and Muckle Roe Island was in place and gate working. Part of the outer net defence was supplied but not yet placed. Five Colliers with a total of 14,942 tons of coal were in harbour and a salvage vessel (*Zepher*) for mooring net defences. The *Gibraltar* had not yet arrived but was expected shortly. Work in connection with the water supply was being proceeded with and communication by means of telephones was in course of arrangement.

The Armed Boarding Steamer *Duke of Cornwall* arrived with despatches from the Commander-in-Chief and was sent to convey orders to *Teutonic* on G Patrol.

[1] *Venus*, *Trondhjemsfjord* and *Llama* were released by Customs without reference to the Contraband Committee.

[2] The identity of the ship is not known; there was no U-boat in the area at the time; possibly the *Trondhjemsfjord* is meant (para. 15).

A submarine with sails set was sighted 15 miles north of St Kilda steering NW. Another submarine was chased by an Auxiliary Patrol Vessel in Lat. 60.15´N, Long. 3.8´W until she submerged.

15. Thursday, 29th July – The Armed Boarding Steamer *The Ramsey* arrived at Swarbacks Minn with further despatches from Commander-in-Chief, and was sent to deliver orders to *Teutonic*.

Duke of Cornwall having returned from meeting *Teutonic* conveyed my despatches to the Commander-in-Chief.

I left Swarbacks Minn in the evening and returned to patrol areas.

Information was received of the sinking of the Norwegian Steamer *Trondhjemsfjord* in Lat. 61.30´N, Long. 3.42´W by a German submarine on 28th July [118]. This vessel which was proceeding to Kirkwall in charge of an Armed Guard from *Hildebrand* was fired at by the submarine at 0.25 p.m., the shot passing over the bows. The Master altered course to bring the submarine astern and proceeded at full speed. After a chase of half an hour the submarine fired a second shot and the *Trondhjemsfjord* which was being rapidly overhauled, stopped. The Master was ordered on board the submarine with the Ship's papers, but before leaving he arranged for the disguise of the Armed Guard, his wife who was on board, providing the Officer (Lieutenant Crawford, RNR)[1] with some of her husband's clothes in place of his own which she packed with her own effects for removal. The rifles etc., belonging to the Guard were concealed in the fore peak. Soon after the Master got on board the submarine she signalled to the crew of the *Trondhjemsfjord* to abandon ship immediately. At 1.25 p.m. when all boats were clear of the ship the submarine fired a torpedo amidships from a distance of about 130 yards, and the *Trondhjemsfjord* listed heavily to port. Amongst other cargo this steamer was carrying a large quantity of sulphuric acid which burst with a loud explosion and flew to the height of the mastheads on ship being hit by the torpedo. She sank at 2.51 p.m.

The submarine then towed the crew and Armed Guard in their boats about four miles to the southward where the Norwegian barque *Glance* was met with and ordered by the German officer to embark them.

The submarine was of the latest type, being about 200 feet long with two masts, fitted with wireless, armed with a 12 pdr gun forward and a 6 pdr gun aft. The hull was grey and her number was painted out. The Commander was a young man about 25 who treated the Master of the Norwegian Steamer with courtesy. He explained that his chief reason

[1]Crawford, Percy P., DSC, RNR, Sub-Lieutenant 1915, Lieutenant 1917.

for sinking the *Trondhjemsfjord* was that she was an English Steamer bought by the Norwegian Company since the commencement of hostilities. He also said that he was looking out for the *Drammensfjord* which he had instructions to sink on account of her British origin.[1]

The Master of the *Trondhjemsfjord* (Captain Bang) and his wife appear to have behaved in a most praiseworthy way throughout. Whilst on board the submarine the former denied that he had an Armed Guard on board his ship or that he had been boarded by a British patrol vessel. Their Lordships will no doubt suitably acknowledge their services.

The Crew and Armed Guard were first transferred to the Swedish Steamer *Orlando*, bound for Sweden, and the Armed Guard eventually reached Thurso in the Trawler *Princess Juliana*, the Master and crew of *Trondhjemsfjord* remained in *Orlando*.

Submarines were again reported to be operating off St Kilda.

16. Friday, 30th July – *India* intercepted the Norwegian Steamer *Kristianiafjord* west bound. Among the passengers were three German men – two over age and one blind – and a number of German and Austrian women, mostly belonging to the theatrical profession.

17. Saturday, 31st July – *Andes* and *Victorian* were met at pre-arranged rendezvous for the purpose of transferring Armed Guards.

18. Sunday, 1st August – *Alsatian* intercepted the Norwegian Steamer *Bergensfjord* from New York to Bergen with a general cargo and 350 passengers, also 24 men working their passage. She was sent in to Kirkwall with an Armed Guard, her Master making the usual protest against this proceeding.[2]

The disposition of the Squadron was as follows:

A Patrol ... *Alsatian*, *Victorian*, *India*, *Andes*, *Digby*.
C Patrol ... *Hildebrand*, *Oropesa*, *Ebro*, *Ambrose*, *Fiona* (Armed Boarding Steamer).
E Patrol ... *Hilary*.
F Patrol ... *Virginian*.
G Patrol ... *Teutonic*, *Patuca*.
Proceeding to Liverpool to coal ... *Cedric*.
Coaling at Liverpool ... *Otway*, *Alcantara*, *Orcoma*, *Arlanza*.
Coaling in Clyde ... *Mantua*, *Patia*, *Motagua*, *Changuinola*, *Orotava*.
Special service ... *Columbella*.

[1]The submarine was *U 41*.
[2]*Bergensfjord* was not detained.

During the past week 69 ships were intercepted and examined, of which 12 were sent in to port with Armed Guards.

A submarine was reported in Lat. 55.30´N, Long. 4.16´W steering West.

19. Monday, 2nd August – *Patuca* reported passing in Lat. 62.31´N, Long. 3 E wreckage, apparently the stem of a small sailing vessel which had been a long time in the water. She also sighted a life buoy with the name *Alarm* on it.[1]

Digby was met at a pre-arranged rendezvous and given orders to proceed to Reykjavik and communicate with HM Consul and Mr Cable with a view to obtaining information as to reported submarine base at Seidisfjord; she was then to return to work on F patrol.

A report was received from the Russian steamer *Dronty* that at 7.30 p.m. on 1st August she sighted a Swedish Steamer painted grey with national colours on her sides in Lat. 59.40´N, Long. 4 W. This vessel which appeared to be about five or six thousand tons and had twin masts, was behaving suspiciously, steaming slowly in circles. She crossed the bows of the *Dronty* at 9 p.m. steering west, and when 10 miles distant showed two powerful white lights, one at the ensign staff and one amidships.

This report was passed to the Commander-in-Chief.

20. Tuesday, 3rd August – *Gibraltar* arrived at Swarbacks Minn where she will be stationed as Guard and Depot Ship.

21. Wednesday, 4th August – *Patuca* was sent in to Swarbacks Minn and ordered to take 1000 tons of coal.

Orcoma and *Patia* were met and given orders for patrol.

22. Thursday, 5th August – Submarines were reported 8 miles NNW from Butt of Lewis, and in Lat. 61.15´N, Long. 0.50´W.

Patia intercepted the Norwegian Steamer *Drammensfjord* Baltimore to Bergen with corn and coal, and sent her to Kirkwall with an Armed Guard. Special directions were given as to the route of this vessel in view of the activity of submarines in the vicinity of the Shetlands.[2]

23. Friday, 6th August – Directions were received from Commander-in-Chief to keep patrols well to the westward in order to clear enemy submarines operating to the west of Orkneys. *Orotava* was

[1]If 'Alarm' is the ship's name, it was a sailing vessel of 267 tons built as recently as 1913; there is no record of it being sunk by a U-boat.

[2]The Contraband Committee had agreed on 3 August that *Drammensfjord* need not be brought in if a guarantee for all the cargo was forthcoming; when it was brought in it was allowed to go on at once; the strong suggestion was made that the ships of this line call at Kirkwall voluntarily.

ordered to Lat. 57 N, Long. 11 W to intercept and warn ships to keep west of Long. 11 W until north of Faroe Islands, and A and C patrols were instructed to send ships intercepted to Lerwick round Muckle Flugga or else round Butt of Lewis on parallel 58.30´N thence to Cape Wrath passing through Pentland Firth in daylight to Kirkwall. They were also directed to warn ships intercepted on passage to Arkhangel to pass west of Long. 11 W.

Andes, *Digby* and *Alcantara* were met at pre-arranged rendezvous and given necessary orders ...

Submarines were reported in Lat. 56.13´N, Long. 6.16´W and 25 miles NW of Muckle Flugga. The Swedish Steamer *Ester* was stopped by a submarine with two guns 46 miles N of Butt of Lewis.[1]

24. Saturday, 7th August – The Danish Steamer *Oscar II* from New York to Copenhagen with a large number of passengers and general cargo was intercepted by *Ebro* and sent in to Lerwick ... Her Master handed in a written protest.[2]

Virginian on G Patrol reported having intercepted and sent to Kirkwall with an Armed Guard the Swedish Steamer *Vollrath Than* with 8000 tons of iron ore from Narvik to Rotterdam, also the *Swarva* with a cargo of the same description for Middlesbrough.[3]

Submarines were reported in Lat. 59.30´N, Long. 4.50´W and in Lat. 61.4´N, Long. 1.42´W where the Trawler *Ocean Queen* was sunk by gun fire.[4]

25. Sunday, 8th August – *Patuca* was met at a pre-arranged rendezvous and reported as to her recent coaling at Swarbacks Minn. Arriving at 5 a.m. on 4th August she took in 1000 tons of coal, filled up with water, received fresh provisions, swept boiler tubes, and left on 7th August. The actual coaling which was carried out with the assistance of 100 RNR stokers from *Gibraltar* occupied 50 hours.

The disposition of the Squadron was as follows:

A Patrol ... *Patia*, *Mantua*, *Victorian*, *Changuinola*, *Hilary*.
C Patrol ... *Hildebrand*, *Orcoma*, *Ebro*, *Ambrose*, *King Orry* (Armed Boarding Steamer).
E Patrol ... *Alcantara*.
F Patrol ... *Digby*.

[1]The identity of the submarine is not known.

[2]*Oscar II*, recorded at Lerwick on 8 August, was apparently released at once.

[3]The owners were asked if they would sell *Vollrath Than*'s cargo to 'England', complied, and the cargo went to Prize Court on 12 August (TS 14/4 of 10 and 12 August 1915); *Swarva* was not detained.

[4]By *U 38*.

G Patrol ... *Virginian*, *India*.
Orotava patrolling in Lat. 57 N, Long. 11 W.
Alsatian patrolling in Lat. 63 N, Long. 4 W.
Proceeding to Liverpool ... *Andes*.
Coaling at Liverpool ... *Cedric*, *Otway*, *Teutonic*.
Coaling in Clyde ... *Oropesa*.
Rejoining Patrol from Liverpool ... *Arlanza*.
Rejoining Patrol from Clyde ... *Motagua*.
Rejoining Patrol from Swarbucks Minn ... *Patuca*.
Special service ... *Columbella*.

Of 64 Ships intercepted and examined during the last week 12 were sent into port with Armed Guards. Submarines were reported to be operating off Muckle Flugga where a British Steamer was sunk by gun fire.[1]

The following items of interest were included in a report made by the Officer of the Armed Guard placed on board Norwegian Steamer *Bergensfjord* when that ship was sent to Kirkwall on 1st August: The *Kristianiafjord* of the same line is fitted with a wireless direction finder, and it is hoped that a similar instrument will be supplied to *Bergensfjord* as soon as condenser can be obtained. The route followed by *Bergensfjord* both outward and homeward passed through Lat. 63 N., Long. 7 W. She usually arrived at this position about 2 p.m. on the Sunday after departure from New York. A passenger stated that he had seen German plans for the manufacture of ammunition machines which he understood were to be sent to Germany either through Greece or Sweden. The orders for these machines stood in the name of a Swedish firm. The Officer of the Armed Guard and the Midshipman accompanying him were treated with great courtesy by the Master, and took their meals with the saloon passengers. On requesting to be allowed to pay for their entertainment they were informed that they were the guests of the Company.

26. Monday, 9th August – The following information as to the conditions at Arkhangel was elicited from the Master of the Norwegian Steamer *Jonas Rein* which was intercepted by *Alsatian*, proceeding to Greenock with timber: Ships are being convoyed into Arkhangel from Isodore Point by British minesweepers flying the Russian Flag, and as many as twenty are brought in at once. Average arrivals are about two or three per diem. Three ships which have struck mines are beached

[1]This appears to be a mistake; no sinking is recorded anywhere on that date.

near the Narrows, they were upright on bottom and appeared to be little damaged. None of their cargo had been removed and they will probably be floated off. Ships arriving are promptly berthed to discharge cargo, but workmen are troublesome and cause delay. There is more war material on shore than the railway can handle and there is a quantity of outward cargo waiting for shipment. The general attitude of the inhabitants is optimistic but they appear to concern themselves little with the war. All ships from the United States were calling at Kirkwall so far as he could judge, as he had not met any Masters whose ships had come direct. His ship had been convoyed clear of the White Sea on the return voyage.

Arlanza reported having intercepted the Norwegian Steamer *Grecian* from Newcastle to Sydney, Cape Breton Island, in ballast. Her Master stated that at 10 p.m. on 7th August he was boarded by a large submarine in Lat. 58.20´N, Long. 1.40´W.[1]

Swedish steamer *Sydic* Baltimore to Malmo with coal was intercepted by *Ambrose* and sent to Kirkwall with an Armed Guard ... .[2]

In the area covered by A Patrol dense fog was experienced.

27. Tuesday, 10th August – Fog still prevalent in A Patrol area.

Information was received that the Danish Steamer *Eleanora Maersk* with an Armed Guard from *Andes* had been stopped by a submarine in Lat. 61 N, Long. 1.22´W on 8th August. The Master was ordered on board the submarine with his papers but was eventually allowed to proceed and arrived at Lerwick. The submarine was about 250 feet in length, painted light grey, with one gun.[3]

At 8 a.m. on Sunday *India* reported her position. At 3 p.m. *Virginian*, being Senior Officer of G Patrol, was told to pass the following signal to *India*: 'German Auxiliary Cruiser *Meteor* sailed from Heligoland Bight early morning 6th August. Maximum speed 14 knots, 2 masts, 1 funnel, carries torpedo tubes on forecastle. She may be bound to mine White Sea'.[4]

At 5 a.m. Tuesday 10th, *Virginian* reported: 'Have been 2¾ hours calling *India*. I closed and searched her patrol, was told by Norwegian patrol that he was informed by passenger boat *India* torpedoed and sunk 67.24´N, 13.44´E, 6.30 p.m. on Sunday. Cargo boat standing by. Norwegian patrol boat searched position, no trace, still searching for

[1]The submarine is not identifiable.

[2]*Sydic* was allowed to proceed after investigation (TS 14/4 of 11 August 1915).

[3]This was probably *U 24*, possibly *U 38*.

[4]*Meteor* had carried out such a mission in the spring, as had some submarines (see page 224, note 3).

survivors. Sent message by patrol boat to *Saxon* and *Newland* to assist in search until time to return to coal ...'.[1]

Virginian also reported that the Norwegian passenger steamer was not near enough to pick up survivors and did not close *India* as the cargo boat was already on the spot. The Norwegian patrol officer thought that the survivors had been taken ashore by the cargo boat. The weather at the time of the incident was calm and the *India* apparently sank slowly [129].

Mantua reported having intercepted the Danish Barquentine *Olga*, Dysart to Reykjavik with coal, whose Master stated that he was boarded by a German submarine in Lat. 60.6´N, Long. 5.31´W on 7th August. He was asked if he had seen any British Men of War and replied 'No'.[2]

Virginian reported that *Tenby Castle* had intercepted the Norwegian steamer *Steotstad*, Narvik to Middlesbrough with ore on 9th August, and had sent her direct to her destination with an Armed Guard as the Master refused to navigate the ship to Kirkwall.

Ambrose was met at a pre-arranged rendezvous and given orders to proceed to Swarbacks Minn to coal.

The Commander-in-Chief informed me that the German Auxiliary Cruiser *Meteor* which was reported to have left Heligoland Bight on 6th August had been sunk.[3]

Several submarines were reported going north along the Norwegian Coast. Ships on G Patrol were warned.

28. Wednesday, 11th August – *Arlanza* intercepted and sent in the Swedish SS *Zamora* with coal from Baltimore to Stockholm, consignee Beijer. The Master stated that he expected to be stopped in the Cattegat and then taken into a German port.[4]

Orcoma intercepted and sent in the Norwegian Sailing Ship *Gouda*, Santa Fe to Copenhagen with quebracho wood consigned to 'M.I. Ballin Sonner'. One of the crew was suspected to be a German ... .[5]

Otway was met at a pre-arranged rendezvous and given orders to take charge of G Patrol off the Norwegian Coast.

[1]*India* was sunk by *U 22*. *India* has been portrayed by E. Keble Chatterton in *The Big Blockade* (London, 1932), as a Q-ship. The account of its work in the Vestfjord area given by Commander Kennedy demonstrates clearly that it was not [129, 130].

[2]The identity of the submarine is not known.

[3]*Meteor*, the formerly British ship *Vienna*, had laid mines in the Moray Firth, and was intercepted on her way home by Commodore Tyrwhitt's Harwich force; *Meteor* was scuttled on interception. *Meteor*'s exploit gained Beatty's reluctant admiration (*Beatty Papers* I, 281).

[4]*Zamora* was allowed to go on after investigation (TS 14/4 of 16 August 1915).

[5]The cargo of *Gouda* was quebrachi wood; it had been reported as being shipped by 'a German firm in Argentina' in a telegram from Buenos Aires of 2 August. The cargo was ordered to the Prize Court and the ship sent to Leith (TS 14/4 of 2 and 18 August 1915).

The following details of the sinking of the Norwegian Steamer *Fimreite* by a German Submarine on 25th July last were contained in a report received from *Motagua* to which ship the Armed Guard on board the Steamer belonged: At 4.14 a.m. when in Lat. 60.17´N, Long. 8.43´W a submarine was sighted on the port bow making for the *Fimreite* at high speed. She fired a gun and ordered the steamer to stop and send a boat. While the Master was on board the submarine, the Officer in charge of the Armed Guard (Mr P.B. Clarke, Midshipman, RNR)[1] ordered his men to take off their uniforms and help to put the boats out. On his return to the ship the Master stated that he had been questioned as to his destination and had given it as Hull; asked if he were going direct, he had replied, 'via Kirkwall'. He was then asked if he had a Prize Crew aboard and answered 'Yes, one officer and four soldiers'. The Germans told him they would sink him for trading with the English and told him not to let the Englishmen get into the boats as they were to be sunk with the ship. The officer of the Guard thinking the Germans might search the boats ordered his men to remove everything uniform and to disguise themselves as much as possible, taking their revolvers in their pockets. As soon as the boats were clear of the ship the submarine opened fire on her with what looked like a 6 or 12 pdr gun. She fired about 15 projectiles one of which struck the boilers, and the *Fimreite* sank bow first.[2]

There were 29 men seen on board the submarine watching the shooting, most of them dressed in duffle suits. The submarine had one mast amidships and a black patch forward where her number had probably been painted out. After sinking the *Fimreite* she dived, heading in a westerly direction. The crew and guard were in the boats from 4.45 a.m. till 3.30 p.m. when they were picked up by the Norwegian Barque *Springbank* which transferred them to the *Caliban* for passage to Stornoway.

Submarines were reported to have been seen off the Norwegian Coast in the latitude of Bergen.

29. Thursday 12th August – Thick fog was experienced on A and F patrols.

Digby reported having intercepted the Trawler *Chamberlain* whose Master stated that when off Buchan Ness on the evening of 9th August his vessel ran over a submerged obstruction which lifted her bodily. He

[1]Clarke, Peter B., DSC, RNR, Midshipman 1914, Sub-Lieutenant 1918.
[2]This was *U 36*; it was clearly worth lying to submarine commanders.

was certain that it was a submarine, and reported the matter to the Minesweeping Trawler *Isle of Lewis* which was in the vicinity.

30. Friday, 13th August – The Swedish Steamer *Gotaland* which was intercepted by *Otway* bound from Narvik to Middlesbrough with iron ore furnished some further information as to the sinking of HMS *India* on 8th August. The torpedo apparently struck the ship abreast the after magazine and she sank in a few minutes, most of the boats being swamped. The *Gotaland* rescued 88 of the crew and the *Saxon* 46. Two boats pulled ashore. The total number saved was about 200 including the Captain, First Lieutenant and Paymaster. The survivors on board the *Gotaland* and *Saxon* were taken to Narvik.

Information was received of the capture by a submarine of the American Sailing Vessel *Pass of Balmaha* while en route for Kirkwall on 4th August. This vessel had an Armed Guard from *Victorian* on board at the time but their fate is not known. The ship herself was taken to Cuxhaven [139].[1]

Thick fog was experienced particularly on A Patrol.

Submarines were again reported on the Norwegian Coast proceeding north.

31. Saturday, 14th August – Fog was prevalent on A and C Patrols.

32. Sunday, 15th August – Disposition of Squadron was as follows:

A Patrol ... *Patia*, *Mantua*, *Ebro*, *Patuca*.
C Patrol ... *Arlanza*, *Orcoma*, *Changuinola*, *Motagua*, *Fiona* (Armed Boarding Steamer)
E Patrol ... *Alcantara*.
F Patrol ... *Orotava*.
G Patrol ... *Otway*, Armed Trawlers *Tenby Castle* and *Rushcoe*.
Alsatian patrolling in Lat. 63 N, Long. 4 W.
Digby patrolling in Lat. 62.30´N, Long. 9 W.
Proceeding to Clyde ... *Hilary*.
Proceeding to Liverpool ... *Virginian*.
Returning to patrol from Liverpool ... *Cedric*.
Coaling at Liverpool ... *Teutonic*, *Victorian*, *Andes*.
Coaling in Clyde ... *Hildebrand*, *Oropesa*.
On special service ... *Columbella*.

[1]The *Pass of Balmaha* was transformed into the German raider *Seeadler* and went on a long surface raid in 1917; she had been captured by *U 36*, which itself was intercepted and sunk by the Q-ship *Prince Charles*; only 15 of her crew were picked up by *Prince Charles*.

At Lerwick ... Armed Trawlers *Saxon*, *Newland*.[1]

During the past week 57 vessels were intercepted and examined, of which 12 were sent in with Armed Guards.

During the past fortnight 21 vessels were intercepted on passage to Arkhangel.

Almost continuous fog prevailed during the week on A, F and E Patrols, and intermittent fog was experienced on G Patrol.

33. Monday, 16th August – Submarines were active in the Liverpool district where a Benzol factory at Lowca, St Bee's Head, was shelled with apparently small damage.[2]

34. Tuesday, 17th August – *Cedric* was met at a pre-arranged rendezvous and communicated with, necessary orders and information being given to Commodore Benson.

Otway reported information received from Armed Trawler *Tenby Castle* on T.2 patrol, to the effect that merchant shipping was passing within territorial waters using Buholm Raasen Channel except in thick weather when ships must pass to seaward of a shoal in Lat. 64.15´N, Long. 9.57´W, at which point only was it possible to intercept them.

In accordance with directions from the Commander-in-Chief, the *Teutonic* which was returning to patrol from Liverpool after coaling, was ordered to proceed to Greenock and coal in readiness for special service.

Wednesday, 18th August.

35. Thursday, 19th August – *Alsatian* intercepted the Danish Steamer *Frederick VIII* New York to Copenhagen with a large number of passengers. She was sent to Kirkwall with an Armed Guard. Efforts were made to identify the Austrian Officer mentioned in Admiralty Telegram No. 597 but he could not be found.[3]

With the approval of the Commander-in-Chief the Armed Trawlers working off the Norwegian Coast were moved to the vicinity of Lat. 64.18´N, Long. 10 E in order to intercept shipping passing outside territorial waters, *Otway* acting as support.

Submarines were reported working off the Norwegian Coast in Lat. 60 N where the Norwegian mail steamer was stopped and mails for Allies seized.

[1]The arrival of the four Armed Trawlers listed here are not noted by de Chair, but they were to be normal members of the Northern Patrol from now on, except in the deepest winter weather [114, 115].

[2]By *U 24*.

[3]*Frederick VIII* was allowed to go on by the Contraband Committee (TS 14/4 of 21 August 1915).

36. *Alsatian* proceeded to Liverpool to coal and when in Lat. 56.27´N, Long. 8.15´W the Armed Trawlers *Walwyn Castle* and *Poyntz Castle* were sighted on patrol, looking out for a suspicious vessel; they had been there 5 weeks.

Friday, 20th August.

37. Saturday, 21st August – I arrived at Liverpool in *Alsatian*.

107. *Lieutenant J.T. Randell, RNR, Commanding Officer* Tenby Castle *to Captain H. E. Purey-Cust,*[1] *Captain i/c Orkney Trawlers*

Longhope, 12 July 1915

About 11.20 a.m. on June 30th Kya Islet bore SW 1/2 S distant about 5 miles, I sighted a steamer coming south from Nerslund, crossed it and saw her name *Pallas* and as she showed me no colours I hoisted the White Ensign and MN of which she took no notice. I then ported and came round and saw she was a German belonging to Flensburg and fired a shot across her bow. She then stopped her engines but put her helm to starboard and headed towards the shore. I then closed her and ordered the Captain to show his colours, he refused. I then ordered him to port and steer west, he refused. I then told him I would give him 5 minutes to make up his mind to either come with me or be sunk. In the meantime I had sent a message to HMS *Victorian* ('German steamer shall I sink her') the answer came back ('Wait'). I then went alongside the *Pallas* and put CPO Rowe and Seaman Hunt on board as Armed Guard and ordered them to take charge, but the Captain of the *Pallas* had rung full ahead, and had his helm over to starboard, and I was forced to fire 2 shots at his steering gear on the poop and so disabled her, he stopped the engines but the ship was gradually drawing towards the shore and when the *Victorian* arrived was about 2 1/2 miles off.

Later the Norwegian gunboat *Freya* came up and demanded her release [89].

[1]Purey-Cust, Herbert Edward, CB, RN, Lieutenant 1878, Captain 1900, Rear-Admiral (retired) 1910, Captain RNR, in command of Orkney Trawlers, 1915, Vice-Admiral (retired) 1915.

108. *Lieutenant J.T. Randell, RNR, Commanding Officer* Tenby Castle *to Captain H.E. Purey-Cust, Captain i/c Orkney Trawlers*

Longhope, 12 July 1915

At 5.50 a.m. on 9th July we were lying off the Huso and Haman group of islets in West Fjord, the weather being thick and rainy, we sighted a large steamer bearing NNW and put on full speed towards her keeping her on our port bow and at 6.10 a.m. signalled him to stop and on closing her saw that she was the Swedish steamer *Malmland wanted*, and ordered him to follow me and steer SW and W. About 6.45 a.m. she put on full speed and drew ahead. I then signalled to him to reduce speed and keep right astern of me.

At 8.20 a.m. we closed HMS *India* and I handed *Malmland* over to armed guard.[1]

She was bound from Narvik with cargo of magnetic ore and carried about 7,000 tons.

109. *Lieutenant J.T. Randell, RNR, Commanding Officer* Tenby Castle *to Captain H.E. Purey-Cust, Captain i/c Orkney Trawlers*

Longhope, 12 July 1915

At 0.20 a.m. on July 8th we were lying off Huso and Haram group of Islets in Vest Fjord and observed a steamer coming from the NE and steered towards same. At 0.52 a.m. we fired a shot across her bows and on rounding to under her stern saw that she was the German steamer *Frederick Arp* of Hamburg and ordered him to stop. At 1.0 a.m. I closed her and hailed the Captain and told him he would have to come along with me, and ordered him to steer SW and W, he refused and steamed towards the land, I then fired a shot into his quarter which stopped him, after he had refused several times to come with me I gave him 5 minutes and told him that he would have to come with me or be sunk, at the end of that time he still refused to come and about two minutes later put his engines ahead and steamed for the shore, and at 1.20 I commenced firing and fired 16 rounds into her star quarter at the water line and she sank at 1.48 in Lat. 67.47´N and Long. 14.15´E.

She was bound to Stettin from Narvik with a cargo of magnetic ore and carried about 4000 tons.

The crew of 13 I handed over to HMS *India* 5 a.m. same date [110].

[1]Nothing reprehensible was found by Customs.

110. *Journal of Sub-Lieutenant F.L. McKeag,*[1] *HMS* India

The *India*'s patrol being on the Norwegian coast, off the mouth of the West Fjord, was a very busy one, and we had the use of two armed trawlers to assist us by acting as scouts. Two German merchant ships were known to be in Narvik waiting their chance to make a dash and we were eagerly waiting for them. They made their dash, and although one got through by moving into territorial waters on the approach of our trawler, the *Tenby Castle*, it was at the expense of her steering gear, which was smashed up by a well-directed shot from the trawler, before the German could cross into safety [107]. The other German ship, the *Friedrich Arp* was sunk by the *Tenby Castle*, and the prisoners to the number of thirteen, who had been allowed to clear off the ship before the trawler opened fire, were handed over to us for safe keeping [109].

After the sinking of the *Friedrich Arp* there were no more German ships left on the Norwegian coast, so that our job in future was just to patrol in the same place, and intercept all ships bound out from Narvik with magnetic ore and send them into Kirkwall, irrespective of where they were bound, for their papers could not be relied on.

111. *Rear-Admiral de Chair to Admiralty*

16 July 1915

Use of Liverpool by Armed Merchant Cruisers

... [O]f the 24 Armed Merchant Cruisers under my command only eight at present use Liverpool as a coaling base, and as a rule two or sometimes three are in harbour at any time. The remaining 16 use the Clyde.

As far as Naval requirements are concerned I do not consider any equally satisfactory arrangement for coaling and storing these ships could be made at any other base, and it must be borne in mind that the efficiency of the Squadron as a whole largely depends on the rapidity with which these operations can be carried out. It is equally important that small repairs should be made good on all possible occasions, and for this Liverpool offers exceptional facilities as being the home port of the ships.

With the establishment of a northern base for the Squadron it may be found practicable to keep these eight ships away from Liverpool for

[1]McKeag, Ernest L., RNR, Midshipman 1915, interned in Norway 1915–1918, Sub-Lieutenant 1918, Lieutenant 1939.

longer intervals, but this will largely depend upon the resources of the new base and the suitability of the plant for coaling ships of this type.

112. *Diary of Dr J. Shaw*

Tuesday 20th July 1915. Heavy sea running so that I did not manage to get on deck. If it were not for our little game of football in the afternoon I think I would be feeling in rather a stale condition. Now that the novelty of this life is wearing off I am beginning to realise the dreadful monotony of it. I am very far from being surprised at the Jack Tar enjoying his [leave] not wisely but too well when he gets ashore. There are rumours of our being out for three months next time. Well, to keep myself from feeling depressed I will have to study as much as possible.

113. *Rear-Admiral Swarbacks Minn to Admiral, Longhope*

20 July 1915

Boom placed and Gate operating. Submit that vessels proceeding hither may be informed that Auxiliary Patrol Trawlers will lead them in. Two Armed Trawlers always at the entrance.

114. *Memorandum by Commander-in-Chief Home Fleets*

HMS *Iron Duke*, 25 July 1915

Orders for Armed Trawlers off the Norwegian Coast

The Armed Trawlers *Tenby Castle*, *Saxon*, *Rosa*, *Newland*, *Arley* and *Mafeking* whilst operating off the Norwegian Coast will be based on Lerwick, and will be under the orders of the Admiral Commanding Orkneys and Shetlands, when at the base.

2. ... It is expected that at least two trawlers, and possibly three, will be maintained on patrol.

***

4. On arrival at the rendezvous and whilst on patrol, the trawlers will be under the orders of the Senior Officer G Patrol who will arrange for a ship of that patrol to meet them at the rendezvous and give them the necessary patrol instructions.

***

8. When possible a ship of the Tenth Cruiser Squadron should be within 100 miles of the trawlers to act as a support.

115. *Orders for Trawlers off the Norwegian Coast*

25 July 1915

Information for Trawlers working off the Norwegian Coast.

The object of adding armed trawlers to the ships of the Tenth Cruiser Squadron on G Patrol is to intercept German and neutral ships carrying iron ore and trade south from Narvik ... .

The trade is difficult to intercept because of the facilities for making the greater part of the passage in Norwegian waters.

2. The patrol areas will be as follows: those lettered T are the trawler areas, and those lettered G are the Tenth Cruiser Squadron areas.

Area T 3. Off Husobarran (Latitude 67.42´N, Longitude 14 E) in West Fjord in such a position outside territorial waters as to intercept the South-bound shipping before passing behind Lande Gode Island.

Area T 2. Northwest of Bjoro Island, in Latitude 64.38´N, Longitude 10.40´E.

Area T 1. Off Standlandet.

G Patrols of the Tenth Cruiser Squadron will usually consist of two or three ships in one or more of the following patrol areas:

G 1. In the neighbourhood of Latitude 63.5´N, Longitude 6.40´E.

G 2. Off Lundo Island (Latitude 64.10´N, Longitude 9.30´E).

G 3. On the parallel of Latitude of 66.30´N, near Traen Island.

G 4. On the parallel of Latitude of 67.25´N between the meridian of Longitude 11.30´E and 13.30´E.

***

3. The three trawler areas selected are in locations where the shipping has to pass outside territorial waters.

4. The crews of the trawlers should endeavour to cultivate friendly relations with the crews of the local fishing craft; the success of the operations will depend largely on their positions and movements not being reported, and the local fishermen can give useful information of the tracks followed by the trade.

5. Attempts are not to be made in any circumstances to intercept shipping inside territorial waters.

116. *Admiralty to Rear-Admiral Commanding Tenth Cruiser Squadron*

26 July 1915

My Lords Commissioners of the Admiralty had under their consideration paragraph 10 of your submission of the 9th inst No. 150/35 [88] regarding the arrangements for using Swarbacks Minn as a Northern Base for the Tenth Cruiser Squadron. In reply I am to point out, with reference to your statement that a frozen meat ship will be required, that the Tenth Cruiser Squadron ships are victualled by the owners and it is understood that the vessels of the squadron will return periodically to Liverpool etc. to replenish. Moreover there is a fresh contract for the supply of meat at Lerwick. It is therefore not understood why a frozen meat ship is required, but if this is so, the question will be considered of arranging for one to be detailed from Scapa as necessary.

2. It is not considered that any Hospital Ship is required at Swarbacks Minn, as the Medical Officers on board each ship under your command can deal with the sick as has been done hitherto. A Medical Officer will be appointed to HMS *Gibraltar* and there is no objection to the sick bay being fitted up for local requirements.

3. Arrangements will also be made for the Hospital Carrier *Magic* from Scapa to visit the base from time to time as necessary, to vacate the sick from HMS *Gibraltar* that require Hospital treatment.

***

117. *Captain G.W. Vivian to Rear-Admiral Commanding Tenth Cruiser Squadron*

HMS *Patia*, 31 August 1915

Report of Proceedings, 26 July–31 August 1915

***

I arrived in Princes Dock, Glasgow at noon on the 26th and commenced coaling that afternoon, finishing the following evening. Such defects as I had, including the provision of extra accommodation for the increased number of stewards and firemen that I now carry, were taken in hand and completed by noon on August 2nd. I left Glasgow at 4 p.m. the same day and proceeded to rejoin the patrol, rounding Cantyre at midnight. On August 4th I met and communicated with your Flagship, and at 6.30 p.m. stopped and boarded the Auxiliary schooner *Fox II* from Ivigtut (Greenland) to Copenhagen with a cargo of cryolite. Sent in to Kirkwall with an Armed Guard.[1] At 6 a.m. on August 5th met the British steamer *Strathdee*, previously boarded. At 7.00 p.m. the same day stopped and boarded the Norwegian steamer *Drammensfjord* from Baltimore to Bergen with grain and coal. The captain of this ship sent me a written protest at being sent to Kirkwall for examination, owing as he said, to what had previously occurred to the *Cubano*. This did not convey much to me as I had no knowledge as to what had happened to that ship. Sent in to Kirkwall with an Armed Guard.[2] On the night of the 7th August Admiralty signalled that this ship need not be sent in, but it was unfortunately too late as far as we were concerned. On August 6th [*sic*: *recte* 8th] intercepted the Russian steamer *Ethelaida* from Barry to Archangel with coal. Told to proceed. On August 9th between two banks of fog sighted a steamer which after a good deal of trouble I eventually boarded in a thick fog. She was the Danish steamer *Botnia* for Iceland from Copenhagen with a general cargo, part of which consisted of 10,000 barrels of petroleum. Sent to Stornoway with an Armed Guard.[3] On Aug. 10 at 4 a.m. intercepted the Russian steamer *Betty* from Barry to Archangel with coal. Told to proceed. Communicated with *Mantua* during the forenoon and received from her two ratings. On Aug 11th it blew hard from the SE and was very thick and from that date to the 17th continual fog and mist of varying intensity was experienced. Occasionally it was very thick but more generally it was patchy with some clearings but visibility was always small. During this period one ship was seen or rather heard, for on the 14th we heard and eventually closed the British steamer *Lovaine* from Manchester to Archangel in ballast. On the 17th, in accordance with your orders I directed *Mantua*, *Patuca* and *Ambrose* to meet me at a rendezvous at 6 a.m. to get Armed Guards from *Ambrose* coming from Swarbacks Minn. Weather was again thick and no sights had been obtained for some time. On reaching the rendezvous by D.R. at 6 a.m. I could find nobody, but shortly afterwards I picked up *Patuca* and then *Mantua*. *Ambrose* could not be found and seemed by her W/T to be still some way distance. During the morning the fog cleared somewhat, becoming more patchy, and the three ships were spread to search for *Ambrose*. At 11.30 *Ambrose*, who had had fog most of her way was found and the Armed Guards were transferred. I left A Patrol that afternoon in accordance with your orders to patrol further South. At 8

[1] *Fox II* was not detained.
[2] See page 188, note 1. The *Cubano* had been sunk in June near the Flannan Islands.
[3] See page 214, note 2.

p.m. intercepted the Russian steamer *Burevestnik* flying the previously boarded flag. On 18th August I passed a mark-buoy which may have been a fisherman's mark-buoy, wreckage possibly from *Ceylon*.[1] At 1 p.m. intercepted and boarded the American oil-tank *Platuria* from Philadelphia to Copenhagen with 5000 tons of petroleum. Sent in to Kirkwall with an Armed Guard.[2] On the 20th and 21st we had a fairly hard blow from the NW. On the 22nd intercepted the Danish sailing-ship *Laurets* from Fowey to Helsingborg with china-clay. Told to proceed. On the 24th at 10 a.m. intercepted and boarded the Swedish steamer *St Andrew* from Baltimore to Goteborg with a cargo of steam-coal. Sent to Kirkwall with an Armed Guard.[3] On Aug. 25th intercepted and boarded the Norwegian steamer *Songa* from San Nicholas (Argentina) to Helsingborg or Malmo with a cargo of Indian corn. Both in the case of this ship and the *St Andrew*, the captains requested to go to Stornoway and not to Kirkwall. The captain of the *St Andrew* said he had no charts to go to Kirkwall and therefore must go to Stornoway, but I put that right by giving the Armed Guard Officer the necessary charts, which did not please the captain at all. The captain of the *Songa* said he had not enough coal to go to Kirkwall and as I had no means of verifying this without holding the ship up for some time I eventually sent him in to Stornoway with an Armed Guard. This marked preference for Stornoway seems rather curious, possibly the Customs examination is not so searching as at Kirkwall.[4] From Aug. 26th to 28th we had strong NW winds with thick misty weather and very poor visibility. On Aug. 28th intercepted the Aberdeen trawler *John Boyle* from Stornoway to the Rockall Banks. Told to proceed. On Aug 29th I met and communicated with *Changuinola* receiving from her one of my Armed Guards. On Aug. 31st I was relieved on my patrol by *Mantua* and left for the Clyde in accordance with my orders.

During this patrol the average daily coal consumption has been reduced somewhat and the ship has consequently been able to keep the sea for a longer period. This was partly due to our having cruised at

[1]No record of the sinking of the *Ceylon* is known.

[2]The Customs at Kirkwall were told by the Contraband Committee to detain *Platuria*. A sister ship, *Wico*, had been taken into Swinemunde by the German Baltic patrols, where some of the cargo had been discharged. The Committee clearly felt that such ships were being intercepted by the German patrol by collusion, and that the Scandinavian destination was a blind. In fact *Wico* had discharged part of her cargo only in order to make repairs and the full cargo was eventually delivered to Sweden. *Platuria* was allowed to go ahead on 27 August (TS 14/4 of 21 and 27 August 1915).

[3]*St Andrew* was allowed to proceed at once (TS 14/4 of 26 August 1915).

[4]*Songa* was not detained.

various times at a reduced speed owing to thick weather, partly to the better quality of the coal, but mainly to the improved efficiency of the Engines and the Engine-Room department generally. We are now able to maintain in moderate weather a speed of 11 knots on 33 tons of coal daily and of 12 knots on 45 tons. After that consumption rises as we are getting near our full-power, 13 knots means 57 tons, 14 knots 67 tons, and 15 knots which is practically our full speed, 78 tons daily. For a ship of this displacement these figures seem low and they would of course be lower at the slower speeds if we had not always got steam for full speed ready.

With reference to my remarks in my last letter of proceedings relative to Armed guards sent in to Stornoway in ships: on Aug. 9th I sent in a steamer to Stornoway. The Armed Guard in that ship rejoined us on Aug. 29th more by good luck than anything else as we happened to meet the *Changuinola* with this Guard on board. The Guard had been at Glasgow since Aug. 13th.

During this patrol, that is from Aug. 2nd to Sept. 1st, the following ships were intercepted (not including trawlers). 11 steamers of which 2 were British, 3 were Russian and 6 were sent in with Armed Guards. 1 Sailing ship from a British Port.

The health of the ship's company has not been as satisfactory as I could have wished, and the sick-list has been rather high. We had one case of scarlet fever early in the trip which did not spread, and we had four bad cases of ptomaine poisoning, all of which have now recovered. I passed Cantyre at 9 p.m. on August 31st and arrived in the Clyde at 3 a.m. on Sept 1st.

118. *Lieutenant Percy P. Crawford RNR to Rear-Admiral HMS* Cyclops*, Scapa Flow*

Thurso, 29 July 1915

I beg to report that at 4 a.m. on the 27th July in Lat. 62.41´N, Long. 13.31´W, I was instructed by Captain H. Edwards, RN of HMS *Hildebrand* to take the Norwegian SS *Trondjemsfjord* to Kirkwall, stated by the Master to have a cargo of Grain, Coke, Cases of Machinery, Automobiles and Cases of Sulphuric Acid.

2. The Master (Bang) set course S 44° E (Mag). On July 28th at 0.53 a.m. Munken Light was abeam, distant 11 miles, altered course SE by E ½ E (Mag). At 0.25 p.m. on the same day a Submarine abaft the port beam fired a shot over the bow within a few feet. At once the master altered course to the Southward to bring her astern and ordered Chief

Engineer to give all steam possible. After steaming for about half-an-hour, the Submarine fired a second shot, which appeared to pass under the ship. The Master then stopped as we were being overhauled very quickly and it being quite impossible to ram her. The submarine then came within hailing distance and ordered the master to go aboard with ship's papers, and whilst he was away he signalled to us to abandon ship immediately. At 1.25 p.m. boats were all clear of ship and submarine fired a torpedo amidships from a distance of about 130 yards. Ship listed heavily to port and sunk at 2.51 p.m.

3. The Submarine towed crew and armed guard for about 4 miles South to a Norwegian barque (*Glance*) bound from Norway to New York, and ordered the master to take us aboard. The submarine then steamed alongside the *Trondjemsfjord* for about 10 minutes, standing by until she sank, and then steamed away at full speed in a South-easterly direction.

The submarine was of the latest type, being about 200 feet long with two masts, a 12 pounder gun forward and a six pounder aft; number painted out and hull grey. Her Commander was a young man, and treated the Master of the Norwegian steamer with all courtesy. He explained that his chief reason for sinking the ship was that she was an English steamer bought over since hostilities commenced. Our position when submarine was sighted was Lat. 61.3´N, Long. 3.42´W by D.R., our course still being SE by E 1/2 E Mag. At 9 p.m. the Master of the barque *Glance* shaped a course for Sule Skerry, which was passed on the port hand about 9 miles at 2 a.m. on the 29th. Then steered close-hauled on starboard tack to try and make Cape Wrath, the wind then being westerly, force 2/3, ship doing about 3 knots and setting fast to the Eastward.

At 1 p.m. on the 29th July Swedish steamer *Orlando* in ballast came alongside bound for Sweden, and took crew and armed guard on board and steered to pass through Pentland Firth. At 3.30 p.m. Trawler *Princess Juliana* came off and armed guard boarded her and put into Thurso.

Until trawler *Princess Juliana* was sighted off Dunnet Head no patrol vessel of any kind was sighted during the whole of the passage.

Whilst in conversation with the Master of barque *Glance* he informed me that on July 26th in Latitude 59 1/2 N, Long. 0 a submarine passed under his stern, but made no signal. She was steering in a North-easterly direction.

I would like to report on the very exemplary manner in which the master of the steamer *Trondjemsfjord* behaved throughout. As soon as the submarine was sighted he ordered that the guard should be rigged out in the crews' clothes, and giving me one of his own uniforms in order to disguise us; stowing rifles away in the fore peak. On my advice instead of stopping after the first shot was fired, he continued at full speed to try and escape, and not until we saw how useless it was, did he stop. Had it not been for his wife being on board I firmly believe that he would have tried to ram her.

Whilst on the submarine he denied that he had an armed guard on board, or that he had been boarded by a British patrol vessel. As he was only on the ship for about three minutes after returning from the submarine, he had no time to save any of his effects and instruments, except for a few things his wife packed.

I am enclosing his address, so that you can take any action you may think necessary for his splendid behaviour. Also a list of the value of clothing lost by crew of the vessel.

The Master and crew of *Trondjemsfjord* remained in SS *Orlando* bound for Sweden, and from there will proceed to Norway.

119. *Admiral S.C. Colville to Commander-in-Chief Home Fleet*

HMS *Cyclops*, 1 August 1915

... I concur in the proposal to use drifters in lieu of tugs as Harbour Service Vessels and also in paragraphs 2 and 3 of the Admiralty Letter. There are, however, great difficulties in procuring drifters, none have been obtained for the Kirkwall Examination Service although enquiries have been made at Ports for a fortnight.

2. As regards the staff required the details given in my letter 16/530A of 25th June [102] still hold good namely:

Naval Examination Staff –
1 Commander (Retired) (must be junior to Commander Alston – a Lieut Commander would do).
1 German Interpreter.
1 Scandinavian interpreter.
1 Assistant Paymaster RNR
messengers, guards etc. to be provided by Shetlands RNR

3. The present Customs House Staff consists of one Surveyor, six Officers and three Preventive Officers. Another Civil Service Officer (Assistant Surveyor) will probably be required.

4. There are Consuls for Denmark, Sweden and Norway but none for the United States.[1]

120. *Andrew Johnsen*[2] *to Under Secretary of State for Foreign Affairs*

Hotel Metropole, London, 2 August 1915

On the 30th of July the tragic news of the loss of our steamer *Trondhjemsfjord* reached London [118]. It was reported that she had been sunk by a submarine on the 28th on 61.30´ north latitude and 3.48´west longitude. I immediately submitted this information to my home office and got last night the following reply:

'Your news regarding *Trondhjemsfjord* extremely lamentable. How has the communication reached you and have you any intimation as to where crew will be landed[?]. Have you ascertained whether steamer was under command of British prize-crew and on way to Kirkwall[?]. In view of what has happened and which is only what we have anticipated all along you must strongly appeal to the Government that they will now be pleased to instruct their patrols not to divert our steamers any more. The system we have established being an evident proof of our cargoes' innocent character and destination. We maintain that British interests are in no way better safe-guarded by the taking of our steamers into British port than were they left to proceed on their voyage. Norwegian Americaline.'

and also this morning the following:

'Captain Bang and crew arrived here tonight after being landed Helsingborg this morning from Swedish steamer *Orlando*. Captain reports *Trondhjemsfjord* had been captured by His Majesty's Cruiser *Hildebrand* and ordered proceed Kirkwall under command of prize-crew. By thus diverting steamer out of her safe course she has been left to the mercy of German submarine. We ask you to bring this to the knowledge of the British Government and to repeat our previous earnest appeal of this morning. Norwegian Americaline'.

which I hasten to bring to His Britannic Majesty's Government's knowledge, and referring to the above expressions and my previous applications I most earnestly and respectfully again beg to request that His Britannic Majesty's Government will dispense with the present system of bringing all our steamers in to British ports for examination.

Judging from the informations now at hand with regard to the

[1]This was agreed by the Commander-in-Chief by letter to the Admiralty next day.
[2]Andrew Johnsen was the agent for the Norwegian–America line in London.

disaster of SS *Trondhjemsfjord* it must be assumed that the sinking of the vessel is only a consequence of the act of bringing her out of her course under command of British prize-crew, and the same may happen any time to our other vessels if facilities are not being granted.

Taking into consideration the experience of the last 3 months I beg to ask whether The Norwegian Americaline is to be blamed for any action contrary to His Britannic Majesty's Government's desires respecting the carrying of passengers or cargo, which should make it necessary to strictly maintain the bringing up of our vessels?

If anything to complain of what is then the gain compared with the loss of time, large expenses and the great risk of diverting the vessels from their safe course, which we with the consent of the Norwegian Government's underwriters prefer to sail in order to avoid the German submarines.

And what would be the loss to His Britannic Majesty's Government, if the steamers were permitted to proceed directly with the understanding, that we consider the Norwegian port of destination equal to a British port of inspection[?].

Can we do anything further to establish full confidence?

Would it facilitate matters if we undertake to collect guarantees for every item carried by our steamers?

I am very anxious to have the question dealt with immediately, as SS *Bergensfjord* now may be in the dangerous waters and SS *Drammensfjord*, which left Baltimore for Bergen on the 22nd ultimo, is not far away.

After what has happened I have still not relinquished the hope that His Britannic Majesty's Government will consider the question carefully and arrive at a satisfactory decision.

Accidents of this nature create ill feelings, not only amongst the 6,000 shareholders of our company (of which about 4,000 Americans) but I dare say the whole nation. On the other side I am sure that any reasonable regard for the interests of a neutral country will be duly appreciated.

121. *Commander-in-Chief Home Fleets to Admiralty*

HMS *Iron Duke*, 3 August 1915

Be pleased to acquaint the Lords Commissioners of the Admiralty that on examination of the blue book (Cd.7698) 'Annual Statement of the Trade of the United Kingdom 1914', Vol. I, it is seen that the decrease in the amount of cotton re-exported to Germany during 1914 compared with that exported in 1913 (35,886 centals decrease) is considerably more than counterbalanced by the increase in the quantity exported to neighbouring neutral countries (Norway 27,451 centals increase, Netherlands 50,451 centals increase). It is further understood that the exports of cotton to Holland, Denmark, Norway and Sweden have increased to a still more remarkable degree during 1915 and it is considered that the presumptive evidence is conclusive that most of the cotton in excess of the normal consumption of that article by the countries in question has an enemy destination.

2. In confirmation of this an extract from an enclosure in Admiralty letter N.L. 14786 of 11 June 1915 may be quoted: 'if goods in transit from the American continents to Germany, carried in vessels bound to Norway, are allowed to pass without confiscation before reaching Norway, there would appear to be little or no prospect of stopping them later, as they are not affected by the Norwegian export prohibitions, and can be sent on by land if danger is apprehended on the sea route to Germany.' It cannot be doubted that the same remarks are applicable to goods carried in vessels bound to Goteborg, Malmo, Copenhagen, and other neutral ports adjoining Germany. The profits on the trade are so great that it is reported that the shippers arrange in certain cases to get their ships captured by the Germans when off Malmo, so as to avoid passing their cargoes through neutral countries (see letter dated 22 April addressed by a Boarding Officer of HMS *Patuca* to the commanding officer of that ship, which was forwarded to the Admiralty through the Rear Admiral Commanding, Tenth Cruiser Squadron) ...[1]

3. As their Lordships are aware, during the recent season ship after ship laden with cotton from America, consigned to Goteborg and other neutral ports near Germany, was intercepted by the Tenth Cruiser Squadron, brought into Kirkwall, examined and allowed to proceed. As a consequence the Germans today are reported to be well provided with cotton. It is earnestly submitted that this policy may be modified during the coming season. It is in our power at this time of the year, at least as far as ships which pass through the North Sea are concerned, 'to prevent commodities of any kind from reaching or leaving Germany', as provided in the terms of the Order in Council of 11 March 1915, and I urge that we may be allowed to do so. The matter directly concerns the fleet, as cotton is believed to be indispensable to the manufacture of the explosives used by the Germans.[2]

[1]Not located; see also page 235, note 2.

[2]'Raw cotton, cotton tenters, cotton waste, and cotton yarns' were declared absolute contraband by Order-in-Council on 20 August 1915.

4. The matter is most urgent, because during the coming winter neutral ships carrying contraband cannot be intercepted with the same certainty as in the summer, or even to so great an extent as was done during last winter, since the increase in the number and size of the German submarines has driven the Tenth Cruiser Squadron patrols west of the longitude 11 W, whereas last winter they were able to work in comparatively sheltered waters.

5. It is rarely practicable to board ships in the Atlantic in winter and the cruiser must therefore accompany the ship to be examined into the submarine danger area in order to board her and she can be attacked with ease by the submarines waiting under the shelter of Faroes, Orkneys, Shetlands or Western Hebrides. The 18-hour winter nights north of Faroe also render evasion easy.

6. An energetic and effective control of the neutral shipping is therefore most desirable in the short period of fine weather and long days which remains.

7. An abstract is annexed of the ships which arrived at Kirkwall and Lerwick for examination between 30 May and 10 July, from which it is seen that only 13% of these vessels were sent south for further examination. I am not aware of the final disposal of the 13%, but it is probable that many of them were allowed to proceed to their destinations.

8. Taking all things into consideration, I am forced to the conclusion that it is doubtful whether the work of the Tenth Cruiser Squadron, and the heavy cost of its upkeep, is producing any effect other than slight inconvenience in Germany.

Abstract of vessels sent into Kirkwall for examination
30 May to 10 July, 1915

A

Total number sent in – 125 (including 16 fishing vessels)

Nationalities

Norwegian	35	
Danish	37	
Swedish	29	(including 1 fishing vessel)
American	9	
Dutch	15	(all fishing vessels)
TOTAL	125	(including 16 fishing vessels).

B

Number sent on for further examination – 17

Nationalities

Norwegian	7
Swedish	5
Danish	3
American	2
TOTAL	17

C

Cargoes of 'B'

General	6
Foodstuffs (Miscellaneous)	1
Maize	1
Coffee and Bran	1
Resin, Cotton and Oil	1
Cotton Grain and Cotton Seed Cake	1
Cotton Seed Cake	1
Barley and Linseed Cake	1
Cocoanut cake and earthnut cake	1
Iron Ore	1
Agricultural Machinery	1
Quebracho	1
TOTAL	17

Abstract of vessels sent into Lerwick for examination

30 May to 10 July, 1915

A

Number sent in – 23 (including 11 fishing vessels)

Nationalities

Norwegian	4	
Danish	2	
Swedish	6	
Dutch	11	(fishing vessels)
TOTAL	23	(including 11 fishing vessels)

B

Number sent on for further examination – Nil.

122. *Commander-in-Chief Home Fleets to Admiralty*

HMS *Iron Duke*, 4 August 1915

Be pleased to lay the following remarks before the Lords Commissioners of the Admiralty in regard to Danish shipping intercepted by the Tenth Cruiser Squadron.

Period (1915)	
7 Mch–19 Apl	33 per cent of the vessels* intercepted were Danes.
19 Apl–30 May	28 per cent ..do..
30 May–8 July	32 per cent ..do..
7 Mch–19 Apl	29 per cent of the vessels* of all nationalities intercepted were to or from Danish ports.
19 Apl–30 May	22 per cent ..do..
30 May–8 July	20 per cent ..do..

* Exclusive of fishing vessels

2. In this connection it is of interest to note that Danish shipping companies have done so well during the War that their shares have risen enormously. According to well recognised Copenhagen financial journals, between July 1914, and 25th May 1915, an average rise of 54.7 per cent took place in the shares of sixteen such companies with an aggregate capital of eighty-nine million kroner.

3. This increase in Danish carrying trade must be made up as follows:

(a) Fresh trade between other neutral countries carried in Danish bottoms;
(b) Fresh trade between other countries and Denmark. The destination or origin of this trade is probably Germany.

4. In these circumstances it is submitted that, as soon as Denmark has received her normal imports, an enemy destination, under the Order-in-Council of 11th March, 1915, may be presumed for all further goods, consigned to Denmark, which may be found on board vessels sent in for examination by the Tenth Cruiser Squadron.

123. *Graeme Thomson,*[1] *Director of Transports, to Commanding Officer HMS* Cedric

Admiralty, 4 August 1915

I have to acquaint you that consideration is being given to the question of standardisation of the rates for Mercantile Ratings in vessels belonging to the Tenth Cruiser Squadron, and in this connection I shall be glad if you will furnish me with a statement showing the rates now being paid for each Rating, and if any ratings performing similar duties are receiving different rates of pay, the number paid at each different rate.

124. *Sir Eyre Crowe, Under-Secretary of State for Foreign Affairs to the Secretary of the Admiralty*

Foreign Office, 4 August 1915

I am directed by Secretary Sir E. Grey[2] to transmit to you herewith, for the consideration of the Lords Commissioners of the Admiralty, a copy of a letter dated August 2nd from Mr Johnsen, relative to the sinking of the Norwegian America Line's SS *Trondhjemsfjord* [120].

Sir E. Grey would be glad to receive such observations as their Lordships may be able to offer on this letter, and he would suggest that, if their Lordships see no objection the SSs *Bergensfjord* and *Drammensfjord* need not be brought in on this voyage.

125. *Admiralty Minute by Director of Trade Division*

8 August 1915

This vessel [*Trondhjemsfjord*] was sunk presumably on account of change of flag [120, 124]. A telegram from H.B.M. Minister, Christiania ... contains the following: 'The German Captain (of submarine) stated that he had orders to sink the vessel on account of her transfer from British to Norwegian flag during the war'.

[1]Thompson, Graeme, GCB, GCMG, CB (1875–1953), Director of Transports 1914, Director of Shipping for Admiralty and Ministry of Shipping 1917–1919, Colonial Secretary Ceylon 1919–1922, Governor of British Guiana 1922–1925, Governor of Nigeria 1925–1931, Governor of Ceylon 1931–1933.

[2]Grey, Sir Edward, Bt, KG, PC, MP (1862–1933); MP 1885–1916, Under Secretary for Foreign Affairs 1892–1895, Secretary of State for Foreign Affairs 1905–1916, Ambassador to USA, 1919, Viscount Grey of Fallodon.

The *Drammensfjord* has been similarly transferred. Neutrals who purchase ships from a belligerent do so well knowing that the other belligerent may refuse to recognise the transfer of flag (Declaration of London, Art. 55 & 56). In the case of these two ships the transfer is a valid one, at least it is probable that most Prize Courts would so hold, but the validity should be tested in a Prize Court. If Germany acts contrary to international usage, it is for the Norwegian Government to protect the rights of its own nationals.

It appears that even if no prize crew or armed guard had been put on board of the vessel, and the submarine could not have known that such a guard was on board, she would still have been destroyed in accordance with the orders of the German Government, therefore no route the vessel might take could be described as safe. The *Drammensfjord* will, in all probability, meet a similar fate, armed guard or not. If vessels are to be given free passage through the patrols, some drastic means must be devised of ensuring that they do not carry contraband. Treating a Norwegian port as a British port for inspection would be derogatory to the sovereign rights of Norway, and would scarcely be recognised by that country, and in any case cargo arrived at its destination would be claimed by the consignee, subject to any definite stipulation to the contrary in the bill of lading.

While the above expresses the opinion of the Trade Division on the general question, in deference to the urgent representations of the Foreign Office, a telegram was sent to the patrols stating that *Drammensfjord* should not be brought in. This telegram sent within an hour of the receipt of Foreign Office letter was not in time to have the desired effect, and the *Drammensfjord* had been already detained and is proceeding to Kirkwall where, as she is already in the war zone, she will be examined in accordance with the usual procedures.[1]

[1]The sinking of the *Trondhjemsfjord*, though the DTD does not say so, is in direct contrast with British practice, as evidenced in the treatment of the former German oil tankers bought by Standard Oil in the USA, where the transfer was accepted. The difference was, of course, a consequence of using submarines rather than surface craft, and a result of the involvement or not of the United States: 'rights' and 'morals' did not enter the issue.

126. *Commander F.H. Walter to Rear-Admiral Commanding Tenth Cruiser Squadron*

HMS *Victorian*, 29 September 1915

Report of Proceedings, 12 August–24 September 1915

1. Ship arrived at base at 8.30 p.m. 12th August, and docked at midnight.

2. Ship undocked at 4 p.m. on 20th ult., and proceeded to patrol with 4242 tons of coal on board and a mean draught of 30ft 10ins, being 18ins down by the bow.

3. Ship rolled heavily (23 degrees) considering the very moderate beam sea, and Port 2 and Starboard 2 guns could not have been fought owing to constant washing down; their height above water being 11 feet.

4. On 22nd ult. communicated with *Orcoma*.

On 25th ult. communicated with *Hilary*.

On 28th ult. communicated with *Mantua*.

On 31st ult. carried out submarine calibre firing from all 6 in. guns.

5. On 1st September communicated with *Arlanza*.

On 9th September communicated with *Alcantara* in dense fog.

On 11th inst met *Otway*. Stopped engines for three hours to repair leaking joints.

6. On Thursday 16th inst left Patrol for Swarbacks Minn, passing north of Faroes and communicated with *Virginian* en route at 10.30 a.m. on 17th.

7. On 18th inst at 6 a.m. anchored at Swarbacks Minn, and Colliers *Dalewood* and *Tournelly* came alongside. 1001 [tons] were received in 30 hours, only one hold being used at first and two hoists. This will be improved in future. Trimming caused much delay.

8. All boats were lowered and Boys etc. were away constantly for sailing and rowing instruction. Many Boys were found who could not row at all.

9. The Rear-Admiral Swarbacks Minn visited ship at 8 a.m. on Thursday 24th inst, and dirty and foggy weather was experienced.

10. Number of Trawlers intercepted since 20.8.15...........10
Number of ships intercepted since 20.8.15...................9
Total number intercepted 19
Ships sent in with Armed Guard..............................Nill

A good deal of foggy and misty weather was experienced.

Ship arrived at Mersey at 7.15 p.m. on 30th September.

127. *Minute by Captain Richard Webb, Director of Trade Division*

13 August 1915

The C.-in-C.'s figures deal only with re-exports from the United Kingdom [121].

The total import figures for the neutral countries are still more striking. The following are supplied by the War Trade Department, who have gone very closely into the matter.

	Imports 6 mos. ending June 1915 Tons	Normal Imports 6 Months Tons
Norway	17,450	1,932
Sweden	116,748	11,796
Denmark	17,925	3,234
Holland	107,520	53,640
	259,643	70,602

Suggest that a copy of C.-in-C.'s letter be sent to the Foreign Office, who now, through the Contraband Committee and Enemy Exports Committee, directly control the disposal of ships and cargoes sent in by vessels of the 10th Cruiser Squadron.

128. *Diary of Dr J. Shaw*

Tuesday, 17 August [1915]. We are meeting quite a number of ships, among them two Russians, who dipped to us out of courtesy. I am taking a watch for intercepted signals. We steer a circle round the ships we board now so as to give submariners as little chance as possible. Sometimes we go to general quarters in fact and train all the guns on the ship we are boarding in case she is a German in disguise supplied with torpedo tubes.

129. *Commander W.G.A. Kennedy, RN*[1] *to Lords Commissioners of Admiralty*

through HM Minister, Christiania, 20 August 1915

It is with extreme regret that I have to report the loss by sinking of HMS

[1]Kennedy, William G.A., RN (1873–1938), Lieutenant 1896, Commander 1907, Captain of *India* 1915, interned in Norway 1915–1918, Captain (retired) 1921.

India, which event took place on Sunday the 8th day of August 1915 at about 5.42 p.m. GMT and was caused by being struck by a torpedo fired from a submarine in the Vest Fjord, off the Norwegian coast at approximately 6 to 7 miles WNW true from Heligver Light under the following circumstances:

Whilst on patrol on the parallel of 67.30´N and between 11.30´E and 13.30´E, a Swedish ship the SS *Gloria* was sighted to the northward accompanied by HM Armed Trawlers *Saxon* and *Newland*, the *India*'s course was altered to meet them and after a most thorough search lasting about one and a half hours she was allowed to proceed at about 10 a.m. and a report by W/T made to the Senior Officer on patrol in HMS *Virginian*. Course was then altered to the Southward speed 14 knots and zigzagging and at about 11 a.m. another ship was sighted making for Taen Island and as she was inside the three-mile limit, I closed her and followed her to the Northward to identify her. She proved to be the Swedish SS *Gotaland*. This had taken the *India* several miles north of her patrol line into the Vest Fiord again. Course was then altered for the patrol line again and at *about 12 o'clock* noon an urgent W/T message was received from HMS *Virginian* ordering me to send the Swedish SS *Gloria* in to Kirkwall. I accordingly altered course so as to steer for the centre of the Vest Fjord and increased speed to 16½ knots with the hope of possibly intercepting her (she was bound to Kirknaes) and at 2 p.m. when North of Husan Baran Islands as nothing could be seen of her, I shaped course to the Southward and steered for the centre of the patrol line speed 14 knots and zigzagging. At about 3 p.m. a steamer was observed inshore just to the northward of Taen Island. Course was altered to intercept her and at about 4 p.m. I came up with her. She was then just north of Heligvaer Light and just inside the three mile limit. I steamed past her and signalled her. She answered that she was the SS *Hillhouse* from South Shields to Arkhangel in ballast and she hoisted the red ensign. She had no name visible anywhere and I considered her very suspicious but could not interfere with her (in view of subsequent events I am of opinion that she was the mother ship and decoy of the submarine). She was a large steamer capable of carrying about 6000 tons of cargo. She was painted black, had one black funnel and two black masts and her inboard upperworks were a dirty yellow colour and the master was wearing a white coat and white peak cap. Smoke was then sighted to the NNW and course was shaped for it. This proved to be HM Armed Trawler *Saxon*. I signalled her and then altered course back to the centre of the patrol line and very shortly afterwards a steamer was reported to the SE and making towards Taen Island so I again altered course so as to try and intercept her. I then left the bridge and went to the W/T house to enquire into a signal they had received FTP to CQ and gave orders that it was not to be answered. I then went down to the hurricane deck (the next deck) and within a very few minutes the 'alarm gongs' sounded. I ran to the bridge and saw the track of a torpedo approaching the ship from an angle of about 30 degrees on the starboard bow. I called out 'Full speed ahead' and 'Hard a-port' and turned and watched the track of the torpedo. I at first thought that the torpedo had gone under the ship as the track of the torpedo reached the ship before the explosion. The torpedo hit the ship right aft between the after companion way and the after gun the starboard side. The ship at once commenced to settle by the stern listing slightly to *port* as she did so. I gave the order to 'abandon ship', the following boats which were kept out were all lowered, the starboard boats were not put into the water, the port boats were lowered into the water.

Starboard	1st cutter (28 ft. service cutter)
	1st lifeboat Ships boats
	3rd " " "
	1st whaler " "
Port	2nd cutter (28 ft. service cutter)
	2nd lifeboat Ships boat
	2nd whaler " "

These boats were all fully manned except the 2nd whaler. There was still a great deal of way on the ship, the 2nd cutter and 2nd whaler got away from the ship, the 2nd lifeboat capsized, the starboard boats were hopelessly thrown into confusion owing to the 1st lifeboat's foremost fall freeing itself and thereby causing her to swing round and foul the 3rd lifeboat and 1st whaler. The 1st cutter it is believed was stove in against the ship's side whilst being lowered, and I very much regret that all the efforts which were made to save life by means of the boats actually caused the great loss of life. Of the number saved, 189 officers and men, 19 officers and 138 men all either dived or went down with the ship. The efforts to get the life rafts out were unavailing, as time did not permit. The ship sank in between 3 and 5 minutes after the explosion. The stern settled rapidly into the water and then appeared to break off and the ship plunged down suddenly stern first. I myself went down with the ship clinging to the foremost davit port side and eventually floated up amongst the wreckage. Before concluding this portion of the report, I wish to place on record my admiration at the magnificent behaviour of the officers and men, as notwithstanding the appalling swiftness of the catastrophe, the most perfect discipline prevailed until the end, and I would like to particularly mention the names of Lieut. Richard G. Groundwater RNR,[1] Acting Lieut. Biggs RNR[2] and Chief Gunner Charles G. Byrne RN. Their work in lowering the boats, endeavouring to get the liferafts out, and in serving out extra liferafts, was beyond all praise, and also the name of Senior Engineer C.W. Nelson RNR (temp),[3] who only left the engineroom as the water swept over the foot plates. This concludes the report so far as the loss of HMS *India* is concerned.

I would respectfully submit that Lieutenant Groundwater RNR, who was saved by a boat from the SS *Gotaland* be asked to furnish a report on the work of rescue performed by the officers and crew of that ship, and that Sub-Lieut. Sidney RNR[4] of HM Armed Trawler *Saxon* should likewise report on the rescue work of his officers and crew. I enclose a copy of a report from Sub-Lieut. E.W. Alltree, RNR,[5] who was the officer of the watch at the time and who was in charge of the 2nd cutter at Heligvar.

For myself I can only state that everything that it was possible for men to do was done by the Captain, Officers and Crew of the *Saxon*; everything they had was placed at our disposal, and I am sure that at least half their belongings were given away to clothe the officers and men.

After I had been taken on board the *Saxon* and as no more could be seen, I directed Mr Sidney to follow the SS *Gotaland* to Narvik and told him to take a pilot who came alongside. My reason for deciding to go to Narvik was to avoid the submarine following us if I went South and made for the *Virginian*.

On arrival at Narvik about 9 a.m. Monday morning we were met by the Norwegian police authorities and by Mr. J.N. Aagaard, HM Vice Consul,[6] when everything possible was done to assist us, medical assistance was sent from the shore and food and clothing was sent on board both ships as soon as possible. The *Saxon* was put alongside the *Gotaland* to receive the 4 bodies, and then she was moored alongside the jetty and a shed put at our disposal for a mortuary for the eleven dead. They were then taken charge of by the authorities.

[1]Groundwater, Richard G., RD, RNR, Lieutenant 1908, interned in Norway from 1915, Lieutenant-Commander 1916.

[2]Biggs, John H., RNR, Sub-Lieutenant 1913, Acting Lieutenant 1915, interned in Norway from September 1915.

[3]Nelson, Charles W., RNR, Engineer Lieutenant-Commander 1915, interned in Norway from 1915.

[4]Sidney, William H., RNR, Sub-Lieutenant 1915.

[5]Alltree, Ernest W., RNR, Sub-Lieutenant 1913, interned in Norway from September 1915, Acting Lieutenant 1919.

[6]Aagaard, Johannes Nikolai, British Vice Consul at Narvik from 1914.

The Officers and men on the SS *Gotaland* were taken under escort to an interment camp at Bjerkvik at 4 p.m. the same day, and we in the *Saxon* were told that we had to remain on board until it was decided whether we had to be interned and at about 9 p.m. Captain E. Einang of the Royal Norwegian Navy informed me that the Officers and men of the *Saxon* belonging to the *India* were to go to the camp that night. I had previously protested against the internment. At about 11 p.m. Capt. Einang asked me to speak to him on shore when we were already in the Norwegian government Vessel *Michael Sars*. He then informed me that if I decided to, I could take the *Saxon* to sea with all she had saved, I then most reluctantly decided that, as there was no accommodation, no food and that everyone was worn out, we had better go to the camp where we arrived at 3 a.m. on Tuesday morning and remained there till Saturday 24th 7 p.m. when the Officers and men saved by the *Saxon* and by the ship's boats were transferred to the present Internment Camp at Jorstadmoen, Faaborg, nr. Lillehammar.

The funeral of the Officers and men who died on board the *Saxon* and *Gotaland* and from the hospital at Narvik, took place on Thursday afternoon, they were buried at the cemetery at Narvik with full military honours, the funeral being attended by all the authorities, Military, Naval and Civil, Mr Gainer[1] and Mr J. Aagaard, HM Consuls. I was represented by Lieut. R. Groundwater RNR (I was laid up with a bad ankle the result of a blow in the water) and a party of the Officers and men from the camp also attended. The funeral was most impressive, the coffins were covered with flowers, evergreens and wreaths sent by districts who all attended to show their sympathy.

I attach lists showing – (1) the officers and men saved by the *Saxon* and ship's boats, (2) the Officers and men saved by the Swedish SS *Gotaland*, (3) the Officers and men buried at Narvik and Bodo, (4) the Officers and men missing, (5) men absent on sailing. Also Sub-Lieut E.W. Alltree RNR report [130].

By the courtesy of the Norwegian Government I have been allowed to send this report to HM Legation without being censored.

[1]Gainer, Donald St Clair, CBE, KCMG (1891–1966), British Vice-Consul in Norway, 1915–1922, at Narvik, Vardo, Christiansand, Tromso, Bergen and Hamar, Chargé d'Affaires Havana 1923 and 1924, Acting Consul General Rotterdam 1925, Vice-Consul Munich 1926–1929, Consul Breslau 1929, Consul General Mexico 1931–1932, Bavaria 1932–1938, Austria 1938–1939, Minister to Venezuela 1939–1944 (finally as Ambassador), Ambassador to Brazil 1944–1947, Ambassador to Poland 1947–1950, Under Secretary of State at the Foreign Office 1950–1951, retired 1951, Chief Executive International Road Federation (London branch) 1951–1957.

130. *Sub-Lieutenant E.W. Alltree RNR to Commander W.G.A. Kennedy RN*

[no date, but about 19 August 1915]

On Aug. 8th at 5.40 pm the ship was steaming at 58 revolutions 14 knots, heading SSW to head off Swedish steamer. Lookout on foc'sle reported 'submarine on starboard bow'. Looking in the direction indicated I saw track of torpedo about 300 yds distant, at the same time Commander Kennedy ran on to the bridge and ordered 'Hard a port' 'Full speed ahead' which orders were immediately carried out by the Navigator and myself. I also sounded war alarm. Torpedo struck the ship in my opinion below No. 3 gun starboard. Orders were given by Commander Kennedy to send messages for assistance, as vessel heeled over about 10° to port and was going down by the stern, Commander gave the order to 'Abandon ship'. I went into No. 2 cutter and found her ready for lowering and apparently full. I got into the boat which was lowered by Chief Gunner Chas G. Byrne RN and a seaman: great difficulty was experienced in getting away from the ship as she was still going through the water at about 10 knots, all the other boats on Port side with the exception of port whaler capsizing in water.

Vessel was sinking rapidly by the stern, bow being lifted right out of the water and guns on foc'sle carrying away, vessel then broke in two by after well deck and sank rapidly. Torpedo struck ship at about 5.41 p.m. and she disappeared at about 5.46 p.m.

In No. 2 cutter I went to edge of wreckage and saw all hands near hanging to spars, wreckage or rafts, whom we left for Swedish steamer which was about 2 miles distant proceeding to assistance, to pick up, considering it not advisable to enter field of wreckage on account of capsizing, having 35 hands in cutter at the time. Port whaler left the ship with 10 hands, picking up 3 more out of the water, she being deep in the water owing to water shipped when leaving ship.

I headed for Swedish steamer, but afterwards headed for the land Helligvar, bearing ESE distant 7 or 8 miles. We also saw trawler *Saxon*, steering to assistance of those in the water.

When about 2 miles from scene of disaster we sighted submarine, submerged all but periscope about half mile distant, steaming towards us, she diving when only about 30 yards distant.

8.30 p.m. arrived at Helligvar where we were well received and served with supper and allotted rooms for the night. 9 p.m. roll call 48 hands all told.

August 9th at 3 a.m. Three bodies, identified immediately as Private L. Marks, RMLI, Petty Officer Prior and Wm Dent, Greaser, were brought ashore by motorboats. Considerable wreckage was also brought ashore and inspected, no confidential books, or papers being amongst it, with the exception of set of charts of coast of Scotland which I burnt. At 6 p.m. I left Helligvar with postmaster on SS *Bodin* for Bodo to report to Consul. 10 a.m. arrived Bodo and reported to Consul who communicated with Narvik and Christiania. I was then sent on Norwegian gunboat *Andenaes*, Lieut. Johannessen, to Helligvar and brought men, bodies and boats to Bodo. On arrival there bodies were placed in coffins and we followed them to mortuary. I also took a doctor to Helligvar to see Seaman Keats who was injured in back and put into hospital at Bodo.

Under direction of Consul we were allotted hotel accommodation. August 10th at 10 am I inspected No. 1 starboard cutter which had been brought into Bodo. She was holed below water-line in 2 planks, the hole being only about 6" square also sternboard had partially carried away. This boat with No. 2 cutter and whaler I left in care of Consul.

Funeral arrangements were made with Consul. The service being our service read by a Norwegian Chaplain in Norwegian, I had previously searched several shops and inquired of Consul for a book of Prayer in English which apparently was not to be obtained anywhere.

The Norwegian Navy supplied a guard of six sailors, a Petty Officer and a Warrant Officer. Amongst the Mourners being the British Consul, Lieut. Arentz Norwegian Navy and Lieut. Johannessen Norwegian Navy. Deep sympathy was shown by the inhabitants both by their presence and many floral tributes. The coffins being covered with flags picked up from the *India* White Ensign, Union Jack and Red Ensign, wreaths being placed on coffins by British Consul also by Lieut. Johannessen for Norwegian Navy also by survivors.

At 3.30 p.m., we left Bodo for Bjerkvik on Gunboat *Andenaes* arriving at camp on August 11th at 4 am.

Whilst at Helligvar and Bodo we had every kindness shown to us by the Norwegian people.[1]

131. *Sub-Lieutenant R.W. Bateman, RNR*[2] *to Admiral Commanding Orkneys and Shetlands*

HMS *Andes*, Longhope [n.d., but late August 1915]

I beg to report that on August 8th at 6.30 p.m. in a position with Muckle

[1]The survivors who were landed in Norway were detained for the rest of the war.
[2]Bateman, Robert W., DSC, RNR, Sub-Lieutenant 1915, Lieutenant 1917.

Flugga bearing 5.33´E (mag) distance 19 miles the above vessel [Danish SS *Eleanora Maersk*] was intercepted by a German submarine. The submarine was first observed at a distance of approximately four miles, periscope alone visible, but on approaching within about one mile rose to the surface, fired a live shell at ship which fell about thirty yards short and then made a signal calling on Master to take his papers to submarine. The Master complied with the order but on being asked denied vessel carried Armed Guard. Ship was then allowed to proceed, the submarine following up astern until 8.15 p.m., Muckle Flugga Light bearing SSW (mag) distance twelve miles, when periscope disappeared and was not again sighted.[1]

At 1.15 a.m. on 9th I was hailed by HM Trawler *Grimsby 113* and I informed her what had occurred, stating time and position and suggested he endeavour to communicate information to Lerwick without delay.

***

132. *Commanding Officer* Tenby Castle *to Commander H.G. Alston, Senior Naval Officer Lerwick*

22 August 1915

The following is an abstract from Boarding Book of above ship, and customs list of ships boarded on T2 Patrol from time of arrival on August 6th until time of leaving 21 August [20 ships listed]:

***

You will observe that we boarded nothing of importance after the 2nd day on the patrol as ships going north would carry the news and ships carrying iron ore would go down inside Rodo Island and inside Kauran Leden, so that we only boarded ships that didn't carry, for instance SS *Flynderborg* should have passed south from Finiedet with a cargo of pyrites for Helsingborg Sweden on the 20th she passed inside, also large Swedish steamer with iron ore to Rotterdam passed inside the same day.

On the evening of the 21st while taking our boat on board and ship tossing about, she lifted in the swell and the stern post came away and as the *Rushcoe*'s boats are too unhandy for boarding ships I approached the Senior Naval Officer 10th Cruiser Squadron Commmodore Booty

[1]The submarine was probably *U 24*, though it may have been *U 38*.

and requested that the *Tenby Castle* should be fitted with a proper boarding boat with a short derrick on the foremast to lift her out of the water and take her in on main deck, as the weather has been rough over on the Norwegian coast prevailing winds on shore and it is absolutely necessary to have a good boat and means of getting her in and out quickly. Commodore Booty[1] agreed with me and sent a signal through to Admiral 10th Cruiser Squadron asking that the matter should be arranged.

It would also make the patrol more efficient if I could have a railing round the wheelhouse for lookout men, as on the Norwegian coast one can see ships at such a distance in fine weather that the higher the lookout the better, also in bad weather it is impossible to keep a man on the fo'c'sle head on account of heavy seas when head on.

[1]Booty, Edward L., CB, MVO, RN (1871–1949), Commander 1903, Captain 1908, Commodore in *Otway* 1915–1917, Naval Assistant to Admiral Commanding Coast Guard and Reserves 1917–1920, Rear-Admiral 1920, retired 1921, Vice-Admiral retired 1925.

5

LIFE ON PATROL, AUGUST–NOVEMBER 1915

The records of the Tenth Cruiser Squadron are very largely reports composed by officers, midshipment and lieutenants sent off in charge of prize crews on suspect vessels [e.g. 138, 154, 156], sent to the two successive admirals in command. There are also useful accounts, as by Dr Shaw, of less official matters, such as his curious record of inter-officer and shipboard sports. There is, however, only one direct record of the attitude of the men on the lower decks that remains, the diary of A/B Style, who had been in *Calyx*, and was then transferred to *Alcantara* – until he was killed in that ship [150, 162, 169]. His diary is here divided into monthly sections, and it provides a glimpse of a life which was clearly hard-working and in many ways extremely tedious. Note the entries for 6 to 30 November, for instance, with virtually nothing to record except the weather. And yet there is a clear contrast between A/B Style and Dr Shaw in their comments on the Shetlands: both men went for a walk and then had tea in a cottage; Shaw was fairly interested in the landscape, but Style thought there was 'not much to see'; in the cottage, however, Style clearly got the housewife talking, and writes a paragraph on her lifestyle; all this Shaw seems not to have noticed.

Other indications of lower deck attitudes came later, but there had been a straw in the wind early on, when Admiral de Chair noted that the early enlistees, on short-term enlistments, were unlikely to re-enlist [28 para. 24]. Much more serious was the festering problem of pay-rates, for men had been enlisted at different rates, and the Admiralty was dragging its collective feet on resolving the difficulties [153], as it had on the issue of the responsibility of the Armed Guards if intercepted by German ships or submarines [136, 139]. Some strains in relationships had surfaced already in the summer of 1915, at Kirkwall between the Armed Guard officers and the officers of the *Caesarea* [90, 94, 95], and Captain Vivian had put through complaints about the food provided to his ship [75]. Both pay and food were issues which would recur.

And all the time, in the face of another North Atlantic winter, the interceptions and boardings went on.

133. *Rear-Admiral de Chair to Admiralty*

HMS *Alsatian*, 15 September 1915

Report of Proceedings, 23 August–15 September 1915

***

1. Saturday, 23rd August – *Columbella* in company with *Acacia* (Sloop), *Arley* and *Mafeking* (Armed trawlers), having visited Bear Island, North Cape and several fjords in Norway and Finland, returned to patrol having found no trace of any submarine base. *Columbella* then proceeded to Clyde to coal and make good defects.

2. The British Trawler *Robinia*, G.Y 114, boarded by *Victorian* on 30th August reported that on 17th August in Latitude 62.13´N, Longitude 6.50´W she saw a German Submarine come to the surface in Fugle Fjord in the Faroe Islands and communicate with a boat from the shore. This information was passed to the Commander-in-Chief.

On the same date, viz: 30th August, *Orcoma* intercepted and sent to Kirkwall with an armed guard the Danish Steamer *Gullfoss*, Reykjavik to Copenhagen with ponies, wool, fish and cod-oil, and twenty-five passengers. Her master said he was proceeding via Kirkwall and then protested against being sent in on account of the danger of submarines but as she was (according to his own statement) calling at Kirkwall, his protest appeared somewhat uncalled for and bears out the suggestion of the Consul General, New York, communicated by Admiralty Letter M.6597 of 8th August, that the operations of this new line to which she belongs should be closely watched.[1]

At this period of the year ships of the Tenth Cruiser Squadron on A, E, F and G patrols are constantly intercepting Norwegian, Swedish and Danish ships carrying cargoes of fish and salted herrings, and a very brisk trade appears to be going on between Iceland and Scandinavian Ports in these food stuffs. From enquiries made by the Boarding Officers when examining these ships there is little doubt but that a large proportion of this important staple of life finds its way to Germany.

3. Tuesday, 31st August – *Alsatian* having completed with coal and effected necessary repairs left Liverpool and proceeded to rejoin patrol.

Wednesday, 1st September.

4. Thursday, 2nd September – *Ebro*, *Arlanza* and *Virginian* were met at pre-arranged rendezvous and given necessary orders.

[1]*Gullfoss* was not detained; but see also page 261, note 1.

In accordance with directions from the Commander-in-Chief C patrol was moved to Long. 13 W.

A report was received that the British Steamer *Roumanie* had been sunk by a large submarine in Lat. 58.15´N, Long. 9.20´W but from an intercepted signal from St Kilda the same steamer was apparently on fire in that position.[1] The British Steamer *Whitefields* was also reported to have been sunk in Lat. 60N, Long. 6.30´W by a submarine with two periscopes.[2]

5. Friday, 3rd September – *Oropesa* reported having intercepted and sent to Kirkwall with Armed Guard the Danish SS *United States* from New York to Copenhagen … This ship had a general cargo and among her passengers were six male Germans over 55 years of age provided with safe conduct.[3]

Cedric and *Hilary* were met at a pre-arranged rendezvous and orders and information were communicated. From information received by *Arlanza* it would appear that after the American SS *Llama* had been chased and captured by ships of the 10th Cruiser Squadron on patrol, and taken to Kirkwall with Armed Guard running the usual risks from submarines, she was given a green clearance and allowed to proceed, and later found her way in to Swinemunde where her cargo of oil probably fetched a good price to a German firm.[4] It seems incredible that after one year of war experience we should be deliberately allowing such supplies to reach the enemy after intercepting the ships conveying them.

6. Saturday, 4th September – *Hildebrand* on being relieved on G patrol by *Virginian* reported that the Trawlers operating on the Norwegian Coast had intercepted and examined three ships but found nothing contraband or suspicious. A large amount of traffic appears to be passing by the inshore channel, inside territorial waters and it is very difficult to get them to come out at all.

7. Sunday, 5th September – The disposition of the Squadron was as follows:

A Patrol … *Alsatian*, *Cedric*, *Hilary*.

C Patrol … *Orotava*, *Patuca*, *Victorian*, *Mantua*, *Motagua*, *Changuinola*, *Ebro*.

[1]Sunk by *U 20*.

[2]By *U 33*.

[3]Guarantees being forthcoming the *United States* was allowed to proceed on her voyage (TS 14/5 of 6 September 1915).

[4]This is presumably a garbled version of the incident of the *Wico* – see Chapter 4, page 235, note 2.

D Patrol … *Alcantara.*
F Patrol … *Andes.*
G Patrol … *Virginian* (*Tenby Castle* and *Newlands*, Armed Trawlers).
Hildebrand – Proceeding to E Patrol.
Proceeding to Swarbacks Minn … *Oropesa.*
Proceeding to Lerwick … *Saxon* and *Carysfort* (Armed Trawlers).
Coaling at Liverpool … *Arlanza* and *Orcoma.*
Coaling in Clyde … *Patia*, *Columbella*, *Ambrose*, *Digby.*
Coaling at Scapa Flow … *Teutonic.*
Rejoining patrol from Swarbacks Minn … *Otway.*

Of 89 vessels intercepted and examined during the past week 14 were sent in with armed guards.

7 vessels intercepted on passage to Archangel.

Otway was met at a pre-arranged rendezvous and given orders and information. A report was received from *Tenby Castle* (Armed Trawler) that she had seen a sea-plane flying East over Kya Island (Lat. 64.23´N, Long. 10.11´E) but its nationality could not be distinguished.

Tenby Castle also reported that on 12th August he fell in with a Norwegian patrol vessel, and on mentioning that his engines required repair, he was invited by the Norwegian Officer to go in and anchor at Bessalier (Chart No. 2308) for the night, which he accordingly did, coming out again on the morning of 13th August.

Fog was prevalent in the area of A Patrol.

8. Monday, 6th September – The Danish Sailing Vessel *Ceres* Greenland to Copenhagen was intercepted and sent to Lerwick with an Armed Guard from *Hilary*. This vessel … carried a cargo of sperm oil and sealskins, and the Master produced a certified statement that she belonged to the Danish Government, and the cargo was guaranteed.[1]

Orotava reported having intercepted the Danish government Vessel *Godthaab*, Copenhagen to East Greenland with a general cargo of German, Austrian and Turkish origin. She was sent to Stornoway with an Armed Guard as her cargo appeared to be a clear case of enemy's export.[2]

Foggy weather continued on A Patrol.

9. Tuesday, 7th September – *Hildebrand* and *Teutonic* were met at pre-arranged rendezvous and communicated with. Thick fog was prevalent at the time and the W/T Direction Finder in *Alsatian* proved

[1]*Ceres* was recorded at Lerwick on 14 September, but was not detained.

[2]As Rear-Admiral de Chair discovered (para. 14), *Godthaab* was not detained; no reference was made to the Contraband Committee.

very useful in determining the positions of these ships. A special report on this instrument is being forwarded.

Ambrose, en route from the Clyde, reported main engines broken down in Lat. 56.13´N, Long. 3.45´W at 10.30 a.m. Necessary repairs were made and ship proceeded at 4.50 p.m.

10. Wednesday, 8th September – On account of the prevalence of fog A Patrol was moved to Long. 11 W thus forming with C Patrol a continuous line from Lat. 34.40´N to 55.20´N, ships 50 miles apart, patrolling 40 miles true North and South, ships being in their southern position at 8 a.m. and every 8 hours.

A second lookout crowsnest on foremast of all ships of 10th Cruiser Squadron has now been placed well above the height of funnels giving a very good range of vision and ensuring that other ships can be sighted before we ourselves are seen. Ships of 10th Cruiser Squadron can be readily recognised by the two crowsnests on foremast.

11. Thursday, 9th September – *Alsatian* arrived at Swarbacks Minn and anchored in Busta Voe. In company with Rear Admiral Fawckner I inspected the coaling and watering plant and other local arrangements of the base. The rate of coaling ships has increased with experience and will no doubt continue to do so; the present average is from 50 to 60 tons per hour. A plentiful supply of water for boilers exists but no drinking water can be procured at present. Ships of 10th Cruiser Squadron are sent in to coal singly, taking about 1000 tons each; when the resources of the base are fully developed several ships can be coaled at once, but to do this more RNR firemen (preferably gas stokers) will be required.

Hilary reported having intercepted the Danish SS *Godafoss* with wool and horses from Reykjavik to Leith and Copenhagen. She was sent in to Kirkwall with an Armed Guard in accordance with Admiralty orders.[1]

12. Friday, 10th September – *Alsatian* left Swarbacks Minn and returned to patrol.

A submarine was reported off Flannan Islands, proceeding north, and another off Statlandet on the Norwegian Coast. Ships in the vicinity were warned.

13. Saturday, 11th September – Dense fog was prevalent on all patrols.

[1]The problem in *Godafoss*'s cargo was the wool; when guarantees that it would be stored were given, the ship was allowed to go on (TS 14/5 of 13 September 1915). The ship's detention caused some shock in Iceland, according to Commander Mahon in his report on his visit.

At 10 p.m. *Oropesa* reported that she was in collision with *Patia* in Lat. 58.8´N, Long 11 W. *Ebro*, *Changuinola* and *Columbella* went to their assistance. *Oropesa* sustained comparatively little damage but *Patia*'s fore compartment was flooded and *Ebro* was ordered to escort her to the Clyde.

14. Sunday, 12th September – At 2.15 a.m. *Patia* reported that her stem was badly damaged and water was up to collision bulkhead which, however was intact and holding well. The bulkhead was shored up and ballast shifted aft to bring her bow up, Captain of ship preferring to steam stern first [144, 145].

Further examination of *Oropesa* at daylight shewed plates and frames from water line to upper deck bent, one beam and stringer plate on water line bent and several rivets on waterline shorn off. Boat deck was cut into but guns were not damaged. As she was leaking slightly I ordered her to proceed to the Clyde for repair.

At 3.0 p.m. as *Patia* appeared to be making little progress I submitted to the Commander-in-Chief that tugs should be sent to meet her off Barra head. Yacht, trawler and tugs were ordered to be sent from Stornoway and the Commander-in-Chief directed *Patia* to proceed to East Loch Roag in the Hebrides for temporary repairs.

The disposition of the Squadron was as follows:

A Patrol … *Alsatian*, *Teutonic*, *Hilary*, *Ambrose*.
C Patrol … *Patuca*, *Orotava*, *Victorian*, *Otway*, *Motagua*, *Changuinola*.
E Patrol … *Hildebrand*.
F Patrol … *Andes*.
G Patrol … *Virginian* and Trawlers *Tenby Castle* and *Newland*.
Coaling in Clyde … *Mantua*, *Digby*.
Coaling at Liverpool … *Arlanza*, *Alcantara*.
Coaling at Swarbacks Minn … *Cedric*.
Returning from Clyde … *Columbella*.
Returning from Liverpool … *Orcoma*.
Proceeding to Clyde … *Patia*, *Ebro*, *Oropesa*.

Of 51 Vessels intercepted and examined during the week 9 were sent into port with Armed Guards.

The work of the patrols was much hampered by fog which prevailed all the week in most of the areas.

Otway reported having intercepted the Danish Steamer *Godthaab*, Stornoway to Greenland. This was the vessel sent in with an Armed Guard on 6th September, having a general cargo of German, Austrian and Turkish origin (see para. 8) but she had been given a green customs clearance and allowed to proceed.

15. Monday, 13th September – At 2.40 a.m. *Ebro* reported that she had sighted a submarine in Lat. 58.5´N, Long. 10.5´W steering north. From detailed reports by both *Patia* and *Ebro* it appeared that they first observed the lights of a supposed steamer which *Ebro* proceeded to investigate. The chase proved to be a submarine but her identity was not established until *Ebro* was so close that she could not fire, when the submarine dived. After a short interval she rose again and showed a light. *Ebro* attempted to ram her but she had disappeared when the ship arrived on the spot [144].[1] Meanwhile the *Patia* which had hitherto been proceeding stern first at 3 knots reversed her engines and went ahead at 12 to 15 knots to clear the dangerous area. At 6.50 a.m. she reported that she was proceeding east at 15 knots and that her shored up bulkhead was intact, collision mats in place and 200 tons of ballast shifted aft [145]. In view of these favourable conditions she requested permission to proceed direct to the Clyde instead of putting in to East Loch Roag, and this course having been approved by the Commander-in-Chief she shaped course to the South with *Ebro* in company.

The British Trawler *Audrey* intercepted by *Columbella* reported the suspicious action of three Dutch Trawlers anchored off Portland, Iceland. One of the trawlers followed a motor boat behind an island and after dark returned and communicated with the other two.

16. Tuesday, 14th September – At 0.50 a.m. *Patia* reported that she was attacked by a submarine in Lat. 56.23´N, Long. 9.32´W. The torpedo was observed on the starboard quarter passing astern.[2] *Patia* arrived in the Clyde at 11 p.m.

A case of acute appendicitis was successfully operated upon on board *Patuca* by the Medical Officers of that ship and *Orotava*.

The Norwegian Steamer *Lokken* reported to the Trawler *Tenby Castle* that a large German submarine was seen in Lat. 57.53´N, Long. 7.30´E proceeding north.

17. Wednesday, 15th September – *Orcoma* on E patrol reported a large number of trawlers leaving Iceland. She was directed to send them in to Lerwick if destination was south of Ekersund.

Arlanza was met at a pre-arranged rendezvous and despatches were received from her.

In accordance with Admiralty Letter M.06474 of 7th September

[1]Despite the circumstantial account here and in [144], there is no record on the German side of a U-boat in the area at the time.

[2]Again there is no record of a submarine in the area.

received to-day [140] this report is being closed now and subsequent reports of the proceedings of the Squadron under my command will be forwarded at intervals of about a fortnight as opportunity offers.

134. *Admiralty to Commander-in-Chief Home Fleets*

25 August 1915

… HMS *Brilliant* will be ordered to proceed to Lerwick as soon as she is ready.

2. A boom defence will be established between Leake Rock and Taing of Horn at the South entrance and between Green Hand and Turra Tang at the North entrance.

3. The defence cannot be commenced before the first week in September, but it is not considered necessary to delay sending the *Brilliant* to Lerwick meanwhile.

4. The Board of Customs have been requested to send an additional Assistant Surveyor of Customs to Lerwick as soon as possible, giving notice to the Admiral Commanding Orkneys and Shetlands when he is due to arrive.

5. The Naval Examination Staff … will be detailed and sent up as soon as possible.

135. *Commander-in-Chief Home Fleets to Admiralty*

HMS *Iron Duke*, 27 August 1915

Captain A. Bromley[1] in *Columbella* arrived at my base today, having carried out a very thorough search of the Norwegian and Russian coast east of the North Cape.

2. Everything points to the fact that German submarines are not operating in the White Sea and that their base is either in the Lofoten Islands or in the vicinity of Tromso.

3. It is submitted that an agent be sent to search this coast thoroughly with a view to making representations to the Norwegian Government should evidence of the base be discovered.

[1]Bromley, Sir Arthur, Bt, KCMG, KCVO, RN (1876–1967), Commander 1908, Captain 1915, Captain in *Columbella*, Captain in *Courageous*, 1916–1919, Flag Captain Light Cruiser Force 1919–1922, retired 1922, Rear Admiral (retired) 1926, Ceremonial and Reception Secretary Dominions and Colonial Office 1931–1952, succeeded as baronet 1957.

136. *Commander-in-Chief Home Fleets to Admiralty*

HMS *Iron Duke*, 28 August 1915

Be pleased to bring to the notice of the Lords Commissioners of the Admiralty the case of the Armed Guard on board the American Sailing Ship *Pass of Balmaha*, as reported in German newspapers, extracts of which have been sent me by the Director of the Intelligence Division …

2. If the German account is true, which is very doubtful, it appears that the *Pass of Balmaha* was intercepted by the *Victorian* on 21st July 1915, and ordered into Kirkwall with an Armed Guard. Whilst on passage thither she was intercepted on 31st July 1915 by a German submarine, placed in charge of a single Petty Officer, and sent into Cuxhaven, where she arrived on 2nd August 1915, with the British Armed Guard still onboard.

3. In view of the fact that this report is forwarded to me from the Admiralty, it is submitted that I may be informed whether their Lordships consider that the British Armed Guard should have resisted and retaken the ship while under neutral colours, as Admiralty letter M.04362 of 18th June 1915 lays down that 'Armed Guard should on no account attempt any belligerent act under a neutral flag'.[1]

4. It is pointed out that the same Admiralty letter states that 'a further reply will be sent regarding the position of Armed Guards on board neutral vessels'. Nearly three months have elapsed since the date of my letter to which this communication refers, and I submit that an early decision may be made and communicated to me [101].

137. *Surveyor D.J. Kelleher to Board of Customs and Excise*

Kirkwall, 2 September 1915

***

The neutral steamer *Sami* owned by the East Asiatic Company of Copenhagen on a voyage from Copenhagen, Norresundby and Gothenburg to the West Indies, thence via Panama Canal to Valparaiso; and the *Dania* owned by the United Steamship Company of Copenhagen on a voyage from Philadelphia, Baltimore and New York to Copenhagen having been diverted by their owners to Kirkwall for examination to meet Admiralty requirements, stranded in Orkney waters during thick fog.

[1]Cf [101] for the C-in-C's transmittal of this amendment.

Both vessels had general cargoes with dutiable goods – that of the *Dania* included unmanufactured tobacco and rum. As both ships were in a position of great danger immediate steps were taken to salve the vessels by discharging part of the cargo into craft brought alongside, and by jettisoning part of the heavier and less valuable cargo. Both vessels sustained serious damage – the *Sami*'s cargo being completely submerged at high water – but have now been refloated.

***

In the ordinary course of their voyage these steamers would not have been in the vicinity of the Orkney Islands and the stranding occurred through their attempts to reach Kirkwall, as directed, for examination purposes. There was no intention that any part of the cargo should be landed in this country.[1]

***

138. *Sub-Lieutenant W. MacFarlane, RNR,*[2] *to Senior Naval Officer Kirkwall*

Kirkwall, 3 September 1915

I have the honour to report that, acting under the instructions of Commander Dugmore, RN,[3] in command of HMS *Ebro* the Danish steamship *Vesta* was boarded by Acting Lieutenant Smiles RNR,[4] boarding officer, and myself at 5.30 p.m. September 1st in Lat. 63.54´N, Long. 11.13´W. Particulars of the ship, her cargo, and passengers were signalled to HMS *Ebro*, and also the fact that she intended calling at Thorshavn and Kirkwall. The reply came back to send our cutter to *Ebro* for an armed guard, to take the *Vesta* to Kirkwall. The master of the *Vesta* protested against being taken out of his route, as he had on board 64 passengers and 4 bags of mail for Thorshavn. Lieutenant Smiles again signalled the *Ebro* to repeat the fact of the passengers being there, and the *Ebro* sent back instructions to me to take the same route as on a former occasion. Lieutenant Smiles then said he would personally speak about the matter on board HMS *Ebro* and in

[1]The general purpose of this letter was to explain why no landing fees had been charged.

[2]MacFarlane, William M.F., RNR, Sub-Lieutenant 1915, Lieutenant 1917.

[3]Dugmore, Eric V.F.R., RN, Commander 1908, Captain of *Ebro* 1915, Captain 1916, retired as Captain.

[4]Smiles, Stephen H., OBE, RNR, Sub-Lieutenant 1914, Lieutenant 1916.

anticipation of any change of orders, the engines of the *Vesta* were not started. After the sea boat was hoisted the international signal TXB was run up (Proceed on your voyage) upon which we set out course for Kirkwall. No other signals were sent from the *Ebro*.

There is nothing to report on the voyage, and I have no complaints to make.

The vessel anchored in Kirkwall Harbour at 7.15 p.m. September 3rd.

[Note added for Admiral Orkneys and Shetlands, Longhope, by Customs Officer N.L. Down]:

The *Vesta* passed a few miles from the Faroes, but these unfortunate men have been brought on here, without any food or shelter (deck passengers) and will now have to be taken probably to Copenhagen, and sent back from there.[1]

139. *Minute by J.W.S. Anderson*[2]

7 September 1915

As regards this particular incident [106 para. 30, 136], a letter received from Sub-Lieutenant Harris[3] states that another German submarine kept touch with the *Pass of Balmaha* until Heligoland, so that it appears the Armed Guard would not have been able to resist effectively.

140. *Admiralty to Rear-Admiral Tenth Cruiser Squadron*

7 September 1915

With reference to your submission of 21st ultimo … [106] forwarding a report of proceedings of Cruiser Force B, I am commanded by My Lords Commissioners of the Admiralty to acquaint you that they would be glad to receive shorter reports rendered (say) about once a fortnight. While the narratives at present forwarded by you are of considerable interest,

[1] A complaint about this was also made by the owners, the Danish United Shipping Co.; the ship was allowed to go on by the Contraband Committee (TS 14/5 of 8 September 1915).

[2] Anderson, John William Stewart, CB, MVO (1874–1920), Admiralty Clerk, Assistant Secretary in the Admiralty from 1917 to his death.

[3] Harris, Charles E., RNR, Sub-Lieutenant 1915 in *Victorian*, captured in *Pass of Balmaha*. It would seem that Harris was able to supply plenty of information in his letter from the POW camp.

they lose much in value owing to its being too late when they are received to take action on any of the matters referred to.[1]

141. *Rear-Admiral de Chair to Admiralty*

HMS *Alsatian*, 1 October 1915

Report of Proceedings, 16 September–1 October 1915

***

1. Thursday, 16th September – The British Trawler *Pericles* H 131, Hull to Iceland reported that a month ago a submarine was stated to have searched Fugle Fjord, Faroe Islands. This rumour probably refers to the report made by *Robinia* GY 1147 mentioned in para. 2 of my letter No. 266/35 of 15th September.

2. Friday, 17th September – *Virginian* which had been relieved in charge of G Patrol was met and communicated with. She reported that she had been unable to capture any south bound ships outside territorial waters on the Norwegian Coast, as in thick weather they anchored within the limits and when the weather was clear they took the inshore passage.

3. Saturday, 18th September – Bad weather greatly interfered with the work of the Squadron and in many cases prevented boarding. Two ships were directed to proceed to Kirkwall without Armed Guards.

A report was received that a large steamer heavily listed to port, with mainmast gone had been sighted on 15th September in Lat. 60 N, Long. 5.55´W. Patrols were warned to keep clear of this derelict which might also prove to be a submarine trap.[2]

A submarine was reported in Lat. 59.50´N, Long. 4.22´W proceeding west.

4. Sunday 19th September – The disposition of the Squadron was as follows:

A Patrol … *Alsatian*, *Teutonic*, *Mantua*.
C Patrol … *Otway*, *Arlanza*, *Motagua*, *Orotava*, *Ambrose*, *Digby*.
E Patrol … *Orcoma*.
F Patrol … *Hilary*.

[1]This request, somewhat overdue perhaps, was complied with to the extent that future reports tended to be produced at shorter intervals; on the other hand, both de Chair and his successor Tupper also allowed their reports to expand – so 'shorter reports' as the Admiralty requested, was not the actual result.

[2]It is possible that this was *Whitefields*, reported sunk on 2 September; otherwise it has not been possible to identify the ship.

G Patrol ... *Columbella* and Armed Trawlers *Robert Smith* and *Rushcoe*.
Joining C Patrol ... *Cedric*.
Proceeding to Liverpool to coal ... *Virginian*.
Proceeding to Lerwick ... Armed Trawlers *Tenby Castle*, *Newland*.
Coaling &c. in Clyde ... *Ebro*, *Oropesa*, *Hildebrand*, *Patia*, *Patuca*.
Coaling at Liverpool ... *Alcantara*, *Andes*.
Coaling at Swarbacks Minn ... *Changuinola*, *Victorian*.

Of 77 vessels intercepted and examined during the past week, 14 were sent in with Armed Guards and 2 without Armed Guards. Four vessels were intercepted on passage to Archangel.

Arlanza reported that one leg of the buffer spring shackle on her steering engine had fractured. As this could not be repaired at sea she was ordered to proceed to Liverpool to make good the defect and return to patrol as early as possible.

Orcoma intercepted the Norwegian Steamer *Aalesund* with 3100 barrels of herrings from Iceland to Copenhagen via Hangesund. As she stated that she must call at the Faroes for coal she was allowed to do so.

It is worthy of note that the Danish Steamer *Oscar II* and Swedish Steamer *Atland* which were intercepted and directed to Kirkwall without Armed Guards (which could not be put on board on account of the weather) arrived at that port.[1]

5. Monday, 20th September – C Patrol was warned that the submarine which passed Muckle Flugga on the night of 17th September had not been sighted off the coast and might therefore be operating in the Patrol area.

6. Tuesday, 21st September – Fog prevailed in the northern patrol areas, and very much hampered the work of the patrols.

7. Wednesday, 22nd September – The Danish Motor Ship *Pacific* which was intercepted west bound by *Mantua* reported having sighted a derelict steamer in Lat. 60.20´N, Long. 7.28´W at 1 p.m. on 21st September. Both masts were gone but the funnel was still standing. This was evidently the derelict referred to in para. 3.

Dense fog again hampered the work of ships in the northern patrol areas.

8. Thursday, 23rd September – *Alsatian* arrived at Swarbacks Minn and commenced coaling.

[1]Two items of the cargo of *Oscar II* were deemed contraband, but could not be reached at Kirkwall; the ship was allowed to go on with a promise that the suspect items would be returned to Britain.

On enquiry as to the disposal of ships sent to Lerwick I learned that six vessels loaded with fish from Iceland to Scandinavian ports south of Ekersund had been released. The Norwegian Sailing Vessel *Bonanza* with paraffin from New York to Bergen had also been released after a German chemist and an Officer had been removed from her, and the Danish Steamer *Ragnhild* from Greenland to Copenhagen with cryolite consigned to Julius Nielsen, a firm with a branch at Altona, had been allowed to proceed.[1] The utility of sending in vessels with fish for further examination appears doubtful.

Dense fog continued on the patrol areas.

9. Friday, 24th September – *Mantua* reported having intercepted the Swedish SS *Helsingborg*, Port Arthur to Aarhus, with a cargo of cotton seed cake. She was sent in to Kirkwall with an Armed Guard in compliance with Admiralty orders received today.[2]

10. Saturday, 25th September – *Alsatian* having taken in 1000 tons of coal left Swarbacks Minn and proceeded to rejoin A patrol.

The average number of tons per hour taken by *Alsatian* was 98 whereas *Cedric* had coaled at the rate of 126. Bags and buckets were used by *Alsatian* but it is hoped to improve the rate of coaling in future by using the large iron 1 ton bucket.

11. Sunday, 26th September – The disposition of the Squadron was as follows:

A Patrol ... *Alsatian*, *Alcantara*, *Victorian*, *Changuinola*.
C Patrol ... *Mantua*, *Arlanza*, *Patuca*, *Digby*, *Ebro*.
E Patrol ... *Orcoma*.
F Patrol ... *Andes*.
G Patrol ... *Columbella*, Armed Trawlers *Robert Smith*, and *Rushcoe*.
Coaling at Liverpool ... *Otway*, *Virginian*, *Teutonic*.
Coaling etc. in Clyde ... *Patia*, *Oropesa*, *Orotava*, *Motagua*, *Hilary*, *Hildebrand*.
Proceeding to Liverpool to coal ... *Cedric*.
Proceeding to Clyde ... *Ambrose*
At Lerwick ... Armed Trawler *Newland*.
At Longhope ... Armed Trawlers *Tenby Castle*, *Saxon*.

Of 39 ships intercepted and examined during the past week 7 were sent into port with Armed Guards.

[1]Both ships' cargoes had been considered by the Contraband Committee (TS 14/5 of 15 and 17 September 1915) before being allowed to proceed.

[2]*Helsingborg*'s cargo was 3310 tons of cottonseed cake; the Contraband Committee sent it to the Prize Court as a test case.

Patrols were much hampered by continuous fog. At 1.20 p.m. *Caribbean* was heard making 'S.O.S.' signals from Lat. 58.48´N, Long. 5.17´W. The position of the nearest ship of Tenth Cruiser Squadron, viz: *Arlanza* in Lat. 59 N, Long. 11.20´W was reported to the Commander-in-Chief and instructions were requested whether she should be sent to assist. The answer was that she was too far off. Meanwhile *Caribbean* continued to report 'water gaining on fires' and 'ship drifting to westward', and the *Birkenhead* was sent to her assistance.[1]

Alcantara was met at a pre-arranged rendezvous and dispatches were received from her; after which she was sent to relieve *Columbella* on G Patrol.

12. Monday, 27th September – *Patuca* reported having intercepted the Norwegian Steamer *Ulf* ...... New York to Bergen and Christiania with .... contraband consigned to the Nitro-...... This vessel was originally the Greek *Olympia* of Argostoli and was transferred at Glasgow on 15th August. She was sent to Kirkwall with an Armed Guard in accordance with the directions contained in Admiralty Telegram 2350 of 22nd September.[2]

The Danish Steamer *Hellig Olaf* bound west was spoken by *Mantua* and allowed to proceed …

At 11.10 p.m. *Hildebrand* which was returning to patrol after coaling in the Clyde reported that she had sprung a leak in No. 1 hold and had 6 feet of water in it. I directed the nearest ship, viz: *Arlanza* to proceed to her assistance if necessary and *Hildebrand* was ordered to report if water gained on the pumps.

13. Tuesday, 28th September – At 1.50 a.m. *Hildebrand* reported that the water in her hold was under control. The leak appeared to be from the sea into No. 1 tank and thence through top of tank under sand ballast into the hold. As the hold could not be pumped out on account of the sand choking the suckers, I ordered *Hildebrand* to return to the Clyde at 3.15 a.m. At 8.56 a.m. the holds were reported clear of water and sand ballast was being got out.

Ebro reported having intercepted the Danish Steamer *Absalom*, Philadelphia to Copenhagen with lubricating oil. She was sent to Kirkwall with an Armed Guard … .[3]

Alsatian intercepted and examined the British SS *Wray Castle* with 600 Belgian Troops and Munitions .... to Archangel.

[1]*Caribbean* survived; whatever had happened was not due to a submarine attack.

[2]The document in the PRO is damaged, hence the gaps in this and later paragraphs. *Ulf* was allowed to go on by Customs at Kirkwall.

[3]*Absalom* was not detained.

With the approval of the Commander-in-Chief, the Armed Trawlers *Rushcoe* and *Robert Smith* on G Patrol were moved to T.1 area with a view to intercepting the German Steamer *J.L. Larsen* which was reported from Trondhjem to be loading ore for Lubeck.

14. Thursday, 30th September – *Patuca* reported having intercepted the Danish Steamer *Minsk*, New York to Copenhagen with a general cargo of foodstuffs. She was sent to Kirkwall with an Armed Guard … *Patuca* also intercepted the Danish Steamer *Frederick VIII*, New York to Copenhagen, with a general cargo, chiefly foodstuffs, and 357 passengers. She was sent in according to orders.[1]

Ebro reported having intercepted the Danish Steamer *Jelling*, Baltimore to Copenhagen, with a cargo of grain. One German trimmer … was discovered on board. The ship was sent to Kirkwall with an Armed Guard.[2]

A German of military age was also discovered in the Swedish Steamer *Avesta* which was intercepted by *Mantua* from Rivadesella to Christiania with coffee, and sent in to Kirkwall.[3]

In all, eight steamers were sent in to Kirkwall and Lerwick with Armed Guards during the day.

15. Friday, 1st October – *Orcoma* on E Patrol north of Iceland reported that information had been received that all shipments of herrings for the season had been [made(?)] and that only a few sailing trawlers were ..... steamers had been seen.

Andes reported having intercepted the Norwegian Steamer *Ledaal*, New York to Archangel, calling at Tromso for coal, with a general cargo including copper consigned to private individuals. She was sent in to Lerwick with an Armed Guard in order that the destination of the copper might be fully enquired into.

German submarines were reported from the Norwegian coast proceeding north and west on 29th September, and on 18th October one was sighted by the Swedish Steamer *Avesta* in Lat. 59.54´N, Long. 10.45´W steering west.

[1]*Frederick VIII* was not detained, but *Minsk* was a complicated matter. Word had come from New York that a discharged stoker claimed there were submarine parts under coal in No. 3 hold. At the same time several items of the cargo were also deemed contraband. The Customs investigated, and soon decided the stoker's story had been sour grapes; but the contraband earned the ship a trip to King's Lynn where the items were to be discharged and stored (TS 14/5 of 2, 4, 5 and 19 October 1915).

[2]No doubt after the German was removed, *Jelling* was released (TS 14/5 of 4 October 1915).

[3]*Avesta* was not detained.

142. *Surveyor D.J. Kelleher to Board of Customs and Excise*

Lerwick, 17 September 1915

I beg to forward herewith a claim for freight and a protest against removing the cargo of the Norwegian sailing ship *Hebe* of Lillesand prior to payment of freight, made on behalf of the shipowner – Henrik Hansen, Lillesand – by the Norwegian Chamber of Commerce London on the instructions of the Norwegian Legation, London.

The *Hebe* sailed from Port Arthur, Texas, on 15 June 1915 with a cargo of 333,450 gallons of Diesel oil for Stockholm. The vessel was diverted by the Admiralty and arrived at Lerwick with a prize crew on board, on 21st August 1915. Particulars of the cargo were reported … [and] it was ordered to be discharged and placed in prize. Instructions were received from the Admiralty Marshal on the 24th August 1915 to order the vessel to Fleetwood for this purpose and to ask the Senior Naval Officer to arrange for a tug.

The vessel left this port on the 4th September 1915 for Fleetwood in tow of the tug *Harrington*.

143. *Diary of Dr J. Shaw*

Saturday 18 [September 1915]. I went on shore [at Busta Voe] in the afternoon again, watched football match between firemen and officers for a short time and then went for a stroll with Pearse and Hayward[1] and got another fine view. This time … could [see] Olna Firth where there was a Whaling Station in peace time. Having got to the top of the hill where there was a collection of stones we returned and had tea in a small farmhouse, which seems to be a regular tea room now since officers come to it from all ships and had a simple tea.

144. *Commander Eric V. Dugmore to Rear-Admiral Commanding Tenth Cruiser Squadron.*

HMS *Ebro*, 18 September 1915

Encounter [with a submarine] took place while escorting HMS *Patia* to harbour after her collision with HMS *Oropesa*. *Patia* was practically stopped or steaming two or three knots astern, and *Ebro* was keeping

[1]Hayward, Charles J.L., DSC, RNR, Midshipman 1910, Sub-Lieutenant 1916, Lieutenant 1918.

Pearse, Cyril A., RNR, Midshipman 1914, Lieutenant 1918.

station on her, following in her wake. Shortly after midnight *Patia* was lost sight of. At 0.55 a.m. a faint white light was seen bearing SSW. This was taken to be the shaded light that *Patia* had been asked to show at intervals or when necessary, and course was altered to take up station. Shortly after, the light was found to belong to a stranger, by the *Patia* shewing navigation and not-under-control lights. About the same time a red bow light was seen on the stranger. From the gradual alteration in bearing and the height of the lights, it was judged that the stranger was a steamer some distance off. From subsequent experience, however, it proved that she was a submarine moving slowly and quite close. At 2.0 a.m. acting under wireless instructions from *Patia* to investigate I proceeded at thirteen knots towards the stranger, then bearing East, which course I steered until fairly close. The stranger's lights were soon lost sight of, but the phosphorescence shewed her wake. On making out her course by this means to be ENE, I altered to steer a parallel course, the stranger being brought about two points on the starboard bow. The *Ebro*'s speed had been reduced in order to avoid making a conspicuous bow wave and the blowing off of steam. I did not consider it advisable to make the presence of a man-of-war known by using the search light, because of *Patia*'s helplessness and her proximity, taking into account the probability that she had a greater chance of being torpedoed than the *Ebro*, especially as she had exhibited not-under-control lights. It was too dark to make out the outline of the stranger. At about 2.35 a.m. I noticed something unusual about her wake, and swung the ship away from it to avoid mines, by starboarding and then porting the helm. Almost immediately after, she established her identity as a submarine by diving almost under *Ebro*'s bow. At the same time an elongated phosphorescent mass appeared beneath the surface, close to the ship. This may have been a mine or a torpedo which failed to run. The guns had orders to fire on making out a submarine, but at this stage she was too close for them to bear. I altered course to NNE and increased to utmost speed, at the same time reporting by wireless the presence of a submarine. A steamer's lights were seen on the port quarter, and these were taken to belong to *Patia*: that ship was informed by wireless that her lights were showing; it appears, however, that this was not the *Patia*, but probably a steamer (the *Rapidan*) which was sighted again later. Shortly after, the submarine came to the surface on the starboard quarter and apparently going at full speed for a few minutes. She then seemed to reduce speed considerably or stop. I turned to attempt to ram her, but her light disappeared at about the same time and no further trace of her was seen. I continued to search at full speed until 4.25 a.m. At 3.57 a.m. the faint glimmer of a white light was seen and steamed for with the intention of ramming. On this occasion, knowing that the *Patia* was in safety, I used a searchlight and discovered that the vessel was a steamer steering S 85° E. She reported herself as the *Rapid* or *Rapidan*. (Evidently the latter, having a swan bow).

At 5.50 a.m. the *Patia* was discovered ahead.

145. *Memoirs of Surgeon Sub-Lieutenant D.A. Knight.*[1]

Patia was once in collision with another ship in our patrol, HMS *Oropesa*, one night. We were rejoining after a week in Glasgow and owing to a mistake in a wireless signal we thought we still had some miles to go. It was a brilliantly starry night in summer, but quite dark, and of course neither ship was showing any lights. Suddenly we struck *Oropesa* a glancing blow on her port beam, tearing a hole in her side above the water line and turning the first 6–8 feet of our bows to one side. Of course we had a huge gap extending well down below the water line, and the forward part was flooded up to the forward bulkhead. *Oropesa* was ordered into port on her own steam. *Patia* was hove to all night and at first light a collision mat was fitted, but the Captain decided it was too risky to steam forwards in case the bulkhead gave way. So all that day we proceeded back to the Clyde stern first at about 2–3 knots, accompanied by a destroyer sent out from Scapa. Then about 1 a.m. a light was sighted some distance away and the destroyer went off to investigate. She found a German U-boat on the surface charging his batteries, got so close to him that she could not depress her guns enough to hit her and watched her do a crash dive. After that the Captain said 'to Hell with the bulkhead' and turned round and steamed ahead at about 10 knots. We arrived in the Clyde late next afternoon escorted by two destroyers and got another fortnight's leave undergoing repairs.

146. *Admiral Longhope to Admiralty*

19 September 1915

Following message has been sent to Commander-in-Chief Grand Fleet and Rear-Admiral Tenth Cruiser Squadron, begins: 'Lerwick examination service is now established, about 50% of vessels should be sent Lerwick remainder to Kirkwall, all passenger ships should be sent invariably to Kirkwall'.

[1]Knight, Dennis A., RNVR, Surgeon Sub-Lieutenant 1914.

147. *Notebook diary of Able Seaman W.C. Style [serving in* Alcantara*]*

September 21, 1915

We left Liverpool today and the weather was splendid. I managed to get a post card ashore to send to you, hope you got it all right.

September 22nd.

but just 24 hours when we picked up a large steamer *Cappella I*[1] which had slipped through the patrol some how, but have sent her into port with a prize crew (Buenos Aires to Goteborg).

September Friday 25th.

We have seen nothing this last 48 hours but have been told that German submarines are about here and we stopped a steamer this morning at 5 o'clock a.m. who informed us that a German submarine had shelled a Norwegian steamer laden with timber and blown both masts out of her, the crew managing to escape in boats. Left her a complete wreck. Derelict, last seen drifting to the westward in the Gulf Stream so I suppose we shall sink her if we drop across her.[2] We have formed a very good brass band on board, with some very decent musicians, so that will help us to pass a good few hours.

P.S. the steamer that the Germans shelled was 50 miles south of St Kilda's when it occurred not far from here as we have not gone to our northern patrol yet, expect to go end of this week. The weather here is quite warm, but we are still getting fogs. (Name of steamer *John Brummer* for Kirkwall, was not on suspected list.) She was bound for Baltimore in ballast.[3]

September 26th

Picked up *Alsatian* our flag ship and sent one or two letters to her as she was going in and received orders, but what for I don't know. Blowing hard. At 7.45 p.m. the northern light was showing beautifully, lit up the whole sky wonderful and continued on and off until about 9 a.m. One thing that I noticed was like a beam of light, something like a beam of a searchlight, but it sprang from nowhere and seemed to hover over the ship right fore and aft her.

September 27th, '15.

10 a.m. picked up the *Columbella* (she is the old *Columba*) send a mail to Liverpool by her and then proceeded to take up her patrol off Tronjheim. Blowing a stiff gale. Received good news from war by

[1]*Cappella*'s cargo was maize, bran, and linseed; the maize was sent to the Prize Court (TS 14/5 of 25 September 1915).

[2]See page 268, para. 3.

[3]The ship was *John Blumer* (see page 291, note 1).

wireless (Poldhu) [wireless station]. I forgot to mention that yesterday (Sunday) at 2 p.m. we got news the *Caribbean* had been torpedoed 20 miles SW off Cape Wrath, and we went to help her but after proceeding a short distance in her direction had a wireless to say she could manage to reach port without aid.[1]

September 28th.

Nothing to mention of importance. We have arrived off the coast of Norway on our patrol. Stiff gale, but began to abate by 5 p.m. Good news again, this morning by wireless (Poldhu).

September 29th.

This morning at 10 a.m. we picked up two trawlers the *Robert Smith* and the *Rusko* in company, having crews on board from one of the patrol vessels. Crews after submarines. Both trawlers are armed with two guns, one 3 pdr forward and one 12 pdr aft.

2 p.m. Picked up a Russian named the *Mary* of Pingu with munitions proecected [*sic*].

October 1st at sea.

At 3 p.m. we ran across the *Durham* of West Hartlepool from Archangel. She had the appearance of a German cruiser, and we went to action stations. She also thought we was a German and tried to escape but she pulled up when we sent a round across her bows. Her skipper was quite delighted to find we were English.

148. *Translation of a Note Verbale from German Government to US Embassy*

Berlin, 21 September 1915

The Danish passenger steamer *United States* which sailed from New York on April 23, 1915, bound for Copenhagen, in the first days of May was stopped by a British auxiliary cruiser about sixty to eighty miles off Kirkwall. While performing this act, as well as during the examination and when departing, the auxiliary cruiser flew the Danish national flag, the same flag also being displayed by the steamer *United States*. These statements are based on the sworn testimony of a reliable witness who has been a seafaring man for many years and can exactly discern the national flags.

That a British auxiliary cruiser was actually concerned, becomes apparent from the fact that a British naval officer accompanied by

[1]See page 271, note 1; there was no submarine in *Caribbean*'s vicinity at the time.

several marines left the cruiser and boarded the *United States*, and that the officer induced the captain to proceed to Kirkwall, whence the steamer was not permitted to leave until May 6 1915. The auxiliary cruiser had a coat of grey paint and a displacement of possibly 8500 tons.

The German Government energetically protests against this unheard of misuse of a neutral flag by the British Navy. At the same time it calls attention to the dangers to neutral shipping arising from this misuse and must leave with the British Government the responsibility for damages to neutral ships resulting from the adoption by British warships of a procedure having the intent to deceive.

The Imperial Foreign Office requests the American Embassy to cause steps to be taken to the end that, through the intervention of the American Embassy at London, the foregoing be brought to the attention of the British Government, and that this Office be informed at the proper time of the latter Government's reply.

The Danish Government has been apprised of this step [160].

149. *Commander-in-Chief Home Fleets to Admiralty*

HMS *Iron Duke*, 29 September 1915

With reference to Admiralty letter M. 26375/15 of 17 September 1915, referring to … remarks [in] a copy of a report dated 21 August 1915 by the captain of HMS *India* [129] upon the sinking of that ship by an enemy submarine, be pleased to inform the Lords Commissioners of the Admiralty that I am not aware what orders, if any, were issued by the Rear-Admiral Commanding Tenth Cruiser Squadron to the *India*.

2. Directions for the areas to be worked by the ships of the Tenth Cruiser Squadron off the Norwegian coast are contained in my W/T signals, copies of which are attached. Those for working in conjunction with the armed trawlers off the Norwegian coast are given in HF 0020/30 of 25 July 1915, copy enclosed, and were issued to the armed trawlers, ships of the Tenth Cruiser Squadron on G Patrol and to the Rear-Admiral Tenth Cruiser Squadron [114, 115].

The orders were drafted for the guidance of the officers commanding the armed trawlers; the patrol areas of the ships laid down in my signal of 2nd June are not altered. Ships are not forbidden to enter narrow waters, but the armed trawlers have been attached to the Norwegian patrol specially to work in the inshore waters; it has not been my intention that heavy ships should intercept vessels in the fjords.

3. From the information before me, I consider that it was unwise on

the part of the Captain of the *India* to remain in sight of the land and in about the same position so long as he did on the afternoon of 8 August, and I infer from the statement in paragraph 2 of Commander Kennedy's report ... that in the forenoon the *Gloria* was boarded by an officer from *India* although two armed trawlers were in company with the *Gloria*, and it appears clear that Commander Kennedy had no suspicion that submarines might be in the vicinity.

4. The *Virginian*'s urgent signal to detain the *Gloria* led the Captain of the *India* to steam into the Vest Fjord and, supposing that he had received no warning of submarines in the fjord, I consider that he was justified in chasing her, as the trawlers were too slow to do so. It would have been more prudent, on giving up the chase at 2 p.m., to have withdrawn the *India* at high speed, leaving the trawlers to intercept shipping emerging or entering the inshore channel, instead of employing the *India* on this work.

150. *Notebook diary of Able Seaman W.C. Style [Serving in* Alcantara*]*

October 2nd 5 a.m.

Picked up *Robert Smith* trawler again and exchanged orders.

At 10 p.m. picked up a Swedish steamer *Phillys* Archangle to Glasgow with timber, allowed to proceed. Her home port was Landskonter.

Shortly after we stopped the *Merridir* of Glasgow, Archangle to London with timber.[1]

At 7 p.m. we stopped a Norwegian named the *Hiso* from Archangle to Newport Mon, with timber, allowed to proceed.

October 3. 3.30 a.m.

Stopped a Russian steamer Blythe to Archangle with coal. Allowed to proceed. 6 a.m. picked up the trawler *Rusko* she was homeward bound. 7 a.m. picked up the trawler *Saxon* and put a crew aboard for submarine spotting.

Monday 4th.

3 a.m. Stopped steamer *Turkey* Archangle to Hull. Allowed to proceed.

Tuesday 5th.

From now to Thursday was foggy. Nothing sighted.

[1]The correct name of '*Merridir*' is not known.

Thursday 7th.

Fine weather again. Noon stopped steamer *Westville* of South Shields from Blyth to Archangle with coal.

Friday 8th.

Fine weather again. Stopped SS *Fyero* Wilson line from Hull to Archangel (just noticed that I have spelt Archangel wrong every time).[1] Skipper of steamer told us that 41 German trawlers had been captured with mines and it was rumoured that Ostend had been retaken. We have been looking out for a ship with a woman on board supposed to be a spy, but have had no luck to date. Submarines reported 20 miles south of here last night.

11.40. Action stations were sounded. We had sighted a ship which looked suspiciously like a German cruiser but she proved to be *Ravenstone* of Newcastle, we were all pretty thankful as it was so dark and she may have been hiding submarines. Archangel to Dundee with timber.

Saturday October 9th, '15.

At 6 a.m. we stopped the *Plutos* Government transport no. 666. Archangel to Portsmouth. Fine weather. 10 a.m. Picked up our trawler *Saxon* and she left with fresh orders.

Sunday October 10th '15.

2 a.m. stopped the Norwegian Steamer *Gudrun* Bergen to Iceland, empty and rolling heavily. Boarding officer had a hard job to get on board. Weather fine.

Monday October 11th

Beautiful morning, but a gale brewing somewhere. About 5 p.m. we stopped a Russian steamer *Sibir* of Martopol, Russia. Archangel to London with red wood sleepers.

Tuesday 12th.

Blowing up pretty stiff in for a good gale. 9 a.m. picked up the Armed liner *Mongolia* [actually *Mantua*] who relieved us of our patrol, and we are proceeding to the coaling base, Bustavo in the Shetlands.

2 p.m. terrible gale running but ship a good sea boat and rides beautifully. Sea looks splendid. If we were in the old *Calyx* still we should have a lively time.

Wednesday 13th.

7 a.m. Sea is pretty well calm again, and we are nearing the Shetlands shall get in about 9 a.m.

9.30 a.m. Arrived and it looks pretty desolate from the ship. Can't see half a dozen houses all told. Plenty of colliers here and also drifters

[1]The correct name of *Fyero* is not known.

used for sweeping purposes. Mail came on board, didn't get a letter, but I was not disappointed, as we have only left Liverpool 25 days today.

Thursday 14th '15.

Started coaling today. Poldhu says we have declared war on Bulgaria.

Friday 15th.

Still coaling but all quiet. *Virginian* came in and started coaling. Saw northern lights tonight from about 9.15 to 9.45, can't describe them as I should like to. They came across the sky in successive waves of lights and also in rays or beams and all seemed to collect over the ship where for a time they hung, became tinted with very pretty colours and then slowly faded away.

Saturday 16th.

Still coaling. Shall finish today. Weather very fine. Had good news by wireless (Poldhu). Should have gone to sea today but are waiting for a prize crew from Liverpool.

Sunday 17th '15.

Prize crew came back today. I went on shore this afternoon, and had a good walk around, not much to see. Had tea in one of the crofters' houses.

Very homely people, the wife of the crofter explained to us how they lived. They have to make all their own woollen cloth right from the wool off the sheep. Shew us (my chums and I) the old fashioned spinning wheel and how they worked it and some of the different woollen gear she had made. She baked some bread in a kettle over a peat fire, but she took the hottest embers from the fire and placed on the kettle lid to assist the baking. She told us how the women have to assist to cut the peat, dig the potatoes, dig the turnips, look after the cattle etc., so altogeth[er] they have a pretty busy time. Got on board and came straight to sea.

Monday 18th Sea.

Beautiful weather. Quiet all day.

Tuesday 19th.

Good weather again. Picked up steam ship *Ripa*, Norwegian, Bergen to the Faeroes with fish at 1 p.m. Allowed to proceed. Good news by wireless.

Wednesday 20th.

Nice day. At 6 p.m. we stopped the steamer *Sappho* Wilson Line from Hull to Archangel. Got some papers dated the 16th. Allowed to proceed.

Thursday 21st.

Fine weather. All quiet. Have got beautiful sky effects at sunset and sunrise. Sometimes the sky looks very angry but taken altogether very beautiful.

Friday 22nd.

Beautiful weather again. All quiet.

Saturday 23rd.

At 9 a.m. we stopped steamer *Weimar* Leith of the Currie Line. Archangel to London. Butter and eggs. Allowed to proceed.

At 2 p.m. we stopped the sailing ship *Gildas* Cardiff to Bergen with coals. Allowed to proceed. Had news this morning from 'Poldhu' of the shooting of Miss Cavell,[1] made our fellows mad. Pity the Germans '---'. Vide Dr Lyttleton.[2]

Sunday 24th.

Good news by wireless. Comments from Yankee press re Miss Cavell same as usual all talk. At 7.30 p.m. we stopped the steamer *Hector* Norwegian bound for Carnarvon with iron ore. Allowed to proceed. At 10 a.m. we stopped the steamer *Draglett* Norwegian from Cardiff with coals. Allowed to proceed.

At 11 a.m. we overtook the *Hector* again and sent her into Kirkwall with a prize crew. At 2 p.m. we stopped a Swedish steamer the *Iberia* of Goteborg, Cadiz to Copenhaven with wines and fruit. Had been stopped before by German submarine. Sent her into Kirkwall with a prize crew.[3]

Monday 25th Sea.

At 3 a.m. we stopped a Norwegian steamer the *Kerlo* from Stavanger to Iceland. Allowed to proceed. Beautiful weather.

At 9 a.m. we ran across the steamer *Romsdalfjord*, Norwegian from Newport News USA to Bergen with 5,000 tons of grain, and after inquiry we sent her into Kirkwall with a prize crew.[4]

Tuesday 26th Sea.

Beautiful morning again. One of those sunrises that you can't really describe. At 8.30 a.m. we picked up the HMS *Manchuria* [actually *Mantua*, again] going in to Liverpool and I believe we took over her

[1]Cavell, Edith, a British nurse who helped Allied soldiers escape in Belgium in 1915, and was caught and executed by the Germans; the execution, quite justified by her activities, was notably stupid, and provided the Allies with a very effective propaganda point.

[2]The editor cannot fathom this reference.

[3]*Hector* was in possession of a Netherlands Overseas Trust certificate, but this had no consignee; the ship was allowed to go on (to Rotterdam, not Carnarvon) on condition that the Trust withheld delivery until the consignee problem was sorted out. *Iberia* had one item, pepper, which was consigned to a black-listed destination and was ordered discharged; the ship resumed its voyage on 26 October (TS 14/5 of 28 and 30 October 1915).

[4]*Romsdalfjord* was inspected and allowed to go on (TS 14/5 of 26 October 1915).

patrol, by this time the sea began to get up rather rough and we found that it was caused by a gale that had occurred to the south of here.

Wednesday 27th. Sea.

Splendid weather again. Did not sight anything until 10 a.m. this morning when we dropped across the trawler *Arley* with one of our crews on board.

At about 5.30 p.m. we ran alongside HMS *Andes* which had brought the two prize crews back.

Thursday 28th. Sea.

9 a.m. stopped steam ship *Rainbow* of London from Hull to Archangel. Allowed to proceed.

Between 10 and 11 a.m. we had two trawlers alongside the *John Newland* and *Rusko*. Gave them some orders and parted company.

About 10 p.m. we had a bit of a shock. I was playing cards when the alarm bell or action bell was sounded and away we all went to our stations. It was quite black on the upper deck and going from the light I could see nothing at first but when my eyes got accustomed to the light that there was from the moon I could make out a big vessel on the port quarter coming up hand over fist. We then got news that one or two German cruisers had got through and most of us on board here thought we were in for a rough time.

We sent out wireless and this cruiser intercepted it and she then made herself known. She was the *Duke of Edinburgh*, a big cruiser of our own and you can guess we were pretty thankful, etc.

Friday 29th.

Rather cold today but still bright, although the sea is beginning to bear up rough. At 3.15 this morning we stopped a big steamer the *Rutherglen* of Glasgow laden with timber Archangel to the Tyne. Allowed to proceed.

At 5.30 p.m. we went to action stations and started steaming as fast as we could go after a packet they had sighted, but it proved to be one of our patrol boats. It gets dark at about 3.45 p.m. and makes it rather difficult to distinguish even your own vessels. By this time it was blowing a good stiff gale.

We are now looking for a German merchantman supposed to have reservists on board.

Saturday 30th Sea.

Blowing hard all night and a stiff sea running. Worst we have had for a long while. Still after the German merchantman. Wonder if we shall get her.

Sunday 31st Sea.

Weather settled and fine.

At 9.30 a.m. we stopped the steamer *Little Emma* Norwegian only loaded with fish. Allowed to proceed. At 4 p.m. we stopped the sailing ship *Sigrid* of Goteborg with cork. Cap Trafalgar to Copenhagen. Allowed to proceed. At 11 p.m. we stopped the steamer *Balto* Norwegian New York to Goteborg laden with copper and machinery oils etc. We put a prize crew on board and sent her to Kirkwall.[1]

151. *Rear-Admiral de Chair to Admiralty*

HMS *Alsatian*, 31 October 1915

Report of Proceedings, 3–31 October 1915

***

1. Sunday, 3rd October – The disposition of the Squadron was as follows:

A Patrol ... *Alsatian*, *Otway*, *Columbella*, *Ebro*, *Virginian*.
B Patrol ... *Motagua*, *Orotava*, *Hilary*.
C Patrol ... *Mantua*, *Arlanza*, *Oropesa*, *Changuinola*, *Patuca*.
E Patrol … *Orcoma*.
F Patrol ... *Andes*.
G Patrol ... *Alcantara*, and Armed Trawler *Newland*.
Coaling in Clyde ... *Hildebrand*, *Patia*, *Ambrose*.
Coaling at Liverpool ... *Cedric*, *Teutonic*, *Victorian*.
Coaling at Swarbacks Minn ... *Digby*.
Rejoining Patrol ... Armed Trawler *Saxon*.
Proceeding to Lerwick … Armed Trawlers *Robert Smith* and *Rushcoe*.
At Lerwick … Armed Trawler *Tenby Castle*.

Of 63 Vessels intercepted and examined during the past week 18 were sent in with Armed Guards, and one without.

2. Monday, 4th October – Fog was prevalent on patrol areas and much hampered the work of intercepting vessels.

Reliable report was received of the presence of a submarine off Hvidingsoe on the Norwegian Coast.

3. Tuesday, 5th October – Thick fog was experienced in area of A Patrol.

4. Wednesday, 6th October – In compliance with orders from the

[1]*Balto* was not detained.

Commander-in-Chief, *Arlanza* was detached from patrol and directed to proceed through Pentland Firth to Cromarty to coal in readiness to convey an Officer to Archangel.[1]

Fog continued in the northern areas.

5. Thursday, 7th October – The British Steamer *Westville* intercepted by *Alcantara* en route from Blyth to Archangel, reported having sighted mines on the surface in Lat. 58.12´N, Long. 0. 35´E on 5th October. This information was passed to the Commander-in-Chief.

6. Friday, 8th October – A report was received from *Almanzora* which was joining the Squadron from Belfast that her trials were satisfactory but that her sailing was delayed on account of trouble experienced in obtaining Engineers. She could give no definite date of departure.[2]

The Commander-in-Chief informed me that *Arlanza* when entering Cromarty Firth had gone ashore on the Nigg side but had been floated off. No damage was sustained. *Cedric* was met at a pre-arranged rendezvous and orders and information were communicated to her. *Otway* reported having intercepted the Swedish Steamer *Orion* (late British *Coningsby*, 2158 tons) Philadelphia to Stockholm with a cargo of caissons.

Some of the crew signed on in America were considered to be suspicious. She was sent to Kirkwall with an Armed Guard.[3]

7. Saturday, 9th October – *Alsatian* intercepted and examined the Danish Trawler *Ymir* GK 448, from Iceland to Fleetwood with fish. This vessel which was painted black with the Danish Flag on her sides and a Yellow funnel with the letter Y painted on it, exactly corresponded with the description given in Admiralty Telegram No. 224 of 3rd June 1915, of the German Trawler *Marsalaymir* or *Erna*. She was in possession of a pass to Fleetwood issued by the British Consul in Iceland but as it was considered possible that she was obtaining information as to the position of the patrols an Armed Guard was placed on board and she was sent to her destination for examination. Admiralty Telegram No. 452 relative to the *bona fides* of this Trawler was not received until three days later.

[1]*Arlanza* had a terrible time on detachment. She was sent to Cromarty to collect several French and British officers, and grounded there. In Russian waters she struck a mine and was beached; repairs took a long time; she was out of action for six months, and another of the Patrol's ships had to be sent to collect her cargo and her passengers; details are in the NMM at NOR/1 'HMS Arlanza'.

[2]*Almanzora* was presumably a replacement for *India*, but another ship, *Ambrose*, is not listed at the next muster (para. 8), though de Chair does not state that she had been removed from his squadron.

[3]*Orion* was inspected and allowed to go on (TS 14/5 of 11 October 1915).

Dense fog prevailed in the northern patrol areas.

8. Sunday, 10th October – The disposition of the Squadron was as follows:

A Patrol … *Orcoma*, *Cedric*, *Orotava*, *Alsatian*.
C Patrol … *Digby*, *Otway*, *Oropesa*, *Motagua*, *Hilary*, *Victorian*.
E Patrol … *Andes*.
F Patrol … *Virginian*.
G Patrol … *Alcantara* and Armed Trawlers *Newland* and *Saxon*.
Proceeding to Swarbacks Minn … *Ebro*.
Coaling at Swarbacks Minn … *Mantua*, *Patuca*.
Coaling &c. at Liverpool … *Teutonic*.
Coaling &c. in Clyde … *Patia*, *Columbella*, *Changuinola*.
Rejoining patrol from Clyde ... *Hildebrand*.
Rejoining patrol from Lerwick ... Armed Trawlers *Rushcoe* and *Robert Smith*.
Detached on special service ... *Arlanza*.
At Belfast ... *Almanzora*.

Of 51 vessels intercepted and examined during the past week 9 were sent in with and 2 without Armed Guards.

A submarine was reported off the Flannan Islands.

9. Monday, 11th October – *Alsatian* proceeded to Liverpool to coal, and during the afternoon the weather became bad and sea so rough as to make it very difficult to board intercepted vessels.

At 11.30 p.m. *Hilary* intercepted the American Steamer *Platuria* with petroleum, but she was unable to board due to heavy sea. She was directed to detain her till weather moderated. This was successfully accomplished next day.[1]

10. A report of the movements of a German Submarine on 1st October as observed by Sub-Lieutenant Easty, RNR[2] of *Mantua* when in charge of an Armed Guard on board the Swedish SS *Avesta* is forwarded as being of interest ... From this account it would appear that the submarine though prepared to deal with merchant shipping, was not anxious to encounter an armed vessel such as she evidently took the *Polarine* to be.[3]

[1]*Platuria* was not, in the event, detained (TS 14/5 of 15 or 16 October 1915).

[2]Eastty, Alfred M., RD, RNR, Sub-Lieutenant 1910, Lieutenant 1917, Lieutenant-Commander (retired), serving in *Pembroke* (Nore Command) 1940.

[3]The account referred to has not been located; the reference to *Polarine* is thus unclear.

11. Tuesday, 12th October – The gale continued during the night.

At 8 a.m. *Motagua* intercepted the Norwegian Steamer *Brode* with a cargo of grain in Lat. 58.54´N, Long. 11.35´W but had to detain her as the sea was too heavy to lower a boat.

12. Wednesday, 13th October – In spite of very bad weather *Digby* succeeded in boarding and sending to Lerwick with an Armed Guard the Norwegian Steamer *Skoglund*, Louisburg to Copenhagen … .[1]

At 3 p.m., as gale was increasing, *Motagua* was ordered to escort *Brode* to Lerwick putting an Armed Guard on board when weather permitted, but at 5.20 p.m. *Motagua* reported steamer had to heave to owing to increasing gale.

During the night all ships on A and C patrols were obliged to lie to on account of the gale increasing, boarding being impossible.

13. Thursday, 14th October – At 6.30 p.m. *Motagua* managed to get an Armed Guard on board Norwegian Steamer *Brode*.[2]

14. Friday, 15th October – *Hilary* intercepted and sent in to Lerwick with an Armed Guard the Danish Steamer *Kentucky*, New York to Copenhagen with general cargo. This vessel was ordered to be sent in ... .[3]

15. Saturday, 16th October – At midnight *Hildebrand* boarded the Norwegian Steamer *Corona*, Baltimore to Bergen, with grain. Her Master having stated that his ship had sprung a leak and was sinking the crew of 19 were taken on *Hildebrand* which then stood by. ... [T]he crew were thoroughly examined and six men who had joined at Baltimore were placed under arrest. In the meantime *Otway* was directed to proceed at full speed and assume charge of possible salvage operations. While carrying out this order *Otway* intercepted and sent to Kirkwall with Armed Guard the Danish Steamer *United States* proceeding east with 312 passengers among whom was the Austrian Aviator Von Georgevitch mentioned in Admiralty Telegrams of 10th and 12th October.[4]

At 8.30 a.m. *Corona* had 18 inches of water above the stokehold plates but as the leak appeared to be a small one and confined to Engine

[1]Several items of *Skoglund*'s cargo went to the Prize Court; there was also some uncertainty about the ship's ownership (TS 14/5 of 18 and 29 October 1915).

[2]*Brode* was not detained.

[3]Several items of cargo were not on the *Kentucky*'s manifest, others were on the consignee Black List; 14 items were directed to be prize-courted, and for others assurances from the company and from the Danish government against re-export were sought (TS 14/5 of 21 October 1915).

[4]Otherwise the *United States* was, as usual, allowed to go on (TS 14/5 of 26 October 1915) once the usual guarantees were forthcoming.

room and Stokehold an attempt at towing was made at 0.45 p.m., *Hilary* being ordered to act as escort. At 4.05 p.m. *Hildebrand* reported that the Steamer's cable which was being used in conjunction with wire hawsers had parted, but in spite of the considerable sea running at the time she was again taken in tow at 8.40 p.m. and headed for Stornoway. It is considered exceptionally good seamanship on the part of Captain Edwards to have managed this on a dark night with such a heavy sea and in submarine area.

16. Sunday, 17th October – By directions of the Commander-in-Chief *Hildebrand* cast off the tow at 6.45 a.m. and at 11 a.m. *Hilary* sank the *Corona* as a danger to navigation.

Ebro intercepted and sent to Lerwick with an Armed Guard the Danish Sailing Vessel *Livingstone* from Iceland ostensibly for Faroe Islands with cargo of salt fish. This vessel had a painted bow wave and was considerably off her course.[1]

Otway intercepted the Danish Steamer *Vulcan*, Philadelphia to Kirkwall and Malmo with oil. She was sent in to Lerwick with an Armed Guard ... .[2]

Digby intercepted the Danish Steamer *Hans Jensen* Baltimore to Goteburg with coal. As it is stated in CMO 270/1915 that this vessel is suspected, she was sent in to Lerwick with an Armed Guard.[3]

The disposition of the Squadron was as follows:

A Patrol … *Orcoma*, *Patuca*, *Cedric*.
C Patrol … *Orotava*, *Digby*, *Otway*, *Victorian*, *Hilary*.
E Patrol … *Andes*.
F Patrol … *Patia*.
G Patrol … *Mantua*, Armed Trawlers *Robert Smith* and *Rushcoe*.
Joining Patrol from Clyde … *Changuinola*.
Joining Patrol from Swarbacks Minn … *Ebro*.
Joining Patrol from Lerwick … Armed Trawlers *Tenby Castle* and *Arley*.
Proceeding to Lerwick … Armed Trawlers *Newland* and *Saxon*.
Proceeding to Stornoway … *Hildebrand*.
Proceeding to Swarbacks Minn … *Motagua*.
Coaling &c. at Liverpool … *Alsatian*, *Teutonic*.

[1]*Livingstone* was not detained.

[2]*Vulcan*'s whole cargo, listed as lubricating oil and diesel oil, was ordered to be placed in the Prize Court, and every barrel tested; it was suspected that the oil was actually castor oil (TS 14/5 of 20 October 1915).

[3]An initial question over the *Hans Jensen*'s owner was answered from Copenhagen that he was 'absolutely reliable' (TS 14/5 of 20 and 23 October 1915).

Coaling in Clyde ... *Columbella*.
Coaling at Swarbacks Minn ... *Alcantara*, *Virginian*, *Oropesa*.
At Belfast ... *Almanzora*.
On special service ... *Arlanza*.

Of 42 vessels intercepted during the week ten were sent in with, and one without Armed Guards. Continuous heavy weather had at times prevented boarding and necessitated ships heaving to.

17. Monday, 18th October – *Victorian* intercepted the Norwegian Steamer *Alstad*, New York to Bergen. As this vessel is stated to be suspicious ... she was sent in to Kirkwall with an Armed Guard.[1]

Orcoma intercepted the Danish Steamer *Island* Reykjavik to Leith and Copenhagen with meat, fish, sheepskins and 15 passengers, one of whom was for Berlin. These passengers were considered suspicious. The ship was sent to Lerwick with an Armed Guard. She was stated to belong to the United Shipping Co. ... having given an undertaking that their vessels should call at a port in the United Kingdom both inward and outward bound, but in view of the suspicious passengers it was thought desirable to make sure of a thorough examination being carried out [187].[2]

18. Tuesday, 19th October – The Armed Trawler *Tenby Castle* which should have left Lerwick on the evening of 17th October for G Patrol, attempted to proceed at daylight but was obliged to return in the evening in consequence of renewed defects.

Almanzora joined the Squadron from Belfast and proceeded on patrol.

Virginian intercepted the Norwegian Steamer *Pollux*, Reykjavik to Bergen, calling at Thorshavn with general cargo, mails and fifteen passengers for Thorshavn, ninety seven for Bergen, some of the latter being considered suspicious. She was sent to Kirkwall in charge of an Armed Guard, the Officer of which was directed to inform the examining officers there of the suspicious circumstances.[3]

Hilary intercepted the Norwegian Steamer *Dratsberg*, Buenos Aires

[1]The *Alstad* was detained only briefly (TS 14/5 of 20 October 1915).

[2]A mistranslation of items on the manifest occasioned a flurry of telegrams about *Island*'s cargo, revealing that the Customs at Lerwick relied on a self-compiled word list, despite translators being supplied [102]. See also Shetland Archives, CE 86 1/20, 87–88. In the end *Island* was allowed to continue her voyage (TS 14/5 of 26 October 1915).

[3]The *Pollux* was in fact a Dutch ship (according to Lloyds Register), but the suspicions of the *Virginian*'s captain were apparently unfounded; the ship was released (TS 14/5 of 19 October 1915).

to Copenhagen with grain. She was sent to Kirkwall with an Armed Guard … .[1]

Midshipman Frank R. Allen, RNR[2] of *Ebro* who had been accidentally shot on 1st October died in hospital at Lerwick.

19. Thursday, 21st October – The weather became bad during the night, ships on patrol were obliged to lie to, but in spite of heavy sea *Oropesa* managed to intercept and place an Armed Guard on board Norwegian sailing vessel *Glance*, cargo petroleum and coke.[3]

Weather improved towards evening.

20. Friday, 22nd October – A submarine was reported by an Auxiliary Patrol Vessel in Lat. 59.37´N, Long. 3.55´W, on the surface at 7.40 a.m.

Victorian intercepted the Danish Steamer *Hellig Olav*, New York to Copenhagen with 242 passengers, 86 of whom were Germans, 12 being men, the remainder women and children. She was sent in to Kirkwall with an Armed Guard … .[4]

21. Saturday, 23rd October – *Columbella* intercepted the Swedish Steamer *Consul Olsson* from Tampa to Helsingborg with phosphate. She was sent in to Kirkwall with an Armed Guard … .[5]

22. Sunday, 24th October – The disposition of the Squadron was as follows:

A Patrol … *Patuca*, *Motagua*, *Cedric*, *Oropesa*, *Ebro*.
C Patrol … *Changuinola*, *Digby*, *Hildebrand*, *Victorian*, *Teutonic*, *Virginian*, *Columbella*.
E Patrol … *Almanzora*.
F Patrol … *Patia*.
G Patrol … *Mantua*, *Alcantara*, Armed Trawlers *Rushcoe*, *Arley* and *Robert Smith*.
Proceeding to Liverpool … *Orcoma*.
Proceeding to Swarbacks Minn … *Hilary*.
Rejoining Patrol from Liverpool … *Alsatian*.
Coaling in Clyde … *Orotava*.

[1]*Dratsberg* was not detained.

[2]Allen, Frank R., RNR, Midshipman 1915, died that year.

[3]*Glance* was permitted to go on after inspection (TS 14/5 of 27 October 1915).

[4]*Hellig Olav* was allowed to proceed, having passed inspection by Customs (TS 14/5 of 25 October 1915).

[5]A query was raised over the consignee, said to be the German consul at Malmo, though nothing resulted against him; the cargo was nevertheless sent to the Prize Court as being likely to reach Germany by being captured before reaching Helsingborg, which is in the Sound, where German ships were active (TS 14/5 of 25 and 26 October 1915).

Coaling at Swarbacks Minn … *Otway*, *Andes*.
At Lerwick … *Tenby Castle*, *Newland*, *Saxon*.
On special service … *Arlanza*.

Of 57 vessels intercepted and examined during the week 18 were sent in with Armed Guards (11 to Kirkwall, 7 to Lerwick).

Alsatian intercepted the Norwegian Steamer *John Blumer* Baltimore to Bergen with wheat and rye. She was sent in to Kirkwall with an Armed Guard in accordance with instructions received from the Admiral Commanding Orkneys and Shetlands.

23. Monday, 25th October – *Alcantara* intercepted the Norwegian Steamer *Romsdalfjord*, Newport News to Bergen with a cargo of rye consigned to the Norwegian Government. Seven of the crew had been shipped in the United States. She was sent to Lerwick with an Armed Guard.[1]

Cedric was met at a pre-arranged rendezvous and I went on board her and made an informal inspection of the ship underweigh.

24. Tuesday, 26th October – *Otway*, *Ebro* and *Digby* were met at a pre-arranged rendezvous and orders and information were communicated.

25. Wednesday, 27th October – *Andes* intercepted the Danish Sailing Ship *Hjalmar* in tow of the Whaler *Funding* from Funding Fjord, Faroes to Stavanger with whale oil. Both vessels were sent to Lerwick in charge of an Armed Guard … .[2]

The wind increasing to a gale from SE at nightfall directions were given to the Squadron to lie to as necessary. Barometer fell to 29.25.[3]

26. Thursday, 28th October – *Andes* intercepted the Danish Sailing Ship *Ofelia* in tow of the Whaler *Magnus* from Funding Fjord, Faroes to Stavanger with whale oil. *Ofelia* was sent in to Lerwick in charge of an Armed Guard in compliance with Commander-in-Chief's signal 0020 of 26th October; *Magnus* was allowed to proceed.[4]

Information was received that on 22nd October *Arlanza* which was on special service had been injured by a mine and towed to Yucanski Roads whither repairing materials and diving plant were being despatched by the Russian Government.[5] During the day the wind

[1]The *John Blumer* and the *Romsdalfjord* were allowed to go on, after consideration by the Contraband Committee (TS 14/5 of 27 October 1915).

[2]*Hjalmar* and *Funding* were not detained.

[3]990 mbs.

[4]*Ofelia* did not reach Lerwick until 16 November, but was then released by order of the Contraband Committee (Shetland Archives CE 85 4/7).

[5]*Arlanza* had to be unloaded for repairs to be made; the ship was *hors de combat* until November.

increased to force 10 Barometer fell to 28.96[1] and the sea increased to 8 making it very difficult to board ships intercepted.

27. Friday, 29th October – *Andes* intercepted the Danish Steamer *Esrom*, New York to Copenhagen with a general cargo including contraband and sent her to Lerwick in charge of an Armed Guard ... On enquiry it was found that this vessel had passed within a mile of the south coast of Iceland in thick weather until in Lat. 65 N. When captured she was intending to put into Bergen for coal.[2]

28. Saturday, 30th October – At 4 a.m. *Columbella* reported that she could hear *Oscar II* calling up Lands End and Bergen, and at 6 p.m. *Cedric* intercepted her en route for Copenhagen with a general cargo and 183 passengers including five German men, eleven women and children. She was sent to Kirkwall with an Armed Guard.[3]

Hildebrand reported that she had intercepted the Danish Sailing Ship *Maracaibo* in Lat. 59.37´N, Long. 10.35´W and had supplied her with eight days' provisions. This vessel which had been originally intercepted on 18th October by *Orotava* had an Armed Guard from that ship on board and was bound for Lerwick but the south easterly gales prevalent during the last week had prevented her making any headway, and her supplies had run very short.[4]

29. Sunday, 31st October – The disposition of the Squadron was as follows:

A Patrol ... *Motagua*, *Ebro*, *Otway*, *Alsatian*, *Oropesa*, *Patia*.
C Patrol ... *Hilary*, *Changuinola*, *Hildebrand*, *Cedric*, *Almanzora*, *Teutonic*, *Columbella*.
F Patrol ... *Andes*.
G Patrol ... *Alcantara*, Armed Trawlers *Arley* and *Saxon*.
Proceeding to Liverpool ... *Virginian*.
Coaling at Liverpool ... *Orcoma*.
Coaling &c. in Clyde ... *Digby*, *Patuca*.
Coaling at Swarbacks Minn ... *Victorian*.
Rejoining squadron from Swarbacks Minn ... *Mantua*.
On detached service ... *Arlanza*, *Orotava*.
At Lerwick ... Armed Trawlers *Rushcoe*, *Robert Smith*.

[1]980 mbs.

[2]*Esrom* was sent to Hull, part of her cargo being deemed contraband (Shetland Archives CE 85 7/7).

[3]*Oscar II* was not detained.

[4]*Maracaibo*'s cargo was sent to the Prize Court; the consignee was on the British Black List (TS 14/6 of 8 November 1915).

Of 64 ships intercepted and examined during the week 18 were sent in to port with, and 1 without, Armed Guards.

Alcantara on G Patrol intercepted the Norwegian Steamer *Balto*, New York to Goteborg with copper, machinery, rifles, motor cars, ammunition and one Lady passenger. Her Master stated that he had kept to parallel 61° until in Long. 14 and had then passed, in thick weather, north of the Faroe Islands. She was, however, intercepted in Lat. 62.18´N, Long. 2.1´E and sent to Kirkwall with an Armed Guard.[1]

30. I attach as an enclosure hereto the report made by Commander William G.A. Kennedy relative to the loss of HMS *India* on 6th August 1915. This report has already been forwarded to the Admiralty but as it forms part of the records of the Squadron under my command it seems desirable to include it in my report of proceedings [129].[2]

152. *Admiral S.C. Colville to the Admiralty*

HMS *Cyclops*, 4 October 1915

… I have just returned from visiting Swarbacks Minn and submit that

(a) the three pounder guns for arming the gate vessels at Swarbacks Minn should be sent there immediately.

(b) I do not consider two 12 pounders mounted on shore would be any real use against a submarine attack; but I have detailed two more Armed Trawlers from the Shetland Patrol for the purpose of guarding the booms and attacking any submarine caught in the nets.

(c) As the *Gibraltar* is principally used as a depot ship for accommodating the coaling parties etc., for the Tenth Cruiser Squadron, she cannot be stationed near the boom for the defence of the entrance owing to the great difficulty and delay in transporting these parties from such an exposed anchorage. The *Gibraltar* therefore cannot be considered as a floating battery for the defence of the boom in addition to her being a depot ship, and if their Lordships consider that there is any fear of the Germans attacking this place with craft for the purpose of breaking the boom, and thereby allowing submarines to enter the harbour and torpedoing any of the Tenth Cruiser Squadron inside, a battery of at least four 5" guns should be established on shore near the boom,

[1]See page 284, note 1.

[2]Note that this report, despite the Admiralty's request for fortnightly reports [140], covers four weeks. De Chair clearly compiled his reports by the cruise not by time.

the site being definitely settled by the proper experts.

3. The establishment of the Naval Base at Swarbacks Minn and of the examination Service at Lerwick has been a very heavy drain on the Shetland Patrol leaving few vessels to patrol the waters of these islands, and I would once more submit the necessity of the additional vessels ...

153. *Commodore R.E.R. Benson to Rear-Admiral de Chair*

HMS *Cedric*, 8 October 1915

I have the honour to submit for your consideration the question of the rate of pay of Mercantile Ratings, as I consider it an important matter for some very necessary adjustments to be made as early as possible.

2. When the Ship commissioned on the 7th December 1914, Engine room complement, cooks, artizans, etc., were signed on at the port rate of Pay which then obtained, plus a war bonus of £1 to each class of ratings. The authority for this procedure was Letter No. T.0574/1914, of 13th November 1914, from the Director of Transports. An extract of this letter is attached ...

3. Since that date however the value of labour has, in consequence of the war, increased, and the result of this has been that men who have joined to fill vacancies, etc., have perforce been signed on at a higher rate of pay, viz: the port rate of pay at the time of entry plus a war bonus. This was necessary as the men would not have signed on at any lower rate of pay. As an example of my meaning, on 7th December 1914, Asst. Stewards were signed on to receive £4.5.0 a month with £1 war bonus, whilst now a man entered receives £5.5.0, and £2 war bonus. The consequence is that an assistant steward, entered at the present time receives more pay (£7.5.0) than the Saloon steward entered on commissioning (£6.10.0) under whose orders he acts. This applies equally to all classes of ratings.

4. I am aware that this matter is receiving the attention of the Director of Transports [123] ... but I would submit in view of these facts, that the matter may be treated as urgent, especially as the men who have served since commissioning feel, and I think reasonably, that circumstances have placed them in a very unfortunate position.

154. *Midshipman Cyril A. Bamford, RNR,*[1] *to Commanding Officer HMS* Orcoma

11 October 1915

I have the honour to report that on the 16th September 1915 in Lat. 66.49´N, Long. 16.0´W, I went, in charge of the Armed Guard, on board the Swedish Topsail Schooner *Valand* of Halmstad from Akureyri, Iceland, to Leith with a cargo of herrings with orders from you to take the schooner to Lerwick, making Muckle Flugga during the dark hours, if possible.

Before proceeding with further details of the voyage, I wish to make it clear that the Captain of the *Valand* retained charge of the sailing of the ship, and when difficulties arose, we invariably consulted together and agreed on the best course to be taken without friction.

We had a light fair wind until p.m. 18th Sept. when the wind began to haul Easterly. At 9.30 p.m. on 19th Myggenaes (Faero Islands) was sighted bearing SE by S. By evening the wind and sea had increased to a strong South easterly gale, and on morning of the 20th, the gale was so strong that we considered it advisable to heave to, our noon position by dead reckoning being Lat. 61.55´N, Long. 9.33´W. As the wind appeared to be increasing I deemed it best to run North and sail down the Eastern side of the Faero Islands. This was accordingly done and at 8 p.m. on 21st Myggenaes was again sighted bearing S by W. At this point the steering gear broke down but fortunately the gale had moderated slightly and in a few hours the necessary repairs were effected. On the 22nd we were becalmed, but the following day had head wind from SSE accompanied by dense banks of fog. On 25th the fog cleared altogether and there was a moderate ENE wind. By this time our provisions were practically exhausted and we had for the greater part to subsist on salt herrings from the cargo. At noon on that day (25th) the wind commenced to blow from the NE and by 6 p.m. a strong North Easterly gale had set in. At 8 p.m. we sighted Muckle Flugga bearing S 56° W, but owing to the Force of the gale the absence of coast lights and the improbability of sighting any of the Patrol near Lerwick we steered a course further seawards rather than attempt to make port. At 1 a.m. on 26th, the fore rigging carried away and the foremast nearly went overboard, but by knocking away the bulwarks on the port side,

[1]Bamford, Cyril A., DSC, RNR, Midshipman 1914, Lieutenant 1918, Lieutenant-Commander RN 1927, serving in Hydrographic Department, 1940, Commander (retired) 1945.

passing wire strops round the ribs of the ship and rigging up temporary stays, the damage was repaired in a few hours. On the evening of 27th, I determined to make an attempt to get to Lerwick and we accordingly sailed Northward on the Port tack. At 4 a.m. on 28th, the starboard anchor was carried overboard, but was eventually got on board without any damage beyond making a dent in the ship's side. At 5 a.m. land was sighted and at 6 a.m. we discovered that the ship was between Fair Island and Sunburgh Head, the North Easterly gale having set us to the Eastward. As it was then impossible to get to Lerwick and dangerous considering the wind to attempt to reach Kirkwall, added to which the ship's gear was in a rotten condition, sails and ropes carrying away incessantly until the lower topsail was the only sound sail onboard, I decided to run before the gale for Leith. On 29th Sept. land was sighted bearing WNW and at 4 p.m. we passed close to a town, which the Master thought was Aberdeen and reduced sail so as to make the Bell Rock by daylight. At 6 p.m. there were two flashing lights in sight, one (four flash light) 2 points on our Starboard bow and the other (red & white flash light on our Port Beam. As these lights were only sighted once and not again, we considered that they were fishing vessels signalling to one another. At 8 p.m. owing to the similarity of these lights to shore lights, I decided to keep the 8 to 12 watch, and at 10 p.m. the aforementioned 4 flash light appeared again about 4 points on the starboard bow. I called the Master, but the light was not visible again. As May Island was the only 4 flash light on the coast, I told the Master to heave to for the night. In the morning (30th) May Island was abaft our Port Beam. The mistake had been caused:

(1) By the absence of proper charts & navigation instruments,
(2) By the sun not having been visible from the time we left the Shetlands.

The town which was sighted, instead of being Aberdeen, must have been Montrose, and the aforementioned lights, May Island on our Starboard Bow and the Bell Rock on our Port Beam.

At 4 a.m. on the 30th September we attempted to go through the Southern Channel of the Forth between May Island and Dunbar light, but were instructed by Destroyers to enter by the Northern Channel. Owing to the wind we did not weather May Island until 5 p.m. that evening. We proceeded up the Forth as far as Largo Bay and anchored for the night in 12 fathoms. In the morning (1st October) we proceeded and arrived in Leith Roads at 4.30 p.m. and docked in the Old Dock at 5.30 p.m. I immediately reported myself to the Senior Naval Officer at Leith.

The Armed Guard, of which I was in charge, consisted of:

A. Seaward, Seaman, RNR 7013A.
G. Bowman, Ord. Seaman, D/J.34840.
R. McGuinness, Stoker, RNR V.663.

I have the honour especially to bring to your notice the name of A. Seaward, Seaman, RNR, who was of the greatest help throughout the voyage, being at all times ready and willing to do everything he could to assist in the working of the ship, and whose ability was of great value.[1]

155. *Commander E.V. Dugmore to Rear-Admiral Commanding Tenth Cruiser Squadron*

HMS *Ebro*, 11 October 1915

I have the honour to report that on 10th October 1915 at 6.50 p.m. the Russian Steamer *Sicilia* from Liverpool to Archangel attempted to ram HM ship under my command. The position was: Lat. 61.58´N, Long. 3.58´W. It was quite dark and slightly hazy.

The *Sicilia* was steering apparently NNE. The *Ebro* was on her starboard beam headed about WSW and her helm had been starboarded in order to give the *Sicilia* a wide berth before turning up on the quarter to examine her. At this stage the *Sicilia* altered course, evidently with the intention of ramming, and a collision was only avoided by *Ebro* reversing her port engine at full speed.

I directed the Boarding Officer to enquire into the reason for this action on the part of the *Sicilia*. The result of the enquiries shows the mate was on watch. He said he thought the *Ebro* was a German, but the Boarding Officer found it impossible to elicit any information as to what kind of German vessel. The mate was very excited, and incoherent. As the Master seems to have taken all possible steps to avoid a collision as soon as the hull of the *Ebro* was visible (which was at very close range), the only conclusion I can arrive at is that the mate seeing nothing but the *Ebro*'s bow wave, mistook her for a submarine.[2]

[1] *Valand* was detained.

[2] The note appended by Admiral Oliver on 26 October is as likely an explanation as any: 'No action seems necessary. The mate may have been drinking, or possibly lost his nerve; much cannot be expected for £4 10. a month.'

156. *Sub-Lieutenant D.L. Edwards, RNR,*[1] *to Commanding Officer HMS* Orcoma

15 October 1915

I have the honour to make the following report re my voyage in the Norwegian Brigantine *Haugar* bound from Iceland to Haugesund with a cargo of herrings:

On 16th Sept. I went on board the *Haugar*, in charge of the armed guard, in Lat. 66.49´N, Long. 15.46´W with instructions from you to proceed to Lerwick, and I set a course accordingly. On 18th Sept., the Faero Islands were sighted at daybreak and, as the wind which had hauled from NE to SE, had risen to a gale, I agreed with the Master re heaving the ship to. The pump had to be worked continually as with the heavy labouring of the ship, which was over 50 years old and leaked badly, the water in her increased rapidly. While her crew manned the pump, the armed guard and myself trimmed the sails as necessary. On 19th Sept. the gale continued, heavy seas being shipped. The topmast backstay carried away and preventer was rigged. On Sept. 20th we were in the vicinity of the Faero Bank and the wind having decreased we proceeded on the Starboard tack. On 21st Sept. 9 a.m. we again sighted the Faero Islands, the ship heading for Dimon Fiord, and the wind being SSE (moderate). Not anticipating a change before we could tack clear of the Faero Islands, which it was essential we should weather, the Master of the *Haugar* and I decided to go through the fiord and thus save considerable time. At 1 p.m. we were due North of Syrderi [correctly Sydero] Island, when we were becalmed and we drifted out to sea again. About 7 p.m., a good breeze sprang up from S.E. and we again attempted to go through the fjord, but when we were only half a mile from the high land, the wind dropped and the tide carried the ship landward, the sea being smooth at the time. By then it was dark and no lights were visible, we were so near the rocks that it seemed almost possible to touch them and we drifted West almost scraping them. To leeward there was a ledge of rocks running out and as it seemed impossible for the ship to clear them, the Master and I decided that the ship must be abandoned. The lifeboat was hoisted out with the topsail halyards and, as it was not provisioned, I put my remaining stores into it. We pulled off a little way, there being no place where a landing was possible, and watched the ship drift towards the rocks, but much to everyone's surprise she drifted through without touching them. We then

[1]Edwards, David L., RNR, Sub-Lieutenant 1915, Lieutenant 1917.

proceeded to re-embark from the boat, which was leaking so badly that one of my guard had to bail as fast as he could with a bucket. On regaining the *Haugar* I found that the Compass had been broken to pieces by Main Boom, but luckily there was a spare Compass, which although small I succeeded in rigging up. A breeze sprang up from the SSE and we proceeded to tack to South of Sydero. On 22nd the provisions which we brought with us, were finished and the ship had not much in the way of stores, we subsisted on hard bread and salt fish. On 23rd Sept. we were becalmed and I sighted the Faero Islands from aloft. At 4 a.m. on the 24th a breeze sprang up from NNE, freshening towards evening. The ship would not head as high up as Muckle Flugga, but our course would take us south of the Shetlands and we could make for Kirkwall instead of Lerwick. On 25th Sept. the wind increased to a moderate gale and at 6 p.m. we hove to. Towards night the weather became worse, and part of the bulwarks were stove in and a jib and staysail were blown away. The ship was labouring heavily and made water fast: the Armed Guard helped at the pump and rendered all possible assistance wherever required. On 26th Sept. the weather moderated slightly and at 3 p.m. land was sighted, which we made out to be Papa Westral [correctly Westray] Island, North of the Orkneys, but being unable to pass north of it we stood out again. On the 27th the wind was still NNE (strong) and at noon became very squally, but I advised the Master to carry on in the expectation of sighting land before dark, which however we did not do. The heavy squalls seemed to strain the ship in every part and she took heavy seas, which made pumping very difficult. At daybreak we sighted Noup Head, the wind being NNE with very violent squalls. We rounded Seal Skerry at 10 a.m. and arrived at Kirkwall at 6 p.m. The Master informed me there were 4 feet of water in the hold.[1]

I have the honour to report that the conduct of the armed guard, which consisted of:

Wm S. Elliott, Sergeant RMLI RFR Plym.1499.
Walter Whalley, Private RMLI 17212 Plym.
Charles Bradder, Stoker 1 C1. RFR SS 102384.

was admirable. They were always ready to render assistance wherever required: They were constantly wet through and frequently had to sleep in their saturated clothes.

I respectfully would mention the name of Sergeant Elliott, whose assistance was most valuable.

[1]*Haugar* was not detained.

157. *Surveyor D.J. Kelleher to Board of Customs and Excise*

Lerwick, 18 October 1915

I beg to forward an application from the Norwegian Vice-Consul here for transmission to the Board of Trade requesting an extension of the time specified in Section 10 Merchant Shipping Act October 1906 with regard to the carriage of deck cargoes in winter, as modified by SC 3 of 27.8.1915 in the case of the Norwegian S/S *Ledaal* still under war detention at this port.

The *Ledaal* was diverted on the 1st inst by HMS *Andes* on her voyage from New York to Archangel, arrived here on the 4th inst ...

The applicant states that the vessel was chartered to take a cargo of timber from a port in the White Sea to Dundee immediately after discharge at Archangel, that owing to her detainment it will be impossible to carry out the contract within the time specified, the 15th November 1915, and that this will involve a loss of freight to the extent of £4,000. Under the exceptional circumstances it is submitted for consideration whether the indulgence requested be granted for the voyage in question.[1]

158. *Memorandum by Alex. Hunt, Admiralty M Branch*

20 October 1915

It has been decided to transfer to the French Authorities the Armed Merchant Cruiser *Digby*, which will be taken over by the French all standing and commissioned and manned by them, the Engineer Officer and some ratings being temporarily left in the ship and the Gunner and a few Petty Officers.[2]

[1]*Ledaal* was carrying machinery. The Contraband Committee made enquiries: the Russian Consul-General in New York explained that most of the cargo was for the Russian government, but the British Ambassador in Washington recommended 'reserve' in dealing with the case. Enquiries were made in St Petersburg, but the answers were slow in arriving; the ship was still at Lerwick at the end of October (TS 14/5 of 5, 22 and 29 October 1915).

[2]*Digby* was renamed *Artois*, and became a problem [163, 195, etc.].

159. *Lieutenant-Commander F. Buckeridge*[1] *for Admiralty Port Officer, Kirkwall, to Admiral Commanding Orkneys and Shetlands*

Longhope, 22 October 1915

I have the honour to submit the following extract from a report made by Sub-Lieutenant H. Stuart Knight, RNR[2] of HMS *Virginian*, the officer-in-charge of Armed Guard which brought in the Norwegian HMS *Pollux*.

'In the course of conversation with some of the members of the crew there, the following rumours were in circulation. Two Swedish ? 'sailing ships' have been chartered to load at one or more of the Iceland ports; I presume in the vicinity of Seidisfjord. Their cargo is to be whale oil and wool, and their destination Germany.

'I was also informed that some of the cargo carried by Danish steamers from Iceland ports in barrels and manifested as herrings is in reality oil.

'Again it appears that some of the Norwegian steamer owners are chartering Swedish and Danish steamers on time charter, on their coasts, and are transmitting goods for enemy destinations from their own ships in their own ports, e.g., Christiania, Bergen.'[3]

160. *Commodore R.E.R. Benson to Rear-Admiral Commanding 10th Cruiser Squadron*

HMS *Cedric*, 28 October 1915

I have the honour to report ... that the Danish steamer *United States*, with 484 passengers and general cargo, from New York to Christiansund and Copenhagen, was boarded by *Cedric* at 1 p.m. on 1st May 1915, Lat. 59 36´ North, Long. 9 4´ West, and proceeded to Kirkwall with armed guard shortly after 2 p.m. [148].

2. At 1.30 p.m. *Cedric* was in visual touch with *Motagua*, and, when that ship made her pendants, the 'Affirmative Flag' was hoisted in *Cedric* in acknowledgement, and then hauled down.

3. The similarity between the 'Affirmative Flag' and the Danish Merchant Ensign undoubtedly accounts for the origin of the statement that belligerent rights were exercised under the Danish Flag. I need

[1]Buckeridge, Frank, RNVR, Lieutenant-Commander 1915, Admiralty Port Office, Kirkwall, from 1915.

[2]Knight, Henry Stuart, RNR, Sub-Lieutenant 1914, Lieutenant 1916.

[3]See page 289, note 3.

hardly add that the British White Ensign was flying in *Cedric* the whole time.

4. I would observe that the Danish Ensign has never been supplied to *Cedric*.

161. *Rear-Admiral de Chair to Admiralty*

HMS *Alsatian*, 15 November 1915

Report of Proceedings, 1–15 November 1915

***

1. Monday, 1st November – With the approval of the Commander-in-Chief A, C and F Patrols were shifted to new positions, and in view of the increased hours of darkness in and out patrol was substituted for line ahead.

The new positions and arrangements were generally as follows:

A Patrol … Centre Line 315° from Lat. 62.30´N, Long. 5 W, ships 40 miles apart, crossing centre line at noon daily, steering to make good 280° turning in time to cross again at midnight, steering 100° until time to turn again.

C Patrol … Centre Line Meridian of 11 W southern ship being in Lat. 58.6´N ships 25 miles apart, crossing centre line at 11 a.m. steering to make good 280°, turning in time to cross again at 1 a.m., steering 100° until time to turn again. The southern ships were ordered not to approach St Kilda or the Flannan Islands within 40 miles.

F Patrol … In the vicinity of Hvalsbak, Lat. 64.36´N, Long. 13.15´´W keeping outside 100 fathom line in thick weather.

A submarine was chased by an Auxiliary Patrol Vessel in Lat. 58.51´N, Long. 5.27´W.

2. Tuesday, 2nd November – *Alsatian* arrived at Swarbacks Minn and proceeded to shift protective and ballast coal as ordered by Admiralty.

The establishment of Lerwick as an examination port being now complete a large percentage of the vessels intercepted by the Squadron has lately been sent there instead of to Kirkwall. Of those sent in since 13th October five have been placed in the Prize Court, four are awaiting decision, and eight have been cleared. The *Esrom* sent in by *Andes* on 29th October was found to be carrying over 1000 tons of copper. Her Master had previously been Chief Officer of the ship and had recently been given the higher rank, an unexpected promotion probably not entirely unconnected with the cargo.[1]

With six ships in port the harbour appeared to be only half full.

I was informed that the boom from The Nab to Taing of Ham on Bressay was in position.

In accordance with directions from the Commander-in-Chief C Patrol was moved to the Westward of Long. 12 W to be clear of the Grand Fleet which was operating to the eastward between Lat. 58.30´N and 61 N.

Columbella intercepted the United States Sailing Vessel *Andrew Welch*, San Francisco to Helmstad with a cargo of beans. She was sent in to Lerwick with an Armed Guard ... .[2]

3. Wednesday, 3rd November – The opportunity was taken of inspecting HMS *Victorian* which had just finished coaling at Swarbacks Minn.

D Patrol was moved still further to the westward (Long. 17 W) in order to keep clear of the Grand Fleet.

4. Thursday, 4th November – *Victorian* intercepted the Danish Schooner *Mette*, Faroes to Stavanger with whale oil. She was sent to Lerwick with an Armed Guard.[3]

Ebro intercepted the Norwegian Steamer *Lyngenfjord*, Philadelphia to Christiania with rye, flour, leather, food stuffs and general cargo. Her Master handed in a written protest against being sent in for examination and refused to navigate his vessel while in the war zone. She was sent to Lerwick with a large Armed Guard.[4]

Teutonic intercepted the United States Steamer *Polarine* (late German *Ems*) belonging to the Standard Oil Company of New York, from Pennsylvania to Copenhagen with oil. Her Second Engineer was a German. She was sent to Kirkwall with an Armed Guard, her Master refusing responsibility for the navigation of his ship in the war zone [177].[5]

Alsatian left Swarbacks Minn and returned to patrol. A report was received from the Officer of the Armed Guard from *Andes* who took charge of the Danish Sailing Vessel *Ofelia* on 28th October that the

[1]See page 292, note 2.

[2]The *Andrew Welch* was not detained.

[3]This name is probably wrong: no *Mette* is recorded at Lerwick, or in Lloyd's Register.

[4]*Lyngenfjord* had to provide guarantees before it was allowed to proceed (TS 14/6 of 8 November 1915).

[5]*Polarine* was allowed to go on (TS 14/6 of 8 November 1915). There is a different account of this at [177].

Master had informed him that he was to receive £100 if he succeeded in running her cargo, or £50 if he failed. The cargo in question consisted of 400 barrels of whale oil.[1]

5. Friday, 5th November – *Patia* was met at a pre-arranged rendezvous and given necessary orders.

6. Saturday, 6th November – *Cedric* and *Orcoma* were met at a pre-arranged rendezvous. The latter brought official correspondence.

The Danish Barque *Maracaibo* with an Armed Guard from *Orotava* which had been placed on board on 18th October arrived at Lerwick [151 para. 28].

The weather became bad with strong wind and heavy sea and prevented boarding.

7. Sunday, 7th November – The disposition of the Squadron was as follows:

A Patrol ... *Motagua*, *Ebro*, *Oropesa*, *Alsatian*.
C Patrol ... *Otway*, *Victorian*, *Hildebrand*, *Hilary*, *Almanzora*, *Teutonic*.
F Patrol ... *Andes*.
G Patrol ... *Alcantara*, *Orcoma* and Armed Trawler *Saxon*.
Proceeding to Swarbacks Minn ... *Cedric*.
Coaling at Swarbacks Minn ... *Changuinola*, *Columbella*.
Coaling at Liverpool ... *Virginian*.
Coaling &c. in Clyde ... *Mantua*, *Patuca*, *Digby*, *Patia*.
At Lerwick ... Armed Trawler *Arley*.
Rejoining Patrol from Lerwick ... Armed Trawlers *Robert Smith* and *Rushcoe*.
On special service ... *Arlanza*, *Orotava*.[2]

Of 43 vessels intercepted and examined during the past week 14 were sent into port with Armed Guards.

Orders were received that *Digby*, on completion of refit in Clyde, should proceed to Devonport preparatory to her transfer to the French Naval authorities at Brest [163].

Almanzora reported an acute case of appendicitis following double pneumonia and requiring immediate operation which was undertaken by the Medical Officer and carried out successfully. This is the third operation for appendicitis carried out in the Squadron at sea.

[1] *Ofelia* was not detained when sent into Lerwick.

[2] *Orotava* had been detached to collect *Arlanza*'s cargo and passengers from Yukanski Fjord, Russia, where the latter had grounded.

Alcantara on G Patrol reported that she was unable to communicate with the Armed Trawler *Saxon* by W/T. As her apparatus appeared to be defective, directions were given for *Saxon* to return to Lerwick on arrival of *Rushcoe* and *Robert Smith* which were ordered to operate on T.3 Patrol.

8. Monday, 8th November – *Otway* reported having intercepted the Danish Steamer *Hellig Olav* bound westward. Among her passengers were three Austrian Poles who were removed. This vessel was not taken into port but the Master was warned that by carrying enemy subjects he rendered his ship liable to detention for further examination.

Andes and *Changuinola* were met at pre-arranged rendezvous and Armed Guards were transferred to their proper ships.

9. Tuesday, 9th November – The wind in the patrol areas increased to a gale and rendered boarding difficult and in some cases impossible. Ships were eventually ordered to lie to as necessary.

Otway intercepted the Swedish Steamer *Drottning Sophia*, … and being unable to board, kept her in company through the night. This ship had a cargo of coffee and was bound for Christiania.

10. Wednesday, 10th November – The gale continuing, *Otway* was directed to take *Drottning Sophia* under the lee of the Faroes in order to put an Armed Guard on board, but the Steamer requested permission to lie to and this was allowed. She was eventually boarded and sent to Lerwick with an Armed Guard.[1]

Teutonic intercepted the Danish Steamer *Tyskland* with a cargo of corn from Baltimore to Gothenburg hove to. *Teutonic* stood by to board as soon as weather moderated as a German was reported to have shipped in this Steamer …

Cedric which had completed coaling at Swarbacks Minn was detained there as the state of the weather made it unsafe for her to attempt to pass the boom.

During the night *Otway* intercepted and sent to Kirkwall the Danish SS *Frederick VIII*, New York to Copenhagen with general cargo and passengers [164].[2]

11. Thursday, 12th November – *Teutonic* succeeded in boarding the

[1]A long series of queries about items of cargo in *Drottning Sophia* stretched on for six weeks; at last, having given an undertaking to return a consignment of coffee to the Prize Court, the ship was released (TS 14/6 of 15 November to 27 December 1915 *passim*).

[2]A problem with bacon in *Frederick VIII*'s cargo had to be solved before the ship could sail on (TS 14/6 of 13 November 1915).

Tyskland during the middle watch and sent her to Lerwick with an Armed Guard.[1]

Alsatian spoke the Russian Volunteer Steamer *Krasnoiarsk* on passage for Archangel from New York and gave her directions as to her route.

The gale continued with unabated violence in the northern patrol areas, but *Cedric* was able to leave Swarbacks Minn and return to patrol.

12. Saturday, 13th November – *Ebro* reported that she had intercepted the Norwegian Sailing Vessel *Songelv* which was in charge of an Armed Guard from *Victorian*, in Lat. 59.16´N, Long. 6.50´W with her rigging crippled by the heavy weather which she had met with in her endeavour to make Lerwick. She was ordered to Stornoway and the Senior Officer at that port was requested to provide a tug to assist her in.[2]

13. Sunday, 14th November – The disposition of the Squadron was as follows:

A Patrol … *Changuinola*, *Virginian*, *Alsatian*, *Teutonic*.
C Patrol … *Cedric*, *Almanzora*, *Hilary*, *Victorian*, *Patuca*.
F Patrol … *Columbella*.
G Patrol … *Orcoma*, Armed Trawlers *Robert Smith* and *Rushcoe* (on T.3).
Proceeding to Clyde … *Ebro*.
Rejoining patrol from Clyde … *Mantua*, *Patia*.
Rejoining patrol from Lerwick … Armed Trawler *Arley*.
Coaling at Liverpool … *Otway*, *Alcantara*, *Andes*.
Coaling in Clyde … *Oropesa*, *Motagua*.
Coaling at Swarbacks Minn … *Hildebrand*.
At Lerwick … Armed Trawlers *Tenby Castle*, *Newland*, *Saxon*.
On special service … *Arlanza*, *Orotava*, *Digby*.

Of 49 vessels intercepted and examined during the past week, 15 were sent into port with Armed Guards.

Teutonic was met at a pre-arranged rendezvous and given orders to proceed to patrol on Long. 40 W between Lat. 61.10´N and 61.50´N in order to intercept the Norwegian Mail Steamer *Kristianiafjord* which it was considered probable would pass through the Faroes or close to the

[1]*Tyskland* was investigated and allowed to go on (TS 14/6 of 15 November 1915). Note the irony of *Teutonic* intercepting *Tyskland* (Danish for 'Germany') to prevent goods reaching Germany.

[2]*Songelv*'s cargo was investigated when she eventually reached Stornoway, but she was then allowed to go on (TS 14/6 of 16 November 1915).

southward of Sydero. *Hildebrand* which was rejoining patrol after coaling at Swarbacks Minn was ordered to patrol in the vicinity of Lat. 61.30´N, Long. 2 E across the probable course of *Kristianiafjord* to Bergen. All patrols were warned to look out for this vessel and signalling by W/T was ordered to be reduced to a minimum.

14. Monday 15th November – *Orcoma* reported that on Saturday, 13th November a Norwegian patrol boat had closed the Armed Trawlers working on T.3, and had made a strong protest against these vessels operating in Vest Fjord interfering with shipping and using W/T. The Norwegian Officer claimed that to the northward of the line Skomvaer Light–Gunna Sound Island they were in territorial waters. *Orcoma* had accordingly ordered the Armed Trawlers to patrol the entrance of Vest Fjord to the southward of Skomvaer Light–Gunna Sound [156].

At 6.25 a.m. a signal was received from *Patuca* forwarding a report from the United States Oil tank steamer *Wico* that she had passed black floating mines 10 miles NE of North Rona and that at 2.30 a.m she had sighted a large steamer proceeding NE at high speed in Lat. 58 50´N, Long. 8 30´W. Considering that the steamer sighted was probably *Kristianiafjord* I directed *Teutonic* to endeavour to cut her off between her present position and Muckle Flugga. At 10.52 p.m. signal was received from *Teutonic* that she had intercepted the *Kristianiafjord* in Lat. 61.10´N, Long. 0.50´W steaming at high speed without navigation lights. She was sent to Kirkwall with an Armed Guard [164, 166, 167, 168].[1]

The action of this passenger steamer in steaming at high speed without lights might have had serious consequences and it is fortunate she was not sunk by gunfire in mistake for a hostile minelayer. As represented on former occasions it is considered that this ship should be seized as strong measures are necessary in dealing with the Norwegian–American Line which is undoubtedly under German influence.

15. Swarbacks Minn in the Shetlands is now in regular use as a coaling base by ships of the Tenth Cruiser Squadron, and its proximity to the patrol areas and its natural advantages for such a purpose make it extremely useful as a means for keeping the maximum number of ships on patrol at one time.

Its utility is however somewhat limited by the small amount of labour available and by the unusual types of ships concerned which are in no wise suitably fitted or designed for coaling in any other place than an enclosed basin. These difficulties have now been overcome to a great

[1]After all that, *Kristianiafjord* was allowed to go on (TS 14/6 of 16 November 1915).

extent and the ships are coaled over all into their fore holds and bunkers from colliers secured one on each bow, although this necessitates a very considerable height of hoist. During this winter weather the use of the side port has not as a rule been found practicable on account of their low position on ship's side and the consequent danger of flooding the bunkers in any lop.

Up to date the average number of ships coaling in any one month is 15, and each ship is at present limited to taking in approximately 1000 tons. This somewhat sparing use of the base is due to the necessity of limiting the stay of the ships in harbour to two days, and also to the lack of labour available when they are there. At the same time the ships are expected to fill up with boiler water, get what provisions they can, and make necessary repairs to their engines.

It is regretted that drinking water is unobtainable, fresh provisions are scarce, and no large repairs can be carried out as there are no facilities for such work at present.

As stated in my telegram No. 181 of 4th November, an additional 100 stokers, RNR are urgently required in *Gibraltar* in order that the ships may complete with coal and be able to return to patrol in the shortest possible time.

162. *Notebook diary of Able Seaman W.C. Style [Serving in* Alcantara*]*

Monday 1 November.

Had a quiet day. Beautiful weather. Tonight saw the northern lights beautifully, wonderful sight.

Tuesday 2nd Sea.

I forgot to say that we heard that the *Andes* had caught the German that we were after [150, 29 October]. At 2 a.m. we stopped the Steamer *Russel* of Leith for Archangel. She was a whaler, chartered by the Admiralty, but I don't know what for.

Wednesday 3rd Sea.

At 4 a.m. this morning we stopped a big steamer the *Hallfried el Magdalene* Skandsness Norway to Middlesbrough with iron ore, put a prize crew on board and sent her to Kirkwall.

Thursday 4th Sea.

At 11 a.m. we stopped the steamer *Silvio* Wilson Line. Hull Archangel to London with timber. Allowed to proceed.

At 12 a.m. we picked up our trawler the *Arley*, gave them provisions and orders and left them again.

Friday 5th.

Beautiful weather but wind knocking about. At 6 a.m. we stopped the steamship *Ledad os Kastergas* of Stavanger Norway, New York to Archangel with motor cars, etc. She had been to Lerwick and was allowed to proceed.[1]

Saturday 6th. Sea.

All quiet today except a strong gale beating up. 4 p.m. big sea rising in for a good time tonight.

Sunday 7th Sea.

Heavy sea still running but gale blew itself out. At 5 p.m. we overtook the *Orcoma* our relief. She took over our patrol and we started home.

Monday 8th Sea.

Fine weather. Sighted the Faeroe Islands at about 6 a.m. and we passed St Kilda's some time late tonight.

Tuesday 9th Sea.

Weather choppy but fine. Saw Barra Head about 5.30 this morning.

November Friday 19th '15.

Left Liverpool today in very fine weather. Passed a new small cruiser under trial steaming very fast.

Saturday 20th '15.

Weather turned out very rough.

Sunday 21st '15.

Gale running. Passed several steamers making very heavy weather of it.

Monday 22nd '15

Gale still running. Picked up the *Alsatian* flagship at 11.30 a.m. and sent a boat away. She had a very lively time. At about 4 p.m. the weather seemed to abate a bit.

Tuesday 23rd.

Heavy sea still running. This heavy weather is beginning to shake the ship up.

Wednesday 24th.

Weather abated and quite fine.

[1]The names *Hallfried el Magdalene* and *Ledad os Kastergas* are unknown to any records, including *Lloyd's Register*; A/B Style is obviously writing up his diary from aural memory; like any Englishman – note the regular misspelling of Kintyre, Sumburgh and 'Loch' by officers – his ear for non-English words and sounds and names is poor. This whole section, to my mind, conveys better than any other document in this volume the tedium of much of the work of the squadron.

Thursday 25th.

Weather still fine. Saw the northern lights tonight.

Friday 26th.

Weather still fine. Had good news by wireless.

Saturday 27th. Sea.

Weather still moderate. Nothing exciting.

Sunday 28th.

Picked up the *Alsatian* again. Captain had to go on board for orders.

Monday 29th.

Picked up the *Andes* who brought out our trawler's crew. It is beginning to beat up rough again.

Tuesday 30th.

We have experienced some very bad weather today. One sea that washed aboard put a gun out of action, washed some ammunition away and a stretcher and we nearly lost a man.

163. *Minute by Admiral H.F. Oliver*

7 November 1915

The 10th CS consists of 22 ships instead of 24. It has been arranged to transfer the *Digby* to the French who will man her. This releases a crew to man another vessel.

The French have stated that the *Atmah*, a yacht which they offered to add to the 10th CS is unfit for service in northern waters. This was expected as it was not likely any yacht would have been of use off the Shetlands in the winter. They now ask for another armed merchant cruiser to be transferred to them to man instead of the *Atmah*.

We need not expect that we shall get as much work out of the ships manned by the French as we do now when the ships are manned by British crews, the French also want to communicate once a month with Archangel by means of the French manned cruisers, this will be to our advantage as frequent communications patrols the route and also enables us to communicate with *Iphigenia* at Alexandrovsk and Captain Kemp[1] at Archangel.

The patrols of the 10th CS for the purpose of stopping trade in the vicinity of the Shetlands will be practically reduced from 22 ships to 20 ships.

[1]Kemp, Thomas Webster, CN, CMG, CIE, Commander 1900, SNO, Persian Gulf 1908, Captain 1906, commanded British force at Archangel 1915–1917, Rear-Admiral (retired) 1917, Vice-Admiral 1922, Admiral 1926.

It is submitted to transfer one of the smallest vessels *Orotava* or *Oropesa* to the French to man and to take up two vessels and man them with the crew of *Digby*, and the second vessel transferred and the balance crew from *Arlanza* who will shortly return from White Sea in *Orotava*.

164. *Lieutenant R. Murchison Jones, RNVR*[1] *to Commander W.L. Down, Admiralty Port Officer Kirkwall*

Kirkwall, 13 November 1915

I have the honour to make the following report.

In course of conversation with the Captain and Officers of the Danish Mail Steamer *Frederik VIII*, I learned that there is much comment upon the fact that the Norwegian Steamers *Bergensfiord* and *Kristianiafjord* are not brought into Kirkwall.

In New York, the Officers of the Danish passenger boats have to submit to considerable chaff, and it is rumoured that when passengers book by the Norway America Line, they are practically told there is no stop at Kirkwall.

The Officers of the *Frederik VIII* informed me that many of their stewards department and some of the sailors have served on board the Norwegian passenger boats, and tell them that the course followed for evading our Patrol is between the Faroe Islands.

One sailor is said to have stated that the Fjord boats lay between the Islands during the hours of daylight and then cover their port holes, Saloon windows, and any opening through which light could pass with blankets of thick curtains. I have been unable to ascertain whether these vessels sail without their steering lights, but they are certainly supposed to use paraffin lights of low power.

It is suggested that the Norwegian Steamers are carrying the bulk of the German passengers who feel pretty confident of getting through, also such passengers who do not care to submit to the rigorous investigation laid down by the Directors of the Danish Mail Steamers before being permitted to buy tickets.

I am informed, in strict confidence, that a Swedish lady passenger named B. Borg, had booked by the *Frederik VIII* and was found to have a large amount of luggage of considerable weight. The Baggage Officer

[1]Jones, Richard Murchison, RNVR, Sub-Lieutenant 1915.

insisted on this being opened, and 8 pieces were found to contain cubes of Nickel of the size sketched.[1]

I have myself seen one of these cubes, but was unable to obtain it, as the Company had given directions that it was to be brought to the Head Office at Copenhagen.

It is suggested that this passenger will in all probability obtain a passage by the *Kristianiafjord* which was billed to leave New York a few days after the *Frederik VIII* and it is estimated that she should arrive in the vicinity of these waters about Monday.

I gathered that any person who appears to have a piece of luggage which would seem to be of excessive weight is required to disclose its contents before being allowed to embark on the Danish Mail Steamers.

[1]Here Jones drew a rough square, about an inch on a side.

6

DE CHAIR'S LAST MONTHS, NOVEMBER 1915–FEBRUARY 1916

Rear Admiral de Chair's tenure of command ended, rather to his surprise, with the one fighting success of his command, when *Alcantara* fought the German raider *Greif*; both ships sank, but the dominance of the Royal Navy in North Atlantic waters was demonstrated by the fact that the fight was conducted in view of another British ship, and a third arrived almost at once [199–203].

Otherwise the winter was another endurance test for the ships and men, a constant tedium of patrolling, coaling, fighting storms, in sixteen or seventeen hours of darkness every day, with intermittent periods of danger for boarding parties, though the patrols were becoming very practised at intercepting ships [166, 167]. The persistent westerly gales of the winter caused several ships to sustain serious damage, notably *Orotava* [179, 189, 190]. The trawlers were withdrawn to British waters [165 paras 14 and 16, 176], and it became almost normal to be unable to send boarding parties to the intercepted ships. Several of the boarded sailing vessels were driven to Norway by the storms [172, 178, 188, 192, 193], where the Norwegian authorities rapidly removed the prize crews by ferries to Newcastle. No doubt they did the same with any Germans who fell into their hands.

There also emerged, from gossip, and from newspaper reports [173], considerable evidence of desperate measures by Germany to move scarce goods from the USA to Germany [97, 181 para. 12]. This could only be encouraging, though there was also evidence of successful 'blockade-running' and it was ominous that the American Ambassador should become involved in a protest over one interception (page 352, note 2).

165. *Rear-Admiral de Chair to Admiralty*

HMS *Alsatian*, 6 December 1915

Report of Proceedings, 16 November–5 December 1915

***

1. ... I beg to draw attention to a report by the Admiralty Port Officer Kirkwall which was forwarded by the Admiral Commanding Orkneys and Shetlands in his submission No. 943/30.C. dated 1st November 1915. From the information contained therein drawn from conversation with the Captain and Officers of the Danish Mail Steamer *Frederick VIII* [164], there is evidence that the Steamers of the Norwegian American Line deliberately lay themselves out to attract German passengers and that luggage containing contraband can be conveyed by this line without much risk of interference by the officials. That these vessels use every endeavour to evade our patrol has already been conclusively proved, and taking all the facts into consideration it appears that they are definitely engaged in non-neutral service and so are liable to seizure.

2. Tuesday, 16th November – Instructions were received from the Commander-in-Chief directing me to visit Scapa Flow in order to confer with him as to arrangements of patrol for the winter.

Cedric intercepted the Danish Steamer *Falkland*, Copenhagen to New York in ballast. This vessel which was originally the German SS *Uriate IV* had been transferred to the Danish Flag and now belongs to Albert Jensen whose ships are German controlled ... She was sent to Kirkwall with an Armed Guard.[1]

3. Wednesday, 17th November – I arrived at Scapa Flow in *Alsatian* and conferred with the Commander-in-Chief, receiving his directions as regards patrols for the winter. *Alsatian* left Scapa Flow at 3 p.m. and proceeded to the east of Orkneys to avoid an enemy submarine reported to have been sighted during the forenoon in Lat. 59.10´N, Long. 20.25´W. Information was received that the American Sailing Ship *Andrew Welsh* in charge of an Armed Guard from *Columbella* had arrived at Christiansund in distress on account of the heavy weather prevailing. She had been ordered to proceed to Lerwick but had apparently been unable to reach that port [161 para. 2].

4. Thursday, 18th November – A signal was received from the Commander-in-Chief to the effect that a German Cruiser with three funnels had passed out of the Skaggerack on the afternoon of 17th November. Directions were given to warn patrol to keep within supportable distance of one another. A and C Patrols were accordingly ordered to close on signal the centre ship to visual signal distance and the former was moved to Lat. 62 N, Long. 10 W. *Orcoma* on G patrol received orders to rendezvous with *Donegal* and to caution the Armed Trawlers working on the Norwegian Coast to remain in the vicinity of

[1] *Falkland* was not detained.

territorial waters. *Teutonic* which had just completed coaling at Swarbacks Minn was despatched to a position in Lat. 61 N, Long. 6 W to work in conjunction with A and C Patrols.

5. Friday, 19th November – A large submarine was reported to be steering WNW on the surface north of Shetlands.

6. Saturday, 20th November – A and C patrols were again spread to 20 miles apart.

Cedric while entering the Mersey grounded at 8.44 a.m. She was floated off during the day and proceeded to Liverpool to be dry docked.

7. Sunday, 21st November – The disposition of the Squadron was as follows:

A Patrol ... *Changuinola*, *Virginian*, *Hildebrand*, *Alcantara*, *Alsatian*.
C Patrol ... *Patia*, *Teutonic*, *Patuca*, *Mantua*.
G Patrol ... *Orcoma*, Armed Trawlers *Rushcoe*, *Arley*, *Tenby Castle*.
Proceeding to Clyde to Coal ... *Hilary*.
Coaling at Liverpool ... *Cedric*, *Andes*, *Otway*, *Almanzora*, *Victorian*.
Coaling in Clyde ... *Motagua*, *Ebro*, *Columbella*.
Proceeding to Lerwick ... Armed Trawler *Robert Smith*.
At Lerwick ... Armed Trawlers *Saxon*, *Newland*.
On special service ... *Arlanza*, *Digby*, *Oropesa*, *Orotava*.

Of 21 vessels intercepted and examined during the week 4 were sent into port with Armed Guards.

With the approval of the Commander-in-Chief the regular patrols of the Squadron were resumed with the exception of G patrol from which *Orcoma* was detached to accompany *Minotaur* and *Donegal* to North Cape.

8. Monday, 22nd November – *Teutonic* intercepted the Danish Steamer *Dansborg*, Savannah to Denmark with oil cake and sent her to Kirkwall with an Armed Guard ... .[1]

Patuca intercepted the Norwegian Steamer *Kong Haakon*, Baltimore to Christiania with rye and wheat. The cargo had shifted and the vessel had a list of 12 degrees to port and only 12 hours coal at four knots in her bunkers. She had been burning red and green flares which were observed and reported by the Norwegian Steamer *Quernstad* boarded earlier in the evening by *Patuca*. One of the crew had been injured by the heavy seas; he was attended to by the Medical Officer from *Patuca*, and an Armed Guard was placed on board and the *Kong Haakon* proceeded for Stornoway in company with *Patuca*.

[1]*Dansborg* was not detained.

9. Tuesday, 23rd November – *Patuca* was ordered to tow *Kong Haakon* if necessary and she proceeded to do so at 9.15 a.m. (Lat. 58.38´N, Long. 10.55´W) as the vessel had exhausted her coal after steaming for eleven days against North Easterly gales. The Senior Officer Stornoway was requested to send tugs to her assistance.

On A patrol area the wind increased to a gale and ships were ordered to lie to as necessary.

10. Wednesday, 24th November – At 3.15 p.m. *Patuca* reported that she had turned over the *Kong Haakon* to the Trawler *Alberia* which together with the *Ophir II*, yacht *Calanthe* and tug *Flying Buzzard* had been sent from Stornoway to meet her. *Alberia* then took *Kong Haakon* in tow and proceeded to Stornoway at 3 knots. *Patuca* then returned to Patrol.

Changuinola intercepted and sent in the Swedish Steamer *Signe*, Rio de Janeiro to Christiania with coffee. It was ascertained that seven German stowaways had been landed by this vessel at Corcubion on the advice of the Swedish Consul.[1]

11. Thursday, 25th November – Information was received of the safe arrival of the Norwegian Steamer *Kong Haakon* at Stornoway.[2]

Orcoma which had been detached, by direction of the Commander-in-Chief, to the North Cape in company with the Seventh Cruiser Squadron, returned to G patrol. She reported that nothing had been seen of any hostile vessel and very bad weather had been experienced.

12. Friday, 26th November – The Armed Trawlers *Newland* and *Saxon* were met at a pre-arranged rendezvous and given orders, the former to patrol east of Faroes examining Skopen and Dimon Fjords by day in order to ascertain whether *Kristianiafjord*, which was known to be proceeding west, passed through or sheltered between the islands in order to avoid the patrol, and the latter to join G patrol working on T.1.

13. Sunday, 28th November – The disposition of the Squadron was as follows:

A Patrol ... *Alsatian*, *Alcantara*, Armed Trawler *Newland*.
C Patrol ... *Otway*, *Patia*, *Mantua*, *Motagua*.
F Patrol ... *Andes*.
G Patrol ... *Orcoma*, Armed Trawler *Saxon*.
Coaling at Liverpool ... *Cedric*, *Teutonic*, *Almanzora*.

[1] *Signe* was not detained.

[2] After investigation *Kong Haakon* was allowed to continue her voyage (TS 14/6 of 25 November 1915).

Coaling in Clyde ... *Ebro*, *Columbella*, *Changuinola*, *Hilary*, *Orotava*, *Hildebrand*.
Rejoining Patrol from Liverpool ... *Victorian*.
Coaling at Lerwick ... Armed Trawler *Robert Smith*.
Proceeding to Lerwick to coal ... Armed Trawlers *Arley*, *Rushcoe*.
Coaling at Swarbacks Minn ... *Virginian*, *Patuca*.
Detached on special service ... *Arlanza*, *Oropesa*, *Digby*.

Of 26 vessels intercepted and examined during the week nine were sent in with and one without Armed Guards.

Patia intercepted and sent to Kirkwall the Norwegian Steamer *Hercules*, New York to Bergen with general cargo, and having on board 13 men and 4 women saved from the Newfoundland Schooner *Swallow* who were picked up in Lat. 46.11´N, Long. 44.37´W.[1]

14. Monday, 29th November – The Armed Trawler *Tenby Castle* being due at Lerwick and not having arrived, *Orcoma* on G patrol was directed to search for her and Armed Trawler *Newland* was sent to assist. *Orcoma* succeeded in getting into W/T touch with *Tenby Castle* and later she met her. *Tenby Castle* reported that she had received considerable damage in the gale of 23rd November, her decks being swept by the seas. She put into Bessiker (Lat. 64.15´N, Long. 10.19´E) on Thursday 25th November to effect repairs, and received assistance from the Norwegian Gunboat *Hidalgo*. She left Bessiker on Sunday 28th November and had arrived at Stadtlandet this morning. She expected to arrive at Lerwick on evening of 30th November or morning of 1st December. The weather becoming worse, boarding was not practicable and it was necessary to follow vessels intercepted and in some cases to lie to while keeping them in company.

15. Tuesday, 30th November – The Squadron remained practically hove to on account of the bad weather especially in the northern patrol areas, with wind at East, force 8, barometer 29.18 and steady.[2]

16. Wednesday, 1st December – *Alcantara* on G patrol reported that the Armed Trawler *Newland* was returning to Lerwick in a leaky condition and with her boats smashed, due to heavy weather encountered.

At 11.15 a.m. *Ebro*, which was on her way out of Clyde to rejoin patrol, reported that her starboard tail shaft was thumping badly. On

[1]*Hercules*' manifest had been telegraphed to the Contraband Committee from New York; Customs were to check everything and the ship could then go on (TS 14/6 of 29 November 1915).

[2]985 mbs.

examining propellers under the lee of Rathlin Island one was found to be badly broken and ship had to return to the Clyde.

Virginian reported that she had made an attempt to board the Danish Steamer *Helmer Morch* with which she had been in company since yesterday. As the weather showed little signs of improving and the Master stated he would call at Kirkwall. *Virginian* was directed to allow her to proceed.[1]

The *Otway* after chasing for 7 hours in very heavy weather came up with and stopped SS *Ovidia* with a cargo of wheat from Baltimore to Norkoping. As the sea was too rough and breaking heavily boats could not be lowered, and *Otway* was directed to hold *Ovidia* till an Armed Guard could be put onboard.[2]

Shortly afterwards *Mantua* intercepted the Sailing Barque *Perm*, Philadelphia to Bergen, cargo petroleum, and was directed to stand by her and board as soon as weather moderated.[3]

In accordance with signal received from Commander-in-Chief ships on C patrol were ordered to shift from their area and form line ahead patrol 360° from Lat. 60 N, Long. 10 W, ships being 30 miles apart patrolling 40 miles. The neutral vessels which were being kept in company were directed to Lerwick and Kirkwall as necessary as boarding was still impracticable.

17. Thursday, 2nd December – A report was received from the officer in charge of the Armed Guard from *Columbella* placed on board the American Sailing Ship *Andrew Welch* on 2nd November giving details of the passage of the ship which was eventually forced to take refuge in the Norwegian Port of Christiansand. After sighting several submarines the *Andrew Welch* rounded Muckle Flugga on 6th November and attempted to make Lerwick. A patrol boat was spoken off Noss Head which directed her to heave to but disappeared without rendering any assistance. The weather getting worse the Master wished to make for Helmstad and on the officer refusing to allow this, the crew struck work. As the Guard were unable to work the ship a compromise was made by running for Aberdeen and the ship arrived off Girdleness on 11th November. Signals were made for a pilot and a small steamer was spoken and promised to send out a tug but no assistance arrived, and a heavy gale from NNW springing up the *Andrew Welch* was forced to remain hove to until 14th November. The crew again refused to work,

[1]*Helmer Morch* was not detained.
[2]*Ovidia* was allowed to continue after investigation (TS 14/6 of 4 December 1915).
[3]*Perm* was not detained.

and as the water was getting low and pumps failed to draw, the officer of the Guard agreed to run for the nearest Norwegian port, Christiansand, where he communicated with the British Consul.

The opportunity was taken to carry out an inspection of *Alsatian* at sea.

18. Friday, 3rd December – *Otway* was met at a pre-arranged rendezvous and given orders for conduct of patrols. Patrols were disposed with a view to the interception of the Norwegian SS *Bergensfiord* on her eastward voyage, three ships being placed on the Atlantic route South of Rockall, 10 W, the remainder of C patrol covering to south and A patrol to northward of Faroe Islands.

19. Saturday, 4th December – *Patuca* intercepted the Norwegian SS *Flora* (ex. *Olaf Kyrre*) from Faroe Islands to Bergen with 500 barrels of fish oil, 3000 barrels of fish and meat, also 52 passengers. She was sent to Lerwick with an Armed Guard.[1]

Alsatian intercepted the Danish Mail Steamer *Hellig Olaf*, New York to Copenhagen with general cargo and 275 passengers including 7 German and 2 Austrian women and one one-armed Austrian man. She was sent to Kirkwall with an Armed Guard.[2]

20. Sunday, 5th December – On southern portion of patrol area barometer fell from 29.26 to 28.74[3] in 10 hours and an Easterly gale sprang up with exceptional violence rendering movement of ships on patrol difficult.

With a view to intercepting *Bergensfjord* the *Patia* was told off to guard Dimon Fjord, between Faroe Islands and *Alcantara* and *Orcoma* on G Patrol extended their ordinary patrol south to cover the track to Bergen.

The disposition of the Squadron was as follows:

A Patrol ... *Alsatian*, *Victorian*, *Patuca*.
C Patrol ... *Otway*, *Virginian*, *Motagua*, *Hildebrand*, *Orotava*, *Changuinola*, *Hilary*.
F Patrol ... *Andes*.
G Patrol ... *Alcantara*, *Orcoma*, Armed Trawler *Saxon*.
Proceeding to Swarbacks Minn ... *Mantua*.
Rejoining from Liverpool ... *Almanzora*.
Coaling at Liverpool ... *Cedric*, *Teutonic*.

[1]*Flora*, after investigation, was allowed to sail on (TS 14/6 of 6 December 1915).

[2]After guarantees against re-export of certain items were obtained, *Hellig Olav* was allowed to go on (TS 14/6 of 6 December 1915).

[3]990 to 973 mbs.

Repairing defects in Clyde ... *Columbella*.
In dock at Belfast ... *Ebro*.
Coaling at Swarbacks ... *Patia*.
At Lerwick ... Armed Trawlers *Newland*, *Tenby Castle*, *Arley*, *Rushcoe*, *Robert Smith*.
Special service ... *Arlanza*, *Oropesa*, *Digby*.

Of 23 vessels intercepted and examined during the past week 7 were sent into port with, and 2 without Armed Guards.

166. *Commander-in-Chief Home Fleets to Admiralty*

HMS *Iron Duke*, 17 November 1915

With reference to the Report of Proceedings of the Rear-Admiral Commanding Tenth Cruiser Squadron dated 15 November 1915 [161] ... be pleased to bring to the notice of the Lords Commissioners of the Admiralty the clever interception of the Norwegian-America Line steamer *Kristianiafjord* by HMS *Teutonic* (Commander Adrian H. Smyth)[1] which was due to the good dispositions of the Rear-Admiral [167].

2. It is submitted that strong representations may be made to the Norwegian government that the *Kristianiafjord* runs great risk of being fired on and sunk in mistake for a German minelayer, if she navigates within the war zone without navigation lights.

3. With regard to clause 14 of the Rear-Admiral's letter, reporting that a Norwegian patrol officer protested on 13th November against our armed trawlers operating in Vest Fjord, I have informed the Rear-Admiral that the contention of the Norwegian officer is untenable and directed him to be guided entirely by the provisions of clause 2, page 1 of the Naval Prize Manual as modified by Admiralty telegram of 10 July no. 671.

[1]Smyth, Adrian Holt, RN (1878–1951), Lieutenant 1901, Commander 1913, Captain of *Teutonic* 1915, of *Moldavia* 1916–1918, Captain (retired) 1918.

167. *Commander A. Smyth, RN to Rear-Admiral Commanding Tenth Cruiser Squadron*

HMS *Teutonic*, 18 November 1915

In accordance with your directions, *Teuton*ic assumed patrol on the 4th Meridian between 61.10´N and 61.50´N at 5.30 p.m. on Sunday the 14th November for the purpose of intercepting *Kristianiafjord.*

The patrol was carried out at 60 revolutions – 16.3 knots.

At 8.25 a.m. on the 15th a signal from the *Patuca* to S.O. 10th CS was intercepted, part of which read: 'American Oiler *Wico* reports a large steamer going NE very fast, 55.14´N, 8.30´W about 2.30 a.m. As *Patuca*'s 2.30 a.m. position was 58.50´N, 5.50´W, 59.04´N, 8.30´W was assumed as 2.30 a.m. position of *Wico.*

Assuming this vessel to be *Kristianiafjord* and knowing her maximum speed to be 16½ knots when driven, I spread a fan from this position on a northerly course, 23°, passing close to Sydero light, and easterly, 60°, passing close north of Muckle Flugga with radii for every even 10° between. Assuming her to have made good an average speed of 15 knots, I plotted the 10, 11, 12, and 13 hour circles. Taking into consideration the absence of W/T signals from 10th CS Ships (by your orders), the knowledge that the Captain of *Kristianiafjord* prided himself on evading the patrol led me to believe that he would push on. I therefore decided to move my patrol position to the Southward without orders. I was steaming South to do this when at 11.19 a.m., I received your directions as follows: 'At 2.30 a.m. 58.50´N, 8.30´W large steamer going North East, possibly *Kristianiafjord.* Endeavour to cut off between your position and Muckle Flugga light'. I immediately increased to 66 revolutions – 18.2 knots.

The weather was bright and fine with occasional snow flurries and rain squalls – assuming therefore the maximum visibility of 10 miles I shaped a course to be at 2.30 p.m. 10 miles from *Kristianiafjord*'s 2.30 p.m. position on the 60° course line. At 2.55 p.m. having sighted nothing, I stood 67½° at the same speed. Although I felt convinced that *Kristianiafjord* had stood up to make Sydero, yet the most easterly course took him furthest ahead and I felt compelled to assume that he had made that at 15 knots.

I now argued as follows: Considering the persistent strong North easterly wind he would not steer to pass less than 5 miles off Muckle Flugga and from a position 9 miles off I would see him – assuming him to have taken a more northerly course he would at least make to touch the limit of visibility of Muckle Flugga Light (25 miles to him) and from 21 miles I would see him. I was influenced also by the knowledge that *Hildebrand* had orders to patrol to the eastward and the conviction that to efficiently patrol a short area is better than to patrol inefficiently a greater space.

At 15 knots and visibility 10 miles he would be in sight of either point for 80 minutes; I must therefore reach either point at 80 minute intervals.

The moon in quadrature crossed the meridian about 7 p.m. and set about 1 a.m., but I had to admit that if he was not burning lights it would be by the greatest good fortune that I could intercept him.

The wind and sea increased considerably between 4 and 6 p.m., and at 7 p.m., I decided that if ahead of me he must be in sight and that he could not possibly be making 15 knots

I therefore reduced to 16.3 knots, and at 8.20 p.m., with Muckle Flugga Light bearing 167° I commenced to patrol 0° and 180° standing to windward proportionately longer than to leeward.

At 10.15 p.m. when at the north extreme, at about 18 miles distant from Muckle Flugga Light, I had just stepped from the Chart House to Bridge to order course to be altered, I heard the Officer of the Watch direct the helm to be ported and the starboard engine stopped – he called out to me that there was a large steamer close to port running fast without lights, but when I observed her she appeared to be stopped. I demanded her name and she replied *Kristianiafjord*. I ordered her to remain stopped and switch on all lights, but as he was slow in switching on and failed to answer a further call I fired a warning 6 pdr blank.

***

The sea being too high to board him, I stood with him in the direction of Kirkwall.

At about 4.15 a.m. the Captain of *Kristianiafjord* having refused to proceed without a guarantee for responsibility and the weather having very slightly moderated – I placed an Armed Guard under a Lieutenant on board and directed her to Kirkwall.[1]

I then left the patrol for Swarbacks Minn.

[1]See Chapter 5, page 307, note 1.

168. *Memorandum by Captain Richard Webb, Director of Trade Division*

26 November 1915

1. It is proposed that copy of the Rear-Admiral's report re the case of the SS *Kristianiafjord*, page 9 [161 paras 13–14] should be sent to the Foreign Office with a request that HM Minister in Christiania should be asked to warn the Norwegian American Line of the danger of such conduct.

It is pointed out, however, that the Norwegian American Line have recently concluded an Agreement with HM Government under which in consideration of receiving adequate supplies of bunker coal, the Company agrees to abide by the Conditions of Supply of bunker coal ... In view of the fact that it is quite possible for the Company to purchase all the bunker coal which they require in the United States, it was considered desirable to meet the wishes of the Company in respect of the two mail steamers *Kristianiafjord* and *Bergensfiord*, and it was therefore agreed these vessels should not be required to call at a United Kingdom port for examination, but that they should be directed to follow a fixed course in order that they could be intercepted and brought in if necessary.

The incident complained of by Rear-Admiral, 10th Cruiser Squadron, occurred before these arrangements had been explained to the Master of the *Kristianiafjord*. The position has now been made clear and the Agent of the Company in London has undertaken that in future the vessels will show electric navigation lights and all the usual deck lights exhibited by a mail steamer and has telegraphed to Norway to that effect ...

2. The Foreign Office should also be informed of the cases of the *Lyngenfjord*, *Polarine* and *Ofelia*.

The case of the SS *Lyngenfjord*, page 3, appears to be in violation of the above mentioned Agreement made with the Norwegian American Line.

In the case of the *Polarine*, the Standard Oil Co. are understood to have given directions to all their Captains to call voluntarily at Kirkwall for examination.

In the case of the *Ofelia*, this vessel was released against a guarantee given to HM Minister, Christiania, that neither the whale oil or any of its products would leave Norway. It is suggested Mr Findlay be informed of the bribery of the Master.

3. The SS *Esrom*, page 2, has been placed in the Prize Court under

the Order-in-Council abrogating Article 57 of the Declaration of London. About half her cargo has also been placed in the Prize Court. Of the copper, 800 tons were en-route for Sweden under the terms of the Copper Agreement.

4. The reports of the Officers in charge of the Armed Guards placed on board the SS *Valand* and *Haugar* [156] are interesting, and it is submitted that these two Officers and the Armed Guards are worthy of commendation.

169. *Notebook diary of Able Seaman W.C. Style* [*serving in* Alcantara]

Wednesday 1st December '15

Weather has abated somewhat and glass rising steadily, so we shall have some good weather.

December Wednesday 1st '15 Sea.

Picked up a motor ship named the *Kronprinzess*? *Margusta*? with leather, coffee, and general cargo valued at roughly £3,000,000 for Norway and Sweden. (I don't think[)]. Anyhow we found one German on board and sent her in with a prize crew. The weather was very bad and I don't think they would have sent her at that time (9 p.m.) but the prize put her lights out and tried to steam away.[1]

Thursday 2nd.

Weather quite calm, but we had a heavy fall of snow tonight and it is very cold.

Friday 3rd.

Nothing exciting up till now (10 p.m.) but still very cold. Had news by wireless. American papers say Germany has lost 58 submarines since start of war and another 20 are still unaccounted for.[2]

Saturday 4th '15 Sea.

The weather has eased again and quite calm. At 3 p.m. we stopped the steamer *Ripa of Berza* from Glasgow to Christiansund, examined and allowed to proceed. At 11.30 p.m. we stopped the sailing ship *Fingland* of Mersden from Setubal Portugal to Udavalla Sweden with salt. Allowed to proceed.[3]

[1]The ship was *Kronprinsessen Margaretha*; many items in its cargo, especially coffee, were deemed contraband; it was only allowed to go on after four items were discharged to the Prize Court; the ship was held up for three weeks (TS 14/6 of 3 and 27 December 1915).

[2]Germany had 26 U-boats in January 1915, built 62 during the year and lost 20; to have lost 78 was impossible.

[3]Style has the names wrong: *Ripa of Berza* is probably *Ripa* of Bergen; *Fingland* is unidentifiable, as is 'Mersden'.

We also ran across one of our trawlers which I forgot to mention at 8 a.m. ran up and gave them some provisions.

Sunday 5th '15.

Nothing to report. Plenty of snow fell during the night but it made the air warmer.

Monday 6th '15.

At 6 a.m. we stopped the steamer *Mary* a Russian, Blythe to Archangel. I don't think we shall get many more up to there as it must be pretty well froze in by now.

Between 9 a.m. and 11 a.m. we ran across our trawlers again, the *Saxon*, the *Tenby Castle* and *Arley* and left orders. I think we are after some big blockade runner as we have been steaming pretty fast ever since we left the trawlers.

Tuesday 7th.

A bit rough this morning but it has become quite calm again tonight. It was a lovely sight to see the ship this morning breaking the sea right over her and the spray blowing right away to leeward but she was very steady with it and not at all uncomfortable.

Wednesday 8th.

We have been very quiet again, but the weather is rather cold.

Thursday 9th.

Today has been very quiet again, we have sighted nothing.

December 10.

At noon today we picked up the trawler *Rushko* and took the Captain on board for some orders, but what I don't know.

Saturday 11th.

Still quiet but beginning to beat up rough. We have had fairly good war news by wireless lately. Snowing hard tonight expecting a heavy storm.

Sunday 12th.

Plenty of snow about but the sea has gone quiet. We are tearing along after some steamer. Don't know where we shall pick her up.

5 p.m. the wind and sea is beating up rough but we are still driving through it.

Monday 13th.

Had a very rough night ship rolling very heavily from 4 a.m. until about 9.30 a.m. At about 4.30 a.m. we pulled up the steamer we were after and made her keep company with us as far as the Shetlands. She was making bad weather of it. We ran with her under the lee of the land about 12 noon examined her. She was a passenger steamer the *United States* of Copenhagen Denmark, full of passengers but she was a suspect although going to New York US and we put a strong prize crew on board and sent her to Greenock.[1]

I think some German officials implicated in the big trial in Yankee land were on board.[2] Weather getting calmer. The Shetlands was covered in snow when we were under the lee of the land, and it was mighty cold, but it looked very pretty.

At 8.30 p.m. we stopped a Norwegian the *Inder* of Christiansund, bound for Blythe in ballast. Allowed to proceed.

Tuesday 14th. At Sea.

Blowing hard and snowing all the forenoon, but eased after noon and became quite fine by dark. We have the moon quite early now. I noticed it at exactly 3 p.m. the other day.

At about 9 a.m. we ran across two trawlers again the *Saxon* and *Tenby Castle*, and left orders and at about 10 a.m. ran across the *Harley* [*sic*] and did the same to her.

Wednesday 15th.

Fine weather but still cold. At about 11.15 a.m. we picked up the *Ebro* just out from Liverpool and she left us despatches and papers. Saw the northern lights again last night and tonight.

Thursday 16th.

Fine weather. This morning we picked up the *Saxon* and another trawler, disguised. I don't know her name but she looked like a boat that had been captured by the build of her. We also saw the *Oropesa* signalling far away on the horizon.

Friday 17th.

At 9 a.m. we picked up our trawler the *Arley* again but we soon left her and at about 10 a.m. we carried out 6" gun firing as the weather was very good for it, but still cold. At 9 p.m. we had a steamer the *Algol* of Bergen from Narvik brought out to us by the trawlers and we put a prize crew on board and sent her to Manchester where she was supposed to be bound for.

[1] *United States* was not detained.

[2] The 'big trial' is probably a reference to the trial of Hamburg–America Line Company officials in New York in November and December 1915 for supplying German ships from American ports. This coincided with the revelation of the involvement of Franz von Rintelen in planting bombs in munition ships; at the same time the United States government insisted on the expulsion of Major Franz von Papen, and Captain Karl Boy-Ed, respectively Military and Naval Attachés at the German Embassy in Washington, for involvement in spying; Rintelen was also expelled, and taken off his ship for detention in Britain; cf. C. Andrew, *For the President's Eyes Only* (London, 1995), 33–36, and, for the wider context, B.W. Tuchman, *The Zimmerman Telegram* (London, 1959), chapters 5 and 6.

Saturday 18th.

Still very cold, but very fine. At 11 p.m. the trawler brought us out another steamer of the same line called the *Deneb*, she was of Bergen and also from Narvik bound for Manchester. We put a prize crew on board and sent her in to Manchester.[1] Had slight fall of snow again tonight.

Sunday 19th.

This morning wireless tells us that the ship *United States* that was captured was a very rich prize. At 2.30 p.m. in a violent snow storm we picked up the Norwegian steamship *Roskva* of Christiania from Port Talbot with coal allowed to proceed. Bitterly cold.

Monday 20th.

Very bright day but very cold.

Tuesday 21st.

Fine day still cold going to meet our trawler. At 1 p.m. picked up the trawler with a big turret ship called the *Nyland* of Goteborg from Narvik to Middlesbrough with iron ore, sent her in with prize crew.[2] We went in very close to the Norwegian coast and it looked very beautiful through the glasses all the hills were clad in snow everywhere you looked, and they rise sheer up from the water we were only about 5 or 6 miles away.

At 9 p.m. we ran across a Swedish steamer the *Urna* of Helsingborg, Sweden, from New York to Helsingborg and Copenhagen with general cargo and a lot of contraband. Prize crew sent into Lerwick.[3]

Wednesday 22nd.

Plenty of snow storms today and ice over the decks. At 11 p.m. had a wireless. Proceed to Liverpool.

Thursday 23rd.

At 9 a.m. we ran across the steamship *Turid* of Tronjheim Norway for Swansea with pit props it was very rough when we boarded her and allowed to proceed. At 4 p.m. we picked up our relief the *Columbella* exchanged signals and started for home. Still very cold.

Friday 24th.

After leaving the *Columbella* we picked up a patrol ship a long distance off and signalled by searchlight to her, then left her. About 40

[1]Neither *Algol* nor *Deneb* was actually carrying contraband, since the cargo was consigned to Britain; that the ships were given armed guards is perhaps an indication of British suspicion.

[2]As *Algol* and *Deneb* (see previous note).

[3]*Urna*'s cargo gave rise to numerous investigations; the ship was sent to Bristol to discharge these items to the Prize Court; this was a slow process, probably deliberately; the ship was reported ready to clear on 7 February, but it was still at Bristol on the 25th, a delay of over two months (TS 14/6 of 23 December 1915 to 25 February 1916 *passim*).

to 50 miles further south we passed another patrol ship going north.
Saturday 25th.

Weather was very rough, but as we were moving with it we did not feel it much. Passed Burra Head this morning. We have just had two submarines reported in the vicinity.

Expect to pass Rathlin Island at about midnight. Very quiet for Xmas Day. Had a bit of a concert tonight.
Sunday 26th.

Arrived quite safe at the Bar at about 5.30 a.m. and proceeded to Liverpool.[1]

170. *Rear-Admiral de Chair to Admiralty*

HMS *Alsatian*, 31 December 1915

Report of Proceedings, 6–31 December 1915

***

1. Monday, 6th December – *Patuca* intercepted the Norwegian steamer *Bergensfiord* New York to Bergen, in Lat. 62.34´N, Long. 5.45´W. The Master made the usual protest against being sent into port and stated that he had always followed the Great Circle track from New York to Bergen and had made no attempt to evade the patrol. His statement was however somewhat at variance with the position in which he was intercepted, as the proper course would have taken him close to Muckle Flugga. Of 784 passengers on board two were identified as German subjects, one being a Doctor Gellhorn … and the other over military age. The ship was sent to Kirkwall with an Armed Guard.[2]

Weather in patrol areas was bad, and boarding a matter of some difficulty.

2. Tuesday, 7th December – The Easterly Gale moderated somewhat; but on *Orotava* attempting to resume patrol after lying to her sea boat was washed overboard. *Teutonic* which was proceeding to rejoin patrol from Liverpool, experienced a whole Westerly Gale and was compelled to shelter in the Minch.

3. Saturday, 11th December – *Victorian* intercepted the Swedish

[1]This is the end of A/B Style's diary, written apparently for his wife. He died in *Alcantara*'s fight with *Greif* at the end of February; his next diary no doubt was lost with him. That this part survived is due to his leave at this juncture.

[2]*Bergensfjord*'s manifest had been sent to the Contraband Committee in advance. Once it had been checked by Customs, the ship was allowed to proceed (TS 14/6 of 2 and 4 December 1915).

steamer *Kronprinz Gustaf*, from Rio-de-Janeiro to Christiania, with a general cargo. One fireman was discovered to be a German subject. She was sent to Kirkwall ... .[1]

The Gale increased again and by 9 p.m. all ships on A and C Patrols had to reduce speed or heave to.

4. Sunday, 12th December – The Disposition of the Squadron was as follows:

A Patrol ... *Cedric*, *Ebro*, *Almanzora*, *Victorian*, *Teutonic*.
C Patrol ... *Changuinola*, *Patia*, *Mantua*, *Hilary*, *Hildebrand*, *Columbella*, *Orotava*, *Otway*.
F Patrol ... *Andes*.
G Patrol ... *Alcantara*, *Orcoma*, Armed Trawlers *Tenby Castle*, *Arley*, *Rushcoe*.
Additional Patrol (Lat. 62.30´N, Long. 9.30´W) ... *Motagua*.
Coaling at Liverpool ... *Alsatian*.
Coaling at Clyde ... *Patuca*.
Coaling at Swarbacks ... *Virginian*.
At Lerwick ... Armed Trawlers *Robert Smith*, *Newland*, *Saxon*.
On special service ... *Arlanza*.[2]

Of 32 vessels intercepted and examined during the week, 4 were sent in with Armed Guards.

5. Monday, 13th December – *Hildebrand* reported that during the Gale on 6th December, the foremost deckhouse had been damaged beyond efficient repair by ship's artificers, and in bad weather water got below and rendered the stokers' quarters uninhabitable. The Captain stated however that the defect was not sufficiently serious as to necessitate the ship's return to her base at once.

Cedric had heard the Norwegian steamer *Oscar II* communicating by W/T the previous day when 400 miles West of Butt of Lewis, and C Patrol was warned that this vessel would probably reach their area on Monday night. She was intercepted by *Hildebrand* at 7.20 p.m., and sent to Kirkwall with an Armed Guard ... .[3]

[1]*Kronprinz Gustaf* was not detained.

[2]The two ships transferred to the French flag (*Digby* and *Oropesa*) are not listed.

[3]*Oscar II* went on after inspection (TS 14/6 of 13 December 1915). This was the Peace Ship referred to in the next paragraph, hired by Henry Ford and carrying a choice group of peace activists and journalists. The activists, as de Chair says, wildly disagreed with each other, and the journalists treated the whole affair with derision. Ford, who paid for them all, was sincere, but lost interest and returned to New York on 23 December from Bergen, via *Bergensfjord* – to be intercepted yet again by the Tenth Cruiser Squadron: see Barbara S. Kraft, *The Peace Ship: Henry Ford's Pacifist Adventure in the First World War* (New York, 1978), or, more briefly, Robert Lacey, *Ford, the Men and the Machines* (London, 1986), chapter 8.

One of the signals from *Oscar II* intercepted on 12th December, was of some interest, as it stated that several members of the Peace Commission were preparing to return to America from Christiania on account of the insulting attitude adopted by the Extreme Pacifists towards those upholding President Wilson's programme of preparedness for war. The Message, which was from 'Charles Stewart', presumably a Press Correspondent, went on to mention the general dissension amongst the members of the Commission which Mr Ford had been unable to dissipate.

Alcantara intercepted the Danish Mail Steamer *United States* Westbound in heavy weather which prevented boarding. She had a parcel mail on board and *Alcantara* was directed to escort her under the lee of the Shetlands where an Armed Guard was placed on board and she was sent to Greenock ... .[1]

The Master of the *United States* stated that the Dutch Steamer *Potsdam* which had left Christiania two hours before him, had German subjects on board travelling to New York. Patrols were directed to keep a good look-out for this vessel.[2]

6. Thursday, 16th December – *Motagua* intercepted the Swedish Steamer *Jemtland*, New York to Goteburg, with a cargo of Copper, Nickel, Antimony, Oil and general. This vessel was not burning navigation lights when sighted. She was only showing a faint binnacle light which was not visible at any distance, and she was apparently steaming at full speed and attempting to evade the Patrol. She was sent into Lerwick with an Armed Guard ... .[3]

Virginian intercepted the Danish Mail Steamer *Frederick VIII*, New York to Copenhagen, with 920 passengers, several being of Enemy nationality and of military age. All the latter claimed to belong to the Red Cross. She was sent into Kirkwall with an Armed Guard ... .[4]

7. Friday, 17th December – *Mantua* intercepted the Norwegian Steamer *Halingdal*, Louisburg to Norresund, with Cotton-seed Cake. She was sent into Lerwick with an Armed Guard ... .[5]

8. Saturday, 18th December – *Hildebrand* reported that a leak had appeared on the starboard side at the bottom of the third frame abaft

[1]See page 326, note 1.

[2]There is no record of *Potsdam* being intercepted.

[3]Many items of the *Jemtland*'s cargo went to the Prize Court, and even the ship itself was threatened with such a fate (TS 14/6 of 18 and 20 December 1915).

[4]Many items of Frederick *VIII*'s cargo were investigated before the ship was allowed to go on (TS 14/6 of 18 December 1915 *et al.*).

[5]*Halingdal* was allowed to go on after Customs inspection.

collision bulkhead, letting in about two tons of water per hour. It was not considered necessary however for the ship to leave patrol.

A Report was received from the Officer of the Armed Guard from *Alcantara* (Lieut. Vivian, RNR)[1] who proceeded to Greenock in the Danish Steamer *United States* that while on board that ship, a Canadian (naturalised US citizen) had informed him that a steamer belonging to Bergen would shortly leave Brazil with Rubber ostensibly for Sweden, but that arrangements had been made for her capture by the Germans. He also stated that German women travelling from the United States to Europe, carried parcels of Rubber as personal luggage.

It is understood that about 1400 postal parcels of German origin were removed from the *United States* before she left Greenock.

9. Sunday, 19th December – The disposition of the Squadron was as follows:

A Patrol ... *Cedric*, *Almanzora*
C Patrol ... *Motagua*, *Teutonic*, *Victorian*, *Hildebrand*, *Hilary*, *Virginian*.
F Patrol ... *Andes*.
G Patrol ... *Alcantara*, *Ebro*, Armed Trawlers *Saxon*, *Walpole*, *Rushcoe*.
Rejoining patrol from Liverpool ... *Alsatian*.
Coaling at Liverpool ... *Orcoma*.
Coaling in Clyde ... *Patia*, *Patuca*.
Coaling at Swarbacks Minn ... *Otway*, *Orotava*, *Columbella*.
Proceeding to Clyde ... *Mantua*.
Proceeding to Swarbacks Minn ... *Changuinola*.
At Lerwick ... Armed Trawlers *Tenby Castle*, *Arley*, *Robert Smith*.
On special service ... *Arlanza*.

Of 57 Vessels intercepted and examined during the week, 22 were sent into port with, and one without Armed Guards. Exceptionally fine and clear weather was experienced.

10. Monday, 20th December – *Hilary* having developed defect in her Tail Shaft, due to engines racing in heavy sea, was sent to the Clyde for repairs and to complete with coal.

Almanzora reported fresh water service pipes frozen and burst. The necessary stores for repair were ordered to be supplied by *Cedric*.

A submarine was reported five miles SE of St Kilda, steering SW at ten knots on the surface.

[1] Vivian, Harold A., RNR, Sub-Lieutenant 1914, Lieutenant 1916.

11. Tuesday, 21st December – *Otway* intercepted the Norwegian Barque *Skomvaer*, Buenos Aires to Flekkefjord with Quebrache. She was sent to Kirkwall with an Armed Guard ... [172].[1]

Almanzora intercepted the American Steamer *A.A. Raven*, New York to Archangel with military and medical stores. She was directed to call at Alexandrovsk ...

12. Wednesday, 22nd December – *Alcantara* intercepted the Swedish steamer *Urna*, New York to Goteborg with general cargo. Seventeen of the crew had been shipped in New York. She was sent to Lerwick with an Armed Guard … .[2]

The Glass fell rapidly, and the Southeasterly Gale increasing accompanied by heavy sea made boarding difficult and in many cases impossible. Ships on patrol were obliged to heave to and could not make headway.

13. Thursday, 23rd December – *Otway* captured the Swedish steamer *Carolina*, New York to Gothenburg with Hides, Copper and general cargo. She was sent to Kirkwall with an Armed Guard ... [171].[3]

Patuca intercepted Norwegian steamer *Frotz Smith* with Oil-cake and Cotton-seed. She was sent to Lerwick with an Armed Guard.[4]

In both these cases great difficulty was experienced in boarding – Wind SE Force 8 – Heavy squalls of snow and hail.

Met *Almanzora* in Lat. 62.47´N, Long. 6 W, and I personally visited her to see if the extent of the damage done to her fresh water service by frost necessitated her leaving patrol for repair. I found the pipes had burst in several places, icicles hanging from them; but considered temporary repairs could be effected.

14. Friday, 24th December – *Ebro* on G Patrol intercepted the Norwegian steamer *Bergensfjord* West bound with thirty bags of Parcel Mails duly certified as not being of enemy origin as laid down in C.I.O. 1316. She had 243 passengers including one German (male) aged 48; and her cargo, which was chiefly fish, was also certified as of neutral origin. *Ebro* was directed to remove the German passenger and allow the ship to proceed.[5]

The weather in A and C Patrol areas improved but boarding was still difficult and in some cases impracticable.

[1]*Skomvaer* was not detained; quebrache (or quebracho) is a South American hardwood.

[2]See page 327, note 3.

[3]The agents assured the Contraband Committee, through the Consul General in New York, that *Carolina*'s master had been instructed to call at Kirkwall; there were many questions about the ship's cargo (TS 14/6 of 24 December 1915 *et al.*).

[4]The *Frotz Smith* was not detained.

[5]See page 328, note 2.

15. Sunday, 26th December – The disposition of the Squadron was as follows:

A Patrol ... *Cedric*, *Almanzora*, *Alsatian*.
C Patrol ... *Otway*, *Changuinola*, *Victorian*, *Orotava*, *Hildebrand*, *Virginian*, *Patuca*.
F Patrol ... *Andes*.
G Patrol ... *Ebro*, *Columbella*, Armed Trawlers *Saxon*, *Walpole*.
Coaling at Liverpool ... *Orcoma*, *Alcantara*.
Coaling in Clyde ... *Mantua*, *Hilary*.
Coaling at Swarbacks Minn ... *Motagua*, *Teutonic*.
Rejoining from Clyde ... *Patia*.
At Lerwick ... Armed Trawlers *Tenby Castle*, *Arley*, *Rushcoe*.
At Longhope ... Armed Trawler *Robert Smith*.[1]

Of 42 vessels intercepted and examined during the week, 11 were sent in with and 3 without Armed Guards.

The Heavy weather experienced interfered with patrols a good deal all the week.

16. Monday, 27th December – Information was received from the Commander-in-Chief that Enemy submarines were again becoming active in Home waters, and ships proceeding to Clyde and Liverpool were to be warned accordingly.

Columbella reported that the Armed Trawler *Walpole* had intercepted the Norwegian Steamer *Sneppe* with Iron ore from Narvik to Middlesbrough and was escorting her; her Master was inclined to give trouble.

Mantua which should have been leaving the Clyde after coaling, was delayed owing to leaks which had developed in the recent severe weather. The Captain Superintendent reported that it would be necessary to dock her and that her repairs would be completed by 12th January.

Hildebrand, having reported further damage discovered in the neighbourhood of the existing leak, and rivets of after support of Collision Bulkhead sheared and support working, the ship was ordered to proceed to the Clyde for repair.

17. Tuesday, 28th December – *Cedric* reported that in Lat. 63.21´N, Long. 6 W she had rescued from a boat the Master (Andrew Smith) and Second Officer (Joe Hansen) of the British steamer *Morning*. This

[1]*Arlanza*, still in the north, is now omitted.

steamer – a Dundee Whaler – was loaded with Ammunition at Brest and was on her way to Arkhangel. She left Queenstown on 21st December and after bunkering in the Faroes was spoken by *Alsatian* on 22nd December during a Southeasterly Gale. The Master stated that after leaking for two days, due to working of ship, she foundered on the morning of 24th December in Lat. 64.15´N, Long. 7 W. With the exception of the Second Mate and himself the crew were drowned, the boats being stove in. Both men were much exhausted having been four days in an open boat in bad and very cold weather. The matter was reported by W/T to the Commander-in-Chief.

The Armed Trawler *Robert Smith* was met at a rendezvous off the Faroes and given orders to thoroughly search the fjords among the Islands for submarines and ships trying to evade patrols.

Orotava intercepted the American steamer *Maumee*, ex *Djursland*, ex *Verhaven*, Copenhagen to New York in ballast. In view of her origin ... instructions were asked whether she should be sent in. She was released in accordance with Commander-in-Chief's directions ...

Orcoma should have left Liverpool this day after completion of coaling and making good small defects, but I was informed by the Senior Naval Officer, Liverpool, that owing to Labour troubles she would not be able to sail until 3rd January. The seriousness of such a state of affairs at a time like the present needs no comment from me; but I would point out that this is not by any means the first time that a ship, urgently required on patrol, has been delayed in port by unpatriotic conduct on the part of the workmen.

The Captain Superintendent, Clyde, reported that ships of the Tenth Cruiser Squadron now completing with all despatch on the Clyde must be delayed in consequence of Christmas holidays to the workmen; this also appears strange at such a time.

Having decided that the Trawler patrol on the Norwegian Coast could be of little use in intercepting vessels during the Winter months, the Commander-in-Chief gave directions for the withdrawal of the Armed Trawlers employed there in connection with G patrol and they were accordingly ordered to return to Lerwick with a view to augmenting the Fair Isle patrol. [176].

18. Wednesday, 29th December – In C patrol area the Gale continued with snow and low visibility and boarding was carried out with great difficulty.

19. Thursday, 30th December – *Motagua* was met at a pre-arranged rendezvous and ordered to proceed to Reykjavik to convey a secret packet from the Foreign Office to the Acting British Consul at that Port.

Teutonic had been keeping the American steamer *Muskogee* in company since yesterday, 29th December, being unable to board on account of the heavy weather. As there seemed little prospect of improved conditions, *Muskogee* was ordered by signal to proceed to Kirkwall and *Teutonic* returned to patrol.[1]

During the height of the Gale, *Orotava* reported her steam steering gear disabled through breaking of rudder chain at 6 a.m. Repairs were with difficulty effected and damage made good by 11.45 p.m.

20. Friday, 31st December – *Changuinola* intercepted the Norwegian Steamer *Aladdin*, New York to Helsingborg with Grain for the Swedish Government. She had Owners' orders to proceed to Kirkwall but she attempted to avoid examination however. She was sent to Kirkwall with an Armed Guard.[2]

21. Attached to this Report will be found diagrammatic Charts and Curves showing the extent and result of the work of the Ships of the Tenth Cruiser Squadron during the past year – patrolling without intermission an area of 220,000 square miles, in all weathers and under circumstances rendered difficult by the attacks of Enemy submarines.

During this time 3,018 ships have been intercepted on the High seas and carefully examined; 677 ships of this number have been found to be carrying contraband and otherwise suspicious cargoes and have been sent to a British port for examination and confiscation of cargo, as considered desirable by the Authorities.

While engaged in this work, the Tenth Cruiser Squadron has lost two ships by submarine attack (*Bayano* and *India*) two by mines (*Arlanza* and *Viknor*), and one by foundering at sea in heavy weather (*Clan Macnaughton*). It is regretted that this has resulted in a loss of some 63 Officers and 800 Men, who went down with their ships.

There is no doubt but that the efficiency of the Patrol has increased as greater experience has been gained, and it can be truly said that far less ships manage successfully to evade the Patrols than at first. It is also evident that the number of ships attempting to get through this area has considerably decreased.

22. A separate Report, dealing with the Wireless Telegraphy work of the Squadron, is attached [182]. Wireless Telegraphy has been the principal means of communication to individual ships spread over a large area, seldom in sight of each other and constantly being moved to

[1]*Muskogee*'s cargo was oil and petroleum and it was a former German-owned vessel; it was allowed to go on after investigation (TS 14/7 of 3 and 6 January 1916).

[2]*Aladdin* was not detained.

more advantageous positions for intercepting neutral vessels as the circumstances of each case required. This would have been impossible without Wireless Telegraphy.

To give some idea of the extent of the Wireless Telegraphy signalling during the year, it may be mentioned that a daily average of 21 signals sent and 46 signals received was made by the Senior Officer of the Tenth Cruiser Squadron, which works out at an average of one signal every 21 minutes throughout the year, and yet the amount of signalling has been restricted to a minimum.

23. Between 1st January and 31st December 1915 *Alsatian* has been 262 days at sea, steaming 71,500 miles, using 40,287 tons of Coal. This may be taken as typical of the work of each ship of the Squadron.

24. The adventures of the Armed Guards sent away to take ships intercepted into a British port, have been the subject of other letters, and on the whole it may be said that remarkably few casualties in their ranks have occurred – only one Guard being taken prisoners; one being carried to Norway (where the vessel of which they were in charge, the American barque *Andrew Welsh*, was retained, while they were allowed to return to England); and two had their prizes sunk under them by submarines. I would draw attention to the cheerful willingness of these young Officers and Men who take this constant risk without the satisfaction of being allowed to strike a blow in defence of their own safety.

171. *Contraband Committee Minutes*

14 December 1915

Telegram from Mr Bayley,[1] 11 December 1915:

'Swedish ship *Carolina* sailed December 9th for Gothenburg.

Whilst this steamer is understood to have omitted to call at Kirkwall on previous voyages her agents advised me that they have warned masters of the seriousness of evading Naval Patrols, and they anticipate vessel will call at Kirkwall on her present voyage.'.[2]

[1]Bayley, Charles Clive (1864–1923), British Consul-General in New York, 1915–1919; he had been Treasurer in the Niger Coast Protectorate, 1894–1899, taking part in the Benin Campaign of 1897, Consul in New York, 1899–1907 and Warsaw 1908–1913, Consul-General in Moscow 1913–1915; he retired in 1919 and died in 1923 (FO List).

[2]See page 332, note 3.

172. *Sub-Lieutenant S.F. Carter*[1] *to Commodore S.L. Booty*

HMS *Otway*, 19 January 1916

I was placed on board the Norwegian Barque *Skomvaer* in Lat. 61.20´N, Long 10.58´W, with an Armed Guard of one Midshipman and 4 Seamen, and 8 days provisions on 21st December 1915 at 3.35 p.m., with orders from you to take her to Lerwick for examination. She had a Crew of 21, Cargo of Quebrachi Wood and left Buenos Ayres on 15th October for Flekkefjord in Norway.

2. We experienced strong Easterly winds until 1st January 1916, and consequently made no headway towards Lerwick. During this time we frequently met Ships of the Patrol, including HMS *Orotava* on 26th December who supplied us with provisions which I estimated were for 8 days, and HMS *Cedric* on 1st January who also supplied us with provisions which I estimated were for 5 days.

3. On 1st January in the afternoon the wind veered to SW and West which enabled us to run for Lerwick. We passed Muckle Flugga on 3rd January at 2.30 p.m., and arrived off Lerwick in the first watch.

4. We were off Lerwick from 3rd to 8th January, but did not get in on account of contrary and baffling winds.

5. On 8th January it was blowing a gale from the Northward, and I decided to run for Kirkwall. The wind fell during the evening and on 9th January backed to the SW, I then again headed for Lerwick.

6. On 10th January it was blowing a gale from WNW. Noon position 59.56´N, 0.53´E. In the forenoon the Master informed me that provisions, water and oil were all running short. I sent Mr Ritson, Midshipman,[2] to inspect the Storerooms with the Steward, he found about 8 days provisions, but only 5 days water and oil. At 1 p.m. the Crew complained to the Master respecting the safety of the Ship; it was then blowing very hard from the NW, with a very high sea. At 5 p.m. the Master insisted that the Ship must run for safety, I reluctantly consented, and we accordingly ran to the SEd. During the first watch the very heavy gale continued.

7. On 11th January we made the Norwegian Coast, and on 12th January at 1.30 p.m. picked up a Pilot. During this and following days calms with heavy snow squalls were experienced. We tried to make Stavanger or Haugesund, but were eventually taken in tow by two small

[1]Carter, Stanley F., RD, RNR, Sub-Lieutenant 1915, Lieutenant 1917.

[2]Ritson, Edward A., RNR, Midshipman 1914, Sub-Lieutenant 1918, Lieutenant-Commander (retired) in 1940.

tugs on 13th January at 10.30 p.m., and towed into Flekkefjord, where we arrived on 14th January at 4.45 a.m.

8. On 14th January at 7.30 a.m. Norwegian T.B.D. boarded ship, and having obtained particulars went away for orders. At noon the Commander of the T.B.D. returned with permission from the Norwegian Government for the Armed Guard to leave the Country as soon as possible. The British Consul arrived immediately afterwards, and with his assistance I arranged to lodge the Armed Guard on shore for the night, and to leave for Stavanger the following day.

9. We left Stavanger on 16th January at 5 a.m. in the Norwegian SS *Rognvald Jarl*, and arrived at Newcastle on 17th January at 4.30 p.m. I took the Armed Guard and reported myself on board HMS *Satellite* that night. On 18th January we proceeded to Liverpool, and rejoined HMS *Otway* at 5 p.m

10. For some days before we arrived at Flekkefjord the Master has been supplying us with bread, milk, tea, &c, but up to our last day on board we still had tinned meat and cocoa remaining. I offered payment for what we had had to the Master. He communicated with the Owner who said he wished to make no claim either for this or for the delay of the Ship.

11. I am of opinion that the Master did his utmost to get the Ship into Lerwick, until we had to run for safety on 10th January, at which time we were also short of food and water. I much regret that I was unable to take the *Skomvaer* into Lerwick in accordance with your orders.

173. *Extract from the Morning Post*

22 December 1915

From our Special Correspondent, Washington, 21st December.

Fancy a woman imagining in these times that she could leave New York on an ocean trip with nearly two tons of personal baggage and escape observation; yet that is what a female agent of the German Government attempted, and, naturally, she has landed in the police net. So desperately hard up are the Germans for rubber, especially for motor car tyres for military use, and so effective is the British Naval blockade, despite German statements that a blockade does not exist, that in their extremity they have tried to smuggle in rubber from the United States as the personal baggage of women travellers. Manufacturers of rubber in this country are permitted to obtain crude rubber for their own use by an agreement made with the British Government, Rubber Association representatives of American rubber consumers pledging themselves not to permit any rubber to be exported. Anna Dekkers, a German woman, who arrived in the United States from Rotterdam a few days ago, was arrested as she was about to return there because she had 3500 lbs of rubber in trunks and eight packing cases, which were declared simply to contain her personal belongings.

It is a violation of the law for a person to export merchandise without previously making a Custom House declaration of the nature and value of the merchandise The arrest of Dekkers has brought to light a plot financed in Germany to smuggle rubber from the United States. The money was furnished by the Deutches Bank, and Max Jaeger was employed on this side to arrange the details. He made his purchases through Richard Wohlberg, a rubber merchant, who was procuring his rubber under the agreement that he would not re-export it. Jaeger had arranged for a stream of women to cross to Holland, each of whom was to carry rubber as personal luggage. At Rotterdam the women were to be met at the dock by a man formerly connected with the German Army, who would be identified by a white chrysanthemum in his button hole. The women were to turn their baggage over to him, and he was to send it to various places in Germany designated by the Deutches Bank. This is one of the most clumsy of all the German plots, and that it should be seriously attempted shows how extreme must be the needs of Germany at the present time.[1]

174. *Rear-Admiral de Chair to Commander-in-Chief Grand Fleet*

25 December 1915

With reference to A[dmiralty] L[etter] M.08900, of the 7th December 1915,[2] (copy of which has been received by me) relative to the conduct of the Norwegian American Line SS *Kristianiafjord* and certain other neutral vessels intercepted by the squadron under my Command, I have the honour to point out that the arrangements referred to in paragraph 2 of that letter, as regards the agreement with HM Government by the Company to abide by the Conditions of supply of bunker coal, do not appear to me in any way to affect the general necessity for intercepting and sending into port these vessels on every occasion when met with.

[1]I include this extract, no doubt massaged to some degree and affected by the wartime censorship, to show that not all the sailors' suspicions were paranoia.

[2]Not printed, but this clearly refers to de Chair's comments in [161 para. 14], Lieutenant Jones's letter [164] and Jellicoe's letter [166].

2. It is clearly proved that passengers by vessels of Norwegian American Line more particularly, are conveying Rubber and other contraband to Europe under the disguise of personal luggage, and it is also a known fact that the passenger ships of this Line frequently carry Enemy reservists or men of military age.

3. In these circumstances, it would not appear that any modification of the treatment hitherto accorded to these vessels can be allowed without seriously impairing the efficiency of the blockade against Germany, unless they are instructed by their Owners to call at Kirkwall.

175. *Admiral Madden*[1] *to Rear-Admiral Swarbacks Minn (Telegram)*

HMS *Iron Duke*, 27 December 1915

For information. The *Champagne* will not be attached to Tenth Cruiser squadron, but it is anticipated that she will be regularly detailed under the orders of the French Admiralty for services between France and Archangel.[2]

176. *Telegrams*

Northern Patrol Trawlers

1. Commander-in-Chief to Rear Admiral 10 Cruiser squadron, 27 December [1915].

Do you see any objection to withdrawal of trawlers from Norwegian patrol during winter. I think they would be better employed in Fair Island Channel.

2. Senior Officer 10 Cruiser squadron to Commander-in-Chief, 27 December.

Consider trawlers would be much better employed in Fair Island Channel during winter. Great benefit to conduct of Northern Patrol if I may communicate direct with Senior Officer patrol in Fair Island Channel through Gibraltar.

3. Commander-in-Chief to Admiral Commanding Orkney and Shetland, 28 December.

Do not let any more armed trawlers leave for Norwegian coast till further orders.

[1]Madden, Charles, Rear-Admiral 1911, Chief of Staff to Admiral Jellicoe 1914–1916, Vice-Admiral 1915, second-in-command Grand Fleet 1916–1919, Admiral 1919, Admiral of the Fleet 1924, First Sea Lord 1927–1930.

[2]*Champagne* is the former *Oropesa*, transferred to the French flag.

4. Commander-in-Chief to Admiral Longhope, 28 December.

Norwegian patrol trawlers have been directed to return to Lerwick. Request you will organise a Fair Island Patrol for them to intercept trade.

5. Admiral Longhope to Commander-in-Chief, 30 December.

It has been customary for the 10th Cruiser squadron to provide an armed guard, one officer and four men, in each trawler to place on board any vessel sent in. Rear-Admiral Tenth Cruiser squadron ... 28 November asked Admiralty to provide this armed guard for each trawler, but he has received no reply. As each trawler will require an armed guard, will 10th Cruiser Squadron provide them as is done now or Admiralty, as requested by Rear Admiral Tenth Cruiser squadron.

6. Commander-in-Chief to Admiralty, 1 January [1916].

Request information whether armed guards will be provided. Trawlers have been withdrawn from Norway and will be stationed in Fair Island Channel. Admiral Commanding Orkney and Shetland has no reserve to draw upon and it is not considered that Rear-Admiral 10th Cruiser Squadron should be required to provide armed guards for trawlers.

7. Admiralty to Commander-in-Chief, 5 January [1916].

Armed guards will be sent.

177. *Please and Sons to Admiralty*

15 Old Jewry Quarters, London E.C., 31 December 1915

***

We have now received a letter from the Standard Oil Company in which they express considerable surprise at the report made by the Authorities that they allege their steamer *Polarine* on the 4th November last endeavoured to proceed to Copenhagen without calling at a British Port. They have taken the matter up with Captain Dart, who was in command of the vessel, and he states that the facts are as follows.[1]

On November 4th at 11 o'clock a.m. the *Polarine* was signalled by a British Cruiser to stop, and this order was at once obeyed. An officer from the British cruiser came on board, examined the ship's papers and requested Captain Dart to take his ship to Kirkwall via the Pentland Firth. Captain Dart protested against going through that passage, and refused to navigate the ship at his own risk, because the lights in the Pentland Firth were not in operation, and as the Spring tides then

[1]*Polarine* had been sent in on 4 November 1915 [161 para. 4].

prevailing caused a current of nine knots with a flood tide. This condition and considering the *Polarine* can only make nine knots under best conditions, and taking into consideration the eddies attendant on the tide, made the steering conditions in Captain Dart's opinion most precarious, as if the vessel should take a sheer in one of these narrow passages there was every chance of her going ashore, and consequent great danger to life and property. These conditions would be accentuated in the event of fog setting in, and this is quite prevalent in these latitudes. Captain Dart stated that while he was in Kirkwall on a previous voyage two ships had gone ashore in the Pentland Firth and were brought in to Kirkwall in a damaged condition after being floated. Captain Dart most emphatically denies that he was endeavouring to go to Copenhagen without calling at Kirkwall, and states that he specifically advised the Officer who boarded him that he was bound for Kirkwall in accordance with instructions from his owners, which instructions were in writing, and which were produced to the officer in question. At the time the *Polarine* was intercepted she was in the latitude of Fair Isle, and Captain Dart had intended to take the Fair Isle passage, which is a clear and unrestricted passage attendant with no difficulties to navigation, and the vessel was heading for Fair Isle at the time. Captain Dart's intention was to act on the advice which he received from a British Naval Officer on a previous voyage, that is to say, that the Fair Isle passage is a proper and safe course to take, and to pass to the northwards of the island and then turn down to Kirkwall. Captain Dart further says that he indicated his unwillingness to resume responsibility for the navigation of the vessel through the Pentland Firth, and the boarding officer returned to the cruiser to report; approximately two hours afterwards another officer with an armed guard came on board to take the vessel to Kirkwall through the Pentland Firth, and to which officer Captain Dart surrendered the command of his ship, requesting at the time that the officer in question put sufficient crew on board to take care of the navigation, both on deck and in the engine room, as Captain Dart felt he could not justify letting his own crew operate the vessel under the circumstances indicated. The Naval Officer represented to Captain Dart that it was most inconvenient to bring a full crew on board, so Captain Dart modified his position to the extent of permitting his officer and engineers to work under the direction of the naval officer, and during the subsequent navigation of the vessel to and through the Pentland Firth. Captain Dart himself offered his own services in the way of advice and assistance to the naval officer, which advice and assistance was welcomed by the latter, and Captain Dart co-operated with the naval officer and gave him all possible advice and assistance, looking to the safe navigation of the ship, but reserving of course his position that he was not in charge. What actually then happened was the vessel reached the western entrance to the Pentland Firth towards evening when it was getting dark a patrol steamer reported that it was getting too late in the day to get through. The vessel therefore had to turn back, and make for open water for the night, going back until they had Cape Wrath Light in sight. The vessel returned to the entrance to the Pentland Firth at daylight next day, at which time the conditions turned out to be favourable, and the vessel went through safely.

While Captain Dart was unwilling as above indicated to assume responsibility for the safe navigation of the ship through the Pentland Firth, he indicated to the naval officer that he would be willing to resume responsibility for the navigation of the steamer to Kirkwall via the Fair Isle passage, and he states further, had he been permitted to take that route Kirkwall would have been reached if anything earlier than by going through the Pentland Firth, taking into account the delay brought about by the vessel having to return to open water and hang up for the night in order to approach the western entrance of Pentland Firth again at daylight.

Having regard to the very serious nature of the charge made against Captain Dart and to the full statement he has made in reference to the matter, we think, in all fairness to him, the naval authorities should be asked to state upon what evidence they accuse him of having endeavoured to proceed to Copenhagen without calling at a British port and their reply should be communicated to us.

It appears to us that the naval officer in charge of the armed guard which boarded this vessel at the time in question jumped to the conclusion that the vessel was going to Copenhagen direct because she was heading for the Fair Isle passage.

While on this subject we think some understanding should be come to with the naval authorities regarding the course our company's vessels should take in making Kirkwall. It strikes us as being manifestly unfair to ask a captain to take his vessel through any particular passage, which, in his opinion, is dangerous to his ship, as he knows the capabilities of his vessel far better than a naval officer who has just come on board. It seems to us Captain Dart was perfectly within his rights to refuse to continue his command in navigating his vessel through the Pentland Firth and if in the future any boarding officer insists on any of our Company's vessels taking a course which the Captain considers dangerous, whether the Captain continues in charge of or assists in the navigation, or not, our Company must hold the naval authorities liable for whatever may happen.

We have had the benefit of talking this matter over with one of our Company's Captains who is now in London, and he tells us that the safest course is to go North of the Shetlands, but if the weather is favourable the Fair Isle passage is considered safe. The Pentland Firth passage is not at any time considered safe, as at the best of times it requires local knowledge, which our Captains do not assume.

We shall be glad to hear further on this matter generally in due course.

178. *Sub-Lieutenant J.H. Potts*[1] *to Commander A.H. Smyth*

19 January 1916

On the afternoon of December 31st, 1915, I boarded the Norwegian Barque *Titania* with instructions to take her to Kirkwall.

The Glass was exceptionally low at the time and although a high sea was running there was very little wind.

On January 1st I was challenged by HMS *Motagua* and asked if 'all was well', I replied in the affirmative.

January 2nd. At 4 p.m. this day it was blowing heavily from the WSW and our position by D.R. was 30 miles West of North Ronaldshay, as it was then dark and taking into consideration that I had 16 hours of darkness in front of me, no lights showing on the land, and it being impossible to heave the ship to on account of wind and sea, I decided to go North of Muckle Flugga.

When North of the Shetlands the wind and sea were so heavy that I was unable to get the Ship on the Southerly course having lost a foresail in the attempt.

January 6th. This day we received our position from a Norwegian steamer and found ourselves to be 30 miles off the Norwegian Coast.

The Captain then being short of provisions and oil wanted to put into Bergen but I persuaded him to have one more try at Kirkwall. The wind then being NW we set a course for Uskerry Is.

But the weather conditions were against our making any further headway towards Kirkwall as the wind began to veer and by 5 p.m. it was blowing a gale from the WSW, and although we tried to beat up to windward the ship became unmanageable and on the morning of January 10th we sighted the Norwegian Coast.

[1]Potts, James H., RNR, Sub-Lieutenant 1916, Lieutenant, 1917.

At 8 a.m. I was informed by the Master that a Man-of-War was heading towards me, looking out of a Scuttle I saw a Submarine about 4 miles off. I immediately hid my uniform, put on some Clothes of the Crew's, went on deck and took the wheel.

The submarine came alongside, she looked a modern vessel well over 200 feet in length, had no distinguishing number and no ensign flying.

The barque was boarded by a German Officer who examined the ship's papers and told the Master to proceed.

The Submarine then left, heading due South, after being alongside 4 minutes.

On January 12th we dropped anchor in Arendal Harbour. I reported at the British Consulate, gave my parole to the Norwegian Naval Authorities not to leave Arendal until I received permission.

The same day I was granted permission to leave for England when I wished. In the meantime I had received orders from the Consul Garston in Christiansand to proceed to Christiania, and made a full report to the British Legation.

At Christiania I received a suit of Mufti and left for Bergen my occupation being stated on my passport as Salesman.

At Bergen I was assisted by the British Consul and managed without difficulty to leave the same night for Newcastle, arriving there the morning of the 17th.

179. *Memoirs of Surgeon Sub-Lieutenant D.A. Knight*

Patia did over 250 days at sea in 1915. From November to March the weather was gales about three weeks in each month, and often it was impossible to lower a boat to board ships. Sometimes we were hove to alongside a ship for a couple of days before we could board her. Occasionally the gales were so severe that some ships were severely damaged. *Patia* once shipped a sea so heavy that it damaged her bridge, injured one officer, smashed fittings in the wheelhouse, bent the forward 6-inch gun platform and strained her hull so that the fresh water tanks were contaminated.

180. *Recorded recollections of Dr J. Shaw (in 1978)*

There was on the *Changuinola* for some time a Roman Catholic padre.

He was a jolly good chap called Calderwood,[1] but I am told that the C. of E. and Scottish Presbyterian padres wouldn't come aboard I was told and this R.C. padre would and he went to sea with us for quite a bit.

We had some French sailors on board. We had a lot of Channel Islanders and French. I think one or two French Canadians. The crew consisted of Newfoundland men and I used to censor with the French letters written in French because I could read French.

We had two code books. A vocabulary and a cipher. A cipher for important things and a vocabulary for things that didn't matter so much. In any case, if it interests you, the Captain gave an order one day. I used to read these messages. I could decypher them just by looking at them. The vocabulary about. I could tell roughly but the Captain made a rule that we would report every wireless message that came through. So we talked among ourselves and I got a message one day from another ship would some ship go to a rendezvous with another ship on which there will be so many tons of potatoes, so many cabbages, so many Brussels sprouts, and so much of this and that and I went down to the Captain's cabin and wakened him and he sort of said get out of my cabin. I was only taking him at his word, you see. I thought it would be a good thing to do. Just to sort of pull his leg a bit. I never heard any more about it. The Captain thought it was a joke afterwards.

[On the submarine menace in the *Changuinola*.] Some of the older men, the old pensioners and other old Marines and old seamen and so on, they did get anxious sometimes. They did and the long nights in which you only had about an hour's daylight. They got on their nerves. The man opposite to my cabin who was a Lieutenant RNVR. A great big healthy strong chap. The strongest man on board. He came into my cabin weeping one morning. He said doctor I can't stand any more of this. He said, I will go mad, I will go crazy, and I saw the Captain next day. I was actually on my own because the P.M.O. was out of order. He came also sort of, I don't know whether you would call him a nervous wreck or what but anyhow … and I said to the Captain you will have to get rid of Lieutenant Inglis. He has broken down. He is no good. I said, you will have to get rid of our principal medical officer because he is no good, and there were two old seamen who came to me to see me one day and they said we can't stand this any longer doctor. We will go daft. So I spoke to the Captain about them and they were discharged to Portsmouth or something like that.

The strain was the perpetual darkness, I think largely. I don't think

[1]Calderbank, Alexius, RN, Roman Catholic Chaplain 1915, General Staff Duties, 1918, retired 1927.

there was much else. Of course, about nearly half the ships were lost of that squadron. About ten of them I think out of twenty or twenty-five or something like that were lost. Just disappeared some of them. There was that strain that you could always be more or less a target for a submarine if one came along.[1]

181. *Rear-Admiral De Chair to Admiralty*

HMS *Alsatian*, 19 January 1916

Report of Proceedings, 1–18 January 1916

***

1. Saturday, 1st January – *Orotava* on C Patrol intercepted and sent to Lerwick with an Armed Guard the Norwegian Steamer *Otta*, Baltimore to Bergen with grain. Her Master raised difficulties and protested against being sent in.[2]

2. Sunday, 2nd January – *Almanzora* on A patrol intercepted the Swedish Steamer *Kronprins Gustav Adolph*, Rio de Janeiro to Malmo with general cargo, and sent her to Kirkwall with an Armed Guard as directed in Admiralty Telegram 1639 of 26 December. As this vessel was caught on Latitude 63.15´ North, Longitude 5.8´ West, it was evident she had tried to evade the patrol.[3]

A submarine was sighted on the surface 15 miles W by S of Muckle Flugga steering West.

The disposition of the Squadron was as follows, the Ships on each patrol being shown from North to South:

A Patrol … *Andes*, *Almanzora*, *Alsatian*, Armed Trawler *Robert Smith*.
C Patrol … *Cedric*, *Changuinola*, *Teutonic*, *Orotava*, *Patuca*, *Patia*.
F Patrol … *Motagua*.
G Patrol … *Columbella*.
Proceeding to Liverpool … *Otway*.
Coaling at Liverpool … *Orcoma*, *Alcantara*, *Virginian*.

[1]I have some doubts about the value of recollections such as these at a distance of sixty years, particularly in the matter of numbers. This passage should be compared with the more detailed, specific and convincing entries in Dr Shaw's diaries.

[2]*Otta* was not detained.

[3]The coffee in *Kronprins Gustaf Adolph*'s cargo was deemed contraband (as in its sister ship (see page 350, note 7)), but this only delayed the ship a few days (TS 14/6 of 13 December 1915).

Coaling to Clyde … *Mantua*, *Hilary*, *Hildebrand*.
Coaling at Swarbacks Minn … *Victorian*, *Ebro*.

Of 20 vessels intercepted and examined during the past week, 9 were sent in with, and 2 without Armed Guards.

3. Monday, 3rd January – Information was received from the Senior Naval Officer, Liverpool, that *Otway* when entering the Mersey had been in collision with the British Steamer *Dominion*, which was at anchor. *Otway* was placed in dock.

The Armed Trawler *Robert Smith* was met at a pre-arranged rendezvous and given orders as to the further investigation of a report that sailing trawlers were leaving the Faroes with contraband destined for Germany.

4. Tuesday, 4th January – I arrived at Swarbacks Minn in *Alsatian* to coal, and found there the French Auxiliary Cruiser *Champagne* (late British Armed Merchant Cruiser *Oropesa*) with some 200 Russian naval ratings from Serbia on board for passage to Archangel. I personally visited the vessel in company with the Senior Officer, Swarbacks Minn, and ascertained that her commanding officer was in possession of the necessary Confidential and Signal Books to enable him to communicate with British Naval authorities.

Orotava again reported her steam steering gear broken down. Hand gear was used until the damage was made good.

Very bad weather was experienced in C Patrol area.

5. Wednesday, 5th January – The gale continued and prevented boarding, several of the Ships having to lie to. Towards evening the weather improved somewhat. Ships coaling at Swarbacks Minn were much hampered in their coaling. The French Auxiliary cruiser *Champagne* in Olna Firth dragged her anchors during the night. She had been warned that she would require more cable out and probably another anchor, but apparently did nothing and was much surprised in the morning to find she had dragged about 5 cables.

6. Thursday, 6th January – I took the opportunity of inspecting *Patuca* and *Ebro* which had completed coaling.

A submarine was reported to be operating in Latitude 58.43´ North, Longitude 40.12´ West.

Heavy weather was again experienced, especially in C Patrol area, where Ships were directed to lie to as necessary.

7. Friday, 7th January – A report was received from the Senior Naval Officer Liverpool, that *Alcantara*'s return to patrol would be delayed as she could not leave Liverpool on account of labour troubles till 10 February.

8. Saturday, 8th January – I left Swarbacks Minn and returned to A Patrol.

The French Auxiliary Cruiser *Champagne* also left and proceeded for Archangel.

The Norwegian Steamer *Bonhemr* was sunk either by mine or submarine in Latitude 58.59´ North, Longitude 4.35´ West. Her Master stated that before the explosion he saw what he took to be a spar moving in a south-easterly direction.[1]

9. Sunday, 9th January – The disposition of the Squadron was as follows:

A Patrol … *Andes*, *Motagua*, *Orcoma*, *Alsatian*.
C Patrol … *Patuca*, *Victorian*, *Teutonic*, *Orotava*, *Hilary*.
G Patrol …*Columbella*, *Ebro*.
Proceeding to Liverpool … *Cedric*.
Rejoining from Liverpool … *Virginian*.
Coaling at Liverpool … *Alcantara*, *Otway*, *Almanzora*.
Coaling etc, in Clyde … *Hildebrand*, *Mantua*.
Coaling at Swarbacks Minn … *Patia*, *Changuinola*.

Of 24 Ships intercepted and examined during the week 5 were sent into port with, and 1 without armed guards. The work of the Patrols was much hampered by the bad weather prevailing.

A report was received from *Orcoma* of the operations of Armed Trawlers attached to B Patrol last November. Among other items of interest it stated that the Norwegian Government claimed the whole of West Fjord inside the line Skomvaer–Gronna as territorial waters, and the officer in command of a Norwegian Patrol vessel admitted that he had given orders to block all W/T communication between our Armed Trawlers and Cruisers …

10. Monday, 10th January – A strong South westerly gale was blowing and orders were given to Ships to lie to as necessary. *Hilary*, which intercepted the Norwegian Steamer *Haugestol* from Galveston with cotton for Gothenburg, could not board, and was directed to follow to the eastward and do so when weather allowed.[2]

11. Tuesday, 11th January – *Alsatian* intercepted the Swedish Steamer *Kronprinsessen Victoria* from Rio de Janeiro to Christiania with coffee and wool. The Ship evidently intended to evade the Patrol

[1]The exact cause is not known, but no submarine seems to have been involved.
[2]*Haugestol* was not detained.

as she was well North of the Faroes when intercepted. She was sent to Lerwick with an Armed Guard.[1]

Hilary intercepted the American Steamer *Ausable* (ex *Laura*), Galveston and Norfolk (USA) to Esbjerg with cotton seed cake. She was sent to Kirkwall with an Armed Guard. This vessel is on the Admiralty 'Black List'.[2]

12. Wednesday, 12th January – *Hilary* intercepted the Swedish Steamer *Stockholm* and found that, in addition to mails and 132 passengers, she carried a cargo of grain, cotton, and copper. She was sent to Kirkwall with an Armed Guard. Admiralty Telegram 1400 of to-day's date, relative to the shipment of milk powder by registered mail in this vessel, was not received until after she had been despatched.[3]

A large proportion of the squadron being absent from Patrol coaling and making good repairs – two or three being delayed by labour troubles and industrial holidays – orders were given to A and C Patrols to revert to line ahead patrol in a generally North and South direction.

Motagua was met at a pre-arranged rendezvous and a report was received of her recent visit to Reykjavik.[4] … I would draw special attention to clause 7, in which Captain Webster states that 'a large amount of goods of enemy origin, such as silks, fine cloth, cutlery, etc, is imported by parcel post – in fact, it is said, some of the shops have been almost entirely supplied in this manner'. This traffic can only be carried on through the medium of one or other of the regular steamship lines trading to Iceland, which it has been decided are not to be interfered with …

Towards nightfall a heavy gale from the North sprang up, increasing to almost hurricane force and veering to the North East. All Ships were compelled to lie to.

13. Thursday, 13th January – *Hilary* on C Patrol intercepted the Danish Steamer *United States*, New York to Christiania, with general

[1]Many queries were made about *Kronprincessen Victoria*'s cargo; the ship was not released until 10 February (TS 14/7 of 11 January 1916 to 10 February 1916 *passim*). See also [187 para. 10].

[2]The ownership of *Ausable* rendered it a candidate for the Prize Court, but the cargo was deemed innocuous; it was allowed to go on after some thought (TS 14/7 of 15 and 19 January 1916). See also [187 para. 10].

[3]Many items in *Stockholm*'s cargo were prize-courted at once, and others were found in a Customs search. The Foreign Office issued a press statement accusing the owners and the ship of suspicious behaviour; the Customs, however, explained the confusion as a result of hurried loading. The publicity was, in fact, part of the general British diplomatic campaign to get Sweden to accept British conditions of trade. The ship was eventully allowed to go on early in February (TS 14/7 of 17 January 1916 *et al.*).

[4]Not printed; it is at ADM 137/298, 21–26.

cargo. She followed her until the weather moderated and sent her to Kirkwall with an Armed Guard ….[1]

Hilary now had five Armed Guards, totalling 6 Officers and 20 men, away from the Ship, and before night she sent another guard on board the Norwegian Steamer *Sif*, New York to Bergen, with a cargo of flour and general.[2]

The Senior Naval Officer, Liverpool, reported that *Alcantara*, which had been at that Port since 26 December, was still delayed owing to labour trouble and stress of weather.

14. Friday, 14th January – The weather again became very bad and the Patrols were forced to lie to, the wind increasing to a hurricane.

15. Saturday, 15th January – During the heavy gale *Orotava*, which was at Swarbacks Minn, dragged both anchors and was unable to complete coaling. The boom gate vessel at that Port having dragged her anchors, the entrance was blocked temporarily. The shore end of the boom net defence, which was secured round a large rock, also carried away due to the rock splitting under the strain.

16. Sunday, 16th January – The disposition of the squadron was as follows:

A Patrol … *Orcoma*, *Alsatian*, *Alcantara*.
C Patrol … *Hilary*, *Patuca*, *Virginian*, *Patia*, *Changuinola*.
G Patrol … *Patuca*.
Special patrol … *Columbella*.
Coaling at Liverpool … *Almanzora*, *Otway*, *Andes*, *Teutonic*, *Cedric*, *Victorian*.
Coaling at Clyde … *Mantua*, *Hildebrand*, *Motagua*.
Coaling at Swarbacks Minn … *Orotava*.
Joining from Liverpool … *Artois* (French).

During the past week 18 vessels were intercepted and examined, and of these 11 were sent in with, and one without, Armed Guards.

***

Virginian on C Patrol intercepted the Norwegian Steamer *Bergensfjord*, New York to Bergen, in Latitude 59.41´ North, Longitude 9 West. She was sent into Kirkwall with an Armed Guard, her Master lodging the usual protest and refusing to take responsibility for the navigation. Shortly before being boarded *Bergensfjord* was heard

[1] *United States* was not detained.
[2] *Sif* was allowed to go on after investigation (TS 14/7 of 19 January 1916).

sending a W/T message to the SS *New Sweden*, probably warning her of the presence of Patrol Cruisers.[1]

17. Monday, 17th January – *Orotava* joining C Patrol intercepted the Norwegian Steamer *Storaker*, Port Arthur, Texas, to Aalborg with oil cake, and sent her in to Kirkwall with an Armed Guard ….[2]

From an intercepted W/T message from Bergen to a passenger on board the SS *United States*, relative to the *Storaker* it would appear that there is a certain amount of gambling on the part of Insurance Companies on the chance of vessels evading or being caught by our patrols.

18. Tuesday, 18th January – *Patuca* intercepted the Danish Steamer *Hellig Olaf*, Christiansand to New York, with 182 passengers, 29 bags of parcel mail and clearance for mails from Danish Government. Her Master presented a printed protest against being sent into port, but an Armed Guard was put on board with orders to take her to Stornoway for examination ….[3]

Columbella intercepted the Norwegian Sailing Ship *Beechbank*, Mejillones, Chile, to Copenhagen, with saltpetre. She had owner's orders to call at Kirkwall and an Armed Guard was put on board to take her there ….[4]

182. *Rear-Admiral de Chair to Commander-in-Chief Grand Fleet*

HMS *Alsatian*, 2 January 1916

I have the honour to forward the following remarks on Wireless Telegraphy in the 10th Cruiser Squadron for your information:

When the present 10th Cruiser Squadron was formed in December 1914, only 4 ships – *Alsatian*, *Otway*, *Teutonic* and *Mantua* – had previously been serving as Armed Merchant Cruisers. In view of the almost entire absence of active service personnel and of officers and

[1] *Bergensfjord* was not detained; *New Sweden* was not intercepted.

[2] *Storaker*'s cargo of cottonseed cake was sent to the Prize Court. This brought protests from both the United States Ambassador and the Danish government. A letter was found in a search of the ship which, it was claimed, showed subterfuge by the owners. The ship was eventually discharged and then immediately chartered by the British government to take coal to Gibraltar (TS 14/7 of 19 January to 28 February 1916 *passim*).

[3] After guarantees were extracted against re-export the *Hellig Olav* was allowed to sail on (TS 14/7 of 20 January 1916).

[4] *Beechbank*'s cargo was nitrate of soda; it was sold to a London company on 3 February, as an alternative to condemnation in the Prize Court (TS 14/7 of 28 January and 3 February 1916).

men with a knowledge of coding work or of the service generally, unusual difficulties were anticipated in getting the Squadron into working order.

I. RATINGS.

The absence of suitable W/T operators in sufficient numbers at first presented very serious difficulties. The ratings drafted from depots were mostly boys or RNR operators who had no experience of watchkeeping at sea: very few competent ratings were available.

2. It was at once decided that an effort must be made to obtain the services of some of the civilian operators who were accustomed to work these ships when in the passenger service. It was ascertained that these men were not willing to come forward and serve in Armed Merchant Cruisers, their objection being that assistant pursers and junior engineers were being granted commissions, whereas they were asked to serve as Chief Petty Officers. As there was no time to waste, and as the men appeared to be socially and intellectually quite as worthy of commissions as the majority of other mercantile officers who had received them, Admiralty was requested by telegraph to approve of these men being engaged as Temporary Warrant Telegraphists, RNR. On approval for this being given, steps were taken to interview a number of operators at the offices of the Marconi Co. at Liverpool and about 25 were secured. These men were just in time to join their ships before they sailed.

3. Such active service ratings as were in the squadron were concentrated in certain ships, so that they should serve together, and the incompetent RNR ratings and Boys received from the depots were borne as supernumeraries temporarily until they had learnt their work.

4. These arrangements worked very well indeed. The Warrant Telegraphists RNR (Tempy) picked up service procedure very quickly, and with one or two exceptions have proved themselves most satisfactory. They are excellent operators, very willing and intelligent, they are in fact drawn from a good class, and in many cases have been highly reported on.

5. After about six months' service, the higher active service ratings who could be spared were discharged to depots without relief, and the remaining active service ratings except Boy Telegraphists were relieved by RNR and RNVR ratings from the Grand Fleet. The W/T Complements on Armed Merchant Cruisers have been raised from 3 to 4, the 4th rating being a Boy Telegraphist to be relieved by a RNR or RNVR rating when available, and there are now no active service W/T ratings higher than Boy Telegraphist serving in the squadron.

These Boy Telegraphists, of whom there are now 14, are discharged to the Grand Fleet on advancement to Ordinary Telegraphist.

6. It might here be mentioned that nearly all the Warrant Telegraphists RNR (Tempy) who form the back bone of the W/T complements are engaged for the period of the war only. It is considered that they form a very valuable reserve to fall back upon, as they follow the same occupation in time of peace. At the close of the war they will be thoroughly conversant with service procedure and methods and it is recommended that they should be formed into some sort of reserve, in case of their services being required on any occasion.

It is observed that they draw the same pay as W/T operators RNR and the only cost to the Admiralty in granting them temporary Warrant rank, in addition to the higher rate of messing, is the outfit allowance.

II. INSTRUMENTS.

When taken over by Admiralty all ships were already fitted with Marconi 1½ W/T apparatus and tuned for the transmission of the Long and Short Commercial waves. Additional instruments were fitted to enable the transmission of 1000 metre waves.

2. The arrangements made between Admiralty and Marconi Co. when these ships were taken over are not known. In the passenger service it is understood that in return for a yearly rental, the Marconi Co. provide the operators and keep the set in a state of repair. Several of the installations, notably those in *Otway* and *Mantua*, have been in use for many years, consequently renewals should not be at Admiralty cost if the sets remain the property of the Marconi Co. All ships have been directed to keep a careful record of new instruments supplied, making a note of any case where the instrument replaced was in a bad or worn condition when the ship was taken over.

3. Experience on patrol shows that the Marconi 1½ KW apparatus is very inferior to the Service Type II installation which employs the same power, considerable difficulty being experienced in maintaining communication between the Senior Officer's ship and the Q wave guard of the Grand Fleet.

4. Three ships, *Alsatian*, *Cedric*, and *Teutonic*, were therefore fitted with Marconi 3 KW sets, no 5 KW sets being available. This resulted in a great improvement in communication. It has been found, however, that the design of this set is not altogether suitable for heavy work such as it has been required to perform in *Alsatian*. The synchronous spark gap on the alternator shaft necessitates the motor alternator being in the W/T Office immediately under the bench on which the instruments are installed. To reduce the noise the machine is shut up in a cupboard, but

this entails rather unfair working conditions for a machine running at 3000 revolutions per minute. The phase adjustment requires constant and careful adjustment, otherwise the note goes off at once. Several cases have occurred of the condenser breaking and this has been traced, in each case to gap adjustment. Safety spark points must be fitted to save the condenser.

5. Generally speaking the Transmitting Instruments and arrangements of the Marconi Co. are much inferior to those in the Service.

6. 1½ KW sets with synchronous gaps are fitted in *Alcantara*, *Motagua*, *Ebro*, *Almanzora*. Admiralty has been asked to approve of *Otway* being similarly fitted.

7. The only receiving instruments supplied at first, except to *Alcantara*, *Ebro* and *Arlanza*, were magnetic detectors. The three above mentioned ships were fitted with Marconi Crystal Receivers Type 26, suitable for the reception of long wave lengths only.

8. Marconi Crystal Receivers Type 16 were supplied to *Ambrose*, *Oropesa*, *Alsatian*, *Teutonic*, *Virginian*, and *Cedric* and subsequently No. 26 receivers were supplied to all the remaining ships which had not got them. These steps were necessary to enable ships of 10th Cruiser Squadron to receive Admiralty messages sent via Cleethorpes. The ships with No. 26 receivers have since been supplied with Type No. 20 receivers in addition, for the reception of the 600 metre wave.

9. The No. 16 detector in *Alsatian* has been found excellent. It can be adjusted to receive over a range of wave lengths from 1000 to 12,000 ft, and it compares very favourably with service receiving instruments.

10. The general arrangements of the Marconi Room whereby the transmitting instruments are enclosed in a silent cabinet and reception takes place in the office itself are bad. In heavy weather partitions etc. creak and other noises very often render reception of weak signals impossible. This was represented, and silent receiving cabinets were fitted in ships where they were most required.

11. All ships except *Cedric*, *Teutonic* and *Digby* have the ordinary roof aerial, and there have been remarkably few cases of these being carried away in the heavy weather which is experienced during the winter months.

12. In *Alsatian* an intercepting aerial running aft from the main, enables press messages to be read with ease.

III. DIRECTION FINDER.

In May 1914 a Marconi Bellini Tosi Direction Finder was supplied to *Alsatian* from *Marlborough*. It was fitted up with the assistance of the

Marconi Engineer at Liverpool and tried on several occasions during two cruises. The results were not very hopeful, due to the fact that no one had ever seen one of these instruments before, and to the difficulty of obtaining first hand information concerning the working of it. Occasionally the instrument gave fairly accurate results, but it was not reliable.

2. In August 1914, a Direction Finder evolved by the National Physical Laboratory at Teddington was sent to *Alsatian* for trial at sea, and Mr Smith[1] its inventor arrived to instal it. He employed an aerial consisting of a wooden cube, 12 ft. square, wound with a large number of turns of insulated copper wire, in four segments. This was supported between the funnels and the instruments were installed alongside the Marconi Bellini Tosi set, in the gymnasium. The receiving device was a Round's Valve and signals could be heard at a great distance. Eiffel Tower and Norddeitch were heard with the listeners lying on the table at the other end of the room. As was to be expected however this form of aerial showed itself very unsuitable for a ship at sea. In bad weather the wires continually carried away and in a winter gale, the cube could not have held together. The instruments were not easy to adjust quickly, which was a great disadvantage as neutral merchant ships seldom give much time for a reading to be obtained when in the neighbourhood of the patrols.

These considerations in addition to the fact that its accuracy was not greater than the Marconi Bellini Tosi instrument led to the latter being decided on as the better of the two.

3. On next arrival at Liverpool, Lieut. Round[2] of the Marconi Co, visited *Alsatian* and altered the circuits of the Marconi Bellini Tosi instrument, providing it with a Round valve receiver and making other improvements.

4. The result of these alterations was an immediate improvement in accuracy and range of the set, and the direction finder may now be regarded as accurate within 5 or 10 degrees, and sometimes less. It has been of great use in rendezvousing with other ships of 10th Cruiser

[1]Smith, Frank Edward, OBE, GCB (1876–1970), at the National Physical Laboratory from its opening in 1900 to 1919; invented magnetic mine, FRS 1918, Director of the Department of Scientific Research and Experiment at the Admiralty 1920–1929, Secretary to the Department of Scientific and Industrial Research 1929–1939, adviser to various ministries 1939–1945.

[2]Round, Henry Joseph (1881–1966), worked in the Marconi Company 1902–1914, installed radio-direction finding equipment for military intelligence on the Western Front and in Britain; with Marconi again from 1919, installing radio transmitters; consultant with the Admiralty 1939–1945, working particularly on submarine detection equipment.

Squadron in thick weather.

5. During the present cruise a ship of the 10th Cruiser Squadron, which it was desired to meet and which was 45 miles out of her proper position was discovered entirely owing to the direction finder.

6. Similar instruments are about to be fitted in *Otway* and *Teutonic*.

7. It is considered probable that great use could be made of this instrument as an aid to navigation in thick weather, if set up on shore.

IV. CODING.

The problem of providing an efficient coding staff, always a difficult one, becomes more difficult still in an Armed Merchant Cruiser supplied with all Codes and Cyphers and with only inexperienced RNR or RNVR officers and men available for using them. To be really efficient the officers and men employed on this important duty must never be changed. It has been found, however, impossible to adhere to such an arrangement as it entails great hardship on officers and men so employed in that they lose touch with their professional duties. Moreover they are actually required from time to time for outside duties with prize crews, etc.

2. On the whole the coding is well done, and this is probably due in part, to the large number of signals made to the squadron, and consequent practice for the coders. The length of time which must elapse before written correspondence can be circulated, owing to the long periods these ships remain at sea, is largely responsible for the number of signals made. When special efforts are being made to intercept certain Scandinavian American Liners fitted with Direction Finders, a general silence is ordered for about 48 hours.

An analysis of the number of W/T signals sent and received by Senior Officer, 10th Cruiser Squadron during the year 1915 gives the following results:

	Received	Sent	Total
For year	16996	7839	24835
Average daily	46	21	67

One every 21 minutes.

183. *Commander-in-Chief Home Fleets to Rear-Admiral commanding Tenth Cruiser Squadron*

4 January 1916

Report in writing any evidence that you have, other than the statement made in the letter of 14th November, No. 943 [cf. 164], from the Admiral Commanding Orkneys and Shetlands to the Admiralty, to support the contention in clause 2 of your letter of 25th December, No. 3, that passengers by the Norwegian-American Line carry contraband in their luggage.

184. *Rear-Admiral De Chair to Commander-in-Chief Grand Fleet*

HMS *Alsatian*, 7 January 1916

… [T]he contention in clause 2 of my letter No. 3 of 25th December last was based on the statement of Lieut. Murchison Jones, RNVR contained in the correspondence quoted above, supplemented by a report from the *Morning Post* Special Correspondent in Washington dated 21st December 1915, which appeared in the issue of the Journal of 22nd December 1915, copy of which is attached [164, 173].

2. The repeated endeavours of these ships to avoid being intercepted – even going to the extent of proceeding without lights – has left little doubt in my mind that the Captains have received inducements to get through without being taken to Kirkwall. The only conclusion that can be drawn is that Contraband or Enemy subjects are conveyed in these vessels.

185. *Commander-in-Chief Home Fleets to Admiralty*

HMS *Iron Duke*, 10 January 1916

Be pleased to inform the Lords Commissioners of the Admiralty that I desire to make the following comments on the Report of Proceedings of the Rear-Admiral Commanding Tenth Cruiser Squadron … of 31 December 1915 [170].

2. In the final portion of his report the Rear-Admiral touches upon the work of the squadron during the year 1915. I am most fully in agreement with all that he writes and consider that the work of officers and men merits the very highest commendation. They deserve all that their country can do for them. If it had been found possible to adopt the

rationing policy in regard to Scandinavian countries which I have so frequently advocated, the work of the Tenth Cruiser Squadron would have reduced the enemy to very serious straits.

3. The statement of the Rear-Admiral in clause 17 of his report, in regard to labour troubles and Christmas holidays having delayed the completion of ships, is a most regrettable indication of the total lack of patriotism shown by men who call themselves Britishers, who are enjoying very high wages, and who yet will not devote their utmost energies towards the defeat of the enemy.

The Grand Fleet has suffered in efficiency from precisely similar causes and such a condition of affairs fills one with apprehension and wonder.

186. *Minute by Captain Richard Webb, Director of Trade Division*

16 January 1916

All vessels of the Norwegian America Line except the *Bergensfjord* and *Kristianiafjord* are under agreement to call at Kirkwall.

The *Bergensfjord* and *Kristianiafjord* should be sent in on each occasion for the removal of the parcel mails and also in order that the Company may set up a plea of '*force majeure*' when resisting action in the Norwegian Courts by the consignees of goods which have been returned to this country.

Arrangements have been made by the New York agents for the inspection of passengers' luggage by the New York Customs in conjunction with the British Consular Inspector. One case of attempted smuggling of nickel was detected in this manner. Two trunks of rubber have recently been detected by the Danish United SS Co., and have been sent back to this country.

A signal was sent out on 3rd January 1916, directing that all vessels carrying parcel mails should be sent into port; this would cover both ships.

Suggest C-in-C be so informed, observing that as soon as the departure of these vessels from United States port is known, an order for their interception will always be sent out by the Admiralty while the present system is in force.

187. *Rear-Admiral de Chair to Admiralty*

HMS *Alsatian*, 7 February 1916

Report of Proceedings, 19 January–6 February 1916

***

1. Wednesday, 19th January – *Duke of Cornwall* which had left Swarbacks Minn to return to Longhope with despatches, was forced to put back to harbour owing to the heavy sea running.

Bad weather was prevalent in all Patrol areas and ships were hove to, reporting a heavy gale. Ships coaling at Busta Voe were obliged to stop coaling and raise steam; some dragged their anchors although all had two anchors down.

2. Thursday, 20th January – *Patia* reported that while hove to she had shipped a heavy sea which had seriously damaged her bridge and injured an Officer. Temporary repairs were effected [179].

The continued bad weather made coaling in Swarbacks Minn a slow and difficult operation. In going alongside *Artois*, the Collier collided with her and damaged her making a hole in the port bow with the crown of her starboard anchor. Temporary repairs having been made, coaling of this ship proceeded.

3. Friday, 21st January – *Orotava* reported wheelhouse and all bridge fittings smashed by heavy sea and that she was obliged to run before the gale endeavouring to use hand steering gear but unsuccessfully. She was directed to run for shelter if possible and to proceed to the Clyde through the Minch if necessary [189, 190].

Patia was also directed to proceed to the Clyde as all her fresh water tanks were contaminated with salt due to the straining of the ship, and the ship's company were reported to be suffering from gastric trouble.

4. Saturday, 22nd January – *Almanzora* intercepted the Swedish steamer *Axel Johnson*, Gothenburg to Monte Video with general cargo and forty bags of parcel mail. She was sent to Stornoway with an Armed Guard as there was the possibility that she was carrying enemy's export.[1]

The Commanding Officer of the *Artois* having requested that a British Officer might be lent temporarily to advise as to the routine and work of the Squadron, Lieutenant Kenyon,[2] the Gunnery Officer on my

[1]*Axel Johnsson* was not detained.

[2]Kenyon, Guy V., RN, Lieutenant 1908, Lieutenant-Commander 1916, Commander (retired) 1928.

staff, was lent for ten days with orders to give assistance and information as necessary [195].

Owing to the heavy weather, the gate of the Boom at Swarbacks Minn was damaged and sank below the surface in the centre and could not be opened. *Alsatian* however, having completed coaling, was able to leave harbour, passing over the gate without mishap.

Information was received that the Norwegian sailing vessel *Skomvaer*, which had been intercepted by *Otway* on 21st December and dispatched to Lerwick with an Armed Guard, had arrived at Flekke Fjord, Norway on 14th January, having been unable to make a British Port owing to contrary winds and shortage of provisions. The Armed Guard was allowed to return to England by the Norwegian Authorities. A full report by the Officer in Charge, Sub-Lieutenant S.F. Carter, RNR, is attached hereto … [172]

Although this ship was beating about off Lerwick for five days she does not appear to have received any assistance which might have enabled her to reach that port.

A report was received from *Orcoma* that as a consequence of the long period of heavy weather recently experienced, the main deck in storeroom passage on starboard side of ship, directly over frames Nos 121–124 had buckled about seven-eighths of an inch. In order to lessen the strain it was decided to replace the door of No. 2 hold, which was removed before the ship commissioned, as this would enable coal in No. 2 hold to be used before that stowed in the reserve bunker.

5. Sunday, 23rd January – The disposition of the Squadron was as follows:

A Patrol … *Alcantara*, *Alsatian*, *Otway*.
C Patrol … *Almanzora*, *Hilary*, *Patuca*, *Columbella*
F Patrol … *Virginian*.
G Patro … *Ebro*.
Rejoining from Clyde … *Mantua*.
Proceeding to Clyde … *Patia*, *Orotava*, *Changuinola*.
Coaling at Liverpool … *Cedric* (paying off), *Teutonic*, *Andes*, *Victorian*.
Coaling in Clyde … *Hildebrand*, *Motagua*.
Coaling at Swarbacks Minn … *Orcoma*, *Artois* (French).

During the past week 19 Vessels were intercepted and examined and 8 of these were sent in with and 1 without Armed Guards; but the continuous bad weather and succession of gales greatly hampered the work of the ships on patrol.

6. Monday, 24th January – The following remarks contained in

Boarding Reports received are of interest:

AMERICAN SS *Ausable* ex *Laura.*

'This ship forms a one ship company called the Ausable Steamship Co. which is managed by the American Transatlantic Co., one of the Directors of which is a man called Wagner, of German descent'.[1]

AMERICAN SS *Brindilla.*

'During passage to Kirkwall ship was hove to in gale two boats stove in and port side of bridge severely damaged. Officer in Charge of Armed Guard, Ship's Officer of Watch and one Marine washed off bridge. None seriously hurt. Ship's medicine chest used.'[2]

Otway, which was met at a pre-arranged rendezvous, reported that she had been fitted with a W/T Direction Finder and that her W/T Installation had been converted to a Disc Discharge type by the supply of $1\frac{1}{2}$ KW Rotary Converter.

Information was received from the Officer of the Armed Guard placed on board the Norwegian Bargue *Alonzo* by *Alcantara* on 19th instant, that owing to stress of weather and damage to the ship, he had been compelled to put into Aalesund [188].

Ebro intercepted the Norwegian Barque *Beechbank* with Armed Guard on board, in Lat. 61.25´N, Long. 1.58´E. This vessel was trying to make Lerwick but had lost her fore and maintop masts and her mizzen-topgallant mast and nearly all her sails and boats were gone. As the ship was tight *Ebro* endeavoured to take her in tow but without success and as weather again became bad, *Ebro* could do nothing but stand by till morning. The crew were difficult to manage and would not go aloft and the cutting away of the mizzen-top sail and other work aloft had to be carried out by the RNR Officer of Armed Guard and the Master of the ship. Lieutenant Wynn, RNR,[3] of Armed Guard took complete charge after the dismasting of the ship.

7. Tuesday, 25th January – The weather continued very bad with a gale from WSW, force 9–10, sea very high, and it was impossible to communicate by boat – *Ebro* being light with only 22% of coal remaining became somewhat unmanageable. This difficulty was overcome by veering an anchor and six shackles of cable. Although a dangerous experiment, this steadied *Ebro* and enabled hawsers to be got on board by a buoyed line drifted to windward, and a rocket. The *Beechbank* was eventually got in tow with a 6" and $5\frac{1}{2}$" wire and 90 fathoms of her chain cable, using a long tow.

[1]See page 350, note 2.

[2]*Brindilla* was not detained.

[3]Wynne, Hugh D., RNR, Sub-Lieutenant 1914.

At 12.35 p.m., *Ebro* reported *Beechbank* in tow and proceeding towards Lerwick – maximum speed 2 knots. I detached *Alcantara* to stand by *Ebro* as a defence against submarines.

Almanzora reported that while assisting to secure the starboard seaboat, Lieut. Commander Harold Philips[1] had fallen overboard and been drowned. This regrettable incident occurred in weather which prevented any attempt being made to save life by lowering a boat.

8. Wednesday, 26th January – At 7.45 a.m. *Ebro* reported that in spite of heavy weather, which made progress slow, she was towing the *Beechbank* at 2 knots, and later as the conditions improved, speed was increased.

9. Thursday, 27th January – *Ebro* reached Lerwick at 10 a.m., left *Beechbank* in charge of the Armed Trawlers and then proceeded to coal at Clyde.[2]

It is considered that Commander Dugmore of *Ebro* did very well in saving this ship, as she was being driven on a lee shore (in Lat. 61 N, Long. 3.25´E) before the gale, when taken in tow.

10. Friday, 28th January – The following information was given in a report received from Lieutenant John A. Douglas, RNVR,[3] the Officer of the Armed Guard which took the Swedish steamer *Kronprincessin Victoria* to Lerwick and subsequently to Newcastle, arriving at the latter port on 17th January:

The *Kronprincessin Victoria* had a cargo of 45,000 bags of Coffee and a deck load of 300 tons of quebracho wood. The freight for the Coffee was 180s/- per ton (before the War freight was 22/- per ton) freight for the deck load was 100s/- per ton. In both cases the freight was paid before the cargo was taken on board.

Lieutenant Douglas was informed by the Examining Officer at Lerwick that the ship had Nickel on board with other cargo.

The Master of the Steamer handed over a Mail bag, and when pressed for other papers, he produced from his cabin several large packets sealed and addressed, remarking that he believed them to contain duplicate manifests but did not know for certain. On being opened it was found that the contents were enclosed in a second cover also addressed. On opening this second cover the papers were found to be manifests which did not agree with those originally produced, part, if not all, of the cargo being consigned to German interests direct.

[1]Phillips, Harold, RNR, Lieutenant 1907.
[2]See page 352, note 4.
[3]Douglas, John A., RNVR, Lieutenant 1915.

The Master of the Vessel, who appeared to be very nervous, informed Lieutenant Douglas that his original intention had been to run as far North as Lat. 64 N, but owing to the bad weather and the presence on board of his wife who was ill, he ran East on Lat. 62.48´N. He regretted not having gone further North as he might have been able to get through. He admitted that the ship had twice been caught. He stated that one ship was to have left Santos two days after he did.

Lieutenant Douglas copied the following positions from the Ship's Log:

5 Jan. Lat.	45.40´N, Long. 22.21´W.
6 Jan. ..	49.45´N, .. 21.55´W.
7 Jan. Lat.	53 N, Long. 21.2´W.
8	56.37´N, Long. 19.2´W.
9	60.4´N, Long. 16.18´W.
10	62.14´N, Long. 11.16´W.
11	62.20´N, Long. 5.29´W.

The Steamers of this Line run to Malmo and no further, in order to avoid possible trouble with the Germans. The Company is understood to be building six more steamers for the purposes of this trade. Two of these are to be 12,000 ton boats burning oil fuel.[1]

11. Sunday, 30th January – The disposition of the Squadron was as follows:

A Patrol … *Andes*, *Otway*, *Alsatian*.
C Patrol … *Hildebrand*, *Almanzora*, *Artois*, *Hilary*, *Orcoma*, *Mantua*.
F Patrol … *Victorian*.
G Patrol … *Alcantara*.
Proceeding to Clyde … *Ebro*.
Coaling &c in Clyde … *Orotava*, *Motagua*, *Patia*, *Columbella*, *Changuinola*.
Rejoining from Clyde … *Patuca*.
At Liverpool … *Teutonic*.
Coaling at Swarbacks Minn … *Virginian*.

During the past week 21 vessels were intercepted and examined, of which 5 were sent into port with Armed Guards. Bad weather greatly hampered the work of the patrols.

[1]See page 290, note 5.

12. Tuesday, 1st February – *Almanzora* in preparing to board the Norwegian steamer *Drammensfjord* had her boat smashed by accident. The after fall took charge when lowering and seven men were injured though none seriously.[1]

13. Wednesday, 2nd February – *Artois* intercepted the Danish sailing vessel *Vigilant*, Goteborg to Morocco in Lat. 59.25´N, Long. 8.10´W, and at the first attempt to board she had an accident with her boat and dropped a man overboard. The man was picked up and *Vigilant* boarded. Her foremast was gone and her rigging was in a bad state and the Master requested that the crew should be taken on board *Artois*. This was done with some difficulty on account of the weather and an attempt was made to tow the derelict which was loaded with wood and leaking. As the weather became worse it was found impossible to get the *Vigilant* in tow and *Artois* was directed to stand by her for the night. *Orcoma* was also sent to assist as it was considered most desirable to get the *Vigilant* to Stornoway, so that she might be well searched, there being strong suspicions of her carrying stores for enemy's submarines to Mediterranean.

14. Thursday, 3rd February – *Artois* continued to stand by the *Vigilant* but she was unable to take her in tow on account of the state of the weather.

Orders were given to patrols to lie to as necessary as the gale increased.

Orcoma succeeded in boarding the Swedish steamer *Sagoland*, Baltimore to Landskrona with wheat. Two of the crew were considered suspicious and the ship was sent to Kirkwall with an Armed Guard.[2]

15. Friday, 4th February – The weather slightly improved and at 9.45 a.m., *Artois* reported that she had the derelict in tow and was proceeding to Stornoway. At noon her position was Lat. 59.57´N, Long. 7.1´W, Speed 4.5 knots. The Rear-Admiral Stornoway was informed of her approach and was requested to provide an escort.

Mantua was directed to meet *Artois* at 8 a.m., on the 5th and protect her from submarine attack until escort from Stornoway arrived.

16. Saturday, 5th February – *Mantua* reported that she was in company with *Artois* at 8.30 a.m. – heavy gale from WSW, speed 1 knot. At 2 p.m., Rear-Admiral Stornoway made a signal that an escort consisting of the Yacht *Calanthe*, two Whalers and a Tug should have

[1]*Drammensfjord* was apparently not sent in on this occasion.

[2]*Sagoland* was allowed to go on after investigation of the cargo of wheat (TS 14/7 of 5 February 1916).

been with *Artois* at 8 a.m., but they apparently took shelter under the land.

At 9.30 p.m., *Artois* having arrived under the lee of the Butt of Lewis., *Mantua* was directed to rejoin patrol.

A submarine was reported in Lat. 58.34´N, Long. 4.12´W, proceeding East on the surface.

17. Sunday, 6th February – At 10.45 a.m., *Artois* with *Vigilant* in tow arrived at Stornoway.[1]

The wind and sea which had been rising during the last twelve hours were now at the force of a full gale (9–10) from WSW, Barometer 28.44.[2]

The Disposition of Patrol was as follows:

A Patrol … *Andes, Virginian, Hilary.*
C Patrol … *Alsatian, Otway, Motagua, Hildebrand, Almanzora, Orcoma, Mantua, Patuca.*
F Patrol … *Victorian.*
G Patrol … *Alcantara.*
Rejoining from Liverpool … *Teutonic.*
At Stornoway … *Artois.*
Coaling &c at Clyde … *Changuinola, Columbella, Orotava, Patia, Ebro.*

During the past week 33 vessels were intercepted and examined – 8 sent in with Armed Guards and 1 towed to Stornoway.

A report was received that a steamer had fired on the periscope of a submarine in Lat. 53.28´N, Long. 3.52´W, not far from Liverpool.

***

188. *Sub-Lieutenant Leonard Stanley, RNR,*[3] *to the Commanding Officer HMS* Alcantara

HMS *Alcantara*, 8 February 1916

In accordance with your orders I have the honour to report that at 6 p.m. on Wednesday, January 19th, 1916, in Lat. 63.0´N, Long. 4.53´W, I went on board the Norwegian four-masted barque *Alonso* in charge of an armed guard, with instructions from you to take her to Lerwick. The

[1] *Vigilant* was not detained, at least not by the Customs.
[2] 963 mbs.
[3] Stanley, Leonard, RNR, Sub-Lieutenant 1915.

weather at the time was a very strong southerly wind and heavy sea. The barque was under lower topsails and heading East.

On Thursday, January 20th, the wind veered to SW, and increased in force, the sea being very high. The barque continued under the same sails heading SSE, shipping heavy water, labouring and rolling heavily. The ship was practically hove to, it being impossible to carry any more sail.

On Friday, January 21st, in Lat. 62.0′N the gale continued with frequent terrific squalls and hail. The whale oil tanks and boilers on deck commenced to work loose, and the Captain was afraid that they would carry away and take the bulwarks with them. Later in the day, the fore topgallant stay, the fore topmast staysail, and jib, carried away. The preventor stanchions supporting the tanks and boilers were broken. Half the crew were sick.

On Saturday, January 22nd, at 11 a.m., Yttero Light, Norway, was sighted bearing East, the wind being WSW, and blowing with renewed violence: and the ship was immediately put on the port tack, heading North. The question of seeking shelter was now discussed as the ship was on a lee shore and in no fit condition to weather the storm. On Sunday, January 23rd, after trying in vain for the last 24 hours to get clear of the coast, and seeing no improvement in the weather, I decided it was necessary to run for shelter. Signals of distress were flown off Rondo Island, and at 11 a.m. a motor-lifeboat came out, the Coxswain of which piloted us into Aalesund, where we anchored at 1.30 p.m.

On arrival I reported myself to the Customs and to the Police and made a joint statement with the Captain to the Police as to the circumstances of the case.

On Tuesday, January 25th, the Norwegian Destroyer *Draug* arrived and took the Armed Guard and myself on board. Later in the day the Commander of the destroyer informed me that we were allowed to proceed to England. We were put on shore and the destroyer then left the wharf on account of the rough weather, and went to an anchorage.

Before going ashore at Aalesund, the men's arms and accoutrements were concealed by wrapping them in sacking.

Owing to the death of the British Vice Consul, the Consulate at Aalesund was shut up. We therefore remained in the town until it was possible to get on board the steamer for Bergen.

On arrival at Bergen, I reported to the British Consul, who made arrangements for our passage to Newcastle, and on Thursday, January 27th we left Bergen in SS *Vega*.

After arriving at Newcastle we proceeded to Liverpool, where I reported myself to the Senior Naval Officer.

189. *Diary of Dr J. Shaw*

23 January 1916. When I was in Glasgow I had an opportunity of seeing the *Orotava*. Bishop, the O.W., showed me the bridge or rather what was left of it. The whole front of it was smashed in, the whole wheelhouse was smashed to matchwood. Everything lying prone on the deck. Angle bars or iron cut across as if by a knife. Her rails twisted in weird shapes and a few of her boats smashed. Her steering gear had gone wrong. Some of her deck plates were loose. She seemed an old wreck and I wondered how she could hold together. I heard that one time she rolled at an angle of 48° … The ship was sending out S.O.S. signals; some passenger steamer went to her help. I don't suppose the weather could have been much worse.

190. *Captain G.E. Corbett*[1] *to Rear-Admiral Commanding Tenth Cruiser Squadron*

HMS *Orotava*, 27 January 1916

I have the honour to report, in consequence of damage sustained, proceedings of this ship in the gale which lasted from Wednesday 19th to Sunday 23rd January (inclusive).

On Wednesday and Thursday, when it was merely blowing a stiff gale (Barometer falling to 28.05)[2] there was no difficulty in laying to as usual.

On Friday about 6 a.m., however, wind increased in force and by 9 a.m., was blowing (I estimated) with hurricane strength, which lasted for more than two hours. It then eased somewhat, but continued blowing very hard and sea became very big, having apparently been flattened down, as it were, previously by the force of the wind.

Until 4 p.m., the ship had been kept head on to the sea, though occasionally falling off a few points, by steaming revolutions for 10 to 13 knots, the ship apparently making no headway.

Just about that time, when ship was actually head to the sea and on an even keel, a heavy sea, which I estimated to be over 35 feet high as I could not see over it, swept past the bows and forecastle and broke abreast of and right on to the bridge and all open decks below it.

[1]Corbett, Godfrey Edwin, RN (1871–1929), Commander 1906, commanding in Tenth Cruiser Squadron, then in charge of convoys, Captain 1919 (retired), Inspector of Imperial Lighthouse Service.

[2]950 mbs.

Practically all bridge fittings and most of wheelhouse were swept away, also considerable damage was done to Standard Compass Platform (45 feet above W.L.) Chart table smashed, bowl of compass dislodged, &c.

Fortunately, notwithstanding the mass of wreckage of iron, stanchions, splintered timber &c., flung in all directions, the only person who received any injury worth mentioning was the Officer of the Watch, he being slightly cut and badly bruised.

By the time Hand Steering gear was connected up, ship had fallen off broadside to sea, and, considering the difficulty of conning from aft to keep ship up to the sea, I decided the safest course would be to try and run, which was accordingly done.

During the night wind and sea moderated, so that it was possible to steer for The Minch; but there was some difficulty in making it, as next forenoon (Saturday) the wind again increased to full gale force (raising a big steep sea) and continued so to blow until Firth of Clyde was reached late on Sunday.

In addition to damage mentioned above, steel casings of Saloon &c., on Upper and Promenade Decks were bent, and also beams supporting deck immediately under where weight of water fell. Deck round after end of engine room casing also showed signs of weakness as a result of working of ship and stringer plate has been found badly corroded and is being replaced.

In addition there are a considerable number of minor defects, some due to the big gale and others to the almost continuous bad weather during the last six weeks.

It is estimated by the Contractor, who has all the defects in hand, that he will require until 12th February to make them good; but he promises to hasten the date of completion if possible.

I might mention that, having received your permission to pass through the Minch, *Orotava* subsequently proceeded via Sounds of Mull and Islay. I should suggest that navigation through the latter would be simplified if a cairn, or some mark, was erected on hill behind and on bearing of about 198° with the Distillery Chimney to give a clearing mark for the 4½ fathom patch near Northern entrance.

191. *Commander-in-Chief Home Fleets to Rear-Admiral Commanding Tenth Cruiser Squadron*

HMS *Iron Duke*, 31 January 1916

With reference to your letter of 19 January 1916, no. 12/3,[1] relative to the list of vessels reported as not intercepted by the patrols during the period 21st April to 5th December 1915, the presumption that many of the vessels which passed without examination took the route south of C Patrol and thence by North Rona or Sule Skerry and Fair Island is concurred in, and the following remarks are made in that connection.

(a) The part of the route included in area I is now well watched by the local patrols, and they have orders to board and examine merchant vessels.
(b) With regard to the Fair Isle Channel, the trawlers stationed there since 1st January will now intercept vessels attempting to pass except when the weather is too bad there even for trawlers to keep the sea.
(c) As regards the passage round Muckle Flugga, a whaler patrol was placed off that point on 4th December last, but it was necesary to withdraw it on 10th December as whalers were found to be of little use in the heavy seas experienced there. That locality, therefore, is not regularly patrolled.

***

192. *Sub-Lieutenant C.C. Logan*[2] *to Rear-Admiral Commanding Tenth Cruiser Squadron*

14 February 1916

I have the honour to render the following report of proceedings from the time I was placed on board the Norwegian Sailing Vessel *Hippalos* – from Savannah to Nykjobing with a cargo of cotton seed cake – at 11.30 a.m. on 1 February in charge of an armed guard, consisting of myself and four ratings, with orders from Captain John F. Grant-Dalton, Royal Navy,[3] of *Hildebrand*, to take her in to Lerwick for Examination.

1. 1 February – 11.20 a.m. Boarded *Hippalos* with an armed guard of

[1]Not located.

[2]Logan, Charles C., RNR, Sub-Lieutenant 1915, Lieutenant 1917.

[3]Grant-Dalton, John Foster (1873–1938), Lieutenant 1894, Commander 1906, Captain 1914, Captain of *Hildebrand* 1915–1917 and of *Armadale Castle* 1917, SNO Zanzibar 1919–1921.

myself and four men in Latitude 60.32´ North, Longitude 7.54´ West. Set course SE by E 3/4 E (Magnetic). Speed 8 knots.

2. 2 February – 7 a.m. Set topgallant sails, speed 9 to 10 knots, high seas, fine and clear, wind WNW. Noon position 60.13´ North, 4.31´West. 4.40 p.m. position 60.3´ North, 3.30´ West. 6 p.m. Furled topgallant sails and foresail, wind increasing and South Westerly.

3. 3 February – 3 a.m. Sunburgh Light North 8 miles (just seen), glass falling fast. Wind backed to SSW. 7.30 a.m. Hove to 4 miles South (Magnetic) off Bressa Sound. Wind shifted to South-east, barometer 29.30.[1] 8 a.m. Headed out ENE. 9.30 a.m. – wore ship and stood in. Weather became thick obscuring the land, wind and sea rising, barometer 29.10. 11 a.m. – Wind shifted to South-west. Boxed ship around and stood out, furled staysails and inner jib. Hove to under 3 lower and upper topsails. 1 p.m. – Furled upper topsails. Midnight – Wore Ship.

4. 4 February – Fierce gale with mountainous seas from SSW, and heavily overcast with violent squalls. Shipping seas fore and aft. Cargo shifted over to starboard and ship listed heavily. The man at the wheel was thrown over the wheel box, but only slightly hurt. 8 a.m. – Barometer 29.01. 12.30 p.m. Observed Out Skerries WNW (Magnetic) about 6 miles. 1 p.m. – Wore Ship. 5 p.m. – Out Skerries W 1/2 N (Magnetic) about 14 miles. Drifted E by N 1/2 N, 10 miles. Set lower staysails, the wind and sea moderating and the barometer rising slowly. 9 p.m. – Set upper topsails. 10.30 p.m. Out Skerries dipped. Heading South-east (Magnetic).

5. 5 February – 8 a.m. – Wore Ship, heading W 1/2 N (Magnetic). Fresh SSW wind and a rough sea, cloudy and fine. Barometer 29.45. 9 a.m. – Set foresail. Noon position 60.28´ North, 0.24´ West. 3 p.m. – Wore Ship. Out Skerries S 50° W, 5 miles. Tried to communicate by signals, but received no answer. 4 p.m. – Wind and sea increasing, barometer falling. 11 p.m. – Fierce SW gale with mountainous seas. Cargo shifted to port causing heavy list. Squalls of hurricane force – furled upper topsails and staysails. Mizzen topsail sheet carried away. Barometer 29.20. Staysails main and mizzen carried away.

6. 6 February – Hard gale, fierce squalls with high seas. Wind WSW. 3 lower topsails and foresail, shipping heavy seas. Barometer at noon 29.20, position 60.22´ North, 1.9´ East. Made good S 80° E, 46 miles. Bressa bore S 80° W, 68 miles. First Mate reported there was only 4

[1]The barometer readings in this report range from 982 mbs (29.01") to 996 mbs (29.42").

days more paraffin. Heading S to S ½ W. 4 p.m. – No change in weather. Ship labouring heavily. Barometer 29.13.

7. 7 February – Wind decreased a little, seas still high. 8 a.m. Barometer 29.35. Noon – 59.32´ North, 3.2´ East. Made S 47° E (True) 76 miles. Barometer 29.25. Lerwick NW by W 129 miles. 4 p.m. Barometer 29.30, wind and sea increasing from WSW to W. Guard's provisions finished. Main Lower Topsail went from foot, clewed up, repaired, and set again. Paraffin and water both getting short. 4 p.m. – sounded 100 fathoms – no bottom.

After due consideration I decided to make for Christiansand, provided there was no change in the weather before the following night. If, however, the wind shifted sufficiently to allow us to make any progress to the Westward, then I should proceed West. Strong adverse gales with high seas had been experienced the whole time. The ship was listed heavily to Port and being driven towards the Norwegian Coast. I was of opinion that to remain under sail close hauled for another 18 hours would put the Ship in a dangerous position, and as it was quite impossible to so long as the weather remained as it was to make a British Port, I decided there was no other course to be taken. The Ship was accordingly put on SSE course (Magnetic).

8. 8 February – The wind moderated a little, but there were frequent squalls of hurricane force with hail and snow, barometer 29.30. Set upper topsails. The wind was still west with a high sea and swell, the Ship labouring and rolling heavily. At 10 a.m. sighted the Norwegian coast about 17 miles distant, and about the same time observed a barque some 5 miles to leeward – this was the first vessel sighted. Noon position 58.25´ North, 5.38´ East, steering S 36° E (True). Made S 60° E 105 miles. Barometer 29.40. Altered course S 31° E (True). 4 p.m. Barometer 29.42, strong wind with high westerly sea and swell, fierce hail squalls at frequent intervals. 7 p.m. – As there was still no sign of any change for the better, the Ship was turned East. 8 p.m. Barometer 29.42. High wind and heavy squalls continued. Reduced sail.

9. 9 February – 2 a.m. – Naze light abeam 9 miles distant. 5 a.m. Ryvingen Light abeam 5 miles. Barometer 29.40. 6.30 a.m. Observed Oxo Light House. 7.30 a.m. Hove to awaiting pilot. 8.30 – Pilot aboard and proceeded. 10.30 a.m. Anchored. Proceeded to the British Consulate and reported myself, communicated with the Legation by telephone and gave full particulars. I was directed by the Consul to

leave the Armed Guard on board, but to stay ashore myself so as to be more accessible if required. The Military General of the Forces gave permission for me to visit the town. A Norwegian guard was sent to *Hippalos*, who sealed all the hatches and remained to see that the Ship did not leave until everything was settled.

10. 10 February – Supplied the armed guard with fresh provisions. A telegram was received stating that the question of our disposal had been referred to the Norwegian and British Foreign Offices, and later the Military General informed me that we were not to be interned, but could sail for England as soon as ready.

11. Formal permission to leave the Country was given the following day, and arrangments were made for our passage to Newcastle in SS *Sterling*, where we arrived at 6 a.m. on 14 February. I immediately proceeded to Liverpool and reported.

193. *Lieutenant J.M. Coates, RNR*[1] *to the Commanding Officer, HMS* Patuca

HMS *Patuca*, 17 February 1916

I have the honour to report that on the 2nd February at 1.30 p.m., I boarded the Danish schooner *Eva* of Marstal in charge of an Armed Guard in Lat. 58.45´N, Long 7.39´W, with instructions from you to proceed to Lerwick with the vessel for examination.

The vessel was bound to Odense, Denmark, from Lisbon, with 130 tons of oil cake in bags.

The wind then blowing from WSW, and increasing in force. Midnight on the 2nd, we altered course to ESE (Mag.).

3rd – 8 a.m. Shortened sail down to double reefed foresail, owing to heavy seas and strong southerly gale.

4th – Hove to under double reefed foresail, Southerly gale blowing and heavy sea running, drifting steadily to the Northward. 8.40 p.m., Set jibs and mainsail.

5th – 0.45 p.m. Picked up Ness of Sound Light in Yell Sound, Shetlands and stood in for it but unable to make it. 9 a.m. Tacked ship and stood out to the Westward. 2 p.m. Tacked ship again to try and make Yell Sound again, but failed to do so, being carried bodily to the Northward by the current and heavy seas. 4 p.m. Shortened sail, strong SSW gale and heavy sea. 8 p.m. Hove to, dangerous sea and heavy gale.

[1]Coates, James M., RNR, Lieutenant 1915.

6th – Hove to and drifting steadily to the NE all the time.

7th – Hove to in Lat. 61.35´N Long 0.8´E heavy sea and strong WSW gale. Ship commenced leaking owing to strain during bad weather and attempting to force the sailing. Then having sprung the jibboom and burst the foresail and inner jib; so at 9 a.m. we decided to set a course for Bergen, Norway, as then there was no chance of making a British port and we were afraid of getting driven too far North with the ship in a leaky condition, and getting short of provisions, so set a course S 53 E (mag.) for Bergen Light.

8th – 0.30 a.m. Picked up Bergen Light and stood in for it. We then discovered that we were about 50 miles further to the Eastward than we anticipated. 10 a.m. We were off the Northern entrance of Bergen and stood in towards the Reefs, and eventually managed to navigate the vessel in through them. This would not have been possible but for the heavy seas breaking over the Reefs, as we had no chart of the Entrance. At noon we had passed all dangers and picked up a pilot who took us to an anchorage in the Sundent Sound, Solen Island. 3.30 p.m. let go anchor in 20 fathoms of water.

I then sent a telegram to the British consul, Bergen, informing him of my position and asking him to send a tug boat to take the schooner in tow to Bergen, as the Master wanted her surveyed. It was impossible to sail there as it is all inland navigation.

At 4.30 p.m. the Norwegian Torpedo boat *Brand* came alongside. The Commander of her asked me to come on board to see him which request I complied with and stated to him my reasons for running in there. He then informed me that he had instructions from his Commander-in-Chief to take myself and the Armed guard on board the Torpedo boat and convey us to Skjaergehaven where we would get a steamer at 5 a.m. in the morning, to take us to Bergen, and told me when I got to Bergen I was free to go back to England.

9th – 11.30 a.m. Arrived at Bergen and was met by a Norwegian Naval Officer who directed me to the British Consulate, arriving there at noon, and reported myself to the Consul who asked me to write him a statement of the case which I did, and at 1 p.m. he sent myself and the Armed Guard down on board the Norwegian Mail steamer *Jupiter* to take passage to Newcastle-on-Tyne.

11th – 10.30 a.m. Arrived at Newcastle and repaired to HM Ship under your command at the Southern Base this evening – 11th February 1916.

I beg to submit that myself and the Armed Guard be paid Hard Lying Money from the 2nd February to the 8th February inclusive, as neither myself nor the Armed Guard had any accommodation. I personally had not a place to lie down and any sleep I got was sitting on a bench in the cabin. The men had to make the best of it in a sail locker which was not large enough for two men. None of us had our clothes off during the passage neither had we water to wash with, as this was getting short; and as for cooking, we had to do this when opportunity offered, as the galley was awash most of the time.

194. *Rear-Admiral de Chair to Admiralty*

HMS *Alsatian*, 28 February 1916

Report of Proceedings, 7–27 February 1916

***

1. A report was received from *Patuca* that after leaving Swarbacks Minn in January last, both condensers were found to be choked with a quantity of small fish about the size of sardines, most of which were blocking the entrance to the tubes and a few had been forced through the tubes by the circulating pumps. It was thought that as the net defence probably restricted the entry of shoals of fish to such times as the gate happened to be open, they were likely to be met in great quantities when passing through.

2. With reference to the export of fish oil from Iceland to Norway for Germany, reported by the British Vice Consul at Akureyri (Iceland) information of which has no doubt reached Their Lordships, the following remarks by Lieutenant A.S. Griffith, RNVR,[1] the Officer of the Armed Guard which took the Danish SS *Godafoss* to Lerwick on 1st February, are of interest:

'The SS *Godafoss* is not to be trusted. She carried 18 barrels contents unknown shipped by the German Consul in Iceland, for Germany. Also I do not believe the Captain of *Godafoss* would have put into Lerwick this voyage had not an Armed Guard been placed on board. The excuse would have been heavy weather. I have good reason to believe this Captain is capable of underhand work and well known to German patrol boats.'

3. Monday, 7th February – *Alcantara* intercepted and sent into Lerwick with an Armed Guard the Norwegian sailing vessel *Dagmar*

[1]Griffith, Arthur S., RNVR, Sub-Lieutenant 1915.

from New Brunswick to Trondhjem with a cargo of resin … .[1] The weather on A and C Patrol areas continued severe and made boarding very difficult. The *Motagua* intercepted the United States steamer *Polarine*, Philadelphia to Goteborg with oil, and as it was too rough to board, she was directed to call at Kirkwall.[2]

4. Sunday, 13th February – The disposition of the Squadron was as follows:

A Patrol … *Teutonic*, *Virginian*, *Changuinola*.
C Patrol … *Otway*, *Columbella*, *Hildebrand*, *Ebro*, *Mantua*, *Motagua*, *Orcoma*.
G Patrol … *Andes*.
Proceeding to Swarbacks Minn … *Almanzora*.
Joining C from A … *Hilary*.
Rejoining from Clyde … *Patia*.
Coaling at Swarbacks Minn … *Victorian*.
Coaling and repairing at Liverpool … *Alsatian*, *Artois* (French), *Gloucestershire*.
Coaling and repairing in Clyde … *Patuca*, *Orotava*.
At Portsmouth repairing … *Moldavia*.[3]

During the week 24 ships were intercepted and examined, of which 5 were sent in with and 1 without Armed Guards. The small number of vessels intercepted may be accounted for by the strong westerly gales which necessitated Patrol vessels being hove to for considerable periods.

The Gale increased during the day (Sunday) and ships on C Patrol were obliged to lie to. An Able Seaman, RNVR, was washed overboard from *Columbella*.

On entering Swarbacks Minn during the Gale, *Almanzora* fouled the Net Defence and both her propellers were disabled. She was able to anchor under the shelter of the land and work was at once commenced to clear them.

5. Monday, 14th February – *Orcoma* intercepted the Danish steamer *Hellig Olaf*, New York to Copenhagen with a general cargo and a large

[1]*Dagmar* was sent to South Shields for investigation, and then to King's Lynn for unloading, being allowed to go on on 2 February (TS 14/7 of 8 January to 2 February 1916 *passim*).

[2]*Polarine* was allowed to continue after inspection and investigation (TS 14/7 of 10 February 1916).

[3]*Gloucestershire* and *Moldavia* are new additions; *Alcantara* is omitted, presumably by mistake.

number of mails and passengers, the latter including 10 of enemy nationality. She was sent to Kirkwall with an Armed Guard.[1]

6. Tuesday, 15th February – Engineer Sub-Lieutenant Reginald H. Ribton, RNR,[2] of *Almanzora*, who had been suffering from Pneumonia, died. Arrangements were made for his burial at Swarbacks Minn.

The following information was from the crew of the American SS *Winneconne* regarding the last trip of that vessel from New York to Europe:

'Leaving New York on 15th December with a general cargo, the ship doused lights to escape interception by British Cruisers off the Hudson River. She then shaped a course by the South of Greenland and North of Iceland to the Norwegian coast, having the assistance of a pilot from the sailing port. The *Winneconne* arrived on 10th January at Gothenburg where a quantity of her cargo was discharged into lighters brought over from Germany to receive it. Amongst the cargo so discharged was a number of large heavy cases. The vessel stayed at Gothenburg for about a fortnight and then proceeded to Copenhagen'.[3]

7. Friday, 18th February – In accordance with directions received from the Commander-in-Chief, Patrols were ordered to work to the Westward by night and Eastward by day as the movements of enemy submarines indicated a possible attempt by enemy raiders to break through.

8. Saturday, 19th February – The Swedish steamer *Hogland* with 330 tons of Copper consigned to the Swedish Government was intercepted by *Patuca* and sent to Kirkwall with an Armed Guard in compliance with Admiralty Telegram 2152 of 19th January 1916.[4]

9. Sunday, 20th February – The disposition of the Squadron was as follows:

A Patrol … *Teutonic*, *Victorian*, *Motagua*.
C Patrol … *Otway*, *Ebro*, *Hilary*, *Mantua*, *Patuca*, *Columbella*, *Patia*.
F Patrol … *Virginian*.
G Patrol … *Alcantara*, *Changuinola*.

[1]*Hellig Olav* went on after inspection, arrest of any enemies capable of fighting, and confiscation of enemy mails (TS 14/7 of 16 February 1916).

[2]Ribton, Reginald H., RNR, Engineer Sub-Lieutenant 1915, died 1916.

[3]It is not clear what is the source of this statement; there is no record of the *Winneconne* being boarded, still less sent in at this time.

[4]*Hoglund* had a varied cargo, including meat, asbestos, leather and mohair as well as the copper mentioned by de Chair; many items were sent to the Prize Court and the ship was held up several weeks (TS 14/7 of 23 February 1916 *et al.*).

Proceeding to Swarbacks Minn … *Hildebrand.*
Coaling at Swarbacks Minn … *Almanzora*, *Andes.*
Coaling and repairing in Clyde … *Orotava.*
Coaling, repairing &c at Liverpool … *Alsatian*, *Artois*, *Gloucestershire*, *Orcoma.*
Repairing at Portsmouth … *Moldavia.*

During the week 47 ships were intercepted and examined, 10 being sent in with Armed Guards.

The weather on A Patrol became squally and at 6.30 p.m., *Victorian* reported the loss of her service Cutter in a snow squall. The boat's crew were all saved.

10. Tuesday, 22nd February – *Columbella* intercepted the Swedish steamer *Stockholm*, Gothenburg to New York. She carried 361 bags of Parcel mails, 448 bags of Russian and Swedish mails and 254 passengers – one of enemy origin – and a general cargo. This vessel was sent to Greenock with an Armed Guard, as on account of her size and the large quantity of parcel mails carried, it was not considered advisable that she should go to Stornoway. The Master protested and refused to accept responsibility for navigation of his ship.[1]

11. Wednesday, 23rd February – In accordance with the directions of the Commander-in-Chief, the ordinary method of patrol was resumed and ships were ordered to turn to the Westward at noon.

Information was received that the *Artois* would be delayed for two or three days at Liverpool owing to damage to capstan and loss of anchor and cable.

12. Thursday, 24th February – In view of the fact that several sailing ships with Armed Guards on board had been unable to make Lerwick or Kirkwall during bad weather and had been driven over to the Norwegian Coast, it was suggested to the Commander-in-Chief that they should be allowed to make any British port except Fleet Bases. This proposal was approved and orders were promulgated accordingly. *Teutonic* and *Otway* were met at a pre-arranged rendezvous and orders and information communicated. *Andes* intercepted *Kristianiafjord* proceeding West with a general cargo, 555 passengers and 16 bags of parcel mails. As she had no Certificate of origin of mails …, she was sent into Kirkwall with an Armed Guard.[2]

An interesting item of information was obtained to the effect that on

[1]The Contraband Committee had still not finished dealing with *Stockholm*'s previous cargo; this time no notice was taken, except with regard to the mails, by the Censor.

[2]*Kristianiafjord* was not detained.

the arrival of *Kristianiafjord* at Bergen on her last voyage a letter mail bag was found to contain a parcel of bacon, flour and cheese. This was disclosed by the attacks of rats on the bag in question.

It appears very desirable that vessels of this Line should be sent into port both East and West bound.

Admiralty Telegram No. 561, relative to contemplated attacks by submarines on the Squadron under my Command was received and ships were warned to take all possible precautions. In accordance with the orders of the Commander-in-Chief, C Patrol was moved 30 miles to the Westward and entry to and exit from Swarbacks Minn was restricted to the dark hours.

Report was made of a submarine proceeding West through Fair Island Channel but this was not substantiated.

13. Friday, 25th February – A submarine with two sails was reported steering West on the surface in Lat. 57.58´N, Long. 8.38´W. This report was considered reliable. C Patrol was ordered not to pass to the Eastward of Long. 9 W till further orders.

At 3.52 p.m., Admiralty message 1340 directing that *Oscar II* should be sent in if met with was received, and later she was caught by *Columbella* bound East with a general cargo mostly flour and oil cakes, and 230 passengers, including one German suffering from spinal disease. She carried 1196 bags of letter mails and 212 of parcel mails. Most of the former were for Germany and Turkey. She was sent to Kirkwall with an Armed Guard.[1]

14. Saturday, 26th February – *Gloucestershire* intercepted and sent to Kirkwall with an Armed Guard the Norwegian steamer *Conrad Mohr*, New York to Bergen with petroleum. Three of the crew were of doubtful nationality.[2]

Having been informed by the Commander-in-Chief that my presence was desired in London by the Admiralty as soon as possible in connection with questions of blockade, I made the necessary arrangements for turning over the duties of Senior Officer on patrol, and as Commodore Benson was at Swarbacks Minn, I met *Otway* at a rendezvous and gave Commodore Booty necessary orders, directing him to communicate with *Teutonic* as soon as she returned to patrol.

15. Sunday, 27th February – The disposition of the Squadron was as follows:

[1] *Oscar II* was not detained.

[2] *Conrad Mohr*'s cargo was naphtha as well as petroleum; the ship was allowed to go on (TS 14/7 of 28 February 1916).

A Patrol … *Virginian, Motagua, Changuinola, Victorian.*
C Patrol … *Patuca, Hildebrand, Otway, Columbella, Ebro, Gloucestershire.*
G Patrol … *Alcantara, Andes.*
Leaving patrol for Liverpool … *Alsatian.*
Coaling &c at Liverpool … *Artois* (French), *Orcoma.*
Coaling &c in Clyde … *Orotava, Hilary.*
Coaling at Swarbacks Minn … *Almanzora, Mantua, Patia, Teutonic.*
Repairing at Portsmouth … *Moldavia.*

During the week 51 vessels were intercepted and examined and 18 were sent in with and 1 without Armed Guards.

195. *Lieutenant G.N. Kenyon to Rear-Admiral Commanding Tenth Cruiser Squadron*

HMS *Alsatian*, 9 February 1916

The Captain [of *Artois*] … has little or no experience as a captain of a ship, and, although I gather that he has considerable capacity for directing and staff work, he does not figure equally well in the capacity of captain [187 para. 4].

There is evidence of a very marked lack of self-confidence, which results in a desire to avoid to the greatest possible extent any unusual work, or any work which might lead to any unusual situation.

Thus when on patrol the sighting of a merchant ship was evidently distasteful, and I know of two cases in which reports of the sighting of ships by night which were not clearly visible were treated as imaginary rather than that the ship should go to investigate.

In this way I am of opinion that the *Artois* will accept only such work as is forced on her, never going out of her way to promote the efficient performance of her duties on patrol, by reason of lack of self-confidence, and the anxiety and nervousness which are felt when any work has to be done.[1]

[1] It must be pointed out, in the interests of fair play, that *Digby*, which became *Artois*, was the oldest and smallest ship on the Northern Patrol, and suffered repeated mechanical problems. Having Lt Kenyon breathing down one's neck was also hardly a help to anyone's self-confidence. Admiral Oliver's comment in sending this report to the Admiralty was resigned: 'the *Artois* does not promise to be of much assistance to the Tenth Cruiser Squadron'.

196. *Commander-in-Chief Home Fleets to Admiralty*

HMS *Iron Duke*, 10 February 1916

Be pleased to lay before the Lords Commissioners of the Admiralty the annexed returns showing the numbers of vessels intercepted by the Tenth Cruiser Squadron and of those examined at Kirkwall and Lerwick during the year 1915 …

***

2. Of the vessels examined at Kirkwall and Lerwick, it will be seen that the total number bound for Denmark is over one-third of the total, and is over one-third greater than the numbers bound to any other country; on the other hand, the percentage of these vessels sent to other ports for further examination and possible prize courting is very considerably less than in the case of Norway and Sweden.

This is particularly noticeable in regard to Foodstuffs and Cattlefood bound for Denmark. Approximately three vessels a week with foodstuffs bound for Denmark arrived during the year for examination, but only one in every ten vessels was prevented from proceeding to her destination; in the case of cattlefood bound for Denmark, while over two vessels a week were examined, only one in every 13 vessels during the 12 months was not allowed to proceed directly to her destination from Kirkwall or Lerwick.

197. *Contraband Committee Minutes*

10 February 1916

Telegram from Findlay [in Christiania]: 'Consul at Bergen reports that schooner *Eva* with prize crew on board has arrived at Sognefjord and has asked for a tug, which has been sent with message that they had better head for Kirkwall, or, if that is impossible, should stay on board until they have reported nature of cargo, and I have had time to consider the case with a view to obtaining guarantees …'

198. *Commodore R.E.R. Benson to Rear-Admiral Commanding Tenth Cruiser Squadron*

HMS *Teutonic*, 22 February 1916

With reference to my letter on the question of standardising the rates of pay of mercantile ratings, and your reply … that the matter was receiving attention, I would again venture to bring this matter to your notice [153].

2. I am persuaded to do this as this question was in the *Cedric*, and is in my present ship, constantly brought to my notice, both in the form of requests from men entered at the lower port rate, and when it is necessary to engage men in vacancies.

3. A different procedure seems to have been followed in various ships of the Squadron. For instance in *Teutonic*'s last commission, the Captains decided that they would continue to sign on men when vacancies occurred at the port rate which obtained when the ship commissioned in September 1914.

4. This undoubtedly disposed of the question of dissatisfaction arising through men in the same ship and in similar ratings being at different rates of pay, but has had a very deleterious effect in regard to the quality of men engaged.

5. I am particularly impressed with this fact by observing the totally different stamp of firemen and stewards in this ship compared with those in the *Cedric*. When last in port, in addition to losing 15 men by desertion, I punished no less than 23 greasers, firemen and trimmers for breaking out, leave breaking, and insubordination, and the cells will be full for the whole cruise in consequence.

6. The Engineer Commander explains this by stating that the men he has been able to engage during the commission are those who are practically the dregs of their class, and whose moral and physical character prevents them from obtaining employment at the prevailing port rate, and I can quite see that this state of affairs must result under the circumstances.

7. Matters came to such a crisis that on the day I proposed to sail, I was eighteen engine room ratings short, and then in order that the ship should be able to sail, I cancelled the previous custom and engaged men at the port rate.

8. In addition to these facts, I would point out that nearly every steward who signed off when the *Cedric* paid off, did so under protest, for the reason that nothing had been done with regard to standardising their pay with that of others who had joined at a later date.

9. I therefore submit that the pressing nature of this question, which is becoming increasingly difficult for Commanding Officers to deal with, may be again laid before Their Lords Commissioners of the Admiralty.[1]

[1]This was forwarded to the Admiralty by de Chair's successor, Vice-Admiral Tupper, on 3 March, remarking that the issue 'is causing discontent among the ships' companies' (ADM 137/298, 179). The Admiralty seemingly paid little attention.

199. *Memoirs of Surgeon Sub-Lieutenant D.A. Knight*

In the last week of February 1916 *Patia* was refuelling at Busta Voe in Shetlands and on 28th February she raised anchors at 7 p.m. to leave to replace HMS *Alcantara* on the Norwegian Coast at 8 a.m. next morning. But when the anchors came up there was a large rock jammed in the flukes. It took four hours to remove it, so we did not leave Shetland till 11 p.m. and consequently did not arrive off the Norwegian coast till midday next day. We had the mortification of reading wireless messages about the action between *Alcantara* and the German raider *Greif*, and when we arrived on the scene at midday, all we saw was some floating wreckage and several destroyers and other warships steaming around. Had we arrived at 8 a.m. we would have been there before the action started and would have taken part.

200. *Captain T.E. Wardle, HMS* Alcantara, *to Commander-in-Chief Grand Fleet*

1 March 1916

I have the honour to report that on Tuesday 29th February, at 9 a.m., I was in approximate position 61.45 N, 0.58 E, having ordered HMS *Andes* to rendezvous with me at 61.50 N, 1.0 E, to transfer secret papers.

At 8.55 a.m., smoke was reported on the Port beam, bearing N 75° W (true), and almost at the same time a signal was received from *Andes* stating enemy in sight, steering NE 15 knots – and also another signal describing her – which I read as stating she had two funnels.

I at once increased to full speed and steered for the smoke.

At 9.10 a.m., I sighted *Andes* hull down bearing N (true), and steering NE (true).

At 9.15 being about 6,000 yards off stranger, I hoisted MN and fired two rounds of blank.

The stranger at once stopped and made a signal 'I am stopped'.

She then hoisted her number M.G.VI., which was not in my copy of 'Signal letters of ships of all countries'.

The Ship's company were at action stations and the guns were kept trained on the stranger.

About this time, 9.20 a.m., a signal was received from *Andes* 'Enemy has altered course to SE', and I saw that *Andes* had also altered to SE and apparently reduced speed. She was thus closing us.

When 4,000 yards off the stranger, I altered course to Port to keep this distance off while signalling her.

It could then be seen that she was flying Norwegian colours and had Norwegian flags painted on her side with the name *Rena*.

I then signalled *Andes* by searchlight 'Am intercepting suspicious vessel, is enemy still in sight?' To this no reply was made.

In response to my signals the stranger signalled that she was from Rio-de-Janeiro to Trondhjem.

These particulars, her size and course, all agreed with Lloyd's Confidential List of Ships.

Getting no reply from *Andes*, I determined to put an Armed Guard on board stranger, who appeared quite normal, and then to proceed to help *Andes* with the enemy, as smoke had been sighted SSE true.

While getting the Guard ready, I reduced to 14 knots, and kept clear of the stranger's stern.

At 9.35, *Andes* signalled 'That is the suspicious vessel.'

At 9.40 the boat was being swung out and I was closing stranger on the port quarters when I noticed her ensign staff drop over the stern, the men clearing away a gun on the poop.

At the same moment stranger fired a shell at our bridge, which put the Telemeter steering gear, Engine-room telegraph, and all telephones on the bridge out of action, besides killing and wounding men.

The flaps with flags on her sides were let down and she fought under no flag.

I at once gave the order 'Full speed and open fire – Range 2,500 yards.'

A messenger was sent aft to order the after steering gear to be connected up and all further steering was done from the after control.

The enemy at once went ahead and turned to Starboard, firing high explosive shell, some of them very short, but several hits were made near the water line amidships, penetrating the No. 1 stokehold bunkers which were half empty, and the Engine-room.

At 10.2, the enemy fired a torpedo which passed under our stern, starboard helm being used to avert it.

The first round from our after 6"-Port, hit the ammunition of the after gun and put it out of action.

The German prisoners state that the third salvo all hit the enemy.

At 10.15, enemy was badly on fire by the bridge, range 3,500 yards, and she apparently stopped.

At 10.22, boats were noticed leaving the enemy who was enveloped in a cloud of steam.

I ordered cease firing. HM Ship was beginning to list to Starboard, and then suddenly listed to Port.

The smoke cleared from enemy, and she fired one more round.

I then ordered 'Open fire', but at 10.35 a.m. Ship was listing badly to Port and sinking. I therefore gave the order 'Cease firing, boat stations, stop engines.' The order to stop engines never reached, but they apparently stopped themselves, when the water rose.

Every effort was made to get the boats out and save wounded; but several falls had been shot through, and the men were precipitated into the water – HM Ship was making about 3 knots through the water with the helm apparently hard a starboard, but the ship turning to starboard.

At 11.2, HM Ship sank.

At least 15 boats and a large raft floated clear.

HMS *Comus* and *Munster* were rapidly coming up. *Munster* commenced saving life, while *Comus* proceeded to *Andes* who all the time had apparently been about 8,000 yards off and reopened fire on the enemy, which was still burning furiously.

I am of opinion that enemy was completely abandoned by 10.30, and that the round fired afterwards was due to a heated gun. The statements of prisoners bear this out.

A wireless message was received from *Comus* but the decoded message never reached the Bridge, and I was therefore unaware that help was on its way.

I have the honour to report that the officers and men of HM Ship fought with great gallantry, and that no one left their stations until ordered to; and I personally witnessed cases of men assisting wounded at great risk.

***

201. *Captain G.B. Young*[1] *to Rear-Admiral Commanding Tenth Cruiser Squadron*

HMS *Andes*, 1 March 1916

I have the honour to report that at 8.30 a.m. on the 29th February, when in a position 61.58´N, 1.2´E, smoke was sighted bearing SW, course was altered towards her at 8.35 a.m. At 8.50 a.m. masts and funnel were above the horizon and it was at first thought to be the *Alcantara* with whom a rendezvous had been ordered for 9 a.m. By 8.55 a.m. vessel was made out to be a steamer painted black with black funnel and two masts, and she was of German appearance; she had Norwegian flags

[1]Young, George B.W., DSO, RN, Commander 1906, Captain 1915, retired as Captain.

painted on her sides and the name *Rena* on the bow in white letters. She was steering North by East, range 24,000 yards. I turned to this course and kept ahead of her making urgent signals at 8.50 a.m. 'Enemy in sight'; at 9.20 a.m. she altered to NE by E and I did the same, range 16,500 yds, steaming a good 16 knots. At 9.40 a.m. course was altered to East. His Majesty's Ship *Alcantara* was sighted at 9.25 a.m. and at 9.50 a.m. signalled she was intercepting ship. I altered course to the Southward and closed, range being about 9,000 yards at 10 a.m. At 10.16 a.m. I turned on Starboard helm to N 70° E, steamer then bearing South 50° West, range 8,000 yds. At 10.25 a.m. steamer opened fire on *Alcantara*. I commenced with my starboard guns, but as my course brought *Alcantara* directly in line of fire on the opposite side of the enemy I turned on Starboard helm and brought Port battery into action at a range of 7,500 yards. I closed to 6,000 yards and maintained the range in order to keep out of Torpedo range. *Alcantara* was seen altering to port and in order to keep my range clear I did the same. I subsequently had to turn twice for the same reason as *Alcantara* was getting into line of fire. At 10.40 a.m. enemy's forebridge was seen to be on fire and she commenced to abandon ship, her engines stopping immediately fire was opened. She drifted ahead, slowly turning to Port, and at 10.50 a.m. was entirely out of action and burning fiercely. At 10.45 a.m. I observed that *Alcantara* had a heavy list to port and was afire amidships and after. At 10.50 a.m. His Majesty's Ship *Comus* and His Majesty's Ship *Munster* were sighted, I ceased fire and proceeded towards *Alcantara*. A hail subsequently reached the bridge 'Submarine Red 50'. I turned away when a further report came from After Control 'Submarine Right Astern', I maintained my course and received a second report 'Submarine Astern'. It was with the greatest reluctance that I turned away from *Alcantara* but in view of the reported presence of submarines I had no alternative. Nothing further was seen of the supposed submarine and subsequent events proved that one could not have been there. At 10.55 a.m. *Alcantara* was observed to be sinking and abandoning ship and at 11.10 a.m. she sank, I turned towards her, when a signal was received from *Comus* to the effect that *Munster* had been ordered to pick up survivors. At 11.35 a.m. enemy was still afloat and had not surrendered and I attacked with *Comus* carrying out deliberate firing, manoeuvring on bearings to avoid hitting enemy's boats which were full of survivors. She did not reply to my fire and at 12.20 p.m. I ceased firing as enemy was burning fiercely and sinking, she sank at 1 p.m. with colours flying. I then proceeded to pick up survivors from *Alcantara* and took Assistant Paymaster James Duffill

RNR[1] and two men from a raft and also the body of Mr Casey Chief Gunner RN. I then got two German boats alongside and while doing so a submarine was reported bearing red 20 and *Comus* was seen to open fire in another direction and signalled submarine in sight, I went full speed ahead towing one boat and stopping again at 1.25 p.m. when it was evident report was caused by floating wreckage. The clearing of the boat was a very slow process owing to the height of the ship's side and the presence of wounded and exhausted men in each boat. I then closed *Comus* and sent seaboats to tow rafts alongside. After rescuing 110 men and one Deck Officer (Second Navigator) of whom 7 men and the Officer are very severely wounded, I thoroughly searched the area and found one additional man making the total rescued 111 men and 1 Officer. At 3.37 p.m. I proceeded for patrol.

The ship was not struck, most of the enemy's shots falling short, but it is known that one just missed the stern and one passed overhead. Hitting commenced at once and a good percentage was apparently maintained.

From the evidence gathered from an English-speaking Petty Officer, who was at the wheel, one of the first shots from this ship hit the bridge beneath him, destroying the steering gear and disabling all Officers on the bridge, another shell about the same time exploded in her engine room, completely wrecking it, and putting everyone there out of action, he states by gas fumes. He also states that tremendous damage was done to the ship in the first few minutes of the action.

WEATHER. Visibility about ten to fifteen miles with passing rain showers, wind W.W.1 sea calm.

I have the honour to report that the behaviour of the Officers and ship's company was excellent and entirely in accordance with the traditions of His Majesty's Navy. The exceptional speed of 92 revolutions was maintained thoughout on the engines.

202. *Commander-in-Chief Home Fleets to Flag Officers, Commodores and Officers in charge of HM Ships present*

HMS *Iron Duke*, 29 February 1916

It is of the utmost importance that no news of the destruction this morning of the German raider should reach Germany. If the fact is known on board any ships in the Fleet, the greatest possible care is to

[1]Duffill, James, RNR, Paymaster Sub-Lieutenant 1915.

be taken that it is not mentioned in any correspondence, or in any conversation. I rely upon Commanding Officers to see that this is carried out. If the matter is discussed at all it will with certainty become known in Germany.

2. No entry in regard to this matter is to appear in any Signal log.[1]

203. *Rear-Admiral de Chair to Admiralty*

HMS *Alsatian*, 6 March 1916

Report of Proceedings, 29 February–4 March 1916[2]

***

1. Tuesday, 29th February – *Andes* intercepted German raider *Greif*, but not being certain of her true character, kept out of range ahead till *Alcantara* came up. *Alcantara* engaged and fought an action with the German raider, details of which are given in the enclosed reports from Captain Wardle (*Alcantara*) [200] and Captain Young (*Andes*) [201]. From personal interview which I had subsequently with these officers I learned the following:

Captain Wardle had not, previous to the action, had an opportunity of seeing the photograph of the raider *Moewe*, but on being shown a copy he stated that the vessel he encountered was very similar in appearance but considerably lower in the water.

Alcantara used pointed common shell throughout the action, and they appeared to be successful in igniting ammunition which German survivors state was placed in rear of the guns. Cordite fires were distinctly observed from *Alcantara*.

The enemy's fire was rapid but a large number of short shots were noted which detonated on striking the water. The majority of the hits were amidships on *Alcantara* but one shell detonated directly below the foremost six-inch gun without however putting it out of action or wounding the crew. Men in the ammunition party on the deck below were wounded.

Torpedoes appear to have been fired from amidships but at long range and they were not seen to enter the water. The torpedo fired at *Alcantara* ran slow and passed under her stern.

[1]According to [217], the news became public by 29 March.

[2]The normal chronological arrangement is disturbed here. The various reports of the sinking of *Greif* are grouped together under de Chair's command; Tupper's assumption of command coincided, but his first report has been placed later [204].

So far as can be judged only small fires occurred in *Alcantara* but details from survivors will probably throw further light on this matter. The action apparently lasted approximately forty minutes and at 11.20, *Alcantara* listed slowly on to her starboard side and remained horizontal, finally sinking without causing any suction. Some of the crew who had remained on her side were able to step into a boat which had floated clear from the boat-deck.

The Diesel engine aft was working throughout the action. The lights in the engine room went out early owing to the dynamo being flooded, but light was obtained throughout the ship by means of the Diesel Engine.

I am of opinion that *Andes* was somewhat over-cautious in approaching the raider and that her signals did not make it clear to *Alcantara* that the vessel the latter was approaching was the 'enemy' referred to in her earlier signals. The reported presence of submarines during the later stages of the action appears to have deterred *Andes* from closing to rescue survivors, and her attack on the *Greif* was more in the nature of a '*coup de grace*.'

It is almost certain that no submarine was in the vicinity at any time during the action.

Considering the distance between *Andes* and *Greif* I am doubtful whether any shots from the former actually hit the raider.

Further report will be forwarded when details are obtained from survivors.

2. Friday, 3rd March – *Andes* arrived at Liverpool having on board one officer and one hundred and ten men, from the German raider *Greif*.

3. Monday, 4th March – As reported separately, I hauled down my Flag in *Alsatian* at sunset, and transferred the command of the Tenth Cruiser Squadron to Vice-Admiral Reginald Tupper, CVO.

4. The usual enclosures will be forwarded separately when the necessary information has been tabulated.

7

TUPPER TAKES COMMAND, MARCH–MAY 1916

The appointment of Vice-Admiral Reginald Tupper to replace Rear-Admiral de Chair is rather odd. De Chair had been doing a competent job in command of the 10th Cruiser Squadron, as had Tupper as flag officer at Stornoway. But Tupper had been promoted in the normal way of seniority, and the Stornoway post, mainly trawlers, was presumably not thought big enough for a Vice-Admiral. Command of the Northern Patrol had been a Rear-Admiral's post for two years, yet Tupper was not given more responsibility than de Chair. His appointment is an example of that tendency of war to enlarge the rank of post-holders – later his deputy was a Rear-Admiral, replacing a Commodore. (Similarly, large numbers of Sub-Lieutenants and Midshipmen RNR and RNVR were raised to Lieutenant by 1918.)

Whatever the reason – and mere seniority does not seem sufficient – Tupper certainly brought a more vigorous style of command than that of de Chair. Tupper's reports are peppered with accounts of inspections of the various ships, interviews with captains, supervisions of firing practices, and presentations of medals. These duties may also have been performed by de Chair, but he rarely mentions them. One small practice may symbolise the difference: Tupper almost always reported the names of both officers and men lost at sea for various accidental reasons; de Chair only ever reported the names of officers.

In the main, Tupper had to continue the work in much the same way as his predecessor. The net was gradually closing on the Norwegian–America Line, principally by the British control of bunker coal [216, 221, 225, 229, 233]. The work of the patrol had become largely routine, which may well be one of the reasons for the manifestations of discontent among the seamen which emerged during 1916: the problem of pay developed into a strike on one ship [210], and the replacement of temporary arrangements for food by a standard system was resisted on several others [215 para. 6]. Commodore Benson's attitudes to mercantile ratings and engine room crews [210] may have promoted trouble; he was, in fact, soon replaced [222 para. 9]. There could be no excuse for surprises: the Admiralty had been warned often enough. Even now, however, it took a sharp memorandum from the First Sea Lord [224] to make the Admiralty attend to the problems affecting morale and discipline [227, 228, 230].

204. *Vice-Admiral Tupper to Admiralty*

HMS *Alsatian*, 7 March, 1916

Report of Proceedings, 27 February–6 March 1916

I have the honour to forward the following additional information – as being of interest – to supplement my predecessor's letter of proceedings, No. 124/35, of the 6th March 1916, copy of which has been received by me [203]. This information did not reach him in time to admit of its being included in his report:

1. Sunday, 27th February – *Otway* boarded the United States Steamer *Corning*, Stockholm to New York in ballast. This ship reported a new German minefield between Lat. 55.18´N and Lat. 55.26´N, and Long. 12.42´E and Long. 13 E.

2. Tuesday, 28th February – An action took place between HM Ships *Alcantara* and *Andes*, and SMS *Greif*, which resulted in the sinking of the latter. Detailed reports have already been forwarded [200, 201, 202].

At 8.40 p.m. *Mantua* intercepted *Bergensfjord* in Lat. 59.42´N, Long. 7.38´W, and sent her to Kirkwall under armed guard. She had 230 passengers on board, of whom three were German ladies, 300 bags of mail for Germany, in addition to mails for other countries. Her Captain said she had no parcel mail for Germany.[1]

It is of interest to note that this vessel was many miles off the track mentioned in Confidential Interim Order No. 100 of 21st January 1916.

3. Wednesday, 1st March – During the night *Hildebrand* reported that when in Lat. 60.11´N, Long. 9.7´W, her Officer of the Watch, and weather look-outs, had smelt a strong smell of burnt petrol, and *Mantua* in Lat. 59.30´N, Long. 9 W, reported a similar phenomenon at 9.40 a.m.

As these reports indicated the possible proximity of submarines, C Patrol was moved westward. Shortly afterwards the Commander-in-Chief, who had been informed of the steps taken, gave directions that all ships were to be withdrawn on to the Iceland–Rockall line. Only ten ships were on patrol at the time, and these were stationed as follows: Eight ships on line of bearing 333° from Lat. 58 N, Long. 13.55´W, 40 miles apart, and two ships on the same line of bearing 20 and 40 miles

[1]*Bergensfjord* was not detained.

to the southward of Rockall. Ships were to cross line at Noon, steering 250° and at midnight steering 70°.

4. Friday, 3rd March – *Patia* boarded the Brazilian Steamer *Saldanha de Gama*, in Lat. 62.1´N, Long. 16.52´W. This vessel cleared Para for New York, but had not called there. Her Master stated that he was bound for Christiania, and admitted that he was trying to evade the patrols. Amongst her cargo was 133 tons of rubber. She was sent to Kirkwall with an armed guard.[1]

5. Saturday, 4th March – At 8 a.m. *Orotava* reported she was in pursuit of a Steamer in Lat. 58.40´N, Long. 12.54´W, she had fired a 6" gun at her, but was out of range, and unable to overhaul.

Mantua and *Gloucestershire* were ordered to her support, but were too far away to arrive in time, as ships on patrol were then 40 miles apart. The steamer gradually drew away and only smoke was visible at sunset.

Shortly after abandoning the chase *Orotava* boarded the American Steamer *Pioneer*, who reported that at 3 p.m. he had passed Danish Steamer *Hellig Olaf*. This seems to establish the identity of the vessel.[2]

6. Sunday, 5th March – In Lat. 62.37´N, Long. 14.20´W, *Patia* boarded Swedish Steamer *Oscar Frederik*, from Buenos Ayres and Rio de Janeiro to Christiania, with a general cargo including coffee and wool. She was sent to Kirkwall with an armed guard ... .[3]

The Norwegian Steamer *Sandefjord* was boarded by *Gloucestershire* in Lat. 57.51´N, Long. 16.32´W, and sent to Lerwick with an armed guard ... .[4]

The Disposition of the Squadron was as follows:

Iceland–Rockall Patrol ... *Teutonic*, *Changuinola*, *Ebro*, *Gloucestershire*, *Hildebrand*, *Mantua*, *Orotava*, *Otway*, *Patia*, *Artois*.

Joining Patrol ... *Columbella*, *Victorian*.

At Liverpool ... *Alsatian*, *Andes*, *Orcoma*, *Virginian*.

At Clyde ... *Hilary*.

[1]The master of *Saldanha de Gama* was quite open that he had made his voyage, heading for any Norwegian port he could reach, because he had heard of the high price rubber was fetching in Germany and Scandinavia. Both cargo and ship were sent to the Prize Court. In this case, Brazil's position geographically and diplomatically was not important enough for any finesse by the British (TS 14/7 of 7 March 1916).

[2]*Pioneer* was not sent in.

[3]Various items in *Oscar Frederick*'s cargo were questioned; the ship was detained until the end of March (TS 14/8 of 9 to 28 March 1916).

[4]*Sandefjord* was not detained.

At Portsmouth ... *Moldavia*.
At Swarbacks Minn ... *Almanzora*, *Motagua*, *Patuca*.
On special service ... *Arlanza*.

During the past week 35 ships were intercepted and examined, of which eight were sent in with armed guards, and one – the *Greif* – sunk. The smallness of the number of ships intercepted and sent in can be attributed to the fact that the patrols were to some extent disorganised while assuming new dispositions.

205. *Vice-Admiral Tupper to Admiralty*

HMS *Alsatian*, 23 March 1916

Report of Proceedings, 6–21 March 1916

***

1. Monday, 6th March – In accordance with Admiralty directions my Flag was hoisted in HMS *Orcoma* at Liverpool for command of the Tenth Cruiser Squadron, in succession to Rear-Admiral Sir Dudley R.S. de Chair, KCB, MVO, whose Flag was hauled down in *Alsatian* at sunset the same day.

2. Tuesday, 7th March – During the forenoon I visited the Senior Naval Officer, Liverpool; I afterwards proceeded on board *Orcoma* and arranged for steel platforms to be fitted locally to the right training brackets for use of the trainer at three of the 6" guns. These are necessary in order to raise the trainer's eye to the level with the telescope. The remaining three 6" guns are still without right hand training gear, and cross connected sights, and I submit that these may be fitted at an early date, as without them the fighting efficiency of the ship is much impaired.

Having transferred my Flag to *Alsatian*, I left Liverpool at Noon to join patrol in cold clear weather with a north easterly wind, being escorted until sunset by HM Torpedo Boat Destroyer *Dove*.

Almanzora, which had been at Swarbacks Minn since the 15th February after fouling the boom defence, reported that her propellers were now clear, and that the engines had been tried under way. As, however, there was a slight knocking of the starboard engines, and taking into consideration the fact that the ship was due at her Southern Base, I directed her to proceed to Liverpool and dry dock to ascertain the full extent of the damage done.

Moldavia, having completed the repairs necessary after collision with Norwegian SS *Correct*, sailed from Portsmouth to join patrol.

3. Wednesday, 8th March 1916 – At Noon I took over command of the patrol from Commodore R.E.R. Benson, of *Teutonic*. The disposition of the ships in the squadron was then as follows:

Iceland–Rockall Patrol ... *Teutonic*, *Artois*, *Orotava*, *Gloucestershire*, *Victorian*, *Mantua*, *Columbella*, *Hildebrand*, *Patia*, *Changuinola*, *Hilary*.
Rejoining from Liverpool ... *Alsatian*.
Rejoining from Swarbacks Minn ... *Motagua*.
Joining from Portsmouth ... *Moldavia*.
Proceeding to Liverpool ... *Almanzora*.
At Liverpool ... *Andes*, *Orcoma*, *Virginian*, *Otway*.
At Swarbacks Minn ... *Ebro*, *Patuca*.
Detached ... *Arlanza*.

In the course of the afternoon orders were received from the Commander-in-Chief to resume A and C Patrols, and ships were directed to proceed to their new stations at daylight the following morning, as follows:

A Patrol cross line 315° from Latitude 62.45´N, Longitude 9 W, at noon and midnight, steering 230° and 50° respectively, 38 miles apart from South: *Patia*, *Alsatian*, *Changuinola*, *Artois*, and *Columbella*; Northern Ship to close the land occasionally in clear weather.

C Patrol cross line 360° from Latitude 58.25´N, Longitude 11 W, at Noon and midnight, steering 250° and 70° respectively, 30 miles apart from South: *Orotava*, *Victorian*, *Hildebrand*, *Mantua*, and *Hilary*.

A submarine was reported in Latitude 58.40´N, Longitude 3.50´W.

4. Thursday, 9th March – In the course of the day *Mantua*, *Teutonic*, *Motagua*, and *Patia*, were met at separate pre-arranged rendezvous, and copies of Cypher H were delivered to them for distribution to Ships of the Squadron not already supplied. Commodore Benson came on board and requested that I would visit *Teutonic* regarding certain proposed alterations for improving the accommodation of Officers and men, which I arranged to do. *Teutonic* was then directed to proceed to Thorshavn with confidential matter from the Foreign Office for the British Consul at that Port.

Information having been received that at least one vessel had evaded the Patrol by passing to the north of Iceland, I obtained permission from the Commander-in-Chief to detach a ship to investigate ice and weather conditions in that region. *Motagua* was accordingly detailed for this purpose, and given orders, after delivering correspondence, to proceed along the south coast of Iceland, through the Denmark Strait, and thence round the north coast, keeping a good look out for raiders attempting to pass out into the Atlantic, and also for neutral vessels carrying contraband.

5. Friday, 10th March – *Teutonic* having completed her visit to Thorshavn, I met her and proceeded on board to inspect the alterations proposed. The ship appeared clean and tidy and the men were well dressed. I consider it very necessary that Officers and men should have a place of Assembly sheltered from the weather, and I forwarded proposals to the Senior Naval Officer, Liverpool, for this to be carried out.

Three of her guns have no right training positions, the sight for a trainer being improvised on the left of the shield. I personally tried the position of layer and trainer and consider that the guns as now fitted are not efficient. I have forwarded separate proposals for dealing with this matter ...

Motagua reported distribution of correspondence complete, and that she was proceeding in execution of her previous orders. Floating mines were reported to have been seen in Lat. 53.53´N, Long. 5.14´W.

6. Saturday, 11th March – *Moldavia* was met in the forenoon and given directions to proceed west to enable me to keep in W/T communication with *Motagua* and to support her in case of necessity.

The Commanding Officer reported that the new stem placed in *Moldavia* by Messrs Harland and Wolff, after collision with SS *Correct*, had developed a leak above the water line, but that it would probably not be necessary to take it in hand until the ship's return to her Southern Base.

An Auxiliary Patrol Vessel reported a submarine in sight Lat. 58.35´N, Long. 6.18´W about noon. Information was also received that a submarine might be expected from the southward on her way to Germany.

7. Sunday 12th March – The Senior Naval Officer Liverpool informed me that *Virginian* had sailed from that port the previous evening, following the South of Ireland route in accordance with Admiralty orders. The Consul at Reykjavik, having reported that the passage to the North of Iceland was still navigable, the Commander-in-Chief directed me to station two ships off Cape North to patrol up to the edge of the ice pack. *Ebro* was detached for this purpose and directed to join *Motagua* off Staalbierg Huk when both ships were to proceed to Cape North. *Moldavia* patrolling off Portland Light to maintain W/T communication and also to intercept ships which might be making the South Coast of Iceland. *Motagua*, who was now patrolling off Staalbierg Huk, reported ice off the coast, but as far as could be seen,

there was a clear passage by the land about 25 miles wide. She also reported that the blades of her port propeller had been bent by striking loose ice in the morning, but that her speed had not been affected to any extent. Arrangements were made for her to dock on return to the Clyde about the 20th instant, to enable spare blades to be fitted.

I walked round the Mess Decks, and the men's quarters in *Alsatian* during Divisions. The Ship appears to be very well kept and clean, and the men smart and well dressed.

The disposition of the Squadron was as follows:

A Patrol ... *Columbella*, *Artois*, *Ebro*, *Alsatian* and *Patia*.
C Patrol ... *Hilary*, *Hildebrand*, *Victorian*, *Oratava* and *Patuca*.
E Patrol ... *Motagua*, *Moldavia*.
Rejoining Patrol from Liverpool ... *Virginian*.
Proceeding to Liverpool ... *Teutonic*.
Proceeding to Swarbacks Minn ... *Changuinola*.
At Liverpool ... *Orcoma*, *Andes*, *Otway*, and *Almanzora*.
At Clyde ... *Mantua*.
At Swarbacks Minn ... *Gloucestershire*.

During the past week 63 vessels were intercepted and examined, of which 13 were sent in with armed guards.

The number of vessels using the Northabout route is now steadily increasing.

8. Monday, 13th March – *Patuca* intercepted Danish Steamer *Frederick VIII* from New York to Copenhagen, with 361 passengers, mails, and general cargo. She was sent in to Kirkwall with an armed guard in accordance with Admiralty Message 0002 of the 9th March.[1]

In the evening *Victorian* boarded the American Steamer *Platuria* bound for New York. The captain reported that a large submarine had been sighted the same morning in Latitude 59.40´N, Longitude 6.50´W. This was passed to the Commander-in-Chief, who directed C Patrol to be moved to Longitude 15 degrees West. Instructions were given accordingly.[2]

A message was intercepted from Danish Motor Ship *Jutlandia* to the effect that she was stopped in Latitude 56.30´N, Longitude 12.30´W, with engines disabled, but would be able to proceed the following day.

9. Tuesday, 14th March – *Virginian* and *Orcoma*, who were rejoining patrol, were ordered to pass through this position, but did not see her,

[1] *Frederick VIII* was allowed to sail on after inspection (TS 14/8 of 15 March 1916).
[2] *Platuria* was not sent in.

and later on a signal was intercepted to say that she was proceeding. The Auxiliary patrols to the Eastwards were warned, but up to the present I have not been able to ascertain whether she was intercepted.[1]

Alsatian carried out fire control drill, and aiming rifle practice with good results.

In accordance with orders received from the Commander-in-Chief, *Motagua* had been directed to work with *Ebro* in the neighbourhood of North Cape and Mevenklint Islands, but owing to the passage between the ice and the land being only 12 miles wide with loose ice near North Cape, it was considered inadvisable for her to proceed further, and she was ordered to resume patrol off Staalbierg Huk.

10. Wednesday, 15th March – *Virginian* was met during the afternoon, and official correspondence received from Liverpool. I interviewed Captain Smith[2] on board *Alsatian*.

At 7.20 p.m. *Crescent* was fired at and missed by a submarine in Latitude 56.12´N, Longitude 7.32´W.

11. Thursday, 16th March – In accordance with instructions received from the Commander-in-Chief, directions were given for ships of the Squadron to use the Tory Island route till further orders, when proceeding to and from their Southern Bases.

Andes, which had left Liverpool the previous evening, was ordered to return in connection with the forthcoming trial by Courtmartial of Captain Wardle and other survivors of *Alcantara*.

About Noon information was received that a trawler was chasing a steamer steering west 90 miles north of Muckle Flugga, and had been unable to stop her by gun fire. Dispositions were accordingly made to cut her off, but I was informed later that she had been intercepted.

12. Friday, 17th March – *Artois*, who was about to proceed to Swarbacks Minn, reported that the brickwork of the furnaces of three boilers required rebuilding, which it was estimated would take 12 days. I am informing the Captain of *Artois* that in my opinion this should not have occurred as he has recently spent 22 days at Liverpool.

In the meantime, with the assistance of *Gibraltar* I am endeavouring to get her to sea as early as possible.

[1]*Jutlandia* was inspected at Kirkwall on 17 March 1916 and, having given guarantees on the oats, leather and nitrate of soda in her cargo, was allowed to go on (TS 14/8 of 17 and 18 March 1916).

[2]Smith, Humphrey Hugh, DSO, RN (1875–1940), Lieutenant 1875, Commander 1909, Captain 1915, Captain of *Virginian* 1916–1917, Flag Captain to VAC 10 CS in *Alsatian*, 1917, Captain of *Argus* 1918, Captain RN College Greenwich, Rear-Admiral (retired) 1926, Vice-Admiral 1931, Commodore Royal Naval Reserve 1940.

As the ice off the North Coast of Iceland was reported to be drifting to the Northward, *Motagua* was ordered to proceed to Langenes Flack, if conditions were favourable. On reaching Long. 19.30´W, however, she reported an ice barrier to the Eastward, which appeared to be impassable. I accordingly directed her to return to Staalbierg Huk, and patrol the passage with *Ebro*, which was now 30 miles wide.

In the afternoon I met *Changuinola* at a pre-arranged rendezvous, and in a personal interview with Commander Brocklebank[1] gave him orders to proceed round the North of Iceland from the Eastward, and endeavour to work his way through to North Cape, relieving *Motagua*. In the meantime *Moldavia* was still patrolling off the South West Coast for the purpose of maintaining W/T communication.

13. Saturday, 18th March – *Gloucestershire* intercepted British SS *Theseus*, Barry to Alexandrovsk, with munitions. She was allowed to proceed ...

During the night a moderate North Easterly gale was experienced.

14. Sunday, 19th March – The disposition of the patrols was as follows:

A Patrol ... *Alsatian*, *Patia*.
C Patrol ... *Hilary*, *Virginian*, *Orcoma*, *Gloucestershire* and *Patuca*.
E Patrol (off North Coast of Iceland) ... *Ebro*, *Changuinola*.
F Patrol (off South West Coast of Iceland) ... *Moldavia*.
Proceeding to Clyde ... *Motagua*.
Proceeding to Swarbacks Minn ... *Columbella*.
At Liverpool ... *Teutonic*, *Otway*, *Almanzora*, *Andes*, *Victorian*.
At Clyde ... *Mantua*, *Hildebrand*.
At Swarbacks Minn ... *Orotava*, and *Artois*.

During the past week 46 vessels were intercepted, of which 12 were sent in with Armed Guards.

The Senior Naval Officer Liverpool, informed me that *Otway* was ready to sail, but had been delayed by Admiralty orders.

During the course of the day *Patia* was detached from A to relieve *Moldavia*, who was running short of coal.

In the afternoon *Changuinola* reported that she had succeeded in getting through to North Cape, after passing through loose pack ice, and

[1]Brocklebank, Henry Cyril Royds, CBE, RN (1874–1957), Lieutenant 1895, Commander 1906, Captain of *Changuinola* 1914–1916, Acting Captain and Naval Attache at The Hague 1917–1919, Captain (retired) 1920.

with *Ebro* was directed to patrol between the edge of the ice field and Straumnaes, a passage 20 miles wide.

The Commander-in-Chief informed me that, according to a report from the Consul at Reykjavik, two Men-of-War, accompanied by ten smaller craft, had been seen in the neighbourhood of Grimsby [correctly Grimsey] Island, steering East on the 13th March. This would not appear to be accurate, and probably originated from our own vessels being sighted off the North West Coast about that time.

15. Monday, 20th March – *Orcoma* intercepted and sent in with an Armed Guard, Danish SS *Kentucky*, from New York to Christiania via Kirkwall, with a general cargo, including machinery, and cotton seed oil. Her captain protested against being sent in.[1]

16. Tuesday, 21st March – At 9 30 a.m. *Motagua*, who was proceeding to the Clyde by the Tory Island Route, sighted a submarine at a distance of 8 miles steering South West on the surface, in Latitude 55.20´N, Longitude 10.7´W. As she was out of range, fire was not opened. The Submarine shortly afterwards dived, and was not seen again. Later in the day a steamer was sunk in Latitude 54.23´N, Longitude 9.49´W, probably by the same submarine.[2]

At 6 p.m. *Otway* was met, and I gave Commodore Booty instructions for the conduct of the patrol while *Alsatian* was in Swarbacks Minn.

During the past few days several reports have been received of submarines being expected to pass Muckle Flugga or Fair Island from the Eastward.

17. Wednesday, 22nd March – A North Easterly gale sprang up in the afternoon and increased in violence during the night. Except for short intervals, the weather throughout the period covered by this report has, however, been fine and clear.

18. From three weeks experience in command of the Tenth Cruiser Squadron, I would urge upon Their Lordships the necessity for maintaining it at its full strength of 24 ships, or even increasing this number.

At the present moment I have under my orders 22 ships, viz:

Alsatian	*Mantua*
Almanzora	*Moldavia*
Andes	*Motagua*

[1]*Kentucky*'s cargo included fruit, which brought the Norwegian quota over the limit agreed between the British and Norwegian governments; after this was discharged to the Prize Court, the ship was allowed to go on (TS 14/8 of 25 March to 18 April 1916).

[2]This was the SS *Ashmore*, sunk by *U 43*.

Arlanza	*Orcoma*
Artois (French)	*Orotava*
Changuinola	*Otway*
Columbella	*Patuca*
Ebro	*Patia*
Gloucestershire	*Teutonic*
Hilary	*Victorian*
Hildebrand	*Virginian*

Of these *Arlanza* has now been absent since October 1st, and it appears unlikely that she will be ready to rejoin for some months.

Unfortunately, since *Artois* was taken over by the French, she has frequently been in harbour with small defects, and has at present spent the same amount of time in port as at sea. I am pointing this out to her Captain, and I trust the present state of affairs will be remedied.

It also frequently occurs that one or two ships are detained in harbour for considerable periods for repairs owing to bad weather and other causes, and occasionally a ship is sent on detached service. The average number of ships actually on patrol (omitting those on passage to or from their coaling bases) during the period of this Report is 11.

Instead of maintaining one ship to the North of Iceland, as was done last year, it has been necessary to station two ships on the North West Coast, owing to the possibility of enemy raiders attempting to break out on to the trade routes; a third has been placed off the South West corner to keep a watch on Reykjavik and the southern coast, and also to maintain W/T communication between *Alsatian* and the ships to the Northward, as it is of vital importance to have early information of an enemy raider. This, when a few ships only were available, had the effect of reducing the important A Patrol to one Ship, as it was considered essential to keep C Patrol intact.

Lastly, I would point out that, with C Patrol moved to the neighbourhood of 15 degrees West, owing to the Submarine menace, a large gap is opened through which vessels can pass without being intercepted.

It is understood that *Avenger*, which was shortly due to join my Flag, is now being detailed for other service. This is much regretted, as I understand she is a fine and well equipped ship.

I would submit, therefore, that a minimum of 24 Ships is absolutely necessary to render the patrol efficient, the proposed distribution of which would be as follows:

A Patrol . . 6.
C Patrol . . 6.
E Patrol . . 2.
Maintaining W/T Communication with E . . 1.
On passage to and from coaling bases . . 1.
Coaling and Refitting . . 8.

It is considered that four good trawlers with W/T, would be a valuable addition for use in Icelandic Waters until further ships are available.

19. I would also bring to Their Lordships' notice the question of the Standardisation of Pay of the Mercantile ratings serving in the Squadron, which I submit requires urgent attention.

A report in this connection was called for by the Admiralty in August last ..., and the question has presumably since then been under consideration.

At the present time there appears to be only one course open to Commanding Officers, i.e. to engage men at the prevailing port wage until compulsory service is applied to the Mercantile ratings.

This undoubtedly causes discontent amongst the other members of the Ship's company, who entered at a lower rate, and consider themselves penalised by having come forward early in the war to serve their Country.

***

206. *Commanding Officer HMS* Ebro *to Vice-Admiral Commanding Tenth Cruiser Squadron*

16 March 1916

Submit I may be furnished with any information available as to the whereabouts or disposal of the following officers and men forming Armed Guard placed on board the Norwegian barque *Olivia* on the 14th January 1916:

Lieutenant A.D. Bennett, RNR (in charge).[1]
A. Pottinger, Leading Seaman, Active Service CSC/J 2350
A. Nears, Ableseaman, RFR, CSC/194978
G. Moore, Ableseaman, RFR, CSC/197038
J. Anderson, Ableseaman, RNR, X 1558.

[1]Bennett, Austin D., Sub-Lieutenant 1914, lost in *Olivia* 1916.

207. *Captain G.E. Corbett to Vice-Admiral Commanding Tenth Cruiser Squadron*

HMS *Orotava*, 20 March 1916

I have the honour to submit for your information the substance of a report made to me by Sub-Lieutenant Bishop, RNR,[1] lately returned from Armed Guard duty in SS *Imo* and *Songa*.[2]

The information was obtained from the Masters of both these vessels in the course of conversation, and as the remarks of one are practically corroborated by the other, it is probable that there is a good deal of truth in them.

According to their statements, it appears that vessels wishing to evade the patrols seldom attempt to do so by the Northern route, but make the Butt of Lewis and proceed thence via Pentland Firth.

They claim that even if stopped they are seldom boarded by the Hebrides patrol vessels, who usually content themselves with hailing, and on being told that the ship is going to call at Kirkwall she is allowed to proceed.

If stopped by the patrol to the eastward of the Pentland Firth, they inform them (the Patrol) that they have just left Kirkwall, and in some cases when asked to show the green clearance they show one of some previous trip. As this is only viewed from a distance it passes muster, for, as in the case of the Hebrides patrol, the patrol vessels seldom actually board.

I submit this procedure sounds very plausible, and would no doubt often be successful if it be the case that these patrols do not make a practice of boarding. Both these Masters stated they knew of one vessel, whose name they would not give, which had slipped through in this manner no less than four times.

208. *Vice-Admiral Tupper to Admiralty*

HMS *Alsatian*, 10 April 1916

Report of Proceedings, 23 March–10 April 1916

***

1. Thursday, 23rd March – A North Easterly gale, which had sprung up the previous afternoon, continued throughout the day.

[1]Bishop, Lieutenant in *Changuinola*, 1915.

[2]*Imo* was taken in to Lerwick, whence she was permitted to continue her voyage after inspection (TS 14/8 of 8 March 1916); of *Songa*, there is no record at this time.

Alsatian, proceeding to Swarbacks Minn, sighted two sailing fishing vessels off the South Coast of the Faroes, but was prevented from boarding owing to the state of the sea.

2. Friday, 24th March – *Alsatian* arrived at Swarbacks Minn at dawn, and coaling was commenced at 8 a.m. Other ships in harbour were *Champagne*, *Artois*, *Moldavia*, and *Patuca*.

During the forenoon the Senior Naval Officer, Rear-Admiral Fawckner, and the Captains of *Champagne* and *Artois* came on board.

Hilary intercepted and sent in the American SS *Morene* from Philadelphia to Copenhagen with a cargo of petroleum. On a previous voyage this ship was reported to have supplied oil to Germany ...[1]

Orders were received for the Swedish Steamer *Stockholm* to be sent in if intercepted. This had, however, already been done by *Gloucestershire* earlier in the day. Her cargo included copper and nickel, and there were Germans amongst her passengers .[2]

The Senior Naval Officer, Liverpool, informed me that *Almanzora*, which had been in harbour since the 10th, would not be able to sail before the 27th March owing to stoppage of labour – a serious matter in war time.

A submarine was reported to have sunk a liner in the neighbourhood of Islay.[3] Another was reported off Muckle Flugga at 6.30 p.m., steering west with Auxiliary Patrol Vessels in chase. *Virginian*, who was approaching Swarbacks Minn, was warned.

3. Saturday, 25th March – Heavy weather with snow was experienced on C Patrol, ships being compelled to lie to.

At 9.30 a.m., I went on board *Champagne* to return her Captain's visit. I was received with a guard and the Ship's company was fallen in, though I had asked that there should be no ceremony. I was invited to walk round, and formed the opinion that the ship was well kept; the crew, who were in working dress, had a strong healthy appearance. The Commanding Officer, *Capitaine de Fregate* de Couedic, gives one the impression of being a smart and capable officer.

I afterwards proceeded on board *Artois* where I was also received with a guard. Here I witnessed a gun's crew at loader drill; the practice was fair – 10 rounds in 61 seconds.

The Captains of both *Champagne* and *Artois* informed me that they

[1]*Morene* was inspected and allowed to go on; she had originally been the *Mappin*; her cargo was naphtha (TS 14/8 of 28 March 1916).

[2]There is no record of *Stockholm*'s treatment on this occasion.

[3]This was SS *Englishman*, sunk by *U 43*.

had not yet carried out target practice with service ammunition. I urged them to do so at the first opportunity.

I also visited *Moldavia* and *Gibraltar*; both appeared to be well kept, especially so the *Gibraltar*, which is very clean.

At 10 p.m. as it was blowing a heavy gale from the South East, I gave orders to Ships to let go a second anchor, and raise steam for slow speed.

Moldavia sailed in the evening and was ordered to join E Patrol off the West Coast of Iceland.

4. Sunday, 26th March – The weather continued bad on C Patrol, and *Orotava*, who had intercepted the Norwegian SS *Sinsen*, was obliged to accompany her as the state of the sea prevented boarding.

Information was received that a German Raider, *Minos*, was possibly attempting to pass out to the westward. The Patrols were warned accordingly.[1]

The Disposition of the Squadron was as follows:

A Patrol ... *Otway*.
C Patrol ... *Columbella*, *Orcoma*, *Orotava*, *Hilary*.
E Patrol (off North West of Iceland) ... *Ebro*, *Changuinola*.
F Patrol (off South West of Iceland) ... *Patia*.
Rejoining from Swarbacks Minn ... *Artois*, *Moldavia*.
Rejoining from Clyde ... *Mantua*.
Proceeding to Swarbacks Minn ... *Gloucestershire*.
At Liverpool ... *Victorian*, *Teutonic*, *Andes*, and *Almanzora*.
At Clyde ... *Hildebrand*, *Motagua*.
At Swarbacks Minn ... *Alsatian*, *Virginian*, *Patuca*.

During the past week 39 Vessels were intercepted and examined, of which 10 were sent in with armed guards. The absence of *Almanzora*, repairing damage done by fouling the boom defence at Swarbacks Minn, and *Andes*, detained in connection with the Court Martial on the survivors of *Alcantara*, has been much felt, reducing the number of ships available to 19 for the time being.

5. Monday, 27th March – At 8 a.m. *Orotava* succeeded in placing an armed guard on board the SS *Sinsen*, and then resumed her station on patrol.[2]

[1]This was the date of a sortie by the British battlecruisers to protect Harwich Force against an attempt by the German Battle Fleet to intercept it. Tupper may be referring to *Moewe* which was returning from its first raid about this time. No German raider called *Minos* is known.

[2]*Sinsen* was not detained.

The *Artois* boarded the Norwegian Steamer *Balto* in Latitude 59.55´N, Long. 12.45´W, bound from New York to Goteborg with a general cargo, and sent her in to Lerwick with an armed guard ... It had been reported that this vessel would probably attempt to evade the patrols.[1]

The Skipper of the British Trawler *Lord Lansdowne*, which was boarded by *Changuinola*, stated that he had heard that a steamer, name unknown, was loading skins at Reykjavik for Germany. This probably referred to the *Gustave Falck*, which had already been ordered to be sent in if intercepted.

At Swarbacks Minn there were very heavy snow and hail squalls from the North East throughout the day.

Alsatian and *Patuca* carried out boat exercise, all boats being lowered and sent away under sail; the evolution was well carried out in spite of the bad weather. Opportunity was taken for the Chaplain of *Alsatian* and the local Presbyterian Minister to hold special services on board *Virginian* and *Patuca*.

I went on board *Virginian* and *Intrepid*, and also visited the Whaling Station at Olna Firth, which is used as a store for the Auxiliary Patrol Vessels.

Rear-Admiral Fawckner has the Base well organised, and is always ready to meet the requirements of the Tenth Cruiser Squadron at short notice.

My opinion was asked as regards the desirability of extinguishing the lights in the neighbourhood of Swarbacks Minn with a view to reducing the risk of submarine attack for vessels entering and leaving the harbour, and only exhibiting them when vessels are expected. Such a course would, I think, be more likely to assist a submarine cruising in the vicinity than to confuse her, as the fact of a light being specially exhibited would probably be taken to indicate that a vessel was approaching. A ship of the Tenth Cruiser Squadron is due at Swarbacks Minn almost every day about dawn, but it is not always possible to keep to the programme owing to delays caused by meeting steamers when inward bound. If, however, the lights are always kept burning, as at present, the time of arrival can be altered as necessary.

The approaches could be made more secure by additional Auxiliary Patrol Vessels.

[1]*Balto*'s cargo produced many queries; the copper brought Norway's allocation over the agreed quota, and the matter took some time to resolve; the ship was eventually told it could sail on once the prize courted goods had been discharged, though this had apparently still not been done by 26 April (TS 14/8 of 31 March to 26 April 1916 *passim*).

Alsatian and *Patuca* put to sea about 7 p.m. in a heavy northerly gale.

6. Tuesday, 28th March – A heavy North Easterly gale was experienced to the North of the Faroes.

Otway proceeded to F Patrol off the South West of Iceland to relieve *Patia* who was shortly due to coal.

The ice off the North West coast was reported to be close to the land.

7. Wednesday, 29th March – Weather misty in A Patrol area; *Mantua* and *Moldavia* continued to examine the icefield off the North West of Iceland.

8. Thursday, 30th March – As there appeared to be a considerable amount of loose ice to the north west of Iceland, which had already caused slight damage to two ships, and with a view to being in a better position to intercept contraband Icelandic trade making its way across to the Norwegian coast, and thence to enemy destination, I represented to the Commander-in-Chief it would be better to shift E Patrol to the neighbourhood of Revsnes Light (Lat. 66.33´N, Long. 16.9´W), and place F off Seidisfiord; this last would also enable me to keep in permanent W/T communication with E.

I met *Virginian* in the course of the afternoon and received official correspondence from the Commander-in-Chief.

Today 18 Ships out of the 21 composing the Squadron are at sea.

9. Friday, 31st March – I met *Virginian* at 10.30 a.m., and *Almanzora* at 4 p.m. The Captains of both ships came on board.

Having received the Commander-in-Chief's approval for the proposals contained in the previous paragraph, I directed *Virginian* and *Victorian* to patrol on a line 360 degrees 60 miles from Revsnes Light, and stationed *Almanzora* on F, to patrol 325 degrees 50 miles from Lat. 65.20´N, Long. 12 degrees West.

About 6 p.m. *Moldavia*, patrolling off Ise Fjord, Iceland, boarded the Norwegian Steamer *Gustave Falck* ... bound for Bergen with wool and skins. Whilst the boarding boat was being lowered the Ship endeavoured to escape into neutral waters, and only stopped when fired on. An armed guard was placed on board and the vessel sent to Lerwick.

Her master stated that he had attempted the passage to the North of Iceland, but had been unable to get through owing to the ice.[1]

10. Saturday, 1st April – I met *Teutonic* at 10 a.m. in thick weather, and received official mails. Commodore reported that whilst at Liverpool he had had serious trouble with the mercantile ratings belonging to the engine room department and had been compelled to

[1]*Gustave Falck* was not detained.

apply for a Court Martial on eight men for open mutiny. I have ascertained that all is now going well on board the *Teutonic*.

A copy of a report sent by Commodore Benson to the Senior Naval Officer, Liverpool, is attached [210] ...

A submarine was reported as being in 56.30´N, Long. 6.42´W, at 8.30 a.m. steering South. *Columbella*, who was proceeding to Clyde, was warned accordingly.

11. Sunday, 2nd April – Very misty weather; *Artois* intercepted the Norwegian SS *Brazil* from New York to Rotterdam with a cargo of wheat for the Belgian Relief Commission. She was sent to Kirkwall with an armed guard ... .[1]

I met *Andes* at 2.30 p.m., having located her by means of the W/T Direction Finder. Captain Young came on board and conferred with me. I hope that he may receive some recognition for the part *Andes* took in the finding and sinking of the Raider *Greif* and the capture of part of her crew.

Virginian and *Victorian* having now been established off Revsnes for 24 hours, I withdrew *Otway*, *Mantua*, and *Moldavia* from the west coast of Iceland, to join up with A and C Patrols.

The disposition of the Squadron at Noon was as follows:

A Patrol ... *Andes*, *Hildebrand*, *Alsatian*, *Teutonic*.
C Patrol ... *Hilary*, *Gloucestershire*, *Patuca*, *Artois*, *Orcoma*.
E Patrol (off Revsnes) ... *Victorian*, *Virginian*.
F Patrol (off Seidisfjord) ... *Almanzora*.
Off West Coast of Iceland ... *Mantua*, *Moldavia*, *Otway*.
Proceeding to Swarbacks Minn ... *Orotava*.
At Clyde ... *Changuinola*, *Motagua*, *Ebro*, *Patia*, *Columbella*.

During the past week 30 vessels were intercepted and examined of which 11 were sent in with Armed Guards. The weather has been misty and stormy, boarding being rendered difficult at times.

At noon *Patuca* boarded the Norwegian Barque *Syvstjerne* from Buenos Ayres to Nykoping with a cargo of maize, and sent her to

[1]*Brazil* was allowed to proceed by the Customs at Kirkwall on 6 April 1916. The Belgian Relief Commission had been organised as early as October 1914, and by agreement with the German occupying forces in Belgium and the Allies, was permitted to import food supplies for sale to the Belgian civilian population. Under the first German occupation commander (von der Goltz) this worked well, but the increasing pressure on Germany by 1916 led to more frequent breaches of the agreement.

Lerwick under armed guard. Orders were subsequently received that this vessel was to be sent in if met with.[1]

12. Monday, 3rd April – I met *Otway* at a pre-arranged rendezvous in the course of the afternoon and went on board. There was a strong breeze and heavy swell at the time. The Ship appears to be comfortable and the mess deck well kept. I inspected the Ship's Company at their General Quarters stations. The arrangements for the supply of ammunition will not be efficient until the motors, which have been applied for, are received. A deflection teacher and an improvised spotting table are also required.

13. Tuesday, 4th April – At 2.40 p.m. *Moldavia* intercepted the Norwegian Steamer *Flora* from Bergen to Iceland in Lat. 62.41´N, Long. 13.26´W. As she had mails on board, and had not called at a British Port, she was sent in to Stornoway under armed guard ... The Master energetically protested.[2]

A submarine was reported in Lat. 58.23´N, Long. 8.2´W, steering WSW.

14. Wednesday, 5th April – *Virginian* proceeded along the North Coast of Iceland as far as North Cape without encountering ice.

15. Thursday, 6th April – The Norwegian Steamer *Romsdalfjord* from New York to Christiania via Kirkwall with a general cargo was intercepted by *Orcoma*. She was also carrying 741 bags of mails, including over 300 for Germany. An armed guard was placed on board.[3]

Information was received shortly after noon that a large steamer had been sighted 20 miles to the North of Muckle Flugga steering WSW. *Orcoma* and *Orotava*, which were proceeding to and from Swarbacks Minn respectively, were ordered to intercept her if possible. The *Patuca*, which was on her way to Clyde was also warned. This steamer has not been met with.

16. Friday, 7th April – *Motagua* left Clyde during the night, but was recalled owing to the Admiralty suspending sailings through the North Channel.

[1]*Syvstjerne*'s cargo was 2000 tons of maize; the destination was Falster, the southernmost Danish island, and this produced grave misgivings in the Contraband Committee. The cargo was covered by a Danish Merchant Guild's guarantee against re-export, but the Committee commented that 'it does not seem possible to rely on' this guarantee since it would not prevent the capture of the cargo in Danish waters by a German ship, which had been done by collusion in other cases, or so it was thought. In the end the ship was permitted to go on – the system of guarantees demanded it – and the British Minister in Copenhagen was asked to report its arrival. Whether he did or not is not clear (TS 14/8 of 5, 17 and 25 April 1916).

[2]*Flora* was not detained.

[3]*Romsdalfjord* was not detained, though the mail was investigated.

About 3 p.m. *Hilary* intercepted the Danish Steamer *United States* in Lat. 58.18´N, Long. 15.10´W, from New York to Copenhagen, with 372 passengers, and a general cargo, and sent her to Kirkwall under armed guard.[1] Her Captain stated that *Bergensfjord* had left New York 48 hours after the *United States*.

Gloucestershire reported that G.C. Carey, AB, RNVR ONWZ 1089, had been lost overboard from the fore rigging. Boats were sent away and the vicinity thoroughly searched, but unfortunately without result.

A submarine was reported to have sunk a steamer in Lat. 56.20´N, Long. 7.56´W.[2]

Almanzora and *Andes* were directed to relieve *Victorian* and *Virginian* on E Patrol, the latter joining A when relieved.

17. Saturday, 8th April – It was blowing a gale from the SW and ships on C Patrol had to lie to later on in the day. I met *Gloucestershire* at 11 a.m. having intended to go on board, but there was too much sea running to lower a boat.

Orcoma, on her way to Swarbacks Minn, reported having struck a 'Heavy submerged substance', when in Lat. 60.48´N, Long. 4.24´W, no apparent damage being done. Arrangements were made for divers to examine her on arrival.

A submarine was again reported active in the neighbourhood of Skerryvore, another steamer being sunk in Lat. 56.34´N, Long. 7.24´W.[3]

Ships of the Tenth Cruiser Squadron proceeding to their Southern Bases have been directed to traverse as much of the route between 10°W and the North Channel as possible by night.

At intervals during the day faint W/T calls were heard from *Kristianiafjord* and *Bergensfjord*, but not continuous enough to obtain a bearing on the Direction Finder. The patrol had been specially warned and organised to intercept these vessels, and a short account of the steps taken, and a tracing showing the area searched, emphasises the fact that they are systematically evading the patrol by avoiding the usual routes. I suggest that they should be intercepted near their terminal ports when they evade the 10th Cruiser Squadron, and thus make sure of their being examined.

Alsatian proceeded for Swarbacks Minn, steering such courses as would be most likely to intercept *Bergensfjord* [216].

18. Sunday, 9th April – The *Motagua*, which had sailed from Clyde

[1] *United States* was allowed to sail on after inspection.

[2] This vessel may be *Merops*, acting as a Q-ship, sunk by *U 87*.

[3] This was SS *Adamton*, sunk by *U 22*.

the previous evening, was again recalled owing to the North Channel being closed by Admiralty orders.

The Disposition of the Squadron was as follows:

A Patrol ... *Virginian, Victorian, Hildebrand, Teutonic, Moldavia.*
C Patrol ... *Orotava, Gloucestershire, Otway, Hilary, Artois, Mantua.*
E Patrol ... *Almanzora, Andes.*
Proceeding to Swarbacks Minn ... *Alsatian.*
At Clyde ... *Motagua, Patuca, Changuinola, Ebro, Patia, Columbella.*
At Swarbacks Minn ... *Orcoma.*

During the past week 35 vessels were intercepted, 7 of which were sent in with armed guards. The weather was again bad during the greater part of the week.

19. Monday 10th April – *Alsatian* arrived at Swarbacks Minn and anchored.

***

209. *Vice-Admiral Tupper to Commander-in-Chief Grand Fleet*

HMS *Alsatian*, 27 March 1916

Submitted for information with reference to my predecessor's submission No. 12/3 of 19 January last [191], commenting on your communication H.F.0020/225 of 9 January relative to eastbound vessels reported to have passed through the patrols.

2. As regards the Hebrides patrols, vessels had strict orders to board unless the weather was too bad, in which case any Ships at all suspicious were to be escorted in.

3. The weekly return of vessels brought into Stornoway shows, I think, that few vessels escape. At the same time it is realized some Skippers are more energetic and trustworthy than others.

4. Copies of *Orotava*'s letter have been forwarded to Vice-Admiral, Orkneys and Shetlands, and Rear-Admiral Stornoway [207].[1]

[1]This was a particularly sensitive matter, since Tupper had been responsible, as Rear-Admiral Stornoway, for some of these auxiliary patrols before his promotion to the Tenth Cruiser Squadron. It is odd, to say the least, that this matter should be raised within the first month of his tenure of the new post; no doubt this helps explain the emphasis on earlier comments in his first paragraph.

210. *Commodore R.E.R. Benson to Senior Naval Officer Liverpool*

HMS *Teutonic*, 28 March 1916

I regret to report, with reference to my letter of this date, in which I am applying for a Court Martial to be held on eight mercantile ratings of this ship for open mutiny, that the stated grievances which the Mercantile crews of ships of the Tenth Cruiser Squadron have from time to time brought forward, came to a head today, and I was obliged to submit this crisis to your jurisdiction, as I was unable to overcome it by summary punishment.

2. A system of general messing commenced in HMS *Teutonic* at noon yesterday, 27th instant, in accordance with Admiralty letter V 475/16, of 20th January 1916, and a daily menu was prepared and carried out on the lines on which other ships and establishments under this system are messed. After careful consideration of the menu prepared, I consider that, in both variety and quantity, it is very similar to that obtaining in other ships, and could not be improved except by exceeding the Admiralty scale of 1s 3d per head per day.

3. A Deputation of greasers, firemen, and trimmers requested to see my executive Officer, Lieutenant-Commander Guy Ronald Dolphin, Royal Naval Reserve,[1] this morning, and, stating they represented the whole of the Engine Room Department, informed him that unless they could be messed on the previous system, that is, at the same scale as they had been victualled by the White Star Line (by contract with the Admiralty), they refused to continue duty in the ship. Lieutenant-Commander Dolphin pointed out to them, not only that their action amounted to mutiny, but also that they had not had an opportunity of judging in so short a time, the system of General Messing. They refused however to resume duty, and Lieutenant-Commander Dolphin reported the matter to me.

4. At 2 p.m. I interviewed the representatives in the presence of the whole of the Engine Room Department. They repeated to me the complaint that the food was not what they had been accustomed to. They also, and this was their chief grievance at this time, complained that the majority of them were being paid at less than the port rate now prevailing, and that, in spite of repeated representations, they had received no redress.

5. I then addressed all the men fallen in and told them that I had, in the strongest possible manner, represented to Their Lords

[1]Dolphin, Guy Ronald, RNR, Commander 1916.

Commissioners of the Admiralty, that the question of standardising the rates of pay was one of immediate importance. With regard to the Messing I told them that it would receive my closest attention, and that if I considered either the amount or quality was such as was insufficient for able bodied men, I would take such steps as were necessary. I informed them, however, that they had all signed articles placing them under Naval Discipline, and they must abide by its laws. The men were then ordered to disperse.

6. They remained nevertheless, on the Upper Deck, and Lieutenant-Commander Dolphin reported that they still refused to resume duty.

7. I again saw them all, and having read such portions of the Naval Discipline Act as related to mutiny, gave them a quarter of an hour to decide whether they would return to duty or have the matter placed in the hands of a higher Authority than mine.

8. At the end of this time the three spokesmen informed me that they all refused duty, and I reported the matter personally to you.

9. As you know, when you mustered the whole of these men at 7.30 p.m. today, after you had, in the presence of a large military armed guard, again explained that they were under Naval Law, and that their present action was mutiny, eight of them refused to take the ship to sea in the morning, and were placed under military arrest and marched to HMS *Eagle*.

10. The above is a short summary of events. In it I have omitted many of the statements made by these ignorant, misguided and illiterate men. All however tended to the same points, that is, that they refused to perform duty, unless

(a) Their pay was placed on a footing equal to the prevailing port rate, plus a war bonus.
(b) Their scale of food remained unchanged.

I have also omitted full particulars of what I said to them, except that I always impressed on them the serious nature of the attitude they were adopting and that *they were under Naval Discipline and liable to its penalties in case of misconduct*.

11. I would, however, respectfully submit that this serious misconduct is to a great extent foreshadowed in the letters I have written on the subject of pay of Mercantile Ratings [e.g., 198] ... I have no hesitation in saying that no Naval Officer, except by actual experience, can have any idea of the difficulty in dealing with these Engine Room Mercantile Ratings.

12. They are almost without exception of the lowest scale of humanity found in Great Britain. They have been accustomed to engage

for a cruise of three weeks under mercantile regulations, to have plenty of food served in any unsystematic way they liked, and untrammelled by discipline or restrictions, except to keep their watches, to be treated not as men in a fighting ship, but as animals necessary to the steaming of an Atlantic liner. They have no patriotic, social, or moral conceptions, and their ideas, ingrained from their earliest training, go no further than lots of food in as savage and uncivilised a way as possible, and the greatest amount of pay that their earning capacity can obtain, to enable them to spend as long as possible away from work when they return to port.

13. I submit that the present development is hardly more than might have been expected, and the alteration in food and pay, in other words what these men consider as 'their rights', has brought the matter to a climax.[1]

211. *Memoirs of Surgeon Sub-Lieutenant D.A. Knight*

In April 1916 we were on patrol from the most Northern of the Faroe Islands (Myggenoes Lighthouse) to the North East tip of Iceland (Landanaes) for a fortnight. There was no ice in the water but the weather was so cold that every bit of spray we shipped over the bows immediately froze. There were some inches of solid ice on the foredeck and icicles yards long hanging down from the lower rigging and from the three 6-inch guns, one in the bows and one on each side in front of the bridge. Quite a lovely sight, but I never had any desire to experience such weather conditions again.

[1]The eight men were tried by court martial for 'mutiny not accompanied by violence' and for 'unlawfully attempting to stir up a disturbance'. No evidence was offered on the second charge, and all eight pleaded guilty to the first. Afterwards one of the men claimed he had been 'told' to plead guilty by his defender, who used the word 'advised', though to the complainant the difference – the adviser was an officer, he was a stoker – was probably inaudible. They were all sentenced to two years' hard labour and dismissed from the service. They served the sentence at Inverness Prison and were released in April 1918 (ADM 156/19). Their experience in the prison cannot have been any worse than two years spent stoking a steamer in the North Atlantic, and they were in much less danger of death.

212. *Commander-in-Chief Home Fleets to Vice-Admiral Commanding Orkneys and Shetlands*

3 April 1916

... [I]t is very desirable that the four trawlers for which the Vice-Admiral Commanding Tenth Cruiser Squadron asks [205] could be provided, and, as no more trawlers can be obtained from the South, it is requested that they be detached from the Orkney Patrols.

2. It is thought that the following would be suitable, and by taking one from each of the several units their loss would be less felt, unless you would prefer to detail a complete unit for this service:

2 trawlers from Northern Patrol, such as *Lysander II* and *Ida Adams*;
1 trawler from Western Patrol, such as *Forward Ho!*;
1 trawler from Southern Patrol, such as *Imperia*.

3. Each trawler will require to be fitted with wireless and cabins.

213. *Commander-in-Chief Home Fleets to Vice-Admiral Commanding Orkneys and Shetlands*

4 April 1916

With reference to the report dated 20 March from the Captain of HMS *Orotava* relative to a means of evading search said to be adopted by some neutral vessels a copy of which has been forwarded to you [207], the following remarks are communicated.

2. It is understood that reports are now made to you of Eastward bound vessels which have been boarded by the Tenth Cruiser Squadron and Stornoway patrols ...

3. The Admiralty will now be requested to direct all ports on the West coast to communicate to you the names of vessels carrying green clearance labels which are taking the Northabout route.

4. With regard to other vessels intercepted in Areas II and III, it is requested that all of them may be examined, weather permitting, by the boarding Trawlers, and that if intercepted by the trawlers which do not carry boarding Officers, each vessel may be escorted to an anchorage where the boarding can be carried out under efficient protection, such as Kirkwall or Lerwick, or to a locality where another vessel is available to support the boarding trawler.

***

214. *Minute by Admiral H.T. Oliver*

7 April 1916

With reference to the question of bringing up the 10th C.S. to the approved strength of 24.

The number of effective British ships is		21
Artois	(French)	1
	Total	22

The *Champagne* (French) nominally belongs to the squadron but is never available for patrols as the French use her for taking Staff Officers etc. to Alexandrovsk and when Archangel is open they will probably use her more extensively for such purposes.

The *Arlanza* may be effective in some six months' time if she can be successfully brought back to England from Yukanskie for repairs.

The *Princess* a newly fitted out A.M.C. will be ready about the end of April and will bring the Squadron up to 23 ships.[1]

No steps have yet been taken to replace the *Alcantara*. It is proposed to remove the mine-laying fittings from the *Orvieto* and convert her into an A.M.C. to replace *Alcantara*. She is very little use as a mine-layer owing to her size and is a very costly ship; we should get more use out of her as an A.M.C.

At present *Orvieto* is the only ship fitted for service mines in Home Waters but we could presently recall *Angora* from the Mediterranean.

215. *Vice-Admiral Tupper to Admiralty*

HMS *Alsatian*, 25 April 1916

Report of Proceedings, 10–25 April 1916

***

1. Monday, 10 April – *Alsatian* arrived at Swarbacks Minn, and commenced coaling.

The Norwegian Sailing Vessel *Lapwing*, which had been sent in by *Gloucestershire* on 18 March, was spoken by *Moldavia* in Latitude 60.9´N, Longitude 5.56´W, steering a course NE, but it was too rough

[1]*Princess* (the former German liner *Kronprinsessin Cecilie*) never did join the squadron.

to board. No signals were noticed. Unfortunately nothing has since been heard of this vessel.[1]

The *Motagua*, which had been delayed several days in the Clyde owing to the closing of the North Channel, sailed for Patrol.

2. Tuesday, 11 April – I visited Lerwick, and conferred with the Senior Naval Officer, Commander Hubert G. Alston, Commander Burrard A. Smith, and Lieutenant-Colonel Frank T. Phillips, RMLI,[2] Commanding the Shetland Section, RNR.

It appears that the Auxiliary Patrol Vessels from Lerwick are nearly always employed to the North of Muckle Flugga or to North East of Out Skerries, and that none can be spared to assist the four Trawlers and four Drifters stationed at Swarbacks Minn to patrol the west coast. These latter, I submit, are hardly sufficient to ensure the safety of the approaches to the Harbour and to patrol off the west coasts of the Shetlands. The establishment of a look-out near Eshaness Light connected by telephone with Busta Voe would be an additional safeguard and is strongly recommended [222 para. 8].

I have forwarded a separate application through the Commander-in-Chief for a tug to be stationed at Lerwick to tow Sailing Vessels sent in for examination into Harbour, and to assist them whilst there. This, in my opinion, is very desirable – lately one of the big Sailing Ships dragged badly during a gale. Trawlers and Drifters are not fitted for towing and generally damage themselves when doing so.

I was glad to find that the *Gustav Falck*, which had attempted to evade the patrols, had been sent to the Prize Court with an incriminating cargo.[3]

Ships on C Patrol were compelled to lie to.

At 11 p.m. *Teutonic* left Patrol for Scapa Flow in connection with a trial by Court Martial of certain mercantile ratings belonging to the Engine Room Department.

With reference to clause 17 of my Report of Proceedings, No. 179/35 of 10 April [208], the Diver who examined *Orcoma* found no marks on the Ship's bottom to indicate that she had struck any hard substance. I think it was very likely to have been a whale.

[1]*Lapwing* was being used to return goods condemned to the Prize Court to Britain; see page 422, note 1.

[2]Smith, Burrard A., RN, Commander (retired) 1915 and later serving under Canadian Government.

Phillips, Frank T., Lieutenant-Colonel RMLI 1914, Commanding Shetland Section RNR, Colonel (retired) 1918.

[3]*Gustave Falck* was not detained.

3. Wednesday, 12 April – *Andes* reported the presence of pack ice in Latitude 67.52´N, Longitude 16.57´W.

Artois and *Otway* arrived at Swarbacks Minn for coaling.

4. Thursday, 13 April – *Virginian* reported having touched 'some submerged substance' at 9.45 a.m., Latitude 60 W, Longitude 12.12´W, no apparent damage being done. Nothing was seen on the surface.

Owing to the presence of ice, and bad weather being experienced, E patrol was moved to the eastward.

I visited *Otway*, and presented Distinguished Service Medals recently awarded to certain members of the Ship's Company for good service performed in the Tenth Cruiser Squadron.

Alsatian sailed from Swarbacks Minn at dusk to rejoin patrol.

5. Friday, 14 April – Two submarines were reported as being expected to pass Muckle Flugga from the eastward.

The weather on C patrol hampered boarding, ships having to escort vessels intercepted for some time before being able to place Armed Guards on board.

Alsatian on her way to rejoin patrol intercepted and boarded two Sailing Vessels which proved to be correct.

6. Saturday, 15 April – At 11 a.m. having met and boarded *Hilary*, I presented medals awarded to men belonging to the Ship. I then went round the Ship and Ship's Company. She is exceedingly clean and well kept, the men being well dressed and cheerful. The guns and arms are in very good condition. The gunnery training, organisation, and general condition of the Ship reflects great credit on Captain Bather, and all concerned. Captain Bather expressed great regret at leaving his Ship.[1]

This vessel is still being victualled by the Owners.

In the afternoon I met and boarded *Gloucestershire* in order to inspect the position of the 6" guns placed on the fore well deck of the Ship. The Commanding Officer had represented to me that it would be impossible to fight these guns efficiently in the weather usually experienced on patrol owing to the well deck being awash. As there was a considerable sea running, I had my boat hoisted in and proceeded in *Gloucestershire*.

From personal observation I fully concur that there would be great difficulty in fighting these guns and consider that they should be placed higher. I have reported separately on this matter ... The mountings of the 6" guns appear to be much worn, and training is almost impossible

[1]Bather, Rowland Henry, CBE, RN (1873–1961), Lieutenant 1896, Commander 1907, Captain 1916, Captain of *Hilary* 1914–1916, Rear Admiral (retired) 1922.

when there is any motion. Application has been made for this to be remedied on the Ship's return to her southern base.

The crew contains a very large proportion of untrained ratings, but these are under instruction and progress is being made.

For a newly commissioned Ship she is comfortable and fairly clean, but the men do not appear to be contented; complaints were made to me regarding the victualling, which is conducted on the General Mess System. The Marines and Stewards appeared satisfied. The Seamen, however, say they do not get enough, and what they apparently wanted was the daily Messing Allowance of 4d a day, which they would get if victualled on the standard ration, to enable them to buy food from the Canteen according to their individual tastes. The firemen also complained that they did not get enough, the men coming off watch finding insufficient food remaining. Steps are being taken to ensure that men who have been on watch shall receive a proper meal. I pointed out that the menu ... appeared generous, but they stated they were not accustomed to the class of food and preferred more meat and sugar amongst other things.

With the present high cost of living it does not appear that 1s 3d per head is sufficient for providing the mercantile ratings with the quantity of food to which they are accustomed and I would strongly recommend that this be increased to 1s 6d.

I am glad to say there was no sign of active discontent, the men representing their grievance respectfully, and in the usual service manner.

I spoke to the whole Ship's Company and while I told them I would represent their complaint, I urged them to do their duty to their Country in a cheerful spirit.

Having spent some two hours on board *Gloucestershire* I returned to *Alsatian*.

7. Sunday, 16 April – Having presented Distinguished Service Medals at Divisions on board *Alsatian*, and located *Ebro* in very thick weather by means of the Direction Finder, I proceeded on board about 1.30 p.m. After presenting a Distinguished Service Medal whilst the men were fallen in at Divisions, I went round the decks.

She seems generally comfortable and efficient. The firemen's quarters are clean and tidy, the seamens' and marines' mess decks fairly so. The men did not look particularly smart. The Officers' quarters are very comfortable.

The messing is carried out by the Owners, and there were no complaints. The general Mess System is to be introduced shortly.

The Gunnery appliances are, generally speaking, good, but there is no Deflection Teacher. Practically all the woodwork in the Ship has been left intact, and her magazines are built of wood.

At 5.36 p.m., I met *Orotava*, and, having proceeded on board, presented a Distinguished Service Medal and went round the Ship. The mess decks are very well kept and very tidy, though the Ship is old and the paintwork poor. There is an air of comfort and contentment and smartness about the Ship, and the men are cheerful and well dressed. A brass band has been organized in the Ship composed of volunteers from the Ship's Company.

The gunnery efficiency is above the average. The guns and arms are clean and there is a deflection teacher and spotting table in use. The magazines are built of wood.

The messing is, at present, done by the Owners, but the General Mess System is shortly being introduced. The Paymaster of the Ship did not think he could manage on the 1s 3d per head allowed.

At 2 p.m. *Mantua* intercepted the Danish Steamer *Oscar II* from New York to Copenhagen with 301 passengers, a general cargo and 1690 bags of mails. Amongst her passengers were ten German women and one man aged 65. An Armed Guard was placed on board and the vessel sent to Kirkwall.[1]

The disposition of the Squadron at noon was as follows:

A Patrol ... *Moldavia*, *Orcoma*, *Ebro*, *Otway*.
C Patrol ... *Changuinola*, *Hilary*, *Mantua*, *Gloucestershire*, *Orotava*, *Alsatian*, *Artois*.
E Patrol ... *Andes*, *Almanzora*.
Rejoining from Swarbacks Minn ... *Victorian*.
Rejoining from Clyde ... *Patia*.
At Liverpool ... *Virginian*.
At Clyde ... *Columbella*, *Patuca*.
At Scapa ... *Teutonic*.
Proceeding to Swarbacks Minn ... *Motagua*, *Hildebrand*.

During the past week, 25 vessels were intercepted and examined, six of which were sent in with Armed Guards.

8. Monday, 17 April – A Northerly gale was experienced throughout the day.

Having obtained the Commander-in-Chief's approval for all Ships, with the exception of those on E, to be placed on a line extending from

[1]*Oscar II* was not detained, though the mails were examined.

Latitude 56.30´N, Longitude 11.30´W to Latitude 63.40´N, Longitude 16.10´W, I re-organized the patrols as follows:

A Patrol – Four ships on a line 340° from Latitude 61 N, Longitude 15 W – 40 miles apart.
C Patrol – Four ships on a line 340° from Latitude 58.10´N, Longitude 12.30´W – 30 miles apart.
D Patrol – Three ships on a line 340° from Latitude 56.35´N, Longitude 11.30´W – 30 miles apart.

Alsatian worked temporarily between A and C.

9. Tuesday, 18 April – Information was received from the Captain Superintendent, Clyde, that *Columbella* had badly damaged her stem by running into the dock wall. Her repairs will probably take three weeks.

10. Wednesday, 19 April – A strong ENE breeze and moderate sea. *Alsatian* carried out 6" Target Practice Firing 32 rounds – range 5400 to 4500 control fire. Considering the weather conditions, the practice was good, but more rapidity of fire is required.

Acting on a signal from the Commander-in-Chief, another vessel was placed on C Patrol, making five on C, and three on A.

11. Thursday, 20 April – Strong NE breeze with a considerable swell.

I met *Teutonic* at 10 a.m. and went on board. Having hoisted my boat, I proceeded on patrol with *Alsatian* in company. I went round the men and the ship. She is clean, and very creditable to all concerned. The men were well dressed, and appeared to be well looked after. Apparently the recent discontent [210] has died down, but the 1s 3d per diem for victualling the men is hardly sufficient to give the Mercantile Ratings what they have been accustomed to.

The recent alterations to the Officers' mess etc. have added greatly to the comfort of the Officers and crew.

At 12.20 p.m., I returned on board *Alsatian*, and proceeded on patrol.

Whilst on board, I saw an ingenious piece of mechanism invented by Engineer-Commander James R. Clay, RNR,[1] to prevent the helm being put over the wrong way. A description of this is being forwarded separately.

12. Friday, 21 April – *Mantua* was met at 1.30 p.m., and I went on board to present Distinguished Service Medals. At the invitation of her Captain, I went round the Ship. I found her neat and clean: the men seem happy and contented and well cared for. I consider she is a credit to Captain Tibbits and the other Officers of the Ship. In the morning two Steamers were boarded by *Alsatian* and sent in with Armed Guards.

[1]Clay, James R., RNR, Engineer Commander 1915.

At 4 p.m. I met *Patuca* and boarded her, presenting a Distinguished Service Medal. As another Steamer came in sight, I had no time to go round the mess decks, but the general appearance of the Ship and Ship's Company was quite satisfactory.

The Commander-in-Chief informed me that six Trawlers would shortly be available for service in Icelandic Waters with the Tenth Cruiser Squadron.

The Dutch Steamer *Selene* was intercepted by *Alsatian* in the first watch and sent to Kirkwall with an Armed Guard.[1]

A submarine was reported as having been seen in Latitude 57.50´N, Longitude 9.7´W on the 19th steering to the westward.

13. Saturday, 22 April – Having met and boarded *Patia* at 10 a.m., I hoisted in my boat and proceeded on patrol. After presenting a Distinguished Service Medal, I went round the men at Divisions and mess decks, etc. She is very clean and well kept: the mess decks airy and lighter than those in most ships. The crew looked happy and were well dressed.

The Victualling is done by the Admiralty. There were no actual complaints, but the men have to supplement the food from their own pockets. The ship reflects great credit on Commander Bowring.[2]

One of the wooden magazines has now been replaced by a steel one, which seems satisfactory: but a great quantity of loose timber and lagging is piled close to it, which I am told they have been ordered to retain on board. I submit this is highly dangerous, and hope to be able to store it temporarily at Swarbacks Minn. Otherwise the gunnery and fighting organisation seems efficient.

At noon, I returned to *Alsatian*, and proceeded to join D Patrol.

14. Sunday, 23 April – *Hindustan* was met in the forenoon steering to the northward.

The disposition of the Squadron at noon was as follows:

A Patrol ... *Otway*, *Orcoma*.
C Patrol ... *Patia*, *Patuca*, *Motagua*, *Victorian*, *Teutonic*.
D Patrol ... *Artois*.
E Patrol ... *Ebro*, *Hildebrand*.
Proceeding to Liverpool ... *Alsatian*.

[1]Advance notice had been received of *Selene*'s cargo by the Contraband Committee, which instructed Kirkwall Customs to let the ship go on if the cargo list was correct. This was the first Dutch ship recorded as being sent in by the Northern Patrol (TS 14/8 of 11 April 1916).

[2]Bowring, Vincent L., RN, Lieutenant 1896, Commander 1909, Captain of *Ambrose* 1915, *Patia* 1916, Captain (retired) 1921.

Proceeding to Clyde ... *Gloucestershire*, *Moldavia*.
Proceeding to Swarbacks Minn ... *Changuinola*, *Andes*.
At Liverpool ... *Virginian*.
At Clyde ... *Columbella*, *Orotava*, *Hilary*.
At Swarbacks Minn ... *Almanzora*, *Mantua*.

During the past week, 44 ships were intercepted and examined, 11 of which were sent in with Armed Guards.

Westerly gales were experienced during the greater part of the week.

At midnight, I turned over the patrol to the Commodore *Teutonic* and *Alsatian* proceeded to Liverpool to coal and refit.

15. Tuesday, 25 April – I arrived at Liverpool.

16. I regret to report that the following Sailing Ships sent in with Armed Guards for examination have failed to arrive in port and no further information has been received regarding them:

Norwegian Barque *Pestalozzi* – This Ship was boarded at 6 p.m. on 13 March in Latitude 58.10´N, Longitude 12.30´W, bound from Helsingfors to Santa Fe, Argentine, and an Armed Guard was placed on board with directions to proceed to Stornoway [222 para. 9, 232].

Norwegian Barque *Lapwing* – Intercepted by *Gloucestershire* in Latitude 56.56´N, Longitude 15.36´W on 18 March, and sent in to Lerwick with Armed Guard. This ship was spoken by *Moldavia* on 10 April in Latitude 60.91´N, Longitude 5.56´N.[1]

The names of Officers and men composing the Armed Guards have already been reported ...

***

216. *Captain J.A. Webster to Vice-Admiral Commanding Tenth Cruiser Squadron*

10 April 1916

Steps taken to intercept Bergensfjord *and* Christianiafjord

The Danish SS *United States*, intercepted in Latitude 58.18´N, Longitude 15.10´W at 3 p.m. on 7 April, stated that *Bergensfjord* had sailed from New York 48 hours after her, bound for Bergen. Assuming

[1]*Lapwing* is recorded as having been reported from Moville, Donegal, on 29 March by Customs (TS 14/8 of 29 March 1916); she was then permitted to go, and the Armed Guard were presumably still making their way from Moville to Swarbacks Minn; the second sighting, by *Moldavia*, did not result in *Lapwing* being sent in (see page 416, note 1).

the speed of *Bergensfjord* as 16 knots, it was calculated that she could not be less than 180 miles astern of *United States*, i.e. in the neighbourhood of 58 North, 21 West.

Permission having been obtained from the Commander-in-Chief, line ahead was adopted for C Patrol – consisting of four ships 360° from Latitude 57.50´N, Longitude 14 W at 9 p.m. on the 7th. *Artois* was ordered from her patrol south of Rockall to take up the southern position on C. Ships to be in position by 8 a.m., 8th.

Alsatian left A patrol on noon 6th April to reinforce C patrol, taking the northernmost position.

During Saturday the 8th *Bergensfjord* was heard working with *Kristianiafjord*, but her signals were very weak and intermittent, and no bearing could be obtained by Direction Finder.

Alsatian left C Patrol noon 8th and proceeded to Swarbacks Minn steering courses to cross traffic route to North of Muckle Flugga, on three legs.

Bergensfjord was again heard about 9 a.m. on Sunday, the 9th, calling Bergen Coast Station, but no bearing could be obtained.

C Patrol was forced to heave to by heavy WNW gale from noon Saturday, the 8th, until weather moderated some hours later. *Mantua* leaving Swarbacks Minn p.m. on the 8th was ordered to proceed to 60 N, and 7 W, and thence steering 250° to join C patrol. *Moldavia*, leaving Swarbacks Minn at the same time, was ordered at 12.30 p.m. on the 9th to patrol 180°, 40 miles from Lat. 61.14´N, Long. 6.30´W, until 4 a.m. Monday, then to patrol in the vicinity of 60 N, 6 W, till 8 p.m. 10th.

Norwegian SS *Maud* intercepted by *Otway* in Latitude 59.7´N, Long. 14.18´W, steering 75°, reported passing *Kristianiafjord* in Latitude 54 N, Long. 27.30´W, p.m. on 6th.[1]

It would appear probable that both *Bergensfjord* and *Kristianiafjord* passed south of Rockall.

The following statement shows the number of trips *Bergensfjord* and *Kristianiafjord* have made since the 1st January 1915, and the number of times they have been intercepted by the 10th Cruiser Squadron between 1st January 1915 and 7th April 1916:

Bergensfjord made 12 journeys East.*
and 11 journeys West.
was intercepted 8 times East,

[1]*Maud*'s cargo had been declared in advance, and guarantees were received concerning all items (TS 14/8 of 13 April 1916). This practice perhaps explains *Maud*'s willingness to assist the Patrol in locating *Kristianiafjord*.

and 5 times West.
Kristianiafjord made 11 journeys East.*
and 12 journeys West.
was intercepted 3 times going East
and 6 times going West.

* Including present journey.

217. *Procurator Fiscal Lerwick to Rear-Admiral Fawckner Swarbacks Minn*

13 April 1916

I have made so far the enquiry as to the body of the man found at Westfirth, Yell, on 27th March last, the result of which is that the body is that of a man clothed in the uniform of a man of the British Navy.

In the *Daily Record* of 27th March I notice in the list there given of men amissing from the British Cruiser *Alcantara* which was sunk in the North Sea on 29th February, the name of Duncan Bain. I think the body must be that of this Duncan Bain, as on his stockings was stamped the name 'D. Ross' [*sic*], and his arms were tattooed as follows:

Right arm: blue and red floral design with a heart, and clasped hands and the words 'true love' above this design, and on the

Left arm, a blue and red floral design with the name 'Duncan' within it.

To enable me to complete my enquiry I will be obliged by your informing me whether the description applies to a man of the *Alcantara*, and, if so, to give me the name, age, rating, and place of abode of deceased, and if possible the name and occupation of his father, and maiden surname of his mother. These are required for the registering by me in the Register of Deaths for North Yell and the completion of my inquiry.[1]

[1] 'Seaman Bain, D.' is buried in the cemetery at St Olaf's Chapel on the island of Yell, the only grave of either World War there; it is, suitably, the most northerly cemetery in the British Isles.

218. *Commander-in-Chief Home Fleets to Vice-Admiral Commanding Tenth Cruiser Squadron [and others]*

HMS *Iron Duke*, 15 April 1916

Muckle Flugga Patrol

In the event of information being received indicating the possibility of a German raider of the *Moewe* type endeavouring to break out to the Northward the available ships of the Tenth Cruiser Squadron may be directed to assume a patrol line to the Northward of the Shetland Islands.[1]

2. Should orders be given to this effect, the vessels available are to spread on the patrol line without delay.

The centre line of the area to be patrolled is to run 360 degrees from Muckle Flugga.

Ships on patrol are to be thirty miles apart, the Southern ship, which is to be one of the smallest vessels, is to be at least forty miles from land.

They are to steer in wide zigzags on courses 315° and 225° alternately for three hours on each beat when proceeding to the Westward, and courses 45° and 135° for similar periods when proceeding to the eastward.

***

219. *Admiralty to the Under Secretary of State at the Foreign Office*

17 April 1916

With reference to your letter of the 10th January last, No. 470/X, forwarding a copy of a letter from the London representatives of the Standard Oil Company [177], in which it is stated that the SS *Polarine* had been alleged by the British Naval Authorities to have attempted to proceed to Copenhagen without calling at a British Port, I am commanded by My Lords Commissioners of the Admiralty to acquaint you, for the information of the Secretary of State for Foreign Affairs, that full enquiries have been made as to these allegations, and it has been ascertained that the Naval Officers concerned in regard to this Vessel specifically deny having made any such statement.

[1]*Moewe* had escaped into the Atlantic in December 1915, and had returned in late March, hence the reference. The Northern Patrol had been instituted originally with the aim of preventing just such break-outs and returns.

2. No report to this effect has reached the Admiralty, and My Lords would be glad if Messrs Please and Sons could be called upon to quote their authority for the statement.

3. There was some question as to the route to Kirkwall which should be followed and the Captain of the ship refused to take the responsibility of navigating the vessel through the Pentland Firth – but this is an entirely different matter.

220. *Vice-Admiral Tenth Cruiser Squadron to Rear-Admiral Swarbacks Minn*

21 April 1916

With reference to the coaling arrangements for the Squadron at the Northern Base, the following ships will, as a rule, only coal once at Swarbacks Minn between their visits to Liverpool and the Clyde:

Andes	*Hilary*
Almanzora	*Hildebrand*
Otway	*Ebro*
Orcoma	*Gloucestershire*

221. *Minute by Captain Richard Webb, Director of Trade Division*

23 April 1916

It is clear that the Master of *Bergensfjord* is not to be trusted to abide by any agreement as to course to be followed [208 para. 17, 216].

Propose to inform Foreign Office of the facts, and to suggest the cessation of all further coal facilities to Norwegian American Line until their mail steamers are ordered to call.

The case of the *Teutonic* is presumably being dealt with on other papers, as report of Commodore Benson was made to S.N.O. Liverpool [210].

222. *Vice-Admiral Tupper to Admiralty*

HMS *Alsatian*, 16 May 1916

Report of Proceedings, 24 April–15 May 1916

***

1. Monday, 24 April – *Otway* intercepted Russian Steamer *Kursk*, New York to Victoria Haven. The ship was allowed to proceed ...

2. Thursday, 27 April – *Patuca* placed an Armed Guard on board the Norwegian Steamer *Knut Hamsun* and sent vessel to Kirkwall. Besides general cargo and neutral mails, this ship was carrying 331 bags of enemy mails.[1]

Later in the day *Patuca* also placed an Armed Guard on board the Danish Steamer *Frederik VIII*. There were on board 896 bags of mails for enemy's country, and, of the 496 passengers 5 were German, including Dr Roy McEllweedd referred to in Admiralty message 1610 of 24 April.[2]

The *Bergensfjord*, bound west, must have passed through the patrol during the night or the next day. Dispositions were made to intercept her but without success. She did not use her wireless, and, had she kept to her arranged route, it is considered she must have been sighted.

3. Friday, 28 April – *Orcoma*, having left A Patrol at 10 p.m., that patrol was now reduced to two ships.

4. Sunday, 30 April – *Artois* left Patrol at noon for Brest to dock and re-victual, and the Admiralty were requested to inform the French Authorities of the fact.

At noon the disposition of the Squadron was as follows:

A Patrol ... *Otway*, *Almanzora*.
C Patrol ... *Patia*, *Patuca*, *Andes*, *Changuinola*, *Motagua*.
D Patrol ... *Mantua*.
E Patrol ... *Hildebrand*, *Ebro*.
At Swarbacks Minn ... *Victorian*, *Teutonic*.
At Liverpool ... *Columbella*, *Orotava*, *Hilary*, *Moldavia*, *Gloucestershire*.
At Liverpool ... *Alsatian*.
Proceeding to Brest ... *Artois*.
Proceeding to Liverpool ... *Orcoma*.
Rejoining Patrol ... *Virginian*.

Fifty six vessels were intercepted during the week of which fifteen were sent in with Armed Guards.

During the day no less than twenty ships were boarded by Ships on patrol, of which five were sent in with Armed Guards. The latter included the *Kristianiafjord*, which was intercepted by the *Motagua* (northern ship of C). The *Kristianiafjord* attempted to escape. A written

[1]*Knut Hamsun* was not detained.

[2]*Frederick VIII* was allowed to go on after inspection (TS 14/8 of 29 April 1916). I cannot trace any other reference to 'McEllweedd'.

report has been called for and further details will be forwarded when received. The suspected Lady mentioned in Admiralty telegram 2240 of 28 April was identified.[1]

The *Virginian*, which left Liverpool the previous evening, proceeded to Reykjavik to land Mr Cable, the British Consul for Iceland.

5. Thursday, 4 May – *Virginian* rejoined C Patrol.

6. Friday, 5 May – As *Hildebrand* reported that area of E Patrol was being known, the patrol was ordered to move thirty miles to the eastward, and the time of the southern position changed.

7. Saturday, 6 May – I left Liverpool in *Alsatian* to rejoin patrol.

8. Sunday, 7 May – I took over the command of the patrol from Commodore Benson at noon, the disposition of the Squadron being then as follows:

A Patrol ... *Teutonic*, *Almanzora*.
C Patrol ... *Andes*, *Changuinola*, *Victorian*, *Virginian*, *Motagua*.
D Patrol ... *Gloucestershire*, *Hilary*, *Mantua*.
E Patrol ... *Hildebrand*.
Proceeding to E Patrol ... *Patia*.
Rejoining from Swarbacks Minn ... *Patuca*.
Rejoining from Liverpool ... *Alsatian*.
Rejoining from Clyde ... *Moldavia*, *Orotava*.
At Swarbacks Minn ... *Ebro*.
At Brest ... *Artois*.
At Liverpool ... *Orcoma*, *Otway*.
At Clyde ... *Columbella*.

Fifty seven ships were intercepted and examined during the week of which seventeen were sent in with Armed Guards.

Victorian intercepted the Norwegian Steamer *Bratland* from Charlestown [*sic*] to Aalborg in Latitude 58.56´N, Longitude 14.21´W with a cargo of oil cake. She was sent in to Kirkwall with an Armed Guard in accordance with Admiralty message 1217 of 27 April.[2]

9. Monday, 8 May – The Admiralty informed me that Lieut. Joe C. Bate, RNR[3] of *Patuca* in charge of the Armed Guard placed on board the Norwegian Barque *Pestalozzi* referred to in paragraph 16 of my Letter of Proceedings No. 208/35 of 25 April [215 para. 16] was a Prisoner of War in Germany. It would appear that this ship was

[1]*Kristianiafjord* was not otherwise detained.
[2]*Bratland* was not detained.
[3]Bate, Joe C., RNR, Sub-Lieutenant 1915, Prisoner of War 1916, Lieutenant 1917.

intercepted by a German Submarine and allowed to proceed, after the armed guard had been taken off, as she was spoken in Latitude 39.15´N, Longitude 19.55´W on 2 April (vide *Lloyds Weekly Index* of 19 April) [232].

It might be possible to obtain further information from the British Consul on the ship's arrival at Santos, if the circumstances under which the Armed Guard were captured are not already known.

The Commanding Officer of *Patuca* reports that Lieut. Bate had in his possession a copy of 'Instructions for Boarding Officers and Prize Officers in War-time', dated February 1914, together with Addenda No. 1.

Teutonic was met at a pre-arranged rendezvous, and back signals, etc., received from her. Opportunity was taken to test the Evinrude engine in the boarding boat, which proved quite a success, and I hope the remainder ordered will be supplied as early as possible to the other ships of the Squadron as its use undoubtedly facilitates and quickens boarding.

Teutonic afterwards proceeded to Liverpool to discharge Commodore Robert R.E.R. Benson, C.B., and to embark Commodore John S. Luard.[1] I am sorry to lose the services of Commodore Benson, who has done excellent work.

10. Tuesday, 9 May – The Trawlers *Arley* and *Saxon* were detailed to work temporarily to the north east of the Faeroes until the other Trawlers for duty off the Icelandic Coast were available.

Having met *Virginian* at 4 p.m. I embarked in her and cruised for a couple of hours, during which I inspected the crew at divisions, and went round the Ship.

The crew were well dressed, healthy, and smart looking and the ship most clean and creditable – firemen's quarters being especially good. The gunnery efficiency appears V.G.

11. Wednesday, 10 May – I cruised in *Alsatian* to the north east of the Faeroes, and back to C Patrol. Nothing was seen.

12. Thursday, 11 May – *Ebro* intercepted the Danish Motor Vessel *Annam* in ballast in Latitude 60.50´N, Longitude 2.10´W, bound from Copenhagen to New York. As her Master stated he was calling at Stornoway, and in view of the repeated warnings that have been issued regarding the conveyance of German correspondence, securities etc, in

[1]Luard, John Scott, CB, RN (1865–1936) Lieutenant 1887, Commander 1899, Captain 1905, Commodore 2nd Class in *Teutonic* 1916–1917, *Virginian* 1917, and *Orvieto* 1917, Rear-Admiral (retired) 1917, SNO Falmouth and in command of Area XIV 1917–1919, Vice-Admiral 1920, Admiral 1925.

neutral vessels, I ordered an Armed Guard to be placed on board to take her to Stornoway.[1]

I visited *Almanzora* – crew healthy, smart and well dressed. Gunnery efficiency appears to be V.G. Ship very well kept and most comfortable.

13. Saturday, 13 May – *Almanzora* boarded and sent in to Kirkwall with an Armed Guard the Dutch Steamer *Westerdijk* from New York to Rotterdam, with a general cargo including copper, explosives and grain.[2]

It is worthy of notice that the Masters of the Dutch Steamers *New York* and *Alcor*, intercepted during the course of the day by *Hilary*, both evinced considerable interest as to whether the *Westerdijk* had been met with, but appeared unwilling to give any reasons for doing so.[3]

The Captain of the *Westerdijk* displayed great annoyance at having his wireless room locked and sealed.

14. Sunday, 14 May – The disposition of the Squadron was as follows:

A Patrol ... *Moldavia.*
C Patrol ... *Almanzora, Orotava, Columbella, Andes.*
D Patrol ... *Patuca, Hilary.*
E Patrol ... *Ebro, Patia.*
Joining B from A ... *Gloucestershire.*
Patrolling between A and C ... *Alsatian.*
Rejoining from Swarbacks Minn ... *Motagua.*
Rejoining from Liverpool ... *Orcoma.*
Proceeding to Clyde ... *Hildebrand.*
At Liverpool ... *Teutonic, Victorian, Otway.*
At Clyde ... *Mantua.*
At Swarbacks Minn ... *Changuinola, Virginian.*
At Brest ... *Artois.*

During the week eighty eight vessels (including 34 trawlers) were intercepted and examined, of which 21 were sent in with Armed Guards. This is a considerable increase partly due to Dutch vessels now proceeding Northabout instead of through the Channel, and also to the re-opening of the White Sea.

[1]*Annam* was allowed to go on.

[2]*Westerdijk*'s cargo included some items which were to be sent to the Prize Court; the ship was allowed to go on on the understanding that these items would be returned to Britain (TS 14/9 of 15 and 17 May 1916). Dutch ships were normally routed through the English Channel; this was one of the first to go northabout.

[3]*Alcor*'s cargo was wheat, covered by the Netherlands Overseas Trust; the ship was allowed to continue her voyage (TS 14/9 of 15 and 16 May 1916); *New York*, carrying petroleum, was allowed to go on (TS 14/9 of 15 May 1916).

15. Monday, 15 May – During the forenoon I cruised in *Andes*, re-joining *Alsatian* at noon. *Andes* is in a high state of efficiency. The men are very well dressed and smart in appearance. The ship is clean and well-kept throughout, the firemen's quarters particularly so. The Sick Bay is especially well arranged and commodious. The Gunnery efficiency of the ship is of a high standard. A deflection teacher and spotting table have been improvised on board.

With reference to my Submission No. 204/30 of 20 April, the small number of guns on a broadside, viz: three 6", is very noticeable in a ship of this size, and there appears to be ample room for two additional guns being mounted aft, one on each side.

The magazines are still rough wooden structures, and A.A. mountings have not yet been fitted to the 6 pdr. guns. The alterations approved by Admiralty ... will be taken in hand during the ship's forthcoming visit to her Southern Base.

Columbella placed an Armed Guard on board the Norwegian-American Steamer *Tanafjord* in Latitude 58.26´N, Longitude 11.50´W, bound from New York to Christiania, and sent her in to Kirkwall. Besides a general cargo, she had 374 bags of mails, mostly destined for the enemy.[1]

The Master and crew at first refused to work the ship unless the Admiralty undertook responsibility for her safety, but later on agreed to do so, and she proceeded on her course. This action would appear to be a breach of the agreement made by the Norwegian-American Line ...

At 4 p.m., in Latitude 58.31´N, Longitude 12.45´W, *Orotava* intercepted the Dutch Steamer *Texel* from Baltimore to Rotterdam with a cargo of maize consigned to the Dutch Government. When intercepted, this vessel was steering 120° which the Master explained was necessary in order to make 83°. The Captain of *Orotava* considered that this statement was incorrect, and that the vessel's movements were suspicious. She was sent in to Kirkwall with an Armed Guard.[2]

As *Hilary* now had five Armed Guards away, I directed *Andes* to relieve her as southern ship of D patrol, and ordered *Hilary* to take the northernmost position on C.

The Skipper of the British trawler *Stormcock*, intercepted by *Patuca*, reported the presence of a two-masted sailing yawl acting in a suspicious manner on Helens reef. The area was searched by *Patuca*, but without result.

[1]*Tanafjord*, after inspection, was allowed to go on (TS 14/9 of 18 May 1916).
[2]*Texel* was permitted to continue her voyage (TS 14/9 of 18 May 1916).

The Master of the Danish SS *Godafoss*, boarded by *Gloucestershire* in Latitude 66.26´N, Longitude 15.10´W, reported that the passage to the North of Iceland was now free from ice.[1]

Information was received of the presence of floating mines in Latitude 59.34´N, Longitude 4.20´W and also in 58.46´N, 13.30´W. *Columbella* was ordered to search the latter locality, and picked up a black cask in the neighbourhood the following day; probably this was the object referred to.

16. A report from the officer in charge of the Armed Guard placed on board the Norwegian steamer *Nordanes* on 23 March forms the subject of a separate submission ...[2]

223. *Lieutenant J.M. Coates to Commanding Officer HMS* Patuca

24 April 1916

I have the honour to report that on the 17th March at 6 p.m. in Lat. 57.30´N, Long 16.0´W, I boarded the Danish Schooner *Carl* in charge of an Armed Guard, with instructions from you to proceed to Stornoway with the vessel for examination purposes.

The vessel was bound from Lisbon to Copenhagen with 130 tons of palm cake in bags.

On boarding I asked the Master to steer a course of N 83° E and for Rockall, and on 18th at 8 a.m. Rockall was abeam 2´ distant, on the 19th at 2 p.m. shortened sail as the wind was increasing with a rising sea. At 5 p.m. we hove to under double reefed foresails with easterly gale and heavy sea running. During the 20th, 21st and 22nd we were hove to, strong easterly gale and high sea, on the 23rd the weather moderated slightly, made sail and steered a course E and N. On the 24th St Kilda was abeam about 15´ distant, 8 p.m. Flannan Islands abeam 5´ distant, at which time it fell a flat calm lasting until midnight when wind freshened a little from SW, otherwise we should have drifted ashore on the Islands as the heavy swell was carrying us steadily on to them during the calm. The 25th at 2 a.m. the wind increased to strong S.W. gale with high confused seas, we therefore shortened sail again for fear of losing it. At 8 p.m. the Butt of Lewis was abeam, signalled Armed Trawler *Kordoma* to tow me. He sent Armed Trawler *Bellona* to tow me, at 10 a.m. we

[1] *Godafoss* was sent in for examination, probably to Lerwick; after consultation the Contraband Committee allowed the ship to go on (TS 14/9 of 19 May 1916).

[2] Not located; *Nordanes* was allowed to proceed after a German discovered on board was removed (TS 14/8 of 28 March 1916).

commenced to tow with grass hawser and wire cable, but tow line parted owing to heavy sea; made another attempt to tow with thirty fathoms chain cable $3^1/_3$" and 45 fathoms $2^1/_4$" steel wire, but this parted also the sea and wind by this time having increased to hurricane force making it impossible to tow whatsoever, so I then signalled the trawler to stand by me as long as possible, as we could do nothing and had to lie to under bare poles. The wind and sea by this time had become very dangerous, in fact we fully expected the little schooner to founder with us at any minute as she was absolutely unmanageable by this time and we were being driven steadily to the NE, at 5 p.m. the wind moderated slightly and allowed us to set out double reefed foresail and jib when we tacked ship and stood in for the land again. At 8 p.m. the wind fell light until midnight when it freshened into a strong gale from the NW with a high pyramidal and dangerous sea, with snow squalls. On 26th at 3 a.m. the trawler *Bellona* left us and proceeded to Stornoway, short of coal. At 6 p.m. we managed to sail to within 5 miles of Tiumpin Head, but the wind increasing in force and the sea becoming worse, we had to heave to as it was dangerous to try and steer a course so we were carried away from the land again and at 10 a.m. we were about 15 miles ESE of Tiumpin Head and unable to make Stornoway so we decided to run for Lough Ewe this being the only harbour of refuge we could make as the wind was gradually hauling to the N and NE with heavy snow squalls and following sea. At 2 p.m. arrived off Lough Ewe and was towed into an anchorage by the trawler on guard duty. At 3.40 let go anchor and repaired on shore to report to the S.N.O. there, who communicated with Stornoway and asked them to send a tug to tow the vessel to that port. On the 28th at anchor awaiting the tug's arrival at Lough Ewe.

On the 28th we left Lough Ewe at 10 a.m. in tow of tug *Flying Buzzard* and at 3.30 p.m. arrived off Stornoway Harbour. At 4.40 p.m. we let go anchor inside harbour.[1]

I beg to submit that the three ratings of the Armed Guard and myself be paid hard lying money at full rates from the 17th March to the 26th March inclusive, as the conditions under which we were living were much below those provided in Torpedo Boats of HM's Navy.

The men had only got a very small locker in the bows of the vessel to rest in, and I had to make the best of it in a paint locker, none of us were permitted to wash during the passage owing to shortage of fresh water, and for the greater part of the time we could not do any cooking owing to bad weather.

[1] *Carl* was not detained.

I returned to HM Ship under your command on 8th April at the Southern Base.

224. *Note by Admiral H.T. Oliver*

26 April 1916

Have the grievances which led to the outbreak on board *Teutonic* been remedied? [210].

225. *O. Murray*[1] *to Under Secretary of State Foreign Office*

29 April 1916

... My Lords suggest, subject to the concurrence of Sir Edward Grey, that no further coal facilities should be granted to these ships until the [Norwegian-America] company undertake that their mail steamers shall call at a British port for examination [208, 216, 221].[2]

226. *Admiralty to Vice-Admiral Commanding Tenth Cruiser Squadron*

29 April 1916

With reference to your submission of the 5th instant, No. 178/71 [206], relative to the disappearance of the Norwegian barque *Olivia*, which was sent in for examination on the 14th January last, in charge of an armed guard under Lt A.D. Bennett, RNR, I am commanded by My Lords Commissioners of the Admiralty to acquaint you that they have no further information as to the present whereabouts of the officer and men in question, but that the Foreign Office are being requested to make enquiry of His Majesty's Ministers in Christiania for any further possible news.

[1]Murray, Oswyn A.R. (1873–1936), joined Admiralty 1897, Director of Victualling 1905–1911, Assistant Secretary 1911–1917, Permanent Secretary 1917–1936.

[2]This method became one of the major coercive powers in Britain's blockade armoury: none of the Northern neutrals had coal of their own, and their only alternative European source was Germany; if they bought German coal they were immediately black-listed by Britain; if they wished to go on trading, British coal was their only choice. They could load up with extra coal at US ports, but this reduced cargo space, and many ships did not have spare coal-storing capacity.

227. *Minute by Fourth Sea Lord*[1]

1 May 1916

Complaints were made under two heads, Pay and Victuals [224]. As regards pay it is contemplated to try and establish a flat rate of £7.10s. but whether this will satisfy the men is doubtful. As regards victuals. Any deficiency is a result of faulty organisation on board. The accountant officer and some of the complainants are attending the informal enquiry by D[irector] of V[ictualling] this week. There are many other fleet auxiliaries who provide themselves with enough food and to spare on the same rate of allowance as that complained of by 10 C[ruiser].S[quadron].[2]

228. *J.H. Brooks,*[3] *Director of Victualling, to Fourth Sea Lord*

2 May 1916

With reference to your minute of yesterday, on M 03469 [227], the case which Admiral Tupper mentioned to you was that of the *Gloucestershire*, not the *Teutonic*. He said that when he asked certain lower deck ratings whether they had any complaints some of the men said that they had not enough to eat. As instructed by you I saw today the Captain, Accountant Officer, and afterwards two representative ratings of the Ship's Company, Admiral Tupper himself being present part of the time.

After questioning the Captain and Accountant Officer and looking at menus and ascertaining approximately the quantities issued at the Meals I am satisfied that an ample dietary within reasonable limits is being provided in the *Gloucestershire*. Of the two representative ratings, one a leading signalman said that the Seamen messes told him that sometimes they ran short of meat and certain other food stuffs, and said they (i.e. the Seamen ratings) would prefer to be on the Standard Ration and Messing allowance.

I explained to him that under the system in force in the *Gloucestershire* the men were being victualled at practically 4d a head more than under the Standard Ration and Messing Allowance; that with the articles of Government Provisions at specially cheap prices the

[1]The Fourth Sea Lord was Captain C.F. Lambert.

[2]The following note was added by Admiral H.T. Oliver: 'I should like to be informed of the results of the enquiry and also when this flat rate is decided on'.

[3]Brooks, James Henry, CB, Principal Clerk and Secretary of Department of Victualling Admiralty 1906–1911, Director of Victualling, 1911–1923.

allowance for victualling was practically equivalent to from 1/9d to 2/- a head if they had to get the things for themselves: that there certainly should not be any shortage except by some fault either of the Steward and Cook Staff or of the messes themselves and that the men in point of fact should be very much better off in the way of food than on board an ordinary Battleship.

The other representative, a Fireman who had been in the Navy previously, had not much to say beyond that the Mercantile Firemen did not get as much as they got in the Merchant Service and that sometimes some of the men had to buy food for themselves from the Canteen owing to there being none left for them in their Messes.

Both the representatives were perfectly respectful and after discussing their allegations with them I came to the conclusion that if there was any shortage it was due to some of the younger men taking a good deal more than their share, and that the whole thing was really a matter of arrangement on board ship, there being no real ground for saying that the allowance was insufficient.

The Captain and Accountant Officer also pointed out that if at any time it occurred that any of the Messes did run short there was always a supply in hand in the Galley or elsewhere to make good, and that any such case will be dealt with if represented at the time. The trouble is that in a good many cases the men do not say anything at the time and grumble about it days afterwards when it is too late to put things right.

Although, as I say, I think the present dietary is quite sufficient I am sure that when it has been running longer the Accountant Officer will find it possible to increase the quantities in certain respects especially if the Canteen is given up and Provisions other than Government Provisions purchased specially by the Director of Contracts as is now being done in all Ships starting under the General Mess System.

After explaining the reason for this both the Lower Deck Ratings were in favour of doing away with the Canteen (speaking of themselves only) but it was decided to let it run for one trip more and if then it is desired to give it up the Commanding Officer will notify this to me before the next return to Port.

The case of the *Teutonic* was quite different – The Firemen complained of the change before they had had any experience of it and therefore had nothing to complain of. I can only add that in their case the remarks of the Commodore in paragraph 12 of his letter of 28th March [210] cover the ground.

229. *Captain J.A. Webster to Vice-Admiral Commanding 10th Cruiser Squadron*

HMS *Motagua*, 8 May 1916

***

At about 12.30 p.m. on 30th April, whilst heading N 46 W, zigzagging to the west, a vessel's masts were sighted dead ahead, a considerable distance off. As the bearing was altering to the eastward, I altered course to head the steamer off and on two funnels being sighted from the masthead increased to full speed as I concluded the vessel was the SS *Kristianiafiord.* My course was N 55° E, which I maintained with the bearing constant and the range decreasing. About 2.15 p.m. the vessel appeared to be altering away from me. I was then some eight miles off and hoisted International Signal MN – 'Stop Instantly' at the same time flashing it on the searchlight. No notice was taken of this signal and after a short interval I hoisted International Signal ID – 'Stop or I will fire into you' also flashing it three times on the searchlight, after which I fired a blank at 2.35 p.m. The steamer then altered course about 6 points to starboard and we closed each other.

The Visiting Officer on inspecting the vessel's Log found that the course from 5.00 a.m. to noon had been S 89° E magnetic, but at noon (1.00 p.m. G.M.T.) the course had been altered to N 75° E and the Captain admitted that on sighting smoke he had altered course to the Northward, as it might possibly be a patrol cruiser.

The *Kristianiafiord*'s course S 89° E from noon took her through the Faeroes between Sydero and Sando Islands. The alteration of course to the Northward, made on sighting this ship, took her north of the Faeroes altogether. In any case the vessel was over 30 miles off the track laid down in C.I.O 100/1915 as that to be followed by steamers of the Norwegian-America Line.

The Officer of the Guard, on returning, reported to me that, after the Visiting Officer left the ship another entry was made in the Log – 'Alteration of course 15 degs to port – i.e. N 60° E – at about 1.15 p.m.' He also heard and it seems quite probable, that vessels frequently run between the Faero Is, and that they had photographs of most of the ships of the 10th Cruiser Squaron and in addition charts showing the disposition of the patrols.

This ship was not identified as a cruiser, at first, but on closing the signal yard on the foremast afforded an easy means of identification. I would suggest that it might be advisable to remove the fore yard and replace it by light iron spurs, which would be invisible from a distance and yet give necessary clearance of halyards from the mast.

230. *J.H. Brooks, Director of Victualling, to First Sea Lord*

9 May 1916

Under Owners Victualling, both Officers and Men were messed by the respective companies at overhead rates ranging from Officers 6s 0d to 7s 6d per head per day; the Men 1s 9d to 2s 6d a head per day. There were also special rates for Chief Petty Officers and Petty Officers ranging from 2s 3d to 3s 6d per head per day.

This is obviously an extravagant system and it was decided at the beginning of this year to substitute gradually in the Ships of the 10th Cruiser Squadron, and other Armed Merchant Cruisers commissioning for abroad, a system of Victualling by the Admiralty.

The complete arrangements which involved a good deal of correspondence were finally approved last month; but the change has been gradually introduced in individual Vessels since February.

Under the Admiralty system the Officers are credited with an allowance of 3s 6d a day, and arrange their own Messing as in all other HM Ships. The Men are Messed under the General Mess System, as in force in Naval Barracks and other Shore Establishments, at a rate *not exceeding* 1s 3d a head.

Paragraph 6 of the Vice-Admiral's letter of the 26th April enclosed refers only to the case of the *Gloucestershire*. Since that was written, by the direction of the Fourth Sea Lord I have seen the Captain, and Accountant Officer of the *Gloucestershire* with two representatives of the Ship's Company, the Vice-Admiral Commanding 10th Cruiser Squadron being also present [228] ...

It transpired at the interview that the Accountant Officer of the *Gloucestershire* had been Victualling the Men at about 1s 0d a head instead of working up to the outside limit of 1s 3d, and although I am sure that the food provided by him was ample, I told him he might work up to the 1s 3d and give rather a larger proportion of Meat and Vegetables. At the same time some other Ships are Victualling their Crews at 1s 0d a head I believe quite satisfactorily (see report of *Motagua* enclosed). In considering the sufficiency of the rate of not exceeding 1s 3d it must be remembered that the Government Provisions are drawn at the prices current before the War, and that the actual cost of the articles in the Standard Ration is now more than half as much again. The 1s 3d really represents about 1s 6d to 1s 7d, and I am confident that with the existing arrangement it is ample, and that there is no case at present on which we could go to the Treasury for an increase to 1s 6d in these Ships. They are already being Victualled at about 4d a head more than the Men in HM Ships generally.

***

231. *Vice-Admiral Tupper to the Admiralty*

HMS *Alsatian*, 1 June 1916

Report of Proceedings, 16–31 May 1916

***

1. Tuesday, 16 May.

2. Wednesday, 17 May – *Alsatian* intercepted the Norwegian Barque *Kosmos* from New York to Christiania with a cargo of petroleum coke. She was sent into Lerwick with an Armed Guard ... .[1]

Her Master reported having sighted a floating mine in Latitude 58.50´N, Longitude 19.0´W, at 8 p.m. on the 15th.

In the afternoon I met *Hilary*, and Captain Dean,[2] who had lately assumed command, came on board to call – he had nothing to suggest.

3. Thursday, 18 May – *Moldavia* reported that while patrolling off the South Coast of Iceland, careful enquiries had been made of the Skippers of British trawlers fishing both to the East and West of Portland Light as to whether any traffic was passing along the coast, and all agreed that there was none beyond local trade.

Moldavia intercepted the Norwegian-American Liner *Kristianiafjord* in Latitude 61.25´N, Longitude 3.50´W, bound for New York, and sent her in to Kirkwall with an Armed Guard.[3]

The Master of the Danish SS *Godafoss* having reported that there was now no ice on the north coast of Iceland [205 para. 15] I obtained permission from the Commander-in-Chief to send the *Gloucestershire* and *Ebro* as far as North Cape to ascertain whether the passage was clear.

The Trawlers *Arley* and *Saxon* were met and their Commanding Officers repaired on board. I explained to them their duties etc. Both

[1]*Kosmos* was detained for some time before being allowed to continue (TS 14/9 of 26 May 1916).

[2]Dean, Frederic W., RN, Lieutenant 1889, Commander 1900, Captain of *Hilary* 1916–1917, Captain 1918, retired 1923.

[3]*Kristianiafjord*, despite the recommendation by the Admiralty to tighten the screw on the Norwegian-America Line [208], was permitted to go on. But there was little point in detaining the ship westbound, other than to intercept any enemy mails.

Lieutenant R.J. Mortimer and Sub-Lieutenant Smith[1] seemed intelligent and efficient [224].

4. Friday, 19th May – Fog was experienced all day in the patrol areas.

About 4 p.m. orders were received from the Commander-in-Chief that owing to the submarine threat, Ships were to take up 'The western Patrol'.

Directions – based on orders previously received – were accordingly issued as follows:

> C Patrol – consisting of five ships thirty miles apart on a line 342° from Latitude 57.30´N, Longitude 19 W.
> D Patrol – consisting of three ships also thirty miles apart on a line 318° from Latitude 55 N, Longitude 15 W.
> E Patrol – remained in its former position, to the north of Iceland, while *Alsatian* patrolled to the north of the Faeroes to maintain W/T communication.

The Russian Sailing Vessel *Emma* from Tralee to the White Sea, was boarded by *Columbella* and searched for stowaways as directed. None were found, however, and she was allowed to proceed.

5. Saturday, 20th May – Fog all day.

6. Sunday, 21st May – *Gloucestershire* reported that the passage round the North Coast of Iceland was clear, but loose ice had been met in Latitude 67.19´N, Longitude 22.43´W.

Alsatian, off Faeroe Islands, proceeding to Swarbacks Minn, endeavoured to intercept *Bergensfjord* by means of the W/T Direction Finder. At one time her position seemed to be 40° on our starboard bow and it appeared certain we should catch her, but her signals when next heard were much fainter. She had passed through the western patrols during fog. It was afterwards ascertained that she had called at Kirkwall under orders from her owners, and her Master stated that his Company had decided to order their vessels to call voluntarily at Kirkwall in future when eastward bound.[2]

The disposition of the Squadron at noon was as follows:

[1]Mortimer, Ronald J., DSC, RNR, Lieutenant 1910, Lieutenant-Commander 1918; as to Sub-Lieutenant Smith in *Saxon* in May 1916, it has proved impossible to identify him more clearly.

[2]*Bergensfjord* was not detained.

C Patrol, on line 340° from Latitude 57.30´N, Longitude 19 W ... *Virginian*, *Hilary*, *Orcoma*, *Changuinola*, *Columbella*.
D Patrol, on line 318° from Latitude 55 N, 15 W ... *Andes*, *Motagua*, *Patuca*.
E Patrol, N.E. Iceland ... *Gloucestershire*, *Ebro*.
Patrolling 300° from Latitude 61.40´N, Longitude 10 W to maintain W/T communication ... *Patia*.
Rejoining from Liverpool ... *Otway*.
Proceeding to Swarbacks Minn ... *Alsatian*.
At Liverpool ... *Teutonic*, *Almanzora*, *Victorian*.
At Clyde ... *Hildebrand*, *Mantua*.
At Swarbacks Minn ... *Moldavia*, *Orotava*.
At Brest ... *Artois*.

In the course of the week, eighty vessels, including nineteen fishing craft, were intercepted, of which twenty three were sent in with Armed Guards. During the latter part, the work of the Patrols was somewhat hampered by foggy weather, and by having to take up new positions further west.

7. Monday, 22nd May – At 1 a.m., *Alsatian* arrived and anchored at Swarbacks Minn. HM Torpedo Boat Destroyer *Sprightly* met her off Eshaness, and escorted her to harbour. This appears to me to be a wise precaution, as it materially lessens the chance of submarine attack on entering St Magnus Bay.

As D Patrol was working in the neighbourhood of Latitude 55 N, Longitude 15 W, I arranged for *Patuca* to proceed to Loch Ewe to coal instead of to Swarbacks Minn, in order to shorten the time she would be off patrol, to save coal, and to lessen the danger from submarines.

As a submarine was reported to be coming south from Muckle Flugga, a Torpedo Boat Destroyer and two Trawlers were sent out to look for her – but without result.

8. Tuesday, 23rd May – Information was received that hostile submarines had been sighted off the Faeroes on the 17th and 20th May, possibly searching for the Tenth Cruiser Squadron. Patrols were warned accordingly.

I visited Lerwick and conferred with Commander Hubert G. Alston, Commander Burrard A. Smith, Lieutenant-Colonel Phillips and the Postmaster. I find that so far no orders have been given to connect up Eshaness and Hillswick Lighthouses by telephone from Hillswick Post Office. I submit this is necessary to enable the presence of a submarine to be quickly reported [215 para. 2, 239 para. 2].

9. Wednesday, 24th May – I interviewed the Commanding Officers

of the Trawlers *Arley*, *Saxon*, *Rushcoe*, *Tenby Castle*, *Robert Smith*, *Walpole* now attached to the Tenth Cruiser Squadron, and explained to them their duties and written orders for patrol. It is proposed to employ Trawlers in pairs off the North-East and East of Iceland, and on the South Coast off Portland Light, working in conjunction with ships of the Squadron [232].

I visited Eshaness Light in company with Rear-Admiral Fawckner and Colonel Phillips. The situation is ideal for observing the Bay and approach from the north and west. The ground is suitable for a cable to be laid for telephone, and I submit it would be quicker and cheaper to have cable (similar to the one I laid at St Kilda) than overhead wire.

At 10 p.m. I left Swarbacks Minn in *Alsatian*, to rejoin patrol, escorted by Torpedo Boat Destroyer *Sprightly*.

10. Thursday, 25th May – The Trawlers *Robert Smith* and *Walpole* left Swarbacks Minn with orders to patrol temporarily to the east of the Faeroes on meridian of 60 W between Latitudes 61.30´ and 62.50´N.

At 4 p.m. I met *Columbella* and went on board, cruising in her until 6 p.m. She is fairly clean; ship's company good: general efficiency good but room for improvement.

At 9 p.m. *Patia* intercepted and sent in to Kirkwall with an Armed Guard the Danish Steamer *Oscar II* bound from New York to Copenhagen. She was carrying a general cargo, and 468 passengers, 17 of whom were German or Austrian Women; also 789 bags of letters, including 545 for Germany, in addition to a parcel mail.[1]

Princess left Belfast to join my Flag, as an addition to replace *Alcantara*.

11. Friday, 26th May – Fog and mist. *Rushcoe* and *Tenby Castle* sailed from Swarbacks Minn at noon for E Patrol.

In the course of the afternoon, I met *Otway* and gave her orders to proceed to, and take charge of, E Patrol.

Columbella reports having fired eight rounds at a supposed submarine in Latitude 60.50´N, Longitude 2.21´W, at 8.45 p.m.

12. Saturday, 27th May – *Princess* informed me she had received orders from the Admiralty to return to Belfast and await further instructions.

Alsatian intercepted Danish Auxiliary Steam Sailing Vessel *Fox II* with cargo of cryolite, and sent her to Kirkwall with Armed Guard.[2]

[1]*Oscar II* was allowed to go on after Customs investigation (TS 14/9 of 27 May 1916).
[2]*Fox II* was not detained.

13. Sunday, 28th May – The disposition of the Squadron at noon was as follows:

C Patrol ... *Mantua*, *Patia*, *Orcoma*.
D Patrol ... *Virginian*, *Moldavia*, *Orotava*, *Teutonic*, *Patuca*.
E Patrol ... *Gloucestershire*, *Ebro*.
Patrolling in neighbourhood of Latitude 62 N. Longitude 5 W. to maintain W/T communication ... *Alsatian*.
Patrolling to east of Faroes ... Armed Trawlers *Robert Smith* and *Walpole*.
Joining E from D ... *Otway*.
Joining E ... Armed Trawlers *Rushcoe* and *Tenby Castle*.
Joining from Clyde ... *Hildebrand*.
Proceeding to Clyde ... *Motagua*, *Changuinola*.
At Liverpool ... *Andes*, *Almanzora*.
At Swarbacks Minn ... *Columbella*, *Hilary* and Armed Trawlers *Saxon*, *Arley*.
At Belfast ... *Princess*.
At Brest ... *Artois*.[1]

Fifty-eight vessels, including seven fishing craft, were intercepted during the week, of which fourteen were sent in with Armed Guards for further examination.

14. Monday, 29th May – *Otway* boarded the Danish sailing vessel *J. Lotz* from Halmstad to Akureyri. Her Master reported having sighted a submarine with two guns in Latitude 57.32´N, Longitude 2.49´W, on the 23rd instant, steering 338°.

I met *Hildebrand* in the forenoon, and embarked for Target Practice, which was good. I then despatched her to A Patrol in the neighbourhood of Portland Light, Iceland.

The Senior Naval Officer, Belfast, informed me that *Princess*, which had returned to that port in accordance with Admiralty orders, had been detailed for foreign service. I hope a vessel may shortly be found to replace her, as the Squadron is still three ships short of its nominal strength. At 8 p.m., *Alsatian* intercepted the Danish barque *Ceres*, stated to belong to the Danish Government State Department of Greenland, bound from Greenland to Copenhagen with a cargo of fish oil, salt fish and hides. As these articles are much needed by Germany at the present time, instructions were requested from the Admiralty as to whether she

[1]*Princess* never did join; *Victorian* has apparently been omitted; the patrol (discounting *Artois* and *Arlanza*) is now down to 20 ships and 4 trawlers.

should be sent in. An answer having been received in the affirmative, an Armed Guard was accordingly placed on board, with orders to take her in to port. Her Master energetically protested.[1]

At 11 p.m., the Norwegian steamer *Flora* was intercepted by *Ebro* in Latitude 63.47´N, Longitude 11 W, steering 100° bound from Reykjavik to the Faroes and Bergen, with a general cargo, passengers, and mails for Bergen. Her Master stated he was calling at Lerwick, but in view of the locality, the course he was steering, and the valuable nature of the cargo – which included oil, fish, and wool, I deemed it advisable to place an Armed Guard on board and send her in.[2]

15. Tuesday, 30th May – At 1 a.m., *Patia*, in Latitude 57.44´N, Longitude 19.32´W, reported she was in pursuit of a suspicious steamer, which had altered course on sighting her and was burning no navigation lights.

She eventually proved to be the British steamer *Cannizaro*, from Hull to New York. Her Master stated he had received orders not to burn navigation lights, and to avoid other steamers; he had mistaken *Patia* for a German raider. She was in possession of a Green Customs Clearance and allowed to proceed.

The Captain of *Ebro* informed me that while on E Patrol from 17 April to 4 May, and 13 to 27 May, the visibility experienced was under three miles for 41% of the time in April and for 53% during May – and in May, usually less than one. Fishermen reported that there was no ice within 240 miles to the North and 60 miles to the North-West of Iceland.

16. Wednesday, 31st May – *Alsatian* boarded and sent in the Danish Sailing Vessel *Thorvaldsen*, from Greenland to Copenhagen with a similar cargo to that of *Ceres* referred to in paragraph 14, and also said to be owned by the Danish Government State Department of Greenland. Her Master sent in a written protest.[3]

***

[1] *Ceres*, trading between two Danish ports, was not detained.

[2] *Flora* was detained for some time. A question was raised about the weight of certain items, then the Norwegian government was asked for a guarantee against the re-export of the goods. The ship was still at Lerwick on 7 June, when the Contraband Committee received a telegram pointing this out and saying that the passengers were 'dissatisfied'. Even so, the Committee insisted on the guarantees, which were finally received on the 12th (TS 14/9 of 1 to 12 June 1916 *passim*).

[3] *Thorvaldsen* was detained until the Danish government gave the usual guarantees (TS 14/9 of 12 and 14 June 1916).

232. *Memorandum by Vice-Admiral Tupper*

HMS *Alsatian*, 23 May 1916

Orders for Trawlers attached to Tenth Cruiser Squadron

The following Armed Trawlers have been detailed to work with the Tenth Cruiser Squadron with a view to intercepting contraband trade in Icelandic Waters, though on occasions it may be necessary to use them elsewhere:

Arley *Saxon*	1	*Rushcoe* *Tenby Castle*	2	*Robert Smith* *Walpole*	3

They will work together in pairs as above and be based at Swarbacks Minn.

2. Two pairs, 1 and 3, will work off the east and north coasts of Iceland, in conjunction with two ships of the Tenth Cruiser Squadron, two trawlers always being on patrol.

No. 2 pair will be employed off the south coast of Iceland near Portland Light and will work with a ship of the Tenth Cruiser Squadron for a period of 14 days.

***

9. Attempts are not to be made in any circumstances to intercept shipping inside territorial waters.

233. *Rear-Admiral de Chair*[1] *to Admiralty*

23 May 1916

In connection with the reported evasion of our patrols by passenger ships of the Norwegian America Line the Foreign Office has lately endeavoured to arrange with the Company for the *Bergensfjord* and *Christianiafjord* to make a voluntary call at Kirkwall.

At the request of Lord Robert Cecil[2] I have twice interviewed the

[1]De Chair was now acting as naval adviser to the Minister of Blockade, Lord Robert Cecil (see next note).

[2]Cecil, Lord Edgar Algernon Robert (1864–1958), son of the Marquess of Salisbury, MP 1906–1910 and 1911–1923; Parliamentary Under Secretary of State at the Foreign Office from May 1915 and Minister of Blockade February 1916–July 1918; Assistant Secretary of State for Foreign Affairs 1918, British delegate at the Peace Conference 1918–1919, but resigned January 1919, Viscount Cecil of Chelwood 1923, Lord Privy Seal 1923–1924, Chancellor of the Duchy of Lancaster 1924–1927, President of the League of Nations Union 1923–1945, Nobel Peace Prize 1937.

Company's agent, Mr Andrew Johnsen, and have fully discussed the question with him. At the last interview he informed me that he had received a telegram from his Directors in which they agreed that as a provisional arrangement for the summer months their passenger steamers should call at Kirkwall voluntarily when eastward bound. Mr Johnsen stated that a call at Kirkwall when going west would seriously interfere with the time-table arranged by the Company.

Lord Robert Cecil would be glad to have expression of opinion from the Admiralty as to whether this is considered satisfactory as a tentative arrangement which might go on until such time as the Company can be induced to order their steamers to call voluntarily on both voyages.

Mr Johnsen was given to understand that neither the Government nor the Admiralty could be committed to any definite agreement that the call on the eastward voyage is considered sufficient, but he was told that it might be tried tentatively. At the same time it was pointed out to him that the ships were still liable to be intercepted by patrols and sent into Kirkwall with an armed guard when proceeding to the westward.

During 1915 these ships were frequently intercepted when going west, but in accordance with Admiralty orders they were generally allowed to proceed. Now, however, it will probably be found necessary to send them in for examination for enemy export or improper use of mails.

Mr. Johnsen stated that his Company were willing to terminate their mail contract with the Norwegian Government if so desired, but the point was not pressed as such a proceeding would not do away with the danger of passengers' luggage containing enemy export or the booking of enemy passengers, which would probably result were it spread abroad that any arrangement giving these steamers immunity from search on the western voyage had been come to.

8

TIGHTENING THE BLOCKADE, JUNE–AUGUST 1916

It is no coincidence that the Jutland battle was followed by a careful consideration of the effects of the blockade by the French government [242], by a new look at the Patrol's dispositions [241, 243], and by a deliberate tightening of the whole system [255]. The institution of 'Navicerts', documents detailing cargoes provided at ports of origin after inspection by British officials, was the decisive moment by which the neutrals were enlisted by Britain to administer the blockade [244], and the use of the supply of bunker coal to neutral ships, particularly Scandinavian ships [252], brought the 'blockade-runners' [e.g., 252] and 'evaders' to heel most effectively. All this is clearly a consequence of Jutland, with the renewed confidence it imparted to the Royal Navy and to the British government [249].

It also enabled the Patrol, increased to 22 fully operational ships by the return of *Artois* and the addition of *Orvieto*, to pay increased attention to the relatively minor matter of Icelandic fish supplies, exported by Icelandic and neutral trawlers [257]. The Icelanders were unable to trade freely with Scandinavia and Germany; being neutral they did not feel that their activities were 'illegal', as the British put it. 1916 was the beginning of the adverse effects of the war on all the Scandinavian neutrals – as it was also on all the belligerents. The fuss made over one vessel which penetrated the blockade [263] may be contrasted with the overall success of the Patrol in making interceptions [264].

234. *Vice-Admiral R. Tupper to Admiralty*

HMS *Alsatian*, 8 June 1916

Report of Proceedings, 31 May–4 June 1916

***

1. Wednesday 31 May – At 6 p.m., a signal was received from the Commander-in-Chief directing the Tenth Cruiser Squadron to take up 'Eastern Patrol', on a line 360° from Muckle Flugga.

The following orders were given for ships to take up their new patrol:

Teutonic to join C, take charge of *Mantua* and *Orcoma*, and pass north of the Faroes.

The remaining Ships of D patrol viz: *Orotava*, *Patuca*, *Victorian* and *Moldavia*, together with *Almanzora* – rejoining from Liverpool – to proceed through the Minch and Pentland Firth.

Hildebrand to join *Otway* on E Patrol, North-East of Iceland.

Hilary on leaving Swarbacks Minn that night, to take up a position 40 miles North of Muckle Flugga.

Gloucestershire, on leaving the following night, to take up position 30 miles to the North of *Hilary*.

Alsatian and *Columbella* to proceed north of Faroes and take station to the North of *Gloucestershire*.

Virginian was directed to join up by the Minch–Pentland Firth route as soon as she had completed coaling.

Patia was running short of coal and provisions and was ordered to proceed to Clyde – usual visit.

It was not anticipated that the remaining Ships in harbour would be able to join up for several days.

At 11 p.m. a message was received from the Admiralty to the effect that the raider *Moewe* had sailed from Wilhelmshaven, and the *Independent* was expected to sail from the same port on 1 June.[1]

The Captain of the Armed Trawler *Robert Smith* informed me that he had received information that a large enemy submarine had been frequently calling at Westmanhavn in the Faroes, and had last been seen on 28 May passing through Sydersfjord and off Froldhoved.

2. Thursday 1 June – *Hilary* arrived in position 40 miles to North of Muckle Flugga at 6 a.m.

At 6 p.m. the Commander-in-Chief directed me to assume 'Muckle Flugga Patrol', which provides for a patrol on a line 360° from Muckle Flugga, ships 30 miles apart, nearest Ship 40 from the land; also two ships to the north of the Faroes with a Cruiser and Armed Boarding Steamer between the Faroes and Shetlands Islands [209].

Teutonic and *Mantua* were directed to proceed to the North of Faroes accordingly.

3. Friday, 2 June – By 7 a.m., there were four Ships in position to the

[1]This was a mistaken assumption. No raider sailed at this time; on the other hand, this was the day on which Scheer's High Seas Fleet sortied to challenge the Grand Fleet off Jutland.

North of Muckle Flugga, viz: from South to North – *Hilary*, *Gloucestershire*, *Columbella* and *Alsatian*, the remainder not being due to arrive until 6 a.m, 3 June. The delay was caused by strong Northeasterly wind and sea.

Donegal and *King Orry* were patrolling between the Faroes and the Shetlands, and *Teutonic* and *Mantua* arrived in position to the North of the Faroes.

4. Saturday, 3 June – At 2 a.m. the Commander-in-Chief directed me to transfer the patrol to a line joining a position in Latitude 59.30´N, Longitude 7.30´W, to the Coast of Iceland. Orders were given accordingly.

The Armed Trawlers *Robert Smith* and *Walpole* were ordered to patrol to the West of the Faroes so as to guard the channels between Stromo and Sydero Island.

5. Sunday, 4 June – The disposition of the Squadron at noon was as follows:

Patrolling on line 145° from Latitude 64.10´N Longitude 14.30´W, 30 miles apart – from North to South.	1	*Almanzora*	2	*Orcoma*
	3	*Virginian*	4	*Mantua*
	5	*Alsatian*	6	*Columbella*
	7	*Gloucestershire*	8	*Hilary*
	9	*Victorian*	10	*Patuca*
	11	*Teutonic*	12	*Moldavia*
E patrol, to North East of Iceland	*Otway*, *Hildebrand* and Armed Trawlers *Rushcoe* and *Tenby Castle*.			
Patrolling West of Faroes.	Armed Trawlers *Robert Smith* and *Walpole*.			
Proceeding to Patrol between Latitude 64.30´ and 65´ North on meridian 13 West.	Armed Trawlers *Arley* and *Saxon*.			
At Liverpool.	*Andes*[1]			

[1]The missing ships – *Motagua*, *Orotava*, *Artois*, *Changuinola*, *Ebro*, *Patuca* – were presumably refuelling or travelling to or from one of the bases; note that *Victorian* has reappeared in the list.

235. *Memoirs of Commander B.T. Brewster RN*[1]

The job of boarding these vessels was an unenviable one. The vessel concerned would be ordered to stop, our ship would lower the boarding boat about 1 mile clear of the other ship, order her to close the boarding boat, and then steam away clear (a mile or so) whilst we boarded.

These precautions were very necessary as there was always the possibility that the suspect vessel might turn out to be a disguised German raider (usual armament 6 or 8 x 4.1 inch guns).

... Boarding another ship in open and heavy seas calls for a high degree of skill and seamanship and these Newfoundland seamen were possessed of both.

Life aboard *Virginian* was very rough and tough on account of the prevailing weather conditions, and the fair number of times we had to man the boarding boat, regardless of those conditions, but the ship being a converted merchantman of 5 or 6000 tons, provided a reasonable degree of comfort off watch, and plenty of good plain grub.

236. *Minute by Captain Richard Webb, Director of Trade Division*

1 June 1916

It is considered any understanding with this Company [Norwegian American Line] that their ships need not call at a British port during western voyages is undesirable [224]; it is therefore submitted that the pressure be continued with a view of inducing the Company to instruct their Captains to call in on all voyages, and that the V.A. 10th CS be instructed to intercept these vessels whenever possible.

237. *Commander-in-Chief Home Fleets to Admiralty*

HMS *Iron Duke*, 7 June 1916

***

It would be a matter for satisfaction to all concerned with the blockade if arrangements could be made for information of all cargoes or part cargoes of ships which are dealt with specially by the Prize Courts to be communicated not only to the local Customs but also by their Lordships to me. It is also desirable that this information should be sent to the Vice-Admiral Commanding Orkneys and Shetlands, the Vice-Admiral

[1]Brewster, Basil T., DSC, RNR, Midshipman 1914, Lieutenant (retired) 1919.

Commanding Tenth Cruiser Squadron, and the Rear-Admiral Stornoway.

***

238. *W. Graham Greene*[1] *to Vice-Admiral Commanding Tenth Cruiser Squadron*

8 June 1916

With reference to your letter of 5th April last, No. 178/71 [cf. 206], requesting information as to the whereabouts and disposal of the officers and men comprising the Armed Guard which was placed on board the Norwegian Barque *Olivia* on 14th January I am commanded by My Lords Commissioners of the Admiralty to acquaint you that the owner has had no news of the ship since her disappearance and the *Olivia* has been posted as missing by the Norwegian Veritas.

239. *Vice-Admiral Tupper to Admiralty*

HMS *Alsatian*, 26 June 1916

Report of Proceedings, 8–25 June 1916

***

1. Thursday, 8 June – There still being no news regarding the Raiders which were expected to attempt to escape, I shaped course for Swarbacks Minn, and arrived off Eshaness at 11 p.m. *Donegal* was met coming out and I ordered Torpedo Boat Destroyer *Sprightly*, which was escorting me in, to proceed in company with *Donegal* until well clear of the land.

I arrived at Swarbacks Minn shortly after midnight.

2. Friday, 9th June – Coaling commenced at 7 a.m.

Otway reported drift ice in the neighbourhood of Latitude 67.12´N, Longitude 23.15´W, moving towards the north-east, and ice-fields extending 238° from Latitude 67.28´N, Longitude 24.12´W. Patrol was arranged so as to block the passage between the ice and the land.

I received in news by the newspapers that His Majesty had been graciously pleased to confer on me the honour of a CB and most

[1]Greene, William Grahame, KCB (1857–1950), Private Secretary to the First Lord 1887–1902, Principal Clerk 1902–1907, Assistant Secretary 1907–1911, Permanent Secretary of the Admiralty 1911–1917, and at the Ministry of Munitions 1917–1920.

respectfully wish to express my gratitude at being considered worthy of this honour.

I proceeded to Lerwick, where I met Commander Hubert G. Alston, Commander Burrard A. Smith and Lieut. Colonel Phillips and conferred with them on various matters. I was glad to see the information that orders had been received to connect Eshaness and Hillswick by telephone at once to post office, and to establish a look-out hut at Eshaness [231 para. 8].

3. Saturday, 10th June – *Alsatian* finished coaling at noon, having taken in 1500 tons.

As a report had been received from the British Trawler *Andromache* that Swedish Fishing smacks had been seen acting suspiciously in the neighbourhood of Lat. 60.50´N, Long. 2.10´W, and Lat. 60 N, Long. 4 W, I directed the Armed Trawlers *Robert Smith* and *Walpole* to proceed to these positions and to examine the vessels.

Having embarked armed guards for five ships of the Squadron I proceeded to sea in *Alsatian* at 10.30 p.m. At 11.15 p.m. *Otway* was met in St Magnus Bay approaching the harbour.

4. Sunday, 11th June – In accordance with orders from the Commander-in-Chief, Ships were directed to resume the Iceland–Rockall Patrol, disposed on a line 340° from Lat. 56.35´N, Long. 11.30´W, as follows:

D Patrol ... 3 Ships 30 miles apart from Lat. 56.35´N.
C Patrol ... 5 Ships 30 miles apart from Lat. 58.6´N.
A Patrol ... 2 Ships 30 miles apart from Lat. 62.50´N.

The disposition of the Squadron at Noon was as follows:

Proceeding to A Patrol ... *Virginian*, *Almanzora*, with Armed Trawlers *Saxon* and *Arley*.
Proceeding to C Patrol ... *Motagua*, *Hilary*, *Gloucestershire*, *Columbella*, *Teutonic*.
Proceeding to D Patrol ... *Orotava*, *Moldavia*, and *Victorian*.
E Patrol, Off North Cape, Iceland ... *Andes* and *Hildebrand*
Working between A and C ... *Alsatian*.
Working between Faroes and Shetland ... Armed Trawlers *Robert Smith* and *Walpole*.
Proceeding to Swarbacks Minn ... *Orcoma*, *Mantua*, Armed Trawlers *Rushcoe* and *Tenby Castle*.
At Liverpool ... *Artois*.
At Clyde ... Patuca, *Changuinola*, *Ebro* and *Patia*.
At Swarbacks Minn ... *Otway*.

During the week 73 vessels, including 30 Fishing craft, were intercepted, of which 17 were sent in for further examination.

At 4 p.m. I met *Moldavia* and had an interview with Commander Adrian H. Smyth. Part of the Armed Guards were discharged to her for distribution, the remainder being put on board *Hilary* at 9.30 p.m. *Alsatian* then proceeded to her position on patrol.

5. Monday, 12th June – During the forenoon I met *Teutonic* and went on board to witness target practice, which was well carried out. Fire was opened at 5800 yards 15 seconds after the order was given. The control was good and salvoes accurate. Break downs, steering from after position, and collision mat were exercised. I further looked into the arrangements for repairing leaks, dealing with fires, and attending wounded. All were considered satisfactory. At noon I returned to *Alsatian*, which had been cruising at a distance of 6 miles during the interval.

The Skipper of the British Trawler *Phoebe*, boarded by *Gloucestershire*, reported having sighted about 7th June a trawler, flying Danish colours, painted grey with a yacht bow and two tall masts, acting suspiciously off the south east coast of Iceland. Fishing No. TG 9 (other figure not obtained.) Nothing more has since been heard of this vessel.[1]

Misty and foggy weather came on.

Ordinary W/T communication was ordered to be resumed for important signals; less important messages to be reserved for transmission until important signals had been sent.

6. Tuesday, 13th June – Fog continued all day. Only two vessels were intercepted.

7. Wednesday, 14th June – Fog and mist all day. *Moldavia* proceeded to Loch Ewe to coal. *Artois* sailed from Liverpool to rejoin my Flag. This ship has been absent from patrol since 1st May.

Virginian was met at 11 a.m., the meeting being effected by means of the W/T Direction Finder. Both ships had been working by D.R. for forty eight hours. After interview with Captain H. Smith, I dispatched *Virginian* to Liverpool with mails.

8. Thursday, 15th June – Fog and mist all day. At 7.15 a.m. *Alsatian* intercepted the British SS *Eriner* from Brest to Archangel with munitions, aeroplanes, and motorcars. Her Master stated he had thrown overboard the confidential Admiralty Instructions regarding the route, and had endeavoured to escape in the fog, fearing *Alsatian* was an enemy raider.

[1] 'TG' will refer to Trangisvaag, Faeroes.

Submarines were reported in the Minch and off Cape Wrath.

9. Friday, 16th June – Clear weather. *Alsatian* intercepted a Danish Schooner and Norwegian Barque during the day. Both bound to America and all correct. Also British SS with munitions for Archangel.

Submarine reported near Butt of Lewis.

10. Saturday, 17th June – *Motagua* boarded the Danish SS *Hellig Olaf* from New York to Christiansund with passengers and a general cargo. She was sent in to Kirkwall in accordance with orders from the Commander-in-Chief – Signal 2225 of 15 June.[1]

In the forenoon I met *Artois*, saw *Capitaine de Fregate* Paul de Marguerye, and gave him orders to proceed to Reykjavik with a letter for the British Consul at that Port, which had been forwarded to me under cover of Admiralty Letter M. of 26 May 1916.

Whilst cruising with *Artois* intercepted Norwegian SS *Fram* with grain. Sent her into Kirkwall with armed guard from *Artois*.[2] *Artois* after leaving Reykjavik was directed to cruise off west and north coasts of Iceland.

11. Sunday, 18th June – The disposition of the Squadron was as follows: Ships from South to North:

A Patrol ... *Orcoma*, *Almanzora*, and Armed Trawlers *Saxon* and *Arley*.
C Patrol ... *Motagua*, *Otway*, *Changuinola*, *Hilary*, *Mantua*.
D Patrol ... *Columbella* and *Victorian*.
E Patrol ... *Andes* and *Ebro*.
Patrolling between A and C ... *Alsatian*.
Proceeding to Reykjavik ... *Artois*.
Joining C from D ... *Patia*.
Joining C from Loch Ewe ... *Moldavia*.
Proceeding to Swarbacks Minn ... *Hildebrand*.
At Liverpool ... *Virginian*.
At Clyde ... *Patuca* and *Gloucestershire*.
At Swarbacks Minn ... *Teutonic* and Armed Trawlers *Robert Smith*, *Rushcoe*, *Walpole* and *Tenby Castle*.
At Loch Ewe ... *Orotava*.

During the week 50 vessels, including 6 Fishing craft, were intercepted, of which 16 were sent in with Armed Guards.

[1] *Hellig Olaf* was not detained (TS 14/9 of 19 June 1916).

[2] *Fram* was inspected – the cargo was wheat – and allowed to go on (TS 14/9 of 20 June 1916).

A good deal of fog was experienced throughout the week which considerably interfered with the work of the Squadron.

I went round the mess-decks and sleeping quarters of *Alsatian* and also inspected the ship's company at Divisions. The ship is clean and well kept. The men are well-dressed, smart looking and well drilled. Considerable care has been taken with the firemen and I was specially pleased with their appearance and the cleanliness of their quarters. Everything is done to make the Petty Officers and men comfortable. The Marine Detachment is very good. The general state of the ship and her gunnery efficiency reflects great credit on Captain G. Trewby, Commander Kiddle[1] and the other Officers.

12. Monday, 19th June – Misty weather. *Artois* at Reykjavik informed me she had received information that the Danish Motor Schooner *Pampa* was due to leave Westmann Island on the 20th for Bergen with 700 casks of cod oil. A Patrol off the south coast of Iceland was accordingly warned to look out for her, and two Trawlers were ordered to cruise in that neighbourhood outside territorial waters.[2]

In the forenoon, I met *Hilary*, and saw her Captain, who reports that his guns shoot wildly. I ordered him to test and correct his gun sights, and will witness his Target Practice in July.

Exchanged signals with *Moldavia*.

13. Tuesday, 20th June – Strong NNW wind, and considerable sea.

Exchanged positions with various ships that had many Armed Guards away.

A message was received from the Admiralty stating that a Motor Vessel, name not known, was reported to have sailed on 7 June from New York with 6,000 tons of cocoa, and would attempt to evade the Patrols by proceeding via the North of Iceland.

14. Wednesday, 21st June – Mist and fog.

Armed Trawlers *Rushcoe* and *Tenby Castle* left Swarbacks Minn with orders to cruise to the west of the Faeroes, and *Robert Smith* and *Walpole* to relieve *Saxon* and *Arley* off the south coast of Iceland.

Norwegian Steamer *Are* was intercepted with salt and casks from Fleetwood for Iceland. A quantity of salt is going to Iceland, and I was

[1]Trewby, George, CMG, DSO, RN (1874–1953), Commander 1907, Captain 1913, Captain of *Alsatian* and Flag-Captain to Rear-Admiral Tenth Cruiser Squadron 1916, Captain of *Egmont* (Malta base) September 1918, Rear-Admiral (retired) 1923, Vice-Admiral 1928.

Kiddle, John, RN, Lieutenant 1898, Lieutenant-Commander (retired) 1911, Captain (retired) 1918, at Mercantile Movements Division, Admiralty 1919.

[2]There is no sign that *Pampa* was intercepted.

under the impression it was desired to stop the import of salt in order to limit fish curing and prevent any Icelandic fish reaching Germany. I have sent in some vessels to Lerwick with salt from Spain for Iceland. Definite instructions as to salt cargoes for Iceland would be useful.[1]

15. Thursday, 22nd June – *Artois* having visited Reykjavik and delivered Armed Guards to *Andes* off North Cape, joined A Patrol to the south of Iceland.

Received mails from *Teutonic*, and gave Commodore instructions regarding the conduct of Patrol during my absence.

During the afternoon, I cruised in *Patia*, and witnessed Target Practice, which was poor. I am taking steps to improve it, and propose that the Lieutenant (G) on my Staff shall embark for a cruise in *Patia* to assist in re-organising and instructing the Officers and men in shooting.

16. Friday, 23rd June – The British Steamer *Lowther Range* reported having passed a supposed mine in Latitude 58.26´N, Longitude 15.2´W, at 6.45 a.m. *Moldavia* was ordered to search the neighbourhood, but found nothing. Probably it was a cask or fisherman's float.

Exercised collision mat, etc., on board *Alsatian*, which was well done.

Reported to Commander-in-Chief I proposed to leave Patrol to take *Alsatian* to dock.

17. Saturday, 24 June – At 11.30 p.m. I turned over the command of the Patrol to Commodore Luard of *Teutonic* and proceeded to Liverpool.

18. Sunday, 25 June – Arrived off Bar, Liverpool, at 7.30 p.m.

19. As *Bergensfjord* called at Kirkwall on 9th June west bound, and *Kristianiafjord* on 12th June east bound, without being sent in by the Patrols, it appears that these vessels have now received orders from their Owners to call at a British Port both on inward and outward voyages.[2]

***

[1] *Are* does not appear to have been sent in; if she was, she was not detained.
[2] Neither ship was detained.

240. *Commodore John Luce,*[1] *East Coast of South America, to Admiralty*

HMS *Glasgow*, 12 June 1916

In confirmation of my telegram No. 48 of 28th May 1916 I have the honour to report that on 28th May the Norwegian barque *Pestalozzi* was intercepted in latitude 35.35´S, longitude 55.18´W, by HMS *Glasgow* and detained in accordance with Admiralty orders.

2. Four ratings from HMS *Patuca* were found on board and were transferred to HMS *Glasgow*, while an armed guard from that ship was sent on board the *Pestalozzi*. I examined the ratings from HMS *Patuca* in turn and from their evidence it appears that after being detained by HMS *Patuca* on 13th March and ordered to proceed to Stornoway, the *Pestalozzi* fell in with north-easterly gales which prevented her making that port and on 23rd March, was stopped by the German submarine *U.28* in latitude 58.18´N, longitude 12.0´W. The master was ordered to proceed on board, bringing with him the ship's papers. There he was forced to disclose the fact that he had on board a British armed guard, and the officer in charge, Sub-Lieutenant J.C. Bate, RNR, and afterwards the remainder of the guard were sent for. The German Commander made prisoners of the officer and Leading Seaman Harry Salter, RNR, took possession of all arms and ammunition and sent the remainder of the guard back to the *Pestalozzi*, giving the master a certificate to the effect that he had taken prisoner the Officer and the Leading Seaman, and ordering him to proceed on his voyage to Santa Fe and there hand over to the German Consul the remaining four of the armed guard. The original certificate I obtained from the master and it is now forwarded together with a translation. No one from the submarine was on board the *Pestalozzi* at any time. Four trips were made between the *Pestalozzi* and the submarine and in making three trips three of the four boats which the barque possessed were either swamped or stove in and had to be abandoned. For this reason the crew refused to proceed anywhere but Santa Fe, for which port they were cleared. It seems that they feared a second attack when they had no boats.[2]

3. During the voyage to the River Plate they met a British steamer, name unknown, whom they stopped and asked to take them back to

[1]Luce, John M.R., CB, RN, Lieutenant 1893, Captain 1907, Commodore 2nd Class 1916, Rear-Admiral 1920.

[2]*Pestalozzi* was intercepted by *U 28*; Sub-Lieutenant Bate had been reported as a prisoner-of-war in May [222 para. 9].

England, but the steamer proceeded when she found they were unable to come on board in their own boat. Later they fell in with the British barque *Elginshire* who was unable to take them on board owing to shortage of provisions.

4. I also questioned the master of the *Pestalozzi* and his story coincided in the main points with that given by the ratings from the *Patuca*. He had had his last ship sunk by a German submarine and, after being told by the officer in command of the submarine that the *Pestalozzi* would be sunk without warning if he found her making for a British port, he was evidently afraid to make the attempt having only one boat left. He attributes his misfortunes to the fact that the officer in charge of the armed guard insisted on his proceeding to Stornoway and would not allow him to make for a North Irish port, such as Londonderry, which he could have reached with a fair wind in a few hours.

5. All the ship's papers were in order as reported in my telegram No. 85 of 29th May, and as far as examination could disclose the cargo corresponded to the manifests.

6. On 3rd June the *Pestalozzi* was released in accordance with Admiralty telegram No. 173 and proceeded on her voyage.

241. *Vice-Admiral Commanding Tenth Cruiser Squadron to Commander-in-Chief Home Fleets*

13 June 1916

I have the honour to submit a tracing showing what appears to me, after 4 months' experience, to be the best normal positions for ships of the 10th Cruiser Squadron on patrol.

In these positions the ships are:

(1) In a good position to intercept raiders attempting either to escape to the trade routes or return to Germany.
(2) Comparatively near the northern coaling base, thus saving coal in going there and back.
(3) In a good position for rapidly taking up the positions ordered in Secret Fleet Order No. 14 when a Naval Action is imminent, or for assuming 'Muckle Flugga Patrol' [218].
(4) In easy touch with the Commander in Chief by W/T.
(5) In good positions for intercepting trading vessels on the ordinary routes from the West and from Iceland, and also those which are attempting to evade the Patrol. By placing two vessels south of Rockall the Admiral can utilise these for intercepting or chasing any

vessel that may have broken through the Patrol during the dark or thick weather.

(6) The trawlers of the West Coast of the Faeroes can give early notice of suspicious vessels sheltering or passing through that group; and the Trawlers off the south coast of Iceland can watch Seydisfjord as well.

The two ships stationed off the north west point of Iceland should be able to intercept any Raider or trading vessel proceeding round the north coast.

(7) It is suggested that the different Patrol Lines should be called as follows:

Muckle Flugga Patrol .... Patrol line 1.
The suggested Normal Patrol .... Patrol Line 2.
Rockall–Iceland Patrol .... Patrol Line 3.
Western Patrol .... Patrol Line 4.

It would then only be necessary to have a signal in Grand Fleet Code for 'Take up Patrol Line indicated' followed by a numeral.

It is undoubtedly useful to vary the position of the Patrol Line from time to time and also to vary the Patrol by slightly altering the angle of crossing the Patrol Line.

242. *Summary of the views of the French Foreign Office*

17 June 1916

Effect of 14 months' Blockade on Enemy Trade

After the first disorganisation caused by the war our enemies recovered themselves, and since the beginning of 1915, the trade of the neutral countries adjacent to Germany was developed to such an extent that it more than counter-balanced the direct trade which Germany had lost.

The enemy is actively engaged in smuggling and often eluded our agents abroad. But nothing can enter Germany except through her neutral neighbours, and that, even if the existing international laws have very often prevented us from stopping suspect goods, the English cruisers have none the less taken their toll of them, and the total is far from corresponding to the enemy's requirements.

On the other hand, we must not forget that the Allies were the enemy's greatest sources of supply. In particular, he obtained from Russia enormous quantities of grain and fodder, which cannot be replaced by imports from Northern countries.

The countries adjacent to Germany have no doubt greatly developed their industries, since Germany buys all their products at a good price, but their powers are small, and they cannot provide everything that Germany used to import from abroad.

There is a shortage of cotton, wool, manure, fats, etc., and, most serious of all, of manures containing nitrogen and phosphates. This causes meagre harvests, for German soil is poor, and requires a large quantity of chemical manure.

Germany will have difficulty in making up the shortage of cereals, if the deficit created by a poor harvest is added to the deficit produced by the shortage of her imports. Germany and Austria used to import annually nearly 6 million tons of various kinds of cereals, and produced about 48 million tons.

In addition to the absence of fodder from Russia, and the oil-cake, of which nearly 800,000 tons used to be imported, there is a bad harvest of straw, and of the fodders which cannot be grown without nitrogenous manures. Thus there will be a decline in livestock, or rather, the animals will waste away; in any case the production of meat, fats, butter and milk will decrease considerably. In a normal year Germany and Austria produce nearly 1,200 tons of butter and animal fats of all kinds, for a total consumption of 1,640,000 tons.

The few cargoes of contraband which get through will not succeed in covering these enormous deficits, particularly now that the principle of rationing the neutrals is admitted.

The enemy's foreign trade in imports from the USA has decreased by at least 60%, and the increased imports from Brazil and the Argentine by no means compensates for this enormous diminution, which is becoming more marked.

During the first months of the war German trade undoubtedly found very important outlets through Switzerland and Italy, but since the entrance of Italy into the war, this door has gradually closed, and we may say that it is now shut.

The export of agricultural produce from the neutral countries surrounding Germany has increased to a large extent, but does not compensate for all that the Central Empires used to receive from the Allies, who alone took 30% of their foreign trade.

If we examine the German exports, the same results are apparent. While the Allied markets were almost entirely closed to enemy products, in the course of the third quarter of 1915 the monthly flow of exports from the group formed by the Central Empires and the Northern neutrals to the three great American Republics had fallen from 185 million francs to about 25 million.

The decline in the German exchange, which is becoming more marked in spite of all efforts to prevent it, the detailed regulations which our enemies continually formulate in order to ward off the internal crisis, which daily becomes more serious, supports our conclusions. A stricter blockade and more energetic restrictive measures might have hastened considerably Germany's economic downfall; but the diplomacy of the Allies was faced by innumerable difficulties.

It was impossible for them to disregard the international laws, of which they had constituted themselves the defenders, and it was only as a reply to the illegal measures adopted by Germany that France and England were led to issue the Order in Council of 11th March 1915, followed by the Decree of 13th March 1915, which permitted the seizure of enemy goods carried by vessels flying a neutral flag, whatever their destination. Taken earlier this measure would have turned the neutrals, jealous of their independence, against the Allies, and would have risked throwing them into the arms of our enemies – whilst, then revolted by Germany's barbarous conduct, they were forced to recognise that this defensive measure was legitimate.

The same argument applies to the rationing of the neutrals, who at first rejected it as an infringement of their sovereignty, but who have now practically all accepted it as a relief from the hindrance which the war has inevitably placed in the way of their commerce.

Thanks to these measures which ration all contiguous neutrals except Sweden, the total quantity of the foodstuffs which can enter or leave Germany is very little indeed, and in any case, even including smuggled goods, the enormous shortage in the enemy's supply of cereals and fats cannot be made up. Sweden though maintaining a sulky attitude towards the Allies, does her best to observe neutrality, and, apart from her agricultural produce, she re-exports comparatively little contraband food to our enemies.

With regard to metals and sulphuric acid, the Germans, though deficient for industrial purposes, yet have all they need for military use, and we cannot effectively cut off their supplies of these products, so long as Sweden continues to provide them with iron ore, and Norway with pyrites, and they still hold the Briey region.

Financially our enemies show the same traces of exhaustion, and we have recently learnt that the sum total of Danish coupons presented for payment to German accounts had decreased by half, the bonds having been sold. Here again the fall in the exchange shows that Germany's investments abroad are at a low ebb.

To sum up, after 14 months of war, we see that the imports of the group formed by the Northern neutrals and the Central Empires have been reduced by more than 60%, and the exports of the same group by still more.

Thanks to accumulated stocks and precautionary measures, the enemy lived without excessive privation for the first year. But these stocks are exhausted, stricter vigilance is being exercised, agreements made with the neutrals enable us to withhold the foodstuffs of which our enemies are most in need and we may hope that the time is approaching when inconvenience will become privation and privation famine.

The German Government knows this; the treasures anticipated from the East have proved illusory, and the fierce attacks which Germany has launched against us at Verdun are undoubtedly undertaken for the sole purpose of breaking the ring of iron which encircles her, before it is too late. We cannot close this report without rendering to the Navy, and above all to the English Navy, the homage which is its due.[1]

243. *Commander-in-Chief Home Fleets to Vice-Admiral Commanding Tenth Cruiser Squadron*

20 June 1916

The arrangements for the normal patrol of the ships of the 10th Cruiser Squadron made in your submission of 13th June [241] are approved generally, but the following modifications are suggested.

2. The line-ahead Patrol A fairly covers the ground now that there is no night; a thin line abreast patrol is preferable however when there is any considerable dark period.

3. When more than 13 ships are available A Patrol should be strengthened and C Patrol brought within 40 miles of the Flannan Islands.

The D patrol line would cover more ground if inclined at 80° and 260° instead of 50° and 230°.

4. Your suggestions to number the patrol lines 1 to 4 is approved. The order to assume patrol line 4 will be accompanied by a longitude on which the patrol is to be centred.

5. You are to vary at your discretion both the position and inclination of the patrol lines, informing me of any material change.

[1]This is a hard-headed assessment of the position. The emphasis on the lack of fats and fodder is notable, for this was clearly the main cause of the food shortage Germany later suffered; cf. A. Offer, *The First World War, an Agrarian Interpretation* (Oxford, 1989), part 1.

244. *Contraband Committee Minutes*

20 June 1916

... [T]he Committee considered that the time had fully come when they should begin to take notice of cargoes from the United States to Scandinavia that were not covered by letters of assurance from the Trade Department at Washington. They suggest, therefore, that a telegram should be sent to His Majesty's Ministers at Christiania, Stockholm and Copenhagen informing them that the Navicert Scheme may now be considered to have become definitely established. Hitherto His Majesty's Government have not discriminated against cargoes not covered by Navicerts, but they feel that the time has come for them to detain or hold up for enquiries cargoes from the United States which are not covered by Navicerts, with the object of compelling as many people as possible to submit their booking to us in advance ...[1]

245. *Vice-Admiral Tupper to Admiralty*

HMS *Alsatian*, 16 July 1916

Report of Proceedings, 25 June–15 July 1916

***

1. Sunday, 25 June – The disposition of the Squadron at noon was as follows:

B Patrol ... *Artois*, *Orcoma* and Armed Trawlers *Robert Smith* and *Walpole*.
C Patrol ... *Patia*, *Mantua*, *Changuinola*, *Hildebrand*, *Teutonic*.
D Patrol ... *Orotava*, *Columbella*.
E Patrol ... *Andes*, *Ebro*.
Faeroe Island Patrol ... Armed Trawlers *Rushcoe* and *Tenby Castle*.
Proceeding to join E ... *Patuca*.
Proceeding to Liverpool ... *Alsatian*, *Otway*.
Proceeding to Clyde ... *Moldavia*.
Proceeding to Swarbacks Minn ... *Almanzora*, Armed Trawlers *Arley*, *Saxon*.
At Liverpool ... *Virginian*.

[1]This is provoked by the case of the Swedish ship *Hellenic*, whose cargo had been announced to the Committee and which included antimony and aluminium. A Navicert would have prevented the loading of these items in the first place. The ship was ordered to be sent in – see [245 para. 6] and page 465, note 2.

At Clyde ... *Gloucestershire*, *Hilary*.
At Swarbacks Minn ... *Victorian*, *Motagua*.

Eighty two vessels, including 26 fishing craft, were intercepted and examined during the course of the week, of which 20 were sent in with Armed Guards.

Alsatian arrived off Liverpool at 7.30 p.m.

2. Monday, 26 June – In the course of the forenoon, I visited *Virginian*, which was being rearmed with 6" guns. I ascertained that it had been decided to place two of these in the fore well deck of the Ship, where owing to weather usually experienced on patrol they would be of little use except in the finest weather. I represented this at the Admiralty, and obtained permission for them to be mounted in a more suitable position.

Patuca (having relieved *Andes* on E Patrol) reported that new field ice had closed passage round North Cape. E Patrol formed to the southwards of Lat. 66.35´N, Long. 23.14´W.

No less than 26 vessels were intercepted during the day, six of which were sent in with Armed Guards.

3. Tuesday, 27 June – I attended at Buckingham Palace with Captain Trewby and other Officers from *Alsatian* for the honour of being decorated by His Majesty.

Andes relieved *Teutonic* at 6 a.m. as Northern Ship of C Patrol, and *Teutonic* resumed cruising between A and C Patrols.

The weather remained fine, with good visibility, and a large number of ships were again boarded.

4. Wednesday, 28 June – At 9 a.m. Lat. 62.57´N, Long 14.15´W *Artois*, Southern Ship of A Patrol, reported that she had been chasing at thirteen knots the smoke of a westbound steamer since 7.30 a.m.

She was directed to follow the vessel at full speed, *Teutonic* from the south, and *Orcoma* from the north, steering at high speed to intercept her. The course of the suspicious vessel was about 230°.

The chase continued all day, the *Artois* being able to keep in touch but not to gain. At 7 p.m. *Orcoma* sighted the chase in Lat. 61.43´N, Long. 18.40´W, and reported the vessel as a steamer with two masts and two funnels at a distance of about sixteen miles.

Necessary directions were given to *Orcoma* in case the vessel was considered suspicious and at 11 p.m. – *Teutonic* then being in Lat. 60.34´N, 18.25´W – the vessel stopped and was boarded by *Orcoma*. She was the Russian steamer *Czar*, from Archangel to New York, in ballast, with 145 passengers. She was directed to proceed and ships returned to their patrols.

In the forenoon the *Nascopie*, bound from Archangel to Brest, called up the Senior Officer, Tenth Cruiser Squadron, by W/T in code, and asked route to Brest. She was directed to keep a hundred miles to westward of Ireland until in Lat. 48 North, Long. 10 West, and then proceed direct.

5. Thursday, 29 June – *Teutonic* took northern Ship on C Patrol, which was now reduced to four ships, while D Patrol was temporarily discontinued.

Andes intercepted and sent Swedish Steamer *Stockholm* to Kirkwall with an Armed Guard. This vessel was carrying, besides 737 passengers, a large number of enemy and neutral mails and a general cargo.[1]

6. Friday, 30 June – *Artois* left A Patrol for Swarbacks Minn, reducing A Patrol to one Ship. *Gloucestershire* sailed from Clyde and was directed temporarily to D Patrol.

Mantua, on passage to Swarbacks Minn, placed an Armed Guard on board the Swedish Steamer *Hellenic*, New York to Goteburg, with a general cargo. This vessel was ordered to be sent in by Admiralty W/T message 2120 of 28 June, and had evaded C Patrol.[2]

Victorian intercepted and sent to Kirkwall with Armed Guard, Danish Steamer *United States*, New York to Christiania. This vessel had a general cargo, and was carrying 464 passengers of whom 19 were Germans, also enemy and neutral parcel and letter mails.[3]

7. Saturday, 1 July – In the afternoon *Victorian* reported intercepting *Kristianiafjord*, which had been cleared from Kirkwall the previous day. This vessel refused to answer signals or hoist the Flag of the Day, until *Victorian* opened fire. A separate report is being forwarded regarding this incident [250].

8. Sunday, 2 July – As the Northern Ship of C Patrol had intercepted no shipping during the week, orders were given for the southern position to be moved to Lat. 56.6´N, Long. 12.30´W. The line of Patrol was at the same time extended slightly to the east as the area was probably becoming known to merchant ships.

At noon, the disposition of the Squadron was as follows:

[1]*Stockholm* was not detained beyond the minimum.

[2]It was the case of *Hellenic* which provoked the Contraband Committee to issue the ultimatum summarised in [244] insisting on Navicerts. This system was the beginning of the end for the Northern Patrol, since a Navicert necessarily meant there was no point in intercepting a vessel, unless there was a suspicion of 'fraud'.

[3]*United States* was not held up.

A Patrol ... *Hildebrand*, Armed Trawlers *Robert Smith*, *Walpole*.
C Patrol ... *Andes*, *Victorian*, *Motagua*, *Almanzora*, *Teutonic*.
D Patrol ... *Gloucestershire*.
E Patrol ... *Ebro*, *Patuca*.
Faeroe Islands Patrol ... Armed Trawlers *Rushcoe*, *Tenby Castle*.
Joining E from Swarbacks Minn ... *Patia*.
Proceeding to Liverpool ... *Orcoma*.
At Liverpool ... *Alsatian*, *Otway*, *Virginian*.
At Clyde ... *Columbella*, *Hilary*, *Moldavia*, *Orotava*.
At Swarbacks Minn ... *Artois*, *Changuinola*, *Mantua*, Armed Trawlers *Arley* and *Saxon*.

Eighty nine vessels (including thirty four fishing vessels) were intercepted and examined during the course of the week, of which twenty five were sent in with Armed Guards.

Seven ships were sent in during the day, including the *Bergensfjord* and *Drammensfjord* (Eastbound) and Swedish Steamer *Varing* ordered to be sent in by Admiralty telegram of 25 June.[1]

9. Monday, 3 July – *Hilary* was directed to relieve *Gloucestershire* on D Patrol, and this Ship, after meeting *Victorian* on following day and transferring an appendicitis case for hospital treatment, was ordered to relieve *Ebro* on E Patrol.

10. Tuesday, 4 July – Information was received from the Commander-in-Chief Grand Fleet, that submarines, possibly laying mines, might pass Fair Isle from the Eastward any time after 4 a.m. the following day, or Muckle Flugga six hours later. Orders were, therefore, given for C Patrol to move sixty miles to the westward, assuming the new positions next day.[2]

Teutonic left C Patrol and proceeded to Swarbacks Minn to coal.

11. Thursday, 6 July – Considerable W/T interference was experienced by *Teutonic* from Auxiliary Patrol Vessels and continuous communication with Ships on Patrol could not be maintained. *Almanzora* was, therefore, directed to patrol on 10th meridian west between Lat. 59.30´N and Lat. 60.30´N to act as a W/T link for Senior Officer, Tenth Cruiser Squadron.

Hildebrand suggested altering disposition of A Patrol to line ahead 205° from Lat. 63.41´N, Long. 13.56´W, ships being forty miles apart,

[1] *Varig* (correct name) and *Bergensfjord* were not detained; *Drammensfjord* was examined and allowed to go on (TS 14/10 of 4 July 1916).

[2] *U 75* was in fact busy laying mines at the time, and on 5 July one of them sank the cruiser *Hampshire*, with Lord Kitchener on board, off the Orkneys.

patrolling sixty miles. Trawlers to patrol to the north of this line ten miles apart. This was approved as a temporary measure with a view to intercepting Dutch fishing vessels with cargoes for Holland.

The Commander-in-Chief informed me there were indications of submarines becoming more active, and that it would probably be necessary to move the Patrols to the westward.

12. Saturday, 8 July – *Hildebrand* was directed to resume the former line abreast formation on A Patrol. The Armed Trawlers *Robert Smith* and *Walpole* left A Patrol at 8 a.m. for Swarbacks Minn.

13. Sunday, 9 July – Information was received from the Captain of the *Hildebrand* that the Officer in charge of the Armed Guard placed on board the Dutch Trawler *Eveline*, IJM 15 (sent to Lerwick with Armed Guard, 2 July) had ascertained each barrel of cod liver fetched between £8 and £9 on arrival at Ymuiden, and that they were bought for transmission to Germany.[1]

At noon the disposition of the Squadron was as follows:

A Patrol ... *Hildebrand*, *Artois*, Armed Trawlers *Arley*, *Saxon*.
C Patrol ... *Victorian*, *Mantua*, *Motagua*, *Changuinola*, *Almanzora*.
D Patrol ... *Moldavia*, *Hilary*.
E Patrol ... *Gloucestershire*, *Patia*.
Faeroe Island Patrol ... Armed Trawlers *Rushcoe*, *Tenby Castle*.
Between A and C Patrols ... *Teutonic*.
Proceeding to Swarbacks Minn ... *Ebro*, Armed Trawlers *Robert Smith*, *Walpole*.
Joining D Patrol from Swarbacks Minn ... *Andes*.
Rejoining Patrol to relieve *Teutonic* ... *Otway*.
At Swarbacks Minn ... *Patuca*.
At Liverpool ... *Alsatian*, *Orcoma*, *Virginian*.
At Clyde ... *Columbella*, *Orotava*.

112 Ships (including 40 Fishing vessels) were intercepted and examined during the week of which 27 were sent in with Armed Guards.

This very large number may be accounted for by the continued fine and clear weather as well as the fishing season being at its height. Nevertheless, with fewer ships than usual available for Control, the figures are very remarkable.

[1]*Eveline* was one of 27 neutral fishing vessels which were sent in about this time by various patrols. It was decided that their cargoes were believed to be destined for Germany, and they were all made prize. It is clear that suspicion alone was enough for condemnation, proof was not required (TS 14/9 of 15 June 1916).

At 10 p.m. *Teutonic* met *Otway* in Lat. 60.20´N, Long. 13.0´W, and Commodore Edward L. Booty, M.V.O., assumed charge of the Tenth Cruiser Squadron on patrol, *Teutonic* proceeding to Liverpool.

14. Monday, 10 July – The Norwegian Steamer *Flora* was intercepted by Armed Trawler *Saxon* in Latitude 63.20´N, Long. 18.40´W, bound from Reykjavik to Bergen, via Seidisfjord, other Icelandic Ports, and the Faroe Islands. Her cargo consisted of fish and fish oil for Bergen, and passengers for island ports. Commodore Booty reports that, although on 26 February last this Ship was allowed to proceed when on a similar voyage on the distinct understanding that she called at Lerwick, in view of Admiralty message 2345 of 23 June, he did not think he was justified in again allowing her to do so, and sent her to Lerwick with an Armed Guard.[1]

Almanzora reported that an operation for appendicitis was being performed on Midshipman Marshall, RNR, and in the afternoon his condition was extremely critical. The Admiralty was informed to this effect.

As *Alsatian* was delayed by defects in the Engine Room Department, and could not be ready to sail until p.m. on the 15th, I enquired from the Commander-in-Chief whether I should proceed in *Columbella* leaving Glasgow the following day. To this I received an answer in the affirmative, and at the same time the Commander-in-Chief informed me that an enemy Raider of the *Moewe* type might be expected to attempt to pass through the patrols at any time after daylight on the 12th instant.

I proceeded to Glasgow accordingly and embarked in *Columbella* the following morning.

15. Tuesday, 11 July – *Columbella* being somewhat delayed I did not get to sea until the evening.

In the meantime in order to be in a better position to intercept the raider, I directed Ships to assume Patrol Line No. 2, steering 325° from Latitude 59.40´N, Longitude 7.50´W, to the Coast of Iceland, two ships being maintained to the north west of Iceland and two to the south of Rockall. W/T Silence was ordered to be maintained.

16. Wednesday, 12 July – I relieved Commodore Booty in *Otway*, and resumed command of the patrol.

At 5 p.m. *Columbella* boarded the Swedish Steamer *Roxen*, bound

[1]The complicated destinations of *Flora* caused confusion, but the cargo was ordered to be prize-courted; the ship was then only permitted to go on to Iceland if the Norwegian government guaranteed that the cargo to be collected in Icelandic ports would not be discharged in Norway without a further guarantee against re-export (TS 14/9 of 14 to 29 June 1916 *passim*).

from Goteborg to Cape Town. Her Master stated that it had been his intention to call at Kirkwall, but when off Auskerry on 11 July he was closed and hailed by a Torpedo Boat marked G.47 who, after enquiring his destination and asking some further questions, ordered him to proceed to Cape Town, without boarding him. As the Ship had a general cargo – which was partly consigned 'to order' – and a deck cargo of timber, I sent her in to Buncrana for further examination.[1]

In accordance with previous arrangements, *Patia*, on being relieved on E Patrol, was directed to proceed to Reykjavik to embark the British Vice-Consul and take him to Siglufiord, afterwards proceeding to Swarbacks Minn. This has since been done, the Vice-Consul (Mr Olsen) being saluted with 7 guns on landing at Siglufjord to impress the Natives. The herring fishing is commencing there, and a large number of craft are assembling for the purpose.

17. Thursday, 13 July – I took the opportunity of witnessing target practice by *Columbella* – the firing was good.

At 11.20 p.m. a message was received from *Hildebrand* reporting that the Danish Sailing Vessel *Hossana*, intercepted by *Saxon*, had sighted a submarine in Latitude 64.40´N, Longitude 12.38´W, and that the presence of the submarine had been confirmed by fishermen in the vicinity. I reported this to the Commander-in-Chief, at the same time moving B Patrol 30 miles to the westward.

18. Friday, 14 July – *Columbella* intercepted the Danish Government Vessel *Hans Egede* with cargo of oil and skins from Greenland to Copenhagen. I directed her to be sent in to Lerwick with an Armed Guard. The Captain stated that he wished to call at Thorshavn, but the only reason that he gave for wishing to do so was to enable him to send a telegram. The wife of the Governor of Greenland was on board this vessel. The Captain sent me a written protest … .[2]

As no news had been received regarding the Raider, I obtained permission from the Commander-in-Chief to resume normal patrol the following day.

19. Saturday, 15 July – The weather, which had been misty during the past few days, now became very thick.

Alsatian having returned to Patrol, I arranged a rendezvous and transferred my Flag. This meeting was effected by means of the Direction Finder installed in *Alsatian*, which once again proved its

[1] *Roxen* was not detained.

[2] *Hans Egede* became hostage for problems concerning three other ships; in the end the Danish government gave guarantees covering Greenland products and the ship was released (TS 14/10 of 17 and 27 July 1916).

value, neither ships having had sights for over 24 hours owing to the fog and misty weather. The meeting was delayed some three hours.

As *Almanzora* reported it was considered essential that fresh milk should be obtained for Midshipman Marshall to enable him to recover after the operation for appendicitis, she was directed to proceed to Loch Ewe and land him.

20. During the period of my stay in harbour before embarking in *Columbella*, I took the opportunity of visiting the Admiralty and Foreign Office to discuss matters in connection with the work of the Tenth Cruiser Squadron, and transact other business.

I also visited Poplar and went round the *Orvieto*, which is fitting out for service in the Squadron.

On 5 July, I went down to Roehampton with Major Macworth,[1] of the Royal Flying Corps, from whom I received much valuable information as to the working of Kite Balloons. I ascended in one of these to a height of about 1000 feet, and also witnessed trials in towing the latest pattern experimental Balloon for work afloat. I consider that such a Balloon would be of great value if fitted in one of the Ships of the Squadron, as there are not sufficient Ships to adequately patrol the space between Iceland and the Hebrides. At present intervals amounting to some 120 miles have to be left open in the line where it is thought that little traffic is passing, but of course it is through these gaps that vessels attempting to evade the blockade have a chance of getting through. It is there that Kite Balloons would be of great use for, at any rate, seven months in the year. Recent experience has shewn that the working of Kite Balloons in mercantile vessels does not require any great amount of structural alteration in these Ships. A flat uninterrupted space 90' by 30' with moveable wind screens would suffice, if plant for making and storing hydrogen is carried.

On 7 July, I proceeded to Glasgow and in company with Captain Brian H.F. Barttelot, M.V.O.,[2] the Captain Superintendent, inspected the

[1]Mackworth, J.D., CBE, RFC, Major RFC 1917, Lieutenant Colonel RAF 1918, Deputy Director of Kite Balloons 1919, retired 1919. Tupper's investigation of balloon capabilities was perhaps the result of a conference at the Admiralty on 20 June, where, as Jellicoe summarised its conclusions, '... arrangements were in progress for supplying kite balloons to two ships of the 10th Cruiser Squadron' (*Jellicoe Papers*, II, 23). In fact they never were supplied, no doubt because, on reflection, weather conditions in the North Atlantic were thought unsuitable.

[2]Barttelott, Brian Herbert Fairbairn, KBE, CB, MVO, RN (1867–1942), Commander 1901, Captain 1906, SNO Clyde District 1914–1917, in command of HMS *Resolution* 1917–1918, Rear-Admiral 1918, Admiral Superintendent in Malta 1918–1921, Vice-Admiral (retired) 1923, Director of Dockyards and Repairs 1923–1928, Admiral (retired) 1927.

alterations being carried out to the magazines of *Moldavia*, *Orotava*, and *Columbella*.

While at Portsmouth, I visited the Gunnery School at Whale Island in order to obtain information on gunnery matters connected with the squadron, especially regarding the use of 6" Q.F. and B.L. guns against aircraft.

***

246. *W. Grahame Greene to Commander-in-Chief Home Fleets*

Admiralty, 29 June 1916

... [A]rrangements are being made for the compilation of a weekly return showing the decisions of the Contraband Committee in regard to all ships which are dealt with by the Committee and that copies of these returns will be forwarded to the following officers)[1]:

The Commander-in-Chief, Home Fleets (4 copies).

The Vice-Admiral Commanding Orkneys and Shetlands (2 copies).

The Vice-Admiral Commanding Tenth Cruiser Squadron (24 copies).

The Rear-Admiral Stornoway (1 copy).

The Senior Naval Officer Ramsgate (1 copy).

This return will include the following particulars in regard to the vessels mentioned therein.

1. Name.
2. Nationality.
3. Date before Committee.
4. Port of Examination.
5. Declaration.
6. Cargo.
7. Remarks stating action taken.

2. I am at the same time to refer to the general question of the policy which is being followed for the purpose of exerting economic pressure upon Germany, and to state that it would appear to Their Lordships that some misapprehension exists as to the exact character and scope of the measures which have been adopted in pursuance of that policy. It would appear that doubts are entertained as to the effectiveness of restrictions which permit the passage of a number of neutral vessels through the areas patrolled by HM Ships, and that the assumption exists that such

[1]This is in response to the request by the Commander-in-Chief on 7 June [237].

permission amounts to acquiescence in breaches of blockade, which could be altogether prevented by arresting and detaining all vessels bound for neutral countries contiguous to Germany.

3. I am to point out, however, that, for geographical and other reasons, no blockade of Germany in the strict and technical sense of the term has been declared, and that consequently under existing circumstances there can be no question of vessels breaking the blockade. The measures which have been adopted aim at achieving a result similar that intended by a regular blockade by restricting as far as possible the importation of commodities into Germany through the conclusion of agreements and the development of the rationing system in the adjacent neutral countries, and as regards direct maritime pressure, through the provisions of the Order-in-Council of the 11th March 1915 and the extension of belligerent rights of visit and search and the principles relating to contraband.

4. It is clear, therefore, that it would be impossible and undesirable under the existing procedures to detain every vessel bound for a neutral port which is encountered by HM Ships, as though a strict blockade were in force, and that the present policy, so far as neutral countries are concerned, necessarily involves granting them certain facilities for the importation of goods required for their own home consumption in return for the arrangements which they have accepted for restricting the exportation of commodities to Germany.

247. *W. Grahame Greene to Under Secretary of State Foreign Office*

30 June 1916

With reference to the letter from Rear-Admiral Sir Dudley R. de Chair of the 23rd ultimo [233], relative to a suggested provisional arrangement with the Directors of the Norwegian-America Line, whereby, during the summer months, their passenger steamers shall call at Kirkwall voluntarily, when eastward bound, I am commanded by My Lords Commissioners of the Admiralty to acquaint you for the information of the Minister of Blockade that they consider that any understanding with this Company that their ships shall be exempted from calling at a British port during the voyage westwards is undesirable, and that in their opinion pressure should continue to be brought to bear upon the company with a view to inducing the Directors to call at a British port on all voyages. In conformity with this command Their Lordships have issued instructions to the Commander-in-Chief Home Fleets and the Vice-Admiral Commanding Tenth Cruiser

Squadron that the vessels belonging to this line are to be intercepted whenever possible.

248. *W. Grahame Greene to Vice-Admiral Commanding Tenth Cruiser Squadron*

Admiralty, 1 July 1916

... I am commanded by My Lords Commissioners of the Admiralty to acquaint you that they consider that it is desirable that pressure be brought to bear upon this Company to induce them to issue instructions to the Captains of their vessels to call at Kirkwall on all voyages, and you are accordingly to intercept the SS *Kristianiafjord* and *Bergensfjord* whenever possible.

249. *Commander-in-Chief Home Fleets to Admiralty*

HMS *Iron Duke*, 1 July 1916

Be pleased to represent to the Lords Commissioners of the Admiralty that advantage should be taken of the effect on neutrals of the recent action [i.e., the battle of Jutland] to render the blockade more stringent than it has been made hitherto.

2. In my view, the object at which we should aim is to prevent, as far as we are able, commodities of all kinds from reaching or leaving Germany, as laid down in Order-in-Council of 11th March, 1915. I am of course aware that there is a danger of driving neutral powers, upon whom we are dependent for many necessities, into allying themselves with the enemy if this policy is fully carried out. This contingency would not seem, however, to be more remote than before, and, as the present is the time when the effect of this policy upon the power of endurance of the enemy should be most marked, I venture to urge its acceptance.

3. The great difficulties that have been faced, the opposition that has been overcome and the valuable results that have been achieved by diplomatic means, more especially in the matter of rationing of the neutral States through whom the enemy draws his supplies, are most fully recognised by me. It must not be supposed, therefore, that I lose sight of this when I venture to indicate the direction in which it appears that action, above all if taken at this time, would have the most far-reaching effects.

4. For convenience of reference the more important points which I have represented from time to time with a view to increasing the efficiency of the blockade are enumerated below:

(a) Ration not only commodities of which the enemy is in need, but all those capable of use as substitutes or alternatives, as well as their products and the raw materials from which they are derived.
(b) Reduce rations drastically to a minimum and provide for their further reduction when affected by reduced exports, reduced home consumption or other such contingencies.
(c) Take into consideration, when rationing an article, any supplies available in the form of by-products from other commodities.
(d) Abandon the policy of allowing storage of goods in neutral countries until the end of the war.

250. *Commander F.H. Walter to Vice-Admiral Commanding Tenth Cruiser Squadron*

HMS *Victorian*, 2 July 1916

***

1. A large and fast ship, with two funnels, was sighted about 3.30 p.m. on 1st July, bearing Green 50° and speed was increased to cut her off. The ship was then about ten miles off, but weather was misty with light showers of fine drizzle, and ship was repeatedly lost sight of. She looked somewhat like *Mantua*.

2. At 4 p.m., I hoisted International EC, 'What ship is that', range being about 3000 yards. I increased to Extra Full Speed as the stranger was steaming very fast. I also blew a long blast on my syren, and shortly after fired a blank charge (which the Captain admitted he heard). By this time I was able to make out her name and hoisted MV as she was steaming faster than I was.

3. No notice was taken of my signals and I then fired a shot across her bows, when she stopped, and two minutes after hoisted the wrong flag of the day. This was hauled down and the correct flag was then hoisted. I then closed her and dropped my boat with the Boarding Officer.

4. I instructed the Boarding Officer to inform the Captain he was to obey signals without any unnecessary delay, and that had he shown the correct flag of the day on sighting me half-an-hour previously he would not have had to stop or ease down at all; as it was he was delayed possibly half-an-hour.

5. As there were no less than 1000 passengers and crew on board I think it was a very good object lesson to Neutrals that we still hold command of the sea.

6. The Red Pendant was not used as I did not intend to board,

believing her to be the ship denoted, and I knew SS *Kristianiafjord* was expected. The Captain's excuse was that his orders were to take no notice of signals unless accompanied by the Red Pendant.

7. If this is the correct procedure it is respectfully submitted that HF 0020/323 of 13.3.16 should be amended accordingly. I have intercepted five ships since the order came into force, without once using the Red Pendant which, according to Notice to Mariners No 555 of 23.5.16 is only for special boarding procedure.

8. It is submitted that *Kristianiafjord* has been a blockade runner since the Tenth Cruiser Squadron was instituted.

251. *Vice-Admiral Tenth Cruiser Squadron to Senior Naval Officer Swarbacks Minn*

7 July 1916

In view of Confidential Admiralty Interim Order No. 916 of 1916, it has been found necessary to revise the present arrangements by which coal and fresh provision requirements of ships of the squadron about to visit the Northern Base are reported by W/T.

Orders are accordingly being issued ... that in future ships are not to communicate this information until after arrival in harbour, and in order to facilitate coal arrangements, a list showing the approximate coal requirements of each ship of the squadron visiting the Northern Base is enclosed.

252. *Sir Maurice de Bunsen*[1] *to Admiralty*

Foreign Office, 11 July 1916

As a result of the subsequent negotiations the Directors of the Norwegian-American Line have now notified their intention of complying with our request that these vessels should call regularly at a British port on their outward as well as their homeward voyages and in this understanding the Coal Exports Committee have been requested to resume the former practice of granting general licences for the export of the coal required for the bunkering of their vessels to Norway.

[1]De Bunsen, Sir Maurice William Earnest, PC, GCMG, GCVO, CB (1852–1932), Assistant Under Secretary of State at the Foreign Office 1915–1918; he had had postings to Washington, Berne, Madrid, Paris, Lisbon, Tokyo, Bangkok, Constantinople, as Minister to Lisbon 1905–1906, Ambassador to Madrid 1906–1913 and Vienna 1913–1914; retired 1918.

253. *Vice-Admiral Tupper to Admiralty*

HMS *Alsatian*, 30 July 1916

Report of Proceedings, 16–29 July 1916

***

1. Sunday, 16 July – Misty weather.

Almanzora arrived at Loch Ewe at 11 a.m., landed her patient, and sailed at 2 p.m.

During the forenoon, I met *Otway* and received a report from Commodore Booty for the period during which he was in charge of the Patrol.

At noon, the disposition of the Squadron was as follows:

A Patrol ... *Patia*, *Otway*, *Artois*.
B Patrol (Off SE Coast of Iceland) ... *Patuca*, Armed Trawlers *Arley* and *Saxon*.
C Patrol ... *Moldavia*, *Columbella*, *Ebro*, *Andes*, *Alsatian*.
D Patrol ... *Orotava*, *Mantua*.
E Patrol (Off North Cape Iceland) ... *Hilary*, *Gloucestershire*.
Joining A Patrol from Swarbacks Minn ... *Motagua*.
Joining D Patrol from Loch Ewe ... *Almanzora*.
Joining E Patrol from D ... *Orcoma*.
Proceeding to Clyde ... *Hildebrand*.
Proceeding to Swarbacks Minn ... *Changuinola*.
At Liverpool ... *Teutonic*, *Victorian*, *Virginian*.
At Swarbacks Minn ... Armed Trawlers *Rushcoe*, *Tenby Castle*, *Robert Smith*, *Walpole*.

During the course of the week, 78 vessels – including 26 Fishing Craft – were intercepted, of which 22 were sent in with Armed Guards.

At 4 p.m., I met *Patia*, and Commander Bowring came on board. *Patia* has lately been stationed on the Iceland Patrol, and recently conveyed the British Vice-Consul – Mr Olsen – from Reykjavik to Siglufiord ... The *Edith* referred to on page 2 appears to have escaped the vigilance of the Patrol, who had been specially warned to look out for her.[1]

2. Monday, 17 July – Misty weather.

At 10 a.m., I met *Orcoma*, and in an interview with Commander Coppinger,[2] who has lately assumed Command, explained to him his

[1]Note also the case of *Pampa* at page 455, note 2 above.

[2]Coppinger, Robert Henry, CBE, RN (1877–1967), Lieutenant 1898, Commander 1910, Captain 1916, Captain of *Orcoma* 1916, Rear-Admiral (retired) 1927.

duties, and my views on various matters in connection therewith. On parting company, I gave him orders to join E Patrol and relieve *Gloucestershire*, who was now due to proceed to Swarbacks Minn for coal.

Patuca having reported that Surgeon-Probationer Henry Morrison[1] was suffering from appendicitis, and that, though an immediate operation was not necessary, it was considered very desirable that he should be landed at an early opportunity, I arranged for him to be transferred to *Patia*, and directed that Ship to land him at Stornoway, on her way to Swarbacks Minn.

3. Tuesday, 18 July – *Artois* boarded the Roumanian Steamer *Jiul*, Bordeaux to Archangel, with ammunition for the Roumanian Government. Her Master reported that another vessel of the same Company was due to leave in few days on a similar mission.

During the afternoon, I cruised in *Artois* and witnessed Target Practice, which was good. The system adopted was similar to that used in the British Navy, viz. – 'salvo' firing until hitting was established, then 'controlled independent'. The first salvo was fired from the starboard guns, 48 seconds after the order 'commence', the second salvo 56 seconds later, and the third salvo after a further interval of 56 seconds. 'Controlled independent' was then ordered. The range at the commencement 5900 yards.

The port guns did somewhat better, fire being opened 48 seconds after order 'commence', and the second salvo 42 seconds later. 'Controlled independent' was then ordered.

After the second salvo in each case, the target was straddled, and this was maintained.

This is the first occasion on which *Artois* had fired her guns since commissioning, though I had on several occasions urged her Captain to do so. He seemed pleased with the results, and said he could now meet a Raider with confidence.

Patia arrived off Stornoway at 7 p.m., and having landed Mr Morrison, proceeded to Swarbacks Minn.

With a view to varying the position of the patrols, I obtained permission from the Commander-in-Chief to take up the Iceland–Rockall Line, and the necessary orders were given for Ships to assume their new stations.

[1]Morrison, Henry, RN, Surgeon Sub-Lieutenant 1916, Surgeon-Lieutenant 1918.

Mines were reported off Skerryvore in the neighbourhood of Lat. 56 8´N, Long. 7 W.

4. Wednesday, 19 July – Fog generally.

I gave orders for E Patrol to move to the neighbourhood of Langanaes, so as to be in a better position for intercepting the fishing trade from the westward.

Ebro intercepted the Norwegian Steamship *Imo* chartered by the Belgian Relief Commission from Portland, USA to Rotterdam, with wheat. She was sent in with an Armed Guard … .[1]

The Armed Trawlers *Tenby Castle* and *Rushcoe* left Swarbacks Minn at noon to cruise to the west of the Faeroes, and *Robert Smith* and *Walpole* to relieve *Arley* and *Saxon* off the south east coast of Iceland.

5. Thursday, 20 July – Fog generally.

As *Columbella* had now six Armed Guards away, I directed her to exchange position on patrol with *Ebro*.

6. Friday, 21 July – Fog was again prevalent.

Arley and *Saxon*, having been relieved by *Robert Smith* and *Walpole*, returned to Swarbacks Minn.

7. Saturday, 22 July – Fog in morning.

At noon, I met *Andes* with the help of the W/T Direction Finder. All satisfactory on board. Despatched her to Liverpool to dock.

In the evening, *Motagua* was met. I have recommended Captain Webster to apply for an additional 25 boys, as he appears short handed, and at present has only two on board. All is satisfactory.

8. Sunday, 23 July – At 8 a.m. *Ebro* intercepted and sent in to Kirkwall the Norwegian-American Liner *Kristianiafjord*, from New York to Bergen. She was carrying a general cargo, including foodstuffs, letter and parcel mails, and had on board 648 passengers.[2]

At 9 p.m. I met *Patia*, rejoining patrol from Swarbacks Minn, and gave her directions to relieve *Hilary* in charge of E Patrol.

The disposition of the Squadron at noon was as follows: Ships on patrol being in order from south to north:

A Patrol ... *Alsatian*, *Otway*.

B Patrol ... *Changuinola* and Armed Trawlers *Robert Smith* and *Walpole* (Off SE of Iceland).

[1] *Imo* was not detained.

[2] *Kristianiafjord* was not detained.

C Patrol ... *Patuca*, *Ebro*, *Motagua*, *Columbella*.
D Patrol ... *Orotava* (South of Rockall).
E Patrol ... *Hilary*, *Orcoma* (Off Langanaes, Iceland).
Faeroe Islands Patrol ... Armed Trawlers *Rushcoe* and *Tenby Castle* (Off West Coast).
Rejoining from Swarbacks Minn ... *Patia*.
Proceeding to Liverpool ... *Andes*.
Proceeding to Swarbacks Minn ... *Moldavia*, Armed Trawlers *Arley* and *Saxon*.
At Liverpool ... *Teutonic*, *Virginian*, *Victorian*, *Almanzora*.
At Clyde ... *Mantua*, *Hildebrand*.
At Swarbacks Minn ... *Gloucestershire*, *Artois*.

69 Vessels – including 20 Fishing Craft – were intercepted during the course of the week, of which 15 were sent in with Armed Guards.

I consider the reduction in the number of vessels intercepted is due to the fog experienced.

9. Monday, 24 July – With the Commander-in-Chief's approval C Patrol was moved to the longitude of 10° W, Ships patrolling at a distance of 30 miles apart across a line stretching 360° from Lat. 58.50´N.

10. Tuesday, 25 July – Dense fog prevailed almost throughout the entire day, only three vessels being intercepted by the Patrols.

The Commander-in-Chief informed me that *Campania* would be available to carry out experiments with a kite balloon between the Faeroes and Shetlands on 28 & 29 July, but this had to be postponed owing to engine defects developing in *Campania*. It is proposed that *Alsatian* should attend these experiments when they take place.

11. Wednesday, 26 July – Fog during the day with clear intervals.

Alsatian intercepted and sent into Lerwick with an Armed Guard a small Swedish Steamer *Solve* returning to Gothenburg from Reykjavik with a cargo of salt cod. The Commander-in-Chief had informed me on 29 June that this vessel had sailed from Trondhjem with German coal or salt for Iceland.[1]

Alsatian also intercepted the Sailing Vessel *Amor*, with salt for Iceland, with green clearance from Stornoway.[2]

Patia sighted the Swedish Steamer *William* (207 tons), which is on

[1]*Solve* was on the British Black List, but in view of the agreement made with Iceland on 28 June the vessel was allowed to go on (TS 14/10 of 29 July and 3 August 1916).

[2]*Amor* had given guarantees through Consul Cable (TS 14/10).

the Admiralty Black List, but as she was in territorial waters, it was not possible to board her. She eventually put in to Oeefiord (Iceland).

12. Thursday, 27 July – During the forenoon, *Alsatian* intercepted the French Steamer *Melbourne* and the British Steamers *Benue* and *Dorothy* referred to in Admiralty Message 1207 of 19 July in approximately Latitude 62 N, Longitude 11.30´W, bound for Brest with Russian Troops. The Admiralty were informed of the fact by W/T. The Russian Troops cheered on proceeding.

Orcoma intercepted the Norwegian Steamer *Jokul* from Haugesund to Iceland, with 80 tons of coal as ballast, for which her Master produced a Certificate guaranteeing its use visé by the British Consul. It is noticed that this vessel is shewn in the Admiralty 'Ships' White List' as being confined to one or other of the 'approved trades'.

The Commanding Officer of the *Patia*, who called in at Siglefiord, reported that the Vice-Consul at that Port had informed him that a very large trade was now being carried on in fish oil, and many ruses were being adopted to avoid the Icelandic laws regarding its export ...

I am sending two Trawlers as soon as possible to assist the vessels stationed on E Patrol in dealing with the fish and oil trade from Iceland.

13. Friday, 28 July – Fog in afternoon and evening.

I met *Orotava* at 5 a.m. in order to transfer Armed Guards, afterwards sending her in to Swarbacks Minn to coal.

The Senior Naval Officer, Liverpool, informed me that the anticipated date of completion of *Virginian* is 19 August. This Ship has been absent from Patrol since 16 June for the purpose of being re-armed with 6" guns, which appears to be an abnormally long period.

14. Saturday, 29 July – *Gloucestershire* was despatched to relieve *Patia* on E Patrol, the latter being then ordered to proceed to Clyde via the West Coast of Ireland.

15. During the week, a large number of small vessels have been intercepted with cargoes of salt, barrels, etc, for Iceland ...

***

254. *Vice-Admiral Tupper to Admiralty*

HMS *Alsatian*, 16 August 1916

Report of Proceedings, 30 July–15 August 1916

***

1. Sunday, 30th July – *Patia* boarded and sent in to Lerwick with an Armed Guard the Swedish Steamer *Helge*, which is included in the Admiralty 'Ship Black List' ... Her cargo consisted of 2848 barrels of herrings.[1]

The disposition of the Squadron at noon was as follows:

A Patrol ... *Changuinola.*
B Patrol ... *Hildebrand*, *Robert Smith*, *Walpole* (Off SE of Iceland).
C Patrol ... *Victorian*, *Ebro*, *Otway*, *Moldavia.*
D Patrol ... *Mantua*, *Artois* (South of Rockall).
E Patrol ... *Gloucestershire*, *Orcoma* (NE of Iceland).
Off West of Faeroes ... Armed Trawlers *Rushcoe* and *Tenby Castle.*
Rejoining Patrol from Swarbacks Minn ... *Columbella.*
Joining from London ... *Orvieto.*
Proceeding to Clyde ... *Motagua*, *Patia* (latter via West of Iceland).
Proceeding to Swarbacks Minn ... *Alsatian.*
At Liverpool ... *Andes*, *Almanzora*, *Virginian*, *Teutonic.*
At Swarbacks Minn ... *Orotava*, *Hilary*, Armed Trawlers *Saxon* and *Arley.*
At Loch Ewe ... *Patuca.*

98 vessels (including 37 Fishing Craft) were intercepted by the Patrol during the course of the week, 19 of which were sent in with Armed Guards. Fog was experienced on three days out of the seven.

2. Monday, 31st July – I arrived at Swarbacks Minn in *Alsatian* at 2 a.m. and anchored.

I visited Lerwick and conferred with Commander Hubert G. Alston and Commander Burrard A. Smith. I find that the Hulk *John*, which had been sent in by *Saxon*, with a cargo of salt and coal, the origin of which was suspected to be German, for Siglefiord, Iceland, had been permitted to proceed [cf. 269].[2]

Arley and *Saxon* left Swarbacks Minn in the evening to reinforce E

[1]*Helge* was detained, pending instructions from the Foreign Office. Like the *Hans Egede*, she was a vessel being used to bring pressure on its home government (TS 14/10 of 5 and 6 August 1916).

[2]*John* was not referred to the Contraband Committee.

Patrol, and assist in dealing with the large amount of traffic caused by the herring fishery season in the neighbourhood of Siglefiord.

At 11 p.m. orders were received from the Admiralty for the Swedish Steamer *Thure* from Stockholm to be sent in, if met with. The Ship had, however, been intercepted and sent to Lerwick by *Changuinola* an hour previously. She had on board 1359 barrels of salt and 2827 empty barrels, 200 of which were certified as being of British origin. There was also one passenger.[1]

Information was received that *Orvieto* had left the Thames to join my Flag, thus raising the strength of the Squadron to 22 Ships.

During the night it came on to blow, and *Alsatian* had to let go a second anchor.

3. Tuesday, 1st August – A south-westerly gale with rain was experienced at Swarbacks Minn.

Alsatian completed coaling at noon.

4. Wednesday, 2nd August – In the forenoon, I exercised the Ship's Company of *Alsatian* at various drills, and at 10 p.m. the Ship sailed for patrol in thick weather.

A message was received from the Commander-in-Chief to the effect that the submarine *Deutschland* had sailed from New York p.m. on 1 August, and that she would be due to pass the patrols about the 12th.[2]

5. Thursday, 3rd August – At 4.50 a.m. *Alsatian* hit some submerged object, or perhaps a sea struck the Ship, but she vibrated very considerably. No leak was reported.

Gloucestershire reported having intercepted the Norwegian SS *Cikto* in Latitude 66.26´ North, Longitude 15.9´ West, from Christiansund to Siglefiord with 600 barrels of salt without guarantee and also a cargo of timber, but had been obliged to allow her to proceed owing to her being unseaworthy and short of coal. As, however, information had been received from the Consul at Christiansund, through the Vice-Admiral Commanding Orkneys and Shetlands that this vessel was carrying salt and machinery of German origin, I ordered *Gloucestershire* to re-intercept her, and arranged for *Walpole* to tow her to Lerwick.[3]

[1] *Thure* was not detained.

[2] *Deutschland* was the first of the U-cruisers, unarmed but with a great range and large size. It took a cargo of precious stones and dyestuffs from Kiel to Baltimore and returned with metals – copper, nickel, silver, zinc – and rubber. The development and use of such expensive vessels is a good indication of the effectiveness of the British blockade. The ship returned to Bremen on 24 August, and made a second voyage in the autumn. (Cf. R. Compton-Hall, *Submarines and the War at Sea, 1914–1918* (London, 1981), 255–259.)

[3] This name is wrong; no *Cikto* is in *Lloyd's Register*, nor does it feature in the Contraband Committee minutes. I cannot trace which ship it really is.

6. Friday, 4th August – A report was received from Thorshavn, Faroe Islands, that mines had been seen some 23 miles SE of Sydero, also that a submarine had been sighted on 1 August about five miles west of Farmien Island, steering west.

Since leaving Swarbacks Minn, I had been proceeding north and in the evening met *Gloucestershire*, from whom I received a report regarding the herring fishery to the north of Iceland. A report on the same subject was also received from *Patia* ...

In view of the manifest hardship that would result in certain cases by sending Ships in, that have not obtained consular guarantees before leaving for Iceland, e.g., small sailing vessels that had arrived at the fishing grounds (as a temporary measure ...) I have directed Commanding Officers to obtain a 'Ship Guarantee' on the lines suggested by Mr Olsen, the British Vice-Consul, as stated in *Gloucestershire*'s letter of 1 August 1916 (Swedish Vessels excepted). Under the new Icelandic Proclamation, our Consul appears to be able to prevent export of goods the destination of which appears suspicious.[1]

As regards the point raised in the last paragraph of *Patia*'s letter dated 27 July ..., it would undoubtedly be useful to have a decision as to whether a vessel – other than of Danish Nationality – with an Armed Guard on board would be entitled to obtain fuel or effect sufficient repairs in Iceland to take her to a British port. At the same time, it is quite understood that a vessel should not put in except in the case of absolute necessity.

With reference to the second paragraph of *Patia*'s Report it will be noticed that the *Fenris* was intercepted, and again released (*Gloucestershire*'s letter of 1 August).

Trawlers were despatched on 31 July to assist on E Patrol.

7. Saturday, 5th August – C patrol line was shifted so as to run 340° from Latitude 58.6´ North, Longitude 12.30´ West.

I met *Almanzora*, and gave him instructions as to dealing with the vessels engaged in Icelandic Trade. The Ship has lately come under General Messing, and the men have not yet got accustomed to it.

I also met *Orvieto* and made the acquaintance of Commander

[1]The 'Ship Guarantee' is explained by *Patia*'s captain (ADM 137/298, 328–330): the British consul is 'now enabled to force the Captains of ships trading to Iceland to sign a declaration that they will call at a British port, under a penalty to the Icelandic government. This penalty, in one case of which I am cognizant, was a fine of £5,000 on a ship called the *Edith* which was actually lying at Reykjavik while I was there, and the Consular Staff were hoping that if stopped by any of the patrols it would be in such a position as to prove that she was not carrying out her contract to call at a British port'. There is, in fact, no record of *Edith* being intercepted.

England.[1] The Ship appears to be well turned out, and will be a very useful addition to the Tenth Cruiser Squadron when she has shaken down.

At 8 p.m. in Latitude 59.29´ North, Longitude 14.24´ West *Columbella* intercepted the Russian SS *Ekaterinoslav* referred to in Admiralty message 1504 of 4 August.

8. Sunday, 6th August – Whilst on her way to Lerwick with the Norwegian SS *Cikto* in tow, the Armed Trawler *Walpole* intercepted the Swedish Motor Vessel *Pedro Christopherson*, from Buenos Aires to Stockholm, in Latitude 62.50´ North, Longitude 7.30´ West, and placed an Armed Guard on board. This vessel was reported to be carrying letters for enemy destination ... and from the position in which she was intercepted it would appear probable she was attempting to avoid the patrols. She was sent to Kirkwall with an Armed Guard from *Orvieto*.[2]

During the afternoon, *Columbella* intercepted the French Steamships *Djemnah* and *Natal*, bound from Brest to Archangel, with munitions for the Roumanian Government.

The Master of the Norwegian SS *Conrad Mohr*, boarded by *Mantua* reported having sighted a mine with one horn, 10 miles to the westward of Inistrahull on the morning of Saturday, 5th August.[3] The Commander-in-Chief was informed.

The disposition of the Squadron at noon was as follows: Ships in order from south to north.

A Patrol ... *Orvieto*, *Almanzora*.
B Patrol ... *Hildebrand* (SE of Iceland).
C Patrol ... *Victorian*, *Patuca*, *Moldavia*, *Columbella*, *Alsatian*.
D Patrol ... *Mantua*, *Artois*, *Orotava*.
E Patrol ... *Gloucestershire*, *Hilary*, and Armed Trawlers *Saxon* and *Arley* (NE of Iceland).
Rejoining from Liverpool ... *Teutonic*.
Proceeding to Swarbacks Minn ... *Orcoma*, Armed Trawlers *Robert Smith* and *Walpole*.
Proceeding to Clyde ... *Changuinola*.
At Liverpool ... *Andes*, *Virginian*.
At Clyde ... *Ebro*, *Patia*, *Motagua*.

[1]England, George Plunkett, RN, Lieutenant 1899, Commander 1910, Captain of *Orvieto* 1916–1917 and 1917–1919, and of *Armadale Castle* 1917, Captain 1917, retired 1922.

[2]*Pedro Christopherson* was not detained.

[3]*Conrad Mohr* was either not sent in, or was quickly examined and released by Customs.

At Swarbacks Minn ... *Otway*, Armed Trawlers *Rushcoe* and *Tenby Castle*.

During the week 106 vessels (including 23 Fishing Craft) were intercepted, of which 28 were sent in for further examination.

9. Monday, 7th August – At 10 a.m., having met *Moldavia*, I went on board and cruised in her to witness target practice. This was very well carried out. The shooting was rapid and good – opening range 5800 yards, speed 14 knots. Three salvoes were fired in the first minute after the order to open fire, and hitting established. The Ship is well kept, and the men look well cared for. I consider her efficient. On parting company, I despatched her to Loch Ewe to coal.

10. Tuesday, 8th August – *Otway* sailed from Swarbacks Minn at 12.30 a.m., and shortly after reported that the valve casing of the first I.P. cylinder of her starboard engine had fractured, necessitating that engine being temporarily stopped. By 11 a.m., however, the cylinder had been 'cut out', and she was enabled to proceed at 14 knots using the port engine and three cylinders of the starboard engine.

I arranged to meet her in the evening, in order to investigate the cause and extent of the damage by a Court of Enquiry. The weather, however, came on very thick, and I deemed it advisable to postpone the meeting until the following morning.

Fog was also experienced on other parts of the patrol.

11. Wednesday, 9th August – Having met *Otway*, my Flag Captain, accompanied by the Engineer-Commander on my Staff and the Engineer-Commander of *Alsatian* proceeded on board to investigate the accident. They reported that it was very desirable that *Otway* should return to Harbour as soon as possible, as she could not remain on patrol without undue risk of the crack in I.P. Cylinder extending. Arrangements were made for her to return to Liverpool accordingly. The report of the Court etc. have already been forwarded to the Admiralty ...

Before leaving, I went on board and, having seen the defective valve casing etc, witnessed target practice. The practice was exceedingly good – the best I have so far seen in the Squadron. The Ship is in good order and efficient.

In the evening, I met *Almanzora* for the purpose of transferring Armed Guards, and despatched her to relieve *Gloucestershire* on E Patrol, with orders to send *Gloucestershire* to take her place on A.

With a view to doing all that was possible to intercept the Submarine Liner *Deutschland* and her supposed escort – the Norwegian SS *Haugland* – I directed all vessels, with the exception of the two on E

Patrol and *Andes*, to assume Patrol Line No II by midnight 11–12 August, ships being spread on a line 325 from Latitude 59.10´ North, Longitude 7 West, 30 miles apart, and steering 245 and 65.[1]

The Trawlers *Tenby Castle* and *Rushcoe* were ordered to patrol to the west of the Faeroes between Mygenaes and Sydero, as it was possible the *Deutschland* might meet a German Submarine in that locality as an escort.

The Commander-in-Chief also provided four Trawlers from the Stornoway Patrol to keep watch on Rockall Bank and to support these *Andes* was given orders to patrol 360, 60 miles from Latitude 56.40´ North, Longitude 15.30´ West, i.e. about 40 miles to the westward of Rockall Bank – the idea being that the *Deutschland* would make for Rockall and, on sighting *Andes*, would dive, and break surface on Rockall Bank when the Trawlers should make her dive again, and be able to keep her down until her batteries were exhausted. She would then be an easy prey.

12. Thursday, 10th August – Misty.

In the forenoon, *Alsatian* intercepted the Swedish Sailing ketch *Ture* in Latitude 63.30´ North, Longitude 9.17´ West with a cargo of salt and deal for Iceland. She had, in addition, 38 fifty-gallon barrels of oil for her auxiliary engine. As she had called at Lerwick, and obtained a green Customs clearance on 5 August, she was allowed to proceed, but as these barrels represented about 2,000 gallons of oil, which would be decidedly useful to a Submarine, the policy of allowing these small craft to cruise with such a large deck cargo of engine oil seems a little dangerous. She was not using her engines, and said the oil was for her voyage to Sweden after fishing.

13. Friday, 11th August – Fog all day and all night. A South-westerly gale sprang up in the course of the afternoon, and Ships to the southward reported they were unable to board vessels intercepted. There was a nasty sea, the weather being thick, with heavy rain.

The Squadron assumed the Patrol referred to in paragraph 11, twelve ships being spread on a line stretching from Latitude 59.10´ North, Longitude 7 West to the Coast of Iceland.

14. Saturday, 12th August – Mist and fog, considerable sea running.

15. Sunday, 13th August – Mist early, then clear.

The disposition of the Squadron at noon was as follows:

A, C and D Patrols disposed on line running 325° from 59.10´ North, 7 west – from south to north	*Patuca*, *Columbella*, *Orotava*, *Teutonic*, *Moldavia*, *Orcoma*, *Alsatian*, *Mantua*, *Victorian*, *Orvieto*, *Hildebrand*, *Gloucestershire*.

[1]There is no evidence that *Haugland* was so acting; in fact no ship of that name is in *Lloyd's Register*.

E Patrol – Off Langanaes *Almanzora* and Armed Trawlers *Saxon* and *Arley*.

Off North Cape ... *Hilary*.

Patrolling 60 miles, 360 degrees from Latitude 56.40´ North, Longitude 15.30´ West. } *Andes*.

Patrolling to the west of Faeroes ... Armed Trawlers *Tenby Castle* and *Rushcoe*.

Rejoining A Patrol from Clyde ... *Motagua*.

At Liverpool ... *Otway*, *Virginian*, *Artois*.

At Clyde ... *Changuinola*, *Ebro*, *Patia*.

At Swarbacks Minn ... Armed Trawler *Walpole*.

Docking at Aberdeen ... Armed Trawler *Robert Smith*.

During the week 60 vessels, including 13 Fishing Craft, were intercepted and examined, 19 of which were sent in for further examination. Fog greatly hampered the work of the Patrols throughout the week.

I met *Mantua* in the afternoon, and received despatches from her. Captain Tibbitts reports that so far the Officers and men seem satisfied with the new system of messing.

The Captain Superintendent Clyde informed me that the workmen at Clyde are taking holidays from 19th to 28th August. This will certainly interfere with the refits of four ships belonging to this Squadron, which is unfortunate.

16. Monday, 14th August – *Columbella* intercepted and sent in to Lerwick with an Armed Guard, the Dutch SS *Waalhaven* shewn on the Admiralty 'Ship Black List' ... bound from Rosario to Rotterdam.[1]

Her master reported having sighted a supposed submarine 25 miles to the westward of St Kilda, at 9 a.m. that morning. This might have been the *Deutschland*, but unfortunately she does not appear to have been seen by any Patrol Vessels.

At midnight, three ships were permitted to leave Patrol for coal and docking.

17. Tuesday, 15th August – During the course of the day, A, C and D Patrols were re-arranged as follows:

A Patrol, consisting of *Motagua*, *Orvieto* and *Hildebrand*, to work in line ahead, 360° from Latitude 62.40´ North, Longitude 7 West, ships

[1] *Waalhaven* was not detained.

40 miles apart, and patrolling 120 miles. The object of this was to intercept small vessels proceeding from Iceland to Scandinavia with fish, etc. The weather is clearer out at sea than near the land.

C Patrol, consisting of *Orcoma*, *Mantua*, *Teutonic*, *Victorian*, to work on line 325° from Latitude 59.30' North, Longitude 7.30' West, ships 30 miles apart.

D Patrol, consisting of *Moldavia*, to work 310°, 80 miles from Latitude 56 North, Longitude 10.30' West, to intercept trade from South America and the Mediterranean.

I met Andes in the forenoon, and gave her orders to join E Patrol, sending Hilary to G.

255. *W. Grahame Greene to Commander-in-Chief Home Fleets*

Admiralty, 1 August 1916

I have laid before My Lords Commissioners of the Admiralty your letter of the 1st July last [249] ... relative to the additional measures that might be taken to render the blockade more stringent than hitherto, and thus to prevent commodities of all kinds from reaching or leaving Germany.

My Lords have given the fullest consideration to the points emphasized in your letter, and I am commanded to inform you that arrangements have recently been made,

(i) to purchase a proportion of the home supplies of Holland with a view to their export to this country, and

(ii) to ensure that the season's catch of fish as well as the supply of fish oil and of wool from Iceland shall either be sent to countries from which they will not find their way into Germany or in the alternative be bought up by this country.

In addition efforts are also being made,

(i) to induce Denmark to send a larger proportion of the Danish home supplies to this country.

(ii) to induce Sweden to take more effectual measures to prevent re-export of overseas goods to Germany, and

(iii) to induce Switzerland to prevent goods belonging to German subjects and stored in that country from being sent to Germany as demanded by the German government.

I am further to add that the rationing of commodities to Holland and Scandinavia is proceeding steadily and each week fresh articles are being added to the list.

Letters of assurance for flour to Norway from the United States have been stopped for the present in view of the stocks already in Norway, and the question of the storage of commodities in Denmark and Holland is being reconsidered in view of the danger of the pressure which Germany might possibly bring to bear on those countries.

256. *O. Murray to Commander-in-Chief Home Fleet*

6 August 1916

... In these circumstances [248] the orders conveyed to you ... as to the intercepting of all vessels belonging to the Norwegian-American Line are now to be regarded as withdrawn.

***

In conclusion I am to state that the special arrangement with Mr P.A. Welin in regard to ships of the Lulea Ofoten Coy has been extended to the 31st December and that in future the vessels of this line will call at Lerwick both on their Eastward and Westward passages.

257. *Vice-Admiral Tupper to Admiralty*

HMS *Alsatian*, 30 August 1916

Report of Proceedings, 16–29 August 1916

***

1. Wednesday, 16 August – I met *Gloucestershire* during the forenoon and saw Captain Stanley.[1] The opportunity was taken of sending the Lieutenant (G) on my Staff to look into various matters connected with the gunnery efficiency of the Ship. On parting company I despatched her to the Clyde to coal.

In case the report of submarines being sighted in the neighbourhood of the Faroes should prove correct Ships on Patrol were ordered to be in the Southern position at midnight instead of at Noon in order that the southern Ship should only approach the Faroes during dark hours.

The Armed trawlers *Rushcoe* and *Tenby Castle* left the Faroe Islands Patrol to coal and refit.

2. Thursday, 17 August – During the forenoon I met the Armed Trawler *Robert Smith* at sea. I had her Commanding Officer – Lieutenant James Macintosh, RNR[2] – on board and explained to him

[1]Stanley, Norman L., RN, Lieutenant 1894, Commander 1905, Captain of *Oropesa* 1914–1915, of *Gloucestershire* 1916. Captain 1919, retired 1923.

[2]Macintosh, James, RNR, Sub-Lieutenant 1915.

what his duties would be whilst in Icelandic Waters; he appears to be an intelligent officer.

Patia intercepted and sent in to Kirkwall with an Armed Guard the Swedish Steamer *Kratos* in Latitude 57.50´ North, Longitude 13.57´ West, bound from New Orleans to Bergen with a general cargo. The Ship was reported to be carrying provisions and correspondence for Germany … .[1]

Almanzora reported she had visited Siglefiord, Iceland, the previous afternoon and communicated with the Vice-Consul, who stated that the system of guarantees referred to in clause 6 of my previous report of proceedings ... was working well.

Alsatian arrived and anchored at Swarbacks Minn at 11 p.m. The night was so dark that the Destroyer told off to find and escort *Alsatian* in from Eshaness failed to pick her up.

Orotava and *Victorian* were at anchor.

Information was received from *Orcoma* that the Danish Steam Whaler *Talkna* boarded by her on the 6th August, reported having sighted submarines twice during the month of May in the neighbourhood of the Faroes. In view of the fact that no steamers have been sunk near the Faroes the accuracy of this report is doubtful but all possible precautions are taken in the vicinity.

3. Friday, 18 August – The *Alsatian* performed the best coaling so far at Busta Voe – 153 tons per hour for 1200 tons – and hopes to do still better.

With reference to paragraph 5 of my Submission No.442/35 of 16 August [254], divers examined the neighbourhood of the stem on each side but did not discover any evidence of the Ship having struck anything. I do not recommend docking until the usual time as there is no leak anywhere but the blow received was certainly severe.

4. Saturday, 19 August – *Almanzora* reported that the American Auxiliary Schooner *Speedwell* bound East with fish had been intercepted in the neighbourhood of Langnaes by the armed trawler *Saxon* and sent in to Lerwick with an armed guard. She had no Consular Certificate and refused to sign a guarantee.[2]

[1]*Kratos* was in fact on the White List, and was allowed to go on after inspection (TS 14/10 of 19 and 23 August 1916).

[2]*Speedwell*'s cargo was salted herrings and 41 tons of salt; in the rummage the Customs at Lerwick found ten rubber mats, which roused their instant suspicions. However, they were explained as being left over from when the ship had been used as a yacht, and on consideration concealment was not suggested (TS 14/10 of 24 and 28 August 1916). In the end the ship was allowed to go on.

Orvieto intercepted the Norwegian Trawler *Namdal* with an armed guard on board from *Arley*[1] who reported they had sighted a suspicious vessel with the appearance of a submarine, at 10 a.m., on 18 August in Latitude 65 North, Longitude 12.40´ West steering 135°. It had disappeared suddenly.

At 9.15 p.m., a signal was received from *Ebro* that a very distinct wake such as would be formed by a submarine had been observed in Latitude 65.30´ North, Longitude 12 West steering 90°, and that it was considered unlikely to be that of a whale. The wake showed a sudden alteration of course near *Ebro*. A favourable opportunity of using a depth charge did not occur. I did not consider it necessary to alter *Ebro*'s orders and have not since then received any further evidence that a submarine was in that neighbourhood.

A submarine was reported in Latitude 56.22´ North, Longitude 9.24´ West at 6 p.m.

I left Swarbacks Minn in *Alsatian* at 10 p.m., to rejoin patrol, *Victorian* having previously sailed at 9.30.

5. Sunday, 20 August – *Moldavia* boarded the Danish Sailing Vessel *Rjukan* about noon in Latitude 56.40´ North, Longitude 10.10´ West with a cargo of maize from Buenos Aires to Copenhagen, and sent her in to Stornoway with an armed guard.[2]

Orders were subsequently received from the Admiralty for this vessel to be sent in if met with ...

At 4.30 p.m., the Swedish Sailing Ship *G.D. Kennedy* with an armed guard on board was met becalmed to the South of the Faroes. As the Officer in charge reported he had only 5 days' provisions, I placed another 14 days' on board.[3]

At 7 p.m., in Latitude 63.51´ North, Longitude 10.10´ West *Hilary* intercepted and sent in to Lerwick with an Armed Guard the Danish Motor Schooner *Venus*, bound from Copenhagen to Iceland. Captain Dean informed me that he considered her movements extremely suspicious and believed she was a submarine supply ship. A separate

[1]*Namdal* provided guarantees against re-export, and was allowed to go on (TS 14/10 of 22 August 1916).

[2]The Contraband Committee ordered the cargo to be discharged and *Rjukan* searched for contraband (TS 14/10 of 25 August 1916).

[3]*G.D. Kennedy*'s men scarcely needed provisions for 14 days: the ship and its cargo (2000 tons of linseed) were examined at Lerwick, and the Contraband Committee allowed it to go on by 24 August (TS 14/10 of 24 August 1916). The ship must have reached Lerwick only a day or two after interception by *Alsatian*.

report has been forwarded regarding this vessel...[1] [cf. also 265 para. 24].

At 10 p.m., I met *Columbella* for the purpose of transferring armed guards.

The disposition of the Squadron at noon was as follows:

A Patrol ... *Motagua*, *Orvieto*, *Hilary*.
B Patrol ... *Orotava*.
C Patrol ... *Orcoma*, *Mantua*, *Teutonic*, *Patia*, *Columbella*.
D Patrol ... *Moldavia*.
E Patrol ... *Andes*, *Ebro*, and Armed Trawlers *Robert Smith* and *Walpole* (Off Langanaes, Iceland).
Proceeding from E to A ... *Almanzora*.
Rejoining Patrol from Swarbacks Minn ... *Alsatian*, *Victorian*.
Rejoining Patrol from Clyde ... *Changuinola*.
Proceeding to Swarbacks Minn ... Armed Trawlers *Saxon* and *Arley*.
At Liverpool ... *Otway*, *Artois*, *Virginian*.
At Clyde ... *Gloucestershire*, *Patuca*.
At Swarbacks Minn ... *Hildebrand*, Armed Trawler *Tenby Castle*.
At Aberdeen (Docking) ... Armed Trawler *Rushcoe*.

During the course of the week 105 vessels, including 11 fishing craft were intercepted, of which 35 were sent in for further examination.

6. Monday, 21 August – The Swedish Steamer *Ada* which had successfully evaded the patrols on her Eastward voyage was intercepted by *Orcoma*, from Goteborg to New York and sent in to Stornoway [267].[2]

During the afternoon I met *Hilary* and went on board to witness target practice. The Captain had complained that his gun mountings were not laid true and that the shooting of the guns was erratic in consequence. I took Midshipmen on board to note the sightsetting, and *Alsatian* observed fall of shot with a rake. The result proved that the sightsetting was inaccurate and that there was not much wrong with the guns or mountings. The practice was fair; steps are being taken to improve this. *Hilary* afterwards proceeded to Clyde.

In the evening *Orvieto* was met, and Lieutenant Guy V. Kenyon – the Gunnery Officer on my staff – was sent on board to advise as regards the target practice and general gunnery organization.

[1] *Venus* was cleared by the Customs on examination. The report referred to has not been located.

[2] Despite the ship's record, there is no indication that she was detained on this occasion.

A report was received from *Hilary* covering the period spent on E Patrol of which the following is an extract:

'On 8th instant about 5.30 p.m., coming out of a dense fog bank intercepted Norwegian Steam Trawler *Assistent* trying to escape from *Saxon* which ship had fired several shots at her after usual warnings but had failed to hit or bring her to. Her owner was on board, she had no guarantee, I informed her owner and the Master through Boarding Officer, that unfortunately I was obliged to send her to Kirkwall because she had tried to evade capture, which they did not attempt to deny. They advanced shortage of coal as reason they could not go, I said that what they had was sufficient if used economically. Ultimately as an afterthought they urged shortage of food and water, I supplied some of both and warned Armed Guard Officer to report that ship was considered suspicious' [262].[1]

7. Tuesday, 22 August – The Master of the Russian Steamer *Kamenetz-Podolsk* from Sunderland to New York boarded by *Virginian* reported having sighted a submarine on the surface in Latitude 59.36´ North, Longitude 6.22´ West, the previous day.

A patrol was moved 40 miles 360°.

8. Wednesday, 23 August – At 9.30 a.m., I met *Virginian*, who has just rejoined patrol after being absent since 16 June for the purpose of having her 4.7 inch guns exchanged for 6". I cruised in her for about two hours. Though there was some sea and a considerable swell, the guns took no spray over them, which demonstrated the value of placing them in their present position. I consider the Ship is now efficiently armed.

C patrol was moved to work on a line 340° from Latitude 58 North, Longitude 12.30´ West.

9. Thursday, 24 August – Two British trawlers for fishing grounds and one steamer for Archangel were examined by *Alsatian* and allowed to proceed.[2]

[1]*Assistent* was in the event allowed to continue her voyage (TS 14/10 of 14 and 22 August 1916).

[2]This is the date *Deutschland* reached Bremen. Her sister-ship, *Bremen*, was due to reach the United States early in September, but disappeared en route. I mention this only to point out that Compton-Hall's attribution to *Alsatian* and *Mantua* of *Bremen*'s killing is impossible – particularly when he says they 'modestly' did not claim it. No Royal Navy ship would have failed to claim a U-boat kill; indeed they claimed kills which did not happen, all too often. Further, neither ship was at any time in this summer 'south of Ireland', and only on very rare occasions, as on 25 August, were they even in company. It is noticeable that Compton-Hall gives no source for his information (*Submarines and the War at Sea, 1914–1918*, 258). Whatever happened to *Bremen*, it was not the doing of any ship on the Northern Patrol.

10. Friday, 25 August – East-south-Easterly gale.

The Commanding Officer of *Andes* informed me he had ascertained from the Vice-Consul at Siglefiord that the herring fishery season was now practically over, and it was anticipated that in about a week's time the Scandinavian fishing craft would return home without filling up.

The sea was so bad in the afternoon that I had to defer transferring Armed Guards to *Mantua*, after having previously arranged a rendezvous.

11. Saturday, 26 August – Fine clear weather again.

A patrol was moved to the meridian of 10 West, on a line 360° from Latitude 63 North.

About 11 a.m., the Armed Trawler *Tenby Castle*, patrolling to the west of the Faroes, intercepted the British trawlers *Aries* and *Lord Shrewsbury*. The skipper of the former stated that, according to the Consul at Klaksvig, five floating mines had been picked up 22 miles 135° from Sydero on 11 August. Though there have been persistent rumours of mines being sighted in this neighbourhood, I have been unable to obtain any confirmation of this.

The skipper of *Lord Shrewsbury* stated that he had been told by natives that submarines had been seen amongst the islands on 11 August, and also that a tank was moored in Skuofjord. This appears to confirm the information contained in Admiralty Message No. 572 of 22 December 1914 addressed to the Commander-in-Chief, Grand Fleet. *Tenby Castle* searched for the tank, but without result.

A submarine was reported 25 miles to the west of St Kilda.

12. Sunday, 27 August – At 3 p.m. the *Virginian* boarded the Swedish trawler *Alexander*, G.G.249, in Latitude 64.31´ North, Longitude 9.49´ West, bound from Iceland to Goteborg, with 19 barrels of herrings and 500 lbs of salt fish – the property of the crew. *Virginian* reported that the crew had preferred to throw the fish overboard rather than go in to Lerwick, and he had allowed her to proceed under these conditions, permitting her to keep 12 barrels of fish. I consider that the Captain of *Virginian* was mistaken in allowing this to be done, owing to the capital that it is possible to make out of an incident of this nature, and owing to the possibility of the vessel herself being German owned though under Swedish colours. He should, in my opinion, have sent her in for examination.

Virginian was informed as above, and ordered to endeavour to re-intercept her, but was unable to find her. Commander Wilding[1] has so

[1]Wilding, Michael Henry, CBE, RN (1875–1933), Commander 1911, Captain of *Virginian* 1916, Captain 1918 (retired).

far had but little experience in this work, but is a zealous Officer.

At 5.30 p.m., I met *Orvieto* and went on board for the first time since she joined my flag. The mess decks were very tidy; the hammocks well lashed up and well stowed. She appeared to me to be in very good order (considering the short time she has been in commission) and reflects credit on Commander England and his Officers.

At noon the disposition of the Squadron was as follows: (Ships on patrol being shown from South to North)

A Patrol ... *Virginian*, *Victorian*, *Orotava*, and *Hildebrand.*
C Patrol ... *Orcoma*, *Artois*, *Teutonic*, *Patia*, and *Changuinola.*
D Patrol ... *Columbella.*
E Patrol ... *Ebro*, *Andes*, and Armed Trawlers *Robert Smith* and *Walpole.*
Patrolling between A and C ... *Alsatian.*
To West of Faroes ... Armed Trawlers *Tenby Castle* and *Rushcoe.*
Rejoining C from Swarbacks Minn ... *Orvieto.*
At Liverpool ... *Otway.*
At Clyde ... *Moldavia*, *Gloucestershire*, *Patuca*, and *Hilary.*
At Swarbacks Minn ... *Mantua*, *Almanzora*, *Motagua*, Armed Trawlers *Arley* and *Saxon.*

During the past week 100 vessels, including 15 fishing craft, were intercepted, of which 24 were sent in for further examination.

13. Monday, 28 August – Lovely weather.

During the forenoon I met *Patia* and later *Teutonic*. Commodore Luard came on board and I gave him detailed instructions regarding the conduct of the Patrol during my absence.

Victorian boarded and sent in to Lerwick the Norwegian trawler *Fisk*, bound from Iceland to Haugesund, with herrings. The Vice-Consul at Siglefiord had already informed *Andes* that this vessel was owned by the German Consul at Stavanger.[1]

The following extract from a report of the officer in charge of the armed guard put on board the Danish schooner *Laurits* – Midshipman Francis J. Scott-Stokes, RNR,[2] of *Alsatian* – is given as being of interest:

'One of the crew of the name of Jansen stated that he had formed part of the crew of SS *Saxon Prince*, the last ship sunk by the raider *Moewe*,

[1]*Fisk* was not detained.

[2]Scott-Stokes, Francis J., RNVR, Midshipman 1915, Sub-Lieutenant RN 1918, Commander (retired) 1940.

had been taken prisoner to Germany, and on his release and return to England had made a statement to a British Naval Officer. He mentioned to me that the ketches fitted with auxiliary motors were much used nowadays for the purpose of conveying petrol, the pretence being that it was used for the engine, while as a matter of fact the engine was very little used at all – he hinted at the probability of the surplus being carried to supply the needs of submarines if met with.'

14. Tuesday, 29 August – *Alsatian* left patrol for Liverpool and at midnight 29th–30th I turned over the Command of the Squadron to Commodore Luard.

15. Wednesday, 30 August – *Alsatian* arrived at Liverpool Bar at 10 p.m.

***

258. *Vice-Admiral Tupper to Admiralty*

HMS *Alsatian*, 17 August 1916

D Patrol has for some time past been stationed to the South-East of Rockall with a view to intercepting such traffic: but a great deal depends on the Trawler Patrol off St Kilda and the Butt of Lewis. The Tenth Cruiser Squadron is ordered not to cruise within thirty miles of the 100-fathom line, and many ships pass north inside this line.

If the six trawlers now working with the Tenth Cruiser Squadron for service off Iceland and the Faroes can be detailed to continue work with the Squadron for the winter, I can make good use of them between St Kilda and the 100-fathom line. The Commanding Officers are very good and understand their work with the Tenth Cruiser Squadron.

3. It is submitted that the statement regarding the *Muskovee*'s (*Muskagee*) alleged evasion of the patrols may be further investigated.

It is noticed that Captain Tiedemann of '*Muskokee*' is suspected of being a German, and of introducing papers and documents into Germany ...

259. *Midshipman T.N. Heap, RNR*[1] *to Commander E.V.R. Dugmore, RN*

HMS *Ebro*, 21 August 1916

I have the honour to report that, whilst in charge of Armed Guard on board the Norwegian SS *Breifond* the Master stated that he was

[1]Heap, Thomas N., RNR, Midshipman 1914, Sub-Lieutenant 1918; the ship he was in, *Breifond*, was not detained; the ship he was told about was actually *Muskogee* – see [266].

informed by the master of a Swedish vessel in Kirkwall that he could evade the patrols by keeping to the Southward of Latitude 58 and proceeding Northward fairly close in to the British coast as the patrols were always well to the Westward. He was also informed by the master of the SS *Muskovee* (?) in Philadelphia that the said vessel was German owned and traded under the American flag. On her previous voyage the *Muscovee* evaded the patrols by proceeding to the northward of Iceland and down the Norwegian coast. Further he states that two vessels of the same line have been taken a prize [258].

260. *Lieutenant W.J. Canner RNR*[1] *to Commanding Officer HMS* Hilary

22 August 1916

I have the honour to submit the following Report:

On August 10th, 1916 in Lat. 56.38´N, Long 15.5´W, the Norwegian Steam Drifter *Hareid* of Aalesund was intercepted and boarded by HMS *Hilary*. An Armed Guard was placed on board with orders to proceed to Lerwick.

The Master of the Trawler informed me that his compass had a big error, but he did not know how much this was. The weather at the time, and during the whole of the passage to Lerwick, was such that an observation was unobtainable. There were no Navigation Instruments on board of any kind except the patent log. I made a lead line from some cod line and by continuous soundings eventually reached Lerwick after being five days on board – the latter two of which we were without fresh water. As I had no idea of the whereabouts of the ship, this fact was a serious problem. The whole of the Ship's Company were complaining of thirst.

The course by compass should have brought us to the westward of the Shetland Islands, and the soundings, which I first obtained agreed with those NW of Muckle Flugga. On Sunday morning we sighted a Swedish sailing trawler who told us that our position was about 30 miles NW of Muckle Flugga. The course was continued until such time as I thought we should be about 12 miles NW of that point. The distance run by log should have put us well in close to the land. At this time (noon on Sunday) the Chief Engineer reported that there was only sufficient coal to last for another 24 hours, and that the fresh water was nearly finished and would only last a few more hours. The course was then

[1]Canner, William J., RNR, Sub-Lieutenant 1915, Lieutenant 1917.

altered to SSW by compass (South true) to keep us to the westward of the Shetlands, as we then thought that by steering east, after running 25 miles to the southward, we would surely make the land. By the soundings obtained I was confirmed in my opinion that the vessel was to the westward of the Shetlands so altered course to the eastwards (true). After steaming for about 25 miles in this direction and still finding no land, but on the contrary that the soundings increased suddenly to about 107 fathoms – about 3 a.m. on Monday, it was decided to stop until daybreak to save the coal as we only had sufficient for 9 hours steaming, trusting the fog would lift. During this time we were stopped it was concluded that the vessel must – first by the course steered with no results, secondly by soundings obtained – be about 60 miles from the Norwegian coast, and about 90 miles to the eastward of the Shetlands. As before stated, there was no water on the Ship and just barely sufficient coal to reach Norway, and the food was also getting scarce. At daybreak we proceeded, steering west until noon when we again stopped to try and fix a definite position, but without results. The Master then made a statement to the effect that, having very little coal left, only a hazy idea of the ship's position, and no water, he would cease to have any further responsibility for the safety of the Ship and the lives on board, if we continued to steer west. He pointed out that by steering east we would certainly sight the Norwegian coast and in the event of our being on the west side of the Shetlands (as at first we had every reason to believe) we would in the latter case sight the Shetlands. The Master agreed to sign a written statement to the effect that everything possible had been done to reach Lerwick but for humanity's sake we were forced to proceed on an easterly course to Norway. As the crew were then suffering from thirst, the Ship's Company were assembled and the position explained to them. The crew were of opinion that as the Ship's position was so doubtful it was quite likely that the vessel – by steering west – would actually steer further out into the Atlantic ocean, and eventually, having burnt everything available (as we were now burning empty barrels) there was quite a probability of their dying of thirst. The Master and crew finally agreed to leave things in my hands.

I was of opinion by the soundings that the vessel was to the eastward, but position so uncertain that I fully realised the risk and responsibility in steering to the westward was great but determined that the ship should not go to Norway so continued on a westward course. We continued soundings until 2 a.m. on Tuesday when I considered we should be close to land. I then steamed dead slow, steering SW to stem the ebb tide and await daylight. At 6 a.m. I proceeded west again, still in a dense fog. At 8.30 a.m. land was sighted about 200 yards on the port bow, which we eventually found to be Helli Ness. From this position, we steered for Lerwick, arriving there about 10 a.m. 15th inst.

There is nothing further to report.[1]

261. *Captain F.W. Dean to Vice-Admiral Commanding Tenth Cruiser Squadron*

HMS *Hilary*, 23 August 1916

Submitted herewith Reports from Acting Lieutenants W.J. Canner [260] and S.B. Groome RNR (Temp) [262][2] of their proceedings in the Norwegian Steam Trawlers *Haried* and *Assistent* respectively when taking them in with Armed Guards. I submit that the conduct of these Officers appears to have been very creditable to them both, and I would specially point out that it was only by questioning Mr Groome, having anticipated that he might have trouble with *Assistent*, that I found out about the difficulties he has successfully encountered.

262. *Lieutenant S.B. Groome to Commanding Officer HMS* Hilary

23 August 1916

I have the honour to submit my report of the Steam Trawler *Assistent* with a cargo of herrings which I boarded at 6 p.m. 8 August 1916, in Lat. 66.6´N, Long. 14.6´W, with my Armed Guard with orders to proceed to Kirkwall. On arriving aboard the Captain told me that he had not enough coal to take the Ship to Kirkwall, but as they had 30 tons on board and only burned 5 tons a day for a speed of 9 knots, I ordered him to proceed in on easy steam, a speed of 7 knots. At 6.45 p.m. on the same day, the Captain informed me that he had only one day's provisions and two days water on board, as the Ship was supposed to reach Lodmunder Fiord, Iceland, the following morning. I confirmed this statement and decided to steam for HMS *Hilary* and obtain water and food. I reached her about 7.15 p.m. and was supplied with 75 gallons of water and 4 days' food. At 8 p.m. we set course S 21° E mag., to sight the north of Faroe Island. The following morning, August 9th, we discovered that the patent log had carried away, and as there was not another aboard we had to judge our speed, nor were there any

[1] *Haried* was allowed to go on after investigation (TS 14/10 of 16 and 31 August 1916). Note the fortnight's delay.

[2] Groome, Sydney B., RNR, Sub-Lieutenant 1915, Lieutenant May 1917.

instruments or books of any description to ascertain her position or error of the compass. The weather was fine and clear and a smooth sea, and at 4 p.m. August 10th, we ought to have been abeam of Fugle Island, Faeroes, we decided it was best to set a course due south, and try and pick up land. At 6 p.m. after steaming 14 knots on this course, we still could not see any land and it came on a very thick fog; the Captain stated that he was absolutely unfit to navigate his vessel, and asked me to take charge; I refused to take any responsibility but would give him every assistance in my power; he said it was hopeless for him to try but if I would do all the navigation he would hold himself responsible in case of accident. I then set a course S 16° E mag. to make Fair Island. The following morning, August 12th, the Captain informed me that he had absolutely no idea how his compass was but thought it was about two points out to the northward, so I altered the course to South mag. to allow for this. At 6 p.m., August 12th, we sighted land about $^1/_4$ miles ahead, there still being a thick fog. I stopped the Ship and endeavoured to discover what land it was, by the bearing of the lay of the land I concluded I was off Wats Ness, Burrier Head, Shetlands, soundings giving us 49 fathoms. I was unable to tell whether it was a current that had set us in here, or the compass out, not having any way of finding how the currents were. So, as the weather cleared a little, I set a course south mag. and at 9 p.m. sighted Gruting Voe Light, and half an hour afterwards Oxne Light. I continued this course until midnight, but was unable to pick up Fitfull Head, so I set a course SW $^1/_4$ S mag. for Fair Island, and at 1 p.m. a very thick fog came up, also a strong SSE wind and heavy sea. The vessel rolled terribly and shipped heavy water fore and aft, washing most of the herrings overboard, except those that had been salted in barrels, and stowed down the hold. At 4 a.m. August 13th, the weather was too thick to sight Fair Island, I was allowing 5 knots speed, so I altered the course to SW by $^1/_2$ W, mag. for Start Point, and at 10 a.m. sighted very high land, about 200 yards off, the weather still being very thick and very strong wind and sea. I altered the course and followed the land for about 2 miles, and then lost it. I concluded it was North Ronaldshay Island, and set a course S by W mag. for Start Point; soundings then gave 22 fathoms. At noon, I sighted HM Armed Trawler *Peterborough* and asked the captain for my position. He informed me by semaphore that Mull Head bore SE, and then left me. I was quite at a loss as to my position, not knowing which Mull Head he meant, so I kept her on the same course S by W mag. By this time we had used up our last drop of fresh water, and I was anxious to make port as soon as possible, otherwise I would have anchored until the fog cleared. At 1 p.m. I heard Copinsay Fog Signal and discovered I was ahead of my position, also that the *Peterborough* had given me a wrong bearing, it being NW instead of SE. I then steered NE mag. and at 1.20 p.m. sighted Mull Head the entrance to Stronsay Firth. After rounding Mull Head I steered NW ½ W mag. and at 1.50 p.m. picked up the Kirkwall Pilot Boat, arriving in Kirkwall Harbour and anchoring at 2.30 p.m., August 13th.[1]

263. *Commander-in-Chief Home Fleets to Admiralty*

HMS *Iron Duke*, 28 August 1916

Be pleased to bring to the notice of the Lords Commissioners of the Admiralty the case of the Armed Guard on board the American Sailing Ship *Pass Of Balmaha*, as reported in German newspapers, extracts of which have been sent to me by the Director of the Intelligence Division ...

2. If the German account is true, which is very doubtful, it appears that the *Pass of Balmaha* was intercepted by the *Victorian* on 21st July 1915, and ordered into Kirkwall with an Armed Guard. Whilst on passage thither she was intercepted on 21st July 1915, by a German submarine, placed in charge of a single Petty Officer, and sent into Cuxhaven, where she arrived on 2nd August 1915, with the British Armed Guard still onboard.

3. In view of the fact that this report is forwarded to me from the Admiralty, it is submitted that I may be informed whether their Lordships consider that the British Armed Guard should have resisted and retaken the ship while under neutral colours, as Admiralty letter M.04362 of 18th June, 1915, lays down that 'an Armed Guard should on no account attempt any belligerent act under a neutral flag'.[2]

4. It is pointed out that the same Admiralty letter states that 'a further reply will be sent regarding the position of Armed Guards on board neutral vessels'. Nearly three months have elapsed since the date of my letter to which this communication refers, and I submit that an early decision may be made and communicated to me.

[1] See page 493, note 1.

[2] Not printed, but see [29] and [106]. *Pass of Balmaha* was fitted out as a raider and had a successful career as *Seeadler* before being wrecked in the Fiji Islands in August 1917. The ship had been intercepted by the Northern Patrol, but allowed to proceed, despite being crewed by German Navy men (Norwegian-speaking) captained by a German naval officer, and equipped with two 4.1" guns and two torpedo tubes. The interception is not mentioned in any report, and it is not known which vessel made the boarding.

264. *Admiralty to Commander-in-Chief Home Fleets*

30 August 1916

I am commanded by My Lord Commissioners of the Admiralty to transmit herewith an analysis of the Blockade, principally based on the full returns which have been rendered since the 23rd March of the vessels intercepted by all patrols in Northern waters, for the period up to 30th June. With the further information obtained from other sources, it has been possible to obtain a very correct estimate of the efficiency of the Blockade.

2. It is upon the work of interception performed under arduous and monotonous conditions by the Northern Patrols that the whole of the blockade policy, with its important effects on the course of the war, is necessarily based. My Lords take the opportunity of recording their high appreciation of the skilful and zealous manner in which the work has been carried out.

TABLE A

Neutral Vessels Passing the Blockade

(Period 23rd March–30th June 1916)

Eastbound Vessels .. in Dutch and Scandinavian Ports from Overseas Ports		Westbound Vessels sailing from Dutch and Scandinavian Ports for Overseas Ports	
Passed through the Downs	169	Passed through the Downs	106
Intercepted by the Patrols	180	Intercepted by the Patrols	107
Called Voluntarily at Kirkwall, Stornoway, Lerwick or other British ports	176	Called Voluntarily at Kirkwall, Stornoway, Lerwick or other British ports	154
	525		367
Number of Vessels evading Patrols	11	Number of Vessels evading Patrols	23
	536		390

9

THE EFFECTIVE BLOCKADE, SEPTEMBER–DECEMBER 1916

Tupper's repeated requests for more ships were eventually successful. The *Arlanza* reappeared [288 para. 4], *Avenger* was added [265 para. 19], as were *Armadale Castle* [288 para. 4] and *Kildonan Castle* [276 para. 6]. The removal of the damaged *Mantua* was no real loss, and *Orotava* would have been a liability during another North Atlantic winter [268, 274] – she had been nominated in early 1915 by de Chair as unsuitable for the work, and was perhaps lucky to have survived another winter since then. The main strength of the Patrol was also supplemented by a rising number of armed trawlers. By September 1916 Tupper had six of these useful vessels [265 para. 5], in addition to twenty-two Armed Merchant Cruisers – a total of twenty-eight ships. Yet of these only nine were actually out on patrol at the end of the year. The trawlers were at winter quarters, effectively off Tupper's strength, as a result of the concerted application of their commanders to be transferred to avoid the winter storms further north [273, 277]. Also three ships were sailing to or from patrol; ten cruisers were at one base or another. Tupper then asked for yet more ships [279 para. 15]. And those on patrol were scattered from the Denmark Strait to Rockall.

The blockade was, partly because of these increased numbers, becoming steadily more effective; the various agreements with shipping lines and Scandinavian governments, the British control of bunker coals and the institution of the Navicert system all ensured that ships ceased to carry goods which the British deemed helpful to their enemies. The decreasing proportion of ships being sent in for examination was for a time disguised by the fishing season in the North Atlantic, but when that was over the new situation became clear. By December, Tupper's Report was mainly taken up with reports on rescues and a recapture [283, 288].

265. *Vice-Admiral Tupper to Admiralty*

HMS *Alsatian*, 22 September 1916

Report of Proceedings, 30 August–21 September 1916

***

1. Wednesday, 30th August – I arrived at the Bar at Liverpool in *Alsatian* at 10 p.m., having turned over the command of the Squadron to Commodore Luard of *Teutonic*, the previous day.

2. Thursday, 31st August – During the night a gale came up from the south-west and increased in the course of the day.

Teutonic intercepted British Collier *Dowlais*, from Barry Dock to Archangel, who reported that a lighter she had in tow had broken adrift during the night in approximately Lat. 58 North, Long. 13 West. The Hydrographer of the Navy and also ships on patrol were informed. At 10 p.m. the British Steamer *Saga* reported by W/T sighting an empty barge in Lat. 58.51´ North, Long. 15.50´ West. This was probably the lost lighter.

At 5.30 p.m. orders were received from the Commander-in-Chief to move all patrols to Patrol Line IV during the night. This was in consequence of a submarine having been reported at 7 a.m. 30th August steering west in a position Lat. 60.30´ North, Long. 5 West. Later three further submarines were reported as having been sighted on 29th August North of the Shetlands.

Orders were accordingly given for ships on A, C and D patrols to form in line abreast on the meridian of 18 West. New Southern Positions of D and C being Lat. 55.30´ North, Long. 18 West and Lat. 58 North, Long. 18 West respectively. A gap was left west of Rockall. When these orders had been complied with the disposition of ships on patrol the following day would be:

D Patrol ... *Patuca*, *Motagua*.
C Patrol ... *Artois*, *Teutonic*, *Orvieto*, *Changuinola*, *Virginian*, *Mantua*, *Hildebrand*, *Almanzora*.
E Patrol ... No change.
Proceeding to E to relieve *Andes* ... *Gloucestershire*.
Proceeding to Swarbacks Minn ... *Victorian*.
Proceeding to Liverpool ... *Orcoma*.
Proceeding to Clyde ... *Orotava*.

Boarding was not possible throughout the day in most of the patrol area, and the Danish Barque *Annetta*, Norwegian Barques *Juno* and *Chile* were directed to call at Kirkwall, Lerwick, and Leith respectively.[1] I requested the Admiral Commanding Orkneys and Shetlands to inform me of their arrival.

3. Friday, 1st September – The gale continued during the night. The *Orvieto* intercepted at 8 a.m. the Norwegian Barque *Sagitta* from New York with oil cake for Aarhus. The weather prevented boarding and as the vessel was on the White List, and it was undesirable in view of the submarine menace for *Orvieto* to stand by the ship until weather moderated, she was allowed to proceed and ordered to call at Lerwick.[2]

The weather improved towards night.

4. Saturday, 2nd September – *Ebro* boarded Norwegian Steamer *Ost*, fishing in Lat. 66.19´ North, Long. 20.12´ West, with cargo half filled with salt herrings, ultimately bound for Bergen. The Master refused to sign guarantee to land fish in Iceland but signed a guarantee to call at Lerwick when full.[3] I approved this vessel being allowed to proceed as a test case, and requested Admiral Commanding Orkneys and Shetlands to inform me if the Trawler arrived at Lerwick (Vide also paragraph 11).

During the evening considerable W/T interference was experienced by Norwegian Steamer *Bergensfiord* working with Swedish Steamer *Stockholm*. At 10.55 p.m., *Bergensfiord* called up ML (Call Sign of Senior Officer Tenth Cruiser Squadron) and made, in plain language 'Please wait my turn now'. *Bergensfiord* had been cleared from Kirkwall for New York early in the morning. I have previously represented the interference caused by these vessels making excessive use of their Wireless after leaving Kirkwall.

5. Sunday, 3rd September – At 8.19 a.m. a W/T message was received from the Transport *Huntspill* that she had sighted a large Submarine at 7.30 a.m. in Lat. 59 North, Long. 16.10´ West steering SW. As this was at the eastern extremity of C Patrol and *Teutonic* was not far distant from the reported position, orders were immediately given to all Ships on Patrol to take all possible precautions against submarine attack. Commander-in-Chief Grand Fleet, Rear-Admiral Stornoway, and Butt of Lewis Patrol were informed.

[1]*Annetta* was carrying mahogany and rum from the Danish West Indian island of St Croix to Copenhagen, without a manifest; *Juno* was carrying wheat and rye to Larvik in Norway; *Annetta* was permitted to go on; *Juno* had to wait for guarantees to be obtained before being allowed to sail on (TS 14/11 of 2, 4 and 6 September 1916). There is no record of the treatment of *Chile*.

[2]*Sagitta* was carrying linseed oilcake to a black-listed consignee at Aarhus, ominously close to the German border; yet, after guarantees against re-export were obtained, she was allowed to sail on (TS 14/11 of 7 September 1916).

[3]*Ost* called at Lerwick on 8 September, carrying a catch of 950 barrels of salted herrings; on the 16th she was allowed to go on to Bergen (TS 14/11 of 8 and 16 September 1916).

It occurred to the Commodore that the derelict barge or lighter reported on 31st August in Lat. 58.51´ North, Long. 15.50´ West might have been mistaken for a submarine, and he made further enquiries from *Huntspill*, informing him of its reported position. The Master of the *Huntspill* replied, however, that he was positive about it being a submarine, three hundred feet long, with conning tower amidships. It was sighted at a distance of six miles, and was seen to submerge.

As the Southern Ships of C Patrol were doing by far the most boarding, there seemed a possibility of shipping passing between the Southern Ship and Rockall. The southern position of the patrol was accordingly altered to Lat. 57.30´ North, Long. 18 West.

At noon the disposition of the Squadron was as follows:

C Patrol ... *Artois*, *Orvieto*, *Teutonic*, *Mantua*, *Patia*, *Virginian*, *Hildebrand*, *Almanzora*.
D Patrol ... *Patuca*, *Motagua*.
E Patrol ... *Gloucestershire*, *Ebro*, Armed Trawlers *Rushcoe*, *Tenby Castle*.
Faeroe Island Patrol ... Armed Trawlers *Arley*, *Saxon*.
Rejoining from Liverpool ... *Otway*.
Proceeding to Swarbacks Minn ... *Andes*, *Changuinola*, Armed Trawlers *Robert Smith*, *Walpole*.
At Liverpool ... *Alsatian*, *Orcoma*.
At Clyde ... *Columbella*, *Hilary*, *Moldavia*, *Orotava*.
At Swarbacks Minn ... *Victorian*.

During the week, 128 Ships were intercepted and examined, of which twenty-six were sent in with and five without Armed Guards.

6. Monday, 4th September – *Otway*, out from Liverpool, transferred despatches to *Teutonic* and *Hildebrand* on their patrol lines, and then proceeded to Reykjavik and Thorshavn to deliver the secret packages forwarded to me under cover of Admiralty Letter M. of 19 August. She was directed to obtain any information of interest, especially with regard to the herring fishery season on the North Coast of Iceland, and the reports of submarines in the neighbourhood of the Faeroes. On her way to the rendezvous with *Teutonic*, *Otway* found a lighter painted black, named *Myrtle*, in Lat. 59 North, Long. 14.21´ West. As *Otway* did not consider that it could be towed at the necessary speed for salvage, having in view the reported presence of submarines in the vicinity, the lighter was sunk by gunfire by orders of Commodore *Teutonic*.

After this had been done a signal was received from *Walpole* that the collier *Rustingdon*, boarded in Lat. 66.30´ North, Long. 10 West from Barry Docks to Alexandrovsk, reported that on 30th August, in Lat.

58.50´ North, Long. 15.38´ West, a hundred ton lighter, painted black, parted the tow in a gale and could not be found after two days' search.

The lighter sunk by *Otway* was probably the same, or the one previously referred to in this report as having been lost by *Dowlais*.

7. Tuesday, 5th September – *Victorian*, having arrived on patrol from Swarbacks Minn, was ordered to extend C Patrol a further 30 miles to the south, making the Southern position Latitude 57 North, Long. 18 West.

8. Wednesday, 6th September – *Otway* arrived at Reykjavik at 7 a.m., and left in the evening to rendezvous with a Trawler of the Faroe Island Patrol for the purpose of handing over despatches for Thorshaven.

9. Thursday, 7th September – A Southwesterly gale was experienced which prevented any boarding during this day. *Patia* intercepted the Danish Steamer *Hellig Olaf*, from New York to Copenhagen via Kirkwall. It was not possible to board, so I ordered the vessel to proceed to Kirkwall.[1]

In the evening, HMS *Albemarle*, on passage from Alexandrovsk to Portsmouth was communicated with by W/T and informed of the positions of patrols.

The gale increased during the night.

10. Friday, 8th September – At 6 a.m., with the approval of the Commander-in-Chief, Patrol Line IV was abandoned and ships proceeded to take up their former disposition. This was considered advisable, as no submarine reports had been received since 3rd September, and the number of ships intercepted compared with the previous week showed a large decrease.

The gale increased and boarding was not possible during the day.

At 8.30 p.m. information was received from *Otway* that the French Steamer *Mingrelie* had reported by W/T that her engines were broken down and asked for assistance. *Mingrelie* stated her position was Lat. 62.88´ North, Long. 10.34´ West, and *Otway* proceeded to investigate.

The weather moderated during the night.

11. Saturday, 9th September – During the night W/T communication was regained with E Patrol. This had been lost when the Squadron assumed Patrol Line IV, and boarding reports were received. A very large number of fishing vessels were intercepted by this Patrol during the week and several sent in with Armed Guards.

[1]One item in *Hellig Olav*'s cargo (37 tons of steel pipes) was not covered by a Navicert (out of nearly three hundred items); once assurances were forthcoming, the ship was released (TS 14/11 of 11 September 1916).

With reference to my remarks of 2nd September, *Gloucestershire* reported that the Norwegian Steam Fishing Vessel *Ost*, when again intercepted with a full cargo on 3rd September, attempted to evade the patrol. *Frank Somers*, another Norwegian Steam Fishing Vessel, acted similarly. Armed Guards were placed on board in both cases, and the Admiral Commanding Orkneys and Shetlands was informed.[1]

Otway tried the whole night to find the French Steamer *Mingrelie*, but without success, and *Hilary* was detached from A Patrol in the morning to assist in the search. *Otway*, however, sighted the *Mingrelie* at 10 a.m. On boarding in Lat. 61.56´ North, Long. 11.1´ West, it was ascertained that the vessel had been leaking and pumps had broken down, but that the damage had been repaired and no help was required. The vessel was bound from Arkhangel to Brest and had 1050 Russian Troops on board.

Otway received armed guards from *Virginian* in the evening and then patrolled in vicinity of Faeroes while waiting for the return of the Trawler which had been sent with despatches to Thorshaven the previous day.

12. Sunday, 10th September – At noon the disposition of the Squadron was as follows:

A Patrol ... *Hilary*, *Orvieto*, *Almanzora*.
C Patrol ... *Victorian*, *Motagua*, *Patia*, *Virginian*, *Teutonic*.
E Patrol ... *Hildebrand*, *Patuca*.
B Patrol ... *Gloucestershire*, *Changuinola*, Armed Trawlers *Rushcoe* and *Tenby Castle*.
Faeroe Islands Patrol ... Armed Trawlers *Arley* and *Saxon*.
On Special Patrol ... *Otway*.
Proceeding from C to A Patrol ... *Andes*.
Proceeding to Swarbacks Minn ... *Ebro*.
At Swarbacks Minn ... *Artois*, Armed Trawlers *Walpole* and *Robert Smith*.
At Liverpool ... *Alsatian*, *Orcoma*.
At Clyde ... *Columbella*, *Moldavia*, *Orotava*, *Mantua*.

[1]*Frank Somers* had a cargo of brine and barrels, not having caught any fish before being sent in; it also had a guarantee from Vice-Consul Olsen in Siglufjord. This provoked the Contraband Committee to comment: 'The Admiralty should be asked whether instructions have been forwarded to H.M. Patrols not to interfere with vessels furnished with documents such as is carried by this vessel' (TS 14/11 of 12 September 1916). In fact Tupper had reported the start of the system in his previous report [257 paras 10 and 13].

During the week, 117 vessels were intercepted and examined, of which 27 were sent in with armed guards and 3 without. A large proportion of this total was intercepted by E Patrol, bad weather being experienced on the other patrols for a great part of the week.

13. Monday, 11th September – *Otway*, having received despatches the previous evening from the Trawler which had visited Thorshavn, relieved *Teutonic* at 6 a.m. in charge of C Patrol, and *Teutonic* proceeded to work between A and C Patrols ...

Gloucestershire reported that 12 Armed Guards were away, and the Commodore, therefore, directed *Almanzora* to obtain three Midshipmen and three Ratings from *Andes* and then rendezvous *Gloucestershire* on E Patrol and transfer them for use as armed guards, together with a similar number from *Almanzora*.

In the evening, information was received from the Commander-in-Chief that enemy submarines were in The Minches, Fair Island Channel and East of Orkneys. Neutral Ships with Armed Guards were, therefore, to be sent to Lerwick and Lough Swilly as far as possible. Orders were accordingly given to the Squadron.

14. Tuesday, 12th September – The weather again became too rough for boarding and the gale increased at night. *Motagua* intercepted the Norwegian Barque *Fixstjerne* from Buenos Ayres to Svaneke with linseed: and, as *Motagua* was due at Swarbacks Minn on 14th September, accompanied her in the hope of the weather improving.

15. Wednesday, 13th September – The weather still remained very bad, and at 11 a.m. *Motagua*, having reported she had been unable to board the Norwegian Barque *Fixstjerne*, parted company, ordering her to call at Lerwick.[1]

Information was received from the Admiral Commanding Orkneys and Shetlands that all ships had arrived which during the recent bad weather were ordered to call at either Lerwick or Kirkwall without being sent in with an Armed Guard.

16. Thursday, 14th September – The difficulty of providing armed guards on E Patrol again arose during the day. I, therefore, directed *Artois* (who was meeting *Gloucestershire* in the evening with four armed guards from Swarbacks Minn) to provide Armed Guards for four fishing vessels which had been intercepted and detained, transferring to

[1]*Fixstjerne* had a cargo of linseed, which was ordered to be discharged to the Prize Court. The Contraband Committee suggested an embargo on linseed imports to Sweden, but the Minister of Blockade (Lord David Cecil) only imposed a 'temporary withdrawal of all facilities' to help negotiations along (TS 14/11 of 18 and 25 September 1916).

Gloucestershire for future use, the four armed guards taking passage. *Hilary* was also detached from A Patrol to transfer all available armed guards to *Gloucestershire* and then to return to A Patrol.

The armed Trawlers *Walpole* and *Robert Smith* could not leave Swarbacks Minn until 3 p.m. owing to the gale. *Rushcoe* and *Tenby Castle* being obliged to leave E Patrol noon 15th September to replenish with coal, I approved *Changuinola* being brought east until the Trawlers joining E Patrol arrived.

17. Friday, 15th September – The work on E Patrol continued to be very great and a large number of fishing vessels were again sent in with Armed Guards.

I left Liverpool in *Alsatian* at 1 a.m. to rejoin the Squadron. The Ship had been five days' delayed owing to alterations being carried out in the magazines, and also to fact that workmen's holidays intervened. During the refit, a steam winch was fitted aft on the upper deck for the purpose of working a man lifting Kite or Kite Balloon. The man-lifting Kites have not yet been received.

18. Saturday, 16 September – At 10 a.m., I directed *Teutonic* to cease answering calls for the Senior Officer, Tenth Cruiser Squadron, and took over the Command of the Squadron.

The Commander-in-Chief informed me that the sending of Ships to Kirkwall and Stornoway could now be resumed.

As the Ships on E Patrol were again becoming short of Armed Guards, *Andes* was sent up with three for *Gloucestershire* which had been brought out from Swarbacks Minn, and also four supplied by *Teutonic*. She was further directed to supply any she could spare herself.

19. Sunday, 17th September – At noon, the disposition of the Squadron was as follows:

A Patrol, On line 360° from 63 N. 10 W ... *Artois* and *Hilary*, *Andes* temporarily detached delivering guards to E Patrol.

C Patrol, On line 340° from 58 N. 12.30´ W ... *Patia*, *Moldavia*, *Virginian*, *Columbella*.

D Patrol, On line 330° from 56.30´N. 13 W ... *Orcoma*, *Orotava*.

E Patrol, To North East of Iceland ... *Gloucestershire*, *Changuinola*, Armed Trawlers *Robert Smith* and *Walpole*.

Between A & C ... *Alsatian*.

Proceeding to A ... *Otway*.

Patrolling West of Faeroes ... Armed Trawlers *Saxon* and *Arley*.

Rejoining from Swarbacks Minn ... *Teutonic* (to C), *Ebro* (to E), *Motagua* (to C).

Rejoining from Loch Ewe ... *Patuca* (to C).

Proceeding to Liverpool ... *Almanzora*
Proceeding to Clyde ... *Orvieto*.
Proceeding to Swarbacks Minn ... Armed Trawlers *Rushcoe* and *Tenby Castle*.
At Liverpool ... *Victorian*.
At Clyde ... *Mantua*, *Hildebrand*, *Avenger*.
At London ... *Kildonan Castle* (Fitting out).[1]

During the week 162 vessels were intercepted, of which 58 were sent in with, and 14 without, Armed Guards. Both the number of vessels intercepted and sent in are the largest in any one week since the commencement of the war. The majority were intercepted on E Patrol.

At 2 p.m. *Moldavia*, in Lat. 58.48´N, Long. 12.25´W, informed me that one of the lookouts reported having sighted a small vessel with one mast and a stump funnel at an estimated distance of five miles, but that search had failed to find her – the visibility at the time was 15 miles. In view of the fact that the Commanding Officer considered the report reliable and of the possibility of the vessel proving to be a submarine, I ordered C Patrol to shift to a line running 25° from Lat. 59.38´N, Long. 7.45´W.

I had intended communicating with *Teutonic* during the course of the afternoon but the wind and sea had been rising, and by noon it was blowing hard from the north west with a nasty sea, rendering boat work risky.

20. Monday, 18th September – The gale continued throughout the night and following morning, a number of ships having to lie to. With reference to my letter No. 134/01 of 14 September 1916, forwarded through the Commander-in-Chief, relative to the unsuitability of *Orotava* for the Northern Patrol [268], her Commanding Officer reported that the ship was rolling excessively in the heavy sea, and that it was not possible to maintain her proper course without undue risk.

The weather began to moderate about noon, and at 5 p.m., I was able to communicate with *Teutonic* and receive a report from the Commodore regarding the work of the Squadron during my absence from patrol.

At the same time I received a report from the Commanding Officer of *Gloucestershire* in which he stated that when visiting Siglefiord early in the month the Consul had informed him that a German engineer by the name of Funck had taken passage in *Gullfoss* from Siglefiord to Reykjavik on 4th September.

[1]The addition of *Avenger* and *Kildonan Castle* brought the ship-strength of the squadron to the planned 24 for the first time; plus, of course, 6 armed trawlers.

This man, who is about 25–26 years of age, appears to have arrived in Iceland in September 1915 with a Bulgarian passport prior to the outbreak of hostilities with Bulgaria, and is awaiting opportunity to return to Germany. He is stated to be a very clever engineer: and it is said he has been working for some time on a W/T installation at Seidisfiord.

Changuinola in Lat. 60.5´N, Long. 14.35´W reported it was impossible to go any further with the Hulk *John* which was being taken into Lerwick by an Armed Guard with 1400 barrels of herrings, as she was in a rotten state and quite unseaworthy, and he had to take her crew on board. She was eventually towed into Seidisfiord by *Changuinola* and left there with her crew [269].

D Patrol was moved to a line 325° from Lat. 56 N, Long. 14 W.

21. Tuesday, 19th September – I met *Motagua* at 9 a.m. and boarded her for the purpose of witnessing target practice. This was decidedly good, the first salvo being fired 8 seconds after the order to engage target, second salvo 42 seconds, third salvo, which straddled, 1 m. 15 secs. Controlled independent was then ordered and an accurate fire maintained.

The mess decks were clean and well kept and the firemen's quarters creditable. The men look well and, generally speaking, the Ship is efficient and well kept.

The Russian Steamship *Ekanepeiria II* with 2079 troops on board, from Archangel to Brest, was intercepted and allowed to proceed.

22. Wednesday, 20th September – As E Patrol was once again becoming short of Armed Guards, I arranged for *Patuca* to join that Patrol, after placing four additional Armed Guards on board from *Alsatian*.

When rendezvousing with *Patuca* I took the opportunity of witnessing Target Practice. The target was unfortunately small, and there was a considerable motion on the Ship. Firing was slow and not as accurate as might have been desired; the spotting officer not being bold enough in his corrections. This was disappointing, as the Commanding Officer had taken a lot of trouble and the Ship appears to be in good order. The mess decks were clean and well kept, but the firemen's quarters are less comfortable than any I have seen. A mess place on the Main Deck has been offered them, but they prefer their meals under the poop in their sleeping quarters.

23. Thursday, 21st September – No items of interest to report.

24. With reference to clause 5 of my previous Report of Proceedings ... regarding the suspicious conduct of the Motor Schooner *Venus*, information has been received that this vessel when in the

neighbourhood of the Faeroes sprang a leak and had to be beached in Kvalbo Bay, Sydero Island. Though there is no conclusive evidence it would appear probable that the master was instrumental in scuttling the Ship. A full Report was forwarded by the Officer in charge of the Armed Guard through the Authorities at Kirkwall.[1]

25. During *Alsatian*'s refit at the commencement of this month, I took the opportunity of visiting the Admiralty and the Foreign Office, and on 11 September had an interview with Lord Robert Cecil, when the general work of the Squadron and the procedure for the examination of vessels at the various ports was discussed. I ascertained that certain cases where vessels had been released, after being sent in under suspicion, were being specially enquired into.

I also attended some Paravane experiments from HMS *Nymph* at Spithead on Thursday, September 7th, and received practical instruction in their use and handling. I have submitted a request, through the Commander-in-Chief ... that they may be supplied to Ships of the Tenth Cruiser Squadron as opportunities offer for their docking etc.

26. A Schedule of the Enclosures accompanying this Letter is attached. Amongst these are two reports from Officers in charge of Armed Guards from *Hilary* placed on board the Norwegian Vessels *Haried* [260] and *Assistent* [262]; I consider both these Officers deserve credit for the manner in which they brought their vessels into Port and I submit that it may be noted in their favour at the Admiralty.

266. *Captain Richard Webb, Director of Trade Division, to Vice-Admiral Commanding Tenth Cruiser Squadron*

Admiralty, 8 September 1916

... [P]revious to March 1916 there were several instances of vessels evading the blockade by keeping close along the land, in the manner described in the first portion of the letter from Midshipman Heap dated the 21st August [259].

2. The institution since of a more vigorous inshore patrol, and the examination of the armed trawlers of every individual vessel proceeding through these areas, has had a good effect. As shown by the recent returns, evasion of the blockade by these routes now seems to have been entirely stopped.

[1]See Chapter 8, page 492, note 1.

3. As regards the alleged evasion of the blockade by the SS *Muskogee*, this statement, like many others made by neutrals, is incorrect. This vessel called voluntarily at Kirkwall on 3rd January 1916, and was allowed to proceed on 6th January, her cargo being in accordance with the Oil Agreement, and forming part of the ration of fuel oil allowed to Sweden.

4. At the outbreak of war this vessel was the German SS *Triton*, belonging to the Deutsche Amerikasche Petroleum Gesellschaft. She was transferred to the American Flag by permission of HM Government.

267. *Contraband Committee Minutes*

9 September 1916

... [T]he consignors ... were the shippers of the larger part of the cargo of the steamship *Ada*, who intentionally evaded His Majesty's patrols. Most of these items, shipped in the steamship *Ada* by Messrs Hamilton and Hansell, were either for suspect consignors or would have been held up by His Majesty's Government owing to the nature of the commodity [257 para. 6].

268. *Vice-Admiral Tupper to Commander-in-Chief Grand Fleet*

HMS *Alsatian*, 14 September 1916

I have the honour to represent that I consider it advisable that *Orotava* and *Mantua* should be sent to some smooth water station such as mid-Atlantic. Both these vessels were built for fine weather service in warm climates. Apart from this they were both severely strained in the gales of last winter and *Mantua* has also been strained by grounding.

If therefore they can be exchanged for two Armed Merchant Cruisers accustomed to North Atlantic work for the winter it would be a great advantage. Neither *Orotava* nor *Mantua* are considered fit to face the heavy gales and weather normally experienced during the winter on the Northern Patrol.

269. *Captain H.E.R. Brocklebank to Vice-Admiral Commanding Tenth Cruiser Squadron*

HMS *Changuinola*, 19 September 1916

***

On Saturday 16th Sept., at 7.30 pm I boarded the Norwegian SS *Hodd* near Langanaes and turned her over to *Gloucestershire*, Captain Stanley being S.O. of E Patrol. I was ordered by him to put an armed guard in charge of a petty officer on board any ship that should be sent in, with instructions to the petty officer to keep the ship near Langanaes Point and under the orders of Lieutenant Cook RNR[1] who had been put aboard *Hodd* for the purpose. At 8.45 p.m. I placed CPO A.J. Bagnall (Official No. P.148415) on board the Norwegian SS *Sele* towing the hulk *John*, turned him over to Lieutenant Cook and proceeded to my patrol. On Sunday 17th Sept. at 7.55 a.m. and 9.10 a.m. I placed petty officer's guards on board Swedish SS *Hero* and Norwegian Brigantine *Maagen* respectively and accompanied them to Langanaes where I boarded the Norwegian SS *Tampen* and took all three ships some ten miles to the southward where I met *Gloucestershire* and got some armed guards from him, sending *Hero* and *Tampen* into Lerwick whilst *Gloucestershire*, with some difficulty on account of rising wind, did the same with *Maagen*.[2] By 8.0 p.m. it was blowing a gale from the North with a rising sea and I felt considerable anxiety concerning *Sele*, but an intercepted W/T message from Trawler *Robert Smith* in whose charge she then was, said they were endeavouring to anchor her in Eidis Bay. At 8.40 p.m. I intercepted a message from *Robert Smith* saying that *Sele* was in trouble and I proceeded with *Gloucestershire* to find them. At 11.8 p.m. we found *Sele* and I remained standing by whilst *Gloucestershire* proceeded. *Sele* had *John* in tow and was holding her against the gale.

On Monday 18th Sept. at 5.45 a.m. the tow rope parted and I attempted to get a line on board *John*. It was too rough for boat work; several attempts were made with rockets and heaving lines from windward. At 8.0 a.m. the mist cleared and showed we were about 2 miles NNE of Biarnarey Lat 65.47´N, Long 14.16´W which was unpleasantly close in a Northerly gale. I succeeded in getting a $4\frac{1}{2}$"

[1]Cook, Sub-Lieutenant 1916.

[2]Neither *Hero* nor *Tampen* were detained; *Maagen*'s cargo, however, was sent to the Prize Court since the canning company (the cargo was herrings) was on the Black List (TS 14/11 of 29 September to 10 October 1916, *passim*).

wire aboard but *John*'s crew were too exhausted to handle it, and could not haul in the eye: next time I got a 3" wire on board which parted after tearing away the fair lead and bulwarks on the port side of her forecastle. At 10.0 a.m., the weather having moderated, I sent a boat under Acting Lieutenant Tom Smith RNR[1] who reported that the ship was leaking badly and in a rotten condition; with great difficulty he disembarked the crew and brought them to me. I recovered Chief Petty Officer Bagnall and his Armed Guard from *Sele* and allowed her to proceed. At 1.0. p.m., there being considerable improvement in the weather and having drifted into Hierars Floin clear of Biarnarey, I decided to try again and sent Act. Lieutenant T. Smith RNR with a strong party on board. At the second attempt I got a 4½" wire on board and at 3.0 p.m. when one mile north of Osfles I had her in tow and proceeded to Seidisfiord. At 5.0 p.m. in a slight swell and light Northerly wind towing at five knots her cable parted. I had hold of her again in half an hour and proceeded accompanied by *Robert Smith* who had been standing by since 2.0 p.m. At 9.30 p.m. I cast off the tow abreast of Strandberg in Seidisfiord and directed *Robert Smith* to go alongside her and take her up to a berth in shallower water. He anchored her about 11.0 p.m with her own crew on board and we both proceeded to rejoin our patrols.

I wish particularly to bring before you the names of Acting Lieutenant Tom Smith RNR who showed energy, resource, courage, and thorough seamanship and to whom the success of the salvage was largely due; and also Acting Lieutenant Percival RNR,[2] who handled his boat, when taking over the lines in his usual masterly manner: the arrangements on board *Changuinola* under Lieutenant F.H.D. Clarke, RNR the Executive Officer, were efficiently carried out. Petty Officer William Baker (Official No. 163292) and Act. Leading Seamen Shute R.N.V.R. (Official No. Z.263C) performed excellent work on board *John*. Credit is due to Chief Petty Officer Bagnall for the way in which he stuck to his tow when aboard *Sele*.

[1]Smith, Tom, RNR, Midshipman 1913, Lieutenant 1917.
[2]Percival, Herbert, RNR, Sub-Lieutenant 1914, Lieutenant 1916.

270. *Comment by Rear-Admiral de Chair during discussions on awards for Artois*

19 September 1916

It is true that on first joining the Tenth Cruiser Squadron, *Artois* only evinced a moderate desire to keep the sea, but this state of affairs rapidly improved after a British Naval officer had been attached to her for a period, and her officers and men had learnt what was expected of them.

I concur in the desirability of including *Artois* in the award of decorations, etc., to the Tenth Cruiser Squadron. This would no doubt have a good effect, politically.

271. *Diary of Dr J. Shaw*

21 September 1916. One of the armed guard officers and a few others foregathered in our cabin and we had a little conversation. The armed guards made slighting remarks about engineer officers. Since I have joined the ship I have found there is a great antipathy between officers and engineers in the merchant service.

It does not end there; these RNR officers bring it into the Navy with them; they consider themselves to be of a higher social status than the engineers as probably they are to a certain extent, though I have observed as intelligent men among the engineers as among the deck officers; in fact I may say about the most intelligent talker among the junior officers to be one of the engineers. The engineers have recently got a [ruling] denoting that they are of executive rank. This has caused quite a wave of indignation among the deck officers RNR, some of the latter formerly mates on tramp steamers.

272. *Vice-Admiral Tupper to Admiralty*

HMS *Alsatian*, 1 October 1916

Report of Proceedings, 22 September–1 October 1916

***

1. Friday, 22nd September – Misty and thick weather was experienced.

At 5 a.m. *Otway* intercepted the Norwegian Steamer *Lyngenfiord*, from Narvik to Philadelphia, with a cargo of ore and wood flour. She was allowed to proceed ...

In the course of the forenoon, I met *Avenger*, which had left Clyde on 19th September to join my flag, and went on board. I inspected the Ship's Company at Divisions, and visited the Mess Decks, etc. The men look healthy and well set-up. The ship is clean and well kept, mess decks and crew's quarters being very creditable. The Gunnery efficiency is, however, low – she has no Deflection Teacher or Spotting Table, and has not done Target Practice with Service Ammunition since her Gunnery Trials on commissioning, some five or six months ago. The Lieutenant (G) on my Staff will be sent to her for a week shortly. She is a beautiful ship, and an ideal one for duty with the Tenth Cruiser Squadron.

At 7 p.m., the Commander-in-Chief informed me that several enemy submarines had been sighted in the Northern part of the North Sea, and ordered me to move the patrols to the westward.

Orders were accordingly given for C Patrol to proceed at once to work on a line 340° from Latitude 58 North, Longitude 12.30´ West, and A Patrol on a similar line of bearing from Latitude 61.30´ North, Longitude 15 West.

2. Saturday, 23rd September – D Patrol was moved to line from Latitude 54.30´ North, Longitude 12 West.

Thick fog was encountered during the greater part of the day. In the evening, however, *Alsatian* intercepted the Danish SS *Fox II*, with cryolite on board, and sent her to Kirkwall. This steamer, on her previous voyage, was detained at Lerwick for a very considerable time.[1]

3. Sunday, 24th September – The disposition of the Squadron at noon was as follows:

A Patrol, 340° from Lat. 61.30´ North, Long. 15 West ... *Artois*, *Patia*.
C Patrol, on line 340° from Lat. 58 North, Long. 12.30´ West ... *Motagua*, *Teutonic*, *Avenger*, *Moldavia*.
D Patrol, on line 310° from Lat. 54.30´ North, Long. 12 West ... *Orotava*, *Orcoma*.
E Patrol, off NE of Iceland ... *Hilary*, *Ebro*, *Patuca*, and Armed Trawlers *Robert Smith* and *Walpole*.
Patrolling between A and C ... *Alsatian*.
Joining D from A ... *Andes*.
Joining E from Swarbacks Minn ... *Changuinola*.
Joining C from Clyde ... *Hildebrand*.
Proceeding to Swarbacks Minn ... *Otway*, *Columbella*.

[1]*Fox II* was investigated and then allowed to go on (TS 14/11 of 29 September 1916).

At Liverpool ... *Victorian*, *Almanzora*.
At Clyde ... *Mantua*, *Orvieto*.
At Swarbacks Minn ... *Virginian*, *Gloucestershire*, and Armed Trawlers *Rushcoe*, *Tenby Castle*, *Arley*, and *Saxon*.
At London (Fitting out) ... *Kildonan Castle*.

During the week, 126 vessels were intercepted, of which 33 were sent in with Armed Guards. The majority of these ships were again intercepted by E Patrol.

I met *Otway* about noon, and had a short interview with Commodore Booty.

Passed through foggy patches during the day.

4. Monday, 25th September – *Alsatian* carried out Target Practice with service charges. The practice was good, three salvoes being fired under the minute, and the target straddled – speed of ship, 18 knots.

Hildebrand, who was bringing out ratings for various ships, from the Clyde, reported that two cases of Measles had developed on board. She was directed to isolate the cases, and retain all ratings for the time being.

5. Tuesday, 26th September – I arranged for the Armed Trawler *Rushcoe*, which was leaving Swarbacks Minn, to call at Thorshavn to obtain from the British Consul a translation of the guarantee to be used when boarding Danish fishing vessels off the Faroes and Iceland.

I met *Hildebrand* at 1 p.m., in misty weather, and received mails. The W/T Direction Finder was most useful, as both ships were using D.R., owing to thick weather.

The news that His Majesty had bestowed a C.B. on Commodore Booty, and Decorations on other officers and men of the Tenth Cruiser Squadron, was received with great pleasure and gratitude.

6. Wednesday, 27th September – Thick fog.

Owing to the presence of enemy submarines in the Fair Island Channel ships were ordered to send in vessels for examination to Lerwick, Stornoway, and Lough Swilly as far as possible. The Commander-in-Chief informed me that, for the time being, it was inadvisable to place Armed Guards on board sailing ships unless the Cargo was considered suspicious and of considerable value to the enemy.

Hilary reported that *Robert Smith* had intercepted, sent to Kirkwall with an Armed Guard, the Norwegian Steamer *Alf*, with the Ketch *Polen* in tow, authorizing her to call at the Faroe Islands for coal. *Robert Smith* had been ordered to overtake her, if possible, cancel this permission, and conduct her to the nearest ship of the Tenth Cruiser Squadron in order that she might be supplied with sufficient coal to take her to Kirkwall, direct – but unfortunately, owing to thick weather, the *Robert Smith* was unable to find her.[1]

7. Thursday, 28th September – The weather continued misty.

At 4 p.m., I met the Armed Trawler *Rushcoe* (Lieutenant John T. Randell, RNR) at a rendezvous North West of the Faroes, and received a report or his visit to Thorshavn ...

8. Friday, 29th September – At noon, I moved C Patrol to a line 340° from Latitude 58 North, Longitude 14 West, and D, which had now been reduced to one ship, to 230° from Latitude 58.6´ North, Longitude 11.35´ West.

At 2.30 p.m., *Rushcoe* reported that the white metal of the H.P. crank head had run, and that another bearing was heated. I ordered her to direct *Robert Smith*, or one of the other Trawlers, to tow her to Swarbacks Minn, if necessary; otherwise to anchor and effect repairs if this would not take too long.

9. Saturday, 30th September – Having obtained permission from Admiralty, I ordered *Almanzora*, who was rejoining from Liverpool, to proceed to join E Patrol via the West and North Coasts of Iceland, calling at Reykjavik on her way to obtain the latest information from the British Consul as to cargoes of oil, skins, etc, awaiting shipment at Icelandic Ports.

The Admiral Commanding Orkneys and Shetlands informed me that the Norwegian SS *Tongen* and *Bordeyri*, which had been intercepted by *Gloucestershire* on 16th September, and allowed to proceed on the understanding that they called at Lerwick, ... had failed to call.[2] It is possible that there is some reason for this as the Norwegian SS *Havornen* and Swedish Ketch *Water Lily* sent into Lerwick with armed guard, also by *Gloucestershire* on the same day, have not yet arrived. Further enquiries are being made with regard to the latter [275].

At 4.25 p.m., a signal was received from the Admiralty Oiler *Califol* stating she was attacked by a submarine in Latitude 59.48´ North, Longitude 50.5´ West. I immediately ordered the Armed Trawlers *Arley* and *Saxon*, who were patrolling in the neighbourhood of the Faroes, to proceed to her assistance. Shortly afterwards, however, signals were intercepted that Destroyers were on their way to her, and later that the

[1]*Polen* called at Kirkwall anyway, and, having posted a bond for the cargo of 110 barrels of herrings, was allowed to sail on to her destination (TS 14/11 of 2 and 5 Octember 1916).

[2]*Bordeyri* had in fact been reported to the Contraband Committee on 22 September and was given leave to continue her voyage at once (TS 14/11 of 22 September 1916). There is no record of *Tongen*.

submarine had been evaded. The orders to the Trawlers were therefore countermanded.

As I was unable to get into touch with *Rushcoe* by W/T, I directed *Robert Smith* to search for her in Westmanhavn: she was however unable to find her.

10. Sunday, 1st October – At 9 a.m., having met the Armed Trawler *Robert Smith* to the North-East of the Faroes, and supplied her with provisions, I gave her directions to search for *Rushcoe*, in conjunction with *Arley* and *Saxon*; at 10 p.m., I received a signal from *Arley* to say that *Rushcoe* had repaired damage and was proceeding to patrol, having left Westmanhavn the previous day, before the arrival of *Robert Smith*.

As *Victorian* and *Orvieto* were now joining D, I directed patrol to be formed on a line 340° from Latitude 56.8´ North, Longitude 12.45´ West.

At 7 p.m., information was received from the Commander-in-Chief that a submarine had been sighted in Latitude 60 North, Longitude 4.20´ West, at 1 p.m. on 30th September, steaming West at slow speed, in company with a cargo steamer of about 2000 tons with the word Holland painted in white letters on her side. Patrols were warned accordingly, and directed to take special precautions in case these vessels should be acting in company. As 30 hours had elapsed since the steamer and submarine were seen in the position given, I did not consider it was any use searching for her in *Alsatian*, and I therefore proceeded towards Swarbacks Minn.

The disposition of the Squadron at noon was as follows:

A Patrol, on line 340° from Lat 61 N, Long 14 W ... *Gloucestershire*, *Artois*.
C Patrol on line 340° from Lat. 58 N, Long. 14 W ... *Orcoma*, *Columbella*, *Avenger*, *Otway*.
D Patrol, on line 340° from Lat. 56.8´N, Long. 12.45´W ... *Patia*.
E Patrol, off NE Coast of Iceland ... *Virginian*, *Changuinola*, and Armed Trawler *Walpole*.
Patrolling off Faroes ... Armed Trawlers *Rushcoe*, *Tenby Castle*, *Robert Smith*, *Arley* and *Saxon*.
Joining A from C ... *Hildebrand*.
Joining A from Swarbacks Minn ... *Moldavia*.
Joining D from Liverpool ... *Victorian*.
Joining D from Clyde ... *Orvieto*.
Proceeding to Reykjavik ... *Almanzora*.
Proceeding to Swarbacks Minn ... *Alsatian*.
Proceeding to Clyde ... *Ebro*.

At Liverpool ... *Teutonic*, *Andes*.
At Clyde ... *Mantua*, *Motagua*.
At Swarbacks Minn ... *Hilary*, *Orotava*, *Patuca*.
At London (Fitting out) ... *Kildonan Castle*.

During the past week 79 vessels were intercepted, of which 18 were sent in to port for further examination. This big decrease in the numbers intercepted is accounted for by thick and foggy weather, and the fact that far fewer ships were met with proceeding from Iceland to Scandinavian ports, and it is understood that the herring fishery season is now practically at an end and that the British Vice-Consul, Mr Olsen, has left Siglefiord.

It is proposed to reduce E Patrol to two vessels next week.

I passed the boom at the entrance to Swarbacks Minn at 11.30, and anchored at midnight.

11. With reference to Paragraph 20 of my previous report of proceedings ... I enclose a report from the Commanding Officer of *Changuinola* regarding the assistance rendered to the Norwegian SS *Sele* and hulk *John*. I consider that good seamanship was shown on the part of Captain Brocklebank, and that credit is due him, and to the officers and men mentioned in the last paragraph of the report [269].

***

273. *Lieutenant J.T. Randell RNR to Commanding Officer HMS* Gibraltar

HMT *Rushcoe*, 23 September 1916

I have the honour to submit that this my application to be transferred from this base may be forwarded to the Vice-Admiral Commanding Tenth Cruiser Squadron for his favourable consideration.

I have been 21 months in command of Armed Trawlers in Far Northern Waters covering two winters and feel that in view of the experience gained at the services I have endeavoured to render, I may be qualified for command of a patrol vessel working at a more southerly base.[1]

[1]A similar application was made by Lt J. MacIntosh of *Robert Smith* on 8 September. The difference between these, clearly concerted, applications, and the 'mutiny' of the stokers on *Teutonic* (ADM 137/1218, 157) is a matter of form only: the officers knew the correct procedure, the stokers didn't.

274. *Admiralty to Commander-in-Chief Home Fleets*

Admiralty, 24 September 1916

With reference to your submission of the 16th inst, No. 2133/HD 0010 I am commanded by My Lords Commissioners of the Admiralty to acquaint you that they approve of HM Ships *Mantua* and *Orotava* being detached from the Tenth Cruiser Squadron [268].

2. HMS *Mantua* is found to have sustained serious damage through grounding. She will not therefore rejoin the Tenth Cruiser Squadron.

3. HMS *Orotava* should be detached as soon as either *Armadale Castle* or *Arlanza* have joined the Tenth Cruiser Squadron, probably about the beginning of November.

275. *Midshipman A.J. Bell*[1] *to Commanding Officer HMS* Hilary

28 September 1916

I have the honour to submit the following report.

The Norwegian Motor Ketch *Catherine* was intercepted by HMS *Gloucestershire* off Langanaes Iceland and I with an armed guard from HMS *Hilary* was placed on board with orders to proceed to Lerwick in company with a Swedish Ketch who also had an armed guard on board from HMS *Hilary* with similar instructions.

She kept company for 24 hours until Sunday 17 September at 6.0 p.m. Lat. 64.25´N, Long. 9.45´W, when we were half a mile distant hove to in a heavy Northerly gale. I went below for ten minutes to confer with the Master and on returning on deck could not see the Swedish Ketch in sight, the visibility being three miles. Being hove to it was impossible for me to go in search of her at once, but I did so when the first opportunity offered, which was 28 hours later, Monday 10.30 p.m. I beat around for two hours but could not find traces of her or wreckage, but my position was now uncertain, having drifted in my estimation fifty miles. I could do no more so continued my course to Lerwick. The Officer in charge of Armed Guard on Swedish Ketch was Midshipman W.N. Seal, RNR,[2] but I do not know the vessel's name.

We were ordered to keep company by HMS *Gloucestershire* because my compass was so unreliable. The remainder of the passage is uneventful. On arriving at Birewick anchorage 6.30 p.m. Thursday 21st

[1]Bell, Arthur J., RNR, Midshipman 1914, Acting Sub-Lieutenant 1919, Lieutenant serving in *Arpha* 1940.

[2]Seal, William N., RNR, Midshipman 1916.

September I discovered the Swedish Ketch had not arrived, which was strange to me as she was a larger vessel and of greater speed than the *Catherine*.[1]

276. *Vice-Admiral Tupper to Admiralty*

HMS *Alsatian*, 18 October 1916

Report of Proceedings, 2–18 October 1916

***

1. Monday, 2 October – *Alsatian* commenced coaling about 6 a.m. and by 6 p.m. had received 1200 tons of coal at an average of 149 per hour.

Achilles sailed to patrol the Archangel route; her Captain showed me his orders.

A site was selected for the erection of a Church Army Recreation hut which will be a great boon to the men of the Tenth Cruiser Squadron when they are able to land.

2. Tuesday, 3 October – *Artois* arrived about 6 a.m. Captain de Marguerye reported that her boilers and condensers were in a very bad state and would require a week to be put in order. I sent the Engineer Commander on my staff to investigate the cause of this unlooked for breakdown and find it was due to fair wear and tear.

The news was received that the four Commanders in Command of *Patuca*, *Victorian*, *Changuinola* and *Ebro*, who had been recommended for the acting rank of Captain, had been promoted. I desire respectfully to thank Their Lordships for so quickly granting my request which has given the recipients great satisfaction.

Hilary and *Patuca* sailed to rejoin patrol.

3. Wednesday, 4 October – Information was received that enemy submarines disguised as fishing vessels were operating off North Cape, Norway. Vessels met with on their way to Archangel were warned accordingly.

I met and conferred with Captain Eustace la T. Leatham,[2] of HMS *Cochrane*, during the day.

At 1 p.m., I left Swarbacks Minn in *Alsatian* to rejoin patrol.

[1] *Catherine*'s cargo was salt and herrings; she was allowed to go on (TS 14/11 of 23 and 30 September 1916).

[2] Leatham, Eustace la Trobe, CB, RN (1870–1935), Lieutenant 1892, Commander 1903, Captain 1909, Rear Admiral (retired) 1922.

4. Thursday, 3 October – At 3 p.m., I met *Changuinola* at rendezvous to the North of the Faroes ...

I went on board *Changuinola*, and inspected the crew and mess decks. She appears to be in very good order, but there is apparently no organised recreation room for the ship's company. I consider this essential for long winter nights: No. 2 hold can be fitted for the purpose, and I have arranged with the Captain Superintendent Clyde, for this to be done.

5. Friday, 6 October – As the herring-fishery season on the North East Coast of Iceland is now at an end, and – further – as a report had been received that vessels were evading the patrols by keeping as near to the Greenland Coast as possible and passing well to the North of Iceland – and so to the Norwegian coast, I ordered *Almanzora* and *Hilary*, on E Patrol, to proceed and patrol Denmark Strait between Iceland and the edge of the ice pack. The two Trawlers were, however, left off Langanaes to intercept any vessels that might be bringing the remainder of the season's catch of fish, herring oil, etc., from Icelandic Ports.

Orcoma intercepted and sent in to Kirkwall the Danish mail steamer *Oscar II*, from New York to Christiansund and Copenhagen. There were 13 Germans and Austrians amongst the passengers, and she was carrying 1253 bags of mails, some of which were destined for Germany.[1]

The weather had been very thick all day; cold, and blowing hard from the South East.

6. Saturday, 7 October – At 6 a.m. *Alsatian*, in Latitude 61.24´ North, Longitude 11.44´ West, intercepted the British Collier *Trowbridge* (Owners – W. Doxford & Sons, Sunderland), bound from Barry to Archangel with a cargo of coal. The Master, Mr William R. Marrs, had sustained a simple fracture of the leg during the rough weather of the previous day, and, as he was in need of medical assistance, was brought on board *Alsatian*. It was found advisable to send him to hospital at first opportunity, and he was accordingly transferred to *Virginian* the same afternoon for passage to Liverpool.

Lieutenant John E. Jones, RNR,[2] of *Alsatian*, was placed on board *Trowbridge* to take her to Archangel, the mate of the vessel not feeling competent to do so.

At 11 a.m., *Kildonan Castle*, which has just joined the Squadron,

[1]*Oscar II* was not detained.

[2]Jones, John Edward, RNR, Sub-Lieutenant 1915, Lieutenant 1917.

was met. I embarked, and cruised in her for an hour, inspecting the mess decks and ship's company. The ship promises well, and is a valuable acquisition, but so far she has no Gunnery instructional appliances. I left the W/T Officer and Lieutenant (G) on my staff on board to advise the Captain and Officers as to the general routine and duties in connection with the work of the Squadron – especially as regards W/T and Gunnery.

7. Sunday, 8 October – During the night, the patrol lines were moved to the eastward by order of the Commander-in-Chief, and at noon the disposition of the Squadron was as follows:

A Patrol, on line 310° from Lat. 60.31´N, Long. 12.48´W ... *Gloucestershire*, *Moldavia*.
Off Portland Light Iceland ... *Hildebrand*.
C Patrol, on line 325° from Lat. 59.38´ N, Long, 7.45´W ... *Columbella*, *Orotava*, *Avenger*, *Kildonan Castle*, and *Otway*.
D Patrol, on line 360° from Lat. 57.5´N, Long 12 W ... *Patuca*, *Victorian*.
E Patrol, Off N.W. of Iceland ... *Almanzora*, *Hilary*.
Off Langanaes ... Armed Trawlers *Rushcoe* and *Tenby Castle*.
Between A and C ... *Alsatian*.
Joining A from D ... *Orvieto*.
Patrolling to E of Faroes ... Armed Trawlers *Saxon* and *Arley*.
Proceeding to Liverpool ... *Virginian*.
Proceeding to Clyde ... *Changuinola*.
Proceeding to Swarbacks Minn ... *Orcoma*.
At Liverpool ... *Teutonic*, *Andes*.
At Clyde ... *Patia*, *Motagua*, *Ebro*.
At Swarbacks Minn ... *Artois* and Armed Trawlers *Robert Smith* and *Walpole*.[1]

105 vessels were intercepted during the course of the week of which 26 were sent in with armed guards. A large number of ships were intercepted bound for Archangel.

About noon, *Alsatian* intercepted the Norwegian Barque *Cedarbank* in Latitude 61.31´ North, Longitude 15.53´ West, bound from New York to Leith with 4300 tons of barley. As, from the position in which she was intercepted, she appeared to be much out of her course, and as it was very undesirable that this valuable cargo should go to Norway or Germany, I placed an Armed Guard on board with orders to take her to

[1]The number of ships is again below establishment, at 23, and *Orotava* is due to leave.

Lerwick, or the nearest port, in order that she might be towed to her destination [279 paras 1, 3 and 21].

In the afternoon *Moldavia* was met for the purpose of transferring armed guards. The Engineer Commander on my staff went on board to inspect the steering engine, which had badly broken down, and had been temporarily repaired in a creditable manner.

8. Monday, 9 October – Since the previous evening, *Alsatian* had been proceeding north to supply the trawlers off Langanaes with armed guards and to get into W/T communication with *Almanzora* and *Hilary*, who were specially on the look out for the SS *Ada* off the North West of Iceland.

About 9 p.m. in Latitude 65.13´ North, Longitude 10.42´ West, *Alsatian* intercepted the Norwegian Steamer *Hercules* from New York to Archangel, with a cargo of oil, copper, railway materials, etc. The master stated that, if unable to pass Vardo Island by 15 October, he was permitted to discharge his cargo in Norway: apparently he intended to do this, as he was heading for Norway, and said he could not reach Vardo Island by the date given. Having recently read in a weekly Bulletin of Trade Information that it is not desirable to allow any more copper to go to Norway, and the bearing of the master being suspicious, I considered it advisable to send her in to Lerwick with an armed guard. Her crew was entirely composed of Chinese, the officers being Norwegian.[1]

The weather was bad to the Southward, ships on A and C Patrols being unable to board in a number of cases.

9. Tuesday, 10 October – At 6.30 p.m., *Moldavia* reported that the steering engine had again broken down, the crankshaft bearings having fractured. As the vessel could then only be steered by hand wheel, I ordered her to proceed to Clyde to effect repairs.

Having communicated with the trawlers *Rushcoe* and *Tenby Castle* off Larganaes, *Alsatian* supplied them with three armed guards, and provisions, etc., and then proceeded South.

The weather off Langanaes was fine and clear, a good deal of snow on the high land making the air cold.

10. Wednesday, 11 October – About 6 p.m., I met *Artois* to the North of the Faroes; gave her orders to patrol off Langanaes and to maintain W/T communication with *Almanzora*. I received several armed guards from *Artois*, and proceeded South-West to distribute them. A heavy westerly gale sprang up during the first watch.

[1]*Hercules* was allowed to go on, the problem of her apparent wish to discharge in Norway being handed over to the Navy (TS 14/11 of 14 and 16 October 1916).

11. Thursday, 12 October – Strong westerly gale, with heavy sea. As boarding was rendered impossible, ships were obliged to accompany vessels on which it was desired to place armed guards, until the weather moderated.

12. Friday, 13 October – Gale had abated, but heavy hail showers and confused sea during the day made boarding only just possible.

Avenger intercepted the Danish Sailing Vessel *Laurits* in Latitude 59.40´ North, Longitude 9 West, from Reykjavik to Barcelona, with a cargo of fish. She was sent in to Stornoway with an armed guard, in compliance with the Admiralty messages 0215 and 1750 of 9th October.[1]

The Swedish SS *Baltic*, referred to in N.I.D/O.L. of 30 September as possibly carrying German correspondence, was also sent in with an armed guard, by *Orotava*.[2] The SS *Dania*, referred to in the same communication, had previously been sent in, on 10th October, by *Orotava*.[3]

At 4.30 p.m., *Patuca* boarded the Russian SS *Australia* from Cardiff to Archangel with a cargo of coal. Her master reported that owing to the bad quality of coal supplied for steaming purposes, his ship was only able to attain a speed of 5 knots. This is the second case of this description that has been brought to my notice in the past week – the master of the *Trowbridge*, intercepted on 7 October, making the same complaint.

In view of the submarine menace on the Archangel route, it would appear to be a matter of some importance for such ships to be supplied with coal of very good quality, to enable them to attain as high a speed as possible in case of necessity.

Hildebrand and *Gloucestershire* were met during the day, and armed guards distributed. I regret to report that a mercantile steward, James Chisholm, was found to be missing from *Hildebrand* – presumably lost overboard; the Court of Enquiry could find no reason to account for his disappearance. The Admiralty were informed by W/T.

[1]*Lauritz* was detained because her manifest did not reach the Contraband Committee; otherwise there was no problem (TS 14/11 of 14 and 20 October 1916).

[2]*Baltic*'s cargo raised many small issues, some of which were covered by letters of assurance, though some of *those* were out of date; nevertheless the Contraband Committee was prepared to let the ship go on if guarantees were forthcoming. In the end these were acquired, and the further revelation that one of the consignees had imported German silver to the USA did not alter the decision (TS 14/11 of 16 to 26 October 1916).

[3]*Dania* was on the White List, but there were questions over the precise ownership of some items in the cargo on this occasion. The ship was still delayed near the end of the month (TS 14/11 of 13 to 26 October 1916).

13. Saturday, 14 October – After the temporary lull, a bad south-easterly gale sprang up during the morning, and considerably hampered the work of the patrol being efficiently carried out.

At 2.45 p.m., the Commander-in-Chief informed me that a submarine had been sighted at 3.30 p.m. the previous day, in Latitude 59.50´ North, Longitude 6.49´ West, steaming in a westerly direction, and ordered me to move the patrol to the westward. C Patrol was accordingly directed to take up a line 340° from Latitude 58 North, Longitude 14 West.

Orders were also received from the Admiralty and Commander-in-Chief to warn the Roumanian SS *Jiul*, if met with, that a submarine was probably lying in wait for her, and direct her to alter her course to the Northward. With a view to intercepting her, *Orvieto* was ordered to patrol on the meridian of 14 West between 60 and 61 North, and *Kildonan Castle* between 63.30´ and 64 North on the meridian of 7 West, but so far no news has been received of her. Three steamers – *Adenwell*, *Stellina* and *Westgate* – bound for Archangel, were warned to communicate the Admiralty message to *Jiul* if they saw her.

14. Sunday, 15 October – The gale continued throughout the night, the wind backing to the North West, with a high sea; about noon, however, the weather began to moderate. I met *Motagua* at 4 p.m., and was able, in spite of the heavy sea, to obtain despatches and ratings from her.

At 8 p.m., *Alsatian* intercepted the British Collier *Westgate*, from Cardiff to Archangel, returning to Londonderry owing to the master having broken his leg, besides sustaining injuries to his head, and two men being also injured during the gale. Surgeon Ernest J. Cooke, RN,[1] of *Alsatian*, was put on board to attend to the injured, and accompany the vessel into harbour.

The disposition of the Squadron at noon was as follows:

A Patrol, on meridian of Long 14 W between Lat. 60 and 61 N ... *Orvieto*.
Off Portland Light ... *Hildebrand*.
C Patrol, on line 340° from Lat. 58 N, Long. 14 W ... *Victorian*, *Avenger*, *Orcoma*, *Otway*.
D Patrol ... *Alsatian*.
E Patrol, off N.W. of Iceland ... *Almanzora*, *Hilary*.
Do off Langanaes ... Armed Trawlers *Rushcoe* and *Tenby Castle*.

[1]Cooke, Ernest J., RN, Surgeon-Sub-Lieutenant 1916.

Patrolling to East of Faroes ... Armed Trawlers *Saxon* and *Arley*.
Special Patrol North of Faroes ... *Kildonan Castle*.
Joining A from E ... *Artois*.
Rejoining E from Clyde ... *Motagua*.
Rejoining E from Swarbacks Minn ... Armed Trawlers *Robert Smith* and *Walpole*.
Proceeding to Clyde ... *Gloucestershire*, *Patuca*.
Proceeding to Swarbacks Minn ... *Orotava*.
At Liverpool ... *Virginian*, *Andes*, *Teutonic*.
At Clyde ... *Changuinola*, *Ebro*, *Patia*, *Moldavia*.
At Swarbacks Minn ... *Columbella*.

63 vessels were intercepted during the week, of which 25 were sent in with, and 1 without, Armed Guards.

Nothing has been heard of the SS *Ada*. With the Patrols NW of Iceland and off Portland Light, it seems improbable she got through there. A Patrol has been fairly strong, too, but *Moldavia* had to leave owing to steering engine defects. The space of 30 miles between the 10th Cruiser Squadron and the 100 Fathom Line off Hebrides appears to me to be a probable route for vessels evading patrol for unless they happen to be met by 10th Cruiser Squadron Ships proceeding to, or coming from, Swarbacks Minn, there is nothing to prevent their following the 100 fathom line till they reach the area patrolled by the Cruiser and Armed Boarding Steamer. They could probably get past these to the Coast of Norway in the dark. Now that the Iceland Fishing Season is over, I hope shortly to patrol this space with two or three Trawlers based on Oban.

15. Monday, 16th October – With reference to paragraph 9 of my Report of Proceedings (Submission No. 553/35) of 2 October 1916 and my Submission No. 579/3 of 4 October 1916, *Motagua*, just out of Clyde, informed me that she had the armed guard of *Water Lily* on board.

Gloucestershire was met, proceeding to the Clyde, and despatches placed on board. Engineer Commander Bell[1] on my Staff was also sent in her to join *Virginian* at Liverpool to run full power trial on her leaving to rejoin patrol, as she has not been able to attain her reputed speed.

It came on to blow again from South West, but was just able to transfer armed guards to *Avenger* at dusk, and get boats up before the sea became too bad.

[1]Bell, Henry F., RN, Engineer Commander 1908, Engineer Commander on Vice-Admiral Tupper's Staff in *Alsatian*, 1916, Engineer Captain (retired) 1923.

16. Tuesday, 17 October – The visibility was very low throughout the day, and much wind and sea. Except for a trawler, no vessels were intercepted. I got into W/T communication with E Patrol, and the trawlers off Iceland, but they had nothing to report.

17. Wednesday, 18 October – About 2.30 p.m., a message was received from the Commander-in-Chief to the effect that numerous submarines had been sighted to the North of the Shetlands, and ordering me to move the patrol to line No. IV. Orders were given accordingly for ships on A, C and D Patrols to form on line 360° from Latitude 55.38´ North, Longitude 18 West, one ship remaining off Portland Light, Iceland.

Alsatian arrived at Swarbacks Minn about 10 p.m. No submarines were sighted.

18. The following extract from a report of Lieutenant John A. Douglas, R.N.V.R., of *Alsatian*, containing information obtained when acting as officer in charge of an armed guard on board the Norwegian SS *Alf*, sent in on 27 September, is forwarded as being of interest:

'The owners of the ship and cargo were Messrs Falk, Stavanger. Up to four months ago they acted as German Consul, but found this interfered with their shipping arrangements in England so gave this appointment up. The family has represented Germany at Stavanger for many years'.[1]

Lieutenant Douglas states that he was also informed that the Hamburg agents of Messrs Falk are Theodore Eimbeki, and Stettin agents, Gustave Metzler; also that they have 42 agents in Great Britain, and 22 in Germany.

***

NOTE – I specially wish to draw attention to the large number of ships intercepted, and sent in, off the North East of Iceland as shown by the Chart for September ...

277. *Vice-Admiral Tupper to Commander-in-Chief Grand Fleet*

HMS *Alsatian*, 4 October 1916

In acknowledging with thanks your approval of the proposal that the six trawlers now working with the Tenth Cruiser Squadron should remain attached to the Squadron during the winter months ... I have the honour

[1] *Alf* was not detained.

to request your approval that these trawlers, viz., *Arley*, *Rushcoe*, *Robert Smith*, *Walpole*, *Tenby Castle*, and *Saxon*, may be based at Oban during the winter, as I very much want to use them to patrol the space between the southern ends of D and C Patrols, and the 100 fathom line. They would work between the western limits of Patrol Area No. 1 and Rockall Banks.

2. It will be seen by the enclosed applications that the officers in command – who are all excellent officers, and now thoroughly understand their duties with the Tenth Cruiser Squadron – feel they want a change [273]. They tell me that the week spent at Swarbacks Minn is no recreation, and they might as well be at sea. Oban, however, would be a real change for them; there is a wharf to secure to, and a barrier round the wharf to prevent townspeople from going on board, and also men breaking out of the ship. If the trawlers have 14 days out and 7 days in harbour, they would be well off and, I fancy, quite contented.[1]

278. *Memorandum.*[2]

[n.d., but about 14 October 1916]

In view of the large number of neutral sailing vessels which have been sent in by Northern patrols for examination with an armed guard on board but which, nevertheless, due to heavy weather or other causes have been driven into a Scandinavian port and so failed to reach the port of Examination, it is considered necessary to reduce, as far as possible, the number of armed guards sent away in sailing vessels.

Sailing vessels and sailing fishing vessels coming under following categories need not be sent in unless the Commanding Officer of the Boarding Vessel entertains any suspicion of their bona fides:

(a) Vessels carrying Cargoes for the British Grain group to Denmark of Norway.
(b) Certain vessels with grain cargoes for Denmark covered by the guarantee of the Danish Merchants Guild.
(c) Certain Vessels carrying Salt from Italian, Spanish, or Portuguese Ports to Norway, whose owners have given satisfactory guarantees to HM Minister, Christiania.

[1]This was approved on 9 October 1916.

[2]The authorship and date of this document is unknown, but its position in the file implies composition in October 1916; the author was based in the Admiralty, perhaps in the Trade Division; it may well be by Captain Webb.

(d) Certain sailing fishing vessels bound for Norwegian ports, whose owners are under bond that the vessels will land their catch in Norway.
(e) Any other small sailing vessels met with in such a position and under such weather conditions as to render improbable that they will be able to reach a Port of Examination. In the case, however, of sailing vessels which have been specially ordered by Admiralty telegram to be sent in, every endeavour should be made to comply with the order, and to send them to the most convenient port having regard to the position of the vessel and the direction and force of the wind.

The names of vessels coming under categories (a) (b) (c) (d) will be promulgated from time to time by signal, addressed to the Commander-in-Chief Home Fleets, Vice-Admiral Commanding Orkneys & Shetlands, Vice-Admiral Commanding 10th Cruiser Squadron and Rear-Admiral, Stornoway. Names of vessels so released under this order should be reported to the Admiralty by signal, and in case of (e) the cargo should also be reported if possible.

It is most essential that this order should be kept secret, and, when a vessel is so released, no explanation should by given which could lead to the inference that any general order of this nature is in force or is being acted upon.

***

279. *Vice-Admiral Tupper to Admiralty*

HMS *Alsatian*, 5 November 1916

Report of Proceedings, 19 October–5 November 1916

***

1. Thursday, 19th October – *Hildebrand* arrived at Swarbacks Minn at dawn. At 8 a.m. *Alsatian* commenced coaling, taking in 1800 tons.

With reference to clause 7 of my previous report of proceedings, No. 622/35 of 18 October [276], no news has yet been received of the arrival of the Norwegian Barque *Cedarbank*, sent in to Lerwick by *Alsatian* on 8th October. It appears that she had been sighted off the South East Coast of the Shetlands, and later, after a barque arriving at Lerwick had reported she was off the harbour, a tug was sent to tow her in, but she could not then be found.

2. Friday, 20th October – I visited Lerwick, and saw Commander

Hubert G. Alston, the Senior Naval Officer, and Commander Burrard A. Smith, the Examination Officer.

I found the Norwegian SS *Hercules*, referred to in clause 8 of my previous report [276], still in harbour, and telegraphed to the Director of the Trade Division at the Admiralty asking that she might be detained pending the receipt of the report of Lieutenant Arthur S. Griffith R.N.V.R., the Officer in charge of the armed guard that took her in, which I had the opportunity of seeing. I consider that she was undoubtedly behaving in a suspicious manner, and intended to proceed to Norway, and not to Archangel.[1]

About 1 p.m., a signal was intercepted from *Cabotia* to the effect that she was attacked by a submarine in Latitude 55.6´ North, Longitude 11.58´ West, and, later, that the crew were taking to the boats.[2]

On weighing to leave Swarbacks Minn, *Kildonan Castle*'s bow being caught by the wind before she gathered way, she fouled the colliers *Bengarth*, *Sagonite*, and *Largo*, and grounded by the stern at about 7.45 p.m. I immediately went on board; fortunately she was refloated at 12.45 a.m., without apparent damage. The collier *Largo* also grounded, and refloated about 2 a.m. A full report of the grounding, together with the minutes and finding of the Court of Enquiry held to investigate the accident, have already been forwarded ...

3. Saturday, 21st October – *Avenger* arrived at Scapa Flow to complete with oil fuel.

At 11.40 a.m. *Patia* reported having sighted an enemy submarine in Latitude 55.20´ North, Longitude 16.46´ West, steering to the Eastward. The submarine submerged before fire could be opened, and apparently no Depth Charge was dropped. This was possibly the *U.53* returning from the United States.

Information was received from Leith that the Barque *Cedarbank* had arrived there.[3]

Alsatian left Swarbacks Minn at 6 p.m., to rejoin patrol.

Having obtained permission to base the six Trawlers attached to the 10th Cruiser Squadron on Oban, I left orders for *Rushcoe* and *Tenby Castle*, on leaving harbour, to proceed to patrol between St Kilda and Rockall.

4. Sunday, 22nd October – At noon the disposition of the Squadron was as follows:

[1]*Hercules* had already been given permission to go on – see page 527, note 1.

[2]The submarine was *U 69*.

[3]*Cedarbank* was not detained.

A, C, and D Patrols, on a line 360° from Lat. 55.38´N., Long. 18 W .... *Patia*, *Orcoma*, *Victorian*, *Columbella*, *Ebro*, *Orotava*, *Teutonic*.
Off Portland, Iceland ... *Artois*.
E Patrol, Off NW Coast of Iceland ... *Motagua*.
Off Langanaes ... Armed Trawlers *Robert Smith* and *Walpole*.
Between Iceland and Faroes ... *Alsatian*.
Joining E from Liverpool ... *Andes*.
Joining A from Clyde ... *Changuinola*.
Proceeding to Liverpool ... *Otway*.
Proceeding to Clyde ... *Hilary*.
Proceeding to Swarbacks Minn ... *Almanzora*, *Orvieto*.
At Liverpool ... *Virginian*.
At Clyde ... *Gloucestershire*, *Patuca*, *Moldavia*.
At Scapa Flow ... *Avenger*.
At Swarbacks Minn ... *Kildonan Castle*, *Hildebrand*, Armed Trawlers *Rushcoe* and *Tenby Castle*.
At Aberdeen ... Armed Trawlers *Arley* and *Saxon*.
At Belfast (Fitting out) ... *Arlanza*.[1]

During the week, 58 vessels were intercepted, of which 20 were sent in with, and 2 without, Armed Guards.

At 4 p.m., in Latitude 58.28´ North, Longitude 14.38´ West, *Orvieto* intercepted the French SS *Ione* ..., with Russian troops from Archangel to Brest.

A 4.30 p.m., *Columbella* intercepted the Swedish SS *Stockholm* in Latitude 57.49´ North, Longitude 16.24´ West, from New York to Goteborg with a cargo of grain and copper. There were six women of German nationality amongst her passengers and she was also carrying mails destined for the enemy.[2]

5. Monday, 23rd October – I had ordered *Kildonan Castle* to carry out a full power trial on leaving Swarbacks Minn. Her engines worked well and she averaged 16.8 knots for four hours; she does not appear therefore to have received any damage.

6. Tuesday, 24th October – Mist varied by thick fog at intervals.

Alsatian proceeded North to rendezvous with the Armed Trawlers off Langanaes, and supply them with Armed Guards and provisions.

[1]This is the first time *Arlanza* has appeared in these weekly lists since her grounding in October the year before; her return brought ship numbers back to 24, plus trawlers.

[2]*Stockholm* was not detained.

As no vessels have been intercepted by *Alsatian* since leaving Swarbacks Minn, it would appear that the traffic from Iceland is once again in its normal state.

7. Wednesday, 25th October – Misty, with strong easterly wind.

As *Ebro* now had eight Armed Guards away I arranged for her to exchange places on patrol with *Orotava*.

Alsatian, having rendezvoused with *Robert Smith* and *Walpole* and supplied them with Armed Guards and provisions, proceeded South.

Robert Smith was ordered to call at Thorshaven on her way to Swarbacks Minn to pick up an Armed Guard from *Alsatian* on board the Norwegian SS *Dina Lea*, which had been obliged to put into port owing to the leaky state of the vessel.

Easterly gale off Iceland whilst the patrols to the Westward experience a heavy South-westerly gale.

8. Thursday, 26th October – The bad weather continued on the Western Patrol line, the wind veering to the Northwest and blowing with gale force. Further east a heavy South-easterly gale and heavy seas were met with, and I was unable to communicate with *Virginian*, who was returning to patrol from Liverpool, until the following day.

No boarding was possible.

9. Friday, 27th October – The gale subsided and lovely weather ensued.

Virginian was met and despatches received. The Engineer Officer on my staff, Engineer-Commander Bell, returned on board after carrying out a full speed trial in that vessel. Only 15 knots was obtained instead of 17 with which she is credited. A full report is being forwarded ...

At 2.25 p.m., *Kildonan Castle*, patrolling in Latitude 63.13´ North, Longitude 18.30´ West, was attacked by a submarine, two torpedoes being fired almost simultaneously at a range of between 600 and 1000 yards; both most fortunately missed by the stern as the helm was hard over and the engines put at full speed. There was no time to open fire, as the periscope was not sighted until after the wake of the torpedoes had been seen and whilst the submarine was in the process of diving. *Kildonan Castle* was carrying out Aiming Rifle practice at the time. A full report is being forwarded ... .[1]

A Patrol was immediately moved to a line 320° from Latitude 61.30´ North, Longitude 20.30´ West, and the Trawlers *Rushcoe* and *Tenby Castle*, which were on their way to patrol between St Kilda and Rockall, were despatched to the neighbourhood of Portland Light to search for and destroy the submarine.

[1]The identity of the submarine is not known.

It appears possible that this submarine had been detailed to intercept traffic proceeding to Archangel from the United States, which might be passing along the South Coast of Iceland before striking over to the Norwegian Coast. On the other hand, it is possible she was cruising round Iceland with a view to ascertaining what force we have to prevent a raider from getting through; in that case it is a good thing *Kildonan Castle* was seen and missed.

10. Saturday, 28th October – At 10.30 a.m. *Avenger*, in Latitude 66.16´ North, Longitude 26.30´ West, reported having sighted the periscope of a submarine. A later report stated that this had been seen from the Fore Bridge by a reliable Midshipman and Yeoman of Signals 2 points on the Port quarter at a range of about 3000 yards, and that shortly afterwards a report had been received from aft that 'an object' had been sighted in the same direction. The range – 3000 yards – would appear to be somewhat great for sighting a periscope; the weather conditions however are not known, as the written report has not yet been received. It is doubtful if this submarine is the same one that attacked *Kildonan Castle*, as it would have only just been possible for her to have reached *Avenger*'s position steaming 14 knots.

E Patrol was moved to a line bearing 360° from Latitude 64.40´ North, Longitude 27.40´ West.

At 8 p.m. *Patuca*, rejoining patrol from Clyde, boarded the Dutch SS *Dubhe*, in Latitude 56.54´ North, Longitude 10.50´ West, from Buenos Aires to Rotterdam.[1] The Master reported having been stopped and examined by a German submarine at 1.30 that afternoon, when in Latitude 56.42´ North, Longitude 11.12´ West. The submarine was about 250 feet long, and painted grey; she had no distinguishing mark, and apparently only mounted one gun. On leaving, she proceeded at about 10 knots on the surface steering 30°.

I obtained permission from the Commander-in-Chief to move C and D Patrols each day for about 60 miles, either eastward or westward, and alter the angle of course, as I think this would have the effect of making it more difficult for submarines to locate the patrols, without in any way lessening the chance of intercepting ships.

11. Sunday, 29th October – C Patrol was moved to work on a line 340° from Latitude 57 North, Longitude 17 West, ships 30 miles apart, and D on a line 340° from Latitude 55.30´ North, Longitude 15 West, ships 40 miles apart.

At noon, the disposition of the Squadron was as follows:

[1]It is not known if *Dubhe* was sent in.

A Patrol on line 320° from Lat. 61.30´N, Long. 20.30´W ... *Almanzora*, *Changuinola*, *Kildonan Castle*.
C Patrol, on line 340° from Lat. 57.0´N, Long. 17.0´W ... *Victorian*, *Virginian*, *Orotava*, *Ebro*, *Teutonic*.
D Patrol on line 340° from Lat. 55.30´N, Long. 15.0´W ... *Orcoma*, *Hildebrand*.
E Patrol on line 300° from Lat. 64.0´N, 26.0´W ... *Andes*, *Avenger*.
Off Langanaes ... Armed Trawler *Walpole*.
Between A and C ... *Alsatian*.
Off Portland Light, Iceland ... Armed Trawlers *Rushcoe* and *Tenby Castle*.
Rejoining C ... *Patuca* (from Clyde), *Orvieto* (from Swarbacks Minn).
Proceeding to Clyde ... *Columbella*.
Proceeding to Swarbacks Minn ... Armed Trawler *Robert Smith* (via Thorshavn), *Patia*.
At Liverpool ... *Otway*, *Artois*.
At Clyde ... *Hilary*, *Gloucestershire*, *Moldavia*.
At Swarbacks Minn ... *Motagua*.
At Aberdeen (Docking) ... Armed Trawlers *Arley* and *Saxon*.
At Belfast (Fitting out) ... *Arlanza*.

During the week, 71 vessels were intercepted, 23 of which were sent in with, and 2 without, armed guards.

A communication was received from the Commander-in-Chief asking me to convey his congratulations to the officers and men under my command for the success that had attended the efforts of the Squadron between 1st to 21st September, when 435 vessels were dealt with, and 123 sent in. This has been received by all concerned with the greatest satisfaction.

Lieutenant John A. Douglas, and the Armed Guard, who had been placed on board the Norwegian Barque *Cedarbank*, returned to *Alsatian* from Leith. They had a very strenuous and unpleasant experience, ending almost with starvation. The complete report has been referred to the Commander-in-Chief, Rosyth.[1]

I would submit that orders may be given that armed guards be landed and sent to their ships as soon as possible after the vessel anchors and that Auxiliary Patrol Vessels should endeavour to tow, or escort, into port sailing vessels met at sea with armed guards on board.

[1]This report has not been located.

12. Monday, 30th October – At 2 a.m. *Orcoma*, in Latitude 55.27´ North, Longitude 15.56´ West, intercepted the French SS *Circassie* ..., with troops, from Archangel to Brest.

I moved A Patrol (3 Ships) to a line 320° from Latitude 61.30´ North, Longitude 17 West, and D Patrol (2 Ships) to line 270° from Latitude 55 North, Longitude 11.45´ West.

13. Tuesday, 31st October – I met *Changuinola* in the forenoon. The weather was inclined to be bad, with strong easterly breeze. Carried out Range Finder and Sightsetter Exercise, manoeuvring the vessels for an hour between 10,000 and 4,000 yards.

At 5 p.m. a message was received from the Commanding Officer of *Rushcoe* stating that he had visited Westmann Island, and obtained information from the Consul at Reykjavik by telephone that the British trawler *Nellie Bruce* had been sunk by an enemy submarine at 10 a.m., the previous day, 8 miles to the North of Hvalsbak Rock. The crew of 15 had been landed at Berufiord, but as the place was small, the Consul wished them to be recovered.[1]

Rushcoe and *Tenby Castle* were accordingly directed to proceed to Berufiord and embark the crew, warning any British Trawlers met with en route of the presence of submarines. It was intended to transfer the rescued crew to a homeward-bound trawler.

Information was received that the neighbourhood of Ailsa Craig was dangerous, owing to mines. Ships proceeding to Clyde were warned accordingly.

Stormy night.

14. Wednesday, 1st November – I met *Almanzora* in the forenoon, carried out Range Finder and Sightsetter Exercises, and gave Captain Church[2] orders to take charge of E Patrol on 5th November relieving *Avenger*, and to work round the North of Iceland from the westward to the Latitude of Seidisfiord, keeping the Senior Officer informed of his movements.

A further report was received of submarines being off the Coast of Iceland, a trawler having been chased by two submarines a.m. on the 29th, position not given.

Very strong Telefunken signals were heard about 10 p.m., and some weak ones apparently in answer – they were probably from the two

[1]The submarine responsible may be *U 35*, though this is not certain.

[2]Church, William Drummond, CBE, RN (1866–1937), Lieutenant 1891, Commander 1903, Captain 1910, Captain of *Almanzora* 1915–1919, Rear-Admiral (retired) 1921, Vice-Admiral 1926.

submarines one of which could not be far from, and might have been close to, *Alsatian*; extra precautions were accordingly taken.

I submit that the despatch of anti-submarine vessels would appear to be desirable should the enemy continue to operate in this vicinity.

15. Thursday, 2nd November – During the forenoon, I met *Teutonic* and carried out Rangefinder and Sightsetter exercises. Commodore Luard then came on board and received general instructions regarding the working of the patrol during my absence.

I have left orders for the position and character of the Patrols to be altered frequently with a view to confusing enemy submarines as much as possible; I consider this can be done without impairing the efficiency of the Patrol.

I submit that it would be a great advantage if more Auxiliary Patrol Vessels could be attached to the Squadron. In view of the Ships working off the Coast of Iceland, and the number of British Fishing Trawlers in those waters, it appears very desirable to have anti-submarine craft working in the vicinity. In addition, the Faeroes may require watching, if possible, and it is my intention to use Trawlers to patrol between St Kilda and D Patrol which normally works somewhat to the eastward of Rockall. Two Trawlers – *Rushcoe* and *Tenby Castle* – ought to have been in that locality now, but I had to send them to Iceland to deal with the submarine that attacked the *Kildonan Castle*, and they have done excellent work there, in guarding and warning the Trawlers fishing. Lieut. John T. Randell, D.S.C., RNR has again performed excellent service.

I had some anxiety regarding the safety of *Kildonan Castle*, as she had not been heard for 24 hours and was the Ship nearest to the dangerous area; it turned out, however, that her W/T was temporarily out of order.

Ebro, on C Patrol, reported having seen a bright light low down in the water about 7 p.m., and considered it was a submarine – Latitude 58.15´N, Longitude 16.41’W. It was only visible for a very short time. She proceeded at high speed whilst in the locality.

In the course of the day, I slightly altered the positions of A and E Patrols.

During the past three days a number of reports have been received of submarine activity in the vicinity of the line joining Muckle Flugga and the Flannan Islands.

16. Friday, 3rd November – At 1.30 a.m., *Patuca* boarded and sent in to Kirkwall the Danish SS *United States*, from New York to

Christiansund. She was carrying 257 passengers, and 1131 bags of mails, including 350 parcels and mails for enemy countries.[1]

Rushcoe, on arriving at Berufiord, found that the crew of *Nellie Bruce* had been taken round to Eskefiord, and arranged to proceed there the following morning.

The weather, which except for very short intervals had been remarkably fine during the past week, now broke up and a heavy NE gale sprang up.

17. Saturday, 4th November – Bad weather continued. *Ebro* reported that damage had been caused to bow plates and a scuttle by the sea, but repairs were soon effected. *Kildonan Castle* reported she had lost two boats.

Mines were reported between the Isle of Man and Liverpool. A vessel was sunk by either mine or torpedo in Latitude 53.39´N, Longitude 4.50´W at 3 p.m.[2]

At 7 p.m. I ceased answering calls for the Senior Officer, Tenth Cruiser Squadron, and having turned over the command of the Squadron to Commodore Luard of *Teutonic* I proceeded towards Liverpool.

18. Sunday, 5th November – *Alsatian* arrived at the Bar, Liverpool, at 6 p.m.

19. The following extract from a report received from *Otway* regarding the boarding of SS *Pioneer* on 20 October, is forwarded for information:

'I ascertained from the Master that upon the three previous voyages he had not been intercepted as he had taken the route inside the Flannan Islands and round Butt of Lewis, but was now forbidden to take this route.'[3]

***

[1] *United States* was not detained.

[2] If the cause was a torpedo, the submarine was possibly *U 17*, the only one in the area at the time.

[3] The Contraband Committee recommended that *Pioneer* should be permitted to sail on unless there was a specific query over the cargo (TS 14/11 of 14 October 1916).

280. *Memorandum by Vice-Admiral Tupper*

HMS *Alsatian*, 21 October 1916

... [T]he Armed Trawlers attached to the Tenth Cruiser Squadron will be utilized during the winter months for patrolling between St Kilda and the areas patrolled by the Tenth Cruiser Squadron.

2. During this time they will be based on Oban, and will work in units of two or three [273, 277].

281. *Sub-Lieutenant L.C. Bach RNR*[1] *to Admiralty Port Officer Kirkwall*

1 November 1916

I beg to report that I was sent aboard the Swedish SS *Manningham* on October 29th [19]16 at 11.30 a.m. with orders to proceed to Kirkwall.

On October 31st [19]16 in Latitude 60.01´N, Longitude 4.16´W at 12.30 p.m. the master of the *Manningham*, Captain Anderson, reported to me that he had heard gunfire to the North East.

At 12.45 p.m. a shot was seen to fall in the water a distance of about 200 yards on our port beam, and on reaching the bridge I observed a submarine on the surface steering a parallel course to the SS *Manningham* at a distance of about seven miles. We immediately stopped and I requested the Captain to deny the presence of a British armed guard aboard the *Manningham* if questioned by the submarine commander. I then ordered my men to remove all gear appertaining to the armed guard to the coal bunkers, and obtaining overalls from the Chief Engineer myself and the two men disguised ourselves as firemen, the two men hiding in the coal bunker, while I remained on deck. The submarine then fired a second shot, which fell a distance of 100 yards on our starboard beam, and hoisted a signal ordering the master to lower a boat and present himself with the ship's papers to the submarine commander.

While a boat was being lowered, the submarine approached to a distance of about 400 yards, and fired a third shot which fell about 70 yards over us. The Captain of the *Manningham* then went aboard the submarine and on returning he told me that he had asked if a British armed guard was present, and also if he had been stopped by a British

[1]Bach, Leslie C., RD, RNR, Midshipman 1914, Sub-Lieutenant 1917, Acting Lieutenant January 1919, Commander 1938, serving at Maidstone from August 1939.

Cruiser. His answer to both questions was in the negative, and after looking at the ship's papers the submarine granted permission for the *Manningham* to proceed. The Captain then returned to the ship, and at 2.25 p.m. we proceeded to Kirkwall. The submarine was last seen on the surface steering east, apparently with the intention of stopping a three-masted barque which could just be seen on the horizon. The submarine's speed was approximately ten knots.

Before closing this report I should like to add that I cannot speak too highly of the Master of the SS *Manningham*, who did everything in his power to assist me and to hide the presence of the armed guard.[1]

282. *Lieutenant H. Shotton*[2] *to Rear-Admiral Swarbacks Minn*

HMT *Walpole*, 4 November 1916

Submitted – while on patrol duty to the eastward of Seides Fiord (Iceland), 4 to 5 miles off the land on the 31st October 1916, 10.30 a.m., a steamer was reported bearing to SE (mag), and apparently steering N Eastward. I proceeded to intercept the steamer and found her to be steering to westward. My course was altered to SW to cut her off. The vessel had a W/T aerial, and a fore and main trysail set. I took her for a possible raider working from territorial waters and I hoisted a large size International Code Signal MN (stop immediately). This was not obeyed. I then fired 2 blanks and 1 shot well ahead of the steamer which stopped her. Upon closing I distinguished vessel was flying Danish Naval Ensign and signal numbers GRCK, these were difficult to distinguish on account of the main trysail forming a background and weather. The Officer of the vessel hailed me – 'How dare you fire upon a Danish Man of War'. I found her to be the Danish Fishery Cruiser and replied by hauling down MN and hailed that I had mistaken her identity which however he may not have heard. The vessel went ahead towards the land and then returned and hailed that I was in territorial waters, my vessel retiring to the Eastward having sighted the land Hornaes through the mist. The Danish vessel in reply to my flag signal 'I wish to communicate' passed a W/T message 'Please explain what you want' (CQCQ) – reply 'Sorry I mistook your identity' – answer 'Alright Mr. so am I' – reply 'Thanks' – answer 'Very well'. Trawler dipped ensign and resumed patrol [290].

[1]*Manningham* was permitted to go on at once (TS 14/11 of 25 October 1916); the submarine was probably *U 24*.

[2]Shotton, Harold, RNR, Lieutenant 1916.

283. *Vice Admiral Tupper to Admiralty*

HMS *Alsatian*, 23 November 1916

Report of Proceedings, 5–22 November 1916

***

1. Sunday, 5 November – The disposition of the Squadron at noon was as follows:

A Patrol ... *Otway, Moldavia, Patia.*
C Patrol ... *Virginian, Orvieto, Patuca, Ebro, Teutonic.*
D Patrol ... *Motagua, Hildebrand.*
E Patrol ... *Almanzora, Andes.*
East Coast, Iceland ... *Rushcoe, Tenby Castle.*
Proceeding to Liverpool ... *Alsatian, Avenger.*
Proceeding to Swarbacks Minn ... *Kildonan Castle.*
Rejoining from Swarbacks Minn ... *Changuinola.*
At Liverpool ... *Artois, Orcoma.*
At Clyde ... *Columbella, Gloucestershire, Hilary.*
At Swarbacks Minn ... *Robert Smith, Walpole.*
At Loch Ewe ... *Victorian.*
At Belfast ... *Arlanza.*
At Aberdeen ... *Arley, Saxon.*[1]

During the week 44 vessels were intercepted and examined, of which 14 were sent in with, and two without, Armed Guards.

Rushcoe reported leaving Eskefjord at 10 p.m. with crew of *Nellie Bruce*. The Skipper of the *Nellie Bruce* stated that the submarine sank the trawler by gunfire without giving any warning. The crew took to the boats when firing commenced and the submarine did not attempt to close the boat.

2. Monday, 6 November – Boarding continued impossible all day.

The disposition of C and D Patrols was slightly altered.

3. Tuesday, 7 November – The gale increased during the forenoon. *Teutonic* had been endeavouring since the previous day to communicate with *Otway* to obtain despatches and ratings, but was obliged to abandon the attempt, and left patrol for Swarbacks Minn.

The Commander-in-Chief, Grand Fleet, informed me there was no objection to moving patrols to Patrol Line II, shifting the centre line

[1] *Orotava* has now been removed.

daily as before. Orders were given accordingly, and during the night ships proceeded to their new positions.

A, C, and D Patrols were hove to all the day. The weather commenced to improve at 10 p.m. and steadily improved during the night. No boarding had been possible since Friday afternoon, a very unusual circumstance for so long a period.

Victorian rejoined from Loch Ewe having completed there with coal and water, and also having effected necessary repairs to a 6" gun which had been damaged.

4. Wednesday, 8 November – During the day, Ships proceeded to their new patrols but, although the weather was better, speed had to be reduced when steering to the eastward.

5. Thursday, 9 November – *Teutonic* arrived at Swarbacks Minn at 7 a.m. *Otway* reported boarding Norwegian Steamer *Sneltoppen*, North Shields to New York, Lat. 59.29´ North, Long. 12 West. This was the first Ship boarded by the Patrols during the week.

In the afternoon, *Otway* reported boarding the Mercantile Fleet Auxiliary Collier *Westgate*, from Barry via Londonderry, with coal, to White Sea. She was returning to Londonderry on account of damage caused by gale. The various Port Authorities were informed by Land Wire.

Rushcoe when in Lat. 59.20´ North, Long. 11.25´ West, reported leaving patrol the previous morning for Oban, with crew of the trawler *Nellie Bruce*.

In the evening, *Moldavia* reported intercepting the Norwegian Steamer *Patria*, bound for Reykjavik, with engines broken down, Lat. 61.50´ North, Long. 14.15´ West. The owner who was on board, requested to be towed. As there was too much sea to board in the darkness, *Moldavia* stood by, and requested instructions. The question was referred to the Commander-in-Chief, Grand Fleet, who directed that *Moldavia* was not to tow *Patria* during daylight, but offer to take the crew off, reporting if the offer was refused, when the Consul, Reykjavik, would be informed of the vessel's position.

6. Friday, 10 November – In accordance with instructions received from the Commander-in-Chief, *Moldavia*, having taken off the owner and crew of 14 men, sank *Patria* at 8 p.m.

In the afternoon, *Orvieto* boarded and sent to Lerwick with an Armed Guard the Norwegian Steamer *Sarpfos*, New York to Bergen, with barley, Lat. 59.19´ North, Long. 11.18´ West.[1] The Master reported the

[1] *Sarpfos* was sent in, but was allowed to go on (TS 14/12 of 13 and 16 November 1916).

wreck of a Sailing Vessel in Lat. 59.12´ North, Long. 12.40´ West with about 5 feet of two masts only showing.[1] The Hydrographer of the Navy was informed.

7. Saturday, 11 November – There was again too much sea to board on C Patrol in the afternoon. The *Shannon*, Flagship of the Rear-Admiral Commanding, 2nd Cruiser Squadron, was in harbour during the time *Teutonic* was at Swarbacks Minn, and the Commodore explained to the Rear-Admiral the areas and work of the 10th Cruiser Squadron, and also informed him of the positions of the patrols as now constituted.

The Captain of *Hilary* – joining patrol from Clyde – reported that in Lat. 55.20´ North, Long. 5 West, he personally observed at 9 a.m. an object, which he believed to be a spent torpedo, break surface 200 yards off starboard beam, pointing at the Ship. *Hilary* had been on port leg for five minutes which presumably put ship out of range: no periscope was seen. This was reported to the Commander-in-Chief, Grand Fleet.

Teutonic proceeded to sea from Swarbacks Minn at dusk.

8. Sunday, 12 November – At noon, the disposition of the Squadron was as follows:

A Patrol ... *Moldavia*, *Patia*.
C Patrol ... *Motagua*, *Victorian*, *Orvieto*, *Otway*.
D Patrol ... *Hilary*, *Virginian*.
E Patrol ... *Almanzora*, *Changuinola*.
Rejoining Patrol from Swarbacks Minn ... *Teutonic*, *Kildonan Castle*.
Proceeding to Clyde ... *Hildebrand*.
At Liverpool ... *Alsatian*, *Artois*, *Avenger*, *Arlanza*, *Orcoma*.
At Clyde ... *Columbella*, *Gloucestershire*.
At Swarbacks Minn ... *Andes*, *Ebro*, *Patuca*, *Tenby Castle*, *Walpole*.
At Oban ... *Rushcoe*, *Robert Smith*.
At Aberdeen ... *Arley*.
At Thurso ... *Saxon*.

Only 17 vessels were intercepted and examined during the week, of which 5 were sent in with, and two without, Armed Guards, very bad weather being experienced on all patrols.

As *Moldavia* was leaving the next day for Swarbacks Minn, the owner and crew of the *Patria* were transferred to *Patia*. Orders were given that they were to be transferred to the first intercepted vessel

[1]The ship is not identifiable.

bound to Norway or Iceland: and, failing that, endeavour was made to arrange for the first armed trawler available to convey them to Reykjavik.

9. Monday, 13 November – *Teutonic* proceeded to D Patrol to obtain ratings from *Hilary* for distribution to C Patrol.

10. Tuesday, 14 November – *Orvieto* boarded Danish Sailing Vessel *Dannebrog*, Lat. 59.18´ North, Long. 11.51´ West, from Reykjavik to Liverpool, with a cargo of salt fish. She had been damaged in the recent gale, the Captain being dead and several of the crew injured. An Armed Guard was not placed on board and, at her own request, was directed to call at Stornoway.[1]

Changuinola carried out heavy gun practice during the day.

11. Wednesday, 15 November – *Gloucestershire* proceeded to relieve *Changuinola* in charge of E Patrol. *Teutonic* carried out heavy gun practice.

12. Thursday, 16 November – *Saxon* sailed at noon, and was directed to rendezvous *Patia* and obtain owner and crew of *Patria* for conveyance to Reykjavik, and, after obtaining any information of interest from the British Consul, Reykjavik, to leave immediately for patrol.

Southern position of C Patrol was altered to 20 miles further south.

During the day, a gale got up from the south, and, in the evening, ships on A, C, and D Patrols were obliged to heave to. *Andes*, joining C Patrol from Swarbacks Minn, reported losing a boat.

13. Friday, 17 November – At 7.30 a.m. *Victorian* reported she was standing by an unknown steamer, Lat. 58.4´ North, Long. 11.2´ West, which had lost her propeller. This ship subsequently proved to be the Russian Steamer *Slavonik*, and had been searched for by Stornoway and Queenstown Patrols since 11th instant, when signals had been intercepted that she was in Latitude 56.47´ North, Long. 9.30´ West, and had lost her screw.

Victorian was directed to stand by, orders for him to proceed to Liverpool being cancelled, and the Commander-in-Chief, Admiral Commanding Queenstown, and Rear-Admiral Stornoway informed.

In the afternoon, information was received from the Rear-Admiral Stornoway that two tugs, with an escort, were being sent. The Commander-in-Chief Grand Fleet also signalled that he had requested Admiralty for an ocean-going tug.

At 8.30 a.m. the French Troopship *Mingrelie* sent an urgent message

[1]*Dannebrog* was not detained.

using Allied Fleet Signal Book, that in Lat. 61.15´ North, Long. 15.32´ West, bound from Archangel to Brest, she was 'obliged to scud', course N 70° W. The message was not clear and he was asked by W/T if he were disabled or required assistance. He replied that he was not in want of assistance but that if the bad weather continued he would be in want of coal. In answer to a further signal he said he had sufficient coal for 10 days' steaming at 9 knots.

The Commodore told him that should he find when the weather moderated he had not sufficient coal to reach Brest, he was to inform him. At 8.45 p.m. *Mingrelie* signalled that the weather had improved, and he had resumed his course since 2 p.m.

The Armed Trawler *Saxon* had left Swarbacks Minn the previous day to rendezvous *Patia*, and take owner and crew of *Patria* to Reykjavik. Owing to the gale, however, *Saxon* was directed to shelter under the lee of Faeroes, and, although an attempt was made to bring off the rendezvous at night, it had to be abandoned owing to the weather and *Saxon* having small engineroom trouble.

At 9.30 p.m. the British Steamer *San Tirso* informed *Teutonic* that he was disabled and asked for assistance. His position was asked for.

In the meantime, information was received that two tugs with escort had been despatched by Rear-Admiral Stornoway, and *Victorian* reported that these would be sufficient to tow *Slavonik*.

During the night, the weather improved, although some sea and a heavy swell continued.

14. Saturday, 18 November – At 3 a.m. *San Tirso* signalled that her position was Lat. 59.13´ North, Long. 17.19´ West by dead reckoning, and as *Teutonic* – being north of C Patrol – was in the nearest position, the Commodore decided to proceed to his assistance.

San Tirso was sighted at 7 p.m. in Lat. 59.47´ North, Long. 13.8´ West, *Teutonic* having located him by means of the Direction Finder.[1] He had previously signalled his rudder was broken, and he further reported visually that three of his crew had died and six were sick.

The Executive Officer and a Probationary Surgeon of *Teutonic* were sent on board. The former reported that the rudder head was completely fractured below stuffing box and he hoped it was capable of being made effective the following day: and the latter that the men who were sick were suffering from a form of malarial fever and ague, and that one appeared to be in a critical condition. Nothing could be done to effect repairs or, due to the heavy swell, taking in tow, till daylight, and, after

[1]Note the discrepancy in position.

the invalids had been treated the boat returned and *Teutonic* stood by. Details were reported to the Commander-in-Chief.

At 4.30 p.m. *Patia* reported that the owner and crew of *Patria* had been transferred to *Saxon*, who then proceeded Reykjavik to land them. The Commander-in-Chief was requested to inform the Consul Reykjavik of the fact.

At 7.42 p.m. *Otway* reported that in Lat. 59.18´ North, Long. 11.58´ West, at 1.45 p.m. he had boarded German Prize Norwegian Steamship *Older*, flying Norwegian colours, which had been captured by a German Submarine on 13th November in Lat. 47.8´ North, Long. 9.6´ West. He had been unable to prevent the German prize crew – consisting of 1 Lieutenant, 1 Warrant Officer and 7 men – from exploding bombs and opening cocks to sink the Ship.

He took everyone off, consisting of 22 crew, 25 of Italian Steamer *Lela* sunk on 14 November in Lat. 47.8´ North, 9.6´ West, 8 crew of British Steam Trawler *Hatsuse* sunk on 14 November in Lat. 50.14´ North, Long. 11 West, also the 9 Germans.

Otway was standing by till daylight as the steamer had not sunk and there was too much sea for boat work in the dark.

He ascertained the German Submarine was in company with the *Older* up to yesterday (Friday, November 17th) evening, both being said to be bound for Kiel.[1]

The Commander-in-Chief was informed fully of this Report and a general warning issued to the Tenth Cruiser Squadron as to the presence of the submarine.

***

15. Sunday, 19 November – At 1 a.m. *Victorian* reported tugs had arrived to take *Slavonic* in tow in Lat. 59.50´ North, Long. 12.8´ West, and *Victorian* then proceeded to Liverpool.

At 8.32 a.m. *Otway* reported that the *Older* appeared the same as the previous evening. Examination shewed she was little damaged, with only 3 feet of water in bilges. Steam was raised, Italian and British crews were placed on board, and at 1.15 p.m. she proceeded to Stornoway with an Armed Guard from *Otway*.

Commander-in-Chief Grand Fleet, directed she was to make Butt of Lewis, and Rear-Admiral Stornoway was informed of her departure and requested to warn the inner patrols.

A full report regarding the *Older* has been forwarded separately ... [287].

[1]The submarine appears to have been *U 50*.

At noon, the disposition of the Squadron was as follows:

A Patrol ... *Ebro*, *Artois*.
C Patrol ... *Patuca*, *Andes*, *Otway*, *Motagua*.
D Patrol ... *Virginian*, *Hilary*
E Patrol ... *Gloucestershire*, *Moldavia*.
Between A & C Patrols ... *Teutonic*.
Proceeding to Liverpool ... *Orvieto*, *Victorian*.
Proceeding to Clyde ... *Kildonan Castle*.
Proceeding to Swarbacks Minn ... *Patia*.
Rejoining Patrol ... *Alsatian*.
Proceeding to Reykjavik ... *Saxon*.
Proceeding to Patrol between 20 West and Seydesfjord ... *Arley*.
At Liverpool ... *Almanzora*, *Avenger*, *Orcoma*, *Arlanza*.
At Clyde ... *Columbella*, *Hildebrand*.
At Swarbacks Minn ... *Changuinola*.
At Aberdeen ... *Tenby Castle*, *Walpole*.
At Oban ... *Robert Smith*, *Rushcoe*.

Teutonic and *Otway* standing by British Steamship *San Tirso*, Norwegian Steamship *Older*, respectively.

Of 24 Ships intercepted and examined during the past week, 5 were sent in with, and one without, Armed Guards. Continuous thick or heavy weather was experienced on all patrols throughout the week.

In the course of the day, *Teutonic* made various attempts to repair the rudder of *San Tirso*, and also to take her in tow. All these attempts failed, the gear twice carrying away when hawsers were being placed in position. The heavy swell considerably interfered with the work.

After dark, these attempts ceased, the Engine Room Staff being employed during the night on adapting fittings for repair of the rudder.

At 7 p.m., *Kildonan Castle* reported having intercepted in Lat. 62.50´ North, Long. 11´ West, the British Collier *Margarita*, Archangel to Garston, which was standing by the Danish Sailing Vessel *Dannebrog*, which the Master of *Margarita* considered to be in distress (See reference to this vessel on 14th November). *Kildonan Castle* did not, after examination, consider *Dannebrog* to be greatly damaged, and therefore proceeded.

At 10 p.m. *Teutonic* took in a W/T message addressing 'Any British Man-of-War' from the Norwegian Steamship *Mexicano*, on passage from Galveston to Copenhagen. The Master reported that he had taken on board the crew of the Norwegian Barque *Musselcrag* which had been dismasted in Lat. 59.1´ North, Long. 19.51´ West when bound from Leith to Monte Video. He had attempted to destroy the Ship by setting fire to her, but was not sure whether she had sunk. He requested she might be sunk by gunfire. The Admiralty was informed (for Hydrographer of the Navy), but it was not considered immediately practicable to detail any vessel to search for the derelict, as the patrol was rather weak.[1]

I had left Liverpool in *Alsatian* at 4 a.m. to rejoin patrol.

During the time *Alsatian* had been refitting, I had visited the Admiralty, and also the Foreign Office where I had an interview with Lord Robert Cecil and Rear-Admiral Sir D.R.S. de Chair, K.C.B. M.V.O.

I also visited HMS *Vernon*, and was shewn a new searchlight Shutter which is light tight and will be most useful for Ships of 10th Cruiser Squadron when examining Ships at night so that the light can be focused, kept screened, and then exposed for a couple of seconds. I have asked that Ships of the Squadron may be supplied with these shutters ...

16. Monday, 20 November – The Commander-in-Chief Grand Fleet, informed me that the tug *Sarah Jolliffe* had left Clyde to meet *Teutonic* and tow the *San Tirso*. *Kildonan Castle* (on passage to Clyde) was directed to get into W/T communication with the tug.

At 11 a.m. *Otway* reported that in Lat. 59.29´ North, Long. 12.33´ West, he had passed *Slavonic* in tow of one tug making only 3 knots, and that another tug would be of great assistance. Rear-Admiral Stornoway was informed accordingly.

With reference to the submarine reported to have been in company with the *Older*, *Otway* further reported that the submarine probably parted company 4 p.m. 17th November in Lat. 57.22´ North, Long. 9.45´ West, steering 8°, Masters of British Steamship *Arabia* and United States steamship *Columbian* being said to be on board.

At daylight, *Teutonic* made a further attempt to tow the *San Tirso*, and at 2 p.m. got the hawser in position and commenced towing making good 5 knots. Repairs to rudder head proved impracticable owing to the position of the fracture.

Another of the crew of *San Tirso* died during the forenoon and was buried at sea.

At 4.45 p.m. *Kildonan Castle* informed me that the position of the *Sarah Jolliffe* was Lat. 55.23´ North, Long. 7.44´ West.

17. Tuesday, 21 November – At 9.30 a.m., I met *Teutonic* at a pre-

[1] *Mexicano* came in with the 21 rescuees; the ship was not then detained (TS 14/11 of 23 and 25 November 1916).

arranged rendezvous and took over the command of the Patrol from Commodore Luard.

Having heard that the German Prisoners from the SS *Older* were still on board *Otway*, I decided to rendezvous with her and obtain Commodore Booty's Report.

I left *Teutonic* in charge of *San Tirso* and ordered the Trawlers *Rushcoe* and *Robert Smith* to join her and act as escort to Tug and *San Tirso*.

Arlanza left Liverpool to join my Flag.

18. Wednesday, 22 November – At 4 a.m. *Teutonic* reported that the Tug *Sarah Jolliffe* had arrived on the scene and would take the *San Tirso* in tow at daybreak. *Teutonic* remained in company awaiting the arrival of *Rushcoe* and *Robert Smith*, which were delayed by the weather.

During the morning watch, *Alsatian* had a long chase after a steamer which proved to be the United States SS *Wico*, already boarded by *Motagua* and westbound.[1]

News was received of the arrival of the Norwegian SS *Older* with rescued crews of *Lela* and *Hatsuse*.

I met *Otway* at 11 a.m., and saw Commodore Booty. Having read his report, which has been forwarded, regarding the SS *Older* and having had the principal documents taken from the prisoners roughly translated, which appeared to contain nothing of immediate importance, I asked permission from the Commander-in-Chief to send *Otway* to Loch Ewe by 26 November, and land the prisoners, requesting arrangements might be made for their disembarkation.

The Senior Naval Officer Swarbacks Minn, informed me that the intermediate cross-head of starboard engine of *Patia* had cracked, and that the Court of Enquiry held to investigate the circumstances recommended that the Ship should be sent to the Southern Base for repairs. Arrangements were made for her to proceed to Clyde accordingly.

Motagua was directed to search for, and destroy if found, the Danish two masted Schooner *Danneborg*, which the SS *San Francisco* had reported derelict, leaking and abandoned by her crew in Lat. 59.24´ North, Long. 12.40´ West. *Alsatian* proceeded to search for the wreck of the Norwegian Barque *Musselcrag* referred to in paragraph 15 of this Report.

[1]*Wico* was covered by the blanket permission to other vessels (such as *Polarine* and *Pioneer*) to trade (TS 14/12).

A Patrol was moved to work on a line 360° from Lat. 62.30´ North, Long. 10 West.

The Russian SS *Slavonic* arrived at Stornoway in charge of tugs.

During the course of the day a gale sprang up from the westward.

19. The following extract from a report received from the Commanding Officer of the Armed Trawler *Robert Smith*, dealing with an interview he had with the British Consul at Thorshavn, when on a visit to that port on 30 October, is forwarded for information:

'We went into the matter of Faroese Fishing Vessels who had signed agreements and found that many I had on my list, which was complete up to last October, had failed to report to the Consulate, so I left my list with the Consul and suggested that he should write to the Owners for an explanation, which he promised to do. The consul informed me that there were several sailing vessels loading at various ports in the Islands and that he had reported them to the Foreign Office, also Kirkwall.'

***

284. *Captain T. Dannreuther*[1] *to Vice-Admiral commanding 10th Cruiser Squadron*

HMS *Patuca*, 14 November 1916

I have the honour to report that at 7.30 p.m, on the 30th October 1916 in Lat. 58.14´N, Long. 19.28´W, I boarded the United States schooner *Ethel Mildred*, then becalmed, on a voyage from New York to Aakrahaven for sale in Norway in ballast, the ballast being coal and old furniture. Being a small vessel I decided to ask if the Master would guarantee calling at a British port if the vessel were released. This the Master agreed to do, but requested that an officer might be put on board to pilot him into port as he was unacquainted with the navigation of the British coast. As, however, on investigation it was found that the vessel had no consular certificate, and was said to be one of 6 similar vessels (one of which was named *Norseman*) all being sent for sale to Norway with their papers not quite clear as to whether the sale had already been effected, nor the characters of the new owners known to me, I decided to send this vessel into Lerwick with a small armed guard consisting of an officer to act as a pilot and one man as a reduced armed guard.

This vessel was stopped by a German submarine whilst making for

[1]Dannreuther, Tristan, RN, Lieutenant 1893, Commander 1905, Captain 1908, Captain of *Patuca* 1915–1916, retired 1923.

Stornoway to which port the armed guard officer had my authority to vary his route if desirable.

Herewith is attached the armed guard officer's report of his proceedings, and I submit that under the circumstances this armed guard should be paid Hard Lying Money at half rates for the period they were on board this vessel viz: 31st October to 6th November 1916 inclusive [285].

285. *Lieutenant I.W. Gallop RNR*[1] *to Commanding Officer HMS* Patuca

HMS *Patuca*, 14 November 1916

I have the honour to report that in compliance with your instructions, accompanied by one Stoker, RNR (J.R. Stevens) I boarded the American Schooner *Ethel Mildred* as an Armed Guard, with instructions to conduct her to Lerwick or any other British port, which might prove more convenient in view of the prevailing weather conditions.

2. The *Ethel Mildred* was on a voyage from New York to Aakrahaven (Norway) in ballast consisting of about 30 tons of coal and old cabin furniture. Her normal crew when employed as a fishing vessel would have been about twelve hands, but on this occasion as she was on passage to Norway for sale, it consisted of the Master and five hands. The Master was a naturalised American (born in Newfoundland), the crew consisting of 2 Newfoundlanders, 1 Canadian, and 2 Norwegians.

3. Owing to variable winds I requested the Master to make for the Butt of Lewis, with a view to being towed to Stornoway for examination.

4. About 8.20 a.m. on 5th November, when in Lat. 58.26´N and Long. 7.8´W, steering ENE magnetic and making 5 knots, a submarine was seen to appear from the port quarter at a distance of about one mile with conning tower awash going at a speed of about 12 knots. She had no masts or guns on deck and periscopes were lowered, but later one mast was erected on fore side of conning tower and close to it and German man of war Ensign was hoisted at the mast-head. The submarine was about 200 feet in length, and the deck which was subsequently seen to be flush corresponds to the silhouette of U.17–20, but the masts and exhaust pipe could not have been as shewn in the silhouette. The hull

[1]Gallop, John W., RNR, Sub-Lieutenant 1914, Lieutenant 1916.

and conning tower were newly painted black with no distinguishing marks. No wireless apparatus was seen, and only two officers in German uniform were seen on deck.

5. The submarine passed within 100 yards of the stern and when *Ethel Mildred* hove to she passed ahead and lay off. The American colours were flying in *Ethel Mildred* at the time.

6. The submarine then lowered his mast, dived and disappeared, steering in a NE direction towards the smoke of a west bound steamer whose funnel was just visible. The visibility at the time was about 5 miles. The operation of diving took about 30 seconds and no periscope was erected before so doing.

7. The submarine did not hail the *Ethel Mildred* or ask any questions nor was I molested.

8. At 4 p.m same day when close under the lighthouse on the Butt of Lewis in thick weather the *Ethel Mildred* was stopped by HM Armed Trawler *Sasebo* who offered to take the ship in tow but this course was not necessary as wind then served. I immediately reported the fact of my having been visited by a submarine to the Commanding Officer of *Sasebo* with the request that the information should be immediately communicated to the Rear-Admiral Stornoway which *Sasebo* proceeded at full speed to do.

9. I arrived at Stornoway at 11 a.m. on the 6th November and turned the vessel over to the local authorities and rejoined HM Ship under your command via Kyle of Lochalsh, Thurso and HMS *Vienna* on the 14th November at 4 p.m.

10. The Master and crew of *Ethel Mildred* were friendly and prepared to say that there was no Armed Guard on board if asked. The conditions for accommodating the Armed Guard were about such as might be expected in one of HM Destroyers, but the vessel was short of drinking water and washing could not be allowed.[1]

286. *Admiralty to Vice-Admiral commanding Tenth Cruiser Squadron*

Admiralty, 15 November [1916]

With reference to paragraph 11 of your Letter of the 5th instant, No. 670/35 [279], relative to the proceedings of the Tenth Cruiser Squadron from 18th October to 4th November 1916, I am commanded by My Lords Commissioners of the Admiralty to acquaint you that standing

[1] *Ethel Mildred* was not detained.

orders that Auxiliary Patrol Vessels are to leave their patrols, or abandon their escorts, in order to tow sailing vessels are very undesirable, and it is considered sufficent to direct Senior Naval Officers that Patrol Vessels should render assistance when necessary and when this does not interfere with more important duties. An order to this effect is being issued to Officers in charge of Auxiliary patrol Vessels in Scotland.

2. As regards paragraphs 14 and 15, I am to state that, under present circumstances, there does not seem to be any sufficient reason to tell off Armed Trawlers specially for duty off Iceland, though should the enemy continue to operate in these waters the necessity for a Patrol may arise.

3. My Lords concur in the desirability of providing additional Auxiliary Patrol Vessels to work under your orders, and directions are being given for four Trawlers from the Orkneys area to be despatched to Oban to work with the six vessels at present based on that port, which patrol between the Hebrides and the Tenth Cruiser Squadron.

287. *Commodore E.L. Booty to Vice-Admiral Commanding Tenth Cruiser Squadron*

HMS *Otway*, 19 November 1916

I have the honour to report that HM Ship under my command sighted the Norwegian SS *Older* of Bergen at about 0.10 p.m. on the 18th instant. On approaching it was seen that she was flying Norwegian colours. In reply to my signals she said she was from Halifax to Leith with a general cargo, as, however, Lloyds Weekly Index of 26th October 1916 last reported her at Havre on the 19th October my suspicions were roused and I decided to board although I really thought there was too much sea to do so.

2. I ordered her to stop and placed this ship in position for boarding which was effected at about 1.45 p.m. in Lat 59.19´N, Long 11.58´W.

The Boarding Officer found the *Older* in possession of a German prize crew consisting of one Lieutenant, one Warrant Officer and seven Seamen from a German submarine which had captured her on the 13th November about noon in Lat. 47.8´N, Long. 9.5´W. She sailed from Newport (Mon.) on the 11th November bound to Gibraltar with a cargo of coal.

3. There were also on board:

(i) The crew of 25 of the Italian SS *Lela* of Genoa which was sunk by gunfire by the same submarine on the same day, and in the same position as the *Older* was captured. The Master of the *Lela* was taken on board the submarine. The *Lela* was from Glasgow to Genoa with a cargo of coal.

(ii) The crew, numbering 8, of the British steam trawler *Hatsuse* (CF 18) which was also sunk by gunfire from the same submarine on the 14th November in Lat. 50.14´N, Long 11.0´W.

4. The Boarding Officer made a brief report of the facts of the case by signal; I directed him to send the Germans on board in our boat, he replied 'they have bombs placed ready to blow up the ship.' As, in addition to the Boarding Officer, I had only a Midshipman and two men who were armed on board *Older* and the Germans numbered nine, it was a difficult situation. I signalled that I would take off all hands and that one German should be sent in each boatload. I lowered a second boat and transshipped them as fast as possible – only about six men could be brought at a time on account of the heavy sea.

At about 4.0 p.m the Boarding Officer signalled that they had about half-an-hour (before the bombs were timed to explode). The *Older* then lowered one of her own boats which with one of ours brought off the remainder.

5. The persons taken off the *Older* consisted of:

Master, Officers and Crew of *Older*	22
Officers and Crew of *Lela*	25
Skipper and Crew of *Hatsuse*	8
German Prize Crew	9
Total	64

6. The last boat left *Older* at 4.20 p.m. and by the time everyone was on board *Otway* it was rapidly getting dark.

The German Officer of the Prize Crew told me that the bombs would explode at any moment and that before leaving they had opened the sea-cocks in the Engine room.

7. I had intended to retake possession of the *Older* immediately but there was undoubtedly too much sea for a boat in the dark. *Otway* stood by all night steaming round and round the abandoned ship.

8. At daylight today there was no difference in her appearance, I therefore sent the Boarding Officer, an Engineer Officer, Carpenter and party on board to take charge of her and ascertain if there was any damage, if she was making water and if possible to raise steam. No bombs were found and there was only three feet of water in the bilges, fires were lit and steam was ready for slow speed by noon.

9. I saw the Master – John T. Mohn – of *Older* and informed him that I would conditionally restore his ship to him and gave him a written statement to this effect ...

I then proceeded to re-embark first the Norwegian crew followed by the Italian and British survivors, and an armed Guard in charge of Sub-

Lieutenant S.F. Carter, RNR, to whom I gave orders to take the ship to Stornoway. She proceeded at 1.13 p.m. 19th November.

10. It appears that the German Prize Crew did not form part of the crew of the submarine by which it was placed on board *Older*, but had been on board a Swedish ship (*Varing*?) which was being used in the same way for survivors of other sunken ships in the Bay of Biscay. The Swedish ship being short of water had been permitted to go and the prize crew taken on board the other submarine. The skipper of *Hatsuse* was taken on board the submarine before being sent to the *Older*; he states that the submarine was 60 metres in length, had two guns, was six years old and was homeward bound.

11. The submarine kept company with *Older* and as far as could be ascertained they only parted company in the afternoon or evening of the 17th instant. They were both said to be bound for Kiel. The *Older* apparently had only a vague idea of his position on account of the recent bad weather.

12. The German prisoners were thoroughly searched immediately on being received on board. Nothing of importance was found on them. There is no doubt that they had opportunity of throwing overboard any papers, etc., of importance before leaving the *Older* and they threw their arms overboard at the last moment.

No diaries or letters were found on the prisoners. Such papers as were found are forwarded herewith ...

13. The Officers have been separated from each other and from the men and no intercourse is possible between Officers and men.

14. ... [N]o information of importance has been derived from the prisoners. From conversation with the Lieutenant it appears that his submarine had been about 7 weeks out from Germany and lately has been operating in the Bay of Biscay. He states that on a previous occasion he has been in the neighbourhood of Iceland and on one occasion a trip of 30 days was spent looking for this squadron.

15. The following German papers and gear were removed from the *Older*:

(i) Papers including Prize Crew Officer's rough log and sight book.
(ii) Chart (Blue black) originally the property of the Italian ship *Lela* which shows the presumed track of *Older* up to p.m. of the 17th November.
(iii) A wireless receiving set.
(iv) A case containing 3 fuzes or detonators, presumably for use with bombs.

(v) An empty wooden case which had contained something of the same sort as (iv).
(vi) Six pistol holsters (some containing ammunition clips).
(vii) One pair of binoculars.
(viii) One flashing signal lantern.

These are being forwarded herewith.

16. With reference to paragraph 4, my appreciation of the situation was that if I took any precipitate action from the ship my small party on board *Older* could be overwhelmed by the Germans, who largely outnumbered them and (the Boarding Officer signalled) defied them. They would probably then sink the ship and I should be able to pick up very few of the large number on board on account of the heavy sea.

My plan of getting the Germans away one at a time and then overpowering the remainder seemed likely to succeed, when everyone left on board abandoned the ship together at 4.20 p.m.

17. From the markings on the Chart found an board *Older* (par. 15 ii) it appears that the German submarine probably parted company with *Older* at 4 p.m. on the 17th instant in Lat. 57.22´N, Long. 9.44´W steering 8° ...

18. From information received from the Norwegian and Italian Officers, the Masters of the P. & O. SS *Arabia* and United States SS *Columbian* are on board the submarine; this may help to identify her. She may be U.50 or 58 and a cap ribbon belonging to one of the men is marked 'IV UNTERSEEBOOTS = HALBFLOTTILLE. IV'. She is said to have three guns (Skipper of *Hatsuse* said 2), to be 230 feet long, speed 14 knots on surface and 9 knots submerged, and to be able to remain submerged for 5 days. The *Hatsuse* is said to have been the 11th ship she sank on this voyage.[1]

19. The return for the Prisoners of War Information Bureau will be forwarded when instructions as to the disposal of the prisoners are received, direct to Sir J.D. Rees, MP KCIE CVO[2] in accordance with C.M.O. 108/16 xl 14.

A nominal list of the prisoners is submitted herewith.

20. The W/T apparatus found on board *Older* is purely a receiving set, and could in no circumstances send signals. It was in the Chart

[1]*Lela* and *Hatsuse* were sunk by *U 50*, which also captured *Older*; *Columbian* was sunk by *U 49*.

[2]Rees, Sir John David, MP, KCIE, CVO (1854–1922), Indian Civil Service 1875–1901 (interpreter of Tamil, Telugu, Persian, Hindustani, Russian), M.P. 1906–1910 and 1912–1922, Chairman of numerous companies, Director of the Prisoners of War Information Bureau 1915–1920, Baronet 1919.

House and was undoubtedly used for receiving instructions from the submarine. The Germans said it was taken from an American ship (*Columbian*?) which had been sunk but it appears to be of German make and was probably carried by the submarine for the purpose of putting on board whatever ship they employed as receiving ship for survivors of vessels sunk – which was the role forced on *Older*.

21. I would bring to your notice the good work of the Boarding Officer, Lieutenant Howard Uncles, RNR.[1] He has been the regular Boarding Officer for 1 year 8 months now. He handled the matter on board the *Older* with good judgment and I think it is due to the way he effected the removal of the Germans that they left the ship without ensuring her sinking.

The boats' crews are also deserving of notice, especially George F. Reddings, Leading Seaman, RNR, A 2702, coxswain of one of the boats. They worked hard in a very heavy sea both on Saturday and Sunday, especially so on the former day, when the sea was almost impossible. On Saturday 64 men were taken off and on Sunday 55 men re-embarked, in addition to our own armed guards on both days and a working party on Sunday.

22. A list of articles sent with this letter under separate cover is attached.

288. *Vice-Admiral Tupper to Admiralty*

HMS *Alsatian*, 5 December 1916

Report of Proceedings, 23 November–4 December 1916

***

1. Thursday, 23 November – The Armed Trawler *Saxon* reported she had landed the crew of *Patria* at Reykjavik and had returned to her patrol.

The tow between the tug *Sarah Jolliffe* and *San Tirso* parted during the night, and some difficulty was experienced in renewing it.

Alsatian cruised in search of the derelict *Musselcrag*, referred to in paragraph 18 of my previous report ...

2. Friday, 24 November – Armed Trawler *Arley* reported that water was finding its way into the fore compartment, but that the leak could not be traced. She was directed to proceed direct to Oban where she was due on 29 November in the ordinary course of events.

[1]Uncles, Howard, DSC, RNR, Sub-Lieutenant 1914, Lieutenant 1916.

At 8 p.m. *Teutonic* reported she had been relieved by *Rushcoe* and *Robert Smith* who then took over the escorting of *San Tirso*. I informed the Commander-in-Chief of the state of affairs and as progress was somewhat slow, represented that an additional tug would be of great assistance.

3. Saturday, 25 November – I met *Otway* about 10 a.m. and sent her to Loch Ewe to land the nine German Prisoners captured from SS *Older*.

During the day E Patrol was moved from the North East coast of Iceland to the neighbourhood of Denmark Strait.

Nothing was seen of either of the derelicts *Musselcrag* or *Danneborg*.

Clear weather with strong North Westerly breezes and a heavy swell.

4. Sunday, 26 November – *Otway* arrived at Loch Ewe and left in the evening for Swarbacks Minn.

In the evening the Rear Admiral, Stornoway, informed me that the tug *Gladstone*, escorted by the Armed Trawler *Armageddon* had sailed to assist in the towing of *San Tirso*. Owing to bad weather little progress was made during the course of the day.

At noon *Motagua* intercepted and sent in to Kirkwall with an Armed Guard the Norwegian SS *Kristianiafjord* which was carrying 507 bags of enemy mails.[1]

Alsatian continued to search for *Musselcrag*. The weather was bad on all patrols, and considerably interfered with boarding operations.

At noon the disposition of the Squadron was follows:

A Patrol (On line 360° from 62.30´N, 10´W) ... *Ebro*, *Artois*, *Moldavia*.
C Patrol (On line 235° from 59.17´N, 8.30´W) ... *Patuca*, *Andes*, *Motagua*, *Avenger*.
D Patrol (On line 320° from 56.30´N, 13.0´W) ... *Arlanza*, *Hilary*.
E Patrol (Denmark Strait, Iceland) ... *Gloucestershire*, *Changuinola*.
Between A & C ... *Alsatian*.
Rejoining Patrol ... *Virginian*.
Proceeding to Oban ... *Saxon*, *Arley*.
Escorting *San Tirso* ... *Rushcoe*, *Robert Smith*.
At Liverpool ... *Orvieto*, *Almanzora*, *Orcoma*, *Victorian*.
At Clyde ... *Patia*, *Kildonan Castle*, *Hildebrand*, *Columbella*.
At Loch Ewe ... *Otway*.

[1] *Kristianiafjord* was not detained.

At Aberdeen ... *Tenby Castle*, *Walpole*.
At Swarbacks Minn ... *Teutonic*.
Fitting out at Liverpool ... *Armadale Castle*.[1]

During the course of the week 44 vessels were intercepted of which sixteen were sent in with, and one without, armed guards. Better weather was experienced than during the previous two weeks.

5. Monday, 27 November – The weather continued bad with the wind in the south west.

At noon I met *Virginian* and delivered some steam pipes which had been repaired. She was then sent to relieve *Arlanza* on D patrol.

About 7 p.m. *Alsatian* intercepted the Danish Schooner *Hertha* from Reykjavik to Copenhagen. There was too much sea to board and she was allowed to proceed. D Patrol was moved to work on a line 270° from 57 N, Longitude 11 W.

During the day HMS *Renown* passed through the patrols.

6. Tuesday, 28 November – During the night the wind veered to the Westward and a heavy gale was experienced throughout the day. With the high sea running no boarding was possible.

Little progress was made with *San Tirso*.

7. Wednesday, 29 November – Gale subsiding, though still a heavy sea running.

About noon *Motagua* came across a wooden derelict keel up in Latitude 59.35´N, Longitude 10.57´W, probably *Danneborg*. She fired 50 rounds into the wreck in an attempt to sink it, but did not succeed in doing so before dusk.

At 3.30 p.m. *Alsatian* sighted a derelict in Latitude 59.42´N, Longitude 13 W, which proved to be the sailing vessel *Musselcrag*. Opportunity was taken to carry out target practice with practice projectiles. The range was between 6000 and 7000 yards, but owing to the heavy swell and bad light the practice was difficult and, although the target was frequently straddled, she only appeared to be hit twice. *Alsatian* then closed and fired 12 lyddite shells at short range. All the shells detonated and very soon caused *Musselcrag* to disappear.

At 7 p.m. *Alsatian* intercepted Norwegian SS *Kristiania* from Baltimore to Christiania with a cargo of grain and sent her to Kirkwall with an armed guard.[2]

8. Thursday, 30 November – From 1 a.m. till daylight *Alsatian* followed a steamer which proved to be the British SS *Cannizaro* from

[1]This returns the ship numbers to 24.
[2]*Kristiania* was not detained.

Hull to New York. It would save a great deal of time and trouble as well as some anxiety if such vessels could be given a clearance flag based on the system at present in vogue in the Grand Fleet. A separate submission to the Commander-in-Chief is being forwarded regarding this ...

Avenger completed the destruction of *Danneborg*.

The tug *Gladstone* having joined up, better progress was being made with the towing of *San Tirso*, but at 7.30 p.m. the hawsers of both tugs again parted.

News was received by Poldhu Telegram that Sir David Beatty, GCB, KCVO, DSO, had been appointed to command the Grand Fleet.

9. Friday, 1 December – *Gloucestershire* reported that on 29 November in Latitude 66.7´N, 26.44´W a track apparently that of a torpedo had been observed passing astern of the ship. Nothing else was seen.

E patrol had been moved to work on a line 45° from Latitude 64 N, Longitude 27 W.

Information was received from the Senior Naval Officer Liverpool, that owing to the boiler makers refusing to work overtime the sailing of *Orcoma* would be delayed – a deplorable state of affairs in time of war. These delays in the refitting of ships causes a shortage in the number on patrol. At the present moment I have only 13 at sea out of a total of 24 instead of 17 as there should be. In consequence I am obliged to keep ships out from the Southern bases beyond the usual 50 days.

The Admiralty informed me that *Kildonan Castle* at present at Clyde, was required for special service, and would be absent from the squadron for about one month.

10. Saturday, 2 December – At 7 a.m. in Latitude 61.18´N, Longitude 11.40´W *Alsatian* intercepted the Swedish SS *Ada* from Gothenburg to New York ... which had succeeded in evading the patrols on her Eastward voyage. As it was dark and blowing hard at the time she was shadowed till daylight and then successfully boarded in a very heavy sea. She was sent into Stornoway with an armed guard.[1]

At 3 p.m. I met *Otway* rejoining from Swarbacks Minn, and gave her orders to relieve *Gloucestershire* in charge of E patrol in Denmark Strait.

11. Sunday, 3 December – C Patrol was moved to Patrol Line III, working on a line of bearing 345° from latitude 58.20´ North, longitude 14 West.

San Tirso arrived Lough Swilly at 3 a.m. towed by the tugs *Sarah*

[1]*Ada* was not detained.

Joliffe and *Armageddon* and escorted by the Armed Trawlers *Rushcoe* and *Robert Smith*.

I consider that the Commanding Officer of *Rushcoe* Lieutenant John T. Randell, DSC, RNR, who took charge of towing operations on *Teutonic* leaving for Swarbacks Minn on 24 November did very well in bringing the vessel safely into port.

I arrived at Swarbacks Minn in *Alsatian* at 10 p.m.

At noon the disposition of the squadron was as follows:

A Patrol (On line 360° from 62.30´N, 10 W) ... *Ebro*, *Arlanza*.
C Patrol (Proceeding to line 345° from 58.20´N, 14 W) ... *Andes*, *Hilary*, *Avenger*, *Teutonic*.
D Patrol (Cruising between Rockall and 10 W) ... *Virginian*.
E Patrol (Denmark Strait) ... *Changuinola*, *Gloucestershire*.
Proceeding to E ... *Otway*.
Proceeding to Swarbacks Minn ... *Alsatian*.
Proceeding to Clyde ... *Motagua*.
At Swarbacks Minn ... *Artois*, *Moldavia*.
At Clyde ... *Patia*, *Hildebrand*, *Columbella*.
At Liverpool ... *Orvieto*, *Almanzora*, *Orcoma*, *Victorian*.
At Loch Ewe ... *Patuca*.
At Obam ... Armed Trawlers *Saxon*, *Arley*.
At Aberdeen ... Armed Trawlers *Tenby Castle*, *Walpole*.
At Loch Swilly ... Armed Trawlers *Rushcoe*, *Robert Smith*.
Fitting out at Liverpool ... *Armadale Castle*.
Fitting out for special service at Clyde ... *Kildonan Castle*.

During the week, 49 vessels were intercepted of which 12 were sent in with and 4 without Armed Guards. Westerly winds and heavy seas were encountered throughout the week.

Monday, 4 December.

***

10

THE SUBMARINE MENACE RENEWED, DECEMBER 1916–MARCH 1917

In late 1916 a new Commander-in-Chief, Beatty, and a new First Lord, Carson, were appointed. The latter had no discernible effect on policy, the former only a little effect, both running up against the Admiralty bureaucracy which was a past master at delay and refusal [e.g., 296, 308]. But by the end of the year the Tenth Cruiser Squadron was being faced by a newly active enemy once more, the German submarine fleet. Despite frequent scares and many sightings (or mistaken sightings), there had been few attacks on the ships of the Patrol for a year and more [294 para. 18]. This began to change a month or so before the Germans began unrestricted submarine warfare on 5 February 1917 [307, also 316, 319]; note also the use of wireless detection [294].

Tupper responded by insisting on more firing practices and submarine drills on his visits to various ships. He was also fertile of ideas and expedients – hoping to use a trawler as a Q-ship [298, 299, 304], a mine barrage [289 para. 2] – and he had substantial support from the Commander-in-Chief [305]. Both were blocked by the Admiralty, for their ideas demanded ships, and there were simply no more suitable vessels available [306]. Tupper, in fact, had more ships than ever, when detachments returned and fitting-out was completed, and was promised more trawlers [317 para. 1].

289. *Vice-Admiral Tupper to Admiralty*

HMS *Alsatian*, [19] December 1916

Report of Proceedings, 4–20 December 1916

***

1. Monday, 4 December – *Alsatian* commenced coaling at 8 a.m.

Information had been received the previous evening from the Admiral, Orkneys and Shetlands, that the Dutch SS *Gamma*, which had been reported as 'out' from Holland on the 29th November, had been cleared from Kirkwall at 11 a.m. that morning. It was noticed however that a vessel purporting to be the *Gamma* had been intercepted by *Teutonic* and *Avenger* in the early morning of 2 December, and allowed to proceed.[1]

The facts were reported to the Admiral Orkneys and Shetland, who was asked if he was able to identify the vessel. He replied he was unable to do so and had reported particulars to the Admiralty and Commander-in-Chief.

A full report of the incident has been forwarded to the Commander-in-Chief with a view to an Enquiry being held on *Avenger*'s arrival at Scapa Flow …

I informed *Capitaine de Fregate* Paul de Marguerye, of *Artois*, that His Majesty had conferred upon him the decoration of the Distinguished Service Order. I pinned the ribbon to his breast and said I hoped that His Majesty would be able to decorate him at some future date. Monsieur Paul de Marguerye seemed greatly impressed as well as proud and grateful of the honour.

Having landed and met Admiral Fawckner and the Captains of *Shannon* and *Cochrane*, the question was discussed of maintaining a swept channel across St Magnus Bay from the boom defence as far as Eshaness Light. I have in consequence forwarded a recommendation to the Commander-in-Chief … that six minesweeping trawlers or drifters should be stationed at Swarbacks Minn, instead of two as at present.

Moldavia left harbour at 4 p.m.

2. Tuesday, 5 December – At 3.30 a.m. orders were received from the Commander-in-Chief to move the patrols to Line No. IV, owing to possible submarine menace. Directions were given accordingly for Ships to form on a line 360° from Latitude 55.30´ North, Longitude 18 West.

Alsatian completed coaling during the day, having taken in 1800 tons. The weather was bad, but I visited Lerwick and conferred with Commander Alston and the Examination Officers and also was instructed in the latest pattern of Indicator Nets with Mines.

In connection with my suggestion forwarded to the Commander-in-Chief … for laying nets with mines across the North Sea from Buchan Ness to Lister Fiord, Norway, it seems practicable to put the firing battery in a Mine Case painted a Special colour and, if this was moored some distance from the nets, it would not be necessary to keep drifters out watching after the nets had once been laid.

[1]This caused a minor crisis in the squadron – [291, 292, 293, 295].

3. Wednesday, 6 December – *Hilary* arrived at Swarbacks Minn at dawn and commenced coaling.

During the afternoon, men were landed for exercise from *Alsatian*. The Church Army Hut has not yet been erected, though all the material is ready. As there appeared to be some delay regarding the renting of a site, I telegraphed to the Admiralty asking that the necessary authority might be given.

Artois left harbour about 5 p.m., and at 9 p.m. I followed in *Alsatian*.

4. Thursday, 7 December – Strong South Easterly wind and considerable swell.

The *Duke of Edinburgh* with an Armed Boarding Steamer in company was sighted to the North of the Faroes about 2 p.m.

5. Friday, 8 December – Orders were received from the Admiralty, through the Commander-in-Chief, to detach four ships of the 10th Cruiser Squadron for special service in pursuit of a Raider. As it was necessary for these vessels to have a large radius of action and be suitable for steaming in the tropics, *Almanzora*, *Orvieto*, *Orcoma* and *Arlanza* were selected for the purpose. The first three were already at Liverpool, and *Arlanza* was ordered to proceed there with despatch to complete with stores and provisions.[1]

Gloucestershire, at Swarbacks Minn, was selected as a stand-by ship in the event of one of the others not being immediately available. Later in the day the Rear-Admiral Swarbacks Minn informed me that she had been ordered to Clyde, presumably to replace one of the other vessels. She sailed soon after midnight.

At 3 p.m. in Latitude 59.25´ North, Longitude 15.55´ West, *Ebro* intercepted the Danish trawler *Bragi*, from Santander to Reykjavik, via Falmouth, with salt and other cargo. She was sent in to Stornoway with an Armed Guard … .[2]

Owing to the shortage of ships on patrol, I obtained permission from the Commander-in-Chief to temporarily abandon E, and directed *Otway* and *Moldavia* to join the main patrol line.

[1]This was in pursuit of *Moewe*, which 'escaped', for the second time, in November. She overheard *Artois* and *Moldavia* arranging a rendezvous and was thus able to avoid meeting them, to go on for a four-month cruise in the Atlantic. The pursuit was vain, and *Moewe* captured or sank 34 ships. The diversion of four ships from the Northern Patrol was justice, since it was the Patrol's ships' carelessness which let her through; it was also an extra benefit for the Germans. It is worth remembering, in this connection, that the Patrol's original function had been to block the egress of German ships from the North Sea, and on this day it failed to do so. *Arlanza*, one of the diverted ships, had only been back on the Patrol for a month.

[2]*Bragi* was not detained.

At 8 p.m., orders were received from the Commander-in-Chief to take up Patrol Line No. 2.

6. Saturday, 9 December – A heavy North Easterly gale, which had sprung up in the course of the night, considerably delayed ships taking up their new positions, and made all boarding impracticable.

I had intended meeting *Teutonic* to receive her report regarding the incident of the SS *Gamma*, but was obliged to abandon the rendezvous and despatch her to Liverpool, as she was running short of coal.

7. Sunday, 10 December – Gale had moderated and Patrol Line No. 2 was taken up during the forenoon.

At 9 a.m., *Avenger* in Latitude 60.27´ North Longitude 9.11´ West, intercepted a Norwegian Sailing Vessel *Maletta* from Copenhagen to St Thomas, in ballast. Her Master reported having been boarded by an enemy submarine at 1.30 p.m. on 8 December when in Latitude 62.10´ North, Longitude 2.12´ West; the submarine was steering west.[1]

About the same time the Commander-in-Chief ordered special precautions to be taken against submarine attack.

The Master of the Norwegian Sailing Vessel *Veetdal* (ex *Olav*), boarded by *Artois*, reported having sighted several mines in Latitude 57.24´ North, Longitude 5.50´ East on 30 November.

The disposition of the Squadron at noon was as follows:

A Patrol, 90 miles 325° from Lat. 62 N, Long. 14 W … *Moldavia*.

C Patrol, on line 325° from Lat. 59.17´N, Long. 8.30´W … *Patuca*, *Artois*, *Otway*, *Ebro*, *Avenger*.

Between A & C … *Alsatian*.

Patrolling off St Kilda … Armed Trawlers *Arley* and *Tenby Castle*.

Rejoining from Clyde … *Columbella*.

Rejoining from Swarbacks Minn … *Hilary*.

Proceeding to Liverpool … *Teutonic*, *Virginian*, *Arlanza* (for special service).

Proceeding to Clyde … *Gloucestershire* (for special service).

At Liverpool … *Orvieto*, *Victorian*, *Andes*, *Almanzora* (for special service) *Orcoma* (for special service), *Armadale Castle* (fitting out).

At Clyde … *Changuinola*, *Motagua*, *Patia*, *Hildebrand*.

At Swarbacks Minn … Armed Trawler *Saxon*.

At Aberdeen (Docking) … Armed Trawler *Walpole*.

At Fleetwood (Docking) … Armed Trawlers *Rushcoe* and *Robert Smith*.

Special service … *Kildonan Castle*.

[1]The submarine is not identifiable.

During the week, 38 vessels were intercepted, 16 of which were sent in with Armed Guards for further examination.

Attention has already been drawn to the large number of ships at the Southern Bases. Until the five vessels, which are at present detached, rejoin, it is of urgent importance that all work which will delay a ship in harbour beyond the normal period of 10 days, should be deferred until succeeding Visits, as otherwise it is impossible to maintain the efficiency of the patrol.

The delay at the Southern Bases entirely upsets the relief programme, and vessels have to be kept on patrol, and away from their refitting ports, beyond the normal 50 days, which is bad for their boilers, etc.

8. Monday, 11 December – Strong Easterly breezes, with snow squalls and considerable sea.

At 1.30 p.m., having met *Avenger*, and received a written report regarding the interception of the Steamer purporting to be the Dutch SS *Gamma*, I ordered her to proceed to Scapa to oil, according to programme, and with a view to the Enquiry, ordered by the Admiralty, being held.

Intercepted messages had already led me to believe that it was anticipated a Raider would shortly be making an attempt to break out into the Atlantic, and about 3 p.m. the Commander-in-Chief informed me a Raider was possibly proceeding via the North of Iceland or the Faroes. At the same time he directed me to place a Ship on E patrol to the North of Iceland, and to strengthen A and B Patrols at the expense of C and D. By countermanding order for *Avenger* to oil and by ascertaining that *Ebro* – already overdue for overhaul and coaling – could remain out two or three days more, 8 Ships were then available for the work, and these were disposed as follows:

A Patrol, on line of bearing 310° from Latitude 62.33´ North, Longitude 8 West, 40 miles apart … *Columbella* and *Alsatian*.
B Patrol, between 64.20´ North and 65.20´ North, on meridian of 12 West … *Avenger*, orders to proceed to Scapa being cancelled.
C Patrol, on line 325° from Latitude 59.17´ Longitude 8.30´ West … *Hilary*, *Patuca*, *Otway*; *Ebro*, on her way to Clyde, was recalled to join C.
E Patrol, on line between 66 and 67 North, on meridian of 13 West … *Moldavia*.

Arley reported that the Commanding Officer, a Petty Officer, and Leading Seaman were unfit for duty, owing, it was believed, to

Influenza. I gave permission for her to proceed to Oban, leaving only one Trawler to patrol between St Kilda and 10 West.

Received news by Poldhu that Sir Edward Carson had been selected for First Lord of the Admiralty.[1]

A north easterly gale sprang up during the afternoon.

9. Tuesday, 12 December – The gale continued throughout the day, the weather being misty and visibility consequently low.

Hilary on being relieved on C by *Ebro* was directed to join A patrol.

10. Wednesday, 13 December – The weather moderated during the night but in the afternoon the wind again freshened to a gale.

The Second Light Cruiser Squadron having taken up patrol on a line joining Sydero and Noup Head, C Patrol was reduced to two Ships, and A and B Patrols ordered to work on a line 360° from Latitude 61.30′ North, Longitude 9 West, Ships 45 miles apart from South in the following order: *Hilary*, *Columbella*, *Alsatian*, *Avenger*. This was the best I could do with a view to intercepting a Raider passing North of Faroes and making for Icelandic territorial waters.

The armed trawlers *Tenby Castle* and *Saxon* were directed to patrol between St Kilda and 10 West with a view to their working across the route followed by Dutch Vessels proceeding to and from Holland and Falmouth. I submit that the route at present used by these vessels, viz: passing to the west of Ireland, Skerryvore, St Kilda, through positions 60 North, 6 West and 61 North, 6 West, and thence along the parallel of 61 North as far as 3 East, generally carries them clear of the 10th Cruiser Squadron patrols. Probably this fact is known to the enemy, and if so, he may thus be provided with a key to a comparatively safe passage through the patrols. I intend using the trawlers attached to the 10th Cruiser Squadron to block this passage as far as possible, but I would suggest that Dutch Vessels should in future be instructed to pass to the west and north of Rockall from the position 61 North, 6 West. This should ensure their being intercepted in the majority of cases, and thus give the impression that the whole area is thoroughly patrolled. The trawlers *Tenby Castle* and *Saxon* intercepted two of the Dutch Steamers between St Kilda and 10 West today.

[1]This is the only reference in these documents to the political crisis which broke the Asquith government and brought in the Lloyd George coalition in December 1916. Carson had been Attorney-General in Asquith's government, and had been responsible for prosecuting Prize Court cases sent there by the Customs and the Contraband Committee; he could be assumed to be *au fait* with the general status for the blockade. He was not, however, in the small War Cabinet. Lord Robert Cecil, who had been Under-Secretary of State at the Foreign Office received the title of Minister of Blockade; it was a renaming only; he had already done the job as Under-Secretary. But his chief was now Arthur Balfour, not Sir Edward Grey.

Owing to mines being reported off Skerryvore I cancelled the orders which I had given to *Ebro* to proceed through the Minches, and directed her to use the Tory Island Route. She would also be patrolling on that route.

11. Thursday, 14 December – North easterly gale throughout the day.

At 7 p.m. the Commander-in-Chief informed me that no further news had been received regarding the supposed Raider, and that ordinary patrol was to be resumed.

Avenger was ordered to proceed to Scapa Flow, and *Moldavia* withdrawn from E to take her place on A. *Columbella* and *Hilary* were directed to join C, making four vessels on C and two on A.

12. Friday, 15 December – Still blowing strongly from the North East with heavy snow storms.

About 6.30 a.m. the Admiral Orkneys and Shetlands informed me that a suspicious vessel had been sighted in the vicinity of Muckle Flugga steering to the westwards. This proved later to have been the *Minotaur* and C Patrol which had been moved to the Eastward to intercept her, was directed to resume normal patrol.

13. Saturday, 16 December – At 7 a.m. *Alsatian* met Danish Fishery Cruiser *Island Falk* who made her name by flash lamp. She was kept in sight until daylight in order that she might be identified. I then signalled to her that 'The Admiral wishes to thank the Captain for his courtesy to the Armed trawlers in Iceland waters and for his kindness to the crew of *Nellie Bruce* sunk by German submarine on 30 October'. The *Island Falk* replied – 'Captain wishes to thank Admiral for his compliment.'

Communicated by boat with *Moldavia*.

Alsatian intercepted in Latitude 62.42´ North, 8.40´ Russian SS *Yaroslavl* from Liverpool to Yukanski, munitions, Aeroplanes, 44 French Officers, etc.

Otway reported intercepting the Russian Steamer *Tzesarevich Alexis* from Archangel to Glasgow, with 17 passengers, including Rear-Admiral Phillimore and Brigadier-General Jackson.[1] As she was proceeding via the Minches she was warned of the presence of mines in the vicinity of Skerryvore.

[1]Phillimore, Richard Fortescue, GCB, KCMG, MVO, RN (1864–1940), Commander 1899, Captain 1904, Rear-Admiral 1915, attached to Russian Imperial Headquarters 1915–1916, in Command of First Battle Squadron 1916–1918, Admiral commanding Aircraft Carrier HMS *Furious* March 1918, Vice-Admiral 1920, in command of Reserve Fleet 1920–1922, Admiral 1924, Commander-in-Chief Plymouth 1923–1926, retired 1929.

Jackson, Robert Whyte, Royal Inniskilling Fusiliers, Colonel 1902, Brigadier-General and Director of Ordnance Services 1915, was also attached to Russian Imperial HQ, 1915–1916.

14. Sunday 17 December – At noon the disposition of the Squadron was as follows:

A Patrol on line 360° from Latitude 61.30´ North, 9 West ... *Alsatian*, *Moldavia*.
C Patrol, on line 325° from Latitude 59.17´ North, 8.30´ West ... *Patuca*, *Otway*, *Hilary*, *Columbella*.
Rejoining Patrol ... *Orvieto*, Armed Trawler *Arley*.
Patrolling between St Kilda and 10 W ... Armed Trawlers *Saxon*, *Tenby Castle*.
At Liverpool ... *Teutonic*, *Virginian*, *Victorian*, *Andes*, *Armadale Castle* (Fitting out).
At Clyde ... *Ebro*, *Changuinola*, *Motagua*, *Patia*, *Hildebrand*.
At Scapa ... *Avenger*.
At Brest ... *Artois*.
At Swarbacks Minn ... Armed Trawler *Walpole*.
At Fleetwood ... Armed Trawlers *Robert Smith*, *Rushcoe*.
Special service ... *Almanzora*, *Arlanza*, *Orcoma*, *Gloucestershire*, *Kildonan Castle*.

During the week 44 Ships were intercepted, of which five were sent in with, and three without, Armed Guards. Bad weather was experienced most of the week.

15. Monday, 18 December – *Moldavia* left patrol. I had kept her out to the limit of her coal endurance, and she would only have 250 tons on board on arrival at the Clyde.

In spite of a very heavy sea, *Alsatian* managed to put an Armed Guard on board the Norwegian SS *Kronprinsesse Victoria*.[1] The Danish SS *Gullfoss* and two British Trawlers were also intercepted and allowed to proceed.

16. Tuesday, 19 December – The Master of the Dutch Steamer *Celebes* from Amsterdam to Falmouth, boarded by Trawler *Arley* reported that the vessel had been stopped by an enemy submarine a.m. on 17 December in Latitude 60.56´ North, Longitude 3.5´ East.[2]

With a view to watching the Faroes and the passage between there and Iceland, I moved *Columbella* from C and arranged for her, together with *Alsatian*, to patrol on a line joining 60 North, 11´ West and 64 North, 8 West. This left three Ships on C Patrol and two Armed Trawlers

[1]*Kronprinsesse Victoria* was not detained, though it had been regarded as suspicous in the past.

[2]The submarine is not identifiable.

patrolling between St Kilda and 10.30´ West, which is the best that can be done, with the Ships at present available.

Otway having been relieved by *Avenger* on C proceeded to Liverpool. *Patia* at last sailed from Clyde, her date of departure having been postponed four times.

17. Wednesday, 20 December – North Easterly gale with thick Strong North Easterly winds and snow squalls have been more or less continuous since 9 December.

On arrival of *Patia* on patrol, I decided to take *Alsatian* in for coal at Swarbacks Minn, *Patia* taking *Alsatian*'s place on A.

If the Ships leave Clyde and Liverpool according to their programme dates, it is hoped that nine Ships will be on patrol towards the end of next week.

***

290. *Commander-in-Chief Grand Fleet to Admiralty*

HMS *Iron Duke*, 6 December 1916

***

2. The tracing mentioned in letter from Vice-Admiral Tenth Cruiser Squadron No. 87/02 of 13th June 1916 [241] attached shows the various patrol lines:

Patrol Line No 1. A line 360° from Muckle Flugga.
Patrol Line No 2. A line joining the Butt of Lewis to the coast of Iceland in Long. 15.0´W.
Patrol Line No 3. A line joining a position in Lat. 56.45´N, Long 11.0´W to the coast of Iceland in Long. 17.0´W.
Patrol Line No 4. A line joining the South-west point of Iceland through Lat. 57.0´W, Long. 19.0´W to Lat. 55.0´N, Long. 15.0´W.

3. The Tenth Cruiser Squadron normally occupy Patrol Line no 2. The vessels are arranged in groups A, B, C, D, and E and occupy positions along the line as follows:

A Patrol: ships cruise normally in line ahead about the centre of the line on courses 325° and 145°.
B Patrol: ships cruise normally in line abreast to the northward of and near the south coast of Iceland on courses 40° and 220°.
C Patrol: Ships cruise normally in line ahead to the Southward of A on courses 255° and 55°.

D Patrol: ships cruise normally in line abreast on courses 80° and 260° through a position in Lat. 56.30´N, Long. 13.0´W.
E Patrol: Ships cruise normally to the Northward of Iceland. The distance between the ships on patrol is usually about thirty miles, but this, of course, varies according to the number of vessels on patrol.

291. *Commander Arthur L. Ashby*[1] *to Vice-Admiral Commanding Tenth Cruiser Squadron*

HMS *Avenger*, 7 December 1916

In accordance with your W/T message timed 1100 of this date, I have the honour to make the following report:

2. Between 1.0 a.m. and 2.17 a.m. on December 2nd I was boarding a Norwegian steamer *Artemis* in Lat. 59.35´N, Long. 12.32´W. During this period the lights of a vessel were observed to the North-eastward, steering to the South-westward and passing to the North and West of me. I estimate that this vessel was over five miles away when first sighted by me.

3. After hoisting my boat on return from boarding I proceeded to intercept this steamer.

4. At 3.45 a.m. I commenced making signals to the vessel by asking 'What ship', and the reply was *Gamma*, after which I proceeded to enquire 'Where from' and 'Where bound' and received the replies 'Amsterdam' and 'New York', respectively. The next signal 'What was last port of call', was replied to by 'Kirkwall'. The signals from the vessel were bad throughout, the main difficulty appearing to be the taking in of my signals. I could not get her to take in the signals 'What cargo' and 'Have you flag of day'. All signals were made 'en clair', and the time occupied in signalling was nearly an hour and a half.

5. During this period the head wind had increased in force and the sea risen considerably, and the vessel's speed which had previously been ten knots or over was reduced to about four knots. Boarding was entirely impracticable.

6. In order to see whether she was flying any flag and whether she was laden I used my searchlight, my position then being on her bow, and distant a half to three quarters of a mile.

7. She had no flag flying, and appeared to be light, pitching very considerably in the head sea.

[1]Ashby, Arthur L., CMG, RN, (1876–1956), Lieutenant 1897, Commander 1909, Captain of *Avenger* 1915–1917, Captain (retired) 1922.

8. She had a black hull, distinctly a red bottom, and white upperworks, two masts and one funnel with Dutch flag on the bows – I did not see any lettering on the side. As far as I remember the funnel was black, but I am not certain on this part, and the Officer who was on watch at the time is at present away on Armed Guard duties. She had good navigation lights burning and other lights were showing.

9. I sent the message 'Intercepted Dutch steamer *Gamma* Amsterdam to Kirkwall to New York Lat. 59.28´N, Long. 12.24´W, steering 240°. Too rough to board. Request instructions 0515'. Not having seen any flag, and not having received replies to my last two signals (I had concluded she was unable to read them) I did not include any reference to flag of day or cargo in my message to you.

10. On receipt of your message 'Permit ship which has been detained to proceed', timed 0555, I left the vessel in order to get into touch with another vessel coming from south-westward.

292. *Commodore J.S. Luard to Vice-Admiral Commanding Tenth Cruiser Squadron*

HMS *Teutonic*, 7 December 1916

In accordance with your W/T message 1100 of 7th instant, I have the honour to report the following details in connection with intercepting the supposed Dutch steamer *Gamma*:

2. At 0.15 a.m. on 2nd December a steamer showing the usual steaming lights together with several lights from curtains and ports, was sighted right ahead about five miles distant. *Teutonic* was then steering 55°.

3. It was a dark night and there was a strong breeze with a rough sea. Zigzag course was stopped to close the steamer to within signalling distance. Her position was then Lat. 59.50´N, Long. 11 West.

4. In reply to the flashing signal 'What ship?' the steamer replied '*Gamma*' (very indistinctly), and to further signals from *Teutonic* she stated she was from Holland to Falmouth and also what was understood to be 'Ballast'. Her signalling throughout was very bad.

5. … I concluded she was the Netherlands Overseas Trust vessel … The state of the sea and extreme darkness being such as to make boarding dangerous, also her replies being considered satisfactory, I directed her to proceed.

293. *Finding of the Court of Enquiry into the Circumstances attending the Interception of a Supposed Enemy Raider by HMS* Avenger *and* Teutonic

18 December 1916

***

2. We find that the vessel intercepted by *Teutonic* at 0.25 a.m. on 2 December 1916 [291] and by *Avenger* later the same morning [292] was not the *Gamma*, as she represented. From the description as to size, etc, by the various officers and men who saw her it would seem that, if an enemy, she was probably a supply ship than a raider [295].[1]

294. *Vice-Admiral Tupper to Admiralty*

HMS *Alsatian*, 7 January 1917

Report of Proceedings, 21 December 1916–7 January 1917

***

1. Thursday, 21 December – At 4 p.m. I gave charge of the Patrol to *Hilary* and shaped course for Swarbacks Minn. I had intended arriving there about midnight, but owing to the weather becoming thick, and a gale blowing, this was postponed until the following morning.

A mined area was reported between the Isle of Man and Liverpool.

Owing to the heavy misty weather no ships were intercepted during the day.

2. Friday, 22 December – I arrived at Swarbacks Minn in *Alsatian* at 8.30 a.m. Coaling was commenced at 9.30 a.m. I conferred with the Rear-Admiral Swarbacks Minn and the Senior Officer of Second Cruiser Squadron.

3. Saturday, 23 December – Coaling was completed at 2 p.m., 1600 tons having been taken in at an average of 123.8 tons per hour.

The foundations of the Church Army Hut are now laid.

4. Sunday, 24 December – Held Divine Service. Petty Officers and

[1]The problem with this finding, at least from an historian's viewpoint, is that it leaves the precise identity of the ship unclear. The idea that it was a supply ship for U-boats may be discounted, since there is no sign that the Germans used them. It seems, in fact, probable that the ship really was the Dutch SS *Gamma*, and the whole affair was a command mistake. However, if the ship really was going from Amsterdam to New York, or even Falmouth, the positions recorded by *Avenger* and *Teutonic* show she was going the wrong way.

men from *Alsatian* were landed during the afternoon for recreation.

At 4 p.m. left Swarbacks Minn for patrol.

At 6 p.m. *Avenger* intercepted the Swedish SS *Anglia* in Latitude 58.43´ North, Longitude 11.12´ West, bound from New York to Goteborg with a cargo of Cotton Seed Oil. She was sent in to Kirkwall with an Armed Guard … .[1]

The Captain Superintendent Clyde informed me that *Moldavia* was showing signs of structural weakness and that it was considered essential to strengthen her hull before she put to sea. This is probably due to the Constructors having removed the expansion joint when fitting the ship to carry guns. In consequence she will not be available until the 17th of January.

At noon, the disposition of the Squadron was as follows:

A Patrol, on line 20° from 60 North, 11 West … *Patia*, *Columbella*.
C Patrol, on line 325° from 59.17´ North, 8.30´ West … *Orvieto*, *Avenger*, *Hilary*.
Patrolling Between St Kilda and 10 West … Armed Trawler *Walpole*.
Rejoining Patrol … Armed Trawler *Saxon*.
At Swarbacks Minn … *Alsatian*.
At Liverpool … *Teutonic*, *Otway*, *Virginian*, *Andes*, *Victorian*.
At Clyde … *Patuca*, *Moldavia*, *Ebro*, *Changuinola*, *Motagua*, *Hildebrand*.
At Brest … *Artois*.
At Oban … Armed Trawlers *Tenby Castle*, *Arley*.
At Fleetwood … Armed Trawlers *Robert Smith*, *Rushcoe*.
On special service … *Almanzora*, *Arlanza*, *Orcoma*, *Gloucestershire*, *Kildonan Castle*.
Fitting out at Liverpool … *Armadale Castle*.

During the week 31 vessels were intercepted, of which 10 were sent in with Armed Guards.

5. Monday, 25 December – Fine day, mild weather.

Kildonan Castle, whose special Service had been postponed, rejoined patrol, and was directed to work in an area contained by the following positions:

Latitude	57.15´	North,	Longitude	13 West.
”	56.35´	”	”	13 ”
”	50.35´	”	”	10.30´ West.
”	58.15´	”	”	10.30´ ”

[1]*Anglia* was not detained.

with a view to supporting the Armed Trawlers working between St Kilda and Longitude 10.30´ West.

Hilary was met at 9.30 a.m. for the purpose of transferring Armed Guards.

Christmas day passed pleasantly. In the evening a concert was given in *Alsatian* to those not on duty which was greatly appreciated.

6. Tuesday, 26 December – *Victorian*, which had left Liverpool on 24 December, reported that shortly before sailing she had discharged 17 cases of measles, two of which had subsequently died, and that two further cases had developed during the past 24 hours. I directed her not to send any Armed Guards away for the present, and arranged for her to join A Patrol where fewer ships would be intercepted.

At 7.45 a.m. *Alsatian* intercepted fragments of a W/T message from an American Steamer to the SS *Kroonland* in which she referred to having heard S.O.S. calls and to a ship being hit by shells. The signals were, however, weak.[1]

Alsatian carried out Aiming Rifle practice and Anti-Submarine practice with good results.

C Patrol was shifted 30 miles to the Eastward.

7. Wednesday, 27 December – Several Ships having rejoined from the Southern bases, A Patrol was formed on a line 360° from Latitude 62 North, Longitude 9 West, consisting of *Patia*, *Virginian*, *Andes*, and *Victorian*, ships 45 miles apart. The Senior Officer was directed to move the Patrol one degree of Longitude each day within the limits of 90 West and 12 West.

Ebro and *Changuinola* were ordered to proceed to E Patrol on line of bearing 300° from Latitude 62.30´ North, Longitude 25 West.

I met *Victorian* at 9.30 a.m. and received despatches. It had been my intention to proceed on board and witness target practice but owing to the recent epidemic of measles, and two fresh cases being reported, I decided to defer my visit.

With reference to paragraph 1 of my previous report of proceedings No. 804/35 of 21 December, the Commander-in-Chief informed me to the effect that owing to the deep water in St Magnus Bay, a swept channel was not essential, but that frequent searches should be carried out in the immediate approaches to the harbour and that the isolated shallow patches should also be occasionally searched. These latter should, however, be avoided by Ships making or leaving the port. He

[1] I can make nothing of this; perhaps it may be taken as a good sample of the fog which war generates.

also informed me that sufficient mine-sweeping gear was being sent to Swarbacks Minn so that all six trawlers stationed at the base could carry out minesweeping duties.

8. Thursday, 28 December – Ships on C Patrol experienced a SW gale which interfered with boarding operations.

Hildebrand should have sailed to rejoin patrol but it was reported that the gun trials had shown a weakness in the mounting of the forecastle 6" gun and that she had had to return to harbour. She will not now be ready until 11 January.

C Patrol was moved 60 miles to the westward.

9. Friday, 29 December – Fine again. About 3.30 a.m. the Armed Trawler *Arley* in Latitude 58.10´ North, Longitude 9.10´ West, reported she was unable to overhaul a large four masted steamer which she had been endeavouring to intercept. The steamer's course was about 240° and speed 14 knots.

At 9 a.m. *Kildonan Castle*, which had steered to intercept her, reported that she had not been sighted, which it was estimated should have been done about 7 a.m.

Kildonan Castle was ordered to chase, and *Ebro* and *Changuinola* on their way to E Patrol were diverted to endeavour to cut her off.

At 7 p.m. the Rear Admiral Stornoway, informed me that the Danish Motor Ship *Panama* had cleared from that Port at 12.15 p.m. the previous day, bound for Panama. As this Ship has four masts, and should have reached the position in which *Arley* saw her, it is considered she is most probably the vessel in question.

Kildonan Castle, *Ebro*, and *Changuinola*, were later directed to resume patrol as they had not sighted the vessel.

I afterwards ascertained from *Arley* that she had fired a blank charge from her 12 pdr, the gun then jamming, and two shells from the 6 pdr accompanied by red Very's Lights. It is suggested that, when *Panama* is next at a British Port, if it is found she is the vessel referred to, an explanation should be requested as to why she did not stop.

10. Saturday, 30 December – Fine weather with heavy swell.

I left Patrol in *Alsatian* for Scapa Flow to visit the Commander-in-Chief, leaving *Andes* in charge during my absence.

11. Sunday, 31 December – *Alsatian* arrived and anchored at Scapa Flow at 9 a.m., leaving again at 5.30 p.m. for patrol. Various matters were discussed with the Commander-in-Chief in connection with the 10th Cruiser Squadron, notably the question of reducing the number of colliers, and the possibility of using Scapa Flow instead of Swarbacks Minn as a Northern coaling base, or the alternative of abandoning a Northern base and using Liverpool and the Clyde only.

The visit to Scapa was greatly appreciated by both Officers and men. I heard many remarks as to the great interest taken all round in seeing the Grand Fleet, which they hardly ever had an opportunity of doing, and feeling that the 10th Cruiser Squadron really belonged to it. From that point of view I am greatly in favour of allowing each Ship of the Squadron to visit Scapa occasionally for coaling, etc. The Commander-in-Chief honoured *Alsatian* with a short visit, and went round the Officers' quarters, mess decks, etc.

At noon, the disposition of the Squadron was as follows:

A Patrol on line 360° from Lat. 62 N between Long. 9 and 12 W … *Patia*, *Virginian*, *Victorian*.
C Patrol on line 325° from Lat. 59.17´N, Long. 8.30´W … *Motagua*, *Columbella*, *Orvieto*, *Avenger*.
D Patrol (see clause 5) … *Kildonan Castle*, *Hilary*.
Between A & C … *Andes*.
Joining E Patrol … *Changuinola*, *Ebro*.
Rejoining Patrol from Clyde … *Patuca*.
Between St Kilda and Long. 10.30´W … Armed Trawlers *Saxon*, *Walpole*, *Arley*.
At Swarbacks Minn … Armed Trawler *Robert Smith*.
At Liverpool … *Teutonic*, *Otway*.
At Clyde … *Moldavia*, *Hildebrand*.
At Scapa … *Alsatian*.
At Brest … *Artois*.
At Fleetwood … Armed Trawler *Rushcoe*.
At Oban … Armed Trawler *Tenby Castle*.
On special service … *Almanzora*, *Arlanza*, *Orcoma*, *Gloucestershire*.
Fitting out at Liverpool … *Armadale Castle*.

During the week 49 vessels were intercepted, of which 20 were sent in with Armed Guards.

12. Monday, 1 January – Messages were received from the Admiralty to the effect that directional Wireless had placed a submarine in Latitude 58.20´ North, Longitude 8.5´ West at 8 p.m. the previous evening, and in Latitude 58.8´ North, Longitude 10.5´ West at 12.15 a.m. Ships were warned as necessary.

C Patrol was shifted 30 miles to the Eastward during the day, and *Changuinola* and *Ebro* were ordered to abandon E Patrol and join A.

News was received that the Captain of *Ebro* and First Lieutenants of *Teutonic* and *Arlanza* had been promoted, which gave great satisfaction to the 10th Cruiser Squadron.

13. Tuesday, 2 January – At 9 a.m. I met *Patuca* and *Virginian*. Commodore Luard who had come out from the Clyde in *Patuca*, came on board, and I gave him general orders for the conduct of the Patrol during *Alsatian*'s absence in Liverpool for refit. He afterwards transferred to *Virginian*, where he is temporarily flying his Broad Pendant.

I took the opportunity of proceeding on board *Virginian* to witness target practice. The weather was fine with a South-Westerly breeze and confused swell; the light was good. The practice was very good, first salvo being fired 10 seconds and second salvo 35 seconds after my order to engage target. The target was straddled at 50 seconds, when 'Controlled Independent' was ordered. The fire was rapid and accuracy good; range 5000 to 4000. I also tested the arrangements for dealing with fires and stopping leaks, afterwards going round the mess decks and sleeping quarters. I consider the Ship to be efficient and creditable to all concerned.

Victorian was ordered to proceed to E Patrol, working between Latitude 65 and 67 North, Longitude 8 and 13 West.

A and C Patrols were also re-organised.

14. Wednesday, 3 January – I met *Andes* at 10 a.m. and went on board for firing. Weather fine with a westerly breeze and heavy confused swell. Practice V.G.; first salvo was fired 6 seconds after the order to engage the target, second salvo 34 seconds; straddled at 50 seconds. 'Independent' was then ordered. The firing was rapid and accuracy good in spite of heavy swell which made target difficult to see; range 5000 to 4000. Mess decks and Ship generally clean and efficient; fire parties and leak parties know their work well.

Virginian intercepted the Norwegian Steamer *Fram* in Latitude 60.1´ North, Longitude 11.42´ West, from New York to Christiania, and sent her in to Kirkwall with an Armed Guard. Besides a general cargo, she was carrying 958 bags of mails mostly for enemy countries.[1]

At 6.50 p.m., *Patuca* boarded the Russian Steamer *Voronej*, from Archangel to Bordeaux, in Latitude 63.52´ North, Longitude 10.12´ West. The thrust block and starboard shaft were broken, and the Master requested instructions as to where he should proceed for repairs. He was directed to make for Stornoway and Admiralty were requested to send him orders there.

15. Thursday, 4 January – The Admiralty informed me that the

[1] *Fram*, after investigation and having provided the usual guarantees, was allowed to sail on (TS 14/13 of 8 January 1917).

French Auxiliary Cruiser *Champagne* would join the Tenth Cruiser Squadron for the winter months, leaving Brest about the 5th of January for Liverpool.

At 9.30 a.m. I met *Orvieto* and went on board to witness 6" gun practice. There was a fresh North westerly breeze with considerable sea and hail squalls. Range 5000 to 4000. The target was rather small and difficult to see but the practice was nevertheless V.G. First salvo was fired 15 seconds after order to engage target, second salvo 55 seconds, third salvo 1 minute 35 seconds. The target was then straddled and 'Independent' ordered. Fire was rapid, accuracy good. Later, I tested the Anti-Submarine defence which was capital. I then visited mess decks and consider the ship clean and efficient. Fire parties and leak stopping parties were exercised.

Alsatian proceeded to D Patrol.

A submarine was reported to have been seen off the West Coast of Hebrides, near Haskeir Reef.

About 6.30 p.m. information was received that the approaches to Kirkwall and Lerwick had been mined. Ships were warned and ordered to send vessels in to Stornoway or Lough Swilly until further orders.

16. Friday, 5 January – North Westerly wind, force 6–7, considerable sea and hail squalls.

About 9.30 a.m. *Avenger* was met and I went on board for target practice, but the state of the sea and squalls, etc made it very difficult to see the target at 5000. In addition the Ship had a considerable motion. Some firing was carried out from the Port Battery and I then decided to postpone the test until a more favourable opportunity. 15 rounds 'Controlled Independent' were fired with fair results as regards accuracy but firing was slow – if target had been a ship it would have been easier for spotters and gunlayers. The practice was, however, good on the whole considering the conditions.

The mess decks were very clean and comfortable. I also visited the Engine Room and Boiler Room which are excellent. The Ship is efficient.

Kildonan Castle proceeded to Loch Ewe to coal.

17. Saturday, 6 January – At 7.30 a.m. *Avenger* reported that *Tenby Castle* had sighted a large steamer in Latitude 58.10´ North, Longitude 8.30´ West at 6.30 a.m., steering 40°. She proceeded in chase, but had lost sight of her in the fog.

I ordered *Motagua* to endeavour to intercept her, but although smoke was sighted, she reported she had been unable to gain on it. The Admiral Orkneys and Shetlands was requested to warn his patrols.

The Rear-Admiral Stornoway, informed me a submarine had been sighted by a Norwegian Steamer at 2 a.m. the previous morning in Latitude 59.6´ North, Longitude 6.48´ West, steering West-South-West.

At 10 a.m. I ordered Commodore Luard in *Virginian* to take charge of the patrols and proceeded to Liverpool via the Tory Island Route.

Alsatian carried out a full power trial, a speed of 19.5 knots being attained.

18. Sunday, 7 January – *Alsatian* arrived at the bar, Liverpool at 8.30 a.m. and proceeded up harbour.

***

… [D]uring 1916 some 3388 vessels were intercepted of which no fewer than 889 were sent in with Armed Guards for further examination. The increase shown on the preceding year, when the figures were 3098 and 743 respectively is probably due to the large number of vessels intercepted off the North East Coast of Iceland during the herring fishery season. Owing to the submarine menace the patrols had frequently to be moved far to the westward and were then not in such a favourable position for intercepting shipping as in the previous year.[1]

The loss in personnel and material during these operations was fortunately very much smaller than in 1915.

The *Alcantara* was sunk in action off the Norwegian Coast with the German Raider *Greif*, 2 Officers and 67 men being lost as a result of this engagement. One Officer and 5 men belonging to *Ebro*, were also lost in the Norwegian barque *Olivia* which had been sent in under Armed Guard, and was not again heard of.

In addition, one Officer and a Leading Seaman, belonging to *Patuca*, were removed by a German submarine from the Norwegian barque *Pestalozzi* and taken to Germany as Prisoners of War.

The remainder of the Armed Guards have returned to their Ships but several have experienced great hardships and very considerable risk from shipwreck, as well as the usual risks from submarines. The Officers and men of Armed Guards are, I submit, worthy of special commendation for having so successfully performed their arduous duties.

As a set off to our losses the German *Greif* was sunk by *Alcantara* and *Andes* on 29 February, the surviving Officers and men being made prisoners. A German Prize, the Norwegian SS *Older* was also captured

[1]But see [298, 299].

by *Otway* while attempting to break through the patrols, with an Armed Guard of one Officer and 8 men on board.

Several Ships were fired at with torpedoes by enemy submarines on various occasions, happily without success. Submarines were operating much farther afield during the latter part of the year, *Kildonan Castle* being fired at and missed, off the Coast of Iceland in Longitude 18 West. Submarines were also reported at other places round the Coast of Iceland.

Unfortunately the enemy mercantile Submarines proceeding to and from America, were not sighted by any Tenth Cruiser Squadron Ships.

The zeal, energy and cheerfulness of the Commanding Officers and crews of the Ships of the Tenth Cruiser Squadron excites my warm approbation.

295. *Commander-in-Chief Grand Fleet to Admiralty*

HMS *Iron Duke*, 22 December 1916

Circumstances Attending the Interception of a Supposed Armed Raider

It would appear from the facts elucidated at the Court of Enquiry that both the *Avenger* and *Teutonic* [291, 292, 293] failed to carry out the instructions regarding the examination of merchant vessels in their entirety – the *Avenger* in that she did not insist on seeing the flag of the day after ascertaining that the supposed 'German' had a clearance from Kirkwall – the *Teutonic* in that she did not detain the vessel for being a long way from the track laid down for vessels of the Netherlands Overseas Trust; she was very far from the position a ship proceeding to Falmouth should have been in [331].

2. Neither in the *Teutonic* nor *Avenger*'s report is there any reference to the special signal (cone six feet high) arranged with the Netherlands Overseas Trust …

It would appear that this distinguishing mark is being disregarded. The attention of the Netherlands Overseas Trust should be called to this fact and to the instructions which state that vessels are not to call at any port between Falmouth and Holland whether outward or homeward bound, and that the routes laid down must be strictly adhered to.

3. It is considered, however, that the best method of preventing a recurrence of this regrettable incident is to insist on all vessels showing the flag of the day, and should this be adopted the recommendation in paragraph 2 of these remarks will not apply.

This will involve a change of route for outward bound vessels of the Netherlands Overseas Trust as there would be obvious objections to giving them the flag of the day at a Dutch port.

All outward bound ships from the North Sea should therefore call at Kirkwall and receive the flag of the day. This would apply to Norwegian and other neutral traffic similarly, with Lerwick as an alternative port of call, and any vessel which cannot shew the flag of the day should be treated with grave suspicion and sent in for examination.

This is considered the only single means of preventing a recurrence of vessels' breaking out.

296. *Commander-in-Chief Home Fleets to Admiralty*

HMS *Iron Duke*, 30 December 1916

Be pleased to lay before the Lords Commissioners of the Admiralty the following remarks relative to the arrangements now in force for maintaining the blockade of Germany and preventing the escape of enemy raiders from the North Sea into the Atlantic.

2. The squadron which is chiefly concerned in carrying out both these duties is the 10th Cruiser Squadron. This squadron nominally consists of 25 vessels. Of these at the present moment

(a) four of the best ships have been withdrawn to hunt an enemy raider.
(b) another, the *Kildonan Castle*, is about to be withdrawn for special service;
(c) another, the *Armadale Castle*, has not yet joined;
(d) the *Artois* and *Champagne* can never be relied on;
(e) about one-third of the remainder are coaling or refitting.

With the present force, therefore, only from 12 to 13 vessels are on patrol.

3. The recent reduction in numbers of this important blockade squadron most gravely compromises the general efficiency of the patrol, and the present composition of the squadron is inadequate for the work of containing, with any degree of reliance,
(i) the passage North of Iceland,
(ii) the passage between Iceland and the Faeroes,
(iii) the passage between the Faeroes and the Orkneys.

This is the more serious if, as would appear, no advance information of the possible passing out of raiders by the enemy is in future to be expected; in fact it may be said that, under present circumstances, the chances are favourable to the raider. Nor can we ensure a strict blockade.

4. The strategic reasons which prompted a reduction of the blockade squadron are not clear to me, bearing in mind the probability that

determined efforts would be made during the dark nights to pass out additional raiders, and, further, that such reduction lessens the stringency of the blockade at the time when it is most important to maintain it at its full efficiency.

5. The only enemy surface vessels on the high seas which can operate against our trade are those which escape the vigilance of the 10th Cruiser Squadron Patrol. The chief part of the overseas supplies for countries bordering on Germany has to pass through the 10th Cruiser Squadron patrol. On both these accounts it is urgent and vital that the 10th Cruiser Squadron should be in numbers adequate for efficiency. An increase in present numbers is therefore imperative.

6. So far as I am aware, the forces at present employed for the protection of trade outside the 10th Cruiser Squadron are as given in Appendix I. Exclusive of gunboats there are in the Atlantic, Pacific and Indian Ocean

26 cruisers,
13 armed merchantmen.

7. The following definite proposals are suggested for consideration in order to strengthen the 10th Cruiser Squadron, it being observed that patrol work in all distant waters, no matter how important, is at the moment insignificant compared with the requirements of tightening the blockade and preventing the escape of enemy merchantmen.

(a) Withdraw *Ophir*, *Orotava*, *Marmora*, *Laurentic* and *Calgarian* from the Atlantic trade routes. Place the Second Cruiser Squadron (five ships) on the North American trade route for convoy work. Ask the French Government to spare the *Waldeck Rousseau*, *Ernest Renan*, *Edgar Quinet* (endurance 11,000 miles) to assist on the West Indian trade routes.
(b) Withdraw *Avoca*, *Orbita*, *Otranto* from Pacific and ask the Japanese Government if they will take over the Pacific.
(c) Withdraw *Macedonia*, *Orama*, *Edinburgh Castle* from South America. Replace by *Suffolk*, *Essex*, *Cumberland*, *Bacchante*, pressing on with the refits of these ships.
(d) Withdraw *Princess* from East Coast of Africa.
(e) Withdraw *City of London* from China and ask Japanese Government to assist with another cruiser if necessary.

The ships thus withdrawn should, if suitable to the work, be absorbed in the 10th Cruiser Squadron. Any entirely unsuitable should be released for mercantile work.

8. The above scheme in outline will actually result in greater strength on the trade routes, and ships will be ready for immediate convoy work

should a raider get through. All organisations for convoy and routes must be prepared in readiness to place in immediate operation. The scheme will enable a permanent patrol of about 24 vessels to be kept up by the 10th Cruiser Squadron, that is, an increase in efficiency of about 100% may be expected in the operations of this Squadron.

9. The pooling of the naval resources of the Allies, as has already taken place with the military and financial resources, is involved. A combined staff should discuss and work at these problems. The allied naval forces must exert their maximum strength. At present the employment of vast naval forces, British, French and Italian, in Mediterranean waters to deal with the comparatively small Austrian and Turkish navies cannot be reconciled with the pressing need for personnel and cruisers elsewhere. Nor does it appear that the maximum strength of the Japanese navy is being thrown into the conflict.

10. I have not touched, in the above, on the employment of the Third Battle Squadron. The role which this Squadron is intended to fulfil and the motives which led Their Lordships to sanction its present base are unknown to me.[1] It is certain, however, that a large number of highly trained officers and men are employed in it, and a considerable number of destroyers maintained for screening purposes, and it is for consideration whether the above could not be more usefully employed. No reason is seen why these ships with reduced and less highly trained officers and crews on board should not be usefully employed in certain distant points of the trade routes. Failing this, however, it is recommended the ships should be paid off and the whole of the valuable personnel released to positions where their services are urgently required.

297. *Vice-Admiral Tupper to Commanding Officer HM Trawler* King Lear

HMS *Alsatian*, 31 December 1916

Being in all respects ready for sea you are to proceed to rendezvous with the Senior Officer Tenth Cruiser Squadron in Lat. 61.30´N, Long. 10 W, reporting the time and date of your expected arrival.

[1]The Third Battle Squadron consisted of *Dreadnought* and a group of predreadnoughts, the *King Edwards*, and was stationed in The Swin (the mouth of the Thames, by the Nore lightship). Admiral Jellicoe, now First Sea Lord, replied in a personal note on 4 January 1917, pointing out that the four ships detached from the 10th Cruiser Squadron would be away for some time. Clearly speaking from experience he also noted that 'I do not think a single patrol line with 10th C.S. can ever serve against a raider getting out' (*Jellicoe Papers* II, 136).

In the absence of further orders you should then proceed to 64.30´N, 13 W, and patrol along the South Coast of Iceland between that position and the Vestmann Islands.

2. As far as possible arrangements will be made for a ship of the Tenth Cruiser Squadron to be within W/T touch at all times.

3. Your principal duties will be to intercept and examine shipping, guard our fishing trawlers and keep a good look-out for enemy submarines in the neighbourhood. In carrying out these duties you should be guided by the attached 'Orders for Trawlers attached to the Tenth Cruiser Squadron'.

4. You will in future be based on Oban and when necessary for you to leave patrol to coal and provisioning you should report the fact to the Senior Officer Tenth Cruiser Squadron four days previously.

298. *Commander-in-Chief Home Fleets to Vice-Admiral Commanding Orkney and Shetland*

1 January 1917

… [I] refer to the proposed use of a 'Q' trawler in Icelandic waters [297]. The primary object of this class of vessel, viz: the attack of enemy submarines, appears to have been somewhat overlooked, but if you concur in these orders, I request you will issue the necessary instructions to the vessel concerned and inform the Vice-Admiral Commanding Tenth Cruiser Squadron of date she will sail.

299. *Vice-Admiral Commanding Orkney and Shetland to Commander-in-Chief Grand Fleet*

Longhope, 5 January 1917

I regret that I am unable to concur in the suggested orders for the 'Q' trawler attached to this base [297, 298, 304]. If this vessel is attached to the Tenth Cruiser Squadron for the duties suggested by Vice-Admiral Tupper, the whole object of her disguise is cancelled, as the hidden armament must of necessity be discovered.

2. It was understood from a verbal message from the Chief of your Staff, that the Vice-Admiral Commanding Tenth Cruiser Squadron was suggesting that this vessel should be sent as a decoy on the route usually employed by such vessels in the course of their fishing. I have already sent her on this route on several occasions and propose to do so again in the near future, following the course which is generally used by vessels proceeding to Fleetwood with their catch. As the *King Lear*

(now named *Enid*) is a fish carrier and much larger than the majority of trawlers, it is advisable to use her as a decoy only on routes followed by such carriers.

3. When this vessel is not employed on decoy duties she has been used on ordinary trawler patrol work in strengthening the Fair Island Channel patrol.

300. *Vice-Admiral Tupper to Admiralty*

HMS *Alsatian*, 24 January 1917

Report of Proceedings, 6–23 January 1916

***

1. Saturday, 6 January – At 8.25 p.m. *Columbella* reported that his boarding boat with Armed Guard had capsized alongside the Norwegian S.V. *Glance*, which had been ordered to be sent to Stornoway. The boat was recovered by *Columbella* and the Armed Guard and boat's crew were saved and remained in *Glance*. The Chief Officer of *Glance* jumped overboard at great personal risk and saved one of the boat's crew.[1]

***

During the day swept channels were opened to Lerwick and Kirkwall through mined areas and traffic was resumed.

I was informed by Vice-Admiral Commanding Orkneys and Shetlands, that the Special Service Trawler *King Lear* had sailed at 8.30 a.m. with orders to proceed through Fair Island Channel to a point South of Iceland, thence to a position West of St Kilda and from there pass Butt of Lewis through Pentland Firth to Longhope. The Squadron was informed as it was possible she might be encountered.

2. Sunday, 7 January – At 1.30 a.m. the Commander-in-Chief Grand Fleet, ordered *Achilles* to proceed with all despatch to patrol 330° from Muckle Flugga till noon to intercept the steamer reported by *Tenby Castle* and *Motagua*. Later in the day, however, he signalled that this vessel had proved to be the Danish steamer *Oscar II* which had since arrived at Kirkwall …[2]

At 9.30 a.m. *Columbella* reported he was engaging an enemy

[1]*Glance* was not detained.
[2]*Oscar II* was not detained.

submarine in Latitude 60 North, Longitude 8.10´ West. The submarine submerged immediately fire was opened. Subsequently it was ascertained the submarine was sighted on the surface at a distance of 3,500 yards and did not fire a torpedo.[1] Orders were given at once for all ships on patrol to increase speed, and, with the Commander-in-Chief's approval, ships were moved to patrol Line 3. The position of sighting submarine was afterwards corrected to Latitude 59.59´ North, Longitude 7.57´ West by observation.

The disposition of the Squadron was as follows:

A Patrol ... *Andes*, *Changuinola*, *Patuca*.
C Patrol ... *Columbella*, *Orvieto*, *Otway*; Joining from A: *Ebro*.
D Patrol ... *Avenger*.
Between A and C ... *Virginian*.
St Kilda Patrol ... Armed Trawler *Tenby Castle*.
Proceeding to Swarbacks Minn ... *Motagua*, *Victorian*.
At Swarbacks Minn ... Armed Trawler *Rushcoe*.
At Clyde ... *Hildebrand*, *Hilary*, *Moldavia*.
At Liverpool ... *Alsatian*, *Armadale Castle* (fitting out), *Teutonic* (Care and maintenance party).
At Brest ... *Artois*.
At Loch Ewe ... *Kildonan Castle*.
At Oban ... Armed Trawlers *Robert Smith*, *Arley*, *Saxon*, *Walpole*.
Special Service ... *Almanzora*, *Orcoma*, *Arlanza*, *Gloucestershire*.[2]

Forty-four Ships were intercepted and examined during the week, of which fifteen were sent in with Armed Guards.

At 2 p.m. in Latitude 9.13´ North, Longitude 6.10´ West, *Motagua* boarded and sent to Kirkwall with Armed Guard, the Norwegian SS *Jethou*, from Pisagua via St Thomas to Aarhus, with a cargo of nitre shipped by a German firm. The Captain of *Motagua* reported that he considered the capture an important one. The Vice-Admiral Commanding Orkneys and Shetlands, was informed of his suspicions. He later communicated to me that the Shippers were Wessel and Duval, Broadway, New York, who at one time had been considered suspicious,

[1]No submarine is recorded in the area at the time.

[2]*Patia* is omitted; with four ships detached, *Armadale Castle* and *Teutonic* out of action and *Champagne* not yet joined, the squadron was reduced to 17 ships (including *Moldavia*, whose removal had apparently been cancelled).

but later had appeared to clear their reputation, having been removed from the General Black List on January 1916.[1]

3. Monday, 8 January – *Patuca* reported that at 3.30 a.m. a white light was seen for 5 minutes at a distance of about 3 miles in Latitude 62.56´ North, Longitude 15.54´ West. There was a bright moon and he searched the vicinity but found nothing. I agree with the Captain of *Patuca* that there is reason to suppose the light was shown by a submarine. Details were reported to the Commander-in-Chief, Grand Fleet. At 3.35 p.m. in Latitude 56.44´ North, Longitude 10.8´ West, *Avenger* reported intercepting the Dutch SS *Frisia* from Amsterdam to Falmouth, General cargo, flying a black cone. As there was too much sea to board, *Avenger* was instructed to follow the vessel and direct her to Lough Swilly. If weather continued to prevent boarding *Avenger* was to turn *Frisia* over to Inner Patrol vessel and then proceed to Liverpool.

4. Tuesday, 9 January – *Avenger* reported at 6.30 a.m. that *Frisia* had been turned over to an Inner Patrol vessel. *Avenger* then proceeded to Liverpool.[2]

Orders were received from Admiralty for *Kildonan Castle*, now at Loch Ewe completing with coal and effecting repairs to a defective armature to return to Greenock as soon as possible and she was given orders accordingly and reported that she would arrive at Greenock on the morning of 11 January.

At 10.45 p.m. in Latitude 61.8´ North, Longitude 10.20´ West, *Orvieto* reported observing during a heavy rain squall, a bright white light about one mile distant. It disappeared on being approached and the vicinity was searched without success. The Captain of *Orvieto* thought it was probably a submarine proceeding South East.

The Commander-in-Chief Grand Fleet was informed of this report.

A possible theory with regard to these lights is that they are challenges by enemy submarines who are expecting to meet a supply ship and that, on seeing a ship approach without answering, they dive.

5. Wednesday, 10 January – The Captain of *Victorian* reported he still had nine cases of measles on board. He sailed from Swarbacks Minn in the evening and was directed to join A Patrol. The distance apart of *Andes* and *Victorian* was reduced to 30 miles so that, in case *Victorian* intercepted a ship requiring an Armed Guard, *Andes* could close and supply it.

[1] *Jethou* was allowed to sail on (TS 14/13 of 9 January 1917); despite the information from the Vice-Admiral Orkney and Shetlands, the vessel's cargo was referred to the Contraband Committee.

[2] *Frisia* was not detained, but some discussion took place (TS 14/13 of 10 January 1917).

6. Thursday, 11 January – At 4.30 p.m. in Latitude 58.44´ North, Longitude 14.38´ West, *Otway* intercepted the Swedish S.V. *Olga*, from Galveston to Goteborg, with sulphur. There was too much sea to board and *Otway* was directed to follow until daylight. In the night, however, during a very heavy rain squall, *Otway* parted company with *Olga* and, as search proved unsuccessful, was directed to return to patrol.[1]

7. Friday, 12 January – No events of interest. Bad weather was experienced on C Patrol.

8. Saturday, 13 January – Gale continued during the night, but weather improved in the evening.

At 7 p.m. *Ebro* reported intercepting the Danish S.V. *Sokoto*, from Baltimore to Aarhus, with phosphate. As the sea was too rough to board, *Ebro* followed till morning when vessel was sent to Stornoway with an Armed Guard.[2] *Otway* reported an Officer had developed measles.

9. Sunday, 14 January – At noon the disposition of the Squadron was as follows:

A Patrol ... *Andes*, *Victorian*.
C Patrol ... *Hildebrand*, *Ebro*, *Motagua*, *Otway*, *Patuca*.
D Patrol ... *Patia*, Armed Trawlers *Rushcoe*, *Tenby Castle*, *Saxon*, *Walpole*.
Between A and C ... *Virginian*.
On special service ... *Almanzora*, *Arlanza*, *Gloucestershire*, *Orcoma*.
Proceeding to Swarbacks Minn ... Armed Trawler *Arley*.
At Swarbacks Minn ... *Changuinola*, *Columbella*, *Orvieto*.
At Clyde ... *Kildonan Castle*, *Moldavia*, *Hilary*.
At Liverpool ... *Alsatian*, *Teutonic*, *Armadale Castle*, *Avenger*, *Champagne*.
At Brest ... *Artois*.
Rejoining Patrol ... Armed Trawler *Robert Smith*.

During the week 24 ships were intercepted and examined, of which 12 were sent in with Armed Guards and one escorted to Lough Swilly.

At 6 a.m., with the approval the Commander-in-Chief Grand Fleet, A and C Patrols moved to the Eastward, A Patrol being in line ahead

[1]*Olga* was later sent in by *Rushcoe*; her cargo was 'crude sulphur', and a question arose over its real destination; the ship was permitted to go on after a fortnight, and the Contraband Committee noted that this shipment completed Sweden's sulphur ration (TS 14/13 of 17 January and 3 February 1917).

[2]*Sokoto* was allowed to go on, but enquiries were to be made as to why the ship had no Navicert (TS 14/13 of 24 January 1917).

330° from Latitude 62 North, and Longitude 12.30´ West and C Patrol crossing centre line 360° from Latitude 58.30´ North, Longitude 10 West.

In the afternoon *Rushcoe* placed an Armed Guard on board the Swedish S.V. *Olga*, Latitude 57.47´ North, Longitude 9.24´ West. This was the Vessel *Otway* had lost during Thursday night (see paragraph 6).[1]

At 4.25 p.m. *Otway* placed an Armed Guard on board the Norwegian SS *Kristianiafjord*. This vessel reported one death from small pox before leaving New York and another developed amongst the crew on the 10 January during the passage. The Admiral Commanding Orkneys and Shetlands, was informed as necessary.[2]

Motagua boarded the British SS *Oswego* in Latitude 59.57´ North, Longitude 10.33´ West, from Middlesbrough to New York, in ballast. The steamer, which showed no lights, was only stopped after a three hours' chase, and the Master reported he had received orders from Middlesbrough, that, after passing Longitude 10 West, he was neither to show lights nor stop for anybody.

This information was reported to Admiralty as, in carrying out such orders, a British Ship runs considerable risk of being fired on by the Patrol.

10. Monday, 15 January.

11. Tuesday, 16 January – At 7.25 a.m. in Latitude 59.53´ North, Longitude 8.43´ West, *Ebro* reported observing a bright white light which was visible for less than a minute at an estimated distance of five to six miles. *Ebro* proceeded to the spot at high speed and, finding nothing, dropped a depth charge in approximately the position in which the light was seen. At 12.30 p.m., however, he boarded the British SS *Gallileo* from Hull to Boston, in Latitude 59.50´ North, Longitude 10 West, and reported that the movements and position of this vessel pointed to the probability of the white light having been accidentally shown by her.

Whether this was the case or not, I consider *Ebro* took correct action at the time, as previous orders had been given by Commodore Luard, who was in charge of the Patrols, that, in cases of this nature use was to be made of the depth charge.

12. Wednesday, 17 January – At 8 p.m. *Rushcoe* reported boarding Norwegian barque *Arlastor* in Latitude 57.39´ North, Longitude 9.6´ West, from Galveston to Aarhus, with cargo of cottonseed cake and an

[1]See page 592, note 1.
[2]*Kristianiafjord* was not detained (TS 14/13 of 16 January 1917).

Armed Guard was placed on board. The Master reported sighting an enemy submarine at noon 16 January in Latitude 56.40´ North, Longitude 7.50´ West, steering 160.[1] The Commander-in-Chief Grand Fleet and Rear-Admiral Stornoway, were informed.

13. Thursday, 18 January – At 10 a.m. St Kilda reported a submarine being sighted 5 miles to the Southward, steering East. *Hilary* was directed to move to the Western limit of D Patrol and the Armed Trawlers to search for submarine. Submarine was again seen by St Kilda 10 miles to the Northeastward, steering North-east. Trawlers were informed but were unable to sight the enemy.

14. Friday, 19 January – Admiralty telegraphed that in future only names of Dutch vessels, cleared from Falmouth to Holland, would be signalled. I consider this to be an advantage, as it will prevent any Dutch outward steamers being allowed to pass without being boarded.

I left Liverpool in *Alsatian* at 3 a.m. to rejoin Patrol.

The Swedish SS *Japan* from Bordeaux to Goteborg, intercepted by *Robert Smith*, reported she had been boarded by an enemy submarine in Latitude 50.34´ North, Longitude 12.54´ West at 11 a.m. on 17 January.[2]

15. Saturday, 20 January – Strong South, South-West breezes; rain and mist. A Patrol was placed on meridian of 9 West with Southern position 62.20´ North, Longitude 9 West, ships being 35 miles apart, patrolling 120 miles.

I met *Otway* at 3 p.m. and Commodore Booty came on board with disposition of Squadron and back signals. I informed him of his appointment to Assistant Admiral Commanding, Coastguard and Reserves, and thanked him for his valuable services which I am sorry to lose. On parting company *Otway* proceeded to D Patrol until time to proceed to Liverpool.

A German Press message was intercepted which stated that SS *Yarrowdale* has reached Swinemunde which is very disappointing [320].[3]

[1]*Arlastor* was detained because another ship, *Vigo*, also going to Esbjerg (not Aarhus) had reportedly been captured by a German ship, the implication being that this was by collusion. Other vessels became involved before *Vigo* was reported to have arrived at Esbjerg with a full cargo after all. Meanwhile *Alastor*'s cargo (1225 tons of cottonseed cake) and the ship itself were ordered to the Prize Court; this was then 'suspended', and after a delay for thought, argument, or the Contraband Committee's *amour propre*, the ship was allowed to go on undischarged (TS 14/13 of 23 and 27 January and 3 and 8 February 1917).

[2]*Japan* was compelled to discharge to the Prize Court its cargo of soya, soya bean oil and lacquer goods before being allowed to go on (TS 14/13 of 22 January 1917). No submarine is recorded in the position at which *Japan* was reported boarded.

[3]*Yarrowdale* was one of *Moewe*'s captures, and carried 400 prisoners from other ships captured to Germany.

16. Sunday, 21 January – At 2.45 a.m., in accordance with instructions received from the Commander-in-Chief, orders were given for C Patrol to move to the Westward of 12 West, forming on a line 345° from 58.20´ North, 14.10´ West.

At 9 a.m. in fine mild weather I met *Virginian* and took over the Command from Commodore Luard, who then proceeded in *Virginian* to take charge of A Patrol which I strengthened with a view to intercepting SS *Gyldenpris*.[1]

At 8.35 a.m. in Latitude 57.53´ North, Longitude 9.14´ West, the Armed Trawler *Walpole* was attacked by an enemy submarine, a torpedo, which passed close under the stern, being fired at a range of about 500 yards. Fire was opened by *Walpole* and the submarine, which was only showing her periscope, submerged immediately after the first round.[2]

The four Armed Trawlers in the vicinity were ordered to concentrate and search for her and at 2.30 p.m. she was again sighted on the surface by *Saxon* in Latitude 58.18´ North, Longitude 9 West at a distance of 3 miles. *Saxon* proceeded to chase, but the submarine submerged soon afterwards and was not again seen.

The Master of the Danish schooner *Norden* from Setubal to Helsingborg, intercepted by *Otway* reported that the vessel had been stopped by an enemy submarine at 3 p.m. on 20 January in Latitude 55 North, Longitude 10.45´ West.[3]

The submarine which had one gun mounted before the conning tower then proceeded to the Northward.

The Master of the Swedish Motor-vessel *Suecia* boarded by *Columbella* from Caleta Buena to Helsingborg, stated that on 18 January, when in Latitude 50 North, Longitude 31 West, he sighted a steamer without lights. Shortly afterwards the steamer hoisted two red

[1]*Gyldenpris*, a Norwegian ship, is not referred to again by Tupper and was apparently not intercepted by the squadron; it was intercepted by someone, however, and sent in. It was regarded with enough suspicion to be sent on to Weymouth to discharge suspect cargo, before being allowed to sail on (TS 14/13 of 5 February 1917).

[2]The submarine cannot be identified.

[3]*Norden* was sent in, and a query arose over her cargo, 400 tons of salt; in the end she was allowed to go on (TS 14/13 of 25 January and 8 February 1917).

lights but on *Suecia* approaching she extinguished them and disappeared.[1]

Information was received that a mine had exploded in a sweep at the entrance to Swarbacks Minn. The sailing of *Andes* and *Ebro* was accordingly postponed, and arrangements made for *Patia*, who was due to coal there, to proceed to Loch Ewe instead.

At noon the disposition of the Squadron was as follows:

A Patrol, taking up patrol on line 360° from Lat. 62.20´ North, Long. 11 West … *Patia*, *Victorian*, *Orvieto*; Joining: *Victorian*, *Motagua*.
C Patrol, taking up patrol across line 345° from Lat. 58.20´ North, Long. 14.10´ West … *Patuca*, *Columbella*, *Changuinola*, *Hildebrand*, *Moldavia*.
D Patrol, taking up patrol across line 360° from Lat. 56.30´ North, Long. 13 West … *Champagne*, *Hilary*.
Between A and C … *Alsatian*.
St Kilda Patrol … Armed Trawlers *Robert Smith*, *Walpole*, *Arley*.
At Swarbacks Minn … *Ebro*, *Andes*.
Rejoining from Liverpool … *Avenger*.
Proceeding to Liverpool … *Otway*.
At Brest … *Artois*.
At Oban … Armed Trawlers *Tenby Castle*, *Rushcoe*.
At Liverpool … *Armadale Castle* (fitting out), *Teutonic* (Care and maintenance).
Special Service … *Almanzora*, *Orcoma*, *Arlanza*, *Gloucestershire*, *Kildonan Castle*.

During the week 65 Ships were intercepted, of which 16 were sent in with Armed Guards for further examination.

17. Thursday, 22 January – Strong Southwest Breeze heavy swell. The Admiralty having directed me to embark the Consul at Reykjavik on board a ship of the Tenth Cruiser Squadron about to return to her Southern base, *Victorian*, due at Liverpool on 27 January was selected for the purpose and left A Patrol that night for Reykjavik. *Champagne* was ordered up from D Patrol to take her place.

[1]*Suecia* was sent in. Her cargo was 5500 tons of nitrate of soda, and the immediate decision of the Contraband Committee was that it could not be allowed to reach Sweden. The recommendation was to discharge it in Britain and put it into storage until the end of the war. But it proved impossible to find storage space and the search was overtaken by the German government's declaration that all ships approaching Britain would be liable to be sunk. The consignees offered to hold the cargo in Sweden, but the Committee rejected this. Eventually purchase by the Ministry of Munitions and the Board of Agriculture was decided on (TS 14/13 of 25 January to 20 February 1917 *passim*).

A Patrol was moved to cross a line 360° from Latitude 63.10´ North, Longitude 9 West at noon and midnight, steering 295° and 115°, 40 miles apart from South – *Moldavia*, *Virginian*, *Motagua*, *Victorian*, and *Orvieto*.

A large submarine was reported to be passing Muckle Flugga at noon, steering Southwest.

18. Tuesday, 23 January – South West wind; moderate and fine.

In the middle watch the Armed Trawler *Robert Smith* reported that when in Latitude 57 North, Longitude 9.29´ West, although using all available means, she had been unable to stop a large four masted steamer which had passed her, steering to the Southwest. *Avenger* and *Champagne* steered to cut her off, and at 8 a.m. the latter intercepted the Danish steamer *Fionia*. On being boarded and questioned the Captain stated that the trawler had not been seen, but judging from the description given by *Robert Smith* and the course and speed, she must have been the vessel referred to. It is suggested that the matter be brought to the notice of the owners of the vessel, and the fact pointed out that she lays herself open to a considerable risk of being fired on and injured if she does not obey the orders to stop [322].[1]

Alsatian chased and at 7.30 p.m. examined a large Hull trawler *Conan Doyle* bound for Iceland. The experimental rockets which had been supplied for the purpose of illuminating shipping at night, were tried. The first rocket fired exploded directly it left the tube. The second, however, fired correctly, but did not have a very good illuminating effect; it also has the disadvantage of being seen from a great distance. A separate report will be forwarded when further experience has been gained.

***

301. *Admiralty to Vice-Admiral Commanding Tenth Cruiser Squadron*

6 January 1917

With reference to paragraph 10 of your submission of the 21st ultimo … [289], forwarding a report proceedings of the Tenth Cruiser Squadron for 4th December to 10th December 1916, I am commanded by My Lords Commissioners of the Admiralty to acquaint you that the proposal that Dutch vessels to and from Holland and Falmouth should be instructed to pass to the west and north of Rockall would entail the

[1] *Fionia* was not sent in.

vessels keeping at least 180 miles to the westward of their present course, which now takes them fairly close past St Kilda. It is considered doubtful whether the Dutch vessels could be induced to take this route, and it would be difficult to supply any reason for this order if one were demanded by the Dutch government. Moreover, if under the present conditions an outward bound Dutch vessel were intercepted on a westerly course in the neighbourhood of Rockall, it would be a fair presumption that she was endeavouring to break her agreement to come to Falmouth.

2. With reference to your remarks in paragraph 7 of your submission, on the delays to vessels of the Tenth Cruiser Squadron at the Southern Bases, I am to enclose for your information, a copy of a letter on the subject which has been addressed to the Senior Naval Officer Liverpool and the Captain Superintendent Contract Built Ships Clyde District [302].

302. *Admiralty to Senior Naval Officer Liverpool and Captain Superintendent Clyde District*

6 January 1917

I am commanded by My Lords Commissioners of the Admiralty to acquaint you that the Vice-Admiral Commanding Tenth Cruiser Squadron has reported that it is impossible to maintain the efficiency of the patrol carried out by the Squadron, if vessels remain at their Southern Bases more than ten days.

2. It is therefore of importance that work which will delay a vessel for more than the normal ten days should be deferred until succeeding visits, and I am to request that this may be done in future.

3. I am to request that you will report any delays which may be due to labour troubles.

303. *Admiralty to Under Secretary of State, Foreign Office*

7 January 1917

With reference to your letter of the 28th December No. 259268, forwarding reports from the Danish Minister respecting the Danish Naval Police ship *Islands Falk*, which was stopped by a British trawler, I am commanded by My Lords Commissioners of the Admiralty to enclose herewith, for the information of the Secretary of State, copy of a report from HM Trawler *Walpole*, explaining the circumstances under which the incident occurred [282].

2. I am to request that suitable apologies may be presented to the Danish government for the quite unintentional affront to the *Islands Falk*.

3. It should be added that the Commanding Officer of the *Walpole* was informed by his Admiral that he should have endeavoured, after the incident, to go on board the *Islands Falk* and express his regrets.

304. *Commander-in-Chief Grand Fleet to Vice-Admiral Commanding Tenth Cruiser Squadron*

10 January 1917

… [T]he Vice Admiral Commanding Orkney and Shetland has informed me that he does not concur in the duties suggested for the 'Q' trawler; the sailing orders have therefore not been issued [299].

It was not the intention that the trawler should be placed permanently under your orders.

The employment you propose would not give scope to her special attributes.

305. *Admiralty to Commander-in-Chief Home Fleets*

15 January [1917]

I have laid before My Lords Commissioners of the Admiralty your letter of the 30th December [296] …, proposing certain measures for strengthening the Tenth Cruiser Squadron by the withdrawal of Armed Merchant Cruisers from service abroad. Their Lordships note that these proposals are put forward on the ground that no patrol work in distant waters, however important, can compare with the urgency of tightening the blockade at home and preventing the escape of enemy merchantmen.

2. In reply, I am to acquaint you that the importance of keeping the Tenth Cruiser Squadron at the fullest possible strength is fully realised by Their Lordships, and every effort will be made to do so. It must, however, be appreciated that patrol work is by no means the only duty carried out by our Squadrons abroad. They are called on to perform other essential duties, i.e. to prevent the escape of enemy interned vessels, to escort transports and to carry gold to the United States. At the present time there are eight cargoes of gold in England and seven in South Africa awaiting shipment. Many transports are awaiting convoy, and a German raider is still at large, and it is of urgent necessity to bring her to action.

3. In view of these facts, Their Lordships have decided that no Ships can be spared from abroad at present, and while the Tenth Cruiser Squadron continues to be below its normal strength the Light Cruisers of the Grand Fleet must be used as far as is possible and consistent with other duties to lessen the chances of further raiders escaping.

4. I am to enclose, for your information, a Memorandum dealing specifically with the suggestions made in paragraph 7 of your letter.

5. With the views expressed in paragraph 9 respecting co-operation between the Allies Their Lordships are in entire accord. The subject is receiving the closest possible attention, but the practical difficulties of inducing the Allies to carry out these proposals are very great.

6. The question of the employment of the Third Battle Squadron, to which you refer in paragraph 9 of your letter is now under Their Lordships' consideration.

306. *Admiralty Memorandum [on proposed reinforcements for Tenth Cruiser Squadron]*

[15 January 1917]

PROPOSALS OF COMMANDER IN CHIEF	REMARKS
1. Replace *Laurentic* and *Calgarian* on North American Station by two vessels from Second Cruiser Squadron.	*Laurentic* and *Calgarian* are continually required for cross-Atlantic trips, convoying troops, carrying gold, etc. There are at present seven gold cargoes waiting for them. Men-of-War, except sometimes *Drake* and *Leviathan*, cannot keep up with the big fast Canadian transports and are much more hampered by gales.
2. Replace *Ophir*, *Orotava* in Ninth Cruiser Squadron and *Marmora* in Cruiser Force (D) by three vessels from Second Cruiser Squadron.	*Ophir*, *Orotava* and *Marmora* are not fit for the Tenth Cruiser Squadron, though most useful in the finer weather down South. Vessels in these waters may be required to steam very long distances while on convoy or other duties; Sierra Leone to Devonport 2750 miles; to Cape Town 3185 miles; to Bermuda 3200 miles.

3. Ask the French to provide *Waldeck Rousseau*, *Ernest Renan*, *Edgar Quinet* for service on West Indian routes.	The French have already provided five vessels *Jeanne d'Arc*, *Dupetit Thouars*, *Gueydon*, *Montcalm* and *Descartes*, for service in the West Indies and three others *Kleber*, *Dupleix* and *Desaix*, on the West coast of Africa (the last is temporarily detached to Halifax). The French also sent the *Gloire* across the Atlantic to Halifax following the trade route, as soon as the raider was known to be at large. The *Amiral Aube* is also assisting the North American Squadron temporarily. The French are not able to undertake further oversea duties, and a request that they should do so would lead to no useful result.
4. Withdraw three Merchant Cruisers from the Pacific and one from China, asking the Japanese to take over the Pacific and supply another Cruiser to China Station.	The Pacific Station is worked under very difficult conditions, Esquimalt being the only British base. The large radius of action of the Merchant Cruisers is a great asset, as if a Collier miscarries they have enough coal to enable them to wait or to reach another supply. The withdrawal of British ships from the Pacific and their replacement by Japanese would strike a serious blow against British prestige on the Western coast of both North and South America, particularly in Chile, where the Japanese are feared and disliked. The proposal would also entail certain duties being dropped, as the Japanese will not enforce our rules against enemy subjects. A reduction in the already small number of British Men-of-War in China and the Bay of Bengal would invite the enemy to recommence his schemes in India, which have hitherto been successfully combated.

5. Withdraw *Macedonia*, *Orama*, *Edinburgh Castle* from South America, and replace by *Suffolk*, *Essex*, *Cumberland* and *Bacchante*.	Of the four Cruisers suggested to be sent out *Suffolk* and *Cumberland* will be required to relieve other vessels now abroad which will become due for large refits, while *Bacchante* and *Essex* are not suitable for service in the Pacific, South and Mid Atlantic, where the coaling difficulties are great and possible coaling places few in number and far apart. There are 49 enemy merchant ships in North and South American ports in the Pacific, and the effect of removing our ships would be to enable the enemy ships to trade at a large profit and cause corresponding loss to British firms. The question of repairs is also important. Armed Merchant Cruisers usually last much longer without repairs than men-of-war, and Simon's Town Dockyard, which has also to keep up the Cape Squadron, could not cope with the County Class Cruisers as well.
6. Withdraw *Princess* from East Coast of Africa.	The *Princess* (a German prize) was originally fitted out for the Tenth Cruiser Squadron. When completed at Belfast she only steamed 13½ knots on her trials. A second trial showed no improvement. She was accordingly sent to East Africa and the *Armadale Castle*, a 17 knot ship, was brought home for the Tenth Cruiser Squadron.
7. Withdraw *City of London* from China and ask Japanese government to assist with another cruiser, if necessary.	The Japanese will not carry out our rules as regards merchant ships, and the substitution of a Japanese Cruiser would not result in the work, now carried out by the *City of London*, being continued.

307. *Sub-Lieutenant F.W. Brooke to Captain L.L. Dundas*[1]

HMS *Motagua*, 17 January 1917

On Friday January 5th 1917 whilst taking the Norwegian steamer *Marjoen* towards Stornoway with Armed Guard, consisting of one officer and three men, we were stopped at 11.30 a.m. by a German Armed submarine firing shells at us from port quarter. The vessel was stopped immediately, but firing was continued until lifeboat was lowered into water, several shells falling perilously close to the steamer, four at least being within ten feet of the ship. Mr. H. Brock, captain of the *Marjoen*, put off on the submersible with the ship's papers, and being bound for Aarhus, Denmark, received a clearance from the German Commander. He was told to stand by to pick up the crew of the Danish Barque *Perngland* which was lying about three miles north of us, if the Germans sank her. Her papers, however, were apparently correct, both the Barque and ourselves being ordered to proceed direct to discharging ports at 2.00 p.m.

The submarine then proceeded about WSW, position at 2.00 p.m. being 59.6´N, 6.48´W, a position which was verified shortly after by getting a bearing of Sulisker Rock.

The *Marjoen* proceeded E x N until darkness set in, when after some little persuasion I finally prevailed on the Captain to carry out my original orders, which were to proceed to Stornoway, which port we reached on January 6th.[2]

***

308. *Commander-in-Chief Home Fleets to Admiralty*

HMS *Iron Duke*, 19 January 1917

Be pleased to submit to the Lords Commissioners of the Admiralty the following remarks in regard to the general Naval situation of the

[1]Brooke, Frank W., RNR, Sub-Lieutenant 1916, Lieutenant 1918.

Dundas, Lawrence Leopold, CMG, RN, Commander 1907, Captain 1916, Captain of *Motagua* 1917, Trade Division, Admiralty 1918, retired 1923.

[2]*Marjoen* carried a cargo of linseed oil cake; the ship was allowed to sail on after examination by a decision of the Contraband Committee. So far as can be seen the incident of the submarine played no part in that decision (TS 14/13 of 8 January 1917); the submarine is not identifiable.

moment and developments which may be expected in the critical months to come.[1]

2. Victory will be achieved by the Power which can impose the most effective blockade upon the enemy. We, therefore, must make every effort to:

(a) tighten and increase our blockade upon the enemy.

(b) minimise and reduce the enemy's blockade upon us.

3. Our blockade of the enemy is imposed by the Tenth Cruiser Squadron, the use of surface vessels for this purpose being made possible by our command of the sea.

The enemy impose their blockade upon us by submarine warfare upon merchant shipping, which bids fair to bring us to defeat.

4. For a means of effecting (a) 'tighten and increase our blockade' I refer to my letter of 30th December 1916 No. 3106/HF 0020 [296] advocating an increase in the numbers of the Tenth Cruiser Squadron and to my letter of 15th December 1916 No 2975/HF 0020 on the subject of reducing the restrictions imposed by a too scrupulous adherence to international agreements; agreements which are being treated as scraps of paper by the enemy.

5. I say, without fear of contradiction, that the Tenth Cruiser Squadron is at present doing more than any other unit of the fleet to bring the war to a successful conclusion. So far, they have been immune from attack. We cannot expect this immunity to continue, and must be prepared for a concerted effort against them by enemy submarines. The maintenance of our blockade must therefore depend on the efficacy of the measures taken to deal with enemy submarines.

6. It is vital to us 'to minimise and reduce the enemy's blockade upon us'. Both considerations demand the defeat of the enemy's submarine campaign. The success of our armies, indeed of all the armies of the Allies, is endangered and will become impossible if the enemy submarine campaign continues with the success which attends it at present. This is no doubt well recognised but I would point out that, the enemy submarine campaign has not been developed in a month; it has been the growth of two and a half years of war, and was foreseen and considered.

7. I am aware that the anti-Submarine Division of the War Staff provides an organisation which it is hoped will be effective in dealing with the problem, and no doubt success will be obtained. But isolated

[1]It is worth noting that this is a letter from Beatty as Commander-in-Chief to Jellicoe, now First Sea Lord, who was his predecessor as Commander-in-Chief.

successes do not provide the cure. Our failure in the past is due to the lack of a sound policy. So in the future, unless all that we do is based on sound policy we shall again fail to achieve that success which is absolutely essential if we are to win the war.

8. The Grand Fleet is being depleted of auxiliaries to meet the losses caused by enemy submarines. It is also being deprived of destroyers to meet requirements to deal with enemy submarines in southern waters. I take no exception to this measures; indeed, if necessary, the whole resources of the Grand Fleet must be given up to deal with the menace.

9. But I submit that as the officer responsible to their lordships for the maintenance of the sea blockade, and viewing as I do, with apprehension, the danger to the Tenth Cruiser Squadron in the near future, I may be kept fully informed of the policy which it is intended to put into force, in order that dispositions may be made accordingly in advance, and that any suggestions regarding policy I may have to offer may be formulated in good time.

309. *Admiralty to Commander-in-Chief Grand Fleet*

22 January 1917

With reference to your submission of the 26th ultimo … suggesting that all neutral ships should call at a British port before crossing the line of the Tenth Cruiser Squadron Patrol, I am commanded by My Lords Commissioners of the Admiralty to inform you that the disadvantages of carrying out the procedure you recommend would outweigh the advantages, and it is therefore not proposed to adopt it.

310. *Vice-Admiral Tupper to Admiralty*

HMS *Alsatian*, 24 January 1917

I have the honour to report that for the sake of convenience it is proposed to reorganise the divisions of the Tenth Cruiser Squadron as shown below; and it is submitted that they may be shown in this manner in the Secret Supplement to the Navy List:

First	Second	Third
Alsatian (Flag)	*Teutonic* (Broad Pendant)*	*Otway* (Broad Pendant)
Almanzora	*Motagua*	*Hildebrand*
Andes	*Arlanza*	*Orcoma*
Kildonan Castle	*Patuca*	*Ebro*
Columbella	*Victorian*	*Hilary*
Gloucestershire	*Changuinola*	*Orvieto*
Virginian	*Avenger*	*Armadale Castle*
Moldavia	*Patia*	*Artois*
		Champagne

*Temporarily flown in *Virginian.*

311. *Admiralty to Commander-in-Chief Home Fleets*

January 1917

Analysis of Blockade, 1 July–31 December 1916

***

It will be observed that the number of Neutral ships which, during the above period, passed through without being examined or intercepted, is 63. These of necessity would be making the Northern Passage, as no vessel could get through the Dover Straits without examination in the Downs. If therefore the number shown in the Table as proceeding Southabout – i.e., examined in the Downs – viz 886, is deducted from the total of 2422, it gives 1536 ships proceeding by the Northabout route, of which only 63, or 4.1%, failed to be intercepted by the Patrols.

TABLE A
Neutral Vessels Passing the Blockade.
(Period 1st July–31st December 1916)

Eastbound Vessels arriving in Dutch and Scandinavian Ports from Overseas Ports		Westbound Vessels sailing from Dutch and Scandinavian Ports for Overseas Ports	
Passed through the Downs	404	Passed through the Downs	482
Intercepted by the Patrols	419	Intercepted by the Patrols	214
Called Voluntarily at Kirkwall, Stornoway, Lerwick or other British ports	409	Called Voluntarily at Kirkwall, Stornoway, Lerwick or other British ports	431
Number of Vessels not		Number of Vessels not	

intercepted by Patrols	32	intercepted by Patrols	31
	1264		1158

Total number of Vessels passing through	2422
Less number of Vessels not intercepted	63
Total number of vessels dealt with	2359[1]

312. *Vice-Admiral Tupper to Admiralty*

HMS *Alsatian*, 31 January 1917

Report of Proceedings, 24–30 January 1917

***

1. Wednesday, 24 January – *Changuinola* in Latitude 59.42´ North, Longitude 15.2´ West, reported having sighted about midnight a white light at an estimated distance of 4 miles; the light was visible for about 10 minutes and then disappeared. She searched the vicinity but found nothing.

About 8.30 p.m. a message was received from the Admiralty that a Ship thought to be an enemy auxiliary cruiser had passed Vyl Lightship on the afternoon of 23 January steering to the Northward, and shortly afterwards, in accordance with orders received from the Commander-in-Chief, Ships of the Tenth Cruiser Squadron were ordered to take up the following patrols:

A Patrol, consisting of 7 Ships, to cross line 30° from Latitude 62.50´ North, Longitude 6.30´ West at noon and midnight, steering 110° and 290°, 30 miles apart. Order of Ships from South ... *Ebro*, *Champagne*, *Andes*, *Moldavia*, *Virginian*, *Motagua*, *Orvieto*.
C Patrol, consisting of 4 Ships to cross line 345° from Latitude 50.20´ North, Longitude 14.10´ West at noon and midnight steering 70° and 250°, Ships 30 miles apart, from South ... *Hilary*, *Patuca*, *Changuinola* and *Hildebrand*.
D Patrol ... *Avenger* patrolling between Rockall and 10.30´ West to support Armed Trawlers working in neighbourhood of St Kilda.
West of Faroes ... *Alsatian* patrolling on meridian of 8.30´ West between Latitude 61.20' North and 63 North.

[1]The precision of these statistics is unlikely to reflect reality. The number of vessels which were not stopped by the patrols is very likely to be considerably higher, particularly with regard to smaller craft. Jellicoe exhibited a greater scepticism over the efficacy of the blockade than did Beatty: 'I think you are wrong in assuming that the blockade will ever cause the enemy to give in', he wrote in a letter to Beatty on 4 February in reply to Beatty's early comments (*Jellicoe Papers* II, 143–144).

Cruiser and Light Cruiser Squadrons together with Armed Boarding Vessels and Destroyers were detailed to patrol to the North of Muckle Flugga and on the Sydero-Noup Head line.

2. Thursday, 25 January – South Easterly gale with heavy seas.

Ships were in position on the main patrol lines by noon, W/T silence being maintained.

Columbella being short of coal was ordered to proceed to Clyde.

3. Friday, 26 January – The weather improved though there was still a gale with a fairly heavy sea running.

No news of Raider being received, I obtained the Commander-in-Chief's permission to despatch *Hildebrand* and *Avenger* to Denmark Strait off Staalburg Huk to intercept the Raider in the event of her evading the Patrols and passing to the North of Iceland.

At noon *Alsatian* boarded with some difficulty and risk the Norwegian SS *Dana*, bound from Reykjavik to Spain, via Thorshaven and Troon, with a cargo of salt fish. As she had a Consul's Certificate from Reykjavik she was allowed to proceed on the Master giving a guarantee that he would proceed direct to Troon on leaving the Faroes.

Information having been received that HMS *Laurentic* had been torpedoed off Lough Swilly,[1] *Columbella* and *Victorian* which were approaching from Westward were warned accordingly.

4. Saturday, 27 January – *Virginian* left patrol to coal at Swarbacks Minn, *Patia* which had left Loch Ewe the previous evening being directed to take her place after delivering despatches to *Alsatian*.

Admiralty Letter M.011624 of 21 January 1917 was received approving the proposals for Ships of the Squadron to proceed more frequently to their Southern Bases instead of coaling at Swarbacks Minn. The information called for as to the coal requirements at the various Ports, etc. is being transmitted with this mail …

About 5 p.m. *Alsatian* intercepted the Swedish sailing vessel *Ragnhild* in Latitude 61.30´ North, Longitude 9 West, bound for Lerwick in charge of an Armed Guard from *Motagua*. Provisions were supplied as the Officer reported they were short of food.

5. Sunday 28 January – The Commander-in-Chief having ordered normal patrol to be resumed at 7.30 a.m., Ships were directed to take up the patrols shown in the following disposition.

At noon the disposition of the Squadron was as follows:

A Patrol, being taken up across line 360° from Lat. 65.40´ North, Long. 9.30´ West … *Andes*, *Orvieto*.

[1]In fact, *Laurentic* struck a mine laid by *U 80*.

B Patrol, being taken up on line ahead from Lat. 62 to 64.40´ North, Long. 9.30´ West … *Champagne*, *Moldavia*.
C Patrol, crossing line 345° from Lat. 53.20´ North, Long. 14.10´ West … *Hilary*, *Patuca*, *Changuinola*, *Patia* (joining from A).
D Patrol between Rockall and 10.30´ West … *Ebro* (joining from A).
St Kilda Patrol … Armed Trawlers *Tenby Castle*, *Rushcoe*.
E Patrol Denmark Strait, Iceland … *Avenger*, *Hildebrand*.
Between B and C … *Alsatian*.
Proceeding to Swarbacks Minn … *Motagua*.
Proceeding to Liverpool … *Victorian*.
At Swarbacks Minn … *Virginian*, Armed Trawler *Saxon*.
At Clyde … *Columbella*.
At Liverpool … *Otway*, *Artois*, *Teutonic* (C & M) *Armadale Castle* (fitting out).
At Oban … Armed Trawlers *Walpole*, *Arley*, *Robert Smith*.
On special service … *Almanzora*, *Orcoma*, *Arlanza*, *Gloucestershire*.[1]

During the week 43 vessels were intercepted, of which 12 were sent in with Armed Guards.

A submarine was reported in Latitude 60.32´ North, Longitude 1.55´ West, at 1.45 p.m., steering South West. *Motagua*, who was due to arrive at Swarbacks Minn the following morning was directed to take Special Precautions.

6. Monday, 29 January – Fine weather.

At 7.30 a.m. *Motagua* reported that when 8 miles from Eshaness she had been fired at and missed by a torpedo, presumably from a submarine. Further information showed that the submarine had not been sighted, but had apparently fired a torpedo when astern of the Ship; this was seen to break surface 400 yards on the port quarter and sink on the port bow, the helm having been put hard aport and the starboard engine full speed astern.[2]

In accordance with signals from the Commander-in-Chief, *Avenger* and *Hildebrand* were recalled from Denmark Strait and ordered to join A Patrol. Although I was directed to use my discretion as to keeping one Cruiser in Denmark Strait, I decided not to leave a Ship in so isolated a position especially as she would be out of W/T touch.

Avenger reported that the South Eastern limit of the ice field was

[1]*Kildonan Castle* omitted.

[2]This submarine is not identified, if, in fact, a torpedo had actually been seen; at 7.30 a.m. in January off Shetland, it is pitch dark.

situated in Latitude 66.45´ North, Longitude 24.30´ West, from thence running 360°. The weather in that locality was fine and clear, visibility 26–30 miles, but thick fog was encountered off North Cape.

When more vessels are available to meet the requirements of A and C Patrols, I strongly advocate having two Ships permanently guarding the West and North-west Coast of Iceland with a view to preventing the passage of raiders.

C Patrol was moved to the Eastward to take up patrol across line 325° from Latitude 59.18´ North, Longitude 8.30´ West.

7. Tuesday, 30 January – Information was received that Midshipman Raymond L. Priest, RNR,[1] of *Otway* in charge of the Armed Guard placed on board the Dutch SS *Gaasterland*, en route for Falmouth, had been removed from that Ship by a German submarine.

8. A number of British trawlers have been met with by *Alsatian* during the past few days, fishing in Icelandic waters and off the Faroe bank and I would again submit that Armed Trawlers may be provided to work with them, or perhaps a better plan would be to arm all these fishing trawlers with at least a 6 pdr or 12 pdr gun. It is quite possible they would account for some submarines as well as render their useful occupation less risky.

***

313. *Vice-Admiral Tupper to Admiralty*

HMS *Alsatian*, 13 February 1917

Report of Proceedings 31 January–11 February 1917

***

1. Wednesday, 31 January – *Ebro* again reported sighting a white light in the distance, at 2.20 p.m., in Latitude 57.20´ North, Longitude 13.6´ West, and also at 2.55 a.m. A search of the area, however, produced no result.

I directed Commodore Luard to proceed to Liverpool in *Orvieto* to pay off *Teutonic* and hoist his broad pendant in *Armadale Castle*.

I arrived at Swarbacks Minn in *Alsatian* at 9.30 p.m. 6 Auxiliary Patrol Vessels were patrolling St Magnus Bay and approaches. Bright moonlight.

[1]Priest, Raymond L., RNR, Midshipman 1914, Prisoner of War 1917.

2. Thursday, 1 February – I discussed with Rear-Admiral Fremantle,[1] Commanding Second Cruiser Squadron, and Rear-Admiral Fawckner, various proposals for rendering the approaches to Swarbacks Minn safer for Ships entering and leaving the harbour. As a result certain recommendations were forwarded to the Commander-in-Chief.

A Court of Enquiry was held under the Presidency of Rear-Admiral Sydney R. Fremantle, MVO, to investigate the manner in which the Examination Service was conducted at Lerwick. The Flag Captain of *Alsatian* was a member of the Court, and several Officers attended as witnesses.[2]

3. Friday, 2 February – *Alsatian* completed coaling having taken in 1600 tons at an average of 178 per hour. This beats all previous records by 24 tons per hour.

Avenger patrolling on A to North-East of Iceland reported that the telemotor pipes of her steering gear had frozen up, the temperature being 17[degrees F] and falling.

4. Saturday, 3 February – *Moldavia* arrived at dawn and commenced coaling. I went on board in the afternoon and presented a Distinguished Service Medal to J. Longman, Greaser …

All boats were lowered and exercised but heavy snow storms somewhat interfered with the programme.

The Commander-in-Chief having informed me he desired, if possible, to see me before resuming patrol, I left Swarbacks Minn at 9.30 p.m. for Scapa Flow. A heavy northerly gale was experienced with snow storms.

5. Sunday, 4 February – Very cold with heavy snow showers. *Alsatian* arrived at Scapa at 9.30 a.m. Various matters in connection with the Tenth Cruiser Squadron were discussed with the Commander-in-Chief and verbal orders were received by me to forward a letter putting forward proposals for additional Armed Trawlers to be attached to the Tenth Cruiser Squadron with a view to increasing the efficiency of the patrols.

[1]Fremantle, Sydney Robert, GCB, MVO, RN (1867–1958), Commander 1899, Captain 1903, Rear-Admiral 1913, commanded Ninth Cruiser Squadron 1916, Second Cruiser Squadron 1917, Aegean Squadron 1917–1918, Deputy Chief of Naval Staff and Lord Commissioner of Admiralty 1918–1919, Vice-Admiral 1919, Commander First Battle Squadron 1919–1921, Admiral 1922, Commander-in-Chief Portsmouth 1923–1926, retired 1926, author of *My Naval Career* (London, 1949)

[2]The enquiry, in fact, was much more specific, concerning the behaviour of Lt Griffith and the problem of the *Hercules*; cf. [279 para. 2].

In the afternoon I paid a visit to Vice-Admiral Sir F. Brock[1] and discussed matters in connection with the Examination Service, Armed Guards, etc, also Defences of Swarbacks Minn.

I left Scapa at 10 p.m. for patrol.

The disposition of the Squadron at noon was as follows:

A Patrol, crossing line 360° from 65.40´ North, 9.30´ West ... *Virginian*, *Andes*, *Avenger*.

B Patrol, Line ahead from 62 North, 9.30´ West to 64.40´ North, 9.30´ West ... *Changuinola*, *Hildebrand*.

C Patrol, crossing line 325° from 59.18´ North, 8.30´ West ... *Hilary*, *Motagua*, *Artois*.

D Patrol, between Rockall and 10.30´ West ... *Patia*.

St Kilda Patrol ... Armed Trawlers *Tenby Castle*, *Rushcoe*, and *Walpole*.

Proceeding to Swarbacks Minn ... *Champagne*.

Proceeding to Clyde ... *Ebro*.

At Swarbacks Minn ... *Moldavia*, Armed Trawler *Saxon*.

At Liverpool ... *Otway*, *Almanzora*, *Victorian*, *Orvieto*, *Arlanza*, *Teutonic* (C & M), *Armadale Castle* (Fitting out).

At Clyde ... *Columbella*.

At Scapa ... *Alsatian* (Proceeded to C Patrol on leaving).

At Loch Ewe ... *Patuca*.

At Oban ... Armed Trawlers *Arley*, *Robert Smith*.

On special service ... *Orcoma*, *Gloucestershire*, *Kildonan Castle*.

During the week 48 vessels were intercepted, of which 15 were sent in with, and 1 without, Armed Guards.

6. Monday, 5 February – Experienced very cold stormy weather and heavy sea during the night.

C Patrol was moved to work across line 360° from Latitude 58.45´ North, Longitude 10.30´ West.

The Master of the Danish SS *Rosborg*, from Baltimore to Esbjerg, intercepted by *Motagua*, reported that the Danish Ships *Belgien* and *Europa* intended to evade the patrols by Owner's orders. Both these

[1]Brock, Frederick E.E., KCMG, CB, RN (1854–1929), Commander 1893, Captain 1898, Rear-Admiral 1908, commander Portsmouth Division Home Fleet 1909–1910, SNO Gibraltar 1912–1915, Vice-Admiral 1913, Admiral Commanding Shetland and Orkneys 1916–1918, retired 1918, Admiral (retired) 1919, serving with Ministry of Munitions.

vessels had, however, been intercepted by *Motagua* on 2nd and 3rd February respectively and sent in with Armed Guards… [314].[1]

7. Tuesday, 6 February – South Westerly gale moderating during the afternoon when *Motagua* was met. The Lieutenant Commander (G) and Engineer Commander on my staff, spent an hour on board dealing with questions of armament and engines.

Admiralty informed me that owing to lack of accommodation in *Armadale Castle*, and for other reasons, Commodore Luard would hoist his broad pendant in *Orvieto*.

About 10 p.m. *Alsatian* intercepted the Norwegian Sailing Vessel *Hermes*, bound from Savannah to Randers (Denmark), with a cargo of Cottonseed Oil Cake and sent her to Lerwick with an Armed Guard.[2]

Stornoway was reported closed owing to mines.

8. Wednesday, 7 February – The wind freshened again to a gale from the South-West, misty weather being experienced on all patrols.

I intended meeting *Changuinola* at 10 a.m. but owing to the thick weather did not do so until 4 p.m.; the W/T direction finder proved very useful.

Changuinola reported having lost two boats and having had the platform of her bow gun washed away in the gale of the previous day. On parting company *Changuinola* was sent to relieve *Avenger* on A Patrol.

The Commander-in-Chief warned me that a steamer had been torpedoed off the South-West of Ireland, possibly by another steamer, which passed close, under Norwegian colours.[3]

9. Thursday, 8 February – Still blowing from the South-West with a heavy sea. Intercepted the British Trawler *Braeriach*, UY 922, making quite good weather of it.

I received by W/T … a list of some 170 Trawlers engaged in fishing off the Faroes, Iceland and Rockall. I submit that at least 24 of the best of these fine trawlers are much needed to work with the Tenth Cruiser Squadron. A separate letter has been forwarded to the Commander-in-Chief on this subject …

The gale was very heavy during the night, but subsided in the morning.

[1]*Rosborg*'s cargo was 'corn' for Esbjerg, a port always regarded with suspicion because of its proximity to Germany; also there were other similar cargoes *en route*; *Rosborg* had to wait until the cumulative totals became clear; it was allowed to go on after a three week delay (TS 14/13 of 8 and 28 February 1917).

[2]*Hermes* was not detained.

[3]This was probably the Norwegian *Storstag*, heading for Queenstown from Buenos Aires, sunk by *U 60*.

10. Friday, 9 February – At 11.15 a.m. *Moldavia* intercepted the Italian SS *Famiglia* in Latitude 58.38´ North, Longitude 10.8´ West with a German Armed Guard on board consisting of 1 Lieutenant and 5 ratings; there were also 3 Englishmen and 9 Italians in the Ship. As soon as they realised capture was imminent the Germans exploded bombs in the engine room and forehold and the Ship sank shortly afterwards, the Armed Guard and crew being taken on board *Moldavia*.[1]

The Admiralty and Commander-in-Chief were informed, and *Moldavia* was at once ordered to proceed to Loch Ewe to land prisoners and other persons.

Later, the Commanding Officer informed me he had been fortunate enough to obtain the German Officer's diary and also important orders for German submarine patrols and instructions for communication.

I directed him to transmit full reports to the Admiralty and Commander-in-Chief on arrival, and send the captured documents direct to the Admiralty. I also asked that one of the Commander-in-Chief's Staff Officers should meet *Moldavia*'s Officer at Inverness on his way South.

Kirkwall being reported closed owing to mines, Ships with Armed Guards were sent to either Stornoway or Lerwick as most convenient.

11. Saturday, 10 February – *Moldavia* arrived at Loch Ewe at 2.30 a.m., disembarked prisoners, etc., and Officer with important documents and sailed again at 4.30 a.m.

At 9.40 a.m. Armed Trawler *Walpole* in Latitude 57 North, Longitude 9.24´ West reported she was chasing a submarine steering North on the surface and throwing off heavy black smoke. She was lost sight of at 10.40 a.m.

In the meantime *Arley*, *Saxon* and *Robert Smith* had been ordered to assist in the chase. These Trawlers reported sighting and engaging submarines as follows:

(1) *Arley* at 12.30 p.m. in Latitude 57.34´ North, Longitude 9.05´ West, sighted submarine submerged. Two depth charges were dropped without result.
(2) *Saxon* at 1.45 p.m. engaged submarine in Latitude 57.48´ North, Longitude 9.17´ West.
(3) *Robert Smith* in Latitude 57.56´ North, Longitude 8.50´ West, engaged two submarines at extreme range, steering North-East.

[1] *Famiglia* had been captured by *U 43*; the function of this 'Armed Guard' was clearly as captors more than 'guards'; the use of the term is indicative of the way the British also saw their 'prize-crews' and 'armed guards'.

The following signal from *Walpole* which is armed with 2 x 6 pounder guns, is quoted for information:

'Wish to report to you morning 10th February engaged enemy submarine, Lat 57.0´N, Long. 9.24´W, fired 21 rounds, all fell short, gun range 5000. I beg to request you to order inspection of guns. Confident if had 12 pounder gun on board could easily have had submarine ...'[1]

I consider it highly advisable she should be armed with a 12 pounder placed on the 'fiddley', and am forwarding a separate submission in this connection ...

Having sighted *Artois* in the afternoon, I took the opportunity of proceeding on board and presented three Distinguished Service Medals, awarded to members of the crew in recognition of their work in the Tenth Cruiser Squadron. On arrival, I was received with a guard and the Officers were presented to me. I made a short speech in French, congratulating the Captain, Officers and men on the good work done by *Artois*, and then decorated the following Petty Officers in the name of the King – P.K.Y.M. Stephan, A.F. Dorleans, & J. Ollivier. *Capitaine* de Marguerye expressed his gratitude to me for having performed the ceremony.

I placed *Artois* on B Patrol so as to guard North-West approaches to the Faroes.

12. Sunday, 11 February – I met *Moldavia* at 8 a.m. and received Commander Smyth's report of the interception of SS *Famiglia*. The documents secured by him and transmitted to the Admiralty certainly appeared to be important.

Ports of Kirkwall and Stornoway were re-opened to traffic.

A submarine was reported off the Isle of Man and *Virginian* who was on her way to Liverpool, was warned accordingly.

At noon the disposition of the Squadron was as follows:

A Patrol, crossing line 360° from Lat. 66.5´ North, Long. 9.30´ West ... *Andes*, *Changuinola*, *Hildebrand*; joining – *Moldavia*.

B Patrol, on line 360° from Lat. 61.30´ North, Long. 10.0´ West ... *Alsatian*, *Artois*.

C Patrol, on line 360° from Lat. 58.45´ North, Long. 10.30´ West ... *Columbella*, *Patuca*, *Champagne*.

D Patrol, Lat. 57 North, Long. 8.30´ to 10.30´ West ... *Hilary*.

St Kilda Patrol ... Armed trawlers *Arley*, *Robert Smith*, *Saxon*,

[1]None of these submarines can be identified.

Walpole.
Rejoining Patrol ... *Victorian.*
Proceeding to Liverpool ... *Virginian.*
At Liverpool ... *Otway*, *Orvieto*, *Almanzora*, *Arlanza*, Fitting Out – *Armadale Castle.*
At Clyde ... *Motagua*, *Patia*, *Ebro.*
At Scapa ... *Avenger.*
At Oban ... Armed Trawlers *Rushcoe*, *Tenby Castle.*
On special service ... *Kildonan Castle.*

During the week 24 vessels were intercepted, of which 15 were sent in with Armed Guards.

13. Of the 24 Cruisers now forming the Tenth Cruiser Squadron, 3 are detached – leaving 21 available.

Of these it is hoped shortly to keep 14 actually on patrol, the other 7 being in harbour coaling and refitting, and it is proposed to dispose them as follows:

Two Ships with large coal endurance in Denmark Strait,
8 Ships between the Faroes and the North of Iceland,
Four Ships between Faroe Bank and North of Rockall, the idea being that more traffic will now pass North of the Faroes owing to the German declaration of a prescribed zone round the British Isles.

At the same time, it is considered necessary to retain some vessels on C and D Patrols – normally placed in area between Latitudes 57 and 61 North, Longitude 8 and 14 West in case of Raiders or vessels with German prize crews on board attempting to get through. Both the *Older* and *Famiglia* were intercepted by Ships on C Patrol.

***

314. *Captain L.L. Dundas to Vice-Admiral Commanding Tenth Cruiser Squadron*

HMS *Motagua*, 5 February 1917

Re Danish SS *Belgien* and *Europa* sent to Kirkwall with Armed Guards 2nd & 3rd February.[1]

I have the honour to report that on Lieutenant Andrew Hardie, RNR,[2] boarding Danish SS *Rosborg* at 1230 this day, he was particularly

[1]Both ships were permitted to sail on, *Belgien* on 5 and *Europa* on 6 February (TS 14/13). Both ships were usually employed by the Belgian Relief Commission.

[2]Hardie, Andrew, RNR, Sub-Lieutenant 1915, Lieutenant 1917.

questioned as to whether the Danish Steamers SS *Belgien* and *Europa* of A.P. Moller of Copenhagen had been sent to Kirkwall, as they both sailed from Baltimore on the same date (11th January), having conveyed generally amongst the Shipmasters of Baltimore they intended to evade the patrol and that this was by the owners' orders.

The Captain of the *Rosborg* stated that the Captains of the above ships, personally, told him of their intentions and he, apparently, resented this very much – expressing the view that if certain vessels on the White List did this, it would be detrimental and taking away the privileges of other ships on the same list.

The Boarding Officer is of the opinion that Captain Petersen of *Rosborg* who has been trading from Narvik to Middlesboro since hostilities commenced – is sincerely pro-British and complained bitterly of A.P. Moller of Copenhagen being on the White List.

315. *Vice-Admiral Tupper to Admiralty*

HMS *Alsatian*, 23 February 1917

Report of Proceedings, 12–20 February 1917

***

1. Monday, 12 February – Very good weather. At 2 p.m. I met *Victorian* just out from Liverpool and went on board to witness target practice and go round the Ship. The result may be briefly summarised as follows:

6" TARGET PRACTICE – Good without being particularly so.
First salvo fired 14 seconds after order to engage target.
Second salvo 52 seconds – straddle. Third salvo 1 minute 40 seconds.
The intervals between the salvoes were somewhat too long.
ANTI-SUBMARINE PRACTICE – Fair. Stations for dropping depth charges had not been exercised. This was explained and then carried out.
FIRE QUARTERS – Fire exercised in ammunition hoist. Water on fire in 1 minute 50 seconds.
MESS DECKS & SLEEPING QUARTERS – Clean and tidy.
REMARKS – Considered generally efficient.

In the evening experiments were carried out with star shell and rockets, concerning which a separate report has been forwarded …

By the mail received from *Virginian* I heard that Rear-Admiral Morgan Singer[1] is likely to succeed Commodore Luard as second-in-command of the Tenth Cruiser Squadron.

2. Tuesday, 13 February – Misty weather, heavy south-west swell and strong breeze.

About 5 p.m. I met *Andes* and sent in a sick Officer and mails to Liverpool by her. At 6 p.m. I rendezvoused with *Avenger* in order to receive a letter from the Commander-in-Chief, containing instructions regarding the disposition of the patrols, the contents of which were at once complied with (see paragraph 3 below).

Loch Ewe having been reported closed owing to mines, arrangements for *Moldavia* to coal there on 16 February had to be cancelled.

3. Wednesday, 14 February – Clear weather, strong south, south-westerly breeze. A, B and E Patrols were modified as follows:

> A Patrol … *Avenger* to work on wide zig-zags between Latitude 64 and 65.30´ North, between Longitude 11 and 12 West, being in southern position at midnight daily.
> B Patrol … consisting of *Artois*, *Alsatian*, and *Moldavia*, 40 miles apart, to work on a line bearing 325° from Latitude 61.30´ North, Longitude 9 West, ships in southern position at midnight daily.
> E Patrol … *Hildebrand* and *Victorian* to proceed to North West of Iceland and establish patrol off Isafiord.

At 5.30 a.m. *Alsatian* intercepted and sent in to Troon with an Armed Guard the Norwegian SS *Stralsund*. Unfortunately the vessel was caught and sunk by an enemy submarine 16 miles from St Kilda (vide paragraph 5). The report of the Officer in charge of the armed guard is being forwarded separately ….[2]

4. Thursday, 15 February – At 3.30 a.m. *Columbella* reported she had been in collision with the British Steamer *Fife* in Latitude 59.56´ North, Longitude 8.50´ West.

The Rear-Admiral, Stornoway, was requested to send tugs but at 5.30 a.m. *Columbella* informed me the Fife had sunk; the crew having been previously taken off.

[1]Singer, Morgan, CB, RN (1864–1938), Commander 1898, Captain 1903, Captain of *Excellent* 1912–1914, Rear-Admiral 1914, DNO 1914–1916, Second in Command Tenth Cruiser Squadron 1917–1918, Vice-Admiral 1919, Commander-in-Chief North America and West Indies 1919–1920, Admiral commanding Coast Guards and Reserves 1921–1923, Admiral (retired) 1924.

[2]That report is not located, but see [316], [319] and [345]. The submarine was *U 78*.

As *Columbella*'s stem had been somewhat extensively damaged and the fore peak flooded, I directed her to proceed to Clyde for repairs. The Captain Superintendent was requested to order a Court of Enquiry to investigate the circumstances attending the collision. A written report of the accident has not yet been received, but *Columbella* arrived safely at the Clyde passing through the Minches and the Sound of Mull. I directed the Trawlers *Arley* and *Saxon* to meet her off the 100 fathom line and escort her past the Butt of Lewis. This service they performed well.

5. Friday, 16 February – The Senior Naval Officer, Liverpool, informed me that *Arlanza* had damaged her port propellers which necessitated docking the Ship, her sailing being consequently delayed. Unfortunate accidents have thus deprived the Patrol of the services of two Ships in the past 24 hours.

At 4 a.m. the Armed Trawler *Rushcoe* reported she had picked up the crew and Armed Guard from the Norwegian Steamer *Stralsund*, which had been sunk by an enemy submarine at 6 p.m. the previous evening 16 miles from St Kilda. *Rushcoe* was ordered to land the guard and crew at Stornoway.

6. Saturday, 17 February – Dull misty weather. Ships were specially warned to look out for the Danish Steamship *United States* which was reported as attempting to evade the patrols and *Artois*, which was about to proceed to Swarbacks Minn was ordered to patrol to the East of the Faroes across her probable route until time to go in.

7. Sunday, 18 February – At 12.15 a.m. *Orvieto* reported she had boarded the Norwegian SS *Tricolor* in Latitude 62.40´ North, Longitude 11.12´ West, bound from Bergen to Newport News in ballast, and requested instructions. The vessel had not called at a British Port and had no Consular certificate.

Whilst waiting for a reply, *Orvieto* proceeded to examine another light, which proved to be a British Trawler.

Tricolor in the meantime extinguished her lights and proceeded on her voyage. She was again intercepted, however, and an armed guard placed on board to take her to Kirkwall. The crew then refused to work the Ship, and the Master stated they had been engaged on the understanding that they should not enter the War Zone. The matter was referred to the Admiralty, who directed that the vessel was to be allowed to proceed, if the Master gave an undertaking to proceed to Halifax; this he agreed to do [318].

At 4.30 p.m. I met *Otway*, flying the broad pendant of Commodore Philip H. Colomb,[1] who has recently been appointed vice Commodore Booty.

I received him on board *Alsatian*, and having explained his duties, I detailed him to take charge of C and D Patrols.

At noon the disposition of the Squadron was as follows:

A Patrol, cruising between Lat. 64 and 65.30´N and Long. 11 and 12 W … *Avenger*.

B Patrol, Line ahead 325° from Lat. 61.30´N, Long. 9 West … *Moldavia*, *Orvieto*, *Alsatian*.

C Patrol, 360° from Lat. 58.45´N, Long. 10.30´ West … *Patia*, *Ebro*, *Champagne*, *Patuca*.

E Patrol, North-West Iceland, off Isafjord … *Hildebrand*, *Victorian*.

St Kilda Patrol … Armed Trawlers *Saxon*, *Tenby Castle*, and *Rushcoe*.

Rejoining Patrol from Liverpool … *Otway*, *Armadale Castle*, *Almanzora*.

At Swarbacks Minn … *Artois*.

At Liverpool … *Andes*, *Arlanza*, *Virginian*.

At Clyde … *Changuinola*, *Hilary*, *Motagua*, *Columbella*.

At Oban … Armed Trawlers *Walpole*, *Arley* and *Robert Smith*.

On Special Service … *Orcoma*, *Gloucestershire*, *Kildonan Castle*.

During the week 35 vessels were intercepted, of which 9 were sent with Armed Guards.

8. Monday, 19 February – During the night two Westbound Steamers with cargo for Halifax and Newport News were intercepted and allowed to proceed, as they each had a British Consular Certificate to the effect that they had no cargo of enemy origin.

At 3.15 p.m., *Armadale Castle* reported she had intercepted the British S.V. *Ainsdale* in Latitude 56.58´N, Longitude 10 W, in charge of the First Mate of SS *Basuta*. This vessel had been picked up abandoned in Latitude 49 North, Longitude 15.47´ West, with a cargo of grain from the River Plate. Trawlers *Tenby Castle* and *Saxon*, were directed to escort her to Stornoway and the Rear-Admiral Stornoway was directed to send a tug. This vessel appears in 'Overdue and Capture List of British Vessels' dated 14 February 1917.

The Norwegian SS *Segovia* was intercepted by *Alsatian* with a fruit

[1]Colomb, Philip H., CB, RN (1867–1957), Lieutenant 1890, Commander 1900, Captain 1906, Commodore in *Otway* 1917, Rear-Admiral 1918, retired 1923.

cargo for Bergen, in Latitude 62.33´ North, Longitude 10.55´ West, and sent in to Lerwick with an Armed Guard: the Master protested.[1]

9. Tuesday, 20 February – I left Patrol in *Alsatian* for Scapa Flow.

At 11 a.m. *Alsatian* intercepted the Norwegian Motor Ship *Brazil* in Latitude 62.26´ North, Longitude 4.50´ West, from Christiania to New York, with a cargo of Wood Pulp. As she had not called at a British Port, an Armed Guard was placed on board and she was sent to Lerwick, the Master protesting.[2]

The Admiralty having informed me that it was desired to send the British Consul of Reykjavik back to Iceland, arrangements were made for him to embark in *Andes* leaving Liverpool about 25th.

***

316. *A.T. Moller & Co to Admiralty*

30/32 Elbe Street, Leith, Edinburgh, 20 February 1917

37430/c SS Stralsund

We regret to have to inform you that the above steamer was torpodoed [*sic*] on the 15th instant, although we are thankful to say the officers and crew were saved and landed at Stornoway by a British Patrol Steamer, but what surprises us more than anything is the contents of the following telegram received from the Norwegian Consul at Stornoway acting by our instructions for the time charterer, Francesco Giordano:

> '*Stralsund* stopped by British Patrol on thirteenth ordered Stornoway for inspection with prize crew on board, fifteenth sunk by German submarine, steamers crew and prize crew who were concealed under clothes had to take steamers boats, crew lost everything, rescued after being several hours afloat by British Patrol Steamer and brought here.'

because according to same it seems that a price [*sic*] crew was on board, and the steamer, on the quick arrival of which the Italian Government reckoned, had been diverted from its course, although

[1] *Segovia* was not detained.

[2] *Brazil* was permitted to continue (TS 14/13 of 22 February 1917) after the usual queries were made and guarantees given.

1. a favourable treatment has been granted to same in virtue of the undertaking we had given on behalf of the Italian time-charterer.
2. she carried cargo from a neutral country to our allies.
3. has been occupied in this particular trade almost uninterrupted for a year and a half which we should have imagined would have secured to her examination in the open sea, more especially as she was bound for verification of papers at Troon.

There are no doubts about it, that U boats are now lurking near the routes which steamers have to follow when taken into Stornoway and if the *Stralsund* had been allowed to proceed on her voyage, the chances are she would have arrived safely at Troon the same as did her sister ship *Dana*, also with cargo for the Italian government.

Might we in this connection be permitted to call attention to the great pluck and foresight of Captain Ommundsen, in dressing up the prize crew as common sailors, when danger was at hand, because had it been discovered, he would probably have been shot, and the British sailors in any case made prisoners. This act on the part of the captain ought to be commented upon, and we think at least, he is worthy of a gold watch and chain, and the crew to be recompensed for giving their spare clothes to the British sailors, more especially, as one and all lost their belongings, the submarine taking, not only the ship's papers and mail, but also all the provisions [319].[1]

317. *Vice-Admiral Tupper to Admiralty*

HMS *Alsatian*, 8 March 1917

Report of Proceedings, 21 February–6 March 1917

***

1. Wednesday, 21 February – *Alsatian* arrived at Scapa Flow at 7 a.m., to replenish with coal.

During the forenoon I visited the Commander-in-Chief and submitted to him the reply I proposed to send in answer to Admiralty message 801 of 20 February, relative to the action to be taken in the case of neutral vessels whose crews refused to work their ship into a port in the United Kingdom, namely:

[1]*Stralsund* was sunk by *U 79*.

'... In case of ships refusing to go in for examination, propose to place Armed Guard on board, endeavour to persuade Master to take her in, and inform him he will be escorted. If crew still absolutely refuse, suggest offering each individual a bonus, to take her in. In case of refusal of bonus, crew to be transferred to Cruiser and ship to be sent in with Prize Crew. Desirable to remove crew to reduce size of Prize Crew, also act as deterrent. Very desirable to prevent neutral ships being sunk whilst on passage to British ports, and for this reason considered necessary system of escort be instituted through War Zone'.

The Commander-in-Chief agreed with my suggestions in the main, but did not anticipate that the proposal to offer a bonus to the crews would be approved.

The suggestion that ships sent in with Armed Guards should be escorted was put forward as it is considered most desirable to prevent such Ships being sunk by enemy submarines, and it was hoped that perhaps some vessels might be found for the purpose. If Ships sent in are sunk it is bound to act as a deterrent to other Ships' crews proceeding in of their own accord.

I have already been using the six Trawlers attached to the 10th Cruiser Squadron and working off St Kilda to escort any vessels intercepted until they could be turned over to the Stornoway Patrols, and, with the advent of the 12 additional Trawlers, which are about to be added to my Command, it will be possible to further extend this to a certain degree by escorting low powered steamers intercepted in other areas.

As the result of a Conference with the Commander-in-Chief and Vice-Admiral Commanding Orkneys and Shetlands, it was decided that Ships should be sent into Kirkwall instead of Lerwick, and that they should be directed to arrive at a position 20 miles to the westward of Noup Head at dawn and thence be escorted in by vessels of the Orkneys Patrol.

The Admiralty informed me that the sailing of HM Ships with the exception of Destroyers, via the North Channel was suspended until further orders, and the Senior Naval Officer, Liverpool reported that the departure of *Virginian* had been delayed in consequence.

2. Thursday, 22 February – A Tug arrived from Stornoway and took the *Ainsdale* in tow (vide paragraph 8 of my previous Report of Proceedings), Trawlers attached to the 10th Cruiser Squadron acting as escort.

Vice-Admiral Sir F.E.E. Brock, KCMG, CB, visited me and

discussed various matters relating to treatment of vessels sent in and detained, etc.

Alsatian completed coaling at 5 p.m., 2000 tons having been taken in at an average of 136 tons per hour, which is considered good work.

3. Friday, 23 February – At 1.15 a.m., the tug towing *Ainsdale* parted tow and proceeded to Stornoway, presumably for the purpose of obtaining a second hawser. As the sails were in ribbons, *Rushcoe* sent two officers and nine men on board to clear away the canvas and get the vessel round on to the starboard tack. In the afternoon, however, the tug returned, accompanied by three trawlers, who took charge of *Ainsdale* in approximately Latitude 58.45´ North, Longitude 5.45´ West, *Rushcoe* and *Tenby Castle* returning to patrol.

The Master of the Danish sailing vessel *Skirner*, boarded by *Patuca* in Latitude 58.44´ North, Longitude 9.55´ West, en route to Uddevalla from Setubal, reported having been stopped by an enemy submarine 30 miles West of St. Kilda the previous day.[1]

The Grand Fleet left harbour between 3.30 and 5.30 p.m. – a most impressive sight, which was an education to all officers and men of *Alsatian.*

Alsatian left Scapa Flow at 6 p.m. to rejoin patrol.

The Special Service Trawler *King Lear*, having been placed under my orders for a month by the Commander-in-Chief, I gave her directions to proceed via the Whiten Channel to North Rona and thence along the 100 fathom line to Swarbacks Minn, where I arranged for her to alter her disguise to that of the small Swedish Vessel *Temis*.

4. Saturday, 24 February – Traffic was resumed through the North Channel.

A, B, and C Patrols were modified as follows:

A Patrol, consisting of 3 Ships, in line ahead, 40 miles apart, 340° from Latitude 63 North, Longitude 10 West, Ships in southern position 6 a.m. and 8 p.m.

B Patrol, consisting of 3 Ships, 30 miles apart; 330° from Latitude 62.20´ North, Longitude 9 West, steering 240° and 60°. C Patrol was moved 40 miles to the eastward.

The Norwegian SS *Bergensfiord* outward bound was intercepted by *Armadale Castle* North of Faeroes, and allowed to proceed on the understanding that she called at Halifax.

5. Sunday, 25 February – Westerly gale, moderating towards evening.

[1]*Skirner*'s cargo was salt and the ship was delayed until a satisfactory reply was received from Sweden as to its destination (TS 14/13 of 27 February 1917). The submarine is not known.

At 9 a.m., I met *Orvieto*, and received back signals. On parting company, I despatched her to take charge of B, *Alsatian* taking her place on A Patrol.

At noon, the disposition of the Squadron was as follows:

A Patrol, Line ahead 340° from Lat. 63 N, Long. 10 W … *Moldavia*, *Alsatian*, *Avenger*.
B Patrol, On line 330° from Lat. 62.20´N, Long. 9 W, steering 240° & 60° … *Orvieto*, *Artois*, *Armadale Castle*.
C Patrol, On line 360° from Lat. 58.45´N, Long. 10.30 W, steering 240° & 60° … *Patia*, *Ebro*, *Otway*.
E Patrol … *Almanzora*, *Hildebrand*.
St Kilda Patrol … Armed Trawlers *Tenby Castle*, *Rushcoe*, *Walpole*.
Proceeding to Liverpool … *Victorian*.
Rejoining Patrol from Liverpool … *Virginian*.
At Swarbacks Minn … *Champagne*.
At Liverpool … *Andes*, *Arlanza*.
At Clyde … *Patuca*, *Columbella*, *Changuinola*, *Hilary*, *Motagua*.
At Oban … Armed Trawlers *Saxon*, *Arley*, *Robert Smith*.
On special service … *Orcoma*, *Gloucestershire*, *Kildonan Castle*.

During the week, 32 vessels were intercepted, of which 8 were sent in with Armed Guards.

6. Monday, 26 February – About 7 a.m. *Armadale Castle* intercepted the American Oil Steamer *Polarine* in latitude 63 North, Longitude 8.45´ West, in ballast, from Goteborg to Halifax. As this vessel's name had not been communicated to me as having permission to omit calling at a British port, I directed an Armed Guard to be placed on board to take her to Halifax. The Master stated that his London Agents had instructed him to proceed to that port. Before allowing her to proceed, however, I requested instructions from the Admiralty, but the reply that an Armed Guard was unnecessary was not received until late in the afternoon. As wind and sea were rising and it was getting dark I decided to allow the Armed Guard to proceed in the vessel.

The Senior Naval Officer, Liverpool, informed me the completion of *Arlanza* had been delayed owing to the failure of the shore engineers to work over the week end.

In the course of the day *Artois* cruising to the West of the Faroes intercepted and sent to Kirkwall with an Armed Guard the Norwegian Steamer *Locksley*, from Portland, USA, to Rotterdam with a cargo of wheat, and *Delfinus* from Bergen to Philadelphia with iron ore. Neither ship gave any trouble.[1]

Andes left Liverpool at 6 a.m. with Mr E.G. Cable, HM Consul for Reykjavik, on board.

7. Tuesday, 27 February – South Westerly gale with thick weather, veering to the westward in the evening.

At 10.30 p.m. *Virginian* in Latitude 62.17´ North, Longitude 13.20´ West reported intercepting the Norwegian SS *Aztec* from Aarhus to New York and informed me that it was too rough to board. I directed her to keep in touch until the weather moderated.

Sixteen vessels out of an available 21 were on patrol on this date.

8. Wednesday, 28 February – The gales continued throughout the day, the weather however being much clearer.

During the forenoon *Hilary* lost a boat, which was swamped alongside after communicating with *Patia*; the crew were fortunately picked up.

At 3 p.m. *Virginian* succeeded in boarding *Aztec* and having found her correct allowed her to proceed after obtaining a guarantee that she would call at Halifax.

A telegram – brought out by *Champagne* – was received from the Admiralty in reply to my 458, quoted in paragraph 1 of this letter, informing me that no escort is available for Ships sent in by the Tenth Cruiser Squadron. The suggestion of offering a bonus to neutral crews for taking the Ship in was not approved. The crews or any portion of the crews of neutral vessels that refuse to work the Ship in are to be removed, their place being taken by men supplied from the Cruiser.

9. Thursday, 1 March – Still blowing from the South-West with a heavy sea. During the forenoon, after a lull, the wind backed to the Southward, and blew with increasing force throughout the day, a very heavy sea running.

In the forenoon I managed to get on board *Armadale Castle* and inspected the crew at Divisions and General Quarters. I also went round the mess decks and the men's sleeping quarters. The seamen and firemen are berthed in small compartments which were very damp and uncomfortable. Of course I saw them under the worst conditions, but they very much need heating apparatus, the fitting of which for some unknown reason was refused during her recent refit. The men, however, seemed healthy. There was one bad case of pneumonia and another of catarrh.

[1]Neither ship was detained.

The steering gear is entirely exposed to shell fire, no armour plate having been fitted round it as in other Armed Merchant Cruisers.

The hatchways leading to the Magazines are caulked to prevent water getting below, but the Magazine shoots made of thin deal are not watertight, and any water on the decks would pour down them.

I consider *Armadale Castle* has been very poorly fitted out; she is not nearly as comfortable as the majority of ships in the Squadron and I was agreeably surprised to find the crew so cheerful.

The weather was too bad for any attempt at Target Practice, but the gunnery organisation appears good.

Robert Smith reported sighting and chasing a submarine at 12.15 p.m., 10 miles to the north of St Kilda. The submarine was steering North-East on the surface at the time.

Another submarine was reported in Latitude 55.56´ North, Longitude 9.43´ West, steering to the North-West.

Andes arrived at Reykjavik and having disembarked the Consul, left to join *Almanzora* in Denmark Strait.

A Patrol was moved to a line 320° from Latitude 63.20´ North, Longitude 8.45´ West.

10. Friday, 2 March – Fine day with heavy confused swell, the gale having died down during the night.

Armadale Castle intercepted the Norwegian barque *Polarstjernen* in Latitude 62.50´ North, Longitude 9.12´ West from Frederickshaven to Galveston, in ballast. She was allowed to proceed on giving guarantee to call at Barbadoes.

Orvieto informed me that the Officer of the Armed Guard who had taken in the Danish sailing vessel *Rosenhjem* reported that the Master had told him that he was approached at New York with a view to signing on as part of the crew German Officers from Ships interned in America. He further stated that he knew of similar cases where Germans had succeeded in getting through in this manner.

I met *Patuca* about 6 p.m. and conferred with Captain Dannreuther, whilst a telegraphist rating from *Patuca* was being examined by the W/T Officer on my Staff, *Alsatian* and *Patuca* continuing on patrol.

11. Saturday, 3 March – The weather again became threatening, and by the evening it was blowing hard from the South-East.

The Armed Trawler *Walpole* intercepted the Norwegian barque *Durban* in Latitude 58.18´ North, Longitude 6.65´ West, from Santa Cruz to Copenhagen, and escorted her in to Stornoway. This vessel had been fired on and holed by a German submarine, and her rigging also carried away in places.[1]

The Norwegian steamer *Opland* from Bergen to Norfolk, USA, intercepted by *Patuca* in Latitude 62.19´ North, Longitude 8.50´ West, was allowed to proceed on giving a guarantee that she would call at Halifax.

The Sailing Vessel *Frederick Lawrence* from Frederickshaven to Savannah was also allowed to proceed on undertaking to call at either Halifax or Bermuda, whichever proved to be most convenient.

At 1 p.m. I met the Special Service Trawler *King Lear* at a pre-arranged rendezvous and gave her orders for patrol, a copy of which are attached. Unfortunately her disguise, that of the small Swedish SS *Temis*, was not very good, the Swedish colours on her side being painted wrongly. The Officer in command appears smart and intelligent [310].

12. Sunday, 4 March – The gale continued, several ships being obliged to lie to, *Ebro* reported losing a life raft overboard in the heavy sea.

Some difficulty was experienced in dealing with Ships that could not be boarded owing to the weather. At 3 p.m. *Ebro* intercepted the Norwegian Sailing Vessel *Najade* from Galveston to Aalborg and was obliged to stand by her until 8 a.m. on 6 March before being able to board [322 para. 12].

At 7 p.m. *Armadale Castle* on her way in to Swarbacks Minn reported intercepting the Norwegian Steamer *Bonna* with a general cargo from Christiania to Boston. As she was unable to board I directed her to turn the vessel over to *Patuca* and then proceed in accordance with previous orders.

I met *Arlanza* at 9.30 a.m. and succeeded in getting a boat to her for despatches in spite of the heavy sea. *Arlanza* then proceeded to B Patrol.

I inspected the Ship's Company of *Alsatian* at Divisions and also went round the mess decks and sleeping quarters, etc. The men are very well dressed and their quarters very clean and well kept, the general state of the Ship reflecting great credit on Flag Captain Humphrey H.

[1]*Durban*'s troubles had only just begun. Her cargo was mahogany, and she was given formal permission to sail on to Copenhagen (presumably after being repaired), but then held up because no ships were being permitted to sail for Denmark at the time. The delay lasted all through April as well (TS 14/14 of 12 March 1917 *et al.*). The submarine which fired on her is not known.

Smith, Commander Norman M.C. Thurstan and Lieutenant Commander Alfred Freer, RNR (First Lieutenant).[1]

The disposition of the Squadron at noon was as follows:

A Patrol, line ahead 320° from Lat. 63.20´N, Long. 8.45´W, steering 320° and 140° … *Changuinola*, *Avenger*, *Virginian*.
B Patrol, crossing line 320° from Lat. 62 N, Long. 10 W, steering 320° and 60° … *Patuca*, *Armadale Castle*, *Otway*.
C Patrol, crossing line 360° from Lat. 58.45´N, Long. 10.30´W, steering 260° and 80° … *Motagua*, *Hilary*, *Ebro*, *Champagne*.
Between B and C Patrols … *Alsatian*.
D Patrol, between Rockall & 10 W … *Artois*.
E Patrol, off NW Iceland … *Almanzora*, *Andes*.
St Kilda Patrol … Armed Trawlers *Walpole*, *Arley*, *Robert Smith*, *Saxon*.
Special Patrol … Special Service vessel *King Lear*.
Joining Patrol … *Arlanza*, *Orvieto*.
Proceeding to Clyde … *Moldavia*.
At Liverpool … *Victorian*.
At Clyde … *Gloucestershire* (from Special Service), *Hildebrand*, *Columbella*.
At Scapa … *Kildonan Castle* (from Special Service).
At Swarbacks Minn … *Patia*.
At Oban … Armed Trawlers *Rushcoe*, *Tenby Castle*.
On Special Service … *Orcoma*.

During the week 58 vessels were intercepted, of which 7 were sent in with, and 8 without, Armed Guards.

13. Monday, 5 March – The SE gale increased somewhat accompanied by heavy snow squalls and occasional mist. The majority of ships were hove to.

At 2 p.m. *Patuca* took over the *Bonna* from *Armadale Castle* in Latitude 61 North, Longitude 12.53´ West, and later in the evening made an attempt to board, but without success.

Kildonan Castle left Scapa at dusk to rejoin Patrol having been absent on special service since 10 January.

About 11 p.m. *Champagne* reported she had intercepted the Norwegian Steamer *Ro*, *Norge* in Latitude 58.53´ North, Longitude 8.54

[1]Thurstan, Norman M.C., DSO, RN, Lieutenant 1906, Commander 1916, Commander (retired) in *Fervent* 1940.

Freer, Alfred, RNR, Lieutenant 1907, Lieutenant-Commander July 1915, Commander 1919.

West, steering 60°, and allowed her to proceed as she was flying the correct Flag of the day and it was too rough to board. As the vessel could not be traced I directed *Hilary*, *Kildonan Castle*, and *Cochrane* to endeavour to cut her off, and asked *Champagne* for further details, to which she replied that the vessel, besides the Norwegian colours, had RO painted on her side followed by the word NORGE, was a ship with one funnel and two masts, and was fully loaded. As the flag of the day which *Champagne* reported she was flying has been checked and found correct, it is considered possible that for some reason *Champagne* only made out the first two letters of the ship's name. She did not ascertain the port of departure nor to what port the ship was bound.

14. Tuesday, 6 March – The gale moderated somewhat, but it was still blowing hard and misty with snow squalls. *Armadale Castle* reported intercepting the Norwegian SS *Ranenfjord* in Latitude 62.55´ North, Longitude 7.28´ West from Christiania to New York with wood pulp and a general cargo. The American Minister from Roumania, with his Staff, was on board. She was allowed to proceed on giving a written guarantee to call at Halifax.

At 8 a.m. *Patuca* boarded *Bonna* and, having found her correct, allowed her to proceed after obtaining a guarantee that she would call at Halifax.[1]

I met *Orvieto* and transferred orders to Commodore Luard regarding the conduct of Patrols during my absence.

At 11.50 a.m., *Kildonan Castle* reported sighting a periscope in Latitude 61.13´ North, Longitude 3.40´ West.

At 6.10 p.m. *Hilary*, in Latitude 59.22´ North, Longitude 9.15´ West also reported that a supposed periscope had been sighted several times by a Midshipman at a distance of about one mile. Earlier in the day – about 6 a.m. – in about the same position, she had reported sighting a bright light for the space of about two minutes, which then disappeared. A search of the area produced no result.

I accordingly ordered C Patrol to move 60 miles to the Westward.

At dusk, as neither *Hilary*, *Kildonan Castle* nor *Cochrane* had seen anything of Norwegian SS *Ro*, I ordered them to resume patrol.

At 9.30 p.m. I received a priority message from the Commander-in-Chief to move all Patrols to the Westward of 17 West. Ships of A, B and C Patrols were thereupon ordered to take up the following disposition:

A Patrol, consisting of *Changuinola* and *Virginian*, 30 miles apart, to

[1]The Contraband Committee considered *Bonna* several times during March and April, apparently expecting the ship to be brought in (TS 14/14).

cross line 300° from Latitude 62.45´ North, Longitude 20 West, steering 240° and 60°.
B Patrol, consisting of *Arlanza*, *Patuca*, *Otway*, *Patia*, and *Avenger*, 30 miles apart, to cross line 360° from Latitude 60.30´ North, Longitude 18 West, steering 240° and 60°.
C Patrol, consisting of *Motagua*, *Hilary*, *Ebro* and *Kildonan Castle*, 30 miles apart, to cross line 360° from Latitude 57.30´ North, Longitude 18 West, steering 240° and 60°.
Between B and C … *Orvieto*.

Two Trawlers were ordered to work in the neighbourhood of Rockall to maintain W/T touch with the Squadron, the remainder patrolling between Latitude 57.15´ North and 58.30´ North, and Longitude 8.30 West and 10 West.

Today I completed one year in Command of the Tenth Cruiser Squadron. During this period 3478 Ships have been intercepted of which 877 were sent in with Armed Guards for further examination. Although several attacks have been made on individual Ships by submarines, no Ship has been hit by torpedo. There has been one collision, viz: between HMS *Columbella* and SS *Fife*, resulting in damage to the bow of the Cruiser and the sinking of *Fife*.

In spite of the dangerous nature of the work carried out by the Squadron, cruising without lights, intercepting ships night and day in all weathers, boarding them, placing Armed Guards on board, and conducting them in safety to their various destinations, there has been no loss of life and only one Cruiser has received injuries, though two Officers and one man have unfortunately been taken prisoners by enemy submarines while performing Armed Guard duties.

I would respectfully submit that great credit is therefore due to Officers in Command of Cruisers and Trawlers, Navigating Officers, Officers of Watch, Boarding Officers, Boarding boats' crews and Officers and men of Armed Guards, for admirable seamanship and conspicuous courage.

318. *Contraband Committee Minutes*

21 February 1917

Quote from Neutral Tonnage Committee, 19 February 1917:

'Steamship *Tricolor* proceeding in ballast to Newport News, is reported by the Admiralty as having been intercepted by the patrols while attempting to evade the blockade. She was ordered into

Kirkwall, but the crew refused to work the ship. Owing to the impossibility of providing a large enough prize crew to work the ship in face of these difficulties, no course was left open but to allow her to proceed on a written undertaking from the master that she would call at Halifax. It was stated that the crew was engaged for the voyage on articles which excluded the vessel from calling at United Kingdom ports.'

Halifax should be asked to ascertain whether this applies to the homeward voyage as well as to the outward voyage, as if so this is a distinct break of the undertaking given by the owners. In the meantime a telegram should be sent to His Majesty's representative in Christiania to ascertain whether the articles on which the crew were engaged undertakes that the vessel shall not call at a British port, and the owner should be asked for an explanation, and until a satisfactory explanation is given the steamship *Artemis* should be detained at Halifax.[1]

319. *Sub-Lieutenant Chas E. Elliot, RNR (Ty)*[2] *to Commanding Officer, HMS* Alsatian

HMS *Alsatian*, 22 February 1917

I have the honour to report that on the 18th February 1917 in Lat. 61.24´N, Long. 12.20´W, I boarded the Norwegian SS *Stralsund* of Haugesund, from Reykjavik, bound for Genoa via Troon, with a cargo of dried fish, and in accordance with your orders directed the Master to proceed for the latter port.

Course was set to pass 10 miles west of St Kilda. We proceeded on this course – south – until 9 a.m. next day, during which time we were boarded by HMS *Patuca* and allowed to proceed. The weather then being overcast and heavy, so that the possibility of getting observations appeared to be improbable, course was altered to S by E, to enable me to check our position by the lead. Wind freshening speed had decreased from eight to six and a half knots. At 12.30 p.m. on the 15th St Kilda was sighted on the port bow and abeam at 2 p.m., distance 7 miles. Course was continued S by E, to pass 10 miles off Barra Head.

At 4.20 p.m. I was in the Captain's cabin, when I heard the engine room telegraph ring. Immediately going up to the bridge, I was just in

[1]Investigations continued. *Tricolor* turned out to be owned by the 'British Consul at Tonsberg', and had been given instructions to call at Halifax on her outward voyage; *Artemis* had already been released (TS 14/14 of 12 March 1917).

[2]Elliott, Charles E., RNR, Sub-Lieutenant 1916, Lieutenant 1918.

time to hear a gun fired, heard a shell pass overhead, and saw it fall about 200 yards on our starboard beam. With the aid of binoculars I saw a submarine on our port beam at 5 miles distance steering 270° – straight for us, apparently coming from the lee of Monarch Island. Seven more shots followed in rapid succession all passing over the ship, which was then stopped. The closest shot appeared to pass at least 60 yards over. At 4.35 p.m. submarine submerged. I at once asked the Master to go full speed and try to escape, but he refused to get underway for fear he should be torpedoed. All hands were by this time on deck and the two life boats were lowered. Leading Seaman Lewis, RNR, who was with me as armed guard came to me on the bridge, and I ordered him to go below and disguise himself, which he proceeded to do with considerable success. I then lashed all my written orders and papers, charts, etc., to our rifle and revolvers, ready to throw overboard if boarded. I gathered that the submarine was on her way towards us, and on Leading Seaman Lewis's return to the bridge, leaving instructions to be told if anything was sighted, I went below, and taking a better uniform from a case, placing the old one inside with overcoat and cap, hid same in the coal bunkers. Then putting some old clothes I found in a cabin, over my uniform as a disguise, I returned to the bridge.

At 5 p.m. I saw a periscope 12 or 15 hundred yards away coming towards us at about 5 knots. At 10 or 15 yards away the submarine turned and went some 200 yards astern where she came to the surface.

Meanwhile I tried to get hold of the Master's papers to destroy the crew lists, etc., but without success – he was in a most excitable state and refused to allow me to touch his papers. I then warned him not to mention the fact that he had been intercepted by a British man-of-war, and under no circumstances whatever to give away the presence of an armed guard on board. I found that my suggestion that he would have a bad time in England if he got there without me seemed to have some effect upon him.

I then gave Leading Seaman Lewis particulars of the position and description of the submarine, where she had appeared from, etc., with orders that, in the event of my being taken prisoner, he should report same immediately to the authorities on shore. It was then that I noticed that I had left £10 advanced in *Alsatian* in my suit case below.

The submarine lay to, and the Master, without direct orders left the ship with three of his men and proceeded with all his papers on board. She meanwhile hoisted International Code Signal AB, which I got the Mate to look up, and obeyed by promptly abandoning ship. I told Lewis to get into the remaining life boat with six of the crew, and as the boat was not large enough to hold any more, I and the three remaining men swung out a small boat on the starboard side, where, being out of sight of the enemy I dropped bundle of papers and firearms overboard. I abandoned ship at 5.40 p.m. The Master had meanwhile reached the submarine and one Officer and a German seaman left her in the same boat (as I learned from the Master afterwards) with four bombs, and went on board *Stralsund*. 20 minutes later, from a distance of 200 yards I heard two explosions, and a quarter of an hour after that the vessel sank by the stern. It was now getting dark; the Master left the submarine with his three men, hailed and joined us, and the three men in the dinghy transferred to the Master's life boat and set the dinghy adrift.

I then asked the Master what information he had given to the submarine officer and he assured me our presence was not disclosed. All his papers, however, including lists of crew, had been taken, and he had been given what appeared to be a receipt for the vessel of which I afterwards took a tracing. Fearing the submarine might approach to count the crew in the boats, I gave instructions for Lewis to keep out of sight in the bottom of the boat, and also kept out of sight myself. At 6.30 p.m., I noticed submarine making off on the surface steering a course of about 90° – apparently going back towards Monarch Island.

Having made fast the painter to one another we hoisted sail in each boat and set course for St Kilda. The wind was SSW, force 3 to 4, sea 3 or 4 also. To keep ourselves from getting chilled in our wet clothes all hands took spells at the oars. We continued hard rowing and sighted St Kilda about 12 p.m. The Master insisted on trying to pass between the islands and only after nearly capsising did he consent to beat round. At 2.20 p.m. on 16th we were under lee of St Kilda, finding no opportunity of landing, the weather promising, we decided to make for Flannan Islands in the hope of meeting a patrol boat on passage. After another hour's pulling we saw the lights of a vessel. Tying my handkerchief to a boat hook, I got the boatswain to pour some paraffin over it, and setting it alight he waved it over his head. The vessel, which proved to be HM Trawler *Rushcoe* promptly switched off lights and turned away. We then all joined in hailing her and were picked up at 3.30 p.m. The Lieutenant in command was very good to us and made us all comfortable with dry clothes and food, etc.[1]

We reached Stornoway at 10.30 p.m, and at 12 p.m. a drifter took all hands ashore. The crew of *Stralsund* and Ldg Seaman Lewis were provided for and I reported in the S.N.O.'s Office. I left Stornoway with Lewis on the morning of the 19th having drawn the necessary money to

[1]This was, of course, the successful John T. Randell.

provide clothing, etc., and reached *Alsatian* at Northern Base at 10.30 p.m. on 21st Feby.

I would mention that the submarine appeared to be about 300 feet in length; she was painted dark grey, had one periscope, no masts, but a guard wire running up from the bow to the conning tower and down to the stern, one gun between the conning tower and the stern which appeared to be a 12 pdr, 8 cwt, and was seen to be in position as the submarine came to the surface. At one time I noticed five Germans on board and one man in the conning tower keeping a careful lookout with binoculars.

From the Master I learned that she had two decks below. She has wireless (of which I could see nothing however). The Master told me he had been closely questioned in Danish by the submarine Officer as to the latest news from America and her attitude towards Germany. He was asked whether he knew of Germany's last declaration with regard to the prohibited area round Great Britain, and was told that on that account his ship and in fact, everything else afloat in the area would be sunk. The submarine Officer went on to say he had been out for 40 days and intended to return to Germany in 10 days' time. He inquired whether any of the shots had hit the *Stralsund* and said he intended hitting her. The Master was given his position and course to steer for Monarch Island.

I was instructed by the SNO Stornoway, to state herein that the Master of the *Stralsund* had been given £30 as a reward for not disclosing the presence of armed guard.

320. *Vice-Admiral Tupper to Commander-in-Chief Home Fleets*

HMS *Alsatian*, 22 February 1917

In accordance with your Minute HF 0220/633 of 21 February 1917 I have the honour to submit the following remarks on the case of the SS *Yarrowdale* [cf. 300 para. 15].

1. The principal cause of the *Yarrowdale* being able to get through undetected would undoubtedly appear to be the small number of ships actually on patrol at the time, which unfortunately at the period had reached its lowest mark, being only five.

2. *Columbella* up to within 24 hours of *Yarrowdale* passing the Faroes, was in fact patrolling across the route she is supposed to have taken, but it was then necessary to send her in to coal – without being able to fill her place immediately – as she had already been kept out beyond her proper date.

3. A table showing the disposition of the Tenth Cruiser Squadron at midnight 24–25 December is attached. From this it will be seen that five ships (including *Kildonan Castle*) were absent from patrol owing to their having been detailed for special service, one ship was reduced to Care and Maintenance Party, and one was still fitting out.

Of the remaining 17, five were absent refitting under the ordinary routine, which should have left twelve available for actual patrol work. No less than *six* of these, however, had been delayed at their Southern Base beyond their normal time. In two cases, the delay was due to a strike of Boilermakers at Liverpool, and in three others owing to the time taken to mount new guns, the shortage in the labour market possibly being responsible for the delay to some extent.

I have previously drawn attention to the delays which have occurred in the overhaul and refit of vessels belonging to the Tenth Cruiser Squadron in my submission No. 782/29 of 5 December 1917 addressed to the Secretary of the Admiralty, a copy of which was sent to you.

4. A tracing showing the movements of ships actually in the Patrol areas during 24th and 25th December is also enclosed.

Disposition of Tenth Cruiser Squadron, 24–25 December [1916]:

A Patrol … *Patia*, *Columbella*.
C Patrol … *Orvieto*, *Avenger*, *Hilary*.
Rejoining from Swarbacks Minn … *Alsatian*.
Rejoining from and at Southern Bases –
Rejoining from Liverpool … *Andes*, *Victorian*, *Virginian*.
At Liverpool … *Otway*, *Teutonic*, *Armadale Castle*.
Rejoining from Clyde … *Kildonan Castle*.
At Clyde … *Hildebrand*, *Motagua*, *Changuinola*, *Ebro*, *Patuca*, *Moldavia*.
At Brest … *Artois*.
On Detached Service … *Almanzora*, *Arlanza*, *Orcoma*, *Gloucestershire*.

321. *Surveyor F. Atkinson to Collector Aberdeen*

Lerwick, 27 February 1917

Formal protests against seizure for Prize Court [have been made] by:

Dauntless, Danish sailing ship, arrived 13 October 1916.[1]
Herlo, Norwegian steamship, arrived 7 October 1916.[2]
Godthaab, Danish steamship, arrived 27 October 1916.[3]
Glenesk, Norwegian sailing ship, arrived 23 October 1916.[4]
Guri, Norwegian sailing ship, arrived 30 January 1917.[5]
Arlastor, Norwegian sailing ship, arrived 22 January 1917.[6]

322. *Admiralty to the Under Secretary of State, Foreign Office*

3 March 1917

I am commanded by My Lords Commissioners of the Admiralty to acquaint you, for the information of the Secretary of State for Foreign Affairs, that they have received a report to the effect that on the 23rd January, HM Trawler *Robert Smith* sighted, in Latitude 57 N, Longitude 9.27´W, a large four-masted steamer which refused to stop when ordered, but passed the *Robert Smith* steaming to the South West. Steps were then taken to intercept her, and the French Cruiser *Champagne*, which is attached to the Northern Patrol, eventually boarded the Danish SS *Fionia*. On being questioned, the master stated that the trawler had not been seen, but, judging from the description given by the *Robert Smith* and from the course and speed of the vessel first sighted, My Lords are convinced that the *Fionia* must have been the vessel referred to [300 para. 18].

I am accordingly to request that, if Mr Balfour sees no objection, the matter may be brought to the notice of the owners of this vessel, whose

[1]*Dauntless*, carrying a cargo of salt fish and fish oil, fell foul of the ration of such products for Norway, and its cargo went to the Prize Court (TS 14/11 of 14 October 1916).

[2]*Herlo*, with 70 tons of fish from the Faeroes to Norway, was ordered to be discharged to the Prize Court, because the consignee (who was not the one named on the manifest) refused to cease trading with Germany (TS 14/11 of 10 and 21 October 1916).

[3]*Godthaab*, carrying fish and other goods, had the fish sent to the Prize Court (TS 14/11 of 23 and 24 October 1916).

[4]*Glenesk*'s problem cannot be located; no doubt its cargo was prize-courted like the rest in this list.

[5]*Guri*, carrying fish from the Faeroes to Stavanger, also fell foul of the Norwegian fish embargo and the cargo went to the Prize Court (TS 14/13 of 31 January and 3 February 1917) with the comment that it was believed to be destined for the enemy.

[6]See page 594, note 1.

attention should be drawn to the fact that the ship is laid open to considerable risk of being fired upon, if the master refused to stop when ordered.

323. *Vice-Admiral Tupper to Commanding Officer HMS* King Lear

3 March 1917

On parting company you are to proceed to shape course as if making for Kirkwall, arranging to cross the 100 fathom line in the afternoon. After dark you should alter course to the westward, and at noon the following day shape course for the Butt of Lewis, crossing the 100 fathom line about 3 p.m. After dark you should again put out to sea and this time approach St Kilda from the North West as if en route for the Clyde, arranging as before to cross the 100 fathom line four or five hours before dark. Then proceed to Oban via the Sound of Mull, reporting yourself on arrival to Lt-Col Heaton Ellis,[1] the Competent Naval Authority, who will give you any assistance you require as regards coaling, obtaining provisions etc, and altering your appearance.

2. After coaling and provisioning etc, at Oban and two days' rest, you should put to sea and on the lines laid down in paragraph 1 arrange to cross the 100 fathom line from the Westward

(1) Towards Tory Island.
(2) Towards St Kilda.
(3) At various points further north as time permits.

When necessary to return to harbour you should proceed to Swarbanks Minn, requesting Admiral Fawckner to report your arrival to me, and await further orders after completing with coal and stores.

3. Your speed whilst on patrol should not as a rule exceed 8 knots.

4. Owing to mines, you should not approach Skerryvore within 16 miles. A copy of the latest Admiralty Message relative to the use of Sound of Mull and Firth of Lorne is also enclosed for your information.

[1]Heaton-Ellis, Charles Henry Brabazon, Kt, CBE (1864–1945), Bedfordshire Regiment from 1885, Indian Civil Service 1875–1901 (interpreter of Tamil, Telugu, Persian, Hindustani, Russian), served under Admiralty 1914–1919.

11

THE SUCCESSFUL BLOCKADE, MARCH–JUNE 1917

The Patrol's effectiveness increased, so much so that in the spring of 1917 it was probably at its least penetrable. This was, in part, due to the increased number of ships on patrol, but also to the use of Halifax, Nova Scotia, as an examination port. At the same time the number of ships which had to be sent in for examination steadily reduced [e.g., 324 para. 18 compared with 357 para. 2]. The Navicert system, the control and rationing of British bunker coal supplies to neutrals and, above all, from April 1917 the participation of the United States in the war, meant that most vessels had been placed under control before they sailed.

The steadily increasing effectiveness of the British measures contributed to the German decision to wage an equally increasingly effective submarine campaign. As a result the spring of 1917 saw the vessels of the patrol much more at risk from attack than ever before, and two were sunk, *Hilary* [349], and *Avenger* [360], while *Motagua* was damaged by a mine as she approached Swarbacks Minn [324 para. 7]. More time was spent in rescue and in fighting off submarines than ever before – but this was, in a sense, what the patrol's original purpose had been. One of Tupper's responses was to ask for a Seaplane Carrier [344, 348, 359], an imaginative response considering the decisive effect of air power on the submarine campaign in Hitler's War.

These two developments in fact also signalled the beginning of the end of the Northern Patrol. As the control of shipping at the ports became complete, the Patrol's usefulness on the high seas began to decline, and the vulnerability of the ships to submarine attack became steadily more obvious. Already in early June it was noted in the Admiralty that sending in sailing ships was hardly worthwhile [353], and steamers were effectively controlled by their need for fuel and docking accommodation. This was a sign that the whole Northern Patrol was under consideration once more.

324. *Vice-Admiral Tupper to Admiralty*

HMS *Avenger*, 29 March 1917

Report of Proceedings, 8–29 March 1917

***

1. Thursday, 8 March – *Avenger* succeeded in boarding the Norwegian Steamer *Skogland*, from Narvik to Philadelphia, with a cargo of minerals, and obtained a written guarantee from the Master to call at Halifax. *Avenger* had been standing by this vessel since 6th instant, having been prevented from boarding and identifying her by the heavy weather.

At 11.30 p.m., orders were received from the Commander- in-Chief, Grand Fleet, through the Admiralty, to move the 10th Cruiser Squadron to Patrol Line IV, all vessels keeping to the westward of Longitude 20 West. The Admiralty message ordering this movement was timed at noon, but owing to the distance to the Westward, W/T communication was difficult and messages were delayed in transmission.

Orders were accordingly given for C and B Patrols to move forthwith to centre line Longitude 21 West, nine ships patrolling for three hours on each side of this line from Lat. 57 N to Lat. 61 N. A Patrol was placed in line ahead 340° from Lat. 61.30´ N, Long. 21 W, the two ships being forty miles apart.

On the assumption that the movement of the patrols to the westward had been ordered on account of the submarine menace, W/T Communication was suspended in the Squadron, except for urgent messages.

As it was impossible for the Armed Trawlers, working in the vicinity of St Kilda, to be supported any longer by a Cruiser, the Senior Officer of the Trawlers was directed to take charge, withdrawing from Rockall the trawler stationed to maintain touch with *Motagua*. He was further directed to employ the trawlers in case of necessity for escorting to the Butt of Lewis Patrol any vessels intercepted.

Virginian left patrol for Swarbacks Minn and was warned to take extra precautions against submarine attack during passage.

2. Friday, 9 March – The patrols got into station on their new lines during the forenoon.

As difficulty in obtaining W/T communication with the Commander-in-Chief Grand Fleet, continued, permission was asked to employ *Orvieto* as W/T link, patrolling at high speed on meridian of 11 W.

3. Saturday, 10 March – At 10 a.m. orders were given to resume normal W/T communication.

At the same hour, *Hildebrand*, in Lat. 55.40´N, Long. 9.54´W, picked up a boat with the Master and fifteen men from the Defensively Armed British Steamer *Newstead*, which had been torpedoed by German Submarine *U-39* on 3 March in Lat. 51.54´N, Long. 13.23´W.[1] The survivors were suffering from exhaustion and unable to be moved for some days, so directions were given to *Hildebrand* to relieve *Almanzora* on B Patrol and transship them for passage. Admiralty and Commander-in-Chief, Grand Fleet, were informed, and a full report from *Hildebrand* has already been forwarded …

Changuinola left A patrol at midnight for Swarbacks Minn thus reducing A Patrol to one ship, which was ordered to patrol sixty miles, 340° from Lat. 61.30´N, Long. 21 W.

4. Sunday, 11 March – At 5 a.m. the Commander-in-Chief's approval was received for *Orvieto* to patrol on 11th meridian of West Longitude and act as a W/T link. *Orvieto* proceeded East accordingly.

At noon the disposition of the squadron was as follows:

A Patrol, 340° from Lat. 61.30´N, Long. 21.00´W ... *Patia*.

B Patrol, 360° from Lat. 59.30´N, Long. 21 W, steering 250° and 70°, patrolling three hours each side of centre line … *Arlanza*, *Patuca*, *Otway*.

C Patrol, 360° from Lat. 57 N, Long. 21 W, steering 250° and 70°, patrolling three hours each side of centre line … *Motagua*, *Hilary*, *Ebro*, *Kildonan Castle*.

E Patrol, North-West of Iceland, off Isafjord … *Almanzora*, *Andes*.

Proceeding to Patrol on Meridian of 11 W, between Lat. 60 N & 61 N … *Orvieto*.

St Kilda Patrol … Armed Trawlers *Rushcoe*, *Saxon*, *Tenby Castle*.

Proceeding to Liverpool … *Avenger*.

Proceeding to Swarbacks Minn … *Changuinola*.

Rejoining Patrol … *Hildebrand* (from Clyde), *Armadale Castle* (from Swarbacks Minn).

At Swarbacks Minn … *Virginian*.

At Clyde … *Artois*, *Champagne*, *Moldavia*, *Gloucestershire*, *Columbella*.

At Oban … Armed Trawlers *Arley*, *Walpole*, *Robert Smith*.

[1]The submarine was actually *U 44*.

Special Service Vessel ... *King Lear*.
On Special Service ... *Orcoma*.[1]

During the week, 23 vessels were intercepted and examined, of which 3 were sent in with Armed Guards and 6 signed guarantees to call at Halifax or other British Colonial port outside the United Kingdom.

Armadale Castle reported boarding, in Lat. 62.39´ North, Long 14.14´ West, at 2 p.m., the Swedish SS *Helsingborg*, from New York to Landskrona with barley. The firemen refused to work on an Armed Guard being placed on board to take the Ship to Kirkwall, and *Armadale Castle* stood by awaiting instructions.

... [D]irections were issued to *Armadale Castle* that such firemen as absolutely refused to work the ship should be taken on board the cruiser, being first warned of the danger they were thus running, and the fact pointed out that, when approaching Kirkwall, *Helsingborg* would be escorted into port. Orders were also given for a minimum naval crew to be placed on board to replace the firemen, and to deal with those remaining in case of trouble, and for the ship thereafter to be sent to Kirkwall.

The Master and entire crew of *Helsingborg* eventually refused to work the ship, and a naval crew was accordingly put on board. The Master protested against being taken into a United Kingdom Port, on account of the German proclamation. *Armadale Castle*, whose W/T apparatus had been temporarily out of action owing to a small fire, reported that the Master and crew of *Helsingborg* had not been taken on board the cruiser, as it was considered that they would probably assist, to some extent, in working the ship, the crew of 23 included 3 women, and further, the weather was unfavourable for transferring them. In the circumstances, *Armadale Castle* was directed to chase the ship whilst Admiralty instructions were requested. W/T communication with Admiralty could not, however, be established, and in the meantime, *Armadale Castle* reported sighting another vessel. Orders were issued to her to intercept the latter and then to resume patrol [325].[2]

On coming into W/T touch with Admiralty (4.10 a.m. the following morning) the circumstances of this case were reported ...

I concur in the action Commander England took in the matter. Taking into consideration the fact of women forming part of the crew, the bad weather for transfer and the submarine menace during transfer, the

[1]Tupper has omitted *Victorian* and *Alsatian*, his own flagship, from the list.

[2]See page 655, note 1. The behaviour of the crew naturally fuelled British suspicions, but need not have been any the less fearful for all that.

patrols being West of 20 West owing to submarine activity, the proper course was, I consider, to send the ship to Kirkwall without delay. She arrived safely on 15 March.

5. Monday, 12 March – *Otway*, *Ebro* and *Motagua* left patrol during the day for Liverpool, Clyde and Swarbacks Minn respectively, and C patrol was therefore disposed in line ahead 360° from Lat. 57.30´ N, Long. 21 W, two ships – and the distance apart of the three ships remaining on B patrol altered to forty miles.

In the afternoon information was received from the Senior Naval Officer, Swarbacks Minn, that the trawler sweep had sunk three mines off Eshaness. *Changuinola*, which was due to arrive at Swarbacks Minn next morning, was ordered to patrol in a position North West of the Faeroes.

At midnight orders were received from the Commander-in-Chief Grand Fleet, to take up Patrol line III and directions were given accordingly.

6. Tuesday, 13 March – During the day ships proceeded east to take up Rockall–Iceland patrol. A large number of ships (eighteen) were intercepted by the patrols during the day.

Information was received from the Senior Naval Officer, Swarbacks Minn, in the evening, that channels were considered clear. *Virginian* left Swarbacks Minn and *Changuinola* and *Motagua* were given orders to arrive on 15th March.

7. Wednesday, 14 March – At 6.30 a.m. the British Steamer *Tortuguero* made a signal in plain language that she was being chased and shelled by a submarine in Lat. 56.10´N, Long. 11.12´W. *Moldavia* answered the call as 'any British-man-of-war', directed the *Tortugeuro* to steer for Rockall and proceeded at full speed towards the vessel in distress. *Moldavia*'s position at 9 a.m. was Lat. 58.12´N, Long. 13.14´W (i.e. after steering south for 1½ hours), as she had been stationed south of C patrol during the night to carry out rendezvous with ships of that patrol early in the morning.

Moldavia was immediately ordered to abandon chase and carry out her previous orders.[1]

At 4.35 p.m. *Saxon* reported sighting a submarine on the surface in Lat. 57.10´N, Long. 9.37´W, steering East. *Rushcoe* and *Tenby Castle* were ordered to proceed to the position, but they were too far away to attempt to be of any help. It was not possible to obtain further details owing to *Saxon*, who was proceeding to Fleetwood, getting out of W/T touch.

[1]It would seem that *Tortuguero* escaped.

At 11.20 p.m., information was received from the Senior Naval Officer Swarbacks Minn, that a loud explosion had been heard after dark in St Magnus Bay and he did not consider ships should enter or leave until the Bay had been thoroughly swept. Orders were therefore immediately issued to *Changuinola* and *Motagua* – which were due to enter during the dark hours of the night, to stand off. Similar orders were subsequently given them by Commander-in-Chief Grand Fleet.

8. Thursday, 15 March – *Almanzora*, *Virginian* and *Moldavia* joined B patrol during the day, and *Patuca* left for Loch Ewe. B patrol was therefore disposed in line abreast forty miles apart, with centre line 340° from Lat. 60.20´N, Long. 15.10´W, five ships.

In the afternoon, information was received from the Senior Naval Officer, Swarbacks Minn that he considered the entrance to that port clear, so *Changuinola* and *Motagua* proceeded to enter during the dark hours in accordance with the previous orders of the Commander-in-Chief, Grand Fleet.

9. Friday, 16 March – At 3 a.m., *Changuinola* arrived safely at Swarbacks Minn.

At 4.15 a.m. an 'Urgent' signal from *Motagua* was received reporting being struck by a torpedo forward. Subsequent messages, however, showed that at 3.15 a.m. in a position S 35 W magnetic, 6½ miles from Eshaness, she had struck a mine. Although extensively damaged, she managed to reach Swarbacks Minn at 7.30 a.m. *Motagua*'s full report of this occurrence has already been forwarded. Three mines were subsequently found by the sweep near the position in which *Motagua* struck, and the port was then closed by Admiralty order until extensive sweeping operations had been completed.[1]

Gloucestershire had reported the previous day that the Navigating Officer was suffering from appendicitis and, although not acute, his condition necessitated hospital treatment. *Gloucestershire* had accordingly been ordered, on the way to E Patrol, to transfer him to *Patia* for passage, but, owing to thick fog, these ships were unable to effect a rendezvous. *Orvieto*, however, succeeded in meeting *Gloucestershire* in spite of the fog, and took the sick Officer for transfer to *Patia* the following day. *Gloucestershire* then proceeded to E Patrol.

At 7 p.m. a signal was intercepted from *Achilles* to Commander-in-Chief, Grand Fleet, stating that *Achilles* and *Dundee*

[1]Admiral Fremantle describes this incident in his autobiography, *My Naval Career*, London, 1949, 215–216, implying that he had only just arrived, though it seems clear (from e.g. [313]) that he had been at Swarbacks Minn since January or February.

had been in action with a raider in Lat. 64.54´N, Long. 0.23´E, at 4 p.m. The last six groups read 'Raider (four groups missed owing to interference) escaped'.

On this information being received, a W/T silence was ordered in the Tenth Cruiser Squadron.

10. Saturday, 17 March – In the middle watch it was ascertained from intercepted signals that *Achilles* and *Dundee* had sunk the raider. Normal W/T communication was accordingly resumed.[1]

The wind and sea got up from the Westward towards evening and ships on patrol had to reduce speed.

11. Sunday, 18 March – *Almanzora* reported that one of the survivors from the British steamer *Newstead* had died of heart failure. He was buried at sea and *Almanzora* was directed to inform the owners on arrival at Southern Base.

At noon the disposition of the squadron was as follows:

B Patrol, 340° from Lat. 60.20´N, Long. 15.10´W, steering 250° and 70° ... *Almanzora*, *Armadale Castle*, *Virginian*, *Moldavia*.
C Patrol, 340° from Lat. 58.30´N, Long. 14 W, steering 250° and 70° ... *Hilary*, *Kildonan Castle*.
E Patrol, North West of Iceland off Isafjord ... *Andes*, *Gloucestershire*.
Patrolling between 63 N, 10 W and 65 N, 10 W ... *Orvieto*.
St Kilda Patrol ... Armed Trawlers *Rushcoe*, *Tenby Castle*, *Walpole*.
Rejoining Patrol ... *Artois*, *Champagne* (From Clyde.)
Proceeding to Loch Ewe ... *Hildebrand*.
At Swarbacks Minn ... *Changuinola*, *Motagua*.
At Liverpool ... *Otway*, *Avenger*, *Alsatian*, *Victorian*.
At Clyde ... *Ebro*, *Columbella*.
At Oban ... Armed Trawlers *Arley* and *Robert Smith*, Special Service Vessel *King Lear*.
At Loch Ewe ... *Patuca*.
At Fleetwood (Refitting) ... Armed Trawler *Saxon*.
On Special Service ... *Orcoma*.[2]

Thirty-nine ships were intercepted and examined during the week, of

[1]The raider was *Leopard*, the former British ship *Yarrowdale* which had been taken by *Moewe* and had reached Germany by the northabout route [300, para. 15; 320]. *Dundee*'s RNR commander was promoted for the action, becoming almost the only RNR officer to reach the rank of captain.

[2]*Alsatian* and *Victorian* have been returned to the list; *Patia* and *Arlanza* are now missing; this last was certainly on patrol (see para. 13).

which two were sent in with, and four without, armed guards. Of this number sixteen were Eastbound and nine Westbound Neutrals.

The weather remained bad during the day and prevented boarding.

12. Monday, 19 March – In the afternoon *Arley* and *Robert Smith* reported having proceeded to Tobermory for shelter.

Robert Smith having received damage to forward gun platform and pedestal, was directed to return to Oban for repairs.

13. Tuesday, 20 March – At 4.30 a.m. *Arlanza* reported observing in Lat. 60.54´N, Long. 13.40´W, a very bright light, three miles distant, which disappeared suddenly.

At 10.45 a.m. *Arlanza* intercepted in Lat. 60.45´N, Long. 13.31´W, the small Danish Schooner *Rolf* (about 200 tons) from Cadiz to Bergen with a cargo of salt. This ship had been previously intercepted by *Armadale Castle* and, as the weather prevented boarding and the *Armadale Castle* was proceeding to Liverpool, the ship had been directed to call at Kirkwall. It seemed, however, when again intercepted, that the *Rolf* might possibly have some connection with the bright light seen by *Arlanza*, so directions were given for an armed guard to be placed on board, the Vice-Admiral Commanding Orkneys and Shetlands being informed of the circumstances and requested to have a thorough examination of the vessel carried out on arrival. Information has since been received that the *Rolf* arrived Kirkwall on the 25th March.[1]

The *Artois*, *Champagne* and *Patuca* arrived in the patrol area during the day, so arrangements were made to dispose B and C patrols in line abreast with four and three ships respectively.

14. Wednesday, 21 March – *Changuinola* left Swarbacks Minn in the evening to rejoin patrol.

Having obtained permission from the Commander-in-Chief Grand Fleet to do so, I transferred my flag to *Avenger* as *Alsatian* could not be ready for sea until 31 March.

At 9 p.m. *Avenger* undocked and anchored in the Mersey.

During the time the *Avenger* had been preparing for sea I visited the Admiralty and conferred with the First Lord, First Sea Lord, Chief of Staff and Director of Trade Department on various matters connected with the Blockade and the Tenth Cruiser Squadron generally.

Although in Weekly Bulletin of Trade Information No. 6 page 2, paragraph 1, it is stated that it is most necessary that all Neutral Ships proceeding West in ballast should be sent in with a view to making them

[1]*Rolf* was not detained.

carry cargoes of coal to our various coaling stations en route, I was instructed verbally that it is not advisable to send in vessels in ballast for examination especially during the present submarine activity. I am adopting this policy and allowing ship in ballast to proceed until I hear to the contrary …

I also paid a visit to the Foreign Office and conferred with Rear-Admiral Sir D.R.S. De Chair on Blockade matters.

A visit to Portsmouth was also paid by me to see three of the Trawlers at present fitting out at that port for service with the Tenth Cruiser Squadron. This enabled me to ask for certain small alterations and additions which will render them more efficient for the special work they have to perform.

I have asked that the 12 new Trawlers should in the first instance call at Oban and there receive their Patrol Orders so that they can be doing useful work on their cruise North to Swarbacks Minn.

Auxiliary Patrol Craft are urgently necessary in the neighbourhood of the 100-fathom line between St Kilda and Sulisker. I submit it is most desirable to have two or three 'P' vessels, if they can be spared, working in that locality which is a highway for German Submarines. The Trawlers are not fast enough to deal efficiently with them, but are of course much better than nothing.

15. Thursday, 22 March – At 6 a.m. I left Liverpool in *Avenger* to rejoin Patrol. Some trawlers and drifters were seen sweeping off Donaghadee and the Yacht *Zara* near Rathlin Island; no other men-of-war were seen. *Avenger* proceeded by N channel (crossing 100-fathom line 2 a.m. 23 March).

At 6 p.m. *Hilary* left patrol for Clyde, *Changuinola* being directed to take her place on C patrol.

Hildebrand arrived at Loch Ewe at daylight and, after Captain Grant-Dalton had transferred command to Captain H.C. Watson,[1] left in the evening to rejoin Patrol.

In the evening, *Robert Smith* sailed from Oban to rejoin Patrol, having completed repairs to gun and pedestal.

16. Friday, 23 March – At noon *Hildebrand* boarded in Lat. 58.53´N, Long. 9.30´W the Norwegian SV *Edderside* from Buenos Aires to Nyborg with a cargo of Oilcake, and sent her in to Stornoway with an Armed Guard. The Master reported that his ship had been boarded by a German raider of about 6000 tons on 6th March, in approximately Lat.

[1]Watson, Horace Cradock, RN, Commander 1911, Captain 1916, Captain of *Hildebrand* 1917–1919, retired 1922.

26 N, Long. 47 W, and was allowed to proceed.[1] This report was passed on to Admiralty and Commander-in-Chief …

At 4 p.m. I met *Orvieto* and took over charge Patrol from Commodore Luard and said good-bye to him. I am sorry to lose his services and trust Their Lords Commissioners of the Admiralty will see fit to acknowledge his good work during the eleven months that he has assisted me as Senior Commodore. During the 5 intervals of about 14 days each whilst my flagship has been coaling and refitting at Southern Base, Commodore D.S. Luard has commanded the blockading squadron in an efficient manner.

On parting company with *Orvieto*, I despatched her to cruise between B and C patrols during the night, thence to proceed to take charge of C patrol.

About 6 p.m., *Arlanza* boarded the British Admiralty oiler *Mina Brea* in Lat. 60 N, 12.16´W bound from Port Arthur to Kirkwall. The Master reported having heard the Raider distress signal BBT from MNT (apparently the SS *Cambrian*) in approximately Lat. 46.20´N, Long. 42.35´W, on 17 March, the signal being repeated continually for 20 minutes, and then suddenly stopping. This was reported to Admiralty and Commander-in-Chief, Grand Fleet ….[2]

At 8 p.m., a signal from *Shannon* to the Vice-Admiral Commanding Orkneys and Shetland was intercepted, stating that the Norwegian Motor Ship *Nosted IV* had been boarded in Lat. 62.32´N, Long. 3.40´W, bound for Bergen with a cargo of salt, and allowed to proceed. This vessel had been intercepted on 2nd March by *Alsatian*, and sent to Stornoway with an Armed Guard, but the Armed Guard were forced to relinquish the vessel at Thorshavn on 12 March owing to the refusal of the crew to work the ship to a British Port. I do not know why *Shannon* let her proceed, but probably as Admiralty had released her at Thorshavn it was not considered good policy to put an Armed Guard again on board.

Directions were given to the Armed Trawlers to move their patrol area North, in accordance with orders received the previous evening from the Commander-in-Chief Grand Fleet, to keep them working off the Hebrides to the Northward of Lat. 58.30´N, between Saturday 24 March and Friday 30 March.

[1]*Edderside* was inspected and investigated and allowed to sail on (TS 14/14 of 26 March 1917); the German ship was presumably *Moewe*, which returned to Wilhelmshaven on 22 March after cruising the mid-Atlantic since November.

[2]If this was a raider's deed, it will have been *Moewe*, but that ship reached Kiel on 22 March, so it seems unlikely; otherwise no raider is known in the area. *Cambrian* may, in fact, simply have used the 'raider' signal to get rapid help.

Since the ships were moved to Patrol Line IV and subsequently to Patrol Line III, the trawlers have ceased to be supported by a ship on C patrol and it was not considered advisable, both on account of shortage of ships and the reports of submarines north of Lat. 56 North, to station D Patrol. A ship in support has, however, not been required, all traffic now apparently passing further North on account of Germany having declared a war area.

The weather was rough during the day; strong South-Westerly wind and considerable sea.

17. Saturday, 24 March – *Artois* reported at 9 a.m. sighting a flat floating object at a distance of 3 miles, which disappeared after a few seconds.

At 10 a.m. met *Hildebrand* with a view to conferring with her new Captain, and explaining to him his duties, but the state of the sea rendered it inadvisable to communicate by boat.

At 11 a.m., *Champagne* intercepted the Norwegian four-masted barque *Leif Gunderson* in Lat. 62.39´N, Long. 14 W, bound from Baltimore to Odense with Corn and reported that the sea was too rough to permit of boarding, requesting instructions. … I directed *Champagne* to detain the barque until able to board, and then to send her to Kirkwall or Stornoway with strong Armed Guard. The interception of this vessel was reported to Admiralty …

Shortly before noon, *Virginian* reported having intercepted in Lat. 62.20´N, Long. 13.41´W, the Danish SS *Lilleborg*, from Copenhagen to New York, via Halifax, in ballast. As it was too rough to board, I directed *Virginian* to accompany the vessel till dusk, and if then still too rough to board, to make her lie to with lights. In the meantime Admiralty instructions were requested … .

Otway (rejoining from Liverpool) was ordered to cruise between Lat. 62 and 63 N on meridian of 11 W until *Champagne* and *Virginian* finished dealing with the respective vessels they were detaining and were able to resume patrol.

In the evening, received Admiralty Telegram 915 Q, stating that the Port of Liverpool had been closed pending further orders.

18. Sunday, 25 March – At 4 a.m., Admiralty Telegram 1805 of the previous evening was received, requesting fuller details of the raider which had intercepted the Norwegian SV *Edderside*. As no further particulars were known to me, and the vessel had arrived at Stornoway, the contents of this Admiralty Message were passed to the Rear-Admiral Stornoway, Admiralty being informed accordingly … .[1]

[1]*Edderside* sailed on to Rotterdam next day – page 648, note 1.

At 8 a.m., a signal was received from *Champagne* reporting that she had succeeded in boarding, and sending to Stornoway with Armed Guard the *Leif Gunderson*. The Tenth Cruiser Squadron Armed Trawlers off Flannan Islands were ordered to look out for the vessel and escort her to port, if met. *Walpole* subsequently picked her up, and escorted her to safety, Rear-Admiral Stornoway sending a Tug and Whaler to relieve *Walpole*. By this system of escorting from 100-fathom line it is hoped to get all vessels in safety to examination ports [334].[1]

At 9.30 a.m., *Otway* reported having boarded, in Lat. 62.8´N, Long 11.8´W the Dutch SS *Westerdijk* and *Gallia*, from Rotterdam to Sandy Hook, in ballast. A German Stowaway was found on board *Westerdijk* who stated that he had been a foreman in a German Munition factory and had deserted. I gave orders for him to be made prisoner. The two vessels were allowed to proceed, having given guarantees to call at Halifax.

At 10 a.m. *Ebro* was met. Her new Commanding Officer, Commander Charles A.W. Wrightson[2] – whom I had not previously seen – came on board. I conferred with him as to his duties on blockade and then despatched *Ebro* to E patrol to relieve *Andes* who was now due to return to Liverpool.

At 11 a.m. *Virginian* boarded the *Lilleborg* and having obtained from the Master a Guarantee to call at Halifax, allowed her to proceed ….[3]

Shortly before noon, *Avenger* boarded the Norwegian SS *Feistein*, a Belgian Relief Ship, in Lat. 61.27´N, Long. 13.50´W, from Philadelphia to Rotterdam, with a cargo of wheat. The vessel having a Green Clearance from Halifax, was given the flag of the day, and allowed to proceed to Rotterdam.

At noon, the disposition of the Squadron was as follows:

[1]Concealed mail was found [see 334], and partly as a result the French government claimed the ship as prize on the grounds that it was a capture by *Champagne*. Vice-Admiral Tupper's report was decisive, as quoted in the Contraband Committee minutes: 'the course of the vessel when intercepted in Lat. 62.39´N, Long. 14 W was 90°, speed 11 knots, wind WSW, carrying press of sail, and that the Master appeared to have had no intention to call at a British port, and was very angry at being sent in to Stornoway'. If the ship was moving at such a speed, no doubt the Master's chagrin was based on more than annoyance at British blockade rules. But one can sense Tupper's seaman's admiration beneath it all (TS 14/14 of 10 to 24 April 1917).

[2]Wrightson, Charles Archibald Wise, CBE, RN (1874–1953), Commander 1909, Captain 1917 in *Ebro* 1917, retired 1922.

[3]*Lilleborg*'s failure to appear was commented on by the Committee, but mainly in respect of future cargoes (TS 14/14 of 31 March 1917).

B Patrol, Crossing Line 360° from Lat. 61.30´N, Long 15 W at 1400 and 2200, steering 240°, 30 miles apart ... *Hildebrand*, *Virginian*, *Champagne*, *Moldavia*, *Patuca*, *Otway* (Joining)
C Patrol, Crossing line 360° from Lat. 58.30´N, Long. 13.30´W at 0900 & 0300, steering 255° & 75°, 40 miles apart ... *Artois*, *Arlanza*, *Orvieto*, *Changuinola*.
E Patrol, North-West of Iceland off Isafjord ... *Andes*, *Gloucestershire*, *Ebro* (Joining.)
Between B & C Patrols ... *Avenger*.
St Kilda Patrol ... Armed Trawlers *Arley*, *Walpole*, *Robert Smith*.
Rejoining Patrol ... Special Service Vessel *King Lear* (from Oban).
At Swarbacks Minn ... *Motagua*.
At Liverpool ... *Alsatian*, *Almanzora*, *Armadale Castle*, *Victorian*.
At Clyde ... *Hilary*, *Kildonan Castle*, *Columbella*, *Patia*.
At Oban ... Armed Trawlers *Rushcoe*, *Tenby Castle*.
At Fleetwood (Refitting) ... Armed Trawler *Saxon*.
On Special Service ... *Orcoma*.

During the week, 47 ships were intercepted, of which 9 were sent in with Armed Guards, and 4 signed guarantees to call at Halifax. Of the total number intercepted, 7 were West-bound and 13 East-bound Neutrals.

At 6 p.m., *Ebro* reported boarding in Lat. 61.34´N, Long. 15.6´W, the Dutch SS *Noordijk*, from Rotterdam to New York. On a guarantee being given to call at Halifax, she was allowed to proceed. The master stated that there were two German stowaways on board the Dutch SS *Oostdijk* – due to pass through the patrols shortly. Ships were informed accordingly, but so far this steamer has not been seen.[1]

At 10 p.m. *Orvieto* left patrol for Liverpool.

Between 10 p.m. 23rd and 6 p.m., 25th March reports have been received of no less than 11 Dutch, 1 Belgian and 1 Danish steamships having been intercepted west-bound for Halifax, in ballast, and 1 Norwegian and 1 Belgian Relief Ship east-bound cleared from Halifax. As it appears probable that these west-bound vessels may communicate the positions in which they were intercepted to East-bound vessels, with a view to aiding the latter to arrange their passage through the patrols during darkness and thus have a better chance of evading them, the Commander-in-Chief was asked and approved that the Tenth Cruiser Squadron be moved to Patrol Line II, and then back to Patrol Line III during this week.

[1]*Oostdijk* was in fact considered by the Contraband Committee (TS 14/14).

I visited the Mess decks and sleeping quarters of *Avenger* and also inspected the men at divisions and was greatly pleased both with the appearance of the men and the cleanliness and tidiness of the ship. Below, the accommodation is most comfortable and well ventilated and warm.

19. Monday, 26 March – Weather improved; heavy swell.

At 11 a.m., *Avenger* intercepted in Lat. 61.38´N, 14.32´W, the Norwegian Oil Tank steamer *Conrad Mohr*, from Bergen to Halifax, in ballast. She was flying the correct flag of the day – having apparently been previously intercepted by the Second Cruiser Squadron Patrol, and was allowed to proceed.

Virginian was then met, despatches were transferred and Commander Wilding came on board to confer with me. I gave him orders to proceed to Liverpool.

Information was received early in the evening, from Oban, that the special service vessel *King Lear* was returning to that port in a damaged condition, caused by heavy weather.

At night, in accordance with the approval of the Commander-in-Chief, B and C patrols were moved to Line II, being disposed as follows:

B Patrol ... Crossing Line 320° from Lat. 62 N, Long. 11.10´W, at 2300 and 1300, steering 70° and 250°, four ships thirty miles apart.
C Patrol ... Crossing Line 320° from Lat. 59.40´N, Long. 7.30´W, at 0300 and 0900 steering 60° and 240°, three ships, 30 miles apart.

Avenger continued to cruise between B and C.

I stationed one ship on A patrol, steering 320° and 140° from Lat. 62.40´N, Long. 15 W to intercept vessels attempting to hug the South coast of Iceland.

During the day, several reports were received of submarines in the vicinity of St Kilda.

20. Tuesday, 27 March – Strong South Westerly Wind; heavy sea and snow squalls.

Vessels were now disposed on Patrol Line II.

In the middle watch, information was received that the port of Liverpool had been re-opened to traffic.

Virginian left patrol at 7 a.m. for Liverpool, and, at about 10 a.m., *Patia* sailed from Clyde to rejoin patrol.

During the forenoon *Moldavia* reported that her rudder post and blade were completely fractured at upper gudgeon rivets, rudder head and engine lifting two inches. She was ordered to leave patrol for the

Clyde, and *Avenger* proceeded to meet her in order that the details and extent of the damage might be more fully ascertained.

Moldavia was steering by engines only, and unable to maintain a speed of more than 10 or 12 knots, or to manoeuvre, and I considered it desirable that she should be escorted through the more dangerous portion of her route, a signal was made to the Commander-in-Chief Grand Fleet, and repeated to the Admiralty, requesting an escort, if possible, to meet her in Lat. 57.10´N, Long. 10.48´W, at 2 p.m., 29th March, and the assistance of a tug through the narrows off Rathlin at 6 a.m. 30 March.

Shortly before midnight the Commander-in-Chief informed me that two destroyers were being despatched to screen *Moldavia* to Clyde as requested, and a tug arranged for.

The Captain Superintendent Clyde has been requested to hold an enquiry into the cause of the damage on *Moldavia*'s arrival.

Hildebrand was directed to take *Moldavia*'s place on C patrol, *Avenger* relieving *Hildebrand.*

21. Wednesday, 28 March – Very fine day; light westerly wind, heavy swell.

At 4 a.m. information was received that Liverpool was again closed to traffic, owing to mines, and shortly afterwards, a signal from the Senior Naval Officer, Liverpool was intercepted diverting *Andes*, *Orvieto* and *Virginian* to Belfast.

At 9.15 a.m., *Patia* reported a case of enteric on board which had developed since leaving Clyde the previous day. The patient was transferred to *Virginian* for passage south.

At 9.20 a.m., in Lat. 62.10´N, Long 10.19´W, *Avenger* intercepted and sent to Stornoway with an Armed Guard the Danish 3-masted schooner *M. Hay* from Cadiz to Mandal (Norway) with a cargo of salt.[1]

Later in the forenoon *Avenger* intercepted the small Danish Ketch *William Martin* (TN 131) in Lat. 62.5´N, Long. 10.31´W from Iceland to Faeroes, with a cargo of salt cod fish. Out of a crew of 15, 10 were suffering from measles. Medical assistance was offered, but not required. The vessel was allowed to proceed.

About noon, *Orvieto* arrived at Belfast.

Early in the afternoon, *Moldavia* intercepted the Belgian Relief ship *Adolph Deppe* (1680 tons) in Lat. 60.4´N, Long. 14.41´W, but being unable to stop and board her she allowed her to proceed. *Changuinola*

[1]*M. Hay* was allowed to continue after inspection (TS 14/14 of 2 April 1917).

was ordered to endeavour to intercept the vessel, and subsequently succeeded in doing so [330, para. 1].[1]

Information was received that *Kildonan Castle* had sailed from Clyde during the forenoon, to rejoin patrol.

At 4 p.m., *Avenger* in Lat. 62.3´N, Long. 12.26´W boarded the Dutch SS *Leersum* from Baltimore to Amsterdam with a cargo of corn. The vessel had a green clearance from Halifax and was allowed to proceed.

Hildebrand was met, and her Captain came on board to confer with me, and then *Hildebrand* resumed patrol.

In the evening, information was received from Oban that *Walpole* had arrived at, and *Rushcoe* and *Tenby Castle* sailed from, that port.

***

325. *Contraband Committee Minutes*

19 April 1917

Letter from HMS *Armadale Castle*, dated 12th March [1917]: 'I have the honour to submit the following report on the interception of the Swedish steamer *Helsingborg*.

'The vessel was boarded at noon, the 11th inst., in Latitude 62.30´ North, Longitude 14.14´ West, steering 90.

'Her papers were in order, except that she had no Charter Party. The Master stated he had been informed by telegraph that ship was under charter to G. August Olssen, of Landskrona.

'Cargo of Californian barley. She had not called at a British port. On my placing a small armed guard on board, the Master informed my Officer that he could not proceed, as the firemen refused to work. He also handed in attached protest in duplicate.

'On receiving your cypher message timed 1540 (attached) I informed Master through Boarding Officer that I was prepared to take such firemen as refused to work on board *Armadale Castle* and replace them by my own men, also that ship would be escorted into Kirkwall etc.

'He then stated that neither he nor any of his crew would assist to work the ship in.

'With reference to his written protest, I made the following enquiries:

'1. Why, if he objected to being sent into a British port, did he not seek information from His Britannic Majesty's Consul at New York

[1] *Adolph Deppe*'s cargo was wheat; she was allowed to sail on, having been reported in advance (TS 14/14 of 10 March 1917).

before sailing? He replied: "Oh, he would have probably have told me to go to Halifax."

'2. Why did he object to calling at Halifax? Reply: Because he had no instructions from his owners to do so. I then had him informed that his apparent objection to going to Halifax for examination, coupled with his protest against being sent to a British port, caused me to look upon his cargo with suspicion and that as far as my responsibility went, I was determined to send him in for examination.

'My wireless had been broken down from 2.50 p.m. to 6.30 p.m., and with night coming on I decided to place on board 1 lieutenant and 1 sub-lieutenant, 6 seamen, 1 engineer lieutenant, 1 engineer sub-lieutenant, and 6 firemen, to take the ship to Kirkwall.

'The sea had been uncommonly bad for a boat all day, and it was with difficulty that the officers and men and their provisions were put on board.

'With reference to your 1540 and 1925, I had no doubt that the firemen refusing to work was only part of the scheme of passive resistance taken up by the Master and crew, and that when approaching the submarine area all hands would assist in view of the common danger.

'It appeared extremely probable that the crew would object to being transshipped on account of the weather, and that force might be necessary.

'There was distinct risk to life and limb getting into the boat alongside *Helsingborg*, and I therefore considered this course undesirable, in view of the complications which would ensue if one of them fell overboard and was drowned.'

A copy of this letter should be sent to the Procurator-General, together with a copy of the telegram from the S.O., 10th Cruiser Squadron to the Admiralty, stating that it certainly appears that the *Helsingborg* did not intend to call at a British port, and that if further information is required Captain England in *Orvieto* should be approached direct.[1]

[1]*Helsingborg*'s cargo of 2500 tons of barley was deemed by the Contraband Committee to be in reality destined for Germany, and was ordered to be discharged to the Prize Court; this was done at Leith on 2 April. Meanwhile the Committee raised with the Admiralty the issue of whether the ship was going to call at a British port without being instructed to do so, and this provoked the letter from Captain England. The matter reached the Procurator-General who wondered if the vessel should be prosecuted. The Committee thought not but recommended a detailed inspection of the ship's bunkers by the Customs. All this most satisfactorily took time, from 11 March to the end of April – and delaying the ship was probably the main object (TS 14/14 of 16 March to 26 April 1917 *passim*).

326. *Captain L.L. Dundas to Vice Admiral Commanding Tenth Cruiser Squadron*

HMS *Motagua*, 20 March 1917

… I attach reports of the Armed guard Officers who took the vessels in question into Kirkwall.

I am still more of the opinion that the SS *Belgien* and SS *Europa* had no intention of calling at Kirkwall and that they intended to evade the Patrol, since receiving the reports of Sub-Lieuts Loram and Johnson,[1] subsequent to my letter No. 1304, 5th February 1917 [327, 328, 329].

327. *Sub-Lieutenant A.J. Johnson, RNR to Captain L.L. Dundas, RN*

HMS *Motagua*, 20 March 1917

I have the honour to report that I was sent on board Danish SS *Europa* in charge of Armed Guard with orders to proceed from Patrol in Kirkwall on the 3rd February.

Shortly after arriving on board, the Captain asked the name of the patrol vessel I was attached to and as to whether her name was HMS *Hilary*. He also said, 'If the snow squall had lasted half an hour longer the *Europa* would have evaded the patrol and been able to proceed to her destination.'

On the passage to Kirkwall, during conversation, the Captain informed me that following instructions he had 'shut out' a portion of the cargo at Baltimore, thereby enabling the *Europa* to carry sufficient bunkers for the return passage to the USA; but on account of rough weather on the first passage, he thought he would hardly have sufficient. The Captain also said: 'All vessels stopped by German submarines in the North Sea were sunk, if they had called at Kirkwall on the voyage.'

He was very inquisitive as regards the movements of the patrols, and asked if the vessel I was attached to went to Glasgow sometimes, but I evaded giving an answer.

[1]Loram, Douglas S., RD, RNR, Midshipman 1912, Sub-Lieutenant 1916, Lieutenant 1919, Commander (retired) in 1940.

Johnson, Albert T., RNR, Sub-Lieutenant 1916.

328. *Sub-Lieutenant D.S. Loram, RNR, to Captain L.L. Dundas, RN*

HMS *Motagua*, 22 March 1917

I have the honour to report that during the time I was on board the Danish SS *Belgien* taking her from patrol to Kirkwall for examination, I was in conversation with the Captain of SS *Belgien* who informed me that he had no orders from his owners to call at Kirkwall and therefore he had no intention of calling there until I boarded him.

On our arrival at Kirkwall at 11.05 a.m. on Sunday, February 4th, 1917, the examination officer boarded, and the Captain of the SS *Belgien* informed him that although he had no orders from his owners to call at Kirkwall he intended to do so, even if he had not been boarded by the Patrol, he also stated that the vessel had enough coal for fuel purposes to take the vessel back to America after reaching his terminal port, Copenhagen, without calling at a British port.

The statement of the Captain of the SS *Belgien* made to the Boarding Officer at Kirkwall re calling at Kirkwall was in direct contradiction to the statement he made to me before arriving at Kirkwall. I informed the Boarding Officer of this when he boarded.

329. *Admiralty Report, by Flag Captain for Vice-Admiral*

26 March 1917

Interception of Danish SS Europa and Belgien

***

2. The positions in which these vessels were intercepted and the courses they were steering do not in themselves suggest that they were attempting to evade the patrols.

Europa was intercepted at 12.30 p.m. on 3 February in Latitude 59.20´N, 9.30´W, steering 85° and *Belgien* at 12.30 p.m. on 2 February in Latitude 59.58´N, 8.6´W, also steering 85°.

330. *Vice-Admiral Tupper to Admiralty,*

HMS *Alsatian*, 9 April 1917

Report of Proceedings, 29 March–8 April 1917

***

1. Thursday, 29 March – Heavy NE–ENE gale accompanied by frequent snow squalls.

At 9 a.m. *Changuinola* reported having intercepted the Belgian Relief Ship *Adolph Deppe* in Latitude 61.17´ North, Longitude 10.22´ West (vide paragraph 21 of my Report of Proceedings No. 246/35 of 29 March [324]), but was unable to board. In the afternoon, however, the weather had sufficiently moderated to permit this being done, when the vessel was found to be in possession of a green clearance from Halifax, and was accordingly allowed to proceed. *Changuinola* then returned to her position on patrol.[1]

At 9.30 a.m. information was received that *Virginian* had arrived at Belfast, and during the afternoon, that *Orvieto*, *Virginian* and *Andes* had sailed from that Port for Liverpool. At about 9 p.m., however, news was received that Liverpool had been again closed owing to mines and that the three latter vessels had been diverted by Admiralty Orders to Clyde. For the same reason *Armadale Castle* and *Almanzora*, which were both now due to leave Liverpool for patrol, were detained in port.

At about 6.30 p.m. *Artois* intercepted in Latitude 59.53´ North, Longitude 6.45´ West, the Danish Sailing Vessel *Havila*, from Buenos Ayres to Svenborg, with a cargo of maize, and sent her to Stornoway with an Armed Guard.[2]

During the course of the evening, I gave orders for B Patrol to move 30 miles to the Westward, Ships to be in their new position at 6 a.m. next morning.

Patia was ordered to relieve *Patuca* on A Patrol but she had to lay to as did most of the Ships.

2. Friday, 30 March – The gale continued throughout the day.

At 6 a.m. *Moldavia* reported that she had been joined by her Destroyer escort and was progressing favourably. She arrived safely at Clyde at 11 a.m.

Owing to the congestion at Liverpool and Clyde, due to the closing of the former Port, and the consequent shortage of Ships on patrol, I

[1]See page 654, note 1 and [324, para. 21].

[2]*Havila* was not detained.

ordered *Arlanza*, who was now due to return to Liverpool, to proceed to Loch Ewe and take in 60% of coal. She accordingly left C Patrol at 2 p.m., her place being taken by *Changuinola*.

Kildonan Castle rendezvoused with *Avenger* in the course of the forenoon to deliver despatches, but was unable to communicate. Owing to the state of the sea throughout the day, no boarding could be done.

3. Saturday, 31 March – Gale still very heavy with violent snowstorms.

At 2.30 a.m. *Robert Smith* reported having lost sight of the Norwegian Sailing Vessel *Fiskaa* in a blizzard, in Latitude 58.25´ North, Longitude 8.50´ West. This vessel had been intercepted on 26 March by *Changuinola* and sent to Stornoway with an Armed Guard. She had been picked up by *Robert Smith*, in accordance with orders, on 30 March, and was being escorted to the Butt of Lewis when lost sight of. *Robert Smith* and *Arley* were ordered to search for her during the remainder of the day, and resume escort, if found. They did not, however, succeed in doing so.[1]

At 8 a.m. *Patia* (rejoined from Clyde) communicated with *Patuca* and transferred ratings for Ships on E Patrol. This transfer had been delayed owing to the weather being too severe to permit of boarding. *Patia* then relieved *Patuca* on A Patrol, *Patuca* proceeding south to transfer the ratings to *Avenger* where they could await a favourable opportunity for transshipment to the Ships now working on E Patrol.

During the forenoon there was a short lull in the gale, and I met *Kildonan Castle* and received despatches. On parting company *Kildonan Castle* was ordered to take the Northern position on C Patrol, in charge.

Shortly afterwards the gale again increased in violence with a very heavy sea.

In the afternoon *Otway* intercepted the Belgian Relief Ship *Otta* in Latitude 63 North, Longitude 13.47´ West, from Halifax to Rotterdam with wheat, and *Hildebrand* the Belgian SS *Liege*, in Latitude 62.5´ North, Longitude 12.36´W, with provisions. In both cases, the weather was reported too rough to board, and I directed *Otway* and *Hildebrand* to shadow the respective Ships until it moderated sufficiently to permit of boarding.

Arley and *Robert Smith* left patrol for Oban during the evening.

At 11 p.m., information was received that the Port of Liverpool had

[1]*Fiskaa* had great difficulty in getting to Stornoway, and was sunk in the attempt (para. 11).

been re-opened to traffic. During this day the decks and masts of *Avenger* were covered in snow and ice, the Ship pitching and rolling heavily.

4. Sunday, 1 April – Gale still very heavy.

During the middle watch, Admiralty telegram No. 847 was received, requesting information as to whether the Norwegian Sailing Vessel *Leif Gunderson*, which had been sent to Stornoway with an Armed Guard by *Champagne* on 25 March, was intercepted in such circumstances as to suggest that she did not intend to call at a British Port for examination. On enquiries being made from *Champagne*, she reported that the course of the vessel when intercepted in Latitude 62.39´ North, Longitude 14 West, was 90°, speed 11 knots, wind WSW carrying press of sail, and that the Master appeared to have no intention of calling at a British Port and was very angry at being sent in to Stornoway … .[1]

At 8.30 a.m. *Kildonan Castle* reported sighting a supposed submarine about an hour previously, in Latitude 60.6´ North, Longitude 9.55´ West, 400 yards on her port quarter. On further enquiries being made, it was ascertained that the origin of the report was the sighting of 'steam rising from a submerged object' by the Officer of the Watch. *Avenger* had sighted a whale the previous day under similar conditions, and I consider that the object sighted by *Kildonan Castle* was almost certainly a whale also.

Patuca was met at 9 a.m. during a lull after heavy snow, and ratings for E Patrol transferred to *Avenger*. On parting company, *Patuca* was ordered to proceed to Clyde.

At 10.20 a.m. information was received that *Almanzora* and *Armadale Castle* had sailed from Liverpool to rejoin patrol. During the forenoon, C Patrol was ordered to move 60 miles to the Westward.

At noon, the disposition of the Squadron was as follows:

C Patrol, Proceeding to a line 360° from Lat. 59 N, Long. 10.30´ crossing 0200 steering 80°, and 1000 steering 260°, Ships 30 miles apart … *Artois*, *Changuinola*, *Kildonan Castle*.

B Patrol, Crossing line 320° from Lat. 62 N, Long. 11.10´W at 0200 steering 60°, and 1000 steering 240°, Ships 30 miles apart … *Hildebrand*, *Champagne*, *Otway*.

A Patrol, Steering 320° and 140° from Lat. 62.40´N, Long. 15 W in southern position noon and midnight daily … *Patia*.

Between B & C Patrols … *Avenger*.

[1]See [324 para. 17] and page 650, note 2.

E Patrol, North-west of Iceland, off Isafjord … *Gloucestershire*, *Ebro*.
St Kilda Patrol … Armed Trawlers *Rushcoe*, *Tenby Castle*.
Rejoining Patrol … *Almanzora*, *Armadale Castle*, from Liverpool.
Proceeding to Clyde … *Patuca*.
Proceeding to Oban … Armed Trawlers *Arley*, *Robert Smith*.
At Swarbacks Minn … *Motagua*.
At Liverpool … *Alsatian*, *Victorian*.
At Clyde … *Orvieto*, *Andes*, *Virginian* (whilst Liverpool closed to traffic).
At Oban … Armed Trawler *Walpole*, Special Service Vessel *King Lear*.
At Loch Ewe … *Arlanza*.
At Fleetwood (refitting) … Armed Trawler *Saxon*.
On Special Service … *Orcoma*.[1]

During the week 50 Ships were intercepted, of which 6 were sent in with Armed Guards and 8 signed guarantees to call at Halifax. Of the total number intercepted, 12 were westbound and 19 eastbound neutrals.

Liverpool now being open *Orvieto*, *Andes* and *Virginian* left Clyde for that Port.

Patuca at about 8 p.m. intercepted the Danish Sailing Vessel *Ebenezer*, in Latitude 58.54´ North, Longitude 11.33´ West, from Savannah to Aalborg, with a cargo of oilcakes. As the weather was too rough for boarding, and *Patuca* was proceeding to her Southern Base, I directed *Artois* to relieve her, and to stand by the Ship until able to board.

At night, as *Hildebrand* was still following the *Liege* eastwards until able to board, *Avenger* took *Hildebrand*'s place on B Patrol.

5. Monday, 2 April – The weather having moderated somewhat, *Artois* was able to board the *Ebenezer*, and put an Armed Guard on board with orders to take the Vessel to Stornoway [337].

Hildebrand also succeeded, during the forenoon, in boarding the *Liege* in Latitude 62.25´ North, Longitude 8.34´ West. The Vessel had a green clearance from Halifax and was accordingly allowed to proceed on her voyage, *Hildebrand* being ordered to return to her position on B Patrol and relieve *Avenger* who had been taking her place.

At noon, information was received that *Orvieto*, *Andes* and *Virginian* had arrived at Liverpool.

[1]Three ships – *Moldavia*, *Hilary* and *Columbella* – omitted.

During the course of the afternoon, *Otway* boarded the *Otta* and, her papers proving correct, allowed her to proceed.

Orders were received from the Admiralty for *Andes* before leaving Liverpool, to embark the French Consul at Reykjavik and Mr George Copland[1] for Passage to Iceland …

During the course of the day *Columbella* reported intercepting the Norwegian Sailing Vessel *Fiskaa*, hove to, in Latitude 57.11´ North, Longitude 11 West, see paragraph 3 of this letter, and *Patuca* the Danish Sailing Vessel *Thalassa*, which had been sent in by *Andes* in Latitude 57.30´ North, Longitude 11 West.[2] The Rear-Admiral Stornoway, was informed with a view to Auxiliary Patrol Vessels picking up and escorting the vessels, if possible.

Information was received that the Norwegian Sailing Vessel *M. Hay* sent in by *Avenger* on 28 March had arrived safely at Stornoway. She had been picked up by *Tenby Castle* on 31 March in Latitude 58.33´ North, Longitude 7.29´ West, and escorted to Butt of Lewis.[3]

6. Tuesday, 3 April – I took the opportunity while in *Avenger* to witness target practice. Four runs of Aiming Rifle were first of all carried out, and then heavy gun practice took place, 5 rounds per gun being fired. There was a considerable improvement in the manner in which the firing was carried out on this occasion.

At noon information was received from Liverpool that *Orcoma* had arrived at that Port, after an absence of nearly 4 months on detached service and later that *Alsatian* having satisfactorily completed her gun trials, had sailed for patrol. During the evening *Columbella* took *Changuinola*'s place on C Patrol to enable her to rendezvous *Avenger* before proceeding to Clyde. *Almanzora*, rejoined from Liverpool, took *Kildonan Castle*'s place on C Patrol, the latter vessel being ordered to cruise between B and C patrols during the night.

In the course of the day *Avenger* intercepted 5 vessels, none of which, however, had to be sent in under Armed Guard.

7. Wednesday, 4 April – At 10 a.m. *Changuinola* was met and I went on board to witness target practice. In spite of a somewhat heavy sea, the practice was very good. I went round the messdecks and inspected the crew's sleeping quarters, and was well satisfied with the general appearance and cleanliness of the Ship. The Ship was generally efficient.

[1]I have not been able to identify Copland.

[2]For *Fiskaa* see also paras 3 and 11 and page 659, note 1; *Thalassa* was not detained.

[3]See page 653, note 1.

At noon *Armadale Castle* (rejoined from Liverpool), relieved *Champagne* on B Patrol. *Champagne* then left for Swarbacks Minn.

During the afternoon *Kildonan Castle* was met and Captain Warton,[1] whom I had not previously seen, came on board. I conferred with him as to his duties on Blockade work in the Tenth Cruiser Squadron. On parting company *Kildonan Castle* was despatched to rendezvous *Patia* on A Patrol to transfer ratings, thence to take Southern position on B Patrol.

When *Kildonan Castle*'s boat returned and was about to be hoisted it was swamped owing to the fault of the winchman. Fortunately, no one was hurt.

At 5.p.m. *Alsatian* heard distress signals S.O.S and B.B.T from an unknown steamer being chased by an enemy submarine in Latitude 55.33´ North, Longitude 13 West. Owing to the 'Raider' distress signal being used, *Alsatian* which was about 50 miles away, turned and proceeded to the position indicated. Shortly afterwards, however, a further signal was intercepted to the effect that the steamer had escaped from the submarine, and *Alsatian* then resumed her former course. The signal B.B.T was evidently made in error.

8. Thursday, 5 April – Cold with strong NE breeze.

At 6 a.m. *Arlanza* boarded in Latitude 59.57´ North, Longitude 6.57´ West, the British Oiler *Tuscarora* from Immingham to New York, in ballast. *Arlanza* reports that the vessel had been 3 days out, but had only been given the clearance flag for 2 days.

Rushcoe and *Tenby Castle* having intercepted a message from St Kilda stating that an enemy submarine had been sighted on the surface steering towards a Sailing Vessel about 9 miles North of St Kilda at once proceeded to that locality. Whilst on their way, another submarine was sighted steering NE, which altered course to westward. *Rushcoe* opened fire but her shots fell short. The submarine fired 6 shots in return none of which, however, did any damage and then submerged.[2]

The Sailing Vessel in distress was sighted shortly afterwards, being shelled by a submarine, and while the trawlers were 6 miles off, she was observed to sink. The Vessel proved to be the Danish Sailing Vessel *Ebenezer*. *Rushcoe* picked up a boat containing the Armed Guard from

[1]Warton, John Fenwick, CMG, CBE, RN (1877–1950), Commander 1908, Captain 1916, Captain in *Kildonan Castle* 1916–1919, took part in the British mission to North Russia and White Sea, Rear-Admiral 1928.

[2]The identity of this submarine is not known; it may have been *U 46*, which sank *Fiskaa* on the 8th.

Artois, and the crew, but nothing further was seen of the submarine [337].[1]

Rushcoe was directed to land the survivors at Oban. Shortly before noon, orders were received from the Admiralty to despatch *Kildonan Castle* to Clyde, using O Channel and directions were issued accordingly.

At noon I met *Alsatian* and transferred my flag, *Avenger* being despatched to relieve *Gloucestershire* on E Patrol. During the period spent in *Avenger*, I was very satisfied with the efficient manner in which the duties as Flagship were performed. These duties entailed a considerable amount of extra work on the Captain and Officers which was performed with zeal and ability.

At 6.30 p.m. in Latitude 61.4´ North, Longitude 14.8´ West, *Alsatian* intercepted what proved to be the Dutch Cruiser *Holland*, returning to Holland from Vigo. In view of the many ruses adopted by the enemy during the course of this War, I did not approach within 8000 yards and I considered it my duty to make absolutely certain as to her identity. With this end in view I asked that I might be allowed to send an Officer on board to see the Captain, whose name I ascertained to be *Kapitein ter Zee* J.H. Zeeman. Having received permission to do so, I sent one of the Officers on my staff, Lieutenant-Commander Kenyon RN, to give my compliments to the Captain and ask whether I could be of any service to him. He was received in a friendly manner.

***

9. Friday, 6 April – At 8 a.m. *Columbella* in Latitude 59.24´ North, Longitude 8.18´ West intercepted the Admiralty Oiler *Powhatan*, bound for Kirkwall, and reported that an escort was required. The Admiral Commanding Orkneys and Shetlands was informed accordingly.

Rushcoe in Latitude 56.5´ North, Longitude 8.5´ West intercepted the Danish Sailing Vessel *Havila* which was proceeding to Stornoway with an Armed Guard from *Artois* on board. As *Rushcoe* reported that the mainsail and lower topsail of the *Havila* had carried away, I ordered her to escort the vessel and turn her over to the Barra Head Patrol. The Rear-Admiral Stornoway, was informed.

At 11.30 a.m. a signal was received from the Commander-in-Chief Grand Fleet, directing that the orders which had been conveyed in his Message 2140 of the 22 March relative to the Patrol area of the Armed Trawlers (vide paragraph 16 of my previous Report of Proceedings No.

[1]This submarine was *U 57*.

246/35 of 29 March 1917 [324]) were to be resumed and that the Trawlers were not to go South of Latitude 58.30´ North, unless for rescue work or on receipt of distress calls. The Trawlers were accordingly directed to work in an area between Latitude 58.45´ North and 59.13´ North and Longitude 7 West and 8 West until further orders.

During the course of the forenoon *Motagua*, having completed the temporary repairs rendered necessary by her recent accident, sailed from Swarbacks Minn for Liverpool.

At 4 p.m. *Alsatian* in Latitude 61.30´ North, Longitude 12.33´ West, intercepted the Norwegian SS *Bollsta* from La Plata to Christiania via Las Palmas with a cargo of salt and Meat, steering 65°. The Master stated that he intended calling at Lerwick, but in view of the position and course of the vessel when intercepted this was considered doubtful, and an Armed Guard was placed on board with orders to take the Vessel to Kirkwall.[1]

At about 5.30 p.m. *Tenby Castle* and *Walpole* sighted and engaged a submarine on the surface in Latitude 58.22´ North, Longitude 8 West, steering 80°, which immediately submerged. About 6 p.m. submarine was again sighted and fired on, *Tenby Castle* claiming to have made two hits with her 12 pounder, one of which struck the bottom of the Conning Tower and apparently caused the submarine to heel over and sink. A large quantity of oil extending over 1/2 mile was found on the surface, and *Walpole* fired a Depth Charge over the spot where the submarine was last seen – Latitude 58.24´ North, Longitude 7.44´ West. A further report will be forwarded when full information has been received [336].

During the day I reorganized A, B and C Patrols as follows:

> A Patrol to steer 10° for 120 miles from Latitude 63 North, Longitude 12.20´ West, in southern position 180° daily, one Ship.
> B Patrol to cross line 360° from Latitude 61.20´ North, Longitude 14 West at 1000 steering 260° and 0200 steering 80°, 4 Ships 30 miles apart.
> C Patrol to cross line 360° from Latitude 59 North, Longitude 12 West at 0900 steering 270° and 0300 steering 90°, three Ships 30 miles apart.

Gloucestershire reported that the passage to the North West of Iceland was about 40 miles wide, the ice pack extending from the South West through Latitude 66.35´ North, Longitude 25.50´ West, Latitude

[1] *Bollsta* was allowed to sail on (TS 14/14 of 10 April 1917).

66.55´ North, Longitude 24.30´ West, Latitude 67.5´ North, Longitude 22.40´ West, and thence to the Northward.

10. Saturday, 7 April – During the day the wind got up from the South West and by nightfall it was blowing hard.

At 1 a.m. *Otway* boarded the Norwegian SS *Mexicano* in Latitude 62.20´ North, Longitude 15.5´ West, from Christiania to Halifax. She was allowed to proceed on giving a written guarantee that she would call at the latter Port.

At 10 a.m. *Otway* was met and I went on board. As it was Saturday routine I did not go round the mess decks, but the Ship did not appear to be so clean as when I was last on board.

Information was received that the Port of Liverpool had again been closed to traffic owing to mines.

Motagua sank a floating mine by gun fire in Latitude 57.31´ North, Longitude 6.49´ West.

11. Sunday, 8 April – The wind veered to the North-west and blew with a great violence throughout the day accompanied by a very heavy sea. Snow was failing and the visibility was low.

During the middle watch a message was received from St. Kilda stating that the *Fiskaa* had been sunk by a submarine 10 miles WNW of the island, and that the crew had been landed. *Walpole* and *Tenby Castle* were ordered to proceed to St Kilda in order to embark *Changuinola*'s Armed Guard and the crew of the vessel, and take them to Stornoway.[1]

In the morning a signal was received from St Kilda as follows:

> 'Following received by visual from submarine – begins: Have been instructed to request you to report me to HMS *Fearless*. Am here in name of *Vennino*, not giving name of vessel – ends – did not answer demand.'

I passed this message to the Commander-in-Chief Grand Fleet, at the same time informing him that the Armed Trawlers *Walpole* and *Tenby Castle* were in the neighbourhood engaged in embarking the crew of the *Fiskaa* from St Kilda.

At 5.30 a.m. *Tenby Castle* sighted a submarine during a rain squall, in Latitude 57.33´ North, Longitude 8.50´ West, which immediately submerged and was not again sighted.

At 11 a.m. *Arlanza* in Latitude 61.14´ North, Longitude 13.35´ West, intercepted the Belgian Relief Ship *Colombier*, but as the weather rendered it too rough to board at that time, *Arlanza* was ordered to

[1]See page 659, note 1.

shadow the vessel until able to do so. About 7.30 p.m. however, owing to the prevailing heavy weather and poor visibility, the vessel was lost sight of.[1]

At noon the disposition of the Squadron was as follows:

C Patrol, Crossing line 360° from Lat. 59 N, Long. 12 W at 0900 steering 270° and 0300 steering 90°, ships 30 miles apart … *Columbella*, *Almanzora*.
B Patrol, Crossing line 360° from Lat. 61.20´N, Long. 14 W at 1000 steering 260°, and 0200 steering 80°, ships 30 miles apart … *Arlanza*, *Gloucestershire*, *Otway*, *Armadale Castle*.
A Patrol, Steering 10° for 120 miles from Lat. 63 N, Long. 12.20´W in southern position at 1800 daily … *Patia*.
E Patrol, Northwest of Iceland, off Isafjord … *Ebro*, *Avenger*.
Between B & C Patrol … *Alsatian*.
St Kilda Patrol … Armed Trawlers *Walpole* and *Tenby Castle*.
Rejoining Patrol … *Artois* (from Swarbacks Minn) Armed Trawler *Arley*.
Proceeding to Clyde … *Hildebrand*.
Proceeding to Liverpool … *Motagua* (from Swarbacks Minn).
At Oban … Armed Trawlers *Saxon*, *Rushcoe*, *Robert Smith*.
At Swarbacks Minn … *Champagne*.
At Clyde … *Moldavia*, *Hilary*, *Patuca*, *Changuinola*, *Kildonan Castle*.
At Liverpool … *Orvieto*, *Andes*, *Virginian*, *Victorian*, *Orcoma*.

During the week 58 Ships were intercepted, of which 2 were sent in with Armed Guards and 5 signed guarantees to call at Halifax. Of the total number intercepted, 7 were westbound and 10 eastbound neutrals.

***

NOTE – It will be observed from the Chart accompanying this letter that the number of ships sent in during March was very small when compared with previous months. This is due to the adoption of Halifax as an Examination Port, and the consequent reduction in the number of ships to be examined at a Port in the United Kingdom. The number of vessels intercepted was normal.[2]

[1] *Colombier* had been notified to the Contraband Committee on 22 March (TS 14/14); it would no doubt have been sent in, but then released at once.

[2] A further interpretation is that this is the beginning of the end of the usefulness of the Northern Patrol, even before the entry of the United States into the war finally closed off German access to neutral ports.

331. *W. Grahame Greene to the Commander-in-Chief Grand Fleet*

Admiralty, 30 March 1917

***

2. I am commanded by their Lordships to acquaint you that they concur in your opinion that both the *Avenger* and *Teutonic* failed to carry out in their entirety the instructions regarding the examination of merchant vessels, the *Avenger* in that she did not insist on seeing the flag of the day after ascertaining that the stranger had a clearance from Kirkwall, and the *Teutonic* in that she did not detain the vessel for being a long way from the track laid down for vessels of the Netherlands Overseas Trust [291, 292, 293, 295].

3. I am to request that Commodore John Luard may be informed that he ought not to have allowed the ship to pass without making further enquiries as to why a ship from Holland to Falmouth was some 150 miles to the westward of the track prescribed for Netherlands Overseas Trust vessels using that route.

4. My Lords consider that Commander Arthur L. Ashby, RN, was very much to blame for not ascertaining that the ship had the correct flag of the day if he accepted a reply that the ship had been into Kirkwall, although such a visit was contrary to the latest arrangements made with the Netherlands Overseas Trust. Moreover, if the ship had really left Kirkwall for New York the position in which she was met should have aroused his suspicions. I am to request that Commander Ashby be informed that he has incurred their Lordships' displeasure.

5. My Lords do not concur with the Court of Enquiry that Lieutenant Commander Guy V. Kenyon, RN of HMS *Alsatian* was justified in the action taken by him in directing HMS *Avenger* to allow the ship to proceed.

332. *Consul E.M. de Garston,*[1] *to Sir M. de G. Findlay, HM Minister*

British Consulate, Kristiansand, 2 April 1917

… [T]he cargo of 3,058,580 lbs American Cotton Seed Cake carried by the Norwegian barque *Thekla*, which arrived yesterday at Gamle

[1]De Garston, Edward Mervyn (1869–1939), British Consul at Christiansand, 1915–1918; earlier consular appointments had been to Leghorn, Palermo, Spezia, Santo Domingo, Port-au-Prince, Ragusa, Bahia, Puerto Rico and Christiania; subsequently he was Consul-General at Milan, Turin and San Marino, retired 1923.

Hellesund with a British armed guard on board, was shipped by The New Orleans Export Co. Ltd, for delivery to J.J. Larsen of Odense, and is to be discharged at Copenhagen.

This consignment is covered by guarantees numbered 96877 and 96878 given by the Merchants Guild of Copenhagen.

The *Thekla* belongs to Messrs J. Samuelson and B. Olsen of Farsund, and is commanded by Olaf Tobiasson of Farsund whose action in successfully concealing from the German submarine which stopped them on March 28th, the presence on board of the British armed guard appears worthy of commendation.

The Master reports that the submarine was very large and roomy and about 350 feet in length, that it had no marks or distinguishing letters and was armed with two guns, one in the bow and one in the stern which appeared to him to be of 105 mm. calibre. Three shells were fired at his ship, the first from aft falling short astern, the second exploded about 6 feet off the port beam, considerably damaging the only remaining lifeboat, and the third passing through the upper topsail. The projectiles used were apparently shrapnel. After the third shot the crew was ordered to leave the ship and the Mate and 12 hands repaired on board the submarine in the damaged lifeboat, leaving the Master alone on board with the armed guard. The Mate and crew succeeded in persuading the Commander of the submarine to allow them to return to their ship and proceed on the voyage on convincing him that the ship was in reality bound to Copenhagen with neutral cargo.

The Master informs me that considerable damage was done to the rigging, in addition to that caused to the lifeboat, by the fragments of the shells fired.

The ship was flying the Norwegian colours from the moment of first sighting the submarine, and moreover signalled her name, voyage and cargo, and being a sailing vessel, she could not be presumed to be attempting to escape, and the Master believes that all these particulars were already previously known to the Commander of the Submarine which apparently only fired on his vessel out of sheer wantonness.[1]

[1]It is not clear from which ship the Armed Guard came – no report has been found – but the submarine was *U 60*.

333. *Lieutenant J.T. Randell to Vice-Admiral Commanding Tenth Cruiser Squadron*

HMT *Rushcoe*, 6 April 1917

I have the honour to report that at 10.30 a.m. 5th April when about ten miles West Flannan Island (*Tenby Castle* in company) we received message from St Kilda as follows: Submarine on surface four miles NNW Steering NE ten knots. I immediately ordered *Tenby Castle* proceed full speed towards position of submarine and we steered W/N with intention opening opposite course to Submarine. At 11.00 a.m. we sighted another submarine bearing west, and steering NE. When about five miles distant she altered course to West. We appeared to be gaining on her at first, and then as she appeared to be getting away, we opened fire 11.30 a.m. extreme range with 12 pounder. We had to alter course three points to fire gun being abaft funnel, and owing to heavy rolling (there was strong breeze from NNE and heavy sea) firing was slow as often Gunner would lose sight of submarine. We fired ten rounds just under half an hour, direction good, but all shots fell short. Submarine opened fire about 11.40 a.m. and fired about eight rounds, could see flashes but not shell. We landed last shot within about 200 yards of submarine and she submerged almost immediately. She was then bearing about WSW and we altered course that direction. Submarine only showed conning tower, no mast, and appeared to be painted brown, evidently rust. At 12.5 p.m. we sighted a schooner bearing SW/W about ten miles distant and altered course towards her. Shortly after we saw shots falling between the schooner and us, and knew that she was being shelled by submarine from SW. Had we had another two or three knots speed and 12 pounder mounted on fo'c'sle head we could have saved vessel and would have had a good chance of hitting the first submarine. We did our best speed and as we got nearer could see the shells dropping nearer the vessel, and shortly after could see submarine from the masthead astern of vessel; we altered course three points and fired three shots from 12 pounder extreme elevation and submarine dived almost immediately and was seen no more. At 12.40 p.m. we saw vessel sink by the head. After firing about 50 or 60 shots at the vessel submarine headed for boat and fired shrapnel just as we fired the three rounds, and I have no doubt but that the random shots prevented submarine from closing boat and the French Armed Guard from *Artois* from being taken prisoner. At 1.45 p.m. we picked up boat with one

Officer and three men Armed Guard French cruiser *Artois*; Captain and four men crew of vessel sunk Danish three masted schooner *Ebenezer*.[1]

***

334. *R. Stokes to Surveyor Stornoway*

[n.d., but *c*. 9 April 1917]

I beg to report the following circumstance in connection with the discovery and seizure of undeclared letters on the above vessel. The *Leif Gunderson* is a four-masted Norwegian barque owned by Gunderson and Gjeste Porsgrad and diverted to this port by the French cruiser *Champagne* on 25th March while in course of a voyage from Baltimore to Odense with a full cargo of maize. Report under O 2305 was made on March 28th, the date of the arrival in this port. The vessel arrived in Baltimore on 24th December 1916 after a ballast voyage from France and departed on the present journey 25th February.

On 30th March the vessel was ordered to proceed to Greenock for examination of cargo … Owing to the necessity of waiting for an Armed Guard and a tug and to the subsequent suspension of all traffic between the Clyde and the Minches and vice versa it was not possible for the *Leif Gunderson* to sail before Saturday April 7th. About noon on that day the Armed Guard took possession of the vessel. Straightway the steward, Henrik Alick (or Ulick) of Hammerfest, told the officer in charge of the guard that on opening a case of apples on Good Friday in order to provide dessert for the ship's officers he found concealed under one layer of apples a bag (produced) containing letters addressed to firms in Germany. He then stove in the heads of four casks and a cursory examination led him to believe that these receptacles also held letters. He did not communicate the fact of his discovery to the master nor, so far as can be ascertained, to anyone else on board. Ulick produced to the Armed Guard officer a receipted bill (attached) which, he alleged, was furnished by the suppliers of the goods. He interprets 'Reg' as meaning 'small', 'Calas' as 'bacon' and 'clean breast' as 'breast of bacon'. In his story related to this officer Ulick said that the three barrels of ham and bacon and one box and one barrel of apples (not two boxes as invoiced) were bought as ship's stores for use on the *Leif Gunderson*.

During this recital the master of the *Leif Gunderson*, O.D. Hansen, was on shore conducting Ship's business. My attention was drawn to the

[1]This was *U 57*.

discovery by the Senior Naval Officer, to whom the Armed Guard officer had reported. Before setting off with a rummage crew to make a detailed examination of the stores, the master was interrogated as to his knowledge of the business. He expressed his great astonishment and vexation, protested his innocence and promised to render every assistance to the search to be undertaken.

Immediately after boarding the vessel the rummage crew entered the strictly guarded lazarette and with the help of the steward discharged the contents of an unmarked barrel and three barrels … on the heads:

Armour and Co
Balti Md
Hams
Calas A – C

The first barrel was filled with letters. Each of the marked barrels had one layer of small old looking rancid hams at each end. The space between was packed with letters, many loose and some in small dirty sacks. Many of these letters were addressed to the Hamburg America line, Hamburg, and such letters all bore a number. Unavailing search was made for a document on which it was suspected these letters might be scheduled. So far as could be seen all letters had an enemy destination and only one bore postage stamps. The whole of the loose letters and sacks were retained and dealt with under Circular O 983, paragraph 9.

As the result of a cross-examination of Ulick it was elicited that he had paid 131 dollars for the goods, believing them to be as invoiced; that such purchase constituted a private trade contract having no relation to ship's stores; and that the master was ignorant of this transaction and of the presence of the goods on board. According to his story Ulick desired to ship the invoiced goods to Norway in order to avoid the high prices obtaining there. He did not deal with Henry A. Kessel and Co, 2121 So Gay St, Baltimore, suppliers of the boxes, because he was informed by a Jew, S. Rachman, 2616 Guilford Avenue, Baltimore, that by employing him as a middleman a saving of 9 cents a pound could be effected on some of the goods. Rachman is described as an old Jew, resident for forty years in America although he states he had at the time of meeting Ulick resided in Baltimore for two months only. He is employed as assistant to a tailor and outfitter named Goldstein from whom the crew bought articles of clothing. Rachman seems to have put himself in the way of Ulick and they used to meet every day at the butcher's and in the market. The master states that to the best of his knowledge and belief Ulick did not land before the 28th December. The 'goods' were shipped on 1st January and the money paid the following day. The steward and the mate both declare that the packages came on board during the absence of the master on shore and without his knowledge and consent. The mate states he was informed that the goods consisted of provisions. It is made to appear that Armour and Co, 335 West Pratt St, Baltimore, were the suppliers. For his intervention Rachman is stated to have received ten dollars from the Steward. During the whole of this cross-examination and during such times as this the master upbraided him for alleged duplicity. Ulick protested his innocence and declared that not until he went in quest of apples on 6th April did he become aware of the actual contents of the packages.

The master states Ulick has sailed with him for 18 months and is within measurable distance of completing the round trip, Scandinavia to Melbourne, and thence to Chili to load nitrates for France – from France to Baltimore in ballast – thereafter this present voyage. Ulick had a brother, Hans P. Ulick, 617 W 145th St, New York, who is reputed to be wealthy and is connected with the firm of H.P. Ulick and Co, Paper Bones (?) 40 and 442 Princes St New York. Henrik M. Ulick states it was from this brother he borrowed the money to make his purchases. The brother visited the *Leif Gunderson* while she lay in Baltimore.

I enclose certain letters from Henrik M. Ulick's brother.

There is also on board a crated 'Perfection Stoves' which Ulick represented as being a gift from his brother and which is being stored with the master's permission in the lazarette.

Certain barrels of flour and pickled beef (ship's stores) were also subjected to internal examination but nothing suspicious found.

335. *Vice-Admiral Tupper to Admiralty*

HMS *Alsatian*, 24 April 1917

Report of Proceedings, 9–22 April 1917

***

1. Monday, 9 April – Strong Northerly gale accompanied by very cold weather and frequent falls of snow. *Arlanza* reported that owing to the very severe weather, fall of snow, and low visibility nothing further had been seen of the Belgian Relief Ship *Colombier* which had been lost sight of the previous evening (vide paragraph 11 of my last report of proceedings). *Arlanza* was accordingly ordered to resume patrol, the Admiralty being informed of the incident in my message No. 504. *Champagne* rejoining from Swarbacks Minn was ordered to endeavour to intercept her, but did not succeed in doing so.

Walpole arrived at Stornoway about 1 p.m. and having landed *Changuinola*'s Armed Guard and the crew of the Norwegian Sailing Vessel *Fiskaa*, sailed again to rejoin patrol.

About 4.30 p.m. *Otway*, in Latitude 62.12´ North, Longitude 14.44´ West, intercepted the Norwegian SS *Augusta* bound for Reykjavik from Hoganas with a cargo of timber. The vessel had sprung a leak and requested a tow. As this request could not be safely complied with owing to possible danger from submarines, an offer was made to take off the crew, which was accepted. They were accordingly disembarked and transferred to *Otway*, who was directed to stand by during the night, and endeavour to enlist the services of a British Trawler to tow her to Iceland the following day, if the weather had sufficiently moderated [338].

Gloucestershire, in Latitude 61.30´ North, Longitude 14.50´ West boarded the Norwegian Sailing Vessel *Audun* from Norfolk News to Bergen via Lerwick with a cargo of coal.

Owing to the heavy sea which was running at the time, *Gloucestershire*'s boat sustained damage alongside the *Audun* and broke adrift, but was safely recovered without any loss of life. An Armed Guard was placed on board with orders to take her to Stornoway, or other more convenient Port.[1]

About 6.30 p.m. *Arlanza* in Latitude 61.51´ North, Longitude 10.14´ West, intercepted the Norwegian Sailing vessel *Vigo*, but was unable to board owing to the heavy sea. *Arlanza* was directed to keep in touch with the vessel and board when possible. Later in the evening, however, she reported that the *Vigo* had been lost sight of in the dark. I ordered her to continue the search at daybreak, but she did not succeed in picking her up.

Information was received that *Motagua* and escort had safely arrived at Liverpool.

2. Tuesday, 10 April – Gale moderated during the day.

The Master of the British Trawler *Hilaria* (GY 698), intercepted by *Alsatian* during the afternoon, expressed his willingness to make an attempt to take the *Augusta* in tow and was given directions for proceeding to the vessel's position, *Otway* in the meantime being ordered to remain by the vessel and await the arrival of the Trawler.

[1] *Audun*'s cargo was 3000 tons of smokeless steam coal. The Contraband Committee discussed whether the entry of the USA into the war made the cargo acceptable where it would not have been earlier. Then a request that the ship be allowed to sail to avoid the risk of sinking had to be discussed and refused. *Audun* was eventually allowed to go on to Bergen with its full cargo (TS 14/14 of 18 April 1917).

At 7 p.m *Otway* succeeded in boarding *Augusta*, who was now settling down, and found 13 feet of water in the hold. Lights were placed on her as necessary; without which it was considered she would be a danger to navigation by night.

Arlanza was met at 11 a.m., despatches were transferred, and the Captain came on board to confer with me. Opportunity was also taken to send the Gunnery Officer on my staff – Lieutenant-Commander Guy V. Kenyon, RN on board *Arlanza* to look into various matters in connection with gunnery drills and organization. On his return he reported everything very satisfactory.

On parting company *Arlanza* was given orders for proceeding to Liverpool.

During the afternoon *Alsatian* intercepted and boarded in Latitude 62.99´ North, Longitude 1.55´ West, the Dutch Steamers *Elve* and *Bernisse*, from Rotterdam to Rufisque, West Africa. As they were found to be in ballast, and their papers correct, they were allowed to proceed …

In the evening *Patia* was met and despatches were transferred. *Patia* was then ordered to proceed to Swarbacks Minn to coal.

3. Wednesday, 11 April – Soon after midnight the wind again got up and blew hard from the North-East throughout the day.

About 12.30 a.m. *Alsatian* in Latitude 62.28´ North, Longitude 10.30´ West, boarded the Danish SS *Island* from Copenhagen to Iceland and Faroes carrying 73 passengers and a considerable quantity of letter mails and parcels, in addition to a cargo of provisions and petroleum. The vessel was in possession of a certificate from the British Legation at Copenhagen giving permission to proceed direct to Iceland without calling at a United Kingdom Port. She was allowed to continue on her voyage in accordance with Admiralty message 2224 of 31 March. She was also informed of the whereabouts of SS *Augusta* in case she wished to tow her to Iceland.

At noon, *Otway* reported that there was no apparent change in the condition of *Augusta*, but that the Trawler which was to take her in tow had not arrived. I then directed *Otway* that, if at 7 p.m. the Trawler had not arrived, the Master of *Augusta* should be given the option to return to his vessel, and that if he then definitely and finally elected to abandon her, she should be sunk by gunfire as a danger to navigation. About 2 p.m., however, the vessel went on her beam ends and slowly sank. *Otway* then resumed patrol.

***

During the evening *Columbella* intercepted the *Vigo*, which had been lost sight of by *Arlanza* on the 9th instant (vide paragraph 1). She was directed to keep in touch with the vessel until the condition of the sea permitted of boarding.

Armadale Castle in Latitude 62.30´ North, Longitude 16.54´ West, boarded the Danish Motor Ship *Fiona*, from Halifax to Svendbord with a cargo of Maize. The vessel was in possession of a green clearance and was allowed to proceed on her voyage. H.R.H. Prince Eric of Denmark[1] was a passenger on board.

4. Thursday, 12 April – *Columbella* succeeded in boarding *Vigo* and having ascertained that she was bound for New York, and in ballast, allowed her to proceed; her papers being in order.

Champagne in Latitude 60.12´ North, Longitude 11.53´ West, intercepted the Norwegian SV *Audun*, which was proceeding to Stornoway with an Armed Guard placed on board by *Gloucestershire* on the 9th instant (vide paragraph 1). The vessel had lost most of her sails in the heavy weather and was unable to proceed until the conditions moderated. *Champagne* was directed to inform her that she should make for Butt of Lewis or Barra Head, when possible, and there pick up escort for Stornoway, or alternatively, to proceed to Lough Swilly.

During the forenoon I met *Gloucestershire* and went on board. I inspected the men at Divisions and also went round the mess decks. Target practice was also carried out. Everything was quite satisfactory and I consider her in a very efficient condition and a credit to Captain Stanley and his Officers.

With the approval of the Commander-in-Chief I gave orders for B and C Patrols to move to patrol line II, disposing them as follows:

> B Patrol – To cross line 325° from Latitude 62 North, Longitude 11 West, at noon, steering 250°, and at midnight steering 70°, four ships, 30 miles apart.
>
> C Patrol – To cross line 325° from Latitude 59.40´ North, Longitude 8 West, at 1000, steering 250°, and 0200 steering 70°, three ships, 30 miles apart.

Senior Naval Officer, Liverpool, informed me that *Andes*, when weighing to sail for patrol during the morning, had damaged her windlass, the necessary repairs to which would cause a delay of the vessel in port for several days. Arrangements were accordingly made

[1]Eric of Denmark (1890–1980), Prince, son of Prince Waldemar, uncle of King Christian X; his brother Axel was a Lieutenant in the (British) Royal Navy.

for the passengers and despatches for Iceland to be transferred to *Changuinola* for passage, the latter vessel being due to sail for the Clyde on the 13th instant.

Otway intercepted the Norwegian SS *Granfos* during the evening bound from Halifax to Rotterdam. As the vessel was in possession of a green clearance from Halifax and was thus being allowed to proceed, the opportunity was taken of transferring the crew of *Augusta* for passage to Rotterdam, the Master of the *Granfos* being willing to perform this service.

About 7 p.m. *Alsatian* intercepted the Norwegian SS *Hovland* in Latitude 61.37´ North, Longitude 12.55´ West, bound from Christiania to Baltimore via Halifax. As this vessel had not been signalled as outward bound for Halifax, a written guarantee was obtained that she should call at that Port before allowing her to proceed.

Several vessels intercepted lately bound for Halifax have been found to be considerably south of the route laid down in Admiralty Letter N.L. 1/32422 of 17 March 1917 …

Orvieto sailed from Liverpool for patrol during the day with Rear-Admiral Morgan Singer, C.B., on board. Information was also received that three of the new trawlers detailed for service with the 10th Cruiser Squadron, viz *Marconi*, *Faraday* and *Macleay* had sailed from Portsmouth for Swarbacks Minn.

5. Friday, 13 April – Fairly rainy fine weather but cold North-east wind and snow showers.

At 10 a.m. *Patuca* was met, despatches were transferred, and Captain Dannreuther came on board to confer with me. On parting company, *Patuca* was despatched to A Patrol to relieve *Artois*.

A letter was received from the Admiralty acquainting me that His Majesty had been pleased to bestow decorations and medals on certain Officers and men of the 10th Cruiser Squadron in recognition of Services rendered. The honour is greatly appreciated by all.

During the afternoon information was received from the Senior Naval Officer, Liverpool, that *Virginian* who was now proceeding to rejoin patrol, had been diverted to Belfast owing to the presence of mines on the North Coast of Ireland.

Almanzora in Latitude 60.25´ North, Longitude 10.18´ West, boarded and allowed to proceed the British ammunition carrier *Umtali*, from Romanoff to Liverpool, with a number of British wounded and several important passengers on board.

At about 5.30 p.m., *Columbella* reported hearing S.O.S. call in Latitude 59.15´ North, Longitude 10.38´ West, and being near that position proceeded towards two British oil tank steamers which were in sight and from which the distress call had apparently emanated. On getting in touch with one of these steamers (*Oiler No. 169*), the Master stated that a supposed submarine had been sighted, and that he had fired one shot at her, the fall of which had been observed by *Columbella*. In the meantime I had ordered C Patrol to move to the Westward, to Line 3, and I directed *Columbella* to keep in touch with the steamers until dark, manoeuvring at high speed. The Armed Trawlers *Saxon* and *Walpole*, who were then working off the Flannan Islands, were also directed to proceed with despatch to the position indicated, in order to render any assistance required. The Oilers proceeded West and were not heard of again after dark.

The Commander-in-Chief, Grand Fleet, was informed of this incident.

6. Saturday, 14 April – An exceptionally heavy North-Easterly gale was experienced by Ships on A and B Patrols.

At 10 a.m. *Gloucestershire* was met and given directions to proceed to Clyde by N Channel. It was too rough to send despatches by her.

During the afternoon C Patrol was redisposed in the following manner, viz: At 1600, to be spread 360° from Latitude 59.30´ North, Longitude 16 West, three ships, 30 miles apart, steering 120°; on reaching meridian 12.30´ West to alter course to 75°; on reaching meridian 8.45´ West to turn to Westward, following reverse courses; Ships to keep approximate station, arranging to be on meridian 12.30´ West daily at 4 a.m., steering Eastward and Westward.

At 5 p.m. *Armadale Castle* in Latitude 62.28´ North, Longitude 14.50´ West, intercepted the Swedish SS *B.G. Kronberg*, from Philadelphia to Stockholm, with a cargo of wheat, but was unable to board owing to the heavy sea running. … *Armadale Castle* was directed to keep in touch with the vessel until able to board, and then to send her in to Kirkwall with an Armed Guard.

Walpole reported engaging a submarine in Latitude 58.30´ North, Longitude 7.23´ West, at 5.30 p.m. The submarine submerged immediately.

7. Sunday, 15 April – *Armadale Castle* succeeded in boarding *B.G. Kronberg* and sent her to Kirkwall with an Armed Guard, the Admiralty being informed … .[1]

[1] *B.G. Kronberg* was detained at Kirkwall pending a decision on the quantity of cereals to be permitted to reach Sweden (TS 14/14 of 18 April 1917).

At noon the disposition of the Squadron was as follows:

A Patrol, steering 10° for 120 miles from Lat. 63 North, Long. 12.20´ West, in Southern position at 1800 daily … *Patuca*.
B Patrol, Crossing line 325° from Lat. 62 North, Long. 11 West at noon, steering 250°, and at midnight steering 70°, Ships 30 miles apart … *Orvieto* (joining), *Otway*, *Armadale Castle*, *Artois*.
C Patrol, From a line 360° from Lat. 59.30´ North, Long. 16 West to steer 120° to meridian 12.30´ to steer 75° to meridian 8.45´ West, thence to turn Westward and follow reverse route; Ships 30 miles apart, crossing meridian 12.30´ West at 0400 daily … *Columbella*, *Champagne*, *Alsatian*.
E Patrol. North-west of Iceland, off Isafjord … *Ebro*, *Avenger*, *Almanzora* (joining).
St Kilda Patrol … Armed Trawlers *Arley*, *Saxon*, *Walpole*, *Robert Smith*.
Rejoining Patrol … *Virginian* (from Liverpool and Belfast).
Proceeding to Clyde … *Gloucestershire*.
Proceeding to Oban … Armed Trawlers *Marconi*, *Faraday*, *Macleay*, *Offa II* (from Portsmouth, after fitting out for service with 10th Cruiser Squadron).
At Swarbacks Minn … *Patia*, Special Service Vessel *King Lear*, Armed Trawlers *Rushcoe* and *Tenby Castle*.
At Liverpool … *Arlanza*, *Motagua*, *Orcoma*, *Andes*, *Victorian*.
At Clyde … *Hildebrand*, *Kildonan Castle*, *Moldavia*, *Hilary*, *Changuinola*.[1]

During the week 43 Ships were intercepted, of which 2 were sent in with Armed Guards and 9 were allowed to proceed on account of having guaranteed to call at Halifax or other Colonial Port. Of the total number intercepted 13 were Westbound and 12 Eastbound neutrals.

Early in the afternoon, *Almanzora* having got into W/T touch with the Ships on E Patrol where she was proceeding to relieve *Ebro*, reported that the ice pack extended 40° from Latitude 66.20´ North, Longitude 26.30´ West, to 66.45´ North, 25.30´ West, thence 90° to 66.45´ North, 25 West, thence 55° to 67.3´ North, 23.55´ West, thence about 30°, with large quantities of loose ice between the ice pack and land east of a line 310° from Stigahlid.

At 4 p.m. *Orvieto* was met and Rear-Admiral Morgan Singer, C.B., came on board. I conferred with him generally on Blockade work in the

[1]The squadron now consisted of 24 ships and 11 trawlers.

10th Cruiser Squadron. He finds *Orvieto* quite comfortable and appears to understand the general organization and working of the 10th Cruiser Squadron on Blockade duty.

On parting company *Orvieto* was directed to proceed to B Patrol and take charge.

At 10 p.m. *Champagne* in Latitude 59.15´ North, Longitude 10.33´ West, boarded the British SS *Riverton* from New Orleans to Hull, with Maize. Her steering gear had been damaged, and she requested an escort. I informed the Admiral Commanding Orkneys and Shetlands accordingly, and in the meantime detailed *Saxon* and *Robert Smith* to intercept the vessel if possible and escort her until relieved.

Changuinola sailed from Clyde during this day having on board the passengers and despatches for Iceland …

8. Monday, 16 April – At 10 a.m. *Columbella* in Latitude 58.45´ North, Longitude 11.17´ West, reported sighting and engaging an enemy submarine. Shortly afterwards, however, she stated this report was unreliable, the supposed submarine being most probably a buoy. Orders which had been given to two of the Armed Trawlers to proceed to her assistance, were accordingly cancelled.

Robert Smith found the Norwegian Barque *Audun*, with Armed Guard placed on board by *Gloucestershire* on the 9th April and escorted her to the Butt of Lewis.

During the day, the following modifications were ordered in the disposition of Patrols:

> A Patrol – To work between Latitude 64 and 65 North, on meridian of 12 West.
> B Patrol – To move 30 miles to the Eastward.
> C Patrol – To keep West of the meridian of 12.30´ West.

9. Tuesday, 17 April – Fine day; smooth sea; Westerly breeze.

During the forenoon, *Saxon* reported that she was in touch with the Russian SS *Czar* bound from Alexandrovsk to Liverpool with troops, 20 miles North-North-West of Butt of Lewis. She was directed to escort the vessel and subsequently reported having turned her over to the Stornoway Patrol.

At 4.20 p.m. *Robert Smith*, who was still escorting *Audun*, sighted a periscope in Latitude 59.20´ North, Longitude 6.20´ West. *Saxon* was ordered to join *Robert Smith* but nothing further was seen of the submarine. The escort of even one Armed Trawler seems sufficient to deter the ordinary submarine, but of course some are bolder.

At 9 p.m. *Alsatian* having already left for Swarbacks Minn, I directed Rear-Admiral Morgan Singer, C.B., in *Orvieto* to assume Command of the Patrol during my absence.

At 9 p.m. *Patia* in Latitude 61.58´ North, Longitude 11.4´ West boarded the Danish SS *Hans Egede*, from Copenhagen to Greenland, with a general cargo. As this Ship had evaded the patrol four times … *Patia* was directed to send her to Kirkwall with an Armed Guard.[1]

Patuca had previously reported that one of her Officers was suffering from Appendicitis, and that his condition while not critical, rendered an early operation advisable. Arrangements were accordingly made for the transfer of the patient to *Artois*, due to leave Patrol for the Clyde on 21st April.

Information was received from Liverpool that *Andes* was being detained in Port owing to the presence of enemy submarines in the North Channel.

10. Wednesday, 18 April – I arrived at Swarbacks Minn in *Alsatian* at 3 a.m. Coaling was commenced at 7 a.m.

Robert Smith, still engaged with *Saxon* in escorting *Audun*, reported her rudder damaged and was given permission to proceed to Stornoway to effect repairs. *Audun* was turned over to the Stornoway Patrol at 2.35 p.m. – her safe arrival being subsequently reported[2] – and *Saxon* continued her passage to Swarbacks Minn. This left no Trawlers out on patrol.

During the day Rear-Admiral Sydney R. Fremantle, MVO, Commanding the 2nd Cruiser Squadron, visited me on board *Alsatian* and I discussed with him various matters in connection with the Northern Patrols. I also conferred with Rear-Admiral William L. Fawckner.

I took the opportunity of going on board the Special Service Trawler *King Lear*, and found her in an efficient state. With the concurrence of the Admiral Commanding Orkneys and Shetlands, I have given her sailing orders for another cruise, a copy of which are enclosed for information … [340]

As Submarine E 44 was in harbour I obtained the services of Lieutenant Gilbert E. Venning, RN[3] to assist the Flag Captain of *Alsatian* in holding an Inquiry as regards the result of the action between *Tenby Castle* and an enemy submarine on 6 April. The Court were of opinion that the submarine was sunk.

[1]*Hans Egede* was not detained.

[2]See page 674, note 1.

[3]Venning, Gilbert E., DSC, RN, Lieutenant 1911, Captain of Submarine *E 44* 1917, Lieutenant-Commander 1915, retired 1923.

It further transpired that *E 44* had been fired on by *Rushcoe* the previous day …

I also inspected the Armed Trawlers *Rushcoe* and *Tenby Castle*; they appear clean and efficient.

11. Thursday, 19 April – The Patrols experienced a North Westerly gale, some Ships being obliged to lie to.

Ebro reported having passed an empty boat with mast up in Latitude 55.53´ North, Longitude 7.45´ West at 7.30 p.m.

Tenby Castle, in Latitude 59.58´ North, Longitude 3.15´ West, intercepted the Norwegian Barque *Fiore*, bound from Buenos Aires to Odense. As the sea was too rough to permit of an Armed Guard being placed on board, *Tenby Castle* escorted the vessel and turned her over to the Sunburgh head Patrol.[1]

I inspected the Armed Trawlers *Arley* and *Saxon*; both are well kept.

Kildonan Castle sailed from Clyde to rejoin Patrol after an absence of a fortnight on detached duty.

12. Friday, 20 April – I visited Lerwick and conferred with Commander Hubert G. Alston, RN, Commander Burrard A. Smith, RN, also Commander Harold E. Sullivan, D.S.O..[2] I found the harbour very full. The examination Staff is complete and ready to deal with vessels sent in by the 10th Cruiser Squadron, but owing to the special character of the work being performed by the various vessels stationed at Lerwick, it is considered best for the 10th Cruiser Squadron not to send vessels there for examination except in special circumstances, such as bad weather or contrary winds, other ports closed owing to mines, etc.

Tenby Castle intercepted and sent in the Danish Schooner *Zenitha*, sent in to Lerwick by *Patia* on 19 April, and escorted her towards Sunburgh Head. On relief, she returned to Patrol.[3]

Admiralty informed me … that the Germans have announced the capture of the Norwegian S.V. *Najade*. This vessel was long overdue, having been intercepted and sent in to Kirkwall by *Ebro* on 4th March. *Ebro* has been directed to forward the names of Officer and men composing the Armed Guard, whose fate is unknown [317, para. 12].[4]

Four of the new Trawlers attached to my Command, viz: *Macleay*, *Faraday*, *Offa II* and *Marconi*, arrived at Swarbacks Minn during the

[1] *Fiore* was inspected and then allowed to sail on (TS 14/14 of 21 April 1917).

[2] Sulivan, Harold E., DSO, RN, Commander 1911, Captain 1917, Captain of *Woolwich* (Depot Ship for TBDs) and Captain (D) of Flotilla at Portsmouth 1918, retired 1923.

[3] *Zenitha* was allowed to go on after being inspected (TS 14/14 of 21 April 1917).

[4] *Najade* was captured by *U 59* on 21 March 1917.

forenoon and I had their Commanding Officers on board *Alsatian* to explain to them their duties in working with the 10th Cruiser Squadron.

As it had been brought to my notice verbally that the arrangements for signalling and communicating between Busta House, *Gibraltar*, 2nd Cruiser Squadron and 10th Cruiser Squadron were not quite satisfactory, I ordered a Conference, composed of representatives from each of the above and presided over by Flag Captain Humphrey H. Smith, DSO, to discuss how they could be improved. I have sent their recommendations to the Rear-Admiral Swarbacks Minn, with the request that he will forward them to the Admiral Commanding Orkneys and Shetlands with his remarks.

At 9 p.m. I left Swarbacks Minn in *Alsatian* to rejoin patrol.

13. Saturday, 21 April – *Orvieto* in Latitude 62.23´ North, Longitude 10.18´ West, boarded the Belgian Relief Steamer *Liege*, from Rotterdam to New York via Halifax, in ballast, and allowed her to proceed. The Master reported having sighted, on the afternoon of the 17th April, off Udsire, two Sailing Vessels flying Swedish colours but apparently acting as Depot Ships to five submarines to whom they were signalling. The Sailing Vessels appeared to have large crews, and the Master of *Liege* expressed the opinion that they were fitted with auxiliary engines. On the approach of *Liege*, one of the submarines submerged, and escorted her for several miles … .[1]

At 10 a.m. *Patuca* boarded the Danish Sailing Vessel *Delos* bound from Cadiz to Bergen with a cargo of salt. Her Master reported having been fired on by a small German submarine of the U.C. type at 1 p.m. on 18 March when in Latitude 35.50´ North, Longitude 9.5´ West, which damaged her sails and rigging; there were no casualties. The submarine was painted dark grey and had one gun.[2] The *Delos* being a small vessel with nothing suspicious was allowed to proceed.

At 8 p.m. *Orvieto* was met and I proceeded on board to confer with the Rear-Admiral and take over charge of the Squadron.

On parting company, *Orvieto* was despatched to patrol between A and B, taking charge of these patrols.

Orders were given for the disposition of C Patrol to be modified as follows:

To cross line 360° from Latitude 58 North, Longitude 12.30´ West, at 0400 daily, steering alternately 55° and 300°.

[1]There is no indication of any of this in the German accounts, and it seems on the face of it a highly unlikely occurrence.

[2]The submarine involved is not known.

Fog was prevalent on B Patrol.

14. Sunday, 22 April – A fine day; smooth sea; cold North Easterly breeze.

At 1.50 a.m. *Kildonan Castle* in Latitude 62.15´ North, Longitude 10.13´ West, intercepted nine British Trawlers, steering in company towards the Iceland fishing grounds. Two of them were armed. Their numbers had been previously transmitted to me by W/T.

At noon the disposition of the Squadron was as follows:

A Patrol, working between Lat. 64 and 65 North, on meridian 12 West … *Virginian*.

B Patrol, Crossing line 325° from 62 North, Long 11.0´ West at 1500 steering 235°, and at 2100 steering 55°, ships 30 miles apart … *Kildonan Castle*, *Armadale Castle*, *Patuca*, *Orvieto*.

C Patrol, Crossing line 360° from Lat. 58 North, Long. 12.30´ West at 0400 daily, steering alternately 55° and 300°, ships 30 miles apart … *Champagne*, *Andes*, *Columbella*, *Patia*.

E Patrol, north-west of Iceland, off Isafjord … *Almanzora*, *Changuinola*, *Hildebrand* (joining).

Between B and C Patrols … *Alsatian*.

Patrolling North of Flannans … Armed Trawlers *Rushcoe* and *Tenby Castle*.

Special Patrol … Special Service Vessel *King Lear*.

Proceeding to Clyde … *Artois*.

Proceeding to Swarbacks Minn … Armed Trawler *Robert Smith*.

At Clyde … *Ebro*, *Gloucestershire*.

At Liverpool … *Otway*, *Arlanza*, *Motagua*, *Orcoma*, *Victorian*.

At Swarbacks Minn … Armed Trawlers *Saxon*, *Arley*, *Macleay*, *Faraday*, *Offa II*, *Marconi*.

At Scapa Flow … *Avenger*.

At Fleetwood … Armed Trawler *Walpole*.[1]

During the week 60 Ships were intercepted, of which 6 were sent in with Armed Guards, and 4 were allowed to proceed on account of having guaranteed to call at Halifax or other Colonial Port. Of the total number intercepted, 7 were Westbound and 20 Eastbound Neutrals.

15. During the period of this letter it will be noticed that the 10th Cruiser Squadron's Trawlers have been of great assistance in escorting to safety vessels sent in for examination with Armed Guards.

***

[1]*Moldavia* and *Hilary* omitted.

336. *Sub-Lieutenant James Henry Arnold, RNR*[1] *to Vice-Admiral Commanding Tenth Cruiser Squadron*

HM Trawler *Tenby Castle*, 10 April 1917

I have the honour to report that at 5.50 p.m. on the 6th April 1917, Lat. 58.15´N, Long. 7.59´W, approximate, steering ENE Mag. weather fine and clear, sea smooth, whilst on patrol, in company with HMT *Walpole* sighted a submarine Lat. 58.20´N, Long. 7.57´W approximate, steering W.

I opened fire at extreme range, shells falling at least 500 yards short. Submarine thereupon submerged. HMT *Walpole* 1 mile ahead of me meanwhile engaged another submarine who also submerged. I kept to my course and at 6.35 p.m. sighted a submarine Lat. 58.23´N, Long. 7.43´W, steering N. I immediately altered my course to port to bring my 12 PR into action, meanwhile firing with the three pounder. Shells from 3 PR falling short. The first shell from my 12 PR fired at a range of 7800 yards struck the submarine at the lower part of his conning tower. The second shell range 7750 just cleared to right of conning tower. The third shell struck submarine in practically the same place as the first shell. I saw the submarine heel over and disappear. I ceased firing and proceeded at once to position of submarine and found surface of the water thickly coated with oil. I steamed round the oil and *Walpole* dropped a depth charge. Both vessels remained cruising in the vicinity of oil until 0800 7th Apri1 1917. No further indication of the submarine being seen.

337. *Captain Dannreuther to Vice-Admiral Commanding Tenth Cruiser Squadron*

HMS *Patuca*, 11 April 1917

I have been informed by Lieut. Petit of the French Auxiliary Cruiser *Artois* that on his ship relieving HMS *Patuca* in Lat. 58.34´N, Long. 11.33´W at 1.45 a.m. on 2nd April 1917, the weather then being too rough to board, his ship stood by the Danish Schooner *Ebenezer* which ship I had intercepted at 8 p.m. on the previous evening, bound from Savannah to Aalborg with a cargo of 300 tons of Oil Cake, which had entered the German blockade area of her own accord and was then hove to in a north easterly gale. At 7 a.m. on the 2nd April, the weather

[1]Arnold, James Henry, DSC, RNR, Sub-Lieutenant 1916, Lieutenant 1918.

having moderated somewhat, Lieut. Petit and three of *Artois*' men were placed on board as an Armed Guard to conduct the ship to Stornoway. A strong NNE wind was experienced for the next three days and at 10 a.m. on the 6th April, when the vessel was nine miles NNE true from St Kilda, two periscopes were seen astern, the wind then being light with a heavy swell the schooner being under full sail and making about four knots, steering NNE, maintained her course.

2. The submarine rose to the awash condition put up her foremast with wireless attached, and hoisted the International Flag signals to abandon ship, but showed no colours. He commenced firing shrapnel and shell from two guns of about 4" size and continued firing for about an hour and a quarter whenever the submarine rose to the crest of a swell. Her firing was erratic but she hit the *Ebenezer* occasionally, and did not cease firing when the Armed Guard and crew consisting of five Danish abandoned the ship in a small boat. They fired at the small boat but failed to hit her. The submarine dived about noon, and was not seen again.

3. The Armed Guard covered their uniforms and the Officer burnt his confidential papers. The submarine did not close the boat or ask any questions, and therefore cannot have known there was a French Armed Guard present. At 2 p.m. on the same day HM Trawler *Rushcoe* picked up the boat containing the Armed Guard and crew and conveyed them to Stornoway. There were no casualties.

4. From Lieut. Petit's description the submarine was probably one of the *U 37* to *44* Class, she was unpainted and rusty, she had two periscopes well separated, showed one mast on the fore side of her conning tower with an aerial leading from the masthead to the after side. The guns were placed one before and the other abaft the conning tower which had square edges when seen from abeam, and a guard rail round the fore side of the conning tower. Her speed on the surface was about twelve knots. It is estimated that about 100 shells were fired, mostly shrapnel, before the schooner foundered. Schooner was built of wood and had an oil cake cargo but no fires were seen from German shell.

338. *Commodore P.H. Colomb to Vice-Admiral Commanding Tenth Cruiser Squadron*

HMS *Otway*, 14 April 1917

I have the honour to report that on the 9th April at 2.30 p.m. in Lat. 62.12´N, Long. 14.44´W I fell in with the Norwegian SS *Augusta*, who signalled she was from Hoganos to Reykjavik, laden with timber. The vessel further signalled that she was unmanagable but did not ask for any assistance at first. After a considerable time spent in signalling information was obtained at about 3.30 p.m. that the ship had sprung a leak and she then asked to be taken in tow. This was refused.

At 4.50 p.m. *Augusta* signalled that she wished to abandon ship immediately. At 5.34 p.m. a volunteer boat's crew left *Otway* and making two trips transferred the Norwegian crew (three officers and ten men) to *Otway* by 5.56 p.m. This I consider was a very creditable performance with the state of wind and sea (7) occasional blinding snow and the temperature at 18.

2. From information received from the Master of the *Augusta* it appears that the ship left Gothenburg on 1st April and called at Stavanger on 3rd April. A northerly gale was encountered on Saturday 7th April, and on Sunday 8th April the ship sprang a leak. The hand pumps proving ineffective, the crew had to resort to buckets for bailing out. The rising water eventually put the fires out on Monday morning 9th April and when *Otway* fell in with her there were eight feet of water in the Engine and Boiler rooms.

3. The Master declined to sign a written statement to the effect that he had abandoned the ship. He expressed his willingness to return to her only if a trawler should arrive to tow her if necessary and said he could count on four or five of the crew returning with him and that the remainder would probably follow their example. He, however, refused to return unless either *Otway* or a trawler were in attendance. A certificate to this effect signed by him is attached.

4. *Otway* stood by the derelict during Monday night 9th April. She was lost sight of at times due to heavy snow squalls. On Tuesday afternoon at 4.50 p.m. the weather being improved, a working party was sent to the ship to ascertain her condition. It was found that she had thirteen feet of water in her holds, Engine and Boiler Rooms, etc., but otherwise did not seem to be in a sinking condition, though she had settled down considerably since the previous day and her stern was nearly awash.

On Wednesday there being no sign of the trawler (GY 698) which you despatched vide your signals 1335 and 2240 of 10th April, *Otway* continued to steam in the vicinity of the abandoned ship until 2.10 p.m. when she heeled over on to her beam ends, righted herself and finally sank slowly in Lat. 61.18´N, Long. 15.0´W. The only wreckage observed was a certain amount of timber – deck cargo – and one boat.

5. The Norwegian crew from *Augusta*[1] were transferred to the Norwegian SS *Granfos* at 7.30 p.m. on Thursday 12 April, bound from Halifax to Copenhagen via Stavanger.

339. *Admiralty Minute by F. Fisher 'For DTD'*

17 April 1917

The facts have been considered at the Bunker Committee.

It appears that A.P. Moller, the owner of the *Europa* and *Belgien* [328, 329], sent telegrams to his captains in America directing them to destroy all papers relating to the call at Kirkwall, and that when called upon to explain these telegrams he stated that his object was to remove all documentary evidence of the intentions to call, but that the vessels would in fact call as heretofore.

From the conversations with the captains when intercepted it is clear that Mr Moller's telegram had been misunderstood, and it is possible that Mr Moller drafted his instructions with the deliberate intention that they should be misunderstood. The Bunker Committee felt, however, that the evidence was not strong enough to establish this and that on the circumstances his explanation must be accepted.

340. *Vice-Admiral Tupper to Commanding Officer HMS* King Lear

HMS *Alsatian*, 19 April 1917

Being in all respects ready for sea you are to leave Swarbacks Minn and proceed to the neighbourhood, say within ten miles from shore, of Seidisfjord, Iceland, passing within about ten miles of the North-East coast of the Faeroes. Thence you should cruise along the coast as far as Portland Light and then shape course as if proceeding to Stornoway, crossing the 100 fathom line about four hours before dark. After dark you should again put out to sea and approach and enter Swarbacks Minn in a similar manner.

When in the neighbourhood of the Hebrides you should be careful not to go to the South of Latitude 58.30´ North.

2. You should sail under Norwegian colours, but need not paint Norwegian flags on the ship's side.

3. Any suspicious looking vessels met with should be reported by

[1]Commodore Colomb lists the names of the Master, two Mates, two Engineers, Steward, four Able Seamen, two Firemen and one Boy.

W/T to the nearest Tenth Cruiser Squadron Cruiser when in touch.

Don't go in Area 62–66 North, 0–5 West.

4. The receipt of this Memorandum is to be acknowledged by the signal '039 of 19 April received'.

341. *Vice-Admiral Tupper to Admiralty*

HMS *Alsatian*, 8 May 1917

Report of Proceedings, 23 April–6 May 1917

***

1. Monday, 23 April – *Avenger* rejoining patrol from Scapa reported that at 7 a.m. a submarine had been sighted submerged in Latitude 61.32´, Longitude 4.0´ West.

At 8 a.m *Champagne* in Latitude 58.4´ North, Longitude 11.32´ West intercepted the Norwegian S.V. *Olivebank* from Gulf Port (USA) to London via Stornoway with a general cargo. I directed her to place an Armed Guard on board, and escort the Vessel until able to turn her over to *Rushcoe* and *Tenby Castle* who were directed to proceed to a rendezvous well outside the 100 fathom line.[1]

The Commander-in-Chief, Grand Fleet, having informed me that the two Sailing Vessels met with by the Belgian SS *Liege* (vide paragraph 13 of my last Report of Proceedings) were probably raiders, I asked *Orvieto* if any further details concerning the vessels could be given, but apart from the fact that the ships were large, no additional information is available.

On establishing W/T communication with E Patrol through *Hildebrand* – who was now proceeding thence to relieve *Changuinola* – I was informed that the passengers and despatches referred to in Admiralty Letter M. 03419 of 21 March had been landed at Reykjavik by *Changuinola* on 20 April.

2. Tuesday, 24 April – *Almanzora* through *Hildebrand* reported that the ice extended from Latitude 66.50´ North, Longitude 26.12´ West, to Latitude 67.5´ North, Longitude 22.40´ West, with dangerous lumps 5 to 10 miles to the Southward. Loose ice was reported observed in Latitude 66.10´ North, Longitude 26.20´ West and Latitude 66.20´ North Longitude 25.50´ West.

Alsatian in Latitude 60.52´ North, Longitude 13.15´ West, boarded

[1]*Olivebank* was not detained.

the Danish Schooner *Harriet* bound for Thorshaven with a cargo of salt. As the vessel was in possession of a British Consular Certificate of destination, she was allowed to proceed, but I have asked (in my message 528) for information as to the present policy generally with regard to cargoes of salt for fish curing purposes proceeding to Scandinavia, the Faroes and Iceland respectively.

At 6 a.m. *Champagne* who was still escorting *Olivebank* reported she was chasing a submarine in Latitude 58.42´ North, Longitude 8.50´ West. Several Shots were fired by *Champagne* and the submarine submerged. At 6.30 a.m. *Rushcoe* and *Tenby Castle* arrived on the scene and took over the escort of *Olivebank*, *Champagne* resuming patrol.

I had ordered *Champagne* to escort this vessel instead of keeping her well outside the submarine area as I thought she would be alert enough to deal with a submarine if sighted; and further, as *Olivebank* was so to speak in charge of a French Officer, I considered it best to let him look after the Ship until I could get a trawler escort. Subsequent events proved that my confidence was not misplaced; and I consider the action taken by *Capitaine* Berthelot both smart and creditable.

As the Norwegian Sailing Vessel *Marita* also sent in by *Champagne* the previous morning should have been in the vicinity I directed one of the Trawlers to search for her and escort her in. Shortly afterwards, however, information was received that she had been sunk by an enemy submarine at 11 a.m. on the same day in Latitude 58.30´ North, Longitude 11.20´ West.[1] Fortunately the Armed Guard and crew were picked up by the Armed Whaler *Cowwhale* and taken to Stornoway. The submarine which sank *Marita* was reported to be acting in company with another. *Marita* was bound from Buenos Ayres to Aarhus with a cargo of 2,650 tons of Maize.

In view of these reports, C Patrol was moved to the Westward with centre line on meridian of Latitude 14.30´ West.

Arley returning to patrol from Swarbacks Minn engaged a submarine at 8 a.m. in Latitude 50.20´ North, Longitude 3.34´ West, steering North West by West at 13 knots. The submarine submerged.

During the course of the afternoon *Patia* was met and I went on board. Target practice was carried out and I inspected the Ship's company and mess decks. She appears to be well kept, the mess decks being tidy especially the part belonging to the boys, which is quite separate from the remainder. The firemen's quarters, however, are rather poor.

[1]By *U 82*.

The target practice was quite good being above the average, though the anti-submarine arrangements required some improvement. This latter I exercised three times and also dropped a depth charge close to the target to instruct the Officers and men in their use.

I consider the ship to be efficient and a credit to all concerned.

Orvieto met the Special Service Vessel *King Lear* at 5.30 p.m. in Latitude 63.2´ North, Longitude 13.00´ West, and passed orders to the latter to proceed with despatch and cruise between Latitude 58.30´ North, Longitude 11 West and Latitude 60.30´ North, Long. 4 W, in view of the reports of enemy submarines in that vicinity.

3. Wednesday, 25 April – During the forenoon, orders were given for B Patrol to re-dispose as follows:

To cross line 360° from Lat. 62.20´ North, Long. 12 West, at 1400 steering 270°, and at 2200 steering 90°, 30 miles apart.

Andes was despatched to relieve *Almanzora* on E Patrol, with special orders to look out for SS *Ausable* …

The Armed Trawlers *Marconi* and *Faraday* were directed to proceed to the South-East of Iceland, to work with the Ship on A, and for *Macleay* to patrol on the Meridian of 10 West, between 61 and 62 North.

4. Thursday, 26 April – Overcast; misty; wind in WNW, force 6–7, with heavy sea.

At noon, *Orvieto*, in Lat. 63.17´ North, Long. 10 West, intercepted the Norwegian Sailing Vessel *Yuba*, from Savannah to Aarhus, with a cargo of oilcake. When the weather had sufficiently moderated, an Armed Guard was placed on board … and the vessel sent to Stornoway, escorted by the Armed Trawlers *Faraday* and *Marconi*. Information has since been received that the *Yuba* arrived safely.[1]

5. Friday, 27 April – Overcast and misty, with wind and sea moderating.

At 7 a.m., *Columbella* intercepted a distress signal in Lat. 56.28´ North, Long. 11.50´West, from the SS *Roseleaf*. This steamer was being shelled by an enemy submarine but reported shortly afterwards that the latter had submerged. The SS *Dromore* was, however, torpedoed some three hours later in Lat. 56.48´ North, Long. 11 West.[2]

[1]A question was raised about the size of the shipment of oilcake in *Yuba*, and about the absence of a Navicert for one item; the Customs were told to investigate further; the enquiries were made at the Danish Trade office; altogether the process took five weeks before the explanation of the problem was received and the ship permitted to sail on (TS 14/14 of 30 April and 14/15 of 2 May to 2 June 1917).

[2]The submarine which shelled *Roseleaf* is not identified, but it was *U 58* which sank *Dromore*, and by implication and geography they were probably the same.

In view of these reports, orders were given for the Special Service Vessel *King Lear* to proceed to the locality, and also for the Armed Trawlers *Arley* and *Saxon* to endeavour to find and rescue the crew of *Dromore*. Unfortunately, however, the *King Lear* could not carry out these orders owing to being short of coal.

Orcoma, who was rejoining from Liverpool after an absence of $3^1/_2$ months on special service in South Atlantic, was met during the forenoon. Captain Coppinger came on board to confer with me. On parting company, *Orcoma* was given orders to rendezvous *Orvieto* and transfer despatches which she had for the Rear-Admiral, thence to join B Patrol.

During this day, orders were given for B patrol to take up the following patrol plan:

Ships (four) to assume the following positions at 0600, 28 April, viz, Lat. 64.17´N, Long. 12.37´W; Lat. 62.53´N, Long. 12.22´W; Lat. 62.24´N, Long. 9.25´W; Lat. 63.51´N, Long. 9.43´W; thence to steer, anti-clockwise, round the quadrangle formed by joining these four positions, arranging to be at turning points every 8 hours.

About 8 p.m., I met the Armed Trawler *Macleay* and gave her orders for patrol.

6. Saturday, 28 April – Overcast and misty, with rain and snow; wind in NE, force 4–5.

Columbella intercepted a message from the Armed Trawler *Lord Lister* stating that the British Oiler *Bullmouth* had been torpedoed at 8 a.m. in Lat. 56.20´N, Long. 11.20´W but was still afloat, and requested assistance in towing the vessel.[1] *Arley* and *Saxon* – who were still searching for the crew of SS *Dromore*, but without success – were ordered to proceed and render the required assistance. Unfortunately, however, the Oiler sank shortly before 10 o'clock.

Avenger, at about 4 p.m., reported she had been chasing a two-masted schooner with auxiliary engine, but had lost sight of her 10 miles ahead, in Lat. 64.26´ North, Long. 13.39´ West, during a thick snow-storm. *Avenger* was ordered to steer west along the coast at a good speed, and then search back to the eastward in daylight.

Almanzora, who was then on her way south from E Patrol, was directed to assist in endeavouring to intercept the vessel. Nothing further, however, was seen of her during the remainder of the day.

Admiralty Message No. 896 was received, informing me that vessels carrying salt for the Faroes should be sent in for examination, while

[1]This was *U 58* again.

those for Scandinavia and Iceland should be allowed to proceed, in the absence of suspicious circumstances.

The following vessels bound for Thorshavn with salt had, however, already been allowed to proceed:

Danish Sailing Vessels *Harriet*, *A.H. Friis* and *Proven*, from Setubal.

Danish Sailing Vessel *Ami*, from Lisbon.

Of these, the *A.H. Friis* was re-intercepted and sent in under Armed Guard.[1]

7. Sunday, 29 April – At 5.30 a.m., *Alsatian*, in Lat. 61.30´ North, Long. 14.40´ West, spoke the Danish Fishery Cruiser *Valkyrien* …

Avenger boarded the Icelandic Trawler *Kopur* (BA 138) and, her papers being correct, allowed her to proceed. *Avenger* reports that this vessel is believed to be the one which had been lost sight of the previous day (Vide paragraph 6). It is satisfactory to have been able to find her again.

At 11.30 a.m., *Kildonan Castle*, in Lat. 62.44´N, Long. 11.12´W, boarded the Danish SS *Danebod*, in ballast, from Copenhagen to New Orleans via Halifax. As this vessel was not on the Admiralty List as having been granted permission to call at the latter port, a guarantee was obtained … before allowing her to proceed.

At noon, the disposition of the Squadron was as follows:

A Patrol, Between Lat. 64 & 65 N, on meridian 12 W … *Avenger* (Rejoining from B).

B Patrol, proceeding to a line 330° from Lat. 62 N, Long. 11 W, crossing at noon steering 255° and at midnight steering 75, 30 miles apart … *Kildonan Castle*, *Orcoma*, *Otway*.

C Patrol, proceeding to a line 360° from Lat. 58.30´N, Long. 13 W, to steer 70° till reaching meridian of 9 W, then turning to westward, 30 miles apart … *Patia*, *Columbella*, *Victorian*, *Changuinola*.

E Patrol, On line 298° from Lat. 65.30´N, Long 25.7´W, steering 28 and 208° … *Andes*, *Hildebrand*.

Between B and C Patrols … *Alsatian*.

Engaged on Escort and Rescue Work … Armed Trawlers *Macleay*, *Offa II*, *Tenby Castle*, *Saxon*, *Rushcoe*, *Arley*, *Marconi*, *Faraday*.

Joining Patrol from Clyde … *Ebro* (to C), *Gloucestershire* (to B).

Joining Patrol from Swarbacks Minn … *Virginian* (to B).

Joining Squadron from Lowestoft … Armed Trawlers *Lord Lansdowne*, *Elf King*, *Edwardian*, *Thomas Stratton*, *Stalwart*.

[1] *A.H. Friis* was allowed to sail on to Thorshavn after investigation (TS 14/15 of 5 May 1917).

Joining Patrol from Oban … Armed Trawlers *Sitvel*, *Corrie Roy*, *St Denis*.
Proceeding to Liverpool … *Almanzora*.
Proceeding to Swarbacks Minn … *Orvieto*.
At Clyde … *Champagne*, *Artois*, *Moldavia*, *Hilary*.
At Liverpool … *Armadale Castle*, *Arlanza*, *Motagua*.
At Swarbacks Minn … Special Service Vessel *King Lear*.
At Oban … Armed Trawler *Robert Smith*.
At Loch Ewe … *Patuca*.
At Fleetwood … Armed Trawler *Walpole*[1]

During the week, 78 ships were intercepted, of which 3 were sent in with Armed Guards, and 9 allowed to proceed on account of having guaranteed to call at Halifax or other Colonial Port. Of the total number intercepted, 12 were Westbound and 16 Eastbound Neutrals.

At 5.30 p.m., *Almanzora* was met. Captain Church came on board to report on the work of E Patrol. On parting company, *Almanzora* was given orders to proceed to Liverpool for her routine coaling and refit.

Shortly before midnight, a signal was received from the Commander-in-Chief, directing that patrols should be so disposed to ensure that no westward bound vessel could pass between the South Coast of Iceland and the Northern ship of A Patrol without being sighted.

A Patrol (one ship) was thereupon ordered to take up a patrol of 100 miles on a line 65° from Lat. 63.25´ North, Long. 17 West while B Patrol was moved 20 miles to the North.

The Armed Trawlers on patrol were employed in escorting the British Steamships *Mendip Range*, *Gwladys* and *Hermione*, intercepted during the course of the day by ships on C Patrol.

8. Monday, 30 April – Lovely day with bright sunshine.

Alsatian, in Lat. 60.45´ North, Long. 14 West, boarded the Norwegian Sailing Vessel *Yola*, from Buenos Aires to Odense, with a cargo of wheat consigned to the Merchants Guild. Her papers were endorsed by the Danish Minister, and countersigned by the British Consul at Buenos Aires. In view of the nature of the cargo, however, I ordered an Armed Guard to be placed on board, and directed the Armed Trawler *Macleay* to escort the vessel to Stornoway.[2]

Three Eastbound Steamers were also examined by *Alsatian* in the middle watch.

[1]This total of 43 ships is the largest in the Northern Patrol's history.

[2]*Yola* was allowed to sail on after the Contraband Committee investigated (TS 14/15 of 1 and 3 May 1917).

Orcoma, in Lat. 62.43´ North, Long. 13.20´ West, boarded the Norwegian Sailing Vessel *Vik*, from Buenos Aires to Aarhus, via Azores, with a cargo of 3300 tons of maize. The Master desired to return to Halifax rather than be sent to Stornoway, but I directed *Orcoma* to inform him that it was regretted his request could not be complied with. An Armed Guard was placed on board to take her in.[1]

During this day, *Hildebrand*, on E Patrol, reported the ice conditions to be as follows:

> Main Ice floe extending from Lat. 67.4´ North, Long. 23.30´ West to Lat. 67.39´N, Long. 24.22´ West, to Lat. 66.71´ North, Long. 25.50´ West, thence to Lat. 66.23' North, Long. 26.11' West; loose ice and small lumps extending from 10 to 15 miles to South-east and South of first-named position and about 8 to 10 miles outside remainder of floe.

The Norwegian Steamer *L.O. Stansland* from Bergen to New York in ballast was intercepted by *Orcoma* and allowed to proceed on giving a written guarantee to call at Halifax …

9. Tuesday, 1 May – Very fine clear weather.

The disposition of B Patrol was modified as follows:

To cross line 330° from Lat. 62 North, Long. 12 30´ West at noon steering 60°, and at midnight steering 240°; five ships, 30 miles apart.

Avenger was ordered to continue patrolling midway between the Northern Ship of B Patrol and the Coast of Iceland.

As it appeared that an enemy raider was expected, W/T communication in the Squadron was restricted to urgent messages only.

At 10 a.m. *Kildonan Castle* was met and Captain Warton came on board to discuss various matters with me.

While in company with *Kildonan Castle*, experiments were carried out with smoke producing apparatus, boxes and shell, a separate report on which will be forwarded in due course.

Generally speaking the smoke boxes did not produce sufficient smoke to adequately screen the Ship even from a submarine, though 4 boxes were thrown overboard at the same time. The white smoke producing apparatus, however, proved excellent and the Ship was entirely screened by the smoke produced.

The smoke shells gave out very little smoke and are not considered satisfactory.

[1] *Vik* was allowed to go on after investigation (TS 14/15 of 7 May 1917).

On parting company, *Kildonan Castle* was ordered to proceed [to] B Patrol, extending it to the Southward.

Information was received during the evening that the Firth of Clyde had been closed to traffic owing to mines.

10. Wednesday, 2 May – South-westerly wind with mist and rain.

Information was received that the Norwegian barque *Yola*, sent in by *Alsatian* on 30th April, had reached Stornoway, having been escorted in by trawlers.

During the afternoon *Otway* in Lat. 63 North, Long. 14.7´ West, intercepted the Norwegian SS *Obj* (?) (ex *Lifjeld*), bound from Narvik to Philadelphia, via Halifax, with a cargo of magnetic ore. As this vessel was not on the Admiralty List of Ships excused calling at a Port in the United Kingdom, and was not in possession of any clearance or Consular certificate, she was only allowed to proceed after giving a written guarantee to call at Halifax …

At about 9.30 p.m. the S.O.S call was heard from the British Oiler *San Melito*, who was being attacked by a submarine in Lat. 59.25´ North, Long. 4.50´ West. Shortly afterwards, however, it was ascertained that the Oiler had escaped.[1]

As I had ascertained from the Commander-in-Chief Grand Fleet that a homeward bound raider was expected shortly, Ships on B Patrol were ordered to reverse the times of crossing their centre line, i.e. to cross at noon steering 240° and at midnight steering 60°. The Armed Trawlers *Faraday* and *Marconi*, who were working in support of B Patrol, were given orders to carry out a line ahead Patrol between Lat. 61.30´ North, Long. 8 West, and Lat. 62.20´ North, Long. 9 West, keeping within visual distance of each other.

W/T silence was maintained except for two hours to enable reports to be collected.

11. Thursday, 3 May – South-westerly wind with mist and rain.

Saxon in Lat. 56.50´ North, Long. 9.32´ West, intercepted the British SS *Hubert*, bound for New York. This vessel reported that she had on board 14 of the crew of the American SS *Rockingham* which had been torpedoed on 1st instant by two submarines in Lat. 55.8´ North, Long. 12.13´ West.[2] As it was reported that two boats of the *Rockingham* were still unaccounted for, *Saxon* proceeded to search for them, but without result.

At 3.30 p.m. *Macleay* sighted a large enemy submarine in Lat. 59.6´ North, Long. 8 West, steering North-west, on the surface, and engaged

[1]The identity of the submarine is not known.

[2]By *U 69*.

her firing three shots. The submarine submerged and was not again seen.

12. Friday, 4 May – Lovely weather, clear and sunny.

Columbella proceeding to Clyde, was diverted to Loch Swilly owing to the former Port being still closed to traffic.

Three of the new Armed Trawlers recently attached to my command, viz: *Sitvel*, *St Dennis* and *Corrie Roy* sailed from Swarbacks Minn for patrol. I am very glad that the new trawlers are commencing work as I would point out that they are proving most useful for escorting vessels.

A list of vessels safely escorted in by Trawlers attached to the 10th Cruiser Squadron since 19 April is attached … Several submarines have been reported as operating in the vicinity during the period.

13. Saturday, 5 May – Lovely weather.

The disposition of C Patrol was altered as follows:

To cross line 130° from Lat. 60 North, Long. 12 West at 1800 steering 180° and 0600 steering 360°; three ships, 40 miles apart.

Armed Trawlers *Macleay* and *Offa II* were met and after giving them some fresh provisions, etc., I directed them to cruise on Faroe Bank to protect British fishing Trawlers, several of which I hear are now working there.

At 4 p.m. I met *Orvieto*. The Rear-Admiral came on board *Alsatian* and was given general directions for the conduct of the patrols during my absence.

On parting company, *Orvieto* was directed to proceed to B Patrol, extending it to the Southward.

A letter was received from the Commander-in-Chief Rosyth, informing me that a Naval Sub-Base is about to be established at Oban under the charge of a Commander, RN. I am glad to hear this as it will enable the 10th Cruiser Squadron Trawlers to use it to greater advantage. At the same time I would add that Lieutenant-Colonel C. Heaton-Ellis has looked after the 10th Cruiser Squadron Trawlers exceedingly well and has taken a great deal of trouble to improve the general efficiency as well as the comfort of the Officers and men.

14. Sunday, 6 May – Lovely weather still continues.

I received the approval of the Commander-in-Chief Grand Fleet to proceed to Liverpool in *Alsatian*, leaving the Rear-Admiral in charge.

At noon the disposition of the Squadron was as follows:

> A Patrol, Midway between B Patrol and South Coast of Iceland, conforming to movements of B … *Avenger*.
>
> B Patrol, Crossing line 330° from Lat. 62 North, Long. 12.30´ West at noon, steering 240° and at midnight steering 60°, 30 miles apart …

Orvieto, *Hilary*, *Gloucestershire*, *Orcoma*, *Virginian*, *Otway*.

C Patrol, Crossing line 130° from Lat. 60 North, Long. 12 West, at 1800 steering 180°, and at 0600 steering 360°, 40 miles apart ... *Patuca*, *Ebro*, *Victorian*.

E Patrol, North West of Iceland ... *Andes*, *Hildebrand*.

Between B & C Patrols ... *Alsatian*.

Patrolling SE of Hvalsbuk ... Armed Trawlers *Corrie Roy*, *St. Dennis*.

Patrolling off Faroe Bank ... Armed Trawlers *Sitvel*, *Offa II*, *Macleay* (joining).

Patrolling to North of Flannans ... Armed Trawlers *Saxon*, *Robert Smith*.

Rejoining Patrol from Liverpool ... *Armadale Castle* (to E).

Rejoining Patrol from Swarbacks Minn ... *Changuinola* (to A).

Proceeding to Clyde ... *Columbella*.

Proceeding to Swarbacks Minn ... Armed Trawlers *Lord Lansdowne*, *Elf King*, *Edwardian*, *Thomas Stratton*, *Stalwart* (latter joining Squadron from Lowestoft via Oban), *Marconi*, *Faraday*.

Proceeding to Oban ... Armed Trawlers *Arley*, *Walpole*.

At Clyde ... *Patia*, *Champagne**, *Artois**, *Moldavia*.

At Liverpool ... *Almanzora*, *Arlanza*, *Motagua*.

At Swarbacks Minn ... *Kildonan Castle*.

At Oban ... Armed Trawlers *Rushcoe*, *Tenby Castle*.

*NOTE – The *Artois* and *Champagne* should have left Clyde for patrol on the 1st and 4th May respectively, but have been prevented by mines.

During the week 74 Ships were intercepted (including 37 Trawlers), of which 4 were sent in with Armed Guards, and 9 were allowed to proceed on account of having guaranteed to call at Halifax, or other Colonial Port. Of the total number intercepted, 12 were Westbound and 10 Eastbound Neutrals.

I inspected the Ship's Company of *Alsatian* at Divisions and also went round the mess decks and sleeping quarters. Everything is highly satisfactory. They look better than I have ever seen them and are a credit to the Navy.

15. *Alsatian* being on her way to Liverpool for routine coaling and refit, I turned over Command of the 10th Cruiser Squadron on patrol to Rear-Admiral Morgan Singer, C.B. in *Orvieto* at 6 p.m. 7th May.

16. *Alsatian* arrived at the Bar, Liverpool, at 9 p.m. and proceeded up harbour.

***

342. *Admiralty to Commander-in-Chief Grand Fleet*

5 May 1917

With reference to your letter of the 25th April ... respecting an engagement between HM Trawler *Tenby Castle* and an enemy submarine, I am commanded by My Lords Commissioners of the Admiralty to inform you that the sinking of the submarine on this occasion is considered improbable, but they have been pleased to award the Distinguished Service Cross to Sub-Lieutenant J.H. Arnold, RNR, in respect of this engagement, and that Officer is to be called upon to forward the names of two members of the Crew for the award of the DSM.[1]

343. *Vice-Admiral R. Tupper to Admiralty*

HMS *Virginian*, 25 May 1917

Report of Proceedings, 8–24 May 1917.[2]

***

1. During the period covered by this letter, the patrols have been disposed on and between lines 2 (from the Butt of Lewis to the Coast of Iceland in Long. 15 W) and 3 (from Rockall Bank to the Coast of Iceland in Long. 17 W). A patrol of two ships has also been maintained North West of Iceland, guarding Denmark Strait between North Cape and the ice, which has sometimes been down to 25 miles from the coast.

The Tenth Cruiser Squadron Trawlers have been employed off the South East Coast of Iceland, in the neighbourhoods of Faroe Bank and Flannan Islands, and between Sulisker and Sydero. They have continued to do most useful work in escorting vessels to safety from various positions in areas patrolled, between Iceland and the Hebrides.

2. The number of Ships intercepted during the period (18 days) covered by this letter has been large – 219, of which 13 were sent in

[1]In this the Admiralty assessors were correct.

[2]Tupper from this Report used a more summary format, providing much less detail; the detail is relegated to an 'enclosure', indigestible in style and content; only one of these is printed, at [367]; see Chapter 12, page 731, note 1. The two previous Reports [335, 341] were certainly very long; there is no record, but it would seem likely that the new format was the result of Admiralty complaints.

under Armed Guard, and 25 were allowed to proceed Westward as having guaranteed to call at, and 44 Eastward, as having cleared Halifax or other British Colonial Port.

***

3. Of the ships intercepted during the period under review, the following are of interest:

(1) The Belgian Relief Ships *Gothland* and *Syrie* ..., westbound from Rotterdam, in ballast, were not on the Admiralty List as having been excused calling at a United Kingdom port. Guarantees to call at Halifax were obtained before they were allowed to proceed.
(2) The Danish Sailing Vessel *Mary Boyes* ... from Iceland to Faeroes with fish, had no clearance and refused to sign a guarantee. She was sent to Stornoway with an Armed Guard.[1]
(3) The Norwegian Sailing Vessel *Queen of Scots* ... was intercepted by *Ebro* on 16 May. This vessel was sent in to Stornoway with an Armed Guard from *Ebro*, in accordance with Admiralty Telegram 1710 of 13 March, but has not yet arrived, although every effort has been – and is being – made to regain touch with her, with the aid of the Tenth Cruiser Squadron trawlers and other vessels.

    On May 17th I heard at Admiralty that this vessel probably had a disguised German national on board. Consequently when I resumed charge of the patrols in 23 May and heard that *Queen of Scots* had been intercepted and sent in under Armed Guard, I requested the Commander-in-Chief Grand Fleet that destroyers and other craft operating in the North Sea be warned to send her in if met, as it seems possible she had sailed East with the Armed Guard overpowered [354].
(4) The Dutch SS *Rijndam* ... which was cleared from Halifax for Rotterdam, had 58 German and 146 Austro-Hungarian passengers on board, including the Austrian Ambassador to America, and the German Ministers to China and Cuba, with their respective staffs; also 6 bags of Embassy mails. The Ambassador and Ministers had claimed to be taken to Bergen instead of Rotterdam, and the Master requested advice as to whether he should comply. Admiralty instructions were asked, and in accordance with Message timed 2337 of 17 May, *Orcoma* was directed to advise the Master that he was cleared for Rotterdam only, and not for Bergen.

[1]*Mary Boyes* was considered by the Contraband Committee, but then allowed to go on (TS 14/15 of 18 May 1917).

(5) The Swedish Sailing Vessels *Drott*, *Argo* and *Ines* … were sent to Stornoway with Armed Guards …, giving the names of these three ships and also the *Elin* as having been refused permission to proceed from Scandinavia to Iceland without calling at a United Kingdom Port. The *Elin* has not so far been seen [347, para. 4].

4. *Moldavia* sighted a submarine at 5 p.m, on 13 May in Lat. 56.45´ North, Long. 10.4´ West. The submarine broke surface, but immediately submerged, steering South-East …

The Dutch Steamers *Bernisse* and *Elve* …, with Armed Guards from *Patia* on board, were torpedoed on the morning of 23 May, in approximately Lat. 59.37´ North, Long. 3.20´ West. The former was safely towed in to Kirkwall, but the latter was sunk. Fortunately, however, both Armed Guards are safe.[1]

On 24 May *Saxon*, having previously engaged a submarine in the vicinity, reported that at 6 a.m., in Lat. 58.54´ North, Long. 9.4´ West, HMS *Merops* was attacked by a submarine, and *Merops* sank her. *Merops*, having sustained a certain amount of damage, was taken in tow by *Saxon*, for Longhope.[2] Medical assistance was offered for two men wounded, but was not considered necessary.

5. His Majesty King George V honoured the 10th Cruiser Squadron by Inspecting the Officers and Ship's Company of HMS *Alsatian* in Canada Dock, Liverpool, on Wednesday 16th May. The Vice-Admiral had the Honour of Presenting the principal officers to His Majesty.

***

344. *Vice-Admiral Tupper to Commander-in-Chief Grand Fleet*

HMS *Alsatian*, 15 May 1917

I have the honour to request that a Seaplane Carrier may be lent to the Tenth Cruiser Squadron during the summer months.

I consider that with such a vessel stationed in the neighbourhood of West Loch Tarbet or St Kilda, or in the neighbourhood of Faroe Bank, working in conjunction with the Tenth Cruiser Squadron Cruisers and Trawlers, there would be excellent opportunities of sinking submarines by bombing from seaplanes.

2. During a recent interview with Commodore Paine he suggested that HMS *Riviera*, with four seaplanes, would be a suitable vessel, and

[1]Both torpedoed by *U 87*.
[2]This was *U 87* again.

advised me to ask that she should be lent, at any rate for three or four months, to the Tenth Cruiser Squadron.

If therefore you think fit to forward the application to the Admiralty I have great hopes of good results [348].

345. *Lieutenant Chas E. Elliot, RNR (Ty) to Commanding Officer, HMS* Alsatian

HMS *Alsatian*, 18 May 1917

***

My orders on boarding the SS *Stralsund* were to proceed in her to the port for which she was bound, viz. Troon, and as stated in the first paragraph of my report dated 22nd February 1917 [319] course was set in accordance to pass 10 miles west of St Kilda. It was only after the vessel had been sunk and the crew and armed guard picked up by HM Trawler *Rushcoe* that orders were given for them to be landed at Stornoway, that being the nearest port. I therefore suggest that the statement quoted by Messrs Moller & Co. [316], that the ship had been diverted, is incorrect. The Master stated however that he was undecided whether it would not be better to go to Stornoway in preference to Troon, but no action to that effect was considered practically.

With regard to the last paragraph of the Company's letter I have to state that the Master did promise not to inform the Submarine Commander of the presence of a British armed guard on board, after I had urged him not to do so, but with regard to clothing borrowed, he had no hand in dressing up either myself or the one man who accompanied me as armed guard beyond saying 'Yes' when I asked him to lend us some clothes. Afterwards I asked the steward to lend me some clothes and was informed there were some in the cabin. I thereupon picked up a pair of old trousers and an overcoat – clothes which I suggest had been discarded by their owner.

Leading Seaman Lewis meanwhile went to a Fireman in the stokehold who had already changed into his best clothes, and was holding an old suit of dungarees, coat and trousers, and on his asking for them was given them by the fireman.

When we had been in the boat some time, the steward remarked that he felt cold and I had to give him his overcoat back.

Finally I would mention that, as stated in the last paragraph of my previous report, I was instructed by the SNO at Stornoway to report that the Master of the *Stralsund* had been given £30 as a reward for not disclosing the presence of the armed guard to the submarine commander.

346. *Admiralty to Under Secretary of State, Foreign Office*

24 May 1917

With reference to your letter of the 24th ultimo … enclosing a copy of a despatch from HM Minister at Christiania, relative to the attack on the Norwegian barque *Thekla* by an enemy submarine [332], I am commanded by My Lords Commissioners of the Admiralty to acquaint you for the information of Lord Robert Cecil, that they concur in the view expressed by HM Consul at Christiania as to the action of the Master in concealing the presence of the Armed Guard on board this vessel, and they have decided that a gratuity of £30 should be awarded to him from Naval Funds in recognition of his conduct on this occasion. As however it is improbable that the *Thekla* will be calling at an early date at a port in the United Kingdom, I am to request that if no objection is seen the gratuity of £30 may be awarded to Captain Olaf Tobiasson with an expression of appreciation of his conduct, by HM Minister at Christiania. I am also to ask that Sir M. Findlay may be requested in making the award to impress upon Captain Tobiasson the necessity of maintaining strict secrecy in regard to the incident.

347. *Vice-Admiral Tupper to Admiralty*

HMS *Virginian*, 7 June 1917

Report of Proceedings, 25 May–6 June 1917

***

1. During the period covered by this letter, the Patrols have been disposed on and between Lines 2 (from the Butt of Lewis to the Coast of Iceland in Long. 15 West) and 3 (from Rockall Bank to the Coast of Iceland in Long. 17 West), excepting that on account of the marked submarine activity in the Southern part of the Patrol Area I deemed it advisable, on 5th June, to move C Patrol somewhat West of Line 2. A Patrol of two ships has also been maintained off the North-West Coast of Iceland, guarding Denmark Strait between North Cape and the ice, and since 31st May one ship has been working off the East Coast of Iceland, between Seidisfiord and Langanes.

***

The Armed Trawlers attached to the Squadron have been employed off the South-East Coast of Iceland, in the neighbourhood of Faroe Bank, and between Sulisker and Sydero. They have done very good work in protecting and escorting British and Neutral shipping, and hunting submarines, during a period of almost unprecedented submarine activity.

2. The number of ships intercepted during the period from 25 May to 5 June (12 days) has been 134, of which 41 were trawlers. Out of that total, 3 were sent in under Armed Guard, and 27 were allowed to proceed Westward as having guaranteed to call at, and 29 Eastward as having been cleared from, Halifax or other British oversea port.

***

3. Of the ships intercepted during the period under review, the following are of interest:

(1) The Dutch Schooner *Proefneming* (V.L.134), Case No. 1080, was intercepted by *Moldavia* on 26 May, and, after rigid examination, was allowed to proceed. On receipt of Admiralty message 2220, steps were taken to re-intercept her, this being accomplished the following morning, and the vessel sent to Stornoway under Armed Guard escorted by an Armed Trawler. She had been 30 days out, in water ballast, but had caught no fish, the fishing gear being stowed in the hold. She had provisions for 90 days. Whether she is merely being used for observing and reporting movements of 10th Cruiser Squadron Ships or whether she had brought stores for submarines and had discharged them, is not known. Her crew are not fishermen and she is undoubtedly suspicious.[1]

(2) The Danish Schooner *Rise* (Case No. 1154), from Goteborg to Rabat, Morocco, with timber, was allowed to proceed on guaranteeing to call at Gibraltar without intermediate call.

(3) The Danish Motor Schooner *Kornso* (case No. 1203), from Balearic Isles to Faroes, with salt, was intercepted by *Artois* on 5 June. When ordered to Stornoway with an Armed Guard, the Master and entire crew refused to work the ship, and could not be induced to depart from this decision. They were accordingly taken on board *Artois*, and a Naval crew was installed to take the ship into port for examination [357 para. 4, 358].

With reference to paragraph 3, clause 3, of my last Report of Proceedings, No. 426A/35 of 26 May [343], it has now been ascertained that the Norwegian Sailing Vessel *Queen of Scots* arrived in Norway. I ordered an Inquiry, which has shown that the Officer of Armed Guard

[1]*Proefneming* was detained, but it is not apparent with what result (TS 14/15).

was wanting in firmness and tact. A separate report of this case is being forwarded [354].

4. As stated in paragraph 1, enemy submarines have been particularly active throughout the Patrol Areas during the period covered by this letter.

It was with deep regret that I heard of the loss of HMS *Hilary* on 25 May, torpedoed and sunk in Lat. 60.40´ North, Long. 0.2´ West, while on her way to Swarbacks Minn for coaling. I am informed by the Commander-in-Chief Grand Fleet, that an Enquiry into the circumstances attending this loss was held on 30 May. Details of the proceedings at this Enquiry have not yet reached me, but judging from the Report received from Captain Dean, I submit that the conduct of the Captain, Officers and Ship's Company was highly creditable and in accordance with the best traditions of the Service [349].[1]

On 26 May, while proceeding to Clyde, a torpedo was fired at *Ebro* in Lat. 56 North, Long. 8.51´ West, and narrowly missed astern. A separate report of this incident has been forwarded …

The Armed Trawler *Arley*, on 28 May, whilst towing the Swedish Sailing Vessel *Drott*, encountered a submarine in Lat. 59.2´ North, Long. 6.48´ West. She cast off the tow, engaged the submarine for half an hour, and believes she was successful in sinking her. *Arley* then resumed the towing of *Drott* and succeeded in taking her safely to Stornoway – a very plucky and creditable performance. I asked the Rear-Admiral Stornoway to enquire into *Arley*'s claim to having sunk the submarine, and I understand that a report of that Enquiry has been forwarded to Admiralty and Commander-in-Chief Grand Fleet direct [350].[2]

Andes, whilst rejoining Patrol from Liverpool on 1 June, sighted a submarine on the surface in Lat. 56 North, Long. 11.54´ West. The submarine immediately submerged; no torpedo was fired …

On 4th June, whilst rejoining patrol from Liverpool, *Orvieto* (the 2nd Flag) was attacked by a submarine in Lat. 57.40´ North, Long. 10.33´ West. Fortunately the torpedo missed, although fired at close range … *Ebro*, who was in company with *Orvieto* sighted the submarine shortly afterwards in Lat. 57.35´ North, Long. 10.50´ West, but no further attack was delivered.

Later in the day *Patuca* (rejoining from Clyde) sighted a submarine on surface in Lat. 58.5´ North, Long. 11.3´ West, steering 300° at high

[1]The submarine was *U 88*.

[2]*Drott* was not detained; *Arley*'s opponent is not identified; it was not sunk.

speed. *Patuca* gave chase, and opened fire at 5,000 yards, firing 13 shots from 6" guns, but without effect. The submarine, which had been gaining on her, then got out of effective range.

In view of these attacks, I ordered *Orvieto*, *Ebro* and *Patuca* to proceed Westward at high speed, and Ships on C Patrol were also moved West to the meridian of 17.

I regret to report that, during the period under review, news has been received of the sinking by the enemy of no less than 4 vessels proceeding into port with Armed Guards from the 10th Cruiser Squadron on board. Although I tried hard to provide escorts, owing to contrary winds and inaccurate navigation, the escorts did not succeed in meeting these vessels, viz:

(1) Danish SV *Freden* ..., sunk on 22 May, with Armed Guard from *Champagne*.[1] The Guard and crew were saved by the Danish SV *Cimbria* (also under Armed Guard with Armed Guard from *Champagne*) and taken into Stornoway.[2]
(2) Swedish SV *Argo* ..., with Armed Guard from *Hilary* was found on fire on 29 May in Lat. 59.27´N, Long. 8.50´W; crew and Armed Guard eventually picked up on the Island of North Rona.
(3) Swedish barquentine *Ines* ..., with Armed Guard from *Orcoma*, shelled and set on fire by submarine. Unfortunately the Officer and men of the Armed Guard were taken prisoners by the submarine. Armed Trawler *Saxon* rescued the crew on 29 May.
(4) Danish SV *Consul N. Nielsen* ... sunk by submarine on 29 May. Armed Guard ex *Virginian*, and crew, landed at Stornoway. A report of the bad treatment of the Armed Guard and crew by the Germans is being forwarded separately [359].[3]

These losses are most regrettable. I have made every effort to employ the Armed Trawlers attached to my Command in escorting vessels sent in under Armed Guard, and others – and they have been instrumental in getting many vessels safely to port – also to hunt the submarines, but owing to the limited speed and W/T efficiency of these Trawlers, it is frequently impossible to place adequate force quickly in the locality required. I have accordingly represented to the Commander-in-Chief Grand Fleet, that if two or more oil fuel destroyers could be spared to

[1]By *U 30*, actually, on 23 March 1917.

[2]Enquiries as to *Cimbria*'s cargo of salt were made to the Consul in Iceland, the French Embassy and the Consul at Thorshavn; after satisfactory answers the ship was allowed to sail on (TS 14/15 of 30 May to 13 June 1917 *passim*).

[3]All these ships – *Argo*, *Ines*, *Consul N. Nielsen* – were sunk by *U 69*.

work with the 10th Cruiser Squadron, attached to *Avenger* for fuelling purposes, the chances of dealing successfully with the submarine menace in the Areas referred to would be greatly enhanced.

5. *Avenger*, whilst proceeding to E Patrol on 25 May, called at Reykjavik, and Captain Ashby interviewed the British Consul. The Consul reports that the Northern fishing season will re-open about 10 July. It is considered by him that the fishing will be done almost entirely by local vessels, very few Norwegian and Swedish being expected to participate this year.

6. At 6 p.m. on 6 June, as *Virginian* was then proceeding to Loch Ewe to coal, I turned over the command of the 10th Cruiser Squadron on patrol to the Rear-Admiral in *Orvieto*, during my temporary absence.

348. *Commander-in-Chief Home Fleets to Admiralty*

HMS *Queen Elizabeth*, 26 May 1917

… [I]f a seaplane carrier is available – as suggested in paragraph 2 of the letter of the Vice-Admiral Commanding Tenth Cruiser Squadron [344] – it might be desirable to utilise her, on the understanding that she would be screened by trawlers of the Tenth Cruiser Squadron.

It is doubtful, however, whether the value of seaplanes for detecting submarines in positions where it would be difficult to send local craft to hunt for them, is sufficient to justify their use in the manner suggested.

349. *Captain F.W. Dean to Vice-Admiral Commanding Tenth Cruiser Squadron*

HMS *Gibraltar*, 27 May 1917

I regret to have to report that at about 7.25 a.m. on 25th inst *Hilary* was disabled by a torpedo and subsequently sunk.

During the morning ship had been advancing 165 deg. at 10 knots steaming 12.5 knots and zigzagging 4 and 8 points. At 7.10 a.m., ship being in Lat. 60.33´N, Long. 3 W, course was altered to 103 degrees, and speed reduced to 10 knots to drop P.V.s. At about 7.22 a.m., the P.V.s having gone clear, speed was increased again to 12.5 knots, and very shortly after a torpedo struck ship on port side just before boiler room. I went to port side of bridge and clearly saw remains of its track and the beginning of same which was between 400 and 500 yards away. I ordered helm hard a port, telegraphed to close W.T. Doors, and then full speed, ‘action stations’ being sounded at the same time. A minute later report was telephoned from Engine Room that water was up to the furnaces and putting out the fires. I then ordered 'abandon ship' stations, standing fast the three after gun's crews. Report was brought me that W/T operator was unable to signal as aerial was damaged, he shifted to auxiliary aerial but, dynamo power failing, the emergency batteries were not sufficiently strong to charge it. He then shifted to main aerial again, one wire of which was still in place and the other wire which had been earthing, having now been insulated, he got a spark and sent emergency signal to *Gibraltar* at 7.45 a.m. He did not however get an acknowledgement till 7.55 a.m. owing to chrystal being out of adjustment through shock. The second torpedo wrecked instruments entirely. All hands went quickly to their stations, I kept engines going as long as possible to get a little further from submarine, ship quickly lost her way and at about 8.0 a.m. I ordered the boats to be lowered. This was done and each boat shoved off as soon as loaded. At about 8.05 a.m., No. 3 boat Port being then alongside getting her last few men in, a second torpedo struck ship port side, nearly under this boat which was blown high in air and its passengers scattered. The four men whose names I have already reported were killed and three were injured, but these and the rest of men from this boat were taken into other boats. Meanwhile a few shots were fired at periscope but without effect. I now ordered the after gun's crews to abandon ship and this was done. The S.M.O., Dr Carr,[1] having had the sick placed in boats, examined the two men who were thrown from No. 3 boat on to the boat deck and found them to be dead. At about 8.30 a.m. the officers and men, about 12 in number who had remained on board working, left ship on Carley rafts or boat. Lieut. Com. Wray[2] and Asst Steward H. Edwards were now the only two persons left on board with me. We provided ourselves with lance bombs on the boat deck in case submarine gave us a chance to use them, also with rifles and ammunition. The periscope was observed from time to time cruising round the ship, and Lieut. Com. Wray fired several shots from a 6 pdr at it but without effect. A favourable opportunity offering we then manned A 6" gun but found that training gear had gone wrong through shock and though we pushed the gun round we were unable to align the sights on the moving periscope. At about 8.40 a third torpedo was fired which struck ship on starboard side of boiler room. At about 9.12 it was apparent that ship was going quickly, we then went down to the promenade deck and the water

[1]Carr, George J., RN, Senior Medical Officer in *Hilary* May 1917, Surgeon Lieutenant-Commander 1918, HMS *Attentive* (Dunkirk) RMA Siege Guns, March 1918.

[2]Wray, Charles M., RNR, Lieutenant 1908, Lieutenant-Commander 1916.

having risen to this level, we got in and swam some 20 yards clear when at 9.15, ship sank. Lieut Harris[1] in a boat somewhat overloaded having picked up many of those from torpedoed boat had kept close by ship, and after she sank he closed two boats (which had been stowed inboard and floated clear) and by my order he distributed some men into each of these. One went to take the men from Carley floats, the other took Lieut Com. Wray, Steward Edwards and myself on board. The submarine came to surface soon after ship sank and hunted amongst the wreckage picking up objects, she then went to the two Carley floats in succession and obtained from officers in them particulars of ship's name, tonnage and armament, she then went off towards SW. The boats made their way towards Shetlands under oars and sail, between 3 and 5 p.m. six of them were rescued by Lieut. Rivers, RNR[2] in drifter *Maggie Bruce* 92 BCK, and in the early morning of the 26th, the seventh and last boat was rescued by T.B.D. *Sarpedon*.

I have satisfaction in reporting that the conduct of officers and men was in accordance with tradition.

I do not think anything was left undone which might have saved ship. The submarine was favoured to the utmost extent by bright low sun which partly accounts for periscope not being seen. The alteration of course at 7.10 a.m. enabled submarine to get in perfect position. I attach a list of officers and men whose conduct is considered worthy of special mention.

350. *Sub-Lieutenant Charles W. Forster RNR,[3] to Senior Officer Tenth Cruiser Squadron*

[n.d, but *c*.31 May 1917]

I have the honour to report that on May 28th at 7.30 p.m., whilst towing the Swedish barquentine *Drott*, and when in Lat. 59.2´N, Long. 6.43´W a German submarine appeared on the starboard quarter of that vessel distant about 3500 yards. I had previously instructed her Master to keep a good look out and to signal me by means of his fog horn immediately on sighting a submarine, 1 blast for starboard side, 2 for Port, and 3 for astern, and it was he who first saw her, and immediately made the prearranged signal, as there was no way of slipping the towing hawser

[1]Harris, Frederick C.P., RNR, Lieutenant 1914.
[2]Rivers, Ernest E., RNR, Sub-Lieutenant 1915.
[3]Forster, Charles W., RNR, Sub-Lieutenant 1915, Lieutenant 1917.

quickly I also had an axe placed in a handy position aft, and a heavy block of iron under the wire and we lost no time in getting clear of the towing gear.

We opened fire immediately with both guns, the submarine doing the same and on account of our first round in the 12 pounder being a miss fire she fired the first shot at us, we got her range at 4000 yards with both guns, she continued firing at us very rapidly although making very bad practice, we not being hit at all, and most of her rounds went over as she did not appear to be trying to increase her distance from us at any great speed, until I observed one shot from our 12 pounder explode on her gun or quite close to it, and put it out of action, when she made off at high speed, making a smoke screen behind her. A little later for some reason she altered her course and came out of the smoke she steered a course exposing her beam to us for some minutes, and it was then that we got her range again. I was observing closely all the time and am sure that we hit her several times, but the shot (besides the one which put her gun out of action) and about which there could be no doubt at all, was the last but one round with the twelve pounder, this one hit her, causing an explosion and I observed what looked like steam or white smoke shoot up, after this I still saw her on the top for a few seconds and she disappeared quite suddenly. I am convinced that she did not submerge but sank. The Armed Guard Officer on the *Drott* was observing from there and saw the shot which put the gun out of action. The range we used for our last few shots was 7100 yards; I think the most remarkable thing about the action was the determined way in which the submarine returned our fire and continued to do so until we put her gun out of action, the whole thing made me suspect that there was another one in the vicinity, and that the one we were engaged with was trying to draw us away from the barquetine while the other one torpedoed her, therefore as it would already take us nearly half an hour to get back to the ship, and that as it would mean a further three quarters of an hour were I to proceed to the spot where the submarine sank, and also some of the men in the early part of the action declared they saw another periscope, I felt that I should be doing a very unwise thing were I to stay away from the *Drott* longer than was absolutely necessary, I therefore proceeded back to her at once.

At the time of her first appearing the submarine was quite close to a narrow path of sunlight caused by the sun, then rather low shining on the water, she got into this and when there it was absolutely impossible to see her at all, neither could we see where our shots were going, fortunately for us she did not stay in this very unfavourable position, and I thought at the time she was perhaps manoeuvring with the intention of putting the *Arley* between her and the *Drott*, with the idea that some of the shots which missed us might hit the barquentine, I was therefore careful to keep out of this line. It is difficult to make a definite statement as to the exact number of rounds fired by the enemy but I noticed about ten myself, that is I either saw the splash or heard them passing overhead, I think there must have been many more as their fire was very brisk for a while. We used (including 8 miss fires) 40 rounds of 12 pounder ammunition, and (including 3 miss fires) 31 of six pounder ammunition.

In accordance with Trawler Order No. 40 I herewith fill in the following particulars not included in above account of the action.

Weather fine and very clear, sea smooth.

Wind light variable air.

Submarine was a large one armed with one gun carried forward.

No depth charge used [357].

351. *Commander I.G. Humphreys, RN,*[1] *to Rear-Admiral, Stornoway*

[n.d., but *c*. 31 May 1917]

Information given by Sub-Lieutenant J. Lunnon, RNR[2] Officer of the Armed Guard on board the Swedish schooner *Thekla*.

When first seen Submarine was about 2 points off starboard quarter distant 4 miles. Submarine opened fire immediately. The *Drott* steaming SSE, Submarine steering about SW. Soon after commencement of action submarine altered course to westward pursued by *Arley*. About 10 minutes after action commenced a stream of smoke came from Submarine, apparently from abaft the conning tower. Submarine then being about 9000 yards off Starboard Quarter and *Arley* about 1 mile astern of *Drott*. While observing submarine through binoculars saw a shot strike submarine abreast gun about 20 minutes after action commenced, submarine then ceased firing and in about 10 minutes passed out of sight below horizon.

[1]Humphreys, Ivan Gordon (1862–1920), RN, Lieutenant 1885, Commander (retired) 1907, on staff of SNO Inverness 1916, Captain (retired) 1917.

[2]Lunnon, James, RNR, Sub-Lieutenant 1915, Lieutenant 1917, Commander 1936, captain of *Laird's Isle* 1939.

352. *Rear-Admiral M.F. Boyle*[1] *to Admiralty*

Naval Base, Stornoway, 1 June 1917

I have the honour to forward herewith copy of the report of Sub-Lieutenant Charles R. Foster, RNR, and also the information obtained from Sub-Lieutenant J. Lunnon, RNR (HMS *Hilary*), Officer of the Armed Guard on board the Swedish Schooner *Drott*, relative to an attack on HM Armed Trawler *Arley* by an enemy submarine on 28th May, 1917 [359, 360].

2. There seems no doubt that the Submarine was hit and the gun put out of action, but it does not appear to be quite certain if the submarine sank or submerged voluntarily under control.

3. Sub-Lieutenant Foster would appear to have acted with great coolness and good judgment, and to have made every preliminary arrangement in case of attack, which proved to be effective and promptly brought the submarine to action. The report of the second periscope being sighted justified his returning to his convoy, and he acted in the full spirit of his orders. His statements were given in a clear and moderate manner, and the way in which he carried out his duties is worthy of high commendation …

353. *Minute by Captain Richard Webb, Director of Trade Division*

2 June 1917

Of the 14 vessels sent in by the 10th Cruiser Squadron during the period covered by this report (i.e., 7th to 24th May) seven have arrived, viz: the sailing vessels *Mary Boyes*, *Disa*, *Kalliope*, *Hiawatha*, *Closeburn*, *Emanuel* and *Cimbria*.[2]

One sailing vessel, the *Queen of Scots*, has been driven into Aalesund [354].

Two steamers, the *Elve* and the *Bernisse*, were torpedoed but the Armed Guards were saved, the *Bernis*se being towed into Kirkwall.[3]

One sailing vessel, the *Ines*, was sunk, and armed guard taken prisoners.

One sailing vessel, the *Argo*, was set on fire. No information yet received as to the fate of the armed guard.

[1]Boyle, Hon. Henry F., MVO, RN, Rear-Admiral 1914, S.N.O. Stornoway 1916 – 1918.

[2].Of these ships only the last two were detained for any time; all were allowed to sail on to deliver their cargoes.

[3]See page 701, note 1.

Two sailing vessels, the *Freden*, intercepted on 16th May, and the *Drott*, intercepted on 20th May, have not arrived, no information has been received as to the fate of the vessels or their armed guards.[1]

In addition to the above, two sailing vessels with armed guards on board, the *Karna* and the *Kodan*, were sunk on May 29th; both the Armed guards have landed safely in Lerwick.[2]

In these circumstances the question of the diversion of small sailing vessels in the danger zone would appear to need consideration.

2. It is suggested that F.O. be asked to direct His Majesty's Representatives in Scandinavia and Holland to inform owners of sailing vessels that in order to avoid danger to their vessels, and their crews they should

(i) Only sail their vessels from Scandinavia and Holland after permission for the voyage has been obtained from His Majesty's Government. This will obviate the vessels being sent into the danger zone.

(ii) Order their vessels inward bound to Scandinavia and Holland to call at Kingston (Jamaica) or Halifax (N.S.) for examination.

3. It is further suggested that in secret memorandum enclosed in A.L. N.L.I. 55761/16 of 14/10/16., par. e. should be re-numbered (f) and a new par. (e) inserted as follows:

'In view of the danger to small sailing vessels from enemy submarines such vessels need not be sent in unless carrying contraband goods of an important nature to Scandinavia or Holland.'

354. *Commander C. Wrightson to Vice-Admiral Commanding Tenth Cruiser Squadron*

HMS *Ebro*, 5 June 1917

I have the honour to report in accordance with Captain Superintendent of Clyde orders, that I have held an investigation as to the reason the sailing vessel *Queen of Scots* with Armed guard, did not make Stornoway as ordered, but owing to the weather was carried to Norway.

The evidence shows:

1. Sailing vessel *Queen of Scots* was boarded on 16th May 1917, at 3.25 p.m. in Latitude 61.25´N, Long 14.0´W by Lieutenant S.M. Smiles RNR, Boarding Officer.

[1]See page 706, notes 1 and page 705, note 2 for these ships.
[2]By *U 28*.

The Master on being told that he would have to go to Stornoway, expressed his opinion to the Boarding Officer, that he would be sunk by submarines and was evidently very anxious, although he was told that an escort would be looking out for him. An Armed Guard consisting of Sub-Lieut C. Redfern[1] and six ratings was placed on board with orders to take the vessel to Stornoway, special instructions were given to Sub-Lieut Redfern not to make too much easting, as the ship was a suspicious vessel, and it was essential that she should be taken to Stornoway. The wind was SE when she was boarded, the ship making an ENE course.

2. After parting with *Ebro* the Master of *Queen of Scots* raised objections to making Stornoway, representing to the Armed Guard Officer, that on account of head wind then prevailing, the ship would be in submarine area for a considerable time, and finally prevailing on Armed Guard Officer to make Lerwick as being a more accessible port, the Armed Guard Officer bearing in mind A.M.C. Order no 17, clause 16.

The wind fell light when within sight and north of the Faroes for two days, then a southerly wind sprang up gradually backing to the eastward, the ship still remaining on the starboard tack.

3. On Sunday the 20th May 1917, the ship was spoken by an armed boarding steamer, who enquired what port the vessel was making and on being informed Lerwick, the ship was allowed to proceed. During the same day when the ship was about 170 miles NNE of Lerwick the wind shifted to the SW increasing to a moderate gale, sail was shortened, the ship still remaining with the wind on the starboard side, making a course about east, this continued for two days, the Master stated that he could not lie nearer to the wind as the main topgallant mast was broken, after which the wind fell light and the Master of the ship reported a shortage of fresh water, when it was decided to make the nearest port to replenish; the wind still remained SW and unfavourable for making Lerwick.

The ship was then taken to Alesund, arriving at 7.30 p.m. on the 28th May 1917.

Owing to a log not being kept by the Armed Guard Officer, the dates and times of occurrences are given from memory.

I consider that Sub-Lieut C. Redfern in charge of the Armed Guard did not take strong enough measures in getting the Master to even attempt to make Stornoway, and owing to his lack of experience in

[1]Redfearn, Cyril, RNR, Midshipman 1915, Sub-Lieutenant 1918.

sailing ships, he was bluffed into acquiescing in all the master's proposals.[1]

355. *Vice-Admiral Tupper to Commander C. Wrightson*

HMS *Virginian*, 6 June 1917

I concur in your opinion that Sub-Lieutenant Redfern showed a distinct lack of determination in dealing with this vessel, and propose to express this opinion to Their Lords Commissioners of the Admiralty [354].

2. It is regretted that you did not place an officer in charge of the Armed Guard who was experienced in Sailing Ships, if such an officer was available.

356. *Commander C. Wrightson to Vice-Admiral Commanding Tenth Cruiser Squadron*

HMS *Ebro*, 6 June 1917

Submitted: The only officers who are experienced in Sailing Ships were required on board, for duties as 1st Lieutenant, Boarding Officer, Navigation, Gunnery [355].

This officer had carried out Armed Guard duties before satisfactorily, and was therefore sent.

357. *Vice-Admiral Tupper to Admiralty*

HMS *Alsatian*, 19 June 1917

Report of Proceedings, 7–18 June 1917

***

1. During the period covered by this letter, A and B Patrols have been disposed on and between Lines 2 (from the Butt of Lewis to the coast of Iceland in Long. 15 W) and 3 (from Rockall Bank to the coast of Iceland in Long. 17 W), while C patrol – south of Lat. 60 N – has been

[1]The cunning displayed by the Master is worth noting: Redfearn was clearly up against a true master of guile. *Queen of Scots* was built in 1877 at Stockton-on-Tees and had a displacement of 1400 tons – its failure to be inspected by Stornoway Customs will hardly have harmed the war effort. Compare this document with the attitude displayed in the preceding one.

kept somewhat west of Line 3, owing to the submarine activity between Rockall and the North of Ireland & West Coast of Scotland.

A patrol of two ships has also been maintained off the North-West coast of Iceland, guarding Denmark Strait between North Cape and the ice, and, during the last two days, one ship has been cruising on the East and North-East Coasts of Iceland.

***

The Armed Trawlers attached to the Squadron have been employed in support of A Patrol (off the South-East Coast Iceland), in the neighbourhood of Faroe Bank, and between Rockall and the Butt of Lewis. They have done good work in protecting and escorting British and Neutral Shipping, and on patrol duties generally. There have been six small encounters between trawlers and enemy submarines.

2. The number of ships intercepted during the period from 6 to 18 June (13 days) has been 118, of which 21 were trawlers. Out of that total, 2 were sent in under Armed Guards, and 35 were allowed to proceed westward as having guaranteed to call at, and 34 eastward as having been cleared from, Halifax or other British oversea port.

***

3. Of the ships intercepted during the period under review, the following are of interest:

(1) The Dutch S.V. *Thor* … was intercepted by *Hildebrand* on 16 June, and sent to Stornoway under Armed Guard … This vessel appears suspicious, having been out for 16 days and only caught 2 barrels of fish. She has since reached Stornoway.[1]

(2) *Orvieto* intercepted the Dutch SS *Zeelandia* … from Amsterdam to New York, with a general cargo, 6 German women passengers, and mails.[2]

At the time of interception, no notification had been received from the Admiralty that this vessel was excused calling at a port in the United Kingdom. Further, the fact that she was carrying mails would appear to be in contravention of one of the conditions under which such permission is to remain valid …

Reference was therefore made to Admiralty, and a reply was received stating that the vessel had been excused calling at a port in the United-Kingdom.

[1] *Thor* was not detained.

[2] *Zeelandia* carried linseed as part of her cargo, which caused her to be held up through most of May and June (TS 14/15).

I submit therefore that when vessels *are* permitted to carry mails, it may be so stated in the Admiralty Message, otherwise, according to my present instructions, such vessels have to be detained until instructions are obtained from Admiralty. This not only causes delay to the vessel – which may be innocent – but it also generally means that the Cruiser watching her is withdrawn from her position on patrol for a long period (12 hours or so), and so leaves a gap in the patrol.

4. I much regret to record the loss of HMS *Avenger*. Whilst proceeding to Scapa to oil she was struck by torpedo at 2 a.m. on 14 June, in Lat. 60.47´N, Long. 3.53´W, and it was singularly unfortunate that the two destroyers which I had asked for to screen her to port were within about 30 miles of meeting her when the accident occurred. From shortly after the time she was struck, *Avenger* was unable proceed under her own steam, and in spite of every effort made by destroyers and auxiliary craft to save her, she sank at 2.25 p.m. [360].[1]

I deeply deplore the loss of this fine vessel, which, following so soon on that of the *Hilary*, seriously impairs the strength and efficiency of the Squadron. I am very thankful however that the Captain, Officers, and crew – with the exception of one man killed by the explosion – were rescued.

The Danish Motor Schooner *Kornso*, manned by a crew from *Artois* (Vide my last Report of Proceedings, paragraph 3, clause (3) [347]), was sunk by submarine on 15 June, in Lat. 59.55´N, Long. 5.30´W.,[2] but I am glad to be able to report that the crew was rescued and taken to Kirkwall by the Armed Yacht *Portia*.

On 17 June, *Virginian* in Lat. 58.31´N, Long 15.20´W, intercepted the British Steamers *Mendip Range* and *Queen Adelaide*, bound for Stornoway, and proceeding together in mutual support. I detailed three trawlers to escort these vessels to the Butt of Lewis Patrol. They picked them up fairly quickly, but, whilst proceeding under this escort, the *Queen Adelaide* was torpedoed and sunk shortly after noon on 18 June, in Lat. 58.44´N, Long. 8.35´W.[3] The members of her crew, with three exceptions, were rescued by one of the escorting trawlers – *Tenby Castle* – which then went on to join the other two, and the escort of the *Mendip Range* was safely completed.

This is the first occasion on which a vessel under escort by 10th Cruiser Squadron Trawlers has been successfully attacked.

[1]*Avenger* fell to *U 69*.
[2]*Kornso* was sunk by *U 62*.
[3]By *U 70*.

5. I submit, and respectfully urge, that if two or more destroyers or sloops – or other suitable vessels possessing the requisite speed – could be spared to work with the 10th Cruiser Squadron, the chances of avoiding regrettable incidents such as those recorded above would be greatly increased.

6. I re-hoisted my Flag in *Alsatian* on 11 June, after being in *Virginian* since 21 May, and I wish to record my satisfaction with the efficient manner in which the duties of Flagship were performed by *Virginian*. These duties entailed a considerable amount of extra work on the Captain and Officers, which they carried out with zeal, ability, and success.

7. On arrival at Loch Ewe on 7 June, I received by signal from *Moldavia* the news that His Majesty had been pleased to bestow on me the Honour of KCB. I would like most respectfully to express my gratitude to My Lords Commissioners of the Admiralty for expressing in this manner Their satisfaction at the good work done by the Rear-Admiral, Commodore, and Captains, Officers and men serving under my Flag.

The recommendation to His Majesty is very greatly appreciated by the Vice-Admiral Commanding and all serving in the Tenth Cruiser Squadron.

8. The weather generally has been fine, with occasional misty days. Sea smooth. Southerly and Westerly winds have prevailed.

358. *Contraband Committee Minutes*

8 June 1917

Telegram from Vice-Admiral Tenth Cruiser Squadron, 8 June 1917: 'Danish motor schooner *Kornso* was boarded by French cruiser *Artois* in Lat. 63.8´N, Long. 13.20´W on 5th June p.m. bound for Faroe Islands with salt from the Balearic Islands. The Master and entire crew refused to work the ship to Stornoway, when ordered to proceed there with an armed guard. A naval crew was accordingly placed on board to take the vessel in, the master and crew being taken on board *Artois*.'[1]

[1]This would seem to be good judgement by the master and crew, since *Kornso* was sunk. Note that the ship was carrying salt between two neutral states.

359. *Admiralty to Commander-in-Chief Grand Fleet*

14 June 1917

With reference to your submission of the 26th ultimo [348], … relative to the proposed employment with the 10th Cruiser Squadron of a Seaplane Carrier for Anti-submarine work, I am commanded by My Lords Commssioners of the Admiralty to acquaint you that no Seaplane Carrier is available at present for this service.

360. *Commander Arthur L. Ashby to 'The Senior Naval Officer Afloat, Scapa Flow'*

On board HMS *Vienna*, 15 June 1917

I deeply regret to have to report the loss of HM Ship *Avenger* under my command yesterday morning under the following circumstances.

2. In accordance with instructions received from the Vice-Admiral Commanding Tenth Cruiser Squadron, I was proceeding from patrol·to Scapa Flow for the purpose of completing with oil. In accordance with W/T instructions received from you I was proceeding to a position Lat. 60.00´N, Long. 4.00´W, where I expected to meet HM Ships *Noble* and *Nessus* at 0300 Thursday 14 June 1917 which were to act as escort. My position at noon on Wednesday 13 June 1917 was Lat. 63.22´N, Long. 5.04´W, and at 8 p.m. on that day Lat. 61.55´N, Long. 3.42´W. HMS *Avenger* was torpedoed in Lat. 61.30´N, Long. 3.57´W.

3. Up to 0200 I was proceeding at a speed of 18 knots altering course 90 degrees every ten minutes, the mean course being S 26° W, wind South force 3, overcast, visibility about 6 or 7 miles, sea slight.

4. At 0150 I was on the starboard leg altering course to port to the mean course at 0200.

5. At 0203 the Officer of the Watch, Temporary Acting Lieutenant Robert A. Bingham, Royal Naval Reserve,[1] on hearing a shouted report from the port side of the Fore Bridge looked out to port and saw the track of a torpedo approaching on a bearing of about one point before the port beam, and felt the shock of a torpedo striking the ship immediately afterwards. The said report was made by the Midshipman of the Watch, Temporary Midshipman Ronald V. Edwards, Royal Naval Reserve,[2] who had seen for a very short space of time a portion of the

[1]Bingham, Robert A., RNR, Sub-Lieutenant 1916, sunk in *Avenger*, June 1917, and in *Champagne*, October 1917, Lieutenant 1918.

[2]Edwards, Ronald V., RNR, Midshipman 1916.

conning tower and periscope of a submarine. The Executive Officer, Lieutenant Commander Robert Bannister Lyness, Royal Naval Reserve,[1] who was on the starboard side of the boat deck near the foremost funnel, being then the officer on duty in charge of the Extra Submarine Lookouts, felt the shock of the torpedo and immediately afterwards saw the track. The necessary W/T message sent from the W/T Cabinet to *Noble* and received by her at once. All pumps (which were in the Turbine Room) were put out of action including feed pumps which necessitated putting out the burners of the furnaces. All W/T doors, except Nos. 7 and 9, were closed at the time, and these two were closed on action stations being sounded.

6. The helm was immediately put hard aport and the ship turned away from the direction from which the torpedo had approached, but the turbines stopped immediately and the ship gradually lost her way.

7. The torpedo apparently struck the ship either on or just before the after bulkhead of the Turbine Room killing David Kerr – Greaser, Mercantile – Discharge A. No. 53753 and injuring Engineer Sub-Lieutenant (Temporary) Hugh Kirkland, Royal Naval Reserve,[2] on the thigh and face and Seaman Malcolm Carmichael – O.N. – A.8897 Royal Naval Reserve.

8. The Turbine Room and No. 4 Hold flooded immediately, and I imagine that the bulkhead between Numbers 4 and 5 Holds was damaged by the concussion, or that the pressure of water forced up the floor of Number 5 Hold and water leaked through from the Shaft Tunnel, and Number 5 Hold gradually filled. The After Peak and After Trimming Tank were dry up to the time I left the ship.

9. The Alarm Gongs were put out of action by the concussion, but the 'Action' bugle was sounded and the men went to their Action Stations.

10. It appeared to me that the ship was settling down rapidly and owing to the flooded state of the Turbine Room and Number 4 Hold it was not possible to ascertain the extent of the damage. In order to try and keep the ship on an even keel, I flooded the port magazine at about 0220. About 0230, seeing that the weather was fine and being afraid of receiving another torpedo in my then helpless state I gave the order to abandon ship, which was done in perfect order, four Officers, two ratings and myself remaining on board. Lieutenant-Commander Lyness made as thorough an examination of the ship as was possible in the circumstances and it was obvious that I was powerless to do any thing

[1]Lyness, Robert Bannister, RD, RNR, Lieutenant 1908, Lieutenant-Commander 1916.
[2]Kirkland, Hugh, RNR, Engineer Sub-Lieutenant 1916.

to assist in keeping the ship afloat. The remainder of those remaining on board scattered round the ship keeping a good lookout for the submarine and ready to fire the guns if sighted.

11. At 0320, the motor boat, which was lying off the port side, reported the periscopes of the submarine coming up astern. Lieutenant-Commander Lyness and Lieutenant Bingham attempted to train the port after 6-inch guns, but the shock of the explosion had brought down the net mantles on top of the guns and they could not be used. Lieutenant Charles Hester, Royal Naval Reserve,[1] and Temporary Lieutenant George Ferguson, Royal Naval Reserve,[2] with Petty Officer 2nd class Charles Simeons, Royal Fleet Reserve, O.N. D 118286, manned the port 3-pounder, and fired five or six rounds at the periscopes, which were then at about 200 yards range, unfortunately without making a hit. The submarine thereupon submerged her periscopes and was not afterwards seen by the *Avenger*. I can only imagine that the submarine had not another torpedo to fire, and that he came under the stern to try to ascertain the name of the ship, which, however, has never been put on.

12. At about 0400, HM ships *Noble* and *Nessus* arrived. I ordered them to take the crew out of the boats, and told my motor boat to bring the empty boats alongside the *Avenger*, so that I could use them for re-embarking such men as I should require on the arrival of the tugs. The *Noble* and the *Nessus* then formed a screen at high speed. At about 0530 the *Noble* sighted the periscopes of the submarine, apparently about a mile on the port beam of the *Avenger*, and *Noble* and *Nessus* proceeded to the attack and each dropped a Depth Charge. The Captains of these vessels informed me that they did not know the results of these Charges. On board the *Avenger* we manned such guns as would train, but never sighted the periscopes. Nothing was seen of the submarine after this.

13. Up to this time, the water in Number 4 Hold appeared to be stationary and I had every hope of saving the ship.

14. At about 0730 I got my Carpenter – Chief Carpenter Alexander Fraser – M.M.R. 148240 and two of his mates on board. They did some plugging in the bulkhead between Nos 4 and 5 Holds and sounded. Temporary Engineer Commander John Dunlop, Royal Naval Reserve,[3] and Temporary Engineer Lieutenant-Commander John McKenzie, Royal Naval Reserve,[4] also came on board, but could do nothing. The

[1]Hester, Charles, RNR, Lieutenant 1911, Lieutenant-Commander 1919.

[2]Ferguson, George, RNR, Engineer Sub-Lieutenant 1915, Lieutenant 1917.

[3]Dunlop, John England, RNR, Engineer 1915, Engineer Commander 1916.

[4]MacKenzie John, RNR, Engineer Lieutenant-Commander 1916, Engineer-Commander 1917.

men who formed the boat's crew were taken on board and posted round the ship as lookouts.

15. The wind had been gradually rising, blowing on the starboard side of the ship, which had taken a considerable list to port and was down by the stern.

16. At 0815 it appeared to me that the water was rising in Number 4 Hold and was leaking through the bulkhead between Nos 4 and 5 orlops, the level of the water in Number 5 being then about 2 feet 6 inches lower than that in Number 4. I was afraid of bulkheads giving and taking everything into consideration, I reluctantly decided to abandon the ship at 0830, and went on board the *Noble* with Officers and men, my idea being that I could return to the ship on the arrival of tugs with necessary working parties.

17. At this time the *Relentless* and three other destroyers came to assist in the screen. At 1050 seeing that the ship was undoubtedly settling down, the water then just lapping over the port after end of the shelter deck, I decided that the *Noble* and the *Nessus* should proceed to Swarbacks Minn with the Officers and crew. I had intended to transfer myself to the *Relentless* before they left, but by this time the weather was too bad for boat work. These destroyers arrived at Swarbacks Minn at about 1530 and my Officers and crew were transferred to HMS *Vienna*, in which ship they proceeded to Longhope.

18. I received a W/T message from the *Relentless* that HMS *Avenger* sank at 1225.

19. All Secret and Confidential Documents were thrown overboard in their proper boxes by the Officers and men whose duty it was in each case, except the W/T logs which were burnt, and Secret Package F and Key Memorandum No. 14, which were salved in the Paymaster's Safe, and have been forwarded to the Naval Base Officer, Liverpool.

20. I submit that I may bring to your notice the most excellent state of discipline which was maintained throughout by the Officers and Ship's Company in general during the whole of this period, there being not the slightest signs of panic or confusion, although the ship was torpedoed at 2 o'clock in the morning.

12

THE END OF THE NORTHERN PATROL, JUNE 1917–JANUARY 1918

Once the USA was in the war the Northern Patrol was redundant, but it took a couple of months for this to be fully realised; it also took that long for the blockade system of the USA to be organised. Rear-Admiral de Chair, who had been the Admiralty's man in the Ministry of Blockade, went to Washington with the Foreign Secretary in May 1917, and no doubt gave of his experience. In the Admiralty the effective end of the Patrol was signalled by the decision of a committee on 27 June to begin transferring ships of the Patrol to convoy duties [365, 366], though it had been on the agenda for some time before that [361].

Even so it then took some months to eliminate the Patrol altogether. It was felt at first that the news of its abolition would leave the North Atlantic open to German ships, and to neutral 'evaders' [371]. But the institution of convoys was even more effective against single raiders than against submarines, and neutrals were controlled by the agreements their governments had made with the Allies as well as by American participation in the blockade. A ghost patrol was proposed, to exist mainly as a series of radio codes [406], but the ships involved were obviously of more use in convoys, either as escorts or as carriers, whether Armed Merchant Cruisers or trawlers. Paradoxically it may have been the laying of the minefield of the Northern Barrage which persuaded the Admiralty finally to remove the old Northern Patrol – paradoxically because the evidence suggests that the Barrage was ineffective.

But the Northern Patrol in fact lived on in two ways. It was a term which tended to be used for the small ships, trawlers and drifters, which tended the Barrage. As such, it was both a continuation and a revival, for the Barrage lay across the North Sea more or less on the line of patrol originally adopted by the *Edgars* at the start of the war. The second way was less material: the absence of the Northern Patrol was an even more compelling sign of the sea power of the Royal Navy than its presence. Even without the Northern Patrol's ships its effects lived on, and no ships moved but by the Navy's leave.

361. *Memorandum by Captain Richard Webb, Director of Trade Division*

15 June 1917

Future Activities of 10th Cruiser Squadron

Generally speaking the trade of the blockade runner has come to an end. A variety of causes has brought this about.

(a) Our control of coal.
(b) The introduction of the system of Letters of Assurance in the USA.
(c) The penalties suffered by the Owner of the Offending vessel.
(d) So much money can be made legitimately that it is not worth the while of a Shipowner to engage in risky enterprises.

2. The entry of the USA and Brazil[1] into the War have still further curtailed the opportunities for getting cargoes through to Scandinavia or Holland which have not been approved by H.M. Government.

3. The proclamation of the Danger Zone round the United Kingdom by the enemy had the effect of holding up neutral shipping which lasted until the Overseas Examination Ports (Halifax, etc) were established.

4. At the present time all Neutral vessels trading between North Sea Ports in Scandinavia and Holland and ports abroad sail (by our permission) from their home Ports, passing outside the Danger Zone, to their Oversea Ports of Examination where they are searched. These vessels are usually in ballast on the outward voyage as there is very little export trade from Scandinavia and Holland. From the Ports of Examination they proceed to their ports of loading. On the return voyage, in order to avoid being brought into the Danger Zone, they again call at the Oversea Ports of Examination, whence they proceed direct to their Home Port.

This system has practically abolished the work hitherto carried out by the 10th Cruiser Squadron.

5. As the positions and cargoes of all neutrals are now so closely watched, blockade running by a neutral is almost impossible without discovery.

6. There is of course the possibility of a German vessel escaping and proceeding to a neutral country such as Venezuela or Mexico to load a cargo for Germany but it is thought that we should get information in sufficient time to intercept her homeward bound.

[1]The United States declared war on 6 April 1917; Brazil did not so do until 26 October; Captain Webb was anticipating somewhat.

As the difficulties previously experienced in intercepting vessels on the other side of the Atlantic have now disappeared she could be captured off her port of loading and taken to a USA port.

7. In these circumstances it would seem that the 10th Cruiser Squadron could be materially reduced in strength.

8. The only vessels 10th Cruiser Squadron now send in for examination are small sailing vessels and fishing boats or sealers. Many of these have been burnt or sunk whilst being sent in with armed guards [353].

The last weekly return states that 134 vessels were intercepted; 41 were trawlers, 21 Westbound with approved cargoes, 29 Eastbound which had been examined at Halifax, and 3 sent in for examination.

9. Whilst it is desirable that these vessels should be sent in, it is open to question whether large and valuable Merchant Cruisers should be exposed to the risk of being torpedoed for this purpose alone.

10. The measures taken in order to improve and tighten the blockade have all been taken on the assumption that the 10th Cruiser Squadron would enforce any attempted evasion and it is therefore suggested that any reduction in the numbers of the Squadron should be kept secret and that some vessels should continue to patrol in order to 'show the flag'.

11. The disposition of the 10th Cruiser Squadron according to the latest return was as follows:

On patrol, 9 (including flagship)
Proceeding to Liverpool, Clyde and Loch Ewe, 3.
At Clyde Ports, 5.
At Liverpool, 4.
At Swarbacks Minn (?coaling), 1.
Total 22, of which 9 were on patrol.

The numbers given vary according to circumstances but assuming the strength of the squadron as 22, about one half are on patrol and the other half refitting or proceeding to or from the Clyde and Liverpool.[1]

12. It is suggested that it would be possible to reduce the squadron to 9 ships, 3 on patrol, 3 refitting and 1 proceeding to or from the home port, thus releasing some 14 or 15 vessels for general service [362].

13. In this memorandum no account has been taken of the question of raiders. If the convoy system develops, the 14 ships referred to above would be most useful as convoy vessels and could carry some cargo as well. They should be able to deal with any ordinary raider. If the enemy

[1]Captain Webb has ignored the trawlers recently added to the Patrol.

decides to send out a heavy armed cruiser (such as a Battle Cruiser) to raid, they would of course be incompetent to deal with her but on the other hand they could not stop a Battle Cruiser whilst employed as at present in the 10th Cruiser Squadron.

14. In order to convert these vessels into convoy vessels little or no change of personnel would be necessary. They are commanded by Naval Officers, and have Signal and W/T Ratings conversant with the present situation. The RNR Officers should know all about any cargoes they may be required to carry. The crews are under the Naval Discipline Act.

362. *Appendix to Webb's Memorandum* [361]

[15 June 1917]

Tenth Cruiser Squadron

Vessels that are considered most suitable for patrol duties		Vessels that can best be spared for detached duty	
Name	Approximate sea speed	Name	Approximate sea speed
Alsatian	18	**Andes*	15
Orvieto	17	**Almanzora*	15
Otway	17½	**Arlanza*	15
Ebro	14½	*Note – Can take 8–9000 tons cargo.	
Motagua	14		
Hildebrand	14¼	***Virginian*	15
Patuca	14	***Victorian*	15
Patia	14	***Kildonan Castle*	15
Changuinola	14	***Armadale Castle*	15
Orcoma	14½	***Columbella*	16
Moldavia	17½	***Teutonic*	16[1]
Gloucestershire	14	**Note – Can take 5000–6000 tons cargo.	
Artois	13		
Champagne	14		

[1] *Teutonic* had been in a Care-and-Maintenance condition for several months, and had been paid off in February.

363. *Vice-Admiral Commanding Tenth Cruiser Squadron to Rear-Admiral Commanding Second Cruiser Squadron*

15 June 1917

… [I]t is requested that arrangements may be made for the Senior Officer Tenth Cruiser Squadron to be given particulars by W/T of any Westbound vessels intercepted but not boarded by the Second Cruiser Squadron (except those flying the correct flag of the day), with a view to these ships being subsequently boarded by the Tenth Cruiser Squadron.

364. *Minute on the Future of the 10th Cruiser Squadron*

Trade Division, Admiralty, 19 June 1917

… [W]hen America had adopted the rationing policy the function of the 10th Cruiser Squadron from the point of view of trade with North America disappears.

It is expected that the rationing system will be adopted in America drastically at an early date. Propose to request Admiral Sims[1] on his return to take this matter up with the US Navy Board.

With regard to the remaining question of trade from South America, the meeting considered that our intelligence system would be sufficient to give us warning in time for us to catch any ship trying to get through.

365. *Memorandum by Trade Division, Admiralty War Staff*

19 June 1917

At a meeting held in my room this morning on this subject, Rear-Admiral Osmond de B. Brock[2] (Chief-of-Staff Grand Fleet) stated that the Commander-in-Chief Grand Fleet, was agreeable to giving up 8 ships of the 10th Cruiser Squadron on the understanding that they should be available in the event of any fresh emergency.

On being asked whether, supposing 8 ships were taken away from

[1]Sims, William Sowden, USN (1858–1936), Naval Attaché St Petersburg 1897–1900, commanded Destroyer Flotilla of Atlantic Fleet 1913–1915, commanded US Naval Forces in European Waters 1917–1919, Vice-Admiral, Admiral, retired 1922.

[2]Brock, Osmond de Beauvoir, CGB, KCB, KCMG, KCVO, RN (1869–1947), Lieutenant 1889, Commander 1900, Captain 1904, Rear-Admiral 1915, Chief of Staff Grand Fleet 1916–1919, Vice-Admiral 1919, Deputy Chief of Naval Staff 1919–1921, Commander-in-Chief Mediterranean 1922–1925, Admiral 1924, Commander-in-Chief Portsmouth 1926–1929, Admiral of the Fleet 1929.

the Squadron and, say, 6 left to keep up a patrol (i.e., 3 or 4 out at a time), the Commander-in-Chief's view would be that the balance should go to Scapa to take part in periodical sweeps, Rear-Admiral Brock stated that the C-in-C assumed that 8 ships might be safely taken away leaving 12 for patrol (probably 7 out at a time), but that the C-in-C considered the vessels should remain on patrol and that this course was preferable to periodical sweeps. C-in-C preferred the use of Loch Ewe to Scapa.

Vice-Admiral Sir Reginald Tupper (Commanding the 10th Cruiser Squadron) gave me the following list of 9 ships which he and the C-in-C thought could best be spared, adding that they could all carry sufficient coal to allow them to do a double convoy journey across the Atlantic without re-coaling.

		Approximate sea speed	
17,000 at Full Speed	*Andes*	15	Can take about 9,000 tons cargo.
10,900	*Almanzora*	15	
11,300	*Arlanza*	15	
6,660	*Virginian*	15	Can take 5,000–6,000 tons cargo.
6,200	*Victorian*	15	
	Kildonan Castle	15	
7,930	*Armadale Castle*	15	
8,300	*Columbella*	16	
8,000	*Teutonic*	18	

The question of the desirability of retaining the two French ships in the Squadron was mentioned but not decided upon.

The Foreign Office view is that the reduction in the 10th Cruiser Squadron can be made, but that they would like to defer it until the United States has definitely adopted the rationing policy. This is likely to take place during the next few days, and all preparations for the withdrawal of the ships, the re-organisation of the Squadron and organisation of convoys are to proceed on the assumption that the 9 ships will be available to leave England by the middle of July.

366. *Vice-Admiral Tupper to Admiralty*

HMS *Alsatian*, 12 July 1917

Report of Proceedings, 19 June–12 July 1917

***

1. Owing to the submarine activity the patrols have again been working some way to the westward.

The number of Ships available for patrol during this Period has been generally small, especially so during the latter part. This is principally due to the withdrawal of Ships for convoy service and the absence of *Artois* and *Champagne* recommissioning with British crews.

At first 2 ships were maintained on E Patrol to the North-West of Iceland, and 2 to 3 on C Patrol to the West and North West of the Hebrides, the remainder being employed on A and B covering the area between Iceland and the Faroes.

As the Ships available became less, it was first of all found necessary to abandon C Patrol on 6 July, and on the 8th, the number of Ships actually on patrol now being reduced to 6, the Rear-Admiral decided to abandon the patrol in Denmark Straits, and use the vessels thus released to reinforce B.

Two of the Armed Trawlers attached to the Squadron have been working in conjunction with A Patrol to the South of Iceland, and the remainder westward of the Hebrides. They have continued to do excellent work, especially on the matter of escorting shipping to Stornoway across the route usually traversed by U boats outward and homeward bound.

2. The number of vessels intercepted has been considerable, viz. 219 (including 99 fishing craft) in 22 days. Of these it was only found necessary to send in 2 under Armed Guard to Stornoway.

3. The Russian Steamer *Tambov*, boarded on 27 June reported having seen in Lat. 50.50´ North, Long. 24.36´ West, one large drifting mine with 5 or 6 smaller mines attached to it below the surface.

On 4 July *Otway* boarded the Russian SS *Irtysh* bound for Archangel from Savannah. The master of this vessel reported having encountered on 28 June in Lat. 47.17´ North, Long. 41.23´ West, a German submarine with two sails set distant six miles. *Irtysh* altered course and avoided her. He also reported having encountered two hours previously a steamer which hoisted Norwegian colours and acted suspiciously, attempting to close. The steamer was about 3,000 tons, two masts, one black funnel with red band, white band above and below. The steamer and submarine were steering to the South-West.

***

4. The German – Francisco Baptista – referred to in Admiralty message 2029 of 3 July was removed from SS *Tula* by *Hildebrand* on 7 July.

Two Austrian stowaways – deserters from the Austrian Army – were also removed by *Hildebrand* on 3 July from the Belgian SS *Samland* proceeding from Rotterdam to Sandy Hook.

5. On 8 July *Orvieto* in Lat. 61.7´ N, Long. 12.58´ W, boarded and sent into Stornoway the Spanish SS *Iparraguire* bound from Bergen to Santander with a cargo of wood. The Armed Trawlers *Stalwart* and *Thomas Stratton* were ordered to intercept and escort her in, but no news has since been heard of her and it is feared she has been lost or possibly she has gone straight to Santander in spite of the Armed Guard.[1]

6. On 24 June *Arlanza* whilst rejoining patrol from Liverpool was attacked by an enemy submarine when in Lat. 56.18´N, Long 11.20´W. The attack was fortunately unsuccessful, the torpedo passing some 20 yards astern.

Patuca rejoining from Loch Ewe and *Orvieto* proceeding to coal reported sighting submarines on 22nd and 28th June respectively to the North-West of the Hebrides.

Several submarines were also sighted by the Armed Trawlers attached to the Squadron and when possible engaged.

Walpole on the 9th July rescued the crew of the *Atlantic* sunk in the neighbourhood of St Kilda, and also attacked the submarine.[2]

7. On 21 June I received directions to proceed to Scapa and thence to London to attend a Conference at the Admiralty on the 28th ultimo regarding the composition of the 10th Cruiser Squadron.

As a result of this Conference it was decided to detach 8 vessels for convoy work in the North Atlantic the vessels detailed being:

Almanzora	*Columbella*
Virginian	*Andes*
Kildonan Castle	*Arlanza*
Armadale Castle	*Victorian*

[1] *Iparraguire* was sunk by *U 66*.
[2] *Atlantic* had been sunk by *U 53*.

Of these, *Almanzora*, *Virginian* and *Kildonan Castle* have already left to take up their new duties.

It was also decided that *Artois* and *Champagne* should be paid off and recommissioned with British crews for further service in the 10th Cruiser Squadron. These vessels have already been detached for this purpose.

The number of Ships available for patrol work will thus be reduced to 14.

8. As the result of an interview with the Commander-in-Chief, when at Scapa, it was decided that, owing to the submarine activity in the neighbourhood of Swarbacks Minn, Ships of the Squadron should use Loch Ewe only as a Northern Coaling Base until the nights become longer.

It was also arranged that all vessels sent in for examination should be sent to Stornoway to await orders and not direct to Kirkwall, as it would then be easier to arrange for escort, where necessary.

9. I learn with regret that the members of the Boilermakers' Society at Liverpool went out on strike on 9 July. The Senior Naval Officer informs me that this will seriously affect the completion of 10th Cruiser Squadron Ships now in hand at that Port.

10. During the greater part of the period covered by this letter, viz, 24 June–10 July, during my absence in London, and whilst *Alsatian* was refitting, the Rear-Admiral has been in charge of the patrols.

11. The weather has been generally fine with occasional foggy days.

***

367. *Diary of Tenth Cruiser Squadron Events between 19 June and 10 July 1917*[1]

Tuesday 19 June. Received orders from Admiralty *Gloucestershire* to be at special rendezvous at 1900 on 24 June, to convoy transports *Czar* and *Dwinsk*, in accordance with directions contained in Admiralty Message No. 914; *Gloucestershire* directed accordingly.

Orcoma reported that on 16 June ice from WSW to positions Lat. 66.55´N, Long. 25.10´W; Lat. 67 N, Long. 22.35´W; Lat. 61.6´N, Long.

[1]This is the diary which was the basis for the previous Report [366]; why it reached the Admiralty archives is not clear. It is partly repetitive of [366] but is included here as an example of the squadron's record-keeping; cross-references to [366] are not given. Given that it refers to Tupper in the third person, the compiler was perhaps his secretary, or his Flag Captain.

24.20´W; Lat. 67.12´N, Long. 22.40´W, then to North-Eastward; loose fringe melting ice extending in at least 8 to 10 miles; main pack foggy.

Lord Lansdowne intercepted Dutch SV *Thor* (Case No. 1287), and towed her to Stornoway.[1]

Alsatian met *Hildebrand*; Vice-Admiral proceeded on board and presented a DSM, inspected her, and witnessed Target Practice; ship efficient, but might be cleaner.

Wednesday 20 June. British SS *Merionethshire* intercepted on 18 June by *Victorian* in Lat. 59.26´N, Long. 14.41´W, arrived safely at Stornoway; she had been escorted there by *Lord Lansdowne* and *Elf King*.

About 10 p.m. *Columbella* reported that the periscope of a submarine had been sighted in approximately Lat. 64.8´N, Long. 13.26´W, near a Danish smack. Two trawlers were sent to the vicinity to investigate, but nothing further was seen. The smack, TG 404, was examined, nothing suspicious being found. Report considered doubtful.

Alsatian met *Patia*; Commanding Officer came on board *Alsatian* to confer with Vice-Admiral.

Admiralty Message no. 923 received, stating departure of Russian Troopships *Czar* and *Dwinsk* from Archangel delayed; *Gloucestershire* accordingly recalled to her patrol.

B Patrol ordered to cross line 340° from Lat. 60.56´N, Long. 14 W at noon steering 70°, and at midnight steering 250°; 30 miles apart. A Patrol (one ship) to extend B northward 30 miles.

Alsatian met *Virginian*; Captain Wilding came on board to confer with Vice-Admiral and received his orders for proceeding to Liverpool; sent despatches in *Virginian*.

Received Admiralty Message timed 2032 directing a ship of 10th Cruiser Squadron to be detailed to patrol on Meridian of 25 W, between Lats. 48 & 52 N, for purpose of diverting all shipping from making SW coast of Ireland; *Armadale Castle* detailed for this service.

Thursday 21 June. *Gloucestershire* intercepted Danish Barque *Marie* …, from Goteborg to Port Passages, with wood-pulp. As no notification had been received from Admiralty with regard to vessel, instructions asked in Message No. 590. Vessel allowed to proceed in accordance with Admiralty reply – Message No. 591.[2]

In order to facilitate promulgation of War Warning being issued by *Armadale Castle*, the following addition to the Warning was approved:

[1]See Chapter 11, page 716, note 1.

[2]Arrangements were made for *Marie* to be examined at Gibraltar; her return cargo was cork, not thought to be a problem for the Allied war effort (TS 14/15, *passim*).

'Ships receiving this Message, if they meet when West of 16 W any ships eastbound not fitted with W/T to whom this Warning applies, should pass message to them if possible'. Admiralty informed of this in Message No. 591.

British SS *Warpatrol*, *Warcross* and *Tamarac* bound for Stornoway, intercepted by patrols. Armed Trawlers attached to the Squadron were detailed to pick them up and escort into port.

Signal received from Commander-in-Chief, Grand Fleet directing Vice-Admiral to proceed to Scapa, to arrive 25 June, thence to attend Conference at Admiralty on 28 June.

Captain D'Étouat of *Artois* came on board *Alsatian* and conferred with Vice-Admiral; he appears to be very efficient, and of good physique.

Friday, 22 June. Dull misty weather; strong WSW wind and sea.

Motagua sailed from Liverpool, after an absence from patrol of over three months – refitting after being mined at the entrance to Swarbacks Minn on 16 March.

Patuca (rejoining from Loch Ewe) sighted submarine in Lat. 53.54´N, Long. 9.12´W …

Danish SS *Valur* and British SS *Quernmore*, bound for Grimsby and Liverpool respectively, were intercepted during the day, and escorted in by Trawlers attached to the Squadron.

At 2 p.m. in Lat. 59.1´N, Long. 9.19´W, *Arley* sighted two submarines, out of range, steering North-East at high speed, both submerged. About 1½ hours later, *Arley* again sighted a submarine, on surface, in Lat. 57 N, Long. 8.57´W.

Hildebrand boarded the Dutch SS *Elisabeth* …, from Rotterdam to Halifax in ballast. Master reported two Austrian stowaways on board, both of military age, and requested their removal. Stowaways taken on board *Hildebrand* and searched, then transferred to *Changuinola* for passage to Glasgow; Captain Superintendent Clyde informed.

Saturday 23 June. *Alsatian* met *Patuca*; Captain Dannreuther came on board to confer with Vice-Admiral.

Orvieto was met, and the Rear-Admiral came on board *Alsatian* to receive directions regarding the conduct of patrols during the absence of Vice-Admiral.

Orvieto reported that on 20 and 21 June she had patrolled the Icelandic coast, keeping from 8 to 10 miles off, between the Latitudes of Hvalsbak and Cape Revsnes; weather fine and clear.

Alsatian met *Motagua* and received despatches.

Sunday 24 June. The Rear-Admiral, in *Orvieto*, took over command of the patrols at 8 a.m.

Arlanza unsuccessfully attacked by submarine in Lat. 56.18´N, Long. 11.26´W; torpedo passed 20 yards astern.

Arrangements made for *Arlanza* to carry out, when required, special service mentioned in Admiralty Message No. 914, as *Gloucestershire* shortly due to proceed to Clyde.

Disposition of Squadron at noon was as follows:

A Patrol, Extending B Patrol 30 miles to the Northward ... *Columbella*.
B Patrol, Crossing line 340° from Lat. 60.55´N, Long 14 W, at noon steering 70°, and at midnight steering 250°; 30 miles apart ... *Motagua*, *Gloucestershire*, *Hildebrand*, *Patia*, *Andes*.
C Patrol, In area between Lat. 59 N & 60 N, and Long 14 and 17 W .... *Patuca*, *Artois*.
E Patrol, Off North-west coast of Iceland ... *Ebro*, *Orcoma*.
Between B and C Patrols ... *Orvieto*.
Rejoining Patrol (From Liverpool) ... *Arlanza*.
Leaving Patrol For Scapa ... *Alsatian*.
For Clyde ... *Changuinola*.
For Loch Ewe ... *Victorian*.
At Liverpool ... *Almanzora*, *Otway*, *Virginian*.
At Clyde ... *Moldavia*, *Kildonan Castle*.
At Brest ... *Champagne*.
On Special Service ... *Armadale Castle*.
Trawlers. Two proceeding to work with A Patrol; three engaged escorting; three leaving patrol for Oban; ten in port.

The total number of ships intercepted during the past week was 97, of which 22 were trawlers, 34 westbound neutrals, and 16 eastbound neutrals; no ships were sent in under Armed Guard.

At 10.30 p.m. *Alsatian* arrived at Scapa Flow, to land Vice-Admiral.

Monday 25 June. His Majesty King George V proceeded round Grand Fleet in Cruiser *Comus*; Ships were manned and cheered His Majesty in passing.

Vice-Admiral proceeded on board *Queen Elizabeth*, and conferred with the Commander-in-Chief Grand Fleet.

Tuesday 26 June. Vice-Admiral proceeded to Admiralty for Conference, and *Alsatian* left Scapa for Liverpool.

C Patrol directed to cross line 360° from Lat. 58.30´N, Long. 15.30´W, at noon steering 300° and at midnight steering 60°, morning and dog watches, course South true, 30 miles apart.

Moldavia detained in the Clyde owing to submarine.

Offa II reported at 6 p.m. sighted submarine in Lat. 50.25´N, Long. 8 W; submerged at once.

Wednesday 27 June. B Patrol directed to alter time of crossing line to 0300 steering 240° and 0900 steering 60°.

Russian SS *Tambov* (Case No. 1421) reported having sighted and investigated one large drifting mine with five or six smaller mines attached, below surface, in Lat. 52.50´N, Long. 20.36´W; Admiralty informed.

Vice-Admiral at Admiralty. At Conference it was decided to detach eight vessels for convoy work, viz: *Almanzora*, *Andes*, *Arlanza*, *Armadale Castle*, *Columbella*, *Kildonan Castle*, *Victorian*, *Virginian*. These vessels to remain under Vice-Admiral Commanding 10th Cruiser Squadron for administrative purposes for the present. Also *Artois* and *Champagne* to be manned by British crews.

Tenby Castle at 7.40 p.m., reported submarine in Lat. 58.42´N, Long. 8.44´W, submerging immediately.

Armadale Castle ordered by Admiralty to rejoin patrol from special service.

Thursday 28 June. *Orvieto* left patrol at 4 a.m. for Loch Ewe, command of the patrols being turned over to the Commodore in *Otway*.

Orvieto sighted submarine at 8.30 a.m. in Lat. 59.20´N, Long. 8.38´W.

Friday 29 June. Nothing of special interest to report.

Saturday 30 June. Vice-Admiral had the honour of being invested by His Majesty with the KCB, at Buckingham Palace.

Sunday 1 July. *Virginian* sailed from Liverpool for Halifax, on special service.

Disposition of Squadron at noon was as follows:

A Patrol, Extending B Patrol 30 miles to the Northward … *Motagua*.

B Patrol, Crossing line 340° from Lat. 60.55´N, Long. 14 W, at 0300 steering 340° and at 0900 steering 60° … *Orcoma*, *Kildonan Castle*, *Arlanza*, *Hildebrand*, *Motagua* and *Artois* (joining).

C Patrol, Crossing line 360° from Lat. 52.30´N, Long. 15.30´E, at noon steering 300° and at midnight steering 60° morning and dog watches, course South true; 30 miles apart … *Gloucestershire*, *Patuca*, *Patia*.

E Patrol, Off North-West coast of Iceland … *Almanzora*, *Victorian*.

Between B and C Patrols … *Otway*.

Proceeding to Loch Ewe … *Columbella*.

At Liverpool … *Alsatian*.

Proceeding to Liverpool … *Andes*.

At Clyde ... *Ebro*, *Changuinola*.
At Loch Ewe ... *Orvieto*.
At Brest ... *Champagne*.
On Special Service ... *Armadale Castle*, *Virginian*.
Trawlers. Two working with A Patrol; five engaged on escort and rescue work; two rejoining; two leaving; seven in port.[1]

The total number of ships intercepted during the past week was 94, of which 21 were trawlers, 25 westbound neutrals and 13 eastbound neutrals; no ships were sent in under Armed Guard.

Monday 2 July. Nothing of special interest to report.

Tuesday 3 July. *Orvieto* met *Otway* at 9 p.m., and the Rear-Admiral resumed charge of the patrols.

Submarine reported by *Elf King* in Lat. 58.32´N, Long. 9.34´W.

Wednesday 4 July. *Kildonan Castle* ordered to Clyde – required to sail for Halifax on 12 July, on special service.

Admiralty directed that ship detailed for special service mentioned in Admiralty Message No. 914 would require to reach special rendezvous on 10 July; orders passed to *Arlanza* accordingly.

Patuca picked up empty life-boat in Lat. 57.35´N, Long. 10.38´W, belonging to British SS *Haverford*.[2]

Otway boarded Russian SS *Irtysh* ...; latter reported regarding submarine and suspicious steamer encountered on 28 June ...

Thursday 5 July. British SS *Lowther Range* reported that British SS *Bertrand*, bound for Montreal, had picked up 234 survivors including 168 troops, ex transport *Armadale*: Admiralty informed.[3]

B patrol ordered to cross line 340° from Lat. 61.24´N, Long. 14.20´W, at noon steering 50°, and at midnight steering 230°; 30 miles apart.

Almanzora left patrol for Halifax, on special service.

Friday 6 July. Admiralty Message 0844 was received, relative to the British SS *Barlby* having been chased by suspicious vessel in Lat. 75.20´N, Long. 18.30´E. *Arlanza* (proceeding to White Sea on special service) was informed, and ships of squadron directed to warn all ships intercepted en route for Archangel. It appears possible that this is one of the vessels sighted by SS *Liege* off Udsire on 17 April ...

[1]The removal of eight ships would still leave Tupper with 32 ships for the Patrol (he had 40 on 24 June) which is eight more than the original force.

[2]*Haverford* had been sunk by *U 94* on 27 June 1917.

[3]*Armadale* had been sunk on 27 June by *U 60*.

Saturday 7 July. *Artois* left Loch Ewe for Clyde to pay off, in accordance with Admiralty orders.

Armadale Castle at 9.30 a.m. in Lat. 56.50´N, Long. 7.58´W, passed two boats containing 9 men from unknown Danish ship which had been torpedoed; they reported submarine still in vicinity.[1] *Robert Smith* sent to assist, but subsequently reported they had been picked up. *Walpole* and *Rushcoe* ordered to hunt submarine.

Robert Smith engaged enemy submarine in Lat. 57.15´N, Long. 8.5´W.

Hildebrand boarded Danish SS *Tula* and took off German mentioned in Admiralty Message 233 of 2 July.

Victorian left E Patrol for Liverpool, and at the same time, owing to the shortage of ships on patrol, the Rear-Admiral directed *Otway* to leave E to reinforce B, thus leaving Denmark Strait unguarded.

Directions received *Arlanza* should be informed convoy would be 30 hours late at rendezvous. *Arlanza* being out of touch, request made that message be passed to her through 2nd Cruiser Squadron.

Orvieto boarded Spanish SS *Iparraguire* …

Disposition of Squadron at noon was as follows:

A Patrol, Extending B Patrol to the Northward … *Moldavia.*

B Patrol, Crossing line 340° from Lat. 61.23´N, Long. 14.20´W at noon steering 50° and at midnight steering 230° 30 miles apart … *Orvieto, Orcoma, Ebro, Changuinola.*

E Patrol (about to be withdrawn), Off North-West coast of Iceland … *Otway, Victorian.*

Rejoining from Loch Ewe … *Columbella.*

Proceeding to Loch Ewe … *Patia.*

Proceeding to Clyde … *Hildebrand, Motagua.*

At Liverpool … *Armadale Castle, Andes, Alsatian.*

At Clyde … *Artois* (to pay off French crew), *Gloucestershire, Kildonan Castle, Patuca.*

On Special Service … *Virginian, Almanzora, Arlanza.*

At Brest … *Champagne.*

Trawlers. Two working with A Patrol; ten in area between Lats. 56 & 59.30 N, Long. 8 & 11 W; two leaving; four in port.

The total number of ships intercepted during week was 75, of which 32 were trawlers, 19 westbound and 14 eastbound neutrals; no ships sent in under Armed Guard.

[1]The ship and the submarine have not been identified.

B Patrol ordered to take up line ahead, patrol steering 340° and 160° from Lat. 61.22´N, Long. 14.20´W to be in southern position noon and midnight; thirty miles apart.

Vice-Admiral left Liverpool in *Alsatian* to rejoin patrol.

Monday 9 July. Admiralty approval received for *Orvieto* to be taken in hand on the Tyne on 19 July, Liverpool being unable to accommodate her.

Walpole engaged submarine on Lat. 57.40´N, Long. 8.47´W; had only six rounds of 12 pounder ammunition remaining; picked up crew of *Atlantic* which had been sunk by this submarine.

B Patrol ordered to cross line 350° from Lat 61.30´N, Long. 13.2´W at noon and midnight, steering 24° and 160°, 35 miles apart.

Tuesday 10 July. At 4 p.m. *Alsatian* met *Orvieto* and Vice Admiral resumed command of the patrols.

B Patrol ordered to cross line 335° from Lat. 59.6´N, Long. 14.40´W at noon steering 200° and at midnight steering 110°, 43 miles apart.

With reference to clauses 3 and 10 of Second Cruiser Squadron (Patrol General Order No. 27) it is requested that arrangements may be made for the Senior Officer Tenth Cruiser Squadron to be given particulars by W/T of any Westbound Vessels intercepted but not boarded by the Second Cruiser Squadron (except those flying the correct flag of the day), with a view to those ships being subsequently boarded by the Tenth Cruiser Squadron [363].

368. *F. Atkinson to Board of Customs and Excise*

26 June 1917

Special War Work Performed at the Port of Lerwick

***

I may perhaps observe that Lerwick in peace time was of importance only in relation to the fishing industry in which some 600 or 700 British vessels alone were, in the busy summer season, engaged. The main trade apart from the landing of the fish caught was the shipping of it coastwise in a fresh state, and for direct exportation to Russia and Germany after being cured locally. Many Dutch fishing vessels also called to transship their catches into homeward bound vessels. There was also a steamer service to and from the mainland four or five times weekly with passengers, mail and goods, an irregular coasting trade existed in coal and fishing stock, but the foreign imports, apart from fish caught by foreign vessels, consisted principally in fishing stock.

When war was declared the seasonal fishing was suspended – many of the men employed being called up as Reservists – and it has since been conducted on a very limited scale and the comparatively little export trade has been to Russia only.

Table of foreign trade

Year	Ships inward		Outward	
	Steam	Sail	Steam	Sail
1913	218	181	122	26
1914	153	79	99	30
1915	3	0	6	1
1916	0	4	31	0

During the present year there has been no foreign trade with the port[.] [O]nly about 50 local vessels have been engaged in fishing and the catch has been sent to home markets.

***

[Diverted ships – first arrival October 1914 – 3 neutrals. Since March 1915 main work has been with diverted ships.] On the arrival of a vessel in port she was boarded by the waterguard officers who issued a detention notice to the master and brought the papers to the Customs Office. Here the papers were examined and a detailed analysis of the cargo prepared and telegraphed to the various departments as directed, with full particulars of any matters of importance observed such as, with reference to Certificate of Origin, firms on Black List, etc. [September 1914–May 1917 – 628 diverted ships dealt with.]

... The special departmental instructions as to the rummage of Swedish vessels, whaling vessels, and vessels carrying oil were also observed, and at the request of the naval examining officers rummages were undertaken until the naval search party had gained some experience. In the 60 instances stated in which vessels or cargoes had, on instructions, been seized as prize such were taken over by the Collecter (here the Surveyor) of Customs and Excise who was responsible for their safe custody as substitute for the Admiralty Marshal. Immediately such seizure took place notification by wire was also made and the necessary documents and particulars forwarded in each case to the Procurator General's local representatives.

In 55 cases of seizure the vessels were, owing to lack of local facilities, cleared to other ports for discharge and the Collector at the port of destination advised.

Since the early months of this year there has been a marked decrease in the number of diverted ships falling to be dealt with. This has probably been partly due to a fuller use of the harbour being required by the Admiralty for other traffic. In last month (May) the number of ships diverted to Lerwick was 8 while for last year the average was 41 per month.

369. *Rear-Admiral S.A. Fremantle, Commanding Second Cruiser Squadron to Vice-Admiral Commanding Tenth Cruiser Squadron*

HMS *Minotaur*, 29 June 1917

... I regret I am not able to comply with this request [363].

2. The patrol area of the Second Cruiser Squadron depends upon Geographical considerations and cannot be altered without detriment to the main object of the patrol. This area is also in close proximity to a route much frequented by enemy submarines.

3. For these reasons it is essential to reduce the W/T of the Second Cruiser Squadron to an absolute minimum.

4. With very rare exceptions due to weather, the only ships intercepted but not boarded by the Second Cruiser Squadron are (a) ships flying pass flag, (b) ships met with on or about the parallel of 62.30´N by Second Cruiser Squadron ships on passage to and from patrol area.

5. The pass flag is never given to ships unless boarded; it is not seen, therefore, what the object is of informing Tenth Cruiser Squadron that ships have been intercepted, as it is presumed that the Tenth Cruiser Squadron board all ships which are not flying pass flag [373].

370. *Lieutenant J.M. Kelly, RNR*[1] *to Commanding Officer HMS* Virginian

[n.d., but *c.* 1 July 1917]

I have the honour to submit the following report.

Having been placed on board the Barque *Consul N. Neilson* with Armed Guard at noon on the 28th May 1917 (1550 Tons bound for Copenhagen with Linseed), with your orders to proceed with her to Stornoway, but to look out for escort in about 9 West, and parallels 59 North and 60 North.

[1]Kelly, Joseph M., RNR, Sub-Lieutenant 1917.

I gave the Master the position 59.30´ North and 9.0´ West to make for, and supplied him with a larger scale chart which I had brought with me.

As he had his boats still inboard, I told him it would be for safety of everyone concerned to have them ready for swinging out, to which he agreed, and got them ready.

Nothing eventful happened except for head winds and calms, until the morning of the 29th May, when at 4.0 a.m. GMT, in Lat. 59.55´ North, Long. 9.30´ West, I was called by the guard on watch, who reported a submarine in sight.

When I went on deck I could see a submarine about one and a half points on the Starboard bow, about 3000 yards away, on the surface, and making towards us.

I got my Guard together and made them hide all arms and traces of a Guard being on board, and tore up all confidential papers, assuming they might board us.

We all went forward to the chain locker to hide, knowing that the Master would not give us away.

The submarine started shelling us at a range of about 1500 yards forward and aft, at 4.15 a.m. GMT.

The crew took to the boats, myself and guard disguising ourselves as much a possible.

During this time one member (the First Mate) of the Barque's crew was wounded by a shell.

At 4.30 a.m. we had the boats in the water, but the enemy continued shelling until we were well clear, when he commenced fire at us with small arms, again wounding the First Mate in the arm.

At 4.45 a.m. the enemy ceased firing at us, and continued to shell the Barque until she fell over on her side and sank, at 5.15 a.m.

At 5.30 a.m. the submarine came alongside our boat, and her Commander asked in German, the name of the ship, where from, where bound, and what cargo.

The Second Mate replied in German 'Buenos Ayres to Copenhagen with linseed', and then asked for medical assistance, for the wounded man who was bleeding heavily, but the Captain of the submarine took no notice and steamed away to a Swedish schooner which was in company with us about 3 miles off.

Whilst the submarine was alongside us, our boat's crew were scutinised with glasses.

The submarine was about 300 feet long, and newly painted, but flew no ensign.

She had U.66[1] painted in black letters on the forepart of the Conning Tower, which was horse-shoe shaped.

She mounted one gun about 4 inch, on the fore part, and had masts fore and aft for wireless, but not rigged, no guard wires were visible.

The Captain of the submarine was tall and dark, and had a brown moustache, and wore a uniform with distinction lace.

There were only four or five men on deck in jerseys and leather coats and cape, one marine and one seaman being at the gun.

At 5.45 a.m. the submarine left us, and proceeded to the Swedish Schooner, and we made for the Hebrides with warm, calm weather, both boats being connected by a line.

At 6.0 a.m. submarine was observed to be going alongside schooner, and at 6.15 a.m. flames were seen to be coming from the after part of the ship.[2]

The submarine left the schooner at 6.30 a.m. and proceeded across our bow with her wireless up, steering about South by West true, at about 10 knots, on the surface, and remained on the same course until out of sight.

As we had not observed any boats leaving the schooner we proceeded towards her, and at 8.10 a.m., whilst approaching her, another submarine appeared to the North, about three miles off, steaming on the surface.

He came alongside our boats and ordered the Captain to go on board the submarine, from his boat.

The Captain of the submarine asked the Master if he belonged to the schooner, and when told what ship the Master belonged to, asked where *Consul N. Neilson* was from, and where bound.

He then asked to what ship did our boat belong, and after being told that it also belonged to the *Consul N. Neilson*, said ‘Must have been a big ship as you have a big crew’.

The Master of the Barque gave the number as 23 instead of 19.

The submarine Commander also remarked ‘You know very well that you are in the war zone, and will be shot down at sight’, to which the Master replied that he had been driven South by northerly winds.

The submarine Commander then said to the Master ‘Don’t bring so much butter from Denmark to England’, and then shewed him his chart, and indicated his position, telling him to steer South East when he

[1]Actually *U 69*.

[2]This was the Swedish barque *Ines*, from which an Armed Guard from *Orcoma* had been taken prisoner [347, para. 4(3)].

would make land, and when near a steamer would always be found.

The Master then asked for medical aid for the wounded First Mate, and was given two small bandages, and told he could bring the mate on board for treatment.

As myself and guard were in the same boat as the First Mate, the Master thought it inadvisable to bring the boat alongside, and said he would attend to the Mate himself.

The Captain of the submarine pointed to one my guard (Private C.H. Roberts, RMLI, disguised) and asked Master if that was the Chief Officer, who replied that it was the steward.

The submarine Commander then asked about the submarine that sank us, if she had one or two guns, and what course she steered when leaving, and then bid the Master 'Good bye', adding 'You have a long way to go', and left for the Southward (about South by West true).[1]

The Master noticed on the chart he was shown, that there were two areas marked on it in blue colour, triangular in shape extending over the North Minch.

The Base of this triangle extended from about Stornoway to the Mainland, and the apex, in about 58.35´ North, 5.45´ West, the other area, irregular in shape covered an area extending about thirty miles to the Westward from the West coast of the Mainland, and Hoy Island, in the Orkneys.

The Captain of the submarine spoke in German, and the Master of the Barque can speak a little German.

This Captain was about 32 years old, round faced and had a pleasant manner.

One other officer was a thick stout man, about 45 years of age, and had a fat round face, and a dark brown moustache. They wore black overalls, looking like leather, and their faces were very dirty.

One Officer, and twelve men were on deck of the submarine, which was about 250 feet long, fitted for wireless, no number, and had one small gun in front of conning tower (which was round in shape), the gun appeared to be about a 3 inch Automatic, and very short.

She had no guard wires along the deck, was a dirty grey in colour, and flew a dirty ensign.

At 9.0 a.m., the submarine left, and we set sail, keeping a sharp lookout.

At 10.0 a.m. we sighted a small sailing boat to the northward which may have been the Swedish Schooner's boat.

[1]The identity of the second submarine is not known.

The wind up till now had headed us to the Eastward, but at 1.0 a.m. on the 30th June, it gradually went to the West, with a heavy sea and thick misty rain.

We then altered course South True, and kept on until wind and sea became too heavy, when at 4.0 p.m., we ran before the wind and sea with reefed sail.

At 10.0 a.m. weather became clearer, and we sighted the Butt of Lewis Light House, about 6 points on the Starboard Bow about 8 miles distant.

We hauled up as much as it was safe to do, for the sea was still very heavy and breaking on board at times.

About 2.0 p.m. we passed an armed yacht, not a quarter of a mile off, who took no notice of our signals to attract their attention.

At 3.0 p.m. we sighted Tiumpan Light House, which we steered for, the sea being calmer inside, and at 4.15 p.m., I landed at the Signal Station and wired to the Admiral at Stornoway for a tow to take us there, and also gave full details of the occurrence.

A steam drifter eventually arrived, and landed us at Stornoway at 10.30 p.m.

The wounded man was taken to Hospital, and myself and guard reported to the Senior Naval Officer.

In making this report I beg to bring to your notice, Leading Seaman J. Reid, RNR, C/2917, Stoker D. Cunningham, R.F.R., D/288914, and Private C.H. Roberts RMLI, Po/19330, the conduct of these ratings was splendid.

I especially commend Leading Seaman Reid, for his assistance in giving me local information after sighting land.

Private Roberts seemed to begin to suffer mentally on the morning of the 30th June, but the Surgeon at Stornoway says there are no ill effects.

371. *Note by Vice-Admiral Tupper*

6 July 1917

It seems very inadvisable to further reduce the strength of the Tenth Cruiser Squadron for the following reasons:

1. If neutrals find that there is nothing on this side to force them into a British port for examination, it is possible they would avoid visit and search at Halifax, Kingston, Sierra Leone and other ports.

2. If the enemy find that our patrol has been abandoned they will make capital out of it, and put it down to success of Submarine Campaign. They will also be encouraged to despatch surface craft Raiders.

3. Neutrals will probably consider that our Naval Power is weakening.

4. Therefore it is hoped that *Artois* and *Champagne* when commissioned with British Crews will still work in the Tenth Cruiser Squadron and that *Teutonic* will join up in latter part of August.

372. *Vice-Admiral Tupper to Admiralty*

HMS *Alsatian*, 5 August 1917

Report of Proceedings, 12 July–5 August 1917

***

1. The patrols have continued to work to the westward. Since my last report the *Victorian*, *Gloucestershire*, *Columbella*, *Arlanza*, *Motagua*, and *Moldavia* have been detached for convoy service, making 9 in all. Owing to this, and the fact that *Artois* and *Champagne* have not yet rejoined, there have been few ships available for patrol.

One Ship and two armed trawlers have been working on A patrol immediately to the south of Iceland between Long. 15 and 19 W, and since 14 July, except whilst *Motagua* was detached, vide paragraph 2, a Ship has been maintained on in Denmark Strait. The remainder, varying between 3 and 4 ships, have been employed on B and C patrols south of A. *Alsatian* has been southern Ship working between North of Rockall Bank and Lat. 61 N, between Long. 12 and 16 W.

The armed trawlers, with the exception of the 2 referred to above have been working to the west of the Hebrides, between Lat. 59 and 57 N, and from 100-fathom line to about 15 W.

2. On 17 July I received orders from the Commander-in-Chief, Grand Fleet, to direct *Motagua* – then on E Patrol – to sweep towards Lat. 67.30´N, Long. 9.30´W where a suspicious motor vessel was reported to be operating. Nothing, however, was seen and on 22 July I directed *Motagua* who was getting short of coal to abandon the search and join B patrol, *Hildebrand* taking her place on E.

There are very few fishing craft working on the north coast of Iceland.

3. During the period covered by this letter – 24 days – 136 vessels, including 15 fishing craft, have been intercepted, of which two were sent in under Armed guard. This number is somewhat small for the time of year, and appears to be due to the following causes:

(1) The reduction in the number of ships on patrol.
(2) Fewer ships trading to Scandinavia.
(3) Few vessels taking part in the Iceland herring fishery season.

4. With reference to paragraph 5 of my previous report of proceedings, I regret to state that information has now been received that the Spanish SS *Iparraguire* was sunk by an enemy submarine on 9 July, the Officer in charge of the armed guard being taken prisoner. The men however were picked up with the crew of the steamer.[1]

5. The Danish Sailing Vessel *Hariet* … with an armed guard placed on board on 8 July by *Ebro* to take her to Stornoway, arrived at Thorshavn, her intended destination, on 16 July. The armed guard were recovered by the armed trawler *Corrie Roy* and taken to Stornoway. No written report of this incident has yet been received.[2]

6. The following ships from Holland were reported to be carrying German Coal owing to the impossibility of obtaining British. In each case a Consular Certificate to this effect was carried, viz:

Belgian SS *Syrie* from Rotterdam to Sandy Hook, via Halifax …

Belgian SS *Gothland*, from Rotterdam to Sandy Hook, via Halifax ….

Belgian SS *Kurland* from Rotterdam to Halifax …

Belgian SS *Algerie* from Rotterdam to Sandy Hook, via Halifax …

7. There has been considerable submarine activity lately off the west coast of Scotland.

I much regret to have to report the loss of HMS *Otway*, which was torpedoed in Lat. 58.54´N, Long. 6.28´W, at 2225 on 22 July whilst rejoining patrol from Loch Ewe.[3] On being struck course was at once altered towards North Rona, but the Ship sank in approximately Lat. 59.2´N, Long. 6 W before land could be reached. The boats and rafts containing survivors were picked up by the armed whaler *Rorqual* at 0600 the following day [377].

Fortunately the loss of life was comparatively small, only 10 men being unaccounted for out of a total of 380 Officers and men. Five others were seriously injured. No written report of the occurrence has yet been received, all news I have is from W/T sources.

At 1940 on 20 July, *Changuinola* sighted a submarine on the surface in Lat. 59.10´N, Long. 8.18´W at a distance of about 10 miles. The submarine fired 4 rounds at *Changuinola*, all of which however fell

[1]See page 730, note 1.
[2]If one was ever made, it has not been located.
[3]By *UC 49*.

some 6000 yards short. Submarine dived when still about 15,000 yards away.

A number of submarines have been sighted at various times by the trawlers patrolling to the westward of the Hebrides.

8. At 0636 on 30 July distress signals were heard by *Alsatian* from the British SS *Devona* to the effect that she was being attacked by an enemy submarine in Lat. 59.10´N, Long. 11 W, and was steering to the South-west.

Three trawlers were immediately despatched to her assistance, but shortly afterwards she reported she had been obliged to alter course to the North-west.

As this took her away from the trawlers, and as from her position at 1 p.m. she was only some 40 miles from *Alsatian*, course was altered and *Alsatian* proceeded at full speed to her assistance.

The submarine, a large one with two guns, ceased shelling *Devona* at 1340 and disappeared to the South-east about an hour and a half before *Alsatian* arrived.[1]

It is thought that the W/T signals from *Alsatian* to *Devona* and perhaps smoke being observed – the visibility being very great – caused the submarine to desist.

Devona had two men wounded, one having to be transferred to *Alsatian* for treatment.

A separate report has been forwarded regarding this incident … recommending that the Master and crew of *Devona* should be rewarded for the gallant defence of their vessel.

9. I regret to have to record that the armed trawler *Robert Smith* has been missing since 0330 on 21 July, when she was sighted by *Offa II* in Lat. 59.14´N, Long. 9.40´W. A full report regarding this has already been forwarded … .[2]

10. On 2 August the armed trawler *Corrie Roy* discovered moored mines in the neighbourhood of Barra Head. She remained in the vicinity to warn traffic until relieved by local patrols.

11. On 22 July, *Hildebrand* called at Reykjavik on her way to E patrol to deliver correspondence for the French Consul. Captain Watson visited the British Consul, Mr. Olsen, who informed him that the blockade appeared to be most effective. Owing to the decision of the Icelandic Government not to issue supplies to Scandinavian and Dutch

[1]The submarine's identity is not known.

[2]The fate of *Robert Smith* remains unknown; there is no record of her being attacked by a submarine and the position recorded by *Offa II* is rather far out for a mine.

vessels fishing from Iceland, it was anticipated that very few of these would be able to partake in the herring fishery season.

He also stated that the German Engineer Funk … is at present employed in the Icelandic Lighthouse Department. He considered that this should be represented as the lighthouses in Iceland are very isolated, and opportunity might arise for him to install wireless with a view to communicating with enemy vessels.

12. On 3 August *Hildebrand* visited Siglefiord. The information obtained at Reykjavik regarding the herring fishery season was corroborated by the Consul, who reported that the catch was so far very small. Only a few Icelandic fishing vessels were seen in the neighbourhood.

13. In accordance with orders from the Commander-in-Chief, Grand Fleet, the armed trawlers *Corrie Roy*, *Saxon* and *Edwardian* visited Thorshavn to bring any crews of British trawlers sunk by enemy submarines.

***

373. *Commander-in-Chief to Flag Officers of Tenth Cruiser Squadron and Second Cruiser Squadron*

15 July 1917

… [I]t is considered that the Senior Officers on patrol … should mutually inform each other of any vessels which have not been boarded, and in regard to which any possible doubt or suspicion exists [363, 369].

2. These cases will be few in number, and in view of the great importance of intercepting such vessels, and that both Squadrons are maintained for this purpose, the objection to use of W/T must be disregarded.

374. *Commander-in-Chief Grand Fleet to Admiralty*

23 July 1917

With reference to the sinking of HMS *Otway* [377] it is for consideration whether services rendered by ships of Tenth Cruiser Squadron justify the increasing risk entailed in proceeding to Loch Ewe for coal.

Under present circumstances the number of Grand Fleet destroyers available precludes any escort.

As an alternative it is suggested that vessels of Tenth Cruiser

Squadron should meet North Atlantic convoys at a rendezvous and proceed to Loch Swilly with the convoy continuing voyage to Clyde if necessary.

375. *Admiralty to Commander-in-Chief Grand Fleet*

24 July 1915

No objection to Tenth Cruiser Squadron ships meeting convoys and proceeding to Lough Swilly or Clyde [374].

376. *Vice-Admiral Tupper to Commander-in-Chief Grand Fleet*

HMS *Alsatian*, 24 July 1917

In view of the loss of the *Otway* from submarine attack following closely upon that of *Hilary* and *Avenger*, I have the honour to submit that the provision of a destroyer escort for ships of the Tenth Cruiser Squadron proceeding to and from their coaling bases may receive further consideration. Screening by trawlers does not seem quite efficient and they are too slow for escort.

2. Arrangements have already been made with the Rear-Admiral Buncrana for escort to be provided *when available* between Rathlin Sound and about 11 West for Tenth Cruiser Squadron Cruisers proceeding to and from Liverpool and the Clyde, and it is thought that if two, or perhaps three, additional destroyers were placed under his orders escort could then be *always* provided.

3. There then remains the question of escort for ships making use of Swarbacks Minn and Loch Ewe, but as these would involve further destroyers being detailed, it is submitted for consideration that the use of a Northern coaling base should be abandoned for the present, ships remaining on patrol as long as their coal will admit, and returning to their Southern base when necessary to replenish. It has been calculated that neither the number of ships on patrol nor the number of days spent by them at sea will be decreased.

***

377. *Commodore P.H. Colomb to Commander-in-Chief The Nore*

Royal Naval Barracks, Chatham, 25 July 1917

I deeply regret that I have to report the loss of H.M. Ship *Otway* under the circumstances which are mentioned below, but before setting down these circumstances I desire to point out that I may find it necessary to amend, modify, or correct this before a Court of Enquiry as due to the stress and strain of the last three days, there may be lapses of memory, and having lost all documents, I have only my memory to trust to.

2. On Sunday 22nd July when lying at anchor in Lock [*sic*] Ewe, I received orders from the Senior Officer 10th Cruiser Squadron to rejoin patrol, crossing the 100 fathoms line in the hours of darkness, and also that I was to request the Rear Admiral Stornoway, to direct 10th Cruiser Squadron trawlers to screen me as far as possible on passage.

3. This order was carried out, and at 8 p.m. I was in a position with Butt of Lewis bearing 270° distant 8 miles, and shaped course 320°. At 9 p.m. GMT I altered course to 325°, the revolutions at this hour were 75 giving a speed of 16.2 knots, and at 10 p.m. GMT speed was increased to 80 revolutions giving a speed of 17.4, a three point zig-zag was maintained all the time.

4. At about 10.13 p.m. GMT the signalman of the watch reported a periscope on the port beam distant about 1000 yards. Helm was put hard aport, and port engineroom telegraph put to maximum power. The guns were ordered to open on the periscope, but neither gunlayers nor myself could see the periscope. The 6-pdr gun, however, fired one round in the direction pointed out. The Navigating Officer and signalman kept their glasses on the periscope, and when the Navigating Officer reported the submarine right astern, I put the helm amidships and steadied on 49° with submarine astern.

5. After what seemed quite an appreciable time, a torpedo was reported coming on the port quarter, I saw the track, and the course of torpedo was crossing mine at about 18°. The torpedo appeared to be heading for a point in the ship which may be represented as the upper bridge; this is practically the turning point of the ship.

6. Helm was put hard a port in the hope to get the ship parallel with the course of torpedo, or, alternatively, that wash of screws might deflect torpedo, or that torpedo might pass under the port counter.

7. The latter result was nearly achieved, but I estimate the torpedo struck the ship in the port A bracket and exploded, at about 10.18 p.m. GMT. The Nos. 4 and 5 holds quickly filled with water and the ship settled by the stern.

8. Sometime afterwards the Engineer Commander and the Carpenter

having completed their inspection, reported that the ship was flooded abaft the engineroom, the port screw shafting was bent and this had badly strained the after engineroom bulkhead, and in spite of bilge pumps and main circulating engines being on the engineroom bilge, the engineroom was being flooded and the ship was bound to sink.

9. I then directed the Engineer Commander to go as fast as he could with both engines, and I would make for the nearest land. He stated that to work port engine would be dangerous, but I said as the ship was bound to go in the end, we must take the risk and endeavour to make for shallow water. It was also most desirable to get away from the vicinity of the submarine to avoid another torpedo.

10. Course was shaped for North Rona Island which also meant leaving the submarine astern. A speed of about 15 knots was maintained, but later the port shaft broke, tearing engineroom bulkhead further open, and control of ship with helm was lost.

11. Orders were then given to abandon ship, and telegraph put to stop, and after the way was off the ship the Officers and Crew were got into the boats and sent away clear of the ship, the 1st Lieutenant having previously reported that all men except those lost were on deck.

12. The 1st Lieutenant and my steward Croucher were selected from amongst many volunteers to remain in the ship with me to the last with a view to firing on or bombing submarine should she appear. She however, never showed again.

13. At about midnight as the ship seemed to have a chance of floating, and there being no sign of the submarine, I called the W/T operator, Mr Morris, and the coding officer, Sub-Lieutenant Parnell, RNVR,[1] back again on board, and a signal was made stating condition of ship, but this, I believe, did not reach any ship.

14. At about 12.05 a.m. 23rd July the ship showed sudden and evident signs of sinking, so got all Officers and my steward into the boat and shoved off at about 12.10 a.m. The ship was then sinking rapidly by the stern, and about 12.15 threw her nose high in the air and sank.

15. I did not consider it advisable to show any lights during the night, as it might bring the submarine to the neighbourhood for information and prisoners, but at daylight the boats hoisted flags, and at about 6.30 a.m. the boats were picked up by HM whaler *Rorqual*, whose officers and crew vied with each other in making the very large number of men comfortable in every way. Later the crew was distributed between three whalers, and landed at Stornoway in the afternoon of the 23rd July.

[1]Parnell, Harold S., RNVR, Sub-Lieutenant 1916, Acting Lieutenant 1919.

16. I regret to report that 10 of the Seamen complement, whose names were forwarded to the Admiralty on my arrival at Stornoway, lost their lives in the explosion, and there were also 5 men severely wounded, and slightly wounded. These latter men received every attention from Surgeon Page[1] until he had seen them into the hospital at Stornoway; this including the giving of morphia while in the boats, and it is worthy of remark that within some 10 minutes of the explosion taking place, Surgeon Page was able to report all casualties were in the boats at the davits.

17. I desire to place on record the extraordinary steady discipline maintained by all Officers and Men in this critical time, despite darkness and the difficulty of issuing orders owing to the roar of escaping steam, every order issued by me or by any officer was explicitly and accurately carried out, and boats were lowered down close to the water, and later put in the water, and men got in the boats as though at drill.

18. I beg to attach list of Names of Officers whose services I consider worthy of mention and recognition.

378. *Admiralty to Vice-Admiral Commanding Tenth Cruiser Squadron*

26 July 1917

I am commanded by My Lords Commissioners of the Admiralty to acquaint you that it has been decided that the Tenth Cruiser Squadron is in future to consist of twelve ships which should allow of eight being on patrol at a time.

2. As soon as *Artois* and *Champagne* rejoin the Squadron, two more Armed Merchant Cruisers from the Tenth Cruiser Squadron are to be detached for service with Atlantic convoys.

3. On completion of her repairs, HMS *Teutonic* (or another Armed Merchant Cruiser from the Tenth Cruiser Squadron detached in her place) is also to be detached for service with Atlantic convoys.

[1]Page, John F., Surgeon Lieutenant 1915.

379. *Commander-in-Chief Grand Fleet to Vice-Admiral Commanding Tenth Cruiser Squadron*

5 August 1917

... [A]rrangements [have been] made either with the Senior Naval Officer Buncrana or Admiralty direct for incoming vessels [of Tenth Cruiser Squadron] to join one of the North Atlantic convoys at a pre-arranged rendezvous [374, 375].

2. Outgoing vessels should make use of the destroyer escorts leaving Lough Swilly to meet incoming convoys.

3. It is not possible to detail Grand Fleet destroyers for the particular purpose of escorting ships of the Tenth Cruiser Squadron. Twelve Grand Fleet destroyers are now stationed at Buncrana and this number cannot be increased.

380. *Vice-Admiral Tupper to Admiralty*

17 August 1917

Report of Proceedings 6–17 August 1917

***

1. There has been no change in the general disposition of the patrols since my last report.

Owing to 10 Ships being detached for convoy work, and others undergoing long refit which has been lengthened by strikes, the average number on patrol has only been 4 to 5 but an improvement in this respect should shortly take place.

It has now been definitely decided that the Squadron shall in future consist of only 12 large Ships besides the Trawlers. It is hoped to have approximately 8 of these at any one time on patrol subject to the time taken for refit and time lost in awaiting escort.

It will be seen that the Trawlers are still doing excellent work and an increase in their numbers would have good results.

2. The number of vessels intercepted – 33 in 12 days – has been very much below the normal. This is partly due to indifferent weather and low visibility, and partly to the small number of Ships on patrol. Of these, one – the Swedish steamer *Jarl*, bound from Goteborg to Passages, North Spain, with a cargo of wood pulp ... – was sent in to Stornoway under Armed Guard, for examination. Unfortunately this ship was sunk on 7 August by an enemy submarine whilst on her way

in, in Lat. 59.50´N, Long. 9.40´W.[1] Armed Trawlers had been detailed to meet her in Lat. 60 N, Long. 10 W, and escort her in, but had failed to pick her up. The crew and Armed Guard were saved.

In view of the fact that a large proportion of the ships recently sent in under Armed Guard have been attacked by submarines, I submit that Q ships operating to the West and North-West of the Hebrides would have a reasonable prospect of success.

3. At 0430 on 6 August, *Changuinola* picked up 46 survivors from *Chagford* in Lat. 56.54´N, Long. 9.36´W.[2] As the ship was still reported to be afloat in the vicinity with 15 persons on board, the Armed Trawler *Saxon* was ordered to search for her.

At 0750 *Saxon* picked up a boat containing a Petty Officer and 13 men, and at 0940 another boat with survivors. At the same time she reported she had found the ship afloat, but badly damaged, having been struck by 3 torpedoes. She succeeded in taking her in tow, but after proceeding about 7 miles *Chagford* began to break up and finally sank at 0750 the following morning.

Saxon then proceeded to Oban to land survivors.

4. At 1005 on 12 August, signals were received from a British steamer, which proved to be the *Roanoke*, that she was being chased and heavily shelled by an enemy submarine in Lat. 58.40´N, Long. 9.30´W.[3]

The Armed Trawlers *Macleay* and *Edwardian* were at once despatched to her assistance, and at 2145 found her abandoned and with a slight list. *Edwardian* stood by while *Macleay* searched for boats.

At 0500 the following morning as the result of investigating *Macleay* reported that it was considered *Roanoke* could be saved. The Rear-Admiral Stornoway, was asked to send tugs or trawlers, but replied that the tug was already on salvage duty and that he had no trawlers available. Later, *Edwardian* reported *Roanoke* caught fire at 1330 and sank about 1400. The crew were picked up by vessels of the Stornoway Patrol.

5. *Artois* was unsuccessfully attacked by enemy submarine in Lat. 57.6´N, Long. 14.52´W at 0620 on 9 August whilst rejoining patrol from the Clyde, two torpedoes being fired both of which missed – one ahead and one astern.

6. During the period covered by this report, with the exception of the first two days, the Rear-Admiral, in *Patia*, has been in immediate

[1]By *U 22*.
[2]*Chagford* was probably sunk by *U 44*, but this is not wholly certain.
[3]The submarine is not identified.

command of the ships on patrol. I resumed command at 9 a.m. on 16 August.

7. Whilst *Alsatian* was coaling at Liverpool, I visited the Admiralty, when the question of providing escorts for ships of the 19th Cruiser Squadron was considered and arrangements made for vessels proceeding to their Southern Bases to join one of the North Atlantic convoys proceeding via the North of Ireland. Outgoing vessels will proceed to Buncrana to await destroyer escorts leaving to meet incoming convoys: ships with small coal supply will occasionally coal there [379].

Waiting for escorts will have the result of somewhat reducing the time spent actually on patrol, and it is hoped that later on special escorts may be provided to avoid any delay.

8. *Alsatian* left Liverpool on 14 August and joined patrol without escort, by permission of Admiralty, as none was available without entailing several days delay. When in Lat. 55.39´N, Long. 7.11´W, a heavy stress came on the P.V's causing chain to surge and again in Lat. 56 N, Long. 8.14´W, after which the starboard P.V. was found to be missing.

9. Whilst in harbour, *Alsatian* was painted on the 'dazzle' system, which from reports received appears to be efficient.

***

381. *Vice-Admiral Tupper to Admiralty*

HMS *Alsatian*, 7 August 1917

I have the honour to request that I may be informed if the ten Cruisers now detached from the Tenth Cruiser Squadron for Convoy work will remain for Administrative purposes under my orders. Also whether these will be interchangeable with the rest of the Tenth Cruiser Squadron.

2. I would suggest that this course be adopted as I believe it would make for efficiency and also enable Commanding Officers and men to have a change from the somewhat monotonous work of Blockade Patrol [383].

382. *Vice-Admiral Commanding Tenth Cruiser Squadron to Admiralty*

14 August 1917

With reference to Admiralty letter … of 26 July 1917 [378], informing me that the squadron is in future to consist of twelve ships, the position at present is as follows:

On Convoy Duty – 10

Armadale Castle, *Almanzora*, *Arlanza*, *Victorian*, *Columbella*, *Gloucestershire*, *Kildonan Castle*, *Moldavia*, *Motagua*, *Virginian*.

Tenth Cruiser Squadron proper – 12

Alsatian (flag), *Orvieto* (flag), dock.
Andes dock.
Orcoma, *Artois*, *Champagne*, *Changuinola*, *Ebro*, *Patuca*, *Patia*, *Hildebrand*, *Teutonic* (paid off).

2. From this it will be seen that, including *Teutonic*, the number of ships left for patrol work has already been reduced to twelve. It is therefore presumed that on *Teutonic* joining no further vessel is to be detached for Convoy Service as directed in paragraph 3.

***

383. *Admiralty to Vice-Admiral Commanding Tenth Cruiser Squadron*

15 August 1917

… I am to acquaint you that the detached ships will remain under your orders for administrative purposes [381]. To what extent, if at all, they are to be considered as interchangeable with the rest of the Tenth Cruiser Squadron cannot be decided at present. It may, for example, be found most undesirable to lose Captains with experience in the management of convoys.

384. *Vice-Admiral Tupper to Admiralty*

10 September 1917

Report of Proceedings, 17 August–10 September 1917

***

1. There has been no change in the general disposition of the patrols, except that, since 24 August, they have been working to the westward of 15 W, by orders of the Commander-in-Chief, in view of expected submarine activity.

Up to 3 September, the Trawlers, with the exception of two on A Patrol, were working between Barra Head and Rockall.

As, however, ships of the Squadron have, by order of Admiralty, lately been making considerable use of the Minch route when proceeding to and from their Coaling Bases, the Trawlers have been moved to a line running 280° from Lat. 58.44´N, Long. 6.20´W, so as to afford some protection to ships approaching and leaving the Butt of Lewis.

2. During this period 80 vessels were intercepted, of which one – the Swedish Sailing Vessel *India*, on the 'Black List' – was sent in under Armed Guard … She was escorted by two trawlers and has arrived safely at Stornoway.[1]

On 29 August, *Orvieto* was able to render assistance to the Danish Motor Ketch *Sjoloran* … which was intercepted, becalmed, in Lat. 62.32´N, Long. 20.5´W. The vessel was leaking badly, and endeavouring to make Reykjavik for repairs. As the carpenter of *Orvieto*, who was sent on board, found that the stern post was sprung, and was unable to stop the leak, *Orvieto* towed the ketch during the night to within reach of land.

3. On 21 August, *Virginian* (on detached service) whilst proceeding with a convoy from Lough Swilly, in charge of *Changuinola*, was torpedoed by an enemy submarine in Lat. 55.29´N, Long. 8.30´W. She opened fire on submarine with two 6" guns at 500 yards range, and claims to have sunk it.[2] The excellent work and good discipline made it possible to keep her afloat, and she was brought safely back to Buncrana.

I regret to report that three men lost their lives. Two merchant ships in the convoy – the *Devonian* and *Roscommon* – were torpedoed and

[1]*India* was not detained.

[2]*Virginian* was attacked by *U 102*; both survived.

sunk. A full report of this has already been forwarded … .[1]

Changuinola, whilst proceeding to patrol, sighted a submarine the same day in Lat. 55.0´N, Long. 10.32´W. The destroyers *Mandate* and *Nicator*, being in the neighbourhood, were ordered to hunt her.

4. At 1545 on 20 August, a signal was intercepted from the destroyer *Mandate* that the oiler *Bulysses* had been torpedoed in Lat. 58.34´N, Long. 10.53´W. The Armed Trawlers *Macleay* and *Corrie Roy*, who were immediately despatched to her assistance, reached and endeavoured to tow her, but she was too badly damaged to salve, having been struck by two torpedoes, and sank at 0500 the following morning.[2]

Mandate reported that possibly *Nicator* sank the submarine, as one of her paravanes fired whilst sweeping after the second attack. No debris was seen, however.

5. At 1.30 on 26 August, a signal was received that the SS *Durango* was being shelled by an enemy submarine in Lat. 56.40´N, Long. 9.15´W. Tenth Cruiser Squadron Trawlers were ordered to proceed to her assistance, but failed to intercept her, and she was abandoned and sunk about 1630 in Lat. 57.45´N, Long. 8.40´W.[3] The crew were picked up by *Lord Lansdowne* at 1900, and taken to Oban.

The failure of the trawlers to locate her was probably due to the conflicting reports received regarding her position, viz:

At 1130, reported by Malin Head as Lat. 56.40´N, Long. 9.15´W.
At 1352, by *Durango* as Lat. 56.15´N, Long. 9.30´W.
At 1500 " " " Lat. 57.00´N, Long. 9.25´W.
At 1629 " " " Lat. 57.45´N, Long. 8.40´W.

I submit that it would be advantageous if I could be informed when unescorted steamers are passing through the area covered by the 10th Cruiser Squadron Patrols and approaching a Rendezvous for Stornoway or Scapa Flow (and also when outward bound), as I could often arrange for trawlers to escort or screen them.

Several cases have lately occurred where such steamers have been encountered or heard by W/T, e.g. SS *Pearleaf* was heard on 4 September informing Stornoway she was arriving at Rendezvous (position not indicated) at 6 a.m. on 5 September.

6. On 21 August *Ebro* visited Sandvik to land the Icelandic delegates … and on 4 September *Hildebrand* put in to Reykjavik to deliver

[1] *Devonian* and *Roscommon* were sunk by *U 53*.
[2] *Bulysses* was sunk by *U 52*.
[3] *Durango* was probably sunk by *U 52*.

Foreign Office despatches to the British and French Consuls.

Mr Olsen, the British Vice-Consul, informed Captain Watson of *Hildebrand* that the Iceland Herring Fishery Season had been a failure and was practically over now.

7. Arrangements have now been made for a ship of the 10th Cruiser Squadron to coal at Buncrana every 10 days, if necessary.

Swarbacks Minn has been abandoned as a Base for the trawlers attached to the Squadron. All trawlers now proceeding to Oban for coaling and refit.

8. A Boiler-makers' Strike commenced at Liverpool on 16 August, which seriously delayed the work on *Andes*, *Armadale Castle* and *Teutonic*.

As an instance of the manner in which ships have been delayed, *Andes* arrived at Liverpool for long refit on 2 July, and should have been ready to proceed on 22 July. Owing, however, to the boilermakers having come out on strike on two occasions, the ship will not sail until 9 September.

9. The weather, on the whole, has been fair, but has commenced to break up for the winter; two somewhat heavy gales were experienced, each lasting three days.

10. The system of Ships of the 10th Cruiser Squadron joining inward and outward bound mercantile convoys has not proved altogether satisfactory, owing to the amount of time lost to patrol. I have forwarded a separate communication on this subject … [386].

***

385. *Surveyor O.H.L. Tudor to Senior Naval Officer Lerwick*

30 August 1917

Neutral vessels, with certain exceptions* have to apply for bunkers, stating particulars of their intended voyage, cargo, etc. The Board of Customs then lay down certain conditions which as a general principle amount to a written understanding by the owners that the ship will carry out a round voyage in the interests of the allies.

* e.g., *all* Danish vessels, also the vessels of two Norwegian lines (the Bergenske and Nordenfeldske Companies) may bunker unconditionally. These concessions are temporary and are frequently modified.

386. *Vice-Admiral Tupper to Commander-in-Chief Grand Fleet*

HMS *Alsatian*, 1 September 1917

… [T]he present system of ships joining mercantile convoys has not proved altogether satisfactory, as it involves a comparatively large reduction in the amount of time spent by ships on patrol [379].

2. In the case of inward bound ships, owing to the large detour and the slow speed of the convoy, ships are obliged to leave patrol some 24 or 48 hours earlier than would have been the case had they proceeded to their destination.

As regards outward bound ships the delay is liable to be considerably greater as ships first of all have to proceed to the point of assembly for the convoy. The convoy may not leave for two or five days after their arrival, and there is then the additional delay involved in proceeding at slow speed some 200 or 300 miles to the westward before being able to proceed to patrol.

***

3. Under these circumstances I submit it is preferable to accept the submarine menace and that ships should proceed to and from their bases without escort until such time as destroyers can be detailed for the purpose. It is thought that two TBDs or at most three would be quite sufficient if detailed to work under my orders [389].

4. As regards a Northern Coaling Base for those ships of the Squadron which are unable to keep the sea for an extended period, it is considered that Loch Ewe or Lough Swilly would be preferable to Swarbacks Minn, so long as the patrols are working in their present westerly position.

387. *Vice-Admiral Tupper to Commander-in-Chief Grand Fleet*

HMS *Alsatian*, 1 September 1917

***

2. I submit that ships should be interchangeable [383], so as to give as many Captains of the Squadron as possible experience of convoy work, and also to give Captains, officers and ships' companies a change from the somewhat monotonous work of the Blockade.

388. *Vice-Admiral Tupper to Admiralty*

25 September 1917

Report of Proceedings, 10–25 September 1917

***

1. Of the eleven ships available for patrol duties, three have been temporarily detached on convoy service, viz:

Andes to the White Sea on 12 September;
Patuca to Halifax on 22 September;
Orcoma to the White Sea on 23 September.
Andes arrived at Scapa on 23rd instant, and, after completing with coal, etc., will rejoin patrol.

2. An average of five ships has been maintained actually on patrol, and these have been disposed as follows:

One ship on E Patrol, North-West of Iceland, until 21 September, when *Orcoma* was withdrawn for special service.

Four ships on A and B Patrols, working to the westward of 15 W, between Lat. 60 N and the coast of Iceland.

Two trawlers have been working with A Patrol in the neighbourhood of Portland Light, and the remainder spread on a line running 280° from Lat. 58.44´N, Long. 6.20´W.

3. During this period, 51 vessels were intercepted by the patrols. None were sent in under Armed Guard.

4. Very little of interest has occurred, except that, on 19 September, when *Alsatian* was in Lat. 57.18´N, Long. 7 W, proceeding to patrol, she apparently passed through a minefield, as a dull red horned object was observed to come to the surface on the port quarter, being apparently a moored mine swept up by the port P.V. A subsequent examination of the P.V.s disclosed signs of both of them having cut wire. A separate report of this incident is being forwarded …

5. Heavy westerly weather has been experienced on patrol – interfering somewhat with boarding operations.

6. Between 8th and 20th September, the Rear-Admiral, in *Orvieto*, was in charge of the patrols.

***

389. *Commander-in-Chief Grand Fleet to Vice-Admiral Commanding Tenth Cruiser Squadron*

HMS *Queen Elizabeth*, 14 September 1917

… [I]t is regretted that Grand Fleet destroyers are not at present available for escort duties with the Tenth Cruiser Squadron [386].

2. With the approach of the winter months, the value of destroyer escorts in Atlantic Waters would be considerably reduced; the best safeguard for ships approaching the land is to utilise the dark hours to the utmost extent.

390. *Vice-Admiral Tenth Cruiser Squadron to Commander-in-Chief Grand Fleet*

HMS *Alsatian*, 20 September 1917

Within the last 24 hours, orders have been received from the Admiralty to send one ship to Dakar and another to meet vessels from Archangel, both being required for convoy duties. This is *in addition* to the 11 ships (including *Andes*) already detached on convoy service [388].

2. The number of ships available for patrol work is consequently for the time being reduced to 8 and during the next fortnight it is not anticipated that there will be more than an average of 5 ships actually on patrol if present dates for docking, etc., are kept …

3. *Patuca* has been detailed to proceed to Dakar and *Orcoma* to meet Archangel vessels.

391. *Vice-Admiral Tupper to Admiralty*

HMS *Alsatian*, 8 October 1917

Report of Proceedings, 25 September–8 October 1917

***

During this period, *Patuca* and *Orcoma* have been detached for temporary convoy service. Of the remaining nine vessels available, an average of five has been maintained on patrol, being disposed as follows:

One ship on E Patrol, North-East of Iceland, working from Lat. 65 to 66.40´N, between the meridians of 11 and 13 W, since 26 September.

Four ships on A and B Patrols, to the South of Iceland.

With the concurrence of the Commander-in-Chief, E Patrol has been moved from the North-West to the North-East of Iceland. This change was considered desirable, as the passage between the ice and the land in Denmark Strait is now over 100 miles wide, and a ship stationed there is generally out of W/T touch.

Between 25 September and 3 October, A and B Patrols were working to the westward of 15 W, between Lat. 60 N and the Coast of Iceland.

On 3 October the Admiralty informed me a report had been received that the Swedish SS *Ellen* had left Kiel on 2 October to operate as a submarine depot ship off the American Coast. In view of this report, A and B Patrols were disposed on a line running 320° from Lat. 60.15´N, Long. 14.30´W, ships patrolling 40 miles apart. E Patrol remained as before.

Two trawlers have continued to work between A Patrol and the Icelandic Coast, the remainder being spread on a line running 315° from Lat. 58.45´N, Long. 6.30´W.

2. On 2 October, the convoy with which *Hildebrand* was proceeding to the Clyde was attacked by an enemy submarine in the neighbourhood of Rathlin Island, the *Drake* being torpedoed;[1] two other ships were mined in the vicinity. *Hildebrand* arrived safely at the Clyde.

3. On 28 September, *Ebro* called at Reykjavik to land the British Consul, Mr E.G. Cable, who had taken passage from Glasgow. She then proceeded to take up new E Patrol passing West and North of Iceland.

4. After being laid up since December last, *Teutonic* re-commissioned on 2 October for further service in the 10th Cruiser Squadron, thus increasing the number of vessels available for patrol duty to twelve. She has, however, been temporarily detailed for convoy service to the White Sea.

5. Fifteen vessels were intercepted by the patrols. None were sent in under Armed Guard.

6. Except for three days' fog, strong westerly gales and heavy seas have been prevalent, the weather being generally unsuitable for keeping an efficient watch on so large an area with so few ships.

***

[1]By *U 79*.

392. *Captain Percy G. Brown, RN,*[1] *to Commander-in-Chief Plymouth*

Royal Naval Depot, Devonport, 14 October 1917

I regret to report the loss of HMS *Champagne* torpedoed by enemy submarine in the following circumstances.[2]

On the 9th October at 6.10 a.m. mean course N 21°E (mag) zig-zagging, Latitude 54.17´N, Longitude 5.10´W, speed thirteen knots, the ship was struck by a torpedo in the engineroom the starboard side. The lookout at the starboard after gun saw a periscope and gave the order 'Close up', we were struck by the torpedo almost instantaneously, and the periscope disappeared.

Ship's company automatically went to action stations – the leading torpedo man put the depth charges to safe and reported to me, the confidential books were locked up in the steel safes by the decoding Officers and other confidential papers destroyed. All steam was cut off by the explosion. I believe the Engineer Officer of the watch was blown to pieces and there were several other casualties in the engineroom.

The senior Warrant Telegraphist reported to me that the W/T gear, both main and anxiliary, was out of action, and the two Warrant Telegraphists assisted by the electrician then endeavoured to repair the auxiliary W/T set, both of the Warrant Telegraphists unfortunately lost their lives by their devotion to duty.

The main engines were stopped by the explosion, and we could not go astern, but the ship lost way almost at once, the wind was WNW Magnetic, squally, force 5 to 7, state of sea 6.

The 1st Lieutenant asked me to give the order to abandon ship, I said 'No, not yet, as the ship may float for a considerable time, and we may bag the submarine if he comes up.' Almost immediately after this there was a second explosion on the port side in the fore part of the after well deck. I at once gave the order 'Abandon ship'; up to this time not a single gripe had been cast off, nor any attempt made to go to the boats.

The ship remained on an even keel but began to settle rapidly.

The boats with the exception of the collapsibles were got away smartly, although difficulty was experienced owing to the rough sea.

The 1st Lieutenant left by the last boat, the upper deck being then awash, and he only left by my order. He had to jump for it and got in the water.

[1]Brown, Percy G., RN, Lieutenant 1896, Commander 1908, Captain of *Patia* 1915, and of *Champagne* 1917, Captain (retired) 1919.

[2]This is extracted from the Court Martial enquiring into the loss of HMS *Champagne*, 12 November 1917. The submarine was *U 96*.

Four men, Oliver Ward, Able Seaman RNVR, Able Seaman Ryan RNVR, Leading Seaman Watkins RNR, and W.J. Cox, Leading Seaman RNR, volunteered to remain by foremost pair of guns, just after the second explosion. Ward saw a submarine come to the surface about 300 to 400 yards away on the port beam. The port foremost 6" gun was fired at once, projectile apparently went just over. The submarine at once dived and the gun was reloaded and a tube inserted. These men remained by their gun, and I regret to say that Cox was the only one who was picked up.

The collapsible boats were stowed abreast of other boats which had to be lowered, the davits turned in, purchases rounded up, before collapsibles could be turned out. I had asked for a separate pair of davits to be fitted for them but this had not been done. As the other boats had to be got away first there were only the two collapsible boats' crews to do this, there being no steam for the winches, it was found to be impossible to move them.

Sub-Lieutenants Nalder and Hyslop RNR,[1] the Officers of these boats, were endeavouring to turn the boats out, Sub-Lieutenant Nalder was eventually picked up, but Sub-Lieutenant Hyslop was drowned. I ordered Petty Officer W.J. Ware, RFR, to get spars to lever them over the side which he did, and the port boat was half over when we were struck again by a torpedo on the port side before the funnel, the explosion can only be described as tremendous, the ship broke in two complete parts and sank in about thirty seconds, the port collapsible boat fell clear and some men succeeded in scrambling aboard, the starboard one floated bottom up and a few men clung on to it, others got aboard rafts and wreckage. Some men must have been killed by wreckage coming to the surface, which it did with great force.

The final torpedo sank us at 6.30 the first struck us at 6.10. I am unable to give exact times of events which occurred between these times. Owing to the heavy weather, the loaded condition of the boats, and the amount of wreckage, the boats experienced very great difficulty in picking up survivors. Leading Seaman Cox (one of the gun's crew) and myself managed to support ourselves by holding on to an empty biscuit tank for a sea boat, about 5 feet by 3 feet, which came up near us, and we were picked up after several attempts by Lieutenant Bingham, RNR, in one of the boats, somewhere between 7.30 a.m. and 8.0 a.m.

[1]Hyslop, John W., RNR, Sub-Lieutenant 1917, killed 1917.
Nalder, Albert McC., RNR, Skipper 1915, Sub-Lieutenant 1917, Acting Lieutenant 1919.

After I was picked up a sail on our boat was hoisted and we ran before the wind followed by another boat, the sea was very heavy but we made Port Erin, Isle of Man, between 11.30 and noon when I landed and telephoned to the Coast Guard to wireless for help, other boats could not sail, being too overcrowded, and were eventually towed into Port St Mary, Isle of Man, by two trawlers, where they arrived about 1.30 p.m. A collapsible was towed into Peel by the Peel lifeboat in the evening. Two rafts, Sub-Lieutenant Nalder being on board one, were picked up by merchant vessels and crews landed between Liverpool and Manchester. The casualties among saved men were slight, one being left in Hospital, and one in bed in his home in the Isle of Man, remainder returning to Liverpool on Thursday, 11th Oct. 1917.

I held an informal enquiry before reaching Liverpool, and attached are copies of statements made to me by Officers and ratings whom I questioned.

Our total complement was 305 all told and as far as can be ascertained at present, 5 Officers and 53 men are missing. Considering the weather, distance from land, shortness of time between first attack and our sinking, I consider we were extremely fortunate to save so many. The behaviour of the Officers and ship's company was excellent, the First Lieutenant's stations were good, the men knew their stations, and there was an entire absence of panic throughout, and during the time we were in the Isle of Man, where the inhabitants were extremely hospitable, not a single case of drunkenness or other misdemeanour was brought to my notice.

The ship went down with a portion of her guns manned and ready to fire and traditions of the Service were upheld.

At the time of attack we were going as fast as we could keep up, lookouts were stationed all round the ship and were alert.

We had no escort.

393. *Vice-Admiral Tupper to Admiralty*

HMS *Alsatian*, 16 October 1917

Report of Proceedings, 8–16 October 1917

***

1. Between 5th and 9th October patrols were disposed as follows for intercepting German Raider reported to be outward bound:

Five ships South of Iceland on a line running 320° from Latitude 60.45´N, 15.30´W, ships patrolling on parallel courses 40 miles apart, steering to Eastward in daylight and Westward in dark hours.

One ship working from Latitude 65 to 66.40´ North between meridians of 11 and 13 West. On 7 October this Ship was moved to the neighbourhood of Revsnes Light as the Third and Fourth Light Cruiser Squadrons had been ordered to patrol off Langanaes and Storkeness respectively.

NOTE: The Light Cruiser Squadrons were withdrawn on the evening of the 9th.

Orvieto joined patrol from Liverpool on 6 October, and was ordered to sweep West and North of Iceland with a view to ultimately relieving *Ebro* on E.

Two Trawlers off Portland Light and the remainder on line 315° from Latitude 58.45´N, Longitude 6.30´W.

2. At 1225 on 10th October a report was received from *Patia* that at 1130 the Armed Trawler *Walpole* was chasing a large steamer in Latitude 63.18´N, Longitude 19.47´W, which was steering 240° and attempting to evade the patrol. The steamer was reported as having one funnel, a clipper bow, and cruiser stern, and to be proceeding at high speed. *Patia*, whose noon position was Latitude 62.45´N, Longitude 19.25´W, was directed to chase at full speed. *Alsatian* also proceeded at full speed to the westward to cut her off in case she should head South.

Changuinola was already on her way to A Patrol with orders to relieve *Patia* and would thus be in a position to intercept the steamer should she double back to the Eastward and also act as repeating ship for *Alsatian*.

No other Ships were available for chasing, *Andes* and *Artois* having left patrol earlier in the day to coal at Liverpool and Loch Ewe respectively.

The Commander-in-Chief was informed of action taken.

The Trawlers finally lost sight of the steamer about 1700, steering approximately 300°. They had previously endeavoured to stop her by gun-fire, *Walpole* firing one round and *Edward Williams* five, but were out of range. *Walpole* was ordered to proceed to Reykjavik and ascertain whether anything was known of the steamer, while *Edward Williams* patrolled in Faxe Bay.

Meanwhile at dusk *Patia* was directed to steer for Latitude 61.40´N, Longitude 28 W, *Alsatian* continuing on her course to the westward towards this position.

As nothing further had transpired by daylight on 11th, *Alsatian* and *Patia* carried out a curve of search as shown in the accompanying tracing …, *Alsatian* proceeding as far as Latitude 61.20´N, Longitude 32.30´W, being then obliged to return as coal was running short.

Nothing, however, was seen of the steamer. Strong North-Westerly and Northerly winds with heavy hail squalls and rough seas were encountered; the visibility varied from 6 to 15 miles in daytime and nights were dark.

On 13 October a report was received from *Walpole* stating that she had put in to Reykjavik on the 11th, but owing to the state of the weather landing had been impracticable. There was no steamer in the harbour.

3. On 13 October, the patrols having become somewhat disorganized by the operations referred to in the previous paragraph, were redisposed as follows:

One Ship accompanied by two Trawlers on A Patrol between Latitude 62.50´N and the coast of Iceland from Longitude 17 to 21 West.

Four Ships on B Patrol on line running 330° from Latitude 60 N, Longitude 15 West.

Owing to the shortage of Ships on patrol – 2 of the 4 on B having to leave within 36 hours – E patrol had to be temporarily abandoned. It is my intention, however, to maintain a Ship on E whenever five or more are available for patrol as *Orvieto* reports fine, clear, calm weather North of Iceland and no ice.

4. I regret to report that HMS *Champagne* was torpedoed and sunk by an enemy submarine about 6.0 a.m. on 9 October when in Latitude 54.10´N, Longitude 5.32´W whilst rejoining patrol from Liverpool. According to the latest information in my possession – received by W/T – the Commanding Officer, Acting Captain Percy G. Brown, RN, 31 Officers, and 175 Men were picked up. No detailed report has, however, been received [392].

5. 23 Vessels were intercepted by the patrols. None were sent in under Armed Guard.

6. *Patuca* has been absent on convoy duty during the whole of the period covered by this report. *Teutonic* and *Ebro* have also been detailed to proceed to the White Sea on escort duty but have not yet started.

7. Continuous heavy weather has been experienced.

***

10. At 1800 on 14 October I turned over the command of the Ships on Patrol to Rear-Admiral Morgan Singer CB, in *Orvieto*. *Alsatian* then proceeded to Liverpool to complete with coal, provisions, etc., where she arrived at 9.0 a.m. on 16 October.

394. *Vice-Admiral Commanding Tenth Cruiser Squadron to Commander-in-Chief Grand Fleet*

16 October 1917

I submit for your consideration that H.M. Ships *Artois*, *Changuinola*, *Patuca*, and *Patia* should be transferred from Tenth Cruiser Squadron patrol to convoy duties and replaced by ships capable of remaining at sea for at least 25 to 30 days.

2. At present the vessels referred to are obliged to coal at the Northern Base after being 18 to 20 days at sea, and as a rule have to proceed to and from the coaling base without escort.

In view of the recent sinking of Tenth Cruiser Squadron ships, viz. *Hilary*, *Avenger*, *Otway* and *Champagne*, and attacks on other vessels it is considered highly desirable to reduce as far as possible the number of times a ship has to pass through the more dangerous waters to coal, provision, etc. This could be done if the suggestion in clause 1 was adopted, these vessels being relieved by *Gloucestershire*, *Almanzora*, *Arlanza*, and *Armadale Castle*.

These latter vessels were originally chosen for convoy work owing to their cargo carrying capacity. In view, however, of the decision that vessels on convoy duties should not in future carry cargo, this reason no longer holds good.

The employment of vessels to keep the sea for extended periods would also have the advantage of increasing the percentage of time spent on patrol by ships of the Tenth Cruiser Squadron.

3. *Artois*, *Changuinola*, *Patuca* and *Patia* would appear to be suitable for convoy work as it is understood that neither high speed nor large cargo capacity is essential – the last three, however, are good for 14½ knots and *Artois* for 13.

4. Further I submit that *Artois* is not fast enough for patrol work. Her maximum sea speed is only some 13 knots, and she often has difficulty in overhauling vessels on patrol. This is accentuated now that the Squadron has been reduced and the distance between ships on patrol is greater than it was. Her low speed also renders her more liable to successful torpedo attack when proceeding without escort to and from the various coaling bases.

5. It is also requested that a suitable Armed Merchant Cruiser may be detailed to replace *Champagne*, sunk on 9 October in order that the Cruisers detailed for patrol duties may be maintained at at least 12.

395. *Vice-Admiral Tupper to Admiralty*

HMS *Alsatian*, 8 November 1917

Report of Proceedings, 16 October–8 November 1917

***

1. In addition to *Patuca*, previously detached on convoy service, the following ships have also been temporarily detached during the period covered by this Report:

Artois to Sydney, Cape Breton, on 17 October;
Teutonic to White Sea on 17 October;
Patia to White Sea on 18 October.

All the above, with the exception of *Artois*, have since returned, and are now completing with coal at Liverpool or Clyde preparatory to rejoining patrol.

With these ships away, it has not been possible to maintain more than an average of three to four ships on patrol, and these have been disposed to the South of Iceland.

Two trawlers have been working between the Northern cruiser and the coast, and the remainder on a line running North-West from the Butt of Lewis.

2. 49 vessels were intercepted by the patrols; none were sent in under Armed Guard.

On 31 October, when in Lat. 63.15´N, Long. 19.36´W, *Hildebrand* intercepted the Danish Sailing Vessel *Ester*, from Copenhagen to Faskrudfjord, with a general cargo. She had been disabled by a gale on the 29th ultimo, her boat being washed away and sails, hatches, and rigging damaged. She supplied her with water and petrol for auxiliary motor, and as her Captain did not consider she would survive another gale, *Hildebrand* towed her to the Vestmannaeyjar Islands. Information has since been received that she was wrecked there the following day.

3. I regret to report that the Armed Trawler *Thomas Stratton* was sunk with the loss of eight of her crew, by an explosion, probably a mine, in Lat. 58.33´N, Long. 6.23´W, on the 20th October, whilst patrolling in company with *Lord Lansdowne* and *Arley*. A Court of Enquiry was held by the Rear-Admiral Stornoway, and the finding and minutes forwarded by him through the Commander-in-Chief Rosyth.

4. The weather continued bad until 31 October, since when there has been some improvement. On 22 October, *Hildebrand*, whilst standing by the Belgian Relief Ship *Kurland*, was struck by a heavy sea. The two foremost boats on the starboard side and three davits, were carried

away, the gig smashed and the two remaining boats on the starboard side damaged; a few scuttles were smashed in. Fortunately no one was injured.

5. Whilst *Alsatian* was undocking at Liverpool on the 29th October preparatory to leaving for patrol, one watch of firemen and trimmers left the Stokehold to request an increase of pay. They immediately returned to duty, however, when ordered to do so by the Commander, who was supported by part of the Marine Detachment …

6. Rear-Admiral Morgan Singer, CB, in *Orvieto*, was in charge of the patrol between 6 p.m. 14th October, and 10 a.m., 1st November, during absence of *Alsatian* coaling and refitting at Liverpool.

***

396. *Captain H.H. Smith [Flag Captain to Vice-Admiral Commanding Tenth Cruiser Squadron] to Senior Naval Officer Swarbacks Minn*

24 October 1917

As Tenth Cruiser Squadron ships and trawlers are not now using Swarbacks Minn, it is requested that you will return Tenth Cruiser Squadron Orders and Memos supplied to the Rear-Admiral Swarbacks Minn and *Gibraltar*.

397. *Memorandum for the Commander-in-Chief*

[n.d., but 6 November 1917][1]

The question has been raised as to whether it is necessary to keep the 10th Cruiser Squadron at its present strength and if not, whether the squadron might be abolished or materially reduced in numbers, and a patrol maintained by means of 12 trawlers; supplemented by three ships of 10th Cruiser Squadron and the 2nd Cruiser Squadron, held available to proceed to sea when the circumstances require it.

The duties devolving on the 10th Cruiser Squadron have been mainly:

(a) The economic blockade of Germany by intercepting vessels carrying goods destined for that country either direct or through Neutral countries.
(b) To endeavour to intercept armed enemy auxiliaries trying to leave

[1]There is no indication of authorship on this document; the date is derived from the reference to it in [386].

Germany with the object of attacking our trade in distant waters or carrying supplies and arms to E. Africa, Mexico or Ireland.

(c) Vessels of the 10th Cruiser Squadron have also been used for voyages to Northern Russia either with important personages or as ocean escort to troopship convoys.

Dealing with (a) the blockade, the present position as regards goods from overseas to Scandinavia and Holland may be briefly described as follows:

(i) USA – No goods can leave US Ports without a licence from the U.S. Government and (at present) in addition, a letter of assurance from the British Government. The vessels carrying these goods go to Halifax for examination and are released by order from London. The names of the vessels are notified to the Patrols by the Admiralty.

(ii) South American Countries: The Scandinavian and Dutch Steamship Lines trading to South American Ports submit their proposed cargoes to the Foreign Office for approval before loading. Any goods that are not approved are refused by the Steamship Companies in order to save difficulties to their vessels at the Ports of examination.[1]

(iii) Dutch East Indies: Endeavours have been made to institute a similar system but so far have not been completed. In practice no goods are coming forward as the vessels all go to USA Ports for bunkers and are detained under the US Bunker regulations.

(iv) Mediterranean, Spanish and Portuguese Ports – Vessels all go to Gibraltar for examination. Pressure is being put on Portugal to stop her exports to Scandinavia and Holland.[2] The Steamship Companies in this trade are practically all under agreement with us and call voluntarily at Gibraltar for examination. This also applies to all salt cargoes for Norway, Iceland and Faroe.

2. At present owing to:

(a) Our Agreements with Neutral Steamship Lines,

[1]There had been a small rush of Latin American states to join the war once the USA did so: Cuba and Panama on 7 April, and Brazil on 26 October; Bolivia, Dominican Republic, Peru and Uruguay had also broken off diplomatic relations with Germany at various times between April and October. Of these states, however, Cuba, Panama and the Dominican Republic were under United States occupation or strong political influence. One could scarcely call this an enthusiastic participation. In addition the United States had bought the Danish West Indian islands in 1917.

[2]Portugal had been at war with Germany since March 1916.

(b) The bunker policy of the UK and USA, it is practically impossible for a vessel to carry out a voyage which has not been approved by us. In any case, if attempted, we should soon get to know of it, and steps could be taken to capture the offending vessel.

3. There has been no serious attempt to run the Blockade since the autumn of 1916, when the SS *Ada* got through twice and the SS *Atlanten* once: on each occasion from an US Port. The *Ada* was captured outward bound late in 1916 and the *Atlanten* off Rio in the Spring 1917. Experience of the last three years has shown that if a really determined attempt is made to run the Blockade during the winter months, it is almost impossible to capture the vessel in Northern latitudes owing to long hours of darkness and the prevailing bad weather. It is therefore much easier to capture the vessel near her port of loading as was done in the case of the *Atlanten*. As practically the whole of America, North and South, is either actually or tacitly on the side of the Allies, this should present no difficulty.

4. There is a small trade from Iceland to Denmark carried on by small schooners. These vessels are often missed by the Patrols but owing to the control of Iceland produce that we have secured by the Iceland Agreement, their cargoes when East-bound can be considered as negligible.

5. The number of neutral vessels intercepted by the 10th Cruiser Squadron during the period 4th August 1917 to 14th October 1917 was 147 (including 14 for Belgian Relief); the number sent in for examination was 2 (one of which was sunk by submarine), the remainder having previously called at Ports of examination or, in the case of outward bound vessels, being on approved voyages.

6. There are at present a large number of neutral vessels detained in US and Canadian Ports pending the completion of satisfactory agreements between the USA and their respective countries. The numbers are as follows:

Dutch	98	of which	12	are in	Canadian	Ports
Norwegian	111	"	7	"	"	"
Swedish	39	"	5	"	"	"
Spanish	55	"	0	"	"	"

These vessels when released will of course use the Northern route but their cargoes will have been passed and the vessels and their crews examined. The future employment of these vessels will presumably be governed by the terms of the Agreements, and it is hoped to get a number of them into Allied trades.

Dealing with (b) the intercepting of enemy Raiders.

Experience has shewn that when an enemy raider is being sent out or is returning a certain amount of warning has been obtained on most occasions from the fact that certain signals are made, which it is presumed give the raider information of the position of our patrols. This information is obtained either by intercepted signals or by radiogoniometric bearings or signals made by the Squadron. Any such warning is of great value and it is therefore important that the volume of W/T used by the 10th Cruiser Squadron should not be materially reduced as otherwise the enemy will realise that the squadron has been withdrawn and not trouble about the position of the patrol line. It is essential therefore that a few trawlers with good W/T should simulate the old patrol.

With regard to (c) the squadron if reduced as proposed would still be able to provide an escort for troopships as required.

398. *Vice-Admiral Tupper to Admiralty*

HMS *Alsatian*, 24 November 1917

Report of Proceedings, 8–24 November 1917

***

1. *Patuca* and *Artois*, instead of rejoining patrol, have again been detached on convoy service. With *Teutonic* also detached and *Orcoma* undergoing long refit only seven Cruisers have been available for Patrol duties.

2. An average of four ships has been maintained on patrol, all of which have been disposed to the South of Iceland and manoeuvred to cover as large a space as possible having regard to mutual support, etc.

There has been no change in the disposition of the Trawlers, viz. two working with A patrol off south coast of Iceland, and the remainder varying between five and seven on a line running North West from the Butt of Lewis.

No Trawler has yet been detailed to replace *Thomas Stratton*. As the number of Cruisers on patrol is so reduced an increase in Trawler numbers is very desirable.

3. 22 Vessels were intercepted by the patrols, two of which – the Swedish SV *Regulus* … [406][1] and Danish SS *Danmark* …[2] were sent in under armed guard … Each was escorted through the danger zone by two trawlers attached to the 10th Cruiser Squadron and reached port in safety.

4. On 12th November *Andes* called at Reykjavik to deliver letters for the French Consul forwarded under cover of Admiralty Letters M of 10th and 29th October to the Naval Base Officer, Liverpool.

5. I proceeded to Scapa Flow in *Alsatian* on 23rd November in accordance with directions from the Commander-in-Chief, leaving Rear-Admiral Morgan Singer, CB, in charge during my absence.

6. The weather has been generally unfavourable for intercepting shipping, a succession of gales and misty weather being met with and there are now only about 9 hours of daylight per diem.

***

399. *Commander-in-Chief Grand Fleet to Admiralty*

15 November 1917

Composition of the Tenth Cruiser Squadron

The views expressed in the Memorandum enclosed with the Admiralty letter under reply, as regards the utility of the 10th Cruiser Squadron, are concurred in [397]. Their role so far as contraband is concerned has passed, and as regards interception of Raiders, their success has not been marked.

2. I therefore concur in the abolition of the 10th Cruiser Squadron, and in the formation of a small squadron of

3 ships of 10th Cruiser Squadron.
2 *Minotaur* class.
2 Armed Boarding steamers.

[1]*Regulus* carried corkwood and salt, and the former was at once ordered to be discharged to the Prize Court. Customs were asked to make a careful search. It emerged that the Master had tried to 'evade' the patrol [474], and the Contraband Committee ordered the vessel itself to be sent to the Prize Court, which in turned occasioned a protest from the Swedish Foreign Office. The Committee went ahead, claiming it to be a test case (TS 14/18 of 1 to 7 December 1917 *passim*).

[2]*Danmark*'s cargo was mining machinery, with graphite carried apparently as ballast, and it was this which caused enquiries to be made before the ship was allowed to sail on (TS 14/18 of 9 to 26 November 1917).

3. Of the three possible places to base this Squadron, viz, Swarbacks Minn, Loch Ewe, and Scapa, I consider the last-named to be preferable. The most likely points at which to intercept Raiders are off Iceland, at Stalbak Huk (NW corner) or Stokanaes (SE corner); there is little to choose so far as distance from the above-mentioned bases is concerned, on the other hand facilities of every nature exist at Scapa and would have to be re-instituted at Loch Ewe or Swarbacks Minn. It is therefore recommended that the Squadron should be based on Scapa.

4. It is proposed to carry out periodical sweeps with two vessels at a time – say one Armed Merchant Cruiser and one *Minotaur* class – towards Iceland, vessels remaining at sea for about a week. Destroyer escort would be provided as far as Butt of Lewis, which would be passed about dusk thus permitting a good offing to be made before daylight the next morning.

5. As regards the Armed Trawlers, I propose discussing the question of their employment with the Vice-Admiral Commanding 10th Cruiser Squadron. It is noted that it is proposed to retain only 11 trawlers instead of 18 with the newly-formed Squadron. This reduction appears feasible, but, if so, I am strongly of opinion that the vessels released should be employed on the Lerwick–Bergen Convoy route, for which they would be eminently suitable during the winter months.

6. The question of the release of Grand Fleet destroyers from convoy duties on the Lerwick–Bergen route is an urgent one, and will form the subject of a separate letter.

400. *Vice-Admiral Tenth Cruiser Squadron to Senior Naval Officer Shetlands*

24 November 1917

As under certain circumstances it will still be necessary for ships of the Tenth Cruiser Squadron to coal at Swarbacks Minn, it is desired to bring up to date the information regarding the Base entered in the Tenth Cruiser Squadron orders.

I should therefore be obliged if you would cause the attached draft order to be corrected as necessary and returned to me.

2. It is also requested that any future alterations and additions that may be considered sensible may be communicated to me.

401. *Arrangements at Swarbacks Minn*

[November 1917][1]

Officer in charge at base is Captain (Act.) A.H. Oldham[2] in *Gibraltar*. All local orders issued by him should be complied with as necessary.

2. *Arrangements for Entry*. Particulars of the boom defences and the procedure for entering the port will be found in CB 0173 'Instructions for the entry of H.M. Ships into defended ports, etc.', but care should be taken to comply with AMC Order No. 8 as regards obtaining the latest information.

3. *Anchor Berths*. Ships on arrival will be ordered to anchor in one of the following berths:

Busta Voe

No. 1. 770 yards 86 from Busta House F S and 227 from Free Church.

No. 2. 800 yards 111 from Busta House F S and 214 from Free Church.

No. 3. 300 yards 135 from Busta House F S and 214 from Free Church.

Olna Firth

No. 4. S 63 W 5.4 cables from Whaling Station Chimney.

No. 5. S 45 W 4.1 cables from Whaling Station Chimney.

No. 6. S 14 W 3.4 cables from Whaling Station Chimney.

No. 7. S 20 E 3.6 cables from Whaling Station Chimney.

4. *Movements when approaching and leaving Harbour.* Ships approaching during dark hours are to inform the Senior Naval Officer of their movements at least two hours before sunset, in order that they may be directed to exchange positions, if necessary, with other ships in the neighbourhood.

Before sailing, ships should enquire of the Senior Naval Officer as to whether any ship is approaching the Harbour.

5. *Depot Ship*. *Gibraltar* is moored in Busta Voe and acts as Depot and Guardship.

6. *Coaling and Watering Arrangements*. A stock of about 5000 tons of coal is maintained at the Port in two colliers. Requirements are to be signalled to the Senior Naval Officer on arrival.

[1]No example of earlier 'arrangements' survives. This document is clearly the result of experience and the final version – the anchorage was virtually abandoned soon after.

[2]Oldham, Arthur H., RN, Lieutenant 1893, Commander 1904, Captain of *Gibraltar* and SNO Swarbacks Minn 1917–1918, Captain (retired) 1919.

Report of damage to collier (S.1307) duly completed is to be forwarded to the Senior Naval Officer before sailing, care being taken to obtain the Master's signature, whether the collier has sustained damage or not.

There are two water boats attached to the Base, but no tug.

7. *Fresh Provisions*. Fresh provisions can be obtained from Mr T.M. Adie, the Contractor at Voe, who requires 24 hours notice if possible. W/T must not be used for the purpose as there is ample time to make arrangements after arrival. A limited quantity Frozen Meat can be obtained from *Gibraltar* on demand, requirements being signalled on arrival in port.

8. *Mail Arrangements*. Mails arrive and leave twice a week by Fleet Mail Steamers; the programme is set out from time to time in GFOs.

The Post Offices at Brae and Voe (Olna Firth) are not to be used for posting letters.

9. *Church Services*. Ships desiring to avail themselves of the services of the Presbyterian Minister – Rev. W. Fairbairn – should communicate with him direct. Commanding Officers should endeavour to arrange for a service to be held during the stay in harbour, at which it is hoped Wesleyans will also attend.

With reference to AMO 630/1917, ships having a Roman Catholic Chaplain on board are to report the fact on arrival to the Senior Naval Officer, who will make the necessary arrangements for the ministrations mentioned in the Order.

***

402. *Vice-Admiral Commanding Tenth Cruiser Squadron to Commander-in-Chief Grand Fleet*

25 November 1917

As a result of our Conference respecting the future of the Tenth Cruiser Squadron, I submit for your consideration that the three ships to be retained should be:

1. *Alsatian*.
2. *Teutonic*.
3. *Almanzora* or *Orvieto*.

If four can be obtained, then keep these four, making six with the two cruisers from Second Cruiser Squadron.

I would suggest they should work in two squadrons, namely,

i. Three Armed Merchant Cruisers.

ii. Two Cruisers and four Armed Boarding Steamers.

These would cruise alternately, but the Armed Merchant Cruisers – being able to remain out longer – would do the more distant cruises to the westward, examining east and westbound Merchant ships and making W/T signals to disclose their presence, the Cruisers and Armed Boarding Steamers doing the less distant cruises between the Faroes and Norway.

Whilst in harbour at Scapa the three Armed Merchant Cruisers could be fitted by dockyard hands for carrying numerous aircraft – a sketch is attached regarding *Alsatian* to carry say 18 aeroplanes and two kite balloons …

2. As to the 12 trawlers based at Oban, I recommend that they should work in pairs in the space between the Flannan Islands, Rockall Bank and west coasts of Hebrides. An Aerodrome should be organised on West Loch Roag and sea planes from there should work with the 12 trawlers on an organised plan, using St Kilda as a centre.

3. It would probably be best for the Armed Merchant Cruisers to go periodically, say every two months or so, to Southern Bases for boiler cleaning and provisioning as organisation exists there for dealing with them.

403. *Vice-Admiral Tupper to Admiralty*

HMS *Alsatian*, 21 December 1917

Report of Proceedings, 20 November–20 December 1917

***

1. On 24 November, I arrived at Scapa Flow in *Alsatian*, to confer with the Commander-in-Chief regarding the future of the 10th Cruiser Squadron. I remained there until 27 November, and then proceeded to Liverpool, arriving midnight 31 November–1 December, being delayed 48 hours in Belfast Lough owing to the presence of enemy submarines in the Irish Sea.

While *Alsatian* was coaling and cleaning boilers at Liverpool, the accommodation for the crews was raised up one deck to reduce the chance of heavy loss of life in case of accidents from mines or torpedos.

I took the opportunity of visiting the Admiralty to confer respecting the reconstitution of the 2nd Cruiser Squadron, and the administration of the vessels formerly comprising the 10th Cruiser Squadron.

2. Between 24 and 28 November, there were five ships on patrol to the south of Iceland, between 18 and 23 W.

At 11 a.m. on 28th, *Teutonic* reported sighting the conning tower and periscope of a submarine in Lat. 62.25´N, Long. 19.32´W. As the Captain considered the report reliable, the patrol was moved to the westward of Long. 23 W.

3. On 28 November, I received Admiralty Telegram 1130 of the previous day, addressed to the Commander-in-Chief Grand Fleet, approving his proposals for the reduction of the 10th Cruiser Squadron. The ships still employed on patrol duties on that date were *Alsatian*, *Orvieto*, *Andes*, *Teutonic*, *Orcoma*, *Ebro*, *Hildebrand*, *Patia* and *Changuinola*.

In compliance with orders contained in the telegram referred to, and in others subsequently received, ships were detached as follows:

Changuinola to Halifax, from patrol, on 29 November,

Patia to Dakar, from Loch Ewe via Clyde, on 29 November.

Hildebrand to Halifax, from Clyde, on 30 November.

Ebro to Clyde from patrol on 2 December, to await orders, being subsequently directed to proceed to Sierra Leone.

Andes, at Liverpool, was detailed for taking officers and men for *Glory* to Murmansk.

Orcoma, to Liverpool, was ordered to be ready to proceed to Halifax about 9 December.

4. This left *Alsatian*, *Orvieto* and *Teutonic* still under my orders for patrol duties. On 8 December, the situation as regards these ships was as follows:

Alsatian at Liverpool;

Teutonic at Scapa Flow, having left patrol on 5 December;

Orvieto proceeding to Scapa Flow from patrol.

The trawlers attached to the Squadron were patrolling a line running North-West from the Butt of Lewis, those on A Patrol having been withdrawn on 29 November in accordance with instructions from the Commander-in-Chief, Grand Fleet.

5. Fourteen vessels were intercepted by the patrols during this period; none were sent in under Armed Guard.

6. The Armed Trawler *Tenby Castle* visited Reykjavik on 27 November, to deliver the envelope for the French Consul referred to in Admiralty Letter M, of 12 November 1917.

7. On 8 December, by orders of Admiralty, the 10th Cruiser Squadron ceased to exist as such, and I assumed command of the 2nd Cruiser Squadron, consisting of the Armoured Cruisers *Shannon* and *Minotaur*, the Armed Merchant Cruisers *Alsatian*, *Orvieto* and *Teutonic*,

the Armed Boarding Steamers *Amsterdam* and *Duke of Cornwall*, and twelve Armed Trawlers, the other five formerly attached to the 10th Cruiser Squadron being detained for Lerwick–Bergen Convoy work.

A copy of a confidential farewell Memorandum to the Rear-Admiral, and Captains, Officers and Men of the 10th Cruiser Squadron is enclosed; it will be observed that I have avoided mentioning that the 10th Cruiser Squadron has been abolished.

8. On 14 December Rear-Admiral Morgan Singer struck his Flag in *Orvieto*, having been appointed to assist the Commander-in-Chief, North America & West Indies.

9. On 16 December, *Alsatian* – having completed alterations, coaling, etc. – undocked and put to sea from Liverpool, being escorted by T.B.D. *Pelican* until shortly after passing Rathlin Island when, the weather becoming too bad, she was sent to Buncrana, *Alsatian* proceeding to rendezvous with *Teutonic* in Lat. 62 N, Long. 18 W.

10. Bad weather, with gales and snowstorms, were experienced until the morning of 20 December, when the rendezvous was effected. Orders having been received on the previous evening for *Alsatian* to reach Scapa on 21st, course was shaped for that destination after Captain Arnold-Forster[1] had been on board and received orders for patrol until 25 December – when he was directed to leave for Liverpool.

11. I arrived and anchored in Scapa Flow, in *Alsatian* at noon on 21 December.

12. A schedule of the enclosures accompanying this Submission is attached. Included is a Graph showing the number of ships intercepted, and those sent in, each week between 1 January and 8 December 1917, together with the average number of ships (including Trawlers) on patrol.

From this it will be seen that 2079 vessels were intercepted, of which 176 were sent in under Armed Guard.

This shows a considerable reduction in the numbers dealt with in 1915 and 1916, which is mainly due to the following causes:

(1) The smaller number of Armed Merchant Cruisers on patrol. Since the beginning of July, an average of 12 were detached on convoy and other services.

[1]Arnold-Forster, Forster Delafield, CMG, RN (1876–1958), Commander 1908, Captain 1916, Captain *Teutonic*, January 1916–December 1917, Admiralty Anti-Submarine Division 1918–1919, Captain in charge at Simonstown Dockyard, 1921–1923; retired 1923; Author of *The Ways of the Navy* (London, 1931), and *At War with the Smugglers* (London, 1936).

Though the number of trawlers attached to the Squadron was increased early in the year, these of necessity were employed in areas where little shipping would normally be intercepted, being principally used to patrol the line of approach of ships sent in under Armed Guard, and to escort them in if met.

(2) The entry of America into the War, and the greater restrictions consequently imposed on the sailing of neutral vessels for Scandinavian countries.

(3) The unrestricted submarine warfare, which has led to the establishment of oversea examination ports, the number of ships requiring to be sent in to British Ports being thus very considerably reduced.

(4) The number of vessels visiting the fishing grounds off Iceland has been very small, the absence of Scandinavian fishing craft during the herring fishery season, due to the restrictions imposed, being very marked.

13. The operations of the Squadron during the year have unfortunately not been unattended by loss, the Armed Merchant Cruisers *Hilary*, *Avenger*, *Otway* and *Champagne* having been sunk by enemy submarines, and the Armed Trawlers *Robert Smith* and *Thomas Stratton* lost from unknown causes. The *Motagua* was also mined off Swarbacks Minn, and the *Virginian* torpedoed in the vicinity of Lough Swilly whilst proceeding on convoy duty; both these last two however were brought safely into harbour.

It is regretted that, as a result of the above, 8 officers and 101 men lost their lives.

In addition, 4 officers and 2 men were removed by enemy submarines from ships being taken in under Armed Guard, and taken to Germany as prisoners of war.

***

404. *Commander-in-Chief Grand Fleet to Admiralty*

28 November 1917

Duties of Tenth Cruiser Squadron

After conferring with the Vice-Admiral Commanding 10th Cruiser Squadron it is proposed that in the immediate future the 12 trawlers released from the 10th Cruiser Squadron should be employed as at present to the Westward of the Hebrides on anti-submarine operations and for convoy work as requisite.

2. It is recommended for this purpose that the trawlers should be based to commence with on Stornoway and work under the immediate direction of the Rear-Admiral Stornoway. They should not, however, be absorbed in the Auxiliary Patrol craft of that area but should be shown as 'Trawlers for Special Service attached to the Grand Fleet'. It may be found necessary later to change their base and their area of operations. This will depend on the general submarine situation in Northern waters and would be ordered by me if required.

3. It is recommended that an Officer should be appointed to command this trawler force and to be responsible for the general organisation and training.

Lieutenant-Commander J.T. Randell, DSC, RNR, now in *Rushcoe* is strongly recommended by the Vice-Admiral Commanding 10th Cruiser Squadron for this duty. Another Commanding Officer should be appointed to *Rushcoe* so as to leave Lieutenant-Commander Randell free to proceed to sea independently and superintend the operational work of all units.

4. The latest anti-submarine equipment should be installed in this Trawler force including the fish hydrophone.

5. With reference to Paragraph 6 of the enclosure to A.L.M. 014609 of 6th November, W/T signals will be made by the ships of 10th Cruiser Squadron attached to the Grand Fleet when these ships are carrying out cruises to the Westward and also by the trawlers when on antisubmarine operations.

405. *Admiralty to Commander-in-Chief Grand Fleet*

29 November 1917

With reference to your letter No 2831/M.F. 0020 of the 15th November 1917 [399], relative to the composition of the Tenth Cruiser Squadron, I am to acquaint you that Their Lordships approve of the abolition of the Tenth Cruiser Squadron and of the formation of a Squadron consisting of HMS *Alsatian*, HMS *Orvieto*, HMS *Teutonic*, HMS *Minotaur*, HMS *Shannon*, HMS *Amsterdam*, and HMS *Duke of Cornwall*. This reconstituted Squadron will be known as the Second Cruiser Squadron, and you are to report on what date you propose this change of title should come into effect. This Squadron will be based on Scapa, and should be employed as proposed by you in paragraph 4 of your letter.

2. Vice-Admiral Sir Reginald G.O. Tupper, KCB, CVO, will be retained in command of this Squadron (until he has completed two years combined service in the Tenth Cruiser Squadron and new Second

Cruiser Squadron. A further communication will be made regarding Rear-Admiral Singer).

3. As regards Trawlers, Their Lordships approve of 12 Trawlers being retained as part of this new Squadron. The names of the Trawlers selected for retention are to be reported. A separate communication will be sent to you regarding the remainder.

4. The present Second Cruiser Squadron will cease to exist as a separate Squadron, and the Senior Officer, HMS *Shannon*, will follow the orders of Vice-Admiral Sir Reginald Tupper. I am to request that the Senior Officer, HMS *Shannon*, be so informed.

5. I am to state that the Armed Merchant Cruisers released from the Tenth Cruiser Squadron will be allocated in accordance with telegraphic or other orders which may be given from time to time. The administration of these Armed Merchant Cruisers, together with the administration of the Armed Merchant Cruisers that were previously detached from the Tenth Cruiser Squadron for Convoy work, will no longer fall upon Vice-Admiral Tupper. Separate arrangements will be made for this, but in the meantime those that are based for storing purposes in the Clyde or at Liverpool will remain so based.

6. The question of the Naval Base Office at Liverpool will require consideration, and I am to request that Vice-Admiral Tupper may forward suggestions in this connection. If the Office at Liverpool, as seems probable, is not required in connection with the Ships of the new Second Cruiser Squadron, it possibly will be found expedient to use it as a central office for ocean escorts.

406. *Commander-in-Chief Grand Fleet to Vice-Admiral Commanding Tenth Cruiser Squadron*

14 December 1917

Admiralty desires to simulate strong patrol of Tenth Cruiser Squadron between Iceland and Scotland. Following procedure is therefore to be carried out during the forthcoming cruise of *Alsatian* and *Orvieto*. Code messages to be made from positions representing patrol lines and to be similar in form to those ordinarily made by Tenth Cruiser Squadron including position course and speed message. Call signs note frequency and operator to be changed on each occasion. No call sign to be used in more than one position. Call signs to be as follows FS, FI, YR, JT, VI, XR. One or two messages to be made for Longhope to answer. Group 3 will send dummy messages to Senior Officer Tenth Cruiser Squadron by interception at 1310, 0910, 1510 during period you are at sea.

407. *Vice-Admiral Tupper to Admiralty*

HMS *Alsatian*, 6 January 1918

Report of Proceedings, 22 December 1917–5 January 1918

***

1. *Orvieto* left Scapa Flow for patrol at noon 22 December 1917, *Alsatian* following on 24 December to relieve *Teutonic*, who left for Liverpool on the 25th December 1917.

As far as possible endeavour is being made to maintain two ships on patrol especially during the moonlight periods, and make use of W/T so as to simulate the presence of a strong patrol line.

Unfortunately *Teutonic*, which was due to leave Liverpool on 7 January 1918, has been delayed with Windlass defects, and the Senior Naval Officer, Liverpool, informs me that she will not be ready to proceed until 17 January 1918.

In consequence it will not be possible to maintain more than one ship on patrol between now and 18 January 1918.

2. During the period covered by this Report *Alsatian* and *Orvieto*, working 60 miles apart, have made wide sweeps between Lat. 58.30´N and the coast of Iceland and Long. 12 and 20 W keeping a sharp look out for the German raider *Wolf* and the captured Japanese Vessel *Hitachi Maru*, which are shortly expected to make an attempt to get through to Germany.[1]

***

The Trawlers attached to the Squadron have been working between the Butt of Lewis and Bill Bailey's Bank.

3. 11 Vessels were intercepted, all of which were allowed to proceed after examination.

4. *Minotaur* and *Shannon* have been working under the direct orders of the Commander-in-Chief Grand Fleet, and the Admiral Commanding 1st Battle Squadron, in connection with the Lerwick–Bergen convoy.

5. I left patrol in *Alsatian* on 5 January for Scapa Flow, where I arrived and anchored at 12.30 p.m. on 6 January.

***

[1] *Wolf* returned to Germany (after a 15-month cruise) on 17 February 1918.

408. *Vice-Admiral Tupper to Admiralty*

HMS *Alsatian*, 31 January 1918

Report of Proceedings, 6–30 January 1918

***

1. I arrived at Scapa Flow in *Alsatian* at 12.30 p.m on 6th January, leaving *Orvieto* on patrol. That afternoon, however, I was informed by the Commander-in-Chief, Grand Fleet, that *Orvieto* would be required to proceed to Bermuda and was to coal immediately. Orders were accordingly given for her to proceed to Liverpool. As, however, it was found that she could not be ready by the date required, these arrangements were afterwards cancelled.

Unfortunately *Orvieto* on entering the Mersey on the morning of 9th January, collided with the Steamers *British Viscount* and *Regent*, sustaining damage which it was estimated would take six weeks to repair.

2. The stay of *Alsatian* at Scapa was prolonged by very bad weather interfering with the coaling. Advantage was taken of being at that Port to carry out night firing and other drills. The Commander-in-Chief arrived on the 15th and detained *Alsatian* another day to enable him to have an interview with the Vice-Admiral Commanding Second Cruiser Squadron, as to the future work, etcetera, of the Squadron.

3. *Alsatian* left Scapa Flow at 1300 on 16th January to patrol to the Westward in conjunction with *Teutonic* due to leave Liverpool on 17th January. *Teutonic*, however, was delayed by minor accidents and did not join until 21st.

The same afternoon, directions were received to detach her to Halifax to bring back a convoy leaving there on 4th February. I met *Teutonic* the following morning to receive despatches and gave her the necessary orders.

4. Shortly before midnight, 22–23 January, *Alsatian* intercepted the Norwegian Sailing Vessel *Sierra Miranda*, said to be bound from Copenhagen to Hampton Roads; the weather was then too rough to board. As this vessel was not on the list of 'Outward' bound ships, and there was no recent news of her, I asked the Admiralty for instructions … and received orders to send her in … Bad weather prevented boarding until the evening of 23rd, when a strong Armed Guard, under Lieut. John E. Jones, RNR, was placed on board. As after thorough search, nothing suspicious was found and explanations given by the Master appeared to be satisfactory, I requested further instructions from Admiralty.

In the meantime, I decided to detail the Trawlers *Marconi*, *Faraday* and *Sitvel*, who were on their way to Reykjavik with mails and despatches, to escort the vessel in, as no others were available.

Sierra Miranda was accordingly turned over to these Trawlers about 1400 on 25th January, and *Alsatian* having embarked mails and despatches for Reykjavik, proceeded there, arriving at 11.30 a.m. on the 23th.

Some difficulty was experienced in landing the mails and despatches, on account of the ice in the harbour, and as a NE wind sprung up during the afternoon and drove more ice into the harbour, the services of a local steam vessel had to be obtained to tow the motor and other boats through the ice to return to *Alsatian*.

5. I visited the British Consul, Mr E.G. Cable, and the Administrator of the Island, and entertained the British and French Consuls at Luncheon and Dinner.

I was informed that the winter had been exceptionally severe and that there was no passage northabout – the whole of the coast from Staalbjerg Huk to Seidisfjord being icebound.

Alsatian left Reykjavik at 2030.

6. Meanwhile, instructions had been received from the Admiralty to release *Sierra Miranda*. The Trawlers were accordingly directed to take off the Armed Guard and let the vessel go. Unfortunately, this message, though timed 1250 on 24th January, did not reach me until 02.55 a.m. on 26th.

7. During the period covered by this report 10 vessels were intercepted, all of which have been allowed to proceed.

No sign of enemy Raiders, cruisers or submarines passing through the area patrolled has been observed or heard of.

8. *Shannon* and *Minotaur* have been working under the orders of the Commander-in-Chief Grand Fleet, and Admiral Commanding 1st Battle Squadron, in connection with the Lerwick–Bergen convoy.

Shannon left Scapa for Liverpool on 12th January for periodical refit, and, as it has been found that the refit cannot be completed in under eight weeks and that men living on board would interfere with the work to be carried out, it has been decided to reduce the ship to care and maintenance party.

9. On 11th January I received orders from the Admiralty to send six of the twelve Trawlers attached to the Second Cruiser Squadron to Larne, for service in Auxiliary Patrol Area XVII. *Walpole*, *Elf King*, *Stalwart*, *Corrie Roy*, *Rushcoe* and *Offa II* were selected and given directions accordingly.

10. I left patrol on 30th January for Liverpool, leaving four Trawlers

at sea off the Butt of Lewis. Two of these will visit Thorshavn taking despatches for the British Consul and then return to patrol.

Alsatian arrived at the Bar Light, Liverpool, at 1138 on 31st January.

***

SOURCES OF DOCUMENTS

Unless otherwise specified documents are from the collection in the Public Record Office; the other collections used are:

IWM – Imperial War Museum, London.
Liddle Collection – Brotherton Library, University of Leeds.
NMM – National Maritime Museum, Greenwich.
ORO – Orkney Record Office, Kirkwall.
RNM – Royal Naval Museum, Portsmouth.
SRO – Shetland Record Office, Lerwick.

No	*Description*	*Date*	*Reference*
1 THE FIRST PATROL: THE EDGARS.			
1	de Chair to Admiralty	27 August 1914	ADM 137/185, 11–21
2	Revised Arrangements for Cruiser Force B	19 August 1914	ADM 137/185, 24–5
3	de Chair to 'Officers Commanding HM Ships and Vessels under my orders'	22 August 1914	ADM 137/185, 26
4	C-in-C Grand Fleet to de Chair	26 August 1914	ADM 137/414, 78
5	de Chair to Admiralty	1 October 1914	ADM 137/185, 30–41
6	C-in-C Home Fleets to Rear Admiral 10th CS	29 August 1914	ADM 137/1943, 176
7	Slayter to Rear-Admiral 10th CS	6 September 1914	ADM 137/185, 42–3
8	C-in-C Grand Fleet to Rear-Admiral 10th CS	18 September 1914	ADM 137/1989, 35
9	de Chair to Admiralty	1 November 1914	ADM 137/185, 49–62

10	Rosoman to Miller	17 October 1914	ADM 137/997, 14–15
11	C-in-C Home Fleet to Rear Admiral 10th and 3rd CSs HMS *Alsatian*	17 October 1914	ADM 137/1989, 58
12	de Chair to Admiralty	3 December 1914	ADM 137/185, 74–80
13	Journal of Commander Bowen Bowen Papers,		IWM DS/MISC/87 Bowen Papers, pp. 1–3
14	C-in-C Home Fleets to Admiralty	7 November 1914	ADM 137/989, 339
15	C-in-C Home Fleets to Admiralty	11 November 1914	ADM 137/989, 374
16	Admiralty to C-in-C Home Fleets	18 November 1914	ADM 137/989, 390
17	Admiralty to C-in-C Home Fleets and Rear-Admiral HMS *Crescent*	20 November 1914	ADM 137/414, 385

2 THE ARMED MERCHANT CRUISERS

18	de Chair to Admiralty	25 January 1915	ADM 137/185, 87–103
19	Contraband Committee to Spring-Rice	4 December 1914	TS 14/1
20	Walter to Rear-Admiral 10th CS	9 January 1915	ADM 137/989, 596–8
21	Memorandum by Webb	24 December 1914	ADM 137/989, 566–9
22	C-in-C Home Fleets to Admiralty	1 January 1915	ADM 137/1081, 10–12
23	Vivian to Rear-Admiral 10th CS	2 February 1915	NMM VIV/4
24	Contraband Committee Minutes, Statement by Webb	9 January 1915	TS 14/1
25	Contraband Committee Minutes	12 January 1915	TS 14/1
26	Contraband Committee Minutes	18 January 1915	TS 14/1

27	Haughton to Customs and Excise	18 January 1915	ORO, CE 55 3/20, 79
28	de Chair to Admiralty	9 March 1915	ADM 137/185, 121–43
29	Vivian to Rear-Admiral 10th CS	7 March 1915	NMM VIV/4
30	de Chair to Admiralty	5 February 1915	ADM 137/1081, 55
31	C-in-C Home Fleets to Admiralty	10 February 1915	ADM 137/1081, 21
32	Whiting to First Sea Lord	10 February [1915]	ADM 137/1081, 26–7
33	Superintendent of Contract Work to Third Sea Lord	14 February 1915	ADM 137/1081, 75–7
34	Contraband Committee Minutes	15 February 1915	TS 14/1
35	Contraband Committee Minutes	15 February 1915	TS 14/1
36	Contraband Committee Minutes	15 February 1915	TS 14/1
37	Contraband Committee Minutes	16 February 1915	TS 14/1
38	Contraband Committee Minutes	16 February 1915	TS 14/1
39	Contraband Committee Minutes	20 February 1915	TS 14/1
40	Contraband Committee Minutes	22 February 1915	TS 14/1
41	de Chair to Admiralty	23 February 1915	ADM 137/1081, 89–92
42	Note by Whiting	24 February 1915	ADM 137/1081, 97
43	Contraband Committee Minutes	26 February 1915	TS 14/1
44	Contraband Committee Minutes	1 March 1915	TS 14/1
45	de Chair to Admiralty	5 March 1915	ADM 137/1081, 99–100

46	Walter to Rear-Admiral 10th CS	6 March 1915	ADM 137/1085, 39
47	Minute by Webb	12 March 1915	ADM 137/1081, 93

3 THE PATROL ESTABLISHED

48	Vivian to Rear-Admiral 10th CS	14 April 1915	NMM [VIV/4]
49	de Chair to Admiralty	20 April 1915	ADM 137/185, 151–68
50	de Chair to Admiralty	13 March 1915	ADM 137/185, 117
51	C-in-C Home Fleets to Admiralty	15 March 1915	ADM 137/1081, 103–5
52	de Chair to Admiralty	20 March 1915	ADM 137/1081, 42
53	Contraband Committee Minutes	22 March 1915	TS 14/1
54	Contraband Committee Minutes	22 March 1915	TS 14/1
55	C-in-C Home Fleets to Admiral Orkneys and Shetlands and Rear-Admiral 10th CS	28 March 1915	ADM 1/8415/80
56	Contraband Committee Minutes	29 March 1915	TS 14/1
57	Contraband Committee Minutes	30 March 1915	TS 14/1
58	Contraband Committee Minutes	31 March 1915	TS 14/1
59	Contraband Committee Minutes	31 March 1915	TS 14/1
60	Contraband Committee Minutes	31 March 1915	TS 14/1
61	C-in-C Home Fleets to Admiralty	4 April 1915	ADM 137/1081, 108
62	Contraband Committee Minutes	5 April 1915	TS 14/1
63	Contraband Committee Minutes	5 April 1915	TS 14/1
64	de Chair to Admiralty	6 April 1915	ADM 137/1081, 191–6

65	Minute by Webb	12 April 1915	ADM 137/1081, 111
66	Contraband Committee Minutes	14 April 1915	TS 14/1
67	Contraband Committee Minutes	8 April 1915	TS 14/1
68	Diary of Dr Shaw		Liddle Collection: RNMN/Shaw, J
69	Vivian to Rear-Admiral 10th CS	20 May 1915	NMM VIV/4
70	C-in-C Home Fleets to Admiralty	16 April 1915	ADM 137/1081, 200
71	de Chair to Admiralty	31 May 1915	ADM 137/185, 177–95
72	Diary of Dr Shaw		Liddle Collection: RNMN/Shaw, J
73	Extract from Memorandum of Hudson	25 April 1915[?]	ADM 137/1081, 267
74	Note by Dumas	3 May 1915	ADM 137/1081, 262
75	Vivian to Admiralty	4 May 1915	NMM VIV/4
76	de Chair to Oliver	5 May 1915	ADM 137/1081, 203–6
77	Contraband Committee Minutes	8 May 1915	TS 14/2
78	Note by Learmonth	15 May 1915	ADM 137/1081, 211–12
79	Contraband Committee Minutes	17 May 1915	TS 14/2
80	C-in-C to Admiralty	21 May 1915	ADM 1/8415/80
81	Admiralty to C-in-C Home Fleet	21 May 1915	ADM 137/1081, 215
82	Contraband Committee Minutes	24 May 1915	TS 14/2
83	MacLure to Down	26 May 1915	ADM 137/1081, 327–8

84	Vivian to Rear-Admiral 10th CS	17 June 1915	NMM VIV/4, ADM 136/1081, 409–12
85	Colville to C-in-C Home Fleets	29 May 1915	ADM 137/1081, 324–6
86	C-in-C Home Fleets to Admiralty	4 June 1915	ADM 137/1081
87	Rear-Admiral 10th CS to C-in-C Home Fleets	7 June 1915	ADM 137/1081, 279

4 A NEW BASE; SUBMARINES

88	de Chair to Admiralty	9 July 1915	ADM 137/185, 203–24
89	Walter to Rear-Admiral 10th CS	6 July 1915	ADM 137/1101, 52–4
90	Royds to Vivian	13 June 1915	NMM VIV/4
91	Diary of Dr Shaw		Liddle Collection: RNMN/Shaw, J
92	[Vivian to Admiralty]	14 June 1915	NMM VIV/4
93	Webster to Rear-Admiral 10th CS	14 June 1915	ADM 137/1081, 387–9
94	Clark to Vivian	15 June 1915	NMM VIV/4
95	Vivian to Royds	16 June 1915	NMM VIV/4
96	Diary of Dr Shaw		Liddle Collection: RNMN/Shaw, J
97	Vivian to Rear-Admiral 10th CS	26 July 1915	NMM VIV/4
98	Fawckner to Admiralty	19 June 1915	ADM 137/1081, 235–40
99	Webster to Rear-Admiral 10th CS	19 June 1915	ADM 137/1081, 386
100	Diary of Dr Shaw		Liddle Collection: RNMN/Shaw, J

101	C-in-C Home Fleets to Admiral Orkneys and Shetlands, and Rear-Admiral 10th CS	21 June 1915	ADM 1/8415/80
102	Colville to C-in-C Home Fleets	25 June 1915	ADM 137/1081, 341–2
103	C-in-C Home Fleets to Admiralty	29 June 1915	ADM 137/1081, 340
104	Admiralty to C-in-C HM Ships and Vessels Devonport	30 June 1915	ADM 137/1081, 225–6
105	Walter to Rear-Admiral 10th CS	12 August 1915	ADM 137/1101, 56–7
106	[de Chair to Admiralty]	21 August 1915	ADM 137/185, 232–55
107	Randell to Purey-Cust	12 July 1915	ADM 137/1101, 13
108	Randell to Purey-Cust	12 July 1915	ADM 137/1101, 14
109	Randell to Purey-Cust	12 July 1915	ADM 127/1101, 15
110	Journal of McKeag		IWM P 389, McKeag, 7–8
111	de Chair to Admiralty	16 July 1915	ADM 137/1081, 397–8
112	Diary of Dr Shaw		Liddle Collection: RNMN/Shaw, J
113	Rear-Admiral Swarbacks Minn to Admiral Longhope	20 July 1915	ADM 137/1910, 22
114	Memorandum by C-in-C Home Fleets	25 July 1915	ADM 37/1976, 36–40
115	Orders for Trawlers	25 July 1915	ADM 137/1976, 41–2
116	Admiralty to Rear-Admiral 10th CS	26 July 1915	ADM 137/1910, 30–31
117	Vivian to Rear-Admiral 10th CS	31 August 1915	NMM VIV/4
118	Crawford to Rear-Admiral HMS *Cyclops*	29 July 1915	ADM 137/1101, 116–19

119	Colville to C-in-C Home Fleet	1 August 1915	ADM 137/1081, 370–71
120	Johnsen to Under Secretary Foreign Affairs	2 August 1915	ADM 137/1101, 191–2
121	C-in-C Home Fleets to Admiralty	3 August 1915	ADM 137/1101, 205–9
122	C-in-C Home Fleets to Admiralty	4 August 1915	ADM 137/1101, 213–14
123	Thomson to CO *Cedric*	4 August 1915	ADM 137/298, 176
124	Crowe to Secretary of Admiralty	4 August 1915	ADM 137/1101, 190
125	Admiralty Minute by Director of Trade Div	8 August 1915	ADM 137/1101, 193
126	Walter to Rear-Admiral 10th CS	29 September 1915	ADM 137/1101, 327–9
127	Minute by Webb	13 August 1915	ADM 137/1101, 211
128	Diary of Dr Shaw		Liddle Collection: RNMN/Shaw, J
129	Kennedy to Lords Commissioners of Admiralty	20 August 1915	ADM 137/185, 331–7
130	Alltree to Kennedy	19 August 1915[?]	ADM 137/185, 338–40
131	Bateman to Admiral Orkneys and Shetlands	late August 1915[?]	ADM 137/1101, 177
132	CO *Tenby Castle* to Alston	22 August 1915	ADM 137/1101, 309–12

5 LIFE ON PATROL

133	de Chair to Admiralty	15 September 1915	ADM 137/185, 279–88
134	Admiralty to C-in-C Home Fleets	25 August 1915	ADM 137/1081, 359
135	C-in-C Home Fleets to Admiralty	27 August 1915	ADM 137/1910, 80

136	C-in-C Home Fleets to Admiralty	28 August 1915	ADM 1/8415/80
137	Kelleher to Customs and Excise	2 September 1915	ORO, CE 55 3/20, 123
138	MacFarlane to SNO Kirkwall	3 September 1915	ADM 137/1911, 317–18
139	Minute by Anderson	7 September 1915	ADM 1/8415/80
140	Admiralty to Rear-Admiral 10th CS	7 September 1915	ADM 137/185, 266
141	de Chair to Admiralty	1 October 1915	ADM 137/185, 295–302
142	Kelleher to Customs and Excise	17 September 1915	SRO, CE 85 4/9, 1
143	Diary of Dr Shaw		Liddle Collection: RNMN/Shaw, J
144	Dugmore to Rear-Admiral 10th CS	18 September 1915	ADM 137/1101, 317–18
145	Memoirs of Surgeon Knight		Liddle Collection: RNMN/Knight/2
146	Longhope to Admiralty	19 September 1915	ADM 137/1081, 371
147	Diary of A/B Style		RNM Ms 1983/292 JD 51
148	Translation of Note Verbale from German Govt to US Embassy	21 September 1915	ADM 137/1101, 358–9
149	C-in-C Home Fleets to Admiralty	29 September 1915	ADM 137/1101, 245–6
150	Diary of A/B Style		RNM Ms 1983/292 JD 51
151	de Chair to Admiralty	31 October 1915	ADM 137/185, 308–21
152	Colville to Admiralty	4 October 1915	ADM 137/1910, 33
153	Benson to de Chair	8 October 1915	ADM 137/298, 174–5
154	Bamford to CO *Orcoma*	11 October 1915	ADM 137/185, 361–2

155	Dugmore to Rear-Admiral 10th CS	11 October 1915	ADM 137/1101, 369–70
156	Edwards to CO *Orcoma*	15 October 1915	ADM 137/185, 363–4
157	Kelleher to Customs and Excise	18 October 1915	SRO, CE 85 4/9, 1
158	Memorandum by Hunt	20 October 1915	ADM 137/1101, 372
159	Buckeridge for Admiralty Port Officer Kirkwall to Admiral Orkneys and Shetlands	22 October 1915	ADM 137/1081, 284
160	Benson to Rear-Admiral 10th CS	28 October 1915	ADM 137/1101, 301
161	de Chair to Admiralty	15 November 1915	ADM 137/185, 347–56
162	Diary of A/B Style		RNM Ms 1983/292 JD 51
163	Minute by Oliver	7 November 1915	ADM 137/1101, 495
164	Murchison Jones to Down	13 November 1915	ADM 137/1164, 109–10

6 DE CHAIR'S LAST MONTHS

165	de Chair to Admiralty	6 December 1915	ADM 137/185, 386–95
166	C-in-C Home Fleets to Admiralty	17 November 1915	ADM 137/185, 372
167	Smyth to Rear-Admiral 10th CS	18 November 1915	ADM 137/185, 376–9
168	Memorandum by Webb	26 November 1915	ADM 137/185, 365
169	Diary of A/B Style		RNM Ms 1983/292 JD 51
170	de Chair to Admiralty	31 December 1915	ADM 137/185, 403–16
171	Contraband Committee Minutes	14 December 1915	TS 14/6
172	Carter to Booty	19 January 1916	ADM 137/298, 51–3

173	Extract from *Morning Post*	22 December 1915	ADM 137/1164, 118–19
174	de Chair to C-in-C Grand Fleet	25 December 1915	ADM 137/1164, 114–15
175	Madden to Rear-Admiral Swarbacks Minn	27 December 1915	ADM 137/2250, 423
176	Telegrams		ADM 137/1951, 617
177	Please and Sons to Admiralty	31 December 1915	ADM 137/1164, 132–6.
178	Potts to Smyth	19 January 1916	ADM 137/298, 85–6
179	Memoirs of Surgeon Knight		Liddle Collection: RNMN/Knight/2
180	Recollections of Dr Shaw		Liddle Collection: RNMN/Shaw, J
181	de Chair to Admiralty	19 January 1916	ADM 137/298, 10–18
182	de Chair to C-in-C Grand Fleet	2 January 1916	ADM 137/185, 422–31
183	C-in-C Home Fleets to Rear-Admiral 10th CS	4 January 1916	ADM 137/1164, 116
184	de Chair to C-in-C Grand Fleet	7 January 1916	ADM 137/1164, 117
185	C-in-C Home Fleets to Admiralty	10 January 1916	ADM 137/185, 437
186	Minute by Webb	16 January 1916	ADM 137/1164, 120
187	de Chair to Admiralty	7 February 1916	ADM 137/298, 36–48
188	Stanley to CO *Alcantara*	8 February 1916	ADM 137/298, 88–9
189	Diary of Dr Shaw		Liddle Collection: RNMN/Shaw, J
190	Corbett to Rear-Admiral 10th CS	27 January 1916	ADM 137/1218, 33–5

191	C-in-C Home Fleets to Rear-Admiral 10th CS	31 January 1916	ADM 137/1905, 61–2
192	Logan to Rear-Admiral 10th CS	14 February 1916	ADM 137/298, 90
193	Coates to CO *Patuca*	17 February 1916	ADM 137/298, 95–8
194	de Chair to Admiralty	28 February 1916	ADM 137/298, 72–80
195	Kenyon to Rear-Admiral 10th CS	9 February 1916	ADM 137/1218, 22–7
196	C-in-C Home Fleets to Admiralty	10 February 1916	ADM 137/1164, 13–14
197	Contraband Committee Minutes	10 February 1916	TS 14/7
198	Benson to Rear-Admiral 10th CS	22 February 1916	ADM 137/298, 177–8
199	Memoirs of Surgeon Knight		Liddle Collection: RNMN/Knight/2
200	Wardle to C-in-C Grand Fleet	1 March 1916	ADM 137/298, 108–12
201	Young to Rear-Admiral 10th CS	1 March 1916	ADM 137/298, 113–16
202	C-in-C Home Fleets to Flag Officers, Commodores and Officers	29 February 1916	ADM 137/466, 376
203	de Chair to Admiralty	6 March 1916	ADM 137/298, 105–7

7 TUPPER TAKES COMMAND

204	Tupper to Admiralty	7 March 1916	ADM 137/298, 122–5
205	Tupper to Admiralty	23 March 1916	ADM 137/298, 128–41
206	CO *Ebro* to Vice-Admiral 10th CS	16 March 1916	ADM 137/1218, 62
207	Corbett to Vice-Admiral 10th CS	20 March 1916	ADM 137/1164, 355–6

208	Tupper to Admiralty	10 April 1916	ADM 137/298, 153–65
209	Tupper to C-in-C Grand Fleet	27 March 1916	ADM 137/1164, 356
210	Benson to SNO Liverpool	28 March 1916	ADM 137/298, 170–3
211	Memoirs of Surgeon Knight		Liddle Collection: RNMN/Knight/2
212	C-in-C Home Fleets to Vice-Admiral Orkneys and Shetlands	3 April 1916	ADM 137/1951, 615
213	C-in-C Home Fleets to Vice-Admiral Orkneys and Shetlands	4 April 1916	ADM 137/1164, 357
214	Minute by Oliver	7 April 1916	ADM 137/298, 148
215	Tupper to Admiralty	25 April 1916	ADM 137/298, 196–207
216	Webster to Vice-Admiral 10th CS	10 April 1916	ADM 137/298, 216
217	Procurator Fiscal Lerwick to Rear-Admiral Fawckner	13 April 1916	ADM 137/2250, 491
218	C-in-C Home Fleets to Vice-Admiral 10th CS	15 April 1916	ADM 137/1961, 215
219	Admiralty to Under Secretary of State Foreign Office	17 April 1916	ADM 137/1164, 144–5
220	Vice-Admiral 10th CS to Rear-Admiral Swarbacks Minn	21 April 1916	ADM 137/2250, 499
221	Minute by Webb	23 April 1916	ADM 137/298, 191
222	Tupper to Admiralty	16 May 1916	ADM 137/298, 216–28
223	Coates to CO *Patuca*	24 April 1916	ADM 137/298, 248–50
224	Note by Oliver	26 April 1916	ADM 137/298, 192–3

225	Murray to Under Secretary of State Foreign Office	29 April 1916	ADM 137/1218, 82
226	Admiralty to Vice-Admiral 10th CS	29 April 1916	ADM 137/1218, 68
227	Minute by Fourth Sea Lord	1 May 1916	ADM 137/298, 189–90
228	Brooks to Fourth Sea Lord	2 May 1916	ADM 137/298, 193–4
229	Webster to Vice-Admiral 10th CS	8 May 1916	ADM 137/1218, 123–5
230	Brooks to First Sea Lord	9 May 1916	ADM 137/298, 214–15
231	Tupper to Admiralty	1 June 1916	ADM 137/298, 235–43
232	Memorandum by Tupper	23 May 1916	ADM 137/1976, 56–7
233	de Chair to Admiralty	23 May 1916	ADM 137/1218, 127–8

8 TIGHTENING THE BLOCKADE

234	Tupper to Admiralty	8 June 1916	ADM 137/298, 256–60
235	Memoirs of Brewster		IWM PP/MCR/237
236	Minute by Webb	1 June 1916	ADM 137/1218, 129
237	C-in-C Home Fleets to Admiralty	7 June 1916	ADM 137/1164, 71
238	Greene to Vice-Admiral 10th CS	8 June 1916	ADM 137/1218, 77
239	Tupper to Admiralty	26 June 1916	ADM 137/298, 269–77
240	Luce to Admiralty	12 June 1916	ADM 137/1218, 97–9
241	Vice-Admiral 10th CS to C-in-C Home Fleets	13 June 1916	ADM 137/1218, 401
242	Views of French Foreign Office	17 June 1916	ADM 137/1164, 382–5
243	C-in-C Home Fleets to Vice-Admiral 10th CS	20 June 1916	ADM 137/1218, 402

244	Contraband Committee Minutes	20 June 1916	TS 14/9
245	Tupper to Admiralty	16 July 1916	ADM 137/298, 287–99
246	Greene to C-in-C Home Fleets	29 June 1916	ADM 137/1164, 81–2
247	Greene to Under Secretary of State Foreign Office	30 June 1916	ADM 137/1218, 131
248	Greene to Vice-Admiral 10th CS	1 July 1916	ADM 137/1218, 134
249	C-in-C Home Fleets to Admiralty	1 July 1916	ADM 137/1164, 95–6
250	Walter to Vice-Admiral 10th CS	2 July 1916	ADM 137/1218, 146–7
251	Vice-Admiral 10th CS to SNO Swarbacks Minn	7 July 1916	ADM 137/2250, 506
252	Bunsen to Admiralty	11 July 1916	ADM 137/1218, 138
253	Tupper to Admiralty	30 July 1916	ADM 137/298, 314–22
254	Tupper to Admiralty	16 August 1916	ADM 137/298, 336–47
255	Greene to C-in-C Home Fleets	1 August 1916	ADM 137/1164, 104–5
256	Murray to C-in-C Home Fleet	6 August 1916	ADM 137/1218, 140–41
257	Tupper to Admiralty	30 August 1916	ADM 137/298, 355–64
258	Tupper to Admiralty	17 August 1916	ADM 137/1218, 152
259	Heap to Dugmore	21 August 1916	ADM 137/1218, 155
260	Canner to CO *Hilary*	22 August 1916	ADM 37/298, 404–7
261	Dean to Vice-Admiral 10th CS	23 August 1916	ADM 137/298, 403
262	Groome to CO *Hilary*	23 August 1916	ADM 137/298, 408–10
263	C-in-C Home Fleets to Admiralty	28 August 1916	ADM 1/8415/80

264	Admiralty to C-in-C Home Fleets	30 August 1916	ADM 137/1212, 217–20

9 THE EFFECTIVE BLOCKADE

265	Tupper to Admiralty	22 September 1916	ADM 137/298, 372–87
266	Webb to Vice-Admiral 10th CS	8 September 1916	ADM 137/1218, 158
267	Contraband Committee Minutes	9 September 1916	TS 14/11
268	Tupper to C-in-C Grand Fleet	14 September 1916	ADM 137/1218, 210
269	Brocklebank to Vice-Admiral 10th CS	19 September 1916	ADM 137/298, 431
270	Comment by de Chair	19 September 1916	ADM 137/1218, 179
271	Diary of Dr Shaw		Liddle Collection: RNMN/Shaw, J
272	Tupper to Admiralty	1 October 1916	ADM 137/298, 381–7
273	Randell to CO *Gibraltar*	23 September 1916	ADM 137/1218, 290–2
274	Admiralty to C-in-C Home Fleets	24 September 1916	ADM 137/1218, 214
275	Bell to CO *Hilary*	28 September 1916	ADM 137/1218, 277
276	Tupper to Admiralty	18 October 1916	ADM 137/298, 441–52
277	Tupper to C-in-C Grand Fleet	4 October 1916	ADM 137/1218, 289
278	Memorandum	14 October 1916[?]	ADM 137/1218, 267
279	Tupper to Admiralty	5 November 1916	ADM 137/298, 471–83
280	Memorandum by Tupper	21 October 1916	ADM 137/1976, 60
281	Bach to Admiralty Port Officer Kirkwall	1 November 1916	ADM 137/1208, 302–3

282	Shotton to Rear-Admiral Swarbacks Minn	4 November 1916	ADM 137/1218, 357–8
283	Tupper to Admiralty	23 November 1916	ADM 137/298, 493–508
284	Dannreuther to Vice-Admiral 10th CS	14 November 1916	ADM 137/1218, 345–6
285	Gallop to CO *Patuca*	14 November 1916	ADM 137/1218, 347–9
286	Admiralty to Vice-Admiral 10th CS	15 November [1916]	ADM 137/298, 490
287	Booty to Vice-Admiral 10th CS	19 November 1916	ADM 137/1218, 376–83
288	Tupper to Admiralty	5 December 1916	ADM 137/298, 517–24

10 THE SUBMARINE MENACE RENEWED

289	Tupper to Admiralty	[19] December 1916	ADM 137/298, 531–42
290	C-in-C Grand Fleet to Admiralty	6 December 1916	ADM 137/1961, 229
291	Ashby to Vice-Admiral 10th CS	7 December 1916	ADM 137/3169, 495–6
292	Luard to Vice-Admiral 10th CS	7 December 1916	ADM 137/3169, 504
293	Court of Enquiry into interception of raider by *Avenger*, *Teutonic*	18 December 1916	ADM 137/3169, 470
294	Tupper to Admiralty	7 January 1917	ADM 137/299, 11–23
295	C-in-C Grand Fleet to Admiralty	22 December 1916	ADM 137/1212 217, 283
296	C-in-C Home Fleets to Admiralty	30 December 1916	ADM 137/1275, 41–3
297	Tupper to CO *King Lear*	31 December 1916	ADM 137/1951, 625
298	C-in-C Home Fleets to Vice-Admiral Orkney and Shetland	1 January 1917	ADM 137/1951, 624
299	Vice-Admiral Orkney and Shetland to C-in-C Grand Fleet	5 January 1917	ADM 137/1951, 627

300	Tupper to Admiralty	24 January 1917	ADM 137/299, 33–44
301	Admiralty to Vice-Admiral 10th CS	6 January 1917	ADM 137/298, 551
302	Admiralty to SNO Liverpool and Capt Superintendent Clyde District	6 January 1917	ADM 137/298, 552
303	Admiralty to Under Secretary of State Foreign Office	7 January 1917	ADM 137/1218, 369
304	C-in-C Grand Fleet to Vice-Admiral 10th CS	10 January 1917	ADM 137/1951, 628
305	Admiralty to C-in-C Home Fleets	15 January [1917]	ADM 137/1275, 64
306	Admiralty Memorandum	[15 January 1917]	ADM 137/1275, 65–7
307	Brooke to Dundas	17 January 1917	ADM 137/1218, 327–8
308	C-in-C Home Fleets to Admiralty	19 January 1917	ADM 137/1275, 71–2
309	Admiralty to C-in-C Grand Fleet	22 January 1917	ADM 137/1212, 217, 290
310	Tupper to Admiralty	24 January 1917	ADM 137/1275, 80
311	Admiralty to C-in-C Home Fleets	January 1917	ADM 137/1212, 230
312	Tupper to Admiralty	31 January 1917	ADM 137/299, 56–61
313	Tupper to Admiralty	13 February 1917	ADM 137/299, 68–76
314	Dundas to Vice-Admiral 10th CS	5 February 1917	ADM 137/1275, 95
315	Tupper to Admiralty	23 February 1917	ADM 137/299, 84–9
316	Moller & Co to Admiralty	20 February 1917	ADM 137/1275, 124–5
317	Tupper to Admiralty	8 March 1917	ADM 137/299, 95–109
318	Contraband Committee Minutes	21 February 1917	TS 14/13

319	Elliot to CO *Alsatian*	22 February 1917	ADM 137/1275, 155–9
320	Tupper to C-in-C Home Fleets	22 February 1917	ADM 137/1275, 20–23
321	Atkinson to Collector Aberdeen	27 February 1917	SRO, CE 85 4/9, 84
322	Admiralty to Under Secretary of State Foreign Office	3 March 1917	ADM 137/299, 52
323	Tupper to CO *King Lear*	3 March 1917	ADM 137/299, 113

11 THE SUCCESSFUL BLOCKADE

324	Tupper to Admiralty	29 March 1917	ADM 137/299, 119–41
325	Contraband Committee Minutes	19 April 1917	TS 14/14
326	Dundas to Vice Admiral 10th CS	20 March 1917	ADM 137/1275, 101
327	Johnson to Dundas	20 March 1917	ADM 137/1275, 102–3
328	Loram to Dundas	22 March 1917	ADM 137/1275, 104–5
329	Admiralty Report by Flag Capt for Vice-Admiral	26 March 1917	ADM 137/1275, 100
330	Tupper to Admiralty	9 April 1917	ADM 137/299, 156–70
331	Greene to C-in-C Grand Fleet	30 March 1917	ADM 137/3169, 515
332	de Garston to Findlay	2 April 1917	ADM 137/1275, 251–2
333	Randell to Vice-Admiral 10th CS	6 April 1917	ADM 137/1275, 271–2
334	Stokes to Stornoway	9 April 1917[?]	Scottish Record Office, CE 86/1/24–169–73
335	Tupper to Admiralty	24 April 1917	ADM 137/299, 183–200

336	Arnold to Vice-Admiral 10th CS	10 April 1917	ADM 137/1275, 279
337	Dannreuther to Vice-Admiral 10th CS	11 April 1917	ADM 137/1275, 268–70
338	Colomb to Vice-Admiral 10th CS	14 April 1917	ADM 137/1910, 196–9
339	Admiralty minute by Fisher	17 April 1917	ADM 137/1275, 106
340	Tupper to CO *King Lear*	19 April 1917	ADM 137/299, 205
341	Tupper to Admiralty	8 May 1917	ADM 137/299, 211–26
342	Admiralty to C-in-C Grand Fleet	5 May 1917	ADM 137/1275, 288
343	Tupper to Admiralty	25 May 1917	ADM 137/299, 234–7
344	Tupper to C-in-C Grand Fleet	15 May 1917	ADM 137/1275, 432
345	Elliot to CO *Alsatian*	18 May 1917	ADM 137/1275, 146–7
346	Admiralty to Under Secretary of State	24 May 1917	ADM 17/1275, 255
347	Tupper to Admiralty	7 June 1917	ADM 137/299, 254–9
348	C-in-C Home Fleets to Admiralty	26 May 1917	ADM 137/1275, 431
349	Dean to Vice-Admiral 10th CS	27 May 1917	ADM 137/3216, 383–6
350	Forster to SNO 10th CS	31 May 1917[?]	ADM 137/1275, 443–6
351	Humphreys to Rear-Admiral Stornoway	31 May 1917[?]	ADM 137/1275, 447
352	Boyle to Admiralty	1 June 1917	ADM 137/1275, 442
353	Minute by Webb	2 June 1917	ADM 137/1275, 436
354	Wrightson to Vice-Admiral 10th CS	5 June 1917	ADM 137/1275, 483–4
355	Tupper to Wrightson	6 June 1917	ADM 137/1275, 485
356	Wrightson to Vice-Admiral 10th CS	6 June 1917	ADM 137/1275, 485

357	Tupper to Admiralty	19 June 1917	ADM 137/299, 278–82
358	Contraband Committee Minutes	8 June 1917	TS 14/15
359	Admiralty to C-in-C Grand Fleet	14 June 1917	ADM 137/1275, 434
360	Ashby to 'The SNO Afloat, Scapa Flow'	15 June 1917	ADM 137/3671, 513–15

12 THE END OF THE NORTHERN PATROL

361	Memorandum by Webb	15 June 1917	ADM 137/1275, 623–8
362	Appendix to Webb's Memorandum	[15 June 1917]	ADM 137/1275, 629
363	Vice-Admiral 10th CS to Rear-Admiral 10th CS	15 June 1917	ADM 137/1961, 262
364	Minute on future of 10th CS	19 June 1917	ADM 137/1275, 621–2
365	Memorandum by Trade Div Admiralty War Staff	19 June 1917	ADM 137/1275, 623–5
366	Tupper to Admiralty	12 July 1917	ADM 137/299, 298–302
367	Diary of 10th CS events		ADM 137/299, 304–12
368	Atkinson to Customs and Excise	26 June 1917	SRO, CE 85 4/9, 125–34
369	Fremantle to Vice-Admiral 10th CS	29 June 1917	ADM 137/1961, 263
370	Kelly to CO *Virginian*	1 July 1917]?]	ADM 137/1275, 677–9
371	Note by Tupper	6 July 1917	ADM 137/1373, 203
372	Tupper to Admiralty	5 August 1917	ADM 137/299, 319–24
373	C-in-C to Flag Officers of 10th CS and 2nd CS	15 July 1917	ADM 137/1961, 265
374	C-in-C Grand Fleet to Admiralty	23 July 1917	ADM 137/1910, 218

375	Admiralty to C-in-C Grand Fleet	24 July 1915	ADM 137/1910, 218
376	Tupper to C-in-C Grand Fleet	24 July 1917	ADM 137/1910, 209–11
377	Colomb to C-in-C The Nore	25 July 1917	ADM 137/3311, 289–93
378	Admiralty to Vice-Admiral 10th CS	26 July 1917	ADM 137/1910, 362
379	C-in-C Grand Fleet to Vice-Admiral 10th CS	5 August 1917	ADM 137/1910, 217
380	Tupper to Admiralty	17 August 1917	ADM 137/299, 246–9
381	Tupper to Admiralty	7 August 1917	ADM 137/1910, 365
382	Vice-Admiral 10th CS to Admiralty	14 August 1917	ADM 137/1910, 363
383	Admiralty to Vice-Admiral 10th CS	15 August 1917	ADM 137/1910, 367
384	Tupper to Admiralty	10 September 1917	ADM 137/299, 360–4
385	Tudor to SNO Lerwick	30 August 1917	SRO, CE 85 3/11, 86
386	Tupper to C-in-C Grand Fleet	1 September 1917	ADM 137/1910, 219
387	Tupper to C-in-C Grand Fleet	1 September 1917	ADM 137/1910, 367
388	Tupper to Admiralty	25 September 1917	ADM 137/299, 381–2
389	C-in-C Grand Fleet to Vice-Admiral 10th CS	14 September 1917	ADM 137/1910, 230
390	Vice-Admiral 10th CS to C-in-C Grand Fleet	20 September 1917	ADM 137/1910, 229
391	Tupper to Admiralty	8 October 1917	ADM 137/299, 395–7
392	Brown to C-in-C Plymouth	14 October 1917	ADM 137/3696, 332–3
393	Tupper to Admiralty	16 October 1917	ADM 137/299, 408–12
394	Vice-Admiral 10th CS to C-in-C Grand Fleet	16 October 1917	ADM 137/1910, 368
395	Tupper to Admiralty	8 November 1917	ADM 137/299, 425–7

396	Smith to SNO Swarbacks Minn	24 October 1917	ADM 137/2250, 570
397	Memorandum for C-in-C	6 November 1917[?]	ADM 137/1910, 372–5
398	Tupper to Admiralty	24 November 1917	ADM 137/299, 441–2
399	C-in-C Grand Fleet to Admiralty	15 November 1917	ADM 137/1910, 379
400	Vice-Admiral 10th CS to SNO Shetlands	24 November 1917	ADM 137/2250, 572
401	Arrangements at Swarbacks Minn	[November 1917]	ADM 137/2250, 573–4
402	Vice-Admiral 10th CS to C-in-C Grand Fleet	25 November 1917	ADM 137/1910, 382
403	Tupper to Admiralty	21 December 1917	ADM 137/299, 454–8
404	C-in-C Grand Fleet to Admiralty	28 November 1917	ADM 137/1910, 384
405	Admiralty to C-in-C Grand Fleet	29 November 1917	ADM 137/1910, 300
406	C-in-C Grand Fleet to Vice-Admiral 10th CS	14 December 1917	ADM 137/1910, 235
407	Tupper to Admiralty	6 January 1918	ADM 137/299, 473–4
408	Tupper to Admiralty	31 January 1918	ADM 137/299, 484–7

BIBLIOGRAPHY

Most reputable histories of the Great War contain at least a reference to the blockade, and perhaps a mention of the Tenth Cruiser Squadron or the Northern Patrol. Only the Official Histories have much to say on either. Specialist studies of the economic aspects of the war say more, but are of little use in matters relating to the sea. I list here some books and articles found particularly useful on both subjects, and a list of works on the neutral powers and the blockade.

1. The Blockade

Arnold-Forster, W., *The Blockade, 1914–1919 Before the Armistice and After*, Oxford Pamphlets on World Affairs 17 (Oxford, 1939).

Bell, Archibald C., *A History of the Blockade of Germany and of the Countries Associated with her in the Great War, 1914–1918* (London: Her Majesty's Stationery Office, 1937) (published in 1961).

Beveridge, Sir William, *Blockade and the Civilian Population*, Oxford Pamphlets on World Affairs 24 (Oxford, 1939).

Cochin, Denys (ed.), *Les Organisations du blocus en France pendant la guerre 1914–1918* (Paris, 1926).

Consett, Rear-Admiral Montagu W.W.P., *The Triumph of Unarmed Forces, 1914–1918* (London, 1923).

Devlin, P., *Too Proud to Fight: Woodrow Wilson's Neutrality* (Oxford, 1974).

Fayle, C. Ernest, *Seaborne Trade* (3 vols, London, 1920–1924).

Guichard, Louis, *Histoire du blocus naval, 1914–18* (Paris, 1922).

Jack, D.T. *Studies in Economic Warfare* (New York, 1944).

Lank, Rudolf, *Der Wirtschaftskrieg und die Neutralen, 1914–1918* (Berlin, 1940).

Martini, Peter Albert, *Blockade im Weltkrieg* (Berlin and Bonn, 1932).

May, Ernest R., *The World War and American Isolation, 1914–1917* (Cambridge, Mass., 1959).

Medlicott, W.N., *The Economic Blockade*, Vol. I, *History of the Second World War*, UK Civil Series (London, 1952).

Offer, Alvin, *The First World War, an Agrarian Interpretation* (Oxford, 1989).

Ritchie, H., *The Navicert System during the World War* (London, 1937).

Salter, J.A., *Allied Shipping Control, An Experiment in International Administration,* Economic and Social History of the War, British series, Carnegie Endowment for International Peace (Oxford, 1921).

Siney, Marion C., 'British Official Histories of the Blockade of the Central Powers during the First World War', *The American Historical Review* **58** (1963), 392–401.

Siney, Marion C., 'The Allied Blockade Committee and the Inter-Allied Trade Committees – The Machinery of Economic Warfare, 1917–1918', in K. Bourne and D.C. Watt (eds), *Studies in International History* (Hamden, Conn., 1967), 330–344.

Siney, Marion C., *The Allied Blockade of Germany 1914–1916* (Ann Arbor, 1957).

Vincent, Paul G., T*he Politics of Hunger: the Allied Blockade of Germany 1915–1919* (Athens, Ohio, 1989).

2. The Northern Patrol

Brocklebank, J. (ed.), *Tenth Cruiser Squadron, Northern Patrol* (Liverpool, 1974).

Chatterton, E. Keble, *The Big Blockade* (London, 1932).

Corbett, J.S. and H. Newbolt, *Naval Operations*, 5 vols, *History of the Great War* (London, 1920–1931).

De Chair, Sir Dudley, *The Sea is Strong* (London, 1961).

Dittmar, F.J. and J.J. Colledge, *British Warships 1914–1919* (London, 1972).

Grant, R.M., *U-boats Destroyed* (London, 1964).

Grant, R.M., *U-Boat Intelligence* (London, 1969).

Hoseason, John T., *My Life at Sea*, 1950/1960 (typescript in Shetland Record Office).

Hurd, Sir Archibald, *The Merchant Navy*, 3 vols, *Official History of the Great War* (London, 1921–1929).

Langmaid, K., *The Sea Raiders* (London, 1963).

Liddle, P.H., *The Sailor's War 1914–1918* (Poole, 1985).

Lloyds Reports of Prize Cases (London, 1915–1918).

Marder, A., *From the Dreadnought to Scapa Flow* (5 vols, London, 1961–1970).

Spindler, Arno, *Der Handelskrieg mit U-booten* (5 vols, Berlin and Frankfurt-am-Main, 1932–1966).

The Tenth Cruiser Squadron during the Command of Admiral de Chair 1914–1916 (London, 1921).

Tupper, Sir Reginald, *Reminiscences* (London, 1929).

3. The Northern Neutrals

Derry, T.K., *A History of Modern Norway, 1814–1972* (Oxford, 1973).

Kaarsted T., *Great Britain and Denmark, 1914–1920* (Odense, 1979).

McKercher, B.J.C. and K.E. Nielson, '"The Triumph of Unarmed Forces": Sweden and the Allied Blockade of Germany 1914–1917', *Journal of Strategic Studies* 7 (1984), 178–99.

The Netherlands and the World War, Studies in the War History of a Neutral, vol. II, Economic and Social History of the War, Netherlands series, Carnegie Endowment for International Peace (New Haven, 1928).

Riste, Olav, *The Neutral Ally, Norway's relations with belligerent powers in the first world war* (Oslo, 1965).

Scott, F.D., *Sweden, the Nation's History* (Minneapolis, 1977).

Sweden, Norway, Denmark and Iceland in the World War, Economic and Social History of the World War, Carnegie Endowment for International Peace (New Haven, 1930).

Vigness, Paul G., *The Neutrality of Norway in the World War* (Stanford, 1932).

INDEX

Most writers and recipients of letters and documents in this collection are not indexed; nor are the places and ships from which letters were addressed. This information will be found at the heads of the documents, some of it conveniently listed in 'Sources of Documents'. Placenames such as Kirkwall, Lerwick, Stornoway, and Swarbacks Minn, which occur on almost every page, are indexed only selectively.

Ships' names are listed in italics and are identified by the initial letter of their country of registration in brackets:

B – Belgium
D – Denmark
D(I) – Denmark (Iceland)
F – France
G – Germany
N – Norway
NL – Netherlands
R – Russia
S – Sweden
UK – United Kingdom
US – United States

Naval vessels are similiarly identified with the addition of the letter 'N' (for 'Navy'), with the exception of 'RN' for 'Royal Navy'.

Ships which served in the 10th Cruiser Squadron are in capitals.

NAVY RECORDS SOCIETY
(FOUNDED 1893)

The Navy Records Society was established for the purpose of printing unpublished manuscripts and rare works of naval interest. Membership of the Society is open to all who are interested in naval history, and any person wishing to become a member should apply to the Hon. Secretary, Professor A. D. Lambert, Department of War Studies, King's College London, Strand, London WC2R 2LS, United Kingdom. The annual subscription is £30, which entitles the member to receive one free copy of each work issued by the Society in that year, and to buy earlier issues at reduced prices.

A list of works, available to members only, is shown below; very few copies are left of those marked with an asterisk. Volumes out of print are indicated by **OP**. Prices for works in print are available on application to Mrs Annette Gould, 5 Goodwood Close, Midhurst, West Sussex GU29 9JG, United Kingdom, to whom all enquiries concerning works in print should be sent. Those marked 'TS', 'SP' and 'A' are published for the Society by Temple Smith, Scolar Press and Ashgate, and are available to non-members from the Ashgate Publishing Group, Gower House, Croft Road, Aldershot, Hampshire GU11 3HR. Those marked 'A & U' are published by George Allen & Unwin, and are available to non-members only through bookshops.

Vol. 1. *State papers relating to the Defeat of the Spanish Armada, Anno 1558*, Vol. I, ed. Professor J. K. Laughton. TS.
Vol. 2. *State papers relating to the Defeat of the Spanish Armada, Anno 1588*, Vol. II, ed. Professor J. K. Laughton. TS.
Vol. 3. *Letters of Lord Hood, 1781–1783*, ed. D. Hannay. **OP**.
Vol. 4. *Index to James's Naval History*, by C. G. Toogood, ed. by the Hon. T. A. Brassey. **OP**.
Vol. 5. *Life of Captain Stephen Martin, 1666–1740*, ed. Sir Clements R. Markham. **OP**.
Vol. 6. *Journal of Rear Admiral Bartholomew James, 1752–1828*, ed. Professor J. K. Laughton & Cdr. J. Y. F. Sullivan. **OP**.
Vol. 7. *Holland's Discourses of the Navy, 1638 and 1659*, ed. J. R. Tanner. **OP**.

Vol. 8. *Naval Accounts and Inventories in the Reign of Henry VII*, ed M. Oppenheim. **OP**.

Vol. 9. *Journal of Sir George Rooke*, ed. O. Browning, **OP**.

Vol. 10. *Letters and Papers relating to the War with France 1512–1513*, ed. M. Alfred Spont. **OP**.

Vol. 11. *Papers relating to the Spanish War 1585–1587*, ed. Julian S. Corbett. TS.

Vol. 12. *Journals and Letters of Admiral of the Fleet Sir Thomas Byam Martin, 1773–1854*, Vol. II (see No. 24), ed. Admiral Sir R. Vesey Hamilton. **OP**.

Vol. 13. *Papers relating to the First Dutch War, 1652–1654*, Vol. I, ed. Dr S. R. Gardiner. **OP**.

Vol. 14. *Papers relating to the Blockade of Brest, 1803–1805*, Vol. I, ed. J. Leyland. **OP**.

Vol. 15. *History of the Russian Fleet during the Reign of Peter the Great, by a Contemporary Englishman*, ed. Admiral Sir Cyprian Bridge. **OP**.

*Vol. 16. *Logs of the Great Sea Fights, 1794–1805*, Vol. I, ed. Vice Admiral Sir T. Sturges Jackson. **OP**.

Vol. 17. *Papers relating to the First Dutch War, 1652–1654*, ed. Dr S. R. Gardiner. **OP**.

*Vol. 18. *Logs of the Great Sea Fights*, Vol. II, ed. Vice Admiral Sir T. Sturges Jackson.

Vol. 19. *Journals and Letters of Admiral of the Fleet Sir Thomas Byam Martin*, Vol. II (see No. 24), ed. Admiral Sir R. Vesey Hamilton. **OP**.

Vol. 20. *The Naval Miscellany*, Vol. I, ed. Professor J. K. Laughton.

Vol. 21. *Papers relating to the Blockade of Brest, 1803–1805*, Vol. II, ed. J. Leyland. **OP**.

Vol. 22. *The Naval Tracts of Sir William Monson*, Vol. I, ed. M. Oppenheim. **OP**.

Vol. 23. *The Naval Tracts of Sir William Monson*, Vol. II, ed. M. Oppenheim. **OP**.

Vol. 24. *The Journals and Letters of Admiral of the Fleet Sir Thomas Byam Martin*, Vol. I, ed. Admiral Sir R. Vesey Hamilton. **OP**.

Vol. 25. *Nelson and the Neapolitan Jacobins*, ed. H. C. Gutteridge. **OP**.

Vol. 26. *A Descriptive Catalogue of the Naval MSS in the Pepysian Library*, Vol. I, ed. J. R. Tanner. **OP**.

Vol. 27. *A Descriptive Catalogue of the Naval MSS in the Pepysian Library*, Vol. II, ed. J. R. Tanner. **OP**.

Vol. 28. *The Correspondence of Admiral John Markham, 1801–1807*, ed. Sir Clements R. Markham. **OP**.

Vol. 29. *Fighting Instructions, 1530–1816*, ed. Julian S. Corbett. **OP**.

Vol. 30. *Papers relating to the First Dutch War 1652–1654*, Vol. III, ed. Dr S. R. Gardiner & C. T. Atkinson. **OP**.

Vol. 31. *The Recollections of Commander James Anthony Gardner, 1775–1814*, ed. Admiral Sir R. Vesey Hamilton & Professor J. K. Laughton.

Vol. 32. *Letters and Papers of Charles, Lord Barham, 1758–1813*, ed. Professor Sir John Laughton.

Vol. 33. *Naval Songs and Ballads*, ed. Professor C. H. Firth. **OP**.

Vol. 34. *Views of the Battles of the Third Dutch War*, ed. by Julian S. Corbett. **OP**.

Vol. 35. *Signals and Instructions, 1776–1794*, ed. Julian S. Corbett. **OP**.

Vol. 36. *A Descriptive Catalogue of the Naval MSS in the Pepysian Library*, Vol III, ed. J. R. Tanner. **OP**.

Vol. 37. *Papers relating to the First Dutch War, 1652–1654*, Vol. IV, ed. C. T. Atkinson. **OP**.

Vol. 38. *Letters and Papers of Charles, Lord Barham, 1758–1813*, Vol. II, ed. Professor Sir John Laughton. **OP**.

Vol. 39. *Letters and Papers of Charles, Lord Barham, 1758–1813*, Vol. III, ed. Professor Sir John Laughton.

Vol. 40. *The Naval Miscellany*, Vol. II, ed. Professor Sir John Laughton.

*Vol. 41. *Papers relating to the First Dutch War, 1652–1654*, Vol. V, ed. C. T. Atkinson.

*Vol. 42. *Papers relating to the Loss of Minorca in 1756*, ed. Captain H. W. Richmond, R. N. **OP**.

*Vol. 43. *The Naval Tracts of Sir William Monson*, Vol. III, ed. M. Oppenheim.

Vol. 44. *The Old Scots Navy 1689–1710*, ed. James Grant. **OP**.

Vol. 45. *The Naval Tracts of Sir William Monson*, Vol. IV, ed. M. Oppenheim.

*Vol. 46. *The Private Papers of George, 2nd Earl Spencer*, Vol. I, ed. Julian S. Corbett. **OP**.

Vol. 47. *The Naval Tracts of Sir William Monson*, Vol. V, ed. M. Oppenheim.

Vol. 48. *The Private Papers of George, 2nd Earl Spencer*, Vol. II, ed. Julian S. Corbett. **OP**.

*Vol. 49. *Documents relating to Law and Custom of the Sea*, Vol. II, ed. R. G. Marsden. **OP**.

*Vol. 50. *Documents relating to Law and Custom of the Sea*, Vol. II, ed. R. G. Marsden.

Vol. 51. *Autobiography of Phineas Pett*, ed. W. G. Perrin. **OP**.

Vol. 52. *The Life of Admiral Sir John Leake*, Vol. I, ed. Geoffrey Callender.

Vol. 53. *The Life of Admiral Sir John Leake*, Vol. II, ed. Geoffrey Callender.
Vol. 54. *The Life and Works of Sir Henry Mainwaring*, Vol. I, ed. G. E. Manwaring.
Vol. 55. *The Letters of Lord St Vincent, 1801–1804*, Vol. I, ed. D. B. Smith. **OP**.
Vol. 56. *The Life and Works of Sir Henry Mainwaring*, Vol. II, ed. G. E. Manwaring & W. G. Perrin. **OP**.
Vol. 57. *A Descriptive Catalogue of the Naval MSS in the Pepysian Library*, Vol. IV, ed. Dr J. R. Tanner. **OP**.
Vol. 58. *The Private Papers of George, 2nd Earl Spencer*, Vol. III, ed. Rear Admiral H. W. Richmond. **OP**.
Vol. 59. *The Private Papers of George, 2nd Earl Spencer*, Vol. IV, ed. Rear Admiral H. W. Richmond. **OP**.
Vol. 60. *Samuel Pepy's Naval Minutes*, ed. Dr J. R. Tanner.
Vol. 61. *The Letters of Lord St Vincent, 1801–1804*, Vol. II, ed. D. B. Smith. **OP**.
Vol. 62. *Letters and Papers of Admiral Viscount Keith*, Vol. I, ed. W. G. Perrin. **OP**.
Vol. 63. *The Naval Miscellany*, Vol. III, ed. W. G. Perrin. **OP**.
Vol. 64. *The Journal of the 1st Earl of Sandwich*, ed. R. C. Anderson. **OP**.
*Vol. 65. *Boteler's Dialogues*, ed. W. G. Perrin.
Vol. 66. *Papers relating to the First Dutch War, 1652–1654*, Vol. VI (with index), ed. C. T. Atkinson.
*Vol. 67. *The Byng Papers*, Vol. I, ed. W. C. B. Tunstall.
*Vol. 68. *The Byng Papers*, Vol. II, ed. W. C. B. Tunstall.
Vol. 69. *The Private Papers of John, Earl of Sandwich*, Vol. I, ed. G. R. Barnes & Lt. Cdr. J. H. Owen, R.N. Corrigenda to *Papers relating to the First Dutch War, 1652–1654, Vols I–VI*, ed. Captain A. C. Dewar, R.N. **OP**.
Vol. 70. *The Byng Papers*, Vol. III, ed. W. C. B. Tunstall.
Vol. 71. *The Private Papers of John, Earl of Sandwich*, Vol. II, ed. G. R. Barnes & Lt. Cdr. J. H. Owen, R.N. **OP**.
Vol. 72. *Piracy in the Levant, 1827–1828*, ed. Lt. Cdr. C. G. Pitcairn Jones, R.N. **OP**.
Vol. 73. *The Tangier Papers of Samuel Pepys*, ed. Edwin Chappell.
Vol. 74. *The Tomlinson Papers*, ed. J. G. Bullocke.
Vol. 75. *The Private Papers of John, Earl of Sandwich*, Vol. III, ed. G. R. Barnes & Cdr. J. H. Owen, R.N. **OP**.
Vol. 76. *The Letters of Robert Blake*, ed. the Rev. J. R. Powell. **OP**.

*Vol. 77. *Letters and Papers of Admiral the Hon. Samuel Barrington*, Vol. I, ed. D. Bonner-Smith.
Vol. 78. *The Private Papers of John, Earl of Sandwich*, Vol. IV, ed. G. R. Barnes & Cdr. J. H. Owen, R.N. **OP**.
*Vol. 79. *The Journals of Sir Thomas Allin, 1660–1678*, Vol. I (1660–1666), ed. R. C. Anderson.
Vol. 80. *The Journals of Sir Thomas Allin, 1660–1678*, Vol. II (1667–1678), ed. R. C. Anderson.
Vol. 81. *Letters and Papers of Admiral the Hon. Samuel Barrington*, Vol. II, ed. D. Bonner-Smith. **OP**.
Vol. 82. *Captain Boteler's Recollections, 1808–1830*, ed. D. Bonner-Smith. **OP**.
Vol. 83. *Russian War, 1854. Baltic and Black Sea: Official Correspondence*, ed. D. Bonner-Smith & Captain A. C. Dewar, R.N. **OP**.
Vol. 84. *Russian War, 1855. Baltic: Official Correspondence*, ed. D. Bonner-Smith. **OP**.
Vol. 85. *Russian War, 1855. Black Sea: Official Correspondence*, ed. Captain A.C. Dewar, R.N. **OP**.
Vol. 86. *Journals and Narratives of the Third Dutch War*, ed. R. C. Anderson. **OP**.
Vol. 87. *The Naval Brigades in the Indian Mutiny, 1857–1858*, ed. Cdr. W. B. Rowbotham, R.N. **OP**.
Vol. 88. *Patee Byng's Journal*, ed. J. L. Cranmer-Byng. **OP**.
*Vol. 89. *The Sergison Papers, 1688–1702*, ed. Cdr. R. D. Merriman, R.I.N.
Vol. 90. *The Keith Papers*, Vol. II, ed. Christopher Lloyd. **OP**.
Vol. 91. *Five Naval Journals, 1789–1817*, ed. Rear Admiral H. G. Thursfield. **OP**.
Vol. 92. *The Naval Miscellany*, Vol. IV, ed. Christopher Lloyd. **OP**.
Vol. 93. *Sir William Dillon's Narrative of Professional Adventures, 1790–1839*, Vol. I (1790–1802), ed. Professor Michael Lewis. **OP**.
Vol. 94. *The Walker Expedition to Quebec, 1711*, ed. Professor Gerald S. Graham. **OP**.
Vol. 95. *The Second China War, 1856–1760*, ed. D. Bonner-Smith & E. W. R. Lumby. **OP**.
Vol. 96. *The Keith Papers, 1803–1815*, Vol. III, ed. Professor Christopher Lloyd.
Vol. 97. *Sir William Dillon's Narrative of Professional Adventures, 1790–1839*, Vol. II (1802–1839), ed. Professor Michael Lewis. **OP**.
Vol. 98. *The Private Correspondence of Admiral Lord Collingwood*, ed. Professor Edward Hughes. **OP**.
Vol. 99. *The Vernon Papers, 1739–1745*, ed. B. McL. Ranft. **OP**.

Vol. 100. *Nelson's Letter to his Wife and Other Documents*, ed. Lt. Cdr. G. P. B. Naish. R.N.V.R. **OP**.
Vol. 101. *A Memoir of James Trevenen, 1760–1790*, ed. Professor Christopher Lloyd & R. C. Anderson. **OP**.
Vol. 102. *The Papers of Admiral Sir John Fisher*, Vol. I, ed. Lt. Cdr. P. K. Kemp, R.N. **OP**.
Vol. 103. *Queen Anne's Navy*, ed. Cdr. R. D. Merriman, R.I.N. **OP**.
Vol. 104. *The Navy and South America, 1807–1823*, ed. Professor Gerald S. Graham & Professor R. A. Humphreys.
Vol. 105. *Documents relating to the Civil War, 1642–1648*, ed. The Rev. J. R. Powell & E. K. Timings. **OP**.
Vol. 106. *The Papers of Admiral Sir John Fisher*, Vol. II, ed. Lt. Cdr. P. K. Kemp, R.N. **OP**.
Vol. 107. *The Health of Seamen*, ed. Professor Christopher Lloyd.
Vol. 108. *The Jellicoe Papers*, Vol. I (1893–1916), ed. A. Temple Patterson.
Vol. 109. *Documents relating to Anson's Voyage round the World, 1740–1744*, ed. Dr Glyndwr Williams. **OP**.
Vol. 110. *The Saumarez Papers: The Baltic, 1808–1812*, ed. A. N. Ryan. **OP**.
Vol. 111. *The Jellicoe Papers*, Vol. II (1916–1925), ed. Professor A. Temple Patterson.
Vol. 112. *The Rupert and Monck Letterbook, 1666*, ed. The Rev. J. R. Powell & E. K. Timings.
Vol. 113. *Documents relating to the Royal Naval Air Service*, Vol. I (1908–1918), ed. Captain S. W. Roskill, R.N.
*Vol. 114. *The Siege and Capture of Havana, 1762*, ed. Professor David Syrett.
Vol. 115. *Policy and Operations in the Mediterranean, 1912–1914*, ed. E. W. R. Lumby. **OP**.
Vol. 116. *The Jacobean Commissions of Enquiry, 1608 and 1618*, ed. Dr A. P. McGowan.
Vol. 117. *The Keyes Papers*, Vol. I (1914–1918), ed. Professor Paul Halpern.
Vol. 118. *The Royal Navy and North America: The Warren Papers, 1736–1752*, ed. Dr Julian Gwyn. **OP**.
Vol. 119. *The Manning of the Royal Navy: Selected Public Pamphlets, 1693–1873*, ed. Professor John Bromley.
Vol. 120. *Naval Administration, 1715–1750*, ed. Professor D. A. Baugh.
Vol. 121. *The Keyes Papers*, Vol. II (1919–1938), ed. Professor Paul Halpern.

Vol. 122. *The Keyes Papers*, Vol. III (1939–1945), ed. Professor Paul Halpern.

Vol. 123. *The Navy of the Lancastrian Kings: Accounts and Inventories of William Soper, Keeper of the King's Ships, 1422–1427*, ed. Dr Susan Rose.

Vol. 124. *The Pollen Papers: the Privately Circulated Printed Works of Arthur Hungerford Pollen, 1901–1916*, ed. Professor Jon T. Sumida. A. & U.

Vol. 125. *The Naval Miscellany*, Vol. V, ed. Dr N. A. M. Rodger. A & U.

Vol. 126. *The Royal Navy in the Mediterranean, 1915–1918*, ed. Professor Paul Halpern. TS.

Vol. 127. *The Expedition of Sir John Norris and Sir Francis Drake to Spain and Portugal, 1589*, ed. Professor R. B. Wernham. TS.

Vol. 128. *The Beatty Papers*, Vol. I (1902–1918), ed. Professor B. McL. Ranft. SP.

Vol. 129. *The Hawke Papers: A Selection, 1743–1771*, ed. Dr R. F. Mackay. SP.

Vol. 130. *Anglo-American Naval Relations, 1917–1919*, ed. Michael Simpson. SP.

Vol. 131. *British Naval Documents, 1204–1960*, ed. Professor John B. Hattendorf, Dr Roger Knight, Alan Pearsall, Dr Nicholas Rodger & Professor Geoffrey Till. SP.

Vol. 132. *The Beatty Papers*, Vol. II (1916–1927), ed. Professor B. McL. Ranft. SP.

Vol. 133. *Samuel Pepys and the Second Dutch War*, transcribed by Professor William Matthews & Dr Charles Knighton; ed. Robert Latham. SP.

Vol. 134. *The Somerville Papers*, ed. Michael Simpson, with the assistance of John Somerville. SP.

Vol. 135. *The Royal Navy in the River Plate, 1806–1807*, ed. John D. Grainger. SP.

Vol. 136. *The Collective Naval Defence of the Empire, 1900–1940*, ed. Nicholas Tracy. A.

Vol. 137. *The Defeat of the Enemy Attack on Shipping, 1939–1945*, ed. Eric Grove. A.

Vol. 138. *Shipboard Life and Organisation, 1731–1815*, ed. Brian Lavery. A.

Vol. 139. *The Battle of the Atlantic and Signals Intelligence: U-boat Situations and Trends, 1941–1945*, ed. Professor David Syrett. A.

Vol. 140. *The Cunningham Papers*, Vol. I, *The Mediterranean Fleet, 1939–1942*, ed. Michael Simpson. A.

Vol. 141. *The Channel Fleet and the Blockade of Brest, 1793–1801,* ed. Roger Morriss. A.

Vol. 142. *The Submarine Service, 1900–1918*, ed. Nicholas Lambert.

Vol. 143. *Letters and Papers of Professor Sir John Knox Laughton (1830–1915)*, ed. Andrew Lambert. A.

Vol. 144. *The Battle of the Atlantic and Signals Intelligence: U-Boat Tracking Papers 1941–1947*, ed. Professor David Syrett. A.

Vol. 145. *The Maritime Blockade of Germany in the Great War: The Northern Patrol, 1914–1918*, ed. John D. Grainger. A.

Occasional Publications:

Vol. 1. *The Commissioned Sea Officers of the Royal Navy, 1660–1815*, ed. Professor David Syrett & Professor R. L. DiNardo. SP.

Vol. 2. *The Anthony Roll of Henry VIII's Navy*, ed. C. S. Knighton and D. M. Loades. A.